RECORDS OF CIVILIZATION

SOURCES AND STUDIES

NUMBERS LIV-LVI

INTRODUCTION TO
ORIENTAL
CIVILIZATIONS

INTRODUCTION TO ORIENTAL CIVILIZATIONS

Wm. Theodore de Bary, EDITOR

Sources of
Chinese Tradition

COMPILED BY

Wm. Theodore de Bary

Wing-tsit Chan

Burton Watson

WITH CONTRIBUTIONS BY

Yi-pao Mei   Leon Hurvitz

T'ung-tsu Ch'u   Chester Tan   John Meskill

COLUMBIA
UNIVERSITY
PRESS
NEW YORK
AND LONDON

The addition to the "Records of Civilization: Sources and Studies" of a group of translations of Oriental historical materials, of which this volume is one, was made possible by funds granted by Carnegie Corporation of New York. That Corporation is not, however, the author, owner, publisher, or proprietor of this publication, and is not to be understood as approving by virtue of its grant any of the statements made or views expressed therein.

PREFACE

This book, the last in a three-volume series dealing with the civilizations of China, Japan, and India, contains source readings that tell us what the Chinese have thought about themselves, the universe they lived in, and the problems they faced living together. It is meant to provide the general reader with an understanding of the background of Chinese civilization, especially as this is reflected in intellectual and religious traditions which have survived into modern times. Much attention is also given, however, to political and social questions which the ordinary history of philosophy or religion would not treat. Indeed, as compared to Japan and India, the dominant traditions of Chinese thought have been less markedly religious in character, there being a noticeable disjunction between the popular practice of religion and the intellectual activity of the ruling elite, which had a more secular orientation. To compensate somewhat for this relative neglect of religious matters by the articulators and preservers of formal tradition, a special chapter is devoted to popular religious movements and secret societies.

As in the other volumes of this series, the readings are drawn from contemporary literature as well as classical. Since in the modern period the urgency of political and social problems has been uppermost in the minds of educated Chinese, it is natural that such tendencies as reformism, nationalism, liberalism, and Communism should be the center of attention in contemporary writings. If this means that other currents of thought—the influence of Western religions, formal philosophy, and art—are inadequately represented, we can only regret that a survey which spans so many centuries allows less scope than one might want for dealing with the variety of thought in any given period—with significant undercurrents and counter trends, or with distinctive individual contributions which nonetheless had little general influence. We have striven for variety and balance in the presentation of Chinese thought as a whole, not necessarily of each era and dynasty.

A further word may be needed concerning the rigid selectivity we have thus been forced to adopt. Those with a distaste for metaphysics and mystical psychology may wonder why almost three chapters are devoted to such aspects of Buddhist and Neo-Confucian philosophy (which indeed present formidable problems in translation and interpretation) when much material that is less forbidding and more understandable in the literature of Chinese thought has been left out. The reason is that we have tried to represent the Chinese tradition in all its range and depth, not merely in its most approachable and appealing aspects. To discard centuries of speculative thought, which the Chinese have considered of great significance in their own tradition, would only be to confirm the common stereotype of the Chinese as practical and worldly in outlook. Practical and worldly they are, but they have also manifested a speculative and contemplative quality of mind which few other peoples can match, and which shows itself in the writings of even so "practical" a man as Mao Tse-tung.

In contrast to most anthologies the translations included here are for the most part our own, and a major portion are of texts not previously translated into English. Because of the unfamiliarity and complexity of many subjects dealt with, we have found it necessary to include more historical and explanatory material than is usual in a set of source readings. Nevertheless, the reader who seeks a fuller knowledge of the historical and institutional background would do well to consult a general or cultural history. It is also possible, of course, to find further literature on some subjects dealt with here in only summary fashion. For topics in traditional Chinese philosophy, Wing-tsit Chan's *An Outline and Annotated Bibliography of Chinese Philosophy* (Far Eastern Publications, Yale, 1959), and for topics in modern Chinese thought, the bibliography appended to J. K. Fairbank, *The United States and China,* rev. ed. (Cambridge, Mass., Harvard, 1958), will prove useful as a reading guide.

The preparation of this volume has been forwarded by the generous collaboration of colleagues at both Columbia and sister institutions. Because of the cooperative nature of the project, and the necessity for integrating and adapting diverse contributions to form a coherent whole, there are few chapters for which a single individual can be identified as the sole author, and the general editor must assume the responsibility for the final form in which each appears.

The contributions of various collaborators may, however, be roughly listed as follows: Mr. de Bary is the principal author of chapters 18, 19, 22, 24, 25, 26 and 29. As editor he is also responsible for the general plan of the work and for most of the introductory materials in their present form. Wing-tsit Chan of Dartmouth College has assisted in many different aspects of the editorial work and is also principal author of chapters 14, 16, 17, 20, 21, 23 and 28. Burton Watson, mainly responsible for Chapters 1 and 8 through 13 and the final section of Chapter 19, also devoted the year 1955–56 to editorial tasks of many types in connection with Parts I to IV. Y. P. Mei of the State University of Iowa contributed substantially to Part I (chapters 2 to 7); Leon Hurvitz, now of the University of Washington, to chapters 15 to 17; T'ung-tsu Ch'u, formerly of Columbia and now of Harvard University, to chapters 18 and 19, and Chester Tan of New York University to chapters 26 and 27. John Meskill helped with the final checking of the manuscript, the bibliography, maps, and chronological tables.

Chi-chen Wang, Te-kong Tong, and Paul Hsiang assisted in the preparation of several of the translations. In addition, several others have been made available to us through the generosity of colleagues elsewhere. In Part V the translations from Lin Tse-hsü and Li Ta-chao are taken from *China's Response to the West*, by Ssu-yü Teng and John K. Fairbank. The translation of the Taiping work, *The Principles of the Heavenly Nature,* has been made available from the documentary history of the Taiping Rebellion being prepared by the Modern Chinese History Project of the Far Eastern and Russian Institute, University of Washington, along with an emended version of Medhurst's translation of *The Book of Heavenly Commandments.* Acknowledgment should also be made to A. L. Basham of the University of London for extracts quoted here from his account of Buddhism in the companion volume, *Sources of Indian Tradition.* Royal Weiler of Columbia helped with Sanskrit terms.

Among those to whom we are indebted for reading portions of the manuscript are Karl A. Wittfogel of the University of Washington, whose constructive criticism of the chapter on Chinese Communism was most helpful. Howard Boorman and the staff of the project, "Men and Politics in Modern China," at Columbia were most gracious in providing biographical data and useful criticism of the chapters on modern China. Others who have read and criticized individual sections include Thomas Berry, Richard Howard, Donald Keene, Arnold Koslow, James T. C. Liu, Ruth Fuller Sasaki, and Arthur Wright.

To Eileen J. Boecklen go the editor's deep thanks for her faithful and capable assistance in the long work of processing these materials for publication, as in so many other aspects of the project which has produced them. A similar service has been provided in the stage of publication by Joan McQuary, Eugenia Porter, and Nancy Dixon of Columbia University Press. Lastly, while making these acknowledgments, the editor may perhaps be forgiven if he makes public his unofficial debt to Fanny Brett de Bary for her constant support and encouragement in the preparation of this series—a debt which cannot be expressed but which he can no longer be expected to keep secret.

This series of readings has been produced in connection with the Columbia College General Education Program in Oriental Studies, which has been encouraged and supported by the Carnegie Corporation of New York. For whatever value it may have to the general reader or college student seeking a liberal education that embraces both the East and West, a great debt is owed to two officers of the Corporation, John Gardner and William Marvel, to Dean Emeritus Harry J. Carman and Lawrence H. Chamberlain of Columbia College, and to Jacques Barzun, Provost of the University and General Editor of the Records of Civilization.

WM. THEODORE DE BARY

Columbia College
New York City
August, 1959

EXPLANATORY NOTE

The sources of translations given at the beginning of each selection are rendered as concisely as possible. Full bibliographical data can be obtained from the list of sources at the end of the book. In the reference at the head of each selection, unless otherwise indicated, the author of the book is the writer whose name precedes the selection. Where excerpts have been taken from existing translations, they have sometimes been adapted or edited in the interests of uniformity with the book as a whole.

Chinese words and names are rendered according to the modified Wade-Giles system of romanization which has become standard in American sinological publications. An exception to this appears in the names of certain Neo-Confucian philosophers where the syllable *i* has been converted to *yi* in order to avoid possible confusion for the non-sinologist. Indic words appearing in the chapters on Buddhism as technical terms or titles in italics follow the standard system of transliteration found in Louis Renou's *Grammaire Sanskrite* (Paris, 1930), pp. xi–xiii, with the exception that here ś is regularly used for ç. To facilitate pronunciation, other Sanskrit terms and proper names appearing in roman letters are rendered according to the usage of Webster's New International Dictionary, 2d edition, Unabridged, except that here the macron is used to indicate long vowels and the Sanskrit symbols for ś (ç) and ṣ are uniformly transcribed as sh. Similarly, the standard Sanskrit transcription of c is given as ch.

Chinese names are rendered in their Chinese order, with the family name first and the personal name last. Dates given after personal names are those of birth and death except in the case of rulers whose reign dates are preceded by "r." Generally the name by which a person was most commonly known in Chinese tradition is the one used in the text. Since this book is intended for the general reader, rather than the specialist, we have not burdened the text with a list of the alternate names or titles which usually accompany biographical reference to a scholar in Chinese or Japanese historical works.

W. T. DE B.

CONTENTS

PART ONE

THE CLASSICAL PERIOD

Outline of Early Chinese History

(Dates and entries before 841 B.C.
  are traditional)

B.C.	Dynasty		
2852			Fu Hsi, inventor of writing, fishing, trapping.
2737		Culture Heroes	Shen Nung, inventor of agriculture, commerce.
2697			Yellow Emperor.
2357			Yao.
2255		Sage Kings	Shun.
2205			Yü, virtuous founder of dynasty.
1818	Hsia Dynasty		Chieh, degenerate terminator of dynasty.
1766	Shang or Yin Dynasty		King T'ang, virtuous founder of dynasty.
[c. 1300]			[Beginning of archeological evidence.]
1154			Chou, degenerate terminator of dynasty.
	Three Dynasties		King Wen, virtuous founder of dynasty.
1122			King Wu, virtuous founder of dynasty.
1115	Chou Dynasty	Western Chou	King Ch'eng, virtuous founder of dynasty. (Duke of Chou, Regent to King Ch'eng)
878			King Li.
781			King Yu.

771	Chou Dynasty (cont.)		
722			Spring and Autumn period (722–481).
551			Period of the "hundred philosophers" (551–c. 233): Confucius, Mo Tzu, Lao Tzu (?), Mencius, Chuang Tzu, Hui Shih, Shang Yang, Kung-sun Lung, Hsün Tzu, Han Fei.
403		Eastern Chou	Warring States period (403–221).
4th to 3d cent.			Extensive wall-building and waterworks by Ch'in and other states.
249			Lü Pu-wei, prime minister of Ch'in.
221	Ch'in Dynasty		The First Emperor; Li Ssu, prime minister.
214	(221–207 B.C.)		The Great Wall completed.

CHAPTER I

THE CHINESE
TRADITION IN
ANTIQUITY

Any attempt to describe the thought of the most ancient or pre-Confucian period of Chinese history is immediately faced with two difficulties. The first is the fact that the traditional awe and respect for antiquity typical of the Chinese has led Chinese writers and thinkers of later periods to ascribe the authorship of their ideas and pronouncements to figures of highest antiquity. Modern scholarship has long suspected, if not definitely proved, that many of the texts traditionally supposed to date from the beginnings of Chinese history are actually comparatively late works, but it is still impossible to state with finality exactly which texts and which ideas are genuinely the product of pre-Confucian times. The second difficulty lies in the fact that, although some of the texts at our disposal almost certainly do date from very ancient times, their wording is so archaic and their meaning so overlaid and obscured by later interpretations, that it is very difficult to say just what they may have meant to the men who composed them. With these cautionary remarks in mind, however, we may attempt to outline the beginnings of Chinese history as they have traditionally been accepted by the Chinese and the literature upon which these traditions are based, and venture a brief description of what appear to be genuinely ancient concepts and patterns of thought representative of the pre-Confucian period.

The traditional account of Chinese history begins with a number of vague, semi-divine culture heroes who are said to have first taught the Chinese people the various arts of civilization. These legendary figures are followed by three rulers of exceptional wisdom and virtue, Yao, Shun, and Yü, who figure so importantly in later Confucian writings. Yü in turn was the founder of the first dynasty of Chinese history, the Hsia.

This Hsia dynasty, which is supposed to have lasted some three hundred years, was brought to an end when the last ruler, Chieh, an exceedingly degenerate and incompetent king, was overthrown by King T'ang, who proceeded to found the second dynasty, the Shang or Yin. Up to this point, it may be stated parenthetically, we have no reliable evidence, archeological or literary, to confirm the existence of any of these men or their reigns. For the existence of the Shang, however, we have not only archeological proof but also bone inscriptions that tell us something about the life of the period. The Shang dynasty was in turn overthrown when King Wen and his son King Wu rebelled against the last ruler of the Shang, King Chou, deposed him and set up a new dynasty. This new dynasty, the Chou, lasted until 221 B.C. and for it and its history we have not only considerable archeological evidence but also numerous texts of unquestionable authenticity.

Let us now turn to the most important body of literature traditionally accepted by the Chinese as a heritage of these ancient times, the Confucian Classics. According to the order in which they are customarily discussed, the first of these is the *I ching* or *Book of Changes.* The people of the Shang dynasty practiced divination by means of bones and tortoise shells, but at some time another method of divination by means of stalks of milfoil also became popular. The *Book of Changes* consists of a short text giving clues to the interpretation of the results of this type of divination, followed by a number of appendixes or "wings" which elaborate upon the metaphysical significance of the interpretations. The basic text is attributed to very ancient times, while Confucius is supposed to have written the "wings." Modern scholarship, however, designates the "wings" as the work of much later times (Ch'in or early Han).

The second Classic is the *Shu ching,* the *Book of History,* or *Book of Documents* as it is sometimes called. This work consists of a number of short announcements, counsels, speeches, or similar oral reports said to have been made by the various rulers and their ministers from the times of Yao and Shun down to the early Chou period. Some of these have been identified as forgeries of the Christian era, while others appear to be works of the middle or late Chou, so that it is probable that only those ascribed to the early Chou are historically reliable. Nevertheless most Chinese have until recent times accepted most of them as accurate descriptions of the men and society of ancient China. The collection of texts supposedly was edited by Confucius, who wrote a short introduction to each document explaining the circumstances of its composition.

The third Classic is the *Shih ching,* the *Book of Odes* or *Book of Poetry,* an anthology of some three hundred poems dating mostly from early Chou times. Some of these are folk songs from the various feudal states of early Chou times, while others are songs used by the aristocracy in their sacrificial ceremonies or at banquets or other functions. One section doubtfully purports to be ceremonial songs of the earlier Shang period. Confucius is supposed to have selected and edited these poems from a much larger body of material, and though this tradition is open to question there seems no reason to doubt the authenticity of the songs themselves.

The fourth Classic, the *Ritual,* is actually a collection of texts, the most famous of which is the *Li chi* or *Book of Rites.* These texts cover a vast range of subjects from the broadest philosophical pronouncements to the most minute rules for the conduct of everyday life. It is uncertain when the collections assumed their present form, though the texts themselves appear to date from middle or late Chou times down to early Han. Again Confucius is vaguely ascribed the role of compiler and editor for some of these texts.

The fifth of the Classics, the *Ch'un-ch'iu* or *Spring and Autumn Annals,* is a brief, laconic chronicle of events in or affecting the state of Lu for the years from 722 to 481 B.C. Lu was the native state of Confucius and it has been asserted that Confucius himself compiled the *Annals* from earlier records existing in the archives of Lu. Because the text of the *Annals* is so brief and obscure, a number of commentaries have been appended to explain the background and significance of the events referred to in the basic text. Of these the most important are the *Tso chuan* or *Tso Commentary,* the *Kung-yang,* and the *Ku-liang* commentaries. The exact dating of these commentaries is still a matter of controversy, though they were all apparently in existence by early Han times. It is in the light of these three commentaries that the *Spring and Autumn Annals* has traditionally been read and interpreted.

These works make up the Five Confucian Classics. A sixth, the "Music," is often mentioned in early writing. Whether there was ever a separate text on music we do not know. No such separate work exists today, though an essay on music is now found in the collection of ritual texts.

It will be noted that all of these texts, with the exception of the three commentaries on the *Spring and Autumn Annals,* purport to date from pre-Confucian times and to represent the earliest literature of the Chinese people, although modern scholarship in some cases denies these claims. It will also be noticed that in every case Confucius himself is assigned a personal role as transmitter, editor, and even commentator. It is true that other schools of thought also studied and made use of these early texts, or even put forward texts of their own for which they claimed equal authority and age. But the Confucian school always pictured itself as the particular guardian and transmitter of the old literature, and from the time in the first century B.C. when Confucianism gained general acceptance these Five Classics became for the educated class the chief object of study, and were regarded not only as the final authority upon questions of ancient history and practice, but as the embodiment of the moral law of Confucius and his predecessors, and the source of all wisdom and right knowledge. The *Book of Changes,* interpreted in the light of its "wings," was taken as a description of the metaphysical structure of the universe. The speeches of the *Book of History* were regarded as records of the government and institutions of the ancient sage-kings and models for all later rulers. The folk songs and ceremonial hymns of the *Book of Odes* were interpreted as praises by the people or the officials of good government or satires against misrule. The ritual texts were the final authority upon all questions of procedure and etiquette. Finally it was asserted that Confucius had compiled the *Spring and Autumn Annals* not as an impartial record of historical fact but as a vehicle to convey his personal judgments upon the men and events of the past and thereby to suggest to men certain moral laws and principles that would guide them in the management of their affairs. These moral lessons, however, are by no means apparent in the brief text of the *Annals,* so that the student must avail himself of the help of the commentaries and ponder each subtle shade of wording before he can grasp the true significance of what Confucius was trying to say. These interpretations of the ancient texts may appear to us extravagantly forced and unsound. Yet it is necessary to bear them in mind if we are to understand the gravity which later thinkers attached to the Classics and the lavish claims which they make in favor of a lifetime devoted to a study of the ancient texts.

Let us note now a few of the terms and concepts which seem to be

However, in contrast to the more anthropomorphic conception of Shang-ti, closely identified with the ruling family and its interests, Heaven was a more universalized conception. It represented a cosmic moral order and a being or power, possessing intelligence and will, which guided impartially the destinies of men. The authority of Heaven might therefore be appealed to in situations where the sanctions of clan or nation did not extend.

After the leaders of the Chou tribe had overthrown the Shang dynasty and set up their own rule around 1120 B.C., they issued a number of proclamations, preserved in the *Book of History,* explaining to the defeated Shang people why they should submit docilely to their new conquerors. In their arguments the Chou rulers appealed to a concept called *t'ien-ming* or the mandate of Heaven. Heaven, they said, elected or commanded certain men to be rulers over the tribes of the world, and their heirs might continue to exercise the Heaven-sanctioned power for as long as they carried out their religious and administrative duties with piety, wisdom, and justice. But if the worth of the ruling family declined, if the rulers turned their backs upon the spirits and abandoned the virtuous ways that had originally marked them as worthy of the mandate to rule, then Heaven might discard them and elect a new family or tribe to be the destined rulers of the world. The Shang kings, it was argued, had once been wise and benevolent rulers, and thus enjoyed the full blessing and sanction of Heaven. But in later days they had grown cruel and degenerate, so that Heaven had called upon the Chou chieftains to overthrow the Shangs, punish their evil ways, and institute a new dynasty.

As one of the sacrificial songs of the *Book of Odes* expresses this idea: "Chou is an old people but its charge is new." Since the Chou had received this new charge from Heaven to rule the world, it was useless and perverse for the Shang people to continue to resist its officers. Thus the Chou rulers explained the change of dynasties not as a purely human action by which a strong state overthrew a weak one, but as a divinely directed process in which a new group of wise and virtuous leaders was substituted for an old group whose members, by their evil actions, had disqualified themselves from the right to rule. To reinforce this view, the Chou leaders advised the people of Shang to look back to their own history, in which this same process had taken place when King T'ang, the virtuous founder of the Shang dynasty, had been directed by Heaven

of greatest antiquity and importance in this body of ancient liter.
Not only in the texts of the Classics but also in the inscriptions on
Shang period oracle bones we find frequent references to a deity ca.
Shang-ti or the Lord-on-High. Just who this deity originally was \
cannot tell, but by the time we know much of him he appears as a divin
ruler who watches over human society and regulates the working of the
universe. In view of the close relationship between religious worship
and family or clan, it is quite possible that Shang-ti was the chief god
of the ruling family (perhaps even a deified ancestor) whose ascendancy
in religion closely paralleled the political ascendancy of the family which
was the basis of his cult. Beneath him are a number of lesser deities of
the sun, moon, stars, wind, rain, and particular mountains and rivers.
In addition to these, the ancient Chinese also believed that their ancestors,
upon death, continued to exist in Heaven, the home of the Lord-on-High,
and to exert a very definite influence upon human affairs. All of these
various spiritual beings were sacrificed to from early times, though just
which groups sacrificed to which deities in the ancient society is not
clear. By Chou times, however, it was customary for only the Chou
kings to sacrifice to the Lord-on-High, while lesser feudal lords sacrificed,
as did the Chou, to their ancestors and to the gods of the mountains
and rivers in their territories. Private families probably sacrificed only
to their own ancestors. These sacrifices were of the utmost importance
in securing the blessings and protection of the spirits, and any move to
neglect them, perform them improperly, or perform sacrifices to which
one was not entitled would, it was thought, bring about misfortune and
calamity. The sacrifices to ancestors in particular were of vital importance
to the welfare of the family or clan, for the ancestors had the power to
aid or punish their descendants according to their pleasure.

At some time very early in Chinese history a second concept, that of
t'ien or Heaven, came to be accepted as roughly synonymous with the
Lord-on-High. Heaven, in other words, exercised the same supreme
power over the universe and mankind that Shang-ti, or the Lord-on-High,
was believed to exercise, and for a while the two terms seem to have
been used interchangeably. But the character *ti* of the compound *Shang-ti*
was used increasingly to mean not a supreme deity but the supreme ruler
of human society, the emperor, while the word *t'ien,* or Heaven, was
more often employed to denote the power that governed all creation.

to overthrow the degenerate ruler of the old Hsia dynasty and institute a new rule. Whether or not this interpretation of the founding of the Shang state reflects to some extent historical fact, or is merely a legend invented by the Chous for their own convenience we cannot say. But from Chou times down to the present day, this description of the dynastic cycle and the concept of the heavenly mandate has been accepted by nearly all Chinese as the correct interpretation of history. Chinese historians have been fully aware of the various economic and social factors which contribute to the weakening and downfall of one dynasty and the rise of another. Yet they have never until the most recent times abandoned the idea that behind these factors and underlying them is a deeper problem of the moral qualification of a man or a family to rule. A ruler may, like the last king of the Shang, be extremely powerful and astute, but if he is selfish and cruel and oppresses his people, Heaven will cease to aid and protect him or sanction his rule, and he will fail. On the other hand a state may be comparatively weak and insignificant, as the early leaders of the Chou are traditionally pictured to have been, but if they are wise and benevolent in their administration and care for their people, then all men will flock to their rule and Heaven will aid them to rise to the highest position. Such is the power and gravity of the heavenly mandate and the moral obligation which it implies.

These then were the basic beliefs of the early Chinese people: a belief in a supreme deity or moral force which ruled the world and took a very personal interest in the affairs of mankind; a belief in the existence and power of a number of nature spirits and spirits of ancestors who had to be served and placated with sacrifices; and a belief in the divine sanction of the political order and the grave responsibility of the ruler to fulfill his moral duties to Heaven and to his subjects. The more purely religious belief in the existence and power of intervention of the spirits is probably older, and as time passes comes to have less importance in Chinese life, though reverence for the spirits of ancestors continues to be a vital factor in the Chinese family system. But the concept of the moral responsibilities of the ruler, and the way in which the ruler should discharge these responsibilities so as not to lose the favor and protection of Heaven, became a major concern of thinkers and one of the key problems of Chinese philosophy. Indeed so important did this problem appear to Confucius and his followers that they were led to reinterpret the whole body of ancient literature—the texts of divination, the speeches and pronouncements, the folk songs, the rules of ritual and etiquette, the chronicles of the feudal states—in search of an answer.[1] It is due largely to them that these ancient texts have been preserved and that the ancient concepts and terms, altered though they were by later interpretations, have continued to remain alive and vital in Chinese thought and life.

Book of History

THE CANON OF YAO AND THE CANON OF SHUN

These documents purport to relate the events and pronouncements of the sage-kings Yao and Shun who reigned around the 22d century B.C. Although there is little possibility they represent any such antiquity, they have been accepted by most Chinese until recent times as accurate accounts of these earliest times. Furthermore the virtue, wisdom, and humility which characterized these ancient rulers and their administration, and particularly their practice in selecting a successor of passing over their own sons in favor of more worthy men from among the people, have been held up as ideals for the guidance of later ages.

[From *Shu ching,* Yao tien and Shun tien]

Examining into antiquity, we find that the Emperor Yao was called Fang-hsün. He was reverent, intelligent, accomplished, sincere, and mild. He was sincerely respectful and capable of modesty. His light covered the four extremities of the empire and extended to Heaven above and the earth below. He was able to make bright his great virtue, and bring affection to the nine branches of the family. When the nine branches of the family had become harmonious, he distinguished and honored the hundred clans. When the hundred clans had become illustrious, he harmonized the myriad states. The numerous people were amply nourished and prosperous and became harmonious. Then he charged Hsi and Ho with reverence to follow august Heaven and calculate and delineate the sun, the moon, and the other heavenly bodies, and respect-

---

[1] The term feudal can be applied to Chou-dynasty China only on the understanding that no exact correspondence to Western feudalism is implied. It serves here, and hereafter in these pages, to differentiate, as traditional Chinese historians did, between the Chou and the relatively more centralized and bureaucratic regimes of the imperial dynasties beginning with the Ch'in (221–207 B.C.). However, some of the basic features associated with these later regimes had already made their appearance in Chou society, and distinguish it markedly from the institutional pattern of feudal Europe.

fully to give the people the seasons. . . . The emperor said: "Ah, you Hsi and Ho, the year has three hundred and sixty-six days, and by means of an intercalary month you must fix the four seasons and complete the year. If you earnestly regulate all the functionaries, the achievements will all be glorious." The emperor said: "Who will carefully attend to this? I will raise him up and employ him." Fang Ch'i said: "Your heir-son Chu is enlightened." The emperor said: "Alas, he is deceitful and quarrelsome; will he do?" . . . The emperor said: "Oh, you Chief of the Four Mountains, I have been on the throne for seventy years. If you can carry out the mandate, I shall resign my position to you." The Chief of the Four Mountains said: "I have not the virtue. I would only disgrace the high position." The emperor said: "Promote someone who is already illustrious, or raise up someone who is humble and mean." They all said to the emperor: "There is an unmarried man in a low position called Shun of Yü." The emperor said: "Yes, I have heard of him. What is he like?" The Chief said: "He is the son of a blind man. His father is stupid, his mother is deceitful, his half brother Hsiang is arrogant. Yet he has been able to live in harmony with them and to be splendidly filial. He has controlled himself and has not come to wickedness." The emperor said: "I will try him; I will wive him and observe his behavior towards my two daughters." He gave orders and sent down his two daughters to the bend of the Kuei River to be wives in the House of Yü. The emperor said: "Be reverent!"

. . . .

The emperor said: "Come, you Shun, in the affairs on which you have been consulted, I have examined your words; your words have been accomplished and capable of yielding fine results for three years; do you ascend to the imperial throne." Shun considered himself inferior in virtue and was not pleased. But in the first month, the first day, he accepted the abdication of Yao in the Temple of the Accomplished Ancestor. . . . Then he made *lei* sacrifice to the Lord-on-High; he made *yin* sacrifice to the six venerable ones; he made *wang* sacrifice to mountains and rivers, and he made comprehensive sacrifices to all the spirits. . . . In the second month of the year he went around the east to the fiefs, and came to the Venerable Tai Mountain where he made burnt offering; he made *wang* sacrifice successively to mountains and rivers and he gave audience to the eastern princes. He put into accord the seasons, the months, and the proper days. He made uniform the pitchpipes, the measures of length, the measures of capacity, and the weights. . . . He delimited the twelve provinces and raised altars on twelve mountains and he deepened the rivers.

THE ANNOUNCEMENT TO THE DUKE OF SHAO

The preface to this document attributed to Confucius states: "King Ch'eng, being in Feng and wishing to fix his residence at Lo, sent the Duke of Shao ahead to survey the locality. Thus was made the Announcement to the Duke of Shao." King Ch'eng, at this time still very young, was the third king of the Chou dynasty and the second to actually reign. The Duke of Shao and the Duke of Chou were his chief advisors. It was at this time that the capital of the Chou state was first fixed at the city of Lo.

[From *Shu ching*, Shao kao]

In the second month, third quarter, sixth day *i-wei*,[2] the king in the morning proceeded from Chou and arrived in Feng. The Grand Guardian, the Duke of Shao, preceded the Duke of Chou to inspect the site. In the third month, the day *mou-shen*, the third day after the first appearance of the new moon on *ping-wu*, the Grand Guardian arrived in the morning at Lo and consulted the tortoise oracle about the site. When he had obtained the oracle he planned and laid out the city. On the third day *keng-hsü*, the Grand Guardian with all the Yin people started work on the emplacements at the bend of the Lo River, and on the fifth day *chia-yin* the emplacements were determined. The next day *i-mao*, the Duke of Chou arrived in the morning at Lo and thoroughly inspected the plans for the new city. On the third day *ting-ssu*, he sacrificed two oxen as victims on the suburban altar, and on the next day *mou-wu* he sacrificed to the God of the Soil in the new city one ox, one sheep, and one pig. On the seventh day *chia-tzu* the Duke of Chou by written documents gave charges to all the rulers of the states of the Hou, Tien, and Nan zones in the Yin realm. When orders had been given to the Yin multitude they arose with vigor to do their work. The Grand Guardian then together with all the ruling princes of the states went out and took gifts and entered again and gave them to the Duke of Chou. The Duke of Chou said: "I salute and bow down my head and I extol the king and your Grace. I make an announcement to all Yin and managers of affairs. Oh, august

[2] Designation in the sixty-day cycle. See Chapter IX.

Heaven, the Lord-on-High, has changed his principal son [i.e., the ruler] and this great state Yin's mandate. Now that the king has received the mandate, unbounded is the grace, but also unbounded is the solicitude. Oh, how can he be but careful! Heaven has removed and made an end to the great state Yin's mandate. There are many former wise kings of Yin in Heaven, and the later kings and people here managed their mandate. But in the end [under the last king] wise and good men lived in misery so that, leading their wives and carrying their children, wailing and calling to Heaven, they went to where no one could come and seize them. Oh, Heaven had pity on the people of the four quarters, and looking with affection and giving its mandate, it employed the zealous ones [i.e., the leaders of the Chou]. May the king now urgently pay careful attention to his virtue. Look at the ancient predecessors, the lords of Hsia; Heaven indulged them and cherished and protected them. They strove to comprehend the obedience to Heaven, but in those times they have lost their mandate. Now a young son is the successor; may he not neglect the aged elders. Then he will comprehend our ancient men's virtue, nay still more it will occur that he is able to comprehend and endeavor to follow Heaven. . . . May the king come and take over the work of the Lord-on-High, and himself manage the government in the center of the land. I, Tan, say: having made the great city, he shall from here be a counterpart to august Heaven. He shall carefully sacrifice to the upper and lower spirits, and from here centrally govern. . . . We should not fail to mirror ourselves in the lords of Hsia; we likewise should not fail to mirror ourselves in the lords of Yin. We do not presume to know and say that the lords of Hsia undertook Heaven's mandate so as to have it for so-and-so many years; we do not presume to know and say that it could not have been prolonged. It was that they did not reverently attend to their virtue, and so they prematurely renounced their mandate. We do not presume to know and say that the lords of Yin received Heaven's mandate for so-and-so many years; we do not know and say that it could not have been prolonged. It was that they did not reverently attend to their virtue and so they prematurely threw away their mandate. Now the king has succeeded to and received their mandate. We should then also remember the mandates of these two states and in succeeding to them equal their merits. . . . Being king, his position will be that of a leader in virtue; the small people will then imitate him in all the world. . . . May those above and below [i.e., the king and his servants] labor and be anxiously careful; may they say: we have received Heaven's mandate, may it grandly equal the span of years of the lords of Hsia and not miss the span of years of the lords of Yin."

Book of Odes

THE GREATER ODES AND SACRIFICIAL ODES OF CHOU
[From *Shih ching*, Ta ya, Wen wang; Chou sung, Feng nien]

King Wen

1

King Wen is on high;
Oh, he shines in Heaven!
Chou is an old people,
But its charge is new.
The leaders of Chou became illustrious;
Was not God's charge timely given?
King Wen ascends and descends
On the left and right of God.

. . . .

4

August was King Wen,
Continuously bright and reverent.
Great, indeed, was the appointment of Heaven.
There were Shang's grandsons and sons,
Shang's grandsons and sons;
Was their number not a hundred thousand?
But the Lord-on-High gave his command
And they bowed down to Chou.

. . . .

7

The charge is not easy to keep;
May it not end in your persons.
Display and make bright your good fame.
And consider what Yin had received from Heaven.
The doings of high Heaven

Have no sound, no smell.
Make King Wen your pattern
And all the states will trust in you.

Rich Year

Rich is the year with much millet and rice;
And we have tall granaries
With hundreds and thousands and millions of sheaves.
We make wine and sweet spirits
And offer them to our ancestors, male and female;
Thus to fulfill all the rites
And bring down blessings in full.

AIRS FROM THE STATES

The "Airs" are folk songs from the various feudal states of early Chou times
telling of the joys and sorrows of the common people in their daily lives. Some
of them are love songs, while others lament the hardships of war or complain against the ills of government. Of the two selections given here, "Big
Rat" is clearly such a complaint against high taxes and corrupt officials. The
other is probably a song of love, but it is worth noting that from very early
times it has been given a strictly political interpretation by the Confucian
school. Thus the Confucianists turned even the old folk songs into lessons
on political morality.

[From *Shih ching,* Wei feng, Shih shu]

Big Rat

The farmers of Wei complain of the tax officials.

I

Big rat, big rat,
Do not eat my millet!
Three years I have served you,
But you will not care for me.
I am going to leave you
And go to that happy land;
Happy land, happy land,
Where I will find my place.

. . . .

3

Big rat, big rat,
Do not eat my sprouts!
Three years I have served you
But you give me no comfort.
I am going to leave you
And go to those happy fields;
Happy fields, happy fields;
Who there shall long moan?

The North Wind

This is probably a love song, but it has traditionally been interpreted as the song of the peasants of Pei who, oppressed by a cruel and corrupt government (the cold wind of the song), urge each other to flee to another state.
[From *Shih ching*, Pei-feng, Pei-feng]

1

Cold is the north wind;
The snow falls thick.
If you are kind and love me
Take my hand and we will go together.
You are modest, you are slow,
But oh, we must hurry!

2

Fierce is the north wind;
The snow falls fast.
If you are kind and love me
Take my hand and we will home together.
You are modest, you are slow,
But oh, we must hurry!

3

Nothing so red as the fox,
Nothing black as the crow [omens of evil];
If you are kind and love me,
Take my hand and we will go in the same carriage.
You are modest, you are slow,
But oh, we must hurry.

CHAPTER II

CONFUCIUS

If we were to characterize in one word the Chinese way of life for the last two thousand years, the word would be "Confucian." No other individual in Chinese history has so deeply influenced the life and thought of his people, as a transmitter, teacher, and creative interpreter of the ancient culture and literature, and as a molder of the Chinese mind and character. The other ancient philosophies, the religious systems of Taoism and Buddhism, all have known their days of glory and neglect; but the doctrines of Confucianism, since their general recognition in the first century before Christ, have never ceased to exert a vital influence on the nation down to our own century. Many Chinese have professed themselves to be Taoists, Buddhists, even Christians, but seldom have they ceased at the same time to be Confucianists. For Confucianism since the time of its general acceptance has been more than a creed to be professed or rejected; it has become an inseparable part of the society and thought of the nation as a whole, of what it means to be a Chinese, as the Confucian Classics are not the canon of a particular sect but the literary heritage of a whole people.

Considering his tremendous influence and importance, the life of Confucius is peculiarly human and undramatic. He was born in 551 B.C. in the small feudal state of Lu in modern Shantung province. His family name was K'ung, his personal name Ch'iu. "Confucius" is the Latinized form of "K'ung Fu-tzu" or "Master K'ung," the title commonly used in referring to him in Chinese. It is probable that his ancestors were members of the lesser aristocracy who had, however, sunk to a position of poverty and insignificance by the time of his birth. His father died when he was very young, leaving him to struggle alone with the problem of securing an education and making his way in the world.

The world he faced was not a bright one. China was divided into a number of small feudal states which were constantly bickering or making war upon each other or upon the barbarian tribes that pressed the Chinese people on all sides. The kings of the central court of the Chou dynasty, who had once given peace and stability to the nation, were weak and ineffective before the might of the more powerful feudal lords. Kings were ordered about by their vassals, rulers deposed or assassinated by their ministers, fathers slain by their sons. All was violence and disorder among the ruling class and there seemed to be no higher power, temporal or spiritual, to which men might appeal.

With energy and utter selflessness, Confucius set about to bring order and peace to his age. He believed that his place was in the world of politics and with almost pathetic persistence he sought through the states of China for a ruler who would be willing to employ him and his ideas in the government. He managed to find employment for a while in his native state of Lu and, according to tradition, rose to a fairly high position. But his success was short-lived; on the whole his political career was a failure, and more and more he turned his attention to the teaching of young men who, he hoped, might succeed in public life where he had failed. Judging from all accounts he was a teacher of rare enthusiasm and art; he was said to have had some three thousand students, of whom seventy-two were close personal disciples or known for their virtue. In his old age he retired to devote himself, so tradition says, to the editing of the texts of the Confucian Classics. He died in 479 B.C.

What was the solution which Confucius offered for the ills and evil of his day? It was the same solution which the philosophers and prophets of so many ages and cultures have offered: a return to virtue. Unless men individually embraced the ideal of *jen*—humanity, benevolence, or perfect virtue—there was no hope that society could be spared the evil, cruelty, and violence that was destroying it.

If there is nothing unique or arresting about this solution urged by Confucius, the reasons he used to persuade men of its aptness deserve close attention. First of all, he held out no utilitarian persuasions to attract men to the practice of perfect virtue. He knew too well from his own experience that virtue is often despised and persecuted, and he cautioned his disciples that they must be prepared to face frequent poverty and distress. The pursuit of material profit did not coincide, but more often directly conflicted with the dictates of virtue; it was the concern only of the small and unenlightened mind. The gentleman, mindless of comfort and safety, must fix his attention upon higher things.

Again, he was very sparing in the invocation of divine or supernatural sanction for his teachings. Confucius seems to have been a man of deep personal piety and reverence. But he lived in an age that was still dominated by a primitive fear of the supernatural and marred by gross and cruel superstitions. The rulers of his time firmly believed in the prophetic nature of dreams, the efficacy of the arts of divination, the baleful power of the spirits of the dead, and all manner of weird and unnatural portents and prodigies. Men still cowered before the eclipse and the age when human sacrifices were carried out on the death of a ruler was less than a century past. In such an atmosphere, Confucius chose to direct attention away from the supernatural and toward the vital problems of human society and the ordering of the state. Viewing as much of the history of this period through the pages of the literature of the Confucian school itself, it is difficult to realize how very rare this humanism and rationalism of Confucius and his disciples must have been in their own time.

Confucius had a strong belief in a natural order that was also a moral order. Heaven for him was a guiding Providence, and one's fulfillment as a man came from acting in accordance with the will of Heaven. This will, however, could be best understood through the study of history. In the traditions, customs, and literature of the past, in the collective experience of mankind, there was objective confirmation of the moral law written in the heart of man. From the ancient legends Confucius selected the figures of the sage-kings Yao and Shun, King T'ang, the wise founder of the Shang dynasty, and above all the great ancestors of the ruling house of the Chou, Kings Wen and Wu and the Duke of Chou, to be his ideals. These men had embodied the humanity and perfect virtue that he advocated, and their deeds and their reigns represented all that was wise and good in Chinese history and society. In particular Confucius looked back to an age of peace and order at the beginning of the Chou when its founding fathers, in the depth of their wisdom and virtue, had set up the institutions and organized the complex feudal hierarchy of the new dynasty, and created solemn rites and music for its leaders and people. These rites and music-dance compositions of the old feudal society, the *li* and *yüeh* which figure so prominently in Confucian literature, were regarded

by Confucius with the utmost gravity. For they were the outward embodiment of the wisdom and virtue of their creators, the expression of
reverence and perfect hierarchical order in society. And by the careful observance of these rites, the thoughtful contemplation of this music and its
meaning, one could recreate in oneself the wisdom and virtue of the
ancients and discipline oneself to the perfect order which they had intended. All the ills of his day Confucius attributed to the fact that the
leaders of society had neglected the old rites, were performing them incorrectly, or usurping rites and ceremonies to which they were not entitled. For as a correct observance of the rites was a sign of perfect social
order and the source of all spiritual enlightenment, so their neglect and
abuse must be no more than the reflection of a deeper moral chaos and
the beginning of spiritual darkness. To abuse the forms of the rites was
to abuse the reality, the moral order which they represented. It was this
abuse of the rites and titles of the social order, and the inner spiritual disorder which it represented, that Confucius deplored. Hence his call for a
"rectification of names," that men might be in reality what they claimed to
be in title, and his insistence upon a careful and reverent attention to the
spirit and letter of the rites.

This emphasis upon ritual—an insistence upon it sometimes even when
its original meaning was lost—must strike us as excessively conservative
and formalistic, as indeed Confucianism in its later days often became.
Yet implicit in this view was an idealization of the past that set a high
standard for the present, and provided more of an impetus to reform,
than to maintain, the status quo. Confucius' own life is sufficient evidence
of his reformist spirit. He sought to conserve or restore what was good,
while changing what was bad. Thus more fundamental to him than either
conservatism or reformism in itself was a clear sense of moral values, expressed in his warm humanity, optimism, humility, and good sense. Confucius lived in a feudal society and conceived of society in terms of the
feudal hierarchy. The common people were to be led, cared for, cherished,
even taught, by the rulers; but their position at the base of the social
hierarchy should not be modified, indeed, could not be without upsetting
the whole vertical order.

Confucius' teachings were for the *chün-tzu,* the gentleman, the potential or actual ruler of society who alone possessed the vision to see beyond personal profit and material interest to the broader interests of the state and mankind. Yet he insisted that it was not mere birth or social position, but precisely this power of vision, this keener and more profound moral sense, which distinguished the gentleman, the true ruler. Like Plato he would have the kings be sages, for only a truly wise and virtuous ruler could fittingly head the hierarchy of society and lead all men, by the example and suasion of his own goodness, to perfect order and a practice of similar virtue. Because of this belief in the importance of character over birth, he gave himself to the teaching of promising young men regardless of their origins. He and his school are responsible for the pedagogic tradition which characterizes all of later Chinese history, for the optimistic belief in the perfectibility of man through learning, and for the reverence for the scholar and the man of letters so pronounced in Chinese society. And it is to a large extent the teachings and example of Confucius and his school which have convinced so many of the great men of later Chinese history that the highest career in life is that of the statesman, that the highest concern of the gentleman-scholar is politics and the proper ordering of the state.

Confucius and his teachings were little respected and less practiced by the men of his day, and for centuries the Confucian school remained only one among many rival schools of philosophy with its greatest strength in the area of Confucius' native state of Lu. But gradually Confucius' humanism began to triumph over the superstition and mysticism of other doctrines, his idealistic emphasis on virtue, kindness, and learning to attract more men than the harsh and cynical philosophies of other states. At last, in the second century B.C., Confucianism was declared the official creed of the nation and the Classics became the principal, if not the sole, study of all scholars and statesmen. Through the centuries the teachings of Confucius continued not only to be revered in China, but also to exert a tremendous influence in Korea, Japan and Annam. Confucius was given the title "Supreme Sage and Foremost Teacher" and his tomb and temple in Ch'ü-fu in Shantung became a kind of Mecca for all educated Chinese, while a Confucian temple on less elaborate scale was established in every county seat throughout the land. Under the Nationalist regime his birthday was (and still is on Taiwan) observed as Teachers' Day, a national holiday.

There is a large body of literature in Chinese, of varying degrees of reliability, on the life and teachings of Confucius. Among this the most important work is the record of the Master's activities and conversations compiled probably by his disciples' disciples, the *Analects*. This work is in twenty chapters and 497 verses, some consisting of the briefest aphorisms. From the time when Confucianism became widely accepted, the laconic and provocative sentences of this work, difficult though they often are to interpret, have exercised a profound influence upon the thought and language of the peoples of East Asia, while for the last eight hundred years it has been a basic text in Chinese education known to every schoolboy. We have selected and translated the more important passages and arranged them under a few significant topics.

Selections from the Analects

CONFUCIUS THE MAN

Personality and Character

1. In his leisure hours, Confucius was easy in his manner and cheerful in his expression. [VII:4]

2. Confucius was gentle yet firm, dignified but not harsh, respectful yet well at ease. [VII:37]

3. Confucius fished but not with a net; he shot but not at a roosting bird. [He did not take unfair advantage of inferior creatures.] [VII:26]

4. When the stables were burned down, on returning from court, Confucius asked: "Was anyone hurt?" He did not ask about the horses. [X:12]

5. When Confucius was pleased with the singing of someone he was with, he would always ask to have the song repeated and would join in himself. [VII:31]

6. The Duke of She asked Tzu Lu about Confucius, and Tzu Lu gave him no answer. Confucius said: "Why didn't you tell him that I am a person who forgets to eat when he is enthusiastic about something, forgets all his worries in his enjoyment of it, and is not aware that old age is coming on?" [VII:18]

7. Confucius said: "Having only coarse food to eat, plain water to drink, and a bent arm for a pillow, one can still find happiness therein. Riches and honor acquired by unrighteous means are to me as drifting clouds." [VII:15]

8. Once when Tzu Lu, Tseng Hsi, Jan Yu, and Kung-hsi Hua were

seated in attendance upon him, Confucius said: "You no doubt consider me a day or so your senior, but let us not mind that. When out of office you say among yourselves that your merits are not recognized. Now suppose some prince were to recognize your merits, what would be your wishes?" Tzu Lu without hesitation replied: "Take a kingdom of a thousand chariots, hemmed in by great powers, oppressed by invading troops, and suffering from famine in addition—I should like to take charge of it. In three years' time I could make it brave and make it understand the right course to pursue." Confucius smiled at him. "And how about you, Ch'iu [Jan Yu]?" "Take a district of sixty or seventy li[1] square," answered Jan Yu, "or say, one of fifty or sixty li square. I should like to take charge of it. In three years' time I could make its people live in abundance; but as for the promotion of rites (li) and music, I should have to leave that to a real gentleman." "And how about you, Ch'ih [Kung-hsi Hua]? Not that I say I could do it," he answered, "but I should like to be trained for it. At the ceremonies in the Ancestral Temple [of the Imperial House] or at the conferences of the princes, I should like to wear the ceremonial cap and gown, and be a minor official assisting in the ceremony." "And how about you, Tien [Tseng Hsi]?" Tseng Hsi paused in his playing of the zither. Putting it aside he rose and replied: "I am afraid my wishes are entirely different from those cherished by these three gentlemen." "What harm is there in that?" said Confucius. "We are just trying to let each express his desire." Then he said: "In the latter days of spring, when the light spring garments are made, I would like to take along five or six grown-ups and six or seven youths to bathe in the River Yi, and after the bath go to enjoy the breeze in the woods among the altars of Wu-yi, and then return home, loitering and singing on our way." Confucius heaved a deep sigh and said: "You are the man after my own heart." [XI:25]

His Sense of Mission

9. Confucius said: "Were any prince to employ me, even in a single year a good deal could be done, and in three years everything could be accomplished." [XIII:10]

10. Confucius said: "Ah! There is no one who knows me!" Tzu Kung asked: "Why do you say, sir, that no one knows you?" Confucius said: "I

[1] A li is equal to about one-third of an English mile.

make no complaint against Heaven, nor do I lay the blame on men.
Though my studies are lowly, they penetrate the sublime on high. Perhaps after all I am known—by Heaven." [XIV:37]

11. When Confucius was in jeopardy in K'uang, he said: "Since the
death of King Wen [founder of the Chou dynasty], does not the mission
of culture rest here with us? If Heaven were going to destroy this culture,
a mortal like me would not have been given such a place in it. And if
Heaven is not going to destroy this culture, what can the men of K'uang
do to me?" [IX:5]

12. When [Confucius' most worthy disciple] Yen Hui died, Confucius exclaimed: "Alas, Heaven has destroyed me! Heaven has destroyed me!" [XI:8]

13. Ch'ang-chü and Chieh-ni were cultivating their fields together.
Confucius was passing that way and told Tzu Lu to go and ask them
where the river could be forded. Ch'ang-chü said: "Who is that holding
the reins in the carriage?" Tzu Lu said: "It is K'ung Ch'iu [Confucius]."
He said: "You mean K'ung Ch'iu of the state of Lu?" "Yes," Tzu Lu
replied. Ch'ang-chü said: "If it is he, then he already knows where the
ford is." Tzu Lu then turned to Chieh-ni. Chieh-ni asked: "Who are you,
sir?" Tzu Lu said: "Chung-yu is my name." Chieh-ni said: "You are a
follower of K'ung Ch'iu of Lu, are you not?" He said: "That is so."
Chieh-ni said: "The whole world is swept as by a torrential flood, and who
can change it? As for you, instead of following one who flees from this
man and that, you would do better to follow one who flees the whole
world." And with that he went on covering the seed without stopping.
Tzu Lu went and told Confucius, who said ruefully: "One cannot herd
together with birds and beasts. If I am not to be a man among other men,
then what am I to be? If the Way (*Tao*) prevailed in the world, I should
not be trying to alter things." [XVIII:6]

His Love of Learning

16. Confucius said: "At fifteen, I set my heart on learning. At thirty, I
was firmly established. At forty, I had no more doubts. At fifty, I knew
the will of Heaven. At sixty, I was ready to listen to it. At seventy, I
could follow my heart's desire without transgressing what was right."
[II:4]

18. When Confucius was in Ch'i, he heard the Shao music[2] and for three months he forgot the taste of meat, saying: "I never thought music could be so beautiful." [VII:13]

14. Confucius said: "When walking in a party of three, I always have teachers. I can select the good qualities of the one for imitation, and the bad ones of the other and correct them in myself." [VII:21]

17. Confucius said: "I am a transmitter and not a creator. I believe in and have a passion for the ancients. I venture to compare myself with our old P'eng [China's Methuselah]." [VII:1]

15. Confucius said: "Sometimes I have gone a whole day without food and a whole night without sleep, giving myself to thought. It was no use. It is better to learn." [XV:30]

19. There were four things that Confucius was determined to eradicate: a biased mind, arbitrary judgments, obstinacy, and egotism. [IX:4]

20. Confucius said: "Those who know the truth are not up to those who love it; those who love the truth are not up to those who delight in it." [VI:18]

21. Confucius said: "Having heard the Way (*Tao*) in the morning, one may die content in the evening." [IV:8]

Confucius as a Teacher

23. Confucius said: "By nature men are pretty much alike; it is learning and practice that set them apart."[3] [XVII:2]

22. Confucius said: "In education there are no class distinctions."[4] [XV:38]

24. Confucius said: "The young are to be respected. How do we know that the next generation will not measure up to the present one? But if a man has reached forty or fifty and nothing has been heard of him, then I grant that he is not worthy of respect." [IX:22]

25. Confucius said: "When it comes to acquiring perfect virtue (*jen*), a man should not defer even to his own teacher." [XV:35]

[2] Classical music of the time of the ancient sage-king Shun (2255–2208 B.C.?).

[3] This simple observation by Confucius was agreed upon as the essential truth with regard to human nature and racial difference by a group of international experts in the UNESCO "Statement on Race" published in July, 1950.

[4] These four Chinese characters are often found written over the gates or on the auditorium walls of Chinese school buildings.

26. Confucius said: "Those who are born wise are the highest type of people; those who become wise through learning come next; those who learn by overcoming dullness come after that. Those who are dull but still won't learn are the lowest type of people." [XVI:9]

27. Confucius said: "I won't teach a man who is not anxious to learn, and will not explain to one who is not trying to make things clear to himself. If I hold up one corner of a square and a man cannot come back to me with the other three, I won't bother to go over the point again." [VII:8]

28. Confucius said: "Learning without thinking is labor lost; thinking without learning is perilous." [II:15]

29. Confucius said: "Yu, shall I teach you what knowledge is? When you know a thing, say that you know it; when you do not know a thing, admit that you do not know it. That is knowledge." [II:17]

30. Confucius said: "Worthy indeed was Hui! A single bamboo bowl of millet to eat, a gourdful of water to drink, living in a back alley—others would have found it unendurably depressing, but Hui's cheerfulness was not affected at all. Worthy indeed was Hui!" [VI:9]

31. When Yen Hui died Confucius bewailed him with exceeding grief. His followers thereupon said to him: "Sir! You are carrying your grief to excess." Confucius said: "Have I gone to excess? But if I may not grieve exceedingly over this man, for whom shall I grieve?" [XI:9]

32. Confucius said: "A young man's duty is to be filial to his parents at home and respectful to his elders abroad, to be circumspect and truthful, and, while overflowing with love for all men, to associate himself with humanity (*jen*). If, when all that is done, he has any energy to spare, then let him study the polite arts." [I:6]

33. These were the subjects on which Confucius often discoursed: poetry, history, and the performance of ceremonies—all these were what he often discoursed on. [VII:17]

34. Confucius said: "Personal cultivation begins with poetry, is made firm by rules of decorum (*li*), and is perfected by music." [VIII:8]

35. Confucius took four subjects for his teaching—literature, conduct, loyalty, and truthfulness. [VII:24]

36. Yen Hui heaved a sigh and said: "You look up to it and it seems so high. You try to drill through it and it seems so hard. You seem to see it

in front of you, and all of a sudden it appears behind you. The Master is very good at gently leading a man along and teaching him. He has broadened me with culture, restrained me with ritual (*li*). I just could not stop myself. But after I have exhausted every resource, there still remains something standing distinct and apart from me. Do what I can to reach his position, I cannot find the way." [IX:10]

37. Shu-sun Wu-shu said to the officials at court: "Tzu Kung is a better man than Confucius." Tzu-fu Ching-po told this to Tzu Kung, and Tzu Kung said: "It is like the matter of house walls. My house wall comes up only to the shoulder, and the people outside are therefore able to see my handsome dwelling, whereas the wall of Confucius rises fathoms high, and unless one is let in by the gate, one does not see the palatial beauty of the ancestral temple and the grandeur of the hundred ministrants inside. But few are they who have found the gate. What Shu-sun says is therefore perfectly easy to understand. [XIX:23]

THE TEACHINGS OF CONFUCIUS

The Unitary Principle: Reciprocity or Humanity

38. Confucius said: "Tz'u, do you suppose that I merely learned a great deal and tried to remember it all?" The disciple replied: "Yes, is it not so?" Confucius said: "No, I have one principle that runs through it all." [XV:2]

39. Confucius said: "Shen! My teaching contains one principle that runs through it all." "Yes," replied Tseng Tzu. When Confucius had left the room the disciples asked: "What did he mean?" Tseng Tzu replied: "Our Master's teaching is simply this: loyalty and reciprocity." [IV:15]

40. Tzu Kung asked: "Is there any one word that can serve as a principle for the conduct of life?" Confucius said: "Perhaps the word 'reciprocity': Do not do to others what you would not want others to do to you." [XV:23]

41. Confucius said: "Perfect indeed is the virtue which is according to the Mean. For long people have seldom had the capacity for it." [VI:27]

42. Confucius said: "It is man that can make the Way great, not the Way that can make man great." [XV:28]

43. Chung-kung asked about humanity. Confucius said: "Behave when away from home as though you were in the presence of an important

guest. Deal with the common people as though you were officiating at an important sacrifice. Do not do to others what you would not want others to do to you. Then there will be no dissatisfaction either in the state or at home." [XII:2]

44. Confucius said: . . . "The humane man, desiring to be established himself, seeks to establish others; desiring himself to succeed, he helps others to succeed. To judge others by what one knows of oneself is the method of achieving humanity." [VI:28]

Humanity (jen)

As the reader will already have judged from its frequent occurrence, *jen* is a key term in Confucius' thought. Sometimes rendered "goodness," "benevolence," or "love," it is the supreme excellence in man or perfect virtue. In later Confucian thought the concept was expanded greatly to suggest a cosmic power. To retain its basically and unmistakably humanistic sense, we have used "humanity" for *jen,* or, when some alternative rendering was clearly called for by the context, have added the romanized original in parentheses (*jen*). By observing the various uses of the same term in different texts, the reader should acquire a sense of both its centrality in Chinse thought and its breadth of meaning.

45. Fan Ch'ih asked about humanity. Confucius said: "Love men." [XII:22]

46. Tzu Chang asked Confucius about humanity. Confucius said: "To be able to practice five virtues everywhere in the world constitutes humanity." Tzu Chang begged to know what these were. Confucius said: "Courtesy, magnanimity, good faith, diligence, and kindness. He who is courteous is not humiliated, he who is magnanimous wins the multitude, he who is of good faith is trusted by the people, he who is diligent attains his objective, and he who is kind can get service from the people." [XVII:6]

47. Confucius said: "Without humanity a man cannot long endure adversity, nor can he long enjoy prosperity. The humane rest in humanity; the wise find it beneficial." [IV:2]

48. Confucius said: "Only the humane man can love men and can hate men." [IV:3]

49. Someone inquired: "What do you think of 'requiting injury with kindness'?" Confucius said: "How will you then requite kindness? Re-

quite injury with justice, and kindness with kindness." [XIV:36]

50. Confucius said: "Is humanity something remote? If I want to be humane, behold, humanity has arrived." [VII:29]

51. Confucius said: . . . "Is there anyone who exerts himself even for a single day to achieve humanity? I have not seen any who had not the strength to achieve it." [IV:6]

52. Confucius said: "As to Hui, for three months his mind did not deviate from humanity. The others can do so, some for a day, some even for a month, but that is all." [VI:5]

53. Confucius said: "Riches and honor are what every man desires, but if they can be obtained only by transgressing the right way, they must not be held. Poverty and lowliness are what every man detests, but if they can be avoided only by transgressing the right way, they must not be evaded. If a gentleman departs from humanity, how can he bear the name? Not even for the lapse of a single meal does a gentleman ignore humanity. In moments of haste he cleaves to it: in seasons of peril he cleaves to it." [IV:5]

54. Confucius said: "The resolute scholar and the humane person will under no circumstance seek life at the expense of humanity. On occasion they will sacrifice their lives to preserve their humanity." [XV:8]

55. Ssu-ma Niu, worrying, said: "All people have brothers, but I alone have none." Tzu Hsia said: "I have heard it said [by Confucius] that death and life rest with Heaven's mandate and that wealth and honor depend on Heaven. Let the gentleman be reverent and make no mistake in conduct, and let him be respectful to others and observant of propriety. Then all within the four seas are brothers." [XII:5]

Filial Piety

56. Tzu Yu asked about filial piety. Confucius said: "Nowadays a filial son is just a man who keeps his parents in food. But even dogs or horses are given food. If there is no feeling of reverence, wherein lies the difference?" [II:7]

57. Tzu Hsia asked about filial piety. Confucius said: "The manner is the really difficult thing. When anything has to be done the young people undertake it; when there is wine and food the elders are served —is this all there is to filial piety?" [II:8]

58. Confucius said: "In serving his parents, a son may gently remon-

strate with them. If he sees that they are not inclined to follow his suggestion, he should resume his reverential attitude but not abandon his purpose. If he is belabored, he will not complain." [IV:18]

59. The Duke of She observed to Confucius: "Among us there was an upright man called Kung who was so upright that when his father appropriated a sheep, he bore witness against him." Confucius said: "The upright men among us are not like that. A father will screen his son and a son his father—yet uprightness is to be found in that." [XIII:18]

60. Tsai Wo questioned the three years' mourning and thought one year was long enough: "If the gentlemen for three years abstain from the practice of ritual, ritual will decay; if for three years they make no music, music will go to ruin. In one year the old crops are exhausted and the new crops have come up, the friction-sticks have made the several seasonal fires—one year should be enough." Confucius said: "Would you then feel at ease in eating polished rice and wearing fineries?" "Quite at ease," was the reply. Confucius continued: "If you would really feel at ease, then do so. When a gentleman is in mourning, he does not relish good food if he eats it, does not enjoy music if he hears it, and does not feel at ease in a comfortable dwelling. Hence he abstains from these things. But now since you would feel at ease, then you can have them." When Tsai Wo had gone out, Confucius said: "What lack of humanity in Yü [Tsai Wo]! Only when a child is three years old does it leave its parents' arms. The three years' mourning is the universal observance in the world. And Yü—did he not enjoy the loving care of his parents for three years?" [XVII:21]

Rites and Music

For Confucius the term *li,* which basically means "rites," embraced all those traditional forms which provided an objective standard of conduct. Thus, while *li* may in given instances refer to "rites," "ceremonial," or "rules of conduct," it has the general meaning of "good form" or "decorum." Confucius insisted, however, that the observance of *li* should be neither perfunctory nor rigid and inflexible, but should be in keeping with circumstances and also with that spirit of reverence and respect for others which the ceremonies or rules of conduct were meant to embody. By showing their intrinsic significance, he attempted to reassert the value of these traditional forms at a time when they were increasingly neglected or performed as mere pretense. Where the external form is indicated by *li* we shall render it "rites"; where the inward spirit, "decorum."

61. Tzu Kung proposed to do away with the sacrificial lamb offering at the announcement of each new moon. Confucius said: "Tz'u! You love the lamb, but I love the rite." [III:17]

62. Confucius said: "Courtesy without decorum becomes tiresome. Cautiousness without decorum becomes timidity, daring becomes insubordination, frankness becomes effrontery." [VIII:2]

63. Confucius said: "Rites, rites! Does it mean no more than jades and silks? Music, music! Does it mean no more than bells and drums?" [XVII:11]

64. Confucius said: "A man who is not humane, what has he to do with rites? A man who is not humane, what has he to do with music?" [III.3]

65. Lin Fang asked about the fundamental principle of rites. Confucius replied: "You are asking an important question! In rites at large, it is always better to be too simple rather than too lavish. In funeral rites, it is more important to have the real sentiment of sorrow than minute attention to observances." [III:4]

66. Confucius said: "If a ruler can administer his state with decorum (*li*) and courtesy—then what difficulty will he have? If he cannot administer it with decorum and courtesy, what has he to do with rites (*li*)?" [IV:13]

Religious Sentiment

67. Tzu Lu asked about the worship of ghosts and spirits. Confucius said: "We don't know yet how to serve men, how can we know about serving the spirits?" "What about death," was the next question. Confucius said: "We don't know yet about life, how can we know about death?" [XI:11]

68. Fan Ch'ih asked about wisdom. Confucius said: "Devote yourself to the proper demands of the people, respect the ghosts and spirits but keep them at a distance—this may be called wisdom." [VI:20]

69. Po-niu was ill and Confucius went to inquire about him. Having grasped his hand through the window, Confucius said: "It is killing him.

It is the will of Heaven, alas! That such a man should have such a malady! That such a man should have such a malady!" [VI:8]

70. Though his food might be coarse rice and vegetable broth, Confucius invariably offered a little in sacrifice, and always with solemnity. [X:8]

71. When Confucius observed sacrificial fasting, his clothing was spotlessly clean, his food was different from the ordinary, and in his dwelling his seat was changed to another place. [X:7]

72. Confucius said: "He who sins against Heaven has none to whom he can pray." [III:13]

73. When Confucius was very ill, Tzu Lu asked that prayers be offered. Confucius asked: "Is there such a thing?" Tzu Lu replied: "Yes, there is. In one of the Eulogies it is said: 'A prayer has been offered for you to the spirits of Heaven and earth.'" Confucius said: "Ah, my praying has been for a long time." [VII:34]

74. Tzu Kung said: "The Master's views on culture and refinement we can comprehend. But his discourses about man's nature and the ways of Heaven none of us can comprehend." [V:12]

75. Confucius said: "I wish I did not have to speak at all." Tzu Kung said: "But if you did not speak, Sir, what should we disciples pass on to others?" Confucius said: "Look at Heaven there. Does it speak? The four seasons run their course and all things are produced. Does Heaven speak?" [XVII:19]

76. Confucius sacrificed [to the dead] as if they were present. He sacrificed to the spirits as if they were present. He said: "I consider my not being present at the sacrifice as if I did not sacrifice." [III:12]

77. The Master did not talk about weird things, physical exploits, disorders, and spirits. [VII:20]

The Gentleman

78. Confucius said: "When nature exceeds art you have the rustic. When art exceeds nature you have the clerk. It is only when art and nature are harmoniously blended that you have the gentleman." [VI:16]

79. Confucius said: . . . "If a gentleman departs from humanity, how can he bear the name? Not even for the lapse of a single meal does a gentleman ignore humanity. In moments of haste he cleaves to it; in seasons of peril he cleaves to it." [IV:5]

80. Confucius said: "The gentleman occupies himself with the Way and not with his livelihood. One may attend to farming, and yet may sometimes go hungry. One may attend to learning and yet may be rewarded with emolument. What the gentleman is anxious about is the Way and not poverty." [XV:31]

81. Ssu-ma Niu asked about the gentleman. Confucius said: "The gentleman has neither anxiety nor fear." Ssu-ma Niu rejoined: "Neither anxiety nor fear—is that what is meant by being a gentleman?" Confucius said: "When he looks into himself and finds no cause for self-reproach, what has he to be anxious about; what has he to fear?" [XII:4]

82. Confucius said: "The way of the gentleman is threefold. I myself have not been able to attain any of them. Being humane, he has no anxieties; being wise, he has no perplexities; being brave, he has no fear." Tzu Kung said: "But, Master, that is your own way." [XIV:30]

83. Confucius said: "You may be able to carry off from a whole army its commander-in-chief, but you cannot deprive the humblest individual of his will." [IX:25]

84. Tzu Kung asked about the gentleman. Confucius said: "The gentleman first practices what he preaches and then preaches what he practices." [II:13]

85. Confucius said: "The gentleman reaches upward; the inferior man reaches downward." [XIV:23]

86. Confucius said: "The gentleman is always calm and at ease; the inferior man is always worried and full of distress." [VII:36]

87. Confucius said: "The gentleman understands what is right; the inferior man understands what is profitable." [IV:16]

88. Confucius said: "The gentleman cherishes virtue; the inferior man cherishes possessions. The gentleman thinks of sanctions; the inferior man thinks of personal favors." [IV:11]

89. Confucius said: "The gentleman makes demands on himself; the inferior man makes demands on others." [XV:20]

90. Confucius said: "The gentleman seeks to enable people to succeed in what is good but does not help them in what is evil. The inferior man does the contrary." [XII:16]

91. Confucius said: "The gentleman is broad-minded and not partisan; the inferior man is partisan and not broad-minded." [II:14]

92. Confucius said: "There are three things that a gentleman fears:

he fears the will of Heaven, he fears great men, he fears the words of
the sages. The inferior man does not know the will of Heaven and does
not fear it, he treats great men with contempt, and he scoffs at the words
of the sages." [XVI:8]

93. Once when Confucius was in Ch'en, the supply of food was exhausted, and some of his followers became so weak that they could not
stand up. Tzu Lu came to the Master in disgust, saying: "Then even
a gentleman can be reduced to such straits?" Confucius said: "A gentleman may indeed be so reduced. But when an inferior man is in straits
he is apt to do anything." [XV:1]

Government by Personal Virtue

94. Chi K'ang Tzu asked Confucius about government. Confucius
said: "To govern (*cheng*) is to set things right (*cheng*).⁵ If you begin
by setting yourself right, who will dare to deviate from the right?"
[XII:17]

95. Confucius said: "If a ruler himself is upright, all will go well without orders. But if he himself is not upright, even though he gives orders
they will not be obeyed." [XIII:6]

96. Tzu Lu asked about the character of a gentleman [man of the
ruling class]. Confucius said: "He cultivates himself in reverential attention." Tzu Lu asked: "Is that all there is to it?" Confucius said: "He
cultivates himself so as to be able to bring comfort to other people."
Tzu Lu asked again: "Is that all?" Confucius said: "He cultivates himself so as to be able to bring comfort to the whole populace. He cultivates
himself so as to be able to bring comfort to the whole populace—even
[sage-kings] Yao and Shun were dissatisfied with themselves about this."
[XIV:45]

97. Confucius said: "Lead the people by laws and regulate them by
penalties, and the people will try to keep out of jail, but will have no
sense of shame. Lead the people by virtue and restrain them by the rules
of decorum, and the people will have a sense of shame, and moreover
will become good." [II:3]

98. Chi K'ang Tzu asked Confucius about government, saying: "Suppose I were to kill the lawless for the good of the law-abiding, how

---

⁵ This is more than just a pun. Confucius was trying to get at the root of the matter
by getting at the root of the word.

would that do?" Confucius answered: "Sir, why should it be necessary to employ capital punishment in your government? Just so you genuinely desire the good, the people will be good. The virtue of the gentleman may be compared to the wind and that of the commoner to the weeds. The weeds under the force of the wind cannot but bend." [XII:19]

99. The Duke of She asked about good government. Confucius said: "[A government is good when] those near are happy and those far off are attracted." [XIII:16]

100. When Confucius was traveling to Wei, Jan Yu drove him. Confucius observed: "What a dense population!" Jan Yu said: "The people having grown so numerous, what next should be done for them?" "Enrich them," was the reply. "And when one has enriched them, what next should be done?" Confucius said: "Educate them." [XIII:9]

101. Tzu Kung asked above government. Confucius said: "The essentials are sufficient food, sufficient troops, and the confidence of the people." Tzu Kung said: "Suppose you were forced to give up one of these three, which would you let go first?" Confucius said: "The troops." Tzu Kung asked again: "If you are forced to give up one of the two remaining, which would you let go?" Confucius said: "Food. For from of old, death has been the lot of all men, but a people without faith cannot survive." [XII:7]

102. Duke Ching of Ch'i asked Confucius about government. Confucius replied: "Let the prince be prince, the minister be minister, the father father and the son son." "Excellent!" said the duke. "Indeed if the prince is not prince, the minister not minister, the father not father, and the son not son, then with all the grain in my possession shall I ever get to eat any?" [6] [XII:11]

103. Confucius said: "To have done nothing (*wu-wei*) and yet have the state well-governed—[sage-king] Shun was the one! What did he do? He merely made himself reverent and correctly occupied his royal seat." [XV:4]

[6] For then the country will be ruined.

CHAPTER III

MO TZU: UNIVERSAL LOVE,
UTILITARIANISM, AND
UNIFORMITY

Among the "hundred philosophers" of ancient China, Mo Tzu had a place of special importance. When Mencius felt called upon to defend and revitalize Confucianism in his own time, he singled out the philosophy of Mo Tzu as being among its most dangerous rivals. Although Mo-ism did not hold this strong position for long, its founder and his teachings left an indelible impression on the Chinese mind. Today they serve as a reminder that the eventual supremacy of Confucian thought was not achieved simply by default or intellectual inertia, but was won in a difficult struggle with worthy opponents.

Mo Tzu (470–391 B.C.?), originally known as Mo Ti, was born a few years after Confucius' death and died a few years before Mencius' birth. His native state was probably Sung or Lu. The name Mo has been thought by some to denote a form of punishment, indicating that he came from a class of prisoners or slaves. In any case the text attributed to him often characterizes the Confucianists as pretentious aristocrats who stand very much on their own dignity and on ceremony, suggesting perhaps a degree of plebeian hostility on the part of Mo Tzu. He was, however, well educated in the Classics and may have once followed the Confucian school himself until he took up a position of strong opposition on certain fundamental points. Thus he condemned what he regarded as the skepticism of many Confucianists in regard to Heaven and spiritual beings, their tendency toward fatalism, and their preoccupation with ritual. These criticisms are indeed invaluable testimony as to the direction in which Confucius' thought was taken by his immediate followers.

Mo Tzu's most characteristic doctrine comes very close to asserting that "all men are equal before God." Believing in Heaven as an active power manifesting love for all men, he urged that men follow Heaven in this by practicing universal love. But his standard of action is strictly utilitarian; love for all men is demonstrated by satisfying their immediate, material needs, and by abandoning all forms of activity and expense which do not contribute to the feeding, clothing, and housing of the people. For this reason Mo Tzu condemned all forms of ritual and music, extravagant entertainment, and, above all, offensive warfare. Moreover, to concentrate human energies on the achievement of social goals, Mo Tzu believed that unity of thought and action was necessary, with the people obeying their leaders and the leaders following the will of Heaven.

What we know of Mo Tzu's career shows him to be a rigorist who set the most exacting standards for himself and his followers. In trying to gain acceptance for his principles he drove himself tirelessly and unmercifully. Unlike the Confucianists, who offered advice only when treated respectfully by a ruler and assured of his honorable intentions, Mo Tzu was ready to preach his gospel to anyone who would listen. At times, upon hearing of the plans of a state to make war, he would hasten to dissuade the ruler from perpetrating such an outrage. On one of these peace missions, it is said, he walked ten days and ten nights, tearing off pieces of his garments to bind up his sore feet, as he went. Often, failing in his efforts at conciliation, Mo Tzu and his followers would rush to aid in the defense of the state attacked, gaining a reputation for their skill in siege operations. In this way they became a tight-knit and highly disciplined group, leading an ascetic life and, even after Mo Tzu's death, obediently following the directions of their "elders."

Some of the chapters of the book of *Mo Tzu* are believed to represent the views of his later followers, whose utilitarian aims inevitably led them into the study of more basic questions, of both a philosophical and a technical character. Thus, for instance, their evangelistic approach and readiness to discuss or debate with anyone may explain why the later Mo-ist canon is so much concerned with logic and dialectics. Yet even in the portions believed to represent Mo Tzu's original teaching there is a laborious, almost painful, attention to step-by-step argumentation. For this reason, perhaps, Mo Tzu has been much less admired for his literary style, or even for his ideas, than for the nobility of soul which he revealed in his life of service to others.

Selections from the Mo Tzu

CHAPTER II: IDENTIFICATION WITH THE SUPERIOR (PART I)

Mo Tzu said: In the ancient beginning of human life, when there was yet no law or government, the dictum was, "every one according to his own standard of right and wrong." Hence, if there was one man, there was one standard; if two, two standards; if ten, ten standards—the more the people, the more the standards. Everyone upheld his own standard and condemned those of the others, and so there was mutual condemnation among men. Even father and son and brother and brother entertained mutual dislike and dissatisfaction, and were kept apart by disagreements rather than united in harmony. People in the world tried to undermine each other with water, fire, and poison. When there was unspent energy it was not exerted for mutual aid; when there were surplus goods they were allowed to rot without being shared; those who knew the excellent way would keep it secret and would not instruct others. The world was in great disorder; men were like birds and beasts.

The cause of all this disorder lay simply in the want of a ruler. Therefore [Heaven] chose the most worthy in the empire and established him as the Son of Heaven [i.e., the ruler]. Feeling the insufficiency of his capability, the Son of Heaven chose the next most worthy in the empire and installed them as the three ministers. Seeing the vastness of the empire and the difficulty of attending to matters of right and wrong and benefit and harm among the peoples of far countries, the three ministers divided the empire into feudal states and assigned them to the feudal lords. Feeling the insufficiency of their capability, the feudal lords, in turn, chose the most worthy in their states and appointed them as their officials.

When the rulers were all installed, the emperor issued a mandate to all the people, saying: "Upon hearing good report or evil, one shall inform one's superior. What the superior considers to be wrong all shall consider to be wrong. When the superior is at fault there shall be good counsel; when the subordinates have achieved virtue there shall be popular commendation. To identify one's self with the superior and not to unite one's self with the subordinates—this is what deserves reward from above and praise from below. On the other hand, if upon hearing good report or evil, one should not inform one's superior; if what the superior considers to be right one should not consider to be right; if what the superior considers to be wrong one should not consider to be wrong; if when the superior is at fault there should be no good counsel; if when the subordinates have achieved virtue there should be no popular commendation; if there should be common cause with subordinates but no identification with the superior—this is what deserves punishment from above and condemnation from below." The ruler made this the basis of reward and punishment. He was clear-sighted and won the confidence of his people.

Now the head of the village was the most humane man of the village. He proclaimed to the people of the village, saying: "Upon hearing good report or evil, you shall inform the head of the district. What the head of the district considers to be right, all shall consider to be right. What he considers to be wrong, all shall consider to be wrong. Put away your evil speech and learn his good speech. Remove your evil conduct and learn his good conduct." How then can there be disorder in the district? . . .

Now, how is order brought about in the empire? There was order in the empire because the emperor could unify the standards in the empire. If, however, the people all identify themselves with the Son of Heaven but not with Heaven itself, then the jungle is still unremoved. Now, the frequent visitations of hurricanes and torrential rains are nothing but the punishments from Heaven upon the people for their failure to identify their standards with the will of Heaven.

CHAPTER 9: EXALTATION OF THE WORTHY (PART II)

Mo Tzu said: Now, in ruling the people, administering the state, and governing the country, the rulers desire to have their authority last a long time. Why then do they not realize that exaltation of the worthy is the foundation of government? How do we know that exaltation of the worthy is the foundation of government? When the honorable and wise govern the ignorant and humble, there is order. But when the ignorant and humble govern the honorable and wise, there is disorder. Therefore, we know that exaltation of the worthy is the foundation of government.

The ancient sage-kings greatly emphasized the exaltation of the worthy and the employment of the capable, without showing any favoritism to their relatives, to the rich and honored, or to the good-looking. The worthy were exalted and promoted, enriched and honored, and made governors and officials. The unworthy were rejected and banished, dispossessed and degraded, and made laborers and servants. Thereupon people were all encouraged by rewards and deterred by punishments, and strove one with another after virtue. Thus the worthy multiplied and the unworthy diminished in number. It was in this way that the worthy were exalted. Thereupon the sage-kings listened to their words and observed their conduct, discovered their capabilities and carefully assigned them their offices. It was in this way that the capable were employed. . . .

When the worthy man rules the state, he starts the day early and retires late, judging lawsuits and attending to the government. As a result, the state is well-governed and the laws are fairly administered. When the worthy man administers the court, he retires late and wakes up early, collecting taxes from passes, markets, and on products from mountains and woods, waters and land to fill the treasury. As a result, the treasury is filled and wealth is not dissipated. When the worthy man manages a district, he sets out before sunrise and comes back after sunset, plowing and sowing, planting and cultivating, and gathering harvests of grain. As a result, grain is in abundance and the people are sufficiently supplied with food. Therefore when the country is well-governed the laws are justly administered, and when the treasury is filled the people are well-to-do. For the higher sphere, the rulers have the wherewithal to make clean wine and cakes for sacrifice and libation to Heaven and the spirits. For the surrounding countries they have the wherewithal to furnish the furs and money to befriend the neighboring feudal lords. For the people within [the state], they have the wherewithal to feed the hungry and give rest to the tired, thus to nurture the multitude and cherish the worthy. Therefore from above, Heaven and the spirits enrich them; from without, the feudal lords associate with them; from within, the people show them affection, and the worthy are attracted to them. Hence they will succeed in what they plan and accomplish what they propose to do. In defense they are strong, and in attack victorious. Now the Way that enabled the sage-kings of the Three Dynasties, Yao, Shun, Yü, T'ang, Wen, and Wu, to subdue the empire and take precedence over the feudal lords was nothing else than this [principle of exaltation of the worthy].

However, if there is only the principle while the method of its application is not known, then success would still seem to be uncertain. Therefore there should be laid down three axioms. What are the three axioms? They are: 1) when the rank of the worthy is not high, people will not show them respect; 2) when their emoluments are not liberal, people will not place confidence in them; 3) when their orders are not final, people will not stand in awe before them. So the ancient sage-kings placed them high in rank, gave them liberal emoluments, entrusted them with important charges, and decreed their orders to be final. Was all this done merely to reward the subordinates? It was done to assure successful government. . . .

And when the worthy do not come to the side of the rulers, the unworthy will be found at their right and left. . . . At home the unworthy are not filial to their parents, and abroad they are not respectful to the elders of the community. They move about without restraint and disregard the rules of decorum between the sexes. When entrusted with the administration of the treasury, they steal; when made to defend a city, they raise an insurrection. When their lord is in trouble, they do not stick by him until death; when the lord has to flee the country, they do not accompany him in banishment. . . . Now, the reason that the wicked kings of the Three Dynasties, Chieh, Chou, Yu, and Li, misruled the country and upset their empires was nothing else than this [employment of the unworthy].

Why do the rulers do this? Because they understand petty affairs but are ignorant about weighty matters. When the rulers have a suit of clothes which they cannot fit by themselves, they will employ capable tailors. When they have an ox or a sheep they cannot kill themselves, they will employ capable butchers. In these two instances they know that they should exalt the worthy and employ the capable for getting things done. But when it comes to the disorder of the country and danger of the state, they fail to realize that they should exalt the worthy and employ the capable to attend to them. Instead, they employ their relatives, they employ the rich without merit, and the good-looking. If the relatives, the rich without merit, and the good-looking are employed, will they necessarily prove themselves wise and intelligent? To let them rule the country is to let the unwise and unintelligent rule the country. And we can be sure that disorder in the country will result.

CHAPTER 16: UNIVERSAL LOVE (PART III)

Mo Tzu said: Humane men are concerned about providing benefits for the world and eliminating its calamities. Now among all the current calamities, which are the worst? I say that the attacking of small states by large states, the making of inroads on small houses by large houses, the plundering of the weak by the strong, the oppression of the few by the many, the deception of the simple by the cunning, the disdain of the noble towards the humble—these are some of the calamities in the world. Again, the want of kindness on the part of the ruler, the want of loyalty on the part of the ruled, the want of affection on the part of the father, the want of filial piety on the part of the son—these are some further calamities in the world. Added to these, the mutual injury and harm which the vulgar people do to one another with weapons, poison, water, and fire is still another kind of calamity in the world.

When we come to inquire about the cause of all these calamities, whence have they arisen? Is it out of people's loving others and benefiting others? We must reply that it is not so. We should say that it is out of people's hating others and injuring others. If we should classify one by one all those who hate others and injure others, should we find them to be universal or partial [1] in their love? Of course, we should say they are partial. Now, since partiality among one another is the cause of the major calamities in the world, then partiality is wrong.

Mo Tzu continued: He who criticizes others must have something to offer in replacement. Criticism without an alternative proposal is like trying to stop flood with flood and put out fire with fire. It will surely be worthless.

Therefore Mo Tzu said: Partiality is to be replaced by universality. But how is partiality to be replaced by universality? Now, when everyone regards the states of others as he regards his own, who would attack the other's state? One would regard others as one's self. When everyone regards the cities of others as he regards his own, who would seize the others' cities? One would regard others as one's self. When everyone regards the houses of others as he regards his own, who would disturb

[1] Mo Tzu is critical of the Confucian idea of love according to the degree of relationship. He calls it partial love or the principle of partiality, as against his own universal love or principle of universality.

the others' houses? One would regard others as one's self. Now when the states and cities do not attack and seize each other, and when the clans and individuals do not disturb and harm one another—is this a calamity or a benefit to the world? Of course it is a benefit.

When we come to inquire about the cause of all these benefits, whence have they arisen? Is it out of men's hating and injuring others? We must reply that it is not so. We should say that it is out of men's loving and benefiting others. If we should classify one by one all those who love others and benefit others, should we find them to be partial or universal in their love? Of course we should say they are universal. Now, since universal love is the cause of the major benefits in the world, therefore Mo Tzu proclaims that universal love is right. . . .

Yet the objections from the gentlemen of the world are never exhausted. It is asked: It may be a good thing but can it be of any use?

Mo Tzu replies: If it were not useful, I myself would disapprove of it. But how can there be anything that is good but not useful? Let us consider the matter from both sides. Suppose there are two men. Let one of them hold to partiality and the other universality. Then the advocate of partiality would say to himself: "How could I be expected to take care of my friend as I do of myself, how could I be expected to take care of his parents as my own?" Therefore when he finds his friend hungry he would not feed him, and when he finds him cold he would not clothe him. In his illness he would not minister to him, and when he is dead he would not bury him. Such is the word and such is the deed of the advocate of partiality. The advocate of universality is quite unlike this either in word or in deed. He would say to himself: "I have heard that to be a superior man one should take care of his friend as he does of himself, and take care of his friend's parents as he does his own." Therefore when he finds his friend hungry he would feed him, and when he finds him cold he would clothe him. In his sickness he would minister to him, and when he is dead he would bury him. Such is the word and such is the deed of the advocate of universality.

These two persons, then, are opposed to each other in word and also in deed. Suppose both of them are sincere in word and decisive in deed so that their word and deed are made to agree like the two parts of a tally, every word being expressed in deed. Then let us ask: Suppose here is a battlefield, and one is in armor and helmet, ready to go into combat, and life and death hang in the balance. Or suppose one is sent as an emissary by the ruler to such far countries as Pa, Yüeh, Ch'i, and Ching, and one cannot be certain as to one's safe arrival and return. Now let us inquire, upon whom would one (under such circumstances) lay the trust of one's family and parents, wife, and children? Would it be upon the friend whose code of conduct is universality, or upon him whose code is partiality? It seems to me, on occasions like these, there are no fools in the world. Even though he be a person who objects to universal love himself, he would lay the trust upon the friend believing in universal love all the same. This is rejection of the principle in word but acceptance of it in actually making a choice—this is contradiction between one's word and deed. It is incomprehensible, then, why the gentlemen of the world should object to universal love when they hear of it.

Yet the objections from the gentlemen of the world are never exhausted. It is objected: Perhaps it is a good criterion by which one may choose among ordinary men, but it would not apply to the choice of rulers.

Let us again consider the matter from both sides. Suppose there are two rulers. Let one of them hold to partiality and the other universality. Then the "partial" ruler would say to himself: "How could I be expected to take care of the people as I do of myself? This would be quite contrary to the nature of things. A man's life on earth is of short duration; it is like a galloping horse rushing past a crack in the wall." Therefore when he finds his people hungry he would not feed them, and when he finds them cold he would not clothe them. When they are sick he would not minister to them, and upon their death he would not bury them. Such is the word and such is the deed of the "partial" ruler. The "universal" ruler is quite unlike this either in word or in deed. He would say to himself: "I have heard that to be an intelligent ruler of the empire one should attend to his people before he attends to himself." Therefore when he finds his people hungry he would feed them, and when he finds them cold he would clothe them. In their sickness he would minister to them, and upon their death he would bury them. Such is the word and such is the deed of the "universal" ruler.

These two rulers, then, are opposed to each other in word and also in deed. Suppose both of them are sincere in word and decisive in deed so that their word and deed are made to agree like the two parts of a tally, every word being expressed in deed. Then let us ask: Suppose, now, that there is a disastrous pestilence, that most people are in misery and privation, and that many lie dead in ditches. Now, let us inquire, if a person could choose between the two rulers, which would he prefer? It seems to me on such occasions as these there are no fools in the world. Even though he be a person who objects to universal love himself, he would choose the "universal" ruler. This is rejection of the principle in word but acceptance of it in actually making a choice—this is contradiction between one's word and deed. It is incomprehensible, then, why the gentlemen of the world should object to universal love when they hear of it.

Yet the objections from the gentlemen of the world are never exhausted. It is pointed out that universal love may be humane and righteous, but is it meant to be put into practice? Universal love is as possible as picking up Mount T'ai and leaping over rivers with it. So, then, universal love is but a pious wish, and how can anyone expect it to be materialized? Mo Tzu replied: To pick up Mount T'ai and leap over the rivers is a feat that has never been accomplished since the existence of man. But universal love and mutual aid have been personally practiced by the great ancient sage-kings.

How do we know that they have practiced it?

Mo Tzu said: I am no contemporary of theirs; neither have I heard their voices nor seen their countenances. The sources of our knowledge lie in what is written on bamboo and silk, what is engraved in metal and stone, and what is cut in the vessels that have been handed down to posterity. . . .

Yet the objections from the gentlemen of the world are never exhausted. The question is raised: When one does not pay special attention to the welfare of one's parents, is not harm done to the virtue of filial piety?

Mo Tzu replied: Now let us inquire into the way the filial sons take care of their parents. I may ask, in caring for their parents, whether they desire to have others love their parents, or hate them? Judging from the whole doctrine [of filial piety], it is certain that they desire to have others love their parents. Now, then, what should I do first in order to attain this? Should I first love others' parents in order that they would love my parents in return, or should I first hate others' parents in order that they would love my parents in return? Assuredly I should first love others' parents in order that they would love my parents in return. Hence, is it not evident that those who desire to see others filial to their own parents, had best proceed first by loving and benefiting others' parents? . . . It is then quite incomprehensible why the gentlemen of the world should object to universal love when they hear of it.

Is it because they deem it so difficult and inpracticable? But there have been instances of much harder tasks that have been accomplished. Formerly, Lord Ling of the state of Ching was fond of slender waists. During his life time, the Ching people ate not more than once a day. They could not stand up without support, and could not walk without leaning against the wall. Now, limited diet is quite hard to endure, and yet it was endured, because Lord Ling encouraged it. . . .

Now, as to universal love and mutual aid, they are incalculably more beneficial and less difficult. It seems to me that the only trouble is that there is no ruler who will encourage them. If there were a ruler who would encourage them, bringing to bear the lure of reward and the threat of punishment, I believe the people would tend toward universal love and mutual aid like fire tending upward and water downwards—nothing in the world could stop them.

CHAPTER 28: THE WILL OF HEAVEN (PART III)

Mo Tzu said: What is the reason for the disorder in the world? It is that the gentlemen of the world understand only trifles but not things of importance. How do we know they understand trifles but not things of importance? Because they do not understand the will of Heaven. How do we know they do not understand the will of Heaven? By observing the way people conduct themselves in the family. When a man commits an offense in the family, he might still escape to some other family for refuge. Yet, father reminds son, elder brother reminds younger brother, saying: "Beware, be careful! If one is not cautious and careful in his conduct in the family, how is he to get along in the state?" When a man commits an offense in the state, he might still escape to some other state for refuge. Yet father reminds son and elder brother reminds younger brother, saying: "Beware, be careful! One cannot get along in a state if he is not cautious and careful." Now all men live in the world and serve Heaven. When a man sins against Heaven he has nowhere to escape for refuge. On this point, however, people fail to caution and warn each other. Thus I know that they do not understand things of importance.

And Mo Tzu said: Beware, be careful! Be sure to do what Heaven desires and forsake what Heaven abominates. Now, what does Heaven desire and what does Heaven abominate? Heaven desires righteousness and abominates unrighteousness. How do we know that this is so? Because righteousness is the proper standard. How do we know righteousness is the proper standard? Because when righteousness prevails in the world, there is order; when righteousness ceases to prevail in the world, there is chaos. So, I know righteousness is the proper standard.

Now a standard is never given by a subordinate to a superior, it is always given by the superior to the subordinate. Hence the common people may not take any standard they please; there are the scholars to give them the standard. The scholars may not take any standard they please; there are the ministers to give them the standard. The ministers may not take any standard they please; there are the feudal lords to give them the standard. The feudal lords may not take any standard they please; there are the three ministers to give them the standard. The three ministers may not take any standard they please; there is the Son of Heaven to give them the standard. The Son of Heaven may not take any standard he pleases; there is Heaven to give him the standard. The gentlemen of the world all can see that the Son of Heaven gives the standard to the empire, but they fail to see that Heaven gives the standard to the Son of Heaven. The sages of old, explaining this, said: "When the Son of Heaven has done good, Heaven rewards him. When the Son of Heaven has committed wrong, Heaven punishes him. When the Son of Heaven is unfair in dispensing reward and punishment and not impartial in judging lawsuits, the empire is visited with disease and calamity, and frost and dew will be untimely." Thereupon the Son of Heaven will have to fatten the oxen and sheep and dogs and pigs, and prepare clean cakes and wine to offer prayer to Heaven and invoke its blessing. I have not yet heard of Heaven praying and invoking the Son of Heaven for blessing. Thus I know that Heaven is more honorable and wise than the Son of Heaven.

Therefore, righteousness does not issue from the ignorant and humble, but from the honorable and wise. Who is the most honorable? Heaven is the most honorable. Who is the most wise? Heaven is the most wise. And so righteousness assuredly issues from Heaven. Then the gentlemen of the world who desire to do righteousness cannot but obey the will of Heaven.

What is the will of Heaven that we should all obey? It is to love all men universally. How do we know it is to love all men universally? Because [Heaven] accepts sacrifices from all. How do we know Heaven accepts sacrifices from all? Because from antiquity to the present day, there is no distant or isolated country but that it fattens the oxen and sheep and dogs and pigs, and prepares clean cakes and wine, reverently to do sacrifice to the Lord-on-High, and the spirits of hills and rivers. Hence we know Heaven accepts sacrifices from all. Accepting sacrifice from all, Heaven must love them all. . . .

That Heaven loves all the people in the world is evidenced not only by this. In all the countries in the world and among all the peoples who live on grain, the murder of one innocent individual is invariably followed by a calamity. Now, who is it that murders the innocent individual? It is man. Who is it that sends forth the calamity? It is Heaven. If Heaven really did not love the people, why should Heaven send forth calamities upon the murder of the innocent?

Furthermore, Heaven loves the people dearly, Heaven loves the people inclusively. This we know. How do we know that Heaven loves the people? Because the worthy [Heaven] invariably rewards the good and punishes the evil. How do we know the worthy [Heaven] invariably rewards the good and punishes the evil. We know this from the record of the sage-kings of the Three Dynasties. Of old, the sage-kings of the Three Dynasties, Yao, Shun, Yü, T'ang, Wen, and Wu, loved the world universally and sought to benefit it. They influenced the minds of the people and led them in the worship of the Lord-on-High, and the spirits of hills and rivers. Heaven was pleased because they loved those whom it loved and benefited those whom it would benefit. And Heaven bestowed reward upon them, placing them on the throne, making them Sons of Heaven, upholding them as models for all men, and calling them sage-kings. Here we have the proof of Heaven's reward of the good. Of old, the wicked kings of the Three Dynasties, Chieh, Chou, Yu, and Li, hated all the people in the world and sought to oppress them. They influenced the minds of the people, and led them in blasphemy against the Lord-on-High, and the spirits of hills and rivers. Heaven was offended because they hated those whom Heaven loved, and oppressed those whom Heaven would benefit. And Heaven decreed punishment upon them, letting fathers and sons be scattered, their empire be put to an end, their state be lost to them, and capital punishment fall upon them. Thereupon, the multitude condemned them, the condemnation lasting through countless generations and the people calling them the lost kings. Here we have the proof of Heaven's punishment of the evil.

The gentlemen of the world who desire to do righteousness have no other recourse than to obey the will of Heaven. One who obeys the will of Heaven will practice universal love; one who opposes the will of Heaven will practice partial love. According to the doctrine of universality the standard of conduct is righteousness; according to the doctrine of partiality the standard is force. What is it like when righteousness is the standard of conduct? The great will not attack the small, the strong will not plunder the weak, the many will not oppress the few, the cunning will not deceive the simple, the noble will not disdain the humble, the rich will not mock the poor, and the young will not encroach upon the old. And the states in the empire will not harm each other with water, fire, poison, and weapons. Such a regime will be auspicious to Heaven above, to the spirits in the middle sphere, and to the people below. Being auspicious to these three, it is beneficial to all. This is called the disposition of Heaven. He who follows it is sagacious and wise, humane and righteous, kind as a ruler and loyal as a minister, affectionate as a father and filial as a son, and all such good names in the world are gathered and attributed to him. Why? Because such conduct is in accordance with the will of Heaven.

Now, what is it like when force becomes the standard of conduct? The great will attack the small, the strong will plunder the weak, the many will oppress the few, the cunning will deceive the simple, the noble will disdain the humble, the rich will mock the poor, and the young will encroach upon the old. And the states in the empire will ruin each other with water, fire, poison, and weapons. Such a regime will not be auspicious to Heaven above, to the spirits in the middle sphere, or to the people below. Not being auspicious to these three, it is not beneficial to anyone. This is called the violation of Heaven. He who follows it is a robber and a thief, not humane and not righteous, unkind as a ruler and disloyal as a minister, unaffectionate as a father, and unfilial as a son, and all such evil names in the world are gathered and attributed to him. Why? Because such conduct is in opposition to the will of Heaven.

CHAPTER IV

TAOISM

Next to Confucianism the most important and influential native philosophy of the Chinese has undoubtedly been that of the Taoist school. No other doctrine of the ancient period except Confucianism has for so long maintained its vigor and attractiveness to the Chinese mind. In many ways the doctrines of Confucianism and Taoism complement each other, running side by side like two powerful streams through all later Chinese thought and literature, appealing simultaneously to two sides of the Chinese character. To the solemn, rather pompous gravity and burden of social responsibility of Confucianism, Taoism opposes a carefree flight from respectability and the conventional duties of society; in place of the stubborn Confucian concern for things human and mundane it holds out a vision of other, transcendental worlds of the spirit. Where the Confucian philosophers are often prosaic and dull, moralistic and common-sensical, the early Taoist writings are all wit and paradox, mysticism and poetic vision. As the two streams of thought developed in later ages, Confucianism has represented the mind of the Chinese scholar-gentleman in his office or study, being a good family man, a conscientious bureaucrat, and a sober, responsible citizen; Taoism has represented the same gentleman in his private chamber or mountain retreat, seeking surcease from the cares of official life, perhaps a little drunk, but more likely intoxicated by the beauties of nature or of the world of the spirit.

Without this Taoist leaven of poetry and mysticism Chinese literature and thought would undoubtedly be a much poorer and shallower affair. But this very preoccupation with mystic worlds has proved to be the greatest weakness of the Taoists. After a brilliant beginning Taoism tended to become appropriated by those who wandered off on an interminable search for the secret of eternal life, which led them into such a slough of superstitious hocus-pocus that they eventually lost credit in the eyes of the intellectual class. The early classics of the Taoist school never ceased to be read by the educated, and to exert an influence upon the formation of their ideas. Indeed many of the most important elements of Taoist teaching were absorbed into Confucianism and Chinese Buddhism. But the Taoist school itself became more and more a cult of popular religion, adopting rites and organizational forms from the Buddhist church, absorbing all sorts of popular superstitions and demon lore, until it became an object of ridicule among educated Chinese.

METAPHYSICS AND GOVERNMENT IN THE LAO TZU

The Taoist school is often referred to as the "Teachings of the Yellow Emperor and Lao Tzu" or of "Lao Tzu and Chuang Tzu." The Yellow Emperor is a purely legendary figure, but we possess two books attributed to the other two fathers of the sect, Lao Tzu and Chuang Tzu. Chuang Tzu seems to have been an actual historical person, but who the philosopher called Lao Tzu was, when he lived, or what his connection was with the text that we have, have been questions of doubt since the first history of the ancient period was written. The tales of the philosopher-recluse Lao Tzu need not concern us here, however; what is important is the book—one of the shortest, most provocative, and inspired works in all Chinese literature. Though the quietism, mysticism, and love of paradox that distinguish this work probably represent very old strains in Chinese thought, whether the book itself is any earlier than the third century B.C. is a question still much debated by scholars.

In a sense, the *Lao Tzu* (or *Tao-te ching*), like so many of the works of this period of political chaos and intellectual ferment, proposes a philosophy of government and a way of life for the ruling class, probably the only people who could read its pages. Yet its point of view and approach to the problems of government are vastly broader than this statement would at first suggest. For the teaching of the *Lao Tzu* is based upon a great, underlying principle, the Way or Tao (from which the name of the Taoist school derives) which is the source of all being and governor of all life, human and natural, and the basic, undivided unity in which all the contradictions and distinctions of existence are ultimately resolved. Much of the book deals with the nature and workings of this first principle, while admitting that it must remain essentially indescribable and known only through a kind of mystic intuition. The way of life which accords with this basic Tao is marked by a kind of yielding passivity, an absence of strife and coercion, a manner of action which is completely spontaneous, effortless, and inexhaustible.

In the human sphere the *Lao Tzu* describes the perfect individual, the sage, who comprehends this mystic principle of Tao and orders his own life and actions in accordance with it, humbling himself, pursuing a course of quietude and passivity, free from desire and strife. It is clear that the sage is conceived of as the ideal ruler, for the *Lao Tzu* gives definite instructions as to how the sage is to conduct his government. He is to cease from meddling in the lives of the people, give up warfare and luxurious living, and guide his people back to a state of innocence, simplicity, and harmony with the Tao, a state that existed in the most ancient times before civilization appeared to arouse the material desires of the people and spur them to strife and warfare, and before morality was invented to befuddle their minds and beguile them with vain distinctions.

But such is the vagueness and ambiguity of the *Lao Tzu* text and the subtlety of its thought that it may yield different interpretations and be approached on very different levels. There have been times in Chinese history, notably at the beginning of the Han dynasty, when men attempted to translate the doctrines of the *Lao Tzu* into action through government policies embodying an extreme laissez-faire attitude. But the teachings of the *Lao Tzu* may also be understood as the creed of the recluse, the man of superior wisdom and insight who, instead of taking a part in society, chooses to retire from public life in order to perfect his own purity and intelligence. It is this interpretation of the *Lao Tzu* that has most often prevailed in later Chinese thought. This, perhaps, is largely because of the influence of the second great Taoist teacher, Chuang Tzu, the author of numerous stories about sages and worthies who were entreated by the rulers of their time to accept high political positions, but who rejected all such offers in favor of seclusion and self-cultivation. It is for this reason that Taoism has so often been the philosophy and consolation of the Chinese gentleman in retirement, of the political failure, and of the scholar who abandons human society in search of a mystic harmony with the world of nature.

The style of the *Lao Tzu* is quite unlike that of the works of the other schools. The text appears to be a combination of very old adages or cryptic sayings, often in rhyme, extended passages of poetry, and sections of prose interpretation and commentary. There is extensive use of parallel constructions and neatly balanced phrases; the statements are laconic and paradoxical, intended not to convince the mind by reasoning but to startle and capture it through poetic vision. The writer makes striking use of symbols such as water, the symbol of a humble, self-effacing force that is in the end all-powerful, or the female and the mother, symbol of passivity and creation. It is this symbolism, this paradoxical, poetic view of life which have won for the work the tremendous popularity and influence which it has exercised through the centuries of Chinese literature and these same appealing qualities that have made it the Chinese work most often translated into foreign languages.

Selections from the Lao Tzu (or Tao-te Ching)

I

The Tao [Way] that can be told of
   Is not the eternal Tao;
The name that can be named
   Is not the eternal name.
Nameless, it is the origin of Heaven and earth;
Namable, it is the mother of all things.

Always nonexistent,
   That we may apprehend its inner secret;
Always existent,
   That we may discern its outer manifestations.
These two are the same;
Only as they manifest themselves they receive different names.

That they are the same is the mystery.
Mystery of all mysteries!
The door of all subtleties!

. . . .

3

Refrain from exalting the worthy,
   So that the people will not scheme and contend;
Refrain from prizing rare possessions,
   So that the people will not steal;
Refrain from displaying objects of desire,
   So that the people's hearts will not be disturbed.

Therefore a sage rules his people thus:
   He empties their minds,
      And fills their bellies;
   He weakens their ambitions,
      And strengthens their bones.

He strives always to keep the people innocent of knowledge and desires, and to keep the knowing ones from meddling. By doing nothing that interferes with anything (*wu-wei*), nothing is left unregulated.

4

The Tao is empty [like a bowl],
It is used, though perhaps never full.
It is fathomless, possibly the progenitor of all things.
It blunts all sharpness,
It unties all tangles;
It is in harmony with all light,
It is one with all dust.
Deep and clear it seems forever to remain.
I do not know whose son it is,
A phenomenon that apparently preceded the Lord.

5

Heaven and earth are not humane:
   To them all things are as straw-dogs.
The sage is not humane:
   To him all the people are as straw-dogs.

.   .   .   .

8

The highest good is like water. Water benefits all things generously and is without strife. It dwells in the lowly places that men disdain. Thus it comes near to the Tao.

The highest good loves the [lowly] earth for its dwelling.
It loves the profound in its heart,
It loves humanity in friendship,
Sincerity in speech, order in government,
Effectiveness in deeds, timeliness in action.
Since it is without strife,
It is without reproach.

. . . .

10

In keeping your soul and embracing unity,
    Can you forever hold fast to the Tao?
In letting out your vital force to achieve gentleness,
    Can you become as the new-born babe?
In cleansing and purifying your mystic vision,
    Can you be free from all dross?
In loving the people and governing the land,
    Can you practice nonaction (*wu-wei*)?
In opening and shutting the gates of Heaven,
    Can you play the part of the female?
In perceiving all and comprehending all,
    Can you renounce all knowledge?

To beget, to nourish,
    To beget but not to claim,
    To achieve but not to cherish,
    To be leader but not master—
This is called the Mystic Virtue (*te*).

. . . .

14

You look at it, but it is not to be seen;
    Its name is Formless.
You listen to it, but it is not to be heard;

Its name is Soundless.
You grasp it, but it is not to be held;
   Its name is Bodiless.
These three elude all scrutiny,
   And hence they blend and become one.

Its upper side is not bright;
   Its under side is not dim.
Continuous, unceasing, and unnamable,
   It reverts to nothingness.

It is called formless form, thingless image;
   It is called the elusive, the evasive.
Confronting it, you do not see its face;
   Following it, you do not see its back.

Yet by holding fast to this Tao of old,
   You can harness the events of the present,
   You can know the beginnings of the past—
Here is the essence of the Tao.

· · · ·

16

Attain utmost vacuity;
   Hold fast to quietude.
While the myriad things are stirring together,
   I see only their return.
For luxuriantly as they grow,
   Each of them will return to its root.

To return to the root is called quietude,
   Which is also said to be reversion to one's destiny.
This reversion belongs with the eternal:
   To know the eternal is enlightenment;
   Not to know the eternal means to run blindly to disaster.

He who knows the eternal is all-embracing;
   He who is all-embracing is impartial,

To be impartial is to be kingly,
To be kingly is to be heavenly,
To be heavenly is to be one with the Tao,
To be one with the Tao is to endure forever.
Such a one, though his body perish, is never exposed to danger.

17

The best [government] is that whose existence only is known by the people. The next is that which is loved and praised. The next is that which is despised. . . .

18

It was when the Great Tao declined,
  That there appeared humanity and righteousness.
It was when knowledge and intelligence arose,
  That there appeared much hypocrisy.
It was when the six relations lost their harmony,
  That there was talk of filial piety and paternal affection.
It was when the country fell into chaos and confusion,
  That there was talk of loyalty and trustworthiness.

19

Banish sageliness, discard wisdom,
  And the people will be benefited a hundredfold.
Banish humanity, discard righteousness,
  And the people will return to filial piety and paternal affection.
Banish skill, discard profit,
  And thieves and robbers will disappear.

These three are the ill-provided adornments of life,
  And must be subordinated to something higher:—
See the simple, embrace primitivity;
  Reduce the self, lessen the desires.

.   .   .   .

21

The expression of Vast Virtue (*te*)
  Is derived from the Tao alone.
As to the Tao itself,

It is elusive and evasive.
Evasive, elusive,
　　Yet within it there are images.
Elusive, evasive,
　　Yet within it there are things.
Shadowy and dim,
　　Yet within it there is a vital force.
The vital force is very real,
　　And therein dwells truth.

From the days of old till now,
　　Its name has never ceased to be,
　　And it has witnessed the beginning of all things.
How do I know the shape of the beginning of all things?
　　Through it.

· · · ·

25

There was something nebulous yet complete,
　　Born before Heaven and earth.
Silent, empty,
　　Self-sufficient and unchanging,
　　Revolving without cease and without fail,
　　It acts as the mother of the world.

I do not know its name,
　　And address it as "Tao."
　　Attempting to give it a name, I shall call it "Great."
To be great is to pass on.
　　To pass on is to go further and further away.
　　To go further and further away is to return.

Therefore Tao is great, Heaven is great, earth is great,
　　And the king is also great.
These are the Great Four in the universe,
　　And the king is one of them.
Man follows the ways of earth,
　　Earth follows the ways of Heaven;

Heaven follows the ways of Tao;
Tao follows the ways of itself.

. . . .

28

He who knows the masculine but keeps to the feminine,
  Becomes the ravine of the world.
Being the ravine of the world,
  He dwells in constant virtue,
  He returns to the state of the babe.

He who knows the white but keeps to the black,
  Becomes the model of the world.
Being the model of the world,
  He rests in constant virtue,
  He returns to the infinite.

He who knows glory but keeps to disgrace,
  Becomes the valley of the world.
Being the valley of the world,
  He finds contentment in constant virtue,
  He returns to the uncarved block.[1]

The cutting up of the uncarved block results in vessels,
  Which, in the hands of the sage, become officers.
Truly, "A great cutter does not cut."

. . . .

32

Tao is eternal, nameless. Though the uncarved block seems small, it may be subordinated to nothing in the world. If kings and barons can preserve it, all creation would of itself pay homage, Heaven and earth would unite to send sweet dew, and the people would of themselves achieve peace and harmony.

Once the block is cut, names appear. When names begin to appear, know then that there is a time to stop. It is by this knowledge that danger may be avoided.

[1] The "uncarved block" is a favorite figure used by the author of the *Lao Tzu* in referring to the original state of complete simplicity which is his highest ideal.

[The spontaneous working of] the Tao in the world is like the flow of the valley brooks into a river or sea.

. . . .

34

The great Tao flows everywhere:
  It can go left; it can go right.

The myriad things owe their existence to it,
  And it does not reject them.

When its work is accomplished,
  It does not take possession.
It clothes and feeds all,
  But does not pose as their master.

Ever without ambition,
  It may be called small.
All things return to it as to their home,
  And yet it does not pose as their master,
  Therefore it may be called Great.

Because it would never claim greatness,
  Therefore its greatness is fully realized.

. . . .

37

Tao invariably does nothing (*wu-wei*),
  And yet there is nothing that is not done.

If kings and barons can preserve it,
  All things will go through their own transformations.
When they are transformed and desire to stir,
  We would restrain them with the nameless primitivity.

Nameless primitivity will result in the absence of desires,
Absence of desires will lead to quietude;
The world will, of itself, find its equilibrium.

. . . .

40

Reversal is the movement of the Tao;
Weakness is the use of the Tao.
All things in the world come into being from being;
Being comes into being from nonbeing.

. . . .

42

Tao gave birth to One; One gave birth to Two; Two gave birth to
Three; Three gave birth to all the myriad things. The myriad things
carry the yin [2] on their backs and hold the yang in their embrace, and
derive their harmony from the permeation of these forces.

To be "orphaned," "lonely," and "unworthy" is what men hate, and yet
these are the very names by which kings and dukes call themselves.
Truly, things may increase when they are diminished, but diminish when
they are increased.

What others teach I also teach: "A man of violence will come to a
violent end." [3] This I shall regard as the parent of all teachings.

43

The most yielding of things outruns the most unyielding.
Having no substance, they enter into no-space.
Hence I know the value of nonaction (*wu-wei*). The instructiveness of
silence, the value of nonaction—few in the world are up to this.

. . . .

48

To seek learning one gains day by day;
To seek the Tao one loses day by day.
Losing and yet losing some more,
Till one has reached doing nothing (*wu-wei*).
Do nothing and yet there is nothing that is not done.
To win the world one must attend to nothing.
When one attends to this and that,
He will not win the world.

. . . .

[2] Yin is the passive, negative, or female principle of the universe; yang is the active,
positive, or male principle.
[3] An ancient saying.

51

Tao gives them birth;
  Virtue (*te*) rears them.
They are shaped by their species;
  They are completed by their environment.
Therefore all things without exception exalt Tao and honor Virtue.
Tao is exalted and Virtue is honored,
  Not by anyone's command, but invariably and spontaneously.

Therefore it is Tao that gives them birth;
It is Virtue that rears them, makes them grow, fosters them, shelters them.

To give life but not to own,
To achieve but not to cherish,
To lead but not to be master—
  This is the Mystic Virtue!

. . . .

65

The ancient masters in the practice of the Tao did not thereby try to enlighten the people but rather to keep them in ignorance. If the people are difficult to govern, it is because they have too much knowledge. Those who govern a country by knowledge are the country's curse. Those who do not govern a country by knowledge are the country's blessing. To know these two rules is also to know the ancient standard. And to be able to keep the standard constantly in mind is called the Mystic Virtue.

Penetrating and far-reaching is Mystic Virtue! It is with all things as they run their course of reversal, until all reach Great Harmony.

. . . .

67

All the world says that my Tao is great, yet it appears impertinent. But it is just because it is great that it appears impertinent. Should it appear pertinent, it would have been petty from the start.

Here are my three treasures. Keep them and cherish them. The first is mercy; the second is frugality; the third is never to take the lead over the whole world. Being merciful, one has courage; being frugal, one has abundance; refusing to take the lead, one becomes the chief of all vessels. If one abandons mercy in favor of courage, frugality in favor of abundance, and humility in favor of prominence, he will perish.

Mercy will be victorious in attack and invulnerable in defense. Heaven will come to the rescue of the merciful one and with mercy will protect him.

. . . .

78

Of all things yielding and weak in the world,
    None is more so than water.
But for attacking what is unyielding and strong,
    Nothing is superior to it,
    Nothing can take its place.

That the weak overcomes the strong,
    And the yielding overcomes the unyielding,
Everyone knows this,
    But no one can translate it into action.

Therefore the sage says:
    "He who takes the dirt of the country,
        Is the lord of the state;
    He who bears the calamities of the country,
        Is the king of the world."
Truth sounds paradoxical!

. . . .

80

Let there be a small country with a few inhabitants. Though there be labor-saving contrivances, the people would not use them. Let the people mind death and not migrate far. Though there be boats and carriages, there would be no occasion to ride in them. Though there be armor and weapons, there would be no occasion to display them.

Let people revert to the practice of rope-knotting [instead of writing], and be contented with their food, pleased with their clothing, satisfied with their houses, and happy with their customs. Though there be a neighboring country in sight, and the people hear each other's cocks crowing and dogs barking, they would grow old and die without having anything to do with each other.

SKEPTICISM AND MYSTICISM IN CHUANG TZU

The second great figure of the early Taoist school is the philosopher Chuang Tzu or Chuang Chou, whose dates are tentatively given as 369 to 286 B.C., making him a contemporary of Mencius. Although he was a minor official at one time, he seems to have lived most of his life as a recluse and almost nothing is known about him.

The book which bears his name, actually probably a combination of his own essays and those of his disciples and imitators, is one of the most witty and imaginative works of all Chinese literature. Like the *Lao Tzu* it does not depend for its effect upon methodical argumentation, but upon the use of parable and allegory, paradox and fanciful imagery. A favorite device of the work is to make an actual historical figure like Confucius serve as an illustration of Taoist ideas, thus involving the great men of Chinese history in all sorts of whimsical and purely imaginative anecdotes.

Chuang Tzu shares with the *Lao Tzu* its central conception of the Tao as the principle underlying and governing all existence. He is, however, less concerned with the Tao as a guide in life than as that which possesses a supreme value in itself, transcending all mundane uses. The *Lao Tzu* teaches the Way of the world and the virtues conducive to survival: humility, gentleness, and nonstriving. In this sense it is a philosophy of acceptance. Yet there are also reformist tendencies in the *Lao Tzu* in so far as it sets forth a social ideal, the state of primitive simplicity, to which the ruler is urged to return. Chuang Tzu, on the other hand, is almost indifferent to human society. He seeks neither to reform things nor to keep them as they are, but only to rise above them.

The philosophy of Chuang Tzu is essentially a plea for the freedom of the individual. But it is a kind of spiritual freedom, liberating the individual more from the confines of his own mind than from external restraints. What he must be freed from are his own prejudices, his own partial view of things, his tendency to judge all else in terms of himself. Man is not the measure of all things, as the humanistic philosophy of Confucius had seemed to imply. What is of man, says Chuang Tzu, is artificial and unnatural; what is of nature or the Tao alone is enduringly and universally true. Thus Chuang Tzu is a skeptic where human or worldly values are concerned. Nothing delights him more than to show the relativity of things, and indulge his gift for satire at the expense of conventional belief and behavior. But his ultimate view is a mystical one, revealing the infinite possibilities of the Tao as contrasted to the limited experience of man left to himself, and affirming that absolute, inexhaustible Truth of which all partial truth is a distortion.

The true man, according to Chuang Tzu, is he who comprehends and lives in the underlying unity of the Tao. He has achieved a happiness that is beyond all change, a life that is beyond life and death. The death which men fear he views as no more than the necessary and proper correlative of human life, the natural and even desirable step following life in an eternal process of cosmic change. Indeed Chuang Tzu is led in his enthusiasm to an almost morbidly glorified view of death, the rest after labor, the cure of the sickness which is life.

Such is the vision of Chuang Tzu, sophisticated in its satire of conventional thinking, boldly imaginative in asserting the freedom of the individual to seek his own fulfillment. As the historian Ssu-ma Ch'ien has pointed out, it is essentially a selfish and egotistical vision which can be of little practical use in the governing of the state. Nevertheless, its subtlety and profundity continued to captivate the Chinese mind, and induced others later to attempt a reconciliation between the lofty view of Chuang Tzu and the problems of state and society, which remained as before the chief concern of Chinese philosophy.

Selections from the Chuang Tzu

CHAPTER I: THE CAREFREE EXCURSION

In the northern ocean there is a fish, called the leviathan, which is no one knows how many thousand *li* in size. This fish changes into a bird, called the roc, whose back spreads over no one knows how many thousand *li*.

When the bird rouses itself and flies, its wings are as clouds, hanging over the sky. When it moves itself in the sea, it is preparing to start for the southern ocean, which is the Celestial Lake.

A man named Ch'i-hsieh was a collecter of strange tales. Ch'i-hsieh said: "When the roc travels to the southern ocean, it flaps along the water for three thousand *li,* and then it soars upon a whirlwind to a height of ninety thousand *li,* for a flight lasting six months."

There is the floating air, there are the darting motes—little bits of creatures blowing one against another with their breath. We do not know whether the blue of the sky is its real color, or is simply caused by its infinite height. Whichever it is, the roc will get the same effect when it looks down from above. If there is not sufficient depth, water will not have the power to float large ships. Upset a cup of water into a depression on the mud floor and a mustard seed will float like a boat. Try to float the cup and it will stick because the water is shallow and the vessel is large. If there is not sufficient volume, wind will not have the power to support the large wings. Therefore, at the height of ninety thousand *li,* the roc has all the wind beneath it. Thereupon, mounting upon the wind, with the blue sky overhead, and with no obstacle in the way, it starts for the south.

The cicada and the young dove laugh at the roc, saying: "When we make an effort to get up and fly, we come to rest in the trees. Sometimes we don't get that far and so we just fall to the ground midway. What is the use of going up ninety thousand *li* in order to start for the south?"

He who goes to the neighborhood forest preserve takes only enough food for three meals with him and comes back with his stomach full. But he who travels a hundred *li* must pound his grain while he stops for the night. And he who travels a thousand *li* must supply himself with provisions for three months. What do these two little creatures know?

Small knowledge is not to be compared with great knowledge nor a short life with a long one. How do we know that this is so? The morning mushroom knows not the alternation of day and night. The mole-cricket knows not the alternation of spring and autumn. These are instances of short life. South of the Ch'u state there is a *ming-ling* tree, whose spring lasts five hundred years and whose autumn lasts five hundred years. In high antiquity there was a *ta-ch'un* tree, whose spring lasted eight thousand years, and whose autumn lasted eight thousand years. This is long life. And yet, P'eng-tsu [who lived 800 years] is still renowned for his longevity, and so many men wish to match him—isn't that a pity?

In Chi's answers to the questions put by T'ang, there is a statement as follows: "In the barren north, there is a sea, the Celestial Lake. In it there is a fish, several thousand *li* in width, and no one knows how many *li* in length. It is called the leviathan. There is also a bird, called the roc, with a back like Mount T'ai and wings like clouds across the sky. Upon a whirlwind it soars up to a height of ninety thousand *li*. Beyond the clouds and atmosphere, with only the blue sky above it, it then turns south to the southern ocean.

"A quail laughs at it, saying, 'Where is that bird trying to go? I spurt up with a bound, and I drop after rising a few yards. I just flutter about among the brushwood and the bushes. This is also the perfection of flying. Where is that bird trying to go?' " This is the difference between the great and the small.

Similarly, a man may possess enough knowledge for the duties of some office and his conduct may benefit his limited neighborhood, or his virtue may be comparable to that of the ruler and he may even win the confidence of the whole country—when such a man passes judgment upon himself he is pretty much like the quail. But Sung Yung Tzu [4] would regard him with a contented smile. If the whole world applauded Sung Yung Tzu, he would not be encouraged; if the whole world denounced him, he would not be discouraged. He held fast to the difference between the internal and the external, and he distinguished clearly the boundary of honor and shame, and that was all. In the world such a man is rare, yet there is still something which he did not achieve. Now Lieh Tzu could ride upon the wind and pursue his way, lightly and at ease, staying away as long as fifteen days. Among those who attained happiness, such a man is rare. Yet, although he was able to dispense with walking, he still had to depend upon something. But suppose there is one who chariots on the normality of the universe, rides upon the transformation of the six elemental forces, and thus makes an excursion into the infinite,

[4] Sung Yung Tzu also appears in the *Mencius* (VIB:4) as Sung K'eng and in the *Hsün Tzu* (ch. 6) as Sung Hsing or Sung Chien. He was close to Mo Tzu's school and taught that men's desires should be few.

what does he have to depend upon? Therefore, it is said: the perfect man has no self; the spiritual man has no achievement; the true sage has no name.

[The sage-king] Yao wished to abdicate in favor of Hsu-yü, saying: "When the sun and moon have come forth, if the torches continue to burn, would it not be difficult for them to shine? When the seasonal rains have come down, if one persists in watering the fields, would this not be a waste of effort? Now, you, sir, just stand before the throne, and the empire will be in order. Since I am here occupying the position, I can see how wanting I am. So I beg to proffer to you the empire."

"You, sir, govern the empire," said Hsu-yü, "and it is already in order. Were I to take your place, would I be doing it for the name? Name is but an accessory of reality; and should I trouble myself for an accessory? The tit, building its nest in the mighty forest, occupies but a single twig. The tapir, slaking its thirst from the river, drinks no more than the fill of its belly. Relax and forget it, my friend. I have no use for the empire. Even though the cook were not attending to his kitchen, the impersonator of the dead [at the ancestral rites] and the priest of prayer would not step over the cups and dishes to do the work for him."

Chien-wu said to Lien-shu: "I heard a tale from Chieh-yü which is extravagant and improbable, in which he lets imagination completely run away with him. It struck me that his extravagance is as boundless as the Milky Way and so improbable that it touches human experience not at all."

"What did he say?" Lien-shu asked.

"He told me that in the Miao-ku-she Mountain there lives a divine man whose skin is as white as ice and snow and whose loveliness is like that of a maiden, that he eats not the five grains but lives only on air and dew, that mounted on a flying dragon he rides above the clouds and wanders beyond the four seas, and that his spirit is such that by concentrating its power he can stay the natural process of decay and insure plentiful harvests. To me these claims are entirely beyond credulity."

"I am not surprised," Lien-shu said. "The blind cannot appreciate beauty of line and depth, the deaf cannot appreciate the beauty of drums and bells. But there is not only blindness and deafness of the body but of understanding as well. This applies to you. For the virtue of the divine man you heard about is such that he aims at the fusion of all beings into

one. Why should he concern himself with the affairs of the world, troubled
though it is? Nothing external can harm this being. He will not drown
in a flood that rises up to heaven, he will not be burned in a drought
that melts metal and stone and consumes whole mountains. Out of his
very dust and siftings one can mold a Yao or Shun. Why should he
concern himself with external things?"

A man of the Sung state came with a stock of ceremonial caps to the
Yüeh state. But the men of Yüeh were accustomed to cutting their hair
short and tattooing their bodies, and so they had no use for such caps. So,
Yao ruled the people of the empire, and maintained the government
within the four seas. After he had paid a visit to the four sages of the
Miao-ku-she Mountain and returned to his capital north of the Fen River,
he had a mysterious look and forgot his empire.

Hui Tzu [5] said to Chuang Tzu: "The King of Wei gave me some
seeds from his huge gourds. I planted them and they bore a fruit the size
of five bushels. I used it as a vessel for holding water, but it was not strong
enough to hold it. I cut it in two for ladles, but each of these was too
shallow to hold anything. It looked huge all right, but it was so useless
that I smashed it to pieces."

Chuang Tzu said: "You are certainly not very clever at turning large
things to account. There was a man of Sung who had a recipe for salve
for chapped hands, his family having been silk washers for generations.
A stranger heard of this and offered him one hundred ounces of gold for
the recipe. His clansmen all came together to consider this proposal and
agreed, saying: 'We have been washing silk for generations. What we
have gained is but a few ounces of gold. Now in one morning we can
sell this technique for one hundred ounces. Let the stranger have it.' So the
stranger got it and spoke of it to the King of Wu. When Wu and Yüeh
were at war, the King of Wu gave him the command of the fleet.

"In the winter he had a naval engagement with Yüeh, in which the
latter was totally defeated. The stranger was rewarded with a fief and a
title. Thus while the efficacy of the salve to cure the chapped hands was
the same, yet in the one case a man thereby gained for himself a title,
while in the other, those silk-washers had to keep on washing silk with
its help. This was due to the difference in the use of the thing. Now, you,

---

[5] Hui Tzu or Hui Shih was a renowned logician and a friendly critic of Chuang Tzu.
(See selection below from chapter 33 of *Chuang Tzu*.)

Sir, since you had this five-bushel gourd on your hands, why did you not make of it a great buoy whereby you could float about in rivers and lakes? Instead of this, you regretted that ladles made from it would not hold anything. Isn't your mind a bit wooly?"

Hui Tzu said to Chuang Tzu: "I have a large tree, which men call the ailanthus. Its trunk is so gnarled and knotty that a carpenter cannot apply his marking-line to it. Its branches are so bent and twisted that the square and compass cannot be used on them. Though it is standing right by the roadside, no carpenter will look at it. Now your words, Sir, are also grandiose but useless, and not wanted by anybody."

Chuang Tzu said: "Have you not seen a wild cat or a weasel? It lies, crouching down, in wait for its prey. Hither and thither it leaps about, not hindered by either what is high or what is low, until it is caught in a trap or dies in a net. Then, there is the yak, large as a cloud across the sky. It is huge all right, but it cannot catch mice. Now you have a large tree and are worried about its uselessness. Why do you not plant it in the realm of Nothingness, in the expanse of Infinitude, so that you may wander by its side in Nonaction (*wu-wei*), and you may lie under it in Blissful Repose? There it will not be harmed by bill or ax and nothing will do it any injury. Being of no use—why should anything be troubled by that?"

CHAPTER 2: THE EQUALITY OF THINGS AND OPINIONS

Whereby is the Tao vitiated that there should be a distinction of true and false? Whereby is speech vitiated that there should be a distinction of right and wrong? How could the Tao depart and be not there? And how could there be speech and yet it be not appropriate? The Tao is vitiated by petty virtues. Speech is vitiated by flowery eloquence. So it is that we have the contentions between the Confucianists and the Mo-ists, each affirming what the other denies and denying what the other affirms. But if we are to decide on their several affirmations and denials, there is nothing better than to employ the light of reason.

Everything is its own self; everything is something else's other. Things do not know that they are other things' other; they only know that they are themselves. Thus it is said, the other arises out of the self, just as the self arises out of the other. This is the theory that self and other give rise to each other. Besides, where there is life, there is death; [6] and where there is death, there is life. Where there is impossibility, there is possibility; and where there is possibility, there is impossibility. It is because there is right, that there is wrong; it is because there is wrong, that there is right. This being the situation, the sages do not approach things at this level, but reflect the light of nature. Thereupon the self is also the other; the other is also the self. According to the other, there is one kind of right and wrong. According to the self there is another kind of right and wrong. But really are there such distinctions as the self and the other, or are there no such distinctions? When the self and the other [or the this and the that] lose their contrariety, there we have the very essence of the Tao. Only the essence of the Tao may occupy the center of the circle, and respond therefrom to the endless opinions from all directions. Affirmation [of the self] is one of the endless opinions; denial [of the other] is another. Therefore it is said that there is nothing better than to employ the light of reason.

Using [7] an attribute to illustrate the point that attributes are not attributes in and of themselves is not so good as using a nonattribute to illustrate the point. [8] Using a horse to illustrate the point that a (white) horse is not a horse (as such) is not so good as using nonhorses to illustrate the point. [9] Actually the universe is but an attribute; all things are but a horse.

The possible is possible; the impossible is impossible. The Tao operates and things follow. Things are what they are called. What are they? They are what they are. What are they not? They are not what they are not. Everything is what it is, and can be what it can be. There is nothing that is not something, and there is nothing that cannot be something. Therefore, for instance, a stalk and a pillar, the ugly and the beautiful, the

[6] This clause occurs also in the 4th of Hui Shih's ten paradoxes. In that context our translation runs, "The creature born is the creature dying." (See selection below from chapter 33 of *Chuang Tzu*.)

[7] This short paragraph is a brief refutation of Kung-sun Lung Tzu's logic. The double reference to the attribute and the horse makes the identification certain. See Chapter V.

[8] The title of chapter 3 of the *Kung-sun Lung Tzu* is "Discourse on Things and Their Attributes," and the opening sentence runs, "Things consist of nothing but their attributes. But attributes are not attributes in and of themselves."

[9] The title of chapter 2 of the *Kung-sun Lung Tzu* is "Discourse on the White Horse," and the opening sentence runs, "A white horse is not a horse."

common and the peculiar, the deceitful and the strange—by the Tao this great variety is all brought into a single unity. Division to one is construction to another; construction to one is destruction to another. Whether in construction or in destruction, all things are in the end brought into unity. . . .

He who belabors his spirit and intelligence trying to bring about a unity among things and not understanding that they are already in agreement may be called "three in the morning." What is meant by "three in the morning"? Well, a keeper of monkeys once announced to the monkeys concerning their ration of acorns that each was to receive three in the morning and four in the evening. At this the monkeys were very angry. So the keeper said that they might receive four in the morning but three in the evening. With this all the monkeys were pleased. Neither name nor reality were affected either way, and yet the monkeys were pleased at the one and angry at the other. This is also due to their ignorance about the agreement of things. Therefore, the sages harmonize the right and the wrong, and rest in nature the equalizer. This is called following two courses at once.

The knowledge of the ancients was perfect. In what way was it perfect? They were not yet aware that there were things. This is the most perfect knowledge; nothing can be added. Then, some were aware that there were things, but not yet aware that there were distinctions among them. Then, some were aware that there were distinctions, but not yet aware that there was right and wrong among them. When right and wrong became manifest, the Tao thereby declined. With the decline of the Tao came the growth of love. But was there really a growth and a decline? Or was there no growth or decline?

Now, I have something to say [namely, that there is no such thing as right and wrong]. I do not know whether or not what I say agrees with what others say [namely, that there is right and wrong]. Whether or not what I say and what others say agree [in maintaining right and wrong], they at least agree [in assuming that there is right and wrong]. Then there is hardly any difference between what I say and what others say. But though this may be the case, let me try to explain myself. There was a beginning. There was a no-beginning [before the beginning]. There was a no-no-beginning [previous to the no-beginning before the beginning]. There was being. There was nonbeing [before there was being]. There was no-nonbeing [before there was nonbeing]. There was no-no-nonbeing [before there was no-nonbeing]. Suddenly being and nonbeing appeared. And yet, between being and nonbeing, I do not know which is really being and which is really nonbeing. Just now I have said something, and yet I do not know whether what I have said really means something, or does not mean anything at all.

In all the world, there is nothing greater than the tip of an autumn hair; Mount T'ai is small.[10] Neither is there anyone who was longer lived than a child cut off in its infancy; P'eng-tsu himself died young. The universe and I exist together, and all things and I are one. Since all things are one, what room is there for speech? But since I have spoken of them as one, is this not already speech? One and speech make two; two and one make three. Going on from this, even the most skillful reckoner will not be able to keep count, how much less ordinary people! If, proceeding from nothing to something, we soon reach three, how much further shall we reach if we proceed from something to something! Let us not proceed; we had better let it alone. . . .

Ch'ü-ch'iao Tzu asked Ch'ang-wu Tzu, saying: "I heard from the Master [Confucius] that the sage does not occupy himself with the affairs of the world. He neither seeks gain nor avoids injury. He takes no pleasure in seeking. He does not purposely adhere to the Tao. He says things without speaking and does not say anything when he speaks. Thus he roams beyond the dust and dirt of this world. The Master himself considers this a very inappropriate description of the sage, but I consider it to be the Way of the mysterious Tao. How do you think of it, my dear sir?"

"These points," said Ch'ang-wu Tzu, "would have perplexed even the Yellow Emperor; how should Confucius understand them? Moreover, you are too hasty in forming your estimate. You see an egg, and expect to hear it crow. You look at the crossbow, and expect to find a dove roasting. Let me try speaking to you in a somewhat irresponsible manner, and may I ask you to listen to me in the same spirit. Leaning against the sun and the moon and carrying the universe under his arm, the sage blends everything into a harmonious whole. He is unmindful of the confusion and the gloom, and equalizes the humble and the honorable. The multitude strive and toil; the sage is primitive and without knowledge.

[10] Compare with Hui Shih's ten paradoxes, especially items 3, 4, and 5. See Chapter V.

He comprehends ten thousand years as one unity, whole and simple. All things are what they are, and are thus brought together.

"How do I know that the love of life is not a delusion? How do I know that he who is afraid of death is not like a man who left his home as a youth and forgot to return? Lady Li was the daughter of the border warden of Ai. When she was first brought to the state of Chin, she wept until the bosom of her robe was drenched with tears. But when she came to the royal residence, shared with the king his luxurious couch and ate sumptuous food, she regretted that she had wept. How do I know that the dead do not repent of their former craving for life? Those who dream of a merry drinking party may the next morning wail and weep. Those who dream of wailing and weeping may in the morning go off gaily to hunt. While they dream they do not know that they are dreaming. In their dream, they may even try to interpret their dream. Only when they have awakened do they begin to know that they have dreamed. By and by comes the great awakening, and then we shall know that it has all been a great dream. Yet all the while the fools think that they are awake; this they are sure of. With minute nicety, they discriminate between princes and grooms. How stupid! Confucius and you are both in a dream. And when I say that you are in a dream, this is also a dream. This way of talking may be called paradoxical. If after ten thousand generations we could once meet a great sage who knew how to explain the paradox, it would be as though we met him after only one morning or one evening.

"Suppose that you argue with me. If you beat me, instead of my beating you, are you necessarily right, and am I necessarily wrong? Or, if I beat you and not you me, am I necessarily right, and are you necessarily wrong? Must one of us necessarily be right and the other wrong? Or may we not both be right or both be wrong? You and I cannot come to a mutual and common understanding, and others, of course, are all in the dark. Whom shall I ask to decide this dispute? I may ask someone who agrees with you; but since he agrees with you, how can he decide it? I may ask someone who agrees with me; but since he agrees with me, how can he decide it? I may ask someone who differs with both you and me; but since he differs with both you and me, how can he decide it? I may ask someone who agrees with both you and me; but since he agrees with both you and me, how can he decide it? Thus, you and I and the others all would be unable to come to a mutual and common understanding; shall we wait for still another?

"What is meant by harmonizing things according to the order of nature? It is: right is also not right, and 'so' is also 'not so.' If right were necessarily right, then with regard to the difference between right and not right there should be no dispute. If 'so' were necessarily 'so,' then with regard to the difference between 'so' and 'not so' there should also be no dispute. Whether or not the modulating voices [of the disputants] are relative to each other, they should be harmonized according to the order of nature and left to her changing processes. This is the way for us to complete our years. Let us forget the lapse of time; let us forget the claims of right and wrong. But let us find enjoyment in the realm of the infinite and let us abide there."

The Penumbra asked the Shadow, saying, "At one moment you move; at another you are at rest. At one moment you sit down; at another you stand up. Why this inconsistency of purpose?

"Do I not have to depend upon something else," replied the Shadow, "for doing what I do? Does not that something upon which I depend still have to depend upon something else for doing what it does? Do I not have to depend upon the scales of a snake or the wings of a cicada? How can I tell why I do a thing, or why I don't do it?"

Once upon a time, Chuang Chou [i.e., Chuang Tzu] dreamed that he was a butterfly, a butterfly fluttering about, enjoying itself. It did not know that it was Chuang Chou. Suddenly he awoke with a start and he was Chuang Chou again. But he did not know whether he was Chuang Chou who had dreamed that he was a butterfly, or whether he was a butterfly dreaming that he was Chuang Chou. Between Chuang Chou and the butterfly there must be some distinction. This is what is called the transformation of things.

CHAPTER 3: THE FUNDAMENTALS FOR THE CULTIVATION OF LIFE

There is a limit to our life, but there is no limit to knowledge. To pursue what is unlimited with what is limited is a perilous thing. When, knowing this, we still seek to increase our knowledge, we are simply placing ourselves in peril. Shrink from fame when you do good; shrink from punishment when you do evil; pursue always the middle course.

These are the ways to preserve our body, to maintain our life, to support our parents, and to complete our terms of years.

Prince Wen-hui's cook was cutting up a bullock. Every touch of his hand, every shift of his shoulder, every tread of his foot, every thrust of his knee, every sound of the rending flesh, and every note of the movement of the chopper was in perfect harmony—rhythmical like the dance of "The Mulberry Grove," blended like the chords of the "Ching-shou" movement.

"Ah, admirable," said the prince, "that your skill should be so perfect!"

The cook laid down his chopper and replied: "What your servant loves is the Tao, which I have applied to the skill of carving. When I first began to cut up bullocks, what I saw was simply whole bullocks. After three years' practice, I saw no more bullocks as wholes. Now, I work with my mind, and not with my eyes. The functions of my senses stop; my spirit dominates. Following the natural markings, my chopper slips through the great cavities, slides through the great cleavages, taking advantage of the structure that is already there. My skill is now such that my chopper never touches even the smallest tendon or ligament, let alone the great bones. A good cook changes his chopper once a year, because he cuts. An ordinary cook changes his chopper once a month, because he hacks. Now my chopper has been in use for nineteen years; it has cut up several thousand bullocks; yet its edge is as sharp as if it just came from the whetstone. At the joints there are always interstices, and the edge of the chopper is without thickness. If we insert that which is without thickness into an interstice, then we may ply the chopper as we wish and there will be plenty of room. That is why after nineteen years the edge of my chopper is still as sharp as if it just came from the whetstone. Nevertheless, when I come to a complicated joint, and see that there will be some difficulty, I proceed anxiously and with caution. I fix my eyes on it. I move slowly. Then by a very gentle movement of my chopper, the part is quickly separated, and yields like earth crumbling to the ground. Then I stand up straight with the chopper in my hand, and look all round, and feel a sense of triumph and satisfaction. Finally I wipe my chopper and put it in its sheath."

"Excellent," said the prince, "I have heard the words of this cook, and learned the way of cultivating life."

. . . .

When Lao Tzu died, Ch'in-shih went to mourn. He uttered three yells and left.

A disciple asked him, saying, "Were you not a friend of the master?" "Yes, I was," replied Ch'in-shih.

"If so, is it proper to offer your mourning in the way you have done?"

"Yes," said Ch'in-shih. "At first, I thought the other mourners were his [Lao Tzu's] followers; now I know they are not. When I went in to mourn, there were old persons weeping as if for their sons, and young ones as if for their mothers. I suppose they behave like that because there are always some people who speak when there is no need to speak, and weep when there is no need to weep. This is to violate the principle of nature and to increase the emotion of man, forgetting what we have received from nature. This is what the ancients called the crime of violating the principle of nature. The master came because it was his natural time; he went because it was his natural course. Those who abide by their time and follow their natural course cannot be affected by sorrow or joy. They were considered by the ancients as men released by the Lord from bondage."

CHAPTER 17: AUTUMN FLOODS

"From the point of view of the Tao," said the Spirit of the Ocean, "things are neither noble nor mean. From the point of view of the individual things, each considers itself noble and the others mean. From the point of view of common opinion, nobility or meanness do not depend on one's self.

"From the point of view of relativity, if we call a thing great because it is greater than something else, then there is nothing in all creation which is not great. If we call a thing small because it is smaller than something else, then there is nothing which is not small. To know that the universe is but a tare-seed, and the tip of a hair is as a mountain, is to have a clear perception of relative dimensions.

"From the point of view of function, if we call a thing useful when it fulfills a function, then there is nothing in all creation which is not useful. If we call a thing useless when it does not fulfill a function, then there is nothing which is not useless. To understand that east and west are mutually contrary, and yet neither can exist without the other, then we have a proper determination of function.

"From the point of preference, if we approve of anyone who is approved of by someone [at least himself], then there is no one who may not be approved of. If we condemn anyone who is condemned by someone else, then there is no one who may not be condemned. To know that [sage-king] Yao and [tyrant] Chieh would each approve of himself and condemn the other, then we have a clear realization of human preference. . . .

"A battering-ram can knock down a city wall, but it cannot stop a hole—the uses of different implements are different. The horses Ch'i-chi and Hua-liu could gallop a thousand *li* in one day, but for catching rats they were not equal to a wild cat or a weasel—the gifts of different creatures are different. An owl can catch fleas at night, and see the tip of a hair, but if it comes out in the daytime it may stare with its eyes and not see a mountain—the natures of different creatures are different.

"Therefore it has been said, one who wishes to uphold the right and eliminate the wrong, or uphold order and eliminate disorder, must be ignorant of the great principles of the universe as well as the nature of things. One might as well try to uphold Heaven and eliminate the earth, or uphold the yin and eliminate the yang, which is clearly absurd. Yet notwithstanding, there are people who insist upon talking in this way without cease. They must be either fools or knaves. . . .

"From the point of view of the Tao," said the Spirit of the Ocean, "what is noble, and what is mean? These are but phrases in a process of alternation. Do not be narrowly restricted in your inclination, lest you conflict with the Tao. What is few, and what is many? They are but varying amounts in a process of rotation. Do not be slavishly uniform in your conduct, lest you deviate from the Tao. Be august, like the ruler of a state whose favors are impartial. Be transcendant, like the god of the land at a sacrifice whose benediction is impartial. Be expansive, like the boundlessness of the four directions within which there are no sectional limits. Embrace all creation in your bosom, favoring and harboring none in particular. This is called impartiality. And where all things are equal, how is it possible for some to be short and some long?

"The Tao is without beginning and without end. Things are born and die, without holding to any permanence. They are now empty, now full, without maintaining a constant form. The years cannot be made to abide; time cannot be arrested. Processes of increase and decrease are in operation and every end is followed by a new beginning. Thus may we speak of the great norm [of the Tao] and the principle pervading all things.

"The life of things passes by like a galloping horse. Every movement brings a change, and every hour makes a difference. What is one to do or what is one not to do? Indeed everything will take its own course. . . .

"Therefore it has been said that the natural abides within, the artificial without, and virtue (*te*) resides in the natural. If one knows the course of nature and man, taking nature as the fundamental and abiding by virtue, one may feel free either to proceed or retreat, either to contract or extend, for there is always a return to the essential and to the ultimate."

"What do you mean," inquired the Earl of the River, "by the natural and the artificial?"

"Horses and oxen," answered the Spirit of the Ocean, "have four feet. That is the natural. Putting a halter on a horse's head, a string through a bullock's nose—that is the artificial.

"Therefore it has been said, do not let the artificial obliterate the natural; do not let effort obliterate destiny; do not let enjoyment be sacrificed to fame. Diligently observe these precepts without fail, and thus you will revert to the original innocence."

. . . .

Once Chuang Tzu was fishing in the P'u River when the King of Ch'u sent two of his ministers to announce that he wished to entrust to Chuang Tzu the care of his entire domain.

Chuang Tzu held his fishing pole and, without turning his head, said: "I have heard that Ch'u possesses a sacred tortoise which has been dead for three thousand years and which the king keeps wrapped up in a box and stored in his ancestral temple. Is this tortoise better off dead and with its bones venerated, or would it be better off alive with its tail dragging in the mud?"

"It would be better off alive and dragging its tail in the mud," the two ministers replied.

"Then go away!" said Chuang Tzu, "and I will drag my tail in the mud!"

. . . .

Chuang Tzu and Hui Tzu were strolling one day on the bridge over the River Hao, when the former observed, "See how the minnows are darting about! Such is the pleasure that fish enjoy." "You are not a fish," said Hui Tzu. "How do you know what fish enjoy?"

"You are not I," retorted Chuang Tzu, "so how do you know that I do not know what fish enjoy?" "I am not you," said Hui Tzu, "and so evidently I do not know what you know. But it is also evident that you are not a fish, and so it is certain that you do not know what fish enjoy."

"Let us go back," said Chuang Tzu, "to your original question. You asked me *how* I knew what fish enjoy. The way you put the question shows that you already knew that I knew. I know it just as we stand here over the Hao."

CHAPTER 33: THE WORLD OF THOUGHT

This is not only the earliest survey of thought in ancient China, but one which has become a classic of Chinese philosophical criticism for its succinctness of presentation and penetrating analysis. In it we see reflected a period of intense intellectual excitement, of great variety and vitality of thought, which belies the conclusion that might be drawn from the rather limited literature surviving from this time. For many of the thinkers taken up here, this chapter is the chief, and sometimes only, source of information. The fact that Chuang Tzu's philosophy is among those criticized has given rise to the suspicion that this chapter has been appended to the book by a later hand, a view held by most scholars. It is significant that Lao Tzu and Chuang Tzu are treated separately, and that the latter is regarded as the pinnacle of thought in this period.

There are many in the world who devote themselves to theories of law and conduct. Each man thinks his own is perfect. Where then is to be found what the ancients called the system of Tao? It is everywhere. Whence comes the spiritual? Whence comes the intelligent? There is that which brings forth sages; there is that which produces kings. They all originate in the One. . . .

The men of old were indeed perfect! They were ranked among the gods and they were the equals of Heaven and earth; they nurtured all things and they harmonized the world. Their beneficent influence was extended to all people. Their ways were expressed through the basic measures and involved in the minutest details. Their spirit permeated everywhere in the six directions and the four quarters, and into everything great or small, fine or coarse. That which was expressed in the measures and institutions has been preserved in a number of the official records of ancient laws and traditions. That which was recorded in the Classics of *Odes, History, Rites,* and *Music* has been known to many of the scholars of Tsou and Lu [11] and the intelligentsia. The *Book of Odes* tells of man's longings; the *Book of History* records events; the *Book of Rites* prescribes conduct; the *Book of Music* expresses harmony of the spirit; the *Book of Changes* discusses the principles of the yin and the yang; and the *Spring and Autumn Annals* defines names and duties. As to the rest of the measures that were diffused throughout the world and established in the Middle Kingdom they were sometimes mentioned and discussed by the various other schools.

When the world fell into chaos, sages and worthies no longer manifested themselves, and the Tao lost its power of unity. Many in the world comprehended but one particular aspect of the whole and they were delighted with themselves. . . . So it was that the "Tao of sageliness within and kingliness without" became obscure and unclear, repressed and suspended. Everyone in the world did what he wished and was a rule unto himself. Alas! The various schools of philosophy went their own ways, farther and farther afield, and they could never accord with the truth. Thus students in later times have unfortunately not been able to see the original purity of Heaven and earth or the complete social order of the ancients. The system of the Tao has been scattered in fragments throughout the world!

To leave no examples of extravagance to future generations, to show no wastefulness in the use of things, to indulge in no excess of measures and institutions, but to keep themselves under the restraint of strict rules so as to be prepared for relieving others in emergencies—these were some of the aspects of the system of the Tao among the ancients. Mo Ti (Mo Tzu) and Ch'in Ku-li [12] heard of them and cherished them. But in practicing them themselves they went to extremes and in restricting other people they were too arbitrary. Mo Tzu wrote an essay on "Condemnation of Music" and another on "Economy of Expenditures." There was to be no singing for the living and no mourning for the dead. He taught universal love and mutual benefit and condemned war. His teaching excluded anger. Besides, he was fond of study, and pressed everyone to

[11] Home states of Mencius and Confucius, indicating the Confucian school.
[12] A leading disciple of Mo Tzu.

conform to his teachings. He did not agree with the former kings. He wanted to do away with the rites and music of the ancients. . . .

Men want to sing but he condemns singing; men want to mourn but he condemns mourning; men want to enjoy music but he condemns music—is this truly in accord with man's nature? Any teaching that would have men toil through life and be contented with a bare funeral at death is too austere. It makes men sorrowful and dejected. Its practice would be difficult. I fear it cannot be regarded as the Tao of the sages. It is contrary to human nature and few people can stand it. Though Mo Tzu himself was able to carry it out, how about the rest of mankind? Being alien to mankind, his teaching is far removed from the way of the kings.

Mo Tzu, in arguing for his system, said: "Formerly when Yü dealt with the deluge, channeling the water into streams and rivers and guiding their courses through the four barbarian regions and the nine provinces, there were 300 great rivers, 3,000 tributaries and innumerable streamlets. With his own hands, Yü handled spade and bucket to channel all the streams into the great rivers. His legs were worn thin, and his shins worn hairless; he was bathed by heavy rains, and combed by the fierce winds. Yet he succeeded in pacifying all the states. Yü was a great sage, and yet he toiled so hard for the world." Thus most of the later Mo-ists were led to use skins and coarse linen garments, and straw and wood for sandals; to toil night and day without cease and to consider self-sacrifice as the ideal. They said: "If we cannot do this we are not following the way of Yü and shall be unworthy to be called Mo-ists."

The disciples of Hsiang-li Ch'in, such as Wo Hou, and the Mo-ists of the South, such as K'u Hou, Chi Ch'ih, and Teng Ling Tzu, all recited the "Mo-ist canon" but interpreted it differently, calling each other heretics of Mo-ism. They disputed with each other about "hardness and whiteness," about identity and difference, and answered each other's arguments in strange and contradictory terms. However, they all regarded the Elder Master as a living sage, aspiring to be his medium upon his death, in order to become his successor. To this day these differences are not settled.

The intentions of Mo Tzu and Ch'in Ku-li were right; their practice was wrong. They would make the Mo-ists of later ages feel it necessary to encourage each other in self-sacrifice until their legs were worn thin

and their shins hairless. The effect of such teachings would be to produce
something better than disorder but still far from perfect order. Nevertheless, Mo Tzu was truly a fine man, of whom there are only too few
to be found. Despite all personal hardships, he held fast to his ideal—
a man of excellence indeed!

Not to be encumbered with popular fashions, not to be dazzled by
the display of things, not to be unfeeling toward other men, and not
to be antagonistic to the multitude; to desire peace in the world for
the preservation of the life of the people; to seek no more than is sufficient for nourishing oneself and others, thus setting one's heart at peace
—these were some of the aspects of the system of the Tao among the
ancients. Sung Hsing and Yin Wen heard of them and cherished them.
They adopted a Hua Shan cap [with a flat top to indicate equality] as
their badge. In dealing with things they began to eliminate all prejudices.
They talked about states of mind and called them the inner bases of
conduct. By warmth of affection they sought the harmony of joy, wherewith to blend all people in the world. They wished to establish this as
the principle of all things. They tried to save the people from fighting
by demonstrating that an insult is no disgrace. They would save the
world from wars by condemning aggression and urging disarmament.
With this message they went about the world, counseling the high and
instructing the low. Though the people would have none of it, Sung
and Yin never stopped harping upon it. Hence about them it was said:
"When everybody was wearied of seeing them, they persisted in showing themselves." However, they did too much for others, too little for
themselves. . . .

To be impartial and nonpartisan; to be compliant and selfless; to be
free from insistence and prejudice; to take things as they come; to be
without worry or care; not to rely on one's wits; to accept all and mingle
with all—these were some of the aspects of the system of the Tao among
the ancients. P'eng Meng, T'ien, and Shen Tao heard of them and
cherished them. Their fundamental idea was the equality of things. They
said: "Heaven shelters things but does not support them. The earth supports them but does not shelter them. The great Tao is all-embracing
without making any distinctions." Realizing that all things have their
capacities and limitations, they said: "Selection cannot embrace the whole;
instruction cannot exhaust the ultimate; only the Tao is all-inclusive."

Therefore Shen Tao discarded knowledge and renounced the self; he acted only upon necessity and was indifferent to things. Such were his principles. . . .

He went when he was pushed and followed when he was led, moving round and round like a whirling gale, like a feather tossed in the wind, like a millstone set turning. He thus preserved himself and avoided defects; in motion or at rest he was free from error and above reproach. Why was this so? Because creatures without reason do not trouble about asserting themselves or burden their minds with knowledge; in motion or at rest they do not depart from the principles of nature, and for this reason they never receive any praise [or blame]. Therefore he said: "Let us be just like creatures without knowledge. There is no use for sages and worthies. A clod of earth never misses the Tao."

Capable and spirited men laughed at him and said, "The teachings of Shen Tao are not for the practice of the living; they are the way of the dead. They would make one become nothing but peculiar."

It was just the same with T'ien P'ien. He studied under P'eng Meng and learned what could not be taught. P'eng Meng's master used to say: "Of old, the men of Tao were only trying to reach the state beyond right and wrong. That was all. So subtle is this doctrine that it cannot be expressed in words!"

The teaching of these men is often contrary to human nature and therefore few pay attention to it. They were not free from arbitrary judgments. What they called Tao is not the Tao; what they considered right was often wrong. P'eng Meng, T'ien P'ien, and Shen Tao did not really know the Tao. Nevertheless, they had probably heard something about it.

To regard essences as subtle, to regard things as coarse, to regard all measurable quantities as inadequate [representations of reality], to abide calmly and dispassionately alone with the spirits—these were some aspects of the system of the Tao among the ancients. Kuan Yin and Lao Tan [Lao Tzu] heard of them and cherished them. They built their system upon the principle of eternal nonbeing and based it upon the idea of supreme unity. Weakness and humility were its outward expression and pure emptiness with noninjury to all things were for them the true substance of their teaching. Kuan Yin said: "Give up all your assumptions, and things and forms will appear as they are. In motion, be like water; at rest, be like a mirror; in response, be like an echo. Be subtle and appear as if not to exist; be quiet, and appear like clear water. He who agrees with others enjoys peace; he who gains, loses. Do not ever put yourself forward, but always follow behind."

Lao Tzu said: "Know the masculine but maintain the feminine; become thereby a ravine for the world. Know purity but endure disgrace; become thereby a valley for the world." Men all reach for the first; he alone took the last. He said, "Receive unto yourself the refuse of the world." Men all seek the substantial; he alone took the empty. Because he did not hoard, he had abundance; indeed great was his abundance. His actions were effortless and without waste. He believed in doing nothing, and laughed at the ingenious. Men all seek for happiness; he alone sought self-preservation through adaptation. He said: "Let us be free from reproach." He believed in depth for one's foundation, and simplicity as the rule of outward conduct. He said: "The hard will be crushed; the sharp will be blunted." He was always generous and tolerant toward things. He would not exploit others. This may be considered the height of perfection. Kuan Yin and Lao Tan—they belonged with the great and true men of old!

Silent and formless, changing and impermanent! Are life and death one? Do I coexist with heaven and earth? Where do the spirits move? Disappearing whither, going whence, so mysteriously and suddenly? All things lie spread before me, but in none of them can be found my destiny—these were some aspects of the system of the Tao among the ancients. Chuang Chou [Chuang Tzu] heard of them and cherished them. With unbridled fancies, extravagant language, and romantic nonsense, he gave free play to his ideas without restraint and without partiality. He regarded the world as dense and muddled, so that discussions in a dignified style would be of no avail. Thereupon he employed effervescent words for rambling discussions, "weighty words" for conveying truths, and allegories for broad illustrations. He had personal communion with the spirit of Heaven and earth but no sense of pride over things. He did not quarrel with what others regard as right and wrong, and so he was able to mingle with conventional society. Though his writings have a dazzling style and stagger the imagination, they are not directed against anything and so are harmless. Though his language is full of irregularities, it is ingenious and witty, seeming to gush forth from the fullness of his thoughts in spite of himself. Above, his spirit roams with the creator; below, he makes friends of those who ignore beginning or end, and are indifferent toward life and death. In regard to the fundamental he was comprehensive and great, profound and free. In regard to the essential he might be called the harmonizer of things and adapter to the higher level. Nevertheless, in his response to change and his interpretation of things, his principles were inexhaustible and not divorced from their origin (Tao). He is mysterious, obscure and boundless.

Hui Shih [13] was a man of many ideas. His writings would fill five carriages, but his doctrines were contradictory and his sayings missed the truth. Referring to the nature of the physical universe, he said: [Here follow ten paradoxes, for which see Chapter V].

Through such sayings Hui Shih made a great show in the world and tried to enlighten the debaters. The debaters of the day were delighted with them. They said: [Here follow twenty-one paradoxes, for which see Chapter V].

Such were the questions over which the debaters argued with Hui Shih all their days without coming to an end.

Huan T'uan and Kung-sun Lung, [14] who were among the debaters, turned men's minds and altered their ideas. They were able to subdue people's tongues but not to win their hearts. Here lay the weakness of the debaters.

Day after day, Hui Shih exercised his wit to argue with people, and deliberately presented strange propositions to the debaters of the day. This was his general characteristic. Nevertheless, Hui Shih regarded his own eloquence as the most excellent. He said: "The universe alone is greater!" He wished to maintain supremacy but he did not have a proper system. Once a queer man from the south named Huang Liao asked him why the sky did not fall and the earth sink, as well as about the cause of wind, rain, and the rolling thunder. Hui Shih answered without hesitation and replied without taking time for reflection. He talked about everything in the universe, on and on without end, and imagining still that his words were but few, he added to them the strangest observations. Actually he merely contradicted people, but wished to have the

[13] For Hui Shih, see Chapter V.   [14] For Kung-sun Lung, see Chapter V.

reputation of overcoming them. Therefore he was never on good terms with others. Weak in the cultivation of virtue, strong in the handling of things, his way was a narrow one indeed!

From the point of view of the Tao of the universe, Hui Shih's ingenuity was about as effective as a humming mosquito or a buzzing fly. Of what use was he to the world? It should be enough to recognize the unity of the Tao and advance it with but a few words. But Hui Shih could not content himself with this; he spread himself insatiably over all things, to be known in the end only as a skilled debater. Alas! With all his talents Hui Shih wandered about without achieving anything; he went after all things without reverting to the Tao. He was like one trying to silence an echo by shouting at it, or like one trying to race with his own shadow. How sad!

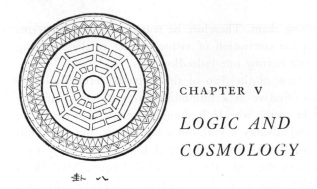

CHAPTER V

LOGIC AND
COSMOLOGY

卦 八

Chinese philosophers as a rule have not interested themselves in logic as an independent discipline. Among the "hundred philosophers" of the classical period there were few logicians. Seven works are listed in the section on logic in the earliest Chinese bibliographical record compiled around the beginning of the Christian era, but of these unfortunately the only authentic text extant is the *Kung-sun Lung Tzu*. Additional material on logic is scattered in the *Mo Tzu,* the *Chuang Tzu,* and the *Hsün Tzu.* The subject matter of these discussions may be called logic only if the term is understood in the broadest sense, for it includes dialectics, sophisms, and paradoxes, as well as logic. The Chinese term for this school is *Ming-chia* or School of Names, the closest English equivalent for which might be "School of Semantics."

HUI SHIH AND KUNG-SUN LUNG

Hui Shih (380–300 b.c.?) and Kung-sun Lung (320–250 b.c.?) are usually regarded as the typical representatives of the school of logic. Not much is known about the life of either of these thinkers. Hui Shih was a man of learning and affairs, an influential minister in one of the feudal states, and the author of a code of laws. He and Chuang Tzu were friends and mutual critics and the *Chuang Tzu* contains several accounts of delightful conversations between the two. Hui Shih wrote a work on logic which is now lost, but a list of ten of his paradoxes has been preserved in the *Chuang Tzu* and is included in our selection. Of the ten items, the first is what might be called an analytical proposition and the last a comprehensive assertion about the nature of existence. Item five seems to be a general statement of the principle of relativity, and the rest are paradoxes based on the relativity of time and space. It is interesting to note that item ten advocates universal love. But in contrast to Mo Tzu, the basis of Hui Shih's doctrine is intellectual rather than religious.

Kung-sun Lung was a scholar who kept a school, had pupils, and often lived under the patronage of one feudal ruler or another. He was chiefly interested in logic and dialectic, and was, like Hui Shih, an advocate of pacifism and disarmament. The *Kung-sun Lung Tzu* is a very brief work, as difficult as it is intriguing. The three chapters we have included in the readings are the best known. Underlying all this intricate argumentation is a method of epistemological analysis, reducing sensory complexes to simple qualities.

A full explanation of these brief selections would require extended analysis and commentary. Some passages, indeed, defy all attempts at elucidation. Nevertheless, even a superficial acquaintance with this type of literature will dispel the thought that logical inquiry is wholly foreign to the Chinese tradition. At the same time its very presence prompts us to ask why, instead of being pursued to a higher stage of development, this line of inquiry should have been relegated to a position of minor importance, in fact of almost complete disregard, by the leading schools of Chinese thought in later times.

The Paradoxes of Hui Shih and the Debaters
[From *Chuang Tzu*, chapter 33]

HUI SHIH

1. The greatest thing has nothing beyond itself; this is called the infinite. The smallest thing has nothing within itself; this is called the infinitesimal.

2. That which has no thickness cannot be increased in thickness; yet in extent it may cover a thousand *li*.

3. The heavens are as low as the earth; mountains are on the same level as marshes.

4. The sun at noon is the sun declining. The creature born is the creature dying.

5. A great similarity differs from a little similarity; these are called the lesser similarities and differences. All things are similar and yet all are different; these are called the greater similarities and differences.

6. The South has no limit and has a limit.

7. I go to Yüeh today and arrived there yesterday.

8. Linked rings can be detached.

9. I know the center of the world; it is north of Yen [the northernmost state], and south of Yüeh [the southernmost state].

10. Love all things equally, for the heavens and the earth are one composite body.

THE DEBATERS

1. The egg has feathers.

2. A chicken has three legs.

3. Ying [the capital of Ch'u] contains the whole world.

4. A dog can be a sheep.

5. The horse lays eggs.

6. The frog has a tail.

7. Fire is not hot.

8. Mountains have mouths.

9. The wheel never touches the ground.

10. The eye does not see.

11. Attributes never reach; the reaching never comes to an end.

12. The tortoise is longer than the snake.

13. T-squares are not right-angled, and compasses cannot make circles.

14. Chisels do not surround their handles.

15. The shadow of a flying bird never moves.

16. There are moments when a flying arrow is neither in motion nor at rest.

17. A puppy is not a dog.

18. A bay horse and a dun cow make three.

19. A white dog is black.

20. An orphan colt has never had a mother.

21. Take a rod one foot long and cut it in half every day, and it will still have something left even after ten thousand generations.

Selections from the Kung-sun Lung Tzu

CHAPTER 2: DISCOURSE ON THE WHITE HORSE

Q: [1] A white horse is not a horse [2]—is this possible?

A: Yes.

Q: Why?

A: "Horse" denotes form: "White" denotes color. What denotes color does not denote form. Therefore it is said, a white horse is not a horse.

Q: There being a white horse, one cannot say that there is no horse. If one cannot say that there is no horse, then why is it not a horse? Since there being a white horse one must admit that there is a horse, how can "white" deny the existence of "horse"?

A · When a horse is wanted, yellow and black ones may all be brought. But when a white horse is wanted, yellow and black ones may not be brought. If a white horse were a horse, then what is wanted in the two instances would be the same. If what is wanted were the same, then a white horse would be no different from a horse. If what is wanted were not different, then why is it that yellow and black horses are satisfactory in the one case but not in the other? What is satisfied and what is not satisfied evidently are not the same. Now the yellow and black horses remain the same, and yet they will do for a horse, but not for a white horse. Hence it should be clear that a white horse is not a horse.

Q: If a horse with color is considered not a horse, then there will be no horses on earth, as there are no colorless horses on earth! Is this possible?

A: Horses, of course, have color. Therefore there are white horses. If horses had no color, there would be merely horses. How could we specify white horses?

But a white horse is not a horse. A white horse is horse united with

---

[1] It is quite evident that this "Discourse" is written in the style of a dialogue between Kung-sun Lung and his common-sense critic. But in the original text there are no indications marking out a question from an answer or one speech from another. Therefore we must be held responsible for the insertion of the Q (question) and A (answer) signs, as well as for punctuation.

[2] "A white horse is not a horse" was evidently a much debated question among the dialecticians of the day.

whiteness, or whiteness united with horse. Therefore, it is said, a white horse is not a horse.

Q: Horse not united with whiteness is horse; whiteness not united with horse is whiteness, as you say. But when horse and whiteness are united, the compound name white horse is applied, which means that they are united. It is not right to refer to them as though they were not united. Therefore it is not right to say that a white horse is not a horse.

Counter-Q: If you should regard a white horse as being a horse, you might as well claim a white horse to be a yellow horse. Would this be possible?

A: No.

A: To hold that a horse is different from a yellow horse is to differentiate a yellow horse from a horse. To differentiate a yellow horse from a horse is to regard a yellow horse as not a horse. Now to regard a yellow horse as not a horse and yet to hold that a white horse is a horse would be like saying that birds fly in lakes or inner and outer coffins are kept in separate places. This would be the most perverse talk and confused argument in the world.

Q: A white horse cannot be said to be no horse, and this is the basis of separating whiteness. Even if it is not separated, still a white horse cannot be said to be no horse. The reason for holding it to be a horse is simply that a horse is invariably a horse, and not that a white horse is another kind of horse. Therefore when we hold that it is a horse, that is not to say that there is one kind of horse and another kind of horse.

A: The whiteness that does not fix itself upon any object may simply be overlooked. But in speaking of the white horse, we refer to a whiteness that is fixed upon its object. Whiteness that is fixed upon an object, is not just whiteness as such.

The term "horse" does not involve any choice of color. Therefore yellow and black ones all will do. The term "white horse" does involve the choice of color. Yellow and black ones are all rejected owing to their color. White horses alone will do. That which does not exclude any color is not the same as that which excludes certain colors. Therefore it is said, a white horse is not a horse.

CHAPTER 3: DISCOURSE ON THINGS AND THEIR ATTRIBUTES [3]

I

Thesis: [4] Things consist of nothing but their attributes. But attributes are not attributes in and of themselves. [5]

Without attributes things cannot be said to be things. Without things, can there be said to be attributes?

2

Antithesis: Attributes are that which do not exist on earth; things are that which do exist on earth. It would be improper to take what does exist as what does not exist.

Thesis. Indeed there are no attributes on earth, and things may not be said to be just attributes [as you say]. Although things may not be said to be attributes, however, are they not that to which attributes are attributed? Attributes are not attributes in and of themselves, but things consist of nothing but their attributes. [6]

Again, there are no attributes on earth, [as you say]. Although things may not be said to be just attributes, certainly neither do they consist of anything other than attributes. Since they do not consist of anything other than attributes, things consist of nothing but attributes. [Ergo], things consist of nothing but their attributes, but attributes are not attributes in and of themselves.

3

Antithesis: That there are no attributes on earth is due to the fact that things have their respective names and are not just attributes. To call them attributes when they are not is to claim all are attributes. It would be improper to take what are not all attributes as what are nothing but attributes.

[3] The term chih, "attribute," may be understood as "to denote," "to designate," "predicate," "quality," and possibly even "universal" and "essence." This "Discourse" endeavors to point out the differences as well as the relationship between the two phases of existence that in Western philosophy are sometimes spoken of as substance and attributes or qualities. In fact, the whole Kung-sun Lung Tzu may be said to revolve around the central theme discussed in this "Discourse."

[4] The insertion of "thesis" and "antithesis" has been made by the translator.

[5] Announcement of the main theme of the discourse.

[6] Reiteration of the main theme.

Thesis: To be sure, attributes are that which does not exist on earth [as you say]. Although there are no attributes on earth, things may not be said to be without attributes. Since they may not be said to be without attributes, things do not consist of anything other than their attributes.[7] Since they do not consist of anything other than their attributes, things consist of nothing but their attributes.[8]

Not that attributes are not attributes, but attributes in things are not attributes in and of themselves. Were there no attributes-in-things on earth, who could say simply there are no attributes? Were there no things on earth, who could say simply there are attributes? Were there attributes but no attributes-in-things, who could say simply there are not attributes or simply that things consist of nothing but their attributes?

Furthermore, attributes are indeed not attributes in and of themselves.[9] And it is only because they adhere to things that they become attributes.

CHAPTER 5: DISCOURSE ON HARDNESS AND WHITENESS

Q: Hardness, whiteness, and stone—may one refer to them as three?
A: No.
Q: May one refer to them as two?
A: Yes.
Q: Why?
A: Hardness being not there, one perceives whiteness: thus what is represented is two [i.e., whiteness and stone]. Similarly whiteness not being there, one perceives hardness: thus what is represented is again two [i.e., hardness and stone].

Q: Having perceived whiteness one cannot say that whiteness is not there; having perceived hardness one cannot say that hardness is not there. Such being the nature of the existence of the stone, are there not three things?

A: When seeing, one does not perceive hardness but perceives whiteness—this is because hardness is not there. When touching, one does not perceive whiteness but perceives hardness—this is because whiteness is not there.

---

[7] A glaringly weak link in the chain of argument.
[8] Reiteration of the first half of the main theme.
[9] Reiteration of the second half of the main theme.

Q: If there were no whiteness on earth, one could not see a stone, and if there were no hardness on earth, one could not feel a stone. Hardness, whiteness, and the stone do not exclude one another; how could [one of] the three be hidden?

A: It hides itself, and is not hidden in or by anything else.

Q: Whiteness and hardness are indispensable qualities permeating each other in the stone. How is it possible for any of them to hide itself?

A: One perceives whiteness and one perceives hardness; what is seen and what is not seen are evidently separate. It is because the one [stone] and the two [qualities] do not permeate each other that they are separate. To be separate is [to be in a position] to hide.

Q: [The whiteness is] the whiteness of the stone and [the hardness is] the hardness of the stone. Although one of them is visible while the other is not, the two together with the stone make three. They permeate one another as width and length do in the case of a surface. Why should they not be all represented together?

A: Something may be white, but whiteness is not thereby fixed upon it; something may be hard, but hardness is not thereby fixed upon it. What is not fixed upon anything is of universal application. How then is it possible to assume that they [hardness and whiteness] must be in and of the stone?

Q: We touch the stone; unless it can be felt, there can be no stone; unless there is the stone there is no sense in referring to the white stone. That the stone and its qualities are not separate is something that is necessarily and infinitely so.

A: Stone is one; hardness and whiteness are two, though they are in the stone. But one of them can be felt while the other cannot; one of them can be seen while the other cannot. Obviously the tangible and intangible are separate; the visible and the invisible hide from each other. There being hiding, who will say that they are not separate?

Q: Because the eye cannot behold hardness nor the hand grasp whiteness, one cannot urge that there is no hardness or whiteness. These organs function differently and cannot substitute for each other. But, just the same, hardness and whiteness both reside in the stone, and how can you insist that they are separate?

A: Hardness is hardness, not necessarily of the stone, as it can be of any other thing. Again, it is not necessarily hardness of any other thing; it can be hardness in and of itself. The hardness that is neither of the stone nor of any other thing does not seem to exist in the world—this is merely to say that it is hidden.

If whiteness could not be whiteness in and of itself, how could it be whiteness of stone and things? If, on the other hand, whiteness is actually whiteness in and of itself, then it is whiteness without having to be whiteness of anything. With yellow and black colors it is the same. Then the stone itself is no more there, and what sense is there in referring to the hard and white stone? These are all separate, and they are separate from the nature of things. It is far better to accept the nature of things than to exert one's perceptive power of feeling and sight.[10]

Furthermore, whiteness is beheld by the eye, but the eye sees by means of light. However, light does not have the faculty of vision. Then neither light nor the eye can by itself see whiteness, and it must be the mind that sees it. Actually the mind alone cannot see it either. Thus the sight of whiteness is something separate.

Hardness is felt by the hand, but the hand feels by means of a hammer. However, the hammer does not have the faculty of feeling. Then neither the hammer nor the hand can feel hardness by itself, and it must be the mind that feels it. Actually the mind cannot feel it either. Thus the feeling of hardness is something separate.[11]

All existences in the world are separate; only when they are treated as independent is it correct.

TSOU YEN: YIN-YANG AND FIVE AGENTS THEORIES

Of the six major schools of classical philosophy, the school of yin-yang and five agents is the only one for which no representative work remains today. The philosopher Tsou Yen (340–260 B.C.?) is often referred

[10] This sentence, like many others, is odd and obscure. We have tried to make out of it the best sense possible.

[11] The last three paragraphs of the chapter are particularly corrupt. It is evident that they try to prove the same point for "hardness" as the preceding paragraphs do for "whiteness." The original text of this particular paragraph was probably in exact parallel form with the preceding one, and the translation is rendered on this assumption.

to as the leading thinker of this school, but his works are lost and all that we know about him is a brief account of his life and thought contained in the *Shih chi* or *Records of the Historian* of Ssu-ma Ch'ien (145?–90? B.C.).

The theories of the yin-yang and of the five agents were probably in their origins quite separate. Both are attempts to explain the workings of the universe in terms of a few basic substances, or more correctly, forces; the pair of complementary agents known as the yin and the yang, and the series of elements called the five powers or five agents (*wu-hsing*). Possibly both of these concepts date from very early times, though they do not seem to be of much importance until mid-Chou times. At that time the need was probably felt for a naturalistic explanation of the working of the universe which would avoid the superstitions and caprices of older interpretations. Thus was developed and elaborated the concept of the basic forces of the yin and yang and the five agents which, operating with complete regularity and spontaneity, motivate and govern all growth and change in the physical world.

We include here two short passages from the *Book of History* which deal with the theory of the five agents. These purport to describe very ancient times, though the actual date of their composition is probably late Chou. These are followed by Ssu-ma Ch'ien's account of the philosopher Tsou Yen. The theories of yin-yang, and the five agents which were just beginning to develop and gain acceptance during the Chou, came to have the greatest importance in the history of both philosophy and popular belief. Because of the lack of adequate illustrative material, however, a detailed discussion of their significance will be postponed until the next section dealing with Han thought.

Selections from the Book of History

THE ANNOUNCEMENT AT KAN

There was a great battle in Kan. The six minister-generals of his hosts were assembled. The king[12] said: "Oh, all ye of my six armies. I have a solemn announcement to make to you.

"The Lord of Hu violates and despises the five agents [metal, wood,

---

[12] Ch'i, the son of Yü and the second king of the Hsia Dynasty; 2197 B.C. is the traditional date of his accession.

water, fire, and earth], and he neglects and discards the three proper spheres [Heaven, earth, and man]. Heaven is about to cut off his mandate; and I am reverently executing the punishment appointed by Heaven."

THE GREAT PLAN

In the thirteenth year the king [13] consulted the Prince of Chi. The king spoke and said: "Oh, Prince of Chi! Heaven, unseen, commands mankind here below and helps it to keep in harmony with its surroundings. I do not know how constant norms achieve their due order."

The Prince of Chi spoke and said: "I have heard that in ancient times [Yü's father] Kun dammed up the inundating waters, and brought disorder into the arrangement of the five agents. God was aroused to anger, and did not give him the Great Plan with its nine categories, whereupon the constant norms were ruined. As to Kun, he was executed, and Yü rose as his successor. Heaven then bestowed upon Yü the Great Plan with its nine categories, and the constant norms were thereby set forth in their due order.

[The nine categories are:] 1) the five agents; 2) reverent attention to the five matters [appearance, speech, vision, hearing, and thought]; 3) earnest devotion to the eight measures of government [food, finance, religious sacrifices, public works, education, justice, diplomacy, and army]; 4) the harmonious use of the five regulators [year, month, day, stars and zodiacal signs, and the calendar]; 5) the establishment and use of the royal standard; 6) the discerning use of the three virtues [correctness, mastery through strength, and mastery through weakness]; 7) the intelligent use of the determinators of doubt; 8) the thoughtful use of the various verifications; and 9) the appreciative use of the five felicities [longevity, wealth, health, love of virtue, and a crowning death] and the awing use of the six extremities [premature death, illness, worry, poverty, evil, and weakness].

"First, the five agents: water, fire, wood, metal, and earth. [As to their nature:] Water is the power to soak and descend; fire, to blaze and ascend; wood, to be crooked and straight; metal, to be malleable; and earth, to take seeds and yield crops. That which soaks and descends produces saltiness; that which blazes and ascends produces bitterness; that

---

[13] King Wu, a co-founder of the Chou Dynasty, eleventh century B.C.

which is crooked or straight produces sourness; that which is malleable produces acridity; that which takes seeds and yields crops produces sweetness."

The Life and Thought of Tsou Yen
[From *Shih chi*, 74:1b–3a]

In the state of Ch'i there were three scholars named Tsou. . . . The second of the Tsou scholars was Tsou Yen, who came after Mencius. He saw that the rulers were becoming ever more dissolute and were not disposed to exalt virtue, like [those ancient rulers recorded in] the Ta ya [section of the *Book of Odes*], embodying it themselves and diffusing it among the common people. Thereupon he scrutinized the operations of the yin and yang and increase and decrease, and wrote about the strange ways of the processes of change, including such essays as "On the Beginning and End," "The Great Sage," etc., totaling more than one hundred thousand words. His words were grandiose and unorthodox. He invariably began by examining small objects, and extended the examination to larger and larger ones till infinity.

He began by tracing from contemporary times back to the time of the Yellow Emperor, as is commonly done by scholars. Then he followed the rise and fall of the ages, noted their good fortune and misfortune as well as their institutions, and extended his survey back to the time before heaven and earth were born, to what was mysterious and unfathomable. . . .

He claimed that from the time of the separation of heaven and earth onward, the five powers [of the five agents] had been in the processes of mutual production and mutual overcoming, and that each temporal reign was in exact correspondence with one of the powers, like parts of a tally. . . .

His theories were all of this sort. But in the final analysis they all came back to the virtues of humanity, righteousness, frugality, and the observance of the proper relations between ruler and subject, superior and inferior, and the six family relationships. It is only at the start that his theories are so extravagant. The rulers and ministers, when they first encountered his theories, were struck with awe and moved to acceptance, but in the end they were unable to practice them.

CHAPTER VI

MOLDERS OF
THE CONFUCIAN
TRADITION

The most important man in the history of Confucianism after its founder
is Meng Tzu or Mencius (372–289 B.C.?), who has been traditionally
regarded by the Chinese people as their Second Sage. He was a native
of the state of Ch'i, near Confucius' old home of Lu, and studied with
a disciple of Confucius' grandson, Tzu Ssu. Like Confucius he spent
most of his life visiting the court of one feudal lord after another in
search of a ruler who would put his teachings into practice. But by
Mencius' time the disintegration of the old feudal order and the moral
decay that had been so apparent in the age of Confucius some two hundred years earlier had reached a crucial stage. Six or seven of the larger
states had succeeded in swallowing up their smaller neighbors and were
locked in a fierce and precarious struggle for supremacy and survival.
The rulers of the day were less than ever interested in hearing sermons
on the efficacy of virtue and the wise ways of the ancients. Mencius'
failure to win political support for his doctrines was even more complete than that of Confucius and, like Confucius, his most significant
work was done as a teacher. By this time, however, rival schools such
as those of Mo Tzu and Yang Chu were active, and Mencius was busily
engaged in refuting their doctrines. His sayings and conversations with
his followers and rivals have been recorded in the book called *Mencius,*
probably by his disciples.

MENCIUS ON GOVERNMENT AND
HUMAN NATURE

Like Confucius, Mencius based his teachings upon the principle of *jen*
or humanity, to which he added a second concept, *i,* "righteousness,"

"propriety," or "duty." Mencius' rival, Mo Tzu, had insisted that equal love should be shown to all men. Mencius argued, however, that in practice one's love for others could not help but be expressed in varying measure according to the degree of personal relationship; that is, according to what is proper and suitable in view of the other person's position and the extent of one's obligation to him. *I*, however, implies a much stronger sense of duty and commitment than our rather mild term "propriety." On the other hand, when using "righteousness" for *i*, we should keep in mind that we are dealing with a sense of obligation intimately bound up with social relations, not an adherence to a universal or Divine moral law such as the word "righteousness" tends to connote in the Western tradition.

Mencius was even more insistent than Confucius that it was these moral qualities of humanity and a sense of duty that mark the true ruler. The governor exists for the sake of the governed, to give the people peace and sufficiency, and to lead them by education and example to the life of virtue. The ruler who neglects this responsibility, or worse, who misuses and oppresses the people, is no true ruler and the people are hence absolved of their fealty to him. It is this championship of the common people and their right of revolution that has caused the *Mencius* to be regarded by some rulers as a "dangerous" book.

Mencius, like Confucius, looked back to the golden ages of the sage-kings Yao and Shun and the early rulers of the Chou dynasty when the world was ruled by virtue and all was peace and order. But he was much more specific in his exposition of the ancient ideal, setting forth in considerable detail the feudal hierarchy, the land system, and other phases of the political and economic institutions that had characterized these glorious reigns of the past. Underlying this seemingly quaint idealism was a realistic appreciation of the material conditions of social order. Mencius insisted that it was the responsibility of the ruler to provide the people with adequate living conditions, without which all moral exhortation and political precept would fail. And he saw the importance of embodying the general principles of social welfare in tangible form, in specific institutions. For instance, upholding the principle of equality in land distribution, he favored the restoration of the "well-field" system. Whether this had actually been widely practiced in ancient times is questionable, but it served so clearly to illustrate Mencius' general principle that later land reformers almost invariably took the well-field system as their model. It is this rare combination of lofty idealism and stubborn realism, as well as Mencius' eye for apt illustration and analogy, that accounts for much of his popularity in later times.

Mencius' famous doctrine of human nature curiously parallels his view of history. In the same way in which he saw the society of his own time as a perversion and corruption of an earlier and perfect age, so he conceived of the character of most men as a distortion and falling away from the state of original goodness into which they had been born. All men are born with the beginnings of virtue and with an inclination toward goodness that is as natural as the inclination of water to flow downward. It is only neglect and abuse of this innate goodness which leads men into evil ways. The individual has only to recover his original goodness, his "childlike heart," as the state has only to return to the purity and order of ancient times, and all evil, both in the individual and in society, will vanish. These in brief are the doctrines of Mencius—idealistic, sometimes even mystical, and yet at the same time quite concrete and practical—which eventually triumphed over those of his successor, Hsün Tzu, to become the orthodox teachings of the Confucian school.

Selections from the Mencius

HUMAN NATURE

Kao Tzu [1] said: "The nature of man may be likened to the willow tree, whereas righteousness may be likened to wooden cups and wicker baskets. To turn man's nature into humanity and righteousness is like turning a willow tree into cups and baskets." Mencius replied: "Sir, can you follow the nature of the willow tree, and make the cups and baskets? Or must you violate its nature to make the cups and baskets? If you must violate the nature of the willow tree to turn it into cups and baskets, then don't you mean you must also violate the nature of man to turn it into humanity and righteousness? Your words, alas, would incite everyone in the world to regard humanity and righteousness as a curse!" [VI A:1]

Kao Tzu said: "The nature of man may be likened to a swift current of water: you lead it eastward and it will flow to the east; you lead it

---

[1] Kao Tzu was a critic and possibly a former pupil of Mencius. In general, Kao Tzu held human nature to be neutral, while Mencius insisted it was good.

westward and it will flow to the west. Human nature is neither disposed to good nor to evil, just as water is neither disposed to east nor west." Mencius replied: "It is true that water is neither disposed to east nor west, but is it neither disposed to flowing upward nor downward? The tendency of human nature to do good is like that of water to flow downward. There is no man who does not tend to do good; there is no water that does not flow downward. Now you may strike water and make it splash over your forehead, or you may even force it up the hills. But is this in the nature of water? It is of course due to the force of circumstances. Similarly, man may be brought to do evil, and that is because the same is done to his nature." [VI A:2]

Kao Tzu said: "Nature is what is born in us." Mencius asked: " 'Nature is what is born in us'—is it not the same as saying white is white?" "Yes," said Kao Tzu. Mencius asked: "Then the whiteness of a white feather is the same as the whiteness of white snow, and the whiteness of white snow the same as the whiteness of white jade?" "Yes," Kao Tzu replied. Mencius asked: "Well, then, the nature of a dog is the same as the nature of a cow, and the nature of a cow the same as the nature of a man, is it not?" [2] [VI A:3]

Kao Tzu said: "The appetite for food and sex is part of our nature. Humanity comes from within and not from without, whereas righteousness comes from without and not from within." Mencius asked: "What do you mean when you say that humanity comes from within while righteousness comes from without?" Kao Tzu replied: "When I see anyone who is old I regard him as old. This regard for age is not a part of me. Just as when I see anyone who is white I regard him as white, because I can observe the whiteness externally. For this reason I say righteousness comes from without." Mencius said: "Granted there is no difference between regarding the white horse as white and the white man as white. But is there no difference between one's regard for age in an old horse and one's regard for age in an old man, I wonder? Moreover, is it old age itself or our respectful regard for old age that constitutes a point of righteousness?" Kao Tzu persisted: "My own brother I love; the

[2] Evidently Mencius here considers he has achieved a *reductio ad absurdum* of Kao Tzu's original proposition. The point of Mencius' complaint is that Kao Tzu has failed to distinguish between the nature of man and the nature of any other being, which Mencius insists must be made.

brother of a man of Ch'in I do not love. Here the sanction for the feeling rests in me, and therefore I call it [i.e., humanity] internal. An old man of Ch'u I regard as old, just as an old man among my own people I regard as old. Here the sanction for the feeling lies in old age, and therefore I call it [i.e., righteousness] external." Mencius answered him: "We love the Ch'in people's roast as much as we love our own roast. Here we have a similar situation with respect to things. Would you say, then, that this love of roast is also something external?" [VI A:4]

The disciple Kung-tu Tzu said: "Kao Tzu says that human nature is neither good nor bad. Some say that human nature can be turned to be good or bad. Thus when [sage-kings] Wen and Wu were in power the people loved virtue; when [wicked kings] Yu and Li were in power the people indulged in violence. Some say that some natures are good and some are bad. Thus even while [the sage] Yao was sovereign there was the bad man Hsiang, even a bad father like Ku-sou had a good son like [the sage-king] Shun, and even with [the wicked] Chou for nephew and king there were the men of virtue Ch'i, the Viscount of Wei, and the Prince Pi-kan. Now, you say that human nature is good. Are the others then all wrong?" Mencius replied: "When left to follow its natural feelings human nature will do good. This is why I say it is good. If it becomes evil, it is not the fault of man's original capability. The sense of mercy is found in all men; the sense of shame is found in all men; the sense of respect is found in all men; the sense of right and wrong is found in all men. The sense of mercy constitutes humanity; the sense of shame constitutes righteousness; the sense of respect constitutes decorum (*li*); the sense of right and wrong constitutes wisdom. Humanity, righteousness, decorum, and wisdom are not something instilled into us from without; they are inherent in our nature. Only we give them no thought. Therefore it is said: 'Seek and you will find them, neglect and you will lose them.' Some have these virtues to a much greater degree than others —twice, five times, and incalculably more—and that is because those others have not developed to the fullest extent their original capability. It is said in the *Book of Odes:*

> Heaven so produced the teeming multitudes that
> For everything there is its principle.

The people will keep to the constant principles,
And all will love a beautiful character.[3]

Confucius said, regarding this poem: 'The writer of this poem understands indeed the nature of the Way! For wherever there are things and affairs there must be their principles. As the people keep to the constant principles, they will come to love a beautiful character.' " [VI A:6]

Mencius said: "All men have a sense of commiseration. The ancient kings had this commiserating heart and hence a commiserating government. When a commiserating government is conducted from a commiserating heart, one can rule the whole empire as if one were turning it on one's palm. Why I say all men have a sense of commiseration is this: Here is a man who suddenly notices a child about to fall into a well. Invariably he will feel a sense of alarm and compassion. And this is not for the purpose of gaining the favor of the child's parents, or seeking the approbation of his neighbors and friends, or for fear of blame should he fail to rescue it. Thus we see that no man is without a sense of compassion, or a sense of shame, or a sense of courtesy, or a sense of right and wrong. The sense of compassion is the beginning of humanity; the sense of shame is the beginning of righteousness; the sense of courtesy is the beginning of decorum; the sense of right and wrong is the beginning of wisdom. Every man has within himself these four beginnings, just as he has four limbs. Since everyone has these four beginnings within him, the man who considers himself incapable of exercising them is destroying himself. If he considers his sovereign incapable of exercising them, he is likewise destroying his sovereign. Let every man but attend to expanding and developing these four beginnings that are in our very being, and they will issue forth like a conflagration being kindled and a spring being opened up. If they can be fully developed, these virtues are capable of safeguarding all within the four seas; if allowed to remain undeveloped, they will not suffice even for serving one's parents." [II A:6]

Mencius said: "Man's innate ability is the ability possessed by him that is not acquired through learning. Man's innate knowledge is the knowledge possessed by him that is not the result of reflective thinking. Every child knows enough to love his parents, and when he is grown up he

---

[3] *Shih ching,* Ta ya: T'ang, Cheng-min.

knows enough to respect his elder brothers. The love for one's parents is really humanity and the respect for one's elders is really righteousness—all that is necessary is to have these natural feelings applied to all men." [VII A:15]

HUMANE GOVERNMENT

Mencius went to see King Hui of Liang. The king said: "You have not considered a thousand *li* too far to come, and must therefore have something of profit to offer my kingdom?" Mencius replied: "Why must you speak of profit? What I have to offer is humanity and righteousness, nothing more. If a king says, 'What will profit my kingdom?' the high officials will say, 'What will profit our families?' and the lower officials and commoners will say, 'What will profit ourselves?' Superiors and inferiors will try to seize profit one from another, and the state will be endangered. . . . Let your Majesty speak only of humanity and righteousness. Why must you speak of profit?" [I A:1]

Mencius said: "It was by virtue of humanity that the Three Dynasties won the empire, and by virtue of the want of humanity that they lost it. States rise and fall for the same reason. Devoid of humanity, the emperor would be unable to safeguard the four seas, a feudal lord would be unable to safeguard the altars of land and grain [i.e., his state], a minister would be unable to safeguard the ancestral temple [i.e., his clan-family], and the individual would be unable to safeguard his four limbs. Now people hate destruction and yet indulge in want of humanity—this is as if one hates to get drunk and yet forces oneself to drink wine." [IV A:3]

Mencius said: "An overlord [4] is he who employs force under a cloak of humanity. To be an overlord one has to be in possession of a large state. A king, on the other hand, is he who gives expression to his humanity through virtuous conduct. To be a true king, one does not have to have a large state. T'ang [founder of the Shang dynasty] had only a territory of seventy *li* and King Wen [founder of the Chou] only a hundred. When men are subdued by force, it is not that they submit from their hearts but only that their strength is unavailing. When men are won by virtue, then their hearts are gladdened and their submission is sincere, as

⁴ The Chinese term *pa*, which during the Spring and Autumn period (722–481 B.C.) meant specifically the chief among the feudal princes.

the seventy disciples were won by the Master, Confucius. This is what is meant in the *Book of Odes* when it says:

> From east and west,
> From north and south,
> Came none who thought of disobedience." [5] [II A:3]

Mencius said: "States have been won by men without humanity, but the world, never." [VII B:13]

Mencius said: "It was because Chieh and Chou lost the people that they lost the empire, and it was because they lost the hearts of the people that they lost the people. Here is the way to win the empire: win the people and you win the empire. Here is the way to win the people: win their hearts and you win the people. Here is the way to win their hearts: give them and share with them what they like, and do not do to them what they do not like. The people turn to a humane ruler as water flows downward or beasts take to wilderness." [IV A:9]

THE ECONOMIC BASIS OF HUMANE GOVERNMENT

Mencius was no advocate of "big government" or extensive economic activity by the state, but in passages like the following he made it clear that the economic welfare of the people was a necessary foundation of political stability, and that therefore the ruler had a responsibility to provide for the material needs of his people.

Mencius said to King Hsüan of Ch'i: . . . "Only the true scholar is capable of maintaining, without certain means of livelihood, a steadfast heart. As for the multitude, if they have no certain means of livelihood, they surely cannot maintain a steadfast heart. Without a steadfast heart, they are likely to abandon themselves to any and all manner of depravity. If you wait till they have lapsed into crime and then mete out punishment, it is like placing traps for the people. If a humane ruler is on the throne how can he permit such a thing as placing traps for the people? Therefore, when an intelligent ruler regulates the livelihood of the people, he makes sure that they will have enough to serve their parents on the one hand and to support their wives and children on the other, so that in good years all may eat their fill and in bad years no one need die of starvation.

[5] *Shih ching,* Ta ya: Wen-wang, Wen-wang yu-sheng.

Thus only will he urge them to walk the path of virtue, and the people will follow him effortlessly. But as the people's livelihood is ordered at present, they do not have enough to serve their parents on the one hand or to support their wives and children on the other. Even in good years life is one long struggle and in bad years death becomes all but inevitable. Such being the case, they are only anxiously trying to stay alive. What leisure have they for cultivating decorum and righteousness?

"If your Majesty wishes to practice humane government, would it not be well to go back to the root of the matter?

"Let the five *mu* [6] of land surrounding the farmer's cottage be planted with mulberry trees, and persons over fifty may all be clothed in silk. Let poultry, dogs, and swine be kept and bred in season, and those over seventy may all be provided with meat. Let the cultivation of the hundred-*mu* farm not be interfered with, and a family of eight mouths need not go hungry. Let attention be paid to teaching in schools and let the people be taught the principles of filial piety and brotherly respect, and white-headed old men will not be seen carrying loads on the road. When the aged wear silk and eat meat and the common people are free from hunger and cold, never has the lord of such a people failed to become king." [7] [I A:7]

THE WELL-FIELD SYSTEM

As the best means of providing for the livelihood of the people Mencius upheld a system of equal landholding which he believed had been maintained by the Chou dynasty. It is doubtful that such a neat and uniform system ever prevailed over the entire Chou kingdom, but on the authority of Mencius (and other Confucian texts dealing with the rites and institutions of the Chou dynasty), this egalitarian system was accepted as the ideal by most later Confucianists. Note, however, how closely it is linked here to a two-class system: the rulers and the ruled.

Duke Wen of T'eng sent Pi Chan to Mencius to learn about the well-field land system. Mencius said: "Now that your prince has made up his mind to put through a humane measure in government and has appointed you to carry it out, you must do your best. At the bottom of all humane government, we might say, lies the system of land division and demarcation.

---

[6] One *mu* or *mou* is approximately one-sixth of an English acre.

[7] This paragraph is recorded also in I A:3 and VII A:22 in the *Mencius,* as if to suggest the importance attached to it in Mencius' thought.

When the land system is not in proper operation, then the well-field farms are not equally distributed among the farmers or the grain for salaries equitably apportioned among the ministers. So a wicked lord or a corrupt magistrate usually lets the land system fall into disuse. When the land system is in proper operation, on the other hand, the distribution of land and the apportioning of salaries can be settled where you sit.

"Although T'eng is a small state, yet there must be those who are gentlemen and those who are countrymen. Without the gentlemen there would be none to rule the countrymen; without the countrymen there would be none to feed the gentlemen.

"In the surrounding country let the land tax be fixed at one part in nine to be paid according to the well-field group plan, while within the limits of the state capital let it be one in ten to be paid individually. For all officers, from the chief ministers down, there should be sacrificial land, in lots of fifty *mu*. For all extra-quota men in a household there should be additional land, in lots of twenty-five *mu*. Whether in burying the dead or in house-moving, a family does not go beyond the district. Within the district those whose farms belong to the same well-field unit befriend one another in their going out and coming in, practice mutual aid in their self-defense, and uphold one another in sickness. Thus the people learn to live in affection and harmony.

"Each well-field unit is one *li* square and contains nine hundred *mu* of land. The center lot is the public field. The eight households each own a hundred-*mu* farm and collaborate in cultivating the public field.[8] When the public field has been properly attended, then they may attend to their own work. This is how the countrymen are taught their status.

"The above are the main features of the system. As to adapting it to your present circumstances, it is up to you and your prince." [III A :3, 13–20]

IMPORTANCE OF THE PEOPLE AND THE RIGHT OF REVOLUTION

[Mencius' disciple] Wan Chang asked: "Is it true that Yao gave the empire[9] to Shun?" Mencius replied: "No. The emperor cannot give the

---

[8] The whole unit has the configuration of the Chinese character 井 (meaning a well).

[9] China before 221 B.C. would be better described as a kingdom than an empire, but the Chinese expression "all under Heaven" suggests that this realm embraced all the known world.

empire to another." Wan Chang asked: "Who then gave it to him, when Shun had the empire?" Mencius said: "Heaven gave it to him." Wan Chang asked: "You say Heaven gave it to him—did Heaven do it with an explicit charge?" Mencius said: "No. Heaven does not speak. It simply signified its will through his conduct and handling of affairs." Wan Chang asked: "How was this done?" Mencius said: . . . "Of old, Yao recommended Shun to Heaven and Heaven accepted him. He presented him to the people and the people accepted him. This is why I said that Heaven does not speak but simply signified its will through Shun's conduct and handling of affairs." Wan Chang said: "May I venture to ask, how was this acceptance by Heaven and the people indicated?" Mencius said: "He was appointed to preside over the sacrifices, and all the spirits were pleased with them: that indicated his acceptance by Heaven. He was placed in charge of public affairs, and they were well administered and the people were at peace: that indicated his acceptance by the people. Heaven thus gave him the empire; the people thus gave him the empire. That is why I said, the emperor cannot give the empire to another. . . . This is what is meant in the Great Declaration [in the *Book of History*] where it is said: 'Heaven sees as my people see, Heaven hears as my people hear.' " [V A:5]

Mencius said: "Men are in the habit of speaking of the world, the state. As a matter of fact, the foundation of the world lies in the state, the foundation of the state lies in the family, and the foundation of the family lies in the individual." [IV A:5]

Mencius said: "[In the constitution of a state] the people rank the highest, the spirits of land and grain come next, and the ruler counts the least." [VII B:14]

Mencius said: "There are three things that a feudal lord should treasure —land, people, and the administration of the government. If he should treasure pearls and jades instead, calamity is sure to befall him." [VII B:28]

Mencius said: "It is not so important to censure the men appointed to office; it is not so important to criticize the measures adopted in government. The truly great is he who is capable of rectifying what is wrong with the ruler's heart." [IV A:20]

Mencius said to King Hsüan of Ch'i: "When the ruler regards his ministers as his hands and feet, the ministers regard their ruler as their heart and bowels. When the ruler regards his ministers as his dogs and horses, the ministers regard their ruler as a stranger. When the ruler regards his ministers as dust and grass, the ministers regard their ruler as a brigand or foe." [IV B:3]

King Hsüan of Ch'i asked: "Is it not true that T'ang banished Chieh and that King Wu smote Chou?" Mencius replied: "It is so stated in the records." The king asked: "May a subject, then, slay his sovereign?" Mencius replied: "He who outrages humanity is a scoundrel; he who outrages righteousness is a scourge. A scourge or a scoundrel is a despised creature [and no longer a king]. I have heard that a despised creature called Chou was put to death, but I have not heard anything about the murdering of a sovereign." [I B:8]

The men of Ch'i made war on Yen and took it. The other feudal lords began plotting to liberate Yen. King Hsüan [of Ch'i] asked: "The feudal lords of many states are plotting war against me; how shall I deal with them?" Mencius replied: "I have heard of one who, with a territory of only seventy *li*, extended his rule to the whole empire. That was T'ang. But never have I heard of the lord of a thousand *li* having to stand in fear of others. It is said in the *Book of History:* 'T'ang launched his punitive expedition, first against Ko. The whole empire had faith in him. When he carried his campaign to the east, the tribes in the west grumbled. When he carried his campaign to the south, the tribes in the north grumbled, saying: "Why should we be last?" ' [Announcement of Chung-hui]. People looked for his coming as they would look for the rain-clouds in time of great drought. Those going to the market were not stopped; those tilling the land were not interrupted. He put their rulers to death and he consoled the people. His visit was like the falling of rain in season, and the people were overjoyed. Thus it is said in the *Book of History:* 'We have been waiting for our lord. When he comes, we shall have a new life.' [Announcement of Chung-hui]." [I B:11]

MENCIUS' DEFENSE OF FILIAL PIETY

Mencius is known in later tradition for his defense of Confucian filial piety against Yang Chu, the individualist, and Mo Tzu, the exponent of universal love. By thus making a special point of it, he gave added importance to filial piety among the Confucian virtues.

Now that sage-kings are no longer with us, the feudal lords yield to their lusts and idle scholars indulge in senseless disputation. The words of

Yang Chu and Mo Ti fill the land, and the talk of the land is either Yang
Chu or Mo Ti. Yang is for individualism, which does not recognize the
sovereign; Mo is for universal love, which does not recognize parents. To
be without sovereign or parent is to be a beast. [III B:9]

Mencius said: "Of services which is the greatest? The service of parents
is the greatest. Of charges which is the greatest? The charge of oneself is
the greatest. Not failing to keep oneself and thus being able to serve one's
parents—this I have heard of. Failing to keep oneself and yet being able
to serve one's parents—this I have not heard of." [IV A:19]

Mencius said: "There are three things which are unfilial, and the greatest of them is to have no posterity." [IV A:26]

Mencius said: "The substance of humanity is to serve one's parents; the
basis of righteousness is to obey one's elder brothers." [IV A:27]

RATIONALISM AND REALISM IN HSÜN TZU

Of the life of the third great Confucian thinker, Hsün Tzu (fl. 298–238
B.C.), we know little except that he was a high official in the states of
Ch'i and Ch'u and the teacher of Han Fei, the representative of ancient
Legalism, and Li Ssu, the prime minister who assisted the First Emperor
of the Ch'in in the unification of the empire. Although the exact dates of
his life are impossible to determine, it is important to note that he lived at
the very end of the Chou period. In his lifetime he witnessed the final
extinction of the royal house of Chou, the gradual destruction of the other
feudal states by the powerful state of Ch'in, and perhaps even the unification of the empire by the First Emperor of the Ch'in. It must have become
clear to him that the optimism of earlier Confucianists concerning a re-
establishment of the old order was no longer warranted, and that some of
their basic assumptions would have to be re-examined. This may account
to some extent for the hardheaded realism which marks his philosophy.

The lateness of the time in which he lived also made it possible for him
to look back upon the solutions offered by all the various schools of
philosophy of the Classical Period, to appraise their writings and adopt
what he found useful in their systems. His writings, collected in the work
called *Hsün Tzu* in thirty-two chapters, differ from the fragmentary
notes of conversations and aphorisms which make up the *Analects* and

Mencius. As time went on, the Chinese philosophers relied not only upon oral instruction to their disciples, but took to writing expository essays in order to preserve their doctrines for later ages, and the *Hsün Tzu* is a series of such essays, well composed and cogently argued.

The historian Ssu-ma Ch'ien has remarked that one reason Hsün Tzu wrote was to attack the superstitious belief in magic, omens, and portents that dominated his age. Certainly he devoted much space to a refutation of the superstitions of his time, arguing for a completely rational and naturalistic view of the universe and man. From the old religious and moral concept of a Heaven which rewards or punishes a ruler according to his deserts, he substituted a purely mechanical process that operates quite independently of the doings of man, while he reinterpreted the ancient sacrifices and funeral rites which had once been intended to propitiate the dead as no more than forms to express the grief of the living.

With this rationalism went a reaction against the excessive idealization of the past. Confucius and Mencius had held up as their ideals the rulers of the early Chou or the more ancient sage-kings Yao and Shun. Rival schools had attempted to outdo the Confucianists by harking back to even more ancient figures of the legendary past until a whole literature had built up describing in detail the lives and institutions of these mythical paragons of virtue. Hsün Tzu employed these conventional historical symbols of virtue in his own discussions, but at the same time he attempted to destroy the gulf of time which the men of his age despairingly imagined separated them from the golden ages of the past. "The beginning of Heaven and earth—it is today. The ways of the hundred ancient kings are those of the later kings." Mankind and human nature are fundamentally the same, past and present. If rulers were wise and virtuous in ancient times, if peace and order prevailed two thousand years ago, then there is no reason why the same situation cannot be brought about again today. The leaders of society have only to comprehend the basic principles of human nature and society, and to discriminate between wise and foolish policies.

The faculty to discriminate between what is wise and foolish, good and bad, is of prime importance in Hsün Tzu's thinking. It is, he declares, what makes man man and distinguishes him from the beasts. He took violent exception to the view of Mencius that all men are born with a nature which is essentially good and that evil is simply an abuse or neglect of this inborn goodness. Hsün Tzu, in a famous essay that has disturbed centuries of later scholars, declared flatly that man's nature is evil and that all goodness is the result of artificial training. While Mencius believed that the purpose of learning was simply to "seek the lost heart" of child-hood innocence, Hsün Tzu saw in education, in the example and leader-ship of the sages, in all art and artifice in society, the only means of salvation for mankind. For Hsün Tzu, all that is good in society—rites, music, the moral worth and teachings of the sages—is the product of social restraint and the faculty of discrimination acting upon, training, and directing the crude animal nature of man.

Hsün Tzu's attack upon Mencius' view of human nature precipitated a long and violent controversy which strikes us today as strangely forced. Both men agreed upon the worth of perfect virtue, both agreed that all men are potentially able to attain it; they even agreed in general that the way to attain it is through the study and imitation of the sages. But where Mencius saw this goodness as something once possessed by all but later lost, Hsün Tzu regarded it as the hard-won achievement of effort and art. Yet later scholars seldom saw the bright hopes for human achieve-ment which Hsün Tzu's doctrine optimistically opened up for mankind; they saw only the blunt initial thesis that the nature of man is evil, and they were instinctively repelled. Although Hsün Tzu enjoyed consider-able popularity in the Han, by T'ang and Sung times he was completely overshadowed by Mencius, whose idealistic doctrines became the orthodox teaching of Confucianism, while Hsün Tzu remained simply one of the classical philosophers.

Selections from the Hsün Tzu

CHAPTER 17: CONCERNING HEAVEN

Heaven operates with constant regularity. It does not prevail because of [a sage-king like] Yao; nor does it cease to prevail because of [a tyrant like] Chieh. Respond to it with good government, and blessings will result; respond to it with misgovernment, and misfortune will result. If the staples of livelihood are built up and used economically, then Heaven cannot impoverish the country; if the sustenance of the people is pro-vided for and their energies are employed in keeping with the seasons, then Heaven cannot afflict the people. If the Way is followed and not deviated from, then Heaven cannot send misfortune. Under such circumstances, flood or drought cannot cause a famine, extreme cold or heat cannot cause any malady, and unnatural apparitions cannot cause disaster. On the other hand, if the staples of livelihood are neglected and used extravagantly, then Heaven cannot cause the country to be rich; if the sustenance of the people is deficient and their energies are employed inordinately, then Heaven cannot make the people healthful. If the Way is violated and conduct becomes unseemly, then Heaven cannot send blessings. Under such circumstances, even if flood and drought do not come, there will be famine; even if cold and heat have not become oppressive, there will be maladies; even if unnatural apparitions do not appear, there will be calamities. Seasonableness and prosperity go together; catastrophe and prosperity do not. It is useless to complain against Heaven, for such is the Way. Hence he who knows the distinctive functions of Heaven and of men may be called a great sage.

To accomplish without exertion [10] and to obtain without effort, this is what is meant by the office of Heaven. Therefore although the mind of the sage is deep, he will not deliberate on the Way of Heaven; although it is great, he will not pass any judgment upon it; although it is minute, he will not scrutinize it—this is what is meant by refraining from contesting with Heaven. Heaven has its seasons; earth has its resources; man has his government. This is how man is able to form a triad with Heaven and earth. If man should neglect his own part in this triad and put all his hope in Heaven and earth with which he forms the triad, he is making a grave mistake.

The fixed stars make their revolutions; the sun and moon alternately shine; the four seasons succeed one another; the yin and yang go through their great mutations; the wind and rain affect all things. The myriad things acquire their proper harmony and thus grow; each thing obtains its proper nourishment and thus attains its full maturity. We do not see the cause of these occurrences, but we do see their effects—we call it the efficacy of spirit. We all know the results achieved, but we do not know the invisible source—we call it the work of Heaven. It is only the sage that does not seek to know Heaven. . . .

Heaven does not suspend the winter because men dislike cold; the earth does not reduce its expanse because men dislike distances; the gen-

[10] A Taoist expression appearing in the *Lao Tzu*, chapter 47.

tleman does not alter his conduct because inferior men make a clamor.
Heaven has a constant way of action; earth has a constant size; the gentleman has a constant demeanor. The gentleman conducts himself according to a constant principle, but the inferior man schemes after results. It is said in the *Book of Odes:*

If a person acts according to the rules of decorum and righteousness,
And does not deviate from them,
Why should he be anxious about people's talk?" [11]

This expresses what I mean.

The King of Ch'u has a thousand chariots following him—this is not
because he is wise. The gentleman eats pulse and drinks water—this is
not because he is foolish. In each case, it is just what is fitting to the
external circumstances. Whereas for a person to have his purpose cultivated, to have his virtuous conduct strengthened, to have his knowledge
and deliberations clarified, to live in this age but to emulate the ancients
—this is what lies entirely within his power. Therefore the gentleman
carefully develops what is within his power, and does not desire what is
from Heaven. The inferior man neglects what is within his power, and
seeks for what comes from Heaven. Because the gentleman carefully
develops what is within his power, and does not desire what comes from
Heaven, he progresses every day; whereas because the inferior man neglects what is within his power and seeks for what comes from Heaven, he
degenerates every day. Therefore, it is one and the same reason why the
gentleman progresses daily and why the inferior man degenerates daily.
And this also accounts for the difference between the gentleman and
the inferior man.

When stars fall or the sacred trees groan, all the people become afraid
and ask: "What is the significance of all this?" I would say: There is no
special significance. This is just due to a modification of Heaven and
earth and the mutation of the yin and yang. These are rare phenomena.
We may marvel at them, but we should not fear them. For there is no
age that has not often experienced eclipses of the sun and moon, unseasonable rain or wind, or occasional appearances of strange stars. If the
ruler is intelligent and the government just, even though these phenomena
should all occur at once, it would do no harm. If the ruler is unintelligent

[11] The quotation does not appear in the present *Book of Odes.*

and his government is bent on evil, although not one of these strange phenomena should occur, still it would be of no help. Hence the falling of stars and the groaning of the sacred trees are due to the modification of Heaven and earth and the mutation of the yin and yang. These are rare phenomena. We may marvel at them, but we should not fear them.

Of all occurrences and phenomena, human portents are the most to be feared. To plow improperly so as to injure the crops, to weed improperly so as to miss the harvest, to govern recklessly so as to lose the allegiance of the people, to leave the fields uncultivated and to harvest poor crops, to let the price of grain rise high and the people starve and die on the roadside—these are what I mean by human portents. When the governmental measures and orders are not clear and just; when decisions of the state are not opportune; when the fundamental tasks are not attended to these are what I mean by human portents. When the ruler of decorum and righteousness are not cultivated, the inhabitants of the inner and outer quarters are not kept apart, and men and women become promiscuous, parents and children distrust each other, the ruler and ruled are at cross purposes, and invasion and disaster arrive at the same time—these are what I mean by human portents.

If people pray for rain and it rains, how is that? I would say: Nothing in particular. Just as when people do not pray for rain, it also rains. When people try to save the sun or moon from being swallowed up [in eclipse], or when they pray for rain in a drought, or when they decide an important affair only after divination—this is not because they think in this way they will get what they seek, but only to add a touch of ritual to it. Hence the gentleman takes it as a matter of ritual, whereas the common man thinks it is supernatural. He who takes it as a matter of ritual will suffer no harm; he who thinks it is supernatural will suffer harm. . . .

You exalt Heaven and meditate on it:
Why not domesticate it and regulate it?

You obey Heaven and sing praises to it:
Why not control its course and employ it?

You look on the seasons with expectation and await them:
Why not seize the seasonal opportunities and exploit them?

You rely on things increasing of themselves:
Why not exercise your ability and multiply them?

You speculate about the nature of things:
Why not manipulate them so that you do not lose them?

You admire the cause of the birth of things:
Why not assist them in their completion?

Hence, I say, to neglect human effort and speculate about Heaven,
Is to miss the true nature of all things.

CHAPTER 23: HUMAN NATURE IS EVIL

The nature of man is evil; his goodness is acquired.

His nature being what it is, man is born, first, with a desire for gain.
If this desire is followed, strife will result and courtesy will disappear.
Second, man is born with envy and hate. If these tendencies are followed,
injury and cruelty will abound and loyalty and faithfulness will disappear. Third, man is born with passions of the ear and eye as well as the
love of sound and beauty. If these passions are followed, excesses and
disorderliness will spring up and decorum and righteousness will disappear. Hence to give rein to man's original nature and to yield to man's
emotions will assuredly lead to strife and disorderliness, and he will revert
to a state of barbarism. Therefore it is only under the influence of teachers
and laws and the guidance of the rules of decorum and righteousness that
courtesy will be observed, etiquette respected, and order restored. From
all this it is evident that the nature of man is evil and that his goodness is
acquired.

Crooked wood needs to undergo steaming and bending by the carpenter's tools; then only is it straight. Blunt metal needs to undergo grinding
and whetting; then only is it sharp. Now the original nature of man is evil,
so he must submit himself to teachers and laws before he can be just; he
must submit himself to the rules of decorum and righteousness before he
can be orderly. On the other hand, without teachers and laws, men are
biased and unjust; without decorum and righteousness, men are rebellious
and disorderly. In ancient times the sage-kings knew that man's nature
was evil and therefore biased and unjust, rebellious and disorderly. Thereupon they created the codes of decorum and righteousness and established
laws and ordinances in order to bend the nature of man and set it right,
and in order to transform his nature and guide it. All men are thus made
to conduct themselves in a manner that is orderly and in accordance with

the Way. At present, those men who are influenced by teachers and laws, who have accumulated culture and learning, and who are following the paths of decorum and righteousness, are the gentlemen. On the other hand, those who give rein to their nature, who indulge in their willfulness, and who disregard decorum and righteousness, are the inferior men. From all this it is evident that the nature of man is evil and that his goodness is acquired.

Mencius says: "The reason man is ready to learn is that his nature is originally good." [12] I reply: This is not so. This is due to a lack of knowledge about the original nature of man and of understanding of the distinction between what is natural and what is acquired. Original nature is a heavenly endowment; it cannot be learned, and it cannot be striven after. As to rules of decorum and righteousness, they have been brought forth by the sages, they can be attained by learning, and they can be achieved by striving. That which cannot be learned and cannot be striven after and rests with Heaven is what I call original nature. That which can be attained by learning and achieved by striving and rests with man is what I call acquired character. This is the distinction between original nature and acquired character. Now by the nature of man, the eye has the faculty of seeing and the ear has the faculty of hearing. But the keenness of the faculty of sight is inseparable from the eye, and the keenness of the faculty of hearing is inseparable from the ear. It is evident that keenness of sight and keenness of hearing cannot be learned.

Mencius says: "The original nature of man is good; but because men all ruin it and lose it, it becomes evil." [13] I reply: In this he is gravely mistaken. Regarding the nature of man, as soon as he is born, he tends to depart from its original state and depart from its natural disposition, and he is bent on ruining it and losing it. From all this, it is evident that the nature of man is evil and that his goodness is acquired.

To say that man's original nature is good means that it can become beautiful without leaving its original state and it can become beneficial without leaving its natural disposition. This is to maintain that beauty pertains to the original state and disposition and goodness pertains to the

---

[12] This saying does not appear in the present *Mencius* but does reflect the doctrine in *Mencius*, VI A:2–6.

[13] This saying does not appear in the present *Mencius* but does reflect the doctrine in *Mencius*. VI A:6 and 8.

heart and mind in the same way as the keenness of the faculty of sight is inseparable from the eye and the keenness of the faculty of hearing is inseparable from the ear, just as we say that the eye is keen in seeing or the ear is keen in hearing. Now as to the nature of man, when he is hungry he desires to be filled, when he is cold he desires warmth, when he is tired he desires rest. This is man's natural disposition. But now a man may be hungry and yet in the presence of elders he dare not be the first to eat. This is because he has to yield precedence to someone. He may be tired and yet he dare not take a rest. This is because he has to labor in the place of someone. For a son to yield to his father and a younger brother to yield to his older brother, for a son to labor in the place of his father and a younger brother to labor in the place of his older brother—both of these kinds of actions are opposed to man's original nature and contrary to man's feeling. Yet they are the way of the filial son and in accordance with the rules of decorum and righteousness. It appears if a person follows his natural disposition he will show no courtesy, and if he shows courtesy he is acting contrary to his natural disposition. From all this it is evident that the nature of man is evil and that his goodness is acquired.

It may be asked: "If man's original nature is evil, whence do the rules of decorum and righteousness arise?" I reply: All rules of decorum and righteousness are the products of the acquired virtue of the sage and not the products of the nature of man. Thus, the potter presses the clay and makes the vessel—but the vessel is the product of the potter's acquired skill and not the product of his original nature. Or again, the craftsman hews pieces of wood and makes utensils—but utensils are the product of the carpenter's acquired skill and not the product of his original nature. The sage gathers many ideas and thoughts and becomes well versed in human affairs, in order to bring forth the rules of decorum and righteousness and establish laws and institutions. So then the rules of decorum and righteousness and laws and institutions are similarly the products of the acquired virtue of the sage and not the products of his original nature. . . .

Man wishes to be good because his nature is evil. If a person is unimportant he wishes to be important, if he is ugly he wishes to be beautiful, if he is confined he wishes to be at large, if he is poor he wishes to be rich, if he is lowly he wishes to be honored—whatever a person does not have within himself, he seeks from without. But the rich do not wish for wealth and the honorable do not wish for position, for whatever a person has within himself he does not seek from without. From this it may be seen that man wishes to be good because his nature is evil. Now the original nature of man is really without decorum and righteousness, hence he strives to learn and seeks to obtain them. . . .

Straight wood does not require the carpenter's tools to be straight; by nature it is straight. Crooked wood needs to undergo steaming and bending by the carpenter's tools and then only will it be straight; by nature it is not straight. As the nature of man is evil, it must be submitted to the government of the sage-kings and the reforming influence of the rules of decorum and righteousness; then only will everyone issue forth in orderliness and be in accordance with goodness. From all this it is evident that the nature of man is evil and that his goodness is acquired.

It may be objected: "Decorum and righteousness and the accumulation of acquired virtues must be in the nature of man so that the sage could bring them forth." I reply: This is not so. Now the potter pounds and and molds the clay and produces earthenware. Are the earthenware and clay then in the nature of the potter? The workman hews a piece of wood and makes utensils. Are furniture and wood then in the nature of the carpenter? So it is with the sage and decorum and righteousness; he produces them in the same way as earthenware is produced. Are decorum and righteousness and the accumulation of acquired virtues then in the original nature of man? As far as the nature of man is concerned, the sage-kings Yao and Shun have the same nature as the wicked King Chieh and robber Chih; the gentleman has the same nature as the inferior man. Should we now regard decorum and righteousness and the accumulation of acquired virtues as being in the nature of man, then why should we prize the sage-kings Yao and Yü and why should we prize the gentlemen? We prize Yao, Yü, and the gentlemen because they were able to transform nature and produce acquired virtue, and from acquired virtue decorum and righteousness issued forth. . . .

There is a saying: "The man on the street can become a Yü." How would you account for that? I reply: All that made Yü what he was that he instituted humanity and righteousness, laws, and government. However, there are principles by which humanity and righteousness, laws and government can be known and practiced. At the same time any man on the street has the faculty for knowing them and has the capacity for practicing them. Thus it is evident that he can become a Yü. Should we assume there were really no principles by which humanity and righteousness, laws and government could be known and practiced, then even Yü would not be able to know them or practice them. Or, should we assume the man on the street really had no faculty for knowing humanity and righteousness, laws and government, or the capacity for practicing them, then the man cannot know, on the one hand, the proper relation between father and son and, on the other, the proper discipline between sovereign and minister. Thus it is evident that the man on the street does have the faculty for knowing and the capacity for practicing these virtues. Now let the man on the street take his faculty for knowing and his capacity for practicing humanity and righteousness, laws and government, and bring them to bear upon the principles by which these virtues can be known and can be practiced—then it is self-evident that he can become a Yü. Yes, let the man on the street pursue the path of knowledge and devote himself to learning, with concentration of mind and a singleness of purpose; let him think, search, examine, and re-examine, day in and day out, with persistence and patience—let him thus accumulate good works without cease, then he may be counted among the gods and may form a triad with Heaven and earth. Hence sagehood is a state that any man can achieve by cumulative effort. . . .

CHAPTER 19: ON THE RULES OF DECORUM (OR RITES, LI)

In these passages Hsün Tzu sometimes uses *li* more in reference to individual and social conduct (in which cases it is rendered "rules of decorum") and sometimes more in reference to religious or social ceremony (in which case "rites" comes closer to the meaning). In either case the underlying idea is conduct in conformity with social, moral, and cosmic order, a central conception of Hsün Tzu.

Whence do the rules of decorum arise? From the fact that men are born with desires, and when these desires are not satisfied, men are bound to pursue their satisfaction. When the pursuit is carried on unrestrained and unlimited, there is bound to be contention. With contention comes chaos; with chaos dissolution. The ancient kings disliked this chaos and set the necessary limits by codifying rules of decorum and righteousness, so that men's desires might be satisfied and their pursuit be gratified. In this way it was made certain that desires were not frustrated by things, nor things used up by desires. That these two should support each other and should thrive together—this is whence the rules of decorum arise. . . .

Rites (*li*) rest on three bases: Heaven and earth, which are the source of all life; the ancestors, who are the source of the human race; sovereigns and teachers, who are the source of government. If there were no Heaven and earth, where would life come from? If there were no ancestors, where would the offspring come from? If there were no sovereigns and teachers, where would government come from? Should any of the three be missing, either there would be no men or men would be without peace. Hence rites are to serve Heaven on high and earth below, and to honor the ancestors and elevate the sovereigns and teachers. Herein lies the three-fold basis of rites. . . .

In general, rites begin with primitive practices, attain cultured forms, and finally achieve beauty and felicity. When rites are at their best, men's emotions and sense of beauty are both fully expressed. When they are at the next level, either the emotion or the sense of beauty oversteps the other. When they are at still the next level, emotion reverts to the state of primitivity.

It is through rites that Heaven and earth are harmonious and sun and moon are bright, that the four seasons are ordered and the stars are on their courses, that rivers flow and that things prosper, that love and hatred are tempered and joy and anger are in keeping. They cause the lowly to be obedient and those on high to be illustrious. He who holds to the rites is never confused in the midst of multifarious change; he who deviates therefrom is lost. Rites—are they not the culmination of culture? . . .

Rites require us to treat both life and death with attentiveness. Life is the beginning of man, death is his end. When a man is well off both at the end and the beginning, the way of man is fulfilled. Hence the gentleman respects the beginning and is carefully attentive to the end. To pay equal attention to the end as well as to the beginning is the way of the gentleman and the beauty of rites and righteousness. . . .

Rites serve to shorten that which is too long and lengthen that which is too short, reduce that which is too much and augment that which is too little, express the beauty of love and reverence and cultivate the elegance of righteous conduct. Therefore, beautiful adornment and coarse sack-cloth, music and weeping, rejoicing and sorrow, though pairs of op-posites, are in the rites equally utilized and alternately brought into play. Beautiful adornment, music, and rejoicing are appropriate on occasions of felicity; coarse sackcloth, weeping, and sorrow are appropriate on oc-casions of ill-fortune. Rites make room for beautiful adornment but not to the point of being fascinating, for coarse sackcloth but not to the point of deprivation or self-injury, for music and rejoicing but not to the point of being lewd and indolent, for weeping and sorrow but not to the point of being depressing and injurious. Such is the middle path of rites. . . .

Funeral rites are those by which the living adorn the dead. The dead are accorded a send-off as though they were living. In this way the dead are served like the living, the absent like the present. Equal attention is thus paid to the end as well as to the beginning of life. . . .

Now the rites used on the occasion of birth are to embellish joy, those used on the occasion of death are to embellish sorrow, those used at sacrifice are to embellish reverence, those used on military occasions are to embellish dignity. In this respect the rites of all kings are alike, antiq-uity and the present age agree, and no one knows whence they came. . . .

Sacrifice is to express a person's feeling of remembrance and longing, for grief and affliction cannot be kept out of one's consciousness all the time. When men are enjoying the pleasure of good company, a loyal minister or a filial son may feel grief and affliction. Once such feelings arise, he is greatly excited and moved. If such feelings are not given proper expression, then his emotions and memories are disappointed and not satisfied, and the appropriate rite is lacking. Thereupon the ancient kings instituted rites, and henceforth the principle of expressing honor to the honored and love to the beloved is fully realized. Hence I say: Sacrifice is to express a person's feeling of remembrance and longing. As to the fullness of the sense of loyalty and affection, the richness of ritual and beauty—these none but the sage can understand. Sacrifice is something that the sage clearly understands, the scholar-gentlemen contentedly per-form, the officials consider as a duty, and the common people regard as established custom. Among gentlemen it is considered the way of man; among the common people it is considered as having to do with the spirits.

CHAPTER 22: ON THE CORRECT USE OF TERMINOLOGY

Now that the sage-kings are no more, the preserving of names has become lax, strange terminology has arisen, and names and their actualities have become confused. As the standards of truth and falsehood are indistinct, even officials who maintain the law and scholars who study by themselves and teach others are likewise in a state of confusion. Should some king arise, he would have to retain certain old names and create certain new names. Thus, it is imperative for him to examine: 1) the reason for having names; 2) the conditions under which agreement and difference in names arise; and 3) the fundamental principles for instituting names.

Different forms are received by the mind and people are equally at a loss [to give expression to these forms]; different things are entangled when names and their actualities are intertwined; [14] noble and base are not clearly differentiated, similarities and differences are not distinguished —if this should be the case, there would certainly be the danger of people's ideas not being understood and their affairs being hampered and handicapped. Therefore, the wise man (the sage-king) institutes names severally to denote their actualities; thus, on the one hand, noble and base are differentiated, and on the other, similarities and differences are distinguished. As noble and base are differentiated and similarities and differences are distinguished, there is no longer the danger of people's ideas not being understood or of people's affairs being hampered and handicapped. This is the reason for having names.

What then are the conditions under which agreement and difference in names arise? They are the natural senses. All [creatures] that are of the same kind and have the same feelings have the same natural senses with which to perceive things. Therefore things are compared and classified, and those that are found to be approximately alike are grouped together. In this way they share the same name and claim each other. Forms and bodies, colors and designs, are distinctions made by the eye. "Clear" and "confused" qualities and big and small volumes of sound, as well as noises, are distinctions made by the ear . . . [and so on with the senses of taste, smell, and touch]. . . . Happy and morose moods,

---

[14] The meaning of the text for the two foregoing clauses is far from clear.

pleasure and anger, sorrow and joy, love and hate, as well as desires, are distinctions made by the mind.

The mind has the faculty of responsive knowledge. By this responsive knowledge it is possible to know sounds through the ear, and to know forms through the eye. However, the faculty of responsive knowledge is dependent on the objects being first noted and classified by the senses. When the five senses note something but do not comprehend it, and the mind responds to it but has no designation, then everyone says there is no knowledge. These, then, are the conditions under which agreement and difference in names arise.

Accordingly, names are given to things. All that are alike are given the same name; all that are unlike are given different names. When a simple term is sufficient to convey the meaning, a simple term is used; when a simple term is insufficient, a compound term is used. When simple and compound concepts do not conflict, the general term may be used; although it is a general term, there is no harm in using it. Knowing that different actualities should have different names, one should let all actualities that are different have nothing other than different terms; thus there could not be any confusion. Likewise one should let all actualities that are alike have nothing other than the same name.

For, although the myriad things are innumerable, there are times when we wish to speak of them all in general, and so we call them "things." "Things" is a great general term. We press on and generalize; we generalize and generalize still more, until we reach that beyond which there is nothing more general; then only we stop. There are times when we wish to speak of things in classes, and so we say "birds and beasts" (i.e., "animals"). "Birds and beasts" is a great particular term. We press on and particularize; we particularize and particularize still more, until we reach that beyond which there is nothing more particular, and then only we stop.

There are no names necessarily appropriate of themselves. Upon agreement things were named. When the agreement has been made and it has become customary, this is called an appropriate designation. That which is different from what has been agreed upon is called an inappropriate designation. Names have no actualities necessarily corresponding to them. Upon agreement things were named. When the agreement has been made and it has become customary, such names are called names appropriate to actualities. But some names are inherently felicitous. When a name is simple, direct, easily understood, and not contradictory, it is called a felicitous name.

There are things which have the same appearance but are in different places; there are things which have different appearances but are in the same place. This distinction is easily made. Things which have the same appearance but are in different places, although they may be classified together, are to be called two actualities. Where the appearance changes, but the thing remains the same and is not different, this is to be called transformation. Where there is transformation but no differentiation, that is to be called one actuality. By this method objects are investigated and their number is determined. These, then, are the fundamental principles for instituting names. If a king some day wanted to define names, it would be imperative for him to examine all these matters.

THE GREAT LEARNING (TA HSÜEH)

The essays known as "The Great Learning" and "The Mean" constitute two chapters of the Confucian Classic, the *Book of Rites*. Even before the Christian era the particular significance and interest of these texts was noted. The Neo-Confucian scholars of the Sung dynasty, claiming to find in them the psychological and metaphysical foundations for their system of thought, elevated these short texts to a position of prime importance in Confucian literature. The great Sung scholar Chu Hsi (A.D. 1130–1200), to emphasize their worth, combined the texts with the *Analects* and the *Mencius* to form the so-called *Four Books* (in the order: *The Great Learning, The Mean, Analects,* and *Mencius*). These four texts became the primer of Chinese education, the first major course of study before a student began his study of the Five Classics; they were read aloud and committed to memory by the students. And for a period of six centuries (A.D. 1313–1905) these four texts served as the basis of the civil service examinations by which Chinese scholars were selected for posts in the government bureaucracy.

The Great Learning is a brief essay of some 1,750 words. Its Chinese title, *Ta hsüeh,* means education for the adult or higher education. It has been variously attributed to Tzu Ssu (483–402 B.C.?), Confucius' grandson, to Confucius' disciple Tseng Tzu, or to one of his pupils. Some scholars, however, especially in the last three decades, have dated it as late as 200 B.C. In all likelihood its basic ideas go back to Confucius, though the essay itself definitely belongs to a later age.

The central theme of the work is self-cultivation. This is, however, no ordinary guide to self-improvement, which can take for granted the intrinsic importance of each man's fulfillment as an individual. Rather *The Great Learning* seeks first of all to establish the value of self-cultivation in terms of accepted social ends, showing its relevance to the problem of good government which underlies much of the thinking of this age. Indeed, the argumentation here often makes sense only if we understand that it is addressed to the ruler and his officials, rather than to any ordinary man in search of moral guidance. Nevertheless, the problem of the ruler proves, upon analysis, to be identical with that of the individual. Not only does good government depend upon the proper conduct of men on the various levels of social organization, and thus upon their individual moral perfection, but also self-cultivation on the part of the ruler must proceed on essentially the same lines as it does for the individual. Before a man can regulate and discipline others he must learn to regulate and discipline himself. To accomplish this *The Great Learning* offers a method or program which became famous for its "eight points," three of them pertaining to social functions and five to personal cultivation. Broad in scope and rather general in meaning, these eight points nevertheless seemed to outline, in neat and concise form, a complete system of education and social organization. No doubt it appealed greatly to the Chinese taste for a balanced, symmetrical, and hierarchical view of things. It served, moreover, as a formulation of those attitudes which are at the very heart of Confucian teaching: the primacy of the moral order, and the delicate balance which must be maintained between individual and social ends. At the same time, however, *The Great Learning* gave impetus to a dangerous form of oversimplification and idealism among Confucianists: the belief that self-cultivation alone could solve all political problems and usher in the perfect society.

It would be difficult to exaggerate the tremendous influence of this short work on Confucian thought, not only in China, but also in Japan, Korea, and elsewhere in the Chinese cultural sphere. Especially in Neo-Confucian thought the interpretation of the "eight points" became one of the central problems of philosophy and ethics. The excerpts which

follow include the basic program of *The Great Learning* and selected passages amplifying two of the eight points.

Selections from The Great Learning

The Way of the Great Learning consists in clearly exemplifying illustrious virtue, in loving the people, and in resting in the highest good.

Only when one knows where one is to rest can one have a fixed purpose. Only with a fixed purpose can one achieve calmness of mind. Only with calmness of mind can one attain serene repose. Only in serene repose can one carry on careful deliberation. Only through careful deliberation can one have achievement. Things have their roots and branches; affairs have their beginning and end. He who knows what comes first and what comes last comes himself near the Way.

The ancients who wished clearly to exemplify illustrious virtue throughout the world would first set up good government in their states. Wishing to govern well their states, they would first regulate their families. Wishing to regulate their families, they would first cultivate their persons. Wishing to cultivate their persons, they would first rectify their minds. Wishing to rectify their minds, they would first seek sincerity in their thoughts. Wishing for sincerity in their thoughts, they would first extend their knowledge. The extension of knowledge lay in the investigation of things. For only when things are investigated is knowledge extended; only when knowledge is extended are thoughts sincere; only when thoughts are sincere are minds rectified; only when minds are rectified are our persons cultivated; only when our persons are cultivated are our families regulated; only when families are regulated are states well governed; and only when states are well governed is there peace in the world.

From the emperor down to the common people, all, without exception, must consider cultivation of the individual character as the root. If the root is in disorder, it is impossible for the branches to be in order. To treat the important as unimportant and to treat the unimportant as important—this should never be. This is called knowing the root; this is called the perfection of knowledge [15]. . . .

What is meant by saying that "the cultivation of the person depends

---

[15] Following the order of the original text as found in the *Li chi*, where it constitutes chapter 42.

on the rectification of the mind" is this: When one is under the influence of anger, one's mind will not be correct; when one is under the influence of fear, it will not be correct; when one is under the influence of fond regard, it will not be correct; when one is under the influence of anxiety, it will not be correct. When the mind is not there, we gaze at things but do not see; we listen but do not hear; we eat but do not know the flavors. This is what is meant by saying that the cultivation of the person depends on the rectification of the mind. . . .

What is meant by saying that "the government of the state depends on the regulation of the family" is this: One can never teach outsiders if one cannot teach one's own family. Therefore the prince perfects the proper teaching for the whole country without going outside his family; the filial piety wherewith one serves his sovereign, the brotherly respect wherewith one treats his elders, the kindness wherewith one deals with the multitude. There is the saying in the "Announcement to K'ang" [in the Book of History]. "Act as if you were rearing an infant." If you set yourself to a task with heart and soul you will not go far wrong even if you do not hit the mark. No girl has ever learned to suckle an infant before she got married.

If one family exemplifies humanity, humanity will abound in the whole country. If one family exemplifies courtesy, courtesy will abound in the whole country. On the other hand, if one man exemplifies greed and wickedness, rebellious disorder will arise in the whole country.[16] Therein lies the secret. Hence the proverb: One word ruins an enterprise; one man determines the fate of an empire. Yao and Shun ruled the empire with humanity, and the people followed them. Chieh and Chou ruled the empire with cruelty, and the people only submitted to them. Since these last commanded actions that they themselves would not like to take, the people refused to follow them. Thus it is that what [virtues] a prince finds in himself he may expect in others, and what [vices] he himself is free from he may condemn in others. It is impossible that a man devoid of every virtue which he might wish to have in others could be able effectively to instruct them.

Thus we see why it is that "the government of the state depends on the regulation of the family."

. . . .

[16] The "one family" and "one man" are the family and person of the ruler.

What is meant by saying that "the establishment of peace in the world depends on the government of the state" is this: When superiors accord to the aged their due, then the common people will be inspired to practice filial piety; when superiors accord to elders their due, then the common people will be inspired to practice brotherly respect; when superiors show compassion to the orphaned, then the common people do not do otherwise. Thus the gentleman has a principle with which, as with a measuring square, he may regulate his conduct.

What a man dislikes in his superiors let him not display in his treatment of his inferiors; what he dislikes in his inferiors let him not display in his service to his superiors; what he dislikes in those before him let him not set before those who are behind him; what he dislikes in those behind him let him not therewith follow those who are before him; what he dislikes from those on his right let him not bestow upon those on his left; what he dislikes from those on his left let him not bestow upon those on his right. This is called the regulating principle of the measuring square.

THE MEAN (CHUNG YUNG)

The Mean has traditionally been ascribed to Tzu Ssu, though it is probably a combination of two or more texts dating in part as late as Ch'in or early Han. The Chinese title of the essay, *Chung yung,* is composed of the elements "centrality" (*chung*) and "normality" (*yung*). The translation "The Mean" suggests the fundamental moral idea of moderation, balance, and suitableness. But in this essay the concept goes much deeper, denoting a basic norm of human action which, if comprehended and complied with, will bring man and his actions into harmony with the whole universe.

The second important concept of this little essay is that of *ch'eng,* sincerity or truth. In one sense *ch'eng* represents the fullness of virtue corresponding to Confucius' concept of humanity (*jen*), sincerity being that moral integrity whereby the individual becomes a genuine or real man. He is "genuine" with others, but also "genuinely" himself, a true human being. The purpose of *The Mean,* however, is precisely to relate what is most essential and real in man to the underlying reality or truth of the universe. Human virtue does not exist or act in a sphere all its own, the "ethical" sphere, which is distinct from the metaphysical. The moral order and the cosmic order are one, and through ethical cultivation the individual not only achieves human perfection but also "realizes" himself in a mystic unity with Heaven and earth. In this way sincerity, as an active and dynamic force, works for the realization not only of man but also of all things. It is the underlying metaphysical principle, corresponding to the "Way" of the Taoists. Indeed *The Mean* may be considered a Confucian response to the challenge of Taoism, which regarded the Way as transcending all relative values, and as being indifferent to the ethical concerns of man. Yet eventually this essay in the direction of a Confucian metaphysics served as a bridge between this school, on the one hand, and Taoism and Buddhism on the other. Its importance was especially great as one of the basic texts of the Neo-Confucian movement in the eleventh century and after.

The contents of *The Mean* are varied. Portions of it deal with the character and duties of the true gentleman, the moral responsibilities of rulership, the performance of social obligations, and the ideal institutions of the sage-kings. Its prescriptions for the regulation of society and the conduct of life are no doubt what prompted inclusion of *The Mean* in the *Book of Rites* (*Li chi*), yet the tone of the work is lofty throughout and breathes the pure Confucian spirit.

Selections from The Mean

I. That which is bestowed by Heaven is called man's nature; the fulfillment of this nature is called the Way; the cultivation of the Way is called culture [or instruction in the truth].

The Way is something that may not be departed from even for one instant. If it could be departed from, it would not be the Way. Hence the gentleman stands cautious and in awe of the unseen and the unheard. There is nothing more evident than what is hidden; there is nothing more manifest than what is minute. Hence the gentleman is watchful when he is alone with himself.

When the passions, such as pleasure and anger and sorrow and joy, have not awakened, the state is called that of centrality. When these passions awaken and each and all attain due measure and degree, it is called the state of harmony. The state of centrality is the great root and the state of harmony is the far-reaching Way of all existence in the world. Once centrality and harmony are realized, Heaven and earth take their proper places and all things receive their full nourishment.

II. Confucius said: "The life of the gentleman is an exemplification of the Mean; the life of the inferior man is a contradiction of it. The life of the gentleman is an exemplification of the Mean, because he is a gentleman and constantly holds to the center. The inferior man's life is a contradiction of the Mean, because he is an inferior man and knows no restraint."

III. Confucius said: "Perfect indeed is the Mean! For long people have seldom had the capacity for it."

. . . .

XIV. The gentleman acts according to the situation he is in and does not desire what is outside of it. If he is wealthy and honorable, he acts like one wealthy and honorable, if poor and lowly, he acts like one poor and lowly. If he is among barbarians, he does what one does among barbarians, if he is in trouble, he acts like one in trouble. There is no situation into which the gentleman enters in which he is not himself. In a superior position he does not abuse his subordinates; in an inferior position he does not hang on his superiors. He makes his own conduct correct and seeks nothing from others, and so he has no resentment. He neither complains against Heaven nor blames men. Thus the gentleman dwells in calm and safety awaiting the commandments of Heaven, while the inferior man walks in danger seeking good luck. The Master said: "In the archer there is a resemblance to the gentleman. When he misses the mark, he turns and seeks the reason for his failure in himself."

. . . .

XX. Duke Ai asked about government, and the Master said: "The government of Wen and Wu is set forth in the historical records on wood and bamboo. If there are the right men, then the government will prosper; if the right men are lacking, the government will collapse. Men must be keen in matters of government, as the earth is keen in making things grow, and then their government will be like a growing reed. Therefore the administration of government depends upon the right men. One gets the right men by the force of one's own personality. One trains one's personality by means of the Way. And one learns the Way through practice of humanity. Humanity is what it is to be a human being, and loving one's relatives is the most important part of it. Righteousness is doing what is right, and honoring the worthy is the greatest part of it. The degree to which one loves one's different relatives and the grades to which one honors various worthy men are dictated by the rules of decorum. . . . Therefore the gentleman may not neglect the training of his personality. If he would train his personality, he must serve his parents. If he would serve his parents, he must understand men. And if he would understand men, he must understand Heaven.

There are five relationships which concern all men, and three virtues by which they are fulfilled. The relationships of ruler and subject, father and son, husband and wife, older and younger brother, and of intercourse between friends—these five are the relationships which pertain to all men. Knowledge, humanity, and courage—these three are virtues which apply to all men, and that by which they are practiced is one. . . .

Confucius said: . . . "Sincerity [17] is the Way of Heaven; the attainment of sincerity is the Way of man. He who possesses sincerity achieves what is right without effort, understands without thinking, and naturally and easily is centered in the Way. He is a sage. He who strives after truth chooses the good and holds fast to it. This involves learning extensively [about the good], inquiring critically into it, pondering carefully over it, distinguishing it clearly, and practicing it earnestly."

. . . .

XXI. Intelligence that comes from sincerity is to be ascribed to nature; sincerity that comes from intelligence is to be ascribed to instruction. Where there is sincerity there is intelligence; where there is intelligence there is sincerity.

XXII. Only he who possesses absolute sincerity can give full development to his nature. Able to give full development to his own nature, he can give full development to the nature of other men. Able to give full development to the nature of men, he can give full development to the nature of all beings. Able to give full development to the nature of all beings, he can assist the transforming and nourishing powers of

[17] The Chinese word *ch'eng* is ordinarily used as an adjective or adverb meaning sincere or sincerely. But in *The Mean* the term is used as a noun in a distinctly metaphysical sense, so that here it might be understood as "Absolute Truth" or "Reality."

Heaven and earth. Capable of assisting the transforming and nourishing powers of Heaven and earth, he may, with Heaven and earth, form a triad.

．．．．

XXV. Sincerity is self-completing, and the way of it is self-directing. Sincerity is the beginning and end of things; without sincerity there is no existence. Therefore the gentleman regards sincerity as the most valuable of all attainments. Sincerity is not only the completion of one's own being. It is also that by which all being is completed. Completing one's own being one attains humanity; completing all being one attains knowledge. These, humanity and knowledge, are the virtues inherent in man's nature, and serve as the means by which the inner and the outer are united. Therefore with sincerity everything done is right.

XXVI. Hence absolute sincerity is unceasing. Being unceasing it is everlasting. Being everlasting it is self-evident. Being self-evident it is extensive. Being extensive it is broad and deep. Being broad and deep it is lofty and intelligent. It is because it is broad and deep that it supports all things. It is because it is transcendental and intelligent that it embraces all things. It is because it is extensive and everlasting that it brings all things to completion. In its breadth and depth it matches earth. In its transcendental intelligence it matches Heaven. Extensive and everlasting, it is infinite. Such being the nature of absolute sincerity, it manifests itself without display; it transforms without motion; it completes without action. The Way of Heaven and earth can be set forth simply: it exists of itself and without duality, and so the manner in which it begets things is unfathomable. The Way of Heaven and earth is broad and deep, transcendental and intelligent, extensive and everlasting.

CHAPTER VII

THE LEGALISTS

Although Legalism is here considered last among the classical schools of thought, and was comparatively late in developing its theoretical position, this school had unquestionably the greatest influence of any upon the political life of its time. Typically its exponents are practicing politicians, more concerned with immediate problems and specific mechanisms of control than with the underlying principles of government. Indeed, there is a strong anti-intellectualism among them and an especial hostility toward the "vain" talk of the philosophers. Shang Yang (d. 330 B.C.), prime minister of Ch'in and the original organizing genius behind that state's long drive to imperial power, is the first of this type to achieve historic importance. A work exists, the *Book of Lord Shang*, which purportedly sets forth the policies which he successfully employed, though there is doubt as to how much of it is authentic. Han Fei (d. 233 B.C.), on the other hand, though less effective as a politician, has left us an excellent statement of the theoretical basis of this school. He was a student of the Confucianist Hsün Tzu who, we recall, taught that human nature is evil, and a schoolmate of Li Ssu who became chief minister to the First Emperor of the Ch'in dynasty. Han Fei was favorably received at the Ch'in court but eventually met death through the machinations of his old associate, Li Ssu. In him all previous teachings of the Legalist thinkers were synthesized and brought to their highest development.

THE THEORIES OF HAN FEI TZU

Legalism in its earliest form was probably the outgrowth of a need for more rational organization of society and resources so as to strengthen the state against its rivals. This was to be accomplished by concentrating power in the hands of a single ruler, and by the adoption of political institutions affording greater centralized control. Kuan Chung in the seventh century, for example, worked to make Ch'i the strongest state of his time by increasing the power of the ruler, but at the same time he upheld many of the traditional moral virtues and supported the old feudal order.

As the struggle among the warring states became more intense, however, technicians of power came forward who put the state and its interests ahead of all human and moral concerns, who in fact glorified power for its own sake and looked upon the human being as having no worth apart from his possible use to the state. Men like Shang Yang completely rejected the traditional virtues of humanity and righteousness which the Confucianists had urged upon rulers, denying that such lofty ideals had any practical relationship to the hard realities of political life. They openly advocated war as a means of strengthening the power of the ruler, expanding the state, and making the people strong, disciplined, and submissive. They conceived of a political order in which all old feudal divisions of power would be swept away and all authority reside in one central administration headed by an absolute monarch. The state would be ordered by an exhaustive set of laws defining in detail the duties and responsibilities of all its members, which would be administered with complete regularity and impartiality. Severe punishments would restrain evil, while generous rewards would encourage what was beneficial to the strength and well-being of the state. Agriculture, as the basis of the economy, would be promoted intensively, while commerce and intellectual endeavor were to be severely restricted, as nonessential and diversionary. The people would live frugal and obedient lives devoted to the interests of the state in peace and war.

These were the principal ideas propounded by Han Fei and to a large extent put into actual practice by the rulers of the state of Ch'in. It will be noticed that, in their complete rejection of ethical values, in their emphasis upon government by law rather than by individual leadership, and in their scorn for the ideals and examples of the past, the Legalists represent the exact antithesis of Confucian thinking. On the other hand the Legalists have obviously learned something from both the Mo-ists and the Taoists. Mo Tzu's stress on uniform standards and on the mobilization of society for the achievement of utilitarian ends is strongly echoed in the totalitarian aims of the Legalists, although they obviously have no use for Mo Tzu's doctrine of universal love and his condemnation of offensive warfare. Moreover Lao Tzu's old idea of nonaction as a way of government is applied to the Legalists' own conception of the ideal ruler, who takes no direct part in the government but simply presides as a semi-divine figurehead while the elaborate legal machinery of government functions of its own accord, obviating the necessity for personal decisions or intervention. Having so regulated the lives of his people that there is no longer any possibility of disorder or need for improvement or guidance, the ruler may retire to dwell, as Han Fei says, "in the midst of his deep palace," far removed from the eyes of the populace, enjoying the luxuries and sensual delights appropriate to his exalted position.

One may imagine the horror and revulsion which such a doctrine aroused among the traditionalists generally, and especially among the Confucianists who attached such importance to personal relations and human values. Their horror no doubt grew as they saw that the policies of the Legalist statesmen succeeded greatly in strengthening the state of Ch'in, whose campaign of conquest moved inexorably onward while the older states decayed and fell victim to its expansions. With the final unification of China by the First Emperor of the Ch'in, it looked as if the harsh policies of Shang Yang and Han Fei had won out over the other schools of political thought. Its exponents were now in a position of power from which, by repressive measures, they could at last deal the death blow to their rivals.

Selections from the Han Fei Tzu

CHAPTER 50: ON THE DOMINANT SYSTEMS OF LEARNING

The dominant systems of learning of the day are Confucianism and Moism. The founder of Confucianism was Confucius; the founder of Mo-ism was Mo Tzu. . . . Since the days of Confucius and Mo Tzu, Confucianism has differentiated itself into eight schools and Mo-ism into three. These schools contradict and disagree with one another in their respective emphases, each claiming to be the true representative of Confucianism or Mo-ism. Now that Confucius and Mo Tzu cannot come to life again, who is to decide among the various schools of the later ages?

Confucius and Mo Tzu both upheld [the sage-kings] Yao and Shun. Though they disagreed in their respective emphases, yet each claimed to be the true representative of Yao and Shun. Now that Yao and Shun cannot come to life again, who is to determine the genuineness as between Confucianism and Mo-ism? The Yü and the Hsia regimes together lasted upwards of seven hundred years, and the Yin and the Chou dynasties upwards of two millennia. Since it is impossible to determine the genuineness as between Confucianism and Mo-ism, if anybody should want now to scrutinize the ways of Yao and Shun which prevailed three thousand years ago, I should imagine it would also be impossible for him to achieve any certainty.

To claim certainty without corroborating evidence is stupid; to refer to anything that one cannot be certain of is self-deceptive. Therefore, those who explicitly refer to the ancient kings and dogmatically claim the authority of Yao and Shun must be either stupid or deceitful. Such stupid and deceptive teachings and such heretical and contradictory actions as these are not to be adopted by the intelligent ruler.

When the Mo-ists attend to a funeral, the deceased is simply clothed in winter clothes in winter and in summer clothes in summer, the coffin is three inches thick and made of soft wood, and mourning is observed for only three months. Regarding the practice as having the merit of frugality, the ruler of the day treats the Mo-ists with respect. The Confucianists, on the contrary, would go into bankruptcy, and even give their sons in pawn in order to accord the proper funeral [to a dead parent]. They would observe three years' mourning till their health breaks down and they have to walk with the aid of canes. Regarding the practice as having the merit of filial piety, the ruler of the day treats the Confucianists also with respect. But as a matter of fact, if one approves the frugality of Mo Tzu one has to reprove Confucius for his extravagance; if one approves the filial piety of Confucius one has to reprove Mo Tzu for his impiety. Now, piety and impiety, frugality and extravagance, are found in the Confucianists and the Mo-ists respectively, and yet the sovereign respects them both alike. . . .

While stupid and deceptive teachings and heretical and contradictory talk are in conflict one with another, the ruler listens to them all equally. As a result, the scholars of the land have neither any definite theory to expound nor any constant standard for their conduct. Just as ice and burning charcoal do not remain long in the same container and as winter and summer do not arrive at the same time, so, heretical and contradictory teachings cannot be expected to prevail simultaneously and result in orderly government. Now that heretical teachings are equally listened to and contradictory talk is absurdly acted upon, how can there be anything else but chaos? Since such is the way the ruler listens to advice, it will also, of course, be the way he will govern the people.

When the learned men today discuss government policies, every so often they say: "Give land to the poor and the destitute, so that even those without property shall not be in want." Now, here is a man just like other men. Yet without the advantage of prosperous years or supplementary income, he has of himself become self-sufficient. This must be due, if not to his diligence, then to his frugality. There again is a man just like other men. Yet without the affliction of any famine, or illness, or calamity, he has of himself become poor and destitute. This must be due, if not to his extravagance, then to his laziness. It is the extravagant and lazy people who have become poor; it is the diligent and frugal people who have become rich. Now the sovereign would tax the rich to give to the poor. This amounts to robbing the diligent and frugal and rewarding the extravagant and lazy. It would be quite impossible then to expect the people to increase their exertion and reduce their expenditures.

Now suppose there is someone who on principle would neither enter any city that is in danger nor join the army, and would not give a hair from his shin even to make a major contribution to the whole world.[1] The ruler of the time will respect him for this, honoring his wisdom, exalting his conduct, and regarding him as a scholar who despises things but esteems life. The reason that the sovereign offers good fields and large pools, and establishes ranks and bounties, is to induce the people to be loyal unto death. But as long as the sovereign honors the scholars who despise things and esteem life, it will be impossible to expect the people to sacrifice their lives and be loyal to their sovereign to the death.

Suppose there again is someone who collects books, practices the art

---

[1] This has reference to Yang Chu, an early spokesman of Taoism.

of speaking, gathers a band of pupils, wears an appearance of culture and learning, and discusses the principles of all things. The ruler of the time will respect him for this, saying: "To show respect to worthy scholars is the way of the ancient kings." Now, those who are taxed by the magistrates are the farmers, while those who are maintained by the sovereign are the learned gentlemen. As long as heavy taxes are collected from the farmers while rich rewards are given to the learned gentlemen, it will be impossible to expect the people to work hard and talk little.

Again, suppose there is someone who holds fast to his principles and his reputation, and conducts himself so that none dares encroach upon his person. Whenever any reproachful word reaches his ear, he will draw his sword. The ruler of the time will respect him for this, regarding him as a self-respecting gentleman. But, as long as the merit of beheading the enemy in war is not rewarded, while bravery in family quarrels is celebrated with honors, it will be impossible to expect the people to fight hard against the enemy but refrain from having private feuds.

In time of peace the literati and the cavaliers are patronized; in time of war uniformed warriors are employed. Thus neither are the ones patronized the ones used, nor are the ones used the ones patronized. This is the reason why there is disorder.

Furthermore, in listening to a learned man, if the ruler approves his words, he should officially adopt them in his administration and appoint the man to office; and if he disapproves his words, he should get rid of the person and put an end to his heretical doctrine. Actually, however, what is regarded as right is not officially adopted in administration, and what is regarded as wrong is not stamped out as heretical doctrine. Thus, what is right is not employed and what is wrong is not eliminated—this is the way to chaos and ruin. . . .

When the sage rules the state, he does not count on people doing good of themselves, but employs such measures as will keep them from doing any evil. If he counts on people doing good of themselves, there will not be enough such people to be numbered by the tens in the whole country. But if he employs such measures as will keep them from doing evil, then the entire state can be brought up to a uniform standard. Inasmuch as the administrator has to consider the many but disregard the few, he does not busy himself with morals but with laws.

Evidently, if one should have to count on arrows which are straight of themselves, there would not be any arrows in a hundred generations; if one should only count on pieces of wood which are circular of themselves, there would not be any wheels in a thousand generations. Though in a hundred generations there is neither an arrow that is straight of itself nor a wheel that is circular of itself, yet people in every generation ride carts and shoot birds. Why is that? It is because the tools for straightening and bending are used. Though without the use of such tools there might happen to be an arrow straight of itself or a wheel circular of itself, the skilled carpenter will not prize it. Why? Because it is not just one person who wishes to ride, or just one shot that the archers wish to shoot. Similarly, though without the use of rewards and punishments there might happen to be an individual good of himself, the intelligent ruler will not prize him. The reason is that the law of the state must not be sidetracked and government is not for one man. Therefore, the capable prince will not be swayed by occasional virtue, but will pursue a course that will assure certainty. . . . .

Now, when witches and priests pray for people, they say: "May you live as long as one thousand and ten thousand years!" Even as the sounds, "one thousand and ten thousand years," are dinning upon one's ears, there is no sign that even a single day has been added to the age of any man. That is the reason why people despise witches and priests. Likewise, when the Confucianists of the present day counsel the rulers they do not discuss the way to bring about order now, but exalt the achievement of good order in the past. They neither study affairs pertaining to law and government nor observe the realities of vice and wickedness, but all exalt the reputed glories of remote antiquity and the achievements of the ancient kings. Sugar-coating their speech, the Confucianists say: "If you listen to our words, you will be able to become the leader of all feudal lords." Such people are but witches and priests among the itinerant counselors, and are not to be accepted by rulers with principles. Therefore, the intelligent ruler upholds solid facts and discards useless frills. He does not speak about deeds of humanity and righteousness, and he does not listen to the words of learned men.

Those who are ignorant about government insistently say: "Win the hearts of the people." If order could be procured by winning the hearts of the people, then even the wise ministers Yi Yin and Kuan Chung would be of no use. For all that the ruler would need to do would be just to listen to the people. Actually, the intelligence of the people is not to be relied upon any more than the mind of a baby. If the baby does not have his head shaved, his sores will recur; if he does not have his boil cut open, his illness will go from bad to worse. However, in order to shave his head or open the boil someone has to hold the baby while the affectionate mother is performing the work, and yet he keeps crying and yelling incessantly. The baby does not understand that suffering a small pain is the way to obtain a great benefit.

Now, the sovereign urges the tillage of land and the cultivation of pastures for the purpose of increasing production for the people, but they think the sovereign is cruel. The sovereign regulates penalties and increases punishments for the purpose of repressing the wicked, but the people think the sovereign is severe. Again, he levies taxes in cash and in grain to fill up the granaries and treasuries in order to relieve famine and provide for the army, but they think the sovereign is greedy. Finally, he insists upon universal military training without personal favoritism, and urges his forces to fight hard in order to take the enemy captive, but the people think the sovereign is violent. These four measures are methods for attaining order and maintaining peace, but the people are too ignorant to appreciate them.

The reason for the ruler to look for wise and well-informed men is that the intelligence of the people is not such as to be respected or relied upon. For instance, in ancient times, when Yü opened the rivers and deepened them, the people gathered tiles and stones [to hit him]; when the prime minister of Cheng, Tzu Ch'an, cleared the fields and planted mulberry trees, the people of Cheng slandered and reviled him. Yü benefited the whole empire and Tzu Ch'an preserved the state of Cheng, but each incurred slander thereby. Clearly the intelligence of the people is not to be relied upon. Therefore, to seek for the worthy and the wise in selecting officials and to endeavor to suit the people in administering the government are equally the cause of chaos and not the means for attaining order.

CHAPTER 49: THE FIVE VERMIN OF THE STATE

In the age of remote antiquity human beings were few while birds and beasts were many, and men were unable to overcome birds, beasts, insects, and serpents. Thereupon a sage arose who fastened trees and branches together and made nests, and all harm was thereby avoided. At this the people were delighted and they made him ruler of the whole world, according to him the title "Nest-Builder." Again, the people in those days lived on the fruits of trees and seeds of grass as well as on mussels and clams which smelled rank and fetid and hurt the digestive organs, and many of the people were afflicted with diseases. Thereupon a sage arose who drilled a piece of wood and produced fire [for cooking], and the fetid and musty smell was thereby transformed. At this the people were delighted and they made him ruler of the whole world, according to him the title "Fire-Maker." In the age of middle antiquity, there was a great deluge in the world, and Kun and his son, Yü, opened channels for the water. In the age of recent antiquity, Chieh and Chou were wicked and disorderly, and T'ang and Wu punished them.

Now, if somebody tried to fasten the trees or drill a piece of wood in the age of the Hsia dynasty, he would certainly be ridiculed by Kun and Yü. Again, if somebody attempted to open channels for water in the age of the Yin and Chou dynasties, he would certainly be ridiculed by T'ang and Wu. For the same reason, if somebody in this present age should praise the ways of Yao and Shun, Kun and Yü, T'ang and Wu, he would certainly be ridiculed by contemporary sages. Hence the sage does not seek to follow the ways of the ancients, nor does he regard precedents as the rule. He examines the circumstances of his own time and plans his course of action accordingly.

There was once a man of Sung who tilled his field. In the midst of his field stood the stump of a tree, and one day a hare, running at full speed, bumped into the stump, broke its neck, and died. Thereupon the man left his plow and kept watch at the stump, hoping that he would get another hare. But he never caught another hare, and was only ridiculed by the people of Sung. Now those who try to rule the people of the present age with the conduct of government of the early kings are all doing exactly the same thing as that fellow who kept watch by the stump. . . .

When Yao held the empire, his reed thatch was left untrimmed and his roof-beams were not planed. The unhusked kernels of cereals were his food and wild greens made his soup. In winter he wore deerskins, and in summer a garment of rough fiber-cloth. Even the food and clothing of a gate-keeper were no worse than his. When Yü held the empire,

he worked with the plow and the spade personally so as to set an example
to his people, till his thighs were without fat and his shins without hair.
Even the toil of the servant and slave was not more arduous than his.
Such being the case, the ancient emperors who abdicated their thrones
were, as a matter of fact, relinquishing but the lot of the gate-keeper
and parting but with the toil of the slave. Therefore even though they
gave up their empire, there was nothing especially praiseworthy. Nowadays, on the contrary, after even a mere district magistrate dies, his descendants can maintain private carriages for many generations. Hence
people value such an office. Thus in the matter of giving up something,
people found it easy to abdicate the throne in ancient times, yet find it
hard to relinquish the post of a present-day district magistrate. This is
because the advantages in each case are so different.

Now, people who dwell in the mountains and have to draw water
from the gorges give water to each other as a gift at festivals; those who
live in swamps and are troubled with too much water hire laborers to
open channels for it. Likewise, in the spring following a year of famine
one is unable to feed one's younger brother, while in the autumn of a
year of plenty even casual visitors are offered food. Not that men neglect
their blood relations and love passers-by, but that the material provisions
on the respective occasions are so different. Hence the ancient indifference
to goods was not due to humanity, but to the abundance of goods. Nor
are the present-day struggles for possession due to niggardliness but to
the scarcity of goods. Men used to decline the position of the emperor
lightly, and this was not because of any inner nobility but because the
power of the emperor was limited. Men now strive fiercely for portfolios
in government, and this is not because of any natural meanness but because the authority of the posts is great. Therefore the sage considers
the condition of the times, whether it is one of plenty or scarcity, abundance or meagerness, and governs the people accordingly. Thus though
penalties are light, it is not due to charity; though punishment is heavy,
it is not due to cruelty. Whatever is done is done in accordance with
the circumstances of the age. Therefore circumstances go according to
their time, and the course of action is planned in accordance with the
circumstances. . . .

Indeed, ancients and moderns have different customs; the present and
the past follow different courses of action. To attempt to apply a benev-

olent and lenient government to the people of a desperate age is about the same as trying to drive wild horses without reins or whips. This is the affliction of ignorance.

Nowadays, the Confucianists and the Mo-ists all praise the ancient kings for their universal love for the whole world, which made them regard the people as parents regard their children. How do we know this was so? Because they say: "When the minister of justice employed punishment the ruler would stop having music; at the news of any capital punishment he would shed tears." In this way they commend the ancient kings. But if you maintain that good government will always prevail whenever the ruler and the ruled act towards each other like father and son, you imply that there are never any wayward fathers or sons. According to the nature of man, none could be more affectionate than one's own parents. And yet in spite of the love of both parents not all children are well brought up. Though the ruler be warm in his affection for his people, how is that necessarily any assurance that there would be no disorder? Now the love of the ancient kings for their people could not have surpassed that of the parents for their children. Since we could not be certain that the children would not be rebellious, how could we assume that the people would definitely be orderly? Moreover, if the ruler should shed tears when a penalty was inflicted in accordance with the law, he might thereby parade his humanity, but not thus conduct his government. Now tearful revulsion against penalties comes from humanity, but necessity of penalties issues from the law. Since even the early kings had to permit the law to prevail and repress their tears, it is clear enough that humanity could not be depended upon for good government. . . .

Now take a young fellow who is a bad character. His parents may get angry at him, but he never makes any change. The villagers may reprove him, but he is not moved. His teachers and elders may admonish him, but he never reforms. The love of his parents, the efforts of the villagers, and the wisdom of his teachers and elders—all the three excellent disciplines are applied to him, and yet not even a hair on his shins is altered. It is only after the district magistrate sends out his soldiers and in the name of the law searches for wicked individuals that the young man becomes afraid and changes his ways and alters his deeds. So while the love of parents is not sufficient to discipline the children, the severe penalties of the district magistrate are. This is because men became naturally spoiled by love, but are submissive to authority. . . .

That being so, rewards should be rich and certain so that the people will be attracted by them; punishments should be severe and definite so that the people will fear them; and laws should be uniform and steadfast so that the people will be familiar with them. Consequently, the sovereign should show no wavering in bestowing rewards and grant no pardon in administering punishments, and he should add honor to rewards and disgrace to punishments—when this is done, then both the worthy and the unworthy will want to exert themselves. . . .

The literati by means of letters upset laws; the cavaliers by means of their prowess transgress prohibitions. Yet the ruler treats them both with decorum. This is actually the cause of all the disorder. Every departure from the law ought to be apprehended, and yet scholars are nevertheless taken into office on account of their literary learning. Again, the transgression of every prohibition ought to be censured, and yet cavaliers are patronized because of their readiness to draw the sword. Thus, those whom the law reproves turn out to be those whom the ruler employs, and those whom the magistrates suppress are those whom the sovereign patronizes. Thus legal standard and personal inclination as well as ruler and ministers are sharply opposed to each other and all fixed standards are lost. Then, even if there were ten Yellow Emperors, they would not be able to establish any order. Therefore, those who practice humanity and righteousness should not be upheld, for if upheld, they would hinder concrete accomplishments. Again, those who specialize in refinement and learning should not be employed, for if employed, they would disturb the laws. There was in Ch'u an upright man named Kung, who, when his father stole a sheep, reported it to the authorities. The magistrate said: "Put him to death," as he thought the man was faithful to the ruler but disloyal to his father. So the man was apprehended and convicted. From this we can see that the faithful subject of the ruler was an outrageous son to his father. Again, there was a man of Lu who followed his ruler to war, fought three battles, and ran away three times. Confucius interrogated him. The man replied: "I have an old father. Should I die, nobody would take care of him." Confucius regarded him as virtuous in filial piety, commended and exalted him.[2] From this we

---

[2] This story about Confucius is not recorded anywhere else and evidently is fabricated out of Confucius' teaching on filial piety.

can see that the dutiful son of the father was a rebellious subject to the ruler. Naturally, following the censure of the honest man by the magistrate, no more culprits in Ch'u were reported to the authorities; and following the reward of the runaway by Confucius, the people of Lu were prone to surrender and run away. The interests of superior and subordinate being so different, it would be hopeless for any ruler to try to exalt the deeds of private individuals and, at the same time, to promote the public welfare of the state.

In olden times when Ts'ang-chieh invented the system of writing, he called self-centeredness "private," and what was in opposition to "private," he called "public." That "public" and "private" were in opposition to each other was from the beginning well understood by Ts'ang-chieh. It is an affliction due to ignorance that nowadays the interests of the two are regarded as identical. . . .

Moreover, what the world regards as virtue consists of devoted and faithful deeds; what it regards as wisdom consists of subtle and mysterious words. Such subtle and mysterious words are hard even for the wisest of men to understand. If laws are set up for the masses in such terms as to be hard for the wisest to understand, then the people will have no way of comprehending them. Just as men who have not even chaff and bran to fill their stomachs would not aim at wine and meat, and just as those who have not even rags to cover their bodies would not insist upon silk and embroidery, so, in the conduct of the government, if the ruler is unable to handle affairs that are most urgent, he should not strive after matters of only distant concern. Now the business of government consists of the affairs of the people. If in dealing with them the ruler should leave alone the ideas that ordinary men and women plainly understand and adopt the theories of the wisest of men, he would be accomplishing just the opposite of proper government. Assuredly, subtle and mysterious theories are no business of the common people.

Men who hold deeds of devotion and faithfulness to be virtuous will of course honor gentlemen who are not deceitful, but those who do so are themselves also devoid of any means for detecting deception. When the ordinary people, clad in plain cloth, make friends among themselves, they seek out men who are not deceitful, as they have neither the wealth to benefit one another, nor the authority to intimidate one another. Now the sovereign occupies a position of authority over his subjects and possesses the wealth of a state. If only he will make rewards great and punishments severe, intensifying thereby the searching light of his statecraft, then even ministers like T'ien Ch'ang and Tzu-han, wicked as they may be, will not dare to deceive him. What need does he have of men who are not deceitful? Today one cannot count even ten men of devotion and faithfulness, yet official posts in the country are counted by the hundreds. If only men of devotion and faithfulness were appointed to office, there would be an insufficiency of candidates, and in that case guardians of order would be few, while disturbers of peace would be many. Therefore the way of the enlightened sovereign consists in making laws uniform and not depending upon the wisdom of men, in making statecraft firm and not yearning after faithful persons, so that the laws do not fail to function and the multitude of officials will commit neither villainy nor deception. . . .

Now the people in the state all talk about proper government. Practically every family keeps copies of the Laws of Shang Yang and Kuan Chung, and yet the state is becoming poorer and poorer. This is because many talk about farming but few follow the plow. Again, people in the state all talk about warfare. Practically every family keeps copies of the books of Sun Wu and Wu Ch'i on the art of war, and yet the army is becoming weaker and weaker. This is because many talk about warfare but few put on armor.

The enlightened sovereign therefore employs a man's energies but does not heed his words, rewards men with meritorious services but without fail bans the useless. Accordingly, the people exert themselves to the utmost in obeying their superiors. Farming is hard toil indeed. Yet people attend to it because they think this is the way to riches. Similarly, warfare is a risky business. Yet people carry it on because they think this is the road to honor. Now if one could just cultivate refinement and learning and practice persuasion and speech, and thereby obtain the fruits of wealth without the toil of farming and receive ranks of honor without the risk of warfare, then who would not do the same? Naturally a hundred men will be attending to learning where one will apply his physical energies. When many attend to learning, the law will come to naught; when few apply their physical energies, the state will fall into poverty. That is the reason why the world is in chaos.

In the state ruled by an enlightened sovereign, one would find no recorded literature and the law would supply the only instruction; one would find no injunctions from the early kings and the magistrates would serve as the only instructors; one would find no [esteem for] bravery in achieving private vengeance, and killing of the enemy would be regarded as the only courageous deed. As a result, the people in the state would all conform to the law in their discourse, would aim at meritorious achievement in their actions, and would offer their services to the army out of bravery. Therefore, in time of peace the state would be rich; in time of war the army would be strong. These might be called the "kingly resources." When the "kingly resources" were stored up, the sovereign could avail himself of any situation that might arise in the state of the enemy. . . .

This then is the customary experience of a disorderly state: the learned men will exalt the ways of the early kings and make a show of humanity and righteousness. They will adorn their manners and clothes and embroider their arguments and speeches so as to scatter doubts on the law of the age and beguile the mind of the sovereign. The itinerant speakers will advocate deceptive theories and utilize foreign influence to accomplish their selfish purposes, being unmindful of the benefit of the state. The free-lance fighters will gather pupils and followers and set up standards of fidelity and discipline, hoping thereby to spread their reputation, but violating the prohibitions of the Five Ministries in the process. The courtiers will congregate in the powerful houses, use all kinds of bribes, and exploit their contacts with influential men in order to escape the burden of military service. The tradesmen and craftsmen will produce inferior wares and collect cheap articles, and wait for good opportunities to exploit the farmers. These five types of men are the vermin of the state. Should the ruler fail to eliminate such people as the five vermin and should he not uphold men of firm integrity and strong character, then he can hardly be surprised if within the seas there should be states that decline and fall, and dynasties that wane and perish.

LI SSU: LEGALIST THEORIES IN PRACTICE

The feudal state of Ch'in, utilizing Legalist practices of strong centralization of power, regimentation of its people and aggressive warfare, had built itself up to a position of forbidding strength in the late years of the Chou dynasty. Finally, under the vigorous leadership of King Ch'eng, it succeeded in swallowing up the last of its rivals and uniting all of China under its rule. In 221 B.C. King Ch'eng assumed the title of *Ch'in Shih-huang-ti,* The First Exalted Emperor of the Ch'in.

He had been aided in his efforts toward unification by a group of astute and ruthless statesmen identified with Legalist doctrines, the most important of whom was Li Ssu (d. 208 B.C.), who became prime minister of the new empire. Thus, for the first time one of the schools of classical thought had its teachings adopted as the orthodox philosophy of a regime ruling all of China.

At Li Ssu's urging the First Emperor carried out a series of sweeping changes and innovations that, in the course of a few years, radically affected the entire structure of Chinese life and society. One of these was the complete abolition of all feudal ranks and privileges and the disarmament of all private individuals. The entire area of China was brought under the direct control of the central court through an administrative system of prefectures and counties. With this unification of the nation came measures for the standardization of weights, measures, and writing script, the destruction of all feudal barriers between districts, and the construction of better roads and communications. Wars were undertaken to subdue neighboring peoples and expand the borders of the nation, great masses of people were forcibly moved to new areas for purposes of defense or resettlement, and labor gangs were set to work constructing the Great Wall out of smaller defensive walls of the old feudal states.

Unprecedented undertakings of such magnitude naturally provoked opposition from many groups. Local loyalties remained strong and men dreamed of throwing off Ch'in domination and restoring the old states. The great public works of road building, construction of defenses and foreign wars brought tremendous suffering to the people who were forced into work gangs or uprooted from their homes. The expenses of the new central government necessitated higher and higher taxes from the farmer. Prime Minister Li Ssu met the threat of opposition with typically Legalist measures. All histories of the other feudal states, all works of rival schools of philosophy—in short all writings which might prompt unfavorable comparison of the Ch'in regime to earlier governments and ways of life—were looked upon as dangerous and ordered to be withdrawn from private hands and burned. All men who dared to criticize the measures of the new regime were to be summarily punished. The people were to be awed and terrorized, and the enforcement of laws made so harsh that all thought of disobedience or revolt would be ruled out.

The First Emperor of the Ch'in was a man of extraordinary vision and demonic energy. He worked tirelessly to build up the power and prestige of his regime, directing campaigns, constructing defenses, erecting magnificent palaces for himself and his court, and traveling on extensive tours of inspection throughout his realm. With the aid of Li Ssu and a few other trusted advisers he managed to carry out his drastic measures and hold down the ever-growing threat of revolt among his subjects. Never before had China been so vast and powerful.

For a while it seemed that Legalism as a theory of government had achieved incontrovertible success. But with the death of this dictatorial emperor the weakness in the Legalist system became apparent. The emperor had ruled from behind the scenes, remaining aloof from his people and ministers. This placed enormous power in the hands of a few trusted officials and eunuchs who were allowed access to him. On his death a struggle for power broke out. Li Ssu and the powerful eunuch, Chao Kao, by concealing the death of the emperor and forging orders in his name, succeeded in destroying their rivals and seizing actual control of the government. The Second Emperor became a helpless puppet, cut off in the depths of the palace from all contact with or information of the outside world. Then Chao Kao turned on Li Ssu and destroyed him and his family, using against him the very Legalist methods that Li Ssu had employed. Popular revolts broke out all over the nation as the people grew increasingly restless under the burden of taxation and oppression. But all news of the seriousness of the situation was kept from the court by officials who had learned to fear the consequences of speaking out. The government was paralyzed by the force of its own autocratic laws. In the end the Second Emperor was forced to commit suicide, Chao Kao was murdered, and the last ruler of the Ch'in submitted meekly to the leader of a popular revolt. In 207, less than fifteen years after its glorious establishment, the new dynasty had come to a violent and ignoble end.

The Ch'in, though short-lived, had a profound effect upon the course of Chinese history. The measures for unification, standardization, and

centralization of power, coercive though they were, destroyed for all time
the old feudal system and gave to the Chinese people a new sense of
unity and national identity. The destruction of the old feudal states, the
shifts of population, and the wars and uprisings which accompanied the
downfall of the dynasty, wiped out the old aristocracy of Chou times and
opened the way for new leaders and new families to rise to power. Nevertheless, the spectacular failure of the Legalists to stamp out rival schools
of thought, to suppress criticism by police control, and to rule the people
by exacting laws and harsh penalties, discredited Legalist policies for
centuries to come. Later regimes might in fact make use of Legalist ideas
and methods in their administrations, but never again did they dare
openly to espouse the hated philosophy of the Ch'in. The First Emperor
and his advisers became the symbols of evil and oppression in Chinese
history, and the dynasty an example to all later rulers of what happens
when the people are exploited and oppressed to the breaking point, when
force and tyranny replace humanity and justice as the guiding principles
of government.

LI SSU

Memorial on Annexation of Feudal States
[From Shih chi, 87:2a–b]

He who waits on others misses his opportunities, while a man aiming at
great achievements takes advantage of a critical juncture and relentlessly
follows it through. Why is it that during all the years that Duke Mu of
Ch'in [659–621 B.C.] was overlord (pa) among the feudal princes, he did
not try to annex the Six States to the east? It was because the feudal lords
were still numerous and the power of the imperial Chou had not yet
decayed. Hence, as the Five Overlords succeeded one another, each in
turn upheld the House of Chou. But since the time of Duke Hsiao of
Ch'in [361–338 B.C.] the House of Chou has been declining, the feudal
states have been annexing one another, and east of the pass there remain
only Six States.

Through military victories, the State of Ch'in has, in the time of the
last six kings, brought the feudal lords into submission. And by now the
feudal states yield obeisance to Ch'in as if they were its commanderies
and prefectures. Now, with the might of Ch'in and the virtues of Your

Highness, at one stroke, like sweeping off the dust from a kitchen stove, the feudal lords can be annihilated, imperial rule can be established, and unification of the world can be brought about. This is the one moment in ten thousand ages. If Your Highness allows it to slip away and does not press the advantage in haste, the feudal lords will revive their strength and organize themselves into an anti-Ch'in alliance. Then no one, even though he possessed the virtues of the Yellow Emperor, would be able to annex their territories.

Memorial on the Abolition of Feudalism
[From *Shih chi,* 6:12b]

Numerous were the sons, younger brothers, and other members of the royal family that were enfeoffed by King Wen and King Wu at the founding of the Chou dynasty. But as time passed, these relatives became estranged and alienated one from another; they attacked each other as if they were enemies. Eventually the feudal lords started wars and sent punitive expeditions against one another, and the king could do nothing to stop them. Now, owing to the divine intelligence of Your Majesty, all the land within the seas is unified and it has been divided into commanderies and prefectures. The royal princes and the meritorious ministers have been granted titles and bountifully rewarded from the government treasury,[3] and it has proved sufficient. When the government institutions have been thus changed and there has been no contrary opinion in the empire, it is evidently the way to keep peace and quiet. To institute a feudal nobility again would not be advantageous.

Memorial on the Burning of Books
[From *Shih chi,* 87:6b–7a]

In earlier times the empire disintegrated and fell into disorder, and no one was capable of unifying it. Thereupon the various feudal lords rose to power. In their discourses they all praised the past in order to disparage the present and embellished empty words to confuse the truth. Everyone cherished his own favorite school of learning and criticized what had been instituted by the authorities. But at present Your Majesty possesses

[3] That is, instead of being granted noble titles and income from a fief, they have received honorary ranks and salaries paid out of taxes.

a unified empire, has regulated the distinctions of black and white, and has firmly established for yourself a position of sole supremacy. And yet these independent schools, joining with each other, criticize the codes of laws and instructions. Hearing of the promulgation of a decree, they criticize it, each from the standpoint of his own school. At home they disapprove of it in their hearts; going out they criticize it in the thorough-fare. They seek a reputation by discrediting their sovereign; they appear superior by expressing contrary views, and they lead the lowly multitude in the spreading of slander. If such license is not prohibited, the sovereign power will decline above and partisan factions will form below. It would be well to prohibit this.

Your servant suggests that all books in the imperial archives, save the memoirs of Ch'in, be burned. All persons in the empire, except members of the Academy of Learned Scholars, in possession of the *Book of Odes,* the *Book of History,* and discourses of the hundred philosophers should take them to the local governors and have them indiscriminately burned. Those who dare to talk to each other about the *Book of Odes* and the *Book of History* should be executed and their bodies exposed in the market place. Anyone referring to the past to criticize the present should, together with all members of his family, be put to death. Officials who fail to report cases that have come under their attention are equally guilty.[4] After thirty days from the time of issuing the decree, those who have not destroyed their books are to be branded and sent to build the Great Wall. Books not to be destroyed will be those on medicine and pharmacy, divination by the tortoise and milfoil, and agriculture and arboriculture. People wishing to pursue learning should take the officials as their teachers.

Memorial on Exercising Heavy Censure
[From *Shih chi,* 87:15a–18a]

The worthy ruler should be one able to fulfill his kingly duties and em-ploy the technique of censure.[5] Visited with censure, the ministers dare

---

[4] The passage from the beginning of the paragraph to this point has been inserted from the fuller account given in *Shih chi,* 6:23b.

[5] Here is the central theme of this memorial. The Chinese term may be more literally translated as "inspection and punishment." To relieve the awkwardness from the repeated use of this cumbersome expression, we have adopted "censure" as a more convenient, though less exact, equivalent throughout the memorial.

not but exert their ability to the utmost in devotion to their ruler. When
the relative positions between minister and ruler are thus defined unmistakably, and the relative duties between superior and inferior are
made clear, then none in the empire, whether worthy or unworthy, will
dare do otherwise than exert his strength and fulfill his duties in devotion to the ruler. Thus the ruler will by himself control the empire, and
will not be controlled by anyone. Then he can enjoy himself to the utmost. How can a talented and intelligent ruler afford not to pay attention
to this point?

Hence, Shen Pu-hai [6] has said: "To possess the empire and yet not be
able to indulge one's own desires is called making a shackles out of the
empire." The reason is that a ruler who is unable to employ censure must
instead labor himself for the welfare of the people as did Yao and Yü.
Thus it may be said that he makes shackles for himself. Now, if a ruler
will not practice the intelligent methods of Shen Pu-hai and Han Fei
Tzu, or apply the system of censure in order to utilize the empire for his
own pleasure, but on the contrary purposelessly tortures his body and
wastes his mind in devotion to the people—then he becomes the slave of
the common people instead of the domesticator of the empire. And what
honor is there in that? When I can make others devote themselves to me,
then I am honorable and they are humble; when I have to devote myself
to others, then I am humble and they are honorable. Therefore he who
devotes himself to others is humble, and he to whom others devote themselves is honorable. From antiquity to the present, it has never been
otherwise. When men of old considered anyone respectable and virtuous,
it was because he was honorable; when they considered anyone despicable
and unworthy, it was because he was humble. Now, if we should exalt
Yao and Yü because they devoted themselves to the empire, then we
would have missed entirely the reason for considering men respectable
and virtuous. This may indeed be called a great misapprehension. Is it
not fitting then to speak of it as one's shackles? It is a fault resulting from
the failure to exercise censure.

Hence, Han Fei Tzu has said: "The affectionate mother has spoiled
children, but the stern household has no overbearing servants." [ch. 50]
And the purpose for saying so is to make certain that punishments are
applied.

[6] A Legalist philosopher, d. 337 B.C.

Hence, according to the laws of Lord Shang [Shang Yang], there was corporal punishment for the scattering of ashes in the streets. Now, the scattering of ashes is a small offense, whereas corporal punishment is a heavy penalty. Only the intelligent ruler is capable of applying heavy censure against a light offense. If a light offense is censured heavily, one can imagine what will be done against a serious offense! Thus the people will not dare to violate the laws. . . .

The fact that intelligent rulers and sage-kings were able for a long time to occupy the exalted position, hold great power, and monopolize the benefits of the empire is due to nothing other than their being able, on their own responsibility, to exercise censure without neglect and to apply severe punishments without fail. It was for this reason that none in the empire dared to be rebellious. If, now, a ruler does not busy himself with what prevents rebellion, but instead engages in the same practices by which the affectionate mother spoils her children, indeed he has not understood the principles of the sages. When one fails to practice the state craft of the sages, what else does he do except make himself the slave of the empire? Is this not a pity?

As a matter of fact, when men who uphold frugality and economy, humanity and righteousness, are installed in the court, then wild and unrestrained revels are cut short. When ministers given to remonstrating and lecturing are admitted to a ruler's side, then abandoned and reckless aims become curbed. When the deeds of patriots and martyrs are given prominence in the world, then all thought of indulgence and comfort has to be abandoned. Therefore the intelligent ruler is one able to keep out these three classes of men and to exercise alone the craft of the ruler, whereby he keeps his obedient ministers under control and his clear laws in effect. Therefore his person becomes exalted and his power great. All talented rulers should be able to oppose the world and suppress established usage, destroying what they hate and establishing what they desire. Thus they may occupy a position of honor and power while they live, and receive posthumous titles that bespeak their ability and intelligence after they die. So, the intelligent ruler acts on his decisions by himself, and none of the authority lies with his ministers. Only thus can he obliterate the path of humanity and righteousness, close the mouths of irresponsible speakers, and keep in confinement the deeds of patriots. Stopping the avenues of hearing and sight, he sees and hears inwardly by himself. Then from without he cannot be moved by the deeds of humane and righteous men and patriots; from within he cannot be carried away by arguments of remonstrance and disputation. Therefore he is able to act according to his heart's desire, and no one dares oppose him.

Thus only may a ruler be said to have succeeded in understanding the craft of Shen Pu-hai and Han Fei Tzu, and in practicing the laws of Lord Shang. I have never heard of the empire falling into disorder while these laws were practiced and this craft understood. Hence, it is said that the way of the king is simple and easily mastered, yet only the intelligent ruler is able to carry it out.

Thus only may the exercise of censure be said to be real. [When the exercise of censure is real,] the ministers will be without depravity. When the ministers are without depravity, the empire will be at peace. When the empire is at peace, its ruler will be venerated and exalted. When the ruler is venerated and exalted, the exercise of censure will be without fail. When the exercise of censure is without fail, what is sought for will be obtained. When what is sought for is obtained, the state will be wealthy. When the state is wealthy, its ruler's pleasures will be abundant. Therefore, when the craft of exercising censure is instituted, then all that the ruler desires is forthcoming. The ministers and people will be so busy trying to remedy their faults that they will have no time to scheme for trouble.

Thus is the way of the emperor made complete, and thus may the ruler be said really to understand the craft between ruler and subject. Though Shen Pu-hai and Han Fei Tzu were to return to life, they would have nothing to add.

PART TWO

THE IMPERIAL AGE: CH'IN AND HAN

B.C.

221–207	Ch'in dynasty.
202–A.D. 9	Former Han dynasty.
202–195	Reign of Kao-tsu.
188–180	Reign of Empress Lü.
179–157	Reign of Emperor Wen.
178	Memorial on encouragement of agriculture by Ch'ao Ts'o.
140	Adoption of first era name, Chien-yüan.
140–87	Reign of Emperor Wu.
136	Doctors for the Five Classics appointed.
124	Increased use of written examinations in selecting officials.
122	Death of Liu An, patron of compilers of *Huai-nan Tzu*.
c.120	Employment of Legalist-minded officials to manage fiscal operations of the state. State monopoly of production of iron and salt; debased coinage and commercial taxes.
115	Campaigns into western regions.
108	Chinese administration in north Korea.
104?	Tung Chung-shu (179?–104?), leading Confucian philosopher.
101	Conquest of states of Tarim Basin.
90?	Ssu-ma Ch'ien (145?–90?), author of *Records of the Historian*.
81	Debate on Salt and Iron.

A.D.

1	Wang Mang regent.
9–23	Hsin dynasty, established by usurper Wang Mang.
25–220	Latter Han dynasty.
79	Collation of the Five Classics by Confucianists in White Tiger Hall.
92	Pan Ku (32–92), principal compiler of *History of the Former Han Dynasty*.
97?	Wang Ch'ung (27–97?), Confucian rationalist.
105	Invention of paper recorded.
175	The Five Classics and *Analects* engraved in stone.
220	Han emperor deposed.
220–280	Period of the Three Kingdoms.

INTRODUCTION

Though China witnessed periods of imperial splendor under several dynasties, we single out the Ch'in (221–207 B.C.) and Han (202 B.C.–A.D. 220) as representing the original "Imperial Age," because in these years the basic pattern for succeeding empires was laid out. The rule of the Ch'in was short-lived but marked a great turning point in Chinese history. By this ruling house the country was brought for the first time under a single unified administration, a centralized state wielding unprecedented power, controlling vast resources, and displaying a magnificence which inspired both awe and dread among its subjects. Achieved after years of steady, systematic conquest, this empire nevertheless proved an unexpected graveyard for the grandiose ambitions of its masters. Yet when the Ch'in collapsed suddenly, it left to the House of Han an important legacy: the idea of empire and the governmental structure to embody it. For almost four centuries under the Han the implications of this great fact were to work their way out in all aspects of Chinese life, not the least in the intellectual sphere. It is this long period of consolidation and co-ordination which we shall be chiefly concerned with here. Though a complex development, this process deserves our attention because in several fundamental respects it shaped the intellectual tradition of China until modern times, and not of China only but of Korea and Japan as well.

The early years of the Han were marked by a long slow struggle to recover for the empire the advantages of the harsh unification effected by the Ch'in, and to establish them firmly in the pattern of Chinese society. The Ch'in had abolished feudalism in one sweeping stroke, yet it arose again among the followers and family of the founder of the Han, whose successors had to set about quietly and patiently whittling away at feudal rights and holdings until they were finally and for all time reduced to an empty formality. The great web of central government, held together by the terror of Ch'in's laws and the personal power of her First Emperor, had quickly disintegrated with the fall of the dynasty. The Han worked gradually to build it up again, unifying, organizing, and standardizing the vast area brought under its control. This effort at standardization extended even to the realm of thought in which again the Han succeeded in accomplishing, by gradual and peaceful means, what the violent proscriptions of the Ch'in had failed to secure.

Reflecting the expanding horizons of the empire was a broadening of intellectual interest and concern with questions of cosmology and the natural order. Hsün Tzu in the century before had written: "Heaven operates with constant regularity. It does not prevail because of a sage-king like Yao, nor does it cease to prevail because of a tyrant like Chieh. Respond to it with good government and blessings will result; respond to it with misgovernment and misfortune will result."

It was thus the duty not only of private thinkers but of the government itself to investigate the natural laws which governed the workings of the universe. The conclusions of the Han philosophers undoubtedly embraced many far-fetched and absurd ideas, as some men of the day were quick to point out. But taken together they reveal to us the powerful urge in the Han to organize all knowledge into a coherent whole, filling in with conjecture where necessary. Han thinkers were deeply convinced that order existed in all things, in the natural world as in society. Their constant efforts were bent upon discovering and classifying everything in this hierarchic order embracing all creation, "so that," as one work puts it, "men may fully understand their whole environment . . . and not be startled by strange things." [1]

The Mean (22) states: "Only he who possesses absolute sincerity can give full development to his nature. Able to give full development to his own nature, he can give full development to the nature of other men. Able to give its full development to the nature of men, he can give full development to the nature of all beings; he can assist the transforming and nourishing powers of Heaven and earth. Able to assist the transforming and nourishing powers of Heaven and earth, he may with Heaven and earth form a triad."

This concept that Heaven, earth, and man form an eternal trinity is basic in Han thought. It was first of all the duty and obligation of man to study and comprehend the laws of Heaven, Heaven in both a religious

[1] *Huai-nan Tzu,* 21:2a.

and a physical sense. Equally strong is the conviction, hardly to be wondered at in an agricultural society, that man, and especially the government, must attend always to concerns of the earth, particularly to matters of irrigation, land usage, flood control, etc. Han thinkers particularly stressed that economic welfare is the basis of popular morality. The scholar or sage might deliberately choose to be poor because he has a sense of values and will refuse to be rich if he cannot become so by virtuous means. But the masses cannot be expected to have such a set of values. They desire material wealth and well-being. If they cannot acquire them justly, they will seek them by unjust means. Therefore the ruler, the enlightened man, must see to it that the people can provide for their needs by just means. The people will follow profit like water flowing downward; they will not so follow virtue. Therefore the course of profit and the course of virtue must be made identical. This is the reason why the government, and eventually the emperor himself, is responsible for the moral conduct of the people. If a poor man steals, it is because he is not able to live honestly. This is not his fault but the fault of the economic and social systems; hence eventually the fault of the emperor. By rectifying these faults, then, the emperor "transforms" the people, that is, makes it possible for them to be virtuous.

Confucianism talks a great deal of this duty of the government to transform or bring to completion the nature of the people, in other words, to civilize them. The first step in the process is to provide peace and prosperity. The second step is moral training or education. This is done through rites (which include everything from the most solemn religious ceremonies to the simplest daily courtesies), music (instrumental music, song, and mimic dance), and literature. Rites and music can be appreciated and learned to some extent by all men, but literature, being a long and difficult study, can be pursued thoroughly only by the intelligent and leisured. The final product of this entire process is the sage, the completely learned man who, because of his learning, possesses the most acute and refined moral sense possible. Ideally, he should be selected to become emperor. But since a constant change of rulers would lead to chaos and the difficulties in selecting successors would be too great, in practice the dynastic principle of hereditary rulership is accepted, and the sage takes up a position as adviser to the emperor. That is, the place of the scholar and sage is in government service. He does not go out to preach in the fields, he does not retire to the wilderness to work out his personal salvation (unless conditions in the government make it impossible for him to render proper service). He operates through the established machinery of the government, which has surveillance over the economic, social, and spiritual welfare of the nation.

This is the philosophy of government and human nature developed and expounded by Confucian thinkers. During the Han this class of scholar officials grew to a position of dominance over the entire Chinese social system, completely replacing the feudal aristocracy of former times. Allying themselves with the imperial system, they succeeded in having Confucianism declared the official state philosophy and in having a state university and system of competitive examinations set up which, in times of peace at least, assured the dominant position of the scholars in the bureaucracy.

Hsün Tzu, the father of Han Confucianism, had written: "Heaven has its seasons, earth its resources, and man his government. This is how man is able to form a triad with Heaven and earth. If man neglects his own part in this triad and puts all his hope in Heaven and earth with which he forms a triad, he is making a grave mistake" (chapter 17). Han thinkers attempted to coordinate what they knew of the "seasons of heaven" (sacrificial rites, astronomy, calendar-construction), the "resources of earth" (economics, agriculture, water-control), and the "government of man" into a single comprehensive science. But their rationalistic urge and love of systematization often drove them further into those realms which Hsün Tzu had warned were unprofitable or dangerous to explore. The result was a wealth of far-fetched beliefs and superstitious practices. In the course of the dynasty, therefore, other thinkers appeared who attempted to combat the grosser absurdities of Han thought and redirect men's attentions to more appropriately human considerations.

CHAPTER VIII

THE IMPERIAL ORDER

The downfall of the Ch'in, more dramatic and sudden even than its rise, had a profound effect upon the thinking of the Chinese. It proved to their satisfaction that terror and strength alone could never rule the world. But the men who wrested from the Ch'in the vast empire it had created were not bent simply on restoring the old order of things.

The aristocratic families of the older feudal states of Chou, which had bitterly resisted the expansion of Ch'in, were seriously weakened by the steps the conqueror later took to prevent their again threatening his power. The opposition which eventually proved fatal to the Ch'in dynasty, therefore, came not from the ranks of the old aristocracy but from the common people. Ch'en She, who led the first major revolt against Ch'in rule, was a day laborer in the fields. Liu Chi, the man who finally set up the Han dynasty after destroying both the Ch'in and rival rebel factions, was likewise of humble origin, as were most of his comrades who fought with him to victory.

THE HAN REACTION TO CH'IN DESPOTISM

As commoners under the Ch'in, these men knew at first hand the suffering that its harsh rule had brought to the people. They were quick, therefore, to abolish its more offensive laws and institutions, while leaving intact much of the rest of its elaborate machinery of government. Under their leadership the new regime of the Han was marked by plebeian heartiness and vigor, simplicity and frugality in government, and abhorrence of the Legalist doctrines of the hated Ch'in.

CHIA I
The Faults of Ch'in

The following excerpt is from the celebrated essay, "The Faults of Ch'in" (*Kuo-Ch'in lun*), by the Han poet and statesman Chia I (201–169 B.C.). Chia I, employing the florid style popular at this time, reviews the history of Ch'in, and analyses the causes which led to its precipitous downfall. His essay, admired as a masterpiece of rhetoric and reasoning, was copied into the two great Han histories, the *Shih chi* and *Han shu,* and has had a far-reaching influence on Chinese political thought.

[From *Shih chi,* 6:41a; *Han shu* 31; *Wen hsüan* 51]

Duke Hsiao of Ch'in, relying upon the strength of the Han-ku Pass[1] and basing himself in the area of Yung-chou, with his ministers held fast to his land and eyed the House of Chou, for he cherished a desire to roll up the empire like a mat, to bind into one the whole world, to bag all the land within the four seas; he had it in his heart to swallow up everything in the eight directions. At this time he was aided by [the Legalist] Lord Shang who set up laws for him, encouraged agriculture and weaving, built up the instruments of war, contracted military alliances and attacked the other feudal lords. Thus the men of Ch'in were able with ease to acquire territory east of the upper reaches of the Yellow River.

After the death of Duke Hsiao, kings Hui-wen, Wu, and Chao-hsiang carried on the undertaking and, following the plans he had laid, seized Han-chung in the south and Pa and Shu in the west, acquired rich land in the east and strategic areas in the north. The other feudal lords in alarm came together in council to devise some plan to weaken Ch'in, sparing nothing in gifts of precious objects and rich lands to induce men from all over the empire to come and join with them in the Vertical Alliance . . . which united all the peoples of the states of Han, Wei, Yen, Ch'u, Ch'i, Chao, Sung, Wei, and Chung-shan. . . . With ten times the area of Ch'in and a force of a million soldiers they beat upon the Pass and pressed forward to Ch'in. But the men of Ch'in opened the Pass and went out to meet the enemy, and the armies of the nine states were blocked and

---

[1] The strategic pass separating the home territory of Ch'in (later the metropolitan area of Ch'ang-an) from eastern China.

did not dare to advance. Ch'in, without wasting a single arrow or losing a single arrowhead, at one stroke made trouble for the whole empire.

With this the Vertical Alliance collapsed, its treaties came to naught and the various states hastened to present Ch'in with parts of their territories as bribes for peace. With its superior strength Ch'in pressed the crumbling forces of its rivals, pursued those who had fled in defeat, and overwhelmed the army of a million until their shields floated upon a river of blood. Following up the advantages of its victory, Ch'in gained mastery over the empire and divided up the land as it saw fit. The powerful states begged to submit to its sovereignty and the weak ones paid homage at its court.

Then followed kings Hsiao-wen and Chuang-hsiang whose reigns were short and uneventful. After this the First Emperor arose to carry on the glorious achievements of six generations. Cracking his long whip, he drove the universe before him, swallowing up the eastern and western Chou and overthrowing the feudal lords. He ascended to the highest position and ruled the six directions, scourging the world with his rod, and his might shook the four seas. In the south he seized the land of Yüeh and made of it the Cassia Forest and Elephant commanderies, and the hundred lords of Yüeh bowed their heads, hung halters from their necks, and pleaded for their lives with the lowest officials of Ch'in. Then he caused Meng T'ien to build the Great Wall and defend the borders, driving back the Hsiung-nu over seven hundred *li* so that the barbarians no longer dared to come south to pasture their horses and their men dared not take up their bows to avenge their hatred.

Thereupon he discarded the ways of the former kings and burned the writings of the hundred schools in order to make the people ignorant. He destroyed the major fortifications of the states, assassinated their powerful leaders, collected all the arms of the empire, and had them brought to his capital at Hsien-yang where the spears and arrowheads were melted down to make twelve human statues, all in order to weaken the people of the empire. After this he ascended and fortified Mount Hua and set up fords along the Yellow River, strengthening the heights and precipices overlooking the deep valleys. He garrisoned the strategic points with skilled generals and expert bowmen and stationed trusted ministers and well-trained soldiers to guard the land with arms and question all who passed back and forth. When he had thus pacified the empire, the First Emperor believed in his heart that with the strength of his capital within the Pass and his walls of metal extending a thousand miles, he had established a rule that would be enjoyed by his descendants for ten thousand generations.

For a while after the death of the First Emperor the memory of his might continued to awe the common people. Yet Ch'en She, born in a humble hut with tiny windows and wattle door, a day laborer in the fields and a garrison conscript, whose abilities could not match even the average, who had neither the worth of Confucius and Mo Tzu nor the wealth of T'ao Chu or I Tun, stepped from the ranks of the common soldiers, rose up from the paths of the fields and led a band of some hundred poor, weary troops in revolt against the Ch'in. They cut down trees to make their weapons, raised their flags on garden poles, and the whole world in answer gathered about them like a great cloud, brought them provisions, and followed after them as shadows follow a form. In the end the leaders of the entire east rose up together and destroyed the House of Ch'in.

Now the empire of Ch'in at this time was by no means small or feeble. Its base in Yung-chou, its stronghold within the Pass, was the same as before. The position of Ch'en She could not compare in dignity with the lords of Ch'i, Yen, Chao, Han, Wei, Sung, and Chung-shan. The weapons which he improvised of hoes and tree branches could not match the sharpness of spears and battle pikes; his little band of garrison conscripts was nothing beside the armies of the nine states; his plots and stratagems, his methods of warfare were far inferior to those of the men of earlier times. And yet Ch'en She succeeded in his undertaking where they had failed. Why was this, when in ability, size, power and strength his forces came nowhere near those of the states of the east that had formerly opposed Ch'in? Ch'in, beginning with an insignificant amount of territory, reached the power of a great state and for a hundred years made all the other great lords pay homage to it. Yet after it had become master of the whole empire and established itself within the fastness of the Pass, a single commoner opposed it and its ancestral temples toppled, its ruler died by the hands of men, and it became the laughing stock of the world. Why? Because it failed to rule with humanity and righteousness and to realize that the power to attack and the power to retain what one has thereby won are not the same.

The Rebellion of Ch'en She and Wu Kuang

This description of the beginning of the first major revolt against the Ch'in dynasty is taken from the biographies of its leaders, Ch'en She and Wu Kuang, in the *Shih chi* and *Han shu*. It clearly illustrates how the severity of the Ch'in laws and institutions drove its people to such desperation that revolt became the only hope of survival.

[From *Han shu*, 31:1a–2b]

When Ch'en She was young he was one day working in the fields with the other hired men. Suddenly he stopped his plowing and went and stood on a hillock, wearing a look of profound discontent. After a long while he announced: "If I become rich and famous, I will not forget the rest of you!"

The other farm hands laughed and answered: "You are nothing but a hired laborer. How could you ever become rich and famous?"

Ch'en She gave a great sigh. "Oh well," he said, "how could you little sparrows be expected to understand the ambitions of a swan!"

In the 7th month of the first year of the reign of the Second Emperor [209 B.C.] the poor people of the village were sent to garrison Yü-yang, a force of nine hundred men. But when they got as far as the district of the Great Swamp in Ch'i, they encountered heavy rain and the road became impassable so that it was evident that they would not reach their destination on time. According to the law, men who failed to arrive at the appointed time were executed. Ch'en She and Wu Kuang plotted together, saying, "If we try to run away we will die, and if we start a revolt we will likewise die. Since we die in either case, would it not be better to die fighting for a kingdom?" . . . When the officer in command of the group was drunk, Wu Kuang made a point of openly announcing several times that he was going to run away. In this way Wu Kuang hoped to arouse the commander's anger, get him to punish him, and so stir up the men's ire and resentment. As Wu Kuang had expected, the commander began to beat him, when his sword slipped out of its scabbard. Wu Kuang sprang up, seized the sword, and killed the commander. Ch'en She rushed to his assistance and they proceeded to kill the other two commanding officers as well. Then they called together all the men of the group and announced: "Because of the rain which we encountered, we cannot reach our rendezvous on time. And anyone who misses a rendezvous has his head cut off! Even if you should somehow escape with your heads, six or seven out of every ten of you are bound to die in the course of garrison duty. Now, my brave fellows, if you are unwilling to die, we have nothing more to say. But if you would risk death, then let us risk it for the sake of fame and glory! Kings and nobles, generals and ministers —such men are made, not born!" The men all answered, "We are with you!"

The Rise of Liu Chi, Founder of the Han

Liu Chi, like Ch'en She, was a man of humble birth who formed a small band of adventurers and opposed Ch'in rule. When his forces grew to a sizeable army, he entered into an agreement with other rebel groups that whoever reached the capital area of Ch'in, Kuan-chung or the land "within the Pass," should become its ruler. In 207 B.C. Liu Chi succeeded in fighting his way to the capital city of Hsien-yang and the Ch'in dynasty came to an end. At this time he issued his famous three-article code (ten characters in Chinese) to replace the elaborate legal code of Ch'in. Though when the dynasty got on its feet a more elaborate set of laws had to be worked out, this three-article code has often been held up as an example of the simplicity and leniency of early Han government. The translations are from the biography of Liu Chi, the "Annals of Emperor Kao-tsu" (his posthumous title) in the *Shih chi*. Liu Chi's various titles have been omitted for the sake of clarity.

[From *Shih chi*, 8:15a–16b]

The army of Liu Chi finally reached Pa-shang [near the capital] ahead of the other lords. The King of Ch'in, Tzu-ying [third ruler of the Ch'in dynasty who had abandoned the title of Emperor] came in a plain carriage drawn by a white horse [2] with a rope about his neck and surrendered the imperial seals and credentials by the side of Brier Road. Some of the generals asked that he be executed, but Liu Chi replied: . . . "It is bad luck to kill those who have already surrendered," and with this he turned the King of Ch'in over to the officials. Then he proceeded west and entered Hsien-yang . . . where he sealed up the storehouses containing Ch'in's treasures and wealth and returned to his encampment at Pa-shang. There he summoned all the distinguished and powerful men of the prefectures and addressed them:

"Gentlemen, for a long time you have suffered beneath the harsh laws

[2] White is the color of mourning.

of Ch'in. Those who criticized the government were wiped out along with their families; those who gathered to talk in private were executed in the market place. I and the other lords have made an agreement that he who first enters the Pass shall rule over the area within. Accordingly I am now king of this territory of Kuan-chung. I hereby promise you a code of laws consisting of three articles only: 1) he who kills anyone shall suffer death; 2) he who wounds another or steals shall be punished according to the gravity of the offense; 3) for the rest I abolish all the laws of Ch'in. Let the officials and people remain undisturbed as before. I have come only to save you from injury, not to exploit or oppress you. Therefore do not be afraid! The reason I have returned to Pa-shang is simply to wait for the other lords so that when they arrive we may settle the agreement." He sent men to go with the Ch'in officials and publish this proclamation in the prefectural villages and towns. The people of Ch'in were overjoyed and hastened with cattle, sheep, wine, and food to present to the soldiers, but Liu Chi declined all such gifts, saying: "There is plenty of grain in the granaries. I do not wish to be a burden to the people." With this the people were more joyful than ever and their only fear was that Liu Chi would not become the King of Ch'in.

Liu Chi Becomes the First Emperor of the Han Dynasty

To insure the loyalty of his comrades and supporters, Liu Chi was obliged to hand out titles and fiefs to them as his conquests advanced. In 202 B.C., when his final success seemed assured, they in turn urged him to assume the old Ch'in title of Exalted Emperor, arguing that if he failed to do so their own titles would lack authority. Like Caesar he modestly declined three times before accepting.

[From *Shih chi*, 8:28b]

The lords and generals all joined in begging Liu Chi to take the title of Exalted Emperor but he said: "I have heard that the position of emperor may go only to a worthy man; it cannot be claimed by empty words and vain talk. I do not dare to accept such a position." Then the courtiers all replied: "Our great king has risen from the humblest beginnings to punish the wicked and violent and bring peace to all within the four seas. To those who have achieved merit he has accordingly parcelled out land and enfeoffed them as kings and peers. If our king does not assume the supreme title, then all our titles also will be called into doubt. On pain of death we urge our request!" Liu Chi declined three times and then, seeing that he could do no more, said: "If you, my lords, all consider it a good thing, then it must be to the good of the country."

THE THEORETICAL BASIS OF THE IMPERIAL INSTITUTION

The Ch'in dynasty had worked out many of the practical problems of bureaucratic organization and administration necessary for the government of a vast empire the size of China. The early Han rulers, while simplifying the legal system and reintroducing a limited feudalism, were careful to keep most of this bureaucratic machinery intact. But since the Ch'in rulers had based their regime upon the now discredited doctrines of Legalism, it was necessary for Han thinkers to work out a new philosophical interpretation and justification for the emperor system. So successful were they at this task that their theories remained the avowed basis of the Chinese imperial institution until its abolition at the beginning of the present century. This concept of empire and the function of the ruler, magnificently comprehensive and, in contrast to the cynicism of Legalist thought, expressed in the loftiest moral terms, constitutes one of the great achievements of Chinese thought.

The early Han was a time of philosophical synthesis. It is difficult to apply old labels to the thinkers of this period, whose ideas are drawn from several of the earlier philosophical schools. In the pages that follow, therefore, we shall make no attempt to deal with Han thought in terms of individual schools, but describe instead the synthesis that formed the orthodox theory of Han rule, largely Confucian in inspiration but containing significant elements borrowed from Taoism, yin-yang thought, and even Legalism.

The rule of the First Emperor of the Ch'in had been characterized by furious regulation of all spheres of national life and the exercise of unlimited autocratic power. Han political theorists, reacting against this situation, favored a government based upon laissez-faire, or "nonaction" as it was expressed, and the delegation of authority. Adroitly surrounding the imperial person with an aura of divine mystery, they urged that the ruler must not trouble himself about specific decisions and actions of government, but leave all such matters to the care of his ministers who were selected, theoretically at least, on the basis of virtue and ability alone. Thus they hoped to forestall the reappearance of the "cult of the individual" that had flourished under the Ch'in. To support this view they stressed the importance of timeliness and flexibility in government. The emperor at the top of the vast pyramid of government might remain inflexibly faithful to certain basic principles of rule. But the formulation and implementation of specific measures must be a day-to-day process carried out by officials personally familiar with the situation. Neither Legalist absolutism, as expressed in the rule of rigid and uniform law, nor old-fashioned Confucianism, clinging tenaciously to the institutions of the past, were acceptable in this new age. Government, though adhering to certain enduring values, must adjust to the times.

This interpretation of the duties of the ruler, in which the emperor was in effect "kicked upstairs" in order to create greater freedom and authority for his ministers, did much to limit the theoretically absolute power of the monarch and assure that, though hereditary right might place an evil or incompetent ruler upon the throne, the government of the nation should not be entirely the victim of his whim. Yet like all political theories, its success was not unqualified. Strong-willed emperors such as Emperor Wu managed to break the power of the ministers and rule directly, while weak-willed ones tended to become virtual prisoners of their own bureaucracy.

The Quietude of the Ruler and the Delegation of Power

The following selections are from the two most important philosophical works of the early Han, the *Huai-nan Tzu* and the *Ch'un-ch'iu fan-lu*. The *Huai-nan Tzu* is a collection of essays written or compiled by scholars at the court of Liu An (d. 122 B.C.), Prince of Huai-nan and grandson of Kao-tsu, the first emperor of the Han. Though largely Taoist in inspiration, the work includes borrowings from other schools and represents an attempt at a synthesis of earlier thought. The *Ch'un-ch'iu fan-lu* or *Deep Significance of the Spring and Autumn Annals* by the famous Confucian scholar Tung Chung-shu (179?–104? B.C.) is likewise a series of short essays on problems of cosmology and political philosophy and was of great importance in the formulation of Han Confucian theory.

[From *Huai-nan Tzu,* 9:1a, 6b–7a]
The craft of the ruler consists in disposing of affairs without action and issuing orders without speaking. The ruler remains still and pure without moving, impartial without wavering. Compliantly he delegates affairs to his subordinates and without troubling himself exacts success from them. Thus though he has his plans in his mind, he allows his counselors to proclaim them; though his mouth can speak, he allows his administrators to talk for him; though his feet can walk, he lets his ministers lead; and though he has ears to hear, he permits the officials to remonstrate with him. Thus among his policies are none that fail and among his plans none that go awry. . . . When the ruler gives ear to affairs of government he is pure and enlightened and without delusion. His mind is empty and his will weak. Therefore his ministers gather about to assist and counsel him, and whether they be stupid or wise, worthy or unworthy, there are none who do not exhaust their talents for him. Only then may he proclaim the rites that will be the basis of his rule. Thus he rides upon the power of the multitude as though it were his carriage, drives the wisdom of the multitude as though it were his horse, and though he traverse dark plains and steep roads, he will never go astray. The ruler of men hides himself far away in the depths to avoid heat and dampness, dwells behind many closed doors to escape rebels and evildoers. He knows neither the shape of the villages about him nor the form of the hills and lakes far away. Beyond his curtains-of-state his eyes see no farther than ten *li,* his ears hear no more than a hundred paces, and yet there is nothing in the whole world that he does not comprehend, for those who come to report to him are many, and those who survey for him are numerous.

[From Tung Chung-shu, *Ch'un-ch'iu fan-lu,* Sec. 18, 6:5b–6a]
Heaven holds its place on high and sends down its blessings, hides its form and shows forth its light. Because it holds a high position it is exalted and because it sends down blessings it is benevolent (*jen*). Because it hides its form it is holy and because it shows its light it is bright. Thus to hold an exalted position and practice benevolence, to hide one's holiness and show forth light, is the way of Heaven. Therefore, he who acts as the ruler of men imitates Heaven's way, within hiding himself far from the world so that he may be holy, and abroad observing widely that he may be enlightened. He employs a host of worthy men that he may

enjoy success, but does not weary himself with the conduct of affairs that he may remain exalted. Loving all creatures, he does not reward in joy or punish in anger, and thereby he may be benevolent. Therefore he who is the ruler of men takes nonaction as his way and considers impartiality as his treasure. He sits upon the throne of nonaction and rides upon the perfection of his officials. His feet do not move but are led by his ministers; his mouth utters no word but his chamberlains speak his praises; his mind does not scheme but his ministers effect what is proper. Therefore no one sees him act and yet he achieves success. This is how the ruler imitates the ways of Heaven.

Political Relativism and the Importance of Timeliness
[From *Huai-nan Tzu*, 13:3a–4b]

If the institutions of the former kings are not suitable, they should be abolished; if the practices of later ages are good, they should be encouraged. Rites and music have never had any constant form. Therefore the sage governs rites and music rather than being governed by them. There is one constant principle in ruling a nation, and that is to consider the well-being of the people as fundamental. There is one thing that is unchanging in theories of government, and that is that the execution of orders is primary. If one benefits the people one need not necessarily copy antiquity; if one accords with the situation of the times one need not invariably follow old practices. In the decline of the Hsia and Shang the laws were not changed, and yet the dynasties perished; the founders of the Three Dynasties did not all copy their predecessors, and yet they became kings. Therefore, under the rule of a sage the laws change with the times and the rites are adapted to popular usage. As clothing and utensils must be fitted to their functions, so laws and institutions must accord with what is proper for the time. Therefore, there is nothing condemnable about modifying ancient ways, and nothing praiseworthy in adhering to fixed principles. Though the hundred rivers rise from different sources they all find their destination in the sea; though the hundred schools of philosophy teach different methods, they all seek the ordering of the state. . . .

A dynasty periodically changes its master; a state often changes its ruler. Each man as he comes to the throne follows his own likes and dislikes and each uses his power to satisfy his own whims and desires. If he would attempt with one fixed system of rites and one fixed set of laws to follow the times and accord with such changes, it is clear that he could never maintain his authority. Therefore the basis of the sage's actions is called the Way, but his actions themselves are called affairs. . . . The Way is like a bell or a chiming stone which has one immutable tone, but affairs are like harps and lyres which change their tones each time they are tuned. In like manner institutions and rites are but tools for governing men, not the reasons behind government. Let humanity be the warp and righteousness the woof, for these are things that never change in a thousand generations. Then if one considers the abilities of his men and notes the exigencies of the times, he may change his ways every day without harm. Why must there be any immutable laws in the world? He who accords with the situation of the times, follows the principles of human nature, and harmonizes with Heaven, earth, and the spirits, may thereby achieve a just rule.

THE MORAL LEADERSHIP OF THE EMPEROR

It should not be supposed on the basis of the selections above, however, that the Chinese emperor was expected to be a passive figurehead seated at the apex of a government in which all actual power was wielded by his officials. In the syncretic view of the ruler as at once exalted above worldly affairs (the Taoist conception) and yet responsible for the welfare of his subjects (the Confucian doctrine), there was a conflict not easily resolved. Although Tung Chung-shu, as we have seen above, at times declared that the ruler should adhere to a policy of nonaction, at other times he urged him to take a very active and personal interest in the direction of national life. Indeed, the emperor in Han thought was far more than the chief officer of a bureaucratic organization. He was the living representative of the whole hierarchical order of mankind, itself a reflection of the larger order of the universe. Since Heaven, earth, and man join in Chinese thought to form an inseparable triad, so the emperor, the head of the third member, is responsible for keeping mankind in harmony with the other members, and of raising all men by the power of his government to the fulfillment of their true human dignity.

The primary instrument by which the ruler accomplishes this exalted task is moral suasion. While delegating the direction of daily affairs to his officials, the ruler is responsible for setting a perfect moral example for them and for his people so that all will be swayed by the power of his goodness and irresistibly drawn to the practice of virtue. In order to reach and be known to his subjects, this goodness and virtue of the ruler are given concrete embodiment in rites and music. If the people are properly exposed to the civilizing influences of rites and music, the Han thinkers insist, they cannot fail to be educated and transformed.

Ch'in Legalist theory had attempted to set up a complex and inflexible set of laws and regulations to govern the entire economic, social, and political life of the nation. Han political theorists, under Confucian influence, desired to substitute education and moral suasion for this system of laws. But the sphere of the ruler's activities was to be no less broad than under Legalism. Upon the government, and eventually upon the emperor himself, rested the responsibility for the economic well-being, education, and moral perfection of every individual in the state.

The Moral Power of the Ruler
[From *Huai-nan Tzu,* 9:8b–9a]

The power to achieve success or failure lies with the ruler. If the measuring-line is true, then the wood will be straight, not because one makes a special effort, but because that which it is "ruled" by makes it so. In the same way if the ruler is sincere and upright, then honest officials will serve in his government and scoundrels will go into hiding, but if the ruler is not upright then evil men will have their way and loyal men will retire to seclusion. Why is it that people often scratch melons or gourds with their fingernails, but never scratch stones or jewels? Because no matter how hard they scratch stones or jewels they can never make an impression. In the same way if the ruler can be made to adhere to right, maintain fairness, and follow a measuring-line, as it were, in measuring high and low, then even though his ministers come to him with evil designs it will be the same as dashing eggs against a rock or throwing fire into water. King Ling loved slim waists and all the women went on diets and starved themselves. The King of Yüeh admired bravery and all the men outdid each other in dangerous feats defying death. From this we may see that he who wields authority can change the customs and transform the manners of his people.

TUNG CHUNG-SHU

The Threefold Obligations of the Ruler
[From *Ch'un-ch'iu fan-lu,* Sec. 19, 6:7a–8a]

The ruler is the basis of the state. In administering the state, nothing is more effective for educating the people than reverence for the basis. If the basis is revered then the ruler may transform the people as though by supernatural power, but if the basis is not revered then the ruler will have nothing by which to lead his people. Then though he employ harsh penalties and severe punishments the people will not follow him. This is to drive the state to ruin, and there is no greater disaster. What do we mean by the basis? Heaven, earth, and man are the basis of all creatures. Heaven gives them birth, earth nourishes them, and man brings them to completion. Heaven provides them at birth with a sense of filial and brotherly love, earth nourishes them with clothing and food, and man completes them with rites and music. The three act together as hands and feet join to complete the body and none can be dispensed with. . . . If all three are lacking, then the people will become like deer, each person following his own desires, each family possessing its own ways. Fathers cannot employ their sons nor rulers their ministers, and though there be walls and battlements they will be called an "empty city." Then will the ruler lie down with a clod of earth for a pillow. No one menacing him, he will endanger himself; no one destroying him, he will destroy himself. This is called a spontaneous punishment, and when it descends, though he hide in halls of encircling stone or barricade himself behind steep defiles, he can never escape. But the enlightened and worthy ruler, being of good faith, is strictly attentive to the three bases. His sacrifices are conducted with utmost reverence; he makes offerings to and serves his ancestors; he advances brotherly affection and encourages filial conduct. In this way he serves the basis of Heaven. He personally grasps the plow handle and plows a furrow, plucks the mulberry himself and feeds the silkworms,[3] breaks new ground to increase the grain supply and

---

[3] Symbolic acts. It is not suggested that the emperor should actually work in the fields.

opens the way for a sufficiency of clothing and food. In this way he serves the basis of earth. He sets up schools for the nobles and in the towns and villages to teach filial piety and brotherly affection, reverence and humility. He enlightens the people with education and moves them with rites and music. Thus he serves the basis of man. If he rightly serves these three, then the people will be like sons and brothers, not daring to be unsubmissive. They will regard their country as a father or a mother, not waiting for favors to love it nor for coercion to serve it, and though they dwell in fields and camp beneath the sky they will count themselves more fortunate than if they lived in palaces. Then will the ruler go to rest on a secure pillow. Though none aid him he will grow mighty of himself, though none pacify his kingdom peace will come of its own. This is called a spontaneous reward, and when it comes, though he relinquish his throne, give up his kingdom and depart, the people will take up their children on their backs, follow him, and keep him as their lord, so that he can never leave them.

How the Way of the King Joins the Trinity

In the following selections Tung Chung-shu likens the task of the ruler in nourishing and perfecting the people to the nourishing activities of the divine and natural worlds, returning always to the conception of the triad of Heaven, earth and man.

[From *Ch'un-ch'iu fan-lu,* Sec. 43, 11:5a–b; Sec. 44, 11:6b–9b]

Those who in ancient times invented writing drew three lines and connected them through the middle, calling the character "king" [王]. The three lines are Heaven, earth, and man, and that which passes through the middle joins the principles of all three. Occupying the center of Heaven, earth, and man, passing through and joining all three—if he is not a king, who can do this?

Thus the king is but the executor of Heaven. He regulates its seasons and brings them to completion. He patterns his actions on its commands and causes the people to follow them. When he would begin some enterprise, he observes its numerical laws. He follows its ways in creating his laws, observes its will, and brings all to rest in humanity. The highest humanity rests with Heaven, for Heaven is humaneness itself. It shelters and sustains all creatures. It transforms them and brings them to birth.

It nourishes and completes them. Its works never cease; they end and then begin again, and the fruits of all its labors it gives to the service of mankind. He who looks into the will of Heaven must perceive its endless and inexhaustible humaneness.

Since man receives his life from Heaven, he must also take from Heaven its humaneness and himself be humane. Therefore he reveres Heaven and knows the affections of father and son, brother and brother; he has a heart of trust and faithfulness, compassion and mercy; he is capable of acts of decorum and righteousness, modesty and humility; he can judge between right and wrong, between what accords with and what violates duty. His sense of moral order is brilliant and deep, his understanding great, encompassing all things.

Only the way of man can form a triad with Heaven. Heaven's will is constantly to love and benefit, its business to nourish and bring to age, and spring and autumn, winter and summer are all the instruments of its will. The will of the king likewise is to love and benefit the world, and his business to bring peace and joy to his time; and his love and hate, his joy and anger, are his instruments. The loves and hates, joys and angers of the king are no more than the spring and summer, autumn and winter, of Heaven. It is by mild or cool, hot or cold, weather that all things are transformed and brought to fruition. If Heaven puts forth these in the proper season, then the year will be a ripe one; but if the weather is unseasonable, the year will be lean. In the same way if the ruler of men exercises his love and hate, his joy and anger, in accordance with righteousness, then the age will be well governed; but if unrighteously, then the age will be in confusion. Thus we know that the art of governing well and bringing about a ripe year are the same; that the principle behind a chaotic age and a lean year is identical. So we see that the principles of mankind correspond to the way of Heaven. [Sec. 44, 11:6b–7b]

The cool and mild, the cold and hot seasons of Heaven are actually one and the same with man's emotions of contentment and anger, sorrow and joy. . . . These four temperaments are shared with Heaven and man alike, and are not something engendered by man alone. Therefore man can regulate his emotions, but he cannot extinguish them. If he regulates them, they will follow with what is right, but if he attempts to suppress them disorder will result. . . .

The spirit of spring is loving, of autumn, stern, of summer, joyous, and of winter, sad. . . . Therefore the breath of spring is mild, for Heaven is loving and begets life. The breath of summer is warm, and Heaven makes glad and nourishes. The breath of autumn is cool, and so Heaven is stern and brings all to fruition. The breath of winter is cold, and Heaven grieves and lays all to rest. Spring presides over birth, summer over growth, autumn over the gathering in, and winter over the storing away. [Sec. 43, 11:5a–b]

The ruler holds the position of life and death over men; together with Heaven he holds the power of change and transformation. There is no creature that does not respond to the changes of Heaven. The changes of Heaven and earth are like the four seasons. When the wind of their love blows, then the air will be mild and the world team with life, but when the winds of their disfavor come forth, the air will be cold and all things die. When they are joyous the skies are warm and all things grow and flourish, but from their wrath comes the chill wind and all is frozen and shut up.

The ruler of men uses his love and hate, his joy and anger to change and reform the customs of men, as Heaven employs warm and cool, cold and hot weather to transform the grass and trees. If joy and anger are seasonably applied, then the year will be prosperous, but if they are used wrongly and out of season, the year will fail. Heaven, earth, and man are one, and therefore the passions of man are one with the seasons of Heaven. So the time and place for each must be considered. If Heaven produces heat in the time for cold, or cold in the season of heat, then the year must be bad, while if the ruler manifests anger when joy would be appropriate, or joy where anger is needed, then the age must fall into chaos.

Therefore the great concern of the ruler lies in diligently watching over and guarding his heart, that his loves and hates, his angers and joys may be displayed in accordance with right, as the mild and cool, the cold and hot weather come forth in proper season. If the ruler constantly practices this without error, then his emotions will never be at fault, as spring and autumn, winter and summer are never out of order. Then may he form a trinity with Heaven and earth. If he holds these four passions deep within him and does not allow them recklessly to come forth, then may he be called the equal of Heaven. [Sec. 44, 11:8b–9b]

Human Nature and Education

Mencius had declared that the nature of man is originally good, Hsün Tzu that it is originally bad. Tung Chung-shu, the first major Confucian thinker to follow these men, attempted to effect a compromise between the two opposing views, teaching that the original nature of man possesses the potentiality for good but is not yet actually good. To achieve actual goodness it must await the transforming and civilizing influence of the ruler's teachings. Thus Tung Chung-shu's doctrine of human nature became one of the cornerstones supporting the exalted Han concept of the dignity and responsibility of the emperor. Indeed as Tung himself writes in a rebuttal of Mencius' view: "If the nature of all men were already good, then what would be left for the king to do when he assumed his calling?"

[From *Ch'un-ch'iu fan-lu*, Sec. 35, 10:3a–5b]

For discovering the truth about things there is no better way than to begin with names. Names show up truth and falsehood as a measuring-line shows up crooked and straight. If one inquires into the truth of a name and observes whether it is appropriate or not, then there will be no deception over the disposition of truth. Nowadays there is considerable ignorance on the question of human nature and theorists fail to agree. Why do they not try returning to the word "nature" itself? Does not the word "nature" (*hsing*) mean "birth" (*sheng*), that which one is born with? [4] The properties endowed spontaneously at birth are called the nature. The nature is the basic substance. Can the word "good," we inquire, be applied to the basic substance of the nature? No, it cannot. . . . Therefore the nature may be compared to growing rice, and goodness to refined rice. Refined rice is produced from raw rice, yet unrefined rice does not necessarily all become refined. Goodness comes from the nature of man, yet all natures do not necessarily become good. Goodness, like the refined rice, is the result of man's activities in continuing and completing Heaven's work; it is not actually existent in what Heaven itself has produced. Heaven acts to a certain degree and then ceases, and what has been created thus far is called the heavenly nature; beyond this point is called

---

[4] Tung is using a favorite Chinese type of argument, that based upon the supposed affinities between characters of similar pronunciation. Such "puns," as we should call them, are intended to be taken in all seriousness.

the work of man. This work lies outside of the nature, and yet by it the nature is inevitably brought to the practice of virtue. The word "people" (*min*) is taken from the word "sleep" (*ming*). . . .

The nature may be compared to the eyes. In sleep the eyes are shut and there is darkness; they must await the wakening before they can see. At this time it may be said that they have the potential disposition to see, but it cannot be said that they see. Now the nature of all people has this potential disposition, but it is not yet awakened; it is as though it were asleep and awaiting the wakening. If it receives education, it may afterwards become good. In this condition of being not yet awakened, it can be said to have the potential disposition for goodness, but it cannot be said to be good. . . . Heaven begets the people; their nature is that of potential good, but has not yet become actual good. For this reason it sets up the king to make real their goodness. This is the will of Heaven. From Heaven the people receive their potentially good nature, and from the king the education which completes it. It is the duty and function of the king to submit to the will of Heaven, and thus to bring to completion the nature of the people.

Rites, Music, and Morality

Music, which originally designated a fairly elaborate performance consisting of instrumental music, singing, and dancing, had from early times been regarded as potentially of great moral benefit or harm. Hsün Tzu and his followers in the Han developed this idea into an elaborate theory of the nature and function of music. By seeing that people listened to the proper music, the ruler could cultivate moral virtue in his people and bring happiness to his kingdom. Music and ritual, therefore, were the means by which the sovereign, fulfilling his sacred duty as the heavenly ordained ruler, transformed and brought to completion the nature of his people.

The following passages are from the essay on music in the *Book of Rites* which expresses the theory of music and ritual so important in this period.

[From *Li chi*, Book 19]

All musical tones arise from the human heart when it is moved by external things. Moving in response to external things, it gives form to its movement in sound. These sounds blend and answer each other, producing modulations, and from these modulations come patterns which form modes. When these modes are combined in a pleasing way and the shields and axes of the war dance, the feathers and pennants of the civil dance are added, we have what is called music. Music is produced by tones and based upon the response of the human heart to external things. Thus when the heart is moved to contentment, its sound is broad and slow; when to joy, it is ebullient and free; when to anger, coarse and shrill; when to reverence, direct and austere; and when to love, harmonious and gentle. These six types of outburst are not innate in man but are produced by the response to external things. Therefore the ancient kings were careful about what affected the heart. . . . Thus the music of a well-ruled state is peaceful and joyous and its government is orderly; that of a country in confusion is full of resentment and anger and its government is disordered; and that of a dying country is mournful and pensive and its people are in distress. The ways of music and of government are thus directly related. . . .

Man is born in stillness, for stillness is his nature given by Heaven. In response to external things he becomes active, activity being the expression of the desires of his nature. He comes to know external things, and with this knowledge his likes and dislikes take form. If these likes and dislikes are not controlled within him and his understanding is beguiled by the external world, then he cannot return to his true self and the principle of Heaven within him will be destroyed. . . . Then his heart will turn to revolt and deception, and his actions will become dissolute and rebellious. The strong will overpower the weak, the many oppress the few; the wise will deceive the ignorant, and the brave coerce the timid. The sick will go untended and the aged and tender, the orphaned and solitary, will find no place. Such is the great disorder that will ensue. Therefore the former kings set up rites and music that men might be controlled by them. . . . Music comes from within, rites from without. Music coming from within is characterized by stillness, while rites which are from without are characterized by order. Great music must be easy, great rites simple. Music induces an end to anger, rites an end to strife. . . . Music is the harmony of Heaven and earth, rites are their order. Through harmony all things are transformed; through order all are distinguished. Music arises from Heaven; rites are patterned after earth. . . . Therefore the sage creates music in response to Heaven, and sets up rites to match earth. When music and rites are fully realized, Heaven and earth function in perfect order.

FILIAL PIETY

Something should be said here about the concept of filial piety, a virtue so much extoled by Confucian thinkers, because of the important role it has played in Chinese life and because of its effect upon political thought and practice. During the Han a brief work known as the *Hsiao ching* or "Classic of Filial Piety" gained great popularity among the educated class. Purportedly written by Tseng Tzu, a disciple of Confucius, it is in the form of a colloquy between Tseng Tzu and the Master. In it Confucius expounds the view that "filial piety is the basis of virtue and the source of all instruction." Only after one has learned how to serve one's parents reverently and obediently can one fulfill one's other duties to ruler and society. In this view filial piety becomes the cornerstone of all morality, and the obligation to love and care for one's parents, to give them a proper burial, and, it should be noted, to reprimand them gently but firmly if they misbehave, takes precedence over all other human responsibilities.

The political effects of such a doctrine were enormous in the Han, as well as in later ages. Since in most cases a ruler came to the throne only after the death of his father, it was in actual practice only his mother that he had to serve and honor; but his duties toward her were a matter of extreme gravity, and any hint that an emperor was failing to fulfill them could cast serious doubt upon his whole character. Many of the empress dowagers in the Han took full advantage of this situation, forcing their sons to make moves which they did not wish to make by fuming, sulking, or even refusing to eat until they had their way. In the Latter Han especially, when most of the rulers succeeded to the throne while still in their teens, the empress dowagers exercised tremendous power. Moreover, as the Han emperors became more and more Confucian in their thinking toward the end of the Former Han, they unwisely adopted the custom of demonstrating their filial piety by honoring their mother's male relatives with fiefs and high government posts. It was in this way that the Wang clan acquired such power and affluence that Wang Mang was able to make himself virtual dictator and finally to overthrow the dynasty and set himself on the throne.

The cult of filial piety was also significant politically as a powerful conservative force at court. It was a mark of respect to his imperial ancestors and especially to the founder of the dynasty that a ruler maintained intact the institutions inherited from them. Especially in later ages this proved a strong deterrent to institutional reform. Innovators could not easily set aside such dynastic precedents when to do so seemed an act of impiety toward the emperor's forebears.

THE THEORY OF PORTENTS

Like the Greeks and Romans, the early Chinese firmly believed in the portentous significance of unusual or freakish occurrences in the natural world. This belief formed the basis for the Han theory that evil actions or misgovernment in high places incite dislocations in the natural order, causing the appearance of comets, eclipses, drought, locusts, weird animals, etc. In more primitive ages, and still at times in the Han, such phenomena were interpreted as direct manifestations of the wrath of an anthropomorphic Heaven and warnings to mankind to reform. At other times they were explained mechanistically as the result of occurrences in the human world which must inevitably produce effects in the interlocking worlds of Heaven and earth. As Tung Chung-shu writes: "All things depart from that which is different from themselves and follow that which is the same," hence, "fair deeds summon all things of a fair nature, evil deeds summon all things of an evil nature, as like answers like." [5]

However interpreted, this theory of portents and omens had a tremendous influence upon Han political thought, for it gave the bureaucracy a method of indirectly censuring the throne when direct criticism was impolitic. It was up to the provincial and court officials how many of the countless and ever-present natural phenomena which the Chinese regarded as portentous should be brought to the attention of the emperor, and a study of the omens and portents recorded in the *History of the*

[5] *Ch'un-ch'iu fan-lu,* Sec. 57, 13:3b.

Former Han Dynasty indicates clearly that the periods when the largest number of such omens are recorded correspond to those times when the bureaucracy had most reason to be dissatisfied with the administration. That the device was in some measure successful is also attested by the large number of imperial edicts also recorded in the *History* in which the emperor, often in real sincerity, begs the ministers and people to inform him wherein he has erred that such phenomena should appear.

The Theory of Portents
[From Tung Chung-shu, *Ch'un-ch'iu fan-lu,* Sec. 30, 8:13b–14b]

The creatures of Heaven and earth at times display unusual changes and these are called wonders. Lesser ones are called ominous portents. The portents always come first and are followed by wonders. Portents are Heaven's warnings, wonders are Heaven's threats. Heaven first sends warnings, and if men do not understand, then it sends wonders to awe them. This is what the *Book of Odes* means when it says: "We tremble at the awe and fearfulness of Heaven!" [6] The genesis of all such portents and wonders is a direct result of errors in the state. When the first indications of error begin to appear in the state, Heaven sends forth ominous portents and calamities to warn men and announce the fact. If, in spite of these warnings and announcements, men still do not realize how they have gone wrong, then Heaven sends prodigies and wonders to terrify them. If, after these terrors, men still know no awe or fear, then calamity and misfortune will visit them. From this we may see that the will of Heaven is benevolent, for its has no desire to trap or betray mankind.

If we examine these wonders and portents carefully, we may discern the will of Heaven. The will of Heaven desires us to do certain things, and not to do others. As to those things which Heaven wishes and does not wish, if a man searches within himself, he will surely find warnings of them in his own heart, and if he looks about him at daily affairs, he will find verification of these warnings in the state. Thus we can discern the will of Heaven in these portents and wonders. We should not hate such signs, but stand in awe of them, considering that Heaven wishes to repair our faults and save us from our errors. Therefore it takes this way to warn us.

[6] Sung, ch'ing-miao; "wo chiang."

According to the principles used in writing the *Spring and Autumn Annals,* if when the ruler changed the ancient ways or departed from what was right Heaven responded and sent portents, then the country was called fortunate. . . . Because Heaven sent no portents and earth brought forth no calamities in his kingdom, King Chuang of Ch'u prayed to the mountains and streams, saying: "Will Heaven destroy me? It does not announce my faults nor show me my sins." Thus we can see how the portents of Heaven come about as a response to errors, and how wonders make these faults clear and fill us with awe. This is because of Heaven's desire to save us. Only those who receive such portents are called fortunate in the *Spring and Autumn Annals.* This is the reason why King Chuang prayed and beseeched Heaven. Now if a sage ruler or a wise lord delights in receiving remonstrances from his faithful ministers, how much more should he delight in receiving the warnings of Heaven!

Portentous Happenings During the Han and Their Significance

The *History of the Former Han Dynasty* contains a long essay, the "Treatise on the Five Agents," devoted to portentous happenings of Han and pre-Han times. Section by section, the treatise takes up such phenomena as fires, earthquakes, droughts, strange animals and birds, etc., lists the known instances of their occurrence, and quotes the opinions of various scholars concerning their significance in relation to the political situation of the time. The compilers of the treatise, with the advantages of historical hindsight, could make their portents and interpretations tally neatly. Their aim, however, was simply to provide a set of examples from past history to guide scholars in the interpretation of similar portents in the future.

[From *Han shu,* 27 B1:16a–b, 31b–32a; B2:9b–10a]

In the 3d month, 8th year of Empress Lü [180 B.C.], the empress was returning from a sacrifice at Pa-shang. As she passed Brier Road, something that looked like a blue dog appeared and bit her in the armpit, and then suddenly disappeared. Divination proved it to be the evil spirit of the King of Chao, Ju-i. She grew ill of the wound in her side and shortly after died. Earlier Empress Lü had poisoned Ju-i and cut off the hands and feet of his mother, Lady Ch'i, put out her eyes, and made her into what she called a "human pig." [B1:31b–32a]

In the 1st year of the era Yüan-feng [80 B.C.] a yellow rat appeared in Yen holding its tail in its mouth and dancing in the main gate of the king's palace. When the king went to see it the rat continued to dance as before. Then he ordered one of his officials to offer it wine and dried meat but still the rat went on dancing without a stop all day and all night until it died. . . . At this time King Tz'u of Yen, Liu Tan, was plotting revolt and this was a sign he would soon die. In the same month the plot was discovered and he was condemned to death. . . .

In the 9th month, 4th year of the era Chien-shih of Emperor Ch'eng [29 B.C.] there were a lot of rats south of the capital of Ch'ang-an which, bringing mugwort and cypress leaves in their mouths, climbed up the cypress and elm trees on the grave mounds of the people and built nests. They were particularly numerous at T'ung-po. There were no babies in any of the nests but only a lot of dried rat dirt. . . . The rat is a small thieving creature which comes out at night and hides during the day. That it should at this time leave its hole in the daytime and climb trees was a sign that someone of humble circumstances was going to ascend to an eminent and noble position. Empress Wei Ssu had her garden at T'ung-po. Sometime after this Empress Chao rose from humble obscurity to the position of highest honor and shared equal glory with Empress Wei. Empress Chao never had any sons and did much mischief. The next year there was the portent of the kite that set fire to its nest and murdered its young. Thus Heaven again showed its meaning. How awesome! [B1:16a–b]

In the 2d month, the day *keng-tzu,* 1st year of the era Ho-p'ing of Emperor Ch'eng [April 18, 28 B.C.] in Mulberry Valley on Mount T'ai, there was a kite that set fire to its nest. A man named Sun T'ung and some others, hearing the noise of flocks of kites and magpies in the hills, went to see what was happening. The nest burned up and fell to the ground and three baby kites were burned to death. . . . The kite is of a greedy and cruel nature. . . . Mount T'ai or Tai-tsung is the first of the five holy mountains and the place where the ruler announces changes in the name or generation of the dynasty. The meaning of Heaven's warning then was this: do not associate with greedy and cruel men or listen to their evil schemes, or you will suffer the misfortune of having your nest burned and your children harmed, your heirs destroyed and your name changed. Shortly after, Chao Fei-yen obtained favor with the emperor and became empress, and her sister, Chao-i, also enjoyed his attentions. Later they heard that Lady Hsü and the concubine Ts'ao Wei-neng had both given birth to imperial sons. Chao-i was very angry and ordered the emperor to have them seized and killed. The princes and their mothers were accordingly all murdered. After Emperor Ch'eng died Chao-i committed suicide and the whole affair came to light. Empress Chao was tried and punished. This was the meaning of the kite which burned its nest and murdered its children. [B2:9b–10a]

THE DYNASTIC MANDATE

The awesome responsibilities imposed upon the ruler in the Han concept of imperial government called for an emperor of extraordinary wisdom and virtue. Rulers were expected to be at the same time philosophers and sages. Ideally the throne should be given to the wisest and most virtuous man in the empire regardless of his birth or social position. Chinese legend cherishes the tales of how the sage emperors of antiquity chose promising young men from among the common people and, when they had demonstrated their worth and ability, relinquished the throne to them rather than to their own sons. This, the philosophers maintained, had been the true golden age, when the empire was shared by all people and virtue alone was the key to kingship.

But the dynastic principle was far too well established in Chinese custom to seriously consider a "return" to the practices of these legendary ages. Accepting the basic principle of hereditary succession, therefore, the Han thinkers confined themselves to defining what qualifications a family needed to assume the position of supremacy.

Chou philosophy had already developed the concept of the "mandate of Heaven" (t'ien-ming), the divine election by which a new dynasty was empowered to set up its rule, and the Han thinkers carried on and elaborated this idea. Naturally enough, they unanimously agreed that Liu Chi had received the mandate of Heaven to found the House of Han. The very fact of his success amply proved this. In addition they cited his intelligence and virtue and numerous portentous happenings associated with his birth and rise to power as additional proofs that he was divinely favored. But in the later years of the dynasty a need was apparently felt for a further justification for Han rule, that of genealogy.

Early Han historians could tell nothing more of Liu Chi's descent than his mother and father's names; later historians provided him with a genealogy going all the way back to the legendary Emperor Yao. This new theory of the distinguished ancestry of the Liu family served both to enhance the prestige of the dynasty and to discourage any commoners who might conceive the idea of imitating Liu Chi's spectacular rise. But anyone with sufficient power may fabricate his own genealogies and proofs of divine election. When Wang Mang became chief minister and overthrew the Han, he provided himself not only with a full set of portents and omens indicating that Heaven had destined him for the throne, but produced a genealogy relating him to the Yellow Emperor, a sage even more ancient than the ancestor of the Liu family.

The Age of Grand Unity and the Rise of Dynastic Rule

This passage from the Book of Rites (Li chi) is one of the most celebrated in Confucian literature. It has been traditionally taken as representing Confucius' highest ideal in the social order, the age of Grand Unity (ta-t'ung), in which the world was shared by all the people (t'ien-hsia wei kung). This ideal has been of special importance in modern China, and the latter motto was often inscribed on public buildings and monuments, such as the tomb of Sun Yatsen. Following the age of Grand Unity came the rise of dynastic rule.

The Book of Rites is a collection of essays compiled during the Han dynasty from earlier writings. The present text is the opening portion of an essay on the "Evolution of Rites" (Li-yün), a subject which assumed the greatest importance in the Han dynasty. Moreover there are strong evidences in this piece of the syncretic tendencies of the Han, which suggest that the primitive ideal of Grand Harmony is actually a Taoist conception, while the age of Lesser Prosperity following it is the original sage-king ideal of Confucius and Mencius downgraded one step. Thus we are surprised to learn that the adoption in this period of typically Confucian institutions and ethics results in the prevalence of intrigue and war. Yet what appealed to the Chinese mind in this scheme was its apparent reconciliation of the primitive ideal and the historical actuality as two aspects of a common process.

[From Li chi, Sec. 9]

Once Confucius was taking part in the winter sacrifice. After the ceremony was over, he went for a stroll along the top of the city gate and sighed mournfully. He sighed for the state of Lu.

His disciple Yen Yen [Tzu Lu], who was by his side, asked: "Why should the gentleman sigh?"

Confucius replied: "The practice of the Great Way, the illustrious men of the Three Dynasties—these I shall never know in person. And yet they inspire my ambition! When the Great Way was practiced, the world was shared by all alike. The worthy and the able were promoted to office and men practiced good faith and lived in affection. Therefore they did not regard as parents only their own parents, or as sons only their own sons. The aged found a fitting close to their lives, the robust their proper employment; the young were provided with an upbringing and the widow and widower, the orphaned and the sick, with proper care. Men had their tasks and women their hearths. They hated to see goods lying about in waste, yet they did not hoard them for themselves; they disliked the thought that their energies were not fully used, yet they used them not for private ends. Therefore all evil plotting was prevented and thieves and rebels did not arise, so that people could leave their outer gates unbolted. This was the age of Grand Unity.

"Now the Great Way has become hid and the world is the possession of private families. Each regards as parents only his own parents, as sons only his own sons; goods and labor are employed for selfish ends. Hereditary offices and titles are granted by ritual law while walls and moats must provide security. Ritual and righteousness are used to regulate the relationship between ruler and subject, to insure affection between father and son, peace between brothers, and harmony between husband and wife, to set up social institutions, organize the farms and villages, honor the brave and wise, and bring merit to the individual. Therefore intrigue and plotting come about and men take up arms. Emperor Yü, kings T'ang, Wen, Wu, and Ch'eng and the Duke of Chou achieved eminence for this reason: that all six rulers were constantly attentive to ritual, made manifest their righteousness and acted in complete faith. They exposed error, made humanity their law and humility their practice, showing the people wherein they should constantly abide. If there were any who did not abide by these principles, they were dismissed from their positions and regarded by the multitude as dangerous. This is the period of Lesser Prosperity."

On the Destiny of Kings

The following essay was written by Pan Piao (A.D. 3–54) of the Latter Han to expound his theory of the divine election of rulers. It was on the basis of

this conception of the divine election of Han Kao-tsu (Liu Chi) and his family
as founders of the dynasty, that Pan Piao and his son, Pan Ku, set about to
continue and rewrite the *Shih chi* or *Records of the Historian* by their predecessor Ssu-ma Ch'ien. This resulted in the first of the so-called "dynastic
histories," the *Han shu* or *History of the Former Han Dynasty*.

[From *Han shu,* 100 A:8a; *Wen hsüan,* 52]

When Emperor Yao abdicated, he said to his successor: "Ah, Shun! The
Heaven-appointed succession now rests in you." Shun used the same
words in transmitting his mandate to Yü.

At this time Chi and Hsieh served as ministers to Yao and Shun,
bringing light to all the world, and their virtue was borne down the
countless generations to their respective descendants, T'ang [founder
of the Shang dynasty] and Wu [founder of the Chou] so that they were
able to rule over the empire. Thus though they encountered troubles
in their own times and their lines of succession were different, yet in
responding to the will of Heaven and according with human kind, they
followed the same principle.

In the same way the family of Liu [Han dynasty] inherited the bless-
ing of Yao, as we see from its genealogy written in the *Spring and Autumn
Annals*. Yao ruled by the virtue of fire, which was handed down to the
Han. When the future emperor, Kao-tsu, first arose in the Marsh of
P'ei, the spirit of the old woman appeared weeping in the night as a
sign from the Red [Fire] Emperor.

For this reason we say that, in order for a man to enjoy the blessing
of rulership, he must possess not only the virtue of shining sageliness
and apparent excellence, but he must be heir to a patrimony of abundant
merit and favor long accumulated. Only then can he, by his pure sincerity, communicate with the divine intelligence and extend his grace to
all living men. Then will he receive good fortune from the spirits and
gods, and all people will come to his rule. There has never been a case
of a man who, the successive generations having passed without showing signs of his destiny or recording the merit and virtue of his family,
has been able to rise to this position of eminence. The mass of people
see that Kao-tsu arose from among the common men and they do not
comprehend the reasons for his rise. They believe that, happening upon
a time of violence and disorder, he was able to wield his sword, as the
wandering political theorists compare the conquest of the empire to a

deer chase in which success goes to the luckiest and swiftest. They do not understand that this sacred vessel, the rule of the empire, is transmitted according to destiny and cannot be won either by craft or force. Alas, this is why there are so many rebellious ministers and evil sons in the world today. To be so mistaken, one would not only have to be blind to the way of Heaven, but totally unobservant of human affairs as well!

Now when famine comes and the people wander from place to place, the starving and cold fill the roads. They think only of getting a coarse coat to cover themselves and a measure of grain to nourish life. Their desires go no further than a few coins, and yet they die and end tumbled in a ditch. If in this way even poverty and misery are meted out by destiny, how much more so the honor of the throne, the riches of all within the four seas, and the blessing of the gods. How could one recklessly try to arrogate to oneself such a position? True, there are some who, happening upon an age of trouble and peril, by bravery, like Han Hsin and Chi Pu; by their powerful situation, like Hsiang Yü and his uncle, Hsiang Liang; or by luck, like Wang Mang, manage to seize authority for a time. Yet all must end cast into the cauldron or bowed beneath the stroke of the ax, boiled alive, or struck down and quartered. How much more damned would be a mean and insignificant man who could not match even these and yet in his blindness hoped to contend for the throne of the sovereign? As a man cannot ride a thousand-mile journey on a crippled jade, as the little swallows and sparrows cannot soar with the great-winged flocks, as the timbers used for corbels and joists cannot bear the weight of beams and ridgepoles, no more can any mere dullard shoulder the burden of imperial rule.

The *Book of Changes* says: "If the leg of the cauldron is broken, the lord's porridge will spill out." That is, the pot is not fit for the purpose.

At the end of the Ch'in dynasty, the strong men in power joined in urging upon Ch'en Ying the title of king. But Ying's mother pressed him not to accept, saying: "From the time I came as a bride into your father's house, I have known only the poverty and lowliness which have been with your family for generations. Now if you were to rise too suddenly to wealth and honor, I fear it would be unlucky. It would be better to take your forces and place them under the command of another. If you are successful you may receive somewhat less profit, but if things go badly then the misfortune will fall on someone else." Ch'en Ying followed her counsel and assured the safety of his family.

The mother of Wang Ling in like manner perceived that the Hsiang family would perish and the Liu family rise to power. At this time Wang Ling was a general of the Han forces [Liu family] but his mother was held captive by Ch'u [Hsiang forces]. An envoy came from the Han camp and the mother of Ling addressed him in these words: "I beg you to tell my son that the King of Han is a superior man and will surely become ruler of the empire. My son should serve him with all diligence and not be of two minds on my account." Then before the envoy of Han she stabbed herself and died, to urge her son on the course he should follow. Later, when it turned out that the Han was victorious, Wang Ling became prime minister and was enfeoffed as a marquis.

Now if a common woman's perception can deduce the course which events will take and can search out the beginnings of good and bad fortune and insure the perpetuation of her family so that the memory of her deeds is handed down in the pages of history, how much more should a great man be able to do? Therefore, though failure and success rest ultimately with destiny, yet it is up to men to choose between the lucky and unlucky. Ch'en Ying's mother understood what would decline, Wang Ling's mother perceived what would prosper. By judging of these, the disposition of the rulership can be determined.

There were five indications of Kao-tsu's rise to the throne. First, he was a descendant of Emperor Yao. Second, his body and face showed many strange markings. Third, there were omens testifying to his divinely inspired conquest. Fourth, he was liberal and of a keen mind, humane and merciful. Fifth, he understood men and knew well how to use their services. In addition, he was trustworthy and sincere, a good strategist who knew how to listen to others. When he saw what was good, he strove for it; when he employed others, he used them as he would himself. He complied with good advice as a boat follows the current, and responded to his opportunities as an echo answering a sound. [There follows a list of references to Kao-tsu's wise and good acts, and the wonders and prodigies accompanying his rise to power.]

If one adds up the successes and failures of history, examines the victories and defeats in the course of human affairs, perceives how the throne has passed from family to family through the generations, and ponders what is meant by the five signs of Kao-tsu's good fortune enumerated above; and if his character does not come up to the requirements for the highest position, and omens and signs do not appear as they did for Kao-tsu, and yet he tries unjustly to seize power and profit, recklessly violating the proper order, failing to weigh external circumstances and in his heart to comprehend the commands of destiny, then must he bring destruction upon the household he should guard, and lose the years Heaven has granted him; his will be like the misfortune of the cauldron with the broken leg and he will go down beneath the punishment of the ax.

But if brave and ambitious men have sincere understanding and awareness; if they fear and heed the warnings of disaster and use transcendent vision and profound judgment; if they employ the perception of Wang Ling and Ch'en Ying and avoid the overblown ambitions of Han Hsin and Chi Pu; rid themselves of the blind notion that the mandate of Heaven can be pursued like a deer in chase and realize that the sacred vessel of rule must be given from on high; if they do not covet that which they could never hope for, in a way that would draw ridicule even from the two simple country women, the mothers of Ch'en Ying and Wang Ling, then will fortune and blessing flow to their sons and grandsons, and the rewards of Heaven will be with them to the end of their days.

On the Auspicious Omens Accompanying Wang Mang's Rise

Wang Mang made the fullest use of the theory of divine election to the throne in his peaceful seizure of the empire from the tottering House of Han, attempting by all means to show that he had received the mandate of Heaven to found a new dynasty. The excerpt which follows is a summary of a number of works on the auspicious omens which were said to indicate Wang's election to the throne. Wang had the works distributed throughout the empire to prove to all his right to rule. Inclusion of the summary in the *Han shu* should not be taken to indicate the historian's approval of its contents.
    [From *Han shu,* 99 B:11a–12b]

When an emperor or ruler receives the mandate, there must be auspicious signs of his virtue and blessing. He must aid and bring to fulfillment the Five Mandators [five agents], that he may repeatedly be answered with tokens of good fortune. After this he will be able to achieve magnificent success and hand down the rule to his sons and grandsons and forever enjoy inexhaustible blessing.

Therefore, when the House of Hsin [Wang Mang] arose, its virtue and blessing became manifest after the twenty-one decades and nine generations of the Han. The emperor first began the mandate with his enfeoffment as Marquis of Hsin-tu; he received an auspicious omen when Annam presented a live rhinoceros; he began his kingship with the stone of Wu-kung; he established his mandate in Tzu-t'ung, and brought it to completion at Tang in Pa. He received repeated good fortune in the twelve answering omens. Thus profound and firm was the way in which Heaven watched over and protected the House of Hsin. In the latter years of the Han Emperor P'ing, the stone inscribed in vermilion appeared at Wu-kung. The period of the power of fire was run out, and that of the power of earth had come. Supreme Heaven, protectively, by the sign of the vermilion stone, cast out the Han and adopted the Hsin, first bestowing the mandate on the emperor. But the emperor, not yet daring to comply with the will of Heaven, humbly declined it, taking up only the position of Regent. Therefore in the autumn of the seventh month, Heaven again sent the three-colored horse. But the emperor once more declined and would not yet accept the throne. Then Heaven sent as the third sign the iron certificate, as the fourth sign the stone tortoise, as the fifth the appearance of the *yü* beast, as the sixth the tablet of dappled jade, as the seventh the black seal, as the eighth the stone book of Mouling, as the ninth the stone of the dark dragon, as the tenth the divine well, as the eleventh the great spiritual stone, and as the twelfth the silk chart with copper seals. These were the repeated omens of the mandate. Gradually they became clearer and more explicit, and when it reached the twelfth, Heaven made a clear announcement to the Hsin Emperor. The emperor deeply pondered the awe of Heaven above, and could not but be fearful. Therefore he cast off the title of Regent, but still he was called only "Acting Emperor." He changed the era name to Ch'u-shih [New Beginning], for he hoped thus to undertake the responsibility of the mandate of Heaven and be able to satisfy the will of the Lord-on-High. But it was not for this that Heaven had earnestly and repeatedly sent down its will by the mysterious commands. Therefore, on this day Heaven, in order once again to make positive its meaning, urged him by the book of the tortoise. Also the courtier Wang Hsü saw a man wearing a plain white robe with a red embroidered collar and a small cap standing in front of the Hall of the Royal Room. He spoke to Wang Hsü, saying: "Today Heaven has united its colors [i.e., the spirits of the five directions are in agreement] and will deliver the people of the world into the hands of the emperor." Hsü was greatly astonished, but when he advanced ten or so paces, the man suddenly disappeared. On the evening of the day *ping-yin* in the Temple of Emperor Kao-tsu of the Han, there appeared the chart of the golden casket, in which Emperor Kao-tsu [founder of the Han] by the mandate of Heaven transmitted the state to the Hsin Emperor. The following morning, the Director of the Imperial Clan, the Marquis of Loyalty and Filial Piety, Liu Hung, hearing of this, summoned the councilors and high ministers for a conference. They had not yet reached a decision when a great divine stone man spoke to them, saying: "You must urge the Hsin Emperor to go to the Temple of Emperor Kao-tsu to receive the mandate. Do not tarry!" With this the Hsin Emperor arose and mounted his chariot and went to the Temple and received the mandate. The day on which he received the mandate was the day *ting-mao*. Now the cyclical sign *ting* belongs to the agent of fire, the power of the family of the Han, while the character *mao* is a part of the character for the name "Liu." This indicates clearly that the Liu family of the Han, ruling by the power of the agent fire, had come to an end and the empire had passed to the House of Hsin.

The emperor was modest and humble and was perfect in his firm refusals of honor, but the twelve portentous responses from Heaven compelled him and made it clear that the mandate could not be refused. He trembled with fear and awe; wretchedly he wept that nothing could be done to prevent the downfall of the family of Han. With the greatest diligence he sought everywhere for some way to aid the dynasty, but he could not achieve his purpose. In his efforts he passed three nights without sleeping and three days without eating. He called together and questioned the councilors and marquises, the high ministers and officials, and all replied: "It is proper that you should respectfully submit to Heaven's awful will." Thereupon he changed the beginning of the year and settled upon a new dynastic name, and throughout the empire changed and began everything anew. After the House of Hsin was set up, the spirits of Heaven and earth were pleased and happy and repeatedly sent blessings in response, so that lucky omens abounded as before.

CONCLUSION

The foregoing selections should give some idea of the philosophical interpretation of the imperial system, the functions of the ruler and his ministers, and the dynastic principles as they were expounded by philosophers in the Han. These philosophers, largely Confucian in education and conviction, were by no means the creators of this system, which was inherited from the Legalist Ch'in. They can hardly be held responsible for the appearance in China of absolute monarchy, the dynastic system or a bureaucratic state, and yet in a sense the Confucian scholars made these their own, both by taking a large share in the actual administration of the empire and by providing an impressive façade for the imperial institution. In this view the emperor was raised to a dignity far transcending his temporal powers; he performed cosmic functions as the central figure in the triad of Heaven, earth, and man, and as the bearer of Heaven's mandate he possessed an aura of divinity worthy of a true Son of Heaven. Indeed the whole hierarchic order of the universe focused upon him, for upon the emperor depended not only the political administration of a vast empire, but also the very fulfillment of man's being and the harmonious functioning of the forces of nature.

The importance of this concept can hardly be overstated, for it remained intimately associated with the exercise of imperial power down to modern times. If the first Westerners to visit China were struck by the almost divine awe in which the emperor was held by his people, and if they were compelled to prostrate themselves before him as a condition of diplomatic intercourse, it was because this attitude had come to be accepted as natural and right from Han times on down. And similarly if the emperors of Japan have been regarded as gods in even more recent years, it is in no small measure due to the influence of this same imperial concept transplanted centuries ago from China. But we should also remember that the Han political theorists offered this interpretation and justification of imperial power, not for its own sake, but to restrain its exercise by defining the heavy responsibilities of imperial rule and by establishing institutions which would serve as a check on the abuse of it.

CHAPTER IX

THE UNIVERSAL ORDER

The Han was heir to the whole range of Chou thought including Confucian ethical doctrines, Legalist political and economic theories, the mystical speculations of the Taoists, and two attempts, like those of early Greek philosophy, to explain all being in terms of a few basic substances, the yin-yang and five-agents theories. Continuing a tendency already apparent in late Chou and Ch'in times, Han thinkers set about to select the best elements from all these systems of thought and combine them into a comprehensive philosophy worthy of the vastness and grandeur of the new empire.

THE INTELLECTUAL SYNTHESIS

In the early Han Taoism enjoyed a period of unusual popularity, perhaps because its emphasis on timeliness, flexibility, and simple, laissez-faire government fitted so well the needs of the time. Thus the two works quoted later, the *Huai-nan Tzu* and the "Discussion of the Essentials of the Six Schools" by Ssu-ma T'an (d. 110 B.C.), though recognizing and adopting the good points of other schools, both proclaim the superiority of Taoist ideas and doctrines. Shortly after the time of these works, however, during the reign of Emperor Wu, the balance shifted in favor of Confucianism. This was largely due to the efforts of scholars like Tung Chung-shu who, equally eclectic in their ideas, were able to produce a system better suited to the needs of the imperial government and its rapidly expanding bureaucracy. Though this new philosophy of Tung Chung-shu and his successors is commonly described as Confucian, it is far removed from the simple ethical doctrines of Confucius and his immediate followers. Its inspiration and the core of its ideas undoubtedly derive from the Confucian school of Chou times, but these have been expanded by borrowings from other schools to embrace many areas of speculation that were hardly touched upon in early Confucianism. For only by offering a complete philosophy of man and the universe was Han Confucianism able to supplant its rivals and achieve, as it did, a position of state-supported orthodoxy.

Conclusion to the Huai-nan Tzu

The final chapter of the *Huai-nan Tzu* summarizes its contents and the reasons why it was written. In the passage below we are given an historical resumé of the Chou period and the schools of thought it produced, showing how each school was a response to the particular problems of its time. Drawing from these schools, but penetrating further into the innermost mysteries of the universe, the *Huai-nan Tzu* aims at a comprehensive synthesis which may serve as a guide to rulers in any place or time.

[From *Huai-nan Tzu*, 21:1a, 6a–8a]

In setting down these writings and discussions, I have sought to illuminate and encompass the Way and its inner power, and to make clear the web of human affairs. I have gazed upward to study Heaven, examined the earth below me, and about me sought understanding of the principles of humanity. Though I have not been able to draw forth the heart of the supreme mystery, from the abundance I have presented one may trace its course and outline. I have covered the essentials and presented a general picture. But my writings have not penetrated into or laid open the pure simplicity, they have not broken open and spread forth the great ancestor of being, and I tremble that men in their blindness may not understand them. Therefore my words have been many and my explanations broad. Again I fear that men may depart from the root and seek after branches. Thus, if I spoke only of the Way and did not mention human affairs, one would not be able to get along in the world today, while if I spoke too much of human affairs and did not discuss the Way, one would not be able to move and rest with the transforming process. Therefore I have written these twenty chapters: Searching out the Way; Beginning the Truth; Patterns of Heaven; Forms of Earth; Seasonal

Regulations; Peering into the Mysterious; Spirit and Soul; The Primal and Constant; The Craft of the Ruler; Erroneous Names; Unifying Customs; The Way and Its Effects; General Discussions; Explanatory Discussions; Military Strategy; Mountain of Discussions; Forest of Discussions; Human Affairs; The Necessity of Training; The Grand Unity.

THE HISTORICAL MISSION OF CONFUCIANISM

In the time of King Wen, Emperor Chou of Shang was the Son of Heaven. Without measure were his taxes and levies, and his killing and slaughtering were without end. Drunken with lust and drowned in wine, he gathered within the palace a great multitude. He made the torture of the burning pillar. He butchered his councilors and cut open pregnant women. All under Heaven were of the same heart and groaned beneath him. King Wen carried on the goodness of four generations, nourishing virtue and practicing righteousness. He lived between Chou and Ch'i and, though his land did not exceed a hundred *li*, yet half of the world turned to him. He wished for the sake of the humble and weak to curb the strong and put down the brigands, and to set up the way of a true king. Thus was born the plan of the Grand Duke [Lü Shang].

King Wen began the undertaking but could not finish it. King Wu succeeded to the undertaking of his father, King Wen. He summoned a small number of troops, himself donned armor and shield, and went to attack the evil and to strike down the unrighteous. In the fields of Mu he made an oath with his army that he would seat himself upon the throne of the emperor. The world was not yet at peace, the land within the seas was not yet at harmony, and King Wu wished to make manifest the excellent virtue of King Wen, to cause the barbarians to take their riches and bring them as tribute. He had not yet been able to penetrate to the far distant regions and therefore he directed the three years' mourning and buried King Wen between the two great pillars of the hall, to await the submission of distant lands.

King Wu reigned for three years and then died. His son, King Ch'eng, was at that time yet in swaddling clothes and could not manage the rule. His uncles, Ts'ai and Kuan, lending support to the heir of Emperor Chou, Lu Fu, planned to start a rebellion. The Duke of Chou carried on the undertaking of King Wen and took over the affairs of the ruler,

acting as a loyal servant to the House of Chou and aiding and supporting King Ch'eng. He feared lest the road of rebellion be not blocked,
lest the subjects should endanger the lord. Therefore he turned out his
horses on Mount Hua, loosed his war oxen in T'ao Forest, smashed his
drums and broke the drumsticks [to show his will for peace] and, grasping the tablets of state, held court, that he might bring peace to the house
of the king and placate the feudal lords. When King Ch'eng grew to
manhood and was able of his own to manage the affairs of government,
Duke Chou received a fief in Lu, where he retired to reform the manners and rectify the customs of the people.

Confucius taught the way of kings Ch'eng and K'ang and transmitted
the admonitions of the Duke of Chou, instructing his seventy disciples
and teaching them to wear the ancient gown and cap and to study the
books and records. Thus were born the teachings of the Confucianists
(*ju*)

THE HISTORICAL MISSION OF MO TZU

Mo Tzu studied the profession of the *ju* and received the arts of Confucius. But he believed that the rites of the Confucianists were too vexatious and complicated, that their elaborate funerals consumed too much
wealth and impoverished the people, their lengthy mournings injured
the living and upset ordinary affairs. Therefore he turned his back upon
the ways of Chou and used the practices of Hsia. At the time of Emperor
Yü [founder of the Hsia], there was a great flood over all the world.
Yü himself carried baskets of dirt and led the people in damming up
the waters. He drained off the rivers and opened up the nine outlets;
he governed their channels and directed them into the nine courses. He
opened the five lakes and settled the eastern sea. In those times, though
it were burning heat, men had no time to rest; drenched, they took not
the leisure to dry themselves. Those who died in the hills they buried
in the hills; those who perished in the swamps they buried in the swamps,
and thus the [Mo-ist] custom of thrifty usage, simple funerals, and brief
mourning began.

CONTRIBUTIONS OF OTHER SCHOOLS

At the time of Duke Huan of Ch'i, the Son of Heaven had become weak
and ineffectual and the feudal lords made wars among themselves. The

I barbarians in the south and the Ti tribes in the north both attacked the Middle Kingdom and the fate of China hung by a thread. The state of Ch'i was backed in the east by the sea and bordered on the north by the Yellow River. Its territory was narrow, its fields few, but its population plentiful and of keen intelligence and skill. Duke Huan took much thought for the troubles of the Middle Kingdom and was greatly pained at the uprisings of the I and Ti. He wished to preserve the perishing, to give continued life to the dying land, and to restore to honor the position of the Son of Heaven and expand the dynastic labors of kings Wen and Wu. Thus for him was written the *Book of Kuan Tzu* [an early Legalist work].

Duke Ching of Ch'i loved music and beautiful women, dogs, and horses. He would go off hunting and forget to return, and indulged himself indiscriminately in sensual pleasures. He built the Terrace of the Grand Hall, collected metal and cast the Great Bell, and so great was its sound that when it was struck it set all the pheasants to squawking in the fields about. In one morning he gave away to his courtiers three thousand bushels of gold. Liang Ch'iu-chü and Tzu Chia-k'uai were his councilors of the left and right. This was the occasion for the "Admonitions" of Yen Tzu (*Yen Tzu ch'un-ch'iu*).

In the days of the twilight age the nobles of the Six States, dividing up each ravine, marking off each valley, barring the rivers, erecting barriers on the mountains, ruled each within his own boundaries and guarded his own territory. Each clung to his own authority, and ruled by his own will, for there was neither provincial official below nor true Son of Heaven above. In campaigns of arms they struggled for power and he who gained the victory was honored. They relied upon protective alliances, exchanging rich presents as guarantees, dividing tallies as warrants of good faith, binding themselves in pacts of mutual assistance in order to preserve their own states and guard their altars of the soil and grain. So were born the Horizontal and Vertical, and the Long and Short Alliances.

Shen Tzu was minister to Chao Li, ruler of the state of Han, which had formerly been part of Chin. Its soil was poor, its people few, and it was surrounded by powerful neighbors. The old customs of the state of Chin had not yet died out when to them were added the new laws of Han. The orders of the former ruler had not yet been abrogated when the new ruler began to issue commands. The new and the old were contradictory, the latter and the former mutually at variance, and the officials were in confusion and knew not what to abide by. Therefore the books on "Laws and Names" were written.

The state of Ch'in had the customs of a ravening wolf. It valued power and belittled righteousness, seeking ever after gain. It could awe the people with its punishments though it could not transform them by goodness; it could move them by rewards though it could not inspire them by its good name. It took the passes and held the rivers, strengthening the four borders. Taking advantage of the land and its natural defenses, it accumulated great wealth. Duke Hsiao hoped, by possessing the power of a tiger or a wolf, to swallow up the other feudal lords, and for him Shang Yang wrote his work on laws [a Legalist classic].

UNIVERSALITY OF THE HUAI-NAN TZU

But books like this of Mr. Liu [Prince of Huai-nan] observe the forms of Heaven and earth, penetrate to the affairs of yesterday and today, weigh the circumstances and set up their systems, measure the situation and set forth what is proper. Seeking the heart of the Way, according with the customs of the Three Kings, it brings together from far and wide. Into the center of the subtlest mystery it skillfully bores to observe its smallest part. Casting away the foul and impure, drawing forth the pure and silent, it unifies the world, brings order to all things, responds to change and comprehends classes and categories. It does not pursue a single path, nor guard but one corner of thought, bound and led by material things and unable to change with the times. Use it in a corner of life and it will never fail; spread it over the whole world and it will never be found lacking.

SSU-MA T'AN
The Discussion of the Essentials of the Six Schools

The following excerpt is from an essay by the historian Ssu-ma T'an in which he discusses the various merits of the six traditional schools of late Chou thought and decides in favor of Taoism.
[From *Shih chi*, 130:3a–4a]

The Great Commentary on the *Book of Changes* says: "There is one moving force, but from it a hundred thoughts and schemes arise. All have the same objective, though their ways are different." [1] The schools of the yin-yang, the Confucianists, the Mo-ists, the Logicians, the Legalists, and the Taoists all strive for good government. It is simply that they follow and teach different ways, and some are more penetrating than others.

It has been my observation that the yin-yang school in its theories puts strong emphasis upon omens and teaches a great many things to be shunned and tabooed. Hence it causes men to feel restrained and bound by fear. But in its work of arranging correctly the all-important succession of the four seasons it fills an essential need.

The Confucianists are very broad in their interests but do not deal with much that is essential. They labor much and achieve but slight success. Therefore their discipline is difficult to carry out to the fullest. But in the way they order the rules of decorum between lord and subject and father and son, and the proper distinctions between husband and wife and elder and younger, they have something that cannot be altered.

The Mo-ists are too stern in their parsimony to be followed and therefore their teachings cannot be fully applied. But in their emphasis upon what is basic [agriculture] and upon frugal usage they have a point that cannot be overlooked.

The Legalists are very strict and of small mercy. But they have correctly defined the distinctions between lord and subject, and between superior and inferior, and these distinctions cannot be changed.

The Logicians cause men to be overnice in reasoning and often to miss the truth. But the way in which they distinguish clearly between names and realities is something that people cannot afford not to look into.

The Taoists teach men to live a life of spiritual concentration and to act in harmony with the unseen. Their teaching is all-sufficient and embraces all things. Its method consists in following the seasonal order of the yin-yang school, of selecting what is good from the Confucian and Mo-ist teachings, and adopting the important points of the Logical and Legalist schools. It modifies its position with the times and responds to the changes which come about in the world. In establishing customs and practices and administering affairs it does nothing that is not appropriate to the time and place. Its principles are simple and easy to practice; it undertakes few things but achieves much success.

[1] Hsi Tz'u, 2:3b.

THE CREATION, STRUCTURE, AND WORKING
OF THE UNIVERSE

Early Confucianism, with its emphasis upon problems of politics and human relations, had devoted little attention to metaphysical or cosmological speculation. The Taoist and yin-yang schools, however, had traditionally been interested in such questions and their explanations of the creation and working of the universe exercised a great influence in Han thought. Thus though in the course of the Han both the Taoist and yin-yang schools as such tended to degenerate into popular cults dealing mainly with necromancy and divination, their cosmological ideas passed into Han Confucianism and became a part of the philosophy of the educated class.

Though the concept of the two primal forces or modes of creation, the yin and the yang, dates from very early times, it was during the Han that it first became a major element in Chinese thought. Gradually, and most notably in the works of Tung Chung-shu, a great body of correspondence was built up relating the two complementary principles of yin and yang to all phases of creation. Thus yang came to connote male, the sun, fire, heat, Heaven, creation, dominance, spring and summer, etc., while yin was related to the idea of female, the moon, cold, water, earth, nourishing and sustaining, recessiveness, autumn and winter, etc. Each force as it reaches its extreme produces its opposite and the two continue to succeed each other in a never-ending cycle. This constant reaction of the two forces on the metaphysical and physical planes was used to explain all processes of growth and change in the natural world.

The yin-yang concept was also developed by Han scholars in their interpretations of the *I ching* or *Book of Changes*. The *I*, being originally a book of divination, had not been banned during the Ch'in and so its line of transmission was not interrupted. Sometime during the Ch'in or Han the original meaning of the *I* was expanded and developed in a series of appendices or "wings" into a comprehensive system of cosmology. The first two of the *I*'s eight basic trigrams, the trigrams of Heaven (*ch'ien*) and earth (*k'un*) were equated with the yang and yin respectively, so that these two metaphysical forces, Heaven and earth, male and female, became the father and mother of all the other trigrams,

and, in turn, of all creation. Themselves springing from the Great Ultimate (*t'ai-chi*), they produce by their interaction all the phenomena of
the world. The eight trigrams, and the sixty-four hexagrams formed
by their combinations, therefore, represent all the possible situations or
mutations of creation, a universe in miniature. By studying these hexagrams and their interpretations the scholar may come to know all the
activities of the universe. Faced with an important decision, he consults
the oracle, which describes to him by means of the symbolic trigrams, as
a modern scientist might describe by mathematical formulae, the condition of the universe in its endless process of change at that particular
moment. It also prognosticates the future course of development, so that
he may judge the best action to take.

Thus the Chinese attempted to describe the universe and its myriad
changes and to reduce them to an ordered and comprehensible system.
The doctrine that extremes produce opposite reactions, that each object
or situation invariably gives birth to its antithesis, cautioned the scholar
to choose a central course, a golden mean between extremes, which would
be timely and in accordance with the situation at the moment. Though
it had its origin in the old superstition of divination by the milfoil stalks,
the *I* was developed by Han thinkers into a cosmological system that
would free men from their ancient dread of the unknown and the supernatural and allow them to live their lives in harmony with and understanding of the basic laws underlying all phenomenal change.

The Creation of the Universe

The following account of the creation is taken from the *Huai-nan Tzu*.
Though mainly Taoist in conception, it was adopted by Han Confucianists
to round out their cosmology, as seen in the *Po-hu t'ung* or *Discussions in the
White Tiger Hall,* a work representing the official Confucian views of the
Latter Han. This same account of the creation was also taken over by the
Japanese and prefaced to their native mythology in the *Nihongi.*

[From *Huai-nan Tzu,* 3:1a, 14:1a]

Before heaven and earth had taken form all was vague and amorphous.
Therefore it was called the Great Beginning. The Great Beginning produced emptiness and emptiness produced the universe. The universe produced material-force [2] which had limits. That which was clear and light

[2] The word *ch'i* translated in our readings as material-force or vital force, in order to
emphasize its dynamic character, plays an important part in Chinese cosmological and

drifted up to become heaven, while that which was heavy and turbid solidified to become earth. It was very easy for the pure, fine material to come together but extremely difficult for the heavy, turbid material to solidify. Therefore heaven was completed first and earth assumed shape after. The combined essences of heaven and earth became the yin and yang, the concentrated essences of the yin and yang became the four seasons, and the scattered essences of the four seasons became the myriad creatures of the world. After a long time the hot force of the accumulated yang produced fire and the essence of the fire force became the sun; the cold force of the accumulated yin became water and the essence of the water force became the moon. The essence of the excess force of the sun and moon became the stars and planets. Heaven received the sun, moon, and stars while earth received water and soil. [3:1a]

When heaven and earth were joined in emptiness and all was un-wrought simplicity, then without having been created, things came into being. This was the Great Oneness. All things issued from this oneness but all became different, being divided into the various species of fish, birds, and beasts. . . . Therefore while a thing moves it is called living, and when it dies it is said to be exhausted. All are creatures. They are not the uncreated creator of things, for the creator of things is not among things. If we examine the Great Beginning of antiquity we find that man was born out of nonbeing to assume form in being. Having form, he is governed by things. But he who can return to that from which he was born and become as though formless is called a "true man." The true man is he who has never become separated from the Great Oneness. [14:1a]

Theories of the Structure of the Universe

Astronomical speculations about the structure of the universe were the subject of much controversy in Han times and were to occupy a large place in later Chinese thought until Western theories were introduced. There were two major theories, with minor variations, regarding the nature of the universe which strove for acceptance among the scholarly world from the end of the Former Han. One of these, the so-called *Hun t'ien* or eccliptical theory, was championed by the scholar Chang Heng (A.D. 78–139). Though most of our

---

metaphysical thought. At times it means the spirit or breath of life in living creatures, at other times the air or ether filling the sky and surrounding the universe, while in some contexts it denotes the basic substance of all creation.

knowledge of these theories is derived from later sources (principally the Treatise on Astronomy of the *Chin shu*), there seems no reason to believe that they do not represent in general the theories as they were expounded in Han times. The following is Chang Heng's explanation of the *Hun t'ien* theory.

[From Chang Heng, *Hun-t'ien-i* in Hung I-hsüan, *Ching-tien chi-lin*, 27:1a–b]

Heaven is like an egg, and the earth is like the yolk of the egg. Alone it dwells inside. Heaven is great and earth is small. Inside and outside of heaven there is water. Heaven wraps around the earth as the shell encloses the yolk. Heaven and earth each are borne up and stand upon their vital force, floating upon the water. The circumference of heaven is 365¼ degrees. This is divided in half, so that 182⅝ degrees are arched above the earth, while 182⅝ degrees are cupped under the earth. Therefore there are 28 heavenly constellations, half of them visible and half invisible. Its two extremes are called the south and north poles. The north pole is the apex of heaven, but it is elevated 36 degrees above the true north of the earth. The north pole is the axis, hence 72 degrees of this upper sphere are constantly visible. The south pole is the other apex of heaven, but it also is deflected 36 degrees below the true south of the earth. It is the axis for the lower half, hence 72 degrees of the lower half are constantly hidden. The two poles are 182+ degrees apart. Heaven turns about the earth like a cart wheel, revolving constantly without stop. Its form is complete and encircling, hence it is called the "encircling heaven" (*hun t'ien*).

To this was opposed a rival theory, the *Kai t'ien* or equatorial theory, described as follows:

[From *Chin shu*, 11A:1b]

Heaven is like an umbrella, earth like an overturned dish. Both heaven and earth are high in the middle and slope down at the edges. The point beneath the north pole is the center of both heaven and earth. This is the highest point of earth, and from here it slopes down on all sides like water flowing downward. The sun, moon, and stars alternately shine and are hidden and this makes the day and night. The highest point in the center of heaven, where the sun is at the winter solstice, is 60,000 *li* from the horizontal line representing the level of the edges of heaven. The height of the earth at its highest point beneath the north pole is also 60,000 *li*. The highest point of the earth is separated from the horizontal line

representing the level of the edges of heaven by 20,000 *li*. Since the highest
point of heaven and earth correspond, the sun is constantly at a distance
of 80,000 *li* from the earth.

There are minor variations on this theory. Both theories seem to have arisen
around the end of the Former Han, but there are precedents for them in
earlier literature. Though the *Hun t'ien* theory gained the ascendancy, there
were many advocates for both sides and the controversy continued until contact
with the West. The great fault of the *Kai t'ien* theory was obviously its failure
to account for the appearance and disappearance of the sun. This led to modifications in the theory, some scholars declaring that the earth was flat, some that
both the earth and heaven were flat, or that the center of the umbrella-like
heaven was inclined so that the edge of heaven revolved a little below the
surface of the earth. Wang Ch'ung of the Latter Han was a follower of the
Kai t'ien theory, with some modifications, and explained the rising and setting
of the sun as follows:
  [From *Lun heng,* Sec. 32, 11:8b–9a]

Heaven is flat just as the earth is flat, and the rising and setting of the
sun is due to the fact that it revolves along with heaven. . . . To the gaze
of men it appears that heaven and earth unite at a distance of no more
than ten *li*. This is only the effect of distance, however, for they do not
actually come together. In the same way when we seem to see the sun
set, it does not actually set. The illusion of setting is the effect of distance. . . .

  As an experiment, let a man take a large torch and walk at night down
a road which is level and without obstructions. By the time he has gone
less than one *li* from the observer the light of the fire will have disappeared. The fire, of course, has not actually gone out. It is only the effect
of distance. In the same way when the sun revolves to the west and disappears from sight, it does not actually set.

The "Great Appendix" to the Book of Changes: The Process of Universal Change
  [From *I ching,* Hsi Tz'u, 1]

Heaven is high, earth is low; thus the *ch'ien* and the *k'un* are fixed. As
high and low are thus ordered, honorable and humble have their places.
Movement and rest have their constancy; according to these strong and
weak are differentiated. Ways coincide according to their species and

things fall into classes. Hence good fortune and bad fortune come about. In the heavens phenomena appear; on earth shapes occur. Through these, change and transformation become manifest. Therefore the strong and the weak [lines in the trigrams] interplay, and the eight trigrams act and react upon each other. Things are roused by thunder and lightning; they are fertilized by wind and rain. Sun and moon revolve on their courses with a season of cold and then a season of heat. The way of the *ch'ien* constitutes the male, the way of the *k'un* constitutes the female. The *ch'ien* knows the great beginning; the *k'un* gives things their completion. The *ch'ien* knows through the easy; the *k'un* accomplishes through the simple. . . .

Therefore the gentleman dwells securely in the emblems of the *Book of Changes* and delights in studying its explanations of the lines. When the gentleman is living quietly he observes the emblems and studies the explanations, and when he is about to act he observes their changes and studies their predictions. Therefore help comes to him from Heaven: good fortune and nothing that is not beneficial. . . .

The successive movement of yin and yang constitutes what is called the Way. What issues from it is good, and that which brings it to completion is the individual nature. The man of humanity recognizes it and calls it humanity; the wise man recognizes it and calls it wisdom. The people use it daily and are not aware of it, for the Way of the gentleman is but rarely recognized. It manifests itself as humanity but conceals its workings. It rouses all things, but is free from the anxieties of the sage. Its glorious power and great reserve are perfect indeed! It possesses everything in abundance: this is its great reserve. It renews everything daily: this is its glorious power. It produces and reproduces, and hence it is called the Changes. As creator of the primal images, it is called *ch'ien*. As giver of the forms in imitation of the images, it is called *k'un*. Because it enables one to explore the laws of number and know the future it is called divination. Because it affords the element of coherence in change it is called the course of affairs. That aspect of it which cannot be fathomed in terms of the yin and yang is called spirit. . . .

Therefore in the Changes there is the Supreme Ultimate. This generates the two primary forms [the yin and the yang]. The two primary forms generate the four modes [major and minor yin and yang]. The four modes generate the eight trigrams. The eight trigrams determine good and bad fortune. . . .

The Beginnings of Human Culture

The passage below relates how the legendary sages of early Chinese history instructed the people in the arts of civilization, and how each of their inventions or discoveries was inspired by the symbolic meanings of the hexagrams of the *Book of Changes*.

[From *I ching*, Hsi Tz'u, 2]

When in ancient times Fu Hsi ruled the world, he looked up to observe the phenomena of the heavens, and gazed down to observe the contours of the earth. He observed the markings of birds and beasts and how they were adapted to their habitats. Some ideas he took from his own body, and went beyond this to take other ideas from other things. Thus he invented the eight trigrams in order to comprehend the virtues of spiritual beings and represent the conditions of all things of creation. He knotted cords and made nets for hunting and fishing. This idea he probably adopted from the hexagram *li*.

After Fu Hsi died Shen Nung arose. He carved a piece of wood into a plowshare and bent another piece to make a handle, and taught the world the advantages of plowing and weeding. This idea he probably took from the hexagram *i*. He set up markets at midday and caused the people of the world to bring all their goods and exchange them and then return home so that everything found its proper place. This he probably took from the hexagram *shih-ho*.

After Shen Nung died, the Yellow Emperor, Yao, and Shun arose. They comprehended change and caused the people to be unwearied, transforming them with spirit so that they were rightly ordered. When the Changes has run one course to its extreme, then it changes, and by changing it is able to continue, and by continuing it achieves longevity. Thus the Changes receives help from Heaven: good fortune and nothing that is not beneficial.

The Yellow Emperor, Yao, and Shun allowed their upper and lower garments to hang down and the world was ordered.[3] This they probably took from the hexagrams *ch'ien* and *k'un*.

They hollowed out logs to make boats and shaved pieces of wood for

---

[3] This would seem to be a description of the invention of traditional Chinese dress. But by advocates of the ideal of "nonaction" it has been used to mean that the sage emperors sat passively upon their thrones without stirring and thereby governed their people.

rudders, and by the advantages of boats and rudders opened up new roads of communication to distant places for the profit of the world. This they probably took from the hexagram *huan*. They yoked oxen to pull heavy loads and mounted horses to go long distances, thus benefiting the world. This they probably took from the hexagram *sui*. They provided double gates and watchmen with wooden clappers to guard against robbers, and this they took from the hexagram *yü*. They split wood to make pestles and scooped hollows in the ground for mortars and thus benefited all mankind by the advantages of mortar and pestle. This they probably took from the hexagram *hsiao-kuo*. They strung a piece of wood for a bow and whittled arrows of wood and introduced the benefits of bow and arrow to awe the world. This they took from the hexagram *k'uei*.

In the earliest times men dwelt in caves and lived out in the open. But the sages of later times substituted houses with ridgepoles and roofs to protect them from wind and rain. This they probably took from the hexagram *ta-chuang*. In the earliest burials the dead were covered thickly with brushwood and buried in the fields with neither mound nor trees to mark the grave, and there was no set period of mourning. But the sages of later times substituted inner and outer coffins. This they probably took from the hexagram *ta-kuo*. In the earliest times knotted cords were used in government but the later sages substituted written documents and tallies so that the officials were kept in order and the people had a clear idea of their duties. This they probably took from the hexagram *kuai*.

THE FIVE AGENTS

Similar in concept to the yin-yang theory is that of the five agents (*wu-hsing*). Like the yin and yang, the agents are not physical substances but metaphysical forces or modes which dominate or control certain periods of time, commonly the seasons, in a fixed succession. It is fairly obvious how the mode or element of wood should be assigned to the season of spring, associated with the color green and the direction east. In like manner fire is assigned to summer, its color red and direction south; metal to autumn, its color white and direction west; and water to winter, its color black and direction north. However, there are five agents and it is accepted that they proceed in the order in which they produce or "beget" each other, i.e., wood produces fire, fire produces earth, earth produces metal, metal produces water, etc. Since there are only four seasons, earth, with the color yellow, is commonly assigned a position in the center, aiding the other elements in their governing of the four seasons.

The correspondences derived by analogy according to this system are too numerous to be explained in detail. The principal ones, illustrating how all facets of the divine and natural worlds were classified by these five agents, are listed in diagram form.

A TABLE OF CORRESPONDENCES FOR THE FIVE-AGENTS SYSTEM

THE FIVE AGENTS

Correspondence	Wood	Fire	Earth	Metal	Water
Seasons	Spring	Summer		Autumn	Winter
Divine Rulers	T'ai Hao	Yen Ti	Yellow Emperor	Shao Hao	Chuan Hsu
Attendant spirits	Kou Mang	Chu Yung	Hou T'u	Ju Shou	Hsuan Ming
Sacrifices	inner door	hearth	inner court	outer court	well
Animals	sheep	fowl	ox	dog	pig
Grains	wheat	beans	panicled millet	hemp	millet
Organs	spleen	lungs	heart	liver	kidneys
Numbers	eight	seven	five	nine	six
Stems	chia / i	ping / ting	mou / chi	keng / hsin	jen / kuei
Colors	green	red	yellow	white	black
Notes	chueh	chih	kung	shang	yu
Tastes	sour	bitter	sweet	acrid	salty
Smells	goatish	burning	fragrant	rank	rotten
Directions	East	South	center	West	North
Creatures	scaly	feathered	naked	hairy	shell-covered
Beasts of the directions	Green Dragon	Scarlet Bird	Yellow Dragon	White Tiger	Black Tortoise
Virtues	benevolence	wisdom	faith	righteousness	decorum
Planets	Jupiter	Mars	Saturn	Venus	Mercury
Officers	Minister of Agriculture	Minister of War	Minister of Works	Minister of Interior	Minister of Justice

THE RECONSTRUCTION OF CHINESE HISTORY

Important also is the application of this theory to history and the succession of dynasties. As each season is ruled by an agent, so, it was believed, each dynasty rules by virtue of an agent which it honors by adopting the color of the agent in its vestments and flags, and by similar ritual observances. The First Emperor of the Ch'in, for instance, believing that his dynasty ruled by the virtue or power of water, adopted black as his official color and even changed the name of the Yellow River to "Powerful Water" (*te shui*).

We have noticed above the order in which the agents produce each other during the year, giving the series: wood—fire—earth—metal—water. There was current, however, another series, with the elements arranged in the order in which they overcome or conquer each other. According to this series, fire is overcome by water, water by earth, earth by wood, and wood by metal, producing the series: fire—water—earth—wood—metal. Because the Ch'in had claimed to rule by the power of water, it was urged by some scholars early in the Han that the Han dynasty should adopt earth, with the color yellow, as its agent, to signify that the Han had conquered the Ch'in. Since, according to tradition, heaven had sent appropriate signs and omens to past dynasties, such as earthworms (earth), knife blades (metal), red birds (fire), etc. to indicate which agent the dynasty should adopt, the reported appearance during the time of Emperor Wen of a yellow dragon was cited by supporters of this theory as additional evidence. Though there were other interpretations offered, the Former Han adopted this idea and honored earth as its patron element.

Toward the end of the Former Han, however, there arose another theory that was eventually used to great political advantage by Wang Mang. According to Liu Hsiang, who wrote a treatise on the five agents, and his son, Liu Hsin, the dynasties succeed each other according to the order in which the agents produce each other. Using this idea newly applied to the interpretation of history, Liu Hsin and his school proceeded to reconstruct a history of past ages that would conform to the theory, assigning a ruling element to each ancient dynasty and inserting "intercalary reigns" of the agent water where necessary to make it consistent. One of the innovations of this system was the assertion that the Han dynasty ruled not by virtue of the agent earth but by that of fire. A second innovation was the extension of history back beyond the legendary Yellow Emperor, who had been the starting point of Chinese history for earlier writers like Tsou Yen and Ssu-ma Ch'ien. It is difficult to say exactly when each step of this new theory was set forth or accepted, but it was substantially completed by the time of Wang Mang, who made use of it in his usurpation of the throne. The final system thus worked out as follows:

Agent	Ruler or Dynasty	Agent	Ruler or Dynasty
Wood	Fu Hsi, T'ai Hao	(Water)	Ti Chih
(Water)	Kung Kung [Intercalary or illegitimate reigns]	Fire	Emperor Yao
		Earth	Emperor Shun
Fire	The Fire Emperor, Shen Nung	Metal	Emperor Yü, Hsia dynasty
Earth	The Yellow Emperor	Water	Shang dynasty
Metal	Shao Hao, Metallic Heaven	Wood	Chou dynasty
Water	Chuan Hsü	(Water)	Ch'in dynasty
Wood	Ti K'u	Fire	Han dynasty

Obviously the next dynasty to follow the Han should rule by the element earth. It is not surprising, therefore, that, as Wang Mang rose to power, it was discovered that, according to certain ancient texts, he was a descendant of the Yellow Emperor and thus fitted to found a new dynasty under the agent of earth.

Though with the downfall of Wang Mang many of his innovations and the doubtful texts used to support them were swept away, this account of the ancient past of China continued to be accepted. It is recorded in the *History of the Former Han Dynasty* by Pan Ku (*Han shu* 21B), who says he is following Liu Hsin, and was generally accepted in China as historical fact until recent times. Thus, using a preconceived philosophical doctrine of historical evolution, the Chinese, with the best intentions and their customary love of order and system in all things, proceeded to rearrange and tailor their ancient legends and records to fit into a neat pattern that should be both immediately comprehensible in its past, and infallibly predictable in its future development.

TUNG CHUNG-SHU

Production and Succession of the Five Agents

Tung Chung-shu made great use of the cosmological theories of the yin-yang and five agents schools in formulating his system of Confucian philosophy. So closely are these concepts woven into all his other ideas that it is impossible to separate his cosmological from his political or ethical theories. In the following selections from the *Ch'un-ch'iu fan-lu* he links the five agents with the five traditional departments of the Chou government. In the original each of the five sections includes an historical example from the Spring and Autumn period, only two of which have been retained in the translation. The excerpt illustrates how Tung combined cosmology, political theory, Confucian ethics and historical examples in setting forth his ideas.

[From *Ch'un-ch'iu fan-lu,* 58, 59]

HOW THE FIVE AGENTS PRODUCE EACH OTHER

The vital forces of Heaven and earth join to form a unity, divide to become the yin and yang, separate into the four seasons, and range themselves into the five agents. "Agent" in this case means activity. Each of the activities is different, therefore we speak of them as the five activities. The five activities are the five agents. In the order of their succession they give birth to one another, while in a different order they overcome each other. Therefore in ruling, if one violates this order, there will be chaos, but if one follows it, all will be well governed. [59]

HOW THE FIVE AGENTS OVERCOME EACH OTHER [4]

Wood is the agent of the Minister of Agriculture. If the Minister of Agriculture becomes corrupt, playing partisan politics and forming cliques, obscuring the wisdom of the ruler, forcing worthy men into retirement, exterminating the high officials, and teaching the people wild and prodigal ways, then the retainers of the lords will wander about and neglect the work of the fields, amusing themselves with gambling, cockfighting, dog racing, and horsemanship; old and young will be without respect, great and small will trespass upon each other; thieves and brigands will arise, perverse and evil men who destroy reason. It is then the duty of the Minister of the Interior to punish him. . . . Now wood is the agent of agriculture, and agriculture is the occupation of the people. If the people are not compliant but revolt, then the Minister of the Interior is ordered to punish the leaders of the rebellion and set things right. Therefore we say metal overcomes wood.

Metal is the agent of the Minister of the Interior. If the Minister of the Interior acts rebelliously, encroaching upon the ruler, taking a high hand with the military forces, seizing authority and usurping power, punishing and slaughtering the guiltless, invading and attacking with

[4] The order of the sections has been rearranged in translation.

ruthlessness and violence, making war and snatching gain, disobeying orders, ignoring prohibitions, disrespecting the generals and leaders, and misusing the officers and troops, then the armies will be exhausted, the land lost, and the ruler will suffer disgrace. . . . Metal is the agent of the Minister of the Interior. If he is weak and does not know how to use the officers and men properly, then the Minister of War must punish him. Therefore we say fire overcomes metal.

Fire is the agent of the Minister of War. If the Minister of War gives himself up to rebellion and scornful talk, libeling and defaming people, then within the palace flesh and blood relatives will be set against each other, faithful ministers driven away, wise and sage men ruined, and the slander and evil will grow day by day. . . . Now fire is the agent of the courtier [i.e., Minister of War]. When he turns to evil and slander, deceiving the ruler, then he who administers the law shall carry out punishment. It is water that administers the law, therefore we say that water overcomes fire.

Water is the agent of the Minister of Justice. If the Minister of Justice turns to false ways, using extravagant respect and petty caution, crafty words and insinuating looks, taking bribes when he hears law suits, prejudiced and unfair, slow to issue orders but quick to punish, punishing and executing the guiltless, then the Minister of Works must correct him. Ying T'ang, Minister of Justice of Ch'i, is an example of this. T'ai Kung, who held a fief in Ch'i, once asked him what were the essentials of ruling a state. Ying T'ang replied: "Simply practice humanity and righteousness, that is all."

"What do you mean by humanity and righteousness?" T'ai Kung asked. Ying T'ang replied: "Humanity means loving men. Righteousness means respecting the aged."

"Loving men and respecting the aged," said T'ai Kung, "just what does that mean?"

"Loving men," said Ying T'ang, "means that, though you have sons, you do not accept any support from them. Respecting the aged means that if a man's wife is older than he, the husband submits to her."

T'ai Kung replied: "I wish to use humanity and righteousness to govern the state of Ch'i, and now you take this so-called humanity and righteousness of yours and throw the country into confusion. I must punish you and bring order to Ch'i again."

Ying T'ang's assertion violates the traditional ethic that a son always serves and supports his father, a wife her husband. The reason T'ai Kung is so outraged at Ying T'ang's statement is that, according to Confucian belief, the slightest violation of the proper order in the ethical, political, or natural worlds will inevitably throw all the others into disorder. This is why Confucianism insists so upon the minutest observance of order and propriety in all things and why it has been led at times into extreme conservatism.

Now it is water that administers the law. If the administrator is prejudiced and unfair, using the law only to punish people, then the Minister of Works must execute him. Therefore we say that earth overcomes water.

Earth is the agent of the servants of the ruler and their head is the Minister of Works. If he is very subtle, then whatever the prince does he will approve; whatever the prince says, he will reply, "Excellent!" Fawning upon the prince and complying with his desires, aiding and carrying out his private whims, he will busy himself with whatever pleases the prince in order to gladden his will, complying with the prince's faults and misdeeds and betraying him into unrighteousness. Great will be such a ruler's palaces and halls, many his terraces and pavilions, with carved ornaments, sculpted and inlaid and resplendent with five hues; but his taxes and levies will be without measure, plundering the people of their means, his expeditions and corvees many and burdensome, robbing the people of their time. He will think up endless projects to wear out the people's strength, and they will groan in oppression and revolt and abandon his land. King Ling of Ch'u was like this, raising the Terrace of the Heavenly Valley, and when after three years it was still not completed, the people were exhausted and spent and they rose up in revolt and killed him. Now earth is the agent of the king's servants. If the king is extravagant and wasteful, exceeding all bounds and forgetting propriety, then the people will rebel and when the people rebel, the ruler is lost. Therefore we say wood overcomes earth. [58]

THE CONCEPT AND MARKING OF TIME

The Chinese conception of history, as we have seen above, was cyclical. This is only natural, since history is no more than a counterpart in the human sphere of the similar cycles of Heaven and earth, those of the planets and the seasons. For this reason Chinese historians, unlike their Japanese, Jewish, or Christian counterparts, have never attempted to assign a temporal beginning or end to the history of the world or the nation. Since time is itself a series of cycles based upon the motions of the planets, it may be conceived as extending indefinitely into the past and future for as long as the planets themselves exist.

Dates in Chinese history are customarily recorded in terms of the years of the reigning monarch. But by Han times there was already in use an additional system of cyclical signs for designating years, days, and hours. The origin of these signs, one a set of ten known as the "ten heavenly stems," another of twelve called the "twelve earthly branches," remains today a mystery, though it is apparent that they are very ancient. It is probable that the ten stems were originally designations for the ten days of the ancient ten-day week, the twelve branches designations for the months. These signs and their associations are listed below:

Five Agents	Ten Stems	Twelve Branches	Beasts	Directions	Hours
wood	chia	tzu	rat	N	11 P.M.–1 A.M.
	i	ch'ou	ox	NNE	1–3
fire	ping	yin	tiger	ENE	3–5
	ting	mao	hare	E	5–7
earth	mou	ch'en	dragon	ESE	7–9
	chi	ssu	snake	SSE	9–11
metal	keng	wu	horse	S	11 A.M.–1 P.M.
	hsin	wei	sheep	SSW	1–3
water	jen	shen	monkey	WSW	3–5
	kuei	yu	cock	W	5–7
		hsü	dog	WNW	7–9
		hai	boar	NNW	9–11

Sometime before the Chou dynasty these two sets of signs were combined to form a cycle of sixty bi-nomial terms used to designate a cycle
of sixty days. Thus in the selection from the *Lü-shih ch'un-ch'iu* which
follows we read that the first two days of spring are *chia* and *i,* which
means that the first term in the bi-nomial designations of the first two
days of the sixty-day cycle beginning in spring will be these two signs
chia and *i.* The season of spring being seventy-two days long, the designations for the first two days of summer will be *ping* and *ting,* the cycle of
ten stems having revolved seven times plus two. In this way the ten
stems which designate the first and second days of each season came to be
associated with the five agents which, as we have seen, correspond to
the seasons.

Again this cycle of sixty bi-nomial terms was used to designate cycles of
sixty years. The twelve branches, as indicated above, were used to designate thirty degree divisions of the circle of the horizon. Observing the
position of Jupiter in the sky for each year of its twelve-year cycle, the
Chinese then employed the sign designating that portion of the sky for
the year, and combined these with the ten stems to form designations for
a sexagenary cycle. This they used to reckon dates independent of the
reigns of emperors, the more common method for indicating dates in
Chinese history. Finally the twelve branches were used to designate
twelve two-hour periods making up the day.

At least by Han times these twelve branches had become associated
with twelve beasts, as indicated above. Because of this, the twelve hours
of the day and the years of the sexagenary cycle were each associated
with one of these beasts. This system of marking time was adopted by
other eastern countries in contact with China. Because of these various
associations with the five agents and twelve beasts, a great deal of
superstitious lore of lucky and unlucky times grew up about the various
cycles. Yet, as we have seen, their basis is essentially rationalistic and
they provided the Chinese with a convenient method of reckoning time
until the adoption of Western time divisions.

HEAVEN, EARTH, AND MAN

The idea that Heaven, earth, and man, in their nature and in all their
workings, form an inseparable trinity is fundamental in Han thought. In

the present chapter and the one preceding, we have attempted to describe separately first the political philosophy and then the cosmological theories of this period. But though this division may be of some convenience in discussion, it is wholly arbitrary and foreign to the Chinese way of thinking. It was the aim of Ch'in and Han philosophers to create a comprehensive, unified system of thought that would at one time explain all questions of the divine, natural, and human worlds. This catholicity of interests is reflected by the treatises of the official history of the period, the *Han shu* or *History of the Former Han Dynasty,* which cover religious affairs, astronomy, the calendar, portents, rites and music, literature, the penal code, economics, geography, and water works. All of these subjects were the direct concern not only of private individuals but of the government, and ultimately of the emperor who was the spiritual and temporal leader of all mankind. It was his responsibility to see that every phase of human activity proceeded properly and remained in harmony with the workings of the other two orders, the divine and the natural.

Lü-shih ch'un-ch'iu: The First Month of Spring

The desire to compile in systematic form all the knowledge of cosmological, ritual, political, and moral questions necessary to the proper conduct of government was a characteristic of this period and is already evident in a work of the Ch'in, the *Lü-shih ch'un-ch'iu* or *Spring and Autumn of Mr. Lü.* This work was written by itinerant scholars and philosophers working under the patronage of Lü Pu-wei, the powerful prime minister of the First Emperor of the Ch'in, and bears, in recognition of its official importance, the name of the prime minister himself. The use of the term "Spring and Autumn" in the title is significant for, though it originally designated merely a court chronicle of the feudal age, from the time when tradition assigned to Confucius the editing of the Lu court chronicle of this name and began to interpret it as a book revealing Confucius' moral and political principles, it took on a new and exalted significance.

The book consists of three large sections representing the trinity of Heaven, earth, and man. The first, that of Heaven, is in twelve chapters. Each chapter, representing one month, begins with a description of the functions of government appropriate to that month. Whether this almanac was original with the work or is of older origin is not clear, but so great was its significance that it was later incorporated into the *Book of Rites* and became a part of the Confucian canon. Each of the twelve chapters is again divided into five subsections, suggesting the influence of the five-agents theory. The second large section is divided into eight chapters of eight subsections each, eight being associated in Chinese numerology with the earth, while the third section is in six chapters of six subsections each, six being the number of man.

The translation of the first section of the almanac of the twelve months which follows will show how closely associated were religion, astronomy, politics, and ethics in Chinese thought. Here we see the characteristic Chinese love of order dividing all things into numerical categories that may be assigned to various times and influences. It should also be noted how misrule or failure to perform the acts proper to the season on the part of the government will cause disturbances in the natural order and bring calamity from Heaven.

[From *Lü-shih ch'un-ch'iu*, 1:1a-4a]

In the first month of spring, the sun is in the constellation Ying-shih. The constellation Shen [Orion] reaches the zenith at dusk, the constellation Wei [Scorpio], at dawn. The first two days of the month are *chia* and *i,* its divine ruler is T'ai Hao, its attendant spirit, Kou Mang. Its creatures are scaly, its musical note *chüeh,* its pitch-pipe *t'ai-ts'ou,* its number 8. Its taste is sour, its smell goatish; its sacrifice is at the inner door for which the spleen of the victim is essential.

The east wind dispels the cold, the hibernating insects and reptiles begin to stir, the fish rise up under the ice where the otter catches them to eat, and the wild geese fly north in season.

The Son of Heaven shall live in the apartment on the left side of the Green Bright Hall. He shall ride in a great belled chariot drawn by dark green dragon horses and bearing green flags. He shall wear green robes with pendants of green jade. His food shall be wheat and mutton, his vessels coarse and open to represent a coming forth. In this month, spring begins. Three days before spring begins, the Grand Astrologer shall report to the Son of Heaven, saying: "On such and such a day spring will begin. The agent of wood is in ascendance." The Son of Heaven shall then fast and purify himself and on the first day in person lead the chief ministers and feudal princes and officials to the eastern suburbs to greet the spring. On his return he shall hold court and bestow rewards upon them. He shall order the three chief ministers to publish abroad his good teachings and to relax the prohibitions of winter, to present awards and bestow alms to all down to the common people so that everyone who is deserving shall receive awards and gifts.

He shall order the Grand Astrologer to cherish the laws and publish the ordinances, to observe the sun and moon, the stars and zodiacal signs so that there will be no error in the calculations of their movements and no mistake in their courses, taking as a model the astronomical laws of ancient times.

In this month, on a favorable day, the Son of Heaven shall pray to the Lord-on-High for abundant harvests. Then, selecting a lucky day, he shall himself bear a plowshare and handle in his carriage, attended by the charioteer and the man-at-arms and, leading the chief ministers, feudal princes, and officials, shall personally plow the Field of God. The Son of Heaven shall plow three furrows, the three chief ministers five, the feudal princes and officials nine. On their return, they shall assemble in the Great Hall where the emperor shall take a chalice and offer it to each of them, saying: "This is wine in recompense for your labors."

In this month the vital force of Heaven descends, the vital force of earth arises; Heaven and earth are in harmony and the grass and trees begin to burgeon.

The ruler shall order the work of the fields to begin. He shall order the inspectors of the fields to reside in the lands having an eastern exposure, to repair the borders and boundaries of the fields, to inspect the paths and irrigation ditches, to examine closely the mounts and hills, the slopes and heights and the plains and valleys to determine what lands are good and where the five grains should be sown, and they shall instruct and direct the people. This they must do in person. When the work of the fields has been well begun, with the irrigation ditches traced out correctly beforehand, there will be no confusion later.

In this month, the Chief Director of Music shall be ordered to open school and train the students in dancing.

The rules for sacrifices shall be reviewed and orders given for offerings to the spirits of the mountains, forests, rivers, and lakes, but for these sacrifices no female creature may be used.

It shall be forbidden to cut down trees, to destroy nests, to kill young insects, the young yet in the womb or new born, or fledgling birds. All young of animals and eggs shall be spared.

Multitudes of people shall not be summoned for any service, nor shall any construction be done on walls or fortifications.

All bones and corpses of those who have died by the wayside shall be buried.

In this month it is forbidden to take up arms. He who takes up arms will surely call down Heaven's wrath. Taking up arms means that one may not initiate hostilities, though if attacked he may defend himself.

In all things one must not violate the way of Heaven, nor destroy the principles of earth, nor bring confusion to the laws of man.

If in the first month of spring the ruler carries out proceedings proper to summer, then the wind and rain will not come in season, the grass and trees will soon wither and dry up, and the nations will be in great fear.

If he carries out the proceedings proper to autumn, then a great pestilence will strike the people, violent winds and torrential rains will come in abundance, and the weeds of orach and fescue, darnel and southernwood will spring up together.

If he carries out the proceedings of winter, the rains and floods will cause great damage, frost and snow will wreak havoc, and the first seeds sown will not sprout.

CHAPTER X

THE ECONOMIC ORDER

Han moralists and philosophers, far from ignoring the mundane problems of man's struggle for livelihood, placed great stress on the material needs of the people. The importance of economic thought in the Han derives both from this basic recognition of the "facts of life" and from the appearance in Han times of acute agrarian crises such as have plagued China down through the centuries. The solutions proposed to these crises, as well as the actual measures taken by the government in the Han, tended to set a pattern for later times.

The wars and uprisings which marked the fall of the Ch'in led to extreme suffering and poverty among the people. What was needed to effect a recovery, the Han was quick to realize, was a period of peace and security with a minimum of government expenditure and interference to allow the people to regain their means of livelihood. The founder of the Han therefore relaxed the harsh laws of Ch'in, reduced the land tax, which under the Ch'in had been as high as two-thirds of the total produce, and kept court expenditures at a minimum. This policy of frugality and laissez-faire was continued more or less consistently by his successors during the early Han with the result that the population increased and the nation recovered with remarkable success.

The government did, however, attempt to take steps to control the amassing of large fortunes by industrialists and traders. Kao-tsu passed sumptuary laws against merchants who had grown rich during the troubled times accompanying the founding of the dynasty, laws designed to turn people from trade, a subsidiary or "branch" activity, back to the fundamental occupation of farming. Though these laws were later relaxed, it was still forbidden for traders or their descendants to hold public office, thus preventing their rise in the social scale. This struggle to keep people in the more productive but less remunerative farming activities from seeking their fortunes in trade and manufacturing continued throughout the Han. A rite was instituted (or, according to some scholars, revived from ancient times) in which the emperor personally performed a ceremonial act of plowing to encourage his people and emphasize the importance of agriculture. During the time of Emperor Wen, the government granted commutation of penalties or honorary court ranks in exchange for gifts of grain, thus making grain a commodity of enhanced value. This policy met with considerable success and, by the time of Emperor Wu, we are told, the government granaries were filled, the government had sufficient funds, and the people lived in ease and plenty.

Economic Distress at the End of the Ch'in Dynasty

The following excerpt from the "Treatise on Food and Money" in the *History of the Former Han Dynasty* describes the plight of the people under Ch'in rule. Though the authors are inclined to be highly critical of the Ch'in, out of partiality to their own dynasty and antagonism to the Legalist policies associated with Ch'in rule, there is no reason to doubt that the conditions described here contributed to the Ch'in collapse.

[From *Han shu*, 7A:7b–8a]

When the world was at last united by Ch'in, the First Emperor set about constructing great public works within the country and driving the barbarians from its borders. He collected in taxes more than half of the people's produce and dispatched half of the men of each village to guard the frontiers. Though the farmers labored in their fields they could not produce enough grain to eat; though the women spun and wove they could not provide enough clothing. The Emperor exhausted the resources of the empire to supply his government, and yet they were still insufficient to meet his desires. All people within the seas grieved and were angry so that at last they fled or revolted.

When the Han arose it inherited the evils of the Ch'in. The nobles rose in revolt, the people were driven from their occupations, and a great famine ensued. . . . People ate each other and more than half of the population perished. . . . The emperor of the Han thereupon relaxed and simplified the laws and lightened the grain taxes to one-fifteenth of the yield.

Edict of Emperor Wen on the Primacy of Agriculture
(163 B.C.)
[From *Han shu,* 4:15a–b]

For the past several years there have been no good harvests, and our people have suffered the calamities of flood, drought, and pestilence. We are deeply grieved by this, but being ignorant and unenlightened, we have been unable to discover where the blame lies. We have considered whether our administration has been guilty of some error or our actions of some fault. Have we failed to follow the way of Heaven or to obtain the benefits of earth? Have we caused disharmony in human affairs or neglected the gods that they do not accept our offerings? What has brought on these things? Have the provisions for our officials been too lavish or have we indulged in too many unprofitable affairs? Why is the food of the people so scarce? When the fields are surveyed, they have not decreased, and when the people are counted they have not grown in number, so that the amount of land for each person is the same as before or even greater. And yet there is a drastic shortage of food. Where does the blame lie? Is it that too many people pursue secondary activities to the detriment of agriculture? Is it that too much grain is used to make wine or too many domestic animals are being raised? I have been unable to attain a proper balance between important and unimportant affairs. Let this matter be debated by the chancellor, the nobles, the high officials, and learned doctors. Let all exhaust their efforts and ponder deeply whether there is some way to aid the people. Let nothing be concealed from us!

CH'AO TS'O

Memorial on the Encouragement of Agriculture

The following memorial, by the eminent Han statesman Ch'ao Ts'o, being dated 178 B.C., cannot be a reply to the emperor's plea above, but was one of a number of suggestions designed to alleviate the conditions of which he complains. The emperor approved Ch'ao's suggestion, with the result that grain became plentiful and the government granaries were filled.
        [From *Han shu,* 24A:9b–13a]

The reason the people never suffered from cold or famine under the rule of the sage-kings was not that these kings were capable of plowing to provide food or spinning to make clothes for them. It was that they opened up for the people the way to wealth. Therefore although emperors Yao and Yü encountered nine years of flood and King T'ang seven years of drought, there were no derelicts or starving within the kingdom, because provisions had been stored up in plenty and all precautions taken beforehand.

Now all within the seas are united. The plenitude of land and people is not inferior to that of T'ang and Yü, and in addition we have not suffered from natural calamities of flood or drought for several years. Why then are the stores of supplies so inferior? Because the land has benefits that have been overlooked and the people have untapped energies. There is still land suitable for growing grain that has not been brought under cultivation, resources of hills and lakes that have not been exploited, and vagrants who have not yet returned to agricultural pursuits. When the people are in poverty, then crime and evil-doing are born. Poverty is bred of insufficiency which is caused by lack of agriculture. If men do not farm, they will not be tied to the land; and if they are not tied to the land, they will desert their villages, neglect their families, and become like birds and beasts. Then although there be high walls and deep moats, strict laws and severe punishments, they still cannot be held in check.

When one is cold he does not demand the most comfortable and warmest garments; when one is starving he does not wait for the tastiest morsels. When a man is plagued by hunger and cold he has no regard for modesty or shame. It is the nature of man that if he does not eat twice a day he will starve, and if in the course of a year he cuts himself no new clothes he will freeze. When the belly is famished and gets no food, when the skin is chilled and has no clothing to cover it, then the most compassionate father cannot provide even for his own child. How then can the ruler keep the allegiance of his people? An enlightened ruler, realizing this, will encourage his people in agriculture and sericulture, lighten the poll tax and other levies, increase his store of supplies and fill his granaries in preparation for flood and drought. Therefore he can keep and care for his people. The people may then be led by the ruler, for they will follow after profit in any direction like water flowing downward.

Now pearls, jewels, gold, and silver can neither allay hunger nor keep out the cold, and yet the people all hold them dear, because they are things used by the ruler. They are light and easy to store, and one who holds them in his grasp may roam the world and never fear hunger or cold. They cause ministers lightly to turn their backs upon their lords and the people easily to leave their villages; they provide an incentive for thieves and a light form of wealth for fugitives.

Grains and fibers, on the other hand, are produced from the land, nurtured through the seasons, and harvested with labor; they cannot be gotten in a day. Several measures of grain or cloth are too heavy for an average man to carry and so provide no reward for crime or evil. Yet if people go without them for one day they will face hunger and cold. Therefore an enlightened ruler esteems the five grains and despises gold and jewels.

At present in a farming family of five not less than two are required to perform labor service [for the state], while those who are left to work the farm are given no more than one hundred *mu* of land, the yield of which is not over one hundred piculs. . . . No matter how diligently they work nor what hardships they suffer, they still must face the calamities of flood and drought, emergency government measures, inordinate tax levies, and taxes collected out of season. Orders issued in the morning are changed before nightfall. Faced with such levies, the people must sell what they have at half price in order to pay, and those who have nothing must take money offered at one hundred percent interest. Thus they are forced to sell their fields and houses, vend their children and grandchildren to pay their debts.

Among the traders and merchants, on the other hand, the larger ones hoard goods and exact a hundred percent profit, while the smaller ones sit lined up in the markets selling their wares. Those who deal in luxury goods daily disport themselves in the cities and market towns; taking advantage of the ruler's wants, they are able to sell at double price. Thus though their men neither plow nor weed, though their women neither tend silkworms nor spin, yet their clothes are brightly patterned and colored, and they eat only choice grain and meat. They have none of the hardships of the farmer, yet their gain is ten to one hundredfold. With their wealth they may consort with nobles, and their power exceeds the authority of government officials. They use their profits to overthrow others. Over a thousand miles they wander at ease, their caps and cart covers filling the roads. They ride in fine carriages and drive fat horses, tread in silken shoes and trail white silk behind them. Thus it is that merchants encroach upon the farmers, and the farmers are driven from their homes and become vagrants.

At present, although the laws degrade the merchants, the merchants have become wealthy and honored, and although they honor the farmers, the farmers have grown poor and lowly. Thus what common practice honors the ruler degrades, and what the officials scorn the law exalts. With ruler and ruled thus at variance and their desires in conflict, it is impossible to hope that the nation will become rich and the law be upheld.

Under the present circumstances there is nothing more urgently needed than to make the people devote themselves to agriculture. To accomplish this one must enhance the value of grain. This may be done by making it possible for the people to use grain to obtain rewards and avoid punishments. If an order is sent out that all who send grain to the government shall obtain honorary rank or pardon from crimes, then wealthy men will acquire rank, the farmers will have money, and grain will circulate freely. If men can afford to present grain in exchange for ranks, they must have a surplus. If this surplus is acquired for the use of the ruler, then the poll tax on the poor can be reduced. This is what is known as reducing the surplus to supply the deficiency. . . . Ranks are something that the ruler may dispense at will; he has only to speak and there is no end to them. Grain is something grown on the land by the people and its supply is continuous. All men greatly desire to obtain high ranks and avoid penalties. If all are allowed to present grain for supplying the frontiers and thereby obtain rank or commutation of penalties, then in no more than three years there will be plenty of grain for the border areas.

TUNG CHUNG-SHU

Memorial on Land Reform

Around 100 B.C. the famous Confucianist Tung Chung-shu submitted a memorial to Emperor Wu advising the limitation of land and slave ownership and other measures to relieve the rapidly developing agrarian crisis. Because of opposition from wealthy families and powerful officials, his suggestions and similar ones made later were never put into effect. It is noteworthy that Tung, while proclaiming the ancient "well-field" system of equal land ownership as the ideal, did not go so far as to advocate its restoration. Not until Wang Mang came to power was the drastic step taken to effect a return to the ideal society enshrined in Confucian tradition.

[From *Han shu*, 24A:14b–15b]

In ancient times the people were not taxed over one-tenth of their produce, a demand which they could easily meet. They were required to give no more than three days of labor a year, which they could easily spare. The people had wealth enough to take care of the aged and look after their parents, serve their superiors and pay their taxes, and support their wives and loved ones. Therefore they took delight in obeying their rulers.

But the Ch'in changed all this. It used the methods of Shang Yang [Legalism], altered the imperial institutions, did away with the well-field system, and allowed the people to buy and sell land. The rich bought up great connecting tracts of ground, and the poor were left without enough land to stick the point of an awl into. In addition the rich had sole control of the resources of rivers and lakes and the riches of hills and forests. Their profligacy overstepped all restrictions and they outdid each other in extravagance. In the cities they commanded as much respect as the rulers, and in the villages their wealth equalled that of the nobles. How could the common people escape oppression? . . . In addition labor services were increased until they were thirty times those of ancient days, while taxes on fields and population and profits from salt and iron increased to twenty times those of old. Those who worked the land of the rich had to give half their crops in rent. Therefore the poor were forced to wear clothing fit only for cattle and horses and eat the food of dogs and swine. On top of this harsh and greedy officials punished and executed them indiscriminately until the people, grieved and deprived of their livelihood, fled to the hills or turned to a life of banditry. Condemned men half filled the roads and tens of thousands were imprisoned each year.

Since the Han began it has followed the ways of the Ch'in without change. Although it would be difficult to restore at once the ancient well-field system, it is proper that present usage be brought somewhat closer to the old ways. Ownership of land should be limited so that those who do not have enough may be relieved and the road to unlimited encroachment blocked. The rights to salt and iron should revert to the people. Slavery and the right to execute servants on one's own authority should be abolished. Poll taxes and other levies should be reduced and labor services lightened so that the people will be less pressed. Only then can they be well-governed.

STATE CONTROL OF COMMERCE AND INDUSTRY

Pan Ku, principal author of the *History of the Former Han Dynasty,* sees the reign of Emperor Wu as the turning point from prosperity to eventual ruin of the dynasty. Though economic life recovered considerably after his reign, the historian is certainly correct in designating this period as the beginning at least of policies and trends which led to the downfall of the Han.

The barbarian tribes bordering China on the north and west had constituted a constant menace to the empire, frequently invading and pillaging as far as the capital itself. Emperor Wu set out upon a series of military conquests that extended Chinese hegemony far out to the northwest, placing the empire for the first time in close contact with the states of Central and Western Asia and eventually Rome. Following these conquests, he undertook vast programs of colonization of the newly acquired areas, as well as extensive canal and road building, repairing of dikes, and other government projects. Famous and glorious as were these military conquests and other undertakings, however, they were bought at the price of the economic health of the nation. Because of the frugality of his predecessors and the prosperity of the empire, he was able to embark upon his grandiose plans. But he soon found it necessary to secure new revenues to sustain them.

The means that he took to secure them were not really in the nature of a state-planned economy to benefit the nation as a whole, though this was claimed for them, but were merely attempts to fill the imperial coffers at any cost. He continued the campaign begun by his predecessors to deprive the remaining feudal lords of their power and wealth, penalizing them for all manner of offenses and confiscating their land and wealth. He sold honorary titles, military ranks, and government offices in such profusion that the official hierarchy was reduced to chaos. He set about to crush individual traders and industrialists and transfer their lucrative enterprises to government control. High taxes were levied upon the rich and a system of spies set up so that, at any suspicion of attempted evasion, their entire estates were confiscated.

Perhaps most famous and widely discussed of his fiscal measures was the setting up of government monopolies in the vital industries of iron, salt, liquor, and coinage of money, and the establishing of government trading. The iron and salt industries had formerly been the source of great wealth to private individuals or feudal lords who controlled them. It was natural therefore that the emperor should see an excellent opportunity to divert these profits to the imperial treasury by making them government monopolies. Moreover he set up, under a bureau of "Equalization and Standardization," a system of government marketing offices which bought up goods at low prices or collected taxes in produce and, transporting them at government expense, sold them in other areas or at other times at an advantageous price. Though it was claimed that this measure, like the salt and iron monopolies, was designed to protect the people from exploitation by unscrupulous private traders, its real purpose was to secure government revenues. These measures were successful in keeping the government treasuries supplied with funds and allowing the emperor to live in splendor and carry out his plans. But they, along with the forced conscription and heavy labor services imposed upon the people, reduced the nation to poverty and brought extreme popular resentment.

Emperor Wu, though professing firm support of Confucian ideals, was in fact pursuing, in the establishing of such government monopolies and speculation, traditional Legalist theories such as the Ch'in had followed. Moreover, to insure the success of his business ventures, he appointed experienced industrialists and financial experts to administer the government monopolies. These men were staunch supporters of the Legalist philosophy.

In 81 B.C., shortly after the death of Emperor Wu, a debate was called at court between these Legalist officials, headed by the Lord Grand Secretary, and a group of Confucian literati representing opinions of the opposition. A record of this famous debate, the *Yen-t'ieh lun* or *Debate on Salt and Iron,* has been preserved and shows clearly the struggle of the Confucian scholars to secure support for their views and gain control of the government from the Legalists whom Emperor Wu had installed. The government rested its case upon several cogent arguments; the fiscal policies were necessary to maintain defensive warfare against the

Hsiung-nu tribes (probably Huns) who threatened the empire. The government by its disinterested control of vital industries was protecting the people from private exploitation. Finally, the trade opened up by the western expansion had brought to the empire a flood of heretofore unknown luxuries such as horses, camels, furs, rugs, precious stones, exotic fruits, etc.

To these arguments the Confucian literati stolidly replied that the Chinese had no business in the barbarian lands of Central Asia, that China should make peace with its neighbors and be content to remain safely within its traditional boundaries. In reply to the second argument they pointed to the fact that corruption and maladministration in the government system of monopolies were forcing the people to use inferior products or at times to do without them entirely. The government, they claimed, was in actuality entering into competition with the people (private enterprise) in trade, an area outside its proper sphere of activity. On the question of increased foreign trade, they noted aptly that the furs, precious stones, and exotic fruits, bought with silk produced at great labor by the common people, found their way only to the houses of the rich and noble. The debate was a lively affair, the government constantly taunting the scholars with their poverty which, it claimed, was proof of their incompetence in worldy affairs, the latter replying with volleys of classical allusions to expose the wayward nature of the government policies.

On the whole the literati were successful. Though all government monopolies could not be abolished because of the need for revenue, the main features of Emperor Wu's fiscal policies were modified to conform more with Confucian ideals.

The Debate on Salt and Iron
[From *Yen-t'ieh lun,* Sec. 1, 1:1a–5b; Sec. 7, 2:2b–3a; Sec. 10, 2:10a–b; Sec. 19, 4:10b]

In the sixth year of the era Shih-yüan [81 B.C.] an imperial edict was issued directing the Chancellor and the Imperial Secretaries to confer with the worthies and literati who had been recommended to the government and to inquire into the grievances and hardships of the people.

The literati responded: We have heard that the way to govern men is to prevent evil and error at their source, to broaden the beginnings of morality, to discourage secondary occupations and open the way for the exercise of humanity and righteousness. Never should material profit appear as a motive of government. Only then can moral instruction succeed and the customs of the people be reformed. But now in the provinces the salt, iron, and liquor monopolies, and the system of equitable marketing have been established to compete with the people for profit, dispeling rustic generosity and teaching the people greed. Therefore those who pursue primary occupations [farming] have grown few and those following secondary occupations [trading] numerous. As artificiality increases, basic simplicity declines; and as the secondary occupations flourish, those that are primary suffer. When the secondary is practiced the people grow decadent, but when the primary is practiced they are simple and sincere. When the people are sincere then there will be sufficient wealth and goods but when they become extravagant then famine and cold will follow. We recommend that the salt, iron, and liquor monopolies, and the system of equitable marketing be abolished so that primary pursuits may be advanced and secondary ones suppressed. This will have the advantage of increasing the profitableness of agriculture.

His Lordship [the Imperial Secretary Sang Hung-yang] replied: The Hsiung-nu have frequently revolted against our sovereignty and pillaged our borders. If we are to defend ourselves then it means the hardships of war for the soldiers of China, but if we do not defend ourselves properly then their incursions cannot be stopped. The former emperor [Wu] took pity upon the people of the border areas who for so long had suffered disaster and hardship and had been carried off as captives. Therefore he set up defense stations, established a system of warning beacons, and garrisoned the outlying areas to insure their protection. But the resources of these areas were insufficient and so he established the salt, iron, and liquor monopolies, and the system of equitable marketing in order to raise more funds for the expenditures in the borders. Now our critics, who desire that these measures be abolished, would empty the treasuries and deplete the funds used for defense. They would have the men who are defending our passes and patroling our walls suffer hunger and cold. How else can we provide for them? Abolition of these measures is not expedient! [Sec. 1, 1:1a–2a]

His Lordship stated: In former times the peers residing in the provinces

sent in their respective products as tribute but there was much confusion
and trouble in transporting them and the goods were often of such poor
quality that they were not worth the cost of transportation. For this reason transportation offices have been set up in each district to handle
delivery and shipping and to facilitate the presentation of tribute from
outlying areas. Therefore the system is called "equitable marketing."
Warehouses have been opened in the capital for the monopolizing of
goods, buying when prices are low and selling when they are high.
Thereby the government suffers no loss and the merchants cannot speculate for profit. Therefore this is called the "balanced level" [stabilization].
With the balanced level the people are protected from unemployment, and
with equitable marketing the burden of labor upon them is equalized.
Thus these measures are designed to insure an equal distribution of goods
and benefit the people and are not intended to open the way to profit and
provide the people with a ladder to crime.

The literati replied: In ancient times taxes and levies took from the
people what they were skilled in producing and did not demand what
they were poor at. Thus the farmers sent in their harvests and the weaving
women their goods. Nowadays the government disregards what people
have and requires of them what they have not, so that they are forced to
sell their goods at a cheap price in order to meet the demands from
above. . . . The farmers suffer double hardships and the weaving women
are taxed twice. We have not seen that this kind of marketing is "equitable." The government officials go about recklessly opening closed doors
and buying up everything at will so they can corner all the goods. With
goods cornered prices soar and when prices soar the merchants make their
own deals for profit. The officials wink at powerful racketeers and the
rich merchants hoard commodities and wait for an emergency. With
slick merchants and corrupt officials buying cheap and selling dear we
have not seen that your level is "balanced." The system of equitable
marketing of ancient times was designed to equalize the burden of labor
upon the people and facilitate the transporting of tribute. It did not mean
dealing in all kinds of commodities for the sake of profit. [Sec. 1:5a–b]

THE LITERATI ATTACK LEGALIST PHILOSOPHY

The literati spoke: He who is good with a chisel can shape a round hole
without difficulty; he who is good at laying foundations can build to a
great height without danger of collapse. The statesman I Yin made the

ways of Yao and Shun the foundation of the Yin dynasty, and its heirs succeeded to the throne for a hundred generations without break. But Shang Yang made heavy penalties and harsh laws the foundation of the Ch'in state and with the Second Emperor it was destroyed. Not satisfied with the severity of the laws, he instituted the system of mutual responsibility, made it a crime to criticize the government, and increased corporal punishments until the people were so terrified they did not know where to put their hands and feet. Not content with the manifold taxes and levies, he prohibited the people from using the resources of forests and rivers and made a hundredfold profit on the storage of commodities, while the people were given no chance to voice the slightest objection. Such worship of profit and slight of what is right, such exaltation of power and achievement, led, it is true, to expansion of land and acquisition of territory. Yet it was like pouring more water upon people who are already suffering from flood and only increasing their distress. You see how Shang Yang opened the way to imperial rule for the Ch'in, but you fail to see how he also opened for the Ch'in the road to ruin! [Sec. 7, 2:2b–3a]

CONFUCIAN LITERATI RIDICULED

His Excellency spoke: . . . Now we have with us over sixty worthy men and literati who cherish the ways of the Six Confucian Disciplines, fleet in thought and exhaustive in argument. It is proper, gentlemen, that you should pour forth your light and dispel our ignorance. And yet you put all your faith in the past and turn your backs upon the present, tell us of antiquity and give no thought to the state of the times. Perhaps we are not capable of recognizing true scholars. Yet do you really presume with your fancy phrases and attacks upon men of ability to pervert the truth in this manner? [Sec. 10, 2:10a–b]

See them now present us with nothingness and consider it substance, with emptiness and call it plenty! In their coarse gowns and cheap sandals they walk gravely along sunk in meditation as though they had lost something. These are not men who can do great deeds and win fame. They do not even rise above the vulgar masses! [Sec. 19, 4:10b]

THE REFORMS OF WANG MANG

Though a brief period of prosperity followed the relaxation of Emperor Wu's fiscal policies, the economic health of the nation gradually worsened.

Corruption spread through the government from top to bottom. In spite of frequent recommendations for the limitation of land and slave ownership, land and wealth became concentrated in the hands of large official or merchant families. As the peasants were deprived of their land or lost it due to natural disasters, they went into slavery or formed bands of robbers. Government-maintained dikes and waterworks fell into disrepair, increasing the menace of flood and drought. It was when conditions had reached a critical stage that Wang Mang managed to seize power and set about to remedy the situation by a series of sweeping reforms.

WANG MANG
Edict on Land Reform

In A.D. 9 Wang Mang ordered the establishment of an equal land-holding system based on the ancient "well-field" ideal. This involved the nationalization of all land, abolition of private land-holding and prohibition of the sale of land or slaves. The attempt proved a complete failure and was repealed three years later. Subsequent proposals for solution of the land problem, which was a chronic difficulty in later dynasties, tended to follow along the lines suggested by these Han reformers, i.e., either simple limitation on landholding, or outright nationalization and redistribution. Note how Wang Mang's edict follows the wording of Tung's memorial above.

    [From *Han shu*, 99B:9a–10a]

The ancients set up cottages and wells with eight families to a "well-unit" (900 *mu*). One husband and wife cultivated one hundred *mu* of land, remitting one-tenth of the produce as tax. Thus the state enjoyed plenty, the people were rich, and the sound of hymns of praise arose in the land. This was the way of Yao and Shun and it was followed and continued by the Three Dynasties. But the Ch'in was without principle and increased the levies and taxes for its own use, exhausting the strength of the people with its inordinate desires. It destroyed the institutions of the sages and abolished the well-field system. Consequently there arose those who encroached upon the lands of the farmers, avaricious and vile men, the strongest of them measuring their fields in the thousands, while the weak were left without enough land to stick the point of an awl into. In addition they set up markets for slaves where people were penned up like cattle and horses. In handling common people and servants they usurped the right to punish even by death. Villainous and tyrannical men, with profit as their sole concern, went so far as to kidnap and sell men and their wives and children, profaning the will of Heaven, destroying human relationships, and perverting the principle that man is the noblest creation of Heaven and earth. . . .

The House of Han lightened the tax on land to one-thirtieth of the produce. However, there were commonly taxes for commutation of military service which even the aged and ill had to pay. In addition the powerful and rich families oppressed the people, alloting lands for cultivation to sharecroppers and plundering them by high rents for borrowed lands. Thus though in name the tax was one-thirtieth, actually it amounted to one-half. Though father and son, husband and wife year in and year out plowed and weeded, yet the produce left to them was not enough to support life. Therefore the rich, whose very horses and dogs had a surplus of meal and grain, grew arrogant and perpetrated evil deeds, while the poor, without even the dregs of grain to satisfy themselves with, were reduced to despair and turned to a life of crime. Both sank into wickedness, and punishments had to be used and could not be set aside.

Formerly, when I occupied the position of Regent, it was my intention to nationalize all land and apportion it into "well-units" according to the population. At that time the empire enjoyed the portentous blessing of the double-headed grain, but because of the unfortunate occurrence of rebellions and banditry, I was forced temporarily to abandon my plans.

Now at this time let the term be altered and the land throughout the empire be designated "king's fields" and slaves be called "private retainers." Neither land nor slaves are to be bought or sold. Those families whose adult males do not number eight, but whose fields amount to more than one "well-unit," shall divide the surplus lands among their near relatives of the nine generations and the people of their townships and boroughs. Thus those who are without lands shall justly receive them according to this system. Anyone who shall dare to criticize the well-field system of the sages, or seek in defiance of the law to delude the populace, shall be cast out beyond the four borders to face demons and evil spirits.

CONCLUSION

Some modern historians have attempted to see in Wang's reforms a sincere attempt to alleviate the sufferings of the people, while others regard

them, like Emperor Wu's policies, as merely plans for securing increased
government revenues. Whatever his real motivation, his reforms were
an undoubted failure.

Wang Mang revived all the monopolies of Emperor Wu on coinage,
salt, iron, liquor, and natural resources, and the system of government
marketing. As formerly, this had the same effect of forcing up the prices
of necessary commodities, lowering the quality, depriving many people
of their livelihood, and imposing an additional tax burden upon the
population. In addition he imposed taxes upon artisans and professional
men, forced the officials to take reductions in salary during bad years,
and demanded voluntary contributions of four-fifths of their salary from
the officials to support military expenses, made necessary by an inept
foreign policy which put him at war with the border tribes. In a series of
rapid changes, he issued a profusion of new coins, withdrew old ones
from circulation, and threw the currency into such chaos that people lost
all confidence in it and secretly traded with old Han money. So great was
the number of persons convicted of violating this rash of new laws and
reforms that it soon became impossible to carry out sentences upon them
all and efforts at punishment of offenders had to be abandoned.

The furious activity of Wang's brief reign served to antagonize all
classes of society and his impractical attempts to revive ancient practices
cost him the backing of the Confucian bureaucracy which had earlier
supported him. Without the confidence of his officials, his measures, however effective they might theoretically have been, were wrecked on the
administrative level by noncooperation and corruption. He tried vainly to
carry on alone, working day and night to handle all administrative matters personally. But the situation was beyond help. Pan Ku, in the *Han
shu,* writes:

"The people could not turn a hand without violating some prohibition.
. . . The rich had no means to protect themselves and the poor no way
to stay alive. They rose up and became thieves and bandits, infesting the
hills and marshes, and the officials, being unable to seize them, contrived
on the contrary to hide their presence so that they grew more prevalent
day by day. . . . Famine and pestilence raged and people ate each other
so that before Wang Mang was finally punished half the population of
the empire had perished. . . . [In A.D. 25] the founder of the Eastern
Han received the mandate of Heaven and, washing away their vexations

and hardships, together with all the people of the empire made a 'new beginning.' "[1]

This "new beginning" carried the Han dynasty until its final fall in A.D. 220. Decimation of the population and the thorough shaking up of the social order accompanying the fall of Wang Mang served naturally to alleviate the economic crisis of the empire and give it a new lease on life. The period which followed was one of relative peace and cultural attainment. Yet the same economic cycle which marked the history of the Former Han repeated itself with ineluctable persistence. Court intrigue, official corruption, the concentration of land in the hands of wealthy families, displacing the people from their fields and turning them to banditry, bred the inevitable warlordism and antidynastic revolution. The reign of Wang Mang, itself only a prolongation and aggravation of the agrarian crisis of the Former Han, had precipitated a peasant revolt known as the Red Eyebrows originating in the eastern province of Shantung. The Latter Han fell victim to a similar revolt which began, under Taoist influence, in Szechwan, led by a group known as the Yellow Turbans. This cycle of agrarian crisis and decay of the central government, climaxed by peasant revolts originating in the border areas, repeats itself over and over in Chinese history, forming a pattern running through the successive rise and fall of each dynastic house.

[1] *Han shu,* 24B:25a-b.

CHAPTER XI

RATIONALISM AND SUPERSTITION

Han thinkers, deeply under the influence of Hsün Tzu's rationalism, labored to work out a rational, naturalistic, and moral scheme embracing all realms of thought and knowledge. They tried to discover a cosmic order working in all things—in the evolutions of history, the rise and fall of ruling houses, the terrors of the natural world—and to reduce this order to a few basic principles that could be comprehended by all thinking men. It is not too much to call their aims scientific in the modern sense, for they sincerely sought by their ordered theories to free men from the fear and darkness of primitive times and to give them an understanding that would make them no longer the victims of the changes and vagaries of history and the natural world. The average man of the twentieth century, unable to comprehend the intricate laws of physics and mathematics which yet, he knows, govern his very existence, is far more a victim in his own mind of the natural world than the Han thinker who believed he could comprehend and predict all processes of change through the action of the yin and yang and the five agents.

That these primitive attempts of Han thinkers to work out a rational science of things in the end only substituted new superstitions for old ones is hardly to be wondered at. The bases of their theories were, from our point of view, hopelessly crude and inaccurate, their generalizations faulty, and their neatly ordered conclusions forced. In the hands of most people of the time, they were put to uses that differ little from other forms of superstition, ancient and modern. The selection given earlier on the miraculous portents marking the rise of Wang Mang to the throne amply illustrates this point. It is an example of the type of humbug which appeared in the Han and did much to discredit the essentially rationalistic systems of thought from which it sprang.

APOCRYPHAL LITERATURE

The so-called apocryphal literature of the Han was of two principle kinds, the *wei* or exegetical books, and the *ch'an* or prophetic books. The exegetical books were of a more respectable nature than the latter, and it was indeed only the excesses to which they went that caused their eventual discredit among scholars. As the Classics are known by the name *ching* which means "warp," so the exegetical books were called *wei* or "woof," and their function was primarily to aid and supplement an understanding of the Classics, giving explanations of obscure passages and background for the events recounted in the older texts, and systematizing the thought into a consistent doctrine. It was the custom for individual scholars or schools to write such commentaries in order to set forth their own particular interpretation of some classic. Tung Chung-shu's work on the *Spring and Autumn Annals,* the *Ch'un-ch'iu fan-lu,* may be regarded as an early and quite respectable example of this type of literature. As Confucianism began to flourish under official patronage, however, it is natural that this production of exegetical material should reach considerable proportions, much of it of a worthless nature. Wang Ch'ung, the eminent thinker of the Latter Han, writes of this situation in his day: "The Confucianists when they discuss the Five Classics often miss the truth. Former Confucianists failed to examine the matter fully but simply made up wild theories, and later Confucianists, trusting in the pronouncements of their teachers, continue to repeat these old stories. They go on vainly learning words and phrases, calling themselves the followers of a particular school, and rush to become teachers themselves. . . . They have no time to search things out for themselves and test the accuracy of their assumptions. Thus these senseless theories are handed on without a break and truth becomes lost and hidden." [1]

In addition to these exegetical writings produced by the scholars, there appeared a mass of books recording prophecies, miracles, mysterious

[1] *Lun heng,* 28:1a.

charts, and diagrams, supposed to have been handed down from high antiquity, which gained currency among lesser scholars and charlatans and often attracted the favorable notice of the emperors. As in most ancient nations, prophecies and prophetic signs played an important part in early Chinese thought. Numerous miracles and prodigies, solemnly recorded in the histories, were associated with the births and early lives of the emperors. Emperor Wu in particular was much under the influence of wonder workers and magicians. Confucianism, as it came to be the dominant philosophy of the bureaucracy, was inevitably involved in this atmosphere of superstition.

It is not certain when the actual prophetic books came into existence. During the Former Han scattered prophetic utterances undoubtedly existed, but these were not collected and compiled into books until some-time around the reign of Wang Mang. The function of these books was to give scriptural basis to certain actions which the emperor or someone aspiring to high position might contemplate. As noted, Wang Mang made free use of them to justify his usurpation. They were also designed to prove by all manner of fantastic means the sacred authority of the Confucian canon and the Confucian philosophy, or rather it might better be said, the Confucian religion, for that is what it was rapidly becom-ing at this time.

Tung Chung-shu and his school maintained that Confucius had been an actual "uncrowned king" who in the *Spring and Autumn Annals* laid down the institutions for a new dynasty and enjoyed all the heavenly approval appropriate to a true ruler. This tendency toward the deifica-tion of Confucius was carried to an extreme in the apocryphal books. Many of these books were attributed to Confucius or his disciples, others were claimed to be of far greater antiquity, having been handed down from such legendary personages as the Yellow Emperor. They were re-plete with fabulous stories of these early rulers, as well as prophecies concerning later times, even down to predictions of the rise and develop-ment of the Han dynasty itself.

Needless to say such a mass of equivocal and fantastic material, cred-ited by a large number, though by no means all, of the officials and peo-ple of the day, was welcomed by any ruler or aspirant to the throne who could thereby "prove" his claims to power. It is not to be supposed, how-ever, that these writings were unanimously accepted. Their absurdities and anachronisms, the grossness of their style and lack of true scholarship branded them as spurious in the eyes of the more discerning scholars of the day, who openly attacked them. It was not until the Sui and early T'ang dynasties, however, that the apocryphal books were finally officially proscribed and copies of them confiscated and burned, so that our knowledge of them today is based only on surviving fragments.

Legends Concerning Confucius

The following selections indicate the sort of legends that grew up about Confucius in the Han. The second account, from a post-Han work, may have been influenced by stories of the birth of Buddha.

[From *Ch'un-ch'iu yen-k'ung-t'u* in *Ku-wei-shu* 8:2b]
The mother of Confucius, Cheng-tsai of the Yen family, was idling about the bank of a large pond when she fell asleep and dreamed that the Black Emperor sent word inviting her to come. When she had gone she had intercourse with him in her dream and he said: "You will give birth in the hollow of a mulberry tree." When she awoke she felt strange. She bore Confucius in a place called Hollow Mulberry.

[From *Shih-i-chi* 3:4b–5a]
The night Confucius was born two azure dragons came down from the heavens and coiled about Cheng-tsai's room. When she had given birth to Confucius as her dream had said, two goddesses appeared in the sky bearing fragrant dew with which they bathed her. The Emperor of Heaven came down and performed the Music of Heavenly Tranquillity, filling the rooms of the Yen family. A voice spoke, saying: "Heaven is moved and gives birth to this sage child. Therefore I have descended and celebrate it with music," and the sound of the pipes and bells was unlike any heard in this world. In addition there were five old men ranged about the court of Cheng-tsai's house who were the spirits of the five stars. Before Confucius was born there was a unicorn which spat up a jade document before some people in Confucius' village of Ch'üeh-li and on it was written: "In the decline of the Chou the descendant of the spirit of water shall be an uncrowned king. Therefore the two dragons encircled the room and the five stars fell in the courtyard." Cheng-tsai, being wise and understanding, recognized these things as holy and wonderful and she took a multicolored cord and bound the horn of the uni-

corn and kept it for two nights, but then it went away. A physiognomist examined Confucius and said: "This child is descended from King T'ang of the Yin dynasty. He shall become an uncrowned king under the power of the agent water and, as the scion of kings, attain the highest reverence."

YANG HSIUNG

The works of the Confucian scholar, statesman, and poet Yang Hsiung (53 B.C.–A.D. 18) represent a reaction against this atmosphere of supernaturalism which was beginning to invade Confucianism, and an attempt to return to earlier concepts of naturalism and spontaneity in the interpretation of the universe. His most significant work, the *Fa yen* or *Aphorisms,* modeled after the Confucian *Analects,* is a series of pronouncements and brief dialogues between the author and an imaginary questioner. In these Yang Hsiung emphasizes the humanism and rationalism which characterized pre-Han Confucianism and attacks the extreme fatalism, the belief in portents and the arts of immortality, and other superstitions and abuses which he believed were corrupting the Confucian tradition of his day.

YANG HSIUNG

Selections from the Aphorisms
[From *Fa yen,* 1, 2, 6, 8, 10, 12, 13]

Someone asked about fate. Fate, I replied, is the will of Heaven and not man's doing. When man acts, it is not fate. What are man's doings? he asked. A man can choose preservation or destruction, life or death; these are not fate. Fate is inexorable. What then of the early deaths of [Confucius' disciples] Yen Yüan and Jan Po-niu? These were inexorable. But a man who deliberately stands under a shaky wall courts injury as he moves and invites death when he walks. Is this fate? So-called "lucky people" often turn their good luck into bad, while "unlucky people" turn their bad luck into good. [6]

Someone asked whether it is true [as Mencius said] that a sage is born every five hundred years. I replied that the sages Yao, Shun, and Yü succeeded one after the other, while King Wu and the Duke of Chou were both sons of King Wen. On the other hand sages like King T'ang and Confucius were born a great many hundreds of years apart. If you try to predict the future on the basis of the past, you cannot tell whether even one sage will be born in the course of a thousand years. [8]

Someone asked if the sage pays attention to strange happenings. I replied that the sage in his practice of virtue considers the observation of strange happenings as of secondary importance. Thus I consider that to practice virtue constantly is fundamental, but to reform suddenly and practice virtue after seeing some wonder is second-rate. [13]

Someone asked about the strange tales concerning the Yellow Emperor. They are merely attributed to his name, I replied. In olden times when Emperor Yü directed the control of the flood he injured his foot and since then all the sorcerers go around limping. The ancient physician P'ien Ch'üeh was a native of Lu and now all doctors claim to be from Lu. People who are trying so sell a fake always endeavor to make it look genuine. [10]

Someone asked whether those who study because they covet long life may be said to love learning. They have no love of learning, I replied, for in learning there is no covetousness. [1]

Someone asked whether immortals really exist as people claim. Ha! I said. I have heard that Fu Hsi and Shen Nung died, that Yao and Shun passed away, that King Wen was buried at Pei and Confucius was buried north of the city of Lu. Should you alone grumble at death? There is nothing man can do about it. Immortality does not apply to the likes of us. . . . The sage worries that in this world there is still something he does not understand; the seeker of immortality worries that in this world he may lose one day of life. Life, life! They call it life but in truth it is death! But, my questioner continued, if there is no such thing in this world as immortality, why do people talk of it? Those who talk so, I said, are idle chatterers! With their idle chatter they try to make what does not exist come into existence. . . . What is born must die, what has a beginning must have an end. That is the way of nature. [12]

Someone asked whether the feudal lords in his day knew that Confucius was a sage. They knew it, I replied. If they knew it, then why did they not employ him? They could not, I said. Can you explain how one can recognize a man as a sage and still not be able to use him? If you employ someone, I said, you ought to follow his advice. If they had

followed Confucius' advice, they would have had to abandon their usual
ways, go against what they were accustomed to and strengthen their
weak points at the expense of their strong ones so that they would have
become very confused. Only a person of great virtue could have employed Confucius. [8]

In ancient times Yang Chu and Mo Ti blocked the road of the true
way, but Mencius refuted them, opening the road and broadening it.
In later times there are again those who block the road. I venture to
compare myself to Mencius. [2]

WANG CH'UNG

In his *Lun heng* or *Critical Essays,* the Latter Han philosopher Wang
Ch'ung (A.D. 27–97?) writes: "Though the chapters of my *Critical Essays*
may be numbered in the tens, one phrase covers them all: hatred of
fictions and falsehoods." [2] He maintains this critical spirit through the
eighty-five extant sections of his work, attacking all types of falsehoods
and superstitions which flourished in his day and wittily and incisively
debunking them. His methods, as well as his object, have been lauded
as the first steps toward a true scientific spirit of investigation. He employs two methods of reasoning to establish what he considers the truth
of the matter. The first is that of actual observation of facts, the true
scientific method, in which the data are not merely observed, he is careful to point out, but thoroughly considered in the mind of the observer
so that their true significance may be comprehended. His second and
more common method, however, is reasoning by analogy, so popular
in Chinese thinking. It is this method which, in spite of his best intentions, often leads him into patent absurdities when he assumes that
things which are analogous in one respect are naturally of the same
class and hence analogous in other respects as well.

Yet to fully appreciate the significance of Wang's insistence upon ex-
perimental proof (however he may have failed in the application of his
ideal) it should be remembered that up until this time, and indeed long
after it, the Chinese thinker was often content to cite in proof of any
idea at all some obscure and frequently irrelevant or spurious ancient

[2] *Lun heng,* 20:11a.

text. Wang is thus attempting to banish some of the falsehoods that had grown up because of misreading or distortion of the old texts. With the literal-mindedness that is one of his failings, however, he frequently misses the point of metaphorical writing in the Classics and calls them to account for what is patently only poetic license, as one might demand of Shakespeare in the name of science how one person's hand could turn the whole ocean red.

Though Wang Ch'ung formulated no systematic philosophy of his own, there are several concepts which dominate his thinking. First is that of the spontaneity of the natural order. Like the earlier Taoists, he insists that the natural order is without consciousness or purpose but creates, sustains and destroys by pure and inevitable spontaneity. His favorite simile for man, opposing the exalted position accorded mankind in orthodox Confucianism, is that of a flea or louse hidden in the folds of the garment of the universe. He therefore vehemently denies that such an insignificant creature could possibly, as had been asserted, influence by his actions the order and harmony of the natural world.

The second outstanding feature of Wang's thought is his extreme fatalism, which he extended to cover not only individuals but whole nations, leading him by analogical reasoning to the rather curious position, especially for a professed Confucianist, that the prosperity or downfall of a dynasty are entirely a matter of its fated span of life.

WANG CH'UNG

Selections from the Critical Essays
[From *Lun heng*, 18:1a, 17:14b–15b]

When the vital force (*ch'i*) of Heaven and earth come together, all creatures are born spontaneously, just as children are born spontaneously when the vital force of husband and wife unite. Among the creatures thus born those with blood in their veins experience hunger and cold. Seeing that the five grains can be eaten, they gather and eat them; seeing that silk and hemp can be worn, they make clothes of them. Some people insist that Heaven produced the five grains purposely to feed man, and silk and hemp to clothe him. But this is to make Heaven the farmer or the mulberry girl of man, which is incommensurate with the principle of spontaneity. Therefore such ideas are suspect and cannot be accepted. [18:1a]

A worthy ruler orders the state as a loving father orders his family. A loving father may instruct and enlighten his children and grandchildren, but he cannot make them all filial and good. When children are good the family will prosper, and when the people are at peace the nation will flourish. But that which flourishes must decay and that which prospers must decline. If prosperity is not caused by the success of virtue, then decline is not caused by its failure. . . . Thus good government is not due to the efforts of worthies or sages nor is disorder the result of immorality. When a nation faces decline and disorder, worthies and sages cannot restore it to glory, and when it is well ordered, evil men cannot bring it to ruin. The fact that an age is ordered or disordered is due to its seasons of growth and not to its government. . . . Whether the ruler be worthy or unworthy, whether his government be enlightened or unenlightened can have no effect. . . . What is the reason an age becomes disordered? Is it not because robbers grow numerous, rebels arise, and the people discard decorum and righteousness and revolt against their superiors? All of these come from the fact that there is a scarcity of grain and people cannot endure hunger and cold. . . . The causes of good and evil conduct lie not in human character but in the dearth or affluence of the year. We may say then that the observance of decorum and righteousness depends upon a sufficiency of grain. As we know, the grain produce depends upon the year. If the year is one of flood and drought then the five grains are spoiled. This is not caused by the government but is the result of seasonal cycles. If one is to say that flood and drought are caused by the government, then in the times of Chieh and Chou there should have been constant flood and drought, for no one governed worse than they did. But as a matter of fact at that time there were no calamities of famine or dearth. Calamities such as these have their cycles of occurrence which on the contrary occasionally come during the reigns of sage rulers. [17:14b–15b]

A Discussion of Death

Among the numerous beliefs of the men of his day that Wang Ch'ung attacked as superstitious and baseless was that in the existence of a conscious life after death. It is apparent that the Chinese from ancient times had believed that the souls of the dead at times assumed human forms, appeared among men, and were capable of doing them conscious injury. Wang does not deny the existence of phantoms which occasionally appear in a form like that of the dead. But he vigorously attacks the idea that such phantoms are actually the souls of the dead or have any consciousness. His denial of a conscious life after death, some of the main points of which are presented in the translation below, is one of the earliest and most detailed discussions of this problem which, with the introduction of Buddhism in the centuries that followed, was to assume major significance in Chinese thought.

[From *Lun heng,* 20:11a–15b]

People say that when men die they become ghosts with consciousness and the power to harm others. If we try to test this theory by comparing men with other creatures, however, we find that men do not become ghosts, nor do they have consciousness or power to harm. . . . Man lives because of his vital force (*ch'i*) and when he dies this vital force is extinguished. The vital force is able to function because of the blood system, but when a man dies the blood system ceases to operate. With this the vital force is extinguished and the body decays and turns to clay. What is there to become a ghost then? If a man is without ears or eyes he lacks faculties of consciousness. Hence men who are dumb and blind are like grass or trees. But when the vital force has left a man it is a far more serious matter than simply being without ears or eyes. . . . The vital force produces man just as water becomes ice. As water freezes into ice, so the vital force coagulates to form man. When ice melts it becomes water and when a man dies he becomes spirit again. He is called spirit just as ice which has melted changes its name to water. People see that the name has changed, but they then assert that spirit has consciousness and can assume a form and harm others, but there is no basis for this assertion.

People see ghosts which in form appear like living men. Precisely because they appear in this form, we know that they cannot be the spirits of the dead. How can we prove this? Take a sack and fill it with millet or rice. When the millet or rice has been put into it, the sack will be full and sturdy and will stand up in clear view so that people looking at it from a distance can tell that it is a sack of millet or rice. Why? Because the shape of the sack bespeaks the contents. But if the sack has a hole in it and all the millet or rice runs out, then the sack collapses in a heap and people looking from a distance can no longer see it. The spirit of man is stored up in his bodily form like the millet or rice in the sack. When he dies and his body decays, his vital force disperses like the grain running out of the sack. When the grain has run out, the sack no longer retains its shape. Then when the spirit of man has dispersed and disappeared, how could there still be a body to be seen by others? . . .

Since the beginning of Heaven and earth and the age of the sage rulers until now there have been millions of people who died of old age or were cut off in their prime. The number of men living today is nowhere near that of the dead. If men become ghosts when they die, then when we go walking we ought to see a ghost at every step. If men see ghosts when they are about to die then they ought to see millions of them crowding the hall, filling the courtyards, and jamming the streets, and not just one or two of them. . . . It is the nature of Heaven and earth that, though new fires can be kindled, one cannot rekindle a fire that has burned out, and though new human beings can be born, one cannot bring back the dead. . . . Now people say that ghosts are the spirits of the dead. If this were true, then when men see them they ought to appear completely naked and not clothed in robes and sashes. Why? Because clothes have no spirits. When a man dies they all rot away along with his bodily form, so how could he put them on again? . . .

If dead men cannot become ghosts, then they also cannot have consciousness. How do we prove this? By the fact that before a man is born he has no consciousness. Before a man is born he exists in the midst of primal force (*yüan-ch'i*), and after he dies he returns again to this primal force. The primal force is vast and indistinct and the human force exists within it. Before a man is born he has no consciousness, so when he dies and returns to this original unconscious state how could he still have consciousness? The reason a man is intelligent and understanding is that he possesses the forces of the five virtues [humanity, righteousness, decorum, wisdom, and faith]. The reason he possesses these is that he has within him the five organs [heart, liver, stomach, lungs, and kidneys]. If these five organs are unimpaired, a man has understanding, but if they are diseased, then he becomes vague and confused and behaves like a fool or an idiot. When a man dies, the five organs rot away and the five virtues no longer have any place to reside. Both the seat and the faculty of understanding are destroyed. The body must await the vital force before it is complete, and the vital force must await the body before it can have consciousness. Nowhere is there a fire that burns all by itself. How then could there be a spirit with consciousness existing without a body? . . .

Confucius buried his mother at Fang. Later there was a heavy rain and the grave mound collapsed. When Confucius heard of this he wept bitterly and said: "The ancients did not repair graves," and he never repaired it. If the dead had consciousness then they would surely be angry that people did not repair their graves, and Confucius, realizing this, would accordingly have repaired the grave in order to please his mother's spirit. But he did not repair it. With the enlightenment of a sage he understood that the dead have no consciousness.

CHAPTER XII

CONFUCIANISM AND THE CONFUCIAN CANON

During the course of the Han dynasty, Confucianism came to hold the supreme position of philosophical orthodoxy in the Chinese political and cultural system, a position which it maintained more or less continuously until the establishment of the Chinese Republic. It is well to trace in some detail the steps by which this transformation came about and the manner in which the ancient literature came to be compiled into the body of works known today as the Classics.

Kao-tsu, the founder of the Han, a commoner with no pretensions to learning, seems to have had a certain antipathy toward pompous Confucian scholars. But he did not hesitate to make use of them and follow their advice when it helped his designs. Above all, he honestly accorded with the Confucian teaching that the emperor acts on the advice of his ministers, setting an important precedent that did much to check possible despotism among his successors. Still, the influence of Confucianism was by no means exclusive. Some of Kao-tsu's most important followers favored Taoism or other schools of thought. The Ch'in system of government was at first taken over and continued by the Han, and only gradually was it modified to conform less with Legalist and more with Confucian principles.

STATE ORTHODOXY

It was not until the time of Emperor Wu that the Confucianists made a serious attempt to secure exclusive imperial patronage for their teachings. The single man most responsible for the acceptance of Confucianism as the orthodox philosophy of the Chinese state was Tung Chung-shu. In his career as teacher and government official during the reign of Emperor Wu he formulated doctrines and brought about the establishment of institutions that had a profound influence on later ages. It was his conviction that the Han should take constructive measures to change what remained of the old order inherited from the Ch'in. His recommendations to the emperor were presented in a series of answers to questions on government policy posed by the emperor himself. One of these advocated the acceptance of Confucianism as the sole orthodox philosophy of the state:

"The great principle of unity of the *Spring and Autumn Annals* is a constant warp binding Heaven and earth, a moral law pervading past and present. But the teachers of today have different doctrines and men expound diverse theories; the various schools of philosophy differ in their ways and their principles do not agree. Thus the ruler has no means by which to achieve unity, the laws and institutions undergo frequent changes and the people do not know what to honor. Your unworthy servant considers that all that is not encompassed by the Six Disciplines and the arts of Confucius should be suppressed and not allowed to continue further, and evil and vain theories stamped out. Only then will unity be achieved, the laws be made clear, and the people know what to follow." [1]

Emperor Wu eventually followed this suggestion, removing official support from the other philosophies and encouraging Confucianism alone. Thus he was able to achieve in effect the unification of thought that the violent proscriptions of Ch'in had sought but failed to produce.

STATE UNIVERSITY

Closely connected with this plan to give official support to Confucianism was Tung Chung-shu's suggestion for the establishment of a government university for the training of officials in which, of course, Confucian ideas would be taught. He writes:

"Among the things paramount for the upbringing of scholars, none is more important than a state university. A university is intimately related to the fostering of virtuous scholars, and is the foundation of edu-

[1] *Han shu.* 56:21a.

cation. . . . Your servant desires Your Majesty to erect a university and appoint illustrious teachers for it, for the upbringing of the empire's scholars." [2]

In 124 B.C. by imperial order a university was established near the capital at which government-appointed teachers gave instruction to students selected and sent to the capital by provincial authorities. The course of study was normally one year and, upon graduation, all those shown to be capable were given positions in the bureaucracy. By the end of the first century B.C. there were some 3,000 students enrolled in the university, and in the Latter Han the number grew to over 30,000. Thus the bureaucracy became filled with men trained in the official Confucian philosophy.

CIVIL SERVICE

As early as the reign of the first Han emperor, the government had sent out requests asking the provincial officials to recommend capable scholars and men of ability to the government as servants. This idea, old in Confucian tradition, gradually increased in power and effectiveness. Tung Chung-shu himself was selected for an official career after having written outstanding answers, quoted from above, to the examination questions set by the emperor. It was natural, and consistent with his plans for the building and shaping of a Confucian bureaucracy, that he should exert his influence to encourage and develop this system which was later to grow into the famous examination system. Thus he recommended that the emperor have "the marquises, governors of commanderies, and officials of 2,000 piculs salary all select those of worth among the officials and common people and once a year send to the capital two men each who will be housed there and taken care of. . . . In this way all will do their best in seeking out men of worth, and scholars of the empire can be obtained, given official posts, and used in the government." [3]

[2] *Han shu*, 56:12b–13a.   [3] *Han shu*, 56:9b.

THE RIVALRY BETWEEN LEGALISM
AND CONFUCIANISM

In spite of these measures taken under his rule, Emperor Wu himself was far from a model Confucian ruler. His system of harsh and detailed laws, heavy taxes, extensive military expeditions, and government monopolies embodies specifically Legalist measures. He disregarded the precedent set by the founder of the dynasty, acting on his own initiative and ignoring the counsel of his ministers. In private life he devoted much time and expense to Taoist pursuits of the elixir of immortality, attempts to communicate with the dead spirits, and other superstitious practices. So averse was he to any criticism of his measures that under his reign an official was executed on the charge of "disapproval in the heart," based on the evidence of a reported "subtle wry twist of the lips" of the victim. Nothing could be further from the Confucian insistence upon outspoken criticism and discussion of all administrative practices as the sacred duty of ministers and scholars.

Emperor Wu's successor, Emperor Hsüan, continued his policies, giving lip service to Confucian doctrines but favoring Legalist absolutism in practice. When once reproached by the Crown Prince for his departure from Confucian principles, he replied angrily: "The House of Han has its own institutions and laws based on a combination of the ways of the overlords and the sage kings. How could we rely solely upon moral instruction and the governmental system of the Chou? The common lot of Confucianists do not understand what is appropriate to the times but applaud everything ancient and criticize the present. They cause people to confuse names and realities so that they do not know what to abide by. How could they be entrusted with responsibility?" [4]

It was not until the reign of his son, Emperor Yüan, that a ruler fully in accord with Confucian ideals for the first time occupied the throne. Unfortunately, by this time the influence of the emperor's maternal relatives and the eunuchs had become so strong that the emperor, though well-meaning, was largely ineffectual and the decay of the dynasty was clearly foreshadowed.

[4] *Han shu*, 9:1b.

Wang Mang, unorthodox though some of his measures were, put himself forward as the most ardent and meticulous follower of Confucian teachings. The emperors of the Latter Han were likewise all supporters of Confucianism and, though the Confucian ministers toward the end of the dynasty were no more effective in preventing the usurpation of power by the eunuch cliques than they had been at the end of the Former Han, the theoretical supremacy of Confucianism was never challenged. Yet during this era occurred two important developments which were later to have the greatest effect upon the fortunes of Confucianism and Confucian thought. One was the official notice of the introduction of the Buddhist faith into China during the reign of Emperor Ming (A.D. 58–75). The other was the rising power of the Taoist religion, a mixture of the philosophical ideas of Lao Tzu and Chuang Tzu and numerous popular superstitions, with rites and institutions imitated from Buddhism. From this time on Chinese thought will often be concerned with questions of the relative merits of the "Three Teachings"—Confucianism, Buddhism, and Taoism.

THE CONFUCIAN CANON

Han thought on the whole shows little of the vitality and originality that characterized the more unsettled times of late Chou. The real accomplishments of Han intellectual activity lay rather in the systematization of earlier ideas, the compilation of great works of history and lexicography, and the impressive labors of editing and annotating the ancient literature carried out by scholars of this age. This latter work was chiefly done by Confucian literati who, with hard toil and devoted scholarship, set about repairing the damage wrought by Ch'in's burning of the books and the fire and destruction that had razed the Ch'in capital during the troubled days of the founding of the new dynasty.

The books of this age were in the form of bamboo slips, inscribed in lacquer with a line of characters and bound together with thongs. It may easily be imagined how, when the thongs had rotted and the slips became jumbled or lost, a work could be damaged or rendered almost unintelligible. Thus, though copies of many of the ancient books ordered destroyed by the Ch'in were found still to exist, a tremendous task was involved in editing them, reconciling varying versions, and establishing a trustworthy text.

As might be expected, however, the scholars could not often agree among themselves upon an authoritative text, and so there existed side by side slightly different versions of the classical works, each with its own traditions, masters, and disciples.

THE OLD AND NEW TEXTS

The situation was made worse by the appearance of still other versions of some of the Classics, reported by legend to have been found sealed in the wall of Confucius' home. These were the famous Old Text versions, so called because they were written not in the style of characters adopted by the Ch'in and used by the Han, but in an archaic orthography used during the Chou. The controversy precipitated by the appearance of these texts has continued down to the present day.

In the Han the New and Old Text dispute involved fundamental philosophical principles. Generally speaking, the New Text School represented the views of Tung Chung-shu and his followers. It made free use of yin-yang theories, and laid great emphasis upon the interpretation of omens and portents. It was this group that attempted to elevate Confucius to a position approaching divinity, and in this labor it made free use of the prophetic literature which grew up within the Confucian school. An opposition group which arose among private scholars, known as the Old Text School, was led by men from the area of Confucius' own state of Lu, one of the most famous, K'ung An-kuo, being himself a direct descendant of the sage. It was the purpose of these men to expel from Confucianism the superstitions which had invaded it, to return Confucius to his proper position as a teacher, to diminish the influence of the yin-yang school, and to restore the original purity of the doctrine. The first important official patron of the Old Text School was Liu Hsin (46 B.C.–A.D. 23), an outstanding scholar whose reputation has suffered because of his association with the usurper Wang Mang. Emperor Kuang Wu, who restored the House of Han after Wang's execution, was extremely superstitious and lent his full support to the New Text School, abolishing the study of the Old Texts which had been established at the end of the Former Han. However, though the Old Text School failed in the Han dynasty to gain ascendance over its rival, its supporters included most of the important thinkers and scholars of the Latter Han and its spirit of rationalism eventually triumphed.

But to return to the history of the canon itself. To bring order to the situation and promote the unification and systematization of thought he strove for, Emperor Wu in 136 B.C. set up an imperial commission for the recovery of classical texts. With Confucianism now established as the state philosophy, imperial interest and support of this work of recovering and editing the ancient literature continued to increase. In 53 B.C., Emperor Hsüan called a conference of scholars to discuss varying interpretations of the Classics, with the emperor himself attending and acting as final judge in the controversies. The conference continued for two years, and the results were published to form the official interpretation, though varying interpretations were not actually proscribed.

Some years later, in the reign of Emperor Ch'eng, a still more ambitious program was undertaken. Under the directorship of Liu Hsiang (79–8 B.C.), court official and eminent scholar, a group of scholars was set to work collecting copies of all the existing literature of the day. For each work a copy of the table of sections and an abstract of its contents was made. When Liu Hsiang died, his work was continued by his son, Liu Hsin, who presented to the throne on the completion of the project a bibliography in seven sections listing all the important books of the empire. This bibliography was incorporated into the *History of the Former Han Dynasty,* forming an invaluable aid to the study of ancient China and its literature.

Something of the situation which prevailed and the task confronting the scholars in bringing order to it may be judged from the following comments of the historian Pan Ku:

"From the time when Emperor Wu set up learned doctors for the Five Classics and appointed disciples for them, established competitive examinations and encouraged men to study for official positions, until the era Yüan-shih (A.D. 1–5) was a period of over one hundred years. During this time the teachers of classical studies increased like the branches and leaves of a spreading tree. The explanations of one Classic ran to over a million words and the number of professors grew to more than a thousand, for this was the way to official position and profit."[5]

[5] *Han shu,* 88:25a-b.

"Scholars of ancient times while farming and taking care of their families were able to complete their study of one Classic in three years because as they went through the text they concentrated only upon the general meaning. Thus they spent little time and reaped great benefit. By the time they were thirty they had mastered all Five Classics. In later times when the Classics and their commentaries had already become diverse and contradictory, the scholars of wide learning forgot the advice of Confucius to 'hear much and put aside the points of which you are in doubt.'[6] They worked to twist the meaning of passages in order to avoid difficulties of interpretation and with glib phrases and contrived theories destroyed the integrity of the text. Explanations of five characters of the text ran to twenty or thirty thousand words. In time this situation became worse and worse until a youth who spent all his time on one Classic could not speak with authority on it until his head had grown grey. Scholars rested complacently upon what they had learned and attacked anything unfamiliar so that in the end they condemned themselves to sterility. This is the great danger of scholarship."[7]

It is no wonder that, after the troubled times of Wang Mang, a council of scholars was again held, modeled on that held under Emperor Hsüan. The results, combined with those of the former council, were compiled and published in a work known as *Discussions in the White Tiger Hall* (*Po-hu t'ung*), representing in final form the orthodox interpretation of the Confucian Classics.

Thus the Classics were established as the basis for all Confucian learning, and, in turn, for entrance into official position. With minor exceptions, this is the canon as it was known in later ages and as it has come down to us. By the end of the Han, silk scrolls had largely replaced the earlier bamboo slips as writing material for books, and in A.D. 105 the invention of paper was officially recorded. But Han scholars, with the chaos wreaked on the ancient texts by Ch'in's laws and the disorders of the early Han and Wang Mang's time still vivid in their minds, trusted to none of these media for the preservation of their sacred books. Toward the end of the dynasty, by imperial order, the complete texts of the Five Classics and the Confucian *Analects* were engraved on stone tablets and

[6] *Analects* II, 18.   [7] *Han shu*, 30:12b–13a.

set up at the imperial university, a monument to the scholarly labors of the Han Confucianists.

THE TRIUMPH OF CONFUCIANISM

Much speculation has been devoted to the question of why Confucianism, of the major schools of thought that flourished in Chou times and continued into the early Han, should have triumphed over its rivals and attained a position of sole authority. Some scholars have suggested that Confucianism supplies a philosophical basis for the divine right of the emperor, a justification for absolutism, and for this reason was enthusiastically supported by the Han rulers. Confucian thought is indeed firmly based upon the concept of an hierarchically ordered society with a supreme ruler at its head. Yet, if it accords the emperor a divine mission, it so hedges his power about with moral restrictions and qualifications that strong-minded emperors such as Emperor Wu, while a patron of the Confucianists, found it necessary to act quite contrary to their tenets in practice. Confucianism, in its political thought, is much more the philosophy of the officialdom, the bureaucrats, accepting the hierarchical form of imperial government and of society as a whole, but insisting upon the moral qualifications of rulership, as well as upon the right to criticize and restrain the exercise of absolute power. In this endeavor it makes full use of the appeal to tradition (of which it, as the guardian and interpreter of the ancient texts, is the arbiter), curbing imperial lavishness by a reminder of the simple life of old, insisting upon the importance of ministers and counselors in government, making not noble birth but scholastic achievement the requisite for entrance into official position, effectively wrecking measures it does not approve by declaring them at variance with ancient practices, and even reserving to itself the right to judge whether a ruler is morally fit to hold the throne. These literati, moreover, as the only men capable of handling records, regulations, edicts, and the other necessary papers of a highly organized central government, were indispensable to any ruler. As a famous Confucianist pointed out to the founder of the Han, though he might have won the empire on horseback, he assuredly could not rule it from horseback.

Finally, the Confucianists were the teachers and guardians of the ancient literature, originally not exclusively Confucian, but including the best in China's entire literary heritage, a mass of writings incorporating ideas borrowed from many different schools and philosophies which had been absorbed into Confucianism. Thus Confucianism gained supremacy not by extinguishing its rivals but by adapting much of their thought to its own system. Once established as the state philosophy, with the examination system and the imperial university to ensure continuance of its teachings, its position was so well consolidated that it was never displaced until the imperial system itself was discarded.

CHAPTER XIII

THE GREAT HAN HISTORIANS

The intellectual and literary glory of the Han found its highest expression in the two great histories of the period, the *Records of the Historian* (*Shih chi*) and the *History of the Former Han Dynasty* (*Han shu*). Few works outside the Classics themselves have been so much admired, studied, and often in part committed to memory by the Chinese. They set the pattern for all later Chinese histories, establishing a precedent which was responsible for giving to the Chinese nation the most complete and unbroken record of its past possessed by any people.

From very early times the Chinese seem to have possessed an extraordinary love and respect for history. According to tradition even the earliest dynasties had their official historians who were closely associated with astronomical affairs and divination. They were also responsible for acting as mentors to the rulers, instructing them in the lessons of the past, and recording their deeds for the judgment of posterity. Confucianism with its humanistic emphasis did much to encourage and develop this sense of history and feeling for the past. Two of the five Confucian Classics, the *Book of History* and the *Spring and Autumn Annals,* traditionally believed to have been compiled and edited by Confucius, are works of history, and the study of history and appeal to historical example have always been among the principal techniques of Confucian instruction and argumentation.

The *History of the Former Han Dynasty* states of these two historical Classics: "The *Book of History* broadens one's information and is the practice of wisdom; the *Spring and Autumn Annals* passes moral judgments on events and is the symbol of good faith." [1]

[1] *Han shu,* 30:12b.

The function of history, as seen in this statement, is twofold: to impart information and to give moral instruction, as embodied in the traditions of the two Classics. These two traditions, one representing the objective transmission of the words and deeds of history, the other the illustration of moral principles through historical incident, run through all Chinese historiography. In practice the former tradition has dominated. The common method of the Chinese historian has been to transmit verbatim as nearly as possible what his sources tell him, adding only such background and connecting narrative as may be necessary. For example, the historian does not tell us that the emperor issued an edict to such and such an effect, but reproduces the edict in part or in whole so that we may read what he said for ourselves. Since the Chinese historian was often working in an official capacity, he had access to government files of memorials, edicts, court decisions, and other papers that made such a procedure possible. His own job then became one of selecting the most pertinent documents and arranging them in a way best calculated to demonstrate the cause and effect of events. If in addition he wished to inject his own personal opinion, he usually marked it clearly by some conventional literary device so that the reader could readily distinguish it.

The tradition of the *Spring and Autumn Annals,* the didactic function of history, was at the same time by no means forgotten. Only a sage might dare actually to record moral judgments in his writing, as Confucius was supposed to have done in the *Spring and Autumn Annals.* But all men were free to, in fact ought to, study the histories of the past carefully and thoughtfully to deduce for themselves the moral lessons embodied there, to descry the pattern hidden beneath the succession of recorded events. For, like all the rest of creation, history, according to Chinese thought, must have an underlying order. Han philosophy of history, influenced by yin-yang and five agents theories, conceived of history as a cyclical succession of eras proceeding in a fixed order. Not only this succession, but all of history is a manifestation of the universal process of change, growth, and decay, constantly coming to realization in the course of human events. Thus, for the Chinese, philosophically and morally, the proper study of mankind is man, and man as revealed in the pages of history.

THE RECORDS OF THE HISTORIAN

During the Chou there were numerous chronicles and works of history compiled by the feudal states and the various schools of philosophy. But until the Han, when the Chinese for the first time acquired a sense of national and cultural unity, no attempt was ever made to produce a comprehensive history of the entire past of the nation. The *Shih chi* or *Records of the Historian* was begun by Ssu-ma T'an (d. 110 B.C.), Grand Historian under Emperor Wu, and carried on and brought to completion by his son, Ssu-ma Ch'ien (145?–90? B.C.), who succeeded his father in the position of Grand Historian. Comprising 130 chapters, it covers the history of the Chinese people from the Yellow Emperor to the time of the historians.

Ssu-ma Ch'ien divided his material into five sections: Basic Annals, Chronological Tables, Treatises, Hereditary Houses, and Memoirs. This arrangement, with various modifications, has been followed by almost all later official historians. In later histories the section called Basic Annals might better be referred to as Imperial Annals, since it deals only with acts of the officially reigning emperors. Ssu-ma Ch'ien, however, did not so confine himself, but included here the account of Hsiang Yü who, though not officially emperor, in actuality ruled the country. The Chronological Tables need little explanation, being tables of dates for important events. The Treatises, one of the most valuable sections of the work, are essays devoted to the history and description of important subjects. Below are listed the eight Treatises of the *Shih chi* together with those of the *Han shu* which were based upon *Shih chi* material.

Shih chi Treatises	*Han shu Treatises*
Rites	The Calendar
Music	Rites and Music
The Pitch-pipes	Punishments and Laws
The Calendar	Food and Money (Economics)
Astronomy	State Sacrifices
Sacrifices of Feng and Shan	Astronomy
The Yellow River and Canals	Five Agents (Portents)
Balance of Commerce (Economics)	Geography
	Land Drainage
	Literature

The Hereditary Houses, being largely accounts of feudal families, were not usually included in histories dealing with later periods. The chapters of the Memoirs are generally devoted to the lives of famous men—military leaders, politicians, philosophers, etc. Some chapters deal with particular groups such as famous assassins, upright officials, tyrannical officials, wandering knights, imperial favorites, merchants, etc. Others treat non-Chinese lands and peoples such as Korea, southeast China, Ferghana, etc. The concluding chapter is the biography of the historians themselves.

SSU-MA CH'IEN
The Sacred Duty of the Historian

The following excerpt from the autobiography of Ssu-ma Ch'ien relates the words of Ssu-ma T'an to his son as he lay dying.
[From *Shih chi* 130:8a–b, 30b–32a]

The Grand Historian [Ssu-ma T'an] grasped my hand and said weeping: "Our ancestors were Grand Historians for the House of Chou. From the most ancient times they were eminent and renowned when in the days of Yü and Hsia they were in charge of astronomical affairs. In later ages our family declined. Will this tradition end with me? If you in turn become Grand Historian, you must continue the work of our ancestors. . . . When you become Grand Historian, you must not forget what I have desired to expound and write. Now filial piety begins with the serving of your parents; next you must serve your sovereign; and finally you must make something of yourself, that your name may go down through the ages to the glory of your father and mother. This is the most important part of filial piety. Everyone praises the Duke of Chou, saying that he was able to expound in word and song the virtues of King Wen and King Wu, publishing abroad the Odes of Chou and Shao; he set forth the thoughts and ideals of T'ai-wang and Wang Chi, extending his words back to King Liu and paying honor to Hou Chi [ancestors of the Chou dynasty]. After the reigns of Yu and Li the way of the ancient kings fell into disuse and rites and music declined. Confucius revived the old ways and restored what had been abandoned, expounding the *Odes* and *History* and making the *Spring and Autumn Annals*. From that time until today men of learning have taken these as their models. It has now been over four hundred years since the capture of the unicorn [481 B.C., end of the Spring and Autumn period]. The various feudal states have merged together, and the old records and chronicles have become scattered and lost. Now the House of Han has arisen and all the world is united under one rule. I have been Grand Historian, and yet I have failed to make a record of all the enlightened rulers and wise lords, the faithful ministers and gentlemen who were ready to die for duty. I am fearful that the historical materials will be neglected and lost. You must remember and think of this!"

I bowed my head and wept, saying: "I, your son, am ignorant and unworthy, but I shall endeavor to set forth in full the reports of antiquity which have come down from our ancestors. I shall not dare to be remiss!" [130:8a–b]

This our house of Han has succeeded the descendants of the Five Emperors and carried on the task of unification of the Three Dynasties. The ways of Chou fell into disuse and the Ch'in scattered and discarded the old writings and burned and destroyed the *Odes* and the *History*. Therefore the plans and records of the Illustrious Hall and the stone rooms, of the metal caskets and jade tablets, became lost or confused.

Then the Han arose and Hsiao Ho put in order the laws and commandments; Han Hsin set forth the rules of warfare; Chang Ts'ang made the regulations and standards; and Shu-sun T'ung settled questions of rites and ceremonies. At this time the art of letters began again to flourish and advance and the *Odes* and *History* gradually reappeared. From the time when Ts'ao Ts'an put into practice Master Kai's teachings of the Yellow Emperor and Lao Tzu, when Chia Sheng and Ch'ao Ts'o expounded the doctrines of the Legalist philosophers Shen and Shang, and Kung-sun Hung achieved eminence for his Confucian learning, a period of some one hundred years, the books that survived and records of past affairs were all without exception gathered together by the Grand Historian. The Grand Historians, father and son, each in turn held and carried on the position. . . .

I have sought out and gathered together the ancient traditions of the empire which were scattered and lost. Of the great deeds of kings I have searched the beginnings and examined the ends; I have seen their times of prosperity and observed their decline. Of the affairs that I have discussed and examined, I have made a general survey of the Three

Dynasties and a record of the Ch'in and Han, extending in all back as far as Hsien Yüan [the Yellow Emperor] and coming down to the present, set forth in twelve Basic Annals. After this had been put in order and completed, because there were differences in chronology for the same periods and the dates were not always clear, I made the ten Chronological Tables. Of the changes of rites and music, the improvements and revisions of the pitch-pipes and calendar, military power, mountains and rivers, spirits and gods, the relationships between heaven and man, the economic practices handed down and changed age by age, I have made the eight Treatises. As the twenty-eight constellations revolve about the North Star, as the thirty spokes of a wheel come together at the hub, revolving endlessly without stop, so the ministers, assisting like arms and legs, faithful and trustworthy, in true moral spirit serve their lord and ruler: of them I made the thirty Hereditary Houses. Upholding duty, masterful and sure, not allowing themselves to miss their opportunities, they made a name for themselves in the world: of such men I made the seventy Memoirs. In all one hundred and thirty chapters, 526,500 words, this is the book of the Grand Historian, compiled in order to repair omissions and amplify the Six Disciplines. It is the work of one family, designed to supplement the various interpretations of the Six Classics and to put into order the miscellaneous sayings of the hundred schools. [30b–32a]

In 98 B.C., because he dared to speak out in defense of a military leader whom Emperor Wu and the rest of the court believed had disgraced himself, Ssu-ma Ch'ien was condemned to suffer the punishment of castration. The following excerpt is from a famous letter which the historian wrote to a friend relating the circumstances of his disgrace and explaining why it was he chose to suffer the ignominy of castration rather than commit suicide. He consoles himself with the memory of the great men of the past who, in the midst of misfortune, produced writings which have guaranteed their everlasting fame, as he believes his history will do for him.

[From *Han shu*, 62:17b–21b]

My father had no great deeds that entitled him to receive territories or privileges from the emperor. He dealt with affairs of astronomy and the calendar, which are close to divination and the worship of the spirits. He was kept for the sport and amusement of the emperor, treated the same as the musicians and jesters, and made light of by the vulgar men of his day. If I fell before the law and were executed, it would make no more difference to most people than one hair off nine oxen, for I was nothing but a mere ant to them. The world would not rank me among those men who were able to die for their ideals, but would believe simply that my wisdom was exhausted and my crime great, that I had been unable to escape penalty and in the end had gone to my death. Why? Because all my past actions had brought this on me, they would say.

A man has only one death. That death may be as weighty as Mount T'ai, or it may be as light as a goose feather. It all depends upon the way he uses it. . . . It is the nature of every man to love life and hate death, to think of his relatives and look after his wife and children. Only when a man is moved by higher principles is this not so. Then there are things which he must do. . . . The brave man does not always die for honor, while even the coward may fulfill his duty. Each takes a different way to exert himself. Though I might be weak and cowardly and seek shamefully to prolong my life, yet I know full well the difference between what ought to be followed and what rejected. How could I bring myself to sink into the shame of ropes and bonds? If even the lowest slave and scullery maid can bear to commit suicide, why should not one like myself be able to do what has to be done? But the reason I have not refused to bear these ills and have continued to live, dwelling among this filth, is that I grieve that I have things in my heart that I have not been able to express fully, and I am shamed to think that after I am gone my writings will not be known to posterity.

Too numerous to record are the men of ancient time who were rich and noble and whose names have yet vanished away. It is only those who were masterful and sure, the truly extraordinary men, who are still remembered. When the Earl of the West was imprisoned at Yu-li, he expanded the *Changes;* Confucius was in distress and he made the *Spring and Autumn Annals;* Ch'ü Yüan was banished and he composed his poem "Encountering Sorrow"; after Tso Ch'iu lost his sight he composed the *Narratives of the States;* when Sun Tzu had had his feet amputated he set forth the *Art of War;* Lü Pu-wei was banished to Shu but his *Lü-lan* has been handed down through the ages; while Han Fei Tzu was held prisoner in Ch'in he wrote "The Difficulties of Disputation" and "The Sorrow of Standing Alone"; most of the three hundred poems of the *Book of Odes* were written when the sages poured forth their anger and dissatisfaction. All these men had a rankling in their hearts, for they were not able to accomplish what they wished. Therefore they wrote of past affairs in order to pass on their thoughts to future generations. . . .

I too have ventured not to be modest but have entrusted myself to my useless writings. I have gathered up and brought together the old traditions of the world which were scattered and lost. I have examined the deeds and events of the past and investigated the principles behind their success and failure, their rise and decay, in one hundred and thirty chapters. I wished to examine into all that concerns heaven and man, to penetrate the changes of the past and present, completing all as the work of one family. But before I had finished my rough manuscript, I met with this calamity. It is because I regretted that it had not been completed that I submitted to the extreme penalty without rancor. When I have truly completed this work, I shall deposit it in some safe place. If it may be handed down to men who will appreciate it and penetrate to the villages and great cities, then though I should suffer a thousand mutilations, what regret would I have?

Methods of the Historian

On the whole Ssu-ma Ch'ien in his handling of sources displays careful judgment and a laudable skepticism not always equalled by his successors. In the following preface to the first of his Chronological Tables he explains some of the methods and ideals which guide his work.

[From *Shih chi*, 13:1a–b]

The chronicles of the Five Emperors and the Three Dynasties extend back to high antiquity. For the Yin dynasty and before, we cannot compile any genealogical records of the feudal lords, though from the Chou on down they can usually be constructed. When Confucius arranged the *Spring and Autumn Annals* from the old historical texts, he noted the first year of a reign, the time when the year began, and the day and month for each entry; such was his exactitude. However, when he wrote his prefaces to the *Book of History,* he made only general references and did not mention year and month. Perhaps he had some material, but in many cases there were gaps and it was impossible to record exactly. Therefore, when there was a question of doubt, he recorded it as doubtful; such was his circumspection. I have read the genealogical records which have complete dates entered from the Yellow Emperor on down. I have examined these chronologies and genealogies, as well as the "Record of the Cycle of the Five Agents." But these ancient texts disagree and contradict each other throughout. I can hardly consider as meaningless the example of the Master in not attempting to assign the exact year and month to events. Thus, basing my work on the "Virtues of the Five Emperors," I have made this chronological table of the generations from the Yellow Emperor down to the era Kung-ho [841 B.C.].

Ssu-ma Ch'ien, however, was no mere copier of ancient texts. In 138 B.C. an envoy, Chang Ch'ien, was sent on a diplomatic mission as far as western Turkestan. The information he brought back from his travels changed the whole Chinese conception of the geography of lands to the west. Ssu-ma Ch'ien used this information as the basis for a chapter on Ferghana and the other countries of central Asia. Following are his concluding remarks to the chapter.

[From *Shih chi*, 123:21a–b]

The "Basic Annals of Emperor Yü" records that the source of the Yellow River is in the K'un-lun Mountains, mountains some 2,500 *li* high, the place where the sun and the moon in turn go to hide when they are not shining. It is said that on their heights are to be found the Fountain of Sweet Water and the Pool of Jade. Now since Chang Ch'ien visited Bactria, the Yellow River has been traced to its source, and no one has found any such K'un-lun Mountains as the "Basic Annals" records. Therefore, what the *Book of History* states about the mountains and rivers of the nine provinces of China is nearer the truth, while when it comes to the wonders mentioned in the "Basic Annals of Emperor Yü" or the *Classic of Hills and Seas,* I cannot accept them.

The historical labors of Ssu-ma Ch'ien were admirably carried on by Pan Piao (A.D. 3–54) and his son Pan Ku (A.D. 32–92), principal authors of the *Han shu* or *History of the Former Han Dynasty*. At the end of his biography of Ssu-ma Ch'ien, Pan Ku assesses the work of his predecessor.

[From Pan Ku, *Han shu*, 62:22a–23a]

When it comes to the way in which he has extracted from the Classics, selected from the commentaries, and assessed and disposed of material from the various schools of philosophy, Ch'ien is often careless and sketchy and takes improper liberties with his sources. With his diligence he had browsed very widely in books, threaded his way through the Classics and commentaries and galloped up and down from the past to the present, covering a period of several thousand years. But his judgments stray rather often from those of the sage. . . . Yet Liu Hsiang, Yang Hsiung, and other men of wide learning all praise Ch'ien as a man of excellent ability as an historian and testify to his skill in setting forth events and their causes. He discourses without sounding wordy; he is simple without being rustic. His writing is direct and his facts sound. He does not falsify what is beautiful, nor does he conceal what is evil. Therefore his may be termed a "true record."

The Writing of the First Dynastic History

The following extracts are from the biographies of Pan Piao and Pan Ku in the *History of the Latter Han Dynasty*. It was apparently Pan Piao's intention only to continue the writing of history from the point at which Ssu-ma Ch'ien had stopped. But Pan Ku conceived the idea of one unified work covering the entire Former Han period. His *Han shu*, covering the complete span of one dynasty, has been the model for all the later so-called "dynastic histories" compiled to cover every reigning house from Pan Ku's time down to the founding of the Republic.

[From *Hou Han shu*, 40A:2b–3a, 11b–12b]

Pan Piao had great talent and was fond of writing, devoting himself solely to histories and chronicles. At the time of Emperor Wu, Ssu-ma Ch'ien wrote the *Shih chi*, but for the period from the era T'ai-ch'u [104–101 B.C.] on, the volumes were lacking or had never been written. Men of later years who were interested in such things had made various attempts to continue the former work and add material on recent times, but for the most part the results were common and tasteless and completely unworthy to act as a continuation of Ssu-ma Ch'ien's work. Piao then took up this work, continuing and selecting material from earlier histories and supplementing it with various traditions, and composed a "Supplementary Chronicle" in several tens of chapters. [40A:2b–3a]

Pan Ku took the continuation of the former history which Pan Piao had written and, since it was incomplete, immersed himself in study and shaped its ideas, intending to bring it to completion. At this time, however, someone sent a letter to Emperor Hsien-tsung informing him that Pan Ku was privately revising and writing a national history. An order was issued to the prefecture for Ku's arrest, and he was bound and placed in prison in the capital and all his personal books were seized. Formerly there had been a man of Fu-feng, one Su Lang, who had been thrown into prison for deceitfully expounding charts and prophecies and had died there. Ku's younger brother, Ch'ao, fearing that in the prefectural inquiry Ku would not be able to make his case clear, hastened to the capital and sent a request to the emperor for an audience. There he explained in detail what Ku's intentions were in writing his work, and the prefecture also sent Ku's book. Emperor Hsien-tsung was amazed at it and summoned Ku to the Department for the Editing of Books where he was appointed one of the official historiographers of the Lan-t'ai. . . . The emperor charged him to complete the former history. . . . He selected material from earlier sources and gathered together oral traditions to complete his *History of the Former Han Dynasty,* beginning with Emperor Kao-tsu [r. 202–195 B.C.] and ending with the execution of Wang Mang [A.D. 22], some twelve generations, a period of 230 years. He ordered all events, imbued them with the spirit of the Five Classics, and penetrated into all things above and below, completing season-by-season Annals, Chronological Tables, Treatises and Memoirs, one hundred chapters in all. From the time when Ku first received the imperial appointment during the Yung-p'ing era, when he was immersed in study and gathering ideas, until the Chien-ch'u era, when his work was finally completed, was a period of over twenty years. His own age greatly honored his work and among men of learning there were none who did not read and praise it. [40A:11b–12b]

PART THREE
NEO-TAOISM AND BUDDHISM

A.D.

c.65	First reference to Buddhism in China.
c.150	An Shih-kao, Buddhist missionary, in China.
220–280	The Three Kingdoms—Wei, Shu, Wu.
280–420	Chin dynasty.
317	North China abandoned to barbarians.
399–414	Pilgrimage of Fa-hsien to Central Asia and India.
403	Hui-yüan argues at court that Buddhist monks be exempted from bowing to the emperor.
405	Kumārajīva (344–413) appointed National Preceptor.
440	State patronage of Taoism.
542	T'an-luan (476–542), patriarch of Pure Land sect.
575	T'ien-t'ai school of Buddhism founded by Chih-k'ai (531–597).
589–618	Sui dynasty.
618–906	T'ang dynasty.
623	Chi-tsang (549–623), exponent of Mādhyamika school and commentator on Three Treatises.
629	Pilgrimage of Hsüan-tsang (596–664) to India begun.
641	Chinese Buddhist princess married to first king of Tibet.
645	Hsüan-tsang returns from India. Death of Tao-ch'o, Pure Land patriarch and author of *Compendium on the Happy Land.*
666	Lao Tzu canonized by T'ang dynasty as Most High Emperor of Mystic Origin.
671	Pilgrimage to India begun by I-ching.
684–705	Reign of Empress Wu.
693	Empress adopts Buddhist title "Divine Empress Who Rules the Universe" (Chakravartin Deva Empress).
699	"Golden lion" sermon by Fa-tsang (643–712).
713	Hui-neng (638–713), Sixth Ch'an Patriarch.
755	An Lu-shan rebellion.
760	Shen-hui (d. 760), Ch'an master.
845	Official repression of Buddhism.
867	I-hsüan (d. 867), founder of the Lin-chi school of Ch'an Buddhism.
868	Printing of Diamond Sūtra.
869	Liang-chieh (807–869), founder of Ts'ao-tung school of Ch'an Buddhism.
972	Printing of Buddhist canon begun.

CHAPTER XIV

NEO-TAOISM

For almost four centuries after the disintegration of the Han dynasty China was to be without that unity and stability which had seemed to be its chief characteristics. Instead, during this period of the Three Kingdoms and Six Dynasties (A.D. 220–589), China's division into numerous contending states and successive ruling houses brought her perilously close to the loss of her national and cultural identity. To some extent the dominant intellectual tradition suffered in this process. Owing to the prevailing disunity and disruption, the situation was hardly favorable to the kind of scholarly enterprise which the imperial court had once encouraged, while at the same time Confucianism was deprived of much of its importance as a state cult. The textual study and systematizing of the Classics, which had absorbed many of the best minds under the Han, shifted to a different plane now that classical scholarship served no vital function to state or society. It was under such circumstances that intellectual interest in Taoism revived and a foreign religion, Buddhism, for the first time gained a foothold among both the masses and the educated class.

We must realize, however, that the revival of "unorthodox" philosophies and the powerful intrusion of a new religion do not signify a complete redirection of Chinese thought, breaking entirely with the past. For in spite of Confucianism's decline as a bureaucratic institution, its ideals and basic principles remained a contributing factor to the new attempts at adapting Taoism and Buddhism to the needs of the age. Thus in this period, as in so many others in Chinese history, there is a strong tendency toward syncretism.

TAOISM IN PHILOSOPHY

Neo-Taoism is a new term applied to a loose but identifiable movement
in the third and fourth centuries centering around the study of the *Lao
Tzu* (*Tao-te ching*) and *Chuang Tzu*. It was a many-sided movement
finding expression in the spheres of metaphysics, aesthetics, and religion.
In the first sphere it was known as *hsüan-hsüeh,* the study of abstruse or
mysterious truths, as pursued by many scholars whose ideas were developed chiefly in commentaries on the *Lao Tzu* and *Chuang Tzu*.
Among the most important of these were Wang Pi (A.D. 226–249), Ho
Yen (d. A.D. 249), and Kuo Hsiang (d. A.D. 312). Although Wang Pi and
Ho Yen were ardent admirers of Lao Tzu and Chuang Tzu, their aim
was to give new meaning to Confucian texts, for which they wrote commentaries using Taoist terms and concepts, while at the same time reinterpreting Taoism in terms of the social and moral philosophy of Confucianism. Hence to them the key concept of Taoism, *wu* (literally,
nonexistence), is not nothingness, but pure being, which transcends
forms and names, and precisely because it is absolute and complete, can
accomplish everything. The sage is not one who withdraws into the life
of a hermit, but a man of social and political achievements, although these
achievements must be brought about through *wu-wei,* "nonaction" or
"taking no [unnatural] action."

KUO HSIANG
Commentary on the Chuang Tzu

In the commentary on the *Chuang Tzu* by Kuo Hsiang and his collaborator,
Hsiang Hsiu (first half of third century), the positive note is struck in the
equal emphasis on both the internal and external life, for to Kuo Hsiang the
sage moves in the realm of human affairs as well as in the transcendental
world. At the same time, Chuang Tzu's ideas of self-transformation and contentment are strongly stressed, becoming Kuo Hsiang's central themes.

NATURE AND NONEXISTENCE
[From Commentary on *Chuang Tzu,* Sec. 1, 1:8b; Sec. 2, 1:21a–23a; Sec.
22, 7:54b–55b]

The music of nature is not an entity existing outside of things. The different apertures, the pipes and flutes and the like, in combination with

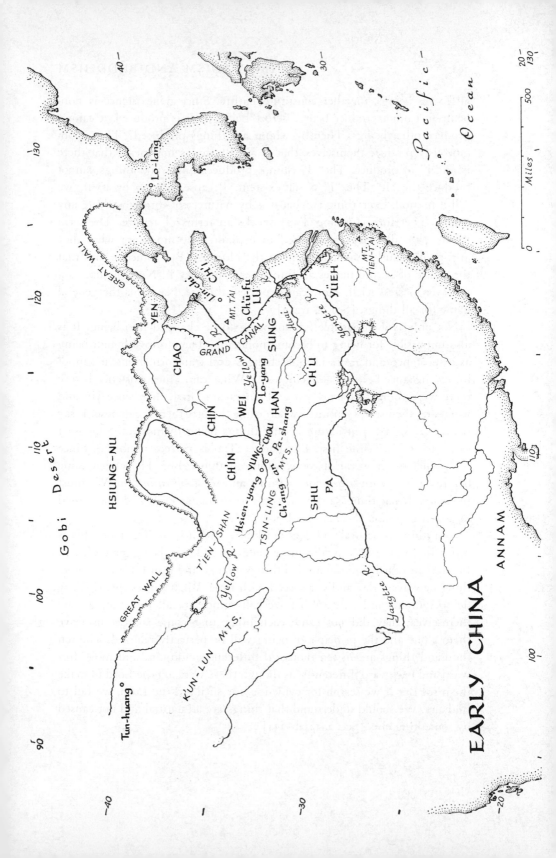

EARLY CHINA

Gobi Desert

Tun-huang °

GREAT WALL

K'UN-LUN MTS.

T'IEN-SHAN

Yellow R.

HSIUNG-NU

CHAO

CHIN

CH'IN

Hsien-yang °

TSIN-LING MTS.

Ch'ang-an ° ° Pa-shang

SHU

PA

Yangtze R.

ANNAM

WEI

Yellow R.

YUNG-CHOU

° Lo-yang

CHOU

HAN

SUNG

Huai R.

CH'U

Yangtze R.

YEN

GRAND CANAL

CHI

° Lin-chih

△ MT. TAI

° Chü-fu

LU

YÜEH

△ MT. TIEN-TAI

° Lo-lang

GREAT WALL

Pacific Ocean

Miles

0   500

90   100   110   120   130

40   30   20

-40   -30   -20

all living beings, together constitute nature. Since nonexistence is non-being, it cannot produce being. Before being itself is produced, it cannot produce other beings. Then by whom are things produced? They spontaneously produce themselves, that is all. By this is not meant that there is an "I" to produce. The "I" cannot produce things and things cannot produce the "I." The "I" is self-existent. Because it is so by itself, we call it natural. Everything is what it is by nature, not through taking any action. Therefore [Chuang Tzu] speaks in terms of nature. The term nature [literally Heaven] is used to explain that things are what they are spontaneously, and not to mean the blue sky. But someone says that the music of nature makes all things serve or obey it. Now, nature cannot even possess itself. How can it possess things? Nature is the general name for all things. [Sec. 2, 1:21a]

Not only is it impossible for nonbeing to be changed into being. It is also impossible for being to become nonbeing. Therefore, although being as a substance undergoes infinite changes and transformations, it cannot in any instance become nonbeing. . . . What came into existence before there were things? If I say yin and yang came first, then since yin and yang are themselves entities, what came before them? Suppose I say nature came first. But nature is only things being themselves. Suppose I say perfect Tao came first. But perfect Tao is perfect nonbeing. Since it is nonbeing, how can it come before anything else? Then what came before it? There must be another thing, and so on *ad infinitum*. We must understand that things are what they are spontaneously and not caused by something else. [Sec. 22, 7:54b–55b]

Everything is natural and does not know why it is so. The more things differ in corporeal form, the more they are alike in being natural. . . . Heaven and earth and the myriad things change and transform into something new every day and so proceed with time. What causes them? They do so spontaneously. . . . What we call things are all that they are by themselves; they did not cause each other to become so. Let us leave them alone and the principle of being will be perfectly realized. The ten thousand things are in ten thousand different conditions, and move forward and backward differently, as though there were a True Lord to make them so. But if we search for evidences for such a True Lord, we fail to find any. We should understand that things are all natural and not caused by something else. [Sec. 2, 1:22b–23a]

The universe is the general name for all things. They are the reality of the universe while nature is their norm. Being natural means to exist spontaneously without having to take any action. Therefore the fabulous *p'eng* bird can soar high and the quail can fly low, the cedrela can live for a long time and the mushroom for a short time. They are capable of doing these not because of their taking any action but because of their being natural. [Sec. 1, 1:8b]

SELF-TRANSFORMATION AND "TAKING NO ACTION"
> [From Commentary on *Chuang Tzu,* Sec. 1, 1:9b–10a; Sec. 2, 2:46b–47a;
> Sec. 11, 4:29a; Sec. 13, 5:25a–b]

If we insist on the conditions under which things develop and search for the cause thereof, such search and insistence will never end, until we come to something that is unconditioned, and then the principles of self-transformation will become clear. . . . There are people who say that the penumbra is conditioned by the shadow, the shadow by the body, and the body by the Creator. But let us ask whether there is a Creator or not. If not, how can he create things? If there is, he is incapable of materializing all the forms. Therefore before we can talk about creation, we must understand the fact that all forms materialize by themselves. If we go through the entire realm of existence, we shall see that there is nothing, not even the penumbra, that does not transform itself beyond the phenomenal world. Hence everything creates itself without the direction of any Creator. Since things create themselves, they are unconditioned. This is the norm of the universe. [Sec. 2, 2:46b–47a]

In the cutting of a tree the workman does not take any action; the only action he takes is in plying the ax. In the actual managing of affairs, the ruler does not take any action; the only action he takes is in employing his ministers. If the ministers can manage affairs, the ruler can employ ministers, the ax can cut the tree, and the workman can use the ax, each corresponding to his capacity, then the laws of nature will operate of themselves, not because someone takes action. If the ruler does the work of his ministers, he will no longer be the ruler, and if the ministers control the ruler's employment, they will no longer be ministers. Therefore when each attends to his own responsibility, both ruler and ruled will be contented and the principle of taking no action will be attained. [Sec. 13, 5:25a–b]

It is he who does no governing who can govern the empire. Therefore Yao governed by not governing; it was not because of his governing that his empire was governed. Now [the recluse] Hsü-yu only realized that since the empire was well-governed he should not replace Yao. He thought it was Yao who did the actual governing. Consequently he said to Yao: "You govern the empire." He should have forgotten such words and investigated into that condition of peace. Someone may say: "It was Yao who actually governed and put the empire in good order but it was Hsü-yu who enabled Yao to do so by refusing to govern himself." This is a great mistake. Yao was an adequate example of governing by not governing and acting by not acting. Why should we have to resort to Hsü-yu? Are we to insist that a man fold his arms and sit in silence in the middle of some mountain forest before we will say he is practicing "nonaction"? This is why the words of Lao Tzu and Chuang Tzu are rejected by responsible officials. This is why responsible officials insist on remaining in the realm of action without feeling any regret. [Sec. 1, 1:9b–10a]

By taking no action is not meant folding one's arms and closing one's mouth. If we simply let everything act by itself, it will be contented with its nature and destiny. To have no alternative but [to rule an empire] is not to be forced into doing so by power or punishment. If only Tao is embraced and simplicity cherished, and what has to be is allowed to run its maximum course, then the world will naturally be contented with itself. [Sec. 11, 4:29a]

CONTENTMENT
[From Commentary on *Chuang Tzu,* Sec. 1, 1:14a; Sec. 3, 2:1a–6b; Sec. 4, 3:28a; Sec. 9, 4:11b]

If a person is perfectly at ease with his spirit and physical power, whether he lifts something heavy or carries something light, it is due to the fact that he is using his strength to a desired degree. If a person loves fame and is fond of supremacy and is not satisfied even when he has broken his back in the attempt, it is due to the fact that human knowledge knows no limit. Therefore what is called knowledge is born of our losing our balance and will be eliminated when ultimate capacity is realized intuitively. Intuitively realizing ultimate capacity means allowing one's lot to reach its highest degree, and [in the case of lifting weights] not adding so much as an ounce beyond that. Therefore though a person carries ten thousand pounds, if it is equal to his capacity he will suddenly forget the weight upon his body. Though a person attends to ten thousand matters [if his capacity is equal to them] he will be utterly unaware that the affairs are upon him. These are the fundamentals for the cultivation of life. . . . If one attains the Mean and intuitively realizes the proper limit, everything can be done. The cultivation of life does not seek to exceed one's lot but to preserve the principle of things and to live out one's allotted span of life. [Sec. 3, 2:1a–2a]

Joy and sorrow are the results of gains and losses. A gentleman who profoundly penetrates all things and is in harmony with their transformations will be contented with whatever time may bring. He follows the course of nature in whatever situation he may be. He will be intuitively united with creation. He will be himself wherever he may be. Where does gain or loss, life or death, come in? Therefore, if one lets what he has received from nature take its own course, there will be no place for joy or sorrow. [Sec. 3, 2:6a–b]

Allow the foot to walk according to its capacity, and let the hand grasp according to its strength. Listen to what the ear hears and see what the eye sees. In knowing, stop at what cannot be known. In action, stop at what cannot be done. Employ [the faculties] as they would use themselves. Do things that would be done by themselves. Be unrestrained within one's lot but do not attempt the least outside of it. This is the easiest way of taking no [unnatural] action. There has never been a case of taking no action and yet of one's nature and life not being preserved, and I have never heard of any principle according to which the preservation of nature and life is not a blessing. [Sec. 4, 3:28a]

The expert driver utilizes the natural capacity of horses to its limit. To use the capacity to its limit lies in letting it take its own course. If forced to run at a rapid pace, with the expectation that they can exceed their capacity, horses will be unable to bear it and many will die. On the other hand, if both worn-out and thoroughbred horses are allowed to use their proper strength and to adapt their pace to their given lot, even if they travel to the borders of the country, their nature will be fully preserved. But there are those who, upon hearing the doctrine of allowing the nature of horses to take its own course, will say: "Then set the horses free and do not ride on them"; and there are those who, upon hearing the doctrine of taking no action, will immediately say: "It is better to lie down than to walk." Why are they so much off the track and unable to return? In this they have missed Chuang Tzu's ideas to a very high degree. [Sec. 9, 4:11b]

If one is contented wherever he goes, he will be at ease wherever he may be. Even life and death cannot affect him, much less flood or fire. The perfect man is not besieged by calamities, not because he escapes from them but because he advances the principles of things and goes forward and naturally comes into union with good fortune. [Sec. 1, 1:14a]

SOCIETY AND GOVERNMENT
    [From Commentary on *Chuang Tzu,* Sec. 1, 1:11b, 14b; Sec. 4, 2:7a–25a;
    Sec. 6, 3:19a; Sec. 13, 5:35a; Sec. 14, 5:42a, 44b]

Man in society cannot get away from his fellow beings. The changes in society vary from generation to generation according to different standards. Only those who have no minds of their own and do not use their own judgment can adapt themselves to changes and not be burdened by them. [Sec. 4, 2:7a]

Events that took place in the past have disappeared with the past. Some may be transmitted to us [in writing], but can this make the past exist in the present? The past is not in the present and even every present is soon changed. Therefore only when one abandons the pursuit of knowledge, lets nature take its own course, and changes with the times, can he be perfect. [Sec. 13, 5:35a]

Humanity and righteousness are principles of human nature. Human nature undergoes changes and is different past and present. If one takes a temporary abode in a thing and then moves on, he will intuit [the reality of things]. If, however, he stops and is confined to one place, he will develop prejudices. Prejudices will result in hypocrisy, and hypocrisy will result in many reproaches. [Sec. 14, 5:44b]

To cry as people cry is a manifestation of the mundane world. To identify life and death, forget joy and sorrow, and be able to sing in the presence of the corpse is the perfection of transcendental existence. . . . Therefore the principles of things have their ultimates, and internal and external reality are to be intuited by means of each other. There has never been a person who has roamed over the entire realm of external reality and yet has not intuited internal reality, nor has there been anyone who could intuit internal reality and yet did not roam over the realm of external reality. [Sec. 6, 3:19a]

Although the sage is in the midst of government, his mind seems to be in the mountain forest. . . . His abode is in the myriad things, but it does not mean that he does not wander freely. [Sec. 1, 1:11b, 14b]

When a thousand people gather together with no one as their leader, they will be either unruly or disorganized. Therefore when there are many virtuous people, there should not be many rulers, but when there is no virtuous person, there should be a ruler. This is the principle of Heaven and man and the most proper thing to do. [Sec. 4, 2:16b]

The ceremonies of ancient kings were intended to meet the needs of the time. When the time has past and the ceremonies are still not cast away, they will become an evil influence to the people and serve to hasten the start of affectations and imitation. [Sec. 14, 5:42a]

When the king does not make himself useful in the various offices, the various officials will manage their own affairs. Those with clear vision will do the seeing, those with sharp ears will do the listening, the wise will do the planning, and the strong will provide protection. What need is there to take any action? Only profound silence, that is all. [Sec. 4, 2:25a]

HSI K'ANG

On Partiality

From the third to the sixth centuries it was fashionable for men of literary and philosophical interests to gather in small coteries and engage in what is called by the Chinese "ch'ing-t'an" or "pure conversation"—conversation which is highly witty, refined, and concerned with philosophical matters transcending the concerns and conventions of the mundane world. Many of the literati such as Wang Pi and Ho Yen were members of such groups, as were many eminent Buddhist monks. The most famous of these groups was the so-called "Seven Sages of the Bamboo Grove" which included Juan Chi, Hsi K'ang, and Hsiang Hsiu. For many years these friends met in the bamboo groves to the north of Lo-yang, the capital of the state of Wei, and behaved with utter disregard for social and intellectual convention. They engaged in philosophical discussions inspired by the freedom and transcendentalism of Neo-Taoist thought. The following excerpts are from the writings of one of this famous group, Hsi K'ang (A.D. 232–262).

[From Shih-ssu lun, in Hsi Chung-san chi, 6:1a–b]

A gentleman is so called because he is not fixed in his mind as to what is right and wrong, but acts without violating Tao. How is this? He whose vital force is tranquil and whose spirit is absolutely peaceful and pure does not occupy his mind with attachments. And he whose physical faculties are clear and whose mental faculties are enlightened does not allow his feelings to be bound by desires. Since his mind is not occupied with attachments, he is able to transcend the established doctrines of social relations and let nature take its own course. And since his feelings are not bound by desires, he is able to discern what is noble and what is lowly and be in harmony with the feelings of people and things. Because he is in harmony with the feelings of people, he does not violate the Great Tao, and because he transcends social ranks and lets his mind take its own course he is not predetermined about what is right and what is wrong. Therefore when we talk about the gentleman, absence of predetermination is the point of fundamental importance and harmony with things is the point of excellence. When we talk about the inferior man, we consider his concealment of feelings as wrong and his violation of Tao as a defect.

On the Nourishment of Life
[From *"Nan 'Yang-sheng lun'"* in *Hsi Chung-san chi,* 4:4b–5a]

Obey laws and follow principles so as not to fall into the net [of the law]. Honor the self for its freedom from crime, and enjoy peaceful leisure in the lack of burden. Roam in the realm of truth and righteousness, and lie down and rest in a humble abode. Be quiet, be at ease, and have nothing to thwart your wishes, and then your spirit and vital force will be in harmonious order. Is it necessary to have glory and splendor before one has honor? Cultivate the field to raise food and weave silk for clothing. When these are sufficient, leave the wealth of the world alone. Do as a thirsty person drinking from a river. He drinks happily enough, but does not covet the voluminous flow. Does one have to depend on an accumulation to be wealthy? This is how the gentleman exercises his mind for he regards rank and position as a tumor and material wealth as dirt and dust. What is the use of wealth and honor to him?

What is difficult to acquire in the world is neither wealth nor glory, but a sense of contentment. If one is contented, though he has only a small plot to cultivate, a coarse garment to wear, and beans to eat, in no case is he not satisfied. If one is discontented, though the whole world supports

him and all things serve him, he is still not gratified. Thus it is that the
contented needs nothing from the outside whereas the discontented needs
everything from the outside. Needing everything, he is always in want no
matter where he goes. Needing nothing, he lacks nothing regardless of
where he may be. If he does not indulge his will because he enjoys
splendor and glory, nor chase after vulgarity because he lives in obscurity,
but moves and has his being with all things as one and cannot be either
favored or disgraced, he is then really honored and wealthy. . . . This is
what the *Lao Tzu* means when it says: "There is no greater happiness
than freedom from worry, and there is no greater wealth than contentment."

The Lieh Tzu

This work, though traditionally attributed to the philosopher Lieh Yü-k'ao
(c.450–375 B.C.) is actually by a Neo-Taoist writer of the third century A.D.
and expresses the attitude of fatalism characteristic of some of the thinkers of
this school.

[From *Lieh Tzu,* 1:1a–b, 6:1a]

[As the *Chuang Tzu* says]: "There is creation which is itself uncreated"
[Ch. 6], and "there is transformation which is itself not transformed" [Ch.
22]. The uncreated is able to create and recreate, and the nontransformed
is able to transform and retransform. That which is created cannot help
producing, and the transformed cannot help transforming. Hence there
is constant production and transformation. By this is meant that there is
no time without production or transformation, as in [the production of]
yin and yang and in [the transformation of] the four seasons. The uncreated, we may assume, is One and has neither beginning nor end. The
nontransformed goes to and fro. The range [of what goes to and fro] is
illimitable. The Way of the One that has neither beginning nor end is
inexhaustible. The *Book of the Yellow Emperor* says: "The Spirit of the
Valley never dies. It is called the Profound Mother. The gate of the
Profound Mother is called the root of Heaven and earth. It is continuous
and seems to be always existing. It can be used forever without being
worn out." [1] Therefore that which creates things is itself uncreated, and
that which transforms things is itself nontransformed. Creation, trans-

---

[1] *Lao Tzu. 6.*

formation, form, appearance, wisdom, energy, decline, cessation—all by itself. It is wrong to say that any of these is achieved through external effort. [1:1a–b]

Effort said to Fate: How can your achievement be compared to mine?

Fate said: What have you done for things that you wish to compare yourself with me?

Effort said: Longevity, brevity of life, obscurity, prominence, honor, humble station, poverty, and success are all within my power.

Fate said: P'eng-tzu's wisdom was not superior to that of Yao and Shun, but he enjoyed a longevity of 800 years. The talent of Yen Hui [Confucius' favorite pupil] was not inferior to those of the multitude, yet he lived for only thirty-two years. . . . If such things are within your power, why is it that you allot long life to P'eng-tzu but short life to Yen Hui; that you award obscurity to the sage and prominence to the stupid, poverty to the good and wealth to the wicked?

Effort said: Is it true then, as you say, that I have no influence over the way things are? Are they under your control?

Fate said: Since I am called Fate, how can I have any control? If a thing is straight, I push it on. If it is crooked, I leave it alone. Longevity, brevity of life, obscurity, prominence, honor, humble station, wealth and poverty—all these come naturally and of themselves. How should I know anything about them? How should I know anything about them? [6:1a]

The "Yang Chu" Chapter of Lieh Tzu

This essay is probably by a contemporary of the unknown author of the *Lieh Tzu,* though it now forms one chapter of that work and like the *Lieh Tzu* expresses the Neo-Taoist tendency toward fatalism. It has been erroneously attributed to the philosopher Yang Chu who lived around 440 to 360 B.C. and is mentioned in the writings of Mencius. A much more pessimistic view of life is expressed here than in the early Taoist philosophers.

[From *Lieh Tzu,* 7:1b–2a]

Yang Chu said: The longest life is but a hundred years, and not one man in a thousand lives to that age. Suppose there is one who does. Half of that time is occupied with infancy and senility. Of the other half, almost half is wasted in sleep at night and naps in the day time. And almost half of the remainder is lost in pain, illness, sorrow, grief, death, and loss [of relatives and friends]. I would estimate that in the ten years or more [that is left to him] a man has hardly one hour in which he is quite content and free from the slightest worry. Then what is the purpose of life? What is the joy of life? Life is only for [the enjoyment of] beauty and wealth, and sound and color. But beauty and wealth cannot always be enjoyed to satisfaction, and color and sound cannot always be indulged in. Instead, we are forbidden by penalties from doing this and are exhorted by rewards to do that. Fame causes us to advance, and the law forces us to retreat. Nervously we struggle for the hollow praise of the moment, and try to arrange things so as to extend our glory after death. In gingerly fashion we exercise the utmost caution over what we hear with our ears and what we see with our eyes. We grieve over the right and wrong of our body and mind. Thus we do but miss the perfect happiness of the years as they go by, and cannot give ourselves free rein even for an hour. What is the difference between this and being doubly chained inside an inner prison?

Yang Chu said: In life the myriad things are different. At death they are similar. In life some are virtuous, some are stupid, some are honored, and some are lowly. This is how they differ. When dead, they stink, rot, disintegrate, and disappear. This is how they are similar. However, all this, from virtue to disappearance, is not of their own doing, and life, death, virtue, stupidity, honor, and lowliness are not what they have achieved for themselves. In these respects the myriad things are ultimately equal. Whether one lives for ten years or for a hundred, and whether one is a benevolent sage or a stupid criminal, everyone dies. In life one may be [as sagely as] Yao and Shun or [as vicious as] Chieh and Chou, but after death everyone turns to rotten bones. And rotten bones are all alike; who can tell them apart? Let us enjoy this life. Why be concerned about the hereafter?

TAOISM IN ART

Chinese art is not exclusively a Taoist province nor that of any particular philosophy or religion. Nevertheless it cannot be denied that Taoism has supplied much of the inspiration in the formulation of the Chinese artistic ideal. The guiding principles for this formulation were set forth during the Chin dynasty (A.D. 265–420), a period of political transition and social change which was characterized, as we have seen, by a generally pessimistic outlook in regard to human affairs but a renewed interest in the world of nature and the spirit. The prevailing intellectual mood was thus especially congenial to the individualism, naturalism, and mysticism of Taoism, which, complemented in certain respects by Buddhism, in turn stimulated creative efforts in the realm of art. In such circumstances emerged the main branches of Chinese painting—Buddhist religious painting, landscape (or "mountain and water" painting as the Chinese call it), flower and bird painting, genre painting—and the basic theories of art. Furthermore, the substitution at the same time of ink for oil-paint and the brush for the reed provided artists with freer media of expression.

Of the several forms of painting, landscape has been regarded as the crowning art of China. It is here that the cardinal principles of Chinese art are embodied and the greatest of Chinese artistic talents immortalized. When the capital of Chin was moved to the present Nanking from the north, the center of Chinese civilization shifted southward. Here the Chinese from the north were deeply impressed by the luxuriant vegetation and scenic charm of the mountains, lakes, and river valleys. Artists responded with a greater interest in landscape painting. More significant than this geographical shift, however, was the growth of Taoism, for the Taoist glorification of nature opened a new vista to artists and imbued them with a new sense of freedom. As a result, landscape advanced from a secondary position as simply the background in portraits to a position of equal and eventually of even greater importance. The harmony of the human spirit and the spirit of nature became the ultimate goal of Chinese art.

This did not necessarily mean, however, that the traditional Confucian social and moral emphasis in art was abandoned. On the contrary, it persisted, but at the same time the Chinese artistic perspective was extended from human society to its natural environment.

The two short essays which follow represent the earliest attempts to express in words the principles of Chinese painting. The authors, Tsung Ping (A.D. 375–443) and Wang Wei (A.D. 415–443), were both distinguished painters though unfortunately none of their works has survived. The writings of these men, brief and obscure though they are, have had a great influence upon later theories of painting. Their belief that painting must represent not only the outward form of nature, but must capture and embody an inner spirit which binds man to the world of hills and streams in mystical harmony, became the basis for the great romantic landscape painters of later ages.

TSUNG PING

Introduction to Landscape Painting
[From *Li-tai ming-hua chi,* 6:3b–4b]

Having embraced Tao the sage responds harmoniously to things. Having purified his mind, the worthy man enjoys forms. As to landscapes, they exist in material substance and soar into the realm of the spirit. Therefore men like the Yellow Emperor, Yao, Confucius, Kuang-ch'eng, Ta-wei, Hsü Yu, and the brothers of Ku-chu [Po I and Shu Ch'i] insisted on traveling among the mountains of K'ung-t'ung, Chü-tz'u, Miao-ku, Chi-shou, and Ta-meng. These are also called the delights of the man of humanity and the man of wisdom.[2] Now the sage, by the exercise of his spirit, follows Tao as his standard, while the worthy man understands this. Mountains and rivers in their form pay homage to Tao, and the man of humanity delights in them. Do not the sage and mountains and rivers have much in common?

I was strongly attached to the Lu and Heng Mountains and had missed for a long time Mounts Ching and Wu, and [like Confucius] did not realize that old age was coming on. I am ashamed that I can no longer concentrate my vital power or nourish my body, and I am distressed to follow the steps of people like the keeper of the Stone Gate [who ridiculed Confucius for attempting to do the impossible]. Therefore I draw forms and spread colors, and create these mountain peaks capped with clouds.

Now, the Principle that was lost in ancient times may, through imagination, be found in the thousand years yet to come. Meanings that are subtle and beyond the expression of words and symbols may be grasped by the mind through books and writings. How much more so in my case, when

[2] A reference to the famous passage in *Analects* VI, 20: "The man of wisdom delights in water; the man of humanity delights in mountains."

I have personally lingered among [the mountains] and, with my own eyes, observed them all around me, so that I render forms as I find the forms to be and apply colors as I see them!

Furthermore, as the K'un-lun Mountain is very large and the pupils of the eye are very small, if the shape of the mountain is forced within an inch of my eyes, I cannot see its form, but if it is placed several miles away, it can be enclosed within the square inch of my pupils. For the truth is that the further the object, the smaller it becomes. Now, as I spread the silk to reflect distant scenery, the form of the K'un-lun and Lang Mountains can be enclosed within the space of a square inch. A vertical stroke of three inches equals a height of several thousand feet, and a horizontal stroke of a few feet embodies an area of a hundred miles. Therefore, in viewing paintings, one's concern is that [the artistic] representation may not be skillful, rather than that small proportion might spoil the likeness, for it is a natural condition [that proportion will preserve likeness]. In this way the sublime beauty of the Sung and Hua mountains and the spirit of the Profound Mother [the Spirit of the Valley] may be reproduced in one picture.

If truth is understood as what is responsive to the eye and appreciable to the mind, then when the representation is skillful, the eye also responds and the mind also appreciates. Such response and appreciation arouse the spirit. As the spirit soars high, truth is attained. What is there to gain by merely searching for the dark crags?

Furthermore, fundamentally spirit has no sign and yet it dwells in all physical forms and acts on all species. As truth enters into a thing, it is reflected, like a shadow, in its manifestations. If one can truly depict them with skill, one can truly be said to have achieved perfection.

And so I live in leisure and nourish my vital power. I drain clean the wine-cup, play the lute, lay down the picture of scenery, face it in silence, and, while seated, travel beyond the four borders of the land, never leaving the realm where nature exerts her influence, and alone responding to the call of wilderness. Here the cliffs and peaks seem to rise to soaring heights, and groves in the midst of clouds are dense and extend to the vanishing point. Sages and virtuous men of far antiquity come back to live in my imagination and all interesting things come together in my spirit and in my thoughts. What else need I do? I gratify my spirit, that is all. What is there that is more important than gratifying the spirit?

WANG WEI

Introduction to Painting
[From *Li-tai ming-hua chi,* 6:5b–6b]

People who discuss painting merely concentrate on the outward aspects and structural effects. Men of ancient times, however, when they produced paintings did not merely record the sites of cities, delineate country districts, mark out the boundaries of towns and villages, or sketch the courses of rivers. Physical appearances are based upon physical forms, but the mind is changing and ever active. But spirit is invisible, and therefore what it enters into does not move. The eye is limited in scope, and therefore what it sees does not cover all. Thus, by using one small brush, I draw the infinite vacuity [the universe in its undifferentiated state], and by employing the clear vision of my small pupils to the limit, I paint a large body. With a curved line I represent the Sung mountain ranges. With an interesting line I represent [the mythical mountain] Fang-chang. A swift stroke will be sufficient for the T'ai-hua Mountain, and some irregular dots will show a dragon's nose. [In the latter], the eyebrows, forehead, and cheeks all seem to be a serene smile, and [in the former], the lonely cliff is so luxuriant and sublime that it seems to emit clouds. With changes and variations in all directions, movement is created, and by applying proportions and measure, the spirit is revealed. After this, things like the temples and shrines, and boats and carriages are grouped together according to kind, and creatures like dogs, horses, birds, and fish are distinguished according to their shape. This is the ultimate of painting.

Gazing upon the clouds of autumn, my spirit takes wings and soars. Facing the breeze of spring, my thoughts flow like great, powerful currents. Even the music of metal and stone instruments and the treasure of priceless jades cannot match [the pleasure of] this. I unroll pictures and examine documents, I compare and distinguish the mountains and seas. The wind rises from the green forest, and foaming water rushes in the stream. Alas! Such paintings cannot be achieved by the physical movements of the fingers and the hand, but only by the spirit entering into them. This is the nature of painting.

RELIGIOUS TAOISM

The central objective of Taoism may be said to be a long and serene life. This, as taught by Lao Tzu, is to be attained through simplicity, tranquillity, and enlightenment; as taught by Yang Chu, through escape from injury and the preservation of the essence of one's being; and as taught by Chuang Tzu, through companionship with nature, spiritual freedom, and indifference to life and death. This philosophical Taoism assumed momentum in the third century B.C. and has continued to the present time.

While the philosophy was developing, another movement led by prac-titioners of the occult was under way, namely, the search for immortality on earth through divination and magic. Since the *Lao Tzu* contains such vague phrases as "the Spirit of the Valley," "the Mysterious Female," "long life," etc., it is understandable why this movement should have utilized the *Lao Tzu* and, for similar reasons, the *Chuang Tzu*. By the first century B.C., a movement developed called "Huang-Lao," after Huang-ti (the Yellow Emperor) and Lao Tzu. This cult enjoyed oc-casional imperial patronage as well as a tremendous following among the masses.

As the movement grew in strength, religious and political reformers competed to incorporate it into their own schemes. One of them, Chang Ling of the second century A.D., made use of the movement to give his own ideas a mysterious and magical character. He collected five bushels of rice from his followers and consequently his teaching became known as the Way (Tao) of Five Bushels of Rice. His followers gave him the title Heavenly Teacher. Thus he became the historical founder of the Taoist re-ligion and his direct lineal descendants held the hereditary title of Heav-enly Teacher. This title was officially approved by the emperor in A.D. 1276, legally abolished in 1368, but popularly continued to this day. The Heav-enly Teacher, who used to abide in the Dragon and Tiger Mountain in Central China where a large domain was granted in 1015, has been spoken of as the "pope" of the Taoist religion. However, he had little control or influence over Taoist priests and was not looked upon as an arbiter of morals or a responsible spiritual leader.

In the second century A.D., a Taoist philosopher, Wei Po-yang (fl. 147–167) wrote a book entitled the *Ts'an-t'ung-ch'i,* which means "The Three Ways of the Yellow Emperor, Lao Tzu, and the *Book of Changes* Unified and Harmonized in the Latter." Thus he attempted to synthesize the Taoist philosophy and occult wizardry with the teachings of the *Book of Changes* and the yin-yang school. The ultimate goal of the book was to prolong life through the practice of alchemy, whereby, it was believed, the universal forces could be harmonized and concentrated in the individual's body. The book became the basis of several important Taoist "Classics," all of which have been regarded as scriptures of Taoism.

The most important development after Wei Po-yang was the philosophy of Ko Hung (A.D. 253–333?) who wrote the *Pao-p'u Tzu (The Philosopher Who Embraces Simplicity)* in an attempt to combine Confucian ethics with Taoist occultism. This is the most important work in religious Taoism from the philosophical point of view. Ko Hung propounded in this book three basic doctrines: immortality on earth, internal and external alchemy, and the merit system in which specific deeds account for the increase or decrease of a specific number of days in one's span of life. All these became basic doctrines of popular Taoism in the centuries following. Representative sections of the *Pao-p'u Tzu* on these three doctrines follow. The work also paved the way for further elaboration of Taoist occultism in K'ou Ch'ien-chih (d. A.D. 432) and T'ao Hung-ching (A.D. 452–536) in whom both doctrinal and organizational developments of the Taoist religion were completed. K'ou Ch'ien-chih regulated the ceremonies and codes of the cult, fixed the names of its deities, and formulated its theology. Through his influence Taoism was made the state religion in A.D. 440 when Buddhism was for a time suppressed.

State patronage was repeated in 574 and 591. Imperial favor reached its height during the T'ang dynasty. The founder of the dynasty was named Li, and because Lao Tzu was supposed to have borne this same surname, he was honored by imperial order as T'ai-shang Hsüan-yüan Huang-ti, or the Most High Emperor of Mystic Origin, ranking above Confucius and the Buddha. Princes, dukes and those below them were required to study the *Lao Tzu,* and Taoist temples were ordered established throughout the empire. In 742, Lao Tzu's illustrious followers, including Chuang Tzu, were canonized. In the following dynasties, however, although

Taoism generally enjoyed imperial respect, it never again existed as a
state cult, but flourished as a religion of the masses, especially of the
illiterate and superstitious.

As a religion of the masses, Taoism is distinguished by several prominent features. It has one of the most thickly populated pantheons in the
world, with deities representing natural objects, historical persons, the
several professions, ideas, and even the whole and parts of the human
body. It has a host of immortals and spirits, and a rich reservoir of
superstitions including an extensive system of divination, fortune-telling,
astrology, etc. It developed an elaborate system of alchemy in its search
for longevity which contributed much to material culture and scientific
development in medieval China. It imitated Buddhism in a wholesale
manner in such things as temples and images, a hierarchy of priests,
monasticism, and heavens and hells. It has often been associated with
eclectic sects and secret societies and so has been an important element in
a number of popular uprisings. Today religious Taoism is rapidly declining, and, in the eyes of many, is virtually defunct. However, its concentration on a good life on earth, its respect for both bodily and spiritual
health, its doctrine of harmony with nature, its emphasis on simplicity,
naturalness, peace of mind, and freedom of the spirit have continued to
inspire Chinese art and enlighten Chinese thought and conduct. Even if
unable to maintain its existence as an organized cult, it has enriched Chinese festivals with the romantic, carefree, and gay carnival spirit of its
cult of immortals, and through its art symbols, ceremonies, and folklore
has given to Chinese folk life a special color and charm.

KO HUNG
The Belief in Immortals
[From *Pao-p'u Tzu,* 2:1a–4a; 12a]

Someone asked: Is it really possible that spiritual beings and immortals
(*hsien*) do not die?

Pao-p'u Tzu said: Even if we had the greatest power of vision, we
could not see all the things that have corporeal form. Even if we were endowed with the sharpest sense of hearing, we could not hear all the sounds
there are. Even if we had the feet of Ta-chang and Hsu-hai [expert

runners], what we had already trod upon would not be so much as what we have not. And even if we had the knowledge of [the sages] Yü, I, and Ch'i-hsieh, what we know would not be so much as what we do not know. The myriad things flourish. What is there that could not exist? Why not the immortals, whose accounts fill the historical records? Why should there not be a way to immortality?

Thereupon the questioner laughed heartily and said: Whatever has a beginning necessarily has an end, and whatever lives must eventually die. . . . I have only heard that some plants dry up and wither before frost, fade in color during the summer, bud but do not flower, or wither and are stripped of leaves before bearing fruit. But I have never heard of anyone who enjoys a life span of ten thousand years and an everlasting existence without end. Therefore people of antiquity did not aspire to be immortals in their pursuit of knowledge, and did not talk of strange things in their conversation. They cast aside perverse doctrines and adhered to what is natural. They set aside the tortoise and the crane [symbols of immortality] as creatures of a different species, and looked upon life and death as morning and evening. . . .

Pao-p'u Tzu answered: . . . Life and death, beginning and end, are indeed the great laws of the universe. Yet the similarities and differences of things are not uniform. Some are this way and some are that. Tens of thousands of varieties are in constant change and transformation, strange and without any definite pattern. Whether things are this way or that, and whether they are regular or irregular in their essential and subsidiary aspects, cannot be reduced to uniformity. There are many who say that whatever has a beginning must have an end. But it is not in accord with the principle [of existence] to muddle things together and try to make them all the same. People say that things are bound to grow in the summer, and yet the shepherd's-purse and the water chestnut wilt. People say that plants are bound to wither in the winter, and yet the bamboo and the cypress flourish. People say whatever has a beginning will have an end, and yet Heaven and earth are unending. People say whatever is born will die, and yet the tortoise and the crane live forever. When the yang is at its height, it should be hot, and yet the summer is not without cool days. When the yin reaches it limit, it should be cold, and yet even a severe winter is not without brief warm periods. . . .

Among creatures none surpasses man in intelligence. As creatures of such superior nature, men should be equal and uniform. And yet they differ in being virtuous or stupid, in being perverse or upright, in being fair or ugly, tall or short, pure or impure, chaste or lewd, patient or impatient, slow or quick. What they pursue or avoid in their interests and what their eyes and ears desire are as different as Heaven and earth, and as incompatible as ice and coals. Why should you only wonder at the fact that immortals are different and do not die like ordinary people? . . . But people with superficial knowledge are bound by what is ordinary and adhere to what is common. They all say that immortals are not seen in the world, and therefore they say forthwith that there cannot be immortals. [2:1a–4a]

Among men some are wise and some are stupid, but they all know that in their bodies they have a heavenly component (*hun*) and an earthly component (*p'o*) of the soul. If these are partly gone, man becomes sick. If they are completely gone, man dies. If they are partially separated from the body, the occult expert has means to retain and restrict them. If they are entirely separated, there are principles in the established rites to recall them. These components of the soul as entities are extremely close to us. And yet although we are born with them and live with them throughout life, we never see or hear them. Should one say that they do not exist simply because we have not seen or heard them? [2:12a]

Alchemy
   [From *Pao-p'u Tzu,* 2:3b–4a; 3:1a, 5a; 4:1a–3a; 6:4a]

The immortals nourish their bodies with drugs and prolong their lives with the application of occult science, so that internal illness shall not arise and external ailment shall not enter. Although they enjoy everlasting existence and do not die, their old bodies do not change. If one knows the way to immortality, it is not to be considered so difficult. [2:3b–4a]

Among the creatures of nature, man is the most intelligent. Therefore those who understand [creation] slightly can employ the myriad things, and those who get to its depth can enjoy [what is called in the *Lao Tzu*] "long life and everlasting existence" [Ch. 59]. As we know that the best medicine can prolong life, let us take it to obtain immortality, and as we know that the tortoise and the crane have longevity, let us imitate their activities to increase our span of life. . . . Those who have obtained Tao are able to lift themselves into the clouds and the heavens above and to dive and swim in the rivers and seas below. [3:1a, 5a]

Pao-p'u Tzu said: I have investigated and read books on the nourishment of human nature and collected formulas for everlasting existence. Those I have perused number thousands of volumes. They all consider reconverted cinnabar [after it has been turned into mercury] and gold fluid to be the most important. Thus these two things represent the acme of the way to immortality. . . . The transformations of the two substances are the more wonderful the more they are heated. Yellow gold does not disintegrate even after having been smelted a hundred times in fire, and does not rot even if buried in the ground until the end of the world. If these two medicines are eaten, they will strengthen our bodies and therefore enable us not to grow old nor to die. This is of course seeking assistance from external substances to strengthen ourselves. It is like feeding fat to the lamp so it will not die out. If we smear copperas on our feet, they will not deteriorate even if they remain in water. This is to borrow the strength of the copper to protect our flesh. Gold fluid and reconverted cinnabar, however, upon entering our body, permeate our whole system of blood and energy and are not like copperas which helps only on the outside. [4:1a–3a]

It is hoped that those who nourish life will learn extensively and comprehend the essential, gather whatever there is to see and choose the best. It is not sufficient to depend on cultivating only one thing. It is also dangerous for people who love life to rely on their own specialty. Those who know the techniques of the *Classic of the Mysterious Lady* and the *Classic of the Plain Lady* [books on sexual regimen no longer extant] will say that only the "art of the chamber" will lead to salvation. Those who understand the method of breathing exercises will say that only the permeation of the vital power can prolong life. Those who know the method of stretching and bending will say that only physical exercise can prevent old age. And those who know the formulas of herbs will say that only medicine will make life unending. They fail in their pursuit of Tao because they are so onesided. People of superficial knowledge think they have enough when they happen to know of only one way and do not realize that the true seeker will search unceasingly even after he has acquired some good formulas. [6:4a]

The Merit System

The doctrine of retribution expounded here resembles in some ways the Buddhist conception of karma. Although it is difficult to establish any definite historical connection between the two, it should be remembered that at this time Buddhism and Taoism borrowed extensively from each other and shared many of the same concepts and terminology.

[From *Pao-p'u Tzu,* 3:7b–10b; 6:5b–7a]

Furthermore, as Heaven and earth are the greatest of things, it is natural, from the point of view of universal principles, that they have spiritual power. Having spiritual power it is proper that they reward good and punish evil. Nevertheless their expanse is great and their net is wide-meshed.[3] There is not necessarily an immediate response [result] as soon as this net is set in operation. As we glance over the Taoist books of discipline, however, all are unanimous in saying that those who seek immortality must set their minds to the accumulation of merits and the accomplishment of good work. Their hearts must be kind to all things. They must treat others as they treat themselves, and extend their humaneness (*jen*) even to insects. They must rejoice in the fortune of men and pity their suffering, relieve the destitute and save the poor. Their hands must never injure life, and their mouths must never encourage evil. They must consider the success and failure of others as their own. They must not regard themselves highly, nor praise themselves. They must not envy those superior to them, nor flatter dangerous and evil-minded people. In this way they may become virtuous and blessed by Heaven; they may be successful in whatever they do, and may hope to become immortal.

If, on the other hand, they hate good and love evil; if their words do not agree with their thoughts; if they say one thing in people's presence and the opposite behind their backs; if they twist the truth; if they are cruel to subordinates or deceive their superiors; if they betray their task and are ungrateful for kindness received; if they manipulate the law and accept bribes; if they tolerate injustice but suppress justice; if they destroy the public good for their selfish ends; if they punish the innocent, wreck people's homes, pocket their treasures, injure their bodies, or seize their positions; if they overthrow virtuous rulers or massacre those who have sur-

[3] The net of Heaven which eventually catches all evildoers in its meshes, a very old concept in Chinese thought.

rendered to them; if they slander saints and sages or hurt Taoist priests; if they shoot birds in flight or kill the unborn in womb or egg; if in spring or summer hunts they burn the forests or drive out the game; if they curse spiritual beings; if they teach others to do evil or conceal their good deeds or endanger others for their own security; if they claim the work of others as their own; if they spoil people's happy affairs or take away what others love; if they cause division in people's families or disgrace others in order to win; if they overcharge or underpay; if they set fire or inundate; if they injure people with trickery or coerce the weak; if they repay good with evil; if they take things by force or accumulate wealth through robbery and plunder; if they are unfair or unjust, licentious, indulgent, or perverted; if they oppress orphans or mistreat widows; if they squander inheritance and accept charity; if they cheat or deceive; if they love to gossip about people's private affairs or criticize them for their defects; if they drag Heaven and earth into their affairs and rail at people in order to seek vindication; if they fail to repay debts or play fair in the exchange of goods; if they seek to gratify their desires without end; if they hate and resist the faithful and sincere; if they disobey orders from above or do not respect their teachers; if they ridicule others for doing good; if they destroy people's crops or harm their tools so as to nullify their utility, and do not feed people with clean food; if they cheat in weights or measures; if they mix spurious articles with genuine; if they take dishonorable advantage; if they tempt others to steal; if they meddle in the affairs of others or go beyond their position in life; if they leap over wells or hearths [which provide water and fire for food]; if they sing in the last day of the month [when the end should be sent off with sorrow] or cry in the first day of the month [when the beginning should be welcomed with joy]; if they commit any of these evil deeds; it is a sin.

The Arbiter of Human Destiny will reduce their terms of life by units of three days or three hundred days in proportion to the gravity of the evil. When all days are deducted they will die. Those who have the intention to do evil but have not carried it out will have three-day units taken just as if they had acted with injury to others. If they die before all their evil deeds are punished, their posterity will suffer for them. [6:5b–7a]

Someone asked: Is it true that he who cultivates the way [to become an immortal] should first accomplish good deeds?

Pao-p'u Tzu answered: Yes, it is true. The middle section of the *Yu-ch'ien ching* says: "The most important thing is to accomplish good works. The next is the removal of faults. For him who cultivates the way, the highest accomplishment of good work is to save people from danger so they may escape from calamity, and to preserve people from sickness so that they may not die unjustly. Those who aspire to be immortals should regard loyalty, filial piety, harmony, obedience, love, and good faith as their essential principles of conduct. If they do not cultivate moral conduct but merely devote themselves to occult science, they will never attain everlasting life. If they do evil, the Arbiter of Human Destiny will take off units of three hundred days from their allotted life if the evil is great, or units of three days if the evil is small. Since [the punishment] depends on the degree of evil, the reduction in the span of life is in some cases great and in others small. When a man is endowed with life and given a life span, he has his own definite number of days. If his number is large, the units of three hundred days and of three days are not easily exhausted and therefore he dies later. On the other hand, if one's allotted number is small and offences are many, then the units are soon exhausted and he dies early."

The book also says: "Those who aspire to be terrestrial immortals should accomplish three hundred good deeds and those who aspire to be celestial immortals should accomplish 1,200. If the 1,199th good deed is followed by an evil one, they will lose all their accumulation and have to start all over. It does not matter whether the good deeds are great or the evil deed is small. Even if they do no evil but talk about their good deeds and demand reward for their charities, they will nullify the goodness of these deeds although the other good deeds are not affected." The book further says: "If good deeds are not sufficiently accumulated, taking the elixir of immortality will be of no help." [3:7b–8a, 10a–b]

Taoism in Relation to Other Schools
[From *Pao-p'u Tzu*, 10:1a–b; 12:1a–b]

Someone said: If it were certain that one could become an immortal, the sages would have trained themselves to be such. But neither Duke Chou nor Confucius did so. It is clear that there is no such possibility.

Pao-p'u Tzu answered: A sage need not be an immortal and an immortal need not be a sage. The sage receives a mandate [from Heaven], not to attend to the way of everlasting life, but to remove tyrants and eliminate robbers, to turn danger into security and violence into peace, to institute ceremonies and create musical systems, to propagate laws and give education, to correct improper manners and reform degenerate customs, to assist rulers who are in danger of downfall and to support those states that are about to collapse. . . . What the ordinary people call sages are all sages who regulate the world but not sages who attain Tao. The Yellow Emperor and Lao Tzu were sages who attained Tao, while Duke Chou and Confucius were sages who regulated the world. [12:1a–b]

Someone asked: Which is first and which is last, Confucianism or Taoism?

Pao-p'u Tzu answered: Taoism is the essence of Confucianism and Confucianism is an appendage to Taoism. First of all,[4] there was the "teaching of the yin-yang school which had many taboos that made people constrained and afraid." "The Confucianists had extensive learning but little that was essential; they worked hard but achieved little." "Moism emphasized thrift but was difficult to follow," and could not be practiced exclusively. "The Legalists were severe and showed little kindness"; they destroyed humanity and righteousness. "The teachings of the Taoist school alone enable men's spirits to be concentrated and united and their action to be in harmony with the formless. . . . Taoism embraces the good points of both Confucianism and Mo-ism and combines the essentials of the Legalists and Logicians. It changes with the times and responds to the transformations of things. . . . Its precepts are simple and easy to understand; its works are few but its achievements many." It is devoted to the simplicity that preserves the Great Heritage and adheres to the true and correct source. [10:1a–b]

[4] Most of the following is quoted from the essay on the six philosophical schools by the Han historian Ssu-ma T'an (d. 110 B.C.).

CHAPTER XV

THE INTRODUCTION
OF BUDDHISM

The coming of Buddhism to China was an event with far-reaching results in the development of Chinese thought and culture and of Buddhism itself. After a long and difficult period of assimilation, this new teaching managed to establish itself as a major system of thought, contributing greatly to the enrichment of Chinese philosophy, and also as a major system of religious practice which had an enduring influence on Chinese popular religion. Indeed, it came to be spoken of along with the native traditions, Confucianism and Taoism, as one of the Three Teachings or Three Religions, thus achieving a status of virtual equality with these beliefs.

By the time Buddhism reached China (according to official tradition, in the first century A.D.), it had already undergone several centuries of development, both in regard to its philosophical doctrines and its religious practices. This is not the place to attempt a summation of that historical development, but a brief statement of the major principles and concepts of Buddhism in India is essential to an understanding of the forms it took in China.[1]

BASIC TEACHINGS OF BUDDHISM

The fundamental truths on which Buddhism is founded are not metaphysical or theological, but rather psychological. Basic is the doctrine of the "Four Noble Truths": 1) that all life is inevitably sorrowful; 2) that sorrow is due to craving; 3) that it can only be stopped by the stopping

[1] This summation is adapted from the account by A. L. Basham in the second volume of this series, *Sources of Indian Tradition*. Readers already familiar with this basic background should turn to the next section, The Coming of Buddhism to China.

of craving; and 4) that this can only be done by a course of carefully disciplined and moral conduct, culminating in the life of concentration and meditation led by the Buddhist monk. These four truths, which are the common property of all schools of Buddhist thought, are part of the true Doctrine (Skt. *dharma*), which reflects the fundamental moral law of the universe.[2]

All things are composite, and as a corollary of this, all things are transient, for the composition of all aggregates is liable to change with time. Moreover, being essentially transient, they have no eternal Self or soul, no abiding individuality. And, as we have seen, they are inevitably liable to sorrow. This threefold characterization of the nature of the world and all that it contains—sorrowful, transient, and soulless—is frequently repeated in Buddhist literature, and without fully grasping its truth no being has any chance of salvation. For until he thoroughly understands the three characteristics of the world a man will inevitably crave for permanence in one form or another, and as this cannot, by the nature of things, be obtained, he will suffer, and probably make others suffer also.

All things in the universe may also be classified into five components, or are composed of a mixture of them: form and matter (*rūpa*), sensations (*vedanā*), perceptions (*saṃjñā*) psychic dispositions or constructions (*saṃskāra*), and consciousness or conscious thought (*vijñāna*). The first consists of the objects of sense and various other elements of less importance. Sensations are the actual feelings arising as a result of the exercise of the six senses (mind being the sixth) upon sense-objects, and perceptions are the cognitions of such sensations. The psychic constructions include all the various psychological emotions, propensities, faculties, and conditions of the individual, while the fifth component, conscious thought, arises from the interplay of the other psychic constituents. The individual is made up of a combination of the five components, which are never the same from one moment to the next, and therefore his whole being is in a state of constant flux.

The process by which life continues and one thing leads to another is explained by the Chain of Causation or Dependent Origination. The root

---

[2] The word *dharma* as employed in Buddhism is strictly untranslatable in English. Besides meaning Law or Doctrine it also represents phenomena in general, as well as the qualities and characteristics of phenomena. Thus the Buddha's last words might be translated: "Growing old is the dharma of all composite things."

cause of the process of birth and death and rebirth is ignorance, the fundamental illusion that individuality and permanence exist, when in fact they
do not. Hence there arise in the organism various psychic phenomena,
including desire, followed by an attempt to appropriate things to itself—
this is typified especially by sexual craving and sexual intercourse, which
are the actual causes of the next links in the chain, which concludes with
age and death, only to be repeated again and again indefinitely. Rebirth
takes place, therefore, according to laws of karma which do not essentially differ from those of Hinduism, though they are explained rather
differently.

As we have seen, no permanent entity transmigrates from body to body,
and all things, including the individual, are in a state of constant flux.
But each act, word, or thought leaves its traces on the collection of the
five constituents which make up the phenomenal individual, and their
character alters correspondingly. This process goes on throughout life,
and, when the material and immaterial parts of the being are separated
in death, the immaterial constituents, which make up what in other systems would be called the soul, carry over the consequential effects of the
deeds of the past life, and obtain another body accordingly. Thus there
is no permanent soul, but nevertheless room is found for the doctrine of
transmigration. Though Buddhism rejects the existence of the soul, this
makes little difference in practice, and the more popular literature of
Buddhism, such as the *Birth Stories* (*Jātaka*), takes for granted the
existence of a quasi-soul at least, which endures indefinitely.

The process of rebirth can only be stopped by achieving Nirvāna, first
by adopting right views about the nature of existence, then by a carefully
controlled system of moral conduct, and finally by concentration and
meditation. The state of Nirvāna cannot be described, but it can be hinted
at or suggested metaphorically. The word literally means "blowing out,"
as of a lamp. In Nirvāna all idea of an individual personality or ego
ceases to exist and there is nothing to be reborn—as far as the individual
is concerned Nirvāna is annihilation. But it was certainly not generally
thought of by the early Buddhists in such negative terms. It was rather
conceived of as a transcendent state, beyond the possibility of full comprehension by the ordinary being enmeshed in the illusion of selfhood,
but not fundamentally different from the state of supreme bliss as de
scribed in other non-theistic Indian systems.

These are the doctrines of the Theravāda or Hīnayāna school, and with few variations, they would be assented to by all other schools of Buddhism. But the Mahāyāna and quasi-Mahāyāna sects developed other doctrines, in favor of which they often gave comparatively little attention to these fundamental teachings.

It was from the first or second century A.D. onward, that Mahāyāna Buddhism arose in India. This new school, which claimed to offer salvation for all, styled itself *Mahāyāna,* the Greater Vehicle (to salvation), as opposed to the older Buddhism, which it contemptuously referred to as *Hīnayāna,* or the Lesser Vehicle. The Mahāyāna scriptures also claimed to represent the final doctrines of the Buddha, revealed only to his most spiritually advanced followers, while the earlier doctrines were merely preliminary ones. Though Mahāyāna Buddhism, with its pantheon of heavenly buddhas and bodhisattvas and its idealistic metaphysics, was strikingly different in many respects from the Theravāda, it can be viewed as the development into finished systems of tendencies which had existed long before.

A tendency to revere the Buddha as a god had probably existed in his own lifetime. In Indian religion, divinity is not something completely transcendent, or far exalted above all mortal things, as it is for the Jew, Christian, or Muslim; neither is it something concentrated in a single unique, omnipotent, and omniscient personality. In Indian religions godhead manifests itself in so many forms as to be almost if not quite ubiquitous, and every great sage or religious teacher is looked on as a special manifestation of divinity, in some sense a god in human form. How much more divine was the Buddha, to whom even the great god Brahmā himself did reverence, and who, in meditation, could far transcend the comparatively tawdry and transient heavens where the great gods dwelt, enter the world of formlessness, and pass thence to the ineffable Nirvāna itself! From the Buddhist point of view even the highest of the gods was liable to error, for Brahmā imagined himself to be the creator when in fact the world came into existence as a result of natural causes. The Buddha, on the other hand, was omniscient.

Yet, according to theory, the Buddha had passed completely away from the universe, had ceased in any sense to be a person, and no longer affected the world in any way. But the formula of the "Three Jewels" or "Treasures"—"I take refuge in the Buddha, I take refuge in the Doc-

trine, I take refuge in the Order"—became the Buddhist profession of
faith very early, and was used by monk and layman alike. Taken literally
the first clause was virtually meaningless, for it was impossible to take
refuge in a being who had ceased to exist as such. Nevertheless the
Buddha was worshiped from very early times, and he is said to have
himself declared that all who had faith in him and devotion to him would
obtain rebirth in Heaven.

A further development which encouraged the tendency to theism was
the growth of interest in the *bodhisattva*. This term, literally meaning
"Being of Wisdom," was first used in the sense of a previous incarnation of the Buddha. For many lives before his final birth as Siddhārtha
Gautama the Bodhisattva did mighty deeds of compassion and self-sacrifice, as he gradually perfected himself in wisdom and virtue. Stories of
the Bodhisattva, known as *Birth Stories* (*Jātaka*) and often adapted
from popular legends and fables, were very popular with lay Buddhists,
and numerous illustrations of them occur in early Buddhist art.

It is probable that even in the lifetime of the Buddha it was thought
that he was only the last of a series of earlier Buddhas. Later, perhaps
through Zoroastrian influence, it came to be believed that other Buddhas
were yet to come, and interest developed in *Maitreya*, the future Buddha,
whose coming was said to have been prophesied by the historical Buddha,
and who, in years to come, would purify the world with his teaching.
But if Maitreya was yet to come, the chain of being which would ultimately lead to his birth (or, in the terminology of other sects, his soul)
must be already in existence. Somewhere in the universe, the being later
to become Maitreya Buddha was already active for good. And if this
one, how many more? Logically, the world must be full of bodhisattvas,
all striving for the welfare of other beings.

The next step up in the development of the new form of Buddhism
was the changing of the goal at which the believer aimed. According to
Buddhist teaching there are three types of perfected beings—*Buddhas,*
who perceived the truth for themselves and taught it to others, *Pratyeka-
buddhas,* "Private Buddhas," who perceived it, but kept it to themselves
and did not teach it, and *Arhants,* "Worthies," who learned it from
others, but fully realized it for themselves. According to earlier schools
the earnest believer should aspire to become an arhant, a perfected being for whom there was no rebirth, who already enjoyed Nirvāna, and

who would finally enter that state after death, all vestiges of his per-- sonality dissolved. The road to Nirvāna was a hard one, and could only be covered in many lives of virtue and self-sacrifice; but nevertheless the goal began to be looked on as selfish. Surely a bodhisattva, after achiev- ing such exalted compassion and altruism, and after reaching such a de- gree of perfection that he could render inestimable help to other striving beings, would not pass so quickly as possible to Nirvāna, where he could be of no further use, but would deliberately choose to remain in the world, using his spiritual power to help others, until all had found salva- tion. Passages of Mahāyāna scriptures describing the self-sacrifice of the bodhisattva for the welfare of all things living are among the most pas- sionately altruistic in the world's religious literature.

The replacement of the ideal of the arhant by that of the bodhisattva is the basic distinction between the old sects and the new, which came to be known as Mahāyāna. Faith in the bodhisattvas and the help they afforded was thought to carry many beings along the road to bliss, while the older schools, which did not accept the bodhisattva ideal, could save only a few patient and strenuous souls.

The next stage in the evolution of the theology of the new Buddhism was the doctrine of the "Three Bodies" (Trikāya). If the true ideal was that of the bodhisattva, why did not Siddhārtha Gautama remain one, instead of becoming a Buddha and selfishly passing to Nirvāna? This paradox was answered by a theory of docetic type, which again probably had its origin in popular ideas prevalent among lay Buddhists at a very early period. Gautama was not in fact an ordinary man, but the mani- festation of a great spiritual being. The Buddha had three bodies—the Body of Essence (Dharmakāya), the Body of Bliss (Sambhogakāya), and the Body of Magic Transformation (Nirmānakāya). It was the latter only which lived on earth as Siddhārtha Gautama, an emanation of the Body of Bliss, which dwelled forever in the Heavens as a sort of su- preme god. But the Body of Bliss was in turn the emanation of the Body of Essence, the ultimate Buddha, who pervaded and underlay the whole universe. Subtle philosophies and metaphysical systems were de- veloped parallel with these theological ideas, and the Body of Essence was identified with Nirvāna. It was in fact the World Soul, the Brahman of the Upanishads in a new form. In the fully developed Mahāyānist cosmology there were many Bodies of Bliss, all of them emanations of the single Body of Essence, but the heavenly Buddha chiefly concerned with our world was *Amitābha* ("Immeasurable Radiance"), who dwelt in *Sukhāvatī,* "the Happy Land" (or "Pure Land" as it was known to the Chinese), the Heaven of the West. With him was associated the earthly Gautama Buddha, and a very potent and compassionate bodhisattva, Avalokiteshvara ("the Lord Who Looks Down").

The older Buddhism and the newer flourished side by side in India during the early centuries of the Christian era, and we read of Buddhist monasteries in which some of the monks were Mahāyānist and some Hīnayānist. But in general the Buddhists of northwestern India were either Mahāyānists or members of Hīnayāna sects much affected by Mahāyānist ideas. The austerer forms of Hīnayāna seem to have been strongest in parts of western and southern India, and in Ceylon. It was from northwestern India, under the rule of the great Kushāna empire (first to third centuries A.D.) that Buddhism spread throughout central Asia to China; since it emanated from the northwest, it was chiefly of the Mahāyāna or near-Mahāyāna type.

THE COMING OF BUDDHISM TO CHINA

As Buddhism spread from its homeland, it became the harbinger of civilization in many of the areas which it penetrated. Many of them had no system of writing before the advent of the new religion. One of the most notable exceptions to this statement, however, was China. By the time Buddhism was introduced China boasted a civilization already very old, a classic canon, time-hallowed traditions, and the conviction that its society was the only truly civilized society in the world. Thus, while Buddhism was the vehicle for the introduction into such a country as Tibet of religion, art, script, literature, philosophy, etc., the Buddhist missionaries found in China a country that possessed these things in an already highly developed state. Buddhism was obliged to compete with indigenous philosophical and religious systems to win the hearts of the Chinese, and the Chinese, for their own part, were hindered in their understanding of Buddhist philosophy by preconceptions based on indigenous philosophical systems.

No one can say when or in what fashion the Chinese first came into contact with Buddhism. It is to be presumed, from conjecture and from what sparse documentation there is, that this contact was with Buddhist icons worshiped by Central Asians coming into China. The Chinese of the time adopted the Buddha into their scheme of things as a demi-god on the order of their own mythical Yellow Emperor and the philosopher Lao Tzu, who was believed to have attained immortality. But the dawn of history for Chinese Buddhism comes with the rendition of Buddhist sacred texts into the Chinese language.

The Chinese were particularly desirous of knowing whether Buddhism could add to their knowledge of elixirs and practices that would contribute to longevity, levitation, and other superhuman achievements. As it happened, Buddhism (like many other Indian religions) prescribed a precise set of practices, varying from school to school, which was believed to enhance the intuitive faculties. The early Buddhist missionaries found that the scriptures containing these prescriptions were what the Chinese wanted most to read and proceeded to translate them. This is the beginning of Buddhist literature in China.

As time went on, and as the interest of China's intellectuals veered toward metaphysical speculation, it became fashionable to seek in Buddhism those sublime truths that persons so inclined were seeking in some of China's own canonized classics. When, in 317 A.D., non-Chinese nations forced the Chinese court to abandon North China for what was to be a period of nearly three hundred years, the South Chinese intelligentsia became more and more effete, and the dominant trend in the Buddhism of the time was toward abstruse philosophic discussion in salons that brought together the cream of secular society and the best wits in the great metropolitan monasteries. A facile interpretation of Buddhism in Neo-Taoist terms prevailed and Buddhism's Indian origins were all but forgotten.

There were contrary trends, however. In the first place, not a few monks, in both North and South China, were earnestly concerned with the true meaning of Buddhism and of Buddhist salvation. The Chinese aversion to foreign languages being what it was, these persons showed their zeal principally in seeking out capable translators or in participating in translation projects themselves. Also, simultaneously with the philosophical salons and the great translation projects there was a trend, more pronounced in the north than in the south, toward a practical and devotional Buddhism. This consisted of an emphasis on contemplative practices as well as on adoration, good works, etc. The erection of temples and statuary soon spread all over China.

The selections which follow are intended to illustrate the general character of Buddhism in this early period and some of the problems encountered in gaining acceptance for it among the Chinese.

MOU TZU
The Disposition of Error

The date and authorship of this work are not known. The surname of the alleged author, Mou, led many persons to identify him with a Latter Han personality named Mou Jung, but subsequent scholarship has demonstrated beyond any reasonable doubt that this cannot be.

As for the date, the general tone of the composition leads one to suspect that the work was written at a time when Buddhism had gained a sufficient foothold to cause many Chinese to fear its influence and to attempt to strike back. While the counterattack against Buddhism in the north took the form of an official persecution or curtailment, under the Southern Dynasties (420–589 A.D.) it usually took the form of polemics. The *Disposition of Error* or *Li-huo lun,* as it is known in Chinese, appears to be an apologia for Buddhism, written in answer to such polemical writings.

The author takes the stand that it is possible to be a good Chinese and a good Buddhist at the same time, that there is no fundamental conflict between the two ways of life, and that the great truths preached by Buddhism are preached, if in somewhat different language, by Confucianism and Taoism as well.

[From *Hung-ming chi,* in *Taishō daizōkyō,* LII, 1–7]

WHY IS BUDDHISM NOT MENTIONED IN THE CHINESE CLASSICS?

The questioner said: If the way of the Buddha is the greatest and most venerable of ways, why did Yao, Shun, the Duke of Chou, and Confucius not practice it? In the seven Classics one sees no mention of it. You, sir, are fond of the *Book of Odes* and the *Book of History,* and you take pleasure in rites and music. Why, then, do you love the way of the Buddha and rejoice in outlandish arts? Can they exceed the Classics and commentaries and beautify the accomplishments of the sages? Permit me the liberty, sir, of advising you to reject them.

Mou Tzu said: All written works need not necessarily be the words of Confucius, and all medicine does not necessarily consist of the formulae of [the famous physician] P'ien-ch'üeh. What accords with principle is to be followed, what heals the sick is good. The gentleman-scholar draws widely on all forms of good, and thereby benefits his character. Tzu-kung [a disciple of Confucius] said, "Did the Master have a permanent teacher?" Yao served Yin Shou, Shun served Wu-ch'eng, the Duke of Chou learned from Lü Wang, and Confucius learned from Lao Tzu. And none of these teachers is mentioned in the seven Classics. Although these four teachers were sages, to compare them to the Buddha would be like comparing a white deer to a unicorn,[3] or a swallow to a phoenix. Yao, Shun, the Duke of Chou, and Confucius learned even from such teachers as these. How much less, then, may one reject the Buddha, whose distinguishing marks are extraordinary and whose superhuman powers know no bounds! How may one reject him and refuse to learn from him? The records and teachings of the Five Classics do not contain everything. Even if the Buddha is not mentioned in them, what occasion is there for suspicion?

WHY DO BUDDHIST MONKS DO INJURY TO THEIR BODIES?

One of the greatest obstacles confronting the early Chinese Buddhist church was the aversion of Chinese society to the shaving of the head, which was required of all members of the Buddhist clergy. The Confucianists held that the body is the gift of one's parents, and that to harm it is to be disrespectful toward them.

The questioner said: The *Classic of Filial Piety* says, "Our torso, limbs, hair, and skin we receive from our fathers and mothers. We dare not do them injury." When Tseng Tzu was about to die, he bared his hands and feet.[4] But now the monks shave their heads. How this violates the sayings of the sages and is out of keeping with the way of the filially pious! . . .

Mou Tzu said: . . . Confucius has said, "He with whom one may follow a course is not necessarily he with whom one may weigh its merits." This is what is meant by doing what is best at the time. Furthermore, the *Classic of Filial Piety* says, "The kings of yore possessed the ultimate virtue and the essential Way." T'ai-po cut his hair short and tattooed his body, thus following of his own accord the customs of Wu and Yüeh

[3] *Ch'i-lin,* a mythical beast like the unicorn, but not actually one-horned.
[4] To show he had preserved them intact from all harm.

and going against the spirit of the "torso, limbs, hair, and skin" passage.[5] And yet Confucius praised him, saying that his might well be called the ultimate virtue.

WHY DO MONKS NOT MARRY?

Another of the great obstacles confronting the early Chinese Buddhist church was clerical celibacy. One of the most important features of indigenous Chinese religion is ancestor worship. If there are no descendants to make the offerings, then there will be no sacrifices. To this is added the natural desire for progeny. For a Chinese traditionally there could be no greater calamity than childlessness.

The questioner said: Now of felicities there is none greater than the continuation of one's line, of unfilial conduct there is none worse than childlessness. The monks forsake wife and children, reject property and wealth. Some do not marry all their lives. How opposed this conduct is to felicity and filial piety! . . .

Mou Tzu said: . . . Wives, children, and property are the luxuries of the world, but simple living and inaction are the wonders of the Way. Lao Tzu has said, "Of reputation and life, which is dearer? Of life and property, which is worth more?" . . . Hsü Yu and Ch'ao-fu dwelt in a tree. Po-i and Shu-ch'i starved in Shou-yang, but Confucius praised their worth, saying, "They sought to act in accordance with humanity and they succeeded in acting so." One does not hear of their being ill-spoken of because they were childless and propertyless. The monk practices the way and substitutes that for the pleasures of disporting himself in the world. He accumulates goodness and wisdom in exchange for the joys of wife and children.

DEATH AND REBIRTH

Chinese ancestor worship was premised on the belief that the souls of the deceased, if not fed, would suffer. Rationalistic Confucianism, while taking over and canonizing much of Chinese tradition, including the ancestral sacrifices, denied the existence of spirits and hence the immortality of the soul.

The Buddhists, though likewise denying the existence of a soul, accepted transmigration, and the early Chinese understood this to imply a belief in an

---

[5] Uncle of King Wen of the Chou who retired to the barbarian land of Wu and cut his hair and tattooed his body in barbarian fashion, thus yielding his claim to the throne to King Wen.

individual soul which passed from one body to another until the attainment of enlightenment. The following passage must be understood in the light of these conflicting and confusing interpretations.

The questioner said: The Buddhists say that after a man dies he will be reborn. I do not believe in the truth of these words. . . .

Mou Tzu said: . . . The spirit never perishes. Only the body decays. The body is like the roots and leaves of the five grains, the spirit is like the seeds and kernels of the five grains. When the roots and leaves come forth they inevitably die. But do the seeds and kernels perish? Only the body of one who has achieved the Way perishes. . . .

Someone said: If one follows the Way one dies. If one does not follow the Way one dies. What difference is there?

Mou Tzu said: You are the sort of person who, having not a single day of goodness, yet seeks a lifetime of fame. If one has the Way, even if one dies one's soul goes to an abode of happiness. If one does not have the Way, when one is dead one's soul suffers misfortune.

WHY SHOULD A CHINESE ALLOW HIMSELF TO BE INFLUENCED BY INDIAN WAYS?

This was one of the objections most frequently raised by Confucianists and Taoists once Buddhism had acquired a firm foothold on Chinese soil. The Chinese apologists for Buddhism answered this objection in a variety of ways. Below we see one of the arguments used by them.

The questioner said: Confucius said, "The barbarians with a ruler are not so good as the Chinese without one." Mencius criticized Ch'en Hsiang for rejecting his own education to adopt the ways of [the foreign teacher] Hsü Hsing, saying, "I have heard of using what is Chinese to change what is barbarian, but I have never heard of using what is barbarian to change what is Chinese." You, sir, at the age of twenty learned the way of Yao, Shun, Confucius, and the Duke of Chou. But now you have rejected them, and instead have taken up the arts of the barbarians. Is this not a great error?

Mou Tzu said: . . . What Confucius said was meant to rectify the way of the world, and what Mencius said was meant to deplore one-sidedness. Of old, when Confucius was thinking of taking residence among the nine barbarian nations, he said, "If a gentleman-scholar dwells in their midst, what baseness can there be among them?" . . . The Commentary says, "The north polar star is in the center of heaven and to the north of man." From this one can see that the land of China is not necessarily situated under the center of heaven. According to the Buddhist scriptures, above, below, and all around, all beings containing blood belong to the Buddha-clan. Therefore I revere and study these scriptures. Why should I reject the Way of Yao, Shun, Confucius, and the Duke of Chou? Gold and jade do not harm each other, crystal and amber do not cheapen each other. You say that another is in error when it is you yourself who err.

WHY MUST A MONK RENOUNCE WORLDLY PLEASURES?

The questioner said: Of those who live in the world, there is none who does not love wealth and position and hate poverty and baseness, none who does not enjoy pleasure and idleness and shrink from labor and fatigue. . . . But now the monks wear red cloth, they eat one meal a day, they bottle up the six emotions, and thus they live out their lives. What value is there in such an existence?

Mou Tzu said: "Wealth and rank are what man desires, but if he cannot obtain them in a moral way, he should not enjoy them. Poverty and meanness are what man hates, but if he can only avoid them by departing from the Way, he should not avoid them." [6] Lao Tzu has said, "The five colors make men's eyes blind, the five sounds make men's ears deaf, the five flavors dull the palate, chasing about and hunting make men's minds mad, possessions difficult to acquire bring men's conduct to an impasse. The sage acts for his belly, not for his eyes." Can these words possibly be vain? Liu-hsia Hui would not exchange his way of life for the rank of the three highest princes of the realm. Tuan-kan Mu would not exchange his for the wealth of Prince Wen of Wei. . . . All of them followed their ideals, and cared for nothing more. Is there no value in such an existence?

WHY DOES MOU TZU SUPPORT HIS CONTENTIONS FROM SECULAR
RATHER THAN BUDDHIST LITERATURE?

The questioner said: You, sir, say that the scriptures are like the rivers and the sea, their phrases like brocade and embroidery. Why, then, do you not draw on the Buddhist scriptures to answer my questions? Why

[6] *Analects* IV, 5.

instead do you refer to the books of *Odes* and *History,* joining together things that are different to make them appear the same?

Mou Tzu said: . . . I have quoted those things, sir, which I knew you would understand. Had I preached the words of the Buddhist scriptures or discussed the essence of nonaction, it would have been like speaking to a blind man of the five colors or playing the five sounds to a deaf man.

DOES BUDDHISM HAVE NO RECIPE FOR IMMORTALITY?

Within the movement broadly known as "Taoism" there were several tendencies, one the quest for immortality, another an attitude of superiority to questions of life and death. The first Chinese who took to Buddhism did so out of a desire to achieve superhuman qualities, among them immortality. The questioner is disappointed to learn that Buddhism does not provide this after all. Mou Tzu counters by saying that even in Taoism, if properly understood, there is no seeking after immortality.

The questioner said: The Taoists say that Yao, Shun, the Duke of Chou, and Confucius and his seventy-two disciples did not die, but became immortals. The Buddhists say that men must all die, and that none can escape. What does this mean?

Mou Tzu said: Talk of immortality is superstitious and unfounded; it is not the word of the sages. Lao Tzu says, "Even Heaven and earth cannot be eternal. How much the less can man!" Confucius says, "The wise man leaves the world, but humanity and filial piety last forever." I have observed the six arts and examined the commentaries and records. According to them, Yao died, Shun had his [death place at] Mount Ts'ang-wu, Yü has his tomb on K'uai-chi, Po-i and Shu-ch'i have their grave in Shou-yang. King Wen died before he could chastise Chou, King Wu died without waiting for King Ch'eng to grow up. We read of the Duke of Chou that he was reburied, and of Confucius that [shortly before his death] he dreamed of two pillars. [As for the disciples of Confucius], Po-yü died before his father, of Tzu Lu it is said that his flesh was chopped up and pickled. Of [the fatal illness of] Po-niu the Master said, "It must be fate," while of Tseng Shen we read that he bared his feet before death. And of Yen Yüan the Master said, "Unfortunately, he was short-lived," and likened him to a bud that never bloomed. All of these things are clearly recorded in the Classics: they are the absolute

words of the sages. I make the Classics and the commentaries my authority and find my proof in the world of men. To speak of immortality,
is this not a great error?

HUI-YÜAN
A Monk Does Not Bow Down Before a King

When an Indian entered the Buddhist clergy, he left his clan, his caste, and
all his worldly possessions. As one standing outside of ordinary society, from
then on he paid no outward signs of veneration to secular potentates. This
practice seems to have accompanied Buddhism eastward. At any rate, we
know that the early Buddhist clerics in China, though they knelt in their
religious ceremonies, displayed no signs of respect to laymen of authority, not
even to the emperor.

At first this constituted no great problem, since only the most eminent
monks were ever likely to meet the emperor, and these were usually foreigners who were not expected to follow full Chinese etiquette. When native
Chinese came to constitute the majority of Buddhist clerics, however, the problem became more serious. The question was brought under discussion at court
during the Eastern Chin period but no settlement was reached until A.D. 403.
At that time the high minister Huan Hsüan (369–404), who had temporarily
usurped the throne, referred the problem to one of the outstanding monks of
the day, Hui-yüan (334–417), for a decision. Hui-yüan replied with a letter
stating that, though Buddhist laymen, like any other laymen, were obliged
to acknowledge their loyalty and respect for their sovereign by the customary
etiquette, the Buddhist clergy, who by the nature of their life and aims were
far removed from ordinary men, could not be expected to go through the
outward signs of obeisance. Huan Hsüan accepted Hui-yüan's argument and
decreed that monks need not bow before the emperor. Shortly after this Hui-
yüan composed a treatise entitled "A Monk Does Not Bow Down Before a
King" (*Sha-men pu-ching wang-che lun*), stating his argument in greater
detail.

[From *Hung-ming chi*, in *Taishō daizōkyō*, LII, 29–32]

BUDDHISM IN THE HOUSEHOLD

If one examines the broad essentials of what the teachings of Buddha
preach, one will see that they distinguish between those who leave the
household life and those who remain in it. Those who remain within
the household life and those who leave it are, in all, of four kinds. In
propagating the doctrine and reaching the beings their achievement is

equal to that of emperors and kings, their transfiguring effect greater than that of the way of government. When it comes to affecting members and enlightening the times, there is no age that is without them. But, as chance has it, they sometimes function and sometimes conceal themselves, retiring or making their appearance as the faith diminishes or prospers. What can be discussed in words I beg to state in brief.

Those who revere the Buddhist laws but remain in their homes are subjects who are obedient to the transforming powers [of temporal rulers]. Their feelings have not changed from the customary, and their course of conduct conforms to the secular world. Therefore this way of life includes the affection of natural kinship and the proprieties of obedience to authority. Decorum and reverence have their basis herein, and thus they form the basis of the doctrine. That on which they are based has its merit in the past. Thus, on the basis of intimacy it teaches love, and causes the people to appreciate natural kindness; on the basis of austerity it teaches veneration, and causes the people to understand natural respect. The achievement of these two effects derives from an invisible cause. Since the cause is not in the present, one must trace it to its source. Therefore the doctrine makes a punishment of sinful karma, causing one to be fearful and thus circumspect; it makes a reward of the heavenly palaces, causing one to be joyous and then to act. These are the retributions that follow like shadows and echoes, and that are clearly stated in the doctrine. Thus obedience is made the common rule, and the natural way is not changed. . . .

Hence one may not benefit by [the ruler's] virtue and neglect propriety, bask in his kindness and cast aside due respect. Therefore they who rejoice in the way of Shākya invariably first serve their parents and respect their lords. They who change their way of life and throw away their hair ornaments must always await [their parents'] command, then act accordingly. If their lords and parents have doubts, then they retire, inquire of their wishes and wait until [the lords and parents] are enlightened. This, then, is how the teaching of Buddha honors life-giving and assists kingly transformation in the way of government.

BUDDHISM OUTSIDE THE HOUSEHOLD

This second part sets forth the core of Hui-yüan's argument as to why the monk should not make a display of respect for worldly potentates. The monk, so the argument goes, is not a disrespectful, much less an impious, person, but he stands completely outside of the framework of lay life, hence he should not abide by its regulations insofar as merely polite accomplishments are concerned.

He who has left the household life is a lodger beyond the earthly [secular] world, and his ways are cut off from those of other beings. The doctrine by which he lives enables him to understand that woes and impediments come from having a body, and that by not maintaining the body one terminates woe. . . .

If the termination of woe does not depend on the maintenance of the body, then he does not treasure the benefits that foster life. This is something in which the principle runs counter to physical form and the Way is opposed to common practice. Such men as these commence the fulfillment of their vows with the putting away of ornaments of the head [shaving the head], and realize the achievement of their ideal with the changing of their garb. . . . Since they have changed their way of life, their garb and distinguishing marks cannot conform to the secular pattern. . . . Afar they reach to the ford of the Three Vehicles,[7] broadly they open up the Way of Heaven and man. If but one of them be allowed to fulfill his virtue, then the Way spreads to the six relations and beneficence flows out to the whole world. Although they do not occupy the positions of kings and princes, yet, fully in harmony with the imperial ultimate, they let the people be. Therefore, though inwardly they may run counter to the gravity of natural relationships, yet they do not violate filial piety; though outwardly they lack respect in serving the sovereign, yet they do not lose hold of reverence.

HE WHO SEEKS THE FIRST PRINCIPLE IS NOT OBEDIENT TO CHANGE

Question: If we examine Lao Tzu's meaning, we see that for him Heaven and earth are great because of their attainment of the One, kings and princes are honored because they embody obedience.[8] [Heaven and earth] have attained the One, therefore they are the source of the myriad changes; [kings and princes] embody obedience, therefore they have the power of moving others [to obey]. Thus the clarification of the First Principle

---

[7] That is, postponing enlightenment in order to bring others closer to salvation, attaining enlightenment by personal exertions in an age in which there is no Buddha, and attaining enlightenment by hearing the Buddha's preaching.

[8] A reference to *Lao Tzu,* 39.

must of necessity reside in the embodiment of the Ultimate, and the embodiment of the Ultimate must of necessity depend upon obedience to change. Therefore the wise men of yore made this the subject of noble discourses, and from this the opinion of the multitude may not differ. If one differs with the opinion of the multitude, one's principles have nothing worth accepting. And yet you speak of not obeying change. Why?

Answer: In general, those who reside within the limits [of ordinary existence] receive life from the Great Change. Although the numerous varieties of things have a myriad of differences and subtle and gross are of different lineage, if one reduces them to their ultimate, there are only the soulful and the soulless. The soulful have a feeling toward change. The soulless have no feeling toward change. If there is no feeling toward change, when change ends, life is finished. Their life does not depend upon feeling. Therefore the form decays and change ceases. If there is feeling toward change, [the feeling being] reacts to things and moves. Motion must depend upon feeling, therefore the life does not cease. If the life does not cease, the change is ever more far reaching and the physical forms pile up more and more. The feelings are more of a handicap and the encumbrances more weighty. The woes are indescribable. Therefore the scriptures say that Nirvāna is changeless, making the cessation of change its home, while the three worlds [9] are in flux, making sin and pain their place. When change is exhausted, then causes and conditions cease forever; when there is flux, then the suffering of pain has no limit. How can we prove that this is so? Life is fettered by physical form, and life depends upon change. When there is change and the feelings react, then the spirit is barred from its source and the intellect is blinded to its own illumination. If one is thus shut up as in a hard shell, then what is preserved is only the self, and what is traversed is only the state of flux. Thereupon the bridle of the spirit loses its driver, and the road to rebirth is reopened daily. One pursues lust in the long stream of time; is one affected thus only once? Therefore he who returns to the source and seeks the First Principle does not encumber his spirit with life. He who breaks out of the grimy shell does not encumber his life with feelings. If one does not encumber one's spirit with life, then one's

[9] The world of desire, form, and no form, a feature of Indian cosmology adopted by the Buddhists.

spirit can be made subtle. The subtle spirit transcending sense-objects—this is what is meant by Nirvāna. The name Nirvāna, can it possibly be an empty appellation? I beg leave to extend this argument and so prove its truth. Heaven and earth, though they are great because they give life to living beings, cannot cause a living being not to die. Kings and princes, though they have the power of preserving existence, cannot cause a preserved creature to be without woe. Therefore in our previous discussion we have said, "[He who has left the household life] understands that woes and impediments come from having a body, and that by not maintaining the body one terminates woe. He knows that continued life comes from undergoing change, and by not obeying this change he seeks the First Principle." Herein lay our meaning, herein lay our meaning. This is why the monk refuses homage to the Lord of the Myriad Chariots [i.e., the emperor] and keeps his own works sublime, why he is not ranked with kings or princes and yet basks in their kindness.

WHEN THE PHYSICAL FORM IS EXHAUSTED THE SPIRIT DOES NOT PERISH

Early Buddhism in India, unlike the Upanishadic philosophy which asserted the identity of the individual soul with the world soul, denied the existence of the soul altogether. Among the Chinese to whom Buddhism was first introduced, however, there was already a widespread belief in spirits, which strongly conditioned their understanding of the new faith. Upon them the Buddhist denial of the soul made less of an impression than other doctrines which seemed to confirm their own beliefs. In the first place, Buddhism preaches reincarnation, which to the Chinese seemed impossible without an individual soul. In the second place, those scriptures that preached the Storehouse of Consciousness and the presence of Buddhahood in all living beings seemed to be speaking of a soul in different language. But basically it seems to have been a belief already strongly held in the immortality of the soul that inclined the Chinese to interpret Buddhism in this fashion and to ignore the many denials of the soul in the canonical texts. Hui-yüan was one of the learned monks influenced by this belief, and no doubt it was shared by many lesser clerics.

Within the Chinese intellectual tradition, however, there were some who took an opposing view, including Confucian rationalists and naturalistic Taoists. Thus, while deeply attached to the custom of ancestor worship as a family rite, the Confucianists tended to deny the survival of the individual soul after the death of the body. From another point of view Chuang Tzu accepted death as a natural and welcome release from life, there being for him no further problem of continued reincarnation or a need to escape it. It is on this basis that Hui-Yüan's fictitious opponent in this final dialogue challenges the Buddhist doctrine of karma and transmigration.

Question: . . . The receipt of spirit is limited to one life. When the life is exhausted, the breath evaporates, and it is the same as nothing. The spirit, though it is more subtle than matter, is still a transformed manifestation of the yin and the yang. When they have been transformed there is life; when they are transformed again there is death. When they come together there is a beginning; when they disperse there is an end. If one reasons from this, one must know that the spirit and the body are transformed together, and that originally they are of the same line. The subtle and the gross are one breath, and from beginning to end they have the same abode. While the abode is whole, the breath comes together and there is a spirit; when the abode crumbles, the breath disperses and the light goes out. When it disperses, it returns what it has received to the Great Origin. When it has perished, it returns to a state of nothingness. Return and termination are natural destinies. Who could create them? . . . Also, the spirit resides in the body as fire is in the wood. While [the body] lives [the spirit] exists, but when [the body] crumbles [the spirit] must perish. When the body departs the soul disperses and has no dwelling. When the tree rots the fire dies out and has nothing to attach to. That is the principle. Even if the matter of sameness and difference were obscure and difficult to clarify, the doctrine of being and nonbeing must rest in coming together and dispersion. Coming together and dispersion is the general term for the change of the breath; it is the birth-and-death of the myriad changes.

In his reply Hui-yüan explains the principle of reincarnation in terms of individual lives or destinies. The key Chinese word here is *shu,* literally "number," which refers to the individual life-span or allotted destiny. At the same time, however, it has Buddhist overtones suggesting the process of multiple causation (karma) which determines the individual lot in life, and thus, in its most general sense, the world of multiplicity subject to endless change and transmigration.

Answer: What is the spirit? It is subtlety that has reached the extreme and become immaterial. The extreme of subtlety cannot be charted by the trigrams and explanations [of the *Book of Changes*]. Therefore the sage calls it "more subtle than matter" and so names it. . . .

The spirit is in perfect accord and has no creator; it is subtle to the extreme and has no name. In response to beings it moves; borrowing an individual lot [i.e., the life of an individual person] it acts. It responds to things but it is not a thing; therefore though the things may change it does not perish. It borrows a lot [in life] but it is not itself that lot; therefore though the lot be run out, it does not end. Having feelings, it can respond to things; having intelligence, it can be found [embodied] in allotted destinies. There are subtle and gross destinies and therefore the nature of each is different. There are bright and dull intellects and therefore their understanding is not always the same. If one reasons from this, then one knows that change is felt by the feelings, and that the spirit is transmitted through change. Feelings are the mother of change, and the spirit is the root of the feelings. The feelings have a way of uniting with physical things, and the spirit has the power of moving imperceptibly. But a person of penetrating perception returns to the Source, while one who is lost in the principle merely runs after physical things[10]. . . .

Feelings and things possessing a destined lot and the changes they occasion have no bounds. Causes and conditions closely interlock, and imperceptibly transmit and transfer. Were it not for those of penetrating vision, who would know of their transformations and who would know of their coming together? I beg leave to prove it for your sake, my worthy opponent, by recourse to fact. The passage of fire to firewood is like the passage of the soul to the body. The passage of fire to different firewood is like the passage of the soul to a new body. If the former firewood is not the latter firewood, then we know that the way in which the finger exhausts its duty is past comprehension.[11] If the former body is not the latter body, then one understands that the interaction of the feelings and the individual destiny is profound. The person in error, seeing the body wither in one life, thinks that the spirit and the feelings perish with it. It is as if one were to see the fire die out in one piece of wood, and say that all fire had been exhausted for all time.

[10] That is, the enlightened person attains Nirvāna (which for Hui-yüan means that the soul returns to its point of origin), while the victim of error suffers endless reincarnation.
[11] This is an allusion to the closing sentence of the *Chuang Tzu*, ch. 3, which reads (according to the traditional interpretation), "If the finger fulfills its duty in adding firewood, then the transmission of the fire knows no exhaustion." Hui-yüan interprets this to mean that, just as the fire moves from the old firewood to the new, so the soul moves from the old body to the new. For him this is very important, since in his view it is a corroboration from a secular Chinese source of the Buddhist theory of reincarnation.

CHAPTER XVI

THE SCHOOLS
OF BUDDHISM I

Sectarian Buddhism developed in China at least three hundred years after Buddhism's presence was first noted there in the first century. It arose, not as a result of schisms, protestant revolts, or individual claims to some new religious revelation, but as a natural outgrowth of tendencies already manifest in the earlier period of indigenous Buddhist thought.

THE GENERAL CHARACTER OF SECTARIAN BUDDHISM

The division of Chinese Buddhism into discreet sects had its origins in the tendency to concentrate on the study of one particular scripture or group of scriptures, as containing the most essential truths of the religion. The Chinese knew almost nothing of the splintering of Buddhism into sects in India and Central Asia. They did not know to what extent the scriptures themselves were sectarian writings, nor did they properly understand the sectarian motivation that lay behind the selection by the various missionaries of the scriptural texts they translated. For them, any Buddhist text translated into Chinese was the word of the Buddha. And since all of the Buddha's pronouncements had to be true, it was necessary to find some way to reconcile the frequently glaring inconsistencies found in the scriptures. A suggestion on how to deal with this problem was furnished to them by the Mahāyāna scriptures themselves.

By the time of the emergence of the Mahāyāna, the Hīnayāna scriptures had already been canonized, and anyone calling himself a Buddhist regarded them as the word of the Buddha. The Mahāyānists composed their own scriptures as they went along, and they found themselves obliged to justify their scriptures as the good coin of Buddhism to a religious community accustomed to reading religious writings of a vastly different tone. To deny the validity of the firmly entrenched Hīnayāna canon was impossible, and the Mahāyānists resorted to a more subtle device. They said that the Hīnayāna was not untrue, but was merely a preparatory doctrine, preached by the Buddha to disciples whose minds were not yet receptive to the ultimate truth. When he had prepared them with the tentative doctrine, he then revealed to them his final truth. Thus the Mahāyāna and the Hīnayāna were both alike the word of the Buddha, and the contradiction between them was only apparent.

The difficulty here, as far as the Chinese were concerned, was the fact that while the Hīnayāna scriptures, having been canonized by a series of ecclesiastical councils, were more or less homogeneous, the Mahāyāna scriptures had never been canonized or coordinated, and frequently contradicted not only the Hīnayāna sacred writings but one another as well. Nevertheless, the scriptures themselves had given them a valuable hint, and some of them proceeded to act on it. The first distinct sects in Chinese Buddhism were, in short, of two kinds: 1) those that concentrated on one scripture or set of scriptures in preference to all others, and 2) those that catalogued the entire canon in such a way as to make one particular scripture appear to contain the Buddha's ultimate teaching. The great T'ien-t'ai and Hua-yen schools are examples of the latter type.

But the sects exemplified by the T'ien-t'ai and the Hua-yen were of a kind that could never have any popular appeal. Their philosophic ideas were of a high-flown variety that the bulk of China's illiterate populace could not hope to understand. In addition, the religious practices prescribed by them for the attainment of salvation could be performed only by monks whose whole lives were devoted to religion. On both accounts these sects tended to be limited to the upper classes, for only they had the leisure and education that was required for the study and understanding of such sophisticated teachings. Among the great masses of people, therefore, it was not doctrine of this type but rather salvationism of the type represented by the Pure Land sect which prevailed.

Furthermore, the attitude that all scriptures represented the word of the Buddha tended to blur, even for the educated specialist, the doctrinal differences which distinguished one sect from another. In the latter half of the T'ang dynasty, from about 750 to about 900, one frequently encounters an eminent Chinese monk going about from one sectarian center to another studying the precepts of all the sects, as if anything short of mastery of all of them was an imperfect knowledge of Buddhism. Some Chinese monks are claimed as patriarchs by as many as three or four different sects. Thus was confirmed in Chinese Buddhism a strong tendency toward syncretism which had long been a marked feature of Chinese thought. Partly for this reason, too, Buddhism shared another characteristic of Chinese religious life: the absence of strong doctrinal tensions and sectarian conflict.

Before taking up the individual schools which illustrate these tendencies, a few general remarks should be made about the later history of sectarian Buddhism in China, and especially concerning its gradual disintegration. From the very beginning, of course, forces were at work which led to the adaptation and transformation of Buddhism in China. Some of these proved to be creative adaptations, not necessarily in conflict with the original spirit of Indian Buddhism. Others were clearly degenerative in the sense that they involved such complete accommodation to the Chinese religious scene as to lose their distinctively Buddhist character. Along with this doctrinal dilution of Buddhism there was the organizational decay which resulted in part from political and social pressures. These included official persecution through the enforced secularization of monks and nuns and the confiscation of monastic land and wealth. The Chinese court kept a jealous, and sometimes covetous, eye on the power and splendor of religious establishments. In addition, the later period of Chinese Buddhism was marked by a deterioration in the standards of the clergy and in monastic discipline. Commercialism infiltrated Buddhist institutions. The general level of education and indoctrination declined, to the point in fact where the average monk might well have been illiterate and in any case knew nothing of Buddhist doctrines. Thus the institutional disintegration of Buddhism was already well advanced before the advent of modern secularism from the West in the late nineteenth and early twentieth centuries. During the early years of the republic this process was greatly accelerated, directly by movements which struck at "superstition" and "obscurantism," and indirectly by the general trend of social and economic decline. Under the Communists the attack has been even more severe and devastating, and such glimmer-

ings of a Buddhist revival as had appeared in reaction to Westernization
in previous decades have now been completely snuffed out. Under present
conditions a Buddhist resurgence in contemporary China is out of the
question.

THE SCHOOLS OF CHINESE BUDDHIST PHILOSOPHY

From the readings in the last chapter it will be apparent that some
of the most fundamental concepts of Buddhism were comprehended and
assimilated by the Chinese with the greatest of difficulty, if at all. Similarly,
our own attempts to understand and translate the more subtle doctrines
of Chinese Buddhism into modern Western terms encounter serious obstacles: textual, linguistic, and historical, as well as conceptual. Concerning many of these problems specialists themselves admit that they are
in the dark, their researches being guided more by caution and diffidence
than by a confident grasp of the subject.

As he takes up the writings of Buddhist philosophers, the reader will
be conscious of having entered another world—not just different from
his own, but different even from the Chinese traditions which preceded
it. For one thing, he will be dealing with metaphysical and psychological
questions which earlier Chinese writers gave less attention to than they
did to the problems of the individual in society. Yet not only are these
questions in their very nature extremely complex, subtle, and elusive,
but also, as discussed by Chinese writers, they presuppose the reader's
familiarity with a vast body of Buddhist doctrine from India. It should
not be forgotten that these writers expounded their ideas to a select group:
those who had some education (always a small minority in China) and
who had dedicated themselves to the pursuit of the religious life, most
often in monasteries. Their audience was not "the general public," nor
the "congregation," nor anything resembling the partakers of modern
mass education. Most often our reader will lack that background knowledge which the writer presupposes in his more specialized audience. For
this reason an attempt has been made to supply it, where possible, in
the introductory matter.

Notwithstanding the difficulties involved in approaching Chinese Buddhist philosophy, the discussion which follows may still provide the reader with some understanding of the type of questions considered most significant by Chinese Buddhists, and some idea also of the range of answers offered to them. In that case the reader will come to appreciate, perhaps not what Chinese Buddhism *is*, but what it is like.

Buddhist philosophy, it will be recalled, first began to flourish in the fourth century A.D. It was interpreted then largely in Taoist terms, on the basis of which "six schools and seven branches" were formed, including Tao-an's theory of Original Nonbeing or the Originally Undifferentiated; the same theory as modified by Fa-shen; Chih Tao-lin's theory of Matter-as-Such; and Fa-wen's theory of No Mind or the Emptiness of Mind. These were simply individual thinkers, not sectarian leaders. As important Indian texts were introduced and translated, as Indian masters arrived, and as Chinese Buddhist scholars finally developed their own systems, differences in opinion appeared and sects came into being. In their zeal to defend their ideas, certain schools of thought denounced others as heretical and established a lineage to earlier masters in order to claim for themselves the authority of tradition. As far as the ordinary Buddhist was concerned, these differences were academic. Thus the sects were essentially different systems of thought rather than contending denominations of religious practice.

Altogether there were ten principal schools, traditionally divided into two main categories, schools of Being and schools of Nonbeing, depending on whether they affirmed or denied the self-nature of the dharmas (here "elements of existence") and the ego. Three of these, the Ch'eng-shih (*Satyasiddhi,* "Establishment of Truth"), the Chü-she (*Abhidharmakośa*), and the Disciplinary (Lü, *Vinaya*), were regarded in China as Hīnayāna schools. The Ch'eng-shih, based on the Satyasiddhi treatise by Harivarman (A.D. c. 250–350), maintained that both dharmas and the ego are unreal. It is not certain whether the school ever existed in India. The treatise was translated into Chinese by Kumārajīva (A.D. 344–413) and was very popular in the fifth and sixth centuries. However, during the eighth century it was absorbed into the Middle Doctrine school.

Another Hīnayāna school, the Chü-she, grew up around the study of Vasubandhu's *Abhidharmakośa,* after it had been translated into Chinese. This school held that "both dharmas and the ego exist." It was active in the sixth and seventh centuries, having replaced the earlier P'i-t'an school which had promulgated the "All Exists" doctrine.

The third Hīnayāna school, the Disciplinary, was based on the Vinaya section of the Buddhist canon. Its doctrine was elaborated and completed by Tao-hsüan (596–667) in the South Mountain. The discipline for which it was known included 250 "prohibitive precepts" for monks and 348 for nuns. Nevertheless, this school hardly existed as an independent sect in China.

None of these three schools exerted much influence or lasted very long. The same may be said of two Mahāyāna schools, the Three-Treatise school and the Consciousness-Only school. They, like the Hīnayāna schools, taught one-sided philosophies, the former reducing everything to Emptiness and the latter reducing everything to Consciousness. Representing such extreme positions, they did not suit the temper of the Chinese. Both the concepts of Emptiness and of the Mind, however, were accepted as basic tenets of the remaining schools, and in this way they have been of great importance in Chinese Buddhist history.

The schools that have formed the spirit and substance of Chinese Buddhism have been the T'ien-t'ai, Hua-yen, Meditation, and Pure Land schools. The common Chinese saying, "The T'ien-t'ai and Hua-yen schools for doctrine and the Meditation and Pure Land schools for practice," accurately describes both the strong influence of these schools in particular and the syncretic nature of Chinese Buddhism in general.

These are essentially Chinese schools because the T'ien-t'ai did not exist in India and while the Pure Land, Hua-yen, and Meditation schools can be traced to India, they developed along characteristically Chinese lines. For this reason they came to overshadow the others and persisted throughout Chinese history.

The following selections have been made from the standard Chinese texts of the six Mahāyāna schools. An attempt is made to include the fundamental ideas of the schools, especially as developed by the Chinese. Chinese translations of Indian works, with the sole exception of the *Scripture of the Lotus of the Wonderful Law,* are not included. Many of these, such as the *Avataṃsaka Sūtra* on which the Hua-yen was founded, are basic philosophical works. Others, like the *Amitābha Sūtra* and the *Diamond Sūtra* have been popular among millions of followers.

While recognizing their fundamental importance to Chinese Buddhists, we must give our primary attention here to products of the native tradition.

The remaining Mahāyāna school, the Esoteric school (Chen-yen, "True Word"), believes that the universe consists of the "three mysteries" of action, speech, and thought. All phenomena represented by these categories of action, speech, and thought are manifestations of the Great Sun Buddha, which is the universe itself. Through secret language, "mystical verse," "true words," etc., the quintessential truth of the Buddha can be communicated to human beings. This doctrine was transmitted to China by several Indian monks and attained a considerable vogue in the eighth century, but rapidly declined thereafter. Its influence was felt mostly in Tibet and Japan, rather than in China.

THE THREE-TREATISE SCHOOL

The Three-Treatise (San-lun) school is the Chinese representative of the Indian Mādhyamika (Middle Doctrine) school of Nāgārjuna (A.D. c. 100 to 200). It was introduced into China by a half-Indian missionary named Kumārajīva (344–413) who translated into Chinese the three Indian works systematizing the Middle Doctrine, two by Nāgārjuna, and the other by his disciple Deva. Hence the name Three-Treatise school.

The Mādhyamika school taught that the phenomenal world has only a qualified reality, as opposed to the Sarvāstivādins, who maintained the ultimate reality of the chain of events or elements which make up the phenomenal being or object. According to the Mādhyamika view, a monk with defective eyesight may imagine that he sees flies in his begging bowl, and they have full reality for the percipient. Though the flies are not real the illusion of flies is. The Mādhyamika philosophers tried to prove that all our experience of the phenomenal world is like that of the short-sighted monk, that all beings labor under the constant illusion of perceiving things where in fact there is only emptiness. This Emptiness or Void (Śūnyatā) is all that truly exists, and hence the Mādhyamikas were sometimes also called Śūnyavādins ("exponents of the doctrine of Emptiness"). But the phenomenal world is true pragmatically, and therefore has qualified reality for practical purposes. Yet the whole chain of existence is only real in this qualified sense, for it is composed of a series

of transitory events, and these, being impermanent, cannot have reality
in themselves. Emptiness, on the other hand, never changes. It is absolute
truth and absolute being—in fact it is the same as Nirvāna and the Body
of Essence, or Dharma-Body, of the Buddha.

Nāgārjuna's system, however, went farther than this. Nothing in the
phenomenal world has full being, and all is ultimately unreal. Therefore every rational theory about the world is a theory about something
unreal evolved by an unreal thinker with unreal thoughts. Thus, by
the same process of reasoning, even the arguments of the Mādhyamika
school in favor of the ultimate reality of Emptiness are unreal, and this
argument against the Mādhyamika position is itself unreal, and so on
in an infinite regress. Every logical argument can be reduced to absurdity
by a process such as this.

The effect of Mādhyamika nihilism was not what might be expected.
Skeptical philosophies in the West, such as that of existentialism, are
generally strongly flavored with pessimism. The Mādhyamikas, however, were not pessimists. If the phenomenal world was ultimately unreal, Emptiness was real, for, though every logical proof of its existence
was vitiated by the flaw of unreality, it could be experienced in meditation with a directness and certainty which the phenomenal world did
not possess. The ultimate Emptiness was here and now, everywhere and
all-embracing, and there was in fact no difference between the great
Emptiness and the phenomenal world. Thus all beings were already participants of the Emptiness which was Nirvāna, they were already Buddha
if only they would realize it. This aspect of Mādhyamika philosophy was
specially congenial to Chinese Buddhists, nurtured in the doctrine of the
Tao, and it had much influence in the development of the special forms
of Chinese and Japanese Buddhism, which often show a frank acceptance
of the beauty of the world, and especially of the beauty of nature, as a
vision of Nirvāna here and now.

For an understanding of this doctrine as it is discussed in Chinese
texts familiarity with certain technical terms is necessary. One is the
concept of "common truth" and "higher truth." It is from the standpoint
of common or worldly truth, i.e., relatively or pragmatically, that dharmas
are said to exist. From the standpoint of "higher truth" they are seen
to be transitory and lacking in any reality or self-nature. Emptiness or
the Void alone represents the changeless Reality. The dialectical process

by which this ultimate truth is reached is known as the "Middle Path of Eightfold Negations," which systematically denies all antithetical assertions regarding things: "there is no production, no extinction, no annihilation, no permanence, no unity, no diversity, no coming in, no going out." Production, extinction, etc. are proved by the school to be unreal by the use of the "four Points of Argument": that is, by refuting an idea as being, as nonbeing, as both being and nonbeing, and as neither being nor nonbeing. The belief in any of the four is an extreme and must be transcended by a higher synthesis through the dialectic method until the Ultimate Void is arrived at, which is the Absolute Middle.

The Middle Doctrine was greatly elaborated and systematized by Chi-tsang (549–623), who had a Parthian father and a Chinese mother. Kumārajīva's introduction of the three treatises had been an effective blow against the metaphysical salons which flourished in the South during the fourth and fifth centuries, interpreting Buddhism in largely Taoist terms. Chi-tsang made the treatises the center of his system of thought and his influence extended to the eighth century. However, the school rapidly declined after the ninth century and soon disappeared.

A large number of Chi-tsang's writings survive, consisting principally of commentaries on Mahāyāna scriptures and treatises, and containing one of the earliest overall attempts at a systematization of Mahāyāna theology.

CHI-TSANG
The Profound Meaning of the Three Treatises

Having set forth his interpretation of the Three Treatises in detailed commentaries to each of them, Chi-tsang here arranges topically what he considers to be the essential doctrine of the treatises as a whole. The stated purpose of his treatise is the "refutation of wrong and demonstration of right." First, he attacks the errors of "outside" or non-Buddhist doctrines among the philosophical schools of India.

[From San-lun hsüan-i, in Taishō daizōkyō, XLV, 1–11]

Altogether in the Western Regions there are ninety-six schools of thought, but among them we may distinguish four basic doctrines which are strongly held. The first is the speculation of erroneous cause and erroneous effect, the second adheres to the doctrine that causes do not exist but effects do, the third sets up the theory that causes exist but effects do not, and the fourth argues that neither cause nor effect exists.

Question: What is meant by "erroneous cause and erroneous effect"?

Answer: There are some heretics who say that the Great Self-existent Heaven (*Maheśvara*) is capable of begetting the myriad beings, and that when the myriad beings perish they return to their Source-Heaven. This is why it is called self-existent. If the Self-existent Heaven is angry all the four kinds of beings [1] suffer, and if the Self-existent Heaven is happy, then all the six stages of existence [2] are in joy. However, Heaven is not the beings' cause, nor are the beings Heaven's effect. They are the imaginings of an erroneous mind. Therefore it is called "erroneous cause and erroneous effect". . . .

To this we [also] object: Good invites a pleasant reward, while evil brings about suffering as a result. For this world is the abode of mutual effect and influence, the place of retribution and response. Only because heretics do not understand these principles have they produced these errors. Furthermore, the species of man begets man, then man in turn resembles man. If the species of things begets things, then things in turn resemble things. This, after all, is the way of self-reproduction. But to say that a single cause, Heaven, can produce the effect of a myriad of species, is this not an error?

Question: What is meant by "nonexistence of cause but existence of effect"?

Answer: There are again certain heretics who, after exhaustive investigation of the myriad things, say that there is nothing from which they originate. Therefore they say that cause does not exist, but that if one actually looks at the various objects, one must know that there are effects. In Chuang Tzu's story about a lump of darkness questioning its own shadow, for example, the shadow exists because of the body, while the body is due to the process of creation [that is, self-transformation]. Since it is due to the process of creation, it has no cause. If the root exists of itself, then the branches are not caused by anything else. Therefore causes are nonexistent and effects existent.

---

[1] Creatures born from the womb, those born from eggs, those supposedly engendered by moisture, and those that come into being through transformation.

[2] Gods, humans, demons, beasts, spirits of the departed, and hell-dwellers.

If we ask, "What difference is there between causelessness and [the Taoist concept of] spontaneity?" they will answer, "'Causelessness' is based on the fact that no cause exists; 'spontaneity' clarifies the fact that the effect exists." While in terms of meaning they are not the same, yet they represent the same adherence to error. And to this we object: Cause and effect produce each other just as length and shortness reveal each other. If there is already an effect, how can there be no cause? If there is no cause, how can there be effect alone? If one insists that there is no cause, and yet there is an effect, then good must bring on the prison of Hell and evil lead the way to Paradise.

Question: What is meant by "there are causes but no effects"?

Answer: According to the school which holds to the [false] view of extinction,[3] there is only a present, but no future. For example, grass and trees all exist for one season only.

To this we object: . . . [As Hui-yüan said], the transmission in firewood is similar to the transmission of the spirit in the body. Fire is transmitted to new firewood as the spirit is transmitted to a new body. . . . [These heretics] seeing the fire die out in one piece of wood, [erroneously] say that fire has perished completely until the end of time. . . .

Question: What is meant by "no-cause and no-effect"?

Answer: [Adherents to this doctrine] deny the existence of both effects produced in the future and causes in the present. . . .

Of the four heresies, this is the most evil. In the present it cuts off good, and for the future it produces an evil state of being. [p. 1]

Having disposed of other philosophies, Chi-tsang now turns his attention to the errors of rival schools within Buddhism. In the section excerpted below he points out some of the errors of the Abhidharma school, a branch of Hīnayāna Buddhism which had appeared in China before the introduction of the Three-Treatise school. The Abhidharmists believed that the dharmas, or ultimate constituents of things, had real existence.

The refutation [of Abhidharma philosophy] has ten divisions. First, it runs counter to the Ultimate Way; second, it abets numerous false views; third, it violates the Great Doctrine [the Mahāyāna]; fourth, it holds to the small fish-trap;[4] fifth, it errs in its own principle; sixth, it has no

---

[3] That existing things are destructible, the death of the body is all-final, etc.

[4] This refers to the famous statement in the *Chuang Tzu* that the purpose of the trap is to catch fish, and that the trap has no intrinsic value whatever. According to

basic faith; seventh, it has stubborn biases; eighth, it does not study fundamentals; ninth, it spoils the words of truth; tenth, it loses the perfect essentials. . . .

Fourthly, "it holds to the small fish-trap": To a man who does not know the source one shows the stream, causing him to trace the stream until he reaches the source. To a man who does not see the moon one points it out with his finger, causing him to follow the finger until he sees the moon. Once the man has traced the stream all the way, he will find that there is one source; once he has gone beyond the finger he finds that there is only one moon. This was the Buddha's meaning in preaching the Small [Vehicle]. Yet the followers of the Abhidharma adhere stubbornly to the Small Principle, and do not turn toward the Great Way. They hold on to the trap and lose the reality, therefore [Nāgārjuna] wrote this discourse to refute them. . . .

Question: Why does one who studies Abhidharma arrive at false views?

Answer: If one says [with the Abhidharma] that the Four Conditions [5] produce the dharmas, then who produces the Four Conditions? If the Four Conditions are born of something else, then that something must be born from something else again, ad infinitum. If the Four Conditions exist of themselves and are not born of anything else, then the myriad things must also not originate from the Four Conditions, and fall into the category of causelessness. Therefore, if beings are born of something else, the process would be unlimited, and if there is a limit there is no cause. From these two points, one may not believe in cause-and-effect. Therefore, if one studies the Abhidharma for long, one arrives at false views. [pp. 2-3]

Of those who misunderstand the Twofold Truth [6] there are, in all, three kinds of men. First are the Abhidharmists, who insist upon the existence of a definite substance, who err in [taking as ultimate what is

---

the Mahāyāna, the Hīnayāna is but an aid toward the understanding of the ultimate truth embodied in the Mahāyāna, but the Abhidharmists make the mistake of adhering to the trap and forgetting about the fish.

[5] Or secondary causes, namely: the Cause Condition, or the chief cause; the Continous Condition which immediately follows a preceding condition; the Objective Condition which has an object or environment as a concurring cause; and the Upheaving Condition which brings all the abiding causes to a culmination.

[6] The Common Truth, that dharmas have a relative or dependent existence; and the Higher Truth, that they are ultimately unreal and Emptiness or the Void alone constitutes changeless reality.

in fact no more than] dependent existence [that is, a thing coming into existence depending on causes and conditions], and who therefore lose [the true meaning of] Common Truth. They also do not know that dependent existence, just as it is, has no existence, and thus they also lose [the true meaning] of the One True Emptiness. Second are those who learn the Great Vehicle and who are called the Men of the Extensive and Broad Way. They adhere to a belief in Emptiness and fail to know dependent existence, hence they lose the [true meaning of] Common Truth. Having adhered to the misunderstood Emptiness, they err with regard to the true Emptiness, and thus also lose the [true meaning of] Higher Truth. Third are those in this very age who, though knowing of the Twofold Truth, in some cases say that it is one substance, in some cases say that it is two substances. The theories are both untenable, hence they lose the [true meaning of both] Higher and Common Truth.

Question: "Higher and Common Truths are one substance." What error is there in this?

Answer: If Higher and Common Truths are one and the same in being true, then Higher Truth is true and Common Truth is also true. If Higher Truth and Common Truth are one and the same in being common, then Common Truth is common and Higher Truth is also common. If Higher Truth is true and Common Truth is not true, then Common Truth and Higher Truth are different. If Common Truth is common and Higher Truth is not common, then Higher Truth and Common Truth are different. Therefore both ways are blocked, and the two cannot be one.

Question: If it is an error to regard the two as one substance, then it should be blameless to regard them as different.

Answer: The scriptures say, "Matter in and of itself is void, void in and of itself is matter." If you say that each has its own substance, then their mutual identity is destroyed. If they have mutual identity, then duality of substance cannot be established. Therefore there is no latitude [for argument] in any direction, and conflicting theories are all exhausted.

Mahāyāna Truth is beyond all predication. It is neither one nor many, neither permanent nor impermanent. In other words, it is above all forms of differentiation or, as its adherents might say, it transcends both difference and identity. In order to make this point clear, San-lun doctrine teaches that each thesis that may be proposed concerning the nature of Truth must be negated by its antithesis, the whole process advancing step by step until total negation has been achieved. Thus the idea of being, representing Common Truth, is negated by that of nonbeing, representing Higher Truth. In turn the idea of nonbeing, now become the Common Truth of a new pair, is negated by the idea of neither being nor nonbeing, and so forth until everything that may be predicated about Truth has been negated.

Question: If the inner [Buddhist Schools] and the outer [Heretics] are both refuted, if the Great [Vehicle] and the Small [Vehicle] are both rejected, then this is the heresy of annihilation. Why call it "true principle"?

Answer: Once the inner and the outer are both obliterated, [the heresies of] annihilation and eternity are thereupon silenced. Once the two extremes are rejected, how can it be other than true principle?

Objection: Now there is [the heresy of] annihilation and there is [the heresy of] eternity; therefore one says that they "are." If there is no [heresy of] annihilation and no [heresy of] eternity, one designates them by saying that they "are not." If they truly "are not," how does [this assertion of their nonexistence] escape [identity with the heresy of] annihilation?

Answer: Once [the heresies of] annihilation and eternity have been silenced, then existence and nonexistence have been equally avoided, and one may no longer charge that [this doctrine] is contaminated by [adherence to the notion of positive] nonexistence.

Objection: Though you have this way out, still you cannot escape rebuttal. Now when there is existence or there is nonexistence, one says that it "is." If there is neither existence nor nonexistence, this itself is "great nonexistence." [7] But once one has fallen into [the idea of] nonexistence, how can [this assertion of nonexistence] escape [identity with the heresy of] annihilation?

Answer: Originally, it was to counter the disease of [belief in] existence that we preached nonexistence. If the disease of [belief in] existence vanishes, the medicine of Emptiness is also useless. Thus we know that the Way of the sage has never held to either existence or nonexistence. What obstacle can there be, then?

Objection: "It *is* existence, it *is* nonexistence,"—one may call this twofold affirmation. "It is *not* existence, it is *not* nonexistence,"—one may call

---

[7] That is, a sort of super-negative, which even negates negation.

this twofold negation. But once one has fallen into affirmation and negation, one has reverted to [the teachings of] Confucius and Mo [Tzu].

Answer: At bottom, it is because it repudiates twofold affirmation that it has twofold negation. But once twofold affirmation has been banished from the mind, twofold negation also ceases. Hence one knows that it is not affirmation, but also that it is not negation.

Objection: "It is *not* affirmation and it is *not* negation." Once again you have fallen into twofold negation. How can you escape negation?

Answer: Twofold affirmation begets a tiger in a dream, twofold negation conjures up a flower in the air.[8] Thus we know that originally there is nothing to affirm, and consequently there is nothing to negate.

Objection: If there is neither affirmation nor negation, then there is also no wrong and no right. Why, then, in the beginning section do you call it "The Refutation of Wrong and the Demonstration of Right"?

Answer: [The idea that] there is affirmation and negation, we consider "wrong." [The idea that] there is neither affirmation nor negation, we call "right." It is for this reason that we have thus called the section explaining the refutation of wrong and the demonstration of right.

Objection: Once there is a wrong to be refuted and a right to be demonstrated, then the mind is exercising a choice. How can one say then that it "leans on nothing"?

Answer: In order to put an end to wrong, we force ourselves to speak of "right." Once wrong has been ended, then neither does right remain. Therefore the mind has nothing to which it adheres [or on which it leans].

Objection: If wrong and right are both obliterated, is this not surely a [positive] view of Emptiness?

Answer: The Treatise on Right Views says:

> The Great Sage preached the Law of Emptiness
> In order to separate [men] from all [positive] views.
> If one still has the view that there "is" Emptiness,
> Such a person even the Buddhas cannot transform.

If water could extinguish fire and then again produce fire, what can be used to extinguish it? [The heresies of] annihilation and eternity are a

---

[8] That is, they are both figments of the imagination.

fire, and Emptiness can extinguish it. But if one clings to Emptiness, then there is no medicine that can extinguish [that disease].[9]

Objection: Once a person is attached to the disease of Emptiness, why, instead of giving him the medicine of existence, do you say that he cannot be converted?

Answer: If one teaches in terms of existence, then one becomes bogged down in existence. At the other extreme, if one banishes words, one becomes attached to annihilation. How can one convert such persons as these?

Question: If the mind has an attachment, what error is there in that?

Answer: If there is an attachment, then there is a fetter, and one cannot obtain release from birth and old age, sickness and death, care and sorrow, pain and suffering. Therefore the *Lotus of the Wonderful Law* says: "I, by means of numberless devices, attract the multitudinous beings, causing them to be separated from all attachments." *Pure Name* says: "To be unattached to the world is to be like the lotus flower. One is never skilled at entering into empty and quiescent action, one attains to the essence of the dharmas without ensnarement or impediment. I bow my head to that which, like space itself, is without any base." The Buddhas of the three ages, because the minds of the beings in the six stages of existence have their attachments, came into the world to preach the scriptures. The Guides of the Fourth Refuge,[10] because the minds of the great and small learners had their props,[11] came into the world to compose their discourses. Hence, when there is a leaning or an obtaining, this is the source of birth and death. To be without any dwelling or attachment is the great principle of the scriptures and treatises. [p. 6]

Question: Why does the scripture set up the Twofold Truth?

Answer: There are two reasons. First it wishes to demonstrate that the Law of Buddha is the Middle Way. Since there is a Common Truth, there is no [heresy of] annihilation [that is, that things have no existence whatever]. Because of the Supreme Truth there is no [heresy of] eternity [that is, that things have eternal existence]. This is why it establishes the Two-

---

[9] That is, the view that Emptiness (the absence of all predication) is a positive attribute, a cardinal heresy from the Mahāyāna point of view.

[10] Those in the final stage of bodhisattvahood who open the way of salvation for others.

[11] What we have rendered "refuge," "prop," and, below, "leaning," all go back to Chinese *i,* the basic meaning of which is "to lean." The truth, according to the Mahāyāna, is supposed to have no substance, nothing on which one can lay hold or lean.

fold Truth. Further, the two wisdoms are the father and mother of the Dharma-Body of the Buddhas of the three ages [past, present, and future]. Because there is the Supreme Truth, true wisdom is produced. Because there is Common Truth therefore [the use of] expedient devices [to save all sentient beings] comes into being. When true wisdom and expedient wisdom are both present, then one has the Buddhas of the ten directions and the three ages. For this reason it establishes the Twofold Truth.

Again, to know the Supreme Truth is to benefit oneself; to know the Common Truth is to be able to benefit others; to know both truths simultaneously is to be able to benefit all equally. Therefore it establishes the Twofold Truth. Also, it is because there is Twofold Truth that the Buddha's words are all true. By virtue of the Common Truth, when he preaches the doctrine of existence, that is true. By virtue of the Supreme Truth, when he preaches the doctrine of Emptiness, that is true. In addition, the Law of Buddha becomes gradually more profound. First he preaches the Common Truth of cause and effect to convert people. Then he preaches the Supreme Truth for them. Also, for the purpose of achieving perfection and achieving the Way he preaches the Supreme Truth to those who possess wisdom and the Common Truth to those who do not. Furthermore, had he not first preached the Common Truth of cause and effect, but preached right away the Supreme Truth, he would have given rise to the heresy of annihilation. For these reasons he preaches both aspects of the Twofold Truth. [p. 11]

THE SCHOOL OF CONSCIOUSNESS-ONLY

The school of Consciousness-Only (Wei-shih) corresponds to the Vijñānavāda or Yogācāra school of Indian Buddhism, which, together with the Middle Doctrine school, represented one of the two main branches of Mahāyāna philosophy. Its great teachers in India were Asanga (fourth century A.D.) and Vasubandhu, of about the same period. When Asanga's works were translated into Chinese in the sixth century A.D., the school was first known as the She-lun, but eventually it was absorbed into the school of the great Chinese monk, translator and philosopher, Hsüan-chuang or Hsüan-tsang (596–664). The latter's school was also known as the Dharma-Character (Fa-hsiang) school after one of the characteristic features of its teaching, as explained below.

The pilgrimage of Hsüan-tsang to the Western regions, in search of the true teachings of Buddhism, is one of the great sagas of Chinese history and literature. After a long and arduous journey he reached the great centers of Buddhist learning in India and Central Asia, where he studied for many years and engaged in debate with the great philosophers of the time. Upon returning home he devoted himself to the monumental task of translating no less than seventy-five basic Buddhist texts into Chinese. Among his most significant accomplishments was the selecting, summarizing, translating, and systematizing of the works of ten great idealists, especially Dharmapāla, in his *Ch'eng-wei-shih lun* (*Vijñapti-mātratā-siddhi* or *Establishment of the Consciousness-Only System*).

The Yogāchāra or Vijñānavāda school was one of pure idealism, and may be compared to the systems of Berkeley and Hume. The whole universe exists only in the mind of the perceiver. The fact of illusion, as in the case of the flies in the short-sighted monk's bowl, or the experience of dreams, was adduced as evidence to show that all normal human experience was of the same type. It is possible for the monk in meditation to raise before his eyes visions of every kind which have quite as much vividness and semblance of truth as have ordinary perceptions; yet he knows that they have no objective reality. Perception therefore is no proof of the independent existence of any entity, and all perceptions may be explained as projections of the percipient mind. Vijñānavāda, like some Western idealist systems, found its chief logical difficulty in explaining the continuity and apparent regularity of the majority of our sense impressions, and in accounting for the fact that the impressions of most people who are looking at the same time in the same direction seem to cohere in a remarkably consistent manner. Bishop Berkeley, to escape this dilemma, postulated a transcendent mind in which all phenomena were thoughts. The Vijñāna-vādins explained the regularity and coherence of sense impressions as due to an underlying store of perceptions (*ālayavijñāna*), evolving from the accumulation of traces of earlier sense-impressions. These are active, and produce impressions similar to themselves, according to a regular pattern, as seeds produce plants. Each being possesses one of these stores of perception, and beings which are generically alike will produce similar perceptions from their stores at the same time. By this strange conception, which bristles with logical difficulties and is one of the most difficult of all Indian philosophy, the Vijñānavādins managed to avoid the logical conclusion of idealism in solipsism. Moreover they admitted the existence of at least one entity independent of human thought—a pure and integral being without characteristics, about which nothing could truly be predicated because it was without predicates. This was called "Thusness" or "Suchness" (*Tathatā*) and corresponded to the Emptiness or Void of the Mādhyamikas, and to the Brahman of Vedānta. Though the terminology is different the metaphysics of Mahāyāna Buddhism has much in common with the doctrines of some of the Upanishads and of Shankara.

For the Vijñānavāda school salvation was to be obtained by exhausting the store of consciousness until it became pure being itself, and identical with the Thusness which was the only truly existent entity in the universe. The chief means of doing this, for those who had already reached a certain stage of spiritual development, was yogic praxis. Adepts of this school were taught to conjure up visions, so that, by realizing that visions and pragmatically real perceptions had the same vividness and subjective reality, they might become completely convinced of the total subjectivity of all phenomena. Thus the meditating monk would imagine himself a mighty god, leading an army of lesser gods against Māra, the spirit of the world and the flesh.

In its more technical formulation, as expounded in China, this doctrine reduces all existence to one hundred dharmas in five divisions, namely, Mind, Mental Functions, Form, Things Not Associated with Mind, and Non-created Elements. Whereas the other schools treated the mind as one dharma, here it is divided into eight consciousnesses. According to this doctrine, the external world is produced when the ālaya (storehouse) consciousness, which is in constant flux, is influenced ("perfumed") by "seeds" or effects of good and evil deeds. As such the phenomenal world is one of appearance or specific characters. It is from this that the school is called Fa-hsiang or Dharma-Character school. But in the final analysis everything is consciousness only, whence comes the other common name for this school.

With regard to the nature of dharmas, the school classifies them into three species. Those of the "character of sole imagination" have only "false existence." Those of the "character of dependence" have "temporary existence," for things produced through causation enjoy neither self-nature nor permanent reality. Only those of the "character of ultimate reality" have "true existence." This ultimate reality is Thusness, the true noumenon transcending all appearance and specific characters. It is Nirvāna. It is the True State of the Tathāgata, the Thus-come One.

In order to reach this state, it is necessary to go through various stages of spiritual development leading to Perfect Wisdom or the Fourfold Wisdom of the Buddha. This is achieved when the first five consciousnesses have become the "wisdom of action," the sense-center consciousness has become the "wisdom of insight," the mind consciousness has become the "wisdom of equanimity," and the ālaya consciousness has become the "wisdom of magnificent mirror."

The school began to decline in China in the ninth century and disappeared several hundred years afterward. This was probably because, like the Three-Treatise school, its philosophy was too subtle, too abstract, and too extreme for most Chinese. Moreover, unlike the Three-Treatise school, it seems to have resisted the tendency to synthesize with other schools. In the twentieth century a new interest was shown in this philosophy by Chinese scholars, and a few Buddhists even made a serious effort to revive it.

The following selection is made from the *Ch'eng-wei-shih lun,* the most important philosophical work of the school, to give an idea of its central concept of consciousness as the only reality.

HSÜAN-CHUANG (OR HSÜAN-TSANG)

Confirmation of the Consciousness-Only System
[From the *Ch'eng-wei-shih lun,* in *Taishō daizōkyō,* XXXI, 7, 10, 22, 25, 37, 38]

The verse [by Vasubandhu] says:

First of all, the storehouse [ālaya] consciousness,
Which brings into fruition the seeds [effects of good and evil deeds].
[In its state of pure consciousness] it is not conscious of its clinging and
  impressions.
In both its objective and subjective functions it is always associated with
  touch,
Volition, feeling, sensation, thought, and cognition.
But it is always indifferent to its associations. . . .

The Treatise says:

The first transformation of consciousness is called ālaya in both the Mahāyāna and Hīnayāna. . . . Why are the seeds so-called? It means that in consciousness itself fruitions, functions, and differentiations spontaneously arise. These are neither the same nor different from the consciousness or from what they produce. . . .

In this way the other consciousnesses which "perfume" [affect] it and the consciousness which is perfumed arise and perish together, and the concept of perfuming is thus established. To enable the seeds that lie within what is perfumed [storehouse consciousness] to grow, as the hemp plant is perfumed, is called perfuming. As soon as the seeds are produced, the consciousnesses which can perfume become in their turn causes which perfume and produce seeds. The three dharmas [the seeds, the manifestations, and perfuming] turn on and on, simultaneously acting as cause and effect. . . .

The verse says:

The second transformation
Is called the mind-consciousness
Which, while it depends on that transformation, in turn conditions it.
It has the nature and character of intellection.
It is always accompanied by the four evil defilements,
Namely, self-delusion, self-view,
Self-conceit, and self-love,
And by touch, etc. [volition, feeling, sensation, thought, and cognition]. . . .

The Treatise says:

"That transformation" refers to the first transformation, because according to the sacred teaching, this consciousness depends on the storehouse consciousness. . . . "It" refers to the consciousness on which this transformation depends, because according to the sacred teaching, this consciousness conditions the storehouse consciousness.

Spontaneously this mind perpetually conditions the storehouse consciousness and corresponds to the four basic defilements. What are the four? They are self-delusion, self-view, and also self-conceit and self-love. These are the four different names. Self-delusion means ignorance, lack of understanding of the character of the self, and being unenlightened about the principle of the non-self. Therefore it is called self-delusion. Self-view means clinging to the view that the self exists, erroneously imagining to be the self certain dharmas that are not the self. Therefore it is called self-view. Self-conceit means pride. On the strength of what is clung to as the self, it causes the mind to feel superior and lofty. It is therefore called self-conceit.

The verse says:

Next comes the third transformation
Which consists of the last categories of discrimination
With subject and object as the nature and character.
They are neither good nor evil.

The Treatise says:

This consciousness is divided into six categories, in accordance with the six different sense organs and the six sense objects. They refer to the consciousness of sight and so on [hearing, smell, taste] in the sense-center consciousness. . . .

The verse says:

Based on the root-consciousness [ālaya]
The five consciousnesses [of the senses] manifest themselves in accordance
    with the conditioning factors.
Sometimes [the senses manifest themselves] together and sometimes not,
Just as waves [manifest themselves] depending on water conditions.
The sense-center consciousness always arises and manifests itself,
Except when born in the realm of the absence of thought,
In the state of unconsciousness, in the two forms of concentration,
In sleep, and in that state where the spirit is depressed or absent.

The Treatise says:

The root consciousness is the storehouse consciousness because it is the root from which all pure and impure consciousnesses grow. . . . By "conditioning factors" are meant the mental activities, the sense organs, and sense objects. It means that the five consciousnesses are dependent internally upon the root consciousness and externally follow the combination of the conditions of the mental activities, the five sense organs, and sense objects. They [the senses] manifest themselves together and sometimes separately. This is so because the external conditions may come to be combined suddenly or gradually. . . .

The verse says:

Thus the various consciousnesses are but transformations.
That which discriminates and that which is discriminated
Are, because of this, both unreal.
For this reason, everything is mind only.

The Treatise says:

"The various consciousnesses" refer to the three transformations of consciousness previously discussed and their mental qualities. They are all capable of transforming into two seeming portions, the perceiving portion and the perceived portion. The term "transformation" is thus employed. The perceiving portion that has been transformed is called "discrimination" because it can apprehend the perceived portion [as the object of perception]. The perceived portion that has been transformed is called the "object of discrimination" because it is apprehended by the perceiving portion. According to this correct principle, aside from what is transformed in consciousness, the self and dharmas are both definitely nonexistent, because apart from what apprehends and what is apprehended, there is nothing else, and because there are no real things apart from the two portions.

Therefore everything created [by conditions] and noncreated, everything seemingly real or unreal, is all inseparable from consciousness.

THE LOTUS SCHOOL: T'IEN-T'AI SYNCRETISM

From the philosophical standpoint, and in terms of its influence on other schools in China and Japan, the Lotus or T'ien-t'ai teaching is of major importance. Moreover, it is distinctively Chinese. Though its basic scripture is the *Lotus of the Wonderful Law* (*Saddharmapuṇḍarīka Sūtra*), a work from North India or Central Asia, the school is founded upon the interpretation given this text by the great Chinese monk, Chih-k'ai (or Chih-i, 538–597), and its alternate name indicates its place of geographical origin, the T'ien-t'ai (Heavenly Terrace) Mountain of Chekiang Province, where Chih-k'ai taught.

For this Grand Master of the T'ien-t'ai, the *Lotus,* one of the most popular of Mahāyāna sūtras, was not merely a theological document but also a guide to religious salvation through practice. He lectured for years on its written text, minutely examining every detail of language and subtlety of meaning, and giving special attention to the methods of religious practice embodied in the *Lotus*. His deliberations were recorded by his pupil Kuan-ting and have come down to us as the "Three Great Works" of the school, namely, the *Words and Phrases of the Lotus* (*Fa-hua wen-chü*), *Profound Meaning of the Lotus* (*Fa-hua hsüan-i*), and *Great Concentration and Insight* (*Mo-ho chih-kuan*).

At Chih-k'ai's time, Buddhist thought in South China was distinctly intellectual in character, while in the north Buddhists were developing a religion of faith and discipline. Himself a product of the South Chinese gentry, but with a northerner, Hui-ssu (514–577), as his teacher, Chih-k'ai came to the conclusion that the contemplative and intellectual approaches to religion were like the two wings of a bird. Consequently, the T'ien-t'ai school is characterized by a strong philosophical content and at the same time a strong emphasis on meditative practice.

The T'ien-t'ai doctrine centers around the principle of the Perfectly Harmonious Threefold Truth. This means that 1) all things or dharmas are empty because they are produced through causation and therefore have no self-nature; but that 2) they do have temporary existence; and that 3) being both Empty and Temporary is the nature of dharmas and is the Mean. These three—Emptiness, Temporariness, and the Mean—involve one another so that one is three and three is one, the relative thus being identified with the absolute.

Furthermore, in the world of Temporariness, there are ten realms of existence—those of the Buddhas, bodhisattvas, buddhas-for-themselves, direct disciples of the Buddha, heavenly beings, spirits, human beings, departed beings, beasts, and depraved men. Each of these shares the characteristics of the others, thus making one hundred realms. Each of these in turn is characterized by ten thusnesses or such-likenesses through which the true state is manifested in phenomena, namely, such-like character, such-like nature, such-like substance, such-like power, such-like activity, such-like causes, such-like conditions, such-like effects, such-like retributions, and such-like beginning-and-end-ultimate. This makes one thousand realms of existence. In turn, each realm consists of the three divisions of living beings, of space, and of the aggregates which constitute dharmas, thus making a total of three thousand realms of existence or aspects of reality.

These realms are so interwoven and interpenetrated that they may be considered "immanent in a single instant of thought." This does not mean that they are produced by the thought of man or Buddha, as taught in some Mahāyāna schools, but rather that in every thought-moment, all the possible worlds are involved. Accordingly the great emphasis in this school is on concentration and insight as a means of perceiving the ultimate truth embodied in such a thought-moment. In short, this is a philosophy of One-in-All and All-in-One, which is crystallized in the celebrated saying that "Every color or fragrance is none other than the Middle Path." Every dharma is thus an embodiment of the real essence of the Ultimate Emptiness, or True Thusness. It follows that all beings have the Buddha-nature in them and can be saved. This is the great message of the *Lotus*.

The school claims that the *Lotus* is the most complete doctrine among all the Buddhist teachings. It classifies the teachings of the Buddha into five periods. The first four, represented by the literature of various schools, are regarded as exploratory or temporary, whereas the teaching contained in the *Lotus* is considered final. Thus a measure of truth is seen in the teachings of other schools, which in certain respects are mutually contradictory, while the *Lotus* is seen as fulfilling and reconciling them in a final synthesis. It is an attempt to replace the Three Vehicles [12] by One Vehicle. In its all-inclusiveness, then, the T'ien-t'ai points again to the doctrine of universal salvation, the outstanding characteristic of the Mahāyāna movement.

The *Words and Phrases,* being a phrase by phrase commentary, does not yield excerpts of a summary character. Those given below are taken from the other two of the "Three Great Works." They are preceded by a short selection from the *Lotus* to give an idea of its message of salvation for all, and a selection from *The Method of Concentration and Insight in the Mahāyāna (Ta-ch'eng chih-kuan fa-men)* by Chih-k'ai's teacher Hui-ssu.

---

[12] Those of the shrāvakas who attain to their own salvation by hearing the Buddha's teaching, the pratyeka-buddhas who attain to their personal enlightenment by their own exertions, and the bodhisattvas who postpone their own Buddhahood for the sake of helping all beings to be saved.

The Scripture of the Lotus of the Wonderful Law

(Ascribed to the Buddha)
      [From *Taishō daizōkyō*, IX, 8–9, 15]

The Buddha appears in the world
Only for this One Reality.
Both the Shrāvaka Vehicle and the Pratyeka-buddha Vehicle [13] are not
   real.
For never by the Small Vehicle
Would the Buddhas save all beings.
The Buddha himself abides in the Great Vehicle,
And in accordance with the Law he has attained,
By meditation and wisdom and the effort and ornament of virtue,
He saves all beings.
I have realized the Supreme Way.
The Law of the Great Vehicle applies to all beings.
If I converted by the Small Vehicle
Even one single human being,
I should fall into stinginess and greed.
Such a thing cannot be done.
If men turn in faith to the Buddha,
The Tathāgata [14] will not deceive them.
O, Shāriputra! you should know that
From the very start I made a vow,
With the desire to enable all beings
To be the same as we are,

                                        . . . .

To convert all beings
And enable them all to enter the Path of the Buddha.
Although I preach Nirvāna,
It is not real extinction.
All dharmas from the beginning
Are always tranquil in themselves and are devoid of appearance.
When the Buddha-son fufills his course,

[13] See the preceding note.
[14] The Thus-Come-One, a name for the Buddha.

He becomes a Buddha in his next life.
Because of my adaptability [to use every suitable means for salvation]
I reveal the Law of Three Vehicles.
Any among the living beings,
Who have come into contact with former Buddhas,
Have learned the Law and practiced charity,
Or have undergone discipline and endured forbearance and humiliation,
Or have made serious efforts at concentration and understanding, etc.,
And cultivated various kinds of blessing and wisdom—
All of these people,
Have reached the level of Buddhahood.

. . . .

Those people who, for the sake of the Buddha,
Installed images,
Or have had them carved,
Have reached the level of Buddhahood.

. . . .

Those who with a happy frame of mind
Have sung the glory of the Buddha,
Even with a very small sound,

. . . .

Or have worshiped,
Or have merely folded their hands,

. . . .

Or have uttered one "Namo" [Praise be . . .],
All have reached the level of Buddhahood.
About the Buddhas of the past—
After they passed away from this world,
They heard the Law,
And all reached the level of Buddhahood.
As to the Buddhas of the future,
Their number will be infinite.
All these Tathāgatas
Will preach the Law by all suitable means.
All these Buddhas,
With an infinite number of suitable means,
Will save all living beings,

And enable them to dwell in the Pure Wisdom of the Buddha.
Among those who have heard the Law,
None will fail to become Buddha.
All Buddhas have taken the vow:
"The Buddha-way which I walk,
I desire to enable all living beings
To attain the same way with me."
Although Buddhas in future ages
Preach hundreds and thousands and tens of thousands
Of methods, beyond number,
In reality there is only the One Vehicle.
All the Buddhas, past and future,
Know that dharmas have no [self-] nature,
And Buddha-seeds [all beings and defilements] are produced by causation.
Therefore they preach the One Vehicle. [pp. 8–9]
All the Shrāvakas
And Pratyeka-buddhas
Cannot by their powers
Penetrate this scripture.
You, Shāriputra,
Can, into this scripture,
Enter only by faith. [p. 15]

HUI-SSU

The Method of Concentration and Insight in the Mahāyāna
[From *Ta-ch'eng chih-kuan fa-men,* in *Taishō daizōkyō,* XLVI, 642–61]

The Mind is the same as the Mind of Pure Self, Nature, True Thusness, Buddha-Nature, Dharma-Body, Tathāgata-Store, Realm of Law, and Dharma-Nature. [p. 642]

Question: Why is [the Mind] called True Thusness?

Answer: All dharmas depend on this Mind for their being and take Mind as their substance. Viewed in this way, all dharmas are illusory and imaginary and their being is really nonbeing. Contrasted with these unreal dharmas, the Mind is called True.

Furthermore, although the dharmas have no real being because they are caused by illusion and imagination, they have the appearance [15] of being created and annihilated. When unreal dharmas are created, this Mind is not created, and when the dharmas are annihilated, the Mind is not annihilated. Not being created, it is therefore not augmented, and not being annihilated, it is therefore not diminished. Because it is neither augmented nor diminished, it is called Thusness. [p. 642]

Although it has been explained above that the Pure Mind is free from the character of all discriminative minds and sense objects, nevertheless this character is not different from the Pure Mind. Why? Although the substance of the Mind is everywhere the same and not differentiated, it originally possesses both functions of remaining pure and being defiled. Furthermore, because of the power, from time immemorial, of ignorance and imagination to influence it, the substance of the Mind is affected by this influence and manifests itself. These unreal appearances have no substance; they are but the Pure Mind. Hence it is said that [substance and appearance] are not different.

But at the same time they are not one. Why? Because, although it possesses the two functions of purity and being defiled, the substance of the Pure Mind does not have the character of distinction between the two; all is everywhere the same and undifferentiated. It is only because of the illusory manifestations caused by the power of influence that differences appear.

But these illusory appearances are created and annihilated, whereas the substance of the Pure Mind is eternal, without coming into or going out of existence, and it endures forever without change. Hence it is said that [substance and appearance] are not one. [p. 645]

Question: When the Tathāgata-Store possesses innumerable dharmas, does it have the character of differentiation or not?

Answer: The substance of the Store is everywhere the same and undifferentiated, and in fact has no character of differentiation. In this respect it is the Tathāgata-Store of Emptiness. However, because this substance of the Tathāgata-Store also has mysterious functions, it possesses all dharma natures to the fullest extent, including their differentiations. In this respect, it is the Tathāgata-Store of Non-Emptiness, that is, the difference in the realm of no-difference.

[15] The Chinese word *hsiang* is a key term in Buddhist philosophy with a wide range of meanings, including specific character or characteristic, appearance, phenomenon, etc. In general here it is translated as "character[istic]" when contrasted with a universal nature, and as "appearance" or "phenomenon" when contrasted with the ultimate reality.

What does this mean? I am not saying that it is like a lump of clay possessing many particles of dirt. Why? The clay is false, whereas the particles of dirt are real. Therefore each particle has its own distinctive material. But since they are combined to form the clay, this possesses the distinctive characteristic of involving many particles. But the Tathāgata-Store is different from this. Why? Because the Tathāgata-Store is the True Law; it is perfect harmony without duality. Therefore the Tathāgata-Store, in its totality, is the nature of a single hair-pore of a single being, and at the same time the nature of all hair-pores of that being. And as in the case of the hair-pore, so in that of the nature of every dharma in the world. [p. 648]

Therefore it is said in the scripture: "In each particle of dirt all the Buddha lands in the ten directions are revealed," and again, "All the Three Worlds and all periods in time can be understood in an instant of thought." This is what it means. Again, "The past is the future and the future is the present." This means that the three times involve one another. [p. 650]

By concentration is meant to know that all dharmas, originally having no self-nature of their own, are never created nor annihilated by themselves, but come into being because they are caused by illusions and imagination, and exist without real existence. In those created dharmas, their existence is really nonexistence. They are only the One Mind, whose substance admits of no differentiation. Those who hold this view can stop the flow of false ideas. This is called concentration.[16]

By insight is meant that although we know that [things] are originally not created and at present not annihilated, nevertheless they were caused to arise out of the Mind's nature and hence are not without a worldly function of an illusory and imaginative nature. They are like illusions and dreams; they [seem to] exist but really do not. This is therefore insight. [p. 642]

As to the function of concentration and insight: It means that because of the accomplishment of concentration, the Pure Mind is merged through Principle with the Nature which is without duality and is harmoniously united with all beings as a body of one single character. Thereupon the Three Treasures [The Buddha, the Law, and the Order] are combined without being three, and the Two Levels of Truth are fused without

---

[16] *Chih* in Chinese, literally "to stop," used as a translation for the Sanskrit *śamatha*, which represents a mental calm that shuts out all distractions.

being two. How calm, still, and pure! How deep, stable, and quiet! How pure and clear the inner silence! It functions without the appearance of functioning, and acts without the appearance of acting. It is so because all dharmas are originally the same everywhere without differentiation and the nature of the Mind is but dharma. This is the substance of the most profound Dharma-Nature.

It also means that because of the accomplishment of insight, the substance of the Pure Mind and the functioning of the objective world are manifested without obstacle, spontaneously producing the capabilities of all pure and impure things. . . . Again, owing to the accomplishment of concentration, one's mind is the same everywhere and one no longer dwells within the cycle of life and death; yet owing to the accomplishment of insight, one's attitudes and functions are results of causation and one does not enter Nirvāna. Moreover, owing to the accomplishment of concentration one dwells in the great Nirvāna, and yet owing to the attainment of insight, one remains in the realm of life and death. Further, owing to the accomplishment of concentration one is not defiled by the world, but owing to the attainment of insight one is not confined to the realm of silence. Further, owing to the accomplishment of concentration, one achieves eternal silence in the process of functioning, and owing to the attainment of insight, one achieves eternal function in the state of silence. Further, owing to the accomplishment of concentration one knows that the cycle of life and death is the same as Nirvāna, and owing to the attainment of insight, one knows that Nirvāna is the same as the cycle of life and death. Further, owing to the accomplishment of concentration, one knows that the cycle of life and death and Nirvāna cannot be attained at the same time, but owing to the attainment of insight, one knows that transmigration is the cycle of life and death and the absence of transmigration is Nirvāna. [p. 661]

CHIH-K'AI
The Profound Meaning of the Scripture of the Lotus of the Wonderful Law

This text, being in the form of a commentary, proceeds by way of an analysis of specific passages in which key concepts are set forth, here, for instance, the term "dharmas."

[From *Fa-hua hsüan-i*, in *Taishō daizōkyō*, XXXIII, 693]

The Master of Nan-yüeh [Hui-ssu] cites three kinds of dharmas, namely, the dharma of the sentient beings, the Buddha-dharma, and the Mind-dharma. The scripture says: "In order to cause the beings to open to view and enter perceptively into the Buddha's knowledge-and-insight". . . . If the beings did not possess the Buddha's knowledge-and-insight, what need to speak of "opening"? It should be known from this that the Buddha's knowledge-and-insight is stored up in the beings. The scripture also says: "With the mere eyes engendered by one's father and mother [eyes of flesh] one can see through the inner and outer Mount Meru [eyes of gods], see deeply into all matter and remain uncontaminated by attachment to any of it [eyes of wisdom], and see matter without error [dharma-eyes]. Though one has not yet attained freedom from defilement, yet one's eye-sense shall be as pure as this, one eye embodying the functions of all eyes [Buddha-eyes]." The above is a passage from this scripture explaining the "subtlety" of the dharma of the beings. The *Mahāparinirvāṇa Scripture* says: "Though one who has learned the Great Vehicle has eyes of flesh, one calls them Buddha-eyes." The other five senses, beginning with those of the ear and nose, by the same token are also thus. The *Aṅgulimālīya Scripture* says: "The so-called eye-sense is ever present in the Buddhas, complete and fully functioning, seeing clearly and distinctly. All the other senses, up to and including the mind-sense, are also thus." The *Prajñāpāramitā Scripture* says: "[The six senses are] six self-mastering kings, for by nature they are pure." It also says: "All dharmas are contained in the eye. They are contained in it and do not exceed it. Even the eye is unattainable [having no substantial existence]. How much the less its containing or not containing! The same is true of all the other senses, up to and including the mind-sense, which in the same way contain all the dharmas." This means that the scriptures declare the "subtlety" of the dharma of the beings.

The subtlety of the Buddha-dharma is as the scripture says: "Cease, cease! No need to speak. My dharma is subtle and difficult to conceive. (The Buddha-dharma does not exceed the tentative and the ultimate.) This dharma is extremely, profoundly subtle, hard to see and hard to understand. Of all the varieties of beings there is none that can know the Buddha. (This refers to the subtlety of His transcendental wisdom.) When it comes to the other dharmas apart from the Buddha, there is also none that can fathom them. (This refers to the subtlety of His immanent wisdom.) As for these two dharmas, only the Buddhas can exhaust the reality of the dharmas. This is called 'the subtlety of the Buddha-dharma.'"

The subtlety of the Mind-dharma is as when in the performance of the four comfortable activities one keeps the mind under control and perceiving all dharmas, neither falters nor retreats, but experiences joy in a single instant, etc. The *Scripture of the View of Samantabhadra* says: "My mind is of itself empty, sin and grace have no subject. When one looks at the mind there is no mind, dharmas are not enduring dharmas. Also, the mind is pure dharma." The *Vimalakīrtinirdeśa* says: "To look at the body, it is reality, and the same is true of looking at the Buddha. The release of the Buddhas is to be sought in the mental activities of the beings." The *Flower Garland Scripture* says: "The Mind, the Buddha, and the beings—these three are without distinction. To destroy the fine impurities of the mind is better than all the rolls of scripture." This is called "the subtlety of the Mind-dharma."

Now, on the basis of these three dharmas, we shall make distinctions of even greater detail.

To detail the dharma of the beings is to discuss the whole range of cause and effect, as well as all the dharmas. To detail the Buddha-dharma is to take the standpoint of effect. To detail the Mind-dharma is to take the standpoint of cause.

The dharma of the beings consists of two parts, the former a statement of the number of dharmas, the latter an interpretation of the appearance of these dharmas.

As for the number, the scriptures sometimes declare that one dharma comprises all dharmas, meaning that the Mind is the three worlds and that there is no dharma apart from it, everything else being merely the creation of the single Mind. They sometimes declare that two dharmas comprise all dharmas, to wit, name and form. In all the worlds there are only name and form. They sometimes declare that three dharmas comprise all dharmas, namely, life, consciousness, and warmth.[17] In this way the number is increased by one at a time until it reaches a hundred thousand. The present scripture uses ten dharmas to comprise all dharmas, namely, the such-like character, such-like nature, such-like substance,

---

[17] The Sarvāstivāda school posits the existence of a life-element which transmits the consciousness and bodily warmth of each being from incarnation to incarnation.

such-like power, such-like activity, such-like causes, such-like conditions, such-like effects, such-like retributions, such-like beginning-and-end-ultimate, and the like of the dharmas. The Master of Nan-yüeh reads these phrases with the word "like" at the end of each, calling them the "ten likes." The Master of T'ien-t'ai says that, if they are to be read for meaning, there are in all three different ways of reading them. The first is "this character's suchness, this nature's suchness, . . . this retribution's suchness." The second is "such-like character, such-like nature, . . . such-like retribution." The third is "their character is like this, their nature is like this, . . . their retribution is like this." Since all readings contain the word "like," the word "like" is common to all of them.

The first reading gives the passage the meaning of Emptiness. If one reads "such-like character, such-like nature, etc.," enumerating the character, nature, etc., of Emptiness, assigning names and titles in a differentiated series, such a reading gives the passage the meaning of Temporariness. If one reads "character is like this, etc.," then one is equating the ten dharmas to the "this" of the reality of the Middle Way. Such a reading gives the passage the meaning of the Mean [of Emptiness and Temporariness]. Distinction makes it easier to understand, hence we specify Emptiness, Temporariness, and the Mean. But if one is to speak from the standpoint of meaning, Emptiness is identical with Temporariness and the Mean. If one explains Emptiness in terms of suchness, then one Emptiness equals all Emptiness. If one details the aspects of suchness into character, etc., then one Temporariness equals all Temporariness. If one discusses the Mean in terms of "this," then one Mean equals all Means. They are not one, two, three, and yet they are one, two, three. They are neither horizontal nor vertical. This is called the true character. Only the Buddhas can exhaust these dharmas. These ten dharmas comprise all dharmas. If one is depending upon meaning, then one may interpret the passage in three senses. If one is depending upon rhythm, then one must read according to the verses, "The meaning of such-like great effect and retribution and of sundry natures and characters."

. . . .

All "dharma-spheres" are so-called in three senses. The number ten depends entirely on the dharma-spheres. Outside of the dharma-spheres there is no other dharma. That which depends and that upon which it depends are joined together in the appellation, hence we speak of the "ten dharma-spheres." Secondly, of these ten kinds of dharmas, each has a different lot. Their several causes and effects are separate from one another, and the common and saintly states have their differences. Therefore the word "sphere" is added to their name. Thirdly, of these ten, each and every dharma-sphere in and of itself comprises all dharma-spheres. For example, all dharmas are contained in hell. This state, without exceeding itself, is substantially identical with Truth, and requires no other point of reliance. Therefore the name "dharma-sphere." The same is true of all the other dharma-spheres, up to and including that of the Buddha. If the number ten depends on the dharma-spheres, then that which depends, accompanying that upon which it depends, enters directly into the sphere of Emptiness. To say that the ten spheres are delimited one from another refers to the sphere of the temporary. To say that the number ten is all the dharma-spheres refers to the sphere of the Mean. Wishing to make this easy to understand we distinguish in this way. If we were to speak from the standpoint of meaning, then Emptiness is identical with Temporariness and the Mean. There is no one, two, three, as we have said before.

This one dharma-sphere contains the ten "such-likes." Ten dharma-spheres contain one hundred "such-likes." Also, since one dharma-sphere contains the other nine dharma-spheres as well, there are thus a hundred dharma-spheres and a thousand "such-likes." One may unite them under five distinctions, the first being evil, the second good, the third the Two Vehicles, the fourth the bodhisattva, and the fifth the Buddha. One may then divide these into two dharmas, the first four being the tentative dharma, the last one being the ultimate dharma. To treat them in detail, each of them comprises both the tentative and the ultimate. We observe this dichotomy only as a practical expedient. But this tentative-and-ultimate, this inconceivable, is the object of the twofold wisdom of the Buddhas of the three periods [past, present, and future]. If one takes this as an object, what dharma is not contained therein? If this object impels wisdom, what wisdom is not impelled thereby? Therefore the scripture says "dharmas." "Dharmas" means that the object understood is broad. "Only the Buddhas can exhaust [them]" means that the wisdom that understands it is deep, reaching its limit, and scouring its bottom.

The Great Concentration and Insight

The *Mo-ho chih-kuan,* from which this portion is quoted, is, as we have indicated above, a manual of religious practice, specifically of the methods of gaining religious intuition. In the following passage Chih-k'ai discusses the method of viewing the realm of the inconceivable, as the first of ten methods of viewing the mind.

[From *Mo-ho chih-kuan,* ch. 5a, in *Taishō daizōkyō,* XLVI, 48–59]

The viewing of the Mind contains ten divisions. The first is the viewing of the realm of the inconceivable. The second is the excitation of the merciful heart. The third is skillful and tranquil concentration and insight. The fourth is the refutation of the dharmas universally. The fifth is the recognition of passage and obstruction. The sixth is the cultivation of the parts of the Way. The seventh is resistance to impediments and ancillary acts of opening one's vision. The eighth is knowledge of order and degree. The ninth is the ability to acquiesce with tranquillity. The tenth is absence of dharma-craving. . . .

First is to see that the Mind is the realm of the inconceivable. Since this realm is hard to explain, let us first make clear the realm of the conceivable, causing that of the inconceivable to be more apparent.

As for the realm of the conceivable, the Small Vehicle also teaches that the Mind gives rise to all dharmas. This refers to the causes and effects of the six lower states of existence and to the endless cycle of reincarnation in the Three Worlds. If one shuns the common and takes delight in the saintly, then one will reject the lowly and emerge upward to the reduction of the body to ashes and the extinction of consciousness. This, then, refers to the constituted Four Truths, which are, in sum, conceivable dharmas. The Great Vehicle also makes it clear that the Mind gives rise to all dharmas, referring to the ten dharma-spheres.

If one views the Mind as existing, then there is good and there is evil. Evil is of three kinds, the causes and effects of the three lowest states of existence. Good is of three kinds, the causes and effects of the states of existence of demons, men, and gods. If one looks at these six kinds, they come into being and perish without permanence, and the mind that views them also does not abide from moment to moment. Furthermore, both the viewer and the viewed come into being subject to causes and conditions. Subject to causes and conditions means empty of substantial reality. These are all the dharmas of cause and effect of the Two Vehicles. If one views Emptiness on the one hand and existence on the other, one will fall into two extremes, sinking into Emptiness and becoming bogged down in existence. Now to evince great mercy, to enter into the temporary and convert the beings, to create a body temporarily where there is in reality no body, to preach Emptiness temporarily where there is in reality no Emptiness and thus to convert and lead—this is the dharma of the cause and effect of bodhisattvahood. To see these dharmas, both the rescuers and the rescued, as dharmas of the reality of the Middle Way, ultimately pure, saying, "Who is good? Who is evil? Who exists? Who does not exist? Who rescues? Who does not rescue? All dharmas without exception are like this!"—this is the dharma of the cause and effect of Buddhahood.

These ten dharmas, ranging from the shallow to the profound, all come out of the Mind. Although in the latter case it is the Greater Vehicle, the doctrine of which we speak is contained within the unlimited Four Truths, and is still within the realm of the conceivable. It is not what the present concentration-and-insight is viewing.

The realm of the inconceivable is as the *Flower Garland Scripture* says: "The Mind, like a skillful painter, creates the various and sundry aggregates. In the midst of all the worlds there is nothing that does not arise from the Mind." The "various and sundry aggregates" are the aggregates of the aforementioned ten dharma-spheres. By "dharma-spheres" we mean three things. The number ten depends, and the dharma-spheres are that upon which it depends. That which depends and that upon which it depends are united in the appellation, hence we say "ten dharma-spheres." Also, of these ten dharmas, the several causes and the several effects do not become confused with another, whence we say "ten dharma-spheres." Also, of these ten dharmas, each and every one is in and of itself the sphere of the dharmas, whence we say "ten dharma-spheres" and so forth.

The name "ten dharma-spheres" applies in each case to the aggregates, objects of perception, and spheres. Their realities are different from one another. The three lowest states of existence are the aggregates, objects of perception, and spheres of tainted evil. The next three states of existence are the aggregates, objects of perception, and spheres of tainted good. The Two Vehicles are taintless aggregates, objects of perception, and spheres. The bodhisattva is both tainted and taintless aggregates, objects of perception, and spheres. The Buddha is neither tainted nor taintless aggregates, objects of perception, and spheres [18]. . . . Since the ten kinds of aggregates are not the same, therefore one calls them "the worlds of the five aggregates." One may take "five aggregates" as a general appellation for the beings, but the beings differ. If one takes the aggregates of the six lowest states of existence, these are the beings of sin and suffering. If one takes the aggregates of men and gods, these are the beings of the enjoyment of pleasure. If one takes the untainted aggregates, these are the beings of true sainthood.[19] If one takes the aggregates of mercy, these are the beings who are the great gentlemen.[20] If one takes the ever-abiding aggregates, this is the Being of the Venerable Ultimate. . . . The dwelling places of the ten varieties of beings are collectively called "lands" or "worlds." By this is meant that hell rests upon a base of red-hot iron; animals dwell on land, in water, and in air; demons dwell on sea-coasts and on the floor of the sea; men dwell on earth; gods dwell in their palaces; the bodhisattvas who have mastered the Six Perfections dwell with men on earth; of bodhisattvas of the Pervasive Doctrine,[21] those whose errors are not yet completely cleansed share the dwellings of men and gods, while those whose errors are completely cleansed dwell in the realm of tentative expedients; of bodhisattvas of the Separate and Rounded doctrines,[22] those whose errors are not yet completely cleansed share the dwellings of men and gods, as well as the realm of tentative expedients, while those whose errors are completely cleansed dwell in the realm of real retribution; and the Tathāgata dwells in the Ever-Quiescent Resplendent Realm. . . . These thirty varieties of worlds all arise from the Mind. Also, of the ten kinds of aggregates, each and every one comprises the ten dharmas. By this we mean their such-like appearance, nature, substance, power, activity, cause, condition, effect, retribution,

[18] The objects of perception are those of the six senses, while the spheres are the six sensory organs, the six senses, and the objects of perception. "Tainted" means giving rise to a process that will maintain existence in the world. Such are the six lowest states of existence. The shrāvaka and pratyeka-buddha, on the other hand, extricate themselves from the world. The bodhisattva does so eventually, but remains in the world for a time. The Buddha, of course, is above all forms of differentiation.

[19] That is, shrāvakas and pratyeka-buddhas.

[20] That is, the bodhisattvas.

[21] The second of the Four Teachings by Law.

[22] The third and fourth, respectively, of the Four Teachings by Law.

beginning- and end-ultimate, and the like. First we shall give a general interpretation of this, then we shall interpret it according to kind.

First, the general interpretation. Character may be distinguished by looking at it. The Explicatory Treatise says: "It is easy to know, hence one calls it 'character.'" For example, the character of water and fire being different, they may be easily distinguished. For another example, men's facial expressions comprise good and bad; when one looks at the external characteristic, one may immediately know what is within. . . . The Mind is also thus, containing all characters. . . . Those who do not observe well do not believe that the Mind comprises all characters. They should follow him who observes things as they are, and believe that the Mind comprises all characters.

As for "such-like nature," nature is situated internally, and has in general three meanings. First, that which does not change is called "nature." The *Scripture of No-Action* calls it "immobile nature." "Nature" has the meaning of "unchanging." Also, "nature" means true nature, and "true nature" means nature by principle, extremely real and without error. It is nothing but another name for Buddhahood. Immobile nature supports Emptiness, discrete nature supports Temporariness, and true nature supports the Mean. Let us now explain how the inner nature cannot change. For example, the fire-nature within bamboo, though it cannot be seen, may not be said not to exist. A kindler with dried grass will burn it all up. The Mind is also thus. It contains the nature of all aggregates. Although they cannot be seen, they may not be said not to exist. If one views it with the eye of wisdom, it contains all natures. . . .

There are also masters who interpret the ten such-likes of the *Lotus of the Wonderful Law* to mean that the five former ones belong to the realm of the common, that is, the tentative, while the five latter ones belong to the realm of the saintly, that is, the ultimate. If we are to rely on their interpretation, then the common man lacks the ultimate, and can never become a saint. The saint also lacks the tentative, and is not rightly and universally wise. This is a narrow and hasty theory, which does nothing but malign the Buddha and disdain the common man. . . .

As for "such-like substance," the principal stuff is called "substance." The aggregates and objects of perception of these ten dharma-spheres all have matter and mind as their substance. By "such-like power" is meant the power to function. For example, a king's acrobat has a thousand myriads of skills, but when he is sick he is said not to have them. When the sickness is healed, he has the skills again. The Mind is also thus. It possesses all powers but, because of the disease of the afflictions, they cannot be exercised. If, however, one looks at it as it really is, it comprises all powers.

As for "such-like activities," to transport and build is called "an act [of creation]." Apart from the Mind, there is nothing to create. Hence one knows that the Mind comprises all activities. As for "such-like causes," that which brings on effect is cause. It is also called karma. The karma of the ten dharma-spheres all arise from the Mind. Only if there is a mind can the karmas be complete. Therefore the scripture says "such-like cause." As for "such-like condition," condition is that by or through which something happens. Anything that helps karma is within the meaning of "condition." Ignorance, lust, and the like can all fertilize karma. Thus the mind in and of itself is condition. As for "such-like effect," attainment is called "effect." Cumulative causes are accumulated in the past and cumulative effect is attained in the future. Therefore the scripture says "such-like effect." As for "such-like retribution," what responds to cause is called retribution. Cumulative cause and cumulative effect are collectively called "cause." They bring on the retribution of a later life. This retribution responds to these causes.

As for "such-like beginning-and-end-ultimate and the like," character is the beginning, retribution the end. Beginning and end all come into being subject to conditions. Since they are subject to conditions, they are empty [of self-substance]. Beginning and end are both empty— this is an interpretation of "like" in the light of Emptiness. Also, character has its own name, retribution has its own name, etc., both temporarily assigned. This is an interpretation of "like" in the light of Temporariness. Also, beginning and end reflect each other. When one looks at the former character, it signals the latter retribution. When one sees the latter retribution, one knows the former character. It is just as when one sees alms one concludes wealth, and when one sees wealth one expects alms. The former and the latter are complementary. This is an interpretation of "like" in the light of Temporariness. Also, character is noncharacter and, while being noncharacter, is character, yet is neither character nor noncharacter. Retribution is nonretribution and, while being nonretribution, is retribution; yet is neither retribution nor nonretribution.

Each and every one of these enters into the extreme of reality-just-as-it-is. This is an interpretation of "like" in the light of the Mean.

Secondly, to interpret according to kind, one may unite the ten dharmas under four types.

The beings in the three lowest states of existence have the display of suffering as their character; the agglomeration of positive evil as their nature; corrupt matter and mind as their substance; the climbing of swords and the entering into cauldrons as their power; the excitation of the ten evils [23] as their activity; tainted evil karma as their cause; lust, clinging, and the like as their condition; the cumulative effect of evil as their effect; the three worst states of existence as their retribution; and a foolish beginning and end as their "like."

The next three states of existence have the display of joy as their character; the agglomeration of positive good as their nature; rising matter and mind as their substance; joyful reception as their power; the excitation of the Five Commandments [24] and the ten goods as their activity; good karma as their cause; the desire for and clinging to good as their condition; the cumulative effect of good as their effect; and existence as men or gods as their retribution. They are "like" in the sense that, as temporary designations, the first and last are mutually complementary.

The Two Vehicles [of the shrāvakas and pratyeka-buddhas] have the display of Nirvāna as their character; release as their nature; the five components [25] as their substance; lack of attachments as their power; the divisions of the Way as their activity; the action of taintless wisdom as their cause; their several actions as their condition; and the Four Fruits as their effect. Having no rebirth in the field of later existence, they have no retribution. . . .

As for the bodhisattva and Buddha, they have secondary cause as their character; the cause of understanding as their nature; direct cause as their substance; the Four Broad Vows [26] as their power; the Six Perfections and all their actions as their activity; the adornment of virtue as

[23] Murder, stealing, adultery, lying, duplicity, slander, foul language, lust, anger, and false views.

[24] The vows taken by the Buddhist laymen not to kill, steal, commit adultery, lie, or take strong drink.

[25] Discipline, contemplation, wisdom, release, and the consciousness of release.

[26] Vows to save limitless beings, extinguish limitless afflictions, learn limitless doctrine, and attain limitless Buddhahood.

their cause; the adornment of merit as their condition; perfect enlightenment as their effect; and great Nirvāna as their retribution. . . .

Now one Mind comprises ten dharma-spheres, but each dharma-sphere also comprises ten dharma-spheres, giving a hundred dharma-spheres. One sphere comprises thirty kinds of worlds, hence a hundred dharma-spheres comprise three thousand kinds of worlds. These three thousand are contained in a fleeting moment of thought. Where there is no Mind, that is the end of the matter; if Mind comes into being to the slightest degree whatsoever, it immediately contains the three thousand. One may say neither that the one Mind is prior and all dharmas posterior nor that all dharmas are prior and the one Mind posterior. For example, the eight characters [of matter] [27] change things. If the thing were prior to the characters, the thing would undergo no change. If the characters were prior to the thing, it would also undergo no change. Thus neither priority nor posteriority is possible. One can only discuss the thing in terms of its changing characters or the characters in terms of the changing thing. Now the Mind is also thus. If one derives all dharmas from the one Mind, this is a vertical relationship. If the Mind all at once contains all dharmas, this is a horizontal relationship. Neither vertical nor horizontal will do. All one can say is that the Mind is all dharmas and that all dharmas are the Mind. Therefore the relationship is neither vertical nor horizontal, neither the same nor different. It is obscure, subtle, and profound in the extreme. Knowledge cannot know it, nor can words speak it. Herein lies the reason for its being called "the realm of the inconceivable."

THE FLOWER GARLAND SCHOOL

The name Flower Garland comes from the *Avataṃsaka Sūtra,* an Indian work purporting to give the teaching of Shakyamuni as a manifestation of the Buddha Vairochana. In Chinese the name is rendered "Hua-yen." This school as such never existed in India. Its nominal founder in China was Tu-shun (557–640), but Fa-tsang, the Great Master of Hsien-shou (643–712), is considered the real founder. Consequently the school is also known as the Hsien-shou school.

---

[27] The primary and secondary characteristics of coming into being, abiding, changing, and perishing (an Abhidharma doctrine).

The main tenet of the school is the Universal Causation of the Realm of Law (*Dharmadhātu*). This means that the entire universe arises simultaneously. All dharmas have the characteristics of universality, speciality, similarity, diversity, integration, and differentiation, and also the Ten States of Thusness or such-like-ness as given in the selection which follows. In other words, all dharmas are in the state of Thusness. In its static aspect, Thusness is the Void, the noumenon, the realm of Principle. In its dynamic aspect, it is manifestation, the phenomenon, the realm of Facts. The two realms are so interpenetrated and interdependent that the entire universe arises through reciprocal causation. As can readily be seen, this concept resembles the T'ien-t'ai idea of "all three thousand realms immanent in an instant of thought," so much so that the teachings of the two schools are often indistinguishable.

In a manner similar to that of the T'ien-t'ai, the Hua-yen school classifies Buddhist sects into five Vehicles. These are: 1) the Small Vehicle, or Hīnayāna, which includes the Chü-she school and advocates individual salvation; 2) the Elementary Great Vehicle, embracing the Three-Treatise and Consciousness-Only schools, which teach universal salvation, assuring human beings that, with some exceptions, all will cross the sea of suffering in a Great Vehicle to the Other Shore; 3) the Final Great Vehicle, that of T'ien-t'ai, which teaches that without any exception all beings, including the depraved, will be saved; 4) the Abrupt Doctrine of the Great Vehicle, identified with the Meditation school, which teaches that salvation can be achieved through abrupt enlightenment; and 5) the Perfect Doctrine of the Great Vehicle, that of Hua-yen, which combines all the other Vehicles. The underlying spirit here, as in the case of T'ien-t'ai, is syncretic. Because of this, the two schools have been able to serve as the philosophical foundation of Chinese Buddhism in general.

FA-TSANG

A Chapter on the Golden Lion

The following treatise is called the *Golden Lion* because it was based on a sermon Fa-tsang preached to the empress in the palace in 699, using the golden lion figure in the imperial hall to illustrate his metaphysical ideas.

[From *Chin-shih-tzu chang*, in *Taishō daizōkyō*, XLV, 663–67]

1. Clarification of Dependent Origination

Gold has no self-nature. Through the agency of a skilled craftsman there is at length the coming-into-being of this phenomenon of the lion. But since this coming-into-being is dependent, therefore it is called "dependent origination."

2. Distinction of Matter and Emptiness

The character [phenomenon] of the lion is empty [of substantial reality]; there is nothing but gold. The lion is not existent, but the substance of gold is not nonexistent. Therefore they are called separately Emptiness. Also, Emptiness, having no self-character and manifesting itself through matter, does not prevent illusory existence. Therefore they are separately called matter and Emptiness.

3. Relation to Three Natures

The Yogāchāra school, whose philosophy influenced the Hua-yen, posited a triad of natures. The first of these is the world of phenomena, that which is "ubiquitously construed and clung to." The second nature is "dependent on something else," that is, the product of causes and conditions. The third nature is "perfect." It refers to the identity of everything with the Absolute.

The lion comes into existence because of our senses. This is called "ubiquitously construed." The golden lion has apparent existence. This is called "dependent on something else." The nature of the gold [of which the lion is made] is unaltered. This is called "roundly perfected."

4. Manifestation of Characterlessness

Since the gold comprises the whole lion, and since there is no lion-character to be found apart from the gold, therefore it is called "characterlessness."

5. Explanation of Not-Coming-into-Being

If one rightly looks at the lion at the time of its coming into being, it is only gold that comes into being. Apart from the gold there is nothing. Although the lion has [the characteristics of] coming into being and extinction, the gold-substance at bottom neither increases nor decreases. Therefore we say that there is no coming-into-being.

6. Treatment of the Five Doctrines

This golden lion is nothing but dharmas of cause and condition, coming into being and perishing every moment. There is in reality no lion-character to be found. This is called the Doctrine of the Shrāvaka Ignorant of the Dharmas. Secondly, these dharmas, born of conditions, are each without self-nature. It is absolutely only Emptiness. This is called the Initial Doctrine of the Great Vehicle. Thirdly, although there is absolutely only Emptiness, this does not prevent the illusory dharmas from remaining as they are. The two phenomena of conditioned origination and temporary or transitory existence subsist side by side. This is called the Final Doctrine of the Great Vehicle. Fourthly, since these two aspects cancel each other out, they both perish, and neither [the result of] our senses nor false existence exists. Neither of the two aspects has any potential power and both Emptiness and existence perish. Then the way of names and words [which gives rise to phenomena] is terminated, and the mind [that contemplates them] has nought to attach itself to. This is called the Sudden Doctrine of the Great Vehicle. Fifthly, when the erroneous consciousness has been annihilated and true substance revealed, all becomes a single mass. Vigorously then does function arise, and on each occasion perfect reality obtains. The myriad forms, in disarray, mix and yet are not confused. The all is the one, both alike having no "nature." [At the same time] the one is the all, for cause and effect clearly follow each other. The [potential] power and the [actual] function involve each other, the folding and unfolding are unhampered. This is called the Rounded Doctrine of the Single Vehicle.

7. Mastering the Ten Profound Theories

The gold and the lion come into being at the same time, full and complete. This is called the Theory of Simultaneous Completeness and Mutual Correspondence. Secondly, the gold and the lion come into being each being compatible with the other, the one and the many each having no obstruction for the other. In this situation the principle [one] and fact [many] are different. Whether the one or the many, each occupies its own position. This is called the Theory of the Mutual Compatibility and Difference of the One and the Many. Thirdly, if one contemplates the lion, then it is only a lion, and there is no gold about it. In this case the gold is hidden and the lion manifested. If one contemplates the gold, then it is only gold, and there is no lion about it. In this case the gold is manifested and the lion is hidden. If one contemplates both, then both are manifested and both hidden. Being hidden, they are concealed and secret. Being manifested, they are evident and revealed. This is called the Theory of the Mutual Completion of the Hidden and the Manifested. Fourthly, the lion's eyes, ears, limbs, joints, and every single pore com-

pletely contain the golden lion. In each pore the lion simultaneously
and all at once enters into a single strand of hair. Each and every strand
of hair contains unlimited lions. Each [of these lions] in turn has hairs
each and every one of which contains unlimited lions, all of which in
turn enter into a single strand of hair. In this way the progression is
infinite, like the celestial jewels on the net of Indra. This is called the
Theory of the Realm of Indra's Net. Fifthly, since this lion's eye completely contains the lion, the whole lion is pure eye. If the ear completely
contains the lion, then the whole lion is pure ear. If all the sense organs
simultaneously contain it, then all are complete, each of them pure and
each of them mixed [with the others]. Also, each one of them is a full
storehouse. This we call the Theory of the Full Possession by the Storehouses of the Faculties of Purity and Mixture. Sixthly, since the lion's
several organs and each and every hair involve the whole lion, each of
them pervading the whole, the lion's ear is its eye, its eye is its ear, its
ear is its nose, its nose is its tongue, its tongue is its body. Each freely
maintains its existence without conflict or obstruction. This is called
the Theory of the Dharmas Mutually Identified While Self-existent.
Seventhly, the gold and lion may be hidden or manifest, one or many,
definitely pure or definitely mixed, powerful or powerless, this or that.
The principle and the comparison illuminate each other. Fact and principle are both revealed. They are completely compatible with each other,
and do not obstruct each other's peaceful existence. When the most
minute are thus established and distinguished this is called the Theory
of the Small and Minute Being Compatible Along with Peaceful Existence. Eighthly, this lion is a created dharma, coming into being and
perishing every instant, dividing into three periods of time, past, present,
and future, without a moment's interval. Of these three periods of time
each contains within itself past, present, and future. By uniting the three
triads of degrees one has nine periods, which again in turn may be united
to form a single dharma. Although they are nine periods, they each have
their differences of coalescence and separation. Yet they exist in mutual
dependence, fading one into the other without obstruction, and all together constituting a single moment of thought. This is called the Theory
of the Distinct Existence of Separate Dharmas in the Ten Periods.[28]
Ninthly, this lion and this gold may be hidden or manifested, one or

[28] The nine periods separately, plus all of them as one period.

many, thus having no self-nature, being evolved out of the Mind. Yet whether spoken of as fact or principle, they are completed and they have existence. This is called the Theory of the Skillful Completion Through the Evolution of the Mind-Only. Tenthly, this lion is spoken of in order to demonstrate ignorance, while the reality of the gold is spoken of in order to manifest the True Nature. These two, principle and fact, explained in conjunction and likened to storehouse consciousness, cause right understanding to be born. This is called the Theory of the Manifestation of the Doctrine with Reference to Facts and the Fostering of Understanding Thereby.

8. Binding Together the Six Characters

The lion is the character of universality. The five sense-organs, being various and different, are the characters of speciality. Since they arise out of a single condition, they are the characters of similarity. The fact that its eyes, ears, etc. do not overlap is the character of diversity. Since the lion is made of the combination of these sense organs, this is the character of integration. The several organs each occupying its own position is the character of disintegration.

9. Achievement of Bodhi

"Bodhi" means the Way, it means enlightenment. When the eye beholds the lion, it sees that all created dharmas, even before disintegration, are from the very beginning quiescent and extinct. By avoiding both attachment and renunciation, one, along this very road, flows into the sea of perfect knowledge. Therefore it is called "the Way." One understands that all of the misconstructions perpetrated since time without beginning have not a single real substance to them. Therefore one calls this "enlightenment." Ultimately, it contains within itself the wisdom that comprises all kinds. This is called "the achievement of bodhi."

10. Entry into Nirvāna

When one sees this lion and this gold, the two characters are both annihilated, the passions do not come into being, and although beauty and ugliness are displayed before the eye, the mind is as calm as the sea. False thoughts vanish completely, there are no pressures. One issues forth from one's bonds and separates oneself from hindrances, and cuts off forever the foundations of suffering. This is called "entering Nirvāna."

渡一遠
江葦舉

CHAPTER XVII

THE SCHOOLS OF BUDDHISM II

In the preceding chapter, four of the major schools of Buddhist doctrine have been presented. Here we shall introduce two of the most important schools of Buddhist religious practice. The first of them, the Pure Land sect, emphasized salvation by faith and became the most popular form of Buddhism in China. The second, the Meditation sect, though appealing to a more limited following, became the most influential form of Buddhism among artists and intellectuals as well as monks. Together they may be taken to represent a general reaction against the scriptural and doctrinal approach to religion, but their growing ascendancy in later centuries should not be regarded as the superseding of older schools by newer ones. In fact, both the Pure Land and Meditation schools existed along with the others, even antedating some like the T'ien-t'ai, and it was only a matter of their surviving better the vicissitudes of religious and social change.

THE PURE LAND SCHOOL

The "Pure Land" (Chinese, Ching-t'u; Sanskrit, Sukhāvatī) is the sphere believed by Mahāyāna Buddhists to be ruled over by the Buddha Amitābha (also known as Amitāyus and Amita). Indian Mahāyānists conceived of the universe as consisting of an infinite number of spheres and as going through an infinite number of cosmic periods. In the present period there is, according to this belief, a sphere called Sukhāvatī, the beauties and excellences of which are described in the most extravagant terms by certain of the Mahāyāna scriptures. Among its advantages is

the fact that it is free of the temptations and defilements which characterize the world inhabited by mortals (for example, the presence of
women).

A common belief among Mahāyāna Buddhists, and one supported by
scripture, was that the earthly reign of each Buddha, terminating in his
attainment of Nirvāna, is followed by a period of gradual degeneration
in his teaching. The period immediately following the Buddha's demise,
known as the era of the True Law, is characterized by the continued
vigor of the Faith in spite of his absence. It is followed in turn by the
era of Reflected Law in which the outward forms of the religion are
maintained but the inner content perishes. Finally comes the era of the
Final Degenerate Law in which both form and substance come to nought.
The scriptures dealing with the reign of Shākyamuni differ considerably
as to the relative length of the periods of the three eras following his
entry into Nirvāna. But it was possible for certain Chinese clerics during
the Six Dynasties to find scriptural justification for their feeling that
the period in which they themselves were living was the very era of
Final Degenerate Law which the sacred writings had predicted. The
confused state of Buddhist doctrine and the difficulty of any but a few
to master it, either in the pursuit of scriptural studies or the practice of
monastic disciplines, helped to convince many clerics and untold numbers
of laymen that their only hope of salvation lay in faith—faith in the saving power of the Buddhas.

In the *Pure Land Sūtra* (*Sukhāvatīvyūha*), one of the principal scriptural bases of Pure Land salvationism, Amita, while yet a bodhisattva
under the name Dharmākara, took forty-eight vows which were instrumental in his attainment of buddhahood. The eighteenth of these, which
came to be considered the most important of them, was: "If, O Blessed
One, when I have attained enlightenment, whatever beings in other
worlds, having conceived a desire for right, perfect enlightenment, and
having heard my name, with favorable intent think upon me, if when
the time and the moment of death are upon them, I, surrounded by and
at the head of my community of mendicants, do not stand before them
to keep them from frustration, may I not, on that account, attain to un-
excelled, right, perfect enlightenment." Since, according to believers in
this scripture, the bodhisattva Dharmākara did in fact become a Buddha
(Amita), the efficacy of his vows is proved, and anyone who meditates

or calls upon his name in good faith will be reborn in his Buddha-world.

Hence the simple invocation or ejaculation of Amita's name (*A-mi-t'o-fo* in Chinese) became the most common of all religious practices in China and the means by which millions sought release from the sufferings of this world. Nor was it simply a sectarian devotion. The meditation upon Amita and his Pure Land became a widespread practice in the temples and monasteries of other sects as well. In religious painting and sculpture too, Amita, seated on a lotus throne in his Western paradise, and flanked by his attendant bodhisattvas (e.g., Kuan-yin, the so-called "Goddess of Mercy") was a favorite theme.

T'AN-LUAN
Commentary to Vasubandhu's Essay on Rebirth

The work from which portions are presented below is a commentary on the Chinese translation of a short essay, partly in prose and partly in verse, ascribed to Vasubandhu and purporting to set forth the essence of the *Pure Land Sūtra* (*Sukhāvatīvyūha*). The author of the commentary is T'an-luan (476–542), a famous patriarch of the Pure Land school. Note how the meditation on Amita is explained in the same terms used for T'ien-t'ai meditative practice, reflecting a close association between this type of devotion and the T'ien-t'ai school.

[From *Wang-sheng lun chu*, in *Taishō daizōkyō*, XL, 827–36]

> Behold the phenomena of yon sphere,
> How they surpass the paths of the three worlds!

The reason that the [Amita] Buddha brings forth the pure merit of these adornments of his sphere is that He sees the phenomena of the three worlds as false, ceaselessly changing in a cycle, and without end, going round like a cankerworm, imprisoned like a silkworm in its own cocoon. Alas for the sentient beings, bound to these three worlds, perverse and impure! He wishes to put the beings in a place that is not false, not ceaselessly changing in a cycle, not without end, that they may find a great, pure place supremely happy. For this reason He brings forth the pure merit of these adornments. What is meant by "perfection"? The meaning is that this purity is incorruptible, that it is incontaminable. It is not like the phenomena of the three worlds, which are both contaminable and corruptible.

"Behold" means "observe." "Yon" means "that happy land." "The phenomena of yon sphere" means "the pure character of that happy sphere". . . . "It surpasses the paths of the three worlds." "Path" means "passageway." By such-and-such a cause one obtains such-and-such an effect. With such-and-such an effect one requites such-and-such a cause. Through the passageway of the cause one reaches the effect. Through the passageway of the effect one requites the cause. Hence "paths". . . . These three worlds, in sum, are the dark house in which the common man, subject to life and death, drifts and goes in a cycle. Though pain and pleasure may differ slightly, though long and short may vary for a time, if one looks at these common men in their totality, there is none without defilement. Holding one another up, leaning on one another, they go in a cycle without end. . . . Now as cause, now as effect, vanity and falsehood succeed each to the other. But happiness is born of the bodhisattva's merciful right view, it is founded on the original vow of the Thus-Come-One's divine power. Those born of womb, eggs, and moisture, as a result of them rise above themselves; the long rope with which karma binds is, by them, forever cut. . . . "It surpasses the Three Worlds,"—truly these are words near to the understanding.

> It is completely like the atmosphere,
> Extensive and great and without limit.

These two verses refer to the perfection of the merit of the quantity of the adornments of this sphere. The reason that the Buddha brings forth this merit of the quantity of these adornments is that He sees the three worlds as narrow and small, in ruins and with gaping holes and bumps. Their shrines and temples are cramped, or their lands and fields are restricting. The road of ambition is short, or the mountains and rivers are insurmountable. Or else countries are divided by boundaries. Such are the various impediments there. For this reason the bodhisattva raised the prayer concerning the merit of the quantity of adornments: "I pray that my land may be like the atmosphere, extensive and great without limits." "Like the atmosphere" means that, though those who come to be reborn therein may be numerous, yet they shall be as if they were nought. "Extensive and great without limits" completes the above meaning of being like the atmosphere. Why like the atmosphere? Because it is extensive and great without limits. "Perfection" means that, though the beings of the ten directions that go to be reborn there, whether those already reborn, those now being reborn, or those going to be reborn, are incalculable and unlimited, basically the place shall ever be like the atmosphere, extensive and great and without limits, never at any time full. Therefore he says, "It is completely like the atmosphere, extensive and great without limit." [pp. 827–28]

Question: Vasubandhu . . . says: "All together with the sentient beings shall go to be reborn in the Happy Land." To which "beings" does this refer?

Answer: If we examine the *Scripture of the Buddha of Limitless Life,* preached at Rājagriha city, we see that the Buddha announced to Ānanda: "The Buddhas, the Thus-Come-Ones of the ten directions, as numerous as the sands of the Ganges, shall all together praise the incalculable awesome divinity and merit of the Buddha of Limitless Life. Then all of the beings that are, if, hearing his name, they shall with a believing heart rejoice for but a single moment of consciousness and with minds intent on being reborn in His land, shall be immediately enabled to go there and be reborn and stay there without return. There shall be excepted only those who commit the Five Violations[1] and malign the True Law." From this we see that even the commonest of men may go thither to be reborn. . . .

Question: The *Scripture of the Buddha of Limitless Life* says: "Those who pray to go thither to be reborn can all go thither to be reborn. Only those who commit the Five Violations and malign the True Law are excepted." The *Scripture of the Contemplation of the Buddha of Limitless Life* says: "They who perpetrate the Five Violations and the Ten Evils,[2] indeed, they who do all manner of evil, may also go thither to be reborn." How are these two scriptures to be reconciled?

Answer: The one scripture specifies two kinds of grave sin. One is the Five Violations, the other is the maligning of the True Law. By virtue of both of these two kinds of grave sin one is unable to go thither to be reborn. The other scripture merely speaks of perpetrating the sins of the Ten Evils and the Five Violations, but says nothing of maligning the

---

[1] These are parricide, matricide, murder of an arhant, introduction of disharmony into the monastic community, and striking a Buddha so as to cause him to bleed.

[2] These are killing, stealing, adultery, lying, duplicity, slander, obscene language, lust, anger, and false views.

True Law. Since one does not malign the True Law, therefore one is able to be reborn there.

Question: Even if a man is completely guilty of the Five Violations, as long as he does not malign the True Law, the scripture allows that he can be reborn there. On the other hand, if there is a man who merely maligns the True Law but is not guilty of the sins of the Five Violations, if he prays to go thither to be reborn, can he be reborn there or not?

Answer: If he merely maligns the True Law, though he might have no other sins, he most certainly cannot be reborn there. Why do I say this? The scriptures say: "Those guilty of the Five Violations descend into the midst of the Hell of Uninterrupted Suffering and there suffer fully one cosmic period of grave punishment. Those who malign the True Law descend into the midst of the Hell of Uninterrupted Suffering, and, when this period is exhausted, turn about and go into the midst of another Hell of Uninterrupted Suffering. In this way they go through hundreds and thousands of such hells." The Buddha records no time at which they are able to leave, because the sin of maligning the True Law is extremely grave. Also, the "True Law" is the Law of Buddha. Once these foolish men have given expression to such calumny, how can they possibly pray for rebirth in Buddha's Land? Even if they were to pray for rebirth there out of a sole desire for the comforts and pleasures of that Land, it would still be like seeking waterless ice or smokeless fire. How could there be any way of obtaining it? [p. 834]

But there are some who call upon His name and bear it in mind, but whose ignorance persists and whose wishes remain unfulfilled. Why? Because they do not practice truly, nor in keeping with His name and its meaning. What is meant by "not practicing truly, nor in keeping with His name and its meaning"? The meaning is ignorance of the fact that the Thus-Come-One is the Body of True Character, the Body that acts for the sake of the beings. Also, "not in keeping" is of three kinds. First is impure faith, since it seems to exist and yet seems not to exist. Second is the lack of unity of faith, since it is not firm. Third is the discontinuity of faith, since it is interrupted by other thoughts. [p. 835]

How does one give rise to a prayerful heart? One always prays, with the whole heart single-mindedly thinking of being ultimately reborn in the Happy Land, because one wishes truly to practice *śamatha* [concentration]. . . .

Śamatha is rendered *chih* [stop] in three senses. First, one thinks single-mindedly of Amita Buddha and prays for rebirth in His Land. This Buddha's name and that Land's name can stop all evil. Second, that Happy Land exceeds the paths of the three worlds. If a man is born in that Land, he automatically puts an end to the evils of body, mouth, and mind. Third, Amita Buddha's power of enlightenment and persistent tenacity can naturally arrest the mind that seeks after lower stages of the Vehicle. These three kinds of *chih* arise from Buddha's real merit. Therefore it is said that "one wishes truly to practice *śamatha* [concentration].

How does one observe? With wisdom one observes. With right mindfulness one observes Him, because one wishes truly to practice *vipaśyanā* [insight]. . . .

Vipaśyanā is translated *kuan* [insight] in two senses. First, while yet in this world, one conceives a thought and views the merit of the above-mentioned three kinds of adornments. This merit is real, hence the practitioner also gains real merit. "Real merit" is the ability to be reborn with certainty in that Land. Second, once one has achieved rebirth in that Pure Land one immediately sees Amita Buddha. The pure-hearted bodhisattva who has not yet fully perceived is now able to perceive fully the Law Body that is above differences and, together with the pure-hearted bodhisattvas and the bodhisattvas of the uppermost station, to attain fully to the same quiescent equality. Therefore it is said that "one wishes truly to practice *vipaśyanā*." [pp. 835-36]

How does one apply [one's own merit] to and not reject all suffering beings? By ever making the vow to put such application first, in order to obtain a perfect heart of great compassion.

"Application" has two aspects. The first is the going aspect, the second is the returning aspect. What is the "going aspect"? One takes one's own merit and diverts it to all the beings, praying that all together may go to be reborn in Amita Buddha's Happy Land. What is the "returning aspect"? When one has already been reborn in that Land and attained to the perfection of concentration and insight, and the power of saving others through convenient means, one returns and enters the withered forest of life and death, and teaches all beings to turn together to the Path of the Buddha. [p. 836]

TAO-CH'O
Compendium on the Happy Land

The compendium from which these extracts are taken was compiled by Tao-ch'o (d. 645), a T'ien-t'ai monk who was particularly devoted to the recitation of the Buddha's name and became one of the great patriarchs of Chinese Buddhism.

[From *An-lo chi*, in *Taishō daizōkyō*, XLVII, 8–11]

The refutation of the misunderstanding of the characterlessness of the Great Vehicle consists of two parts. First is a summary statement of origination, the purpose of which is to enable scholars of later generations to understand right and wrong clearly, to depart from the crooked and face toward the straight. Second is a clarification of right, with reference to the attachments, and consequent refutation. . . .

Question: There are some persons who say that the Great Vehicle is characterless, that it takes no thought of "that" or "this." If one vows to be reborn in the Pure Land, then one is clinging to a characteristic, which ever increases one's impurities and fetters. Why should one seek after this?

Answer: If one reckons thus, it must be said not to be so. Why? The preaching of the Law by all the Buddhas must be accompanied by two conditions. Firstly, it must depend upon the true principles of the dharma-nature. Secondly, it must harmonize with the Twofold Truth. Some people claim that the Greater Vehicle, being free of any false conceptions, is based only on the Dharma-Nature, but they malign the Great Vehicle by saying that there is no condition on which to seek it. This does not harmonize with the Twofold Truth. One who views it in this way falls into the trap of the Emptiness which annihilates[3]. . . .

Question: According to the holy doctrine of the Great Vehicle, if the bodhisattva evinces toward the beings a loving view or great compassion, he should immediately resist it. Now the bodhisattva encourages all beings to be reborn in the Pure Land. Is this not a combining with love, a grasping at character? Or does he escape defiling attachments [in spite of this]?

Answer: The efficacy of the dharmas practiced by the bodhisattva is of

[3] That is, they insist on the Higher Truth (the Absolute) alone and deny relative existence, thus taking Emptiness to mean the denial of all existence.

two kinds. Which are they? One is perception of the understanding of Emptiness and Perfect Wisdom. The second is full possession of great compassion. In the case of the former, by virtue of his practice of the understanding of Emptiness and Perfect Wisdom, though he may enter into the cycles of life and death of the six stages of existence, he is not fettered by their grime or contamination. In the case of the latter, by virtue of his compassionate mindfulness of the beings, he does not dwell in Nirvāna. The bodhisattva, though he dwells in the midst of the Two-fold Truth, is ever able subtly to reject existence and nonexistence, to strike the mean in his acceptances and rejections and not to run counter to the principles of the Great Way. [p. 8]

Refutation of the notion that there are no dharmas outside of the Mind consists of two parts. First is the refutation of the feelings that reckon thus; second is an interpretation in questions and answers.

Question: There are some who say: "The realm of purity which one contemplates is restricted to the inner mind. The Pure Land is all-pervasive; the mind, if pure, is identical with it. Outside of the Mind there are no dharmas. What need is there to enter the West[ern Paradise]?"

Answer: Only the Pure Land of the dharma-nature dwells in principle in empty all-pervasion and is in substance unrestricted. This is the birth of no-birth, into which the superior gentlemen [4] may enter. . . . There are the middle and lower classes [of bodhisattvas], who are not yet able to overcome the world of characters, and who must rely on the circumstance of faith in the Buddha to seek rebirth in the Pure Land. Though they reach that Land, they still dwell in a Land of characters. It is also said: "If one envelops conditions and follows the origin,[5] this is what is meant by 'no dharmas outside the Mind.' But if one distinguishes the Twofold Truth to clarify the doctrine, then the Pure Land does not conflict with the existence of dharmas outside the Mind." Now let us interpret through question and answer.

Question: A while ago, when you said that the "birth of no-birth" is something into which only superior gentlemen can enter, while the middle and inferior ones cannot, were you merely creating this interpretation

---

[4] That is, the bodhisattvas of the upper stages.
[5] Rising above conditioned things to seek the Absolute.

by fitting the doctrine to the man, or is there also proof of this in the Sacred Doctrine?

Answer: According to the *Treatise of the Perfection of Wisdom:* "The bodhisattvas who have newly aroused their minds [to the ultimate goal of Buddhahood] are by receptivity and understanding soft and weak. Though one may say that they have aroused their minds, most of them vow to be reborn in the Pure Land. For what reason is this so? They are like a child which, if not close to the loving care of its father and mother, may descend into a pit, or fall into a well, or suffer calamity at the hands of fire or snake and the like, or may be deprived of milk and die, but which must rely on the care and nurture of its father and mother in order to grow and be able to carry on the heritage of the family. So also is the bodhisattva. If he can arouse his bodhi-mind, pray much for rebirth in the Pure Land, approach the Buddhas, and advance the dharma-body, only then can he properly carry on the household heritage of the bodhisattva and in all ten directions ferry the beings over. For the sake of this benefit, most of them vow for rebirth in the Pure Land." [pp. 8-9]

Fourth is the refutation of the notion that one should vow to be reborn in this filthy land, not in that Pure Land.

Question: There are some who say that one vows to be reborn in this filthy land in order to convert the beings by one's teaching, and that one does not vow to go to the Pure Land to be reborn. How is this?

Answer: Of such persons also there is a certain group. Why? If the body resides in [an estate from which there is] no backsliding, or beyond, in order to convert the sundry evil beings it may dwell in contamination without becoming contaminated or encounter evil without being transformed, just as the swan and the duck may enter the water but the water cannot wet them. Such persons as these can dwell in filth and extricate the beings from their suffering. But if the person is in truth an ordinary man, I only fear that his own conduct is not yet established, and that if he encounters suffering he will immediately change. He who wishes to save him will perish together with him. For example, if one forces a chicken into the water, how can one not get wet? [p. 9]

Fifth is the refutation of the proposition that those who are reborn in the Pure Land mostly take pleasure in clinging to enjoyment.

Question: There are some who say: "Within the Pure Land there are only enjoyable things. Much pleasure in clinging to enjoyment hinders and destroys the practice of the Way. Why should one vow to go thither and be reborn?"

Answer: Since it is called "Pure Land," it means that there are no impurities in it. If one speaks of "clinging to enjoyment," this refers to lust and the afflictions. If so, why call it pure? [p. 9]

Question: The scriptures of the Great Vehicle say that the way of karma is like a scale, the heavier side showing its influence first. How can beings who throughout their lives until this day, whether for a hundred years or for ten, have practiced all evils, how can they, when they approach their end, meet a benevolent person and after ten uninterrupted moments of thought [of the Buddha, etc.] be enabled to go thither to be reborn? If this is so, how can one believe what is said about the heavier side showing its influence first?

Answer: You say that the evil karma of one lifetime is heavy, while you suppose the good of ten moments of thought in the life of an inferior man to be light. Let us now compare their relative lightness and heaviness on the basis of principle precisely to make clear that what matters lies in the mind, in the conditions and one's determination, and not in the distance or length of time involved. In what sense is it in the mind? By that we mean that when such a man commits a sin the sin is born from a vain and perverse mind, while these ten moments of thought are born from hearing the dharma of real character from a benevolent man who by resorting to expedient means comforts him. In the one case it is reality, and in the other it is vanity. How can they be equated? Why do we say this? Suppose a room has been dark for a thousand years. If light enters it for but a moment, it will be clear and bright. How could one say that the darkness, having been in the room for a thousand years, cannot be eliminated? . . . This is what is meant by "in the mind." Secondly, in what sense do we mean "in conditions"? We mean that when that man commits sin, his sin is born from false notions, from among beings who suffer the retribution of the afflictions. But now these ten moments of thought are born out of a mind of supreme faith, out of the name of Amita the Thus-Come-One, a true and pure name of infinite merits. It is as if a man were to be struck by a poisoned arrow, which pierced his sinews and broke his bone, and were immediately to have the arrow removed and the poison cleared away by the mere act of hearing the sound of a drum advertising a remedy. How could one say that, though the arrow was deep and the poison dangerous, he was not able, as soon as he heard the sound of the drum, to pull out the arrow and clear away the poison? This is what is meant by "in conditions." Thirdly, in what sense do we mean "one's determination"? When that man commits sin, the sin is born from a mind that fears consequences and has interruptions, while these ten moments of thought arise from a mind that has neither consequences nor interruptions. This is what is meant by "determination." [pp. 10–11]

Question: If I wish now to practice diligently the concentration of the mindfulness of the Buddha, I do not know what the character and form of this mindfulness look like.

Answer: Suppose a man in an empty and distant place encounters a bandit who, drawing his sword, comes forcefully and directly to kill him. This man runs straight on, looking ahead to cross a river. But before reaching the river he would have the following thoughts: "When I reach the river bank, shall I take off my clothes and cross or wear them and float? To take them off and cross I fear there may not be time. If I wear them and float, then I fear that my life will not be saved." At such a time he has only the single thought of a means to cross the river, and no other thoughts would be mingled with it. So also is the practitioner. When he is contemplating Amita Buddha, he is like the man contemplating the crossing. The thought is continuous, no others being mingled with it. He may contemplate the Buddha's Dharma-Body, or he may contemplate the Buddha's supernatural might, or he may contemplate the Buddha's wisdom, or he may contemplate the Buddha's hair-mark, or he may contemplate the goodness of the Buddha's character, or he may contemplate the Buddha's original vow. In the same way he may recite the name of the Buddha. If one is able to concentrate on it wholeheartedly, continuously and without interruption, one will certainly be reborn in the Buddha's presence. [p. 11]

Question: The *Scripture of the Buddha of Limitless Life* says: "If the beings of the ten directions shall with intense belief and desire for as much as ten moments wish to be reborn in my Land, and if then they should not be reborn there, may I never attain enlightenment." Now there are men in the world who hear this holy teaching and who in their present life never arouse their minds to it, but wait until the end approaches and then wish to practice such contemplation. What do you say of such cases?

Answer: Such cases are not true. Why? The scriptures say: "Ten continuous moments may seem not to be difficult. However, the minds of ordinary men are like a zephyr, their consciousness is more capricious than a monkey's. It runs through the six objects of sensual perception without rest." Everyone should arouse his faith and first conquer his own thoughts, so that through the accumulated practice it will become his nature and the roots of goodness become firm. As the Buddha proclaimed to the great king, if men accumulate good conduct, at death they will have no evil thoughts, just as, when a tree is first bent in a certain direction, when it falls it will follow that bent. Once the sword and the wind arrive, and a hundred woes concentrate upon the body, if the practice is not there to begin with, how can contemplation be consummated? Everyone should form a bond with three or five comrades to enlighten one another. When life's end faces them, they should enlighten one another, recite Amita Buddha's name to one another, and pray for rebirth in Paradise in such a way that voice succeeds upon voice until the ten moments of thought are completed. It is as, when a wax seal has been impressed in clay, after the wax has been destroyed, the imprint remains. When this life is cut off, one is reborn immediately in the Comfortable and Pleasant Land. At the time one enters completely into the cluster of right contemplation. What more is there to worry about? Everyone should weigh this great blessing. Why should one not conquer one's own thoughts ahead of time? [p. 11]

THE MEDITATION SCHOOL

The Meditation school, called *Ch'an* in Chinese from the Sanskrit *dhyāna,* is better known to the West by the Japanese pronunciation *Zen.* As a religious practice, of course, meditation was not peculiar to Ch'an; it had been a standard fixture in all forms of Buddhism, whether Indian or Chinese, from earliest times. Yet no other school attached the exclusive importance Ch'an did to meditation, not only as a method or means for intuiting Ultimate Truth, but indeed as an end in itself, as the Truth realized in action. Nor was any other school prepared to dispense as freely as did Ch'an with scriptural studies or philosophical discussion in favor of a purely intuitive approach to enlightenment. Therefore, where the names of other schools bespoke their scriptural authority (e.g., the Lotus or Flower Garland sects) or their metaphysical position (e.g., Consciousness-Only or Dharma-Character sect), Ch'an's derived from its meditative posture.

From its distaste for book-learning Ch'an became known as the doctrine "not founded on words or scriptures." It was rather a teaching "transmitted from mind to mind," that is, from one master directly to his disciple, without the intervention of rational argumentation or formulation in conceptual terms. However, if in some ways Ch'an seems strongly individualistic and often irreverent and iconoclastic with respect to tradition, it is at the same time highly authoritarian and insistent upon the firmest discipline. Ch'an is, indeed, above all a religious discipline, and one which requires complete submission to the will of the Master, who alone can guide authoritatively and insure the correct transmission of the Truth.

Ch'an teaches "directly pointing to the human mind" and "becoming a Buddha just as you are," believing that the Buddha-nature is inherent in all human beings and that through meditative introspection this nature can readily be seen. By the Buddha-nature is meant the Buddha-mind in its highest attributes and true essence, which transcends all distinctions of object and subject or duality of any kind. It is Emptiness, that is, empty of any specific character. The world of appearances, with all its specific characters, is but a product of the imagination.

To penetrate the Buddha-mind, the great meditation masters variously advocated "absence of thought" in the sense that the mind should be freed from the influence of the external world. They taught "ignoring one's feelings" so as to eliminate all defilements and attachments. They also taught "letting the mind take its course" unhindered among phenomena, the latter being, after all, manifestations of the Buddha-mind

Whatever the approach, the fundamental method has been meditation. This is of two kinds, Tathāgata Meditation and Patriarchal Meditation. The former, the Buddha's way of meditating, involves deliberations of the intellect, while the latter, as taught by the Patriarch Bodhidharma, requires no intellectual effort, but rather direct intuition of the Buddha-mind. The result of meditation is enlightenment, which may come suddenly or gradually. The major tradition has been "sudden enlightenment preceding gradual cultivation," the idea being that cultivation of the religious life must be gradual and guided by Perfect Wisdom.

To bring the mind into sharp focus and to make it alert so that it can immediately intuit Truth, which is everywhere, the mind must be emancipated from old habits, prejudices, restrictive thought processes, and even ordinary thought itself. The horizon must be lifted, the perspective broadened, and the aim always directed toward Ultimate Truth. To this end special methods have been devised to throw off intellection and imagination and to allow the pure mind to make its own discovery. Travel (which usually offers new experience), manual labor, working with nature, etc., are all accepted techniques. But the most commonly used method, especially from the eighth through the eleventh century, has been the "public case" (*kōan* in Japanese), a question-and-answer method in which answers to a disciple's questions may consist of scolding, beating, or strange and illogical utterances. The purpose is to wake up, shock, and sensitize the questioner's mind, so as to help him discover the Truth himself.

Ch'an attributes its mystic beginning to the Buddha himself, who, according to tradition, transmitted the doctrine to his pupil Kāshyapa by merely holding up a flower and smiling. Its founding in China has been attributed to Bodhidharma, the First Patriarch, about A.D. 520. Questions have been raised about his historicity, but recent Chinese and Japanese scholarship has definitely established the fact that such a person was in China during the period 420–479. By that time, however, the meditation doctrine had already become widely accepted and practiced following its advocacy by An Shih-kao (A.D. c. 150). The doctrine of sudden enlightenment had also been advanced earlier by Tao-sheng (d. 434) and had aroused considerable controversy.

The doctrine was ultimately transmitted to the Sixth Patriarch Hui-neng (638–713). At this time the school split into the Southern school of Sudden Enlightenment and the Northern school of Gradual Enlightenment. The Northern school, founded by Shen-hsiu (605–706), soon disappeared, while the Southern school, founded by Hui-neng, has flourished to this day. The two people who perfected the doctrine of the Southern school were indisputably Hui-neng and his immediate pupil Shen-hui (d. 760). But who played the greater role is a matter of debate. Dr. Hu

Shih, looking at the matter from a historical standpoint, maintains that Shen-hui was the key to the development of Ch'an in China. On the basis of newly discovered documents and historical records, he concludes that Shen-hui, in 734, swept aside all forms of sitting in meditation and replaced it with the doctrines of "absence of thought" and "seeing one's original nature." In this way Shen-hui inaugurated a new Ch'an movement which renounced Ch'an itself and is therefore not Ch'an at all. According to Hu, most of the so-called Ch'an sects in the eighth century emphasized knowledge instead of quiet-sitting. The Ch'an masters from 700 to 1000 taught and spoke in plain language and did not resort to enigmatic words, gestures, or acts. The apparently illogical question-and-answer method and other bizarre techniques were not so illogical or ir-rational as they seem, but only methods of educating men "the hard way," so that each individual would have to make the effort to learn for himself.

Dr. D. T. Suzuki agrees with Hu that Chinese Ch'an had almost noth-ing to do with the Indian practice of *dhyāna* (meditation). But he insists that instead of Shen-hui, it was Hui-neng who brought on the revolution, a revolution aimed at the identification of wisdom (*prajñā*) and medita-tion (*dhyāna*). The Ch'an masters understood *prajñā* not as rational knowledge but as intuition. In fact it was Shen-hui's over-rational inter-pretation of *prajñā* that led to the decline of his influence on the historical development of Chinese Ch'an. Later developments such as the questions-and-answers were not rational exercises of the mind but methods con-ducive to *prajñā* intuition. Thus, according to Suzuki, Ch'an is not ex-plainable by mere intellectual analysis.[6]

In any case, the transmission of Ch'an continued without interruption until there were seven sects in the ninth century. After the eleventh cen-tury, however, only two sects, the Lin-chi and Ts'ao-tung, survived. To-gether they have exerted a tremendous influence on Chinese Buddhism at large. The Lin-chi sect was founded by Patriarch I-hsüan of Lin-chi (d. 867) and the Ts'ao-tung sect had Liang-chieh of Tung-shan (807–869) as its First Patriarch and Pen-chi of Ts'ao-shan (840–901) as its Second Patriarch. Hence came the name Ts'ao-tung. Early Lin-chi masters frequently used the "lightning" method of scolding and beating disciples,

---

[6] See Hu Shih, "Ch'an (Zen) Buddhism in China: Its History and Method," *Philosophy East and West*, 3:1 (April, 1953) and D. T. Suzuki, "Zen: a Reply to Hu Shih," *ibid.*

while early Ts'ao-tung masters preferred the question-and-answer or case method. Of the following four selections, two give the basic teachings of the men most responsible for the development of Ch'an in China, namely, Hui-neng and Shen-hui. The other two represent the most commonly used methods in Ch'an teaching, the sermon and the question-and-answer.

The Platform Scripture of the Sixth Patriarch

This short work is traditionally believed to represent a lecture by Hui-neng (638–713), recorded by his pupil Fa-hai. Hu Shih, however, believes it to be the work of an eighth-century follower of Shen-hui, another pupil of Hui-neng. Our translation is from the text discovered in the Tun-huang caves, which is older and much shorter than the traditional version.

[From *Liu-tsu t'an-ching,* in *Taishō daizōkyō,* XLVIII, 337–44]

Monk Hung-jen [601–675] asked Hui-neng: "Whence have you come to pay homage to me? What do you want from me?"

Hui-neng answered: "Your disciple is from Lingnan ["South of the Mountains Ranges," in the region of the present Canton]. A citizen of Hsin-chou, I have come a great distance to pay homage, without seeking anything except the Law of the Buddha."

The Great Master reproved him, saying: "You are from Lingnan and, furthermore, you are a barbarian. How can you become a Buddha?"

Hui-neng answered: "Although people are distinguished as northerners and southerners, there is neither north nor south in Buddha-nature. In physical body, the barbarian and the monk are different. But what is the difference in their Buddha-nature?"

The Great Master intended to argue with him further, but, seeing people around, said nothing. Hui-neng was ordered to attend to duties among the rest. It happened that one monk went away to travel. Thereupon Hui-neng was ordered to pound rice, which he did for eight months. [Sec. 3]

One day the Fifth Patriarch [Hung-jen] suddenly called all his pupils to come to him. As they assembled, he said: "Let me say this to you. Life and death are serious matters. You people are engaged all day in making offerings [to the Buddha], going after blessings and rewards only, and you make no effort to achieve freedom from the bitter sea of life and death. Your self-nature seems to be obscured. How can blessings save you? Go to your rooms and examine yourselves. He who is enlightened use his perfect vision of self-nature and write me a verse. When I look at his verse, if it reveals deep understanding, I shall give him the robe and the Law and make him the Sixth Patriarch. Hurry, hurry!" [Sec. 4]

At midnight Shen-hsiu, holding a candle, wrote a verse on the wall of the south corridor, without anyone knowing about it, which said:

> Our body is the tree of Perfect Wisdom,
> And our mind is a bright mirror.
> At all times diligently wipe them,
> So that they will be free from dust. [Sec. 6]

The Fifth Patriarch said: "The verse you wrote shows some but not all understanding. You have arrived at the front of the door but you have not yet entered it. Ordinary people, by practicing in accordance with your verse, will not degenerate. But it will be futile to seek the Supreme Perfect Wisdom while holding to such a view. One must enter the door and see his self-nature. Go away and come back after one or two days of thought. If you have entered the door and seen your self-nature, I shall give you the robe and the Law."

Shen-hsiu went away and for several days could not produce another verse. [Sec. 7]

Hui-neng also wrote a verse . . . which says:

> The tree of Perfect Wisdom is originally no tree.
> Nor has the bright mirror any frame.
> Buddha-nature is forever clear and pure.
> Where is there any dust?

Another verse:

> The mind is the tree of Perfect Wisdom.
> The body is the clear mirror.
> The clear mirror is originally clear and pure.
> Where has it been affected by any dust?

Monks in the hall were all surprised at these verses. Hui-neng, however, went back to the rice-pounding room. The Fifth Patriarch suddenly realized that Hui-neng was the one of good knowledge but was afraid lest the rest learn it. He therefore told them: "This will not do." [Sec. 8] The Fifth Patriarch waited till midnight, called Hui-neng to come to the hall, and expounded the *Diamond Sūtra*. As soon as Hui-neng heard this, he understood. That night the Law was imparted to him without anyone knowing it, and thus the Law and the robe [emblematic] of Sudden Enlightenment were transmitted to him. "You are now the Sixth Patriarch," said the Fifth Patriarch to Hui-neng, "The robe is the testimony of transmission from generation to generation. As to the Law, it is to be transmitted from mind to mind. Let people achieve understanding through their own effort."

The Fifth Patriarch told Hui-neng: "From the very beginning, the transmission of the Law has been as delicate as a hanging thread of silk. If you remain here, some one might harm you. You had better leave quickly." [Sec. 9]

[Hui-neng, having returned South, said]: I came and stayed in this place [Canton] and have not been free from persecution by government officials, Taoists, and common folk. The doctrine has been transmitted down from past sages; it is not my own idea. Those who wish to hear the teachings of the past sages should purify their hearts. Having heard them, they should first free themselves from their delusions and then attain enlightenment."

Great Master Hui-neng declared: "Good friends, perfection is inherent in all people. It is only because of the delusions of the mind that they cannot attain enlightenment by themselves. They must ask the help of the enlightened and be shown the way to see their own nature. Good friends, as soon as one is enlightened, he will achieve Perfect Wisdom." [Sec. 12]

"Good friends, in my system, meditation and wisdom are the bases. First of all, do not be deceived that the two are different. They are one reality and not two. Meditation is the substance (*t'i*) of wisdom and wisdom is the function (*yung*) of meditation.[7] As soon as wisdom is achieved, meditation is included in it, and as soon as meditation is attained, wisdom is included in it. Good friends, the meaning here is that meditation and wisdom are identified. A follower after the Way should not think wisdom follows meditation or vice versa or that the two are different. To hold such a view would imply that the dharmas possess two different characters. To those whose words are good but whose hearts are not good, meditation and wisdom are not identified. But to those whose hearts and words are both good and for whom the internal and external

---

[7] Technical terms of T'ien-t'ai philosophy denoting two aspects of a single reality.

are one, meditation and wisdom are identified. Self-enlightenment and practice do not consist in argument. If one concerns himself about whether [meditation or wisdom] comes first, he is deluded. Unless one is freed from the consideration of victory or defeat, he will produce the [imagining of] dharmas and the self, and cannot be free from the characters [of birth, stagnation, deterioration, and extinction]." [Sec. 13]

"Good friends, there is no distinction between sudden enlightenment and gradual enlightenment in the Law, except that some people are intelligent and others stupid. Those who are ignorant realize the truth gradually, while the enlightened ones attain it suddenly. But if they know their own minds and see their own nature, then there will be no difference in their enlightenment. Without enlightenment, they will be forever bound in transmigration." [Sec. 16]

"Good friends, in my system, from the very beginning, whether in the sudden enlightenment or gradual enlightenment tradition, absence of thought has been instituted as the main doctrine, absence of phenomena as the substance, and nonattachment as the foundation. What is meant by absence of phenomena? Absence of phenomena means to be free from phenomena when in contact with them. Absence of thought means not to be carried away by thought in the process of thought. Nonattachment is man's original nature. [In its ordinary process], thought moves forward without a halt; past, present, and future thoughts continue as an unbroken stream. But if we can cut off this stream by an instant of thought, the Dharma-Body will be separated from the physical body, and at no time will a single thought be attached to any dharma. If one single instant of thought is attached to anything, then every thought will be attached. That will be bondage. But if in regard to all dharmas, no thought is attached to anything, that means freedom. This is the reason why nonattachment is taken as the foundation.

"Good friends, to be free from all phenomena means absence of phenomena. Only if we can be free from phenomena will the reality of nature be pure. This is the reason why absence of phenomena is taken as the substance.

"Absence of thought means not to be defiled by external objects. It is to free our thoughts from external objects and not to allow dharmas to cause our thoughts to rise. If one stops thinking about things and wipes out all thought, then as thought is terminated once and for all, there will be no more rebirth. Take this seriously, followers of the Path. It is bad enough for a man to be deceived himself through not knowing the meaning of the Law. How much worse is it to encourage others to be deceived! Not only does he fail to realize that he is deceived, but he also blasphemes against the scripture and the Law. This is the reason why absence of thought is instituted as the doctrine.

"All this is because people who are deceived have thoughts about sense-objects. With such thoughts, pervasive views arise, and all sorts of defilements and erroneous thoughts are produced from them.

"However, the school instituted absence of thought as the doctrine. When people are free from [erroneous] views, no thought will arise. If there are no thoughts, there will not even be 'absence of thought.' Absence means absence of what? Thought means thought of what? Absence means freedom from duality and all defilements. Thought means thought of Thusness and self-nature. True Thusness is the substance of thought and thought is the function of True Thusness. It is the self-nature that gives rise to thought. [Therefore] in spite of the functioning of seeing, hearing, sensing, and knowing, the self-nature is not defiled by the many sense-objects and always remains as it truly is. As the *Vimalakīrti Scripture* says: 'Externally it skillfully differentiates the various dharma-characters and internally it abides firmly in the First Principle.' " [Sec. 17]

"Good friends, in this system sitting in meditation is at bottom neither attached to the mind nor attached to purity, and there is neither speech nor motion. Suppose it should be attached to the mind. The mind is at bottom an imagination. Since imagination is the same as illusion, there is nothing to be attached to. Suppose it were attached to purity, man's nature is originally pure. It is only because of erroneous thought that True Thusness is obscured. Our original nature is pure as long as it is free from erroneous thought. If one does not realize that his own nature is originally pure and makes up his mind to attach himself to purity, he is creating an imaginary purity. Such purity does not exist. Hence we know that what is to be attached to is imaginary." [Sec. 18]

"This being the case, in this system, what is meant by sitting in meditation? To sit means to obtain absolute freedom and not to allow any thought to be caused by external objects. To meditate means to realize the imperturbability of one's original nature. What is meant by meditation and calmness? Meditation means to be free from all phenomena and calmness means to be internally unperturbed. If one is externally attached to phenomena, the inner mind will at once be disturbed, but if one is externally free from phenomena, the inner nature will not be perturbed. The original nature is by itself pure and calm. It is only because of causal conditions that it comes into contact with external objects, and the contact leads to perturbation. There will be calmness when one is free from external objects and is not perturbed. Meditation is achieved when one is externally free from phenomena and calmness is achieved when one is internally unperturbed. Meditation and calmness mean that externally meditation is attained and internally calmness is achieved." [Sec. 19]

"All scriptures and writings of the Mahāyāna and Hīnayāna schools as well as the twelve sections of the Canon were provided for man. It is because man possesses the nature of wisdom that these were instituted. If there were no man, there would not have been any dharmas. We know, therefore, that dharmas exist because of man and there are all these scriptures because there are people to preach them.

"Among men some are wise and others stupid. The stupid are inferior people, whereas the wise ones are superior. The ignorant consult the wise and the wise explain the Law to them and enable them to understand. When the ignorant understand, they will no longer be different from the wise. Hence we know that without enlightenment, a Buddha is no different from all living beings, and with enlightenment, all living beings are the same as a Buddha. Hence we know that all dharmas are immanent in one's person. Why not seek in one's own mind the sudden realization of the original nature of True Thusness?" [Sec. 30]

The Great Master said to Chi-ch'eng [pupil of Shen-hsiu]: "I hear that your teacher in his teaching transmits only the doctrine of discipline, calmness, and wisdom. Please tell me his explanation of these teachings."

Chi-ch'eng said: "The Reverend Shen-hsiu said that discipline is to refrain from all evil actions, wisdom is to practice all good deeds, and calmness is to purify one's own mind. These are called discipline, calmness, and wisdom. This is his explanation. I wonder what your views are."

Patriarch Hui-neng answered: "His theory is wonderful, but my views are different."

Chi-ch'eng asked: "How different?"

Hui-neng answered: "Some people realize [the Law] more quickly and others more slowly."

Chi-ch'eng then asked the Patriarch to explain his views on discipline, calmness, and wisdom. The Great Master said: "Please listen to me. In my view, freeing the mind from all wrong is the discipline of our original nature. Freeing the mind from all disturbances is the calmness of our original nature. And freeing the mind from all delusions is the wisdom of our original nature."

Master Hui-neng continued: "Your teacher's teaching of discipline, calmness, and wisdom is to help wise men of the inferior type but mine is to help superior people. When one realizes his original nature, then discipline, calmness, and wisdom need not be instituted."

Chi-ch'eng said: "Great Master, please explain why they need not be instituted."

The Great Master said: "The original nature has no wrong, no disturbance, no delusion. If in every instant of thought we introspect our minds with Perfect Wisdom, and if it is always free from dharmas and their appearances, what is the need of instituting these things? The original nature is realized suddenly, not gradually step by step. Therefore there is no need of instituting them."

Chi-ch'eng bowed, decided not to leave Ts'ao-li Mountain, but immediately became a pupil and always stayed close by the Master. [Sec. 41]

SHEN-HUI

Elucidating the Doctrine

This work by Shen-hui (d. 760) is also entitled *Hymn to the Wisdom that Instantaneously Perceives Noncreation* (*Tun-wu wu-sheng po-jo sung*) in the version found at Tun-huang. In the present translation the text as found in the *Transmission of the Lamp* (*Ching-te ch'uan teng lu*) is emended at certain points in the light of the Tun-huang version.

[From *Hsien-tsung chi,* in *Ching-te ch'uan teng lu,* 30:6b–8a]

"Absence of thought" is the doctrine.
"Absence of action" is the foundation.
True Emptiness is the substance.
And all wonderful things and beings are the function.
True Thusness is without thought; it cannot be known through conception and thought.
The True State is noncreated—can it be seen in matter and mind?
There is no thought except that of True Thusness.
There is no creation except that of the True State.
Abiding without abiding, forever abiding in Nirvāna.

Acting without acting, immediately crossing to the Other Shore.

Thusness does not move, but its motion and functions are inexhaustible.

In every instant of thought, there is no seeking; the seeking itself is no thought.

Perfect wisdom is not achieved, and yet the Five Eyes [8] all become pure and the Three Bodies [9] are understood.

Great Enlightenment has no knowledge, and yet the Six Supernatural Powers [10] of the Buddha are utilized and the Four Wisdoms [11] of the Buddha are made great.

Thus we know that calmness is at the same time no calmness, wisdom at the same time no wisdom, and action at the same time no action.

The nature is equivalent to the void and the substance is identical with the Realm of Law.

In this way, the Six Perfections [12] are completed.

None of the ways to arrive at Nirvāna is wanting.

Thus we know that the ego and the dharmas are empty in reality and being and nonbeing are both obliterated.

The mind is originally without activity; the Way is always without thought.

No thought, no reflection, no seeking, no attainment;

No this, no that, no coming, no going.

With such reality one understands the True Insight [into previous and future mortal conditions and present mortal suffering].

With such a mind one penetrates the Eight Emancipations [through the eight stages of mental concentration].

By merits one accomplishes the Ten Powers of the Buddha.[13]

And one's riches will include the Seven Treasures [of gold, silver, etc.].

[8] Physical eye, heavenly eye through concentration, wisdom eye, Law-eye, and Buddha-eye.

[9] The Buddha's Body of Essence or Law (Dharma-Body), the Body of Bliss, and the Body of Transformation.

[10] Instantaneous view of all existence, ability to hear sound everywhere, ability to know other minds, ability to know former existences, ability to be everywhere and to do anything, supernatural consciousness of the waning of defilements.

[11] Magnificent Great Mirror Wisdom, Wisdom of Equanimity, Wisdom of Great Observation, and Wisdom of All-Accomplishment.

[12] Charity, discipline, patience, effort, calmness, and wisdom.

[13] The power to know what is right and wrong in every condition; to know the karma of all beings; to know all stages of concentration and liberation through wisdom; to know the faculties of all beings; to know the desires of all beings; to know the actual conditions of all beings; to know the directions and consequences of all laws; to know all causes of life and death and good and evil; to know the end of all beings; and to know the destruction of all delusions.

One will enter the Gate of Nonduality
And attain the truth of the One Vehicle.
The Law-Body is the wonder of wonders,
And the Wisdom of the Diamond is the Heaven of Heavens.
Still and always quiet, unlimited in function and response,
It functions but is always empty, it is empty but always functions.
It functions but is not existent; it is True Emptiness.
Being Emptiness it is not nonexistence; it is all the wonderful things
   and beings.
Wonderful Being is the same as great Perfect Wisdom.
The True Emptiness is pure and tranquil Nirvāna.
Perfection of Wisdom is the cause of Nirvāna.
Nirvāna is the result of Perfect Wisdom.
Perfect Wisdom itself is not penetrated, but it can penetrate Nirvāna.
Nirvāna is noncreated but can create Perfect Wisdom.
Nirvāna and Perfect Wisdom have different names but the same real-
   ity.
The names were coined in accordance with certain meanings but the Law
   has no specific character.
As Nirvāna can create Perfect Wisdom, it is called the True Dharma-
   Body of the Buddha.
Perfect Wisdom can penetrate Nirvāna; it is therefore called the knowl-
   edge and insight of the Thus-Come-One.
By knowledge is meant knowing the emptiness and tranquillity of the
   Mind.
Insight means realizing that [one's original] nature is not created.
Knowledge and insight are clear and distinct, but they are neither the
   same nor different.
Hence it is possible that activity and tranquillity are always wonderful,
   and principles and facts are both "thus" [in the true state].
Being "thus," they can prevail everywhere.
In their extensive operation principle and fact are harmonized without
   obstacle.
That the six organs [the five senses and the mind] are free from defile-
   ment is due to the effect of calmness and wisdom.
That the six consciousnesses do not arise is due to the power of True
   Thusness.

If the Mind is in its true state, the sense-objects of consciousness will
  fade out,
And as the sense-objects of consciousness disappear, the mind becomes
  the void.
When the mind and the sense-objects are both no more,
Substance and function will no longer be different.
The nature of True Thusness is pure.
The power of wisdom is infinite.
It is like moonlight reflected in a thousand waves; it can see, hear, under-
  stand, and know.
It can do all these and yet is always empty and tranquil.
Being empty means having no appearance.
Being tranquil means not having been created.
One will then not be bound by good and evil, or be seized by quietness
  or disturbance.
One will not be wearied by life and death or rejoice in Nirvāna.
What is nonbeing is not considered as nonbeing.
What is being is not considered as being.
Whether he walks, stands, sits, or lies down, his mind is not disturbed.
At all times he is empty and possesses nothing.

The teachings of Past, Present, and Future Buddhas are like this and
are transmitted through the compassionate Bodhisattvas. After the Nirvāna of the World-Honored-One, twenty-eight patriarchs of the West
transmitted the doctrine of "mind without attachment" and preached the
knowledge and insight of the Thus-Come-One until Bodhidharma, who
was the first [in the line of transmission] in this land. This transmission
has gone through generations and up to this day has not been terminated.
What is transmitted is an esoteric doctrine and it is essential that a proper
person be found. It is like the pearls of kings, not to be given away foolishly. Only when one possesses the ornaments of blessed virtues and wisdom, and his understanding and conduct are in accord, can he be instituted [as the Patriarch].

The robe is the testimony of the Law and the Law is the doctrine [repre-
  sented by] the robe.
There is only the transmission through the robe and the Law; there is
  no other way.

Internally, the transmission is through the spiritual seal [the intuitive
mind independent of the spoken or written word] which "seals" or
assures the original mind.

Externally, the transmission is through the monk's robe, which is to sym-
bolize the goal of the school.

Without the robe the Law cannot be transmitted.

Without the Law the robe cannot be received.

The robe is the testimony of [the authority of] the Law.

The Law is that which is not created.

Not being created means not having any illusion or delusion,

But possessing the mind of Emptiness and tranquillity.

Knowing Emptiness and tranquillity, one can understand the Dharma-
Body.

Knowing the Dharma-Body, one achieves real emancipation.

I-HSÜAN

A Sermon

This sermon by I-hsüan (?–867), Ch'an Master Hui-chao of the Lin-chi school,
is contained in his *Recorded Sayings*. It is one of the most famous sermons of
the Meditation school. Nowhere else is the doctrine of seeing one's own nature
more forcefully expressed.

   [From *Lin-chi Hui-chao ch'an-shih yü-lu*, in *Taishō daizōkyō*, XLVII,
   497]

The important thing in the study of Buddhism is to achieve a true understanding. If true understanding is achieved, one will not be defiled by life
and death and wherever he may be he will be free. It is not necessary to
achieve anything of particular excellence, but this will come by itself.

   Followers of the Path, from days of yore, worthy masters had their
ways of helping people. As to my way, it is intended merely to help
people from being deceived. If you need to use it, do so and don't hesitate
any more.

   Why are students today not successful? What is the trouble? The
trouble lies in their lack of self-confidence. If you do not have enough self-
confidence, you will busily submit yourself to all kinds of external conditions and their transformations, and be enslaved and turned around by
them and lose your freedom. But if you can stop the mind that seeks
[those external conditions] in every instant of thought, you will then be
no different from the old masters.

Do you wish to know the old masters? They are none other than you who stand before me listening to my sermon. You students lack self-confidence and therefore seek outside yourselves. Even if what you have found is all literary excellence, you will not get the real ideas of the old masters.

Make no mistake! If you miss it in this life, you will have to go through the three worlds [the world of sensuous desire, the world of form, and the formless world of pure spirit] for many, many long periods. If you are carried away by the external world to which you have thrown yourselves, you will be reborn in the womb of an ass or a cow.

Followers of the Path, my views are no different from those of Shākyamuni [the Buddha]. They are being applied in many ways; what is wanting in them? The light emanating from our six senses is never interrupted or stopped. If you realize this, you will enjoy peace throughout life.

Reverend Sirs, there is no peace in the three worlds, which are like a house on fire. They are not places for you to dwell in for long. The devil of impermanence may visit any of us at any time without regard to rank or age. If you do not want to be different from the old masters, don't seek outside yourself. The light of purity which shines out of every thought of yours is the Dharma-Body within you. The light of nondiscrimination that shines out of every thought of yours is the Body of Bliss within you. The light of nondifferentiation that shines out of every thought of yours is the Transformation-Body within you. These Three Bodies are you who are now listening to my talk on the Law. It is only by not seeking or pursuing outside that this can have its effect.

According to scholars of the scriptures, these Three Bodies are to be taken as the Ultimate Principle. But my view is different. They are but names and words and they all depend on something. As the ancients said, the body is dependent on its meaning and the ground is described in terms of its substance. It is clear that the body of Dharma-Nature and its ground are but reflections of light. Reverend Sirs, know and get hold of this person who handles this light, for he is the original source of all the Buddhas and the final abode of truth-seekers everywhere. Your bodily make-up of the four elements [of earth, water, air, and fire] does not understand how to talk or listen. Nor does the liver, the stomach, the kidneys, or the bladder. Nor does vacuity of space. Then who understands how to talk or listen? It is the single light which is formless but very clear before your eyes. It is this that understands how to talk and listen. If you realize this, you will be no different from the old masters. But don't let this realization be interrupted at any time. You will find it everywhere. It is only because wrong imagination is produced, insight is obstructed, thoughts are changed, and essence becomes different that we transmigrate in the three worlds and suffer all kinds of pain. As I view it, you all have a profound realization of this and none will fail to be emancipated.

Followers of the Path, the Mind has no form and penetrates the ten directions. In the eye it sees, in the ear it hears, in the nose it smells, in the mouth it speaks, in the hand it grasps, and in the leg it runs. Originally it is but clear intelligence which divides itself into six natural functions. Let the mind be free from all external searching. You will be emancipated wherever you are.

Why do I say so? What is the idea? It is only because Followers of the Path cannot cut off the thought of seeking outside that old masters play tricks on you.

Followers of the Path, if you view things as I do, you will be able to sit on and break the heads of the Bliss- and Transformation-Buddhas. The bodhisattvas who have successfully gone through the ten stages [toward Buddhahood] will look like hirelings. Those who have attained the stage of full enlightenment will be like prisoners. Arhants [saints in the Hīnayāna] and pratyeka-buddhas [who have attained enlightenment through self-exertion] will be like outhouses. And Perfect Wisdom and Nirvāna will be like a stake to which donkeys are fastened. Why so? It is only because followers of the Path do not understand that all periods of time are empty that there are such hindrances. This is not the case with the one who has truly attained the Path. He follows all conditions and works out all past karmas. He freely wears any garment. He walks wherever he wants to walk and sits wherever he wants to sit. He does not for a single instant think of seeking Buddhahood. Why so? An ancient saying says: "If one seeks after Buddhahood, the Buddha will become the cause of transmigration."

Reverend Sirs, time is precious. Don't make the mistake of following others in desperately studying meditation or the Path, learning words or phrases, seeking after the Buddha or patriarchs or good friends. Followers of the Path, you have only one father and one mother. What else do you want? Look into yourselves. An ancient sage said that Yajnadatta thought he had lost his head [and sought after it], but when his seeking mind was stopped he realized that he had never lost it.

Reverend Sirs, be yourselves and don't pretend anything. There are some old bald-headed fools who cannot tell good from bad and therefore see all kinds of spirits and ghosts, point to the east or to the west, and prefer rain or shine. People like this are sure some day to pay up their debts and swallow burning iron-balls before Old Yama [Lord of Hades]. Sons and daughters of good families become possessed of such fox-spirits and go astray. Poor blind fellows! The day will come when they will have to pay up their board.

PEN-CHI
Questions and Answers

These examples are drawn from the *Recorded Sayings of Ch'an Master Pen-chi* (840–901) of Ts'ao-shan. As explained in the introduction to this section, the question-and-answer or "public case" (*kōan*) method is intended to free the mind from the strait-jacket of intellection by jolting it into an instantaneous intuition of truth. Some answers are obvious, such as the Buddha-mind being everywhere, filling the valleys and streams (No. 21). Others require some reflection, but it is not difficult for an alert mind to gather that "music from dried wood" (No. 20) suggests that there is life in death, and that life and death are identical. Still others are meant to shake up the mind. For the teacher to call his pupil "Teacher Jui" (No. 2) must be shocking. So awakened, the disciple who had appealed for help in his poverty should realize that poverty is virtue and that being worthy enough to be called a teacher, he is in many respects so rich that he is unaware of it, as the drinker does not even realize that his lips are wet. Other answers are similar to the "lightning" technique of the Lin-chi sect, such as "Kill, kill!" (No. 22). But most of them are so enigmatic as to force the questioner to abandon his usual thought processes. These selections follow the original order, but the numbers have been added.

[From *Ts'ao-shan Pen-chi ch'an-shih yü-lu*, in *Taishō daizōkyō*, XLVII, 537–39]

1. Yün-men asked: "If a person who is difficult to change should come to you, would you receive him?"

The Master answered: "Ts'ao-shan has no such leisure."

2. Monk Ch'ing-jui asked: "I am lonely and poor. Please help me, Master."

"Teacher Jui, please come near."

As Jui went near, the Master said: "Someone drank three cups of wine brewed by the House of Pai in Ch'üan-chou, and still said that his lips were not wet."

3. Ching-ch'ing asked: "What is the Principle of Pure Vacuity like, since after all it has no body?"

The Master said: "The Principle is originally like that. Where did facts [the external world, body] arise?"

Ching-ch'ing said: "Principle is the same as facts and facts are the same as Principle."

The Master said: "It is all right to insult Ts'ao-shan himself, but what are you going to do with all the divine eyes [that is, how can you cheat all wise men]?"

4. A monk said: "Your disciple is sick all over. Please cure me."

The Master said: "I shall not cure you."

The monk said: "Why don't you cure me?"

The Master said: "So that you neither live nor die."

5. A monk asked: "Aren't monks persons of great compassion?"

The Master said: "Yes."

The monk said: "Suppose the six bandits [sensuous desires] come at them. What should they do?"

The Master answered: "Also be compassionate."

The monk asked: "How is one to be compassionate?"

The Master said: "Wipe them out with one sweep of the sword."

The monk asked: "What then?"

The Master said: "Then they will be harmonized."

6. A monk asked: "Master, are the eye and the eyebrow acquainted with each other?"

The Master answered: "Not acquainted."

The monk asked: "Why not acquainted?"

The Master said: "They are in the same place."

The monk said: "Why are they not separated?"

The Master said: "The eyebrow is not the eye and the eye is not the eyebrow."

The monk said: "What is the eye?"

The Master answered: "To the point!"

The monk asked: "What is the eyebrow?"

The Master said: "I have my doubts."

The monk asked: "Why do you doubt?"

The Master said: "If I don't doubt, it would mean to the point."

7. A monk asked: "What kind of people are those who avoid the company of all dharmas?"

The Master said: "There are so many people in the city of Hung-chou. Where would you say they have gone?"

8. A monk asked: "In admitting phenomenon, what is true?"

The Master said: "Phenomenon is truth and truth is phenomenon."

The monk asked: "How is that revealed?"

The Master lifted the tea tray.

9. A monk asked: "How is illusion true?"

The Master answered: "Illusion is originally true."

The monk asked: "How is illusion manifested?"

The Master answered: "Illusion is manifestation and manifestation is illusion."

10. Question: "What kind of people are those who are always present?"

The Master said: "It happens that Ts'ao-shan has gone out for a while."

Question: "What kind of people are those who are always absent?"

The Master said: "Difficult to find such."

11. A monk asked: "What did Patriarch Lu indicate by facing the cliff?"

The Master covered his ears with his hands.

12. A monk asked: "An ancient wise man said, 'There has never been a person who, having fallen to the ground, does not rise from the ground.' What is falling?"

The Master said: "The fact is recognized."

The monk said: "What is rising?"

The Master said: "Rising."

13. Question: "In the teachings we have received, it is said, 'The great sea does not harbor a corpse.' What is the great sea?"

The Master said: "It embraces all things."

The monk asked: "Why not harbor a corpse?"

The Master said: "He whose breath has stopped clings to nothing."

The Master continued: "Things are not its accomplishments, and the breathless has its own character."

The monk asked: "With regard to progress toward the highest truth, is there anything else?"

The Master said: "It is all right to say yes or no, but what are you going to do with the Dragon King who holds the sword?"

14. A monk asked: "How can silence be expressed?"

The Master answered: "I will not express it here."

The monk said: "Where will you express it?"

The Master said: "Last night at midnight I lost three pennies by my bed."

15. The Master asked the monk: "What are you doing?"

The monk answered: "Sweeping the floor."

The Master said: "In front of the Buddha figure or behind it?"

The monk answered: "Both at the same time."

The Master said: "Give your sandals to Ts'ao-shan."

16. A monk asked: "What kind of companions in the Path should one associate with so that one may always learn from what one has not learned?"

The Master said: "Sleep in the same bed."

The monk said: "This is still what the monks have learned. How can one always learn from what one has not learned?"

The Master said: "Different from trees and rocks."

The monk asked: "Which is first and which is afterward?"

The Master said: "Not seeing the Path, one can always learn from what one has not learned."

17. A monk asked: "Who is the one who holds the sword in the state?"

The Master said: "Ts'ao-shan."

The monk said: "Whom do you intend to kill?"

The Master said: "I shall kill all."

The monk said: "Suppose you suddenly meet your parents. What will you do?"

The Master said: "Why discriminate?"

The monk said: "But there is yourself!"

The Master said: "Who can do anything about me?"

The monk said: "Why not kill yourself?"

The Master said: "No place to start."

18. A monk asked: "What kind of people are always sinking into the sea of life and death?"

The Master answered: "The second month."

The monk said: "Don't they try to free themselves?"

The Master said: "Yes, they do but there is no way out."

The monk said: "If they are free, what kind of people will accept them?"

The Master said: "Prisoners."

19. A monk raised a case [*kōan*], saying: "Yo-shan asked me how old I was. I said seventy-two. Yo-shan asked, 'Is it seventy-two?' When I said 'yes,' he struck me. What is the meaning of that?"

The Master said: "The first arrow is bad enough. The second one will penetrate even deeper."

The monk asked: "How can the beating be avoided?"

The Master said: "When the imperial edict is in force, all the feudal lords yield the way."

20. A monk asked Hsiang-yen: "What is the Path?"

Hsiang-yen answered: "There is music from [the wind blowing at] the dried wood."

The monk asked: "Who are those in the Path?"

Hsiang-yen answered: "There is an eye-pupil in the skull."

The monk did not understand and went to ask Shih-shuang what is meant by music from the dried wood. Shih-shuang said: "There is still joy there."

The monk said: "What about the eye-pupil in the skull?"

Shih-shuang said: "There is still consciousness there."

The monk did not understand either. He presented the case to the Master, who said: "Shih-shuang is a Shrāvaka [who attains enlightenment on hearing the teachings of the Buddha] and therefore takes such a view." Thereupon he showed the monk the following verse:

When there is music from dried wood, the Path is truly seen.
The skull has no consciousness; the eye begins to be clear.
When joy and consciousness [seem to be] at an end, they are not so.
Who discriminates what is clear amidst what is turbid?

Thereupon the monk again asked the Master: "What does it mean by music from the dried wood?"

The Master said: "Life is not cut off."

Question. "What does it mean by an eye-pupil in the skull?"

The Master answered: "It is not dried up."

Question: "Is there anything more?"

The Master said: "Throughout the world not a single person has not heard."

Question: "From what poem is 'There is music from the dried wood'?"

The Master said: "I don't know what poem." All of those who heard him were disappointed.

21. Question: "What is the basic meaning of the Law of the Buddha?"

The Master said: "Filling all streams and valleys."

22. Question: "Whenever there is any question, one's mind is confused. What is the matter?"

The Master said: "Kill, kill!"

PART FOUR
THE CONFUCIAN REVIVAL

589–618	Sui dynasty.
c.600	Discovery of block printing.
606	*Chin-shih* degree established.
610	Extensive canal system completed.
612–614	Costly campaigns against Koguryŏ.
618	Second Sui emperor murdered by dissatisfied soldiers and officials; T'ang dynasty founded.
618–906	T'ang dynasty.
627–649	Reign of Emperor T'ai-tsung.
7th century	Civil service examinations further developed; system of land nationalization and apportionment according to family size adopted.
684–705	Reign of Empress Wu.
755	An Lu-shan rebellion.
780	Adoption of Twice-A-Year Tax of Yang Yen (727–781).
803	Han Yü's Memorial on the Bone of Buddha.
808	Memorial on Grain Harmonization by Po Chü-i (772–846).
824	Han Yü (786–824).
845	Official repression of Buddhism.
880	Sack of Ch'ang-an by Huang Ch'ao.
907–960	Period of Disunion after collapse of T'ang.
932	First printing of nine classics begun.
960–1279	Sung dynasty.
11th century	Period of Confucian revival: Fan Chung-yen, Hu Yüan, Ou-yang Hsiu, Su Hsün, Shao Yung, Chou Tun-yi, Ssu-ma Kuang, Chang Tsai, Wang An-shih, Ch'eng Hao, Ch'eng Yi, Su Shih.
1055	Conferring of title Holy Duke on descendants of Confucius begun.
1069	Wang An-shih prime minister.
1086	Ssu-ma Kuang prime minister.
1166	Cheng Ch'iao (1108–1166), compiler of *T'ung chih*.
1200	Chu Hsi (1130–1200).
1227	Mongol's destruction of Hsi-hsia. Death of Chingis Khan.
1260–1368	Yüan [Mongol] dynasty.
1313	Adoption by Mongol government of civil service examinations based on Confucian classics.
1319	Ma Tuan-lin (c.1250–1319), compiler of *Wen-hsien t'ung k'ao*.

1368–1644	Ming dynasty.
1416	Chu Hsi's commentaries on the classics and other Neo-Confucian writings published under authority of the Yung-lo emperor.
1433	End of naval expeditions through the southern seas.
1520	Portuguese embassy to Peking.
1529	Wang Yang-ming (1472–1529).
1582	Matteo Ricci at Macao.
1604	Tung-lin Academy established, Ku Hsien-ch'eng (1550–1612), principal founder.
1644–1912	Ch'ing dynasty.
1662–1722	K'ang-hsi reign.
1662	*A Plan for the Prince,* by Ming philosopher and historian, Huang Tsung-hsi (1610–1695).
1682	Ku Yen-wu (1613–1682), leading scholar identified with School of Han learning.
1692	Wang Fu-chih (1619–1692), Ming loyalist and anti-Manchu writer.
1736–1795	Ch'ien-lung reign. Imperial Manuscript Library assembled.
1777	Tai Chen (1724–1777), philosopher and classicist.
1816	Ts'ui Shu (1740–1816), critical historian.
1849	Juan Yüan (1764–1849), bibliophile and patron of scholarship.

CHAPTER XVIII

PRECURSORS OF
THE CONFUCIAN REVIVAL

If today Chinese civilization seems almost synonymous with Confucian culture, we need to be reminded of the long centuries in which China lay under the spell of Buddhism and Taoism. For nearly eight centuries, from the fall of the Han (A.D. 220) to the rise of the Sung (960), Chinese culture was so closely identified with Buddhism that less civilized neighbors like the Japanese and Koreans embraced the one with the other, and thought of great T'ang China, the cynosure of the civilized world, as perhaps more of a "Buddha-land" than the "land of Confucius." The famed centers of learning to which pilgrims came from afar were the great Buddhist temples, where some of the best Chinese minds were engaged in teaching and developing new schools of Buddhist philosophy. The great works of art and architecture, which impressed these same visitors with the splendor of China, were most often monuments to the Buddha. Until the close of this period not even one first-rate mind appeared among the Confucianists who could dispute the pre-eminence of the Buddhist philosophers or slow the progress of the Taoist church, officially supported by the T'ang imperial house.

Indeed, it may be said that during this period, while there were Confucian scholars, there were virtually no Confucianists; that is, persons who adhered to the teachings of Confucius as a distinct creed which set them apart from others. The sense of orthodoxy came much later and only to the educated few. Most people followed Confucius in the home or in the office, but this did not prevent them, high or low, from turning to Buddhism or Taoism in satisfaction of their spiritual or aesthetic needs.

Still it is significant that, if Confucianism could not contend with

its rivals in the religious sphere, neither were they able to displace it
in the social or political sphere. Though in an attenuated and not very
dynamic form, Confucianism remained the accepted political philosophy
in addition to serving as a rather general code of ethics. The family system and the imperial bureaucracy kept Confucian teachings alive during these times, until their validity and relevance to a wider sphere of
thought could be reasserted by more vigorous minds.

The chief means by which these teachings were perpetuated was the
civil service examination system. Under the T'ang dynasty this system
became more highly organized and efficiently administered than ever
before, and the basic subjects were still the Confucian classics. (Because
the imperial house claimed descent from Lao Tzu, there was also one
type of examination based on a knowledge of Taoist texts.) Buddhists
might from time to time win a monarch's favor, eliciting contributions
to religious establishments or securing his participation in their special
rites. Individual monks, too, might occasionally rise high in the government ranks. Still, Buddhism itself, both as a philosophy and a religion, sought to transcend politics and offered nothing in the way of
either a political program or a set of basic principles which might have
been incorporated into the examination system. Therefore the vast majority of those whose education conformed to the requirements of the civil
service system, the great avenue to worldly success in China, submitted
to a curriculum in which the position of the Confucian Classics remained
unchallenged. To many this study of the Classics served only as a method
for achieving a degree of mastery over the language. To others it provided also a treasury of historical lore and prudential maxims which
might be drawn upon in the business of government.

The nature of Confucian scholarship in the T'ang dynasty reflected
the function it served to the bureaucracy. Carrying on in the manner of
the Han classicists, learned men devoted themselves to the kind of textual
annotation and exegesis which would provide more definitive editions
of the Confucian canon used in the examinations. From the scholarly
point of view this work was important, and yet we find in it evidence
only of painstaking study and not of creative thought. In the actual conduct of state affairs, however, we may see quite readily how Confucianism continued to influence thinking on the vital political and economic
issues of the day. The vast problems with which the Han had had to
wrestle confronted the T'ang as well, and the latter showed itself capable

of strong action on a grand scale. At the inception of the dynasty, for instance, it embarked on a program of land nationalization and redistribution, upon which was based the whole system of taxation and military organization, the two most vital operations of the state. So impressive was this system that both the Japanese and Koreans copied it almost to the last detail.

Taking into account, then, the continuing significance of such measures in the development of Chinese society, we pause before taking up the Confucian intellectual revival itself to consider one such example of political reform in the T'ang, and the issues it involved as seen from three different points of view.

A DEBATE ON TAXES IN THE T'ANG

By the middle of the T'ang dynasty (618–906) the system of equalized landholding adopted by its founder had seriously deteriorated. The virtual abolition of private property and resale of land proved impossible to enforce, and over the years concentration of land ownership, though not legally sanctioned, steadily increased. As a direct result the tax system, which had been predicated upon the old scheme of land tenure, became more difficult to administer, more susceptible of evasion, and therefore less productive of revenue for the state. Finally in 780 a new method of taxation was adopted on the recommendation of the statesman Yang Yen (727–781).

Besides greatly simplifying tax collection, Yang's Twice-A-Year Tax introduced for the first time the systematic budgeting of government income and expenditures. After estimating the expenses of local and central governments, each region was assessed its quota of the needed funds, prorated according to local conditions. This also meant adopting money for the first time as the basis for levying taxes. All other forms of taxation were abolished, and this alone collected in two installments during the early summer and late fall.

Despite the success of his reform program and the fact that his Twice-A-Year Tax system was to endure for centuries, Yang Yen suffered a sudden reversal of his fortunes and, in a manner characteristic of the insecurity of high office in China, was banished the following year and forced to commit suicide.

YANG YEN

Memorial Proposing the Twice-A-Year Tax

The following is an excerpt from the *New History of the T'ang Dynasty*, describing the conditions Yang sought to remedy and the solution proposed.
[From *Hsin T'ang shu*, 145:13a–14a]

When the dynastic laws were first formulated, there was the land tax, the labor tax on able-bodied men, and the cloth tax on households. In the K'ai-yüan period [713–741] there was peace and prosperity, and the tax registers were not kept up. Enforcement of the law was lax; people migrated or died, and landed property changed hands [in violation of the ban on sale of land]. The poor rose and the rich fell. Nothing was the same as before. The Board of Revenue year after year presented out-of-date figures [on the taxable population] to the court.

[According to the regulations], those who were sent to guard the frontiers were exempted from the land tax and the labor tax for six years, after which they returned from service. Yet as Emperor Hsüan-tsung was engaged in many campaigns against the barbarians, most of those sent to the frontiers died. The frontier generals, however, concealed the facts and did not report their deaths. Thus their names were never removed from the tax registers. When Wang Kung held the post of Commissioner of Fiscal Census in the T'ien-pao period [742–755] he strove to increase revenue. Since these names appeared on the registers and yet the adults were missing, he concluded that they had concealed themselves to avoid paying taxes. Thereupon he examined the old registers, made allowance for the exemption [of six years] to which they were entitled, and then demanded that the households of these men pay the land and labor taxes which they would have owed the government over the previous thirty years. The people were distressed and had no place to appeal. Thus the tax system had deteriorated badly.

After the Chih-te period [756–762], there were wars all over the empire. Famine and epidemics ensued. All kinds of labor services had to be performed. The population declined and some areas were deserted. The expenses of the state and its armies were drawn from the Commissioner of Funds (*Tu-chih shih*) and the Fiscal Intendants (*Chuan-yün shih*); the local army commanders were supplied by the Regional Commandants (*Chieh-tu shih*) and the Militia Commandants (*Tu t'uan-lien shih*). Thus, there were four offices collecting taxes, and they had no control over each other, so that the system was greatly disrupted. The court had no check on the various commissioners, and the latter had no check on the local perfectures. The special tribute from all parts of the empire went into the inner treasury of the imperial palace [rather than the state treasury]. Powerful ministers and crafty officials took advantage of this and engaged in corrupt practices. The public was given to think that these were gifts to be presented to the emperor; the officials themselves thought of the tribute as so much personal loot. Often it ran into the tens of thousands. In Honan, Shantung, Chien-nan and Hsiang-chou, where large forces were stationed, the military officers all took care of themselves handsomely. Very little of the taxes which should have gone to the emperor was actually presented. Altogether there were several hundred kinds of taxation: those which had been formally abolished were never dropped, and those which duplicated others were never eliminated. Old and new taxes piled up, and there seemed to be no limit to them. The people drained the last drop of their blood and marrow; they sold their loved ones. Month after month they were engaged in the "ten-days" of forced labor on state transport without a rest. Petty officials added to the burden, living at the people's expense. Rich people with many able-bodied adults in their families sought to obtain exemption from labor services by having them become officials, students, Buddhist monks, and Taoist priests. The poor had nothing they could get into [to obtain such an exemption], and continued to be registered as able-bodied adults liable to labor service. The upper class had their taxes forgiven, while the lower class had their taxes increased. Thereupon the empire was ruined and in distress, and the people wandered around like vagrants. Less than four or five out of a hundred lived in their own villages and stayed on their own land.

Yang Yen was concerned over these evils, and petitioned the throne to establish the Twice-A-Year Tax in order to unify the tax system.

"The way to handle all government expenses and tax collections is first to calculate the amount needed and then to allocate the tax among the people. Thus the income of the state would be governed according to its expenses. All households would be registered in the places of their

actual residence, without regard to whether they are native households
or non-native. All persons should be graded according to their wealth,
without regard to whether they are fully adult or only half-adult.[1] Those
who do not have a permanent residence and do business as traveling merchants should be taxed in whatever prefecture or subprefecture they are
located at the rate of one-thirtieth [of their capital holdings]. It is estimated that the amount taken from them will be the same as that paid
by those having fixed domicile, so that they could not expect to gain
from chance avoidance of the tax. The tax paid by residents should be
collected twice a year, during the summer and autumn. All practices
which cause annoyance to the people should be corrected. The separate
land and labor tax, and all miscellaneous labor services should be abolished; and yet the count of the able-bodied adults should still be kept.
The tax on land acreage should be based upon the amount of land cultivated in the fourteenth year of Ta-li [779], and the tax should be collected
equally. The summer tax should be collected no later than the sixth
month, and the autumn tax no later than the eleventh month. At the
end of the year, local officials should be promoted or demoted according
to the increase or decrease in the number of households and tax receipts.
Everything should be under the control of the President of the Board
of Revenue and the Commissioner of Funds."

The emperor approved of this policy and officials in the capital and
the various provinces were informed of it. There were some who questioned and opposed the measure, considering that the old system of land
and labor taxes had been in operation for several hundred years, and
that a change should not be made precipitously. The emperor did not
listen to them, however, and eventually the empire enjoyed the benefits
of the measure.

LU CHIH

Against the Twice-A-Year Tax

Lu Chih (754–805), a close adviser to the Emperor Te-tsung at the end of the
eighth century, possessed rare qualifications as a scholar-official, being admired
for both his moral integrity and literary gifts. Eventually he suffered banish-

---

[1] According to the earlier system of census registration, persons aged sixteen or more
were classified as "half adult" (chung), and those twenty-one or older were classified as
adult (ting). After 744, the ages were raised to eighteen and twenty-two respectively
(See Hsin T'ang shu 51:2a, 6a.)

ment for speaking out against a favorite of the emperor and was not recalled
to court until just before his death.

Politically at odds with Yang Yen, the sponsor of the Twice-A-Year Tax,
Lu wrote a series of three memorials on this subject which exemplify the
essay style for which he was noted. They may also be considered classic statements of the dominant conservative strain in Confucian political thought as opposed to the type of Confucian reformism which advocated strong action by
the state to solve economic and fiscal crises. Characteristic of this conservative
view are a concern for economy in government and simplicity of administration,
as well as a resistance to sudden, drastic changes in time-tested practices. These
attitudes are based on two fundamental principles of Confucian teaching: that
governmental actions should be intended primarily to benefit the people, not
simply the state; and that they should be equitable to all in their application.
Lu Chih finds himself, however, in the typical dilemma of the moderate conservative in regard to drastic reforms already put into effect: to abolish them
altogether would likewise involve great dislocation and confusion. Therefore
he asks only to remedy the most flagrant defects of the new system, rather than
demanding its outright repeal.

[From *Lu Hsüan-kung tsou-i*, KHCPTS ed., pp. 90–93]

According to the established law of the dynasty, there were three kinds
of taxes. The first was known as the land tax, the second, cloth contribution, the third, labor service. This threefold tax system followed the example of former sages and took into consideration the advantages and
disadvantages of the tax measures of previous dynasties. It followed
ancient traditions and embodied profound wisdom; it was just in distribution and encouraged people to remain on the land; it was simple
in general outline and universal in application. For by collecting rent
on the land, exacting cloth from the household and requiring labor from
the individual, the tax was made uniform throughout the empire and
it became impossible for people to evade their share of the tax burden
by moving to another part of the country. Thus, the people were relieved from the feeling of insecurity and the officials freed from the sense
of bafflement which constantly changing tax expedients are likely to give
rise to. As a means of making life secure, it made for permanence of
domicile without restrictive legislation; as a means of imposing labor
service, it became possible to know the population without a vexatious
census; as a means of government, it enabled the rulers to carry out
their duties without complex and exacting laws; as a means of taxation,
it produced enough for those above [the government] without impoverish-
ing those below [the people].

The laws initiated in the Three Dynasties have been, generally speaking, followed by later rulers. Though there are slight differences and modifications in practice, the principles have remained the same. But as a result of the barbarian uprisings in the later years of the T'ien-pao period [742–755], utter confusion reigned in our land and untold suffering came upon our people; the registers and administrative divisions became outmoded due to the shift in population and the tax laws vitiated because of the ever-growing demands of the armies. At the beginning of the Chien-chung period there was an attempt at reform. The government realized the necessity of rectifying the evils but the measures it introduced were not based upon sound principles. It realized the wisdom of simplification, but the methods it adopted were not founded on realities. Thus the new scheme allowed new ills to arise without completely eliminating the old and made a complete paralytic of a man who was before only lame.

Now in undertaking the remedy of old evils, it is necessary to find out their cause. If the times are at fault, it is only necessary to bring order to the times; if the laws are at fault, it becomes necessary to completely revise the laws. The *Book of Changes* says: "One must make sure that what one does is right if one wants to be free from regrets." To make changes without considering causes and consequences would only result in substituting one set of evils for another. One must, therefore, compare the new with the old and anticipate all possible objections and difficulties. And it goes without saying that no scheme should be put into effect before it has been worked out in detail; it also goes without saying that nothing should be changed unless the advantages of the new far outweigh that of the old. For to introduce change without subjecting its premise to a searching analysis and without considering its possible consequences is but to substitute a new evil for the old.

As for the old tax laws, they were instituted by the sage ancestors [of the T'ang dynasty] and had been found workable for a hundred years. It was only after the incidence of the recent military campaigns and the extraordinary expenditures they incurred that the traditional tax laws became inadequate. This is a case of the times being at fault, not the laws. Now without trying first to bring order to the times that are at fault, changes have been made in laws that are free from blame. The traditional measures of cloth contribution and labor service were swept aside and the new scheme of the Twice-A-Year Tax introduced. Being faulty in conception and careless in detail, the new tax scheme has only exhausted the people and made their lot worse every day.

If laws are made with the idea of benefiting the people, it is impossible not to win the support of the people; if they are made with the idea of filling the treasury, it is impossible not to lose the people's support. When Your Majesty came to the throne, you earnestly wished to bring about peace and good government. You issued a gracious proclamation, deeply deploring the existing evils. Concerned with the heavy burden of the multifarious taxes and exactions and grieved by the suffering they had wrought upon the people, you sent out commissioners to announce your benevolent intentions.

To achieve this proper steps should have been taken to take away from those above in order to give to those below, to cut expenses in order to save wealth, to discourage extravagance and greed in order to reverse the trend toward corruption, to eliminate unnecessary outlays in order to relieve the people of heavy exactions. But instead, the provinces have been subjected to great hardship because of the irksome examination of the registers and tax rolls necessary to determine the highest annual tax rate during the Ta-li period [766–780], which the Twice A Year Tax must use as a base. This is in effect the adoption of an unconstitutional expedient as fixed law and the incorporation of oppressive exactions of doubtful origin as regular features of the tax scheme. This amounts to making the extraction of money from the people the primary objective of government; one can hardly say that it is consistent with concern for the people.

To create a law without keeping the welfare of the people in mind —what is this if not a case of faulty conception?

Now surely wealth can only be produced by the labor of men. Skill and industry lead to wealth and plenty; ineptitude and laziness to want and deficiency. It is for this reason that the ancient sage-kings made the able-bodied male the tax unit when they instituted the tax system. They did not demand from a man more than his just portion; nor did they let him escape with less. They did not increase a man's taxes because he worked hard at his crops, nor did they lighten them because he abandoned his tillage. Thus people were encouraged to sow as much as they could. They did not add to a man's taxes because he lived in settled productivity, nor did they exempt a man from his cloth contribution because he wandered about without an established home. Thus stability was achieved. They did not exact more labor from a man because of his industry nor did they accept less from a man because of his laziness. Thus diligence was encouraged. Only by such ways as these can the people be happy in their abode and willingly contribute their best. Even the shiftless and lazy are bound to mend their ways because of the good example of their fellows and the prevailing spirit of fairness and honesty.

The Twice-A-Year Tax works on a different principle. It is based upon property only and not on the able-bodied male. This means that the more property one has, the more one has to pay, and the less property, the less tax. The system entirely fails to take into account the diverse natures of various types of property. For there are things which can be concealed on one's person or hidden away in strong boxes, things of great value though not exposed to curious eyes; there are things heaped up on threshing floors and stored away in bins, things of little value though generally regarded as evidence of wealth. There is property which can be circulated and made to grow, which may be small in amount but on which interest can be collected by the day. There is property in the form of dwellings and utensils which though high in cost bring nothing from one end of the year to the other. But under the Twice-A-Year system, these diverse types of property are all converted into so many strings of money, and it surprises no one that the system should work inequities and encourage evasion. For under this system those who range over the land and traffic in commerce are often able to escape their share of the tax burden while those who devote themselves to the basic vocation [of agriculture] and establish fixed homes are constantly harrassed by ever-increasing demands. This amounts to tempting the people to circumvent the law and forcing them to shirk their just share of labor. It is inevitable that productivity should decline and morals deteriorate, depression come to the village and towns, and a decrease result in the tax collections.

Furthermore, in drawing up the scheme, no effort was made to achieve an equal distribution of the tax burden. The provinces and districts were merely ordered to levy the new taxes according to the old rate. It was not realized that because of the long military campaigns conditions were far from being the same in the different localities. Not only was the nature of the demands made upon one place different from that made upon another, but there was also great disparity in the ability of the administrators. Thus the tax burden varies greatly from place to place, just as opinions differ among the respective commissioners.

In introducing new regulations, existing inequities should have been recognized and changes made wherever necessary; but instead, the officials were more interested in collecting as much in taxes as they could and were loath to eliminate anything. The actual resources and capacities of the various administrative districts were not given any weight at all; the old rate was the only thing that mattered. Thus the new law had the effect of causing ever heavier migrations away from regions where the rate was high and toward the regions where the rate was low. The result was that in the former regions the burden became heavier because the quota had to be shared by fewer people than before, while in the latter regions the burden became even lighter because the quota could be distributed among more people. In this way the situation tends to become more and more inequitable.

Again no policy directive was issued for general guidance. Each of the ten-odd commissioners was given authority to draw up regulations for his own area. Consequently, the inevitable divergence both in the tax rate and the method of collection. When the proposals were reported back to the court, there was no attempt to compare and reconcile them. Under the circumstances it is not difficult to imagine the inconsistencies that the system must entail or the disadvantages that it must evidence when compared with the old.

To create a law without first considering all its possible ramifications and consequences—what is this if not a case of being careless in detail?

Since the law was faulty in conception and careless in detail, it has caused great hardships to a people already sorely tried. They could hardly be expected to stand up under the crushing burden even if the law were administered with the utmost solicitude for their welfare, much less when the officials act as if they are trying to make a confused mass of silk worse confounded or to rip open again an old wound.

Next Lu Chih lists specific abuses which have brought great hardship to the people. One of these is the inflexibility of the new system, which allows of no tax reduction or exemption to meet local emergencies. Another is that, despite the attempt to combine all taxes into this one, additional levies have been superimposed on the Twice-A-Year Tax. Further there is the loss suffered by the people in having to exchange their goods or produce at low rates of commutation for cash in the payment of taxes. Another hidden form of taxation

is the special gifts from each locality to the emperor, which though nominally
sent by officials, are actually paid for by the people. There is also the inequity
resulting from shifts in population, not reported by local governors, which
leave a reduced number of taxpayers to meet the fixed quotas.

Before enumerating the reforms which he believes necessary, Lu reasserts
the basic principles which should govern tax policy as they are found in the
Confucian classics:

Duke Ai inquired of Yu Jo: "It is a year of dearth, and we have not
revenue enough for our needs; what is to be done?" "Why not simply
tithe the land?" replied Yu Jo. "Why, with two-tenths," said the Duke,
"I have still not enough, how could I manage with the one-tenth system?" "If the people enjoy plenty," was the rejoinder, "with whom will
the prince share want? But if the people are in want, with whom will
the prince share plenty?" [2]

Confucius said: "He who rules a state or a household is not concerned
with poverty but with inequity, not with lack of numbers but with want
of harmony." [3] For with equity, there would be no resentment; with
thrift, there would be no poverty; with harmony, there would be no
lack of numbers; with contentment, there would be no upheavals. [4]

All these are examples of regarding the people as the root and wealth
as the branches. If the people are content, there would be a sufficiency
of wealth; if the root is firmly established then the state would be at
peace. Now the people suffer not only want but dire poverty; the taxes
are not only inequitable but many and various; presents not only continue to come but there are numerous additional demands.

This state of affairs not only grieves the heart but threatens the very
safety of the state. What more urgent need for reform could there be
than this?

Your Majesty is cautious in nature and has often warned against innovations. Realizing this, I dare not seek the entire elimination of the
evils and inequities; it would bring some degree of relief if the more
superfluous and more flagrant measures were done away with.

The relief measures recommended by Lu Chih are 1) the elimination of unwise
and unnecessary expenses and the reduction of excessive ones. More specifically

---

[2] *Analects*, XII:9. Translation by W. E. Soothill.

[3] *Analects*, XVI:1. This is not a saying of, but a quotation by Confucius. We have
followed Waley's reconstruction of the text, which is obviously corrupt.

[4] Here Lu Chih paraphrases Confucius instead of quoting, probably because he also felt
that something is the matter with the text.

the surtax of 20 percent must be abolished and emergency levies lifted as soon as the emergency passes. This would bring relief to the extent of 20 or 30 percent. 2) No presents should be accepted from the provinces aside from the traditional requirements. This would not only bring direct relief but also eliminate many attending abuses saddled on the people by unscrupulous officials. This would bring relief to the extent of another 40 or 50 percent. 3) Conversion of tax money units into cloth should be made on the basis of the monthly average price of the respective localities. Since the cloth is inspected by the receiving officials, they should be held responsible for any serious loss due to the poor quality of the cloth, instead of making the people pay again. This would bring relief to the extent of still another 20 or 30 percent.

Lu Chih then makes two positive proposals. The first is a more accurate determination of the number of households in the various provinces, to be carried out by the provincial Twice-A-Year Tax officials in consultation with the ministry of revenue. The second is a classification of the prefectures into two categories after a careful consideration of their respective resources and the drawing up of an appropriate tax schedule for each. Thus, without repealing the Twice-A-Year Tax law, it would be possible to bring about a certain degree of fairness and justice in the distribution of the tax burden, and to make tax collection more effective and evasion less attractive.

PO CHÜ-I

Grain Harmonization

One of China's greatest poets, Po Chü-i (772–846), also had a long and distinguished career as an official. In 808, while a censor at court, he submitted this memorial forthrightly criticizing the revenue-raising devices to which the government had resorted. Grain Harmonization was a euphemism by which the T'ang dynasty version of the ever-normal granary was known. By now a well-established method of stabilizing agricultural prices, it had also been made to serve the often incompatible purpose of raising revenue for the state. As a young man Po had endorsed this system in one of his examination essays. Now he is bitterly disillusioned and calls for its abolition. Also he asks that taxes once again be made payable in grain (in a poem written two years earlier, he had already urged repeal of Yang Yen's Twice-A-Year Tax).

[Adapted from Feifel, *Po Chü-i As a Censor*, pp. 328–33]

I have heard that because of the good harvest this year, the authorities have asked for an imperial order to carry out Grain Harmonization in the metropolitan district and elsewhere, so that the cheap grain may be bought and the farmers may be benefited.[5] As far as I can see, such pur-

[5] Employing the principle of the "ever-normal granary" whereby surplus grain is bought up by the government to set a floor under falling prices.

chases only mean loss to the farmers and do not benefit them at all. Why is this so?

Grain Harmonization means that the government gives out the money and the farmers give out their grain. They bargain together and make the exchange after mutual agreement [on the price]. In recent years Grain Harmonization has not been handled in this way. The prefectures and the districts were allowed to assess each household (according to the number of its members) for a certain amount of grain, to fix the terms and the date of delivery. If there was any delay, the punitive measures of imprisonment and flogging inflicted upon the offenders were even worse than those usually involved in the collection of taxes. Though this was called Grain Harmonization, in reality it hurt the farmers. If these new purchases are carried out in the manner that has become customary, I say that the farmers will only suffer loss and gain nothing whatsoever.

If the authorities established purchasing stations and offered to buy grain at a price slightly better than that which prevailed at the time, the people would certainly want to sell, since they are attracted by profit. Originally this type of transaction was called Grain Harmonization precisely because it would benefit the farmers. If farmers can gain some profit, they will naturally want to come and sell. With this criterion one can judge whether they now expect profit or loss. If the customary abuses were now removed and the advantages of profit offered, we would in truth have a form of Grain Harmonization which would benefit the farmers. Which of these two modes of conducting Grain Harmonization is to be adopted is up to Your Majesty to decide. If neither way is acceptable, then commutation-in-kind would be the next best alternative. Commutation-in-kind means the conversion of taxes payable in cash on growing crops to taxes payable in kind by the farmers. Commutation-in-kind makes it unnecessary for the farmers to sell their grain at a cheap price in order to pay their taxes with cash. This would be a great advantage for the farmers.

In recent years the payment prescribed for Grain Harmonization by the office of public revenues often consisted of bales and rolls of silk or cloth of either an inferior or unpopular quality. It was necessary for the farmer to resell this material in order to obtain cash for paying taxes. When the farmers are paid in this way, cheating and short-changing is inevitable. When the farmers lose more than the original value [of their grain and silk] it is evident that some abuses prevail.

If Your Majesty would consider converting the taxes payable in cash into taxes payable in kind, the farmers would neither suffer loss by selling their wheat and millet for a cheap price, nor would they have the problem of reselling bales of cloth and silk. The profit would go to the farmers, the credit to the emperor. Are the advantages of commutation-in-kind not evident?

If we consider the case from this point of view, it is quite evident that it is better to establish purchasing stations than to assign to each household its share of contribution in grain, and that commutation-in-kind is much better than Grain Harmonization.

I lived for some time in a small hamlet where I belonged to a household which had to contribute its share to Grain Harmonization. I myself was treated with great harshness; it was truly unbearable. Not long ago, as an official in the metropolitan district, I had responsibility for the administration of Grain Harmonization. I saw with my own eyes how delinquent people were flogged, and I could not stand the sight of it.

In the past I have always wanted to write about how people suffered from this plague and to report it to Your Majesty. Since I was a petty and unimportant official in the countryside, I had no opportunity to approach Your Majesty. Now I have had the honor of being promoted to serve Your Majesty and of being listed among the officials who offer criticism and advice. . . .

My arguments may not be strong enough to convince Your Majesty. If this is the case, I hope Your Majesty will, as a test, order one of your trustworthy attendants to inquire incognito among the farmers of the villages and hamlets about Grain Harmonization and commutation-in-kind as to which one involves profit for them and which one involves loss. Then Your Majesty will see that my words are anything but rash and superficial statements. . . .

When the sages make their decisions about some problem, they have the good of the people in mind; they seek only to adopt the most beneficial measures. When loss and gain are in equal proportion, a change is not necessary. When one far outweighs the other, a change must be made. This holds true not only in the present situation, but for all other like instances. I respectfully hope that Your Majesty will be pleased to look into this matter carefully. I have reported with reverence and with respect.

HAN YÜ'S COUNTERATTACK ON TAOISM AND BUDDHISM

Han Yü (786–824) is famous as a literary stylist, whose "ancient-prose" style (as opposed to the elaborate parallel-prose of his day) became a model for later writers. His career as a public official was a stormy one, due in large part to his uncompromising nature and to a deep sense of his mission as a lone defender of Confucian principles in a decadent age. In contrast to that widespread eclecticism which saw Taoism and Buddhism as complementary to Confucianism, Han Yü represented a new and unbending opposition to them as essentially inimical to both Confucianism and Chinese society. This point of view did not gain many adherents in his own time, but Han Yü was "rediscovered" later by one of the early leaders of the Confucian revival in the tenth century and made a virtual patron saint of the new movement. As such he was eulogized in the *New History of the T'ang Dynasty:*

From the Chin through the Sui dynasties, while Taoism and Buddhism were being conspicuously practiced, the Way of the Sages (i.e., Confucianism) was perpetuated as by a thread, and Confucian scholars leaned upon the world's orthodox ideas merely to give support to the strange and supernatural. Han Yü alone grievingly quoted the sages so as to combat the errors of the world, and, though mocked by the stupid, met all rebuffs with renewed ardor. In the beginning no one believed in him, but eventually he gained great renown in his age. Of old, Mencius, who was only two hundred years removed from Confucius, had refuted Yang Chu and Mo Ti. [In the same way] Han Yü, though separated from Confucius by more than one thousand years, rejected the two schools of Taoism and Buddhism. In his destroying of confusion and restoring of orthodoxy, he equals Mencius in merit and doubles him in energy.[6]

His most celebrated memorial, a protest against displaying a supposed relic of the Buddha in the imperial palace, breathes a spirit of fierce hatred for Buddhism not only because it is superstitious and subversive of public

---

[6] Adapted from Bodde in Fung, *History of Chinese Philosophy*, II, 409.

morality but also simply because it is non-Chinese. Anti-foreignism of this sort, which had not previously been characteristic of Confucianism, became an important element in the Neo-Confucian revival later. Han Yü's boldness in opposing the performance of this rite at court so enraged the emperor that Han Yü narrowly escaped execution, and was subsequently banished to southernmost China.

HAN YÜ

Memorial on the Bone of Buddha
[From *Ch'ang-li hsien-sheng wen-chi*, SPTK ed., 39:2b–4b]

Your servant begs leave to say that Buddhism is no more than a cult of the barbarian peoples which spread to China in the time of the Latter Han. It did not exist here in ancient times. . . . When Emperor Kao-tsu [founder of the T'ang] received the throne from the House of Sui, he deliberated upon the suppression of Buddhism. But at that time the various officials, being of small worth and knowledge, were unable fully to comprehend the ways of the ancient kings and the exigencies of past and present, and so could not implement the wisdom of the emperor and rescue the age from corruption. Thus the matter came to nought, to your servant's constant regret.

Now Your Majesty, wise in the arts of peace and war, unparalleled in divine glory from countless ages past, upon your accession prohibited men and women from taking Buddhist orders and forbade the erection of temples and monasteries, and your servant believed that at Your Majesty's hand the will of Kao-tsu would be carried out. Even if the suppression of Buddhism should be as yet impossible, your servant hardly thought that Your Majesty would encourage it and on the contrary cause it to spread. Yet now your servant hears that Your Majesty has ordered the community of monks to go to Feng-hsiang to greet the bone of Buddha, that Your Majesty will ascend a tower to watch as it is brought into the palace, and that the various temples have been commanded to welcome and worship it in turn. Though your servant is abundantly ignorant, he understands that Your Majesty is not so misled by Buddhism as to honor it thus in hopes of receiving some blessing or reward, but only that, the year being one of plenty and the people joyful, Your Majesty would accord with the hearts of the multitude in setting forth for the officials and citizens of the capital some curious show and toy for their amusement. How could it be, indeed, that with such sagely wisdom Your Majesty should in truth give credence to these affairs? But the common people are ignorant and dull, easily misled and hard to enlighten, and should they see their emperor do these things, they might say that Your Majesty was serving Buddhism with a true heart. "The Son of Heaven is a Great Sage," they would cry, "and yet he reverences and believes with all his heart! How should we, the common people, then begrudge our bodies and our lives?" Then would they set about singeing their heads and scorching their fingers,[7] binding together in groups of ten and a hundred, doffing their common clothes and scattering their money, from morning to evening urging each other on lest one be slow, till old and young alike had abandoned their occupations to follow [Buddhism]. If this is not checked and the bone is carried from one temple to another, there will be those who will cut off their arms and mutilate their flesh in offering [to the Buddha]. Then will our old ways be corrupted, our customs violated, and the tale will spread to make us the mockery of the world. This is no trifling matter!

Now Buddha was a man of the barbarians who did not speak the language of China and wore clothes of a different fashion. His sayings did not concern the ways of our ancient kings, nor did his manner of dress conform to their laws. He understood neither the duties that bind sovereign and subject, nor the affections of father and son. If he were still alive today and came to our court by order of his ruler, Your Majesty might condescend to receive him, but it would amount to no more than one audience in the Hsüan-cheng Hall, a banquet by the Office for Receiving Guests, the presentation of a suit of clothes, and he would then be escorted to the borders of the nation, dismissed, and not allowed to delude the masses. How then, when he has long been dead, could his rotten bones, the foul and unlucky remains of his body, be rightly admitted to the palace? Confucius said: "Respect ghosts and spirits, but keep them at a distance!"[8] So when the princes of ancient times went to pay their condolences at a funeral within the state, they sent exorcists in advance with peach wands to drive out evil, and only then would

[7] Acts symbolic of a person's renunciation of the world upon entering Buddhist orders.
[8] *Analects*, VI, 20.

they advance. Now without reason Your Majesty has caused this loathsome thing to be brought in and would personally go to view it. No exorcists have been sent ahead, no peach wands employed. The host of officials have not spoken out against this wrong, and the censors have failed to note its impropriety. Your servant is deeply shamed and begs that this bone be given to the proper authorities to be cast into fire and water, that this evil may be rooted out, the world freed from its error, and later generations spared this delusion. Then may all men know how the acts of their wise sovereign transcend the commonplace a thousand-fold. Would this not be glorious? Would it not be joyful?

Should the Buddha indeed have supernatural power to send down curses and calamities, may they fall only upon the person of your servant, who calls upon High Heaven to witness that he does not regret his words. With all gratitude and sincerity your servant presents this memorial for consideration, being filled with respect and awe.

Discourse on Teachers (Shih-shuo)

Han Yü had little use for the kind of classical training given as a preparation for the civil service examinations. The tutor who merely taught his pupil the literary tricks needed to satisfy the formal requirements was, to his mind, a far cry from the great teachers of the past who had made of Confucianism a living faith. In this essay he argues for a return to the original conception of a teacher and for the necessity of continuing one's education throughout life. So important is this to Han Yü that he believes even considerations of social status and seniority should not stand in the way of a man's pursuit of true learning.
[From Ch'ang-li hsien-sheng wen-chi, SPTK ed., 12:1b–2b]

Students of ancient times all had their teachers, for it is only through the teacher that the Way is transmitted, learning imparted, and doubts dispelled. Unless all men were born with knowledge, who among them could be free from doubts? And if one has no teacher to take his doubts to, they will never be solved. The man who was born before me and truly learned the Way before me I shall follow and make my teacher. The man who was born after me but learned the Way before me I shall also follow and make my teacher. What I seek from my teacher is the Way. What is it to me, then, whether he is older or younger than I? Regardless of high or low station, age or youth, he who has the Way shall be my teacher.

Alas, the teaching of the Way has long been neglected! Hard it is, then, to expect men to be without doubts. The sages of antiquity far excelled ordinary men, and yet they sought teachers and questioned them. But the common people of today, though they are equally far from the level of the sages, count it a shame to study with a teacher. Thus do sages become even wiser, and the stupid more stupid. Indeed is this not why some men are sages and others are stupid?

If a man loves his son he selects a teacher to give the boy instruction, and yet he is ashamed to follow a teacher himself. This is folly indeed. The sort of teacher who only gives a child a book and teaches him to punctuate and read is not what I call a transmitter of the Way and a dispeller of doubts. But at least the child who cannot read goes to a teacher, while the father who is in doubt will not. This is to learn the minor things and neglect the major ones, and I for one fail to see the wisdom of it.

Sorcerers, doctors, musicians, and the various craftsmen are not ashamed to study with teachers. And yet among the families of scholar-officials if you speak of a teacher or a disciple everyone gathers around and begins to laugh. If you ask them why they laugh, they reply: "These two men are practically the same age, and so they must understand the Way equally well." Again if the teacher is lower in social status than the disciple it is considered shameful to study with him, while if he is a high official it is thought that one studies with him only to curry favor. Alas, it is obvious that in such circumstances the teaching of the Way can never be restored. Sorcerers, doctors, musicians, and craftsmen are not considered the equal of gentlemen, and yet gentlemen these days cannot match them in knowledge. Is this not strange?

A sage has no constant teacher. Confucius acknowledged Tan Tzu, Chang Hung, Shih Hsiang, and Lao Tan as his teachers, although Tan Tzu and his like were surely not so wise as Confucius. Confucius said: "When I walk along with two others, they may serve me as my teachers." [9] Thus a disciple is not necessarily one who is inferior to his teacher, and the teacher one who is wiser than his disciples. It is simply that the teacher has learned the Way before others, and has specialized in the art of instruction.

[9] *Analects*, VII, 2.

What Is the True Way? (Yüan Tao)

This brief statement of Han Yü's philosophy is strongly polemical and moves
more by force of rhetoric and emotion than by reasoned argumentation. Han
Yü is most eloquent when asserting his view of Chinese civilization as indebted
to Confucianism for all that is best in it, and of Taoism and Buddhism as
antithetical to these cherished values. All of history since the rise of these two
religions is a process of steady degeneration from the ideal society created by
the ancient sages. These false doctrines must therefore be suppressed in order
that the true Way may prevail and the ideal society be restored.

[From *Ch'ang-li hsien-sheng wen-chi*, SPTK ed., 11:1a–3b]

To love universally is called humanity (*jen*); to apply this in a proper
manner is called righteousness (*i*). The operation of these is the Way
(*Tao*), and its inner power (*te*) is that it is self-sufficient, requiring nothing from outside itself. Humanity and righteousness are fixed principles,
but the Way and its inner power are speculative concepts. Thus we have
the way of the gentleman and the way of the small man, and both good
and evil power. Lao Tzu made light of humanity and righteousness, but
he did not thereby abolish them. His view was narrow like that of a man
who sits at the bottom of a well and looks up at the sky, saying, "The
sky is small." This does not mean that the sky is really small. Lao Tzu
understood humanity and righteousness in only a very limited sense, and
therefore it is natural that he belittled them. What he called the Way
was only the Way as he saw it, and not what I call the Way; what he
called inner power was only power as he saw it, and not what I call
inner power. What I call the Way and power are a combination of humanity and righteousness and this is the definition accepted by the world
at large. But what Lao Tzu called the Way and power are stripped of
humanity and righteousness, and represent only the private view of one
individual.

After the decline of the Chou and the death of Confucius, in the time
of Ch'in's book burnings, the Taoism of the Han, and the Buddhism
of the Wei, the Chin, the Liang, and the Sui, when men spoke of the
Way and power, of humanity and righteousness, they were approaching
them either as followers of Yang Chu or of Mo Tzu, of Lao Tzu or of
Buddha. Being followers of these doctrines, they naturally rejected Confucianism. Acknowledging these men as their masters, they made of

Confucius an outcast, adhering to new teachings and vilifying the old. Alas, though men of later ages long to know of humanity and righteousness, the Way and inner power, from whom may they hear of them? . . .

In ancient times there were only four classes of people, but now there are six.[10] There was only one teaching, where now there are three.[11] For each family growing grain, there are now six consuming it; for each family producing utensils, there are now six using them; for one family engaged in trade, six others take their profits. Is it surprising then that the people are reduced to poverty and driven to theft?

In ancient times men faced many perils, but sages arose who taught them how to protect and nourish their lives, acting as their rulers and teachers. They drove away the harmful insects and reptiles, birds and beasts, and led men to settle in the center of the earth. The people were cold and they made them clothes, hungry and they gave them food. Because men had dwelt in danger in the tops of trees or grown sick sleeping on the ground, they built them halls and dwellings. They taught them handicrafts that they might have utensils to use, trades so that they could supply their wants, medicine to save them from early death, proper burial and sacrifices to enhance their sense of love and gratitude, rites to order the rules of precedence, music to express their repressed feelings, government to lead the indolent, and punishments to suppress the overbearing. Because men cheated each other, they made tallies and seals, measures and scales to insure confidence; because men plundered they made walls and fortifications, armor and weapons to protect them. Thus they taught men how to prepare against danger and prevent injury to their lives.

Now the Taoists tell us that "until the sages die off, robbers will never disappear," or that "if we destroy our measures and break our scales then the people will cease their contention."[12] Alas, how thoughtless are such sayings! If there had been no sages in ancient times, then mankind would have perished, for men have no feathers or fur, no scales or shells to protect them from cold and heat, no claws and teeth to contend for food. Therefore those who are rulers give commands which are carried out by their officials and made known to the people, and the people

[10] The four classes of traditional Chinese society—official, farmer, artisan, and merchant —to which were added the Taoist and the Buddhist clergy.

[11] Confucianism, to which was added Taoism and Buddhism.

[12] *Chuang Tzu,* Sec. 10.

produce grain, rice, hemp, and silk, make utensils and exchange commodities for the support of the superiors. If the ruler fails to issue commands, then he ceases to be a ruler, while if his subordinates do not carry them out and extend them to the people, and if the people do not produce goods for the support of their superiors, they must be punished. Yet the Way [of the Taoists and Buddhists] teaches men to reject the ideas of ruler and subject and of father and son, to cease from activities which sustain life and seek for some so-called purity and Nirvāna. Alas, it is fortunate for such doctrines that they appeared only after the time of the Three Reigns and thus escaped suppression at the hands of Yü and T'ang, kings Wen and Wu, the Duke of Chou and Confucius, but unfortunate for us that they did not appear before the Three Reigns so that they could have been rectified by those sages. . . .

The *Book of Rites* says: "The ancients who wished to illustrate illustrious virtue throughout the kingdom first ordered well their own states. Wishing to order well their states, they first regulated their families. Wishing to regulate their families, they first cultivated their persons. Wishing to cultivate their persons, they first rectified their hearts. Wishing to rectify their hearts, they first sought to be sincere in their thoughts" [*Great Learning, I*]. Thus when the ancients spoke of rectifying the heart and being sincere in their thoughts, they had this purpose in mind. But now [the Taoists and Buddhists] seek to govern their hearts by escaping from the world, the state and the family. They violate the natural law, so that the son does not regard his father as a father, the subject does not look upon his ruler as a ruler, and the people do not serve those whom they must serve.

When Confucius wrote in the *Spring and Autumn Annals,* he treated as barbarians those feudal lords who observed barbarian customs, and as Chinese those who had advanced to the use of Chinese ways. The *Analects* [III, 5] says: "The barbarians with rulers are not the equal of the Chinese without rulers." The *Book of Odes* [Odes of Lu, 4] says: "Fight against the barbarians of the west and north, punish those of Ching and Shu." Yet now [the Buddhists] come with their barbarian ways and put them ahead of the teachings of our ancient kings. Are they not become practically barbarians themselves?

What were these teachings of our ancient kings? To love universally, which is called humanity; to apply this in the proper manner, which is called righteousness; to proceed from these to the Way and to be self-sufficient without seeking anything outside, which is called [inner] power. The *Odes* and the *History,* the *Changes* and the *Spring and Autumn Annals,* are their writings; rites and music, punishments and government, their methods. Their people were the four classes of officials, farmers, artisans, and merchants; their relationships were those of sovereign and subject, father and son, teacher and friend, guest and host, elder and younger brother, and husband and wife. Their clothing was hemp and silk; their dwelling halls and houses; their food grain and rice, fruit and vegetables, fish and meat. Their ways were easy to understand; their teachings simple to follow. Applied to oneself, they brought harmony and blessing; applied to others, love and fairness. To the mind they gave peace; to the state and the family all that was just and fitting. Thus in life men were able to satisfy their emotions, and at death the obligations due them were fulfilled. Men sacrificed to Heaven and the gods were pleased; to the spirits of their ancestors and the ancestors received their offerings. What Way is this? It is what *I* call the Way, and not what the Taoists and Buddhists call the Way. Yao taught it to Shun, Shun to Yü, Yü to T'ang, and T'ang to kings Wen and Wu and the Duke of Chou. These men taught it to Confucius and Confucius to Mencius, but when Mencius died it was no longer handed down. Hsün Tzu and Yang Hsiung understood elements of it, but their understanding lacked depth; they spoke of it but incompletely. In the days before the Duke of Chou, the sages were rulers and so they could put the Way into practice, but after the time of the Duke of Chou they were only officials and so they wrote at length about the Way.

What should be done now? I say that unless [Taoism and Buddhism] are suppressed, the Way will not prevail; unless these men are stopped, the Way will not be practiced. Let their priests be turned into ordinary men again, let their books be burned and their temples converted into homes. Let the Way of our former kings be made clear to lead them, and let the widower and the widow, the orphan and the lonely, the crippled and the sick be nourished. Then all will be well.

Emperor Wu-tsung's Edict on the Suppression of Buddhism

The subjection of Buddhism and other foreign faiths to severe persecution under the Emperor Wu-tsung (r. 841–846) owed nothing directly to the ful-

minations of a Han Yü or to any concerted movement on the part of Confucianists. The emperor, desperately seeking the secret of immortality, was
under the influence of Taoist priests who urged this repression of their rivals
upon him. Still, the justification for this move as set forth in the following
edict is largely of a Confucian character and practical, rather than ideological,
in nature. The obvious advantages to the state of confiscating Buddhist wealth
and secularizing monks and nuns so that they might serve the state as cultivators liable to land and labor taxes had been pointed out long before at the
inception of the dynasty. The edict itself was merely a last step in the process
of suppression which Wu-tsung had been pursuing for some time.

This process did not result in the complete elimination of Buddhism from
China, which would have taken a greater and more sustained effort by Wu-
tsung's successors than it had, but it was a severe setback for the religion. Or-
ganizationally weakened, Buddhism could not maintain its institutional or
doctrinal position as it did in Japan, and tended on the popular level to lose
its identity among the welter of superstitious cults. The edict also served to
reassert with awesome finality a basic principle of the Chinese bureaucratic
state: that a religion maintained its corporate existence only on sufferance of
the state.

[From *Chiu T'ang shu*, 18A:14b–15a]

Edict of the 8th month [845]:

We have heard that up through the Three Dynasties the Buddha was
never spoken of. It was only from the Han and Wei on that the religion
of idols gradually came to prominence. So in this latter age it has transmitted its strange ways, instilling its infection with every opportunity,
spreading like a luxuriant vine, until it has poisoned the customs of our
nation; gradually, and before anyone was aware, it beguiled and confounded men's minds so that the multitude have been increasingly led
astray. It has spread to the hills and plains of all the nine provinces and
through the walls and towers of our two capitals. Each day finds its
monks and followers growing more numerous and its temples more lofty.
It wears out the strength of the people with constructions of earth and
wood, pilfers their wealth for ornaments of gold and precious objects,
causes men to abandon their lords and parents for the company of teachers, and severs man and wife with its monastic decrees. In destroying
law and injuring mankind indeed nothing surpasses this doctrine!

Now if even one man fails to work the fields, someone must go hungry;
if one woman does not tend her silkworms, someone will go cold. At
present there are an inestimable number of monks and nuns in the empire, each of them waiting for the farmers to feed him and the silkworms

to clothe him, while the public temples and private chapels have reached boundless numbers, all with soaring towers and elegant ornamentation sufficient to outshine the imperial palace itself. The exhaustion of goods and manpower, and the corruption of morals that beset the Chin, Sung, Ch'i, and Liang dynasties all were caused by just this situation.

Thus Kao-tsu and T'ai-tsung, the founders of Our dynasty, employed military arts to quell rebellion and disorder, and the arts of peace to bring order to China. Wielding these two rods alone they were able to rule the land. How could anyone think of taking up this religion of the far western wilderness to stand in challenge against Us? During the Chen-kuan and K'ai-yüan eras [627–649, 713–741], steps were already taken for the regulation of Buddhism. But its eradication was not completed and instead it only spread with increasing popularity.

Having thoroughly examined all earlier reports and consulted public opinion on all sides, there no longer remains the slightest doubt in Our mind that this evil should be eradicated. Loyal ministers of the court and provinces have lent their aid to Our high intentions, submitting most apt proposals which We have found worthy of being put into effect. Presented with an opportunity to suppress this source of age-old evil and fulfill the laws and institutions of the ancient kings, to aid mankind and bring profit to the multitude, how could We forbear to act?

The temples of the empire which have been demolished number over 4,600; 26,500 monks and nuns have been returned to lay life and enrolled as subject to the Twice-A-Year Tax; over 40,000 privately established temples have been destroyed, releasing thirty or forty million *ch'ing* of fertile, top-grade land and 150,000 male and female servants who will become subject to the Twice-A-Year Tax. Monks and nuns have been placed under the jurisdiction of the Director of Aliens to make it perfectly clear that this is a foreign religion. Finally We have ordered over 2,000 men of the Nestorian and Mazdean religions to return to lay life and cease from polluting the customs of China.

Alas, what had not been carried out in the past seemed to have been waiting for this opportunity. If Buddhism is completely abolished now, who will say that the action is not timely? Already over a hundred thousand idle and unproductive Buddhist followers have been expelled, and countless of their gaudy, useless buildings destroyed. Henceforth We may guide the people in stillness and purity, cherish the principle of nonaction, order our government with simplicity and ease, and achieve a unification of customs so that the multitudes of all realms will find their destination in Our august rule. Since this eradication of evil began it has daily and in unknown ways worked its effect. Now We send down this edict to the provincial officials that they may further carry out Our will.

CHAPTER XIX

THE CONFUCIAN REVIVAL IN THE SUNG

As dynasties go in China the Sung (960–1279) was not known for its power and stability. It struggled against great odds to bring back under Chinese rule all the lands once held by the T'ang. During the earlier years of the dynasty there was almost constant fighting with "barbarian" tribes in the north and west; during the latter half of the period these invaders held North China, the ancient seat of Chinese civilization, firmly in their grasp until the Mongols swept down to reunify the empire under alien auspices. Even within the Sung domains the nation was beset by chronic fiscal, agricultural, and administrative problems such as had plagued earlier regimes.

Yet in spite of all this Chinese society showed remarkable vitality. Commerce was expanding, and with it a more diversified economy developed. Money, especially the new paper currency, was coming into greater use. As a natural concomitant of such growth there was an increase in the number and size of cities, which at this time attained the wealth, culture, and sheer magnificence soon to impress the Venetian traveler, Marco Polo. In the arts of peace, if not in war, the Sung distinguished itself. Printing for the first time provided the means for more widespread education. Academies, which were centers of higher education, sprang up around the more sizeable collections of books, sometimes endowed by grants of land from the state or private individuals. It was in institutions such as these that the new scholarship, so much an expression of the whole Sung concern for cultural achievement as opposed to military aggrandizement, took its rise. Where for centuries the great Buddhist temples had been the intellectual centers of China, now academies presided over by one or another noted scholar began to attract students in great numbers. Under such circumstances the new scholarship grew and flowered into the new (or as we say, Neo-) Confucianism.

As an example of this new type of scholar and teacher we may cite Hu Yüan (993–1059), who typifies the spirit of the Confucian revival and whose influence was felt among its most prominent leaders. Hu Yüan answered well to the need Han Yü saw for genuine teachers in the tradition of Confucius and Mencius. He was above all a man who took seriously his duties as a moral preceptor of youth and stressed a close teacher-disciple relationship as essential to education. It was regarded as noteworthy in his time that Hu Yüan "adhered strictly to the traditional concept of the teacher-disciple relationship, treating his students as if they were sons or younger brothers, and being trusted and loved by them as if he were their father or elder brother." The Confucianism which he tried to inculcate in this manner was an intensely personal and vital faith, contrasting with the antiquarianism of the old-type scholar and the largely formal training of the bureaucrat. One of his disciples later explained Hu Yüan's contribution in the following terms to the Emperor Shen-tsung:

It is said that the Way has three aspects: substance [or basis, *t'i*], function [*yung*], and literary expression [*wen*]. The bond between prince and minister and between father and son, humanity, righteousness, rites and music—these are the things which do not change through the ages; they are its substance. The *Books of Odes* and *History,* the dynastic histories, the writings of the philosophers—these perpetuate the right example down through the ages; they are its literary expression. To activate this substance and put it into practice throughout the empire, enriching the life of the people and ordering all things to imperial perfection—this is its function.

Our dynasty has not through its successive reigns made substance and function the basis for the selection of officials. Instead we have prized the embellishments of conventional versification, and thus have corrupted the standards of contemporary scholarship. My teacher [Hu Yüan] from the Ming-tao through the Pao-yüan periods (1032–1040), was greatly distressed over this evil and expounded to his students the teaching which aims at clarifying the substance [of the Way] and carrying out its function. Tirelessly and with undaunted zeal, for over twenty years he devoted himself wholly to schoolteaching, first in the Soochow region and finally at the Imperial Academy. Those who have come from his school number at least several thousands. The fact that today scholars recognize the basic importance to government and education of the substance and function of the Way of the sages is all due to the efforts of my Master.[1]

[1] *Sung-Yüan hsüeh-an,* 1:17.

This tribute to Hu Yüan suggests several characteristic features of the Confucian revival in the early Sung. Hu Yüan is both a traditionalist and a reformer. He is more a moralist than a metaphysician, and his primary interest is in the application of Confucian ethics to the problems of government and everyday life. Hu Yüan is also an independent scholar, one whose success came through years of private study and teaching, and who gained official recognition only late in life. Echoing criticism of late T'ang writers of the literary examination system, he condemns it as a perverter of scholarship and as productive of a mediocre officialdom. Finally in the threefold conception of the Way as substance, function and literary expression, Hu Yüan adapts the terminology of Buddhist philosophy (specifically of T'ien-t'ai metaphysics) to the exposition of the traditional Confucian Way, and suggests the manner in which Confucian thought would be enriched and deepened in the process of confrontation with Buddhism and Taoism.

According to this view, the Classics were to be studied as deposits of eternal truth rather than as antiquarian repositories, and the true aim of classical studies was to bring these enduring principles, valid for any place or time, to bear upon both the conduct of life and the solution of contemporary problems. Conversely, no attempt to solve such problems could hope to succeed unless it were grounded on these enduring principles and undertaken by men dedicated to them. Yet neither classical teaching nor a practical program of reform could be furthered except through the mastery of literature and writing—not the intricacies of form and style with which the literary examinations were concerned—but literature as a medium for preserving and communicating the truth in all its forms. Therefore these three concepts, substance, function, and literary expression, were seen as essential and inseparable constituents of the Way, which, as the Sung school exemplified it, embraced every aspect of life. In a sense they may be called the Three Treasures of Confucianism, just as Buddha (Truth), Dharma (Law or Scripture) and Sangha (Monastic Discipline) are the Three Treasures of Buddhism which the Sung Confucianists sought to displace.

With this in mind we should be prepared to recognize the many-sided character of the Confucian revival in the Sung. The broad current of political reform, culminating in the New Laws of Wang An-shih, and the work of the great Sung historians are as much products of this revival as the metaphysical speculations now identified with Neo-Confucianism. Even the work of the great philosopher Chu Hsi must be appreciated as an expression of the Sung spirit in the fields of history and politics as well as in classical scholarship and metaphysics. Such breadth and versatility, indeed, were not uncommon in the great intellectual giants of the Sung: Wang An-shih, whose reputation as an outstanding writer and classicist in his day has been over-shadowed by his fame as a statesman; Ssu-ma Kuang, his chief political antagonist, who is better known today as one of China's great historians; and Su Tung-p'o, the celebrated poet and calligrapher, who was also a man of affairs and played a leading part in the political struggles of that memorable era. These men—to name just a few—are all beneficiaries of the creative and wide-spreading energies of the Sung revival.

Especially in its emphasis upon the practical application of Confucian principles to the problems of the day, Hu Yüan's teaching points to the fact that political, economic, and social thought were to be as integral a part of the Confucian revival as were classical studies and philosophical inquiry. Hu Yüan himself urged practical measures to improve the people's livelihood, to strengthen military defenses against the barbarian menace, to expand irrigation projects in order to increase agricultural production, and also to promote the study of mathematics and astronomy. But Hu Yüan remained a teacher and did not himself engage in politics. At court it was men like Fan Chung-yen and Ou-yang Hsiu who led the reform movement. The latter, a noted poet and historian, proved himself a mighty champion of Confucian orthodoxy who carried on Han Yü's struggle against the twin evils of Buddhist escapism and literary dilettantism. He insisted that "literary activity just benefits oneself, while political activity can affect the situation around us." In him also the Sung school found a vigorous defender of the scholar's right to organize politically for the advancement of common principles. To him, then, we turn for a statement of the need for reform put in its most fundamental terms.

OU-YANG HSIU

Essay on Fundamentals (Pen lun)

Like Han Yü, Ou-yang Hsiu (1007–1070) saw China's ills as due to the forsaking of Confucian teachings in favor of Buddhism, which had corrupted the whole body-politic. Nevertheless, outright suppression of Buddhism, as Han Yü had urged, seemed to him a futile policy. Only a positive program of fundamental reform would remove the underlying causes for the popularity of Buddhism. This called for a complete renovation of Chinese society—and not just the personal moral reformation which Confucianism always looked to for social improvement, but a reform especially of basic institutions to make them conform to the ancient ideal.

[From *Ou-yang Wen-chung-kung chi,* SPTK ed., 17:1a–4b]

The cult of Buddhism has plagued China for over a thousand years. In every age men with the vision to see through its falseness and the power to do something about it have all sought to drive it out. But though they drove it out, it reappeared in greater force; though they attacked and crushed it for a time, it grew only stronger. It has been struck at but not wiped out, and indeed seems rather to grow more prevalent, until in the end it seems as if nothing could be done about it. But is the situation really hopeless, or is it simply that we have not used the proper methods?

When a doctor treats a disease, he tries to ascertain the origin of the sickness and heal the source of the infection. When sickness strikes a man, it takes advantage of the weak spot in his vitality to enter there. For this reason a good doctor does not attack the disease itself, but rather seeks to strengthen the patient's vitality, for when vitality has been restored, then the sickness will disappear as a natural consequence.

In like manner when one seeks to remedy the illnesses of the nation, one must ascertain their origins and heal the areas that are affected.

Buddha was a barbarian who was far removed from China and lived long ago. In the age of Yao, Shun, and the Three Dynasties, kingly rule was practiced, government and the teachings of rites and righteousness flourished in the world. At this time, although Buddhism existed, it was unable to penetrate into China. But some two hundred years after the Three Dynasties had fallen into decay, when kingly rule ceased, and rites and righteousness were neglected, Buddhism came to China. It is clear then that Buddhism took advantage of this time of decay and neglect to come and plague us. This was how the illness was first contracted. And if we will but remedy this decay, revive what has fallen into disuse, and restore once again to the land kingly rule in its brilliance and rites and righteousness in their fullness, then although Buddhism continues to exist, it will have no hold upon our people. This will also come about as a natural consequence.

In ancient times the governments of Yao and Shun and the Three Dynasties set up the well-field system. They made a registry of all subjects, calculated the population, and distributed land to all. Then all men who were capable of farming had land to farm. One-tenth of the produce was taken as tax, while other levies were differentiated in order to discourage indolence and cause all men to devote their full efforts to agriculture and not allow them time for less worthy occupations. Lest the people become weary or neglectful or enter into false ways, they were given meat and wine to nourish their bodies, and musical instruments and ceremonial vessels to delight their ears and eyes. When they were at rest from the work of the fields, they were instructed in rites. Thus for hunting they learned the ceremonies of the spring and autumn hunts, for taking a mate the rites of marriage, for death the rites of funeral and sacrifice, and for banquets and gatherings the rites of the village archery contest. These not only prevented disorder among the people, but also taught them the all-important relationships between superior and inferior, old and young, and all society.

In this way the rules for supporting the living and bidding farewell to the dead were all made to accord with the desires of the people. They were brightened with ceremonial objects and beautifully ordered so that they were a delight to the people and easy to carry out. They were in harmony with the nature and feelings of the people and imparted a restraint which prevented men from going to excess. Still fearing that this might not be enough, the rulers set up schools for the people to teach and enlighten them, so that from the courts of the emperor down to the smallest hamlet there was no place without its school where keen and intelligent men from among the people were sent to study, to discuss with each other, and to lead and encourage the indolent. Ah, how complete was this system of government of the Three Dynasties! Profound was its consideration of the will of the people, complete its provisions for ordering them, comprehensive its measures to protect them, and zealous its ways of encouraging them. Practiced with diligence, it encompassed all things; prevailing steadily, it entered deep into the hearts of men. Thus if the people were not at work in the fields they were engaged in the performance of rites and music; if they were not in their homes they were attending schools. There was nothing they heard or saw but partook of humanity and righteousness. They took to these things with joy and never tired of them, and all their lives they knew nothing different. How had they the leisure then to follow after foreign ways? It is because of this system of government that I say, although Buddhism existed, it could not penetrate [into China].

But when the Chou declined and the Ch'in conquered the world, it discarded the methods of the Three Dynasties and the way of the former kings was cut off. From this time on the rulers of the world were not powerful enough to restore the old ways; they could not perfect their methods of government nor effectively prevent the people from drifting away. It was at this time that Buddhism took advantage of the circumstances to make its appearance and for a period of over a thousand years its adherents daily have grown in number, while our own ways day by day sink into ruin. The well-field system was the first to be abolished, and there arose the evils of encroachment and idle landlordism. After this the rites of the spring and autumn hunts, marriage and funeral ceremonials, sacrifice and archery contests, and all the ways by which the people had been instructed, one by one fell into disuse. Then the wicked among the people found leisure to turn to other things, and the good were confused and lost, and no longer knew the guidance of rites and righteousness. The wicked having leisure began to consider strange and perverse ways, while the good, lacking rites and righteousness, knew not where to go. Then Buddhism, entering at this juncture, trumpeted abroad its grand, fantastic doctrines to lead them, and the people could do no other than follow and believe. How much more so when from time to time kings, dukes, and great men sang its praises, declaring that Buddhism was truly worthy to be believed and followed. Could our people then still doubt and fail to follow?

Haply there may be one man who is not deceived and who, fired with anger, cries, "What is this Buddhism? I shall seize my spear and drive it out!" or another who says, "I shall repulse it with reason!" But Buddhism has plagued the world for a thousand years. What can one man in one day do? The people are drunk with it, and it has seeped into their bones and marrow so that it cannot be vanquished by mouth and tongue.

What then can be done? I say there is nothing so effective in overcoming it as practicing what is fundamental. Long ago, in the period of the Warring States, the teachings of Yang Chu and Mo Tzu were the cause of great confusion. Mencius was grieved at this and devoted himself to preaching humanity and righteousness, for when the doctrine of humanity and righteousness prevails then the teachings of Yang Chu and Mo Tzu will be abandoned. In Han times all the schools of philosophy flourished side by side. Tung Chung-shu was concerned at this and retired to devote himself to the practice of Confucianism, for he knew that when the Way of Confucius was made clear the other schools would cease. This is the effect of practicing what is fundamental in order to overcome Buddhism.

These days a tall warrior clad in armor and bearing a spear may surpass in bravery a great army, yet when he sees the Buddha he bows low and when he hears the doctrines of the Buddha he is sincerely awed and persuaded. Why? Because though he is indeed strong and full of vigor, in his heart he is confused and has nothing to cling to. But when a scholar who is small and frail and afraid to advance hears the doctrines of Buddhism his righteousness is revealed at once in his countenance, and not only does he not bow and submit, but he longs to rush upon them and destroy them. Why? It is simply because he is enlightened in learning and burns with a belief in rites and righteousness, and in his heart he possesses something which can conquer these doctrines. Thus rites and righteousness are the fundamental things whereby Buddhism may be defeated. If a single scholar who understands rites and righteousness can keep from submitting to these doctrines, then we have but to make the whole world understand rites and righteousness and these doctrines will, as a natural consequence, be wiped out.

. . . .

In ancient times Hsün Tzu held the theory that man's nature is basically evil and wrote a book to prove it. I used to favor this idea, but now as I see how the men of my day follow Buddhism, I know that Hsün Tzu's theory is gravely mistaken. Man's nature is basically good, and those who follow Buddhism, abandoning their families and discarding their wives or husbands, are actually going much against this basic nature. Buddhism is a corruption which eats into and destroys men, and yet when the people lead each other on to follow it, it is only because they think that Buddhism teaches the way to do good. Alas, if we could but truly awaken our people to see that it is through rites and righteousness that they may do good, then would they not lead each other on to follow these?

On Parties

As a leading official under the emperors Jen-tsung (r. 1023–1063) and Ying-tsung (r. 1064–1067), Ou-yang Hsiu attempted to recruit and bring into the government able men inspired by Confucian ideals and sympathetic to the reforms he envisaged. Such an attempt to rally the serious scholars of the land in support of a new political program necessarily involved creating an organization much like a political party, committed to the formation of a government composed of like-minded individuals.

Chinese political traditions did not allow for such a development, however. Rulers had always looked with suspicion on any political alignment which might bring pressure on the throne or threaten its security. Any organized opposition was likely to be regarded as a "faction" or "clique," bent on serving its own interests rather than those of the state. One of the main objectives of the civil service examination system was to prevent "packing" of offices with representatives of any single group or faction through favoritism in the recruitment of officials.

Thus the political movements inspired by the Confucian revival, in so far as they were aggressive and well organized, were bound to stir up contention and become involved in bitter factional struggles. Against such attacks Ou-yang Hsiu, in a memorial of 1045, sought to justify the existence of groups dedicated to the best interests of the nation and not to the selfish advantage of their own members.

[From *Ou-yang Wen-chung-kung chi,* SPTK ed., 17:66–8a]

Your servant is aware that from ancient times there have been discussions on the worth of parties. It is only to be hoped that a ruler will distinguish between those of gentlemen and those of inferior men. In general, gentlemen join with other gentlemen in parties because of common principles, while inferior men join with other inferior men for reasons of common profit. This is quite natural. But your servant would contend that in fact inferior men have no parties, and that it is only gentlemen who are capable of forming them. Why is this? Inferior men love profit and covet material wealth. When the time seems to offer mutual advantages, they will temporarily band together to form a party, which is, however, essentially false. But when they reach the stage where they are actually competing among themselves for advantage, or when the advantages they have sought fail to materialize and they drift apart, then they turn about and begin to attack each other, and even the fact that a man is a brother or a relative does not spare him. Therefore your servant maintains that such men have no real parties, and that those which they form on a temporary basis are essentially false. But this is not true of gentlemen, who abide by the Way and righteousness, who practice loyalty and good faith, and care only for honor and integrity. When they employ these qualities in their personal conduct they share a common principle and improve each other, and when they turn them to the use of the state they unite in common ideals and mutual assistance, and from beginning to end act as one. These are the parties of gentlemen. Thus if the ruler will but put aside the false parties of inferior men and make use of the true parties of gentlemen, then the state may be ordered. . . .

The *Book of History* [Chou: T'ai-shih] says: "The King of Shang has thousands and myriads of ministers, but they have thousands and myriads of minds. The King of Chou has only three thousand ministers, but they have one mind." In the time of the King of Shang it may be said that each of the countless ministers had his own mind and there were no parties, and thus the Shang state perished. But the three thousand ministers of King Wu of the Chou formed one great party and therefore the Chou state rose to power. At the time of Emperor Hsien of the Latter Han all the eminent scholars of the kingdom were put into prison on the charge of being partisans. Soon after, with the uprising of the Yellow Turban Bandits, the House of Han was thrown into great disorder. But though the emperor repented of his action and freed all of the partisans, it was too late to save the dynasty. Toward the close of the T'ang dynasty there again began to be much discussion about the advisability of parties until, in the time of Emperor Chao, all the prominent scholars of the court were executed or thrown into the Yellow River with the remark that "This 'stream of purity' is fit only to be dumped in a muddy river!" [2] And with this the T'ang came to an end.

Now of the rulers of the past, none was more successful in causing men to be of different minds and to avoid partisanship than the King of Shang, none so good at suppressing parties of worthy men as Emperor Hsien, none so effective in executing the "pure conduct" parties as Emperor Chao, and yet all these rulers brought confusion and destruction to their states. . . . In the time of King Wu of the Chou, the three thousand

[2] A sarcastic pun made by the high minister Chu Ch'üan-chung who threw the partisans into the muddy Yellow River. The phrase "stream of purity" or "pure stream," denotes a group of persons dedicated to purity of conduct and high moral principles.

ministers of the state formed one great party, larger and more numerous than any party has ever been. And yet through this party the state of Chou was able to come to power, and though it contained a great number of fine men, it was never considered that there were too many. It is hoped that these examples of the rise and fall of states in the past will provide a mirror wherein the ruler of men may profitably gaze.

THE CONFUCIAN PROGRAM OF REFORM

The first steps in the government itself to implement a broad program of reform were taken by the statesman and general Fan Chung-yen (r. 989–1052), who was among those defended by Ou-yang Hsiu when he submitted his memorial on political parties. Fan was an earnest student of the Classics, as well as a man of practical affairs, who became known as a staunch upholder of the Confucian Way and a vigorous opponent of Buddhism. When a young man he had adopted for himself the maxim: "To be first in worrying about the world's troubles and last in enjoying its pleasures," which expresses his high ideal of public service as a dedicated Confucianist. During the reign of Jen-tsung (1023–1063) Fan tried as prime minister to implement a ten-point program including administrative reforms to eliminate entrenched bureaucrats, official favoritism, and nepotism; examination reform; equalization of official landholdings to insure a sufficient income for territorial officials and to lessen the temptation toward bribery and squeeze; land reclamation and dike repair to increase agricultural production and facilitate grain transport; creation of local militia to strengthen national defense; and reduction of the labor service required of the people by the state.

There is nothing startling or revolutionary in this program, but many of the reforms proposed by Fan anticipate changes later made by Wang An-shih which aroused great controversy. To us they represent simply a reorganization of certain governmental activities or practices, and we may fail to appreciate that in a society so dominated by the state and so sensitive to its operations, even administrative changes of this sort could have a deep impact. As it turned out, however, those reforms dealing with education and the examination system had the most significant effect. In his memorial Fan called for the establishment of a national school system through which worthy men could be trained and recruited for the civil service. Though conceived, characteristically enough, more to meet the needs of the government for trained personnel than to make education available to one and all, this system nevertheless represented the first real attempt to provide public school education on a large scale in China. Since nothing of the sort had been undertaken before, it also represented a departure from the established order as embodied in dynastic tradition and precedent. Fan appealed therefore to an earlier and, from his point of view, more hallowed tradition, justifying the change as a return to the system set forth in the classics as obtaining under the benevolent rule of the early Chou kings.

Fan also asked that in the examinations conducted at the capital for the *chin-shih* degree (the highest in the regular system of advancement), more importance be attached to an understanding of the Classics and of political problems than to the composition of poetry. One of his most revealing proposals was to abolish the pasting of a piece of paper over the candidate's name on an examination paper, a practice which had been designed to insure impartial judgment by the examiner. The reasoning behind this suggestion follows from the importance Fan always attached in both teaching and politics to a man's personal integrity. It was just as vital to know the candidate's moral character as his literary and intellectual capacities, and character was impossible to judge except from personal knowledge.

Prompted by Fan's memorial, the emperor called for a general discussion of these questions at court. Fan's proposals were supported by Sung Ch'i and others, who expostulated against the evils of the existing system and urged a "return" to the ancient ideal. As a result a national school system was promulgated by Jen-tsung in 1044, calling for the establishment of a school in each department and district to be maintained and staffed by the local magistrate. At the same time the civil service system was reformed so that the examinations were divided into three parts, with priority given to problems of history and politics, then to interpretation of the Classics, and last of all to poetry composition. Subsequently instruction in the Imperial Academy was also revamped by Hu Yüan, who had been brought to court by Fan Chung-yen, to conform to the methods Hu had used in his private academy.

Few of Fan's reforms survived when he fell from power as a result of bitter factional struggles. Nevertheless, the agitation for reform went on among some of the best minds of the age. The selections which follow are meant to illustrate the types of reform most widely espoused in Confucian circles. To show that this ferment was not confined to persons whose interests and activities were largely political, but instead pervaded the whole Sung school, we have made selections from representatives of the orthodox Neo-Confucian tradition known better as philosophers than as officials. They are, moreover, thinkers whose intellectual antecedents are found among the progenitors of the Sung school already mentioned, and yet whose political and scholarly affinities linked them also to the great reformer Wang An-shih. The first two selections are memorials of the famous Ch'eng brothers, documents which reveal the breadth and variety of reforms advocated. Following them are excerpts from the writings of the philosopher Chang Tsai and the scholar-official Su Hsün, presenting divergent views on a single question: the age-old problem of land reform.

CH'ENG YI
Memorial to the Emperor Jen-tsung

This memorial was presented in 1050, a few years after the fall of Fan Chung-yen and his allies, when Ch'eng Yi (1033–1107) was still only seventeen years old. It is prefaced by a long appeal (abbreviated here) for acceptance of the Confucian Way as the basis of government policy. Only a full return to the ideal society of the sage-kings will suffice to meet the needs of the day. To imitate the Han and T'ang dynasties, great though these were in some respects, would mean succumbing eventually to the same weaknesses which brought them down. This is a recurrent theme of the reformers, who had to overcome widespread skepticism at court that ancient institutions, as well as Confucian moral precepts, could have any practical application in the very different social circumstances of the Sung period. Ch'eng Yi then describes the prevailing economic and social evils which must be remedied, and, like so many other reformers of the time, concludes that the first step in solving them must be a change in the civil service system, so as to bring into the government men with the ability and the determination to rectify these conditions.

[From Yi-ch'uan wen-chi, SPPY ed., I, 14a–16b]

In the Three Dynasties the Way was always followed; after the Ch'in it declined and did not flourish. Dynasties like the Wei and Chin indeed departed far from it. The Han and T'ang achieved a limited prosperity, but in practicing the Way they adulterated it. . . .

In the *Book of History* it says: "The people are the foundation of the nation; when the foundation is solid the nation is at peace." Your servant thinks that the way to make the foundation firm is to pacify the people, and that the way to pacify the people is to see that they have enough food and clothing. Nowadays the people's strength is exhausted and there is not enough food and clothing in the land. When spring cultivation has begun and the seed has been sown, they hold their breath in anxious expectation. If some year their hopes are disappointed, they have to run away [and abandon the land]. In view of these facts, the foundation can hardly be called firm. Your servant considers that Your Majesty is kind and benevolent, loves the people as his children, and certainly cannot bear to see them suffer like this. Your servant suspects that the men around Your Majesty have shielded these things from Your Majesty's discerning sight, and prevented you from learning about them.

Now the government frequently has insufficient funds to meet its expenditures. Having an insufficiency, it turns to the Finance Commission, and the Finance Commission turns to the fiscal intendants of the various circuits. But where are the fiscal intendants to get the money? They simply have to wring it from the people. Sometimes peace is disturbed in all directions at once, and so troops are called out just when the men should attend to the cultivation of their fields, causing still more grievous harm. As these pressing demands are put upon the people, their blood and fat become exhausted; frequently they are brought to financial ruin and their livelihood is lost, while the members of the family are separated and dispersed. Even ordinary men are pained at the sight of this. Surely Your Majesty, who is like a parent to the people, cannot help but take pity on them! The people have no savings and the government granaries are empty. Your servant observes that from the capital on out to the frontiers of the empire, there is no place which has a reserve sufficient to carry over two years. If suddenly there is a famine for more than one year, such as the one which occurred in the Ming-tao period [1032-1033], I do not know how the government is going to deal with it. The soldiers who do no work and yet must be fed number more than one million. Since there is no means to support them, the people will be heavily taxed. And yet the people have already scattered. If strong enemies seize the opportunity to attack from without, or wicked men aspire to power from within, then we may well be fearful of a situation which is deteriorating and threatens to collapse.

Your servant considers that humanity is the foundation of the "Kingly Way." He observes that the humanity of Your Majesty is the humanity of Yao and Shun; and yet the empire has not had good government. This is because Your Majesty has a humane heart but not a humane government. Therefore Mencius [IV A:1] says: "There are now princes who have humane hearts and a reputation for humanity, while yet the people do not receive any benefit from them, nor will they leave any example to future ages—all because they do not put into practice the ways of the ancient kings". . . . . Good government in the empire depends upon obtaining worthy men; misgovernment in the empire derives from a failure to obtain worthy men. The world does not lack worthy men; the problem is how to find them. The purpose of seeking out worthy men is good government, and the way to govern the empire is the way followed by the Five Emperors, the Three Kings, the Duke of Chou, and Confucius. Seeking out those who are familiar with the way of government employed by the Five Emperors, the Three Kings, the Duke of Chou, and Confucius, we should employ each of them according to the degree of his understanding of it. He who knows how to serve as a chief councilor should be made a chief councilor; those who know how to be ministers and high officials should be made ministers and high officials; those who know how to govern a prefecture should be made prefects; and those who know how to rule a subprefecture should be made subprefects. When each of them is employed properly, then all duties will be carried out. And when this is done it could never be that the empire would be without good government.

In the selection of scholars for the civil service, though there are many categories under which men may qualify, yet there are only one or two persons who may be considered [under the category of] "wise, virtuous, square, and upright." [3] Instead, what the government obtains are scholars who possess no more than wide learning and powerful memory. Those who qualify in [the examination on] Understanding of the Classics merely specialize in reciting from memory and do not understand their

[3] A title conferred on a limited number of candidates given a special imperial examination at infrequent intervals.

meaning. They are of little use in government. The most prized and sought after is the category of *chin-shih*, which involves composition of verse in the *tz'u* and *fu* form according to the prescribed rules of tone and rhythm. In the *tz'u* and *fu* there is nothing about the way to govern the empire. Men learn them in order to pass the examination, and after the passage of a sufficient time, they finally attain to the posts of ministers and chancellors. How can they know anything of the bases of education and cultivation found in the "Kingly Way"? They occupy the posts and are expected to fulfill their duties without ever having learned them. This is the same as having a nomad of the North steer a boat or having a riverman of the South be the driver of a horse. How can we possibly expect them to be any good? . . .

For two thousand years the Way has not been practiced. Foolish persons of recent times have all declared that times are different and things have changed, so that it can no longer be practiced. This only shows how deep their ignorance is, and yet time and again the rulers of men have been deceived by their talk. . . . But I see that Your Majesty's heart is filled with solicitude for the people, and if Your Majesty practices the Way of the sage-kings with such solicitude for the people, how can any difficulties stand in the way?

CH'ENG HAO
Ten Matters Calling for Reform

This memorial, presented by Ch'eng Yi's elder brother to the Emperor Shen-tsung (r. 1068–1085), opens with the characteristic assertion that despite the need for adapting institutions to the times there are certain underlying principles of Confucianism which remain valid even for later dynasties like the Sung. He then details ten evils of the day which require bold action. Some of these are urgent problems from almost any point of view—unequal distribution of land, population pressure, inadequate educational facilities, the expense and ineffectiveness of a professional army, the danger of famine and need for increased grain storage, and the need for conservation of natural resources. Other reforms are more doctrinaire in character, though from the Confucian point of view they are the most fundamental of all. These involve the ritual functions of government, and reflect the Confucian conviction that all human evils are attributable in some basic way to improper government. Conversely the moral reformation of mankind is believed possible through the maintenance of a perfectly ordered hierarchy of offices, ranks, and rites. It was, therefore, precisely this belief in the perfectability of man and society which dictated complete conformity to the ancient pattern.

[From *Ming-tao wen-chi,* SPPY ed., 2:6a–7b; *Sung-Yüan hsüeh-an,* 14:332]

Your servant considers that the laws established by the sage-kings were all based on human feelings and in keeping with the order of things. In the great reigns of the Two Emperors and Three Kings, how could these laws not but change according to the times and be embodied in systems which suited the conditions obtaining in each? However, in regard to the underlying basis of government, to the teachings by which the people may be shepherded, to the principles which remain forever unalterable in the order of things, and to that upon which the people depend for their very existence, on such points there has been no divergence but rather common agreement among the sages of all times, early or late. Only if the way of sustaining life itself should fail, could the laws of the sage-kings ever be changed. Therefore in later times those who practiced the Way [of the sage-kings] to the fullest achieved perfect order, while those who practiced only a part achieved limited success. This is the clear and manifest lesson of past ages. . . .

But it may be objected that human nature today is no longer the same as in ancient times, and that what has come down to us from the early kings cannot possibly be restored in the present. . . . Now in ancient times all people, from the Son of Heaven down to the commoners, had to have teachers and friends in order to perfect their virtue. Therefore even the sages—Shun, Yü, [King] Wen, and [King] Wu—had those from whom they learned. Nowadays the function of the teacher and preceptor is unfulfilled and the ideal of the "friend-minister" is not made manifest. Therefore the attitude of respect for virtue and enjoyment in doing good has not been developed in the empire. There is no difference between the past and the present in this matter.

A sage-king must follow Heaven in establishing the offices of government. Thus the functions relating to Heaven, earth, and the four seasons did not change throughout the reigns of the Two Emperors and the Three Kings, and for this reason all the regulations were carried out and everything was well ordered. In the T'ang dynasty these institutions were still preserved in attenuated form, and in its [initial] period of peace and order, the government and regulations of the T'ang had some semblance of correctness. Today, however, the offices and ranks have been thrown into great confusion, and duties and functions have not been performed. This is the reason why the ideal of peace and order has not been achieved. There is no difference between the past and present in this matter.

Heaven created men and raised up a ruler to govern and to guide them. Things had to be so regulated as to provide them with settled property as the means to a flourishing livelihood. Therefore the boundaries of the land had to be defined correctly, and the well-fields had to be equally distributed—these are the great fundamentals of government. The T'ang dynasty still maintained a system of land distribution based on the size of the family.[4] Now nothing is left, and there is no such system. The lands of the rich extend on and on, from this prefecture to that subprefecture, and there is nothing to stop them. Day by day the poor scatter and die from starvation, and there is no one to take pity on them. Although many people are more fortunate, still there are countless persons without sufficient food and clothing. The population grows day by day, and if nothing is done to control the situation, food and clothing will become more and more scarce, and more people will scatter and die. This is the key to order and disorder. How can we not devise some way to control it? In this matter, too, there is no difference between past and present.

In ancient times, government and education began with the local villages. The system worked up from [the local units of] *pi, lü, tsu, tang, chou, hsiang, tsan,* and *sui.*[5] Each village and town was linked to the next higher unit and governed by them in sequence. Thus the people were at peace, and friendly toward one another. They seldom violated the criminal law, and it was easy to appeal to their sense of shame. This is in accord with the natural bent of human feelings and, therefore, when practiced, it works. In this matter, too, there is no difference between past and present.

Education in local schools was the means by which the ancient kings made clear the moral obligations of human relationships and achieved the ethical transformation of all under Heaven. Now true teaching and learning have been abandoned, and there is no moral standard. Civic ceremonies have ceased to be held in the local community and propriety and

---

[4] Under the equal land system of the T'ang, each adult was entitled to hold 30 *mu* of hereditary land and 80 *mu* on assignment from the state.

[5] Units of local administration in ascending order as described in the classic *Rites of Chou.*

righteousness are not upheld. Appointments to office are not based upon
the recommendation of the village communities, and the conduct [of
appointees to high office] not proven by performance. The best talents are
not nurtured in the schools, and the abilities of men are mostly wasted.
These are matters clearly evident, and there is in them no difference between the past and the present.

In ancient times, government clerks and runners were paid by the state,
and there was no distinction between soldiers and farmers. Now the
arrogant display of military power has exhausted national resources to
the limit. Your servant considers that if the soldiery, with the exception
of the Imperial Guards, is not gradually reconverted to a peasant militia,
the matter will be of great concern. The services of government clerks
and runners have inflicted harm all over the empire; if this system is not
changed, a great disaster is inevitable. This is also a truth which is most
evident, and there is no difference between the past and the present.

In ancient times, the people had to have [a reserve of] nine years' food
supply. A state was not considered a state if it did not have a reserve of
at least three years' food. Your servant observes that there are few in the
land who grow food and many who consume it. The productivity of the
earth is not fully utilized and human labor is not fully employed. Even
the rich and powerful families rarely have a surplus; how much worse off
are the poor and weak! If in one locality their luck is bad and crops fail
just one year, banditry becomes uncontrollable and the roads are full of
the faint and starving. If, then, we should be so unfortunate as to have a
disaster affecting an area of two or three thousand square *li,* or bad harvests over a number of years in succession, how is the government going
to deal with it? The distress then will be beyond description. How can
we say, "But it is a long, long time since anything like that has happened," and on this ground trust to luck in the future? Certainly we
should gradually return to the ancient system—with the land distributed
equally so as to encourage agriculture, and with steps taken by both individuals and the government to store up grain so as to provide against
any contingency. In this, too, there is no difference between past and
present.

In ancient times, the four classes of people each had its settled occupation, and eight or nine out of ten people were farmers. Therefore food
and clothing were provided without difficulty and people were spared

suffering and distress. But now in the capital region there are thousands upon thousands of men without settled occupations—idlers and beggars who cannot earn a living. Seeing that they are distressed, toilsome, lonesome, poor, and ill, or resort to guile and craftiness in order to survive and yet usually cannot make a living, what can we expect the consequence to be after this has gone on for days and years? Their poverty being so extreme, unless a sage is able to change things and solve the problem, there will be no way to avoid complete disaster. How can we say, "There is nothing that can be done about it"? This calls for consideration of the ancient [system] in order to reform the present [system], a sharing by those who have much so as to relieve those who possess little, thus enabling them to gain the means of livelihood by which to save their lives. In this, too, there is no difference between the past and the present.

The way the sages followed the will of Heaven and put things in order was through the administration of the six resources.[6] The responsibility for the administration of the six resources was in the hands of the Five Offices. There were fixed prohibitions covering the resources of hills, woodlands, and streams. Thus the various things were in abundance and there was no deficiency in the supply. Today the duties of the Five Offices are not performed and the six resources are not controlled. The use of these things is immoderate and the taking of them is not in due time and season. It is not merely that the nature of things has been violated, but that the mountains from which forests and woods grow have all been laid bare by indiscriminate cutting and burning. As these depredations still go uncurbed, the fish of the stream and the beasts of the field are cut short in their abundance and the things of nature [Heaven] are becoming wasted and exhausted. What then can be done about it? These dire abuses have now reached the extreme, and only by restoring the ancient system of official control over hills and streams, so as to preserve and develop them, can the trend be halted, a change made, and a permanent supply be assured. Here, too, there is no difference between the past and the present.

In ancient times, there were different ranks and distinctions observed in official capping ceremonies, weddings, funerals, sacrifices, carriages, garments, and utensils, and no one dared to exceed what he was entitled to. Therefore expenses were easily met and people kept their equanimity

[6] That is, fire, water, metal, wood, earth, and grain.

of mind. Now the system of rites is not maintained in practice, and people compete with each other in ostentation and extravagance. The families of officials are unable to maintain themselves in proper style, whereas members of the merchant class sometimes surpass the ceremonial display of kings and dukes. The system of rites is unable to regulate the human feelings, and the titles and quantities [7] are unable to preserve the distinction between the noble and the mean. Since there have been no fixed distinctions and proportions, people have become crafty, deceitful, and grasping; each seeks to gratify his desires and does not stop until they are gratified. But how can there be an end to it? This is the way leading to strife and disorder. How, then, can we not look into the measures of the ancient kings and adapt them to our need? Here, too, there is no difference between the past and the present.

The above ten points are but the primary ones. Your servant discusses these main points merely to provide evidence for his belief that the laws and institutions of the Three Dynasties can definitely be put into practice. As to the detailed plans and procedures for their enactment, it is essential that they conform to the instructions contained in the Classics and be applied with due regard for human feelings. These are fixed and definite principles, clearly apparent to all. How can they be compared with vague and impractical theories? May your sage intelligence deign to consider them.

CHANG TSAI
Land Equalization and Feudalism

The philosopher Chang Tsai (1020–1077), an uncle of the Ch'eng brothers, strongly advocated the adoption of the institutions described in the classical books of rites (especially the *Rites of Chou*). Chang long cherished the dream of purchasing some land for himself and his disciples and of dividing it up into well-fields in order to demonstrate the feasibility of restoring the system which the early sage-kings had left to posterity. He died without accomplishing his objective.

Note especially the reasons given by Chang for the superiority of the feudal system and the steps by which he would gradually return to this form of social organization. He is particularly concerned over the problems created by

[7] As stated in the classic *Tso chuan* there was to be a proportionate relation between one's rank and the quantity of goods one might devote to social display within the limits of good form (SPPY ed. 9:8b; Legge I, 97).

the increasing centralization of government, a trend which many recent historians have pointed to as having been greatly accelerated and intensified in
the Sung dynasty and after.

[From *Chang Tzu ch'üan-shu*, KHCPTS ed., 4:83, 84, 85–86]

If the government of the empire is not based on the well-field system,
there will never be peace. The way of Chou is simply this: to equalize. . . .

The well-field system could be put into effect with the greatest ease.
The government only needs to issue an edict and the whole thing can be
settled without having to beat a single person. No one would dare to
occupy and hold land as his own. Moreover, it should be done in such a
manner as to obtain the people's ready compliance, and not cause those
with much land to lose all their means. In the case, let us say, of a high
official holding lands comprising a thousand hamlets, he should be enfeoffed in a state no more than fifty *li* in extent. But for what he possesses in excess of this, he should be assigned jurisdiction as an official [8]
over a proportionate area of land, so that he may have its tax income. [In
this way] people will not lose their former property.

To achieve good government in the empire the only method is to start
with this. The land of the empire should be laid out in squares and
apportioned, with each man receiving one square. This is the basis of the
people's subsistence. In recent times [ie., since the Chou] no provision
has been made for the people's means of subsistence, but only for the
commandeering of their labor. Contrary to expectation, the exalted position of the Son of Heaven has been used for the monopolizing of everything productive of profit. With the government thinking only of the
government, and the people thinking only of themselves, they have not
taken each other into consideration. But "when the people have plenty,
their prince will not be left alone in want. If the people are in want, their
prince cannot alone enjoy plenty." [9]

Chang proceeds to a detailed discussion of the ancient pattern and how it may
be conformed to in the present. Then he returns to the political implications
of this system.

In the case of those families which had formerly held much landed
property, though their land is turned over to the people it is not the

___

[8] Presumably an appointment to terminate at death, and not by hereditary right as in
the case of his fief. The interpretation of this passage is uncertain.

[9] *Analects*, XII, 9.

same as share-cropping or tenancy. Their income may thereby be some-what reduced, yet they will be made land-officials and placed in charge of the people. Once this idea is made clear to them, they will follow along. Even if a few should be unwilling, nevertheless a great majority will be pleased with it and only a minority displeased. Besides how can you pos-sibly take into consideration the feelings of every single individual?

At first we will merely distribute public land to the people, but after ten or twelve years other measures will have to be taken. To start with, land-officials will be appointed [as explained], but later men should be selected for their personal merits. If we really seek to establish the ancient system, we must first study carefully the text [of the *Rites of Chou*] so that we fully understand its underlying meaning and can fill in the gaps to get the overall view. Thus the well-fields may be seen to lead to a restoration of feudalism. For this a determination must be made of the merits of those to be enfeoffed, for only if there are persons of great merit and virtue can we set up the feudal system. Before feudalism was estab-lished the problem was how to govern the well-farms and villages of the empire, and they had to create land officers to govern them. Now, since we cannot yet propose the adoption of a feudal system, much the same thing can be accomplished by appointing lifetime local administrators.

The reason a feudal system must be established is that the administra-tion of the empire must be simplified through delegation of power before things can be well managed. If administration is not simplified [through decentralization], then it is impossible to govern well. Therefore the sages insisted on sharing the management of the empire with other men. It was thus that everything was well-administered in their times. When a sage-king adopts a law, he always thinks in terms of generations to come. If the Duke of Chou were in power, he could personally direct the ad-ministration of the whole empire and everything would be well managed. But how could later rulers hope to achieve this? Besides, why should he who rules the whole empire want to attend personally to the affairs of the whole empire?

If we adopt a feudal system and one of the feudal lords proves un-worthy, he can still be removed and no harm will come of it. How could it be that with the might of a whole empire we could not discipline the ruler of a small state and keep the feudal lords from conspiring to dis-turb the peace of the land? Of course, only if the court is powerful can peace and order be preserved in this way.

Still, in more recent times there have been those who declared that for the Ch'in empire not to maintain a feudal system was the wisest policy. They have just not understood what the sages had in mind!

SU HSÜN

The Land System—A Dissenting View

Su Hsün (1009–1066) was the father of two famous scholar-statesmen including the poet Su Tung-p'o. With the backing of Ou-yang Hsiu he achieved fame himself as a writer and official, without advancing through the regular civil service channels. Widely admired for both the style and sense of his essays, Su here takes up the land problem and attempts to refute two theories widely held: that the distress of the peasantry is due to excessive taxes and that the well-field system should be restored. The essay opens with a discussion (abridged here) of tax rates under the Chou dynasty, which were usually considered to represent the norm.

[From *Chia-yu chi*, SPTK ed., 5:7a–9a]

At the height of the Chou dynasty the heaviest taxes ran to as much as one part in four, the next heaviest to one part in five, and then on down to rates as low as one part in ten or below. Taxes today, though never as low as one part in ten, likewise do not exceed one part in four or one in five, provided that the local magistrate is not rapacious and grasping. Thus there is not a great difference in the rate of taxation between Chou times and our own. . . .

However, during the Chou dynasty the people of the empire sang, danced, and rejoiced in the benevolence of their rulers, whereas our people are unhappy, as if they were extracting their very muscles and peeling off their very skins to meet the needs of the state. The Chou tax was so much, and our tax is likewise so much. Why, then is there such a great difference between the people's sadness today and their happiness then? There must be a reason for this.

During Chou times, the well-field system was employed. Since the well-field system was abolished, the land no longer belongs to the cultivators, and those who own the land do not cultivate. Those who do cultivate depend for their land upon the rich people. The rich families possess much land and extensive properties; the paths linking their fields run on and on. They call in the migratory workers and assign each a piece of their land to till, whipping and driving them to work, and treating them as slaves. Sitting there comfortably, they look around, give commands, and demand services. In the summer the people hoe for them, in the fall they harvest for them. No one disobeys their commands. The landowner amuses himself and yet draws half the income of the land, while the other half goes to the cultivator. For every landowner there are ten cultivators. Thus the landowner accumulates his half share day by day and so becomes rich and powerful; the cultivators eat their half share day by day and so become poor and hungry, without means of appeal. . . .

Alas, the poor cultivate and yet are not free from hunger. The rich sit with full stomachs and amuse themselves and yet are not free from resentment over taxes. All these evils arise from the abolition of the well-fields. If the well-fields were restored, the poor would have land to till, and not having to share their grain and rice with the rich, they would be free from hunger. The rich, not being allowed to hold so much land, could not hold down the poor. Under these circumstances those who did not till would not be able to get food. Besides, having the whole product of the land out of which to pay their taxes to the local magistrate, they would not be resentful. For this reason all the scholars of the empire outdo themselves calling for the restoration of the well-fields. And some people say: "If the land of the rich were taken away and given to those who own no land, the rich would not acquiesce in it, and this would lead to rebellion. After such a great cataclysm, when the people were decimated and vast lands lay unused, it would be propitious for instituting the well-field system all at once. When Emperor Kao of Han overthrew the Ch'in dynasty or when Emperor Kuang-wu succeeded the Former Han, it could have been done and yet was not. This is indeed to be regretted!"

I do not agree with any of this. Now even if all the rich people offered to turn their lands over to the public, asking that they be turned into well-fields, it still could not be done. Why?

Su Hsün proceeds to describe in detail the system of land organization, irrigation, and local administration associated with the well-field system as it is set forth in the *Rites of Chou*. He concludes that such an intricate system could never be reproduced under existing conditions.

When the well-fields are established, [a corresponding system of] ditches and canals would have to be provided. . . . This could not be done without filling up all the ravines and valleys, leveling the hills and mountains, destroying the graves, tearing down the houses, removing the cities, and changing the boundaries of the land. Even if it were possible to get possession of all the plains and vast wildernesses and then lay them out according to plan, still we would have to drive all the people of the empire, exhaust all the grain of the empire, and devote all our energy to this alone for several hundred years, without attending to anything else, if we were ever to see all the land of the empire turned into well-fields and provided with ditches and canals. Then it would be necessary to build houses within the well-fields for the people to settle down and live in peace. Alas, this is out of the question. By the time the well-fields were established, the people would have died and their bones would have rotted away. . . .

Although the well-field [system] cannot be put into effect, nevertheless, it actually would offer certain advantages in the present situation. Now if there were something approximating the well-field [system], which could be adopted, we might still be able to relieve the distress of the people.

At this point Su reviews the proposals made in the Han dynasty for a direct limitation of land ownership, and the reasons for their failure.

I want to limit somewhat the amount of land which one is allowed to hold, and yet not restrict immediately those whose land is already in excess of my limit, but only make it so that future generations would not try to occupy land beyond that limit. In short, either the descendants of the rich would be unable to preserve their holdings after several generations and would become poor, while the land held in excess of my limit would be dispersed and come into the possession of others; or else as the descendants of the rich came along they would divide up the land into several portions. In this way, the land occupied by the rich would decrease and the surplus land would increase. With surplus land in abundance, the poor would find it easy to acquire land as a basis for their family livelihood. They would not have to render service to others, but each would reap the full fruit of the land himself. Not having to share his produce with others, he would be pleased to contribute taxes to the government. Now just by sitting at court and promulgating the order throughout the empire, without frightening the people, without mobilizing the public, without adopting the well-field system, still all the advantages of the well-fields would be obtained. Even with the well-fields of the Chou, how could we hope to do better than this?

THE NEW LAWS OF WANG AN-SHIH

The reform movement which marked time after Fan Chung-yen's fall from power reached its greatest heights during the reign of the Emperor Shen-tsung (r. 1068–1085) under the leadership of Wang An-shih (1021–1086), one of China's most celebrated statesmen. With the sympathetic understanding and patient support of Shen-tsung, who was widely acclaimed for his conscientiousness as a ruler, Wang embarked on a most ambitious and systematic program of reform, designed to remedy the evils already described in the memorials and essays of his Confucian contemporaries. A brilliant scholar and vigorous administrator, Wang had close ties both officially and intellectually with the leading figures in the Confucian revival, and burned with a desire to achieve that restoration of the ancient order which they believed to be the only solution to China's ills. This came out in Wang's first interview with the emperor in 1068, when the latter asked what Wang thought of the famous founder of the T'ang dynasty as a model for later rulers. Wang replied: "Your Majesty should take [the sage-kings] Yao and Shun as your standard. The principles of Yao and Shun are very easy to put into practice. It is only because scholars of recent times do not really understand them, that they think such standards of government are unattainable."

Wang, as a matter of fact, had no thought of completely revamping Chinese society and restoring the institutions described in the classical texts. As the first of the readings to follow makes clear, his aim was rather to adapt the general principles embodied in those institutions to his own situation, making due allowance for vastly changed circumstances. Furthermore, from the manner in which he set about his reforms, we can see that he was no social revolutionary or starry idealist, but rather a practical politician whose first concern was always the interests of the Chinese state and only secondarily the welfare of the Chinese people. Thus his initial reforms were aimed at the reorganization of state finances, with a view to achieving greater economy and budgetary efficiency. And virtually all of the important economic changes later effected by Wang were proposed by a special "brain-trust" assigned to the task of fiscal reorganization, with state revenue very much in the forefront of their minds.

Nevertheless it is to the credit of Wang that he saw how in the long run (which few Chinese statesmen or emperors were willing to consider), the fiscal interests of the state were bound up with the general economic welfare of the people, and both with the promotion of a dynamic and expanding economy. Therefore, even though he did nothing so drastic as the reorganization of Chinese agriculture into well-fields, his approach was bold and visionary in the sense that he saw the problem of reform as reaching into virtually all spheres of Chinese life; and though few of his measures were new or highly original, his program taken as a whole was broader in scope and more diversified in character than anything attempted before or after (until Communist rule).

The first of Wang's "new laws" aimed at achieving greater flexibility and economy in the transportation of tax grain or tribute in kind to the capital. His basic principle was that officials be enabled to resell the goods collected and use funds at their disposal to procure at the most convenient time and place (and with the least transportation cost) the goods required by the government. This was later expanded greatly into a vast state marketing operation which extended to all basic commodities the type of price control and storage system traditionally associated with the "ever-normal granary." In this way the state's assumption of a much more active role in the economy was justified by the common interest of the state and the people in reducing the cost of government and stabilizing prices. So too with the second of Wang's measures, a system of crop loans to provide peasants in the spring with necessary seed, implements, etc., which would be repaid at harvest time. It was designed, on the one hand, to help the peasant stay out of the clutches of usurers at a difficult time of the year, while on the other, it brought revenue to the government through the interest paid on the loans.

Outside the sphere which would be recognized as pertaining to government finance, there were two other activities of the state which vitally affected both the physical well-being of the people and the health of the state. They had to do with the time-honored "right" or "power" of the government to demand from the people both labor service and military service. In the Sung Chinese armies were maintained on a professional basis, with tax revenues providing the means for hiring constabulary and soldiery. To eliminate the great expense of such mercenaries, who were idle much of the time, Wang introduced a militia system whereby each locality would be organized for self-defense and self-policing, with families grouped pyramidally in units of ten, a hundred, and a thousand, taking a regular turn at providing such able-bodied service. Not only did this represent a system of collective security in each locality, but one of collective responsibility as well, the various members of each group being held mutually responsible for the misconduct of any individual. Curiously enough, to achieve the same ends of economy and efficiency in the handling of local government services, Wang used precisely the reverse method. That is, the minor functions of government, which were sometimes menial and often burdensome, had always been performed on an unpaid, draft basis. Wang considered this a system which weighed too heavily on the individuals and households to whom the assignment fell. In place of the draft services, which were essentially a labor tax, he therefore substituted a money tax graduated to "soak the rich," from the proceeds of which men were hired to perform these official services.

The same principle of equalization was applied to the land tax through a new system of land registration and assessment, which was designed to accomplish the same aim as the legendary "well-field" system without any actual redistribution of land or property. This was known as the "square-fields" system, because all taxable land was divided up into units one *li* square, upon which the taxes were graduated in accordance with the value of the land, so that those with less productive land paid proportionately less.

The foregoing examples will serve to indicate the general character and scope of the New Laws having an economic importance. In addition, Wang embarked on a fundamental overhauling of the civil service examination system, which in the early Sung had come in for much criticism from Confucianists who deplored the premium it placed on literary style and memorization of the Classics at the expense of a genuine understanding of Confucian principles and their practical application. In place of the traditional forms of composition and memory testing, Wang substituted an essay on the "general meaning" of the Classics. This raised problems, however, as to how traditional standards of objectivity and impartiality could be maintained in judging the performance of candidates with respect to the handling of ideas and interpretation. Wang solved this in his own way by promulgating a standard essay form and a

complete revision of the Classics with modernized commentary to serve
as an authoritative guide for both candidates and judges.

Almost immediately controversy developed over Wang's interpretations
of the Classics, which were closely bound up with his whole political
philosophy and governmental program. Whether or not Wang's policies
were truly in keeping with the basic teachings of the Confucian tradition
is a question which has been debated right down to modern times. There
can be no doubt that the specific measures he adopted bore a strong resemblance to Legalist-inspired institutions which had vastly augmented
the economic power of the state during the reign of Emperor Wu of
Han. It is equally evident, however, that the benevolent paternalism
ascribed by Confucianists to the ancient sage-kings could be easily construed, as it was by Wang, to justify a vigorous exercise of state power
to promote the general welfare. Wang's memorials are replete with classical precedents for each of the actions he proposes to take. Perhaps nowhere is the close tie between Wang's reforms and classical authority
better illustrated than in his use of the *Rites of Chou,* which he revised
under the title *New Interpretation of the Institutes of Chou (Chou-kuan
hsin-i).* For this classical text Wang made the strongest claims in his
personal preface:

When moral principles are applied to the affairs of government . . . the form
they take and the use they are put to depend upon laws, but their promotion
and execution depend upon individuals. In the worthiness of its individual
officials to discharge the duties of office, and in the effectiveness with which its
institutions administered the law, no dynasty has surpassed the early Chou.
Likewise, in the suitability of its laws for perpetuation in later ages, and in
the expression given them in literary form, no book is so perfect as the *Institutes of Chou (Chou-kuan).*

So effectively did Wang use this book to justify his reforms that his
edition of it became one of the most influential and controversial books in
all Chinese literature. To deny Wang the support he derived from it, his
opponents alleged that the *Institutes of Chou* was itself a comparatively
recent forgery. In later times writers commonly attributed the fall of the
Northern Sung dynasty to Wang's adoption of this text as a political
guide.

Thus Wang's espousal of the *Institutes of Chou* represents the culmination in the political sphere of the long debate in Confucian circles over the applicability of classical institutions, as described in the books of Rites, to conditions obtaining in the Sung dynasty. At the same time, Wang's effort to reinterpret these texts—to discard the Han and T'ang commentaries—and to use a modernized version as the basis for a reformed civil service examination system, stressing the general meaning of the Classics instead of a literal knowledge of them, is a concrete expression of the Confucian urge to break with the lifeless pedantry of the Han and T'ang dynasties, both in the field of classical scholarship and in the form of civil service examinations, in order to return to the essential purity of the classic order. In this respect Wang stands together with the Ch'eng brothers, Chu Hsi, and a host of other Sung scholars in their determination to set aside accepted interpretations and find new meaning in their Confucian inheritance, just as subsequent scholars of a creative or scientific temper were some day to reject the Sung interpretations and press anew their inquiry into the meaning and validity of the Classics.

WANG AN-SHIH
Memorial to the Emperor Jen-tsung

This document, sometimes called the *Ten Thousand Word Memorial,* is famous as Wang's first important declaration of his political views. Those who look to it for a manifesto outlining his later program will be disappointed, for aside from his general philosophy it deals only with the problem of recruiting able officials. Those who recognize, however, that in China any reformer had to wrestle first of all with the intractable bureaucracy, will appreciate why Wang, like many other Sung reformers, should have given first priority to this question. Subsequent readings, including the protests of Wang's critics, will show that in the final analysis this remained the most crucial issue.

Note how Wang strikes a balance between the importance of laws and institutions (the Legalist tendency) and the Confucian view that good government depends ultimately on men of character and ability, unhampered by legalistic restrictions. Observe also his final insistence that the accomplishment of reform may justify coercive measures.

[From *Lin-ch'uan hsien-sheng wen-chi,* SPTK ed., 39:1a–19a]

Your servant observes that Your Majesty possesses the virtues of reverence and frugality, and is endowed with wisdom and sagacity. Rising early in the morning and retiring late in the evening, Your Majesty does not relax for even a single day. Neither music, beautiful women, dogs, horses, sightseeing, nor any of the other objects of pleasure distract or becloud your intelligence in the least. Your humanity toward men and love of all creatures pervades the land. Moreover, Your Majesty selects those whom the people of the empire would wish to have assisting Your Majesty, entrusts to them the affairs of state, and does not vacillate in the face of [opposition from] slanderous, wicked, traitorous, and cunning officials. Even the solicitude of the Two Emperors and Three Kings did not surpass this. We should expect, therefore, that the needs of every household and man would be filled and that the empire would enjoy a state of perfect order. And yet this result has not been attained. Within the empire the security of the state is a cause for some anxiety, and on our borders there is the constant threat of the barbarians. Day by day the resources of the nation become more depleted and exhausted, while the moral tone and habits of life among the people daily deteriorate. On all sides officials who have the interests of the nation at heart are fearful that the peace of the empire may not last. What is the reason for this?

The cause of the distress is that we ignore the law. Now the government is strict in enforcing the law, and its statutes are complete to the last detail. Why then does your servant consider that there is an absence of law? It is because most of the present body of law does not accord with the government of the ancient kings. Mencius said: "There are now princes who have benevolent hearts and a reputation for benevolence, while yet the people do not receive any benefits from them, nor will they leave any example to future ages—all because they do not put into practice the ways of the ancient kings" [IV A:1]. The application of what Mencius said to our own failure in the present is obvious.

Now our own age is far removed from that of the ancient kings, and the changes and circumstances with which we are confronted are not the same. Even the most ignorant can see that it would be difficult to put into practice every single item in the government of the ancient kings. But when your servant says that our present failures arise from the fact that we do not adopt the governmental system of the ancient kings, he is merely suggesting that we should follow their general intent. Now the Two Emperors were separated from the Three Kings by more than a thousand years. There were periods of order and disorder, and there were periods of prosperity and decay. Each of them likewise encountered dif-

ferent changes and faced different circumstances, and each differed also
in the way they set up their government. Yet they never differed as to
their underlying aims in the government of the empire, the state and the
family, nor in their sense of the relative importance and priority of things
[as set forth in the *Great Learning, I*]. Therefore, your servant contends
that we should follow only their general intent. If we follow their intent,
then the changes and reforms introduced by us would not startle the
ears and shock the eyes of the people, nor cause them to murmur. And
yet our government would be in accord with that of the ancient kings.
[1a–2a]

The most urgent need of the present time is to secure capable men. Only
when we can produce a large number of capable men in the empire, will
it be possible to select a sufficient number of persons qualified to serve in
the government. And only when we get capable men in the government,
will there be no difficulty in assessing what may be done, in view of the
time and circumstances, and in consideration of the human distress which
may be occasioned, gradually to change the decadent laws of the empire
in order to approach the ideas of the ancient kings. The empire today is
the same as the empire of the ancient kings. There were numerous capable
men in their times. Why is there a dearth of such men today? It is because,
as has been said, we do not train and cultivate men in the proper way.
[3a]

In ancient times, the Son of Heaven and feudal lords had schools ranging from the capital down to the districts and villages. Officers of instruction were widely appointed, but selected with the greatest care. The affairs
of the court, rites and music, punishment and laws were all subjects
which found a place in the schools. What the students observed and
learned were the sayings, the virtuous acts, and the ideas underlying the
government of the empire and the states. Men not qualified to govern the
empire and the states would not be given an education, while those who
could be so used in government never failed to receive an education. This
is the way to conduct the training of men. [4a]

What is the way to select officials? The ancient kings selected men
only from the local villages and through the local schools. The people
were asked to recommend those they considered virtuous and able, sending up their nominations to the court, which investigated each one. Only
if the men recommended proved truly virtuous and able, would they

be appointed to official posts commensurate with their individual virtue
and ability. Investigation of them did not mean that a ruler relied only
upon his own keenness of sight and hearing or that he took the word
of one man alone. If they wanted to ascertain a man's virtue, they inquired into his conduct; if they wanted to ascertain his ability, they inquired into his utterances. Having inquired into his actions and utterances, they then tested him in government affairs. What was meant by
"investigation" was just that—to test them in government affairs. Yao
employed Shun in exactly this way. How much the more must they
have done this in the employment of lesser personages than Shun? Taking into consideration the great expanse of the nine provinces, the vast
distances within the four seas, and the innumerable lesser posts of administration to be filled, it is obvious that a large number of scholar-
officials are needed. It is not possible for the ruler to investigate each
case personally, nor can he entrust this matter to any other individual,
expecting that in a day or two he could inquire into and test their conduct and abilities and recommend their employment or dismissal. When
we have investigated those whose conduct and ability are of the highest,
and have appointed them to high office, we should ask them in turn to
select men of the same type, try them out for a time and test them, and
then make recommendations to the ruler, whereupon ranks and salaries
would be granted to them. This is the way to conduct the selection of
officials. [5a–b]

[In ancient times] officials were selected with great care, appointed to
posts which suited their qualifications, and kept in office for a reasonable length of time. And once employed, they were given sufficient authority for the discharge of their duties. They were not hampered and
bound by one regulation or another, but were allowed to carry out their
own ideas. It was by this method that Yao and Shun regulated the hundred offices of government and inspired the various officials. [6a–b]

Today, although we have schools in each prefecture and district, they
amount to no more than school buildings. There are no officers of instruction and guidance; nothing is done to train and develop human talent.
Only in the Imperial Academy are officers of instruction and guidance
to be found, and even they are not selected with care. The affairs of the
court, rites, music, punishment, and correction have no place in the
schools, and the students pay no attention to them, considering that rites

and music, punishment and correction are the business of officials, not something they ought to know about. What is taught to the students consists merely of textual exegesis [of the Classics].

That, however, was not the way men were taught in ancient times. In recent years, teaching has been based on the essays required for the civil service examinations, but this kind of essay cannot be learned without resorting to extensive memorization and strenuous study, upon which students must spend their efforts the whole day long. Such proficiency as they attain is at best of no use in the government of the empire, and at most the empire can make no use of them. Therefore, even if students remained in school until their hair turned gray, and spent their efforts the whole day long pursuing the instruction given them, when finally appointed to office, they would not have even the faintest idea of what to do. [6b–7a]

Scholars today think that civil and military affairs are two different things. [They say:] "I know only how to handle civil affairs." The duty of guarding the frontiers and the palace is left to common soldiers, who are usually corrupt, ruthless, and wholly unreliable. Were their ability and behavior such that they could maintain themselves in their own villages, they would never have had to leave their kith and kin to enlist in the army. [8a] [10]

[Of old] . . . those scholars who had learned the way of the ancient kings and whose behavior and character had won the approval of their village communities, were the ones entrusted with the duty of guarding the frontiers and the palace in accordance with their respective abilities —this is the way in which the rulers of ancient times entrusted weapons to men and secured themselves from all danger, both within and without. Today this most important responsibility in the empire, which the ruler should assign only to men selected with great care, is given to those corrupt, ruthless, and unreliable men whose ability and behavior are not such that they can maintain themselves in their local villages. That is why we are always anxious over the security of our frontiers and fearful that the imperial guards may not be depended upon to keep the peace. Indeed, who today is unaware of the fact that the frontier guards and imperial guards cannot be depended on to keep the peace? But since

___

[10] At this time the military establishment of the Sung was separate from the civil administration, and the armies consisted of hired professionals, not militia or draftees.

the educated men of the land regard the carrying of weapons as a disgrace, and since none of them is able to ride, shoot, or has any familiarity with military maneuvers, who is there to take up this responsibility but the hired soldiery? As long as military training is not given, and men of a higher type are not selected for military service, there is no wonder that scholars regard the carrying of weapons as a disgrace, and that none of them is able to ride, or shoot, or has any familiarity with military maneuvers. This is because education is not conducted in the proper way. [8a–9b]

In the present system for electing officials, those who memorize assiduously, recite extensively, and have some knowledge of literary composition, are called "splendid talents of extraordinary accomplishment" or "men of virtue, wise, square, and upright." These are the categories from which the ministers of state are chosen. Those whose memories are not so strongly developed and cannot recite so extensively, yet have some knowledge of literary composition and have also studied poetry in the *shih* and *fu* forms, are called "advanced scholars" (*chin-shih*). The highest of these are also selected as the ministers of state. It can be seen without any question that the skills and knowledge acquired by men in these two categories do not fit them to serve as ministers. And yet those who discuss such matters today hold to the opinion that we have used this method for a long time to select our officials, that through it capable ministers have often been obtained, and that it is not necessary to follow the ancient system of selection in order to obtain scholars. This is defective reasoning. [11b]

In addition, candidates are examined in such fields as: the Nine Classics, the Five Classics, Specialization [in one Classic], and the Study of Law. The court has already become concerned over the uselessness of this type of knowledge, and has stressed the need for an understanding of general principles [as set forth in the Classics]. Nevertheless, those obtained by emphasizing general principles are no better qualified than under the old system. Now the court has also opened up another field of examination, "Understanding of the Classics," in order to promote those proficient in classical studies. However, when we consider the men selected through "Understanding of the Classics," it is still those who memorize, recite, and have some knowledge of literary composition who are able to pass the examination, while those who can apply them to the government of the empire are not always brought in through this kind of selection. [12b]

It has already been made clear that officials are not selected with care, employed in accordance with their competence, and kept in office long enough. But in addition, when entrusted with office, they are not given sufficient authority to fulfill their duties, but find their hands tied by this law or that regulation so that they are unable to carry out their own ideas. Yet your servant is convinced that most of those holding office are not of the right kind, so that if given authority, and not restrained by one regulation or another, they will let go and do whatever they please. Nevertheless, there has not been a single case in history, from ancient times to the present, which shows that it is possible to obtain good government merely by relying on the effectiveness of law, without regard to having the right man in power. On the other hand, there has not been a single case in history, from ancient times to the present, which shows that it is possible to obtain good government even with the right man in power, if he is bound by one regulation or another in such a way that he cannot carry out his ideas. [14a–b]

Your servant also observes that in former times when the court thought of doing something and introducing some reforms, the advantages and disadvantages were considered carefully at the beginning. But whenever some vulgar opportunist took a dislike to the reform and opposed it, the court stopped short and dared not carry it out. Now when a law is set up, it is not for any single individual to enjoy its benefits alone. Therefore, even though the government of the ancient kings was able to benefit all under Heaven, nevertheless, at times following a period of corrupt government, when many men sought for personal advantage, the task of setting up laws and institutions was not without difficulties. . . . Since it was difficult to set up laws and institutions and since the men seeking personal advantages were unwilling to accept these measures and comply with them, the ancients who intended to do something had to resort to punishment. Only then could their ideas be carried out. [17a]

Now the early kings, wishing to set up laws and institutions in order to change corrupt customs and obtain capable men, overcame their feeling of reluctance to mete out punishment, for they saw that there was no other way of carrying out their policy. [17b]

Memorial on the Crop Loans Measure

This memorial submitted to the Emperor Shen-tsung in 1069 calls for the extension to other parts of China of a system of crop loans already experimented with on a limited basis in Shensi province. For this purpose Wang proposes to draw upon the reserves of the government granaries, which he insists would still be able to fulfill their function of stabilizing agricultural prices and storing grain despite the diversion of funds for lending purposes. The memorial is somewhat vague in its wording, and the precise details of the operation of this system are unclear, perhaps because Wang assumed a familiarity with the existing system on the part of those he addressed.

[From *Sung shih*, 176:17b–18b]

In the second year of Hsi-ning [1069], the Commission to Coordinate Fiscal Administration presented a memorial as follows:

The cash and grain stored in the Ever-Normal and the Liberal-Charity granaries of the various circuits, counting roughly in strings of cash and bushels of grain, amount to more than 15,000,000. Their collection and distribution are not handled properly, however, and therefore we do not derive full benefit from them. Now we propose that the present amount of grain in storage should be sold at a price lower than the market price when the latter is high; and that when the market price is low, the grain in the market should be purchased at a rate higher than the market price. We also propose that our reserves be made interchangeable with the proceeds of the land tax and the cash and grain held by the Fiscal Intendants, so that conversion of cash and grain may be permitted whenever convenient.

With the cash at hand, we propose to follow the example set by the crop loan system in Shensi province. Farmers desirous of borrowing money before the harvest should be granted loans, to be repaid at the same time as they pay their tax, half with the summer payment and half with the autumn payment.[11] They are free to repay either in kind or in cash, should they prefer to do so if the price of grain is high at the time of repayment. In the event disaster strikes, they should be allowed to defer payment until the date when the next harvest payment would be due. In this way not only would we be prepared to meet the distress

[11] Interest of 2 percent per month (24 percent per annum) was to be charged for the loans. Private money lenders generally charged more.

of famine, but, since the people would receive loans from the government, it would be impossible for the monopolistic houses [12] to exploit the gap between harvests by charging interest at twice the normal rate.

Under the system of Ever-Normal and Liberal-Charity granaries, it has been the practice to keep grain in storage and sell it only when the harvest is poor and the price of grain is high. Those who benefit from this are only the idle people in the cities.

Now we propose to survey the situation in regard to surplusses and shortages in each circuit as a whole, to sell when grain is dear and buy when it is cheap, in order to increase the accumulation in government storage and to stabilize the prices of commodities. This will make it possible for the farmers to go ahead with their work at the proper season, while the monopolists will no longer be able to take advantage of their temporary stringency. All this is proposed in the interests of the people, and the government derives no advantage therefrom. Moreover, it accords with the idea of the ancient kings who bestowed blessings upon all impartially and promoted whatever was of benefit by way of encouraging the cultivation and accumulation of grain.

This proposal was adopted by the emperor, and put into effect first in the limited areas of Hopei, Ching-tung, and Huai-nan, as suggested by the Commission to Coordinate Fiscal Administration. The results obtained were later considered to justify extension of the system to other areas.

CH'ENG HAO

Remonstrance Against the New Laws

This memorial by Ch'eng Hao, originally a supporter of Wang An-shih, is directed against the crop loan system primarily. Ch'eng contends that the system is generally unpopular and that force is required to compel repayment. It is difficult to determine, however, just what segment of the populace Ch'eng presumes to speak for—whether the peasantry as a whole or only an influential, articulate minority. There is no evidence of any widespread discontent or violence in opposition to Wang, but it is possible that the administration of the system was quite uneven and that certain areas may have been adversely affected. Though the interest charges were less than those of private money lenders, at 20–24 percent per annum they were substantial enough so

[12] Refers here to usurers who seek to monopolize wealth in the form of money, goods or land, but not to industrial monopolists in the modern sense.

that an extensive program might be turned by venal officials into a highly lucrative business.

[From *Ming-tao wen-chi*, SPPY ed., 2:4b–5a]

Recently, your servant has presented repeated memorials asking for the abolition of the advancing of crop loans at interest [13] and abolition of the [Economic] Administrators.[14] Day and night [your servant] waits expectantly, and yet Your Majesty still has not acted upon them. . . .

Now whether the state is secure or insecure depends upon the feelings of the people; whether there is order or disorder hinges upon how things are handled at the start. If great numbers of people are opposed, then whatever one may say, one will not be believed; but if all the people are of one accord, then whatever one does will certainly succeed. It is impossible to bend by force and win by words alone. And what we have heard proposed in recent days only makes matters worse. Your servant reads the memorials of the Commission to Coordinate Fiscal Administration which dispute memorials presented by other high officials and make accusations against officials who have not carried out its orders. This only intensifies the feeling of alarm both inside and outside the court. It is to uphold one particular viewpoint and suppress the public expression of other views; it is to lose the support of the people at the start, all on account of a minor matter. Weighing the relative importance of things, this would hardly seem the proper thing to do.

Your servant considers that Your Majesty already sees clearly into the heart of the matter and fully realizes what is right and what wrong. The mind of Your Majesty does not hesitate to make a change; it is only the minister in charge of the government who still persists in his obstinacy. Thus the people's feelings are greatly agitated and public opinion becomes more clamorous. If one insists on carrying these policies out, certain failure awaits them in the end. [Your servant] hopes that Your Majesty will resolutely exercise your divine judgment and consider in advance what success and failure hinge upon. Rather than pursue one mistaken policy at the expense of a hundred other undertakings, would it not be better to bestow a grand favor and reassure the people's minds by doing away with the disturbances caused by those sent out

---

[13] The text is vague here, referring only to "advance allocations."

[14] Administering the various economic activities of the government, such as the ever-normal granaries, the salt and iron monopolies, etc.

to enforce these decrees, and by manifesting your humanity to the extent of abolishing the interest charged on crop loans? Moreover, when the system of buying and selling grain is put back into effect,[15] our accumulated reserve will expand. The government will then be without fault in its administration and public opinion will have no cause to be aroused. I humbly beg Your Majesty to consider the memorials presented by your servant and act upon them. It would be a most fortunate thing for the whole empire.

WANG AN-SHIH
In Defense of Five Major Policies

In this memorial Wang reaffirms the correctness of his principal policies, while conceding that in three cases much will depend on the effectiveness with which the officials concerned administer them.

[From *Lin-ch'uan hsien-sheng wen-chi*, SPTK ed., 41:4a–5a]

During the five years that Your Majesty has been on the throne, a great number of changes and reforms have been proposed. Many of them have been set forth in documents, enacted into law, and have produced great benefits. Yet among these measures there are five of the greatest importance, the results of which will only be felt in the course of time and which, nevertheless, have already occasioned a great deal of discussion and debate: 1) the pacification of the Jung [Tangut] barbarians; 2) the crop loans; 3) the local service exemption; 4) the collective security [militia]; 5) the marketing controls.

Now the region of Ching-t'ang and the T'iao River [in the northwest] extends over 3,000 *li* and the Jung tribes number 200,000 people. They have surrendered their territories and become submissive subjects of the empire. Thus our policy of pacifying the Jung barbarians has proved successful.

In former times the poor people paid interest on loans obtained from powerful persons. Now the poor get loans from the government at a lower rate of interest, and the people are thereby saved from poverty. Thus our policy on agricultural loans has worked in practice.

It is only with regard to the service exemption, the militia, and the

---

[15] That is, when the reserves of the ever-normal granaries are used for price-support operations rather than being committed to the lending program.

marketing controls that a question exists as to whether great benefit or harm may be done. If we are able to secure the right type of man to administer these acts, great benefits will be obtained, but if they are administered by the wrong type of man, great harm will be done. Again, if we try to enforce them gradually, great benefits will be obtained, but if they are carried out in too great haste, great harm will be done.

The Commentary says: "Things not modeled after the ancient system have never been known to last for a generation." Of these three measures mentioned above, it may be said that they are all modeled after the ancient system. However, one can put the ancient system into practice only when he understands the Way of the ancients. This is what your servant means about great advantages and disadvantages.

The service exemption system is derived from the *Institutes of Chou* [i.e., the *Rites of Chou*] in which the *fu, shih, hsü,* and *tu* are mentioned. They are what the King's System [section of the *Book of Rites*] describes as "the common people who render services to the government."

However, the people of the nine provinces vary in wealth and the customs of the various regions are not the same. The classifications used in the government registration [for local service] are not satisfactory for all. Now we want to change it forthwith, having officials examine every household so that they will be assessed on an equitable basis, and requiring the people to pay for the hiring of men for all kinds of local services, so that the farmers can be released and return to their farms. If, however, we fail to secure the right kind of person for the administration of this measure, the classification of people into five grades [in proportion to their financial status] is bound to be unfair, and the hiring of men to perform services would not be executed in an equitable manner.

The militia act had its origin in the *ch'iu chia* [16] system of the Three Dynasties which was adopted by Kuan Chung in Ch'i, Tzu-ch'an in Cheng, and Lord Shang in Ch'in; and was proposed by Chung Chang-t'ung to the Han ruler. This is not just a recent innovation. However, for hundreds of thousands of years the people of the empire have been free to live together or to disperse and go in all directions as they chose, not subject to any restriction. Now we want to change it forthwith, or-

[16] A system under which units of 128 families each provided men and weapons for military service.

ganizing the people into units of fives and tens, and attaching one village to another. Unlawful activities would thus be kept under observation while benevolence would be manifested to all; the soldiers would be housed in their own homes and ready for any use. If, however, we fail to secure the right kind of person to administer this measure, the people will be alarmed by summonses and frightened by mobilization, and thus the people's confidence will be lost.

The marketing controls originated with the Supervision of the Market in the Chou dynasty and the Price Stabilization and Equalization System of the Han dynasty. Now with a fund of 1,000,000 cash we regulate the prices of commodities in order to facilitate the exchange of goods and also lend the people money on which they must pay the government an interest of several tens of thousands of cash annually. However, we are aware of the fact that commodities and money do not circulate very well in the empire. It is feared that officials eager for personal fame and rewards will seek to achieve speedy results within a year's time, and thus the system will be subverted.

Therefore, your servant considers that the above three measures, if administered by the right kind of person and put into effect with due deliberation, will bring great benefits; whereas, if administered by the wrong men and put into effect with too great haste, they may do great harm.

Thus, if we succeed in carrying out the Service Exemption Law, the seasonal agricultural work of the farmers will not be disturbed and the manpower requirements [of the state] will be borne equally by the people. If the Militia Law is carried out, the disturbances caused by bandits will be brought to an end and our military power will be strengthened. If we succeed in carrying out the Marketing Control Law, goods and money will be circulated and the financial needs of the state will be met.

SU SHIH

Memorial to Emperor Shen-tsung on the New Laws of Wang An-shih

Su Shih (1037–1101), also known by his pen-name Su Tung-p'o, was one of two famous sons of a famous father, Su Hsün. An outstanding poet, calligra-

pher, and painter as well as a public official, Su Shih was initially sympathetic
to the aims of Wang An-shih, but was subsequently driven from court because of his outspoken opposition to the New Laws. In this eloquent memorial, which suggests something of his famous prose style, Su criticizes especially
the new labor service, crop loan, and state marketing systems. Note his complaint that Wang's original proposal concerning the marketing system seemed
to have been deliberately vague and seemingly innocuous, as if to hide Wang's
real intentions.

[From *Ching chin Tung-p'o wen-chi shih-lüeh,* SPTK ed., 24:1a ff.]

What a ruler has to rely upon is only the hearts of men. Men's hearts
are to the ruler what roots are to a tree, what oil is to a lamp, water to
fish, fields to a farmer, or money to a merchant.

Now Your Majesty knows that the hearts of the people are not happy.
Men, whether within the court or outside, whether worthy or unworthy,
all say that from the founding of the dynasty to the present, the fiscal
administration of the empire has been entrusted solely to the commissioner, assistant commissioners, and the supervisors of the Finance Commission, who for more than one hundred years have left no matter untended. Now, for no cause, another commission has been set up in the
name of "Coordinating the Policies of the Three Fiscal Offices." [17] Six
or seven young men are made to discuss fiscal policies day and night
within the bureau, while more than forty aides are sent out to explore
the situation. The vast scale of their initial operations has made people
frightened and suspicious; the strangeness of the new laws adopted has
made officials fearful and puzzled. Worthy men seek for an explanation,
and failing to get any, cannot relieve their anxiety; small men simply
conjecture as to what is going on at court and give voice to slander,
saying that Your Majesty, as the master of 100,000 chariots [i.e., of a
large empire and army] is interested in personal profit, and the official
in charge of the government administration, as the chancellor of the
Son of Heaven, is concerned with controlling wealth. Business is at a
standstill and the prices of goods have been rising. From places as near
as the Huai River region to places as far as Szechwan, hundreds of mouths
are talking and hundreds of views are expressed. Some say that the main
store in the capital [a sarcastic reference to the central government and
its business activities] is considering the establishment of superintend-

[17] The Office of Salt and Iron [Monopolies], the Office of Funds [Disbursements], and
the Office of the Census [Revenue].

encies, that there is going to be a prohibition on [private production of] wine in the mountain wilds of Kweichow, that monks and nuns in permanent residence [at monasteries or nunneries] are to be arrested, and that the salaries of officials and soldiers are to be reduced. Statements like these are countless. And it is even said that the government intends to restore the punishment of mutilation. [3b–4a]

Now the Commission to Coordinate Fiscal Administration has the reputation of seeking for profit, while the six or seven young men and their forty or more aides are instruments for the pursuit of profit. . . . The man who plunges into the forest with a pack of hunting dogs and then protests, "I am not hunting," would do better to get rid of the hunting dogs and then the animals will not be so frightened. The man who takes out fishing nets and heads for the water, but then protests, "I am not going fishing," would do better to get rid of the fish nets and then men would believe him. Therefore your servant considers that in order to expunge the slander, to call forth harmonious feelings, to restore public confidence, and put the nation at rest, nothing better could be done than to abolish the Commission to Coordinate Fiscal Policies. The purpose of Your Majesty in establishing this office was but to promote advantages [or profits] and eliminate disadvantages. So if abolishing it does not promote advantages and eliminate disadvantages, then it should not be abolished; but if abolishing it makes all in the empire happy and puts their hearts at peace, then there is certainly nothing wrong with what promotes such advantages while removing disadvantages. Why, then, should it not be abolished? [4b]

Since ancient times men drafted from the households in each district have always had to be used for local services. It is just the same as the five grains always having to be used for food, hemp having to be used for clothing, boats having to be used for crossing rivers, or bullocks and horses having to be used for traveling on land. Although sometimes other things have been used instead, still in the long run this could not be made a regular practice throughout the empire. Now some people have heard that in the region of Chekiang and Kiangsu, a few prefectures hire men to perform these services, and they want to extend this practice throughout the empire. This is like seeing the dates and chestnuts of Peking and Shansi, or the taro root of Szechwan, and then advocating that the five grains be done away with. How could that be made feasible? Besides, they want the proceeds from government factories to be used for the hiring of public storage and transport officers.[18] Although they are expected to render long-term service, they receive meager payment for their labors. Since they receive so little for such long service, from now on they may be expected gradually to fall away and go elsewhere. How seriously this will affect the whole basis and functioning of local governments can well be imagined! [7b–8a]

Although in recent years, households in the rural districts have been allowed to hire men [to perform these services], nevertheless, if these hired men ran away, the households still had the responsibility [of replacing them]. Now in addition to the Twice-A-Year Tax, another tax item has been introduced called the labor charge, which pays for the government's hiring of men. Thus the government has taken upon itself the responsibility for the hiring of men. Since Yang Yen in the T'ang dynasty abolished the system of [land] taxes in grain, labor taxes [on able-bodied men], and the cloth exaction [on households], and replaced it with the Twice-A-Year Tax, the sum of all taxes collected in the fourteenth year of Ta-li [779] was used as the basis for determining the rate of the Twice-A-Year Tax. Thus the land, labor, and cloth taxes were all combined in the Twice-A-Year Tax. Yet now, while the Twice-A-Year Tax is kept as before, how can a labor tax again be demanded? When a sage introduces a law he always takes thousands of generations into consideration. How can we add another item to the regular taxes? [8b–9a]

Households of which a female is head and those with only a single male are the most unfortunate of all under Heaven. The first concern of the ancient kings was to show them compassion; and yet now the first concern of Your Majesty is to make them [pay for] local services. These are the households in which the family line will be discontinued when its present members die or those in which the only male is still too young. If several years were allowed the latter, he would become an adult, render service, grow old and die, and have his property confiscated by the government [since there is no one to inherit it]. How can a ruler,

---

[18] *Ya-chien*—a type of local service involving responsibility for the storage and transportation of goods or property. Considered extremely burdensome, this responsibility was previously assigned to and rotated among the more well-to-do families, who often tried to evade it.

so rich as to possess all within the four seas, have the hardness of heart not to take pity on such persons? [9b]

There has long been a prohibition against the practice of crop loans. Now Your Majesty has inaugurated the system and made it a regular practice year after year. Although it is declared that there shall be no compulsion to make people take the loans, nevertheless after several generations, if there should be oppressive rulers and corrupt officials, can Your Majesty guarantee that there will be no compulsion? In the days ahead this system will be hated by all under Heaven and it will be recorded in the dynastic history that the crop-loan system began with Your Majesty. What a pity! Besides, when silk was bought in the Southeast, payment was originally supposed to be in cash, while in obtaining horse fodder from Shensi, cash was not allowed in commutation. Edicts were issued by the court and the officials usually enforced them. Nevertheless, salt is always accepted now in payment for silk and cash is allowed in commutation for fodder. From this we can see that the declaration against the use of compulsion in the taking of crop loans is also an empty formality. [10a]

Even if the regulations are strictly enforced and there is really no compulsion, those people and households who would willingly apply for it must be the poor and the families in need, for if they had any surplus of their own, why would they come and do business with the government? But when the [poor] people are whipped and pressed to the extreme, they will run away, and when they have run away, their debts to the government will be apportioned among their neighbors who are collectively responsible. Such a course can have no other outcome; logically it could not be otherwise.

Moreover, of all such measures the ever-normal granary may be considered the best. It is modest in what it seeks to preserve and yet far-reaching in its effects. Suppose a county of 10,000 households has only 1,000 bushels of grain in storage. When the price of grain is high, if the 1,000 bushels are put on the market, the prices of goods are kept stable. When the price of goods in the market is kept stable, there is a sufficiency of food in the land. There is no hoarding of grain by some while others beg for food, no pursuing and pressing by the headman of the village to make people pay back their loans. Now if the ever-normal granary is converted to a crop-loan fund, and one bushel of grain is lent to each household, then what will be done to relieve the hunger of all those besides the 1,000 households [so provided for]? Besides, there is always the fear that the government funds of the ever-normal granary will prove insufficient. If all the funds are used up to buy the grain, then none will be left for money lending; if the fund is held for lending purposes, then very little grain will be bought. Thus we see that the ever-normal granary and the crop-loan system are by nature incompatible. How much can we expect to achieve by it, if we destroy one for the accomplishment of the other? The government will incur a deficit and the people will incur harm. However much we may regret it later, what can be done then? [10b–11a]

During the time of Emperor Wu of Han, the financial resources of the nation were exhausted, and the proposal of the merchant, Sang Hung-yang, to buy commodities when prices were cheap and sell them when prices were dear was adopted. This was called Equal Distribution.[19] Thereupon business came to a standstill and banditry became widespread. This almost led to revolution. When Emperor Chao ascended the throne, scholars all rose up in opposition to the theory of [Sang]. Ho Kuang [the chief minister] heeded the desires of the people and granted their request that the system be abandoned. Then all under Heaven were reconciled to the throne and no further trouble arose. It is surprising to hear this kind of proposal raised again. When this law was first introduced, it sounded as if very little was involved. They said merely that goods bought cheaply here should be transferred elsewhere when prices were high, using supplies near at hand to ease scarcity afar. But offices and staffs have been set up all over, and a large amount of cash has been appropriated. The big and wealthy merchants have all become suspicious and dare not move. They believe that although it has not been openly declared that the government will engage in buying and selling, nevertheless, permission has been given to exchange commodities, and it has never been heard that the government engages in the exchange of goods without competing with the merchants for profit. The business of merchants is very complicated and is difficult to practice. When they buy, they give money in advance; when they sell, they collect the money afterward. Many are the means they use to supplement each other; intricate and involved are their dealings. By these means, their twofold

<hr>

[19] A state marketing system covering all principal commodities. See Chapter X.

profit is obtained. Now for the government to buy such and such a commodity, it must first set up offices and staffs, so that the expense for clerical and fiscal services is considerable at the outset. If not of good quality, an item will not be bought; if not paid for in cash, an item cannot be purchased. Therefore the price paid by the government must be higher than that paid by the people. And when the government sells goods, it will still suffer the disadvantages mentioned before. How can the government get the same profit as the merchant? The court has not taken these factors into consideration, and yet has appropriated 5,000,000 cash for this venture. Once the money is disbursed, I fear it cannot be collected again. Even should there be some slight gain from it, the loss in revenue from taxes on merchants will certainly be greater. [11a–12a]

The preservation or loss of a nation depends upon the depth or shallowness of its virtue, not upon its strength or weakness. The length or shortness of a dynasty depends upon the stoutness or flimsiness of its social customs, not upon its richness or poverty. If its moral virtue is truly deep and its social customs are truly stout, even though the country is poor and weak, its poverty and weakness will not affect its duration and existence. If its virtue is shallow and its social customs flimsy, even though the nation is rich and strong, this will not save it from coming to an early end. When a ruler knows this, he knows what is important and what is not important. Therefore the wise rulers of ancient times did not abandon virtue because the country was weak, nor did they permit social customs to suffer because the country was poor. [12b–13a]

SSU-MA KUANG

A Petition to Do Away With the Most Harmful of the New Laws

Ssu-ma Kuang (1019–1086) was one of the giants among the scholar-statesmen of the Confucian revival in the eleventh century. He had already had a long and distinguished career in high office when he left the government in 1070 out of opposition to Wang An-shih's policies, and devoted himself to writing his monumental general history of China. Following the death of Wang's patron, the Emperor Shen-tsung, Ssu-ma Kuang served briefly as prime minister before his own death, and was responsible for the abolition of many of Wang's reforms.

[From *Wen-kuo wen-cheng Ssu-ma kung wen-chi*, SPTK ed., 46:5b–9b, 47:9b]

Your servant sees that the late emperor was sagacious and intelligent, did his utmost to govern well, and sought to employ an able man to assist him in achieving peace and order. This man was entrusted with the administration of government. His advice was acted upon, and his plans were followed. Nothing could ever come between them. . . . [The late emperor] was indeed an extraordinary ruler, such as not every generation produces and even in a thousand years is rarely met with. Unfortunately the one in whom he placed his trust was a man who largely failed to understand the feelings of men and the principles of things, and who could not fulfill the expectations of his sage master. He was self-satisfied and self-opinionated, considering himself without equal among the men of the past and present. He did not know how to select what was best in the laws and institutions of the imperial ancestors and to bring together the happiest proposals put forth throughout the empire, so as to guide the imperial intelligence and assist in accomplishing the great task. Instead he often adulterated the traditional regulations with his own ideas, which he termed "The New Laws." Whatever this man wanted to do could neither be held up by the ruler nor changed by the people. Those who agreed with him were given his help in rising to the sky, while those who differed with him were thrown out and cast down into the ditch. All he wanted was to satisfy his own ambitions, without regard to the best interests of the nation.

Human inclinations being what they are, who does not love wealth and high rank, and who does not fear punishment and misfortune? Seeing how the wind blew and following with the current, the officials and gentry vied in proposing schemes, striving to be clever and unusual. They abandoned what was right and picked up what was wrong; they supported what was harmful and rejected what was beneficial. In name they loved the people; in fact they injured the people. In name they benefited the nation; in fact they did the nation harm. The crop loans, the local service exemption, the marketing controls, the credit and loan system, and other measures were introduced. They aimed at the accumulation of wealth and pressed the people mercilessly. The distress they caused still makes for difficulties today. Besides, there were frontier officers who played fast and loose hoping to exploit their luck. They spoke big and uttered barefaced lies, waged war unjustifiably and needlessly disturbed the barbarians on our borders. . . . They strewed the wastelands with the skeletons of so many hundreds of thousands of soldiers and abandoned hundreds of millions in weapons and goods in strange lands. Besides, officials who liked to create new schemes which they might take advantage of to advance themselves suggested setting up the collective security militia system (*pao-chia*), horse-raising system, and the horse-care system,[20] as a means of providing for the military establishment. They changed the regulations governing the tea, salt, iron, and other monopolies, and increased the taxes on family property, on [buildings] encroaching on the street,[21] on business, and so forth, in order to meet military expenses. The result was to cause the people of the nine provinces to lose their livelihood and suffer extreme distress, as if they had been cast into hot water and fire. All this happened because the great body of officials were so eager to advance themselves. They misled the late emperor, and saw to it that they themselves derived all the profit from these schemes while the emperor incurred all the resentment. This was not at all what the late emperor had originally intended. . . .

Now the evils of the New Laws are known to everyone in the empire, high or low, wise or ignorant. Thus when Your Majesty revised these laws to even a slight extent, all the people near and far congratulated each other. Yet there are still some measures which are harmful to the people and hurtful to the state, which have many disadvantages and no advantages, such as the collective security militia system, the local service exemption payment, and the general commanderies. These three matters are of immediate and urgent importance, and are the first of the things which should be abolished. Your servant is going to report on them in separate memorials, hoping that it may please your sage will to grant us an early decision and act upon them.

Ssu-ma Kuang presented three separate memorials requesting abolition of each of these measures and summarized his reasons in still another memorial as follows:

Your servant has already pointed out that training and inspection of the militia involves a great expenditure of labor and money for both

---

[20] These systems were designed to provide horses for the army after the old grazing lands had been occupied by hostile tribes. Under the horse-raising system (*hu-ma*) people bought horses which, when raised, were sold to the government. Under the horse-care system (*pao-ma*) the government provided the horses or the funds to buy them and the people were expected to take care of them for the militia. In either case horses that died had to be replaced at the individual's expense.

[21] A tax on roadside stalls, kiosks, etc.

the government and the people, and yet the militia is of no real use in war. To pay money in lieu of local services is easy on the rich and hard on the poor, who must contribute to the support of idlers and vagrants [paid to perform these services]. It results in the peasantry losing their property and being reduced to utter misery, without recourse or appeal. The general commanderies now have absolute control over the army administration, while local civil officials have no authority whatever and no means of coping with emergencies. [47:9b]

The best plan now is to select and keep those new laws which are of advantage to the people and of benefit to the state, while abolishing all those which are harmful to the people and hurtful to the state. This will let the people of the land know unmistakably that the court loves them with a paternal affection. Those officials who are oppressive will be bound to change and serve loyally. Those people who have been estranged and embittered are bound to change and give their support and approbation to the court. This worthy achievement will be crowned with glory, and there will be no end to the blessings it bestows. Would this not be splendid?

CHU HSI

Wang An-shih in Retrospect

Though Wang's New Laws were largely abolished by Ssu-ma Kuang, after the latter's demise, political forces representing Wang's point of view recouped their strength and held power much of the time until the ignominious fall of the Northern Sung dynasty (1126). Many of Wang's policies were briefly revived and some of them—like his public services system, the local security and militia system, and the type of examination essay he introduced into the civil service system—reappeared in later dynasties. Nevertheless, Wang's reputation among later generations of Confucian scholars was generally low, the majority sympathizing with Ssu-ma Kuang, Su Shih, the Ch'eng brothers, and others who had condemned Wang for his flagrant disregard of "human feelings" (which should not necessarily be interpreted to mean "public opinion") and especially for his suppression of criticism at court. Chu Hsi, the pre-eminent philosopher of the Sung school whose views became enshrined as orthodox Neo-Confucianism in later dynasties, was a follower of the Ch'eng brothers. In these excerpts from his recorded conversations, however, he attempts a balanced judgment of Wang An-shih's strengths and weaknesses, trying to rise above the partisan passions stirred up in the great era of reform.

[From *Chu Tzu ch'üan-shu*, 62:30b–33a]

We were discussing Wang An-shih's meeting with Emperor Shen-tsung. "It was a chance that comes only once in a thousand years," I said. "Unfortunately Wang's ideas and methods were not correct so that in the end everything went to pieces the way it did." Someone asked: "When Wang An-shih started, was he so self-assured about his methods and tactics, or did he become so only later?" I replied: "At first he felt only that something should be done. But later when other people began to attack him, he became obstinate and unyielding. Unless one reads his diary one has no way of understanding the full story. As a matter of fact he became so overbearing in argument and so contemptuous of everyone around him that men like Wen Lu-kung [Wen Yen-po] did not dare to utter a word." Someone asked about Ssu-ma Kuang's actions. I replied: "He saw only that Wang An-shih was wrong, and this led him to go too far in the other direction. When the whole matter first came under discussion, men like Su Tung-p'o also felt that reforms should be undertaken, but later they all changed their minds completely." [30b–31a]

The implementation of the reforms was actually planned by all the statesmen together. Even Ch'eng Hao did not consider them to be wrong, for he felt that the time was ripe for a change. Only later, when everyone's feelings had been aroused, did Ch'eng Hao begin to urge Wang An-shih not to do things that went against human feelings. Finally, when Wang had rejected the advice of everyone else and was using all his power to enforce his policies, the other statesmen began to withdraw. Tao-fu asked: "If even the man in the street could tell that the implementation of these reforms would be harmful, why was it that Ch'eng Hao did not consider them wrong?" I replied: "The harm came from the way that Wang put them into practice. If Ch'eng Hao had been doing it, things would certainly not have ended up in the mess they did." It was asked: "What would have been the situation if only [the elder statesmen] Han Ch'i and Fu Pi had been employed in the government?" I replied: "Those two gentlemen would have made no changes at all." "Suppose Ssu-ma Kuang had been in sole charge?" it was asked. "He is altogether a different sort of person again," I said. "If the two Ch'eng brothers had assumed the responsibility," it was asked, "would things not have been different?" I replied: "In the case of Ch'eng Hao things would have been different provided he had full discretion in all matters." [32a–b]

Jen-chieh remarked that the *pao-chia* [militia] system which Wang An-shih put into effect in the capital area naturally aroused opposition at the start. But when the gentlemen of the Yüan-yu party abolished it entirely, what they did was to upset completely a system that was already well established. "That is quite true," I replied. [32b]

It was the opinion of the various worthy men of the Yüan-yu party that in general everything should go according to established ways. Their idea was to correct the mistakes arising from the changes [made by Wang An-shih] during the Hsi-ning and Yüan-feng periods, but they did not realize that they were lapsing into mere stand-pattism. Since the empire exists, soldiers must be trained, abuses must be corrected, and government affairs must be properly ordered. How could one simply do nothing at all? [33a]

ACHIEVEMENTS IN THE WRITING OF HISTORY

Historical thinking and writing during the T'ang and Sung dynasties was, if anything, even more intimately related to the key developments in politics and scholarship than in the great Han dynasty. We have already noted how many of the leading Sung figures were engaged in the writing of history—the statesmen Ou-yang Hsiu and Ssu-ma Kuang, for instance, and the philosopher Chu Hsi—and the breadth of their historical vision reflected the wide range of intellectual inquiry in the Sung. Already in the T'ang, however, we find evidence of a trend toward monumental historical compilations which seem directly to mirror the massive proportions of the T'ang state and empire itself, particularly as shown in its political institutions. It is the encyclopedic character of the great T'ang works, and especially their attention to the details of institutional history, which reminds us that this was a dynasty admired throughout East Asia for its complex bureaucratic organization and its codification of laws. The same concern for order, form, and universality is characteristic of the histories.

After the long period of disunity from the third to sixth centuries, the political unity and stability of the T'ang naturally greatly facilitated the work of keeping detailed and accurate records of government activities, such as the Diaries of Action and Repose. The T'ang also saw the development and elaboration of the *lei-shu* or encyclopedia form of writing. This type of work, first attempted in the Six Dynasties period, consisted of compilations of references to given subjects culled from all possible written sources and arranged by topics. They were designed primarily as handy references for students, writers, and government officials who had not the time to search through voluminous histories and philosophical writings for the facts and allusions they needed in their work. These encyclopedias, which have continued to be compiled up to the present time, not only act in a way as indexes to the staggering volume of Chinese literature, but have also preserved in quotation parts of many books that have otherwise been lost over the centuries. The T'ang also produced the first important work of historiographic criticism, the *Understanding of History* (*Shih t'ung*) of Liu Chih-chi (661–721), a series of essays upon the origin, development, and relative merits of various forms and styles of historical writing. Later the scholar Tu Yu (735–812), who had Legalist leanings, compiled the first great institutional history of China, the *General Institutions* (*T'ung tien*), a work in two hundred chapters containing essays on such subjects as economics, warfare, bureaucratic systems, laws, geography, etc., tracing each subject from its beginnings in the dawn of Chinese history down to the time of the writer. The *Shih chi* and later histories modeled upon it often had included essays devoted to the historical treatment of such topics, but Tu Yu was the first to undertake such a detailed and comprehensive coverage, producing a history centered not upon the ups and downs of political power but upon the long and unbroken development of institutions.

The Sung continued and expanded the historical labors of the T'ang. New and more comprehensive encyclopedic works were compiled, such as the mammoth *Encyclopedia of 977* (*T'ai-p'ing yü-lan*) in one thousand chapters. The old "annal and memoir" style of history, patterned after the *Shih chi* and used for histories of single dynasties, continued to be employed, notably by the scholar-statesman Ou-yang Hsiu (1007–1072) in his *New History of the T'ang Dynasty* and *New History of the Five Dynasties*. Ou-yang Hsiu's works are significant for several reasons. He attempted to broaden the basis of his historical research beyond the government records that had constituted the principal sources for older historical works to include works of fiction, belles lettres, and historical anecdotes. Also, as an ardent advocate of the prose style known as *ku-wen* or ancient prose which had developed in the late T'ang, he employed this style exclusively in his historical writings, even going so far as to rewrite in this style quotations from earlier sources written in a different style. Finally, as a firm believer in the didactic function of history as exemplified in the *Spring and Autumn Annals* of Confucius, he attempted, in imitation of that Classic, to convey by means of careful and precise use of terminology his moral judgments upon the meaning of the events described.

Of even greater importance than the work of Ou-yang Hsiu was that of Ssu-ma Kuang (1019–1086) and his three associates, a history covering 1,362 years of the Chinese past in 294 chapters. The material of this work, gathered from the official histories of preceding dynasties and supplementary sources, was arranged chronologically in the manner of the *Commentary on the Spring and Autumn Annals* (*Tso chuan*), with remarks upon the events and principles by Ssu-ma Kuang inserted at appropriate places in the narrative. Compiled largely under official sponsorship, it was presented to the emperor who conferred upon it the title *General Mirror for the Aid of Government* (*Tzu-chih t'ung-chien*), indicative of the didactic value which the Chinese attributed to the study of history. The work was immediately recognized as a masterpiece of lucid, objective presentation and sound scholarship and has remained to the present one of the most widely read and authoritative of all Chinese histories.

The great merit of the *General Mirror,* as it is referred to, was that it condensed the voluminous works of earlier historians and fused their accounts into one consecutive narrative covering the rise and fall, amalgamation and disunion of all the various dynasties of the past from the fifth century B.C. to the beginning of the Sung. In this respect it was the first major work of political history after the *Shih chi* to preserve the broad continuum of history rather than confine itself to the limits of a single era or state. The focus of Ssu-ma Kuang's narrative was upon political development, which lends itself well to the chronological form which he adopted. The magnitude of the undertaking and the necessity

of arranging all material in chronological order, however, forced him
to neglect questions of institutional development and to break up and
scatter accounts of closely related events because of the dictates of chronology.

The *General Mirror* inspired a number of historians to imitate or attempt to rework Ssu-ma Kuang's material and correct what they regarded
as the defects and shortcomings of his history. Yüan Shu (1131–1205),
distressed at the way material relating to single subjects was broken up
by the chronological form, compiled a work called *Topical Treatment
of Events in the General Mirror (T'ung-chien chi-shih pen-mo)* in which
he rearranged the material of Ssu-ma Kuang's narrative according to
topics, in the manner of the old encyclopedic works. Of more far-reaching significance was the work planned by the philosopher Chu Hsi (1130–
1200) and executed by his disciples, the *Outline and Digest of the General Mirror (T'ung-chien kang-mu)*. This attempted to select only the
most significant points of Ssu-ma Kuang's lengthy narrative, recording
and arranging them in such a way that, like the entries of the *Spring
and Autumn Annals,* they would clearly convey the moral lessons of
history.

This enthusiastic interest in historical writing continued unabated to
the end of the Sung, inspiring several important works of institutional
history as well. Cheng Ch'iao (1108–1166), deeply impressed by the scope
and form of the *Shih chi,* undertook a history of China's entire past using
Ssu-ma Ch'ien's work as a model. The most valuable section of his work,
the *General Treatises (T'ung chih),* is that patterned on the treatises
of the *Shih chi,* fifteen essays covering a variety of subjects, some of them
such as philology, phonetics, and families and clans, never before treated
in essay form. In these he made use of material already collected by the
T'ang historian Tu Yu. Cheng Ch'iao's work was followed by a third
great institutional history, the *General Study of Literary Remains (Wen-
hsien t'ung k'ao)* of Ma Tuan-lin (thirteenth century) which reworked
and added to the material of the *T'ung tien* and *T'ung chih.* These three,
known collectively as the "Three T'ung," are considered the greatest
works of institutional history and were the models for many later con-
tinuations and imitations. The end of the Sung also saw the compilation
of one of the most reliable and comprehensive encyclopedias, the *Jewel
Sea (Yü hai)* of Wang Ying-lin (1223–1296), many of whose ideas and

methods became the inspiration for scholars of the Ch'ing (Manchu) dynasty.

The Sung, in spite of the political weakness and instability of its later days, was one of the most active and significant eras of Chinese scholarship. Like the Han, it was a time in which the Chinese attempted to look back and comprehend in one perspective the whole complex development of their past, to reduce the great mass of material, the fluctuations of political fortunes, the evolutions of institutions, into an ordered unity, and to formulate on the basis of this material certain principles of human society and historical development that would be universally valid. The task facing the Sung historians was monumental, and it is hardly surprising that so many of their works reached monumental proportions. Whatever we may think of their motives and the didactic quality they attempted to instill in their works, we cannot fail to admire the tremendous energy, devotion, and breadth of view with which they undertook the heroic labor of synthesizing and summing up the entire past of China. Government sponsored agencies of later dynasties continued to compile vast collections of historical data, and individual historians continued to produce works of excellent caliber, though of limited scope. But rarely, if ever again, were Chinese scholars to possess the vision and daring to attempt works on a scale to match those of the Sung historians.

Diaries of Action and Repose

From the Latter Han dynasty it had become the practice to have official historiographers at court who attended the emperor when he was engaged in state business and took notes on his words and actions. These notes were then written up and preserved in the archives as the Diaries of Action and Repose (*Ch'i-chü-chu*). The purpose of this was twofold: to provide an accurate and unbiased account of the ruler's deeds which would serve as material for later historians; and to impress upon the ruler that whatever he said or did would be recorded for the approval or condemnation of posterity. During the T'ang it was still the practice, in spite of protests from the emperors, to keep the records strictly out of reach of the imperial glance in order to assure complete objectivity. But in the Sung it became customary to submit the diaries to the emperor for his approval after they had been written up and for this reason their value as historical sources greatly decreased.

[From *Tzu-chih t'ung-chien*, 196:8a–8b, 246:6b–7a]

The year 642, Summer, 4th month. The Emperor T'ai-tsung spoke to the Imperial Censor Ch'u Sui-liang, saying: "Since you, Sir, are in charge of the Diaries of Action and Repose, may I see what you have written?" Sui-liang replied: "The historiographers record the words and deeds of the ruler of men, noting down all that is good and bad, in hopes that the ruler will not dare to do evil. But it is unheard of that the ruler himself should see what is written." The emperor said: "If I do something that is not good, do you then also record it?" Sui-liang replied: "My office is to wield the brush. How could I dare not record it?" The Gentleman of the Yellow Gate Liu Chi added: "Even if Sui-liang failed to record it, everyone else in the empire would"; to which the emperor replied: "True." [196:8a–8b]

The year 839, Winter, 10th month. The Emperor Wen-tsung went to the Official in Charge of the Diaries of Action and Repose, Wei Mo, picked up his notes and began looking at them. Wei Mo objected, saying: "The Diaries of Action and Repose record both good and bad in order to warn and admonish the ruler of men. Your Majesty should only strive to do good. It is not necessary that Your Majesty see the records." The emperor said: "Once before I looked at them." "That," replied Wei Mo, "was the fault of the official in charge of history at that time. If Your Majesty were to examine the records personally, the historiographers would be forced to distort or alter their accounts. Then how could we expect later ages to put any faith in them?" With this the emperor desisted. [246:6b–7a]

LÜ TSU-CH'IEN
A Discussion of History

Lü Tsu-ch'ien (Lü Tung-lai, 1137–1181), historian, classical scholar, and friend of Chu Hsi, began a history covering the period from the end of the Spring and Autumn era to the beginning of the Five Dynasties (484 B.C.–A.D. 907) which, because of illness, he never completed. In the following short essay he makes two points of extreme importance in Sung historiography. The first is that history must be viewed not as a collection of miscellaneous facts but as the continuous record of organic growth and change. This was the concept which inspired Lü and others of his time to undertake the writing of gigantic general histories covering all of the past.

The second point is that the study of history must serve as a basis for action in the present, that only as one imagines himself in the actual setting of history and exercises his own judgment on what course of action would have been appropriate at any given time, can he derive practical benefit from his reading of history. Thus he sums up the concept of the didactic function of history which inspired the works of the Sung historians.

[From *Lü Tung-lai wen-chi,* ESCC ed., 19:431]

Ch'en Ying-chung [Ch'en Kuan] once remarked that the *General Mirror* is like Medicine Mountain: anywhere you pick you always are sure of getting something. But though it may be Medicine Mountain, you must know how to select, for if you do not know how to select, you will end up with nothing more than a vast collection of facts crammed into your memory. Hu Ch'iu Tzu once asked Lieh Tzu why he liked to travel. Lieh Tzu replied: "Other men travel in order to see what there is to see, but I travel in order to observe how things change" [*Lieh Tzu,* 4]. This might be taken as a rule for observing history. Most people, when they examine history, simply look at periods of order and realize that they are ordered, periods of disorder and recognize their disorder, observe one fact and know no more than that one fact. But is this real observation of history? You should picture yourself actually in the situation, observe which things are profitable and which dangerous, and note the misfortunes and ills of the times. Shut the book and think for yourself. Imagine that you are facing these various facts and then decide what you think ought to be done. If you look at history in this way, then your learning will increase and your intelligence improve. Then you will get real profit from your reading.

CHENG CH'IAO
General Preface to the T'ung Chih

In the famous "General Preface" to his history of the entire past of China, Cheng Ch'iao (1108–1166) extols the principle of "meeting and joining"—the continuous stream of history—which he believed should be the foundation of all historical writing. Only when the historian concentrates upon the organic growth of history from age to age, regardless of superficial political divisions, can his work be meaningful to later times. Thus his ideals are Confucius, who in the Classics brought together the records of the first three dynasties of China, and Ssu-ma Ch'ien whose great work spanned five dynasties. With Pan Ku's *History of the Former Han Dynasty,* he laments, it became the custom to write histories covering only single dynasties, and the great principle of continuity was lost. It was no longer possible in such works for the reader to compare and contrast the development of institutions and customs from one age to another, and the whole didactic meaning of history was obscured. Only in his own work, which covers the entire past, is the integrity of history once more restored.

[From *T'ung chih*, 1]

The many rivers run each a separate course, but all must meet in the sea; only thus may the land be spared the evil of inundation. The myriad states have each their different ways, but all must join in the greater community which is China; only then may the outlying areas escape the ills of stagnation. Great is this principle of meeting and joining! From the time when books were first invented, there have been many who set forth their words, but only "Confucius was a sage endowed by Heaven unlimitedly." [22] Therefore he brought together the *Odes* and *History,* the *Rites* and music, and joined them by his own hand so that all the literature of the world met in him. From the deeds of the two emperors Yao and Shun and the kings of the Three Dynasties he created one school of philosophy so that men of later times could fully comprehend the evolutions of past and present. Thus was his way brilliant and enlightened, surpassing all the ages before and all the ages after him.

After Confucius passed away, the various philosophers of the hundred schools appeared and in imitation of the *Analects* each composed a book setting forth his general principles. But no one undertook to carry on the record of the historical facts of ensuing ages. Then in the Han, around the year 140 and later, Ssu-ma T'an and his son Ssu-ma Ch'ien appeared. The Ssu-ma family had for generations been in charge of documents and records and they were skilled at compilation and writing. Therefore they were able to understand the intention of Confucius, to join together the narratives of the *Odes* and *History,* the *Tso Commentary,* the *Narratives of the States,* the *Genealogical Origins,* the *Intrigues of the Warring States,* and the *Spring and Autumn of Ch'u and Han,* to cover the ages from the Yellow Emperor and Yao and Shun down to the Ch'in and Han, and complete one book. It was divided into five sections: the basic annals, which are recorded year by year, the hereditary houses covering the states that were handed down from generation to genera-

[22] *Analects,* IX, 6.

tion, the chronological tables which corrected dates, the treatises which dealt with specific subjects, and the memoirs devoted to the lives of individuals. For a hundred generations the official historians have not been able to depart from this model, nor have scholars ever succeeded in seriously challenging this work. After the Six Classics, there is only this one book. . . .

Confucius took the *Spring and Autumn* form and employed it first and the scholar Tso followed this example, so that their works stand today like the sun and the moon. . . . But since the *Spring and Autumn Annals,* only the *Shih chi* has succeeded in making use of this model of composition. Unfortunately Pan Ku was not the man he should have been, and he failed to grasp the principle of joining and penetrating, and from his time the followers of the Ssu-ma family fell away. . . . Later historians have lost no time in running after the example of Pan Ku, seemingly unable to judge the relative merits of his work and that of Ssu-ma Ch'ien. But Ssu-ma Ch'ien is to Pan Ku as a dragon is to a pig. Why then do all later historians ignore Ssu-ma Ch'ien and follow Pan Ku? . . .

Confucius said: "The Yin dynasty followed the rites of the Hsia; wherein it took from or added to them may be known. The Chou followed the rites of the Yin; wherein it took from or added to them may be known." [23] This is what is known as the continuity of history. But from the time when Pan Ku wrote the history of only one dynasty, this principle of continuity has been ignored. Thus although one be a sage like Confucius he can never know what was taken away or what added in each period. The way of joining and meeting was from this time lost.

MA TUAN-LIN
Preface to the General Study of Literary Remains

In the "General Preface" to his great work on institutional history, Ma Tuanlin (thirteenth century) repeats and elaborates upon the points made earlier by Cheng Ch'iao. Dividing history into two types, political and institutional, he concedes that the former may be treated by separate periods, but maintains, like Cheng Ch'iao, that only a comprehensive survey of the entire past is suitable for dealing with questions of institutional growth and development.

Note Ma's insistence that an understanding of recent institutional history,

[23] *Analects,* II, 23.

not just of the Classics, is essential to the Confucian scholar and fully in keeping with the way of the ancient kings. This is a more sober and realistic view than that of the earlier Sung reformers whose call for a restoration of the ancient order was inspired more by study of the Classics than of recent institutions. At the same time, however, Ma follows in the wake of those Sung Confucianists for whom institutional problems had as much significance as ethical and philosophical questions.

[From *Wen-hsien t'ung k'ao*, 3a]

The philosopher Hsün Tzu long ago remarked: "If you would observe the ways of the ancient sage-kings, they are perfectly obvious, for they are the ways of the later kings. The gentleman studies the ways of these later kings and speaks of the hundred kings of long ago as easily as another folds his hands and begins a discussion." [24] Therefore if one studies institutions, examines laws and statutes, is widely learned and of stout understanding, then truly may he comprehend the affairs of Confucianism.

After the time of the *Odes,* the *History,* and the *Spring and Autumn Annals,* only Ssu-ma Ch'ien deserves to be called a "good historian." He used the annal and memoir, treatise and chronological table form, the annals and memoirs to describe the periods of order and disorder, of rise and fall of states, and the eight treatises to relate matters of law and institutions. Of all the men who have since taken up brush and writing tablet, none has been able to depart from this form. But from the time of Pan Ku and thereafter, histories were written covering only one dynasty so that, much to the distress of the readers, the principle of continuity and development was lost. Finally, however, Ssu-ma Kuang wrote his *General Mirror,* covering the happenings of some 1,300 years in which he selected the narratives of seventeen separate histories and put them all together to form one work. Later scholars who have perused his pages have found all things of past and present therein. But although Ssu-ma Kuang is very detailed on matters of order and disorder, and the rise and fall of dynasties, his treatment of laws and institutions is very sketchy. This is not because of any lack of wisdom on his part, but simply that, his material being so voluminous, he was forced to focus his narrative upon certain problems only and thus neglect others.

It has always been my observation that periods of order or disorder, of the rise and fall of different dynasties, are not interrelated. The way the

[24] *Hsün Tzu,* 3.

Chin came to power, for example, was not the same as the way the Han
came to power, while the fall of the Sui was quite different from the fall
of the T'ang. Each period has its own history, and it is sufficient to cover
in full the period from the beginning to the end of the dynasty without
referring to other dynasties or attempting to draw parallels. Laws and
institutions, however, are actually interrelated. The Yin followed the
rites of the Hsia, the Chou followed those of the Yin, and whoever follows the rites of Chou, though it be a hundred generations after, the way
in which he takes from or adds to them may be known. This was the
prediction made by the Sage, Confucius. Thus from the Ch'in and the
Han down to the T'ang and the Sung, the regulations concerning rites,
music, warfare, and punishments, the system for taxation and selection of
officials, even the changes and elaborations in bureaucratic titles or the
developments and alternations in geography, although in the end not
necessarily the same for all dynasties, yet did not suddenly spring into
being as something unique for each period. Thus the court etiquette and
governmental system of the Han was based upon regulations of the Ch'in;
the military and tax systems of the T'ang were based upon Chou statutes.
Therefore to understand the reasons for the gradual growth and relative
importance of institutions in each period, you must make a comprehensive
and comparative study of them from their beginnings to their ends and
in this way try to grasp their development; otherwise you will encounter
serious difficulties. The type of political history that is not dependent upon
continuity has already been amply covered in Ssu-ma Kuang's book, but
there is no work which deals with institutions which depend for their
understanding upon historical continuity. Is it not fitting that scholars of
our time should turn their full attention to this problem?

Introduction to the Survey on the Land Tax

As if to stress the basic importance of land and taxes in Chinese life, Ma Tuan-
Lin's vast survey of Chinese institutions begins with a study of systems of
land taxation through the ages. His historical viewpoint is typically Confucian in that he regards the ancient feudal society as the ideal and all subsequent institutions as corrupt. Nevertheless he has studied enough of history
to know how thoroughly circumstances have changed since the Chou dynasty,
and he has seen enough idealistic reformers fail to convince him that it is better
to work with existing institutions than to try to change them completely.

[From *Wen-hsien t'ung k'ao*, Author's Introduction, 3c–4a]

The rulers of ancient times did not regard the realm as their own private possession. Therefore the land of the Son of Heaven was a thousand *li* square, while that of the dukes and marquises was a hundred *li* square. Earls held seventy *li*, barons fifty *li*, and within the area of the emperor's territory the high ministers and officials were granted lands and villages from which they received emolument. Each of these held possession of his own land, regarded its inhabitants as his personal charges, and passed it down to his sons and grandsons to possess. He regarded questions of the fertility of the land and the abundance or want of the peasants as of immediate concern to his own family. He took the trouble to examine and supervise things himself so that there was no room for evildoing or deception. Thus at this time all land was under the jurisdiction of the officials, and the people provided support for the officials. The peasants who received land from the officials lived by their own labor and paid tribute. In their work of supporting their parents and providing for their wives and families they were all treated with equal kindness so that there were no people who were excessively rich nor any who were excessively poor. This was the system of the Three Dynasties.

The rulers of the Ch'in were the first to consider all land as their possession and to exercise all power by themselves. The men who filled the posts of district magistrates were shifted about frequently so that they came to regard the land of the district where they were stationed as no more than a temporary lodging. Thus no matter how worthy or wise a magistrate might be, it was impossible for him to know fully the true situation in the villages and hamlets he was supervising. The appointments and terms of office of these local magistrates were subject to time limitations, while evil and corrupt practices in connection with the transfer and holding of land multiplied endlessly. Thus from the time of Ch'in and Han on, government officials no longer had the power to grant land, and as a natural result all land came eventually to be the private possession of the common people. Although there were intervals such as the T'ai-ho period of the Wei [A.D. 227–232] or the Chen-kuan period of the T'ang [627–649] when some effort was made to return to the system of the Three Dynasties, it was not long before their reforms became ineffective. This was because without a revival of feudalism it was impossible to restore the well-field system.

In the ancient times of the Three Dynasties, the Son of Heaven could not hold private possession of the empire, but the Ch'in abolished feudalism and for the first time made the entire empire the domain of one man. In the Three Dynasties period, the common people could not claim the produce of the land as their private possession, but the Ch'in abolished the well-field system and first granted the people the right to the produce of their land. Thus what the Ch'in ought properly to have granted to the feudal lords it took away, and what it ought properly to have taken from the people it granted to them. But this process has already gone on for such a long time that it would be exceedingly difficult to return to the old ways. If one were to try to revive feudalism, it would mean dividing and parceling out all the land again, and this would be the signal for confusion and strife. If one attempted to restore the well-field system, it would only invite resentment and bitterness. This is why the theories of scholars who recommend such a revival cannot be put into practice.

The system of taxing the landholdings of the people but putting no restriction upon the size of their holdings began with Shang Yang [d. 338 B.C.]. The system of taxing people for the land they held, but taking no consideration of whether they were adult or underage [25] began with Yang Yen [d. A.D. 781]. Thus Shang Yang was responsible for abolishing the excellent well-field system of the Three Dynasties, and Yang Yen was responsible for the abandonment of the superior tax system of the early T'ang. Scholars have been very critical of the changes made by these two men, but all later administrations have found it necessary to follow their systems. If they attempted to change back to the old ways, they found that, on the contrary, they only ended up in worse difficulty and confusion and both the nation and the people suffered. This is because the things appropriate to the past and those appropriate to the present are different. Thus I have devoted the first of my surveys to the land tax, tracing the development of systems of land tax through the ages, and adding to it a study of water control, and of military and government farms, making seven chapters in all.

SSU-MA KUANG

A Discussion of Dynastic Legitimacy

From early times the Chinese have viewed their country as a single unit held together by a broad system of customs and moral attitudes common to all its

[25] That is, by incorporating the old labor tax, under which such persons were exempt, into the land tax.

inhabitants and properly ruled by one central authority, the emperor and his court. Yet as the men of the Sung surveyed their past, they could not deny the existence of three periods in Chinese history when this ideal situation did not obtain: the Spring and Autumn and the Warring States eras of the late Chou; the Six Dynasties period between the Han and the T'ang; and the Five Dynasties period between the T'ang and the Sung. During these periods, China was divided into a number of small states, some of them under barbarian or semi-barbarian rule, each struggling for existence and trying to gain mastery of the empire. At such times there were puppet emperors who held only the title but not the actuality of rule, ministers and generals who wielded power far beyond that which properly belonged to their station, usurpations, assassinations, mutual recriminations, and rapid changes of dynasty.

Chinese historians in writing of such periods were faced with serious problems of treatment: were they to regard as rulers those who held the symbolic regalia of rule or those who exercised actual power? Were they to try to single out some states as legitimate dynasties while ignoring others? In other words, where five or six states coexisted in the place of the ancient empire, which one was the real China? Sung historians differed slightly in their beliefs regarding the proper treatment of particular dynasties. But they were almost unanimous upon two vital points: Han theories of dynastic succession based upon the five agents were vain and superstitious and merited no place in serious historical writing; treatment of dynasties must be based upon a frank recognition of historical facts. That is, regardless of whether one approved of the way a dynasty came to power, it could not be ignored or relegated to a minor position; conversely, regardless of how just or orthodox its claims to succession, if a dynasty remained weak and ineffective and failed to unify China, it could not be regarded as the equal of dynasties which had; therefore for the periods of political disunity there was very often no single state that could be regarded as more legitimate than any other.

The Sung historians never denied that the primary function of history was didactic. They continued, like their predecessors of earlier dynasties, to regard the *Spring and Autumn Annals* of Confucius as the supreme model for historical writing and to maintain that the *Spring and Autumn Annals* embodied moral lessons. But they insisted that the *Spring and Autumn Annals,* written during one of these periods of political disunity, taught its lessons precisely because it recognized and recorded facts as facts. If the historian would only follow this example of Confucius and relay the facts of history accurately and carefully, then their didactic import would become clear without forcing the point.

[From *Tzu-chih t'ung-chien,* SPTK ed., 69:7b–8b]

Your servant Kuang observes: Heaven gave birth to the multitudes of people. But conditions make it impossible for them to govern themselves, so that they must have a ruler to govern over them. Anyone who is able to prevent violence and remove harm from the people so that their lives are protected, who can reward good and punish evil and thus avoid disaster—such a man may be called a ruler. Thus before the Three Dynasties the feudal lords had a countless number of states, and anyone who had subjects and possessed altars to the soil and grain went by the name of ruler. But he who united all these countless states and who set up laws and issued commands which no one dared to disobey was called a king. When the power of the king declined, there were rulers of strong states who were able to lead the other feudal lords and enforce respect for the Son of Heaven and such were called "overlords." Thus since ancient times there have been instances when the world was in disorder and the feudal lords contended with each other for power, and for a number of generations there was no king at all.

After Ch'in had burned the books and buried the Confucianists alive, the Han arose, and at this time scholars first began to propound the theory of how the five agents produce and overcome each other according to which the Ch'in was an "intercalary" reign coming between those of wood [Chou] and fire [Han], ruled by an "overlord" and not by a true king. Thus began the theory of legitimate and intercalary dynasties.

After the House of Han was overthrown, the Three Kingdoms ruled simultaneously like the legs of a tripod. Then the Chin lost its control of the empire and the five barbarian tribes swarmed in. From the time of the Sung and the Northern Wei, north and south were divided politically. Each had its own dynastic histories which disparaged the other, the south calling the north "slaves with bound hair," the north calling the south "island barbarians." When Chu Ch'üan-chung succeeded to the T'ang the empire was once again rent to pieces, but when the Chu-yeh clan entered Pien and overthrew him they compared him to the ancient usurpers Yi and Wang Mang and discarded completely the chronology of his dynasty. All these are examples of biased phraseology based on personal interest and do not represent enlightened and just opinions.

Your servant, being stupid, is surely not qualified to know anything about the legitimate and intercalary dynasties of former times. But he would be bold enough to consider that unless rulers were able to unite the nine provinces under one government, although they all bore the name Son of Heaven there was no reality behind it. Although distinctions may be made on the basis of the fact that one dynasty was Chinese and another foreign, one humane and another tyrannical, or that they differed in size and power, yet essentially they were just the same as the various feudal states of ancient times. How can we single out one state for honor and call it the legitimate successor, and consider all the rest as false or usurpers?

Are we to consider those states legitimate which received the throne from the hands of their immediate predecessors? Then from whom did the Ch'en receive the throne, and from whom the Northern Wei? [26] Should we consider as legitimate those who occupied parts of China proper? Then we must recognize the rule of the [barbarian families] Liu, the Shih, the Mu-jung, the Fu, the Yao, and the Ho-lien [of the Five Dynasties period], all of whom ruled territory that had been the domain of the ancient five emperors and three kings. Or are we perhaps to make virtuous ways the criterion of legitimacy? But even the tiniest state must sometimes have its good sovereigns, while in the declining days of the Three Dynasties there were surely unrighteous kings. Thus from ancient times to the present these theories of legitimate dynasties have never possessed the kind of logic sufficient to compel men to accept them without question.

Now your servant in his narrative has sought only to trace the rise and fall of the various states and make clear the people's times of joy and sorrow so that the reader may select for himself what is good and what is bad, what profitable and what unprofitable, for his own encouragement and warning. He has no intention of setting up standards of praise and blame in the manner of the *Spring and Autumn Annals* which could compel a disorderly age to return to just ways.

Your servant does not presume to know anything about the distinctions of legitimate and intercalary, but treats each state only in accordance with its actual accomplishments. Chou, Ch'in, Han, Chin, Sui, and T'ang each in turn unified the nine provinces and transmitted the throne to its descendants. And though their descendants in time grew weak and were forced to move their capitals, they still carried on the undertaking of their ancestors, continued the line of succession, and hoped to bring about a restoration of power. Those with whom rulers contended for power were all their former subjects. Therefore your servant has treated these rulers

[26] Both set themselves up at times of political vacuum.

with all the respect due the Son of Heaven. All other states who were approximately equal in territory and virtue and unable to overcome each other, and who employed the same titles and did not stand in a ruler-subject relationship, have been treated the same as the ancient feudal states, presented equally and without favoritism. This way would seem to avoid doing violence to the facts and accord the fairest treatment.

Nevertheless for times when the empire was split up it is necessary to have some overall chronology in order to distinguish the sequence of events. The Han transmitted rule to the Wei, from whom the Chin received it; Chin passed it on to Sung and thence to Ch'en, whence Sui took it; T'ang passed it to the Latter Liang and so down to the Latter Chou, from whom our Great Sung inherited it. Therefore it has been necessary to adopt the reign titles of these dynasties in chronicling the events that took place in all the various states. This does not mean, however, that one state is being honored and another disparaged, or that any distinction of legitimate or intercalary dynasties is intended.

CHU HSI

General Rules for the Writing of the Outline and Digest of the General Mirror (T'ung-chien kang-mu)

The following are excerpts from a list of general principles (fan-li) which Chu Hsi formulated for the guidance of his disciples in compiling a digest of the *General Mirror*. It was Chu Hsi's conviction in laying down these rules that only by a careful use of terminology and accurate reporting of the facts of history could the moral lessons of the past be clearly and forcefully presented to the ruler.

[From *Chih-yüan k'ao-ting t'ung-chien kang-mu*, Introduction]

The legitimate dynasties are Chou, Ch'in, Han, Chin, Sui, and T'ang. Feudal states are those which have been enfeoffed by legitimate dynasties. Usurpers are those who usurp the throne, interfere with the legitimate line of succession, and do not transmit their rule to their heirs. The periods in which there is no legitimate line appear between Chou and Ch'in, Ch'in and Han, Han and Chin, Chin and Sui, Sui and T'ang, and the Five Dynasties period.

Rulers of legitimate dynasties: those of Chou are called "kings," those of Ch'in, Han, and after are called "emperors." Rulers of feudal states:

those of Chou are referred to by state, feudal rank, and name. Those who unlawfully usurped the title of king are referred to as "so-and-so, the ruler of such-and-such a state"; from the Han on they are referred to as "so-and-so, the king of such-and-such." Those who usurped the title of emperor are referred to as "so-and-so, the lord of such-and-such." Those who revolted and usurped the throne of a legitimate dynasty are referred to by name only.

Ascending the throne, legitimate dynasties: when the Chou kings passed their rule on to their heirs, write: "his son so-and-so was set up" and note that this person then became king so-and-so. When the succession is by natural heir, write: "so-and-so succeeded to the throne." When someone establishes a state and sets himself up as ruler, write: "so-and-so set himself up as king of such-and-such." If someone else sets him up, write: "so-and-so honored so-and-so with such-and-such a title." When someone usurps a state and begins to style himself emperor, write: "so-and-so (title, family and personal name) styled himself emperor." When the rule of a state is transferred to a brother of the ruler, this is called "transmission"; when to someone else, it is called "cession."

Deaths: In cases of rulers of legitimate dynasties, write: "deceased"; and if the death occurred outside the palace, note the place. If the ruler died before his first year of rule was out, write: "departed." If the person was stripped of his honors, write: "died." In cases of grand empress dowagers, empress dowagers, and empresses, write: "Empress so-and-so of such-and-such a family, deceased." In case of suicide, write: "suicide"; where guilty of a crime, add the word "crime." Where the person was innocent but put in prison and died, write: "imprisoned and killed." Deaths of ex-empresses who had been demoted from their position need not be recorded, but if in the course of the narrative they are mentioned, write: "died." In cases where a state perished and the empress lost her rank but continued to maintain virtuous conduct and strive for the restoration of the state, use her former title and write: "deceased." From Ch'in and Han on when a king or peer dies, in all cases write: "died," but if the person was particularly worthy, note his posthumous name. In cases of rulers who usurped states and took the title of emperor, write: "The lord of such-and-such a state, so-and-so, died." For all rulers and chieftains of barbarian tribes, write: "died," as well as for leaders of rebel bands.

When rulers of legitimate dynasties make progresses through the provinces, write: "the emperor went to such-and-such a place." When visiting offices or private houses, write: "honored with a visit," for schools use "inspected" or "observed." If the ruler fled, this must be truthfully recorded.

Diplomatic conferences should all be recorded. If there is a leader, write: "so-and-so met so-and-so at such-and-such a place." If there is no leader, write: "so-and-so and so-and-so met at such-and-such a place."

In the case of legitimate dynasties, when inferiors turn against superiors, it is called "revolt." If it is planned but not carried out, write: "planned revolt." If troops are turned against the palace, write: "raised troops and attacked the palace."

If there is a ruler in China at the time when barbarians invade, write: "invaded and plundered" or "plundered such-and-such a district." If the affair is minor, write: "pillaged such-and-such a place." If there is no ruler in China at the time, then simply say: "entered within the borders" or "entered the passes," etc.

When a legitimate dynasty uses troops against its subjects who have usurped or revolted, it is called "subjugating" or "putting down"; against barbarian tribes who are not subjects, it is called "attacking," etc. When recording wars against enemy states, write: "destroyed them"; against rebels and bandits, write: "pacified them."

It is impossible to record the district, native town, and genealogy of all men; only in the case of worthy men should these be briefly noted. In the case of deaths of ministers, it is only necessary to record those of all prime ministers. For worthy men note their office, honorary title, family and personal names, "died," and add their posthumous name, but for ordinary men omit honorary title, family name, and posthumous name.

All natural disasters and prodigies should be recorded. In cases of lucky omens some may be recorded to show that they are doubtful, others to show that they are frauds.

CHAPTER XX

NEO-CONFUCIANISM: THE SCHOOL OF PRINCIPLE OR REASON

The Confucian revival in the Sung, as we have seen, was distinguished by its breadth of interest and intellectual vigor. But among the many fields of learning into which it penetrated, metaphysics was the one in which it achieved the greatest distinction. Some of the most intense intellectual struggles of the time might have been fought over political and social questions, on the outcome of which the very fate of China, threatened by barbarian conquest, seemed to depend. Yet time quickly deprived these debates of their urgency and point, while the philosophical specula-tions emerging from the academies of the Sung eventually won victories at home and abroad of which the statesman and soldier never dreamed. As a result, when we speak of Neo-Confucianism today what comes to mind first is the great synthesis of the philosopher Chu Hsi, the crowning achievement of the Sung and its most enduring contribution to the civilization of the Far East. This was known as the school of Principle or Reason. Alongside it developed the school of the Mind or Intuition, culminating in the philosophy of Wang Yang-ming during the Ming Dynasty (1368–1644).

The significance of Neo-Confucianism lies in its attempt to formulate answers to some of the most profound problems of human life, problems for which generations of Chinese, including many Confucian scholar-officials themselves, had been turning to Taoism or Buddhism to find a solution. In formulating their own answers the Neo-Confucianists plainly incurred a great debt to both of these schools. The influence of Taoist cosmogony, for instance, is readily apparent in the progenitors of the new movement, while a persistent strain of quietism and subjectivism (most notably in the school of the Mind) may be largely traced to Buddhism and Taoism. Nevertheless, the Neo-Confucian synthesis was by no means a conscious attempt to embrace these divergent philosophies in one vast system, nor did it acknowledge that all three could participate on an equal footing. It was rather predicated on a fundamental rejection of Buddhism and Taoism, and proceeded with a strong consciousness of adherence to an orthodox tradition which should be zealously preserved from the contamination of incompatible ideas. If, in spite of this, we see foreign influences at work, it is not usually through direct borrowing, however disguised, but almost unconsciously in the selection and interpretation of those elements from the earlier Confucian tradition which would best serve in the elaboration of a new synthesis.

This basic reaffirmation of Confucian tradition is reflected in the methods and the literature of the new movement. Problems are discussed most often as they bear upon the interpretation of the Classics, which are considered the fountainhead of all truth. For this reason, also, the terminology employed tends to be drawn from the Classics (with some important exceptions borrowed from the Buddhist lexicon), and much effort is expended on reconciling conflicting views or elucidating obscure concepts in the earlier texts.

Such preoccupations naturally make for less clarity and order in the writings of Neo-Confucianists than we might like today. We cannot help but feel that there is something artificial about this type of combined textual exegesis and philosophical exposition. Still we should not conclude from this that Neo-Confucianism is an imposture upon tradition. It is a new structure, indeed, yet not simply contrived of materials salvaged from the remains of antiquity, but grounded on the solid foundation of Confucian humanism and infused throughout with the optimistic, world-affirming spirit of traditional Chinese thought.

A philosophy concerned very much with this world, at the center of which is always man, Neo-Confucianism reasserts in an even more far-reaching manner what Confucius and his followers had always taught—that man's sense of order and value does not alienate him from the universe but is precisely what unites him to it. The world of human ethics, of social relations, of history and political endeavor is a real one, not just a passing dream or nightmare from which men must be awakened, as the Buddhists said, to the truth of Emptiness. It is this conviction which gave to Neo-Confucianism its abundant vitality, and a degree of universality that recommended it strongly not only to Chinese but also to men in Japan and Korea, who were seeking assurance that their lives had meaning and value.

THE NEW COSMOLOGY AND ETHICS OF CHOU TUN-YI

Chou Tun-yi (or Chou Lien-ch'i, 1017–1073) was the first major Sung scholar to undertake the task of redefining Confucian cosmology and metaphysics. Using a diagram with an accompanying exposition, the "Explanation of the Diagram of the Great Ultimate" translated below, to illustrate his theory, he derived all of the myriad phenomena of creation from what he termed the "Great Ultimate" through the workings of yin and yang and the five agents. In this he was actually only restating ideas already present in the Han appendixes to the *Book of Changes,* the principal source of inspiration for Neo-Confucian metaphysical speculation. But this first principle, the "Great Ultimate," from which all being derives, he also characterized as "Non-ultimate," thus identifying it with the nonbeing or Emptiness of the Taoists and Buddhists. In this way he attempted to explain how the countless differentiated phenomena of existence derive from an original source which is itself pure and undifferentiated, while at the same time refuting Buddhist and Taoist ideas that all being in its particularized manifestations, because so derived, is essentially illusory. Furthermore he developed the idea that "the Many are ultimately One," that "the One is differentiated into the Many," and that "the One and the Many each has its own correct state of being," which also became fundamental concepts of Neo-Confucianism.

Chou Tun-yi's ideas, particularly his concept of the "Non-ultimate," are strongly influenced by Taoism, and it has even been asserted that his cosmogonic diagram was adopted from a Taoist priest. In his ethical thought likewise his emphasis upon tranquillity and "having no desire" shows his indebtedness to Taoist thought. Nevertheless his underlying purpose is typically Confucian, in that he sought to reaffirm the reality and intelligibility of the world of everyday human experience and to provide a rational metaphysical basis for the essential ethical teachings of his school. In this way he laid the foundation for the more searching metaphysical speculations of the Sung Neo-Confucian scholars who followed him.

CHOU TUN-YI

An Explanation of the Diagram of the Great Ultimate
[From *T'ai-chi-t'u shuo*, in *Chou Lien-ch'i chi*, 1:2a–b]

The Non-ultimate! And also the Great Ultimate (*T'ai-chi*). The Great Ultimate through movement generates the yang. When its activity reaches its limit, it becomes tranquil. Through tranquillity the Great Ultimate generates the yin. When tranquillity reaches its limit, activity begins again. Thus movement and tranquillity alternate and become the root of each other, giving rise to the distinction of yin and yang, and these two modes are thus established.

By the transformation of yang and its union with yin, the five agents of water, fire, wood, metal, and earth arise. When these five material-forces (*ch'i*) [1] are distributed in harmonious order, the four seasons run their course.

The five agents constitute one system of yin and yang, and yin and yang constitute one Great Ultimate. The Great Ultimate is fundamentally the Non-ultimate. The five agents arise, each with its specific nature.

When the reality of the Non-ultimate and the essence of yin and yang and the five agents come into mysterious union, integration ensues. The heavenly principle (*ch'ien*) constitutes the male element, and the earthly principle (*k'un*) constitutes the female element. The interaction of these two material forces engenders and transforms the myriad things. The myriad things produce and reproduce, resulting in an unending transformation.

It is man alone who receives [the material forces] in their highest excellence, and therefore he is most intelligent. His corporeal form appears, and his spirit develops consciousness. The five moral principles of his nature (humanity, righteousness, decorum, wisdom, and good faith) are aroused by, and react to, the external world and engage in activity; good and evil are distinguished and human affairs take place.

---

[1] Rendered "vital force(s)" as it appears in earlier sources, *ch'i* is modified to "material-force" in this chapter where its role as the basic matter or stuff of the universe is stressed. Other widely used translations for *ch'i* are "ether" and "matter-energy."

The sage orders these affairs by the principles of the Mean, correctness, humanity, and righteousness, considering tranquillity to be the ruling factor. Thus he establishes himself as the ultimate standard for man. Hence the character of the sages is "identical with that of Heaven and earth; his brilliance is identical with that of the sun and moon; his order is identical with that of the four seasons; and his good and evil fortunes are identical with those of heavenly and earthly spirits." [2] The gentleman cultivates these moral qualities and enjoys good fortune, whereas the inferior man violates them and suffers evil fortune.

Therefore it is said: "The yin and the yang are established as the way of heaven; the elements of strength and weakness as the way of earth; and humanity and righteousness as the way of man." [3] It is also said there: "If we investigate into the cycle of things, we shall understand the concepts of life and death." [4] Great is the *Book of Changes!* Herein lies its excellence!

Selections from *An Interpretation of the Book of Changes*
[From *T'ung shu*, in *Chou Lien-ch'i chi*, 5:1a–b, 17b–19a, 38b]

CHAPTER I: SINCERITY

Sincerity (*ch'eng*) [5] is the essence of sagehood. "Great is the heavenly principle, the Originator. All things obtain their beginning from it." [6] It is the source of sincerity. "The Way of the heavenly principle is to change and transform, so that everything obtains its correct nature and destiny." [7] In this way sincerity is established. It is pure and perfectly good. Therefore, "The successive movement of the yin and the yang constitutes the Way. What issues from the Way is good and that which realizes it is the individual nature." [8] Origination and development characterize the penetration of sincerity, and adaptation and correctness are its completion [or recovery]. Great is the *Changes*, the source of nature and destiny! [5:1a–3b]

---

[2] *Book of Changes*, hexagram 1.   [3] *Book of Changes*, Shuo-kua 2.
[4] *Book of Changes*, Hsi Tz'u 1.
[5] A fundamental concept in the *Mean*, where it represents not only sincerity but also absolute genuineness or realness.
[6] *Book of Changes*, hexagram 1.   [7] *Book of Changes*, hexagram 1.
[8] *Book of Changes*, Hsi Tz'u 1.

CHAPTER 4: SAGEHOOD

"The state of absolute quiet and inactivity" is sincerity. The spirit is that which, "When acted on, immediately penetrates all things." [9] And the state of subtle emergence is the undifferentiated state between existence and nonexistence when activity has started but has not manifested itself in corporeal form. Sincerity is infinitely pure and hence evident. The spirit is responsive and hence works wonders. And emergence is subtle and hence abstruse. The sage is the one who is in the state of sincerity, spirit, and subtle emergence. [5:17b–19a]

CHAPTER 20: LEARNING TO BE A SAGE

Can one become a sage through learning?

Yes. . . . The essential way is to attain oneness [of mind]. By oneness is meant having no desire. Having no desire one is "empty" [absolutely pure and peaceful] while tranquil, and straightforward while in action. Being "empty" while tranquil, one becomes intelligent and hence penetrating. Being straightforward while active, one becomes impartial and hence all-embracing. Being intelligent, penetrating, impartial, and all-embracing, one is almost a sage. [5:38b]

A NUMERICAL UNIVERSE IN THE PHILOSOPHY OF SHAO YUNG

In so far as his ultimate problems are those of human nature and society, and in so far as his main source of inspiration is the *Book of Changes,* Shao Yung (1011–1077) is a true Neo-Confucianist. But actually he is in a class by himself. Like Chou Tun-yi, he was profoundly affected by Taoism, but his conclusions differ widely from those of Chou.

The distinctive characteristic of his philosophy is his theory of number as an essential element of existence. In a rudimentary way this concept is found in the *Lao Tzu,* the *Book of Changes,* and the writings of the Han philosopher Yang Hsiung. But Shao Yung was the first to make numbers the basis of all things and to evolve a definite formula for their production and evolution. Instead of using the number 2 (yin and yang) as in the

---

[9] *Book of Changes,* Hsi-tz'u I.

Book of Changes and Chou Tun-yi, or the number 5 so popular in the apocryphal literature of the Han dynasty, Shao Yung preferred the number 4. This is the number which, by simple progression, will arrive at 64, the number of hexagrams in the *Changes*. Han interpreters had claimed that these hexagrams exercised definite influence over periods of time, physical existence, and all human events. Likewise Shao Yung classified all possible existence into categories of four, such as four heavenly bodies, four periods of time, four kinds of creatures, four types of mandates of Heaven, and so forth, each group corresponding to the other groups and each going through one cycle after another without end. Nowhere else in Neo-Confucianism is this idea of cyclical change so dominant.

The theory of number, with its many charts, is too complicated to be presented adequately without lengthy quotation. From the short selections below it will be clear that the evolution begins with the Great Ultimate, goes through yin and yang, then spirit, then number, then form, and finally reaches materiality. Shao Yung also applied this theory of numerical growth and cycle to history, dividing the past into fixed and distinctive periods and classifying past events according to numerical categories.

These mathematical theories of Shao Yung were too obscure, complex, and arbitrary, it appears, to have any great influence upon the men of his time, who preferred a simpler cosmology such as that of Chou Tun-yi. It is rather in his concept of the sage—the perfect man who, because his mind consciously grasps the underlying unity of all existence, is able with complete objectivity to comprehend and respond to all things—that Shao Yung influenced his contemporaries and successors. This view of man's nature, colored by Taoist ideas of quietude and the unity of existence, played an important part in the development of Neo-Confucian thought.

SHAO YUNG

Selections from the Supreme Principles Governing the World

NUMBER

[From *Huang-chi ching-shih shu,* SPPY ed., 7A:24b–8B:23a]

As the Great Ultimate becomes differentiated, the two primary modes appear. The yang descends and interacts with the yin, and yin rises to interact with yang, and consequently the four secondary forms are constituted. Yin and yang interact and generate the four secondary forms of Heaven; the element of weakness and the element of strength interact and generate the four secondary forms of earth; and consequently the eight trigrams are completed. The eight trigrams intermingle and generate the myriad things. Therefore the One is differentiated into two, two into four, four into eight, eight into sixteen, sixteen into thirty-two, and thirty-two into sixty-four. Thus "in the successive division of yin and yang and the mutual operation of strength and weakness, the six positions [of the lines in each hexagram] in the *Book of Changes* form an orderly pattern." [10] Ten is divided into 100, 1,000, and 10,000. This is similar to the fact that the root engenders the trunk; the trunk, branches; and the branches, leaves. The greater the division, the smaller the result, and the finer the division, the more complex. Taken as a unit, it is One. Taken as diffused development, it is the many. Hence the heavenly principle divides, the earthly principle unites; the *chen* hexagram [symbol of development] augments, and the *sun* hexagram [symbol of bending] diminishes. Augmentation leads to division, division leads to diminution, and diminution leads to unity. [7A:24b]

The Great Ultimate is One. It produces the two [yin and yang] without engaging in activity. The two constitute spirit. Spirit engenders number, number engenders form, and form engenders material objects. [8B:23a]

Forms and numbers in the universe can be calculated, but their wonderful operations cannot be fathomed. The universe can be fully investigated through principles but not through corporeal forms. How can it be fully investigated through external observation? [8A:16b]

HISTORY
[From *Huang-chi ching-shih shu*, SPPY ed., 5:15a–b]

Therefore from the times of old in the administration of their empires rulers have had four kinds of Mandates: Correct Mandate, Accepted Mandate, Modified Mandate, and Substituted Mandate. Correct Mandate is that which is completely followed. Accepted Mandate is that which is followed with certain changes. Modified Mandate is mostly changed but partly followed. Substituted Mandate is that which is changed completely. That which is followed completely is continued completely. That which is followed with certain changes is continued with some deletions.

---

[10] *Book of Changes*, Shuo-kua 2.

That which is mostly changed but partly followed has [a great deal of] deletion followed by continuation. That which is changed completely is deleted completely. That which is changed completely is work meant for one generation. That which is mostly changed but partly followed is work meant for a hundred generations. That which is followed completely is work meant for a thousand generations. That which follows what ought to be followed and changes what ought to be changed is work meant for countless generations. Work meant for one generation, is this not the way of the Five Overlords? Work meant for ten generations, is this not the way of the Three Kings? Work meant for a hundred generations, is this not the way of the Five Emperors? Work meant for a thousand generations, is this not the way of the Three August Sovereigns? Work meant for countless generations, is this not the way of Confucius? Thus we know that the overlords, kings, emperors, and sovereigns had what were called Mandates for a limited number of generations. But the Mandate of Confucius transcends generations.

MAN
　　[From *Huang-chi ching-shih shu,* SPPY ed., 7A:4a–8B:26a]

The origin of Heaven and earth is based on the principle of the Mean [centrality]. Thus the heavenly and earthly principles never deviate from this central principle of existence although they are engaged in incessant transformation. Man is central in the universe, and the mind is central in man. The sun is most glorious and the moon is full when they are in the central position. Therefore, the gentleman highly values the principle of centrality. [7B:4a]

Our nature views things as they are, but our passion causes us to see things subjectively and egoistically. Our nature is impartial and enlightened, but our passions are partial and deceived. When the material endowment in man is characterized by the Mean and harmony, the elements of strength and weakness in him will be balanced. If yang predominates, he will be off balance toward strength, and if yin predominates, he will be off balance toward weakness. As knowledge directed toward the nature of man increases, the knowledge directed toward things will decrease.

Man occupies the most honored position in the scheme of things because he combines in him the principles of all species. If he honors his own position and enhances his honor, he can make all species serve him.

The nature of all things is complete in the human species.

The spirit of man is the same as the spirit of Heaven and earth. Therefore, when he deceives himself, he is deceiving Heaven and earth. Let him beware!

Spirit is nowhere and yet everywhere. The perfect man can penetrate the minds of others because he is based on the One. Spirit is perforce called the One and the Way (Tao). It is best to call it spirit. [8B:16a–17b]

The mind is the Great Ultimate. The human mind should be as calm as still water. Being calm, it will be tranquil. Being tranquil, it will be enlightened.

In the pursuit of prior existence [spiritual culture] sincerity is basic. Perfect sincerity can penetrate all spirits. Without sincerity, the Way cannot be attained.

Our substance and nature come from Heaven, but learning lies with man. Substance and nature develop from within, while learning enters into us from without. "It is due to our nature that intelligence results from sincerity," [11] but it is due to learning that sincerity results from intelligence.

The learning of a gentleman aims precisely at enriching his personality. The rest, such as governing people and handling things, is all secondary.

Without sincerity, one cannot investigate principle to the utmost.

Sincerity is the controlling factor in one's nature. It is beyond space and time.

He who acts in accordance with the principle of Heaven will have the entire process of creation in his grip. When the principle of Heaven is achieved, not only his personality, but also his mind, are enriched. And not only his mind but also his nature and destiny are enriched. To be in accordance with principle is normal, but to deviate from principle is abnormal. [8B:25a–26a]

OBSERVATION OF THINGS

[From *Huang-chi ching-shih shu*, SPPY ed., 6:26a–8B:27b]

When the mind retains its unity and is not disturbed, it can act on, and react to, all things harmoniously. Thus the mind of the gentleman

[11] *Mean*, 21.

is "empty" [absolutely pure and peaceful] and is not disturbed. [8B:29a]

By viewing things is not meant viewing them with one's physical eyes but with one's mind. Nay, not with one's mind but with the principle inherent in things. There is nothing in the universe without its principle, nature, and destiny. These can be known only when principle has been investigated to the utmost, when the nature is completely developed, and when destiny is fulfilled. The knowledge of these three is true knowledge. Even the sage cannot go beyond it. Whoever goes beyond it cannot be called a sage.

A mirror reflects because it does not obscure the corporeal form of things. But water [with its purity] does even better because it reveals the universal character of the corporeal form of things as they really are. And the sage does still better because he reflects the universal character of the feelings of all things. The sage can do so because he views things as things view themselves; that is, not subjectively but from the viewpoint of things. Since he is able to do this, how can there be anything between him and things? [6:26a–b]

When one can be happy or sad with things as though he were the things themselves, one's feelings may be said to have been aroused and to have acted to the proper degree. [8B:26a]

We can understand things as they are if we do not impose our ego on them. The sage gives things every benefit and forgets his own ego.

To let the ego be unrestrained is to give rein to passion; to give rein to passion is to be deluded; and to be deluded is to be ignorant. To follow the natural principles of things, on the other hand, is to grasp their nature; to grasp their nature is to be in possession of spiritual power; and to possess spiritual power is to achieve enlightenment. [8B:27b]

CHANG TSAI AND THE UNDERLYING UNITY OF MATERIAL-FORCE

Chang Tsai (Chang Heng-ch'ü, 1021–1077), the second major thinker in the traditional line of Neo-Confucian succession, continued the efforts of Chou Tun-yi to develop a Confucian metaphysics. As the basis of his system Chang Tsai posited the existence of a single primal substance composing all the universe, *ch'i* or material-force. The concept of *ch'i* had long been a part of Confucian cosmological vocabulary. The Han Confucianist Tung Chung-shu described it as a "limpid, colorless substance" which fills the universe, "surrounding man as water surrounds a fish" and uniting all creation. But Chang Tsai far extended the implications of this basic substance, making of it the sole reality of existence. The world and all its phenomena are not illusory products of mind, as the Buddhists declare, but manifestations of this primal material-force which Chang Tsai identifies with the Great Ultimate, the source of all being. Nor is there, as the Taoists maintain, any dichotomy between nonbeing and being, between the Great Vacuity and the creatures of worldly existence. For this Great Vacuity, which appears to be nonbeing, is for Chang Tsai actually only the primal material-force in its original, undifferentiated state.

The characteristic of this primal force is that it is in a constant process of change, integrating to form human beings and the other creatures of the world, disintegrating again to return to the state of the Great Vacuity. Man's task in the world is to comprehend this process of change and harmonize his action with it, not, like the Buddhists, to try to achieve some state of suspension outside the process, or like the Taoists, to strive by drugs and magic arts to stave off the inevitable disintegration of the human substance and prolong life beyond its natural limits.

CHANG TSAI

Great Harmony
[From *Cheng-meng*, I, in *Chang Heng-ch'ü chi*, 2:3b–10b]

Although material-force in the universe integrates and disintegrates, and attracts and repulses in a hundred ways, nevertheless the principle (*li*) according to which it operates has an order and is unerring.

The Great Vacuity of necessity consists of material-force. Material-force of necessity integrates to become the myriad things. Things of necessity disintegrate and return to the Great Vacuity. Appearance and disappearance following this cycle are all a matter of necessity. When, in the midst [of this universal operation] the sage fulfills the Way to the utmost, and identifies himself [with the universal processes of appearance and disappearance] without partiality, his spirit is preserved in the highest degree. Those [the Buddhists] who believe in annihilation expect departure without returning, and those [the Taoists] who cling to everlasting life and are attached to existence expect things not to change. While they differ, they are the same in failing to understand the Way. Whether integrated or disintegrated, my body remains the same. One is qualified to discuss the nature of man when one realizes that death is not annihilation.

When it is understood that Vacuity, Emptiness, is nothing but material-force, then existence and nonexistence, the hidden and the manifest, spirit and external transformation, and human nature and destiny, are all one and not a duality. He who apprehends integration and disintegration, appearance and disappearance, form and absence of form, and can trace them to their source, penetrates the secret of change.

If it is argued that material-force is produced from Vacuity, then because the two are completely different, Vacuity being infinite while material-force is finite, the one being substance and the other function, such an argument would fall into the naturalism of Lao Tzu who claimed that existence comes from nonexistence and failed to understand the eternal principle of the undifferentiated unity of existence and nonexistence. If it is argued that the countless phenomena are but things perceived in the Great Vacuity, then since things and the Vacuity would not be mutually conditioned, since the form and nature of things would be self-contained, and since these, as well as Heaven and man, would not be interdependent, such an argument would fall into the doctrine of the Buddha who taught that mountains, rivers, and the whole earth are all subjective illusions. This principle of unity is not understood because ignorant people know superficially that the substance of the nature of things is Vacuity, Emptiness, but do not know that function is based on the way of Heaven [law of nature]. Instead, they try to explain the universe with limited human knowledge. Since their undertaking is not thorough, they falsely assert that the universal operation of the principles of Heaven and earth is but illusory. They do not know the essentials of the hidden and the manifest, and jump to erroneous conclusions. They do not understand that the successive movements of the yin and the yang cover the entire universe, penetrate day and night, and form the standards of Heaven, earth, and man. Consequently they confuse Confucianism with Buddhism and Taoism. When they discuss the problems of the nature [of man and things] and their destiny or the way of Heaven, they either fall into the trap of illusionism or are determined that existence comes from nonexistence, and regard these doctrines as the summit of philosophical insight as well as the way to enter into virtue. They do not know how to choose the proper method but instead seek excessive views. Thus they are blinded by onesided doctrines and fall into error.

As the Great Vacuity, material-force is extensive and vague. Yet it ascends, descends, and moves in all ways without ever ceasing. . . . That which floats upward is the yang that is clear, while that which sinks to the bottom is the yin that is turbid. As a result of their contact and influence and of their integration and disintegration, winds and rains, snow and frost, come into being. Whether it be the countless variety of things in their changing configurations or the mountains and rivers in their fixed forms, the dregs of wine or the ashes of fire, there is nothing [in which the principle] is not revealed.

If material-force integrates, its visibility becomes effective and corporeal form appears. If material-force does not integrate, its visibility is not effective and there is no corporeal form. While material-force is integrated, how can one not say that it is temporary? While it is disintegrated, how can one hastily say that it is nonexistent? For this reason, the sage, having observed and examined above and below, only claims to know the causes of what is hidden and what is manifest but does not claim to know the causes of existence and nonexistence.

Material-force moves and flows in all directions and in all manners. Its two elements unite and give rise to concrete stuff. Thus the great variety of things and human beings is produced. In their ceaseless successions the two elements of yin and yang constitute the great principles of the universe.

[The *Book of Changes*] says: "The sun and moon push each other in their course and thus light appears. Winter and summer push each other and thus the year is completed." [12] Spirit is not conditioned by space and change does not assume any physical form. "The successive movement of yin and yang," "unfathomable is the movement of yin and yang" [13]—these describe the Way that penetrates day and night.

[12] Hsi Tz'u, II, 5.   [13] Hsi Tz'u, I, 4-5.

No two of the products of creation are alike. From this we know that although the number of things is infinite, at bottom there is nothing without yin or yang [which differentiates them]. From this we know also that the transformations and changes in the universe are due to these two fundamental forces.

The "Western Inscription" (Hsi-ming)

One section of the work just quoted, *For the Correction of Youthful Ignorance* (*Cheng-meng*), is known separately by the title "Western Inscription" (*Hsi-ming*) because it was inscribed on the western wall of Chang Tsai's study, and achieved extraordinary fame and influence in the Neo-Confucian school. In this brief essay Chang Tsai explores the ethical implications of his theory that all creation is formed of and united by this single underlying substance. In the terms of family relationships, so poignant and meaningful to Chinese readers, he relates how all human beings, all Heaven and earth, must be joined together as though creatures of one flesh and blood, and ruled, as appropriate to their kinship, by the principle of unselfish and humane love. Perhaps nowhere else in all Neo-Confucian literature does lofty metaphysical theory combine so effectively with the basic warmth, compassion, and humanism of ancient Confucianism as in this short passage.

[From *Chang Heng-ch'ü chi*, 1:1a–5b]

Heaven is my father and earth is my mother, and even such a small creature as I finds an intimate place in their midst.

Therefore that which extends throughout the universe I regard as my body and that which directs the universe I consider as my nature.

All people are my brothers and sisters, and all things are my companions.

The great ruler [the emperor] is the eldest son of my parents [Heaven and earth], and the great ministers are his stewards. Respect the aged —this is the way to treat them as elders should be treated. Show affection toward the orphaned and the weak—this is the way to treat them as the young should be treated. The sage identifies his character with that of Heaven and earth, and the virtuous man is the best [among the children of Heaven and earth]. Even those who are tired and infirm, crippled or sick, those who have no brothers or children, wives or husbands, are all my brothers who are in distress and have no one to turn to.

When the time comes, to keep himself from harm—this is the care of a son. To rejoice in Heaven and have no anxiety—this is filial piety at its purest.

He who disobeys [the principle of Heaven] violates virtue. He who destroys humanity (*jen*) is a robber. He who promotes evil lacks [moral] capacity. But he who puts his moral nature into practice and brings his physical existence to complete fulfillment can match [Heaven and earth].

He who knows the principles of transformation will skillfully carry forward the undertakings [of Heaven and earth], and he who penetrates spirit to the highest degree will skillfully carry out their will.

Do nothing shameful even in the recesses of your own house and thus bring no dishonor to them. Preserve the mind and nourish the nature and thus [serve them] with untiring effort.

The great Yü hated pleasant wine but attended to the protection and support of his parents. Border Warden Ying cared for the young and thus extended his love to his own kind.

Emperor Shun's merit lay in delighting his parents with unceasing effort, and Shen-sheng's reverence was demonstrated when he awaited punishment without making an attempt to escape.

Tseng Ts'an received his body from his parents and reverently kept it intact throughout life, while [Yin] Po-ch'i vigorously obeyed his father's command.

Wealth, honor, blessing, and benefit are meant for the enrichment of my life, while poverty, humble station, care, and sorrow will be my helpmates to fulfillment.

In life I follow and serve [Heaven and earth]. In death I will be at peace.

PRINCIPLE AND THE PHILOSOPHY OF HUMAN NATURE IN CH'ENG YI

With the appearance of the Ch'eng brothers, Neo-Confucian thought assumed the outlines of what was to become its final, fully developed form. At the same time the two brothers, though probably unaware of the fact themselves, diverged enough in their thought to foreshadow the two major branches into which the Neo-Confucian school later divided.

Ch'eng Hao, whose doctrines will be taken up later in relation to the school of Mind, and his younger brother, Ch'eng Yi (Ch'eng Yi-ch'uan, 1033–1107), were relatives of Chang Tsai and personally acquainted with both Chou Tun-yi and Shao Yung. They were thus in an ideal position to benefit from the contributions of these eminent exponents of the new philosophical movement that was developing. Ch'eng Yi adopted Chang Tsai's concept of *ch'i,* the material-force which is the stuff of all beings. But to this he added a second concept, that of *li* or principle, the eternal and unchanging laws which inform this basic stuff, defining and giving identity to the individual objects of creation. Material-force thus becomes in Cheng Yi's system no more than the raw matter of creation, inferior to and dependent upon principle for its concrete manifestation. Though in fact the two are always found in combination, principle is logically prior to and independent of the material-force in which it manifests itself.

This dichotomy of principle and material-force provided the basis for Ch'eng Yi's explanation of human nature, which Mencius had declared to be basically good. The principle of man's nature, according to Ch'eng Yi, is indeed eternally good and of equal excellence in all men. But the *ch'i* or material endowment which determines the physical nature or capacity of man differs with the individual and inhibits the full manifestation of his essential nature. Hence arise the evils and inequalities which we observe so clearly among men.

This explanation of evil and inequality as arising from differences in physical capacity, however, did not lead Ch'eng Yi to a fatalistic acceptance of individual limitations. On the contrary, he believed it possible and necessary for every man to overcome these limitations by making a conscious effort to understand the principle of his own nature and the objects of his environment, and by cultivating the moral attitude of "seriousness" or "reverence" *(ching).* This attitude Ch'eng Yi substituted for the "tranquillity" advocated by Chou Tun-yi, a term in his eyes too reminiscent of Buddhist and Taoist quietism. Thus he attempted to direct Neo-Confucianism away from the passive meditation and inward search for enlightenment that characterized Buddhism, toward a positive and vigorous program of moral discipline and inquiry by which all men might manifest more perfectly the goodness that lay in them. At the same time he strongly reinforced, against the Buddhist view of the world as impermanent or illusory, the characteristic Confucian confidence in the essential rationality and stability of the world.

CH'ENG YI

Principle and the Universe
[From *Erh Ch'eng i-shu*, 2A:1a, 19a; 6:2b; 18:9a; and *Erh Ch'eng ts'ui-yen*, 2:4a]

All things under Heaven can be understood by their principle. As there are things, there must be specific principles of their being. [As it is said in the *Book of Odes:*] [14] "Everything must have its principle." [*I-shu* 18:9a]

Due to the interaction of the two material forces [yin and yang] and the five agents, things vary as weak and strong in thousands of ways. What the sage follows, however, is the one principle. People must return to their original nature [which is identical with principle]. [6:2b]

The mind of one man is one with the mind of Heaven and earth. The principle of one thing is one with the principle of all things. The course of one day is one with the course of a year. [2A:1a]

There is only one principle in the world. You may extend it over the four seas and it is everywhere true. It is the unchangeable principle that "can be laid before Heaven and earth" and is "tested by the experience of the three kings." [15] Therefore to be serious (*ching*) is to be serious with this principle. To be humane is to be humane according to this principle. And to be truthful is to be truthful to this principle. [Confucius] said: "In times of danger, a gentleman cleaves to it." [16] [His pupil] also said: "I have not been able to be truthful to it." [17] These are what they said. Principle is extremely difficult to describe. [2A:19a]

The Master said: The principle of Heaven produces and reproduces, continuously without cease. This is because it takes no action. If it had acted by exhausting its knowledge and skill, it could never continue without cease. [*Ts'ui-yen*, 2:4a]

[14] Ta ya, T'ang, Cheng-min.   [15] *Mean*, 29.
[16] *Analects*, IV, 5.   [17] *Analects*, V, 5.

Human Nature
[From *Erh Ch'eng ts'ui-yen,* 3:4a; *Erh Ch'eng i-shu,* 18:17a–b; 19:4b]

The nature cannot be spoken of as internal or external. [*Ts'ui-yen,* 3:4a]

The mind in itself is originally good. As it expresses itself in thoughts and ideas, it is sometimes good and sometimes evil. When the mind has been aroused, it should be described in terms of feelings, and not as the mind itself. For instance, water is water. But as it flows, some to the east and some to the west, it is called streams and branches. [*I-shu,* 18:17a]

The nature comes from Heaven, whereas capacity comes from material-force. When material-force is clear, capacity is clear. On the other hand, when material-force is turbid, capacity is turbid. Take, for instance, wood. Whether it is straight or crooked is due to its nature. But whether it can be used as a beam or as a truss is determined by its capacity. Capacity may be good or evil, but the nature [of man and things] is always good. [19:4b]

Question: Do joy and anger come from our nature?

Answer: Yes. As soon as there is consciousness, there is our nature. As there is our nature, there must be feelings. Without nature, how can there be feelings?

Further Question: Suppose you said that joy and anger come from the outside?

Answer: Joy and anger do not come from the outside. They are due to external influence, but they arise from within.

Question: Are joy and anger to man's nature as waves are to water?

Answer: Yes. It is the nature of water to be clear, still, and smooth like a mirror, but when it strikes sand and stone, or when the ground underlying it is not level, it immediately begins to move violently. Or when wind blows over it, it develops waves and currents. But are these the nature of water? In man's nature there are only the four beginnings [of humanity, righteousness, decorum, and wisdom], and not the various forms of evil. But as without water there cannot be waves, so without nature there cannot be feelings. [18:17b]

Question: Since man's nature is originally enlightened, why is it sometimes obscured?

Answer: This must be investigated and understood. Mencius was correct in saying that man's nature is good. Even Hsün Tzu and Yang Hsiung failed to understand human nature, and Mencius was superior to other Confucianists in that he understood this. Man's nature is universally good. In cases where there is evil it is because of one's capacity. The nature is the same as principle, and principle is the same whether in the sage-emperors Yao and Shun or in the common man in the street. Material-force, which may be either clear or turbid, is the source of capacity. Men endowed with clear material-force are wise, while those endowed with turbid material-force are stupid.

Further Question: Can stupidity be changed?

Answer: Yes. Confucius said: "The most intelligent and the most stupid cannot be changed."[18] But in principle they can. Only those who ruin themselves and cast themselves away cannot be changed.

Question: Is it due to their capacity that the most stupid ruin and throw themselves away?

Answer: Certainly. But it cannot be said that capacity cannot be changed. Since all have the same basic nature, who cannot be changed? Because they ruin and cast themselves away and are not willing to learn, people are unable to change. In principle, if they were willing to learn, they could change. [18:17b]

Seriousness and Humanity

Ching, a basic Neo-Confucian virtue, variously means "serious," "reverent," "respectful," etc. Note that here it applies especially to one's inner moral nature and not simply to external authority.

[From *Erh Ch'eng i-shu,* 2A:13b; 15:1a, 8b, 9a; 18:3a, 5b, 6b; and *Erh Ch'eng ts'ui-yen,* 1:1b, 7b]

As to the meaning of the principle of Heaven. To be sincere is to be sincere to this principle, and to be serious [or reverent] is to be serious about this principle. It is not that there is something called sincerity or seriousness by itself. [*I-shu,* 2A:13b]

For moral cultivation, one must practice seriousness; for the advancement of learning, one must extend his knowledge to the utmost. [18:5b]

Question: What about people who devote all their effort to seriousness

---

[18] *Analects,* XVII, 3.

in order to straighten the internal life, but make no effort to square the external life?

Answer: What one has inside will necessarily be shown outside. Only worry that the internal life is not straightened. If it is straightened, then the external life will necessarily be squared. [18:3a]

If one makes singleness of mind the ruling factor with absolute steadfastness and exercises [what the *Book of Changes* calls] "seriousness to straighten the internal life," [19] he will possess great natural power. [15:1a]

Someone asked whether the will is necessary for seriousness.

Answer: In the initial stage, how can the will be dispensed with? Without the will, nothing can ensue [from consciousness].

Further Question: Is seriousness not tranquillity?

Answer: As soon as you speak of tranquillity, you fall into the doctrine of Buddhism. Only the word "seriousness" should be used but never the word "tranquillity." As soon as you use the word "tranquillity," you imply that seriousness is forgetfulness [or unconsciousness]. Mencius said: "There must be endeavor, but let there be no anxious expectation. Let the mind not forget its objective, but let there be no artificial effort to help it grow." [20] "There must be endeavor" means that the mind is active. Not to forget but to have no anxious expectation means not to try to make it grow. [18:6b]

"When you go abroad, behave to everyone as if you were receiving a great guest. Employ the people as if you were assisting at a great sacrifice." [21] [When Confucius said that], he meant nothing other than seriousness [or reverence]. Seriousness means unselfishness. As soon as one lacks seriousness, thousands of selfish desires arise to injure his humanity. [15:9a]

The Master said: Those who are sincere are always serious. Those who have not yet reached the state of sincerity must be serious before they become sincere. [*Ts'ui-yen,* 1:1b]

The Master said: The humane man regards Heaven and earth and all things as one body. There is nothing which is not part of his self. Knowing that, where is the limit [of his humanity]? If one does not possess [humanity as part of] himself, he will be thousands of miles away from Heaven and earth and the myriad things. [1:7b]

Essentially speaking, the way of humanity may be expressed in one

---

[19] Hexagram 2.   [20] *Mencius,* IIA, 2.   [21] *Analects,* XII, 2.

word, namely, impartiality. However, impartiality is but the principle of humanity; it should not be equated with humanity itself. When man puts impartiality into practice, that is humanity. Because of impartiality, one can accommodate both others and himself. Therefore a humane man is a man of both altruism and love. Altruism is the application of humanity while love is its function. [*I-shu*, 15:8b]

Investigation of Things
[From *Erh Ch'eng i-shu*, 2A:22b; 15:1a, 11a; 18:5b, 8b–9a]

To investigate things in order to understand principle to the utmost does not require the investigation of all things in the world. One has only to investigate the principle in one thing or one event exhaustively and the principle in other things or events can then be inferred. For example, when we talk about filial piety, we must find out what constitutes filial piety. If principle cannot be exhaustively understood in one event, investigate another. One may begin with either the easiest or the most difficult, depending on one's capacity. There are thousands of tracks and paths to the capital, yet one can enter if he has found just one way. Principle can be exhaustively understood in this way because all things share the same principle. Even the most insignificant of things and events have principle. [15:11a]

Someone asked what the first step was in the art of moral cultivation.

Answer: The first thing is to rectify the heart and make the will sincere. The sincerity of the will depends upon the extension of knowledge and the extension of knowledge depends upon the investigation of things. The word *ko* (investigate) means to arrive, as in saying: "The spirits of imperial progenitors have arrived." [22] There is principle in everything, and one must investigate principle to the utmost. There are many ways of doing this. One way is to read about and discuss truth and principles. Another way is to talk about people and events of the past and present, and to distinguish which are right and which wrong. Still another way is to handle affairs and settle them in the proper way. All these are ways to investigate the principle of things exhaustively. [18:5b]

To investigate principle to the utmost does not mean that it is neces-

---

[22] *Book of History*, I chi.

sary to investigate the principle of all things to the utmost or that principle can be understood merely by investigating one particular principle. It means that if one investigates more and more, one will naturally come to understand principle. [2A:22b]

Question: Do observation of things and self-examination mean returning to the self to seek [principles] after principles have been discovered in things?

Answer: You do not have to say that. Things and the self are governed by the same principle. If you understand one, you understand the other, for the truth within and the truth without are identical. In its magnitude it reaches the height of heaven and the depth of earth, but in its refinement it constitutes the reason for being of every single thing. The student should appreciate both.

Further Question: In the extension of knowledge, how about seeking first of all in the four beginnings [of humanity, righteousness, decorum and wisdom]?

Answer: To seek in our own nature and feelings is indeed to be concerned with our moral life. But every blade of grass and every tree possesses a principle which should be examined. [18:8b–9a]

A thing is an event. If the principles underlying all events are investigated to the utmost, there is nothing that cannot be understood.

If one extends knowledge to the utmost, one will have wisdom. Having wisdom, one can then make choices. [15:1a]

The investigation of principle to the utmost, the complete development of human nature, and the fulfillment of destiny are one and only one. As principle is exhaustively investigated, our nature is completely developed, and as our nature is completely developed, our destiny is fulfilled. [18:9a]

Criticism of Buddhism and Taoism
[From *Erh Ch'eng i-shu*, 15:5b, 7b; 18:10b]

The doctrines of Buddhism are not worthy of matching the doctrines of our sage. One need only compare them, and having observed that they are different, leave Buddhism well enough alone. If one tries to investigate all its theories, it is probably an impossible task, for before one has done that, the preoccupation will already have transformed him into a Buddhist. But let us take a look at Buddhism from its practice. In deserting his father and leaving his family, the Buddha severed all human relationships. It was merely for himself that he lived alone in the forest. Such a person should not be allowed in any community. Generally speaking, he did to others what he himself despised. Such is not the mind of the sage, nor is it the mind of a gentleman. The Buddhists themselves will not abide by the principles of the relationship between ruler and minister, between father and son, and between husband and wife, and criticize others for not doing as they do. They leave these human relationships to others and have nothing to do with them, setting themselves apart as a special class. If this is the way to lead the people, it will be the end of the human race. As to their discourse on principle and the nature of things, it is primarily in terms of life and death. Their feelings are based on love of life and fear of death. This is selfishness. [15:5b]

You cannot say that the teachings of the Buddhists are ignorant, for actually they are quite profound. But essentially speaking, they can finally be reduced to a pattern of selfishness. Why do we say this? In the world there cannot be birth without death or joy without sorrow. But wherever the Buddhists go, they always want to pervert this truth and preach the elimination of birth and death and the neutralization of joy and sorrow. In the final analysis this is nothing but self-interest. The teachings of the Taoists even carry with them an element of treachery, as evidenced in their sayings that the purpose of giving is to take away and the purpose of opening is to close.[23] Furthermore, their general intention is to fool the people and to be wise themselves. When [the First Emperor] of Ch'in fooled his people, his tricks probably were derived from the Taoists. [15:7b]

The Buddhists advocate the renunciation of the family and the world. Fundamentally the family cannot be renounced. Let us say that it can, however, when the Buddhists refuse to recognize their parents as parents and run away. But how can a person escape from the world? Only when a person no longer stands under heaven or upon the earth is he able to forsake the world. But while he continues to drink when thirsty and eat when hungry, he still stands under heaven and sets his feet on earth. [18:10b]

[23] *Lao Tzu*, 26.

THE SYNTHESIS OF SUNG NEO-CONFUCIANISM IN CHU HSI

The greatness of Chu Hsi (1130–1200) consists not in any striking originality of mind but in his remarkable capacity to adapt and enfold in one system of thought the individual contributions of his Sung predecessors. For this task he was well equipped by his breadth and subtlety of mind, and by powers of analysis and synthesis which enabled him, while putting ideas together, to articulate each of them with greater clarity and coherence than their originators had done. In this way he defined more precisely such concepts as the Great Ultimate, principle (*li*), material-force (*ch'i*), human nature, and the mind. Of his predecessors it was Ch'eng Yi upon whose philosophy he built most closely. Consequently his school of thought is often identified as the Ch'eng-Chu school, or as the school of Principle (*li*), after the most characteristic feature of their common teaching.

From this central doctrine—that there is an immaterial and immutable principle inhering in all things, which gives them their form and constitutes their essence—derives the fundamental rationalism and optimism of the Ch'eng-Chu school. This principle in man is his true nature, fundamentally good. Man's mind, moreover, is in essence one with the mind of the universe, capable of entering into all things and understanding their principles. Chu Hsi believed in the perfectability of man, in the overcoming of those limitations or weaknesses which arise from an imbalance in his physical endowment. His method was the "investigation of things" as taught by the *Great Learning;* that is, the study of their principles, and also self-cultivation to bring one's conduct into conformity with the principles which should govern it. Eventually, Chu asserted, persistent effort in this direction would result in everything's becoming suddenly clear and the full enlightenment of the sage being attained.

In this type of self-cultivation, broad learning went hand-in-hand with moral discipline. The "things" which Chu Hsi had in mind to investigate may be primarily understood as "affairs," including matters of conduct, human relations, political problems, etc. To understand them fully required of the individual both a knowledge of that literature in which such principles are revealed (the Classics and histories) and active ethical culture which would develop to the fullest the virtue of *jen* (humanity or benevolence). It is through *jen* that the individual overcomes his own selfishness and partiality, enters into all things in such a way as to fully identify himself with them, and thus unites himself with the mind of the universe, which is love and creativity itself. *Jen* is the essence of man, his "humanity," but it is also the cosmic principle that produces and embraces all things.

In contrast to Buddhism there is in Chu Hsi a kind of positivism which affirms the reality of things and the validity of objective study. His approach is plainly intellectual and rationalistic, reinforcing the traditional Confucian emphasis upon scholarship. Chu Hsi himself is probably the most stupendous example of such scholarly endeavor in the Chinese tradition. He wrote commentaries upon almost all of the Confucian Classics, conceived and supervised the condensation of Ssu-ma Kuang's monumental history of China, interested himself in political affairs, education, and agriculture, was a dynamic teacher at his school in the White Deer Grotto, and kept up an active correspondence on a wide variety of subjects. However he had little interest in pursuing his "investigation of things" into the realms of what we would call natural or social science. To the last his humanism manifested itself in a primary concern for human values and ends. The kind of objective investigation which set these aside or avoided the ultimate problems of human life would have seemed to him at best secondary and at worst pernicious.

For this reason we cannot look to Chu Hsi for the beginnings in China of a scientific method, though his philosophy, which stressed the order and intelligibility of things, could in a general way be considered conducive to the growth of science. Chu's influence on later men was felt chiefly through his commentaries on the Four Books—the *Analects,* the *Great Learning,* the *Mean,* and the *Mencius*—which he first enshrined as the basic texts of the Confucian school. In subsequent dynasties these texts, with Chu Hsi's commentary, became the basis of the civil service examinations and thus, in effect, the official orthodoxy of the empire from the fourteenth century down to the turn of the twentieth century. Though subsequent thinkers arose to dispute his metaphysics, few failed to share in his essential spirit of intellectual inquiry, focusing upon the Classics and reinterpreting them to meet the needs of their own time. Moreover, in Japan and Korea his writings were likewise accepted as the most complete and authoritative expositions of Confucian teaching. As such they exerted a significant influence on intellectual movements throughout the Far East, well into modern times.

CHU HSI

Principle and Material-Force
[From *Chu Tzu ch'üan-shu*, 49:1a–8a]

In the universe there has never been any material-force (*ch'i*) without principle (*li*) or principle without material-force.

Question: Which exists first, principle or material-force?

Answer: Principle has never been separated from material-force. However, principle is above the realm of corporeality whereas material-force is within the realm of corporeality. Hence when spoken of as being above or within the realm of corporeality, is there not a difference of priority and posteriority? Principle has no corporeal form, but material-force is coarse and contains impurities. [49:1a–b]

Fundamentally principle and material-force cannot be spoken of as prior or posterior. But if we must trace their origin, we are obliged to say that principle is prior. However, principle is not a separate entity. It exists right in material-force. Without material-force, principle would have nothing to adhere to. Material-force consists of the five agents of metal, wood, water, fire, and earth, while principle contains humanity, righteousness, propriety, and wisdom. [49:1b]

Question about the relation between principle and material-force.

Answer: Ch'eng Yi [24] expressed it very well when he said that principle is one but its manifestations are many. When Heaven, earth, and the myriad things are spoken of together, there is only one principle. As applied to man, however, there is in each individual a particular principle. [49:1b]

Question: What are the evidences that principle is in material-force?

Answer: For example, there is order in the complicated interfusion of the yin and the yang and the five agents. This is [an evidence of]

---

[24] Chu Hsi refers to predecessors by honorific titles which have been converted in the following texts to their ordinary names.

principle [in material-force]. If material-force did not consolidate and integrate, principle would have nothing to attach itself to. [49:2b]

Question: May we say that before Heaven and earth existed there was first of all principle?

Answer: Before Heaven and earth existed, there was certainly only principle. As there is this principle, therefore there are Heaven and earth. If there were no principle, there would also be no Heaven and earth, no man, no things, and in fact, no containing or sustaining [of things by Heaven and earth] to speak of. As there is principle, there is therefore material-force, which operates everywhere and nourishes and develops all things.

Question: Is it principle that nourishes and develops all things?

Answer: As there is this principle, therefore there is this material-force operating, nourishing, and developing. Principle itself has neither corporeal form nor body. [49:3a–b]

K'o-chi asked: When the creative process disposes of things, is it the end once a thing is gone, or is there a principle by which a thing that is gone may return?

Answer: It is the end once a thing is gone. How can there be material-force that has disintegrated and yet integrates once more? [49:3b–4a]

Question: "The Lord-on-High has conferred even on the inferior people a moral sense." [25] "When Heaven is about to confer a great responsibility on any man." [26] "Heaven, to protect the common people, made for them rulers." [27] "Heaven, in the production of things, is sure to be bountiful to them, according to their qualities." [28] "On the good-doer, the Lord-on-High sends down all blessings, and on the evil-doer, He sends down all miseries." [29] "When Heaven is about to send calamities to the world, it will usually produce abnormal people as a measure of their magnitude." [30] In passages like these, does it mean that there is really a master doing all this up in the blue sky or does it mean that Heaven has no personal consciousness and the passages are merely deductions from principle?

Answer: These passages have the same meaning. It is simply that principle operates this way. [49:4a]

[25] *Book of History,* Announcement of T'ang.
[27] *Book of History,* Great Declaration I.
[29] *Book of History,* Instructions of Yi.

[26] *Mencius,* VIB, 15.
[28] *Mean,* 17.
[30] Source unidentified.

Throughout the universe there are both principle and material-force. Principle refers to the Way [Tao], which is above the realm of corporeality and is the source from which all things are produced. Material-force refers to material objects, which are within the realm of corporeality; it is the instrument by which things are produced. Therefore in the production of man and things, they must be endowed with principle before they have their material force, and they must be endowed with material-force before they have corporeal form. [49:5b]

What are called principle and material-force are certainly two different entities. But considered from the standpoint of things, the two things are merged one with the other and cannot be separated with each in a different place. However, this does not destroy the fact that the two things are each a thing by itself. When considered from the standpoint of principle, before things existed their principles of being had already existed. Only their principles existed, however, but not yet the things themselves. . . .

There is principle before there can be material-force. But it is only when there is material-force that principle finds a place to settle. This is the process by which all things are produced, whether large as Heaven and earth or small as ants. Why should we worry that in the creative process of Heaven and earth, endowment may be wanting? Fundamentally, principle cannot be interpreted in the sense of existence or non-existence. Before Heaven and earth came into being, it already was as it is. [49:6a]

The nature of man and things is nothing but principle and cannot be spoken of in terms of integration and disintegration. That which integrates to produce life and disintegrates to produce death is only material-force, and what we call the spirit, the soul (hun-p'o), and consciousness are all the effects of material-force. Therefore when material-force is integrated, there are these effects. When it is disintegrated, they are no more. As to principle, fundamentally it does not exist or cease to exist because of such integration or disintegration. As there is a certain principle, there is the material-force corresponding to it, and as this material-force integrates in a particular instance, its principle is also endowed in that instance. [49:8a]

The Great Ultimate
[From *Chu Tzu ch'üan-shu*, 49:8b–13a]

Question: The Great Ultimate is not a thing existing in a chaotic state before the formation of Heaven and earth, but a general name for the principles of Heaven and earth and the myriad things. Is that correct?

Answer: The Great Ultimate is merely the principle of Heaven and earth and the myriad things. With respect to Heaven and earth, there is the Great Ultimate in them. With respect to the myriad things, there is the Great Ultimate in each and every one of them. Before Heaven and earth existed, there was assuredly this principle. It is the principle that through movement generates the yang. It is also this principle that through tranquillity generates the yin. [49:8b–9a]

Question: [In your commentary on Chou Tun-yi's *T'ung shu*], you said: "Principle is a single, concrete entity, and the myriad things partake of it as their reality. Hence each of the myriad things possesses in it a Great Ultimate." According to this theory, does the Great Ultimate not split up into parts?

Answer: Fundamentally there is only one Great Ultimate, yet each of the myriad things has been endowed with it and each in itself possesses the Great Ultimate in its entirety. This is similar to the fact that there is only one moon in the sky but when its light is scattered upon rivers and lakes, it can be seen everywhere. It cannot be said that the moon has been split. [49:10b–11a]

The Great Ultimate is not spatially conditioned; it has neither corporeal form nor body. There is no spot where it may be placed. When it is considered in the state before activity begins, this state is nothing but tranquillity. Now activity, tranquillity, yin and yang are all within the realm of corporeality. However, activity is after all the activity of the Great Ultimate and tranquillity is also its tranquillity, although activity and tranquillity themselves are not the Great Ultimate. This is why Master Chou Tun-yi spoke only of that state as Non-ultimate. While the state before activity begins cannot be spoken of as the Great Ultimate, nevertheless the principle of pleasure, anger, sorrow, and joy are already inherent in it. Pleasure and joy belong to yang and anger and sorrow belong to yin. In the initial stage the four are not manifested, but their principles are already there. As contrasted with the state after activity begins, it may be called the Great Ultimate. But still it is difficult to say. All this is but a vague description. The truth must be genuinely and earnestly realized by each individual himself. [49:11a–b]

Someone asked about the Great Ultimate.

Answer: The Great Ultimate is simply the principle of the highest good. Each and every person has in him the Great Ultimate and each and every thing has in it the Great Ultimate. What Master Chou called the Great Ultimate is an appellation for all virtues and the highest good in Heaven and earth, man and things. [49:11b]

The Great Ultimate is similar to the top of a house or the zenith of the sky, beyond which point there is no more. It is the ultimate of principle. Yang is active and yin is tranquil. In these it is not the Great Ultimate that acts or remains tranquil. It is simply that there are the principles of activity and tranquillity. Principle is not visible; it becomes visible through yin and yang. Principle attaches itself to yin and yang as a man sits astride a horse. As soon as yin and yang produce the five agents, they are confined and fixed by physical nature and are thus differentiated into individual things each with its nature. But the Great Ultimate is in all of them. [49:13a]

Heaven and Earth
[From *Chu Tzu ch'üan-shu,* 49:19a–24b]

In the beginning of the universe there was only material-force consisting of yin and yang. This force moved and circulated, turning this way and that. As this movement gained speed, a mass of sediment was pushed together and, since there was no outlet for this, it consolidated to form the earth in the center of the universe. The clear part of material-force formed the sky, the sun and moon, and the stars and zodiacal spaces. It is only on the outside that the encircling movement perpetually goes on. The earth exists motionless in the center of the system, not at the bottom. [49:19a]

In the beginning of the universe, when it was still in a state of undifferentiated chaos, I imagine there were only water and fire. The sediment from water formed the earth. If today we climb the high mountains and look around, we will see ranges of mountains in the shape of waves. This is because the water formed them like this, though we do not know at what period they solidified. This solidification was at first very soft, but in time it became hard.

Question: I imagine it is like the tide rushing upon and making waves in the sand. [Is that right?]

Answer: Yes. The most turbid water formed the earth and the purest fire became wind, thunder, lightning, stars, and the like. [49:19b–20a]

Further Question: Can the universe be destroyed?

Answer: It is indestructible. But in time man will lose all moral principles and everything will be thrown together in a chaos. Man and things will all die out, and then there will be a new beginning.

Further Question: How was the first man created?

Answer: Through the transformation of material-force. When the essence of yin and yang and the five agents are united, man's corporeal form is established. This is what the Buddhists call production by transformation. There are many such productions today, such as lice. [49:20a]

Question: With reference to the mind of Heaven and earth and the principle of Heaven and earth. Principle is moral principle. Is mind the will of a master?

Answer: The mind is the will of a master, it is true, but what is called "master" is precisely principle itself. It is not true that outside of the mind there is principle, or that outside of principle there is mind. [49:23a]

Heaven and earth have no other business but to have the mind to produce things. The material-force of the origination [the Great Ultimate including principle and material-force] revolves and circulates without a moment of rest, doing nothing except creating the myriad things.

Question: Ch'eng Yi said: "Heaven and earth create and transform and yet of themselves they have no mind. The sage has a mind but does not take any action."

Answer: That shows where Heaven and earth have no mind. It is like this: The four seasons run their course and the various things flourish. When do Heaven and earth entertain any mind of themselves? As to the sage, he only follows principle. What action does he need to take? This is the reason why Ch'eng Hao said: "The constant principle of

Heaven and earth is that their mind is in all things, yet of themselves they have no mind. The constant principle of the sage is that his feelings are in accord with all creation, yet of himself he has no feelings." This is extremely well said.

Question: Does having their mind in all things not mean to pervade all things with their mind without any selfishness?

Answer: Heaven and earth reach all things with this mind. When man receives it, it becomes the human mind. When things receive it, it becomes the mind of things [in general]. And when grass, trees, birds, or animals receive it, it becomes the mind of grass, trees, birds, and animals [in particular]. All of these are simply the one mind of Heaven and earth. Thus we must understand in what sense Heaven and earth have mind, and in what sense they have no mind. We cannot be inflexible. [49:23b–24a]

When the myriad things are born and grow, that is the time when Heaven and earth have no mind. When dried and withered things desire life, that is the time when Heaven and earth have mind. [49:24a]

Heavenly and Earthly Spirits
[From *Chu Tzu ch'üan-shu*, 51:2a–20a]

Someone asked whether there are heavenly and earthly spirits.

Answer: How can this matter be quickly explained? Even if it could, would you believe it? You must look into all principles of things and gradually understand, and then this puzzling problem will be solved by itself. When Fan Ch'ih asked about wisdom, Confucius said: "To devote oneself earnestly to the duties due to men, and to respect the heavenly and earthly spirits but keep them at a distance, may be called wisdom." [31] Let us understand those things that should be understood. Those that cannot be understood let us set aside. By the time we have thoroughly understood ordinary daily matters, the principles governing the heavenly and earthly spirits will naturally be seen. This is the way to wisdom. When Confucius said: "If we are not yet able to serve man, how can we serve the earthly spirits?" [32] he expressed the same idea. [51:2a]

Is expansion the heavenly spirit and contraction the earthly spirit? [33]

The teacher drew a circle on the desk with his hand and pointing

---

[31] *Analects*, VI, 20.   [32] *Analects*, XI, 12.   [33] A play on words of similar sound.

to its center, said: Principle is like a circle. Within there is differentiation like this. All cases of material-force coming forth belong to yang and are the heavenly spirit. All cases of material-force returning to its origin belong to yin and are the earthly spirit. In the day, forenoon is the heavenly spirit, afternoon the earthly spirit. In the month, from the third day onward is the heavenly spirit; after the sixteenth day, it is the earthly spirit.

T'ung Po-yü asked: Is it correct when speaking of the sun and moon as opposites, to say that the sun is the heavenly spirit and the moon is the earthly spirit?

Answer: Yes, it is. Plants growing are the heavenly spirit, plants declining are the earthly spirit. A person from childhood to maturity is the heavenly spirit, while a man in his declining years and old age is the earthly spirit. In breathing, breath going out is the heavenly spirit, breath coming in is the earthly spirit. [51:6b]

Question about the principles of life and death and heavenly and earthly spirits:

Answer: As the way of Heaven operates, the myriad things develop and grow. There is [logically] principle first and then material-force. Although they coexist at the same time, in the final analysis principle is basic. Man receives it and thus possesses life. The clear part of material-force becomes his vital force, while the turbid part becomes his physical nature. Consciousness and movement are due to yang, while corporeal form and body are due to yin. The vital force belongs to the heavenly aspect of the soul (*hun*) and the body is governed by the earthly aspect of the soul (*p'o*). In his commentary on the *Huai-nan Tzu* Kao Yu said: "*Hun* is the spirit of yang and *p'o* is the spirit of yin." [7:6a] By spirit is meant the master of the body and the vital force. Man is born as a result of the integration of refined material-force. He possesses this material-force only in a certain amount, which in time necessarily becomes exhausted. When exhaustion takes place, the heavenly aspect of the soul and the vital force return to Heaven, the body and the earthly aspect of the soul return to the earth, and the man dies. . . . At death material-force necessarily disintegrates. However, it does not disintegrate completely at once. Therefore in religious sacrifices we have the principle of spiritual influence and response. Whether the material-force of ancestors of many generations ago is still there or not cannot be known. Nevertheless, since those who perform the sacrificial rites are their descendants, the material-force between them is after all the same. Hence there is the principle by which they can penetrate and respond. But the material-force that has disintegrated cannot again be integrated. According to Buddhists, man after death becomes a spirit, and the spirit again becomes a man. If so, then in the universe there would always be the same number of people coming and going, with no need of the creative process of production and reproduction. This is decidedly absurd. [51:18b–20a]

The Relation Between the Nature of Man and Things and Their Destiny
[From *Chu Tzu ch'üan-shu,* 42:2b–5a]

Ch'eng Yi said that destiny is what is endowed by Heaven and the nature is what things receive. Principle is one. As endowed by Heaven in all things it is called destiny. As received by creatures from Heaven, it is called their nature. The difference lies in the points of view. [42:2b]

Question: Destiny is what Heaven endows in man and things and their nature is what they receive from Heaven. But the nature and destiny each have two aspects. From the point of view of their principle, the principle that is destined in man and things by Heaven is called destiny, and the principle received by them from Heaven is called their nature. From the point of view of material-force, the material-force that is destined in man and things by Heaven is also called destiny, and the material-force received by them from Heaven is also called their nature. Is this correct?

Answer: Material-force cannot be called the nature or destiny. They exist because of it, that is all. When the nature of Heaven and earth are spoken of, it refers to principle only; when the physical nature is spoken of, it refers to principle and material-force combined. Material-force is not to be referred to as the nature and destiny. [42:4b]

[The *Book of Odes* says]: "Heaven produces the teeming multitude in such a way that inherent in every single thing there is the principle for its being." [34] This means that at the very time when a person is born, Heaven has already given him his nature. The nature is nothing but prin-

[34] Ta ya, T'ang, Cheng-min.

ciple. It is called the nature because it is endowed in man. It is not a concrete entity by itself, to be destined as the nature, and to exist without beginning and without end. As I once illustrated, destiny or mandate is like an appointment to office by the throne, and the nature is like the office retained by the officer. This is why Ch'eng Yi said that destiny is what is endowed by Heaven and the nature is what things receive. The reason is very clear. Therefore when ancient sages and virtuous men spoke of the nature and destiny, they always spoke of them in relation to concrete affairs. For example, when they spoke of full development of human nature they meant the complete realization of the moral principles of the three bonds [the bond of minister to ruler, son to father, and wife to husband] and the five constant virtues [righteousness on the part of the father, love on the part of the mother, brotherliness on the part of the elder brother, respect on the part of the younger brother, and filial piety on the part of the son], covering the relationships between the ruler and ministers and between father and son. When they spoke of nourishing our nature, they meant that we should nourish these moral principles so as to keep them from injury. This central truth runs through the most subtle principles and the most obvious facts, with nothing left uncovered. These are not empty words. [42:5a]

On being asked about [Chang Tsai's] chapter on moral character failing to overcome material-force, [Chu Hsi] said: Master Chang merely said that both the nature and material-force flow down from above. If my moral character is not adequate to overcome material-force, then there is nothing to do but to submit to material-force as endowed by Heaven. If my moral character is adequate to overcome material-force, however, then what I receive from the endowment is all moral character. Therefore if I investigate principle to the utmost and fully develop my nature, then what I have received is wholly Heaven's moral character, and what Heaven has endowed in me is wholly Heaven's principle. The cases in which material-force cannot be altered are life, death, and longevity or brevity of life, for these, and poverty and wealth, honor and humble station, all depend on material-force. On the other hand, [as Mencius said], though the practice of righteousness between the ruler and his ministers and the exercise of love between father and son are Heaven's mandate [destiny], they are also a part of man's nature. Therefore the gentleman does not say they are Heaven's mandate.[35] They must proceed from myself, not from [Heaven's mandate]. [42:3a–b]

The Nature of Man and Things
[From *Chu Tzu ch'üan-shu*, 42:6a–15a]

The Way [moral law] is identical with the nature of man and things and their nature is identical with the Way. They are one and the same. But we must understand why it is called the nature and why it is called the Way. [42:6a]

After reading some essays by Hsün and others on the nature, the teacher said: In discussing the nature it is important to know first of all what kind of thing it really is. Ch'eng Yi put it best when he said that "the nature of man and things is identical with principle." Now if we regard it as principle, then surely it has neither form nor shadow. It is nothing but this very principle. In man, humanity, righteousness, decorum, and wisdom are his nature, but what shape or form have they? All they have are the principles of humanity, righteousness, decorum, and wisdom. As they possess these principles, many deeds are carried out, and man is able to have the feelings of commiseration, shame, deference, and compliance, and of right and wrong. Take, for example, the nature of drugs, such as the property of increasing heat [vitality]. There is no external form of this nature to be found in the drug. Only after the drug is taken, heat or cold is produced—this is their nature. In man, the nature is humanity, righteousness, decorum, and wisdom. According to Mencius, these four fundamental virtues are rooted in the mind. When, for example, he speaks of the mind of commiseration, he attributes feeling to the mind. [42:6b]

Hu Chi-sui [grandson of Hu An-kuo (1073–1138), founder of the Hu school of Neo-Confucian philosophy], adhering to the doctrine of his school, said: The nature cannot be spoken of as good, for original goodness has no opposite. As soon as you describe the nature as good, you are already contrasting it with evil, and when you speak of it in terms of the opposite of good and evil, it is no longer the original nature you are talking about. Original nature is transcendant, absolute, and beyond comparison, whereas goodness applies to the mundane world. The moment you say it is good, you are contrasting it with evil and you are no longer

[35] *Mencius*, VII B, 24.

talking about the original nature. When Mencius said that the nature is good, he did not mean that the nature is morally good, but simply used the language of admiration, like saying, "How fine the nature!" just as the Buddha exclaimed, "Excellent is the Path!"

In criticizing this theory I say: It is true that original nature is an all-pervading perfection not contrasted with evil. This is true of what Heaven has endowed in the self. But when it operates in man, there is the differentiation of good and evil. When man acts in accord with it, there is goodness. When man acts out of accord with it, there is evil. How can it be said that the good is not the original nature? It is in its operation in man that the distinction of good and evil arises, but conduct in accord with the original nature is due to the original nature. If, as they say, there is the original goodness and there is another goodness contrasted with evil, there must be two natures. Now what is received from Heaven is the same nature as that in accordance with which goodness ensues, except that as soon as good appears, evil, by implication, also appears, so that we necessarily speak of good and evil in contrast. But it is not true that there is originally an evil existing out there, waiting for the appearance of good to oppose it. We fall into evil only when our actions are not in accord with the original nature. [42:9b–10a]

It is said that the word "good" in the expression "The nature is good" is different from the good as contrasted with evil. On that theory I hold that the good at the source of our being and the good in the process of life involving both good and evil are not two different things. They merely refer to two different states before and after it has emerged into activity. But it is the same good whether before it has emerged or afterward when it becomes contrasted with evil. Only after its emergence is it intermingled with evil. But the good in this state is the same good that emanates from the source of our being. [42:13b–14a]

In your [36] letter you say that you do not know whence comes human desire. This is a very important question. In my opinion, what is called human desire is the exact opposite of the principle of Heaven [nature]. It is permissible to say that human desire exists because of the principle of Heaven, but it is wrong to say that human desire is the same as the principle of Heaven, for in its original state the principle of Heaven is free from human desire. It is from the deviation in the operation of the prin-

[36] Ho Shu-ching.

ciple of Heaven that human desire arises. Ch'eng Hao says that "Good and evil in the world are both the principle of Heaven. What is called evil is not originally evil. It becomes evil only because of deviation from the Mean." Your quotation, "Evil must also be interpreted as the nature," expresses the same idea. [42:14b–15a]

The Nature of Man and the Nature of Things Compared
[From *Chu Tzu ch'üan-shu*, 42:27b–30a]

Chi submitted to the Teacher the following statement concerning a problem in which he was still in doubt: The nature of man and the nature of things are in some respects the same and in other respects different. Only after we know wherein they are similar and wherein they are different can we discuss the nature. Now, as the Great Ultimate begins its activity, the two material-forces [yin and yang] assume corporeal form, and as they assume corporeal form, the myriad transformations of things are produced. Both man and things have their origin here. This is where they are similar. But the two material-forces and the five agents, in their fusion and intermingling, and in their interaction and mutual influence, produce innumerable changes and inequalities. This is where they are different. They are similar in regard to principle, but different in respect to material-force. There must be principle, for only then can there be that which constitutes the nature of man and things. Consequently, what makes them similar cannot make them different. There must be material-force, for only then can there be that which constitutes their corporeal form. Consequently, what makes them different cannot make them similar. Therefore, in your *Questions and Answers on the Great Learning,* you said: "From the point of view of principle, all things have one source, and therefore man and things cannot be distinguished as higher and lower creatures. From the point of view of material-force, man receives it in its perfection and unimpeded while things receive it partially and obstructed. Because of this, they are unequal, man being higher and things lower. However, while in respect to material-force they are unequal, they both possess it as the stuff of life, and while in respect to principle they are similar, in receiving it to constitute the nature, man alone differs from other things. Thus consciousness and movement proceed from material-force while humanity, righteousness, decorum, and wisdom proceed from principle. Both man and things are capable of consciousness and movement, but though things possess humanity, righteousness, decorum, and wisdom, they cannot have them completely. . . ." In your *Collected Commentaries* you maintain that in respect to material-force, man and things do not seem to differ in consciousness and movement, but in respect to principle, the endowment of humanity, righteousness, decorum, and wisdom are necessarily imperfect in things. Here you say that man and things are similar in respect to material-force but different in respect to principle, in order to show that man is higher and cannot be equaled by things. In the *Questions and Answers on the Great Learning,* you say that man and things are similar in respect to principle but different in respect to material-force, in order to show that the Great Ultimate is not deficient in anything and cannot be interfered with by any individual. Looking at it this way, there should not be any question. When someone was puzzled by the discrepancies in the *Questions and Answers on the Great Learning* and the *Collected Commentaries,* I explained it in this way. Is this correct?

The Teacher commented: On this subject you have discussed very clearly. It happened that last evening a friend talked about this matter and I briefly explained it to him, but not so systematically as you have done in this statement. [42:27b–29a]

Question: Principle is what is received from Heaven by both man and things. Do things without feelings also possess principle?

Answer: They certainly have principle. For example, a ship can go only on water while a cart can go only on land. [42:30a]

Physical Nature
[From *Chu Tzu ch'üan-shu,* 42:8a; 43:2b–8a]

The nature is principle only. But, without the material-force and solid substance of the universe, principle would have nothing in which to inhere. When material-force is received in its state of clearness, there will be no obscurity or obstruction and principle will express itself freely. If there is obscurity or obstruction, then in the operation of principle, the principle of Heaven will dominate if the obstruction is small and human selfish desire will dominate if the obstruction is great. From this we know that the original nature is perfectly good. This is the nature described by

Mencius as "good," by Chou Tun-yi as "pure and perfectly good," and by Ch'eng Yi as "basic nature" and "the nature traced to the source of our being." However, it will be obstructed if physical nature contains impurity. Hence [as Chang Tsai said], "a gentleman does not consider physical nature as really nature," and, "If one learns to return to accord with his original nature, then the nature of Heaven and earth will be preserved." In our discussion of the nature, we must include physical nature before the discussion can be complete. [43:2b–3a]

The physical nature is no different from the nature of Heaven and earth. The point is that the nature of Heaven and earth runs through the physical nature. For example, the good nature is like water. The physical nature is as though you sprinkled some sauce and salt in it and it then acquired a peculiar flavor. [43:4a]

The nature is like water. If it flows in a clean channel, it is clear; if it flows in a dirty channel, it becomes turbid. When the nature is endowed with material substance that is clear and balanced, it will be preserved in its completeness. This is true of man. When the nature is endowed with material substance that is turbid and unbalanced, it will be obscured. This is true of animals. Material-force may be clear or turbid. That received by man is clear and that received by animals is turbid. Men mostly have clear material-force and hence are different from animals. However, those whose material-force is turbid are not far removed from animals. [43:7a–b]

Someone asked about this inequality in the clearness of the material endowment. The teacher said: Differences in the material endowment are not limited to one kind and are not described only in terms of clearness and turbidity. There are men who are so bright that they know everything. Their material-force is clear, but what they do may not all be in accord with principle. The reason is that their material-force is not pure. There are others who are respectful, generous, loyal, and truthful. Their material-force is pure, but their knowledge is not always penetrating. The reason is that their material-force is not clear. From this you can deduce the rest. [42:8a]

Although the nature is the same in all men, it is inevitable that [in most cases] the various elements in their material endowment are unbalanced. In some men the material-force of wood predominates. In such cases, the feeling of commiseration is generally uppermost, but the feeling of shame, of deference and compliance, and of right and wrong are impeded by the predominating force and do not emanate into action. In others, the material-force of metal predominates. In such cases the feeling of shame is generally uppermost, but the other feelings are impeded and do not emanate into action. So with the material-forces of water and fire. It is only when the yin and yang are harmonized and the five moral natures [of humanity, righteousness, propriety, wisdom, and good faith] are all complete that a man has the qualities of the Mean and correctness and becomes a sage. [43:8a–b]

The Mind
[From *Chu Tzu ch'üan-shu*, 44:1b–13b, 28a–29b]

The principle of the mind is the Great Ultimate. The activity and tranquillity of the mind are the yin and yang. [44:1b]

Mind alone has no opposite. [44:1b]

Question: Is consciousness what it is because of the intelligence of the mind or is it because of the activity of material-force?

Answer: Not material-force alone. Before [material-force] existed, there was already the principle of consciousness. But principle at this stage does not give rise to consciousness. Only when it comes into union with material-force is consciousness possible. Take, for example, the flame of this candle. It is because it has received this rich fat that there is so much light.

Question: Is that which emanates from the mind material-force?

Answer: No, that is simply consciousness. [44:2a]

Question: Mind is consciousness and the nature is principle. How do the mind and principle pervade each other and become one?

Answer: They need not move to pervade each other. From the very start they pervade each other.

Question: How do they pervade each other from the very start?

Answer: Without the mind, principle would have nothing in which to inhere. [44:2a]

Question: Mind as an entity embraces all principles. The good that emanates, of course, proceeds from the mind. But the evil that emanates is all due to physical endowment and selfish desires. Does it also proceed from the mind?

Answer: It is certainly not the original substance of the mind, but it also emanates from the mind.

Further Question: Is this what is called the human mind? [37]

Answer: Yes.

Thereupon Cheng Tzu-sheng asked: Does the human mind include both good and evil?

Answer: Both are included. [44:2b–3a]

Question: The mind is essentially an acting thing. It is not clear to me whether before [feelings] are aroused the mind is completely quiet and tranquil or whether its tranquillity contains within it a tendency toward activity.

Answer: It is not that tranquillity contains within it a tendency toward activity. Chou Tun-yi said that "tranquillity means nonexistence and activity means existence." Tranquillity is not nonexistence as such. Because it has not assumed corporeal form, we call it nonexistence. It is not because of activity that there is existence. Because [activity makes] it visible, we call it existence. Chang Tsai's theory that "the mind unites and commands man's nature and feelings" is excellent. The nature is tranquil while feelings are active, and the mind involves both tranquillity and activity. Whether these refer to its substance or its function depends on one's point of view. While it is in the state of tranquillity, the principle of activity is already present. Ch'eng Yi said that in the state of centrality [i.e., before the feelings are active], the ear hears nothing and the eye sees nothing, but the principles of hearing and seeing must be already there before hearing and seeing are possible. When activity takes place, it is the same tranquillity that becomes active. [44:6b–7a]

In the passage [by Chang Tsai], "When the mind is enlarged, it can enter into everything of the universe," the expression "enter into" is like saying that humanity enters into all events and is all-pervasive. It means that the operation of the principle of the mind penetrates all as blood circulates and reaches the entire [body]. If there is a single thing not yet entered, the reaching is not yet complete and there are still things not yet embraced. This shows that the mind still excludes something. For selfishness separates and obstructs, and consequently the external world

---

[37] The "human mind" is contrasted with the "moral mind" in that the former is in a precarious position because it is liable to mistakes whereas the moral mind always follows moral law. The terms derive from the *Book of History*, Counsels of the Great Yü.

and the self stand in opposition. This being the case, even those dearest to us may be excluded. "Therefore the mind that excludes is not qualified to be one with the mind of Heaven." [44:12b]

Question: How can the mind by means of moral principle (Tao) penetrate all things without any limit?

Answer: The mind is not like a large horizontal door which can be enlarged by force. We must eliminate the obstructions of selfish desires, and then it will be pure and clear and able to know all. When the principles of things and events are investigated to the utmost, comprehension will come as a great release. Chang Tsai said: "Do not allow the mind to be fettered by what is heard or what is seen." "When the mind is enlarged it can enter into everything in the universe." This means that if penetration is achieved through moral principles, there will be comprehension like a great release. If we confine [the mind] to what is heard and what is seen, naturally our understanding will be narrow. [44:13a-b]

Someone asked whether it is true that the Buddhists have a doctrine of observation of the mind.

Answer: The mind is that with which man rules his body. It is one and not a duality, is subject and not object, and controls the external world instead of being controlled by it. Therefore, if we observe the external objects with the mind, their principles will be apprehended. Now, [in the Buddhist view], there is another thing to observe the mind. If this is true, then outside this mind there is another one which is capable of controlling it. But is what we call the mind a unity or a duality? Is it subject or object? Does it control the external world or is it controlled by the external world? We do not need to be taught to see the fallacy of the [Buddhist] doctrine.

Someone may say: In the light of what you have said, how are we to understand such expressions by sages and worthies as "refinement and unity of mind"; "Hold it fast and you preserve it— Let it go and you lose it"; "Fully develop one's mind and know one's nature"; "Preserve one's mind and nourish one's nature"; and "[Standing] let a man see [truthful words and serious action] in front of him, [riding in a carriage] let him see them attached to the yoke"?

Answer: These expressions and [the Buddhist doctrine] sound similar but are different, just like the difference between seedlings and weeds, or between vermilion and purple, and the student should clearly distinguish them. What is meant by the precariousness of the human mind is the budding of human selfish desires, and what is meant by the subtlety of the moral mind is the mysterious depth of the principle of Heaven. The mind is one; it is simply called differently depending on whether or not it is rectified. The meaning of the saying, "Have absolute refinement and unity of mind," [38] is to abide by what is right and discern what is wrong, and to discard the wrong and restore the right. If we can do this, we shall indeed "hold fast the Mean," and avoid the partiality of too much or too little. The saying does not mean that the moral mind is one mind, the human mind another, and that there is still a third one to make them refined and united. By "holding it fast and preserving it" [39] is not meant that one mind holds fast to another and so preserves it. Neither does "letting it go and losing it" [40] mean that one mind lets go another and so loses it. It merely means that if the mind holds fast to itself, what might be lost will be saved, and if the mind does not hold fast but lets itself go, then what is preserved will be lost. "Holding it fast" is another way of saying that we should not allow our conduct during the day to fetter and destroy our innate mind which is characterized by humanity and right-eousness. It does not mean that we should sit in a rigid position to preserve the obviously idle consciousness and declare that "this is holding it fast and preserving it!" As to the full development of the mind, this is to investigate things and study their principles to the utmost, to arrive at broad penetration, and thus to be able fully to realize the principle em-bodied in the mind. By preserving the mind is meant, "Seriousness to straighten the internal life and righteousness to square the external life," [41] a way of cultivation similar to what has just been called refinement, unity, holding fast, and preserving. Therefore one who has fully developed his mind can know his nature and know Heaven, because the reality of the mind is unclouded and he is equipped to search into principle in its nat-ural state. One who has preserved the mind can nourish his nature and serve Heaven, because the substance of the mind is not lost and he is equipped to follow principle in its natural state. Is this the same as using one mind fully to develop another, or one mind to preserve another, like two things holding on to each other and refusing to let go?

[38] *Book of History*, Counsels of the Great Yü.   [39] *Mencius*, VI A, 8.
[40] *Mencius*, VI A, 8.   [41] *Book of Changes*, hexagram 2.

The expressions, "in front of him" and "attached to the yoke" [42] are intended to teach sincerity and truthfulness [in words] and earnestness and seriousness [in conduct], as if saying that if these moral qualities are always borne in mind, we will see them no matter where we may go. But it does not mean that we observe the mind. . . . According to the doctrine of the Buddhists, one seeks the mind with the mind or employs the mind with the mind, like the mouth biting the mouth or the eye seeing the eye. [44:28a–29b]

The Mind, the Nature, and the Feelings
[From *Chu Tzu ch'üan-shu*, 45:3a–19b]

Sometime ago I read statements by Hu Wu-feng [1100–1155] in which he spoke of the mind only in contrast to the nature, leaving the feelings unaccounted for. Later when I read Chang Tsai's doctrine that "the mind unites and commands man's nature and feelings," I realized that it was a great contribution. Only then did I find a satisfactory account of the feelings. His doctrine agrees with that of Mencius. In the words of Mencius: "The feeling of commiseration is the beginning of humanity" [II A, 6]. Now humanity is the nature, and commiseration is feeling. In this, the mind can be seen through the feelings. He further said: "Humanity, righteousness, decorum, and wisdom are rooted in the mind" [VII A, 21]. In this, the mind is seen through the nature. For the mind embraces both the nature and the feelings. The nature is substance and feelings are function. [45:3a–b]

The nature is the state before activity begins, the feelings are the state when activity has started, and the mind includes both of these states. For the nature is the mind before it is aroused, while feelings are the mind after it is aroused, as expressed in the saying: "The mind unites and commands man's nature and feelings." Desire emanates from feelings. The mind is comparable to water, the nature is comparable to the tranquillity of still water, feeling is comparable to the flow of water, and desire is comparable to its waves. Just as there are good and bad waves, so there are good desires, such as when "I desire to be humane" [43] and bad desires which rush out like wild and violent waves. When bad desires are sub-

---

[42] *Analects*, XV, 5.   [43] *Analects*, VII, 29.

stantial, they will destroy the principle of Heaven, as water bursts a dam and damages everything. When Mencius said that "feelings enable people to do good" [VI A, 6], he meant that the concrete feelings flowing from our nature are originally all good. [45:4a]

Question: Is it correct to suppose that sages never show any anger?

Answer: How can they never show anger? When they ought to be angry, they will show it in their countenances. . . . When one becomes angry at the right time, he will be acting to the proper degree. When the matter is over, anger disappears, and none of it will be retained. [45:14b–15a]

Question: How can desires be checked?

Answer: Simply by thought. In learning there is nothing more important than thought. Only thought can check desires.

Someone said: If thought is not correct, it will not be adequate to check desires. Instead, it will create trouble. How about the saying: "Have no depraved thoughts"? [44]

Answer: Thoughts that are not correct are merely desires. If we think through the right and wrong, the ought and ought not of a thing in accordance with its principle, then our thought will surely be correct. [45:19b]

Humanity

As discussed here by Chu Hsi, humanity (*jen*) clearly signifies benevolence or love in the widest sense, both as the essential human virtue and a cosmic force.

[From *Chu Tzu ch'üan-shu,* 47:3a, 19b–20a]

Whenever and wherever humanity flows and operates, righteousness will be fully righteousness and decorum and wisdom will be fully decorum and wisdom. It is like the ten thousand things being stored and preserved. There is not a moment of cessation in such an operation for in all of these things there is the spirit of life. Take, for example, such things as seeds of grain or the pits of peach and apricot. When sown, they will grow. They are not dead things. For this reason they are called *jen* [the word *jen* means both "pit" and "humanity"]. This shows that *jen* implies the spirit of life. [47:3a]

"When man puts impartiality into practice, that is humanity." [45] Hu-

----
[44] *Analects,* II, 2.   [45] *Erh Ch'eng i-shu,* 15:8b.

manity is the principle originally inherent in man's mind. If there is impartiality, there is humanity. If there is partiality, there is no humanity. But impartiality as such should not be equated with humanity. It must be put into practice by man before it becomes humanity. Impartiality, altruism, and love are all descriptions of humanity. Impartiality is antecedent to humanity; altruism and love are subsequent. This is so because impartiality makes humanity possible, and humanity makes love and altruism possible. [47:19b–20a]

CHAPTER XXI

王 守 仁

NEO-CONFUCIANISM:
THE SCHOOL
OF THE MIND
OR INTUITION

The vital role of the Ch'eng brothers in bringing Neo-Confucian thought to maturity has already been mentioned in connection with the younger of the two, Ch'eng Yi, founder of the school of Principle. The older brother, Ch'eng Hao (1032–1085), is a much more shadowy figure. Most of the sayings of the brothers which have come down to us are attributed to the two of them jointly so that it is difficult to determine differences in their respective philosophies. In addition Ch'eng Hao, who died twenty-two years before his younger brother, left few writings in his own name. On the basis of the material we possess, however, we may discern a difference in emphasis between the two which was to have major significance in the later development of Neo-Confucian thought.

CH'ENG HAO AND THE MIND OF HEAVEN AND MAN

Ch'eng Hao was in agreement with his brother on the existence of eternal, unchanging *li* or principles inherent in all creation, and also on their concrete manifestation in *ch'i* or material-force. But, principle being the governing law of both Heaven and man, Ch'eng Hao emphasized the unity of the human mind, which is the embodiment of principle in man, with the mind of the universe. This idea of the unity of Heaven and man has deep roots in the Confucian tradition, and assumed great importance for most Neo-Confucianists. The realization of this unity is humanity (*jen*), and Ch'eng Hao's essay on "Understanding the Nature of Humanity," which follows, is one of the most celebrated in Chinese literature.

For Ch'eng Hao the great virtue (*jen*) of Heaven and earth is that they are life-giving. Man partakes of this virtue in so far as he is one with all that lives. His nature as received from Heaven is originally in a state of balance or harmony with all things, known as the Mean. In the actual nature as embodied in material-force both good and evil may be present, as well as the emotions which naturally and spontaneously react to them. Yet it is only when human feelings are aroused to excess and selfish desires interpose themselves, that the Mean is lost and the identity of man and things is destroyed. The chief task of spiritual cultivation is therefore to stabilize human nature and restore the original unity of the mind with all things. This is done by realizing the essential identity of internal and external existence and by acting with absolute impartiality and unselfishness; in other words by practicing "seriousness to straighten the internal life, and righteousness to square the external life."

Ch'eng Hao based his theories on the *Book of Changes* and the *Great Learning*. As with most other Neo-Confucianists the necessity which he felt to explain himself in terms of these earlier writings accounts for much of the difficulty encountered in interpreting his ideas today. The strong ethical tone of Ch'eng Hao's thought and his vigorous reaffirmation of life and the natural order mark him as truly within the Confucian tradition. At the same time, however, the influence of Taoism and Buddhism, to which Ch'eng Hao had given years of study, is clearly discernible in his subjectivism and his idea of mental composure. It was this latter aspect of his thought which contributed to the second great division of Neo-Confucian thought, the school of the Mind.

Selections from the Complete Works of the Two Ch'engs (*Erh Ch'eng Ch'üan-shu*)

ON UNDERSTANDING THE NATURE OF HUMANITY
[From *Erh Ch'eng i-shu*, 2A:3a–b]

The student must first of all understand the nature of humanity (*jen*). The humane man forms one body with all things comprehensively. Righteousness, decorum, wisdom, and good faith are all [expressions of] humanity. [One's duty] is to understand this truth and preserve humanity with sincerity (*ch'eng*) and seriousness (*ching*), that is all. There is no need to avoid things or restrict oneself. Nor is there any need for exhaustive search. It is necessary to avoid things when one is mentally negligent, but if one is not negligent, what is the necessity for avoidance? Exhaustive search is necessary when one has not found the truth, but if one preserves humanity long enough, the truth will automatically dawn on him. Why should he have to wait for exhaustive search?

Nothing can be equal to this Way [that is, humanity]. It is so vast that nothing can adequately explain it. All operations of the universe are our operations. Mencius said that "all things are already complete in us," that "we must examine ourselves and be sincere and that as a result we will experience great joy" [VII A, 4]. If we examine ourselves but find ourselves to be insincere, there is still an equality and opposition between the two [self and nonself]. Even if we try to identify the self with the nonself, we still do not achieve unity. How can we have joy? The purpose of [Chang] Tsai's "Western Inscription" is to explain this reality [of complete unity] fully. If we preserve humanity with this idea, what more is to be done? [As Mencius said], "There must be endeavor, but let there be no anxious expectation. Let the mind not forget its objective, but let there be no artificial effort to help it grow" [II A, 2]. Not the slightest effort is exerted! This is the way to preserve humanity. As humanity is preserved, the self and the other are then identified. For our innate knowledge of good and innate ability to do good are part of our original nature and cannot be lost. However, because we have not gotten rid of the mind dominated by old habits, we must preserve and exercise our original mind, and in time old habits will be overcome. This truth is extremely simple; the only danger is that people will not be able to hold to it. But if we practice and enjoy it, there need be no worry of our being unable to hold to it.

REPLY TO CHANG TSAI'S LETTER ON THE STABILIZING OF HUMAN NATURE
[From *Ming-tao wen-chi,* 3:1a–b]

I have received your letter in which you said that nature in the state of stability cannot be without activity but must still suffer from the influence of external things. This problem has been ardently pondered by virtuous men. What need is there for a humble person like myself to say anything? However, I have gone over the matter in my mind, and dare present my ideas to you. By the stabilizing of nature we mean that the nature is stabilized whether it is in a state of activity or in a state of tranquillity. One does not lean forward or backward to accommodate things, nor does one make any distinction of the internal and external. To regard things outside the self as external, and drag oneself to conform to them, is to regard one's nature as divided into the internal and external. If one's nature is conceived to be following external things, then while it is outside what is it that is within the self? One may indeed have the intention of getting rid of external temptations, but he fails to realize that human nature does not possess the two aspects of internal and external. As long as one holds that things internal and things external form two different bases, how can one speak of the stabilizing of human nature?

The constant principle of Heaven and earth is that their mind is in all things, yet of themselves they have no mind; and the constant principle of the sage is that his feelings are in accord with all creation, yet of himself he has no feelings. Therefore, for the training of the gentleman there is nothing better than to become broad and impartial and to respond spontaneously to all things as they come. The *Book of Changes* says: "Firm correctness brings good fortune and prevents all occasions for repentance. If he is unsettled in his movements, only his friends will follow his purpose." [1] If, feeling at a loss, one attempts to remove external temptations, then no sooner do some disappear than others will arise. Not only is one's time limited, but the sources of temptation are inexhaustible and therefore cannot be removed.

Everyone's nature is obscured in some way and as a consequence one cannot follow truth. In general the trouble lies in selfishness and intellectual cleverness. Being selfish, one cannot take purposive action to respond to things, and being intellectually clever, one cannot conceive enlightenment as spontaneous. For a mind that hates external things to seek illumination in a realm where nothing exists, is to look for a reflection on the back of a mirror. . . . Mencius said: "What I dislike in your wise men is their forced conclusions" [IV B, 26]. Instead of looking upon the internal as right and the external as wrong, it is better to forget the distinction. When such a distinction is forgotten, the state of quietness and peace is attained. Peace leads to stability, and stability leads to en-

[1] Hexagram 31.

lightenment. When one is enlightened, how can the response to things become a burden? The sage is joyous because according to the nature of things before him he should be joyous, and he is angry because according to the nature of things before him he should be angry. Thus the joy and anger of the sage do not depend on his own mind but on things. Does not the sage in this way respond to things? Why should it be regarded as wrong to follow external things and right to seek what is within? Compare the joy and anger of the selfish and clever man to the correctness of joy and anger of the sage. What a difference! Among human emotions the easiest to arouse but most difficult to control is anger. But if in time of anger one can immediately forget his anger and look at the right and wrong of the matter according to truth, it will be seen that external temptations need not be hated, and he has gone a long way toward the Way.

SELECTED SAYINGS

Principle and the Nature
[From *Erh Ch'eng i-shu*, 1:7b–8a; 6:2a; 11:5a]

Everything has its principle. It is easy [for a thing to function] if it is in accord with its own principle but difficult if it violates it. When everything follows its own principle, what is the necessity for the hard toil of man? [11:5a]

It would be incomplete to talk about the nature of man and things without including material-force, and unintelligible to talk about material-force without including the nature. [6:2a]

"What is inborn is called the nature." [2] Nature is the same as material-force and material-force is the same as nature. They are both inborn. In principle, there are both good and evil in the material-force with which man is endowed at birth. However, man is not born with these two opposing elements in his nature. Due to the material-force with which men are endowed some become good from childhood and others become evil. It is true that human nature is originally good, but it cannot be said that evil is not due to human nature. For what is inborn in man is called his nature. "By nature man is tranquil at birth." [3] The state preceding this

---

[2] *Mencius*, VI A, 3.   [3] *Book of Rites*, 19, "Record of Music."

cannot be discussed. As soon as we talk about human nature, it is already no longer human nature. Actually in our discussion of nature we only talk about [what is described in the *Book of Changes* as]: "What issues from the Way is good." [4] This is what Mencius meant by the original goodness of human nature.

The fact that whatever issues from the Way is good may be compared to the fact that water always flows downward. Water as such is the same in all cases. Yet without any effort on the part of man, some water flows onward to the sea without becoming dirty, while some flows only a short distance and already becomes turbid. Some travels a long distance before becoming turbid, some becomes extremely turbid, some only slightly so. But though they differ in being turbid or clear, we cannot say that the turbid water [evil] ceases to be water [nature]. This being the case, man must make increasing effort to purify the water, as it were. With diligent and vigorous effort, water will become clear quickly. With slow and lazy effort, water will become clear slowly. When it is clear, it is then the original water. Not that clearness has substituted for turbidity, or that turbidity has been taken out and laid in a corner. The original goodness of human nature is like the original clearness of water. It is not true that two distinct and opposing elements of good and evil exist in human nature and that each issues from it. [1:7b–8a]

The Mean, Sincerity, and Seriousness
[From *Erh Ch'eng i-shu*, 11:2a–11a]

The Mean is the great basis of the universe. It is the concrete, obvious, self-evident law of all under Heaven. Any deviation from it will result in error. Only the man of seriousness will not fail but will succeed to the utmost. [11:11a]

[Mencius said]: "All things are already complete in oneself. There is no greater joy than to examine oneself and be sincere [or absolutely real]" [VII A, 4]. If one lacks sincerity, one will violate the principle of things and will not be in harmony with them. [11:9a]

To be sincere is the way of Heaven. To be serious is the basis of human affairs. One who is serious will be sincere. [11:7b]

"Seriousness is to straighten one's internal life and righteousness is to

4 Hsi Tz'u I.

square one's external life." This is the way to unify the internal and external life. [11:2a]

THE UNIVERSAL MIND IN LU HSIANG-SHAN

Even in Chu Hsi's own time his impressive philosophical synthesis, for all its comprehensiveness and clarity, did not win unchallenged acceptance. We have already noted the difference in emphasis which marked the philosophies of Ch'eng Yi and his brother Ch'eng Hao. Lu Hsiang-shan (Lu Chiu-yüan, 1139–1192), a contemporary of Chu Hsi, adopted and elaborated the ideas of Ch'eng Hao on the importance of mind, just as Chu had done with the thought of the younger Ch'eng. As a result a definite cleavage developed between the two wings of Neo-Confucian thought, the school of Principle or Reason and the school of the Mind or Intuition.

Chu Hsi, in order to explain the presence of ignorance and evil among human beings, who by nature are supposed to be good, had distinguished between the original nature of man and his actual nature as embodied in material-force, and had maintained this distinction by carefully differentiating between human nature and the mind, between the principle of Heaven and human desire, and between the so-called "moral mind" and the "human mind." To Lu Hsiang-shan, such distinctions only obscured the essential unity which underlies the universe and man. "Feelings, human nature, the mind, capacity—these are all the same thing; they just happen to be expressed in different words," he declared.[5] Thus he swept aside all of Chu Hsi's subtleties, declaring that mind is identical with principle, with nature, and indeed, with the universe.

Since man's mind is self-sufficient, all-embracing, and originally good, it follows that man posssesses an innate knowledge of the good and an innate ability to do good. He need not investigate the principles of things, which for Chu Hsi had meant the study of the external world, and in particular of the knowledge contained in the Classics. Such a course would only distract and divide the mind, cutting it loose from what is fundamental and setting it adrift among nonessentials. Instead Lu Hsiang-shan advocates turning within to rediscover what is fundamental and to

[5] *Hsiang-shan ch'üan-chi,* 35:10a.

"re-establish the nobler part of one's nature"—man's moral sense. Thus, in their own words, where Chu Hsi's method consists in "following the path of study and inquiry," Lu's consists in "honoring the moral nature."

Selections from the Complete Works of Lu Hsiang-shan

MIND IS PRINCIPLE

[From *Hsiang-shan ch'üan-chi,* 1:3b; 11:5b–6a; 22:5a; 34:1a–b, 21a]

Mencius said: "That whereby man differs from the lower animals is but small. The ordinary people cast it away, while the gentleman preserves it" [IV B, 19]. What is cast away is the mind. That is why Mencius said that some people "cast their original mind away" [IV A, 10]. What is preserved is the mind. That is why Mencius said that "The great man is he who does not lose his child's-mind" [IV B, 12]. [What Mencius referred to as] the four beginnings [of humanity, righteousness, decorum, and wisdom] are this mind. It is what Heaven has endowed us with. All men have this mind, and all minds are endowed with this principle. The mind *is* principle. [11:5b–6a]

The affairs of the universe are my own affairs; my own affairs are the affairs of the universe. [22:5a]

The human mind is most intelligent and principle is most clear. All people have this in mind and all minds contain this principle in full. [22:5a]

The four directions and upward and downward constitute the spatial continuum. What has gone by in the past and what is to come in the future constitute the temporal continuum. These continua, or the universe, are my mind, and my mind is the universe. Sages appeared tens of thousands of generations ago. They shared this mind; they shared this principle. Sages will appear tens of thousands of generations to come. They will share this mind; they will share this principle. Over the four seas sages appear. They share this mind; they share this principle. [22:5a]

The mind is one and principle is one. Perfect truth is reduced to unity; the essential principle is never a duality. The mind and principle can never be separated into two. That is why Confucius said: "There is one central thread running through my doctrines," [6] and Mencius said: "The

---

[6] *Analects,* IV, 15.

Way is one and only one" [III A, 1]. [Quoting Confucius] Mencius also said: "There are but two courses to be pursued, that of humanity and that of its opposite" [IV A, 2]. To act in a certain way is humanity. Not to act in a certain way is the opposite of humanity. Humanity is the mind, the principle. "Seek and you will find it" [VI A, 6] means to find this principle. "Those who know beforehand" know this principle, and "those who are awakened beforehand" [V A, 7] are awakened to this principle. It is this principle that constitutes love for parents, reverence for elders, and the sense of alarm and commiseration when one sees a child about to fall into a well. It is this principle that makes people ashamed of shameful things and hate what should be hated. It is this principle that enables people to know what is right to be right and what is wrong to be wrong. It is this principle that makes people deferential when deference is due and humble when humility is called for. Seriousness (*ching*) is this principle; righteousness is this principle. And what is internal and what is external are all this principle. . . . Mencius said: "The ability possessed by men without having been acquired by learning is innate ability, and the knowledge possessed by them without deliberation is innate knowledge" [VII A, 15]. These are endowed in us by Heaven. "We are originally provided with them," "they are not drilled into us from outside" [VI A, 6]. Therefore Mencius said: "All things are already complete in oneself. There is no greater joy than to examine oneself and be sincere" [VII A, 4]. [1:3b]

The teacher said that the myriad things exist luxuriantly in the mind. What permeates the mind and, pouring forth, extends to fill the universe, is nothing but principle. [34:21a]

The teacher always said that outside of the Way there are no events and outside of events there is no Way. [34:1a]

The theory that principle is due to Heaven whereas desire is due to man is, without saying, not the best doctrine. If principle is due to Heaven and desire due to man, then Heaven and man must be different. This theory can be traced to Lao Tzu. In the "Record of Music" [in the *Book of Rites*] it is said, "By nature man is tranquil at birth. When influenced by external things, he begins to be active, which is desire arising from his nature. As one becomes conscious of things resulting from this impact, one begins to have likes and dislikes. When as a result of these likes and dislikes one is unable to return to his original mind, the principle of Heaven is destroyed." Here is the origin of the theory that principle is from Heaven whereas desire is from man. And the words of the "Record of Music" are based on Lao Tzu. If it be said that only tranquillity is inborn nature, is activity not inborn nature also? It is said in the *Book of History* that "the human mind is precarious, the moral mind is subtle." Most interpreters have explained the human mind [which is liable to make mistakes] as equivalent to human desires and the moral mind [which follows moral law] as equivalent to the principle of Heaven. This interpretation is wrong. The mind is one. How can man have two minds? [34:1b]

METHODS OF CULTIVATION
[From *Hsiang-shan ch'üan-chi*, 11:1a; 14:1a, 32:4a; 34:5a–22a]

Principle exists in the universe without any obstruction. It is only that you sink from it, hide yourself in darkness as in a trap, and lose all sense of what is high and far beyond. It is imperative that this trap be decisively broken and the confining net be pierced and destroyed. [35:15b–16a]

There is concrete principle in the universe. The value of study lies in understanding this principle. If it is understood, concrete behavior and concrete accomplishments will result. [14:1a]

The moral law (Tao) in the universe cannot be augmented or diminished. Neither can it be given or taken away. Man must find this out for himself. [35:3a]

The universe never separates itself from man; man separates himself from the universe. [34:5b]

Students of today pay attention only to details and do not search for what is fundamental. Mencius said: "He who exerts his mind to the utmost knows his nature. He who knows his nature knows Heaven" [VII A, 1]. There is only one mind. My friend's mind, the mind of the sages thousands of years ago, and the mind of the sages thousands of years to come are all the same. The substance of the mind is infinite. If one can completely develop his mind, he will become identified with Heaven. To acquire learning is to appreciate this fact. [35:10a]

Establish yourself and respect yourself. Do not follow other people's footsteps nor repeat their words. [35:22a]

When the teacher resided in Hsiang-shan ["Elephant Mountain"], he often said to his pupils: "Your hearing is by nature keen and your vision is by nature clear. By natural endowment you are capable of serving your father with filial piety and your elder brother with respect. Fundamentally there is nothing wanting in you. There is no need to seek elsewhere. All depends on your establishing yourself." [34:10b]

My learning is different from that of others in the fact that with me every word comes spontaneously. Although I have uttered tens of thousands of words, they are all expressions of what is within me, and nothing more has been added. Recently someone has commented of me that aside from Mencius' one saying, "First build up the nobler part of your nature" [VI A, 15], I had nothing clever. When I heard this, I said, "Very true, indeed." [34:5a]

Mencius said: "First build up the nobler part of your nature and then the inferior part cannot overcome it." It is because people fail to build up the nobler part of their nature that it is overcome by the inferior part. In consequence they violate principle and become different from Heaven and earth. [11:1a]

Principle is endowed in me by Heaven, not drilled into me from the outside. If one understands that principle is the same as master and really makes it his master, one cannot be influenced by external things or fooled by perverse doctrines. [1:3a]

Gather your spirit. Be your own master. "All things are already complete in oneself." What is it that is lacking? When I should be commiserative, I am naturally commiserative. When I should be ashamed, liberal, generous, affectionate, tender, or strong and firm, I am naturally so. [35:18a]

The moral principle inherent in the human mind is endowed by Heaven and cannot be wiped out. Those who are clouded by material desires so as to pervert principles and violate righteousness, have become so because they do not think, that is all. If they can truly return to their true selves and think, their sense of right and wrong and their ability to choose right and wrong will have the qualities of quiet alertness, clear-cut intelligence, and firm conviction. [32:4a]

DIFFERENCES BETWEEN LU HSIANG-SHAN AND CHU HSI
[From *Hsiang-shan ch'üan-chi*, 34:4b–5a, 24ab]

Chu Hsi once wrote to one of his students, saying: "Lu Hsiang-shan teaches people only the doctrine of 'honoring the moral nature.' [7] Therefore those who have studied under him are mostly concerned with putting

---

[7] *Mean*, 27.

their beliefs into practice. But he has neglected to follow the 'path of study and inquiry.'[8] In my teaching is it not true that I have put somewhat more emphasis on following the path of study and inquiry? As a consequence, my pupils often do not approach his in putting beliefs into practice." From this it is clear that Chu Hsi wanted to avoid two defects [failure to honor the moral nature and failure to practice] and combine two merits [following the path of study and inquiry and practicing one's belief]. I do not believe this to be possible. If one does not know how to honor his moral nature, how can he talk about following the path of study and inquiry? [34:4b–5a]

Lu Tsu-ch'ien arranged a meeting at the Goose Lake Temple. My elder brother Fu-chai said to me: "Tsu-ch'ien has invited Chu Hsi to meet us particularly because we differ from him in doctrine". . . . [Chu Hsi] was debating with my brother. I said, "On the way I wrote a poem: . . . 'Work that is simple and easy will in the end be lasting and great/ Understanding that is devoted to fragmentary and isolated details will end up in aimless drifting.'" When I recited my poem up to these lines, Chu Hsi's face turned pale. [34:24a–b]

MORAL INTUITION AND ACTION IN WANG YANG-MING

By the time of the Ming dynasty, a century and a half after Chu Hsi's death, his commentaries on the Classics had been accepted by the state as the orthodox interpretation of the Confucian tradition. This orthodoxy was asserted and maintained in a simple yet highly effective manner—through the civil service examination system. Since the Classics formed the subject matter of the examinations and Chu Hsi's commentaries on the *Four Books* were installed as the standard interpretation, anyone aspiring to office had to master them. In China, where personal success was measured largely in terms of political advancement, most educated men were affected by the requirements of this system.

Even granting Chu Hsi such recognition and support, however, the state could do nothing to insure the continuing intellectual vitality of the Ch'eng-Chu school. By the late fifteenth century this school had

[8] *Mean, 27.*

lost much of its vigor, while the school of the Mind found a new and formidable spokesman in the statesman-general Wang Yang-ming (Wang Shou-jen, 1472–1529). Despite official attempts to close down the private academies in which Wang received an enthusiastic hearing, his ideas elicited a wide response from thinking men and provided the inspiration for the most active schools of thought in the later Ming period.

Four concepts stand out in the philosophy of Wang Yang-ming, two of which derive from his predecessors, Ch'eng Hao and Lu Hsiang-shan. From the former he drew his concept of *jen* or humanity which unites in one body the true sage with the entire universe. Following Lu Hsiang-shan, he equates principle with the mind, in which all things are contained and which is thus one with the mind of the universe. In every man, Wang went on to assert, this original mind manifests itself through innate knowledge, or more literally "good knowledge"—the activity of the mind in its natural purity and perfection. As the principle of human nature this "good knowledge" represents the universal moral law (the principle of Heaven or the highest good) immanent in man and most evident in the individual's innate sense of right and wrong. The fulfillment of one's nature consists simply in remaining true to this innate sense in whatever one does.

The achievement of self-perfection does not require exhaustive investigation into the principles of things external to the mind, or prolonged study of the precepts of the sages in the Classics, as Chu Hsi had indicated. One need only follow the promptings of this innate knowledge, without permitting it to become obscured by the selfish desires and devious rationalizations which alienate man from his true nature and from the universe. Thus the way to sagehood is open to all, humble peasant as well as learned scholar. It is not a profound mystery; but neither is innate knowledge merely a set of truths to be recognized. Rather Wang conceives of it as a continuing function or process, which requires each man actively to seek its realization and extension to all things.

To clarify this point Wang advanced a fourth concept, his doctrine of the unity of knowledge and action. True knowledge must have some practical consequence, just as valid action must be based upon or guided by knowledge. "Knowledge is the beginning of action; action is the completion of knowledge." As an example Wang cites the virtue of filial piety. A man who truly knows or understands the obligations of filial piety will carry them out in practice. At the same time, however, it is only through the actual fullfillment of these obligations that one really comes to know what filial piety means.

Wang's long and active career as a statesman and soldier gave proof of his own primary concern for self-understanding as the key to effective moral action. Nevertheless the language in which he clothed some of his ideas was sufficiently ambiguous to allow conflicting interpretations. Almost immediately his school diverged sharply on basic issues, some viewing innate knowledge as something akin to "conscience," with strong ethical implications, and others conceiving of it more as mystical insight, transcending all ethical norms or values. It was this latter interpretation, so close to the Buddhist view of enlightenment, which won for many of Wang's later followers the appellation, the "Wildcat Ch'an school."

Inquiry on the Great Learning
[From Yang-ming ch'üan-shu, 26:1b–5a]

Question: The Great Learning was considered by a former scholar [Chu Hsi] to be the learning of the great man. I venture to ask why the learning of the great man should consist in "manifesting the clear character"? [9]

Master Wang said: The great man regards Heaven and earth and the myriad things as one body. He regards the world as one family and the country as one person. As to those who make a cleavage between objects and distinguish between the self and others, they are small men. That the great man can regard Heaven, earth, and the myriad things as one body is not because he deliberately wants to do so, but because it is natural with the humane nature of his mind that he should form a unity with Heaven, earth, and the myriad things. This is true not only of the great man. Even the mind of the small man is no different. Only he himself makes it small. Therefore when he sees a child about to fall into a well, he cannot help a feeling of alarm and commiseration. This shows that his humanity (jen) forms one body with the child. It may be objected that the child belongs to the same species [as he]. Yet when he observes the pitiful cries and frightened appearance of birds and animals [about

---

[9] From the original text of the Great Learning.

to be slaughtered], he cannot help feeling an "inability to bear" their suffering. This shows that his humanity forms one body with birds and animals. It may be objected that birds and animals are sentient beings [as he is]. But when he sees plants broken and destroyed, he cannot help a feeling of pity. This shows that his humanity forms one body with plants. It may be said that plants are living things [as he is]. Yet even when he sees tiles and stones shattered and crushed he cannot help a feeling of regret. This shows that his humanity forms one body with tiles and stones. This means that even the mind of the small man necessarily has the humanity that forms one body with all. Such a mind is rooted in his Heaven-endowed nature, and is naturally intelligent, clear, and not obscured. For this reason it is called the "clear character." Although the mind of the small man is divided and narrow, yet his humanity that forms a unity can remain free from darkness like this. This is due to the fact that his mind has not yet been aroused by desires and blinded by selfishness. When it is aroused by desires and blinded by selfishness, compelled by the greed for gain and fear of harm, and stirred by anger, he will destroy things, kill members of his own species, and will do everything to the extreme, even to the slaughtering of his own brothers, and the humanity that forms a unity will disappear completely. Hence if it is not blinded by selfish desires, even the mind of the small man has the humanity that forms a unity with all as does the mind of the great man. As soon as it is obscured by selfish desires, even the mind of the great man will be divided and narrow, like that of the small man. Thus the learning of the great man consists entirely in getting rid of the blindness of selfish desires in order by one's own efforts to make manifest his clear character, so that the original condition of the unity of Heaven, earth, and the myriad things may be restored, that is all. Nothing can be added to this original nature from outside.

Question: Why, then, does the learning of the great man consist also in loving the people?

Answer: To manifest the clear character is to bring about the substance of the unity of Heaven, earth, and the myriad things, whereas loving the people is to put into universal operation the function of that unity. Hence manifesting the clear character must lie in loving the people, and loving the people is the way to manifest the clear character. Therefore, only when I love my father, the fathers of others, and the fathers of all men, can my humanity really form one body with my father, the fathers of others, and the fathers of all men. When it truly forms one body with them, then the clear character of filial piety will be manifested. Only when I love my brother, the brothers of others, and the brothers of all men can my humanity really form one body with my brother, the brothers of others, and the brothers of all men. When it truly forms one body with them, then the clear character of brotherly respect will be manifested. Everything from ruler, minister, husband, wife, and friends to mountains, rivers, heavenly and earthly spirits, birds, animals, and plants, all should be truly loved in order to realize my humanity that forms a unity, and then my clear character will be completely manifested, and I will really form one body with Heaven, earth, and the myriad things. This is what is meant by "manifesting the clear character throughout the empire." This is what is meant by "regulating the family," "ordering the state," and "pacifying the world." This is what is meant by "fully developing one's nature."

Question. Then why does the learning of the great man consist in "abiding in the highest good"?

Answer: The highest good is the ultimate principle of manifesting character and loving people. The nature endowed in us by Heaven is pure and perfect. The fact that it is intelligent, clear, and not obscured is evidence of the emanation and revelation of the highest good. It is the original nature of the clear character which is called innate knowledge [of the good]. As the highest good emanates and reveals itself, one will consider right as right and wrong as wrong. Things of greater or less importance and situations of grave or light character will be responded to as they act upon us. In all our changes and activities, we will entertain no preconceived attitude; in all this we will do nothing that is not natural. This is the normal nature of man and the principle of things. There can be no suggestion of adding to or subtracting anything from them. If any such suggestion is entertained, it means selfish purpose and shallow wisdom, and cannot be said to be the highest good. Naturally, how can anyone who does not watch over himself carefully when alone, and who has no refinement and singleness of mind, attain to such a state of perfection? Later generations fail to realize that the highest good is inherent in their own minds, but each in accordance with his own ideas gropes for it outside the mind, believing that every event and every object has its own definite principle. For this reason the law of right and wrong is obscured; the mind becomes concerned with fragmentary and isolated details, the desires of man become rampant and the principle of Heaven is at an end. And thus the education for manifesting character and loving people is everywhere thrown into confusion.

In the past there have been people who wanted to manifest their clear character, of course. But simply because they did not know how to abide in the highest good, but instead drove their own minds toward something too lofty, they thereby lost them in illusions, emptiness, and quietude, having nothing to do with the work of the family, the country, and the world. Such are the followers of Buddhism and Taoism. There have been those who wanted to love their people, of course. But simply because they did not know how to abide in the highest good, but instead sank their own minds in base and trifling things, they thereby lost them in scheming strategy and tricks, having neither the sincerity of humanity nor that of commiseration. Such are the followers of the Five Overlords [as opposed to true kings] and the pursuers of profit and gain. All of these are due to a failure to know how to abide in the highest good. Therefore abiding in the highest good is to manifesting character and loving people as the carpenter's square and compass are to the square and the circle, or rule and measure to length, or balances and scales to weight. If the square and the circle do not abide by the compass and the carpenter's square, their standard will be wrong; if length does not abide by the rule and measure, its adjustment will be lost; if the weight does not abide by the balances, its exactness will be gone; and if manifesting clear character and loving people do not abide by the highest good, their foundation will disappear. Therefore, abiding in the highest good so as to love people and manifest the clear character is what is meant by the learning of the great man.

Question: "Only after knowing what to abide in can one be calm. Only after having achieved calm can one be tranquil. Only after having achieved tranquillity can one have peaceful repose. Only after having peaceful repose can one begin to deliberate. Only after deliberation can the end be attained." How do you explain this?

Answer: People fail to realize that the highest good is in their minds and seek it outside. As they believe that everything or every event has its own definite principle, they search for the highest good in individual things. Consequently, the mind becomes fragmented and isolated; mixed and confused, it has no definite direction. Once it is realized that the highest good is in the mind and does not depend on any search outside, then the mind will have definite direction and there will be no danger of its becoming fragmented and isolated, mixed, or confused. When there is no such danger, the mind will not be foolishly perturbed but will be tranquil. Not being foolishly perturbed but tranquil, in its daily functioning it will be unhurried and at ease and will attain peaceful repose. Being in peaceful repose, whenever a thought arises or whenever an event acts upon it, the mind with its innate knowledge will thoroughly sift and carefully examine whether or not the thought or event is in accord with the highest good, and thus the mind can deliberate. With deliberation, every decision will be excellent and every act will be proper, and in this way the highest good will be attained. . . .

Now the original substance of the mind is man's nature. Human nature being universally good, the original substance of the mind is correct. How is it that any effort is required to rectify the mind? The reason is that, while the original substance of the mind is correct, incorrectness enters when one's thoughts and will begin to emanate and become active. Therefore he who wishes to rectify his mind must rectify it in connection with the emanation of his thoughts and will. If, whenever a good thought emanates, he loves it as he loves beautiful colors, and whenever an evil thought emanates, he hates it as he hates bad odor, then his will will always be sincere and the mind can be rectified.

However, what emanates from the will may be good or evil, and unless there is a way to make clear the distinction between good and evil, there will be a confusion of truth and untruth. In that case, even if one wants to make his will sincere, he cannot do so. Therefore he who wishes to make his will sincere must extend his knowledge. By extension is meant to reach the limit. The word "extension" is the same as that used in the saying, "Mourning is to be carried to the utmost degree of grief." [10] In the *Book of Changes* it is said that "Knowing the utmost, one should reach it." [11] "Knowing the utmost" means knowledge and "reaching it" means extension. Extension of knowledge is not what later scholars understand as enriching and widening knowledge. It means simply extending

[10] *Analects*, xix, 14.   [11] Hexagram 1.

my innate knowledge of the good to the utmost. This innate knowledge of the good is what Mencius meant when he said: "The sense of right and wrong is common to all men" [VI A, 6]. The sense of right and wrong requires no deliberation to know, nor does it depend on learning to function. This is why it is called innate knowledge. It is my nature endowed by Heaven, the original substance of my mind, naturally intelligent, clear, and understanding.

Whenever a thought or a wish arises, my mind's faculty of innate knowledge itself is always conscious of it. Whether it is good or evil, my mind's innate knowing faculty itself also knows it. It has nothing to do with others. Therefore although an inferior man may have done all manner of evil, when he sees a gentleman he will surely try to disguise this fact, concealing what is evil and displaying what is good in himself. This shows that innate knowledge of the good does not permit any self-deception. Now the only way to distinguish good and evil in order to make the will sincere is to extend to the utmost the knowledge of the innate faculty. Why is this? When [a good] thought or wish arises, the innate faculty of my mind already knows it to be good. Suppose I do not sincerely love it but instead turn away from it. I would then be regarding good as evil and obscuring my innate faculty which knows the good. When [an evil] thought or wish arises, the innate faculty of my mind already knows it to be evil. If I did not sincerely hate it but instead carried it out, I would be regarding evil as good and obscuring my innate faculty which knows evil. In such cases what is supposed to be knowledge is really ignorance. How then can the will be made sincere? If what the innate faculty knows to be good or evil is sincerely loved or hated, one's innate knowing faculty is not deceived and the will can be made sincere.

Now, when one sets out to extend his innate knowledge to the utmost, does this mean something merely apparent, hazy, vacuous, and without substance? No, it means something concrete. Therefore, the extension of knowledge must consist in the investigation of things. A thing is an event. For every emanation of the will there must be an event corresponding to it. The event to which the will is directed is a "thing." To investigate is to rectify. It is to rectify that which is incorrect so as to return to its original correctness. To rectify that which is not correct is to remove evil, and to return to correctness is to do good. This is what is meant by investigation. . . .

If one sincerely loves the good known by the innate faculty but does not in reality act on the thing to which the will is directed, it means that the thing has not been investigated and that the will to love it is not yet sincere. If one sincerely hates the evil known by the innate faculty but does not in reality repel the thing to which the will is directed, it means that the thing has not been investigated and that the will to hate it is not sincere. If within what is good as known by the innate faculty one acts to the utmost degree on the thing to which the will is directed, and if within what is evil as known by the innate faculty one really repels to the utmost degree the evil to which the will is directed, then everything will be investigated and what is known by one's innate faculty will not be deficient or obscured but will extend to the utmost. Then the mind will be joyous in itself, happy and without regret, the emanation of the will will carry with it no self-deception and sincerity may be said to have been attained. Therefore it is said: "When things are investigated, true knowledge is extended; when knowledge is extended, the will becomes sincere; when the will is sincere, the mind is rectified; and when the mind is rectified, the personal life is cultivated." While the order of the tasks involves a sequence of first and last, in reality they are one and cannot be so separated. At the same time, while the order and the tasks cannot be separated into first and last, their operation must be so refined as not to be wanting in the slightest degree. This is why the doctrine of investigation, extension, being sincere, and rectification is a correct exposition of the true heritage of [the sage-emperors] Yao and Shun and why it coincides with Confucius' own ideas.

The Identification of Mind and Principle
[From *Ch'uan hsi lu* in *Yang-ming ch'üan-shu*, 2:4b–5a]

What Chu Hsi meant by the investigation of things is "to investigate the principle in things to the utmost as we come into contact with them." To investigate the principle in things to the utmost, as we come into contact with them means to search in each individual thing for its so-called definite principle. It means further that the principle in each individual thing is to be sought with the mind, thus separating the mind and principle into two. To seek for principle in each individual thing is like looking for the principle of filial piety in parents. If the principle of filial piety is to be sought in parents, then is it actually in my own mind or is it in the person of my parents? If it is actually in the person of my parents, is it true that as soon as parents pass away the mind will then lack the principle of filial piety? When I see a child about to fall into a well [and have a feeling of commiseration], there must be the principle of commiseration. Is this principle of commiseration actually in the person of the child or is it in the innate knowledge of my mind? Perhaps one cannot follow the child into the well [to rescue it]. Perhaps one can rescue it by seizing it with the hand. All this involves principle. Is it really in the person of the child or does it emanate from the innate knowledge in my mind? What is true here is true of all things and events. From this we know the mistake of separating the mind and principle into two.

Such separation is the doctrine of Kao Tzu who taught that righteousness is external to the mind, a fallacy which Mencius strongly attacked. You know [the defects of what you describe as] "devoting oneself to external things and neglecting the internal, and becoming broad but lacking essentials." What is the reason for your saying so? Can we not say that this is trifling with things and losing one's purpose in life? What I mean by investigation of things and extension of knowledge is to extend the innate knowledge of my mind to each and every thing. The innate knowledge of my mind is the same as the principle of Heaven. When the principle of Heaven in the innate knowledge of my mind is extended to all things, all things will attain their principle. To extend the innate knowledge of my mind means extension of knowledge, and all things attaining their principle means investigation of things. In these the mind and principle are combined as one.

The Unity of Knowledge and Action
[From *Ch'uan hsi lu* in *Yang-ming ch'üan-shu*, 1:3ab]

I [Hsü Ai] did not understand the teacher's doctrine of the unity of knowledge and action and debated over it back and forth with Huang Tung-hsien and Ku Wei-hsien without coming to any conclusion. Therefore I took the matter to the teacher. The teacher said: "Give an example and let me see." I said: For example, there are people who know that parents should be served with filial piety and elder brothers with respect, but they cannot put these things into practice. This shows that knowledge and action are clearly two different things.

The teacher said: The knowledge and action you refer to are already separated by selfish desires and no longer knowledge and action in their original substance. There have never been people who know but do not act. Those who are supposed to know but do not act simply do not yet know. When sages and worthies taught people about knowledge and action, it was precisely because they wanted them to restore this original substance, and not just to have them behave like that and be satisfied. Therefore the *Great Learning* points to true knowledge and action for people to see, saying, [they are] "like loving beautiful colors and hating bad odors" [VI]. Seeing beautiful colors appertains to knowledge, while loving beautiful colors appertains to action. However, as soon as one sees a beautiful color, he has already loved it. Smelling a bad odor appertains to knowledge, while hating a bad odor appertains to action. However, as soon as one smells a bad odor, he has already hated it. It is not that he smells it first and then makes up his mind to hate it. A person with his nose stopped up does not smell the bad odor even if he sees a malodorous object before him, and so he does not hate it. This amounts to not knowing bad odor. Suppose we say that so-and-so knows filial piety and so-and-so knows brotherly respect. They must have actually practiced filial piety and brotherly respect before they can be said to know them. It will not do to say that they know filial piety and brotherly respect simply because they show them in words. Or take one's knowledge of pain. Only after one has experienced pain can one know pain. The same is true of cold or hunger. How can knowledge and action be separated? . . . I have said that knowledge is the crystallization of the will to act and action is the task of carrying out that knowledge; knowledge is the beginning of action and action is the completion of knowledge.

The Colloquy at the T'ien-ch'üan Bridge

The two points of view represented in this famous colloquy are those over which the school of Wang Yang-ming eventually divided, one wing emphasizing the importance of moral cultivation and the other intuitive enlightenment. The latter, with obvious leanings in the direction of Ch'an Buddhism, believed that the original reality or inner essence of the mind transcended good and evil, and that spontaneity rather than conscious moral effort was the characteristic of the sage.

[From *Ch'uan hsi lu* in *Yang-ming ch'üan-shu,* 3:20b–21a]

Wang Chi repeated the words of the teacher's instruction as follows: "In the original substance of the mind there is no distinction of good and evil. When the will becomes active, however, such a distinction exists. The function of innate knowledge is to know good and evil, and the investigation of things is to do good and remove evil." Ch'ien Hsü-shan asked: What do you think this means?

Wang Chi said: This is perhaps not the last word [i.e., there is more to it than this]. If we say that in the original substance [or essence] of the mind there is no distinction between good and evil, then there must be no such distinction in the will, in knowledge, or in things. If we say that there is a distinction between good and evil in the will, then in the final analysis there must also be such a distinction in the substance of the mind.

Ch'ien Hsü-shan said: The substance of the mind is the nature endowed in us by Heaven, and is originally neither good nor evil. But because we have a mind dominated by habits, there is in our thoughts a distinction between good and evil. The work of investigating things, extending knowledge, making the will sincere, rectifying the mind, and cultivating the person is aimed precisely at recovering that original nature and substance. If there were no good or evil to start with, what would be the necessity for such effort?

That evening we set ourselves down beside the master at the T'ien-ch'üan Bridge. Each stated his view and asked to be corrected. The teacher said: Here I deal with two types of people. . . . The man of sharp intelligence has already accomplished his task as soon as he apprehends the original substance, penetrating the self, other people, things internal and things external all at the same time. On the other hand, there are inevitably those whose minds are dominated by habits so that the original substance of the mind is obstructed. I therefore teach them definitely and sincerely to do good and remove evil in their will and thoughts. When they become accomplished at this and the impurities of the mind are completely eliminated, the original substance of the mind will become wholly clear. I adopt Chi's view in dealing with the man of sharp intelligence, and that of Hsü-shan for the second type. If you two gentlemen use your views interchangeably, you will be able to lead all people —of the highest, average, and lowest intelligence—to the truth.

CHAPTER XXII

THE LATE HARVEST
OF CONFUCIAN
SCHOLARSHIP

In the late Ming dynasty, after almost five centuries dominated by Chu Hsi's rationalistic metaphysics and Wang Yang-ming's intuitionism, there was a gradual reaction against speculative philosophy and a redirection of thought that set the course of Confucian scholarship down to the nineteenth century. The first signs of this reaction came with the Tung-lin school, organized at Wusih in the lower Yangtze valley by a group of ex-officials deeply concerned over the deterioration of the Ming dynasty and convinced that its cause was a general moral decline in the ranks of scholar-officials. It is significant as the first intellectual movement closely related to politics since Wang An-shih's time; that is, the first attempt to bridge the gap between Neo-Confucian thought as it was actively developed in the schools and the conduct of politics at court.

The Tung-lin Academy was established in 1604 at Wusih in the lower Yangtze valley, as a private (i.e., nonofficial) center for the discussion of philosophical questions. Its principal founder, Ku Hsien-ch'eng (1550–1612), had turned to this type of activity after being forced out of the government for his outspoken criticism of those in power around the throne. Other participants in the discussions of the Academy were identified, like Ku, with the so-called Righteous Circles at court, considered the champions of legality and official integrity in the government. Nevertheless, the purpose of their discussions was not primarily to exert some kind of public pressure upon their political enemies. Rather, as convinced Confucianists, they believed that their efforts should first be directed at intellectual weaknesses which had corrupted the educated class and undermined public life. Their aim was nothing less than the aim of Confucius himself—the moral regeneration of the ruling class. In this respect, then, they thought of themselves, not as breaking new ground or departing from tradition, but as returning to the original spirit of Confucianism. Ku and other leading members of the group still regarded Chu Hsi as the soundest exponent of this tradition, and in fact the stated aims of the school were based on the regulations of Chu Hsi's own academy. Others were more strongly influenced by the philosophy of Wang Yang-ming. While thus differing in their philosophical approach, however, they agreed in reaffirming the fundamentally ethical character of Confucianism and in condemning the more extreme wing of the Wang Yang-ming school, which leaned strongly in the direction of Ch'an Buddhism.

The tendency of this latter group, as we have mentioned, was to interpret Wang's doctrine of innate knowledge as meaning that the original mind of man was endowed with a transcendental perfection, beyond all relative notions of good and evil. To manifest this perfection, man need only rid himself of arbitrary or conventional conceptions of morality, and respond freely to the promptings of this innate, originally pure mind. "Naturalness" and "spontaneity" were the ideals of this group. Conscious moral effort they considered at best a preparatory method for those who still were fettered by ordinary habits of mind.

Initially what the exponents of this point of view appear to have been driving at, following Wang's own revolt against Confucian formalism and scholasticism, was the destruction, not of morality, but of all rigid moralism, prudishness, and hypocrisy. The genuine moral virtues, they assumed, would manifest themselves naturally and without conscious effort. Increasingly, however, the moral subjectivism implicit in this teaching led to a repudiation of traditional Confucian values. In the notorious Li Chih (1527–1602), for example, it brought open contempt for Confucian authority and scoffing at civic virtues as well as at family obligations. Li's adoption of Buddhist garb was only an overt expression of the trend in this group toward an easy syncretism of Buddhism, Taoism, and Confucianism, proclaiming the "three religions to be one." For this his group won the appellation "Wildcat Ch'an school."

In this kind of free-thinking Ku Hsien-ch'eng and his colleagues saw the abandonment of the moral struggle which Confucius had put forward as the highest destiny of man. To it they attributed the moral laxity at court, the readiness of many officials to cooperate with corrupt ministers and powerful eunuchs, and the prevailing fuzziness about right and wrong. Against such opportunism, dignified by the appearance of broad-mindedness, the Tung-lin upheld the moral nature of man, the importance of fixed principles, the necessity for moral effort. The perfection of the sage, they insisted, could only be found in striving. To attain it the "gentleman" or "noble man" of Confucius had to be strengthened by moral training to withstand hardship and temptation. Seeking the true Mean in conduct and character, he had to distinguish it from compromise. He must be prepared to endure disfavor and dare to be different. With this as their aim the Tung-lin leaders returned to the traditional function of the Confucian school: the inculcation of virtue (especially the civic virtues) and a sense of social responsibility. As a corollary to this they emphasized study of the classics—and sound scholarship in general—to counteract the anti-intellectualism of the "Wildcat Ch'an school." Thus Tung-lin reformism in politics was based on a strong conservatism in morals and philosophy.

To its reformist struggle the Tung-lin brought all the fervor and intensity that characterized the bitter battles being waged at court. By their outspoken criticism of those in power, these men risked flogging, official degradation, and perhaps torture and death in the dungeons of the eunuch's secret police. To them the moral issues discussed were of more than pedantic interest—they were matters of life and death. Eventually, in fact, the Tung-lin Academy itself and several affiliated institutions were suppressed (in 1625–1626) by the all-powerful eunuch, Wei Chung-hsien, on the ground that they served as centers of factional opposition.

Though it was a policy of the Tung-lin to discuss only political questions "outside of school," the distinction was actually difficult to draw. Many of the issues discussed centered upon personalities in the government, and the Tung-lin group engaged more in what was called "the judging of other men's characters" than in what we would consider the discussion of national issues or the advancement of a concrete political program. The political battles in which they took part, though they rocked the empire in the early decades of the seventeenth century, are of interest today only as episodes in a struggle for power, fought over such questions as succession to the throne or the propriety of remaining in office instead of retiring to mourn the death of a parent. This is not to say that the Tung-lin and their allies were unconcerned with policy, but only that they made little progress in the study and reform of political institutions—a shortcoming which is perhaps explainable by their almost frenzied concern over China's immediate military plight and the flagrant corruption in public life, as well as by the inescapable fact that no change in policy could be effected without first discrediting and displacing those in power. But whatever the reason, the most notable characteristic of Tung-lin political utterance is its righteous indignation rather than its penetration of political problems. It remained for the next generation to produce men like Huang Tsung-hsi and Ku Yen-wu, who, less directly involved themselves in political contention, were able to approach political questions in the broad light of history and in the most general terms Confucianism allowed.

HUANG TSUNG-HSI'S CRITIQUE OF CHINESE DESPOTISM

Huang Tsung-hsi (1610–1695) was the son of a high Ming official affiliated with the Tung-lin party who died in prison at the hands of the eunuchs. At the age of eighteen, after the fall of the chief eunuch, Wei Chung-hsien, Huang avenged his father's death by bringing to justice or personally attacking those responsible for it. Thereafter he devoted himself to study, took part in a flurry of political agitation at Nanking just before the fall of the Ming dynasty, and then engaged in prolonged, but unsuccessful, guerrilla operations against the Manchus in southeast China. There is evidence that he even took part in a mission to Japan, hoping to obtain aid. After finally giving up the struggle, Huang settled down to a career as an independent scholar and teacher, refusing all offers of employment from the Manchu regime.

Warfare being less total and intensive in those days, Huang was probably not forced to neglect his intellectual interests altogether during those unsettled years. Nevertheless it is remarkable that his most productive years should have come so late in life. His first important work, *A Plan for the Prince* (*Ming-i tai-fang lu*), was written at the age of fifty-two. Thereafter he worked on a massive anthology of Ming dynasty prose and the broad survey of Ming thought, *Ming-ju hsüeh-an,* which is the first notable attempt in China at systematic and critical intellectual history. At his death he was compiling a similar survey for the Sung and Yüan dynasties. Huang's range of interests included mathematics, calendrical science, geography, and the critical study of the Classics, as well as literature and philosophy. In most of these fields, however, his approach is that of an historian, whose underlying bent is reflected further in the fact that his most outstanding disciples and followers in the Manchu period also distinguished themselves in historical studies. Huang was an independent and creative scholar, who re-examined some of the age-old prejudices of the Confucian literati and came to his own conclusions (as, for instance, to the role of Law). Nevertheless, he felt no urge to break with Confucian tradition as a whole; for him it provided the basic principles for the reform of existing evils. Therefore it is not so much as a strikingly original thinker that Huang holds a high place in Chinese intellectual history, but as one who combined the broad scholarship characteristic of the Chu Hsi school with the active interest in contemporary affairs shown by the best of the Wang Yang-ming school. Though a competent classical scholar, he gave more attention to the study of the recent past than did most others of his time, whose interests were increasingly antiquarian. In this sense, *A Plan for the Prince,* which analyzes the political and economic weaknesses of seventeenth-century China in the light of Huang's extensive historical researches, is truly representative of his best work.

HUANG TSUNG-HSI

A Plan for the Prince

A Plan for the Prince (Ming-i tai-fang lu) [1] is probably the most systematic and concise critique of Chinese imperial institutions ever attempted from the Confucian point of view. Besides dealing with the theory and structure of government, it takes up the problems of education, civil service examinations, land reform, taxation, currency, military organization, and eunuchs—all of them closely related to the problem of government or affected by the activities of the state. Huang's views on only a few of these can be set forth here. Though not representative of any sustained or effective movement in Chinese political thinking at the time, Huang's views were not untypical of Confucian scholarly

[1] The Chinese title is not susceptible of literal translation; we give the general sense of it as indicated by Huang's preface to the work.

opinion outside the official class; the great Ku Yen-wu, for instance, expressed himself as in agreement with "sixty or seventy percent of it."

[From *Ming-i tai-fang lu*, 1b–3b]

ON THE PRINCE

In the beginning of human life each man lived for himself and sought to benefit himself. There was such a thing as the common benefit, yet apparently no one promoted it; and there was common loss, yet apparently no one eliminated it. Then a man appeared who did not think of benefit in terms of his own personal gain, but sought to benefit all under Heaven; and who did not think of loss in terms of his own personal disadvantage, but sought to spare all under Heaven of loss. Thus his labors were thousands of times greater than the labors of ordinary men. But to work a thousand or ten thousand times harder without benefiting oneself is certainly not something which human desires seek after. Therefore in those early times some men, considering what was involved in it, refused to become princes—Hsü Yu and Wu Kuang [2] were such. Others undertook it, and then quit—Yao and Shun, for instance. Still others, like Yü, became princes against their own will and later were unable to quit. How could they have felt differently? Indeed, to love ease and hate strenuous labor has always been the natural inclination of man.

However, with those who later became princes it was different. They believed that since they held the power over benefit and loss, there was nothing wrong at all in taking for themselves all the benefits and leaving to others all the loss. They made it so that no man dared to live for himself or seek to benefit himself. Thus the prince made his own private interests the common end of all. At first the prince felt some qualms about it, but his conscience eased with time. He looked upon the world as an enormous estate to be handed on down to his descendants, for their perpetual pleasure and well-being. Of Han Kao-ti it is said that he asked: "Considering the estate I have acquired, which of us, Brother Chung, or myself, has done better for himself?" [3] In these words he betrayed his overweening selfishness. The reason for [these contrasting attitudes] is this: In ancient times the people were considered hosts and the prince was the guest. All of his life the prince spent working for the sake of

[2] Legendary Taoist heroes who refused the throne when it was offered them.

[3] The founder of the Han dynasty, after his conquest of China, asked this question of his father, who had always thought his older brother the more capable of the two.

the people. Now the prince is host and the people are guests. Because of the prince people can find peace and happiness nowhere. In order to achieve his ends, people must be harmed and killed and their families broken up—all for the aggrandizement of one man's fortune. Without feeling the least pity for mankind, the prince says: "I want only to establish this estate for the sake of my descendants." Yet when he has established it, the prince still wrings every drop of blood and marrow from the people and takes away their sons and daughters to serve his excessive pleasures. It seems entirely proper to him. It is, he says, the interest on his estate. Thus the greatest enemy of mankind is the prince and nothing but the prince.

If there had been no rulers, each man would have lived for himself and secured what was to his own benefit. Could it be that the institution of rulership was meant to work out like this? In ancient times men loved their prince, thought of him as a father, likened him to God; and truly this was no more than just. Now men hate their prince, think of him as a mortal foe, call him an "outcast"; and this is perfectly natural. . . .

If it were possible for the latter-day princes to preserve such an estate and hand it down in perpetuity, this selfishness would not be hard to understand. But once the world comes to be looked upon as a personal estate, who in the world does not desire it as much as the prince? Even if the prince could tie his fortune down and lock it up tight, still the watchfulness of one man is no match for the greed of all. At most it can be kept in the family for a few generations, and sometimes it is lost in a lifetime. Sooner or later the spilling of blood and loss of life fall upon his own descendants. . . .

Therefore when the function of the prince is understood, as in the time of T'ang and Yü, everyone would just as soon pass the job on to someone else, and men like Hsü Yu and Wu Kuang are not unique. When the function of the prince is not clearly understood, every man in the market place covets the position. It is for this reason that throughout all subsequent time no one has heard of another Hsü Yu or Wu Kuang.

It is not easy to make plain the function of the prince, but any fool can see that a brief moment of excessive pleasure is not worth an eternity of sorrows.

ON MINISTERSHIP

Here Huang sets forth his conception of the true function and status of state officials. Elsewhere he argues especially for a strong prime ministership. The office of prime minister had been abolished by the founder of the Ming, for fear that it concentrated too much power in the hands of a potential usurper.

[From *Ming-i tai-fang lu*, 4a–5b]

The reason for ministership lies in the fact that the world is too big for one man to govern and that it is necessary to share the work with others. Therefore, when I come forth to serve, it is for the whole world and not for the prince; it is for all men and not for one family. . . .

But those who act as ministers today do not understand this concept. They say that a minister is created for the prince, that he rules only because the prince shares part of the world with him and delegates to him some leadership over the people. They look upon the world and its people as personal property in the prince's pouch. . . .

Whether there is peace or disorder in the world does not depend on the rise and fall of dynasties, but upon the happiness or distress of the people. That is why the fall of Chieh and Chou were occasions for peace and order; why, too, the rise of the Ch'in and Mongol dynasties were nevertheless occasions for disorder; and why the rise and fall of Chin, Sung, Ch'i, and Liang had no effect whatever on the stability or instability of the times.

If a minister ignores the plight of the people, then even if he succeeds in assisting his prince's rise to power or follows him to final ruin, it still can never be said that he has followed the [True] Way of the Minister. The governing of the world is like the hauling of great logs. The men in front call out, "Heave!" those behind, "Ho!" The prince and his ministers are log-haulers working together. If some of them, instead of holding tight to the ropes with feet firmly set on the ground, amuse themselves by cavorting around in front, the others behind will think it the thing to do and the business of hauling logs will be neglected. Alas, the insolent princes of later times indulge themselves [in the same way] and do not tend to the business of the world and its people. From among the men of the country they seek out only such as will be servile errand-boys. And if from the country those alone respond who are of the servile errand-boy type, then when they are protected from cold and hunger for a while, they feel eternally grateful for his majesty's kindness. Such men will not care whether they are treated by the prince with due respect, and will think it no more than proper to be relegated to a servant's status. In the first years of the Wan-li period [1573–1619] Chang Chü-cheng was treated by Shen-tsung with more respect than most ministers are shown, but it was not one-hundredth of what was shown to the counsellors of ancient times. At the time people were shocked because Chü-cheng's acquiescence in these honors seemed unbecoming to a subject. His fault, on the contrary, lay in being unable to maintain his self-respect as a counsellor so that he had to take orders from servant people. Yet he was blamed for exactly the opposite. Why so? Because people's minds had been contaminated for so long by degenerate notions about what a minister was, taking it as the accepted standard. How could they be expected to know that princes and ministers differ in name only, and are in fact the same? . . .

The terms "prince" and "minister" derive their significance from service to mankind. If I have no sense of duty to mankind I am an alien to the prince. If I come to serve him without any consideration for the welfare of mankind, then I am merely the prince's menial servant. If, on the other hand, I have the people's interest at heart, then I am the prince's mentor and colleague. Only then may I really be called a minister.

ON LAW

Huang was rare among Confucianists in the importance which he attached to the form or system of government, rather than simply to the character of the men administering it. Whereas Confucianists had traditionally been hostile to "law," associating with it the concepts of the hated Legalists of old, Huang refused to accept this definition of the term and insisted that "law" could represent something more than the arbitrary and oppressive dictates of despotic regimes.

[From Ming-i tai-fang lu, 6a–7b]

Until the end of the Three Dynasties there was law. Since the Three Dynasties there has been no law. Why do I say so? Because the Two Emperors and Three Kings knew that mankind could not do without sustenance and therefore gave men fields to cultivate. They knew that men could not do without clothes and therefore gave them land on which to grow mulberry and hemp. They knew also that men could not go untaught, so they set up schools, established the marriage ceremony to guard against promiscuity, and instituted military service to guard against disorders. This constituted law [4] until the end of the Three Dynasties. It was never laid down for the benefit of one man alone.

Later rulers, once they had won the world, feared only that their dynasty might not last long and that their descendants would be unable to preserve their empire. To prevent what they feared from happening, they resorted to laws. Consequently, what they called "law" was simply instituted for the sake of one family and not for the sake of all mankind.

Thus the Ch'in abolished feudal fiefs and set up commanderies (*chün*) and prefectures (*hsien*) thinking that this system would better serve their own interests. The Han gave domains to members of the royal house, so as to have them stand guard for the dynasty throughout the empire. The Sung abolished the military commanderies because they caused the dynasty some uneasiness. Such being their laws, how could we expect to find in them the slightest trace of consideration for the general welfare? Indeed, could we call them "law" at all?

The law of the Three Dynasties safeguarded the world for the people. The prince did not monopolize all the wealth of the land nor did he jealously keep the right to punish and reward out of the people's hands. Position at court was not particularly considered an honor; to live an obscure life in the country was not particularly a disgrace. Later this kind of law was criticized for its looseness, but at that time the people were not envious of those in high place, nor did they despise humble status. The looser the law was, the fewer the disturbances which arose. It was what we might call "law without laws." The laws of later times safeguard the world as if it were something in the [prince's] treasure chest. It is not desired that anything beneficial should be left to the lowly, but rather that all blessings be reserved for the one on high. If the prince employs a man, he is immediately afraid that the man will act in his own interest, and so another man is employed to keep a check on the first one. If one measure is adopted, there are immediate fears of its be-

[4] The Chinese term *fa* means "system" as well as legal regulation, and is applied here to the political and social institutions of ancient times, which for Huang represented a kind of basic constitution.

ing abused or evaded, and so another measure must be adopted to guard against abuses or evasions. All men know where the treasure chest lies, and the prince is constantly fretting and fidgeting out of anxiety for the security of the treasure. Consequently, the laws have to be made more comprehensive and detailed, and as they become more detailed, they become the very source of disorder. These are what we might call "unlawful laws."

Some say that each dynasty has its own laws and that succeeding generations of the royal house have a filial duty to follow the ancestral laws. Now the "unlawful laws" were originally instituted because the first prince of a line was unable to curb his own selfishness. Later princes, out of the same inability to curb their own selfishness, may in some cases have broken down these laws. The breaking down of the laws was admittedly a cause for suffering among the people, yet this does not mean that the original enactment of the laws never caused the people to suffer. And still some insist that we get involved in this kind of legalistic muck just to gain a little reputation for upholding the dynastic laws—all of which talk is just the secondhand drivel of petty literocrats.

It might be argued that order and disorder in the world are unrelated to the maintenance or absence of law. Now as to this there has been a great change from the past to the present: one complete upheaval which came with the Ch'in dynasty, and another with the Yüan [Mongol] dynasty. Following these two upheavals nothing at all survived of the sympathetic, benevolent, and constructive government of the early kings. So, unless we take a long-range view and look deep into the heart of the matter, changing everything thoroughly until the original order is restored with its land system, feudal system, school and military system, then even though some minor changes are made there will never be an end to the misery of the common man.

If it should be said that there are only men who govern well, not laws which govern well, my reply is that only if there are laws which govern well, will there later be men who govern well. Since "unlawful laws" fetter men hand and foot, even a man capable of governing well cannot overcome the handicaps of senseless restraint and suspicion. When there is something to be done, he does no more than his share, and since he contents himself with trifling accomplishments, there can be no outstanding achievements. If the law of the early kings were restored, there would be a spirit among men which went beyond the letter of the law. If men were of the right kind, the full intent of the law would be fulfilled; and even if they were of the wrong kind, it would be impossible for them to govern tyrannically and make the people suffer. Therefore I say we must first have laws which govern well and later we shall have men who govern well.

THE SELECTION OF OFFICIALS

For Huang, as for earlier reformers, the operation of the civil service was of crucial importance. Here only his basic principles are set forth, but in the original work he gives a detailed analysis of existing forms of recruitment, examination, and employment, as well as detailed recommendations for their improvement.

[From *Ming-i tai-fang lu*, 17a–18b]

In ancient times the selection of officials was liberal, but the employment of them was strict. Today the selection of officials is strict, but the employment of them is liberal. Under the old system of "state recommendation and village selection," a man of ability did not have to fear that he would go unrecognized. Later on, in the T'ang and Sung, several types of examination were instituted, and if a man did not succeed in one, he could turn around and take another. Thus the system of selection was liberal. . . .

But today this is not so. There is only one way to become an official: through the examination system. Even if there were scholars like the great men of old, such as Ch'ü Yüan, Ssu-ma Ch'ien, Ssu-ma Hsiang-ju, Tung Chung-shu, and Yang Hsiung, they would have no other way than this to get chosen for office. Would not this system of selection be called too strict? However, should candidates one day succeed, the topmost are placed among the imperial attendants and the lowest given posts in the prefectures and districts. Even those who fail [the metropolitan examinations] and yet have been sent up from the provinces are given official posts without having to take examinations again the rest of their lives. Would not this system of employment be called too liberal? Because the system of selection is too confined, many great men live to old age and die in obscurity. Because the system of employment is too liberal, frequently the right man cannot be found among the many holding official rank.

The common man, seeing only that in the past two hundred years a few men of character and achievement have appeared among those chosen, concludes that the examination system is good enough and there is no need to look elsewhere. He does not realize that among the hundreds and thousands taken in by the examination system, some men of character and achievement would inevitably find their way in. This means that men of character and achievement may find their way through the examination system, but the examination system does not find them. If we had scholars draw lots and chose them according to the length of the lot drawn, in the course of several hundred years men of character and achievement would naturally appear among those so chosen. But would we call this a good way to choose officials?

After all, the men of today who have character and ability are a far cry from those of the Han and T'ang dynasties. Today we have only mediocre and shallow men cluttering up the world. But it is surely not because Heaven has ceased to produce men of talent, is it? The system of selection is wrong.

Therefore, I would broaden the system for selecting officials, and choose men [not only] through the regular examinations [but also] through special recommendations, through the Imperial Academy, through the appointment of high officials' sons, through [a merit system for] junior officials in prefectures and districts, through special appointments, through [the recognition of] unique scholarship, and through the presentation of [outstanding] memorials.

LAND SYSTEM

In the following pages Huang gives his views on land reform, which echo the ancient ideal of the well-fields and earlier proposals for land redistribution. The greater part of Huang's discussion of the land problem, however, is a lengthy historical analysis of tax systems (not reproduced here), reflecting his belief that the chief evil was oppressive taxation by the state. Unless this were corrected, even the redistribution of land would not help the peasant. A significant feature of Huang's essay is his discussion of the land problem on the basis of statistical evidence, not just in the abstract. The official statistics available were none too accurate, but at least there were the beginnings here of social science, had Huang's line of inquiry been pursued and more accurate evidence compiled.

[From *Ming-i tai-fang lu*, 26a–27b]

After the abolition of the well-fields, Tung Chung-shu proposed a limitation on the amount of land a man could hold.[5] In accordance with this principle Shih Tan and K'ung Kuang decreed that no one could hold more than thirty *ch'ing* [about 340 acres], and that after a grace period of three years the land of those who violated this decree was to be confiscated.[6] Their intentions were good, but whereas in ancient times the wise ruler distributed land so as to provide for the people; today people own their own land and if an attempt is made to deprive them of it by legal means—if, far from distributing land, the government expropriates it—it is [what Mencius] called "doing an act of unrighteousness" and should not be done.

Some people may say: "If we try to restore the well-field system by seizing the land of the rich, disorders will result. We can restore the well-fields only by taking advantage of strife and bloodshed, when the population is small in relation to the vastness of the land. What a pity, therefore, that it was not done when it might have been: when Han Kao-tsu destroyed the Ch'in dynasty [206 B.C.] or Kuang-wu assumed the throne of Han [A.D. 25]!"

Now the early kings instituted the well-fields in order to provide for the livelihood of the people, in order to make them prosper and multiply. And yet such persons seem to regard the massacre of the people as something fortunate, because this makes it possible for them to advance their own projects. Could it be that they would regard it as a misfortune if, after turning the land into well-fields, the people should thrive and multiply and thus make it difficult for them to carry out their proposed reforms?

Among the scholars of later times, none presented so fully as did Su Hsün[7] the reasons why well-fields could not possibly be restored, and none so cogently as did Hu Han and Fang Hsiao-ju[8] the reasons why the well-fields should be restored. Su Hsün believed that without several hundred years of exhausting labor, it would be impossible to establish a system of rivers and highways, canals and roads, waterways and roadways, ditches and lanes, and trenches and pathways.[9] Now if we

---

[5] See pp. 232–34. [6] At the end of the Former Han dynasty.
[7] See pp. 461–63. [8] Early Ming (late fourteenth century) scholars.
[9] As the system was described in the *Rites of Chou*.

actually distributed land to the people, all routes would be kept open for traffic and all irrigation works could be kept in repair. So why need we get bogged down in the secondary details of the system? All the things that Su Hsün worried about were in no way vital to the well-field system.

Hu Han and Fang Hsiao-ju said well-fields should be restored, but were unable to elaborate an effective method for restoring them. Through a consideration of the military farms,[10] however, I have learned how the well-fields may be restored—in just the same way as the military farms were set up. These days scholars admit, when it comes to military farms, that to operate them is quite feasible, but when it is a question of well-fields, they say it cannot be done. They don't even know that two fives make ten!

Each soldier was allotted fifty *mu* which is equivalent to one hundred *mu* in ancient times.[11] Is it not, then, just the same as the hundred *mu* allotted to each man [under the well-field system] in Chou times? The regular grain tax on fifty *mu* of land was twelve piculs which the soldier-cultivator was permitted to use for his own needs; an additional tax of twelve piculs went to the officers and men of the local garrison for pay and supplies. Thus, actually the tax was just twelve piculs, and this amounts to two pecks (*tou*), four pints (*sheng*) per *mu,* just the same as under the tribute system used in the inner and outer districts during the Chou dynasty.

The total area of military farm land at present is 64,424,300 *mu.*[12] In the sixth year of Wan-li [1578], the total land actually under cultivation was 701,397,628 *mu.* If we find the ratio between them, military farm land is seen to occupy one-tenth of the total. [Since all military farm land is government land distributed to cultivators] that part of the total in which land distribution has not been effected is only nine-tenths. To apply to these nine-tenths of the land what is already true of one-tenth would not seem a difficult thing to do.

All land is either government-owned or private. Government land cannot be bought and owned by an individual. Within the area organ-

---

[10] Farmlands set aside for the support of military households in the Ming dynasty.

[11] Because the unit of measurement was thought to have doubled in the meantime.

[12] Actually Huang's figures are not current but come from the 1587 edition of *The Collected Statutes of the Ming Dynasty* (*Ming hui-tien*).

ized into districts and prefectures, government land occupies three-tenths of the total. Now if we take the total land under cultivation and average it out, with a total of 10,621,436 households in the land, each household would receive fifty *mu* and there would still be 170,325,828 *mu* left over. If the rich were allowed to occupy the remainder, no one need feel that he did not have enough. So why must there be any fuss over property limitations and equalization of land, or this needless to-do about causing the rich to suffer?

WANG FU-CHIH

Wang Fu-chih (Wang Ch'uan-shan, 1619–1692) was born of a scholarly family at the end of the Ming and had already received his first degree when Peking fell to the Manchus. Personally committed to the old dynasty, he raised an armed force and made attempts to support the remnants of Ming rule. When he realized at last the hopelessness of such efforts, he retired to his native place and spent the remainder of his life in seclusion, refusing to have anything to do with the new regime. He wrote and compiled numerous works on the classics, history, philosophy, and literature, employing historical and philological methods of research and at the same time expounding his own political ideas. Because of his isolation and hostility toward Manchu rule, he was little known in his own time. His works were not published until about two centuries after his death when, with the growth and development of anti-Manchu sentiment at the turn of the nineteenth century, they achieved great popularity and influence.

A philosopher of considerable depth and power, Wang Fu-chih reacted strongly against the idealism and subjectivism of the Wang Yangming school and turned back to the Sung master, Chang Tsai, for his basic ideas. He attacked the concept of metaphysical categories or principles as existing above or prior to material forms. According to Wang, function alone determines the form of a thing (not abstract principle) and the two can never be considered apart from one another. As applied to his political philosophy, for instance, this meant that the cardinal Confucian virtues of humanity and righteousness had to be conceived functionally as the means by which the ruler "lovingly cared for his own people" and "regulated his own human relationships" (i.e., performed his obligations to his own kindred).

Having, for a Confucianist, an uncommonly strong sense of racial consciousness, and regarding the preservation of the Chinese people and their culture as the ultimate end of government, Wang insisted that humanity and righteousness were not worth talking about unless they served the preservation of the race. Applying the same principle to political institutions, Wang asserted that there was no ideal system of political, economic, or military organization apart from the geographical conditions or historical circumstances in which they had to function. The institutions appropriate to each age differ, and therefore it is useless to talk of restoring the feudal system or the other institutions described in the Classics, as so many Confucian idealists had urged. Thus despite Wang's realistic attitude in regard to the need for adjusting to changed circumstances, he may be considered a reformer only in a limited sense, since he insisted equally upon the need for reconciling oneself to existing institutions, however defective in certain respects, which had arisen in response to historical changes. Wang, indeed, tended more toward a cyclical or pulsatory view of history than a progressive or evolutionary one. Nevertheless, among reformers of the late nineteenth and early twentieth centuries, his intense nationalism and theory of adaptation to changed circumstances were hailed as anticipating the needs of modern China.

WANG FU-CHIH
Dynastic Rule and the Preservation of the Race

In the following excerpts from the opening portion of his *Yellow Book* (*Huang shu*), Wang argues that the differentiation of species and races is a fundamental principle of nature, and that self-preservation of the people and their culture is the primary duty of the ruler. Because he rejected the Manchus as barbarians and challenged the legitimacy of their rule, great danger attached to the expression of his views. Whether for this reason or for his own idiosyncrasies of literary style, the text is full of cryptic expressions and recondite allusions, as well as censored passages. Because of difficulties in interpretation and reconstruction, the following translation is quite tentative and at some points represents only a rough paraphrase of the original.

[From *Ch'uan-shan i-shu, Huang shu,* 1a–2b]

In the beginning of things how vast and immeasurable were the creative powers of Heaven and earth—metal, wood, earth, fire, wind, and water each producing their appropriate effects as things multiplied and reproduced in the greatest profusion, ebbing and flowing, expanding and contracting, as things were joined together and set apart. Thus the powers of creation and proliferation were limitless in their operation and their end cannot be known. But when the families of things became clearly defined and the lines of demarcation among them were made definite, each was established in its own position and all living things were confined within their own protective barriers. In this way the work of Heaven and earth was accomplished, with the utmost forethought and appropriateness in every detail. For this reason the beasts of the mountain have cloven hoofs, those of the marshlands webbed feet, beasts of burden the power to support things crosswise, and beasts for plowing the power to pull things lengthwise; [those used for] wet cultivation are suited to the southland; [those used for] dry cultivation are suited to the northland. It is not that [Heaven and earth] made these different types because it favored separation and division, but because under the circumstances it was impossible for all things to cooperate and avoid conflict otherwise.

The sage, observing that this was so of all things and that each marked off its own kind from others, took charge of the empire and, serving as its ruler and head, separated the intelligent from the stupid, brought together those who seemed alike, drove out those who would be noxious and contaminating, and raised up walls to keep them apart. In this way he prevented conflict and made it possible for them to cooperate among themselves. Thus the saying that "the sage is co-virtuous with Heaven and earth" was not just empty talk!

Now man partakes of yin and yang, food and breath, equally with other things, and yet he cannot but be distinguished absolutely from other things; the Chinese in their bone structure, sense organs, gregariousness and exclusiveness, are no different from the barbarians, and yet they must be distinguished absolutely from the barbarians. Why is this so? Because if man does not mark himself off from things, then the principle of Heaven is violated. If the Chinese do not mark themselves off from the barbarians, then the principle of earth is violated. And since Heaven and earth regulate mankind by marking men off from each other, if men do not mark themselves off and preserve an absolute distinction between societies, then the principle of man is violated. Thus these three principles are the guardians of the Triad [Heaven, earth, and man].

In ancient times with the decline of the Chou dynasty the bond between the ruler and the people was broken and in their songs poets expressed disrespect for the king. The old capital fell into the hands of the north-west barbarians and the king of Chou took off to the eastern capital where he continued, at least in name, to preserve the dynasty by perform-ing the dynastic rites. The political order broke down completely, as feudal lords conspired among themselves and daily extended their seizure of ter-ritories. Those who cherished the ancient rites and customs and who would have been glad to die for the old order could do nothing but be-moan the disaster which threatened the house of Chou. Yet what the sage [Confucius] was deeply troubled over was something quite different. Writing the *Spring and Autumn Annals,* he strove to make manifest the kingly way. He accepted as his own kind the Chinese within and banished outside the pale of civilization the barbarians without; those who had designs on the Chou throne he censured for their transgressions but took back into the fold; those who pressed in from outside he despised for their meanness and longed to expel from the country. . . .

When kings Wen and Wu had risen up to establish the dynasty, each morning they attended to their duties in caring for the people and each evening they communed with Heaven to learn its will. Preserving the way of the sage-kings and former dynasties, they enfeoffed the various lords in their respective domains so as to hold strategic positions against barbarian incursions. Thus what never ceased to concern the sage-kings was that on the borders of the empire there should be various feudal lords capable of defending against the barbarians, lest the boundary be-tween the Chinese and barbarians not be preserved and the whole empire be thrown into confusion. Now to bring all the feudal states under one ruler, to concentrate in his hands all powers of administration and de-fense, and to reserve for himself alone all glory and honor rather than share these with other lords—would not even the sage-kings, like any other human being, desire this for themselves? Nevertheless, from the outset of the Chou dynasty rule over the various regions of the empire was entrusted to various dukes and barons, so that they might form a con-tinuous line of defense, with each holding his own position while those more and less powerful came to each others' aid. Therefore those who stood on the remote frontiers did not face danger all alone, and despite the vastness of the border regions it was not difficult to control them. By such means the rulers of the Chou at its height took care to maintain a strong defense and hold back the barbarians, so that their power and authority never weakened.

After the reigns of kings Yi [894–879 B.C.] and Li [878–828 B.C.] the feudal lords began to assert themselves, Chou hegemony was weakened and as the country was given over to internal contention, external enemies closed in. . . . However, though the emperor was unable to assert his authority, the strongest of the lords rose up, brought the north and south under control and drove off the barbarian tribes, thus performing the great service of preserving the military power and integrity of China. Though their achievements in war did not by any means measure up to the grand design of the sage-kings for ordering the world, nevertheless the sage recognized their merit and praised them for averting a national disaster and rescuing China from total extermination. . . .

Therefore he who is wise enough to make little of himself yet strong enough to govern the empire and protect his own kind becomes the chief, and he who provides security for his group becomes its ruler. Consequently the sage-king first commanded his people and showed them that he alone was worthy of honor. He guarded those qualities which made him worthy of honor and preserved [the basis of his rule] from destruction, so as to pass [the succession] on from generation to generation, or to some later sage. There might be abdications, successions, and even changes of mandate, yet never should a foreign dynasty be permitted to interrupt the succession [of Chinese sovereigns]. Only after first seeing to this did the sage-king then proceed to assist the weak and encourage the strong; raise up the virtuous and cast down the wicked; introduce the ceremonies of social intercourse to grace the lives of the people, the ceremonies of mourning and sacrifice for the expression of their grief, honors, ranks, and grades to regulate them in the proper order, and punishments and punitive campaigns to keep them under control. . . .

Even the ants have leaders who rule their ant-hills, and if other insects come to attack their nests, the leader gathers the ants together and leads them against their enemies to destroy them and prevent further intrusion. Thus he who would lead the ants must know the way to protect his group. Even so, if the ruler of the empire gives no thought to the future and does not consider well the importance of maintaining its frontiers, then he is unable to command respect or keep order within the empire. When danger threatens from outside, he has no means of warding it off; when natural disasters strike, he has no means of securing the people against them. He is unable to pass the succession on to his own posterity or to protect his own kind. Thus, the kingly way comes to an end. This is what [Confucius in] the *Spring and Autumn Annals* most deplored.

China and the Barbarian Tribes

Here it is clear that Wang is no racist in the modern sense. He does not assert the superiority of Chinese culture over all others, but only that each culture has its own function and each people its own mission.

[From *Tu T'ung-chien lun,* 28:13a–b]

The strength of the barbarians lies in the paucity of their laws and institutions. As long as their shelter, food, and clothing remain crude and barbaric, as long as they continue to foster a violent and savage temper in their people and do not alter their customs, they may enjoy great advantage. And at the same time, because of this China may escape harm. But if they once begin to change and to adopt Chinese ways, then the advantages of their situation will also change. They may thereby in time grow braver and mightier than the Chinese, which will be an advantage gained, but they will also open the way for eventual weakness. Therefore it is said that, as fish forget each other in the rivers and lakes, so men should forget each other and follow their own ways and principles. While the barbarians are content to roam about in pursuit of water and pasture, practicing archery and hunting, preserving no distinctions between ruler and subject, possessing only rudimentary marriage and governmental systems, ranging back and forth over their territory in accordance with seasonal demands, then China can never control or rule them. And as long as the barbarians do not realize that cities can be fortified and maintained, that markets bring profit, that fields can be cultivated and taxes exacted, as long as they do not know the glory of elaborate marriage and official systems, then they will continue to look upon China as a perilous and inhospitable bed of thorns. In like manner the Chinese who are seized and carried off to the lands of the barbarians will regard them with hatred and bitterness and refuse to serve them. The two lands will ignore each other to the advantage of both. It is in accordance with the ordinances of Heaven and the dictates of human feeling that each should thus find delight only in his own ways.

The Way Does Not Exist Outside of Its Practical Application
[From *Ch'uan-shan i-shu; Chou-i wai-chuan*, 5:25a–b]

The whole world is nothing more than an instrument. One cannot say that an instrument is an instrument of the Way, for what is called the Way is simply the way of using an instrument. We know from human experience that if there is no use for an instrument, then the instrument does not exist; conversely, if an instrument actually exists, we need not worry about whether or not it has a use. . . . If there is no instrument, then there is no Way—this statement is seldom made and yet it is absolutely true. . . . Bows and arrows have never existed without the way of shooting them; carriages and carriage horses have never existed without the way of driving them; sacrificial animals and wine, badges and offerings, or bells and chimes, flutes and strings, have never existed without the ways of ritual and music. Therefore the existence of sons demands the existence of the way of a father, or the existence of brothers that of the way of a brother. (There are, however, many "ways" that potentially could exist but actually do not.) Therefore it is quite correct to say that no way exists independent of its instrument.

Many people simply fail to consider the matter carefully enough. Thus the sages of antiquity were able to make use of instruments, but they were not able to make use of the Way, for what is called the "way" *is* the use of instruments. . . . In using them men speak about them and so names come to be fixed to them. These names are fixed to the things from above, as it were, but they also exist among things. One cannot distinguish between a realm of names existing above and one existing among things. So above physical forms there is no so-called realm of the formless. . . . If one tried to set aside instruments and seek for that which existed before the instruments, one might span all the evolutions of past and present, exhaust Heaven, earth, man, and things, and one would not be able to find anything bearing even a name, much less reality. Thus Lao Tzu was deluded when he said that the Way exists in emptiness, for emptiness must be empty of instruments also, and Buddha was likewise mistaken when he declared that the Way exists in nothingness, for nothingness must be a nothingness of instruments. One may propound such wild theories endlessly, but one can never escape from instruments, and if one insists upon pronouncing names that are separated from instruments as though one were some god, whom could one hope to deceive?

On the Inapplicability of Ancient Institutions to Modern Times
[From *Tu T'ung-chien lun,* "IIsü-lun," 5b–6b]

The most effective way of governing is to examine the *Book of History* and temper its pronouncements with the words of Confucius. Surely nothing could be better than this. But the crucial point is whether the ruler's heart is reverent or dissolute, and whether his statutes are too lax or too harsh. Those who fall short are lazy, those who go too far do so from a desire to proceed too rapidly. The principal function of government is to make use of worthy men and promote moral instruction, and in dealing with the people to bestow on them the greatest humanity and love. All governments, from those of Yao and Shun, the Three Dynasties, the Ch'in or the Han down to the present must proceed upon this principle. Examining and selecting men according to principles, apportioning taxes and corvees with fairness, keeping order with arms, restraining with punishments, bringing order with statutes and precedents—these are the means by which all governments have achieved success.

But when it comes to setting up detailed regulations or making up directives, then the authors of the *Book of History* or Confucius offer no guidance. Is this because they ignored reality and paid no attention to details? The ancient institutions were designed to govern the ancient world, and cannot be applied to the present day. Therefore the wise man does not try to set up detailed systems. One uses what is right for today to govern the world of today, but this does not mean that it will be right for a later day. Therefore the wise man does not try to hand down laws to posterity. Thus neither the *History* nor Confucius describe feudalism, the well-field system, the triennial and sexennial meetings of feudal lords, the system for punitive expeditions, the establishment of offices or the awarding of benefices. How then should someone who is not the equal in virtue of the emperors Shun and Yü or Confucius still presume on the basis of his reading to lay down a system of laws for all time? It is quite true that the "Documents of Hsia" contains a section called "The Tribute of Yü." But the system described therein pertains only to the Hsia dynasty; the laws of the Hsia kings were by no means followed in the succeeding Shang and Chou periods. The "Documents of Chou" does in fact contain a section called "Institutes of Chou," but here again these apply only to the Chou. They formed the model for the Chou dynasty and were not carried over from the earlier dynasties of Shang and Hsia. . . .

Times change, conditions are different. How then can a government go along with these changes and keep its people from growing idle? There are crises of the moment to be met in each age, but the expedients used to meet them are not necessarily worthy of constituting a whole theory of government. Before the prefectural system was put into effect the people were supposedly following the principles and practices of the ancient kings, and yet these practices were different from what we read of in the *History* and Confucius. It is not necessary that one consult all the ages of the past and try to follow all their usages. In my writings I have sought the source of success and failure in government and tried to bring my ideas into accord with the fundamental principles of the governments of the sages. But when it comes to questions of particular incidents and laws, then one must follow the times and try to determine what is fitting in each case. Every age has its different points of laxity and strictness [in application]; every affair has its contingent circumstances. It is better therefore to have no inflexible rules, lest one use the letter of the law to do violence to its spirit. Everyone makes mistakes at times, so that one should not try to force the world to follow his own arbitrary views. . . . If these people who try to upset all the established ways of the world and throw everything into panic by putting into effect some private theory derived from their reading are allowed to go on having their way, I cannot say how things will end.

On the Use of Laws..
[From *Tu T'ung-chien lun*, 30:13b–15b]

The nation cannot be governed by laws. Yet if all laws disappear, then the people have no way to maintain their livelihood and rulers no way to guard the people. Therefore if the nation is to be governed, there must first be a leader who will set up laws and institutions to make the people understand that there is a Son of Heaven over them and officials in their midst, and that they are assured of protection so that they may plan for their own livelihood. These laws and institutions that are first set up can never be completely good, and if later ages observe them to the letter, they will bring suffering to the people and incite disorder. In this first and tentative stage, the lawmakers, in an effort to correct evil, may be excessively severe or, following the will of the vulgar, may err in the direction of laxity. They can only make a rough beginning and wait for those who come after to refine and finish. For this reason, the Ch'in laws were not uniformly bad for the people. Ch'in came to power in the confused and chaotic days at the end of the Six States and opened up the way for a new rule by impressing upon the people the fact that laws existed. Then when the Han followed with its broad and tolerant regime, it was able to simplify the laws and abolish those which were oppressive, bringing order to the world. . . .

Therefore I have said that if the nation is to be governed, there must first be a leader to set up laws and institutions. Although they may not be the best, they will be better than no laws at all. Han inherited the laws of Ch'in and reformed them; therefore it could not model its system upon that of the Three Dynasties. T'ang took over the laws of the T'o-pa and Yü-wen dynasties and reformed them, and so its system differed from that of the Former and Latter Han. Sung inherited and reformed the laws of the Kuo and Ch'ai regimes and so could not practice the same ways as the T'ang at its height. When bad laws have once been put into effect and the people have grown accustomed to them over a long period, they will inevitably be intent only upon following these laws. If one can only suppress the evil aspects of these laws and gradually improve them, then the world will eventually attain peace. But if the world is continually in a state of confusion, heir only to the dregs of corrupt government of the preceding dynasty, hastening onward in the decline, completely destroying what was good in the old system, the dissolute attacking each other, military upstarts and petty bureaucrats spreading evil in high positions, and if no one appears to correct or change the laws, then even the wisest of sovereigns will have difficulty in bringing about a speedy reform.

KU YEN-WU, BEACON OF CH'ING SCHOLARSHIP

Ku Yen-wu (1613–1682), born in the last days of the Ming dynasty, had already achieved considerable reputation as a scholar when Peking fell to the Manchus in 1644. The following year he took part in an attempt to defend his native city in Kiangnan against the invading Ch'ing armies. With the fall of the city his foster-mother, who had raised him from infancy, starved herself to death rather than live under the rule of the Manchus, on her deathbed entreating Yen-wu never to serve the new dynasty in any official capacity. Ku remained true to her wishes, spending the rest of his life traveling about North China, working for brief periods at odd jobs of an unofficial nature and carrying on his researches.

During the chaotic days of the end of the Ming, Ku had already become interested in practical subjects such as economics, government, and military defense. The fall of the native dynasty before the Manchu invaders spurred him to pursue these studies with renewed vigor in an effort to find out why the old dynasty had faltered and how its mistakes could be avoided in the future. He bitterly attacked the intuitionism of the Wang Yang-ming school of Neo-Confucianism which, he believed, by its subjectivity and scorn for book-learning had seriously debilitated the intelligentsia of the late Ming. To combat this effete and empty speculation he insisted that scholars must undertake wide and varied research on practical subjects and return to the simple ethical precepts of early Confucianism. He likewise deplored the inordinate attention to literary elegance and belles-lettres that had so often characterized scholars of earlier times, believing that such interests represented only a selfish striving for reputation. When a friend wrote a poem praising him, Ku admonished him with the advice that the writing of such eulogies was no practice for a serious gentleman. "Men must lose themselves and each other in higher principles," he counseled, begging his friend to write no more such poems.[13]

His own works exemplify this new spirit of practical learning. Carrying on the systematic study of phonetics that had developed sporadically in the late Sung and Ming, he perfected the inductive method of research

---

[13] "Letter in Reply to Tzu-te," *T'ing-lin shih-wen chi*, 4:7b.

which was to be applied with such effect by textual critics of the later years of the Ch'ing. Besides important works on phonetics, he produced voluminous studies on historical geography and epigraphy. But his best-known and most significant work is undoubtedly his *Jih-chih lu* or *Record of Daily Knowledge,* a collection of short essays on problems in the Classics, government, economics, the examination system, literature, history, and philology. Carefully composed and revised during the years of his travels and based on personal observation, wide reading and a painstaking collection of evidence, these essays represent not simply a reworking of old material and restating of traditional views, but a new and constructive contribution to the subjects dealt with. They are, as he himself said, not old coin but "copper dug from the hills."

Like many other scholars of the time, Ku believed that one of the fatal weaknesses of the Ming had been an overconcentration of power and authority in the hands of the central government. He therefore recommended a greater decentralization of authority and the strengthening of local self-government in the provinces, even going so far as to suggest the revival of some of the practices of ancient feudalism.

The originality of his researches, and the new ideals of scientific methodology and practical learning which they embodied, had a marked and beneficent influence upon the men of his age. Under his leadership the way was opened for the great movement of critical research and evaluation that characterized the best of Ch'ing scholarship.

KU YEN-WU

True Learning: Broad Knowledge, and a Sense of Shame
[From "A Letter to a Friend Discussing the Pursuit of Learning," *T'ing-lin shih-wen chi*, 3:1a–2b]

It is a matter of great regret to me that for the past hundred odd years, scholars have devoted so much discussion to the mind and human nature, all of it vague and quite incomprehensible. We know from the *Analects* that "fate and humanity (*jen*) were things which Confucius seldom spoke of" (IX, 1) and that Tzu-kung "had never heard him speak on man's nature and the way of Heaven" (V, 12). Though he mentioned the principle of human nature and fate in the appendices to the *Book of Changes,* he never discussed them with others. When asked about the qualities of a gentleman, Confucius said: "In his conduct he must have a sense of shame" (XIII, 20), while with regard to learning he spoke of a "love of antiquity" and "diligent seeking," discussing and praising Yao and Shun and transmitting their tales to his disciples. But he never said so much as a word about the so-called theory of "the precariousness [of the human mind] and the subtlety [of the mind of the Tao] and of the [need for keeping one's mind] refined and undivided," [14] but only said "sincerely hold fast to the Mean—if within the four seas there be distress and poverty, your Heaven-conferred revenues will come to a perpetual end." [15] Ah, this is the reason for the learning of the sage. How simple, how easy to follow! . . . But gentlemen of today are not like this. They gather a hundred or so followers and disciples about them in their studies, and though as individuals they may be as different as grass and trees, they discourse with all of them on mind and nature. They set aside broad knowledge and concentrate upon the search for a single, all-inclusive method; they say not a word about the distress and poverty of the world within the four seas, but spend all their days lecturing on theories of "the weak and subtle," "the refined and the undivided." I can only conclude that their doctrine is more lofty than that of Confucius and their disciples wiser than Tzu-kung, and that while they pay honor to the school of Eastern Lu (Confucius) they derive their teachings on the mind directly from the two sage emperors Yao and Shun. . . .

What then do I consider to be the way of the sage? I would say "extensively studying all learning" [16] and "in your conduct having a sense of shame." [17] Everything from your own body up to the whole nation should be a matter of study. In everything from your personal position as a son, a subject, a brother, and a friend to all your comings and goings, your giving and taking, you should have things of which you would be ashamed. This sense of shame before others is a vital matter. It does not mean being ashamed of your clothing or the food you eat, but ashamed that there should be a single humble man or woman who does not enjoy the blessings that are his due. This is why Mencius said that "all things are complete in me" if I "examine myself and find sincerity." [18] Alas, if a

---

[14] Referring to the *Book of History*, Counsels of Great Yü II, a passage much quoted by Neo-Confucianists.

[15] *Book of History*, Counsels of Great Yü II. [16] *Analects*, VI, 25.

[17] *Analects*, XIII, 20. [18] *Mencius*, VII A, 4.

scholar does not first define this sense of shame, he will have no basis as a person, and if he does not love antiquity and acquire broad knowledge, his learning will be vain and hollow. These baseless men with their hollow learning day after day pursue the affairs of the sage, and yet I perceive that with each day they only depart further from them.

Preface to the Record of the Search for Antiquities
[From personal preface to *Ch'iu-ku lu*]

Ever since I was young I have enjoyed wandering about looking for old inscriptions on metal or stone, although I could not understand them very well. Then when I read Ou-yang Hsiu's "Record of Collected Antiquities" (*Chi-ku lu*) I realized that many of the events recorded in these inscriptions are verified by works of history so that, far from being merely bits of high-flown rhetoric, they are of actual use in supplementing and correcting the histories. For the past twenty years I have traveled widely about the country and whenever I visited some famous mountain or great commercial center, the site of an ancestral shrine or Buddhist temple, I never failed to clamber up to the steepest peak, to search the darkest valley, feeling out the toppled stone markers, tramping about the underbrush, cutting down the old tangled hedges and sifting through the rotten earth. Anything that was legible I made a copy of by hand, and when I came across an inscription that had not been seen by my predecessors I was so overjoyed I could not sleep. I can never forget that with each day that passes more of these remaining inscriptions of the men of ancient times disappear. Most men of later times will probably not share my interest in these things, yet even if they should, in the course of several centuries how many of these inscriptions will have vanished away! . . . Being only a commoner, however, when I went on these expeditions I had neither groom nor horse to accompany me, so that often I found myself wetting the tip of my brush and hesitating in perplexity among the forest birds and monkeys. The men of the north can seldom decipher characters and have only scant information on such matters. I was hampered by lack of daylight, while the mountains were so high and the rivers so deep that there were many places I could not get to. Even in the places I visited there must be things that I missed. Thus it is my hope that other men who share my love will carry on my work and make further recordings of their own.

On the Concentration of Authority at Court

That Ku shared much the same view as Huang Tsung-hsi of the Chinese state as over-centralized is clear from this analysis of the weaknesses of local government under an administrative system more in keeping with the Legalist philosophy than the Confucian.

[From *Jih-chih lu,* 9:15a–16a]

He who is called the Son of Heaven holds supreme authority in the world. What is the nature of this supreme authority? It is authority over all the world which is vested in the men of the world but which derives ultimately from the Son of Heaven. From the highest ministers and officials down to the regional magistrates and petty officers, each holds a share of this authority of the Son of Heaven and directs the affairs of his charge, and the authority of the Son of Heaven is thereby magnified in dignity. In later ages there appeared inept rulers who gathered all authority into their own hands. But the countless exigencies of government are so broad that it is quite impossible for one man to handle them all, so that authority then shifted to the laws. With this a great many laws were promulgated to prevent crimes and violation, so that even the greatest criminals could not get around them, nor the cleverest officials accomplish anything by evading them. People thereupon expended all their efforts in merely following the laws and trying to stay out of difficulty. Thus the authority of the Son of Heaven came to reside not in the officials appointed by the government but in their clerks and assistants [who were familiar with the laws]. Now what the world needs most urgently are local officials who will personally look after the people, and yet today the men who possess least authority are precisely these local officials. If local officials are not made known to the higher authorities, how can we hope to achieve peace and prosperity and prolong the life of the nation?

The Feudal System vs. the Prefectural System
[From *T'ing-lin shih-wen chi,* 1:7a–b]

If we understand why the feudal system changed into the prefectural system, we will also understand that as the prefectural system in turn falls into decay it too must change. Does this mean that there will be a return to feudalism? No, this is impossible. But if some sage were to ap-

pear who could invest the prefectural system with the essential meaning
of feudalism, then the world would attain order. . . . Today the prefectural system has reached a point of extreme decay, but no such sage
appears and people go on doing everything in the same old way. Therefore
with each day the people become poorer, China grows weaker, and we
hasten down the road to ruin. Why is this? The fault of feudalism was its
concentration of power on the local level, while the fault of the prefectural
system is its concentration of power at the top. The sage-rulers of antiquity
were impartial and public-minded in their treatment of all men, parceling
out land to them and dividing up their domains. But now the ruler considers all the territory within the four seas to be his own prefecture, and is
still unsatisfied. He suspects every person, he handles every affair that
comes up, so that each day the directives and official documents pile higher
than the day before. On top of this he sets up supervisors, provincial
governors and governors-general, supposing that in this way he can keep
the local officials from tyrannizing over and harming the people. He is
unaware that these officials in charge are concerned only in moving with
utmost caution so as to stay out of trouble until they have the good fortune
to be relieved of their posts, and are quite unwilling to undertake anything of profit to the people. Under such circumstances how can the
people avoid poverty and the nation escape debilitation? If this situation
is allowed to continue unchanged, I am positive that it will lead only to
chaos with trouble increasing day by day. If, however, the position of local
officials is accorded its proper dignity, and such officials are granted fiscal
and administrative authority, if the post of supervisor is discontinued, the
enticement of hereditary office held out to officials, and a method whereby
they may select their own subordinates put into effect, this will achieve
the goal of imbuing the prefectural system with the essential meaning of
feudalism, and the decay that has come about in the last two thousand
years can be remedied. Rulers hereafter will find that if they hope to
improve the livelihood of the people and strengthen the power of the
nation, they must heed my words.

THE TWILIGHT OF CONFUCIAN THOUGHT

With the firm establishment of the Ch'ing (Manchu) dynasty in the
latter half of the seventeenth century there was a marked change in the

climate of Confucian thought. The reaction against the extreme subjectivism and idealism of the Wang Yang-ming school continued. At its door
was laid the blame for all the weaknesses of the Ming regime; while, on
the other hand, the philosophy of Chu Hsi, confirmed by the Manchu
state as the authoritative teaching and perpetuated as the basis of the
civil service examinations, underwent a strong revival in scholarly circles.

The most significant change, however, did not develop along lines of
the old philosophical rivalries, nor did it bring victory to either of the
established schools. Indeed, they remained in the forefront of intellectual
debate only in so far as both together became targets of attack from a
new direction—from those who pursued further two important tendencies
manifested by the thinkers just discussed, that is, the striving for breadth
of learning and the insistence upon practicality of thought.

Of the two, breadth of learning, especially as embodied in classical
scholarship, set the tone of the new age. And in the field of classical study
no movement had such influence or achieved such remarkable results as
the school of Han Learning, whose name derives from the fact that this
group, dissatisfied like Ku Yen-wu with the metaphysical speculations of
both the Sung and Ming, turned back to the studies of Han dynasty
scholars and commentators as guides to the Classics. In other words, by
the seventeenth century Confucian thought had come around full circle;
where the most creative minds of the Sung had been ready to forego the
meticulous scholarship of the Han and T'ang commentators in the interests of a more vital and expansive approach to the classical tradition,
Ch'ing scholars were now ready to return to historical and exegetical
studies as a corrective to the free-wheeling and mutually conflicting interpretations of the Neo-Confucian schools.

In this process the Han school men made contributions of lasting value
to our knowledge of the Confucian Classics. A discovery which had important repercussions on Neo-Confucian cosmology, for instance, was
that of Hu Wei (1633–1714). Following a line of investigation opened
up by Huang Tsung-hsi and his son, he demonstrated that the diagrams
attached to the *Book of Changes,* upon which the Neo-Confucianists had
based their theories, were late accretions of Taoist provenance rather than
integral parts of the original work. Of equal significance to Confucianism
as a state cult was the demonstration by Yen Jo-chü (1636–1704) that the
so-called ancient text of the "Documents of the Shang Dynasty" in the

Book of History, which had been used for centuries in the official examinations, was a forgery. Much progress was also made by these and
other scholars in re-examining the date and authorship of such classics
as the *Great Learning,* which had been a favorite text of the Neo-Confucianists, as well as in the study of historical geography, philology,
phonetics, epigraphy, and other branches of knowledge having a bearing
on the Classics.

Considering the number of scholars who contributed to these researches
(though not as a formal group), there can be no doubt that the school of
Han Learning represented a truly broad movement in Ch'ing thought
toward a kind of critical scholarship that anticipated modern Western
methods and produced a body of systematic, empirically verified knowledge. Nevertheless, we cannot fail to observe that its achievements were
largely critical and negative in character, rather than productive of new
philosophical speculations (against which, of course, it had turned its
back) or new currents of thought in close touch with the political and
social problems of the time.

Of these limitations in the Han school's work other thinkers, less
representative of the age, were partly aware. There was, for instance, the
so-called Eastern Chekiang historical school stemming from Huang
Tsung-hsi, which stressed the value of studying recent history as well as
ancient. Its leading representatives, such as Wan Ssu-t'ung (1638–1702),
Ch'üan Tsu-wang (1705–1755), and Chang Hsüeh-ch'eng (1738–1801),
kept alive the Confucian view of historical studies as having a practical
bearing on the conduct of government, but as they had little status or influence in the ruling regime, their efforts were devoted largely to upholding the value of private, unofficial historical writing as compared to
state-sponsored projects. In this way they sought to preserve records of
the Ming dynasty which might supplement or correct the Manchu version
of recent events, and they drew attention to the value of local histories or
gazetteers and many other types of records which might contribute to a
fuller, deeper understanding of history than official accounts provided.

Another movement which stressed practicality of thought is identified
with Yen Yüan (1635–1704) and Li Kung (1659–1733), who were equally
critical of the orthodox Neo-Confucian metaphysics of the Ch'eng-Chu
school and of their own contemporaries pursuing the Han learning. Toward the latter their attitude was reminiscent of Wang Yang-ming's con-

demnation of book learning and classical scholarship as a distraction from
the real business of life. Toward the former they had specific objections on
philosophical grounds, in that they considered the Ch'eng-Chu system to
have been deeply influenced by Buddhist and Taoist quietism, particularly
in its view of human nature. The distinction which it had made between
the physical nature of man and his Heaven-bestowed moral nature, Yen
Yüan argued, had fostered the belief that man's actual nature was evil
and that his physical desires had to be repressed so that his ideal nature
might be recovered or restored through a kind of meditative discipline.
Yen contended that this erroneous view of human nature derived from
the fallacious dualism maintained by the Ch'eng-Chu school between
principle (*li*) and material-force (*ch'i*), according to which the true human nature transcended its physical embodiment. Like Huang Tsung-hsi
and Wang Fu-chih, Yen Yüan insisted that there were no principles
apart from things, and that moral perfection could not be achieved except
through the full development of the actual nature in the conduct of
everyday life.

Tai Chen (1724–1777), probably the greatest thinker and scholar of the
Ch'ing dynasty, pursued Yen's line of thought further. He was especially
concerned with the problem of how the truth or principles of things may
be ascertained. The Neo-Confucianists, by asserting that the principles of
things were also contained in the mind and attainable by mental discipline, had led men away from the study of things into introspection
and mysticism. What they called "principle" might be purely subjective,
whereas in fact principle could only be found in things and studied objectively. This required careful observation and analysis, followed by
submission of the results to some kind of public test in order to determine
whether or not the results were confirmed by the observations of others. In
practice, however, the "things" studied by Tai Chen were for the most
part the "affairs" of men with which the Confucian Classics were concerned. In this respect Tai represented also the best traditions of the school
of Han Learning, for he distinguished himself in the same type of classical
scholarship: philology, phonology, historical geography, and mathematical
history.

In Li Kung, too, we can see how this current of philosophical dissent
reconverged with the mainstream of Ch'ing scholarship. "Practical studies"
for him meant the Six Arts spoken of in the Classics, including such things

as archery, music, and ceremonial; and despite his master's condemnation of classical scholarship, Li proceeded to expound his ideas by writing commentaries on classics like the *Book of Changes,* the *Spring and Autumn Annals,* and the *Analects* of Confucius. It is hardly surprising, then, to find that the influence of these men on their own time was more through their scholarship than their philosophy, since the latter won few adherents and found no worthy successors.

In the end, the very attempts of Ch'ing Confucianists to disinherit themselves from Sung and Ming metaphysics demonstrated how much, after all, they were children in spirit of the Neo-Confucianists. Theirs was not a movement to break the bounds of Confucian tradition and explore new intellectual ground. Their fundamental impulse was instead to return, to recover, to restore the ancient truth in its original purity, just as the early Neo-Confucianists of the Sung had thought of themselves as reviving the old order after centuries of disintegration and perversion under the Han and T'ang dynasties. Therefore, the critical spirit they so well exemplified became an instrument for redefining, with greater precision, perhaps, but also within narrower limits, the authentic tradition deriving from the Master of old. Of even the rarest, most critical, most independent of scholars, such as Ts'ui Shu (1740–1816, a translation from whom follows this essay), was this true. Though he dug deeper and deeper into the past, and rejected even Han scholarship in his search for the authentic roots of Confucianism, his achievements in historical study and textual criticism only served as a testimonial of Ts'ui's undiminished faith in Confucius' teaching as the source of all that was worth learning.

What does seem surprising to us, at least from the vantage point of later history, is that an age whose intellectual ideals were breadth of knowledge and practicality of thought, should have been so little stirred by the new knowledge from Europe which the Jesuits brought to China in the sixteenth, seventeenth, and eighteenth centuries. This was certainly not owing to lack of acquaintance with them or of opportunities to learn more. The Jesuits had attracted wide attention by their scientific feats, and had been installed for over a century as the official astronomers of the Ming and Ch'ing courts. They had even made a few important converts to their own faith among scholar officials, and a not inconsiderable number among the common people—enough to cause alarm to men like the xenophobic official Yang Kuang-hsien (1597–1669) who saw in Western science as well as in Christianity a threat to all of Chinese civilization. Yet the net impression made on the Confucian mind was slight.

It is true that interest in mathematics and astronomy among men like Huang Tsung-hsi and others after him in the Han school was greatly stimulated by the revelations of the Jesuits; in fact, a few individuals like Mei Wen-ting (1633–1721) were even ready to acknowledge the great value of the new scientific learning and to assimilate it. More typically, however, this new interest was directed toward a re-examination of China's traditional methods of astronomy, toward recovering much genuine knowledge that had been lost owing to centuries of neglect, or toward defending Chinese tradition by showing, with great ingenuity, that what was valid in the scientific learning of the West was nothing really new but borrowed indirectly from the ancient Chinese, or that, on the other hand, what clearly conflicted with traditional lore must be held invalid. Juan Yüan (1764–1849), a prodigious scholar as well as leading official of his time, testified to the new interest in mathematics and astronomy by his biographies of notable contributors to these sciences, including even Westerners like Ptolemy. Yet his Sino-centric point of view is evident. He contends that, because the knowledge of astronomy attributed to Ptolemy by the Jesuits was so far in advance of the Chinese at the same time (the Han dynasty), the Jesuits must have deliberately exaggerated it in order to deceive the Chinese concerning the accomplishments of the West.[19] Another contention of his is that the revolution of the earth around the sun must be a fallacious theory since it "departs from the Classics and is contrary to the Way." [20]

We should not conclude from this that the attitude of most Confucian scholars toward Western learning was hostile or sharply defensive. More generally it was one of indifference. When in 1818 Juan Yüan sponsored the publication of Chiang Fan's monumental survey of the school of Han Learning in the Ch'ing dynasty (*Kuo-ch'ao Han-hsüeh shih-ch'eng chi*), neither Chiang nor Juan, in their prefatory remarks concerning the significance of this movement, found it necessary to mention its position with respect to Western learning. The great antagonists in Juan's mind are still

[19] *Ch'ou-jen chuan*, 43:6b.
[20] *Ch'ou-jen chuan*, 46:19a.

the old ones—Buddhism and Taoism—and much emphasis is placed on the contribution of the Han school in purging Confucianism of Buddhist and Taoist elements which had infiltrated the original teaching.

What, then, are the reasons for this notable failure to pursue more vigorously their contacts with the West, when by contrast the best minds in Europe were avidly devouring not only curious information about China but the teachings of Confucius himself as related by the Jesuits (from whom we inherit our romanization of his Chinese name, *K'ung Fu-tzu*)? Much has been written on this question, and much more remains to be studied. The Jesuits themselves, from the outset, observed that the general disinterest of the Chinese in Western science was a reflection of their preoccupation with studies which led to official preferment. Trigault, for instance, puts it:

It is evident to everyone here that no one will labor to attain proficiency in mathematics or in medicine who has any hope of becoming prominent in the field of [Confucian] philosophy. The result is that scarcely anyone devotes himself to these studies, unless he is deterred from the pursuit of what are considered to be the higher studies, either by reason of family affairs or by mediocrity of talent. The study of mathematics and that of medicine are held in low esteem, because they are not fostered by honors as is the study of philosophy, to which students are attracted by the hope of the glory and the rewards attached to it. This may be readily seen in the interest taken in the study of moral philosophy. The man who is promoted to the higher degrees in this field, prides himself on the fact that he has in truth attained to the pinnacle of Chinese happiness.[21]

And Du Halde:

The great and only Road to Riches, Honour, and Employments is the study of the *ching* (or canonical books), History, the Laws and Morality; also to learn to do what they call *wen-chang,* that is, to write in a polite Manner, in Terms well chosen, and suitable to the Subject treated upon. By this means they become Doctors, and that Degree once obtained, they are possessed of such Honor and Credit, that the conveniences of life follow soon after, because they are sure to have a Government post in a short time. Even those who return into their Provinces to wait for Posts, are in great Consideration with the Mandarin of the Place; they protect their families against all vexations, and there enjoy a great many privileges. But as nothing like this is to be hoped for by those who apply themselves to the speculative Sciences, and as the Study

[21] Gallagher (tr.), *China in the 16th Century,* pp. 32–33.

of them is not the Road to Honours and Riches, it is no wonder that those sorts of abstract Sciences should be neglected by the Chinese.[22]

What Du Halde says here about the key role of the civil service examination system (the term *wen-chang* refers specifically to the examination essay) only confirms what Confucian reformers themselves had repeatedly pointed to: that education in China, and the capabilities of the educated class, were largely limited by the type of examination system which controlled entrance to official life, and that in a bureaucratic society the alternatives to an official career were few and unattractive. During the first half of the Manchu dynasty, the great influence of the state in intellectual matters was further exerted through its patronage of Confucian scholarship. In an attempt to demonstrate that, though foreigners, their rule was based on a full appreciation of the best in Chinese culture, the Manchus lavished special honors on Confucian scholars recognized for their broad classical learning, and employed large numbers of scholars and scribes in ambitious projects for the preservation, codification, and explication of the classical tradition—projects of such magnitude as the collection of the Imperial Manuscript Library from texts gathered all over the land and the preparation of a compendious critical bibliography for it.

The fact that this collection process also enabled the Manchus to screen out and destroy many works considered hostile to their rule (a process which has been referred to as the "Inquisition of Ch'ien-lung"), was perhaps less significant as a negative factor than the positive support given to a type of classical research which Chinese scholars, pursuing their own line of thought, were already diligently engaged in. Nor should we overlook a more subtle and indirect contribution of the Manchus to the Chinese feeling of self-sufficiency in intellectual matters. This is the sense of well-being and complacency which was fed by the very success of the Manchus as rulers of China in the great K'ang-hsi and Ch'ien-lung reigns. The empire was peaceful and prosperous, the population was growing, and the arts of civilization flourished as never before. In such circumstances it was difficult to take seriously a challenge from the West which had only been tendered at the hands of gentle missionaries and was not as yet backed by overwhelming force.

[22] Adapted from *A Description of the Empire of China* (London, 1741), II, 124, cited in Bernard, *Matteo Ricci's Scientific Contribution to China*, p. 20f.

TS'UI SHU AND THE CRITICAL SPIRIT

One of the finest representatives of the integrity, critical spirit and sound scholarship which marked the best of Ch'ing learning is the historian Ts'ui Shu (1740–1816). Through a long lifetime of scholarly endeavor he worked to refute not only the late Sung and Ming misinterpretations of the Classics, but the similar misinterpretations and errors of the Han Confucianists, attempting by methods of historical research to restore the purity of ancient Confucianism. His most important researches are embodied in a collection of essays entitled *K'ao hsin lu* or *Record of Beliefs Investigated*. In addition he wrote a brief work called *Essentials of the Record of Beliefs Investigated* (*K'ao hsin lu t'i-yao*) in which he expounded in an informal style, interspersed with lively anecdotes, the ideals and methods which guided him in his work.

Ts'ui avoided official life for the most part and preferred to devote himself to independent scholarly research, though this meant inevitably a life of hardship and poverty for himself and his faithful wife. Of his great work, the *Record of Beliefs Investigated*, a famous disciple said: "Since his ideas were of no value in the examination halls, there were few who believed in him. On the contrary there were those who seized upon his most trustworthy conclusions and on his clearest elucidations to discredit him. Within the next century there will surely be some in this broad empire who will truly understand him." [23]

TS'UI SHU

Selections from the Essentials of the Record of Beliefs Investigated

[From *K'ao hsin lu t'i-yao*, A:2–22]

Is it impossible to believe what other people have said? The world is very large and I cannot do and see everything in it. How much more so with the world of a thousand years ago! If I do not accept the accounts of other men, by what means can I find out about it? But is it possible to believe *everything* that others have said? Surely if one did he would end up like the man in the story who took Ma Yüan's lily seeds for pearls.

[23] Ch'en Li-ho, quoted in Hummel (ed.), *Eminent Chinese*, II, 773.

. . . Tongues will grow in people's mouths and there is nothing to restrain them; brushes will find their way into men's hands and there is nothing to hold them back. Whatever comes into a man's head to say he may say, and there is no limit to how far he can go. . . .

In our prefectural town there was a Liu family who had two meteorites. According to the story that was told by everyone around the village some shooting stars had fallen long ago on the Liu mansion and changed into stones. I was still young when I heard of this but I already doubted it. When I was a little older I was playing once with the Liu boys and they showed me the stones and some inscriptions carved on them in seal and ordinary script. When I questioned them very closely they finally said: "That story is not really true. One of our ancestors was an official in the south where he came across these stones. They were such an odd shape that he supposed there were no others like them in the world and so he just carved these inscriptions to give proof, and yet as you see the whole thing was a fake." How then is one to go about ascertaining the truth of what people say?

When the Chou had declined many strange doctrines sprang up. The various schools of Yang Tzu, Mo Tzu, the Logicians, the Legalists, the diplomatic alliances, and the yin and yang all made up sayings and invented incidents to fool wise men and sages. The Han Confucianists were acquainted with these various teachings and, accepting them as quite reliable without even examining them carefully, proceeded to note them down in their books and commentaries. . . . After this there appeared the cults of the prophetic and apocryphal works whose theories were even more absurd, and yet Liu Hsin and Cheng Hsüan made use of them in expounding the Classics so that they have been handed down for ages now. Scholars avidly study all these without ever examining their origins. They suppose only that, since the Han Confucianists were close to antiquity, their assertions must be based upon older traditions and not irresponsibly selected at random. Even among the Sung Confucianists with all their diligence and purity there are many who accepted these theories without alteration. . . . Mencius said: "It would be better to be without the *Book of History* than to believe it all. In the 'Completion of the War' section, I select only two or three passages which I believe" [VII B, 3]. If a sage like Mencius is as cautious as this when reading the Classics, how much more so in the case of commentaries on the Classics, and even more with the various philosophical works. Mencius also said: "In learning extensively and discussing minutely what is learned, the object is to be able to go back and set forth in brief what is essential" [IV B, 15]. One desires a wide range of information not for the sake of extensive learning itself, but only because one wishes by repeated comparisons and revisions of the data to arrive at a single truth. If one simply exhausts all learning without knowing what to select, then although he reads all the books in the world he is not so well off as a stupid and uneducated man who is yet free from serious error. . . .

The Han Confucianist Tung Chung-shu once wrote a work on disasters and portents. Emperor Wu submitted the book to the court officials for their opinion. Lü Pu-shu, one of Tung Chung-shu's disciples, having no idea that the book was written by his teacher, expressed the opinion that it was a work of gross stupidity. As a result Tung Chung-shu was put on trial for his life. To any book written by their own teachers men accord the fullest honor and belief; any book not by their teachers they disparage and revile, without ever inquiring into the merits of the works. . . . When I read the Classics I do not respect them blindly merely because they are Classics. Instead I try only to discover the intentions of the sages, and thereby come to appreciate the loftiness and beauty of their writings so that I cannot be misled by forgeries. . . .

The ancients had a saying: "Are you buying vegetables or looking for something worthwhile?" By this they meant that one should value quality and not quantity. . . . The words and actions of Confucius recorded in the *Analects* are quite numerous. Men of ancient times could have ruled the kingdom with only half of them, much less all. Therefore if scholars wish to put Confucius' examples into practice in hopes of becoming sages themselves, they have only to study this one book. But the scholars feel that this is not sufficient and so in addition they consult the *Sayings of the School of Confucius,* a collection of forgeries by someone in the Chin dynasty. Still dissatisfied because the selections in the *Sayings of the School* are not comprehensive enough, they have selected passages from heterodox and purely fictional works to make up the *Collected Sayings of Confucius* and the *Lesser Analects* to supplement their studies. Without asking whether these stories are true or false they make quantity their only criterion of worth. Alas, is this not seeking something worthwhile in the same way one would buy vegetables? . . .

Neither in the past nor the present has there ever been any lack of people who read books. . . . Among them have been scholars of keen intellect whose intentions were of the loftiest. And yet they were led astray by the fashions of the times. . . . As scholars who valued truth none can compare with the Sung Confucianists. Yet most of them concerned themselves with questions of the nature and principle of things and with moral philosophy. If one looks among them for men who devoted themselves to historical research he will find no more than two or three out of ten. By Ming times scholarship had grown increasingly heterodox and it became so that if one hoped to write anything important he had to be conversant with Ch'an doctrines and interlard his library shelves with Buddhist books. . . . In the past centuries there have been plenty of scholars who devoted their minds to the study of antiquity. Whenever I read works such as Chao Ming-ch'eng's *Record of Inscriptions on Metal and Stone* (with the colophon by Hung Mai) or Huang Po-ssu's *Further Studies of the Tung-kuan,* I never fail to remark with a sigh that the breadth of learning and diligence of research of these former scholars surpass mine a hundred times. By the detail on a plate or a vase, some minute point about a goblet or a ladle, they declare, "This is Chou," "This is Ch'in," "This is Han." The preface to the *Orchid Pavilion Collection* [on the ritual of the lustral sacrifices], written by Wang Hsi-chih, surely has no connection with the practical dos and don'ts of human affairs, and yet scholars ask, "Which is the genuine text?" "Which is the forged text?" so thorough are they in their research and so discriminating in their judgments. Only when it comes to affairs of the rulers and sages of antiquity, which are directly concerned with morals and the human heart, will people listen to anything others say without discriminating between truth and falsehood. Why should this be?

In order to repair some of the omissions of former scholars and supplement certain of their defects, I have written this book, the *Record of Beliefs Investigated* (*K'ao hsin lu*), which I hope will not be found entirely useless.

HUNG LIANG-CHI

China's Population Problem

Hung Liang-chi (1746–1809) was a rather typical scholar-official of the Ch'ing dynasty. He advanced slowly through the civil service system (winning the final degree only at the age of forty-four), was assigned to minor government

posts and projects, and devoted himself to the kind of studies which many of
those identified with the school of Han Learning pursued: geography, local
history, and the Classics. His one distinguishing feature was his candor, which
led to a brief exile in Chinese Turkestan for scolding the emperor in a
memorial. To this same forthrightness, perhaps, is due his frank reconsidera-
tion of a fundamental assumption in Chinese thinking: that a growing population is an index of good government and socially desirable. Hung expressed
his ideas on this subject in a few pages of miscellaneous essays, entitled "Opinions," written in 1793, five years before Malthus' *Essay on the Principle of
Population*. Though Hung's essential insight is the same as Malthus', the
Ch'ing scholar did not think of himself as developing a new science according
to rigorous methods, nor did anyone appear to explore his ideas further.

By Western standards China had been heavily populated since before the
time of Christ—about sixty million, with considerable fluctuation in periods
of extreme distress or prosperity. During the century or more before Hung
wrote, however, the population began to rise rapidly toward its recent several-
hundred-million level. No doubt simple empirical observation and reflection
sufficed to convince this acute and inquiring scholar that China was faced
with a problem of new and frightening proportions.

[From *Hung Pei-chiang shih wen chi,* 1:8a–9b]

There has never been a people which did not delight in peaceful rule,
nor a people who did not wish peaceful rule to endure for a long time.
Peaceful rule having lasted now for more than one hundred years, it
may be considered of long duration. But if we consider the population,
we can see that it has increased five times over what it was thirty years
ago, ten times over what it was sixty years ago, and at least twenty times
over what it was one hundred and some tens of years ago. Or consider
it in terms of a single family: In great-grandfather's time, he had a ten-
room house and a field of one *ch'ing*.[24] There was himself, and after he
took a wife, two persons, With two people occupying a ten-room house
and a plot of one *ch'ing,* they had ample space and something to spare.
Estimating that each man has three children, in the second generation
there would be four people including father and sons, and with each
taking a wife there would be eight. Since they could not do without some
help in the household, there would be no less than ten. With ten people
occupying a ten-room house and feeding themselves from a one-*ch'ing*
plot, we can see that they would barely have space enough to live in
and land enough to get food from. When the children beget grandchil-

---

[24] One *ch'ing* consisted of 100 Chinese acres (*mu*), or roughly fifteen acres.

dren and the latter take wives, then even allowing for the dying off of a few, there would still be at least twenty-odd people, living in a ten-room house and feeding themselves from a one-*ch'ing* plot. Just reckoning the number of mouths to feed and the number of legs taking up room, we can see that there would not be enough space for them all. Carrying the process one generation further and one more after that, then in comparison to great-grandfather's time, the number of mouths would have multiplied at least fifty or sixty times.[25] What in great-grandfather's time was one family would now have divided into at least ten families. Among them some families would be much reduced in size and others would have many able-bodied men, yet the two factors would balance each other off.

It may be argued: "In great-grandfather's time the waste-lands had not been fully developed and the home-sites were not fully occupied." Nevertheless they could not be increased more than double the number, or at most perhaps three or five times what they were. Yet the population has increased ten or twenty times, so that there is a shortage of houses and fields but a surplus of people. And how much worse is it with some families monopolizing land—with one man holding the houses of a hundred men, and one household holding the lands of a hundred households! Who can be surprised at the frequency with which people die from exposure and starvation, exhaustion and despair?

"Does Heaven and earth have no way to take care of this?" one may ask. Flood, drought, and pestilence—that is nature's way of regulating things. But the number of those who suffer misfortune from flood, drought, and pestilence is only a few. "Does the ruler and his government have no way to deal with it?" To have all land utilized and the people exert themselves to the utmost; to move people into newly opened fields in the border lands; to reduce taxes, where they have increased in weight and number, so as to bring them into line with former levels; to prohibit extravagance and stop the monopolizing of land; to open the government granaries in times of flood, drought, and pestilence and give the people food—these are about all that the ruler and his government can do to regulate and ameliorate things.

To sum up, when there has been prolonged peace, Heaven and earth

---

[25] Apparently Hung's rough calculations are meant to apply to the fourth generation rather than the fifth.

cannot but produce people, yet what Heaven and earth has to provide for these people is limited to a certain amount. When peace is prolonged, the ruler and his government cannot keep people from reproducing, yet the means by which they can hope to provide for the needs of the people are limited to these few just mentioned. Now if, out of one family that has ten sons and brothers, there are always one or two who prove incorrigible, how much less, out of the vast number in the empire, can we expect that everyone will restrain himself and comply with the law? If one man's dwelling is insufficient for ten men, how much less will it suffice for a hundred? If one man's food is insufficient to provide for ten, how much less will it provide for a hundred? This is why I consider peaceful rule a cause of anxiety for the people.

LI CHIH-TSAO
Preface to the True Meaning of God

As a final footnote to our survey of the Confucian tradition before modern times, we offer a document that is significant, not as representing any major trend or movement in the later development of Confucian thought, but because it marks the first genuine contact between Confucianism and Christianity as introduced by the Jesuits. It illustrates difficulties encountered in the bridging of cultural traditions, and thus, though untypical of an age still centered on tradition and little interested in the outside world, anticipates rather the characteristic problems of China confronted by the West in the nineteenth century.

Li Chih-tsao (d. 1630), together with Hsü Kuang-ch'i, was a leading Christian convert of Matteo Ricci, the pioneer Jesuit missionary who won a place for himself at court as an astronomer and mathematician. A scholar-official of the late Ming dynasty and holder of the highest regular literary degree (*chin-shih*), Li took an early interest in Western geography and astronomy, and assisted Ricci in disseminating this knowledge in China. His conversion to Christianity came later, after he had already written the following introductory note (in 1607) to Ricci's basic work on the fundamentals of Christianity for the Chinese.

Note especially the attempt to identify God with the Confucian concept of Heaven as presiding over the moral order, and to establish the worship of God as the culmination of the natural loyalties so much stressed in Confucian ethics. Li (and Ricci) emphasizes the convergence of the Confucian moral ideal with the Christian doctrines of divine justice and self-perfection. Christ and the Cross are not in the forefront of discussion; nor, on the other hand, are the speculations of the Neo-Confucianists, which Ricci found less compatible.

[From *T'ien-chu shih-i* in *T'ien-hsüeh ch'u-han*]

In ancient times when our Master [Confucius] spoke of self-cultivation, he said that one should try first to serve his parents diligently and through this come to know Heaven. Then came Mencius who rendered the doctrine of self-cultivation and service to Heaven complete. Now to know is to serve. Serving Heaven and serving parents are one and the same thing. But Heaven is the ultimate basis of all service. In explaining Heaven no book excels the *Book of Changes,* the source of our written [Chinese] characters. It says that the primal power [26] which governs Heaven is the king and father of all. Furthermore, it says the Lord (*Ti*) appears in thunder and lightning, and the master of Tzu-yang [Chu Hsi] identified *Ti* as the ruler of Heaven. Thus the idea of the Lord of Heaven [God] did not begin with Mr. Li.

The popular notion of Heaven is so unenlightened that it is not even worth discussing. The Buddhists, for their part, go too far in abandoning their homes and leaving their parents unattended; furthermore, they disregard Heaven and treat the Lord (*Ti*) with contempt, holding only their own selves as worthy of respect. Would-be Confucianists, on the other hand, are wont to discuss the mandate of Heaven, the principle of Heaven, the way of Heaven and the virtue of Heaven; but, while they are wholly immersed in these [Neo-Confucian] conceptions, the ordinary man neither knows Heaven nor holds it in awe—and it is no wonder!

The teaching of Mr. Li, which is based on serving and glorifying Heaven, explains Heaven quite clearly. Seeing that the world desecrates Heaven and venerates the Buddha, he has spoken out in repudiation of these errors. Basing his arguments on the teachings of the Master [Confucius], he has written a book in ten chapters called *The True Meaning of God* [lit. the Lord of Heaven], wherewith to instruct men in the good and ward off evil.

In this book he says that men know to serve their parents, but do not know that the Lord of Heaven is the parent of all. Men know that a nation must have a rightful ruler, but do not know that the Lord (*Ti*),

---

[26] *Ch'ien-yüan*—the primal male element identified with Heaven in the opening portion of the *Book of Changes.*

who alone "governs Heaven," is the rightful ruler of all. A man who does not serve his parents cannot be a [true] son; a man who does not know the rightful ruler cannot be a [true] minister; a man who does not serve the Lord of Heaven cannot be a [true] man. This book gives particular attention to the question of good and evil, and of retribution in the form of blessings and calamities. Now goodness that is not complete cannot be called perfectly good; [27] and even of the slight imperfections in human nature we speak of "rectifying evils." To do good is like ascending, that is, ascending into Heaven; to do evil is like falling, that is, falling into Hell. The general purpose of the book is to make men repent their transgressions and pursue righteousness, curb their passions and be benevolent toward all. It reminds men of their origin from above so as to make them fear lest they fall down into the place of punishment; it makes them consider the awful consequences and hasten to cleanse themselves of all sin. Thus they might not be guilty of any offense against the Great Heavenly Lord Above.

He [Ricci] crossed mountains and seas to bring precious gifts from a land that since ancient times has had no contact with China. At first he knew nothing of the teachings of [the ancient sages] Fu Hsi, King Wen, the Duke of Chou, or Confucius, and what he said was not based on the commentaries of [the Neo-Confucian philosophers] Chou Tun-yi, the Ch'eng brothers, Chang Tsai, and Chu Hsi. However, particularly in respect to his emphasis on the great importance of knowing and serving Heaven, what he says tallies with the Classics and commentaries. As regards Heaven and hell, obstinate men still refuse to believe in them. Yet Confucianists have always held that the rewarding of the good and the visiting of misfortune upon the wicked was a principle evident from the examination of Heaven and earth. To depart from good and pursue evil is like leaving the high road and plunging into steep mountains or heavy seas. Why is it that some people will not believe anything unless perhaps it concerns their most urgent duties to their rulers or parents, or unless it involves danger in the form of tigers, wolves, dragons, or crocodiles? They insist on having personal experience of everything themselves. Is this not being too stupid and unreasonable? They do not

---

[27] That is, though Mencius and the Neo-Confusianists spoke of human nature as good (in opposition to Hsün Tzu in ancient times and the Buddhists later) the goodness of human nature should not be thought of as wholly perfect.

appreciate the deep sincerity which moved him to come among us. To preach the truth, of course, one need not raise the question of reward and punishment, but if it serves to frighten fools and alarm the lazy, then it is right and proper that the good should be praised and rewarded, while the wicked are berated and punished. Thus his deep and sole concern has been to instruct the people and preach sound doctrine.

I have read some of his books and found that they differ from recent scholars on many points; but have an underlying resemblance to such ancient works as the *Su-wen*,[28] *Chou-pi*,[29] K'ao-kung,[30] and Ch'i-yüan.[31] So, it seems to me, what is spoken in truth does not contradict the truth. In self-examination and obedience to conscience he is most careful and strict with himself. He is what the world calls a "lofty teacher," and none among the Confucian scholars is more worthy of credence than he.

The mind and heart of man are the same in East and West, and reason is the same. What differs is only speech and writing. When this book appeared it was written in the same language as ours, refined and civilized, and thus could serve to open the mind for instruction. Since the purpose of the book was to promote peace and wellbeing, to espouse sound doctrine and improve morals, it is certainly no trifling piece, nothing to be taken lightly or to be put in the same class as the works of earlier philosophers.

My friend Mr. Wang Meng-pu has reprinted this book in Hangchow and I have presumed to write a few words for him. Not that I would dare to publicize a foreign book in order to spread unheard-of ideas, but I am mindful of the fact that we are all under the Majesty of Heaven and owe Him homage. Perhaps too there are things in it which we have been accustomed to hearing but have failed to act upon, and which may now prompt us to re-examine ourselves. Moreover, it may make some contribution to our study and practice of self-cultivation.

---

[28] An ancient text on medicine, attributed to the Yellow Emperor.
[29] Early work on astronomy, attributed to the Duke of Chou.
[30] Final portion of the *Rites of Chou*; here probably a reference to the work as a whole.
[31] A reference to Chuang Tzu, who was said to have been an official of Ch'i-yüan.

華
佗
割
股
療
疾

CHAPTER XXIII

POPULAR RELIGION AND SECRET SOCIETIES

For the most part this book has been concerned with the great movements of thought among the educated elite of China. In such movements, however, the great masses of common people were rarely caught up. What filtered through to them was a much simplified and sometimes distorted view of the teachings which had found favor among those with some education and prestige. Such notions were quickly adapted to the needs of those indigenous, and somewhat heterogeneous, religious cults which have subsisted among the people for centuries.

POPULAR RELIGION

From the earliest times in China we hear of shamans, magicians, interpreters of dreams, and diviners who presided over a variety of religious cults and commanded the respect and awe not only of the common people but even at times of members of the aristocracy. Though Chinese historians, themselves mostly followers of Confucianism, have seldom deigned to notice these popular cults and superstitions, popular literature reveals a widespread belief among the common people of China in a host of benevolent and baleful gods and spirits, and the prevalence of numerous practices such as the making of offerings to win their aid or the observance of taboos to escape their wrath. Government officials have occasionally moved to curb the grosser forms of superstition or have taken active steps toward suppression when some popular cult assumed a dangerously political tone. But generally the ruling class has been content to leave the common people to their own beliefs.

While educated Chinese have paid homage only to Heaven and their ancestors, and sometimes to Confucius, Buddha, Lao Tzu, and a few other historical personages, the common people have believed in the existence of thirty-three Buddhist Heavens, eighty-one Taoist Heavens, and eighteen Buddhist hells, and put faith in astrology, almanacs, dream interpretation, geomancy, witchcraft, phrenology, palmistry, the recalling of the soul, fortune telling in all forms, charms, magic, and many other varieties of superstition. They have regularly visited temples and shrines of all descriptions which the educated generally avoided. Often fatalistically, they have believed that spiritual beings controlled their fortunes and must therefore be continually consulted, coddled, and appeased. While the literati have regarded Confucianism, Buddhism, and Taoism essentially as systems of philosophy, the common people have embraced them as religions and regarded their founders as supernatural beings.

Thus there has been a strong tendency in China for the educated and uneducated to go their separate ways in matters of religion. Unquestionably this has deeply affected the character of popular religion in China, which has been deprived of intellectual guidance and been forced to subsist on a low cultural level. By the same token, scholar-officials have had less influence in religion than they might otherwise have exerted, for the state cult of Confucius, to which they adhered, had little to offer the people at large.

It is clear that neither the intelligentsia nor the common people could be called Confucianists, Buddhists, or Taoists exclusively, for they have accepted all three systems as "different roads to the same destination." Aside from 600,000-odd Buddhist monks and nuns, 3 or 4 million Buddhist lay devotees or "disciples at home," several hundred thousand Taoist priests and "vegetarian women," 20 million or so Muslims, about 3½ million Roman Catholics, and close to 600,000 Protestants, all of whom were identified with a single religion in 1949, the majority of China's millions have "worn a Confucian crown, a Taoist robe, and a pair of Buddhist sandals," as the saying goes.

The pattern of folk beliefs reflects this facile syncretism. Generally their ethical notions have had a Confucian tone, while their views of the supernatural have been derived mostly from religious Taoism, itself more closely related to the complex of primitive Chinese religion than to philosophical Taoism. In spite, however, of these common elements in popular religion, individual cults have varied greatly among themselves, emphasizing this or that aspect of a rather shapeless tradition according to the needs of the particular group or locality concerned.

Perhaps the clearest expression of these beliefs is to be found in two tracts that have for centuries been influential among the Chinese population as a whole, the *Treatise of the Most Exalted One on Moral Retribution,* which is part of the Taoist canon, and *The Silent Way of Recompense,* which, though largely Taoistic, reflects the teachings of all three religions. In these two short treatises, Confucian social and moral ideals, the Buddhist teaching of noninjury to any form of life, the Taoist worship of stars and various gods as well as its merit system, the doctrine of recompense, the worship of Heaven, the belief in Heaven and hell, and the hope for everlasting life are all expressed in short, epigrammatical sentences that for centuries have been familiar to the common people whether literate or illiterate.

The Treatise of the Most Exalted One on Moral Retribution

This popular treatise has sometimes been considered the work of Lao Tzu, though its actual date and authorship are unknown. Since it is listed in the bibliographical section of the *History of the Sung Dynasty,* it dates at least from the thirteenth century and is probably much earlier. Millions of copies of this work, and of *The Silent Way of Recompense* which follows here, have been distributed over the years by men and organizations of good-will. They are standard texts in most popular cults, and would probably be found in any rural village which possessed even a few books.

[From *T'ai-shang kan-ying p'ien, Tao-tsang,* pp. 834–39]

The Most Exalted One said: "Calamities and blessings do not come through any [fixed] gate; it is man himself that invites them."[1] The reward of good and evil is like the shadow accompanying the body. Accordingly there are in Heaven and earth spiritual beings who record a man's evil deeds and, depending upon the lightness or gravity of his transgressions, reduce his term of life by units of three days.[2] As units are taken away, his health becomes poor, and his spirit becomes wasted. He will often meet with sorrow and misery, and all other men will hate

---

[1] *Tso chuan,* Duke Hsiang 23.
[2] There are differing theories concerning the length of the units of time used here and in the following.

him. Punishments and calamities will pursue him; good luck and joy will shun him; evil stars will harm him. When the allotted units are exhausted, he will die.

Furthermore, there are the Three Ministers of the Northern Constellation residing above man's head. They register his crimes and sins and take away from his term of life periods of three hundred or three days. There are also the Three Worm-Spirits residing inside man's body. Whenever the fifty-seventh day [of the sixty-day cycle, the day characterized by severity and change] comes around, they ascend to the court of Heaven and report man's sins and transgressions. On the last day of the month, the Kitchen God does the same. When a man's transgressions are great, three hundred days are taken away from his term of life. When they are small, three days are taken away. Great and small transgressions number in the hundreds. Those who seek everlasting life on earth must first of all avoid them.

Go forward if your deed follows the Way (Tao) but withdraw if it violates it. Do not tread evil paths. Do nothing shameful even in the recesses of your own house. Accumulate virtue and amass merits. Have a compassionate heart toward all creatures. Be loyal to your sovereign, filial to your parents, friendly to your younger brothers, and brotherly to your older brothers. Rectify yourself and so transform others. Be compassionate to orphans and sympathetic to widows. Respect the old and cherish the young. Even insects, grass, and trees you must not hurt. You should grieve at the misfortune of others and rejoice in their good fortune. Assist those in need and save those in danger. Regard others' gain as your own gain and their loss as your own loss. Do not publicize their shortcomings nor boast of your own superiorities. Stop evil and promote good. Yield much but take little. Accept humiliation without complaint and favor with a sense of apprehension. Bestow kindness and seek no recompense. Give without regret.

He who is good is respected by all men. The way of Heaven helps him, happiness and wealth follow him, all evil things shun him, and spiritual beings protect him. Whatever he does will succeed. He may even hope to become a god or an immortal.

He who seeks to become an immortal of Heaven should perform 1,200 good deeds. He who seeks to become an immortal of earth should perform 300.

But if he acts contrary to righteousness or behaves improperly. . . .
[Here follows a long list of sins and crimes to be avoided, similar to
that given in Pao-p'u Tzu [3] concluding with:] if he is insatiably covetous
and greedy or takes oaths and swears to seek vindication; if he loves
liquor and becomes rude and disorderly or is angry and quarrelsome
with his relatives; if as a husband he is not faithful and good, or as a wife
she is not gentle and obedient; if the husband is not in harmony with his
wife; if the wife is not respectful to her husband; if he is always fond
of boasting and bragging; if she constantly acts out her jealousy and
envy; if he behaves immorally toward his wife and children; if she behaves improperly toward her parents-in-law; if he treats with slight and
disrespect the spirits of his ancestors or disobeys the commands of his
superiors; if he occupies himself with what is not beneficial to others
or cherishes a disloyal heart; if he curses himself and others or is partial
in his love and hatred; if he steps over the well or hearth [which should
be taken seriously because water and fire are indispensable to life] or
leaps over food [served on the floor] or a person [lying on a floor mat];
if he kills babies or brings about abortion or does many actions of secret
depravity; if he sings or dances on the last day of the month or year
[when the end should be sent off with sorrow] or bawls out or gets angry
on the first day of the year or the month [when the beginning should
be welcomed with joy]; if he weeps, spits, or urinates when facing north
[the direction of the emperor] or chants and laughs facing the hearth
[which should be treated solemnly because the family depends on it for
food]; and, moreover, if he lights incense with hearth fire [a sign of
disrespect] or uses dirty fuel to cook food; if he shows his naked body
when rising at night or executes punishment on the eight festivals of
the year; if he spits at a shooting star or points at a rainbow; if he suddenly points to the three luminaries or gazes long at the sun and the
moon; if in the spring months [when things are growing] he burns the
thickets in hunting or angrily reviles others when he faces north; if without reason he kills tortoises or snakes [which are honored along with
the Northern Constellation], if he commits these or similar crimes, the
Arbiter of Human Destiny will, according to their lightness or gravity,
take away from the culprit's term of life periods of three hundred or
three days. When these units are exhausted, he will die. If at death there

[3] See pp. 302–3.

remains guilt unpunished, the evil luck will be transferred to his posterity.

Moreover, if one wrongly seizes another's property, his wife, children, and other members of his family are to be held responsible, the expiation to be proportionate up to punishment by death. If they do not die, there will be disasters from water, fire, thieves, loss of property, illness, quarrels, and the like to compensate for the wrong seizure.

Further, he who kills men unjustly puts a weapon into the hands of others who will turn on him and kill him. He who seizes property unrighteously is like one who relieves hunger with spoiled food or quenches thirst with poisoned wine. He will be full for the time being, but death will inevitably follow. . . .

If one has already done an evil deed but later repents of his own accord and corrects his way, refrains from doing any evil and earnestly practices many good deeds, in time he will surely obtain good fortune. This is what is called changing calamities into blessings.

Therefore the man of good fortune speaks good, sees good, and does good. Every day he has three kinds of goodness. At the end of three years Heaven will send down blessings on him. The man of evil fortune speaks evil, sees evil, and does evil. Every day he has three kinds of evil. At the end of three years Heaven will send down calamity on him. Why not make an effort to do good?

The Silent Way of Recompense (Yin-chih wen)
(popularly attributed to the Taoist deity, Wen ch'ang)
[From Chou Meng-yen (ed.), Yin-chih wen kuang-i]

The Lord says: For seventeen generations I have been incarnated as a high official, and I have never oppressed the people or my subordinates. I have saved people from misfortune, helped people in need, shown pity to orphans, and forgiven people's mistakes. I have extensively practiced the Silent Way of Recompense and have penetrated Heaven above. If you can set your minds on things as I have set mine, Heaven will surely bestow blessings upon you. Therefore, I pronounce these instructions to mankind, saying. . . .

Whoever wants to expand his field of happiness, let him rely on his moral nature.

Do good work at all times, and practice in secret meritorious deeds of all kinds.

Benefit living creatures and human beings. Cultivate goodness and happiness.

Be honest and straight, and, on behalf of Heaven, promote moral reform. Be compassionate and merciful and, for the sake of the country, save the people.

Be loyal to your ruler and filial to your parents.

Be respectful toward elders and truthful to friends.

Obey the purity [of Taoism] and worship the Northern Constellation; or revere the scriptures and recite the holy name of the Buddha.

Repay the four kindnesses [done to us by Heaven, earth, the sovereign, and parents]. Extensively practice the three religions.

Help people in distress as you would help a fish in a dried-up rut. Free people from danger as you would free a sparrow from a fine net.

Be compassionate to orphans and kind to widows. Respect the aged and have pity on the poor.

Collect food and clothing and relieve those who are hungry and cold along the road. Give away coffins lest the dead of the poor be exposed.

If your own family is well provided for, extend a helping hand to your relatives. If the harvest fails, relieve and help your neighbors and friends.

Let measures and scales be accurate, and do not give less in selling or take more in buying. Treat your servants with generosity and consideration; why should you be severe in condemnation and harsh in your demands?

Write and publish holy scriptures and tracts. Build and repair temples and shrines.

Distribute medicine to alleviate the suffering of the sick. Offer tea and water to relieve the distress of the thirsty.

Buy captive creatures and set them free, or hold fast to vegetarianism and abstain from taking life.

Whenever taking a step, always watch for ants and insects. Prohibit the building of fires outside [lest insects be killed] and do not set mountain woods or forests ablaze.

Light lanterns at night to illuminate where people walk. Build river boats to ferry people across.

Do not go into the mountain to catch birds in nets, nor to the water to poison fish and shrimps.

Do not butcher the ox that plows the field. Do not throw away paper with writing on it.

Do not scheme for others' property. Do not envy others' skill or ability.

Do not violate people's wives or daughters. Do not stir up litigation among others.

Do not injure others' reputation or interest. Do not destroy people's marriages.

Do not, on account of personal enmity, create disharmony between brothers. Do not, because of a small profit, cause father and son to quarrel.

Do not misuse your power to disgrace the good and the law-abiding. Do not presume upon your wealth to oppress the poor and needy.

Be close to and friendly with the good; this will improve your moral character in body and mind. Keep at a distance from the wicked; this will prevent imminent danger.

Always conceal people's vices but proclaim their virtue. Do not say "yes" with your mouth and "no" in your heart.

Cut brambles and thorns that obstruct the road. Remove bricks and stones that lie in the path.

Put in good condition roads that have been rough for several hundred years. Build bridges over which thousands and tens of thousands of people may travel.

Leave behind you moral instructions to correct people's faults. Donate money to bring to completion the good deeds of others.

Follow the principle of Heaven in your work. Obey the dictates of the human heart in your words.

[Admire the ancient sages so much that you] see them while eating soup or looking at the wall. [Be so clear in conscience that] when you sleep alone, you are not ashamed before your bedding, and when you walk alone, you are not ashamed before your own shadow.

Refrain from doing any evil, but earnestly do all good deeds.

Then there will never be any influence or evil stars upon you, but you will always be protected by good and auspicious spirits.

Immediate rewards will come to your own person, and later rewards will reach your posterity.

A hundred blessings will come as if drawn by horses, and a thousand fortunes will gather about you like clouds.

Do not all these things come through the Silent Way of Recompense?

RELIGIOUS SECTS

For centuries there has been a multitude of religious sects in China. Some are specifically affiliated with the great religions of the past, such as the Ten Schools of Buddhism (now virtually reduced to four) and the Northern and Southern Schools of Taoism. Others are syncretic in character, drawing upon different religious traditions, ancient and modern. In them the drive toward fusion and reconciliation is often far stronger than the desire for clarity or purity of doctrine. This is partly because such sects or societies have drawn most of their support from the uneducated, who have been generally uninterested in or incapable of articulating a systematic body of belief, and who have had difficulty preserving definite traditions. For the same reason, and because they were wholly or in part secret cults, these sects have remained shrouded in mystery, ignored by scholars and historians. A recent study of one area revealed fourteen religious societies previously unknown to the outside world. It is evident that, in recent times at least, such movements have risen to popularity and then disappeared again with astonishing swiftness.

As an example of the newer societies there is the Society of the Way (*Tao yüan*), or Society of the Way and Its Virtue (*Tao-te she*), which originated in Tsinan, North China, about 1921. Its buildings consist of five halls, one each for worship, scripture reading, meditation, preaching, and charity. On its altar are the names of Confucius, Lao Tzu, and the Buddha, and symbols representing Christianity and Islam. Its teachings emphasize the community of Heaven and man in matters of the spirit, and the spirit of world brotherhood. For its members, it urges meditation, cultivation of the inner life, the belief in planchettes,[4] and the use of spirit photography. For others, it practices charity and other forms of social service, operates hospitals, and establishes banks with small deposits for poor people. Its Decalogue reads: 1) Do not dishonor par-

[4] Boards used to obtain mediumistic messages like the Ouija boards of the West.

ents; 2) Do not lack virtue; 3) Do not lack goodness; 4) Do not lack righteousness; 5) Do not lack mercy; 6) Do not conceal the goodness of others; 7) Do not be cruel; 8) Do not have secrets; 9) Do not have envy or spite; and 10) Do not blaspheme.

The Fellowship of Good (*T'ung-shan She* or Society for Common Good) was started around 1918 in Peking. It advocates the "internal meritorious deeds" of worship, meditation, and vegetarianism, and the "external meritorious deeds" of charity and maintaining schools. It follows all three religions but strongly opposes monasticism and the renunciation of the family. Its Ten Ideals are: a straight heart, a high type of service, unrestricted virtue, clear instruction, observance of law, diligence in moral culture, desire for progress, harmony, maintenance of high ideals, and the unification of the soul. It believes that illness can be cured by quiet sitting. Until very recently it had branches in all parts of China, including Manchuria, but now it hardly exists.

Of the old societies, the most important is the White Lotus, chiefly because of its many branches both past and present. According to one account, it was founded in 1133 as a Buddhist sect emphasizing repentance, suppression of desires, vegetarianism, and abstinence from alcohol and the taking of life. It attracted many people, especially peasants, and soon spread from North to East and Central China. In addition to the use of prayers, incense, charms, and incantations, members also practiced boxing and fighting with spears, for the avowed purpose of resisting the invading Jurchen barbarians and supporting the Sung dynasty. In the last seven hundred years the society has rebelled against the Mongols and Manchus a number of times, especially in 1794, 1801, and 1813. In the early decades of this century, the society was strong in North China but rather weak in the lower Yangtze area. It was strongly organized on a local basis, with a leader who exercised absolute power. It is difficult to tell whether any of this has survived vigorous attempts at suppression by the Communists.

The White Lotus has branched into many sects such as the Red Scarf Society, the Eight Trigram Society, the Yellow Society, the notorious Boxers who rose to expel foreigners in 1900, and the Society of the White Robe. One of the more prominent ones in the last several decades has been the Tsai-li (Principle Abiding) Society. It obeyed the Law of Buddhism, observed the practice of Taoism, and followed the social rites of Confucianism. Its members abstained from smoking and drinking, did not burn incense or worship idols, but used many incantations and charms. The sect encouraged its members to be diligent and thrifty, and many poor and lazy people became hard-working and well-to-do under its influence. For this reason it had a strong appeal in rural areas, especially in North and West China. Members were mostly from the artisan and laboring classes, followed by farmers and merchants, and a few intellectuals.

Another important branch of the White Lotus in recent times has been the Way of Pervading Unity (*I-kuan Tao*). While other societies were declining, the Way gained strength and extended its activities during the Second World War. Like the Tsai-li, its origin is traced to the White Lotus but it is more likely that it evolved from secret activities started by some elements of the Boxers after the Revolution of 1911. The sect believes that the One is the root of all things and as a principle penetrates and pervades all existence. The universe evolves from the realm of *li* (principle or law), which is infinite and prior to the realm of *ch'i* (material-force), through its active and passive principles (yin-yang), and then to the phenomenal world. We are now in the midst of the third catastrophe in the history of human existence, and it is through the mercy of the Mother of No-birth, the Creator of all, and our own moral and spiritual efforts that the world will be saved. All systems— Confucianism, Taoism, Buddhism, Christianity, and Islam—with all their sages, gods, and Buddhas, are vehicles for this salvation. In the end all people will be saved.

Followers of the sect have emphasized internal and external meritorious deeds equally. The former includes self-cultivation, purification of the heart, reduction of desires, and control of the mind. The latter includes the use of charms and planchettes, the practice of the "three secrets" of finger signs and magic phrases, abstinence from meat, tobacco, and alcohol, incantation, worship of all religions, offering and sacrifice, study and recitation of Buddhist and Taoist canons, preaching and charity. Like most secret religious societies, it has attracted chiefly the ignorant and illiterate. There is no way of reckoning the number of its followers or its temples. During the Second World War it was very active in almost the entire territory occupied by Japan, especially in North China. Since the war, however, it has been suppressed and its activities have died down. How it has fared under the Communist regime is hard to ascertain.

The Way of Pervading Unity is specially significant for us because it is both old and new, old because of its origin in the White Lotus and new because of its recent appearance. While the literature of other societies either is so cryptic as to be untranslatable or is unavailable to us, that of the Way is accessible and is clearly expressive of the major beliefs and practices of these various religious societies. For these reasons we have translated below excerpts from several of its tracts. Note the various interpretations of Tao, the doctrine of three stages in each historical cycle, the Neo-Confucian philosophy of human nature and natural principle, the Buddhist gospel of universal salvation and its injunction against taking life, the Taoist technique of inner and outer meritorious deeds including alchemy and quiet sitting, the theory of retribution, and the harmony of the three religions.

Questions and Answers on the Way of Pervading Unity
[From *I-kuan tao-li wen-ta*, pp. 1–20]

Friend asked: It has not been very long since I joined the Way. I am ignorant about everything. Please enlighten me as to what the Way (Tao) really is.

I answered: Our Way is called the Way of Pervading Unity. If you ask about its whats and whys, their answers are many. Let me select and comment on the most essential as an introduction for you.

The Way is the general name for all goodness; all charitable work may be called the Way. It is also the ultimate principle; whatever conforms to the principle conforms to the Way. It is also the correct principle, such as parental love for the father, filial piety for the son, righteousness for the husband, obedience for the wife; loyalty, obedience, love, and virtue are all the Way. It is also the natural principle. There is the principle of Heaven in Heaven, the principle of earth in earth, the principle of human nature in human beings. We also say that the nature is the embodiment of the Way. What is inborn in us is born of heavenly nature. The nature of man is originally derived from the principle of Heaven. If we cultivate our nature with the principle of Heaven as our guide, we will fulfill the Way. . . .

I have heard my teacher say that Yao and Shun were born at high noon. Our epoch is at the transition from the high noon [of history] to the next period [1:00 to 3:00 P.M. of history]. When noon reaches its height, sunshine is full and complete. Hence the possibility of universal salvation in three stages and the reclarification of the Way of Pervading Unity. By the three stages is meant that Fu Hsi drew the eight trigrams and inaugurated culture and civilization, thus constituting the first stage. Confucius edited the Classics, formulated rites, developed moral principles, and established social standards, thus constituting the second stage. At present there are many religious societies both at home and abroad, each rectifying man's nature and destiny and probing into the nature and the principle, thus constituting the third stage. Since you, Sir, live in this generation, it means that circumstance brings you and the Buddha together. You should cultivate the Way with special effort, for happy circumstances should not be passed over. The nature is derived from the principle of Heaven; it is shared by all men. Who is he who cannot achieve a good and virtuous life? When one practices the Way, even if he cannot become an Immortal or a sage, he still can avoid bringing shame to his ancestors or causing trouble to his descendants, and become a perfect man. There are now many religious tracts available. If you want the best, search extensively.

Friend said: I have heard you say that Confucianism is a religion. How about Buddhism and Taoism? Are they orthodox or heterodox systems? Kindly tell me.

I said: The Way is in essence the nonultimate and the one principle. The one is divided into three, as a man's person is divided into essence, vital force, and spirit. At first the one is divided into three, and now the three are united as one, which is the sign of perfect culmination.

However, among the three religions, the Law of the Buddha is the highest. For this reason, at all times past and present, the great leaders of religion have been Buddhists. The *Hsien-chieh Scripture* says: "When the universe was formed out of chaos, it was decided that there would be ten Buddhas ruling the universe and there have already been seven." This can be proved by the fact that there are seven Buddhas in the Ta-hsiang Temple in the Fen-yang district of Shansi and also the Temple of Seven Buddhas in Ying Village of Ma-chuang in the Hsiao-i district of Shansi. In early times there was no written language and therefore their names are difficult to find out. The remaining three Buddhas are the Dīpankara Buddha, Tathāgata Buddha and Maitreya Buddha. Dīpankara ruled for 1,500 years and Tathāgata Buddha ruled for 3,000 years. The accounts of Maitreya need not be told here. He has already assumed the rule in his hands.

The Tathāgata Buddha was born on the eighth day, the fourth month, in the year 1027 B.C. His father's name was Ch'a-li [Shuddhodana], meaning pure rice, and his mother's name was Lady Maya. He left home at the age of nineteen. Having received instructions from Dīpankara, he preached for forty-nine years and wrote scriptures and left them for the salvation of the world throughout 10,000 years. His way is to point directly to one's nature and to become a Buddha, to explore directly to the source, to wipe out [the phenomenal characteristics of] sound and color, and to remove the distinction of the self and the other. Later generations call him the Founder of Buddhism. The *Record of the School Sayings of Confucius*[5] says: "There is a sage in the west whose name is Buddha. Without uttering a word, he speaks the truth. He transcends both chaos and order, for his is the way of nonaction (*wu-wei*)." He also left these words: "My way runs in cycles of 3,000 years—1,000 years of Correct Law, 1,000 years of Semblance of Law, and 1,000 years of Decay of Law. After the period of Decay of Law, the period of Correct Law will begin again." This is the same as the principle of jointly observing the three religions today.

Lao Tzu's surname was Li, his name was Erh, his style-name was Po-yang, and his posthumous name Tan. He was born in the Ch'en district in the state of Ch'u in 604 B.C. He was once King Yu's custodian of documents. His father's surname was Han, private name K'un, and style-name Yüan-pi. His mother's name was Ching-fu. She was pregnant for eighty years before he was born under a plum (*li*) tree. For this reason he changed his surname from Han to Li. After Confucius interviewed him about rites, because of the stupidity of King Yu, he mounted a buffalo and rode through Han-ku Pass to the west where he converted the barbarian King Yin-hsi. His way is to nourish the mind through simplicity. Its method is to draw water to supplement fire [to balance the passive and active forces of yin-yang]. When fire and water are harmonized, then one proceeds to refine gold fluid and reconvert cinnabar [after it has been turned into mercury which, in Taoist alchemy, represents the acme of the way to immortality]. He left the *Tao-te ching*, the *Classic of Purity*, the *Treatise of the Most Exalted One on Moral Retribution*.

[5] The *K'ung Tz'u chia-yü*, a spurious work from the Han dynasty.

and the *Silent Way of Recompense,* which now circulate throughout the world. As to Confucius, his work covers both government and religion and need not be recounted here.

The fundamental ways of the three religions are all directed at the nature and the principle. Their ethical standards and moral principles all flow out of the heavenly nature. When the substance of the nature is understood, moral principles will be correctly comprehended even without study. As is often said, when the substance is understood, the function is comprehended, and when the root is firm, the branches flourish. This is only natural.

Unfortunately, Buddhism has lost its wonderful truth and Taoism has lost its practice of alchemy and magic formulas. Their followers merely recite scriptures and chant vows and beg food from people. Confucianism has lost its central principles of the nature and the principle. Even world-renowned writers do nothing more than search for paragraphs and pick up sentences. If you ask them about the practice of "knowing where to rest," "unperturbedness," "tranquillity," and self-introspection, or the method for the investigation of things, or complete development and nourishment and fulfillment of human nature, few can answer. The result is that the three religions have almost completely disappeared.

In our Way all three religions are observed. We practice the social rites and moral principles of Confucianism, utilize the methods of the Founder of Taoism, and follow the rules of Grand Old Buddha. When these are applied on a small scale, one's years will be increased and life prolonged. When applied on a large scale, one will be enlightened in the Way and become a pure being [a saint]. This is the work of reclarifying the principles of Pervading Unity.

Friend said: Since there is Pervading Unity in the three religions, do all of them require vegetarianism?

I said: Abstinence. There are the Five Precepts in Buddhism, and not to kill is the first. Man exists for only a few scores of years and should not become an enemy of animals. The main thing is of course universal salvation. There are, I am afraid, cases where a person is not free [to abstain] and because of his vegetarianism his cultivation of the Way is sometimes hampered. Therefore while the discipline is there, its application must be flexible. Nevertheless, people who are cultivating the Way must hold compassion as fundamental. An insect or a bird shares with us the same heavenly nature. It is only because they differed in merits and demerits in their previous lives that they have changed in this life. If we kill and eat them, we are obstructing the principle of Heaven. [The Immortal] Lü Tsu wrote a poem which says:

> My flesh is the same as the flesh of all creatures;
> Its shape is different but its principle is not.
> Do not let Yama [Ruler of Hell] judge you.
> Ask yourself what you should do.

If you, Sir, are willing to give up some enjoyment of the mouth, please burn incense in front of the altar and take vows [not to eat meat]. I shall report to the Hall of Lao Tzu where your meritorious deed will be recorded. . . .

Friend said: If one wants to go ahead, what should be the first step?

I said: Build up a firm faith. Faith is the mother of the Way and the source of meritorious deeds. If a man has no faith, even divination will not be effective for him. It must be realized that all people are sufficiently endowed with the nature of Heaven, and Taoist immortals and Buddhas are identical in reality. It is due to various degrees of ignorance or enlightenment that we have become different. The round head and square feet of man resemble Heaven and earth. His inhaling and exhaling are symbolic of yin and yang. His two eyes are comparable to the sun and the moon, and his five internal organs correspond to the five elements. His pleasure, anger, sorrow, and joy are no different from wind, clouds, thunder, and rain, and his [four moral virtues of] humanity, righteousness, decorum, and wisdom are basically the [four aspects of] origination, development, adaptation, and correctness [of the universe]. Babies at birth are of the same reality as Heaven and earth, and the sages Yao, Shun, Confucius, and Mencius are no different from the common man. Those who understand the principle will become immortals and Buddhas, while those who violate it will become earthly spirits and wandering souls. Follow it and cultivate it—this is the Way. It is the unalterable principle. Do you believe in it?

Friend said: According to your theory, all scriptures are useless.

I said: Scriptures are a means. The great Way must be cultivated and intuited by oneself. A Buddha can show us the direction but cannot do the cultivation for us. The recitation of scriptures is merely a means whereby we may intuit the Law, that is all. If reciting the scriptures can always lead to an understanding of the Way, then what scriptures did the Buddhas of old have to recite? We should not avoid reading, but should not rely on it. Therefore it is said that reading scriptures is not so good as preaching them, and preaching them is not so good as acting according to them.

Friend said: The Deity we worship is called on the one hand the Twice Shining Lord on High, and, on the other, the Infinite Mother. Please tell me whether the Deity is male or female.

I said: By Twice Shining is meant that the Deity has shone and yet shines again. By being infinite is meant having no limit. It is called Mother because it is its nature to create. Heaven, earth, and man above and below, immortals and Buddhas, heavenly and earthly spiritual beings, and all things with intelligence are creatures of the one Mother. Hence modern scholars speak of the 400,000,000 people as uterine brothers, and in Kuan-ti's altar instructions there is the saying: "Your nature is originally my nature; you and I are essentially no different."

Friend said: In past years when there was no kerosene in this country, our sesame oil and hemp-seed oil were very cheap. When opium poppy was grown everywhere, the price of rice was very low. At that time the cash was the unit and there was much money in circulation. Now that we light our lamps with kerosene, the opium poppy has disappeared, and a copper is worth ten cash, things should be much cheaper. How is it that money is scarce and droughts and floods are unduly severe?

I said: Gold and silver are the spirit of the universe. A person's spirit declines when he gets old. It is the same with the universe, and for the same reason the times are bad. Droughts and floods are determined by the state of the people's mind. Among the five elements, water is produced by Heaven. When rain fails to fall or when it falls at the wrong time, it is all because the people's minds are perverted and no longer in harmony with the mind of Heaven. There is only one way to restore normal conditions: it is goodness or moral character. Heaven can send down calamity, but can also bestow blessings. Just as water can overcome fire, so goodness can deliver us from suffering. Goodness in the person can protect the person. Goodness in the family can protect the family. If everyone is good, the world will be peaceful before sundown.

Chu Hsi said: "Our mind is one with the mind of the universe." If man's mind is good, the mind of the universe is also good. The universe and all things form one body with me. As to things being expensive when they should be cheap—well, it does not matter. People who cultivate the Way only think of good and evil, and therefore what they enjoy is quite free from the price of things. All of us must be good in order to restore normal conditions.

Methods of Religious Cultivation
[From Kuo Ting-tung et al., *I-kuan tao i-wen chieh-ta*, pp. 8a–9b]

How should male and female friends of the Way practice meritorious deeds?

In practicing such deeds, male and female friends should divide the burden but work together, the total membership being mobilized. Some may take up the responsibility of Heaven, earth, and man and write letters to propagate the principles of moral reform. Others may lecture on the teachings of the scriptures and propagate the gospel. Those with money may contribute according to their capacity to print holy scriptures and books of instruction. Those with energy may go in all directions to persuade and lead their good relatives and friends to join the Way as soon as possible. Some may donate money to build Buddha Halls to help a great number of people to practice meritorious deeds. Others may uphold with all their heart the Law of the Buddha so that the work of the Way will expand and grow daily. Some may be determined to practice earnestly and to abide reverently by the orders of the teacher. Some may cultivate the Way all their lives, thus setting an example for others. All these methods should be followed by male and female friends of the Way in their own ways to attain the fruits of goodness. . . .

What are internal meritorious deeds?

Cultivating the person, perfecting the self, seeing to it that all one's conduct conforms to the principle, making one's mind pure and desires few, and "seeking the lost mind"—all these are internal meritorious deeds.

What is the way to seek the lost mind? Can you tell me the method?

The method of seeking the lost mind is simply the way of controlling the mind. Of course, the most important way to control the mind is quiet sitting. For wisdom is born of the spirit, and the spirit is born of peace and quiet. To refine one's essence in order to transform it into energy, to refine energy in order to transform it into spirit, and to refine spirit so that it may return to vacuity, there is no other way than quiet sitting.

To practice quiet sitting, sit cross-legged and erect, both in the morning and in the evening, with eyes closed in order to nourish the spirit, and with the tongue touching the roof of the mouth. Let the mind be calm and breathing be quiet. Get rid of all impure thoughts and erroneous ideas. Think neither of good nor of evil. Neither move nor shake, breathe neither in nor out. When sitting reaches the point that not a single thought arises and all anxieties have ceased, then there will be profound peace and purity and nothing inside or outside [the mind]. . . .

What are external meritorious deeds?

Exhort others to do good and bring them to perfection. Enable all living creatures to be saved and everyone to turn toward the good. Do the work of assisting people and benefiting living beings. Harbor the thought of helping others in misfortune and saving the world. First rectify oneself and then rectify others. Deeds like these are external meritorious deeds.

What is the proper way of practicing an external meritorious deed?

In practicing an external meritorious deed, one must not have any intention of seeking for fame, and, what is more, one must not say any unkind word or show any angry expression. If one does a deed for the sake of fame, there is no merit in it to speak of. If one tries to exhort others with a bad temper or an angry expression, one is no longer a practitioner of the Way. In short, doing a meritorious deed, one must obey the holy teachings of the three religions and make the best real effort. Copying religious tracts, building Buddha Halls, propagating the doctrines of the Way so as to enlighten people—all these are meritorious deeds of the first order. We must realize that to transform a person so that he achieves the Way [and becomes a saint] is to make it possible for his ancestors of nine generations to ascend to Heaven, and to copy a sentence from a religious tract is better than to utter 10,000 words. Even the sages of the three religions did not go beyond this. As to the worldly work of rendering assistance in emergencies, helping people in their misfortunes, relieving others and removing danger, donate money to do it yourself if the need is small, and raise money and work with others if the need is great. Other meritorious deeds that require no money should be practiced whenever and wherever the occasion arises.

SECRET SOCIETIES

Secret societies have existed in China since ancient times but their activity and numbers increased markedly from the time when the Sung dynasty was invaded by barbarians from the North. Because of the secrecy which has surrounded them and because scholars have regarded them as unworthy of attention, little reliable information about these societies has come down to us. However, generally speaking, they are represented by two broad movements, the White Lotus and the Hung Society. The White Lotus Society has predominated in the North. It has been chiefly religious (though it has started and participated in many revolutions) and has a great number of branches loosely organized and related to one another. The Hung Society, on the other hand, has predominated in South, West, and Central China. It has been primarily political, though with a religious coloring, and has branched into several well-organized groups. The White Lotus and some of its offshoots have already been mentioned. In this section, we shall confine ourselves to the Hung Society.

The Hung Society (*Hung men*) may possibly have its origin in the White Lotus, though more probably it was organized in the middle of the seventeenth century by supporters of the Ming dynasty with the avowed purpose of overthrowing the Manchus and restoring Chinese rule. According to the society's own account, it was founded by a scholar named Yin Hung-sheng in 1631, whom its members consider to be their First Founding Father. In the declining years of the Ming, Yin rallied a number of prominent scholars about him in an effort to save the dynasty. His efforts were unsuccessful, however, and he died in 1645. A decade or so later, a group of monks in the Shao-lin Temple in Fukien secretly organized for revolution. In 1672 when the Manchu emperor called for volunteers to fight an invasion by a western tribe, they answered the call and expelled the invaders. But when it was finally discovered that they were actually rebels in search of an opportunity for an uprising, their temple was surrounded and burned. Five monks (later honored as the

"Five Early Founding Fathers") escaped, hid under a bridge, and were saved by five brave men (the "Five Middle Founding Fathers"). These were later joined by five other monks (the "Five Later Founding Fathers"). After much fighting against the Manchus, they met Abbot Ten-thousand-Cloud Dragon (Wan Yün-lung) and Ch'en Chin-nan (the "Great Ancestor"), who started an independent uprising. Ch'en and the Five Early Founding Fathers plotted their revolution in the Red Flower Pavilion in present Hupei province. In the second period (1:00–3:00 A.M.) of the twelve-period day cycle on the twenty-fifth day of the seventh month in 1674 they and their followers formally took a vow to be fraternal brothers, overthrow the Manchus, and restore the Ming. The conspiracy spread to South China. By 1698 Ch'en had died but his successors continued the fight. Members of the society worshiped Heaven as father and earth as mother and for this reason the society is also called the Heaven and Earth Society (*T'ien-ti hui*).

It is doubtful if any of this account is reliable. Even the origin and meaning of the name Hung is in dispute, but the majority opinion holds that it refers to the reign Hung-wu of the founder of the Ming dynasty. At any rate the story of the burning of the Shao-lin Temple has become a colorful and exciting part of Chinese folklore dramatized in endless variations on the popular stage and in story telling, and the Bridge and the Pavilion have been adopted as sacred symbols in the society's ceremonies. The movement, starting in Fukien, spread later to Formosa, to East, South, and West China, and finally to the far Southwest and Northwest. The society participated in many revolts, notably those of 1774 and the Taiping Rebellion.

Like most secret societies, the *Hung men* has developed into many branches, such as the Double Sword Society, Dagger Society, and the Clear Water Society. Their history is vague and their relationships are uncertain. Two branches of the society, however, stand out prominently and are known at least in broad outline. One of these is the Triple Harmony Society (*San-ho hui,* referring perhaps to the harmony of Heaven, earth, and man; or to the three "rivers," also pronounced *ho,* where the rebels met). It is also called the Triad Society (*San-tien hui,* referring perhaps to the three dots on the left side of the Chinese character *hung*). The other branch is the Elders Society (*Ko-lao hui*). The Triad Society was strong in South China, especially among farmers and working people, as well as among the overseas Chinese. In the United States it has branched into or affiliated with the Chih Kung Tong ("Society to Bring About Justice"), which is now no longer secret but a purely charitable organization. In recent years the Triad Society took an active part in the Revolution of 1911 led by Sun Yat-sen, in the revolution against Yuan Shih-k'ai's attempt to become emperor in 1915, and in resisting the Japanese invasion in the Second World War.

The Elders Society, variously named in different parts of China, originated in Fukien somewhat later than the Triad Society. One theory is that in 1853 when the Triad Society was resisting the Manchus in South China, the Elders Society arose in Central and North China in sympathetic response. In any case it spread over most of the country but became particularly strong in Central, North, and West China. It is said to have been so powerful in the nineteenth century that even leading government generals such as Tseng Kuo-fan (1811–1872) and Tso Tsung-t'ang (1812–1885) were obliged to join it. In recent times it was the most extensive, well organized, and influential of China's secret societies.

The ideals of the Hung Society may be summed up as patriotism, chivalry, fraternity, and traditional morality. The spirit of patriotism of the society needs no comment, except to add that the society worships Emperor T'ai Tsung (r. 627–644), founder of the T'ang dynasty. Like other secret societies, it employs pass words, hand signs, signs by arrangement of tea cups, and so on, about which members are pledged to keep absolute secrecy or suffer death. Unlike other secret societies, however, the combined spirit of chivalry, fraternity, and patriotism makes the Hung Society unique. It regards as its model the famous fraternity of the Peach Garden, where Kuan Kung (d. 219, erroneously called in the West the God of War) and two other heroes vowed to be brothers and to defend the Han dynasty, and also the well-known 108 rebels vividly described in the novel *Shui-hu chuan* (*The Water Margin* or *All Men Are Brothers*).

Certain numbers are regarded by the society as sacred. One of these is 108, which may refer to the rebels just mentioned or may be the sum of 36 and 72, which in their turn probably refer to the 36 gods in Heaven and the 72 gods on earth. Hence these numbers are used for the punishments specified below. The documents that have been selected for translation represent those most expressive of the ideals and attitudes of the society.

They are oaths taken by candidates and "commands" given by the Worshipful Master at various stages in the initiation ceremony. Besides oaths and commands, there are many poems, questions and answers, and other sayings used in meetings, most of them so cryptic as to be unintelligible to an outsider. The documents selected below are those common to the Hung Society as a whole.

The Thirty-Six Oaths of the Hung Society
[From Chu Lin, *Hung men chih,* pp. 26–30]

We, sharing fortune and misfortune, are dedicated to the restoration of the Ming dynasty which belonged to Heaven and earth and all existence, to the destruction of the barbarian bandits [the Manchus], and to waiting for the true mandate of Heaven. We reverently worship the Lord of Heaven and the Sovereign of Earth, the spirits of mountains and rivers and grain, the spirits of the Six Powers, the spirits of the Five Dragons in the five directions, and the infinite number of spiritual beings. Since the establishment [of our Society] hundreds of activities have been promoted. What the ancients knew to be worthy of teaching to later generations, we pass on.

Brethren! I shall now lead you again into the midst of loyalty to country and devotion to friends. We swear before Heaven on High in the spirit of sharing life and death. Tonight each of us recommends several new followers to the Heaven and Earth Society, follows the example of the fraternal pledge in the Peach Garden, and vows to be a Brother to the others, takes Hung as his family name, Gold-and-Orchid as his private name,[6] and forms one family. After entering the Hung Society, you must be of one body and one mind, each helping the other, and never allowing any distinction between one another to be made.

Tonight we worship Heaven as our father, earth as our mother, the sun as our brother, and the moon as our sister. We also worship before our First Founding Father, the Five Founding Fathers, Ten-thousand-Cloud Dragon, and others, and all spiritual beings of the Hung family. As we kneel in worship before the altar tonight, our minds and spirits are suddenly pure and clear. Each shall cut his finger, suck his blood, and take the oath of living and dying together.

[6] Gold standing for the solidity of friendship and orchid for its fragrance.

We consider the second period [1:00–3.00 A.M.] of the twenty-fifth day of the seventh month, 1674, as the time of our birth. Spread over the two capitals [Nanking and Peking] and the thirteenth provinces [in South, East, West, and Central China], we form one body and one mind, all seeking happiness for one another and each assuming his burden without any carelessness or failure. As soon as the kings and dukes of the present regime are no longer truly kings and dukes, and generals and prime ministers no longer truly generals and prime ministers, and the people begin to show unrest, that is the sign given us by Heaven that the Ming dynasty is to be restored and the barbarian bandits destroyed. We should be determined to carry out the command of Ch'en Chin-nan, which he gave many years ago, construct pavilions and build bridges [as stations in this lodge], establish the City of Universal Peace, re-enact the drama, travel over the five lakes and the four seas to search for the heroic and the brave, hold firmly in hand the authority of the City of Willows, burn incense and take the oath that will last as long as our land. Let each new member attend to his task in his respective sphere, and carry out the principle [of revolution] according to the will of Heaven. "Those who obey Heaven shall live and those who disobey shall perish."[7] All those who can restore the Ming dynasty, avenge our grievance, wipe out our disgrace, and establish the order of Universal Peace will themselves receive the titles of king and duke and their posterity will be prosperous throughout all generations. Whoever violates this principle shall be destroyed beneath swords and halberds and have his heirs cut off. Only people with a heart of loyalty and spirit of devotion may receive eternal blessing. We receive our lives from Heaven and earth and exist under the light of the sun and the moon. After we join in fraternity, we now suck our blood, make our pledges, and take our vows. We look upward and invite the spiritual beings to descend and bear witness. Each shall show his sincerity and take the Thirty-six Oaths:

1. From the time I enter the Hung Society, your parents are my parents, your brothers and sisters are my brothers and sisters, your wife is my sister-in-law, and your sons and nephews are my sons and nephews. If I violate this oath, may I be destroyed by the five thunders.

2. Whenever [a fellow Brother's] parents or brother pass away and there is no fund for burial, every Brother must immediately make known

[7] *Mencius*, IV A, 7.

the fact as soon as the white silk flies [an emergency call for help arrives] so that those with money may contribute money and those without money may contribute their energy. If a Brother [conceals the fact] and pretends ignorance, may he be destroyed by the five thunders.

3. Whenever any of the Hung family Brothers in the provinces or abroad arrives, whether he be a scholar, farmer, artisan, merchant, or tramp, he must be received, accommodated for the night, and given meals. If a Brother pretends ignorance and treats a fellow Brother as an outsider, may he perish beneath 10,000 swords.

4. Even though a Brother may not be acquainted with a fellow Brother of the Hung family, if the fellow Brother hangs up his signboard or utters a password and he still does not recognize the fellow Brother, may he perish under 10,000 swords.

5. Affairs of the Hung family may not be divulged or confided to one's father, son, brother, or relative. If a Brother privately passes on or tutors others in the Society's underwear [secret documents] or waist-bands [membership certificates], or uses them for the purpose of making money, may he perish beneath 10,000 swords.

6. Brothers of the Hung family may not secretly act as leads for the arrest of a fellow Brother. Even if there is accumulated enmity, the matter should be presented to the Brethren for a just settlement, and by no means should hatred be retained in one's heart. If by chance an arrest is made by mistake, the fellow Brother must be set free at once. If a Brother violates this oath, may he be destroyed by the five thunders.

7. Whenever a fellow Brother is in financial difficulty, a Brother must come to his assistance. He must do his best to provide the fellow Brother with money for his expenses or fare, whether the amount is large or small. If he shows no consideration in this, may he be destroyed by the five thunders.

8. If a Brother fabricates stories about a fellow Brother violating his human obligations, plotting to assassinate the Incense Master [Worshipful Master], or committing a murder, may he perish beneath 10,000 swords.

9. If a Brother violates a fellow Brother's wife, daughter, or sister, may he be destroyed by the five thunders.

10. If a Brother appropriates a fellow Brother's money or property [entrusted to him for safe keeping], or deliberately fails to deliver the same as requested, may he perish under 10,000 swords.

11. If a Brother does not devote all his mind and energy when a fellow

Brother entrusts his wife or children to his care, or important matters to his handling, may he be destroyed by the five thunders.

12. If anyone joining the Hung Society this evening lies about the date and hour of his birth, may he be destroyed by the five thunders.

13. Having joined the Hung Society this evening, one must have no regret or sigh. If a Brother entertains such a state of mind, may he perish beneath 10,000 swords.

14. If a Brother secretly assists an outsider [against a fellow Brother] or robs him of money or possessions, may he be destroyed by the five thunders.

15. A Brother must not force a fellow Brother to sell him goods or force him out in order to make a sale. If he relies on his strength and oppresses a weak Brother, may he perish beneath 10,000 swords.

16. A Brother must return the money or things borrowed from a fellow Brother. If he goes contrary to his conscience and appropriates the money or things, may he be destroyed by the five thunders.

17. When in a robbery a Brother takes money or things from a fellow Brother by mistake, they must be returned at once. If he intends to appropriate them, may he perish under 10,000 swords.

18. If a Brother is captured by a government official, he must bear the consequences for what he has done himself and must not involve a fellow Brother because of any enmity. If a Brother violates this oath, may he be destroyed by the five thunders.

19. When a fellow Brother is murdered or arrested, or when he has gone away for a long time, and the family he has left behind becomes destitute, a Brother must take steps to render assistance. If he pretends ignorance, may he be destroyed by the five thunders.

20. When a fellow Brother is abused by others, a Brother must go forward to help him if he is in the right or arbitrate if he is in the wrong. If a fellow Brother is repeatedly abused by other people, the Brother must not pretend ignorance but must inform the Brethren so they may consult and decide on a course of action, with everyone contributing money and those without money contributing energy to strive for his glory. If a Brother violates this oath, may he be destroyed by the five thunders.

21. Whenever a Brother learns that a fellow Brother from the provinces or from abroad is to be arrested, he must lose no time in informing the fellow Brother so he may escape as soon as possible. If the Brother pretends ignorance, may he perish beneath 10,000 swords.

22. A Brother must not conspire with an outsider to cheat a fellow Brother of money in a place of gambling. If he commits this crime knowingly, may he perish beneath 10,000 swords.

23. A Brother must not fabricate stories or twist the words of fellow Brothers so as to set them apart. If he violates this oath, may he perish beneath 10,000 swords.

24. A Brother must not illegally proclaim himself a Worshipful Master. When the mourning period [period of training] of three years since initiation into the Hung Society is over, if he is truly loyal to the Society and devoted to the Brethren the Worshipful Master will tutor him in the literature of the Society, and eventually he may be promoted to be the Worshipful Master either through transmission or through the recommendation of the three Deacons. If he acts [as a Worshipful Master] without proper authority, may he be destroyed by the five thunders.

25. After joining the Hung Society, all enmity among Brothers must be wiped out. If a Brother violates this oath, may he be destroyed by the five thunders.

26. When a Brother's own brother is involved in a dispute or lawsuit with a fellow Brother of the Hung family, the Brother must try to reconcile them and must not render aid to either side. If he violates this oath, may he be destroyed by the five thunders.

27. A Brother must not, under any pretext, invade the territory held by a fellow Brother. If he pretends ignorance and places the fellow Brother in danger, may he be destroyed by the five thunders.

28. A Brother must not be jealous of the money or things acquired by a fellow Brother or plot to share his spoil. If he has such intentions, may he be destroyed by the five thunders.

29. A Brother must not betray the secret or harbor any bad intention when a fellow Brother makes some fast money. If he violates this oath, may he perish beneath 10,000 swords.

30. A Brother must not secretly help an outsider to oppress fellow Brothers of the Hung family. If he violates this oath, may he perish beneath 10,000 swords.

31. A Brother must not oppress people because of the power or the huge membership of the Hung family, and, what is more, he must not do violence and behave like a despot. Instead he must mind his own business. If he violates this oath, may he perish beneath 10,000 swords.

32. A Brother must not breed hatred of fellow Brothers because they do not lend him money. If he violates this oath, may he be destroyed by the five thunders.

33. If a Brother rapes a fellow Brother's young child, may he be destroyed by the five thunders.

34. A Brother must not accept or buy a fellow Brother's wife or concubine as his own spouse. Neither may he commit adultery with them. If he commits such a crime knowingly, may he perish beneath 10,000 swords.

35. A Brother must be very careful in his speech and may not carelessly use the words, phrases, and other secrets of the Hung family, so as to prevent outsiders from penetrating our mysteries and to avoid inviting trouble with them. If he violates this oath, may he perish beneath 10,000 swords.

36. Whether a Brother is a scholar, a farmer, an artisan, or a merchant, he should attend to his own occupation. Having joined the Hung Society, the first emphasis must be loyalty to the Society and devotion to the Brethren, and the cultivation of fellowship with all Brothers within the four seas. When the time of uprising comes, all Brothers must be of one mind and united effort to destroy the Manchu role, restore the Ming empire as soon as possible, and avenge the burning of the Five Early Founding Fathers. If in an emergency a Brother is hesitant or divided in his mind, escapes from his responsibility, and makes no effort, may he perish beneath 10,000 swords.

The Ten Prohibitions of the Hung Society
[From Chu Lin, *Hung men chih*, pp. 32–33]

1. Wives of Brothers must cultivate correct behavior and married Brothers must not be given to sexual promiscuity. If wives do not cultivate correctness, both of their ears will be cut off. If [married] Brothers are sexually promiscuous, they will be punished by death.

2. When a Brother's parent dies and he lacks money for the funeral and asks Brothers for financial help, all should do their best to help him. Those who refuse will have both ears cut off.

3. When a Brother makes a plea of poverty and appeals for a loan, he may not be refused. Those who hold him in contempt or sternly refuse him will have both ears cut off.

4. Brothers may not purposely cause a fellow Brother to lose money in a place of gambling or secretly cheat him. Those who commit this offense will be beaten with a bamboo 108 times.

5. After joining the Hung Society, no Brother may secretly divulge the Society's regulations to outsiders. Those who commit this offense will be punished by death.

6. When a Brother entrusts money or documents in the course of his business or dealings with people abroad, they may not be secretly used or appropriated. Those who commit this offense will have both ears cut off.

7. When a Brother engaged in a fight with outsiders comes for help, aid must be rendered. Those who pretend not to know him will be beaten with a bamboo 108 times.

8. Any Brother who, because of his superiority, oppresses his inferiors, or because of his strength maltreats the weak, will have both ears cut off. In addition he will be beaten with a bamboo 72 times.

9. When a Brother is in distress, aid should be given immediately. Those who violate this will be beaten with a bamboo 108 times.

10. When a Brother is in danger or has been arrested by a government official, all Brothers must take steps to save him. Those who shirk responsibility under any pretense will be beaten with a bamboo 108 times.

The Ten Disciplines of the Hung Society
[From Chu Lin, *Hung men chih*, pp. 35–36]

1. It is not permitted to injure or destroy a fellow Brother [that is, in the Society's secret language, be disrespectful to him].

2. It is not permitted to curse or scold parents.

3. It is not permitted to stir up a lamp or put out a light [stir up trouble].

4. It is not permitted to oppress others because of one's superiority.

5. It is not permitted to deceive Heaven and cross the river [cheat people].

6. It is not permitted to skim off the fat and leave the soup [take the best for oneself].

7. It is not permitted to be inhumane and unrighteous.

8. It is not permitted to pick the red and take what is submerged in water [take illegal fees or compensation].

9. It is not permitted to struggle to go ahead when walking with others [push ahead for personal glory].

10. It is not permitted to usurp any position in the Society.

The Eight Virtues of the Hung Society
[From Chu Lin, *Hung men chih,* p. 141]

1. Be absolutely loyal and dedicated to the country.
2. Be filial and obedient to parents.
3. Instruct and teach your wife and children.
4. Be harmonious with your brothers.
5. Be harmonious with your neighbors.
6. Help people in distress and save people in danger.
7. Sincerely advise your friends.
8. Protect the rich and help the poor.

PART FIVE
CHINA AND THE NEW WORLD

1935	Establishment of Communist headquarters at Yenan.
1936	Sian incident: kidnapping of Chiang Kai-shek followed by United Front of Nationalist government and Communist Party.
1937	Marco Polo Bridge incident, expanding into Japanese occupation of coastal China and Yangtze valley.
1938	Chungking made wartime capital.
1943	Chiang Kai-shek's *China's Destiny*. Beginning of Communist Party reform movement at Yenan.
1945	End of Pacific War.
1949	Withdrawal of Nationalist government to Taiwan; founding of Communists' "People's Republic." Mao's "Dictatorship of the People's Democracy."
1957	The "Hundred Flowers" campaign launched by Mao Tse-tung's speech on "The Correct Handling of Contradictions Among the People."

CHAPTER XXIV

THE OPENING
OF CHINA
TO THE WEST

The year 1839, which saw the opening of the Opium War between Britain and China, is the great turning point in China between old and new. It marks the end of China's long existence as an independent civilization, free to disregard what took place beyond the borders of the Central Kingdom, and its emergence into a world of rapid, irresistible change. The new China might be slow in coming and still constantly stalked by its past, but the outcome of this historic encounter was to insure that, eventually and inevitably, dynamic forces from the West would have a large part in shaping its future.

Up to this time, for almost three centuries since the first arrival of the Portuguese off South China, the Chinese court had succeeded in dealing with Westerners on its own terms. Trade was confined to a few ports where agents of the court could regulate it strictly and tax it heavily. This indeed was the traditional pattern of state control over commerce, whether foreign or domestic—a system designed to hold it under close supervision, to keep the merchant in an inferior status, to subordinate commerce to the interests of the state, and to obtain a maximum in revenue while assuming a minimum of responsibility on the part of the imperial bureaucracy for the actual conduct of trade (which was handled by licensed merchants in accordance with the age-old practice for state monopolies). Many of the disadvantages of such a system from the trader's point of view were not, therefore, disabilities specially imposed on foreigners and calculated to harrass them, but simply limitations inherent in the "regular" conditions of doing business in China. Chinese merchants, for their part, had long since learned to live with them. Westerners, especially British traders in the early nineteenth century, remained restive under these restrictions and resentful of them. Imbued with the spirit of a rising English middle class, believing in free trade and the near-sacredness of property, they ran up against a regime which recognized neither of these as basic principles and a way of life in which the pursuit of profit was actually scorned as ignoble.

If the established pattern for foreign trade had such disadvantages for the merchant, it involved difficulties for the government as well. Burdensome taxes and restrictions were an invitation for enterprising and resourceful persons to engage in smuggling. Smuggling, moreover, could prove lucrative not only for the direct participants but for local officials as well, who could be bribed to keep hands off the illegal traffic. These factors help to explain why it should have proven so difficult for the government to put an end to the opium trade in spite of repeated bans on its importation and sale. The state was not merely in conflict with foreigners, who found opium from India and the Near East a wonder-drug in curing the chronic imbalance of trade with China, but with its own members whose self-interest led them to "squeeze" the traffic for their personal benefit rather than stamp it out for the good of all.

On the other hand, the "self-interest" of foreigners participating in the China trade was not wholly bound up with the marketing of opium, and it is possible that intelligent negotiation would have brought about gradual reduction in imports of the drug, while other articles, especially manufactured goods, took the place of opium in the trade. Unfortunately, the traditional conduct of foreign relations by the Chinese court was confined largely to tribute-relations with states looked upon as "vassals" of the emperor. There was no inclination to establish equal relations with the Western powers or to enter into negotiations which might lead to an abridgement of the emperor's absolute power to deal with foreigners as he would with his own subjects. For want of such a middle ground on which to meet, the means were lacking whereby to resolve the constant conflicts which arose in contacts between Chinese and foreigners over differing conceptions of justice and equity.

Under these circumstances a stalemate was no solution. The evils of the opium traffic were so far-reaching that the Chinese could ignore them only at great peril. Meanwhile the impossibility of China's maintaining its traditional isolationist policy made imperative the finding of a new *modus vivendi* with the West. Some sort of showdown was inevitable.

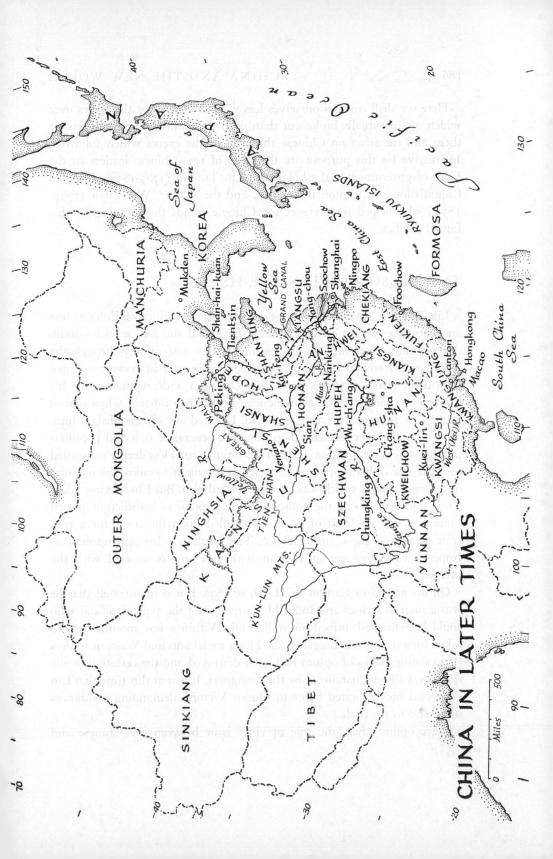

CHINA IN LATER TIMES

Here we shall concern ourselves less with the merits of the issues over which war eventually broke out than with the Chinese understanding of them and the effect on Chinese thinking of the events which followed. Instructive for this purpose are the cases of two Chinese leaders in the fields of government and scholarship: Lin Tse-hsü (1785–1850), Imperial Commissioner at Canton in 1839–40, and the scholar, Wei Yüan (1794–1856), who helped to interpret for Chinese minds the meaning of this fateful conflict.

THE LESSON OF LIN TSE-HSÜ

Lin Tse-hsü, a native of the southeast coastal province of Fukien, was an exemplary product of the Chinese educational and civil service system. After winning the *chin-shih* degree in 1811, he rose rapidly through the official ranks and served with particular distinction in posts concerned with fiscal matters and public works, gaining a wide reputation for his competence, integrity and humaneness. By the late thirties, when opium smuggling became a pressing question, Lin had already established himself as an able governor and then governor-general of rich and populous provinces in Central China. In such a position a man less deeply concerned over the fate of his people might have been content to enjoy the measure of personal success which was already assured him. But Lin, having taken strong measures to end the traffic in his own sphere of jurisdiction, placed himself in the forefront of those who called upon the court for a full-scale assault on the opium menace. The result was his appointment as Imperial Commissioner at Canton with full powers to deal with the problem.

On his arrival in Canton in March of 1839, Lin demonstrated that he was a man of serious and inflexible purpose, not the type of official who could be wheedled, bribed, or stalled off. Within a few months he had taken such strong action against the Hong merchants and Western traders that existing stocks of opium had been destroyed and the cessation of the traffic was all but guaranteed by the foreigners. It was at this time that Lin addressed his celebrated letter to Queen Victoria demanding assurances of an end to the trade.

Were opium, then, the sole or chief issue between the Chinese and

British, there would presumably have been no cause for the outbreak of the first Anglo-Chinese War later that same year. To the British on the scene, however, Lin's uncompromising policies seemed not just firm or tough but arrogant and unreasonable. Though ready to make substantial concessions with regard to the drug traffic in order not to lose all opportunities for trade, for them the lure of profits did not suffice to overcome strong feelings in what they regarded as matters of principle. The lack of treaty relations meant that there was no established procedure for the administration of justice in incidents involving Chinese and foreigners. Commissioner Lin was determined that Chinese authorities should mete out punishment for crimes on Chinese soil of which foreigners had been accused. The British were equally adamant in refusing to turn over suspects, whose guilt was by no means established, to the mercies of Chinese officials whom they considered vindictive and inhumane. When Lin countered with the breaking off of all trade and expulsion of the British from China, full-scale hostilities broke out.

The Chinese, as is well known, were pitifully unprepared on land and sea to resist the force of British arms, and it was only a matter of weeks before the underlying weakness of Lin's "get-tough" policy became fully exposed. Officially disgraced, the erstwhile viceroy and commissioner was eventually banished to Chinese Turkestan. In the meantime, he had become fully persuaded of the need for strengthening China through the adoption of Western arms and methods of warfare, though he could make no progress in gaining acceptance of this view at court. Even when later restored to the official ranks, partly on account of his accomplishments in flood control and land reclamation work, Lin lacked any real opportunity to influence state policy in the direction of greater realism and reform. The lesson he had learned in Canton remained largely his own. It would be decades more before the court could be moved by further misfortunes to take such warnings to heart.

LIN TSE-HSÜ
Letter to the English Ruler

In this celebrated letter to Queen Victoria (1839), Lin argues against the opium trade with all the moral earnestness of the Confucian scholar and lofty condescension of one speaking for the imperial court. On its own terms, of course, Lin's argument is unanswerable. Yet his tone indicates how unready the Chinese were to deal with the British as diplomatic equals or to negotiate outstanding differences on other scores.

Intransigent as he appeared, Lin nonetheless compelled admiration. His likeness appeared later in Mme. Tussaud's Wax Museum in London, and the distinguished British consular official and sinologist, H. A. Giles, said of Lin: "He was a fine scholar, a just and merciful official, and a true patriot."

[From Teng and Fairbank, *China's Response to the West*, pp. 24–27]

A communication: magnificently our great emperor soothes and pacifies China and the foreign countries, regarding all with the same kindness. If there is profit, then he shares it with the peoples of the world; if there is harm, then he removes it on behalf of the world. This is because he takes the mind of Heaven and earth as his mind.

The kings of your honorable country by a tradition handed down from generation to generation have always been noted for their politeness and submissiveness. We have read your successive tributary memorials saying: "In general our countrymen who go to trade in China have always received His Majesty the Emperor's gracious treatment and equal justice," and so on. Privately we are delighted with the way in which the honorable rulers of your country deeply understand the grand principles and are grateful for the Celestial grace. For this reason the Celestial Court in soothing those from afar has redoubled its polite and kind treatment. The profit from trade has been enjoyed by them continuously for two hundred years. This is the source from which your country has become known for its wealth.

But after a long period of commercial intercourse, there appear among the crowd of barbarians both good persons and bad, unevenly. Consequently there are those who smuggle opium to seduce the Chinese people and so cause the spread of the poison to all provinces. Such persons who only care to profit themselves, and disregard their harm to others, are not tolerated by the laws of Heaven and are unanimously hated by human beings. His Majesty the Emperor, upon hearing of this, is in a towering rage. He has especially sent me, his commissioner, to come to Kwangtung, and together with the governor-general and governor jointly to investigate and settle this matter. . . .

We find that your country is sixty or seventy thousand *li* from China. Yet there are barbarian ships that strive to come here for trade for the purpose of making a great profit. The wealth of China is used to profit the barbarians. That is to say, the great profit made by barbarians is all taken from the rightful share of China. By what right do they then in return use the poisonous drug to injure the Chinese people? Even though the barbarians may not necessarily intend to do us harm, yet in coveting profit to an extreme, they have no regard for injuring others. Let us ask, where is your conscience? I have heard that the smoking of opium is very strictly forbidden by your country; that is because the harm caused by opium is clearly understood. Since it is not permitted to do harm to your own country, then even less should you let it be passed on to the harm of other countries—how much less to China! Of all that China exports to foreign countries, there is not a single thing which is not beneficial to people; they are of benefit when eaten, or of benefit when used, or of benefit when resold: all are beneficial. Is there a single article from China which has done any harm to foreign countries? Take tea and rhubarb, for example; the foreign countries cannot get along for a single day without them. If China cuts off these benefits with no sympathy for those who are to suffer, then what can the barbarians rely upon to keep themselves alive? Moreover the woolens, camlets, and longells [i.e., textiles] of foreign countries cannot be woven unless they obtain Chinese silk. If China, again, cuts off this beneficial export, what profit can the barbarians expect to make? As for other foodstuffs, beginning with candy, ginger, cinnamon, and so forth, and articles for use, beginning with silk, satin, chinaware, and so on, all the things that must be had by foreign countries are innumerable. On the other hand, articles coming from the outside to China can only be used as toys. We can take them or get along without them. Since they are not needed by China, what difficulty would there be if we closed the frontier and stopped the trade? Nevertheless our Celestial Court lets tea, silk, and other goods be shipped without limit and circulated everywhere without begrudging it in the slightest. This is for no other reason but to share the benefit with the people of the whole world.

The goods from China carried away by your country not only supply your own consumption and use, but also can be divided up and sold to other countries, producing a triple profit. Even if you do not sell opium, you still have this threefold profit. How can you bear to go further, selling products injurious to others in order to fulfill your insatiable desire? . . .

We have further learned that in London, the capital of your honorable rule, and in Scotland (Ssu-ko-lan), Ireland (Ai-lun), and other places, originally no opium has been produced. Only in several places of India under your control such as Bengal, Madras, Bombay, Patna, Benares, and Malwa has opium been planted from hill to hill, and ponds have been opened for its manufacture. For months and years work is continued in order to accumulate the poison. The obnoxious odor ascends, irritating Heaven and frightening the spirits. Indeed you, O King, can eradicate the opium plant in these places, hoe over the fields entirely, and sow in its stead the five grains [i.e., millet, barley, wheat, etc.]. Anyone who dares again attempt to plant and manufacture opium should be severely punished. This will really be a great, benevolent government policy that will increase the common weal and get rid of evil. For this, Heaven must support you and the spirits must bring you good fortune, prolonging your old age and extending your descendants. All will depend on this act. . . .

Now we have set up regulations governing the Chinese people. He who sells opium shall receive the death penalty and he who smokes it also the death penalty. Now consider this: if the barbarians do not bring opium, then how can the Chinese people resell it, and how can they smoke it? The fact is that the wicked barbarians beguile the Chinese people into a death trap. How then can we grant life only to these barbarians? He who takes the life of even one person still has to atone for it with his own life; yet is the harm done by opium limited to the taking of one life only? Therefore in the new regulations, in regard to those barbarians who bring opium to China, the penalty is fixed at decapitation or strangulation. This is what is called getting rid of a harmful thing on behalf of mankind.

Moreover we have found that in the middle of the second month of this year [April 9] Consul [Superintendent] Elliot of your nation, because the opium prohibition law was very stern and severe, petitioned for an extension of the time limit. He requested a limit of five months for India and its adjacent harbors and related territories, and ten months for England proper, after which they would act in conformity with the new regulations. Now we, the commissioner and others, have memorialized and have received the extraordinary Celestial grace of His Majesty the Emperor, who has redoubled his consideration and compassion. All those who within the period of the coming one year (from England) or six months (from India) bring opium to China by mistake, but who voluntarily confess and completely surrender their opium, shall be exempt from their punishment. After this limit of time, if there are still those who bring opium to China then they will plainly have committed a willful violation and shall at once be executed according to law, with absolutely no clemency or pardon. This may be called the height of kindness and the perfection of justice.

Our Celestial Dynasty rules over and supervises the myriad states, and surely possesses unfathomable spiritual dignity. Yet the Emperor cannot bear to execute people without having first tried to reform them by instruction. Therefore he especially promulgates these fixed regulations. The barbarian merchants of your country, if they wish to do business for a prolonged period, are required to obey our statutes respectfully and to cut off permanently the source of opium. They must by no means try to test the effectiveness of the law with their lives. May you, O King, check your wicked and sift out your vicious people before they come to China, in order to guarantee the peace of your nation, to show further the sincerity of your politeness and submissiveness, and to let the two countries enjoy together the blessings of peace. How fortunate, how fortunate indeed! After receiving this dispatch will you immediately give us a prompt reply regarding the details and circumstances of your cutting off the opium traffic. Be sure not to put this off. The above is what has to be communicated. [Vermilion endorsement:] This is appropriately worded and quite comprehensive (*Te-t'i chou-tao*).

The Need for Western Guns and Ships

This letter to his friend Wu Tzu-hsü, written two years after the debacle at Canton, expresses Lin's realization of the need for adopting modern weapons and methods of warfare. As one in official disgrace, however, Lin dared not speak out nor even communicate his thoughts privately except in guarded fashion. Under such circumstances it is understandable that the advocacy of reform should have been hampered and the taking of concrete steps so long delayed.

[From Teng and Fairbank, *China's Response to the West*, p. 28]

The rebels' ships on the open sea came and went as they pleased, now in the south and now suddenly in the north, changing successively between morning and evening. If we tried to put up a defense everywhere, not only would we toil and expend ourselves without limit, but also how could we recruit and transport so many troops, militia, artillery, and ammunition, and come to their support quickly? . . .

When I was in office in Kwangtung and Kwangsi, I had made plans regarding the problems of ships and cannon and a water force. Afraid that there was not enough time to build ships, I at first rented them. Afraid that there was not enough time to cast cannon and that it would not be done according to the regulations, I at first bought foreign ones. The most painful thing was that when the Hu-men [the Bogue or "Tiger's mouth," the entrance to the Canton River] was broken into, a large number of good cannon fell into the hands of the rebellious barbarians. I recall that after I had been punished two years ago, I still took the risk of calling the Emperor's attention to two things: ships and guns. At that time, if these things could have been made and prepared, they still could have been used with effect to fight against the enemy in Chekiang last fall [1841]. Now it is even more difficult to check the wildfire. After all, ships, guns, and a water force are absolutely indispensable. Even if the rebellious barbarians had fled and returned beyond the seas, these things would still have to be urgently planned for, in order to work out the permanent defense of our sea frontiers. . . .

But at this time I must strictly observe the advice to seal my lips as one corks the mouth of a bottle. However, toward those with identical aims and interests, I suddenly spit out the truth and am unable to control myself. I extremely regret my foolishness and carelessness. Nevertheless, when I turn my thoughts to the depth of your attention to me, then I cannot conceal these things from myself. I only beg you to keep them confidential. By all means, please do not tell other persons.

WEI YÜAN AND THE WEST

The *Illustrated Gazetteer of the Maritime Countries,* by Wei Yüan (1794–1856), is a landmark in China's relations with the West, since it represents the first systematic attempt to provide educated men with a realistic picture of the outside world. A sizeable compilation running to sixty chapters, this gazetteer owed its inception to the pioneering work of Lin Tse-hsü who, while in Canton, made strenuous efforts to gather information about the West, taking notes himself, collecting materials, arranging translations, and compiling a *Gazetteer of the Four Continents,* which Wei used as the basis for his own work after Lin's dismissal.

Wei was exceptional in his alertness to the situation confronting China and his realization of the need for serious study of the West. He was not, however, a man whose intellectual importance derived from inadvertent involvement in what proved to be a momentous issue. A classicist and historian of the first rank, Wei combined the finest traditions of Ch'ing scholarship with the serious concern of the dedicated Confucian official in matters of state. By 1842 he had already published his military history of the Ch'ing dynasty, *Sheng-wu chi,* a work regarded as authoritative and often reprinted. Consequently, he spoke as one commanding scholarly respect, not as a mere opportunist or crackpot, and the tone of his work reflects his serious purpose—to provide information upon which to base practical state policies rather than simply to peddle curious notions about the strange world outside.

Wei's general thesis in the *Gazetteer* is this: the Western barbarians, bent on power and profit, have devised techniques and machines by which to subvert or conquer the civilized world. China, dedicated as she is to virtue, learning, and the ways of peace, possesses a spiritual and moral strength which can yet triumph over the enemy if only the Chinese awaken to the danger and apply themselves to the practical problems involved. Traditional military science suggests that the first requisite is intelligence of the enemy—of his strengths and weaknesses. The second requisite is to match these strengths and exploit the weaknesses. If the natural abilities of the Chinese are devoted to the study and adoption of Western military methods, and there is not too great an impatience with the achievement of immediate results, the time will come when China can reassert herself. In the meantime, she should seek to exploit the prime weakness of the West—its inherent disunity, which derives from the lack of a common moral basis and consequent anarchy of selfish ambitions among the nations. To play the Western powers off against one another is then the obvious strategy.

Despite the violent and contemptuous tone of his language, Wei is careful to state that his is a policy valid either for war or for peace. He admits of the possibility that China's military preparations may not enable her soon to resist or attack the West. Peace negotiations could prove necessary again as they had in the Opium War. Yet a policy of playing the Western powers off against each other, while gaining time for reform and strengthening within, would be appropriate even in these circumstances.

Wei's official career, though one of genuine distinction, was limited to relatively minor posts and matters of more traditional concern to the bureaucratic class: internal (and particularly local) administration, flood control and irrigation, water transport, and salt administration. His *Illustrated Gazetteer of the Maritime Countries* was reprinted many times, expanded and supplemented. Japanese editions of this work and Wei's *Sheng-wu chi* came to the attention of the samurai reformer Sakuma Shōzan, who spoke of Wei as "a comrade in another land." Sakuma also commented, however, that in practical matters like gunnery Wei lacked firsthand experience and his information was often inaccurate.[1]

Thus Wei's approach to the problem of national defense may be said to reflect his Confucian concern for the state, a more realistic estimate of Western power, and the Ch'ing scholar's penchant for works of compilation based on critical, though not necessarily empirical, research. He had neither the opportunity, nor perhaps the inclination, to take up the practical art of war which in the past had proven so uncongenial to Chinese Confucian tastes. Wei's own urgings to the contrary, this same lack of practical efforts remained a weakness of China for years to come.

WEI YÜAN
Preface to the Illustrated Gazetteer of the Maritime Countries

In the preface to his work, Wei, characteristically for the Ch'ing scholar, starts with a discussion of the sources he has drawn upon. Then he explains the nature and purposes of the work, and provides a conspectus of the contents, chapter by chapter. The whole is in a highly rhetorical style, replete with classical allusions and the usual pretensions in regard to Chinese cultural superiority and world sovereignty.

[From *Hai-kuo t'u-chih,* Original Preface, 1a–6b]

The present work, *Illustrated Gazetteer of the Maritime Countries (Hai-kuo t'u-chih)* contains sixty chapters. Upon what is it based? It is based, on the one hand, upon the *Gazetteer of the Four Continents (Ssu chou chih)* which was translated by Secretary [of War], Lin [Tse-hsü], former Governor-General of Kwangtung and Kwangsi, and, on the other hand, upon the histories and gazetteers of different previous dynasties, and the different series of *Island Gazetteers* published since the Ming

[1] Cf. Tsunoda, de Bary, and Keene, *Sources of Japanese Tradition,* pp. 603–16.

period, and also upon many barbarian atlases and books published in recent years. They were brought together, and thoroughly searched. Many difficulties had to be worked out in order that this pioneer work might be published.

At a rough estimate, about eighty percent of the source materials used in this book covering the Southeastern Ocean [Southeast Asia] and the Southwestern Ocean [South and West Asia] and about sixty percent covering the Great Western Ocean [Western Europe], the Little Western Ocean [North Africa], the Northern Ocean [Russia and Eastern Europe], and the Outer Great Western Ocean [North and South America] are new materials supplementing the original [Lin's] book covering the same areas. They are also illustrated with maps, tables, and diagrams. A variety of opinion from different schools is presented in the interests of broad coverage.

In what respect does this work differ from the gazetteers of earlier writers? The answer is that those earlier works all described the West as it appeared to Chinese writers, while this book describes the West as it appears to Westerners.

What is the purpose of the present work? Its purpose is to show how to use barbarians to fight barbarians, how to make the barbarians pacify one another [to our advantage], and how to employ the techniques of the barbarians in order to bring the barbarians under control. The *Book of Changes* says: "Depending upon the mutual influence of love and hate, there may be fortune or misfortune; depending upon the mutual influence of approach and withdrawal, there may be repentance or regret; depending upon the mutual influence of honesty and dishonesty, there may be gain or loss." [2] So it is in defending against an enemy: depending upon whether one knows the enemy's position or not, there may be absolute gain or total loss. In ancient times those who succeeded in driving off the barbarians knew the enemy's position as clearly as if it were spread out upon their own desk or carpet; they were informed of the enemy's condition as intimately as if the enemy were dining or sleeping with them.

With this book in hand, then, will it be possible to drive off the barbarians?

Perhaps so, perhaps not. This book provides only military tactics, not the basic strategy. It provides the tangible means for making war, but not

[2] Hsi hsia 9 (Legge, 405).

the intangible ones. There were ministers of state in the Ming period who said that in order to deal with the menace of Japanese pirates on the high seas, it was first necessary to pacify the hearts of the people, embittered by an accumulation of grievances. But what are the accumulated grievances now? They come neither from flood nor from fire; they are stirred up neither by swords nor by other metal weapons. They are due not to traitorous elements along the coast; nor to the opium smokers or opium smugglers [but to misgovernment]. Therefore the gentleman [as he reads the *Book of Odes*] turns to the chapters of *Yün-han* and *Ch'e-kung* [which were written to praise King Hsüan of the Chou dynasty for his efforts to restore the great virtue of his ancestors] before he reads the chapters of *Ch'ang-wu* and *Chiang-han* [which praise the same king for his successful expedition against the Huai tribes]. By so doing he is able to understand the zealous concern of the poets who wrote the two sections, Ta ya and Hsiao ya, of the *Book of Odes*. In the same way, when he studies the interpretations of King Wen and the Duke of Chou [in the *Book of Changes*] with regard to "adjusting man's inward thoughts and external acts" and "the seasonal rotations of growth and diminution," he is able to understand the anxious concern of the authors and annotators of the *Book of Changes*. Man's zealousness and sense of concern are the means by which Heaven in the natural course of things brings peace out of chaos, by which human hearts are converted from ignorance to enlightenment, and by which man's abilities are turned from what is vain to what is practical.

Previously, the Chun-k'o-erh tribes were very unruly during the periods K'ang-hsi and Yung-cheng (1662–1735), but were suppressed with lightning speed in the middle of the Ch'ien-lung period (1736–1796). Yet the steady poisoning of our people by the barbarians with their opium represents a crime ten thousand times worse than that of the Chun-k'o-erh tribes. However, our present emperor, His Majesty, is so benevolent and diligent. His virtue matches that of His ancestors. The operations of Heaven in time and of man through his own efforts are conjoined for our advantage. Why should we fear that the time is not ripe for extermination of the barbarians; why should we fear that there may be no chance to show our might? Thus all of our courageous people must show their eagerness for the achievement of such a task, and anyone who has not lost his senses must devise some means for its accomplishment. Away with hypocrisy! Away with all window dressing! Away with the dread of difficulty! Away with the nurturing of internal evils and the tolerating of private gain at the expense of the public interest! Then the minds of men will be aroused from their ignorant lethargy.

First of all, through practical projects we must advance practical effort; and through practical effort advance practical projects. The mugwort must be kept in dry storage for three years [before it can be applied as an effective medicine]. Our nets must be made ready before we can go fishing in the lake. We must not try to drown ourselves in the river merely to show our heroism, nor must we try to appease our hunger by drawing picture-cakes. Then we shall no longer be plagued by a dearth of men with practical abilities.

Secondly, once rid of our ignorant lethargy, the sun will shine more brightly in the sky; once the dearth of men with practical abilities is remedied, government orders will be carried out with the speed of wind and lightning. There is a statement in the commentary:[3] "Bring all the waste land in the country under cultivation; let all farms be under good care; so that the people within the four seas will be contented, and even the Yüeh-shang tribes [the most remote barbarians] will be our loyal subjects." With this concern in mind, I wrote this preface for the *Hai-kuo t'u-chih*.

. . . . .

Defensive measures may serve offensive purposes as well as purposes of peaceful negotiation. Use the barbarians to control the barbarians, so that all our borders may be strongly held. Thus the first section of this book deals with maritime defense.

Down through three thousand years [of world history]; over the ninety thousand *li* of the world's circumference, both vertically in time and horizontally in space, with geographical charts and historical data, the second section presents a general survey of historical and territorial changes for all nations in the world.

Neither the barbarian religion nor the barbarian opium can penetrate the borders of our vassal states [to the South]. Alas, that they can show their will to resist [while we cannot]. So the third section deals with the nations along the coast of the Southeastern Seas [i.e., Indo-China, Siam, etc.].

[3] Which "commentary" (*chuan*) is unspecified; we have been unable to locate the source.

The Isles of Luzon and Java [i.e., the Philippines and the East Indies] are equal in extent to Japan, but they are either encroached upon or absorbed [by Western barbarians]. Taking heed of the overturned cart ahead [to avert a similar disaster for ourselves], the fourth section deals with the Isles of the Southeastern Ocean [Southeastern Asia].

The religion has been changed three times, and the land cut into Five Regions. The magpie's nest is now occupied by the turtle doves,[4] which are also a threat to China. The fifth section deals with India.

Both the whites and the blacks are from remote and isolated areas. They are forced to serve as advance guards, collaborating with the seafarers of the West. The sixth section deals with Africa of the Little Western Ocean.

The western part of the Mediterranean Sea is inhabited by many barbarian tribes, who cherish only profits and power, and indeed are as treacherous as the owls. The seventh section deals with the European countries in the Great Western Ocean.

Her [Russia's] tail lies in the East and her head in the West; her northern borders extend to the sea of ice. If we make alliances with the nearby countries in order to attack those afar, she may be our friend in a land war. The eighth section deals with Russia in the Northern Ocean. [In this section Wei sets forth his hope that Russia may distract England by invading India. In the next he suggests that the United States would be a natural ally in naval warfare.]

She has effectively resisted the violent invasion of the English barbarians and faithfully guarded the central plain. If we make alliances with those afar, in order to attack those nearby, she may be of assistance in a sea war. The ninth section deals with the United States in the Outer Great [Western] Ocean.

Every man has Heaven as his source; religious teachings derive from the sages. Though the different teachings meet and part, agree and disagree, they are all orderly and logical. The tenth section deals with religions of the Western nations.

It is China alone which embraces ten thousand *li* under one sovereignty. In contact with one another but unconnected—are Europe and Arabia. The eleventh section presents a chronological table of events in China and the West.

[4] So stupid they cannot make a nest for themselves.

The Chinese calendar has been supplemented by the Western; the Western calendar differs from the Chinese. As a guide for the people in their seasonal labors, ours takes the place of honor. The twelfth section presents a table of similarities and differences between the Chinese and the Western calendars.

In war topography is of first importance, however remote and wild the region. By the gathering of supplies and sketching of plans, a war can be won in the office. The thirteenth section presents a general survey of geographical conditions in each country.

Topography, important though it be, is nothing compared to cooperation among men. Surprise tactics and orthodox strategy are to be used according to circumstances, so that there will be the least expenditure of force and a maximum of concerted planning. The fourteenth section presents a program for controlling the barbarians.

Knowing one's own plans and being familiar with those of the enemy, one may judge whether to wage war or negotiate peace. Without knowing the right medicine, how can one cure the disease of shortsightedness and stupidity? The fifteenth section offers a compilation of data on the barbarian situation.

Maritime warfare depends upon warships, as land warfare depends upon battlements. Without mastering the best techniques, how can the stormy seas be tamed? The sixteenth section presents a detailed discussion of warships.

The Five Elements are able to subdue one another. Among them metal and fire are the most fierce. A thunder blast from the earth can serve both offensive and defensive purposes. The seventeenth section presents a detailed discussion of firearms and their use in warfare.

The languages and conveyances of different peoples are not the same, but their currencies are similar. To make a skillful use of them, one must make the utmost use of one's intelligence. The eighteenth section deals with [Western] currency, goods, and contrivances.

This preface is written by Wei Yüan of Shao-yang, Secretary to the Cabinet, on the 12th moon of the 22d year of Tao-kuang (February, 1843) at Yangchow.

玉　天恩
　　玉　太和
璽　　和　天　救八永
輯　真　天　兄王位定
日　永真王天王世萬乾
　錫王王兄王基幼乾
天　貴興督洪王歲坤
　祿福篤督日王歲坤
璽玉全芳洪王天

CHAPTER XXV

THE HEAVENLY KINGDOM OF THE TAIPINGS

In the writings of Lin Tse-hsü and Wei Yüan we have seen the impact of the West on two men who exemplified the finest traditions of Chinese statecraft and Confucian scholarship—representatives of that elite group which had served for centuries as the custodians of the Chinese government and of Confucian values in thought and scholarship. On another level of society, in these years just after China's defeat in the Opium War, there were signs of an even more powerful and striking reaction to the West in the great Taiping Rebellion, a mass movement so remarkable that it has continued to excite and perplex historians in recent years almost as much as it did Chinese and Western observers in the mid-nineteenth century. If on closer acquaintance this great popular uprising has seemed to reflect less of Western influence than of native traditions and internal unrest, it remains a fascinating example of the interplay between Chinese and Western ideas in an historical event of the first magnitude.

Hung Hsiu-ch'üan (1813–1864), the leader of this rebellion which swept up like a whirlwind from the southernmost regions of China, was the son of a poor peasant family belonging to the Hakka minority group and living not far from Canton. Hung had enough promise as a student so that his family joined together in providing him with an education and sending him on to take the provincial civil service examinations. Though repeatedly unsuccessful, on one of these visits to Canton (1836) Hung heard a Christian missionary preach and picked up some religious tracts. When the following year he failed again at the examinations, he seems to have suffered a nervous collapse and during his illness to have had certain visions. In one of them a fatherly old man appeared to him and complained that men, instead of worshiping him, were serving demons. In another Confucius was scolded for his faithlessness, and repented his ways. In still another a middle-aged man appeared and instructed Hung in the slaying of demons. These apparitions he later understood as signifying that God the Heavenly Father (whom he identified with the supreme god, Shang-ti, of ancient Chinese tradition) and Jesus Christ, his Elder Brother, had commissioned him as the Younger Brother to stamp out demon worship. To some Hung might have appeared to be the victim of his own fevered imaginings, but others were impressed by his quiet earnestness and deep sense of conviction. Perhaps most significant from the Chinese point of view was his ability to persuade members of his own family of the rightness of his cause.

These ideas continued to ferment in Hung's mind, yet it was only seven years later that he took the trouble to read more carefully the tracts given him in Canton, containing translations and summaries from the Bible and sermons on scriptural texts. Later still he spent two months studying in Canton with the Reverend Issachar J. Roberts, an American Southern Baptist missionary, whose fundamentalist teachings provided Hung with what limited knowledge he gained of Christianity. In the meantime, Hung, who earned a livelihood teaching in village schools, had been joined by some of his relatives in idol-breaking missions which aroused local feelings and the displeasure of the authorities. Forced to shift their activities westward, these prophets without honor in their own country met with a far better reception among the Hakkas of Kwangsi. By the late 1840s Hung found himself the leader of a growing band known as the God Worshipers. Here, too, however, the iconoclasm and strange teachings of the God Worshipers provoked official intervention and attempts at suppression.

In the mind of Hung the Manchu regime seems to have become identified quite early with the demonic forces which had to be destroyed in order to establish the Kingdom of Heaven on earth. But it was more than Hung's iconoclasm which led this new religious movement increasingly to take on a political and military aspect. Famine and economic depression in the late 1840s, burdensome taxation, the decline in dynastic prestige as a result of defeat at the hands of the British and the consequent impairment of governmental functions, especially in the more remote regions like Kwangsi, contributed to a situation in which the survival of any group depended upon its ability to defend and provide for itself in the midst of growing confusion and lawlessness. The God Worshipers were only one such group, but they proved better organized and possessed of a greater sense of purpose than most.

Under pressure of constant official harassment, Hung and his closest collaborators finally worked out a plan for full-fledged revolt. In effect it put the God Worshipers on a total-war footing. A military organization was created which would mobilize all of the resources of the community for prosecution of the war effort. Personal property had to be turned over to a communal treasury (the "Sacred Treasury"), religious observances were strictly enforced, and a detailed code of military discipline and ethical conduct was established with heavy penalties for any violations.

Systematically the leaders of the uprising set about consolidating their forces, making weapons, indoctrinating their followers, and training the militia. By December of 1850 the new army was able successfully to withstand a full assault by government troops, and in the flush of this first victory Hung formally proclaimed, at the start of the new year, his rebel regime, the Heavenly Kingdom of Great Peace. He himself assumed the title of Heavenly King, and others of the leaders, including several with military and organizational talents probably superior to those of Hung, were ranked as subordinate kings or princes.

The name of the new regime suggests that it was meant to fulfill the highest ideals of the Chinese political tradition (Taiping, or "Great Peace" designated a period of perfect peace and order according to one cyclical view of ancient history), along with the realization of a Kingdom of Heaven in which all worshiped the one True God. It was thus to be a theocratic state with military, political, and religious authority concentrated in a single hierarchy. Such an all-embracing, monolithic structure was congenial enough to the Chinese political scene and particularly suited to the requirements of a revolutionary situation. As a political venture the Taiping movement had a broad appeal to anti-Manchu, nationalist sentiment. As a program of economic reform, it attracted the overburdened and destitute, particularly among the peasants. As a new community—indeed a great family in which all the members were "brothers" and "sisters"—it had an appeal to rich and poor alike who suffered from the social dislocation and insecurity of the times. The Taiping cause, in other words, became a rallying point for all those elements which traditionally have attached themselves to a new dynastic movement.

Even in the powerful appeal of its religious *mystique* the Taiping Rebellion had something in common with peasant uprisings and dynastic revolutions in the past. Where it differed, however, was in the intensity and sectarian fanaticism with which Taiping religious teachings were insisted upon. Great importance was attached to the indoctrination of new recruits, and volunteers who refused to accept the Taiping faith—however genuine might be their antipathy to the Manchus—were turned away. In fact, the extraordinary discipline of the Taiping armies, the heroism of many in battle, and their readiness to meet death—for which there could be no earthly reward—all suggest that a sense of religious purpose, rather than simply economic gain or political ambition, was what held together this motley assemblage of malcontents and misfits, missionaries and messiahs.

From the military standpoint the Rebellion enjoyed startling success in its early years. It had the advantage of tight organization, firm discipline, talented commanders, and a high degree of mobility which derived from the cutting of all personal ties to home and property. Nevertheless, if Taiping progress northward was devastatingly swift, through Hunan to the central Yangtze valley and thence eastward to Nanking, this rapid advance came about only by the adoption of a strategy which had its own limitations—notably the bypassing of large centers of resistance. The Taipings concerned themselves little with organizing the countryside as they passed through. No permanent envelopment of these bypassed strongholds and eventual reduction of them was seriously attempted. Local opposition and temporary setbacks, instead of suggesting the need for caution and consolidation, were interpreted as signs from God that they should push on in other directions toward new and greater triumphs. The chief military commander, Yang Hsiu-ch'ing, who had the title of Eastern King, frequently claimed direct revelation from God the Father in support of his strategic moves, and Taiping accounts of the campaign make it appear that the triumphal course of the rebellion reflects the direct intervention of God in history through the instrumentality of chosen deputies like Hung and Yang.

Once established in their capital at Nanking, occupied March, 1853, and renamed "Heavenly Capital" (T'ien-ching), the Taipings sent out an expedition to take Peking which again made striking gains initially, but was eventually slowed, isolated, and defeated. A similar expedition to the West was more successful in enlarging the area under Taiping control, but for the most part the new regime found itself engaged in a protracted struggle to maintain its position in the lower Yangtze valley, a rich and populous region which posed formidable problems of defense and administration. For ten years the fortunes of war waxed and waned, with the exploits of some Taiping commanders resulting in heavy defeats for imperial armies, while, on the other hand, increasing pressure was exerted against them by the reorganized and revitalized forces of regional leaders loyal to the Manchu cause—leaders such as Tseng Kuo-fan, Tso Tsung-t'ang, and Li Hung-chang, who were to play a dominant role in the subsequent history of the dynasty.

A significant loss for the Taipings was their failure to enlist the support of the West. There was early sympathy for the rebel cause on the part of some Westerners in the treaty ports, based on a favorable impression of Taiping morale and discipline, as well as the hope that the Taiping religion might prove genuinely Christian. However, contacts with the leaders of the revolt soon disillusioned and alienated them. The fanaticism, ignorance, and arrogant pretensions of the latter to a special divine commission, to which even foreign Christians must submit, quickly dispelled any illusions that the Taipings would be easier for the Western powers to deal with than the Manchus. Subsequently Taiping moves threatening Shanghai brought the active intervention of the West against them.

A far more serious weakness of the Taipings was internal—a failure in political leadership. The Taiping "kings" paid little attention to systematic organization of the countryside, preferring to establish themselves in the larger towns and cities. Moreover, educated men with experience in civil administration, whose services might have been highly useful, were repelled by the Taipings' uncouthness, their superstitious adherence to a "foreign" faith, and apparent repudiation of Confucian orthodoxy. A civil service examination based on official Taiping literature did little to remedy the lack of trained personnel. Increasingly, too, the cohesion and capacities of the Taiping leadership were severely strained. After the capture of Nanking, Hung steadily withdrew from active direction of affairs, and assumed a role reminiscent of the Taoist sage-emperor who ruled by his magic potency—in this case his divine virtue. Yet in fact

Hung's whole personality disintegrated rapid'y, as he devoted himself more and more to the pleasures of the palace. There, in violation of the strict sexual morality and monogamy enjoined upon the Taipings, the Heavenly King kept a virtual harem.

In the meantime, the Eastern King, Yang Hsiu-ch'ing, steadily arrogated greater powers to himself and even aspired to the imperial dignity, before he lost his life in the first of a series of blood-baths which deprived the regime of several top leaders and many of their adherents. Thereafter Hung tended to place his own relatives in key positions, being more concerned for their trustworthiness than their ability. One such relative was Hung Jen-kan, prime minister in the last years of the regime, who had far more acquaintance with Christianity and the West than the other "kings," but who proved unable to effectuate any of his plans for the reorganization of the regime along more Western lines.

One of the great ironies of the Taiping Rebellion was revealed at the time of its final collapse in the summer of 1864. Nanking had been in danger for months when Li Hsiu-ch'eng, an able general whose military successes had not turned his head from a devoted loyalty to Hung, advised abandonment of the capital and escape to the south. The Heavenly King chose to remain, insisting that God would protect and provide for the Taipings. Yet by June of 1864 Hung had himself despaired of his cause, taken poison and died, his body being found later, draped in imperial yellow, in a sewer under the palace. Hung's faithful followers held out another month in the midst of the worst privation and suffering, and when finally overwhelmed by the Manchu forces, gave up their lives in a great slaughter rather than submit. Tseng Kuo-fan, leader of the victorious armies, is authority for the statement that not one surrendered.

There can be no doubt then that an intense, if misguided, religious faith was a crucial element in the Taiping movement, the most distinguishing feature of which was its monotheism. In the past China had not lacked for gods or popular religious movements, nor had the imperial court been without its own cult linking dynastic rule to the will of Heaven. But it was Hung who first proclaimed a belief in one God who was the Father of all, a God who was at once accessible to the prayers of the individual and actively concerned with the governing of the world. In Taiping documents, as will be seen from the selections which follow, this point is particularly stressed: that whereas the old cult of Heaven was a one-family affair, jealously guarded by the ruling house, the True God was the ruler, father and friend of all. His direct accessibility to men, however, proved both a boon and a bane to the Taipings. For if this conception stimulated a genuine piety in many, it also provided a dangerous weapon to a few of their leaders who claimed divine inspiration for their actions and God's sanction for their own ambitions.

Western influence can be clearly seen in some of the practices adopted by the Taipings, such as a calendar with a seven-day week and observance of the sabbath. It may have been responsible in part also for the greater equality accorded to women, the condemnation of polygamy and adultery, and the bans on slavery, foot-binding, gambling, wine, and tobacco. The coincidence, however, of a strait-laced Protestant fundamentalism with a degree of native puritanism among the Chinese peasantry (the latter reflected also in the professedly anti-Christian Communist movement of the mid-twentieth century) makes it difficult to assess precisely the degree of foreign influence.

In its combination of militant monotheism, prophetic inspiration, and drive for power in the name of God, the Taiping movement is perhaps most reminiscent of the rise of Islam in the seventh-century Near East. Where in the latter case, however, cultural traditions were less deeply rooted among the nomadic Arabs who enlisted in Muhammad's cause, even the peasant Chinese who so largely made up the forces of Hung Hsiu-ch'üan were already deeply imbued with ethical and religious traditions rooted in the past. To a considerable extent the Taipings were compelled, in spite of their early hostility to Confucianism, to compromise with many of its customs and values, or, more accurately, unconsciously to accept them without sensing any incompatibility between traditional ethics and the new faith. Such accommodations, nonetheless, proved insufficient to bridge the gap between Taiping ideology and the Chinese tradition, or to equip the revolutionary leadership for the stupendous task of ruling a mature and complex society. In the end it was the defenders of tradition and those schooled in Chinese statecraft who emerged victorious to guide China's destinies for another half-century.

The Book of Heavenly Commandments (T'ien-t'iao shu)

This text, officially promulgated by the Taiping regime in 1852, was probably written several years earlier to serve as a basic statement of the God Worshipers' creed and religious practice when they were first organized. It bespeaks a simple and unpretentious faith, constantly reiterating the hope of Heaven and fear of hell in a manner reminiscent more of the Qur'ān than of the Bible. Much of it is devoted to forms which are to be used in the saying of prayers, grace at meals, etc., and to an explanation of the Ten Commandments. Under the latter we find provisions for segregation of the sexes, and prohibitions against opium smoking and gambling, which reflect a strong puritanical strain in the early Taiping movement.

When a translation of this work by W. H. Medhurst appeared in the English-language *North China Herald* on May 14, 1853, the editor commented: "We cannot help thinking that this is a most extraordinary document, and can see in it little to object against. Two things strike us on reading it carefully through: the one is that with the exception of occasional references to redemption by Christ and apparent extracts from the Lord's Prayer, the ideas seem to be generally taken from the Old Testament, with little or nothing from the New; the other is that it appears to be mainly a compilation drawn up by the rebels themselves, for if a Christian missionary had had anything to do with it, he certainly would not have directed the offering up of animals, wine, tea, and rice even though these offerings were presented to the Great God. As it is, we repeat, it is a most extraordinary production, and were the rebels to act up to everything therein contained, they would be the most gentle and moral set of rebels we ever met with."

The translation given here is adapted and revised from that of Medhurst as emended on the basis of other early editions of the text by members of the Modern Chinese History Project, Far Eastern and Russian Institute, University of Washington, as a part of a documentary history of the Taiping Rebellion, which is soon to be published.

[From Hsiao I-shan, *T'ai-p'ing t'ien-kuo ts'ung-shu*, Series I, ts'e 1, pp. 1a–2b]

Who in this mortal world has not offended against the Heavenly Commandments? If one was not aware of his offense in former times, he can still be excused; now, however, as the Lord God has already issued a gracious proclamation, henceforth whoever knows how to repent of his sins in the presence of the Lord God, not to worship false spirits, not to practice perverse things, and not to transgress the Heavenly Commandments, shall be permitted to ascend to Heaven and to enjoy happiness, and for thousands and myriads of years to enjoy dignity and honor without end. Whoever does not know how to repent of his sins . . . will most certainly be punished by being sent down to hell to suffer bitterness, and for thousands and myriads of years to suffer sorrow and pain without end. Which is gain and which is loss, we ask you to think over. Our brothers and sisters throughout the mortal world, ought not all of you to awaken from your lethargy? If, however, you continue unroused, then are you truly base-born, truly deluded by the devil, and truly is there bliss which you do not know how to enjoy. [1a]

Now, those whose minds have been deluded by the demons always say that only the monarch can worship the Lord God. However, the Lord God is the universal Father of all in the mortal world. Monarchs are his able children, the good his filial children, the commoners his ignorant children, and the violent and oppressive his disobedient children. If you say that monarchs alone can worship the Lord God, we beg to ask you, as for the parents of a family, is it only the eldest son who can be filial and obedient to his parents?

Again it has been falsely said that to worship the Great God is to follow barbarians' ways. They do not know that in the ancient world monarchs and subjects alike all worshiped the Lord God. As for the great Way of worshiping the Lord God, from the very beginning, when the Lord God created in six days Heaven and earth, mountains and seas, man and things, both China and the barbarian nations walked together in the great Way; however, the various barbarian countries of the West have continued to the end in the great Way. China also walked in the great Way, but within the most recent one or two thousand years, China has erroneously followed the devil's path, thus being captured by the demon of hell. Now, therefore, the Lord God, out of compassion for mankind, has extended his capable hand to save the people of the world, deliver them from the devil's grasp, and lead them out to walk again in the original great Way. [1a–b]

A FORM TO BE OBSERVED IN REPENTING SINS

Let the suppliant kneel down in the sight of Heaven and pray to the Lord God to forgive his sins. He may use a written form of prayer, and when the prayer is over, he may either take a basin of water and wash his whole body clean, or he may perform his ablutions in the river, which will be still better. After repenting his sins, let him morning and evening worship the Lord God, beseeching that the Lord God look after him, and grant him His Holy Spirit to transform his heart. When taking his meals, he should give thanks to God, and every seventh day worship and praise God for His grace and virtue. Let him also constantly obey the ten Heavenly Commandments. Do not on any account let him wor-

ship all the false spirits that are in the world, still less let him do any
of the corrupt things of the world. In this manner, the people may become the sons and daughters of the Lord God. While in the world the
Lord God will look after them, and after ascending to Heaven the Lord
God will graciously love them, and in high Heaven they will eternally
enjoy bliss. [2a–b]

THE TEN HEAVENLY COMMANDMENTS

1. Honor and worship the Lord God. . . .[1]
2. Do not worship false gods. . . .
3. Do not take the name of the Lord God in vain. . . .
4. On the seventh day, worship and praise the Lord God for his
grace. . . .
5. Be filial and obedient to thy Father and Mother. . . .
6. Do not kill or injure men. . . .
7. Do not indulge in wickedness and lewdness.

In the world there are many men, all brothers; in the world there
are many women, all sisters. For the sons and daughters of Heaven, the
men have men's quarters and the women have women's quarters; they are
not allowed to intermix. Men or women who commit adultery or who
are licentious are considered monsters; this is the greatest possible transgression of the Heavenly Commandments. The casting of amorous
glances, the harboring of lustful imaginings about others, the smoking
of opium, and the singing of libidinous songs are all offenses against
the Heavenly Commandment.

8. Do not steal or rob.

Poverty and riches are granted by the Lord God, and whosoever
steals or plunders the property of others, transgresses the Heavenly Commandment.

9. Do not tell [or spread] falsehoods.

All those who speak wildly, falsely, or treacherously, and those who
use coarse and vile language trangress against the Heavenly Commandment.

10. Do not think covetous thoughts.

When a man looks upon the beauty of another's wife or daughter

---

[1] The commentary of the Taiping expositor has been omitted except for the last
four commandments.

and then covets that man's wife or daughter; when a man looks upon the richness of another man's possessions and then covets that man's possessions; or when a man engages in gambling and buys lottery tickets and bets on names,[2] all these are transgressions of the Heavenly Commandment. [6b–8a]

A Primer in Verse (Yu-hsüeh shih)

This official text, first published in 1851, offers simple and concise formulations—easily put to memory—of basic religious and moral principles which the Taiping leaders wished to inculcate in their followers. Although opposed to Confucianism in so far as it was identified with the established regime or took on the appearance of a religious cult, the Taipings unconsciously accepted much that is readily recognizable as Confucian in social and political ethics.

[From Hsiao I-shan, *T'ai-p'ing t'ien-kuo ts'ung-shu*, Series I, t'se 4, pp. 1a–5b, 14a-b]

PRAISING GOD

The Lord God-on-High, the divine Being,
Is respectfully worshiped in all countries.
Men and women throughout the world,
Pay homage to Him morning and evening.
All that we see, above and below,
Basks in the Lord's favor.
In the beginning it took only six days
For the creation of all things to be completed.

Is there anyone, circumcised or uncircumcised,
Not created by God?
Give thanks [to Him] for the heavenly favor
That you may obtain everlasting glory.

PRAISING JESUS CHRIST

Jesus was a Crown Prince,
Whom God sent to earth in ancient times.

---

[2] It was a common practice of the time, especially in Kwangtung, to bet on who would succeed in the state examinations. Gambling clubs were established for this purpose. The Kwangtung government first fined such gambling and later collected a gambling tax from the clubs.

He sacrificed His life for the sins of men,
Being the first to offer meritorious service.

It was hard to bear the Cross;
Grieving clouds darkened the sun.
The noble Prince from Heaven,
Died for you—men and women.

Having returned to Heaven after His resurrection,
In His glory, He holds all power.
Upon Him we are to rely—
Be saved and enter Paradise!

PRAISING PARENTS

[Just as] the storing up of grain provides against starvation,
[So] the raising up of children provides against old age.
He who is filial to his parents will have filial sons.
Thus, mysteriously, is recompense made.

You should ask yourself,
How you were able to grow up.[3]
Respect the teaching of the Fifth Heavenly Commandment;
Honor and wealth will shower down on you from the Heavenly Court.

THE IMPERIAL COURT

The imperial court is an awesome place.
With fear and trembling heed the imperial authority as if it reached
  into your very presence.
The power of life and death belongs to the Son-of-Heaven.
Among the officials none should oppose Him.

THE WAY OF A KING

If one man, aloft, upholds the Right,
The myriad states all enjoy repose.[4]
Let the king alone hold power;
And all slander and depravity will disappear forever.

[3] Through the loving care of your parents.
[4] These two lines are adapted from the opening passage of the *Book of Changes*.

THE WAY OF A SUBJECT

The more virtuous the Master, the more honest will be His subjects.
Wise kings produce good officials.
I [Yin] and [Duke] Chou have set the example [for ministers].
Upholding justice, they maintained discipline at court.

THE WAY OF THE FAMILY

> Kinsfolk within the household—
> Be cheerful and happy!
> Be harmonious and united as one body,
> Blessings will shower down upon you from Heaven.

There follow similar maxims for eleven other family relationships from mother,
son, etc., to older and younger sister-in-law, as well as injunctions with regard
to sexual chastity and fidelity, and disciplining of the senses. For the most part
these are of a traditional Chinese character, and largely Confucian, like the
verses above. Finally the primer concludes with the following:

PARADISE

> Whether to be noble or mean is for you to choose.
> To be a real man you must make an effort to improve yourself.
> Follow the teaching of the Ten Commandments;
> You will enjoy the blessings of Paradise.

The Taiping Economic Program

The following selection is taken from *The Land System of the Heavenly
Kingdom* (*T'ien-ch'ao t'ien-mu chih-tu*), which was included in the list of
official Taiping publications promulgated in 1853. Its precise authorship is
uncertain, and there is no evidence of a serious attempt having been made to
put this system into effect in Taiping-controlled areas. Nevertheless, as a statement of Taiping aims the document carried with it all the weight of Hung
Hsiu-ch'üan's authority and that of the Eastern King, Yang Hsiu-ch'ing, then
at the height of his power. It reflects one of the chief appeals which the movement made to the Chinese peasantry.

The plan set forth here amounts to a blueprint for the total organization
of society, and especially of its human resources. If its initial concern is with
the land problem, as the title indicates, it quickly moves on to other spheres
of human activity and brings them under a single pattern of control. The

basic organization is military in nature, reminiscent of the farmer-soldier militia of earlier dynasties. In its economic egalitarianism, totalitarian communism, authoritarian hierarchy and messianic zeal, this Taiping manifesto seems to foreshadow the Chinese Communist movement of the twentieth century, while at the same time it echoes reformers and rebels in the past. Most typically it recalls the fondness of earlier Chinese thinkers for what might be described as the "completely-designed" society—their vision of a neat symmetrical system embodying the supreme values of Chinese thought: order, balance, and harmony.

Nevertheless, we can appreciate how conservative Confucianists would have recoiled at the thought of so much economic regimentation. Tseng Kuo-fan, their great leader in the struggle against the Taipings, commented: "The farmer cannot till his own land and [simply] pay taxes on it; the land is all considered to be the land of the Heavenly King [and all produce goes directly to the communal treasury]. The merchant cannot engage in trade for himself and profit thereby; all goods are considered to be the goods of the Heavenly King."

The organizational note is struck at the outset with an explanation of the system of army districts and military administration (omitted here). We reproduce below only the basic economic program.

[From Hsiao I-shan, T'ai-p'ing t'ien-kuo ts'ung-shu, Series I, t'se 4, pp. 1a–3a]

All officials who have rendered meritorious service are to receive hereditary stipends from the court. For the later adherents to the Taiping cause, every family in each military district (*chün*) is to provide one man to serve as a militia man. During an emergency they are to fight under the command of their officers to destroy the enemy and to suppress bandits. In peacetime they are to engage in agriculture under the direction of their officers, tilling the land and providing support for their superiors.

All land [in the country] is to be classified into nine grades. Land that produces 1,200 catties of grain per *mu* during the two harvest seasons of the year is to be classified as A-A Land. That which produces 1,100 per *mu* during the same periods is to be classified as A-B Land; that which produces 1,000 catties is to be classified as A-C Land, 900 catties as B-A Land, 800 as B-B Land, 700 as B-C Land, 600 as C-A Land, 500 as C-B Land, and 400 as C-C Land.[5]

---

[5] This classification of the land into nine grades follows the form found in the "Tribute of Yü" section of the *Book of History;* the general method of land allocation follows the principle set forth in the *Rites of Chou,* Ti kuan hsia (SPTK ed., 4:24).

[For the purposes of land distribution], one *mu* of A-A Land is equal to 1.1 *mu* of A-B Land, 1.2 *mu* of A-C Land, 1.35 *mu* of B-A Land, 1.5 *mu* of B-B Land, 1.75 *mu* of B-C Land, 2 *mu* of C-A Land, 2.4 *mu* of C-B Land, or 3 *mu* of the C-C Land.

The distribution of all land is to be based on the number of persons in each family, regardless of sex. A large family is entitled to more land, a small one to less. The land distributed should not be all of one grade, but mixed. Thus for a family of six, for instance, three are to have fertile land and three barren land—half and half of each.

All the land in the country is to be cultivated by the whole population together. If there is an insufficiency [of land] in this place, move some of the people to another place. If there is an insufficiency in another place, move them to this one. All lands in the country are also to be mutually supporting with respect to abundance and scarcity. If this place has a drought, then draw upon the abundant harvest elsewhere in order to relieve the distress here. If there is a drought there, draw upon the abundant harvest here in order to relieve the distress there. Thus all the people of the country may enjoy the great blessings of the Heavenly Father, Supreme Ruler, and Lord God-on-High. The land is for all to till, the food for all to eat, the clothes for all to wear, and money for all to spend. Inequality shall exist nowhere; none shall suffer from hunger or cold.

Every person sixteen or over, whether male or female, is entitled to a share of land; those fifteen or under should receive half the share of an adult. For instance, if a person of sixteen is given a *mu* of land in the A-A class, a person under that age can only receive half of that amount, namely, 0.50 *mu* of land of the same class. Or if a person sixteen or over is given 3 *mu* of C-C land, then a person fifteen or under would receive half of that, or 1.5 *mu* of C-C land.

Mulberry trees are to be planted along the walls [of villages] throughout the country. All women are required to grow silkworms, to do weaving, and to make clothes. Every family of the country is required to raise five hens and two hogs, in keeping with the proper breeding seasons.[6]

During the harvest season, the Group Officer[7] should direct [the grain collection by] the sergeants. Deducting the amount needed to feed the twenty-five families until next harvest season, he should collect the rest of the produce for storage in state granaries. The same method of collec-

[6] A paraphrase of *Mencius*, I A, 7.
[7] The *liang ssu-ma*, official in charge of each 25-family group.

tion is applicable to other kinds of products, such as barley, beans, ramie fiber, cotton clothes, silk, domestic animals, silver and copper cash, etc., for all people under Heaven are of one family belonging to the Heavenly Father, the Supreme Ruler, the Lord God-on-High. Nobody should keep private property. All things should be presented to the Supreme Ruler, so that He will be enabled to make use of them and distribute them equally to all members of his great world-family. Thus all will be sufficiently fed and clothed. That is the will of the Heavenly Father, the Supreme Ruler, the Lord God-on-High, who has dispatched the True Ruler of Great Peace to save the men of the world.

The Group Officer must keep a record of the amount of grain and cash he has collected and report them to the Treasurers and Receiving and Disbursing Tellers. A state treasury and a church are to be established among every twenty-five families, under the direct administration of the Group Officer. All expenditures of the twenty-five families for weddings, births, or other festival occasions are to be paid for out of the state treasury. But there is to be a fixed limit; not a penny is to be spent beyond that. For each festival occasion, such as a wedding or the birth of a child, a family is to be allowed 1,000 copper cash and 100 catties of grain, so that there will be a uniform rule throughout the country. In sum, nothing should be wasted, in order that there will be provision against any exigency of war or drought. Thus, throughout the land in the contracting of marriages, wealth need be no consideration.

In the twenty-five family units pottery-making, metal-working, carpentry, masonry and other such skilled work should be performed by the sergeants and militiamen in the off-seasons from farming and military service.

In conducting the different kinds of festival ceremonies for the twenty-five families under his administration, the Group Officer should hold religious services to pray to the Heavenly Father, the Supreme Ruler, and Lord God-on-High. All the bad customs of the past must be completely abolished.

The Principles of the Heavenly Nature (T'ien-ch'ing tao-li shu)

This official work, dated 1854, was written after the Taipings had established their capital at Nanking and the first flush of victory gave way to a seeming let-down in morale, discipline, and zeal for the cause. It served to restate the religious creed of the Taipings and emphasize those qualities—self-sacrifice, loyalty, and solidarity—which had contributed to their amazing successes. The appeal throughout is to a dedicated and crusading military elite.

Another important purpose of the book was to enhance and consolidate the position of the Taiping leadership, especially that of the Eastern King, Yang Hsiu-ch'ing, who was virtual prime minister of the regime and the one who inspired the writing of this document. We see here in a strange new garb the old conception of the ruler as commissioned with divine powers to unite the world and establish peace. Both Hung and Yang are thus represented as in some degree sharing the role of Jesus Christ as saviors of the world. Since it would not have done for any of the "kings" to engage openly in such self-glorification, nominal authorship is attributed to the "marquises" and "chancellors" who constituted the next highest ranks in the Taiping hierarchy.

Extant editions of the text appear to date from about 1858, by which time rivalries and mistrust had split the leadership, Yang had been assassinated, and his assassin, the Northern King, murdered by Hung. Though there are many direct and indirect evidences of dissension, the text has not been amended or adjusted to these later developments except to strip the Northern King of his rank.

The translation here has been adapted from that of C. T. Hu for the documentary history of the Taiping Rebellion being prepared by the Modern Chinese History Project of the Far Eastern and Russian Institute, University of Washington.

[From Hsiao, *T'ai-p'ing t'ien-kuo ts'ung-shu,* ts'e 5, pp. 1–37]

With regard to human life, reverence for Heaven and support of the Sovereign begin with loyalty and uprightness; to cast off the devil's garb and become true men—this must come about through an awakening. Now, the Heavenly Father and the Heavenly Elder Brother have displayed the heavenly favor and specially commanded our Heavenly King to descend into the world and be the true Taiping sovereign of the ten thousand states of the world; they have also sent the Eastern King to assist in court policy, to save the starving, to redeem the sick, and, together with the Western and Northern Kings, [Wei] Ch'ang-hui,[8] and the Assistant King, to take part in the prosperous rule and assist in the grand design. As a result, the mortal world witnesses the blessings of resurrection, and our bright future is the symbol of renewal. [1a–b]

We marquises and chancellors hold that our brothers and sisters have been blessed by the Heavenly Father and the Heavenly Elder Brother,

[8] Former King of the North who, having assassinated the Eastern King and in turn been murdered by Hung, was no longer referred to by his title when this edition was published.

who saved the ensnared and drowning and awakened the deluded; they have cast off worldly sentiments and now follow the true Way. They cross mountains and wade rivers, not even ten thousand *li* being too far for them to come, to uphold together the true Sovereign. Armed and bearing shield and spear, they carry righteous banners that rise colorfully. Husband and wife, men and women, express common indignation and lead the advance. It can be said that they are determined to uphold Heaven and to requite the nation with loyalty. [2a–b]

You younger brothers and sisters have now experienced the heavenly days of Great Peace (Taiping), and have basked in the glory of the Heavenly Father, the Supreme Ruler and Lord God-on-High. You must be aware of the grace and virtue of the Heavenly Father, the Supreme Ruler and Lord God-on-High, and fully recognize that the Heavenly Father, the Supreme Ruler and Lord God-on-High, is alone the one true God. Aside from the Heavenly Father, the Supreme Ruler and Lord God-on-High, there is no other god. Moreover, there is nothing which can usurp the merits of the Heavenly Father, the Supreme Ruler and Lord God-on-High. In the ten thousand nations of the world everyone is given life, nourished, protected, and blessed by the Heavenly Father, the Supreme Ruler and Lord God-on-High. Thus the Heavenly Father, the Supreme Ruler and Lord God-on-High, is the universal father of man in all the ten thousand nations of the world. There is no man who should not be grateful, there is no man who should not reverently worship Him. Have you not seen the Heavenly King's "Ode on the Origin of Virtue and the Saving of the World," which reads: "The true God who created Heaven and earth is none but God; all, whether noble or mean, must worship Him piously"? This is precisely our meaning! [4a–5a]

There follow citations from the Confucian Classics referring to the Lord-on-High (*Shang-ti*) which are taken here as showing that God was known to and worshiped by the ancient Chinese. Subsequently, however, various forms of idolatry arose.

However, worldly customs daily degenerated. There were even those who likened themselves to rulers, and, being deluded in heart and nature, arrogant yet at fault, and falsely self-exalted, forbade the prime minister and those below to sacrifice to Heaven. Then [these men] competed in establishing false gods and worshiping them, thus opening up the ways of the devilish demons. The people of the world all followed in like fashion, and this became firmly fixed in their minds. Thereupon, after a considerable time, they did not know their own errors. Hence the Heavenly Father, the Lord God, in view of mortal man's serious crime of disobedience, at his first anger, sent down forty days and forty nights of heavy rain, the vast waters spreading in all directions and drowning mortal man. Only Noah and his family had unceasingly worshiped the Heavenly Father, the Supreme Ruler and Lord God-on-High; therefore, relying on the heavenly grace, they were fortunate and they alone were preserved. In this, the first instance of the Heavenly Father's great anger, was the great proof of his great powers displayed.

After the Flood, the devilish king of Egypt, whose ambition was mediocrity and who was possessed by the demons, envied the Israelites in their worship of God and bitterly persecuted them. Therefore, the Heavenly Father in his great anger led the Israelites out of Egypt. In this, the second instance of the Heavenly Father's great anger, was the great proof of his great powers displayed.

However, the rulers and people of that time still had not completely forgotten the heavenly grace. But since the emergence of Taoism in the Ch'in [dynasty] and the welcoming of Buddhism in the Han [dynasty], the delusion of man by the demons has day by day increased, and all men have forgotten the grace and virtue of the Heavenly Father. The Heavenly Father's merits were falsely recognized as the merits of demons. Therefore, the Heavenly Father, observing this from above, saw that the people of the mortal world followed the demons and were being transformed into demons; strange and peculiar, they were no longer men. The Heavenly Father once again became greatly angered; yet if he were to annihilate them completely, he could not bear it in his heart; if he were to tolerate them, it would not be consonant with righteousness. At that time, the elder son of the Heavenly Father, the Heavenly Elder Brother Jesus, shouldered the great burden and willingly offered to sacrifice his life to redeem the sins of the men of the world. The Heavenly Father, the Supreme Ruler and Lord God-on-High, sincere in his pity for the world and profound in his love for man, spared not his eldest son, but sent him down to be born in Judea, and to redeem our sins in order to propagate the true Way. At the time of his redemption of our sins, he was falsely accused and nailed upon the cross, so that mortal man could rely upon his precious blood and be cleansed of all sin. Thereby did he make complete the grace of the Heavenly Father, who had sent him down to be sacrificed for the world. [6a–7a]

Let us ask your elder and younger brothers: formerly the people sacrificed only to the demons; they worshiped the demons and appealed to the demons only because they desired the demons to protect them. Yet how could they think that the demons could really protect them? Let us consider one example. During a drought, no man failed to worship the demons and to pray for rain. Certainly they did not realize that this is all within the power of the Heavenly Father; when He decrees a drought, a drought follows; when He decrees rain, rain follows. If the Heavenly Father did not decree sweet rain, then even though they worshiped the demons of the mortal world, one and all, still the drought would continue as before. A popular saying has it: "If beating a drum can bring rain, then mountain peaks can be opened to cultivation; [9] if the burning of incense can bring protection, then a smoking kiln can satisfy opium smokers; if a vegetarian diet can bring immortality, then bulls can ascend to heaven; if taking opium can satiate hunger, then a fart can fertilize a field." Another popular saying goes: "The bean curd is only water, the king of hell is only a demon." In view of this, it can be seen that the demons are not responsive and are unable to protect men. The people pray for rain, yet they cannot send down rain. To worship them is of no avail. However, the men of the world sank even deeper, not knowing how to awaken themselves. Therefore, the Heavenly Father again became angry.

In the ting-yu year [1837], our Heavenly Father displayed the heavenly grace and dispatched angels to summon the Heavenly King up to Heaven. There He clearly pointed out the demons' perversities and their deluding of the world. He also invested the Heavenly King with a seal and a sword; He ordered the Savior, the Heavenly Elder Brother, Jesus, to take command of the heavenly soldiers and heavenly generals and to aid the Heavenly King, and to attack and conquer from Heaven earthward, layer by layer, the innumerable demons. After their victory they returned to Heaven and the Heavenly Father, greatly pleased, sent

[9] That is, it is as unlikely that beating a drum could bring rain as that mountain peaks could be cultivated.

the Heavenly King down upon the earth to become the true Taiping
Sovereign of the ten thousand nations of the world, and to save the people of the world. He also bade him not to be fearful and to effect these
matters courageously, for whenever difficulties appeared, the Heavenly
Father would assume direction and the Heavenly Elder Brother would
shoulder the burden. [8a–9a]

Several instances are then given of the way in which God's power was manifested in the triumphant campaigns of the Taiping forces, and of how His will
was made known to them. The account concludes with these episodes:

In the *jen-tzu* year [1852], at Yung-an-chou, our food supplies were almost exhausted, nor was there even any red powder [gunpowder]. The
demons, several hundred thousand in number, rank upon rank, encircled the city from all directions. There was no avenue of escape. By
this time the devilish demons knew of our situation and became unusu-
ally fierce, all believing their plan would succeed. In the third month,
the Heavenly Father greatly displayed his powers and ordered us younger
brothers and sisters, one and all, to uphold the true Sovereign and attack
Kuei-lin. We then moved the camps and broke through the encirclement; and, because the Heavenly Father had changed our hearts, we
one and all with utmost energy and disregard for our persons struck
through the iron passes and copper barriers, killing innumerable devilish demons, and directly arrived at the Kwangsi provincial capital. Thereupon Kuei-lin was encircled. Later, because the people of the city came
out and spoke to the Eastern King, reporting that the city granaries were
empty and that provisions were deficient, the Eastern King, seeing that
their strength was exhausted, showed great mercy and immediately ordered a temporary lifting of the siege until another good plan of attack
could be contrived.

You all should know of the Heavenly Father's power, his omniscience,
omnipotence, and omnipresence. Why was it that the one city of Kuei-
lin alone could not be attacked and secured? This was because our Heavenly Father secretly made it so—something not easily understood by
man.

Thereafter, from Kuei-lin we moved on to capture Hsing-an, Ch'üan-
chou, Tao-chou, Ch'en-chou, and other moated cities. Wherever the
Heavenly Army went, battles were won and objectives taken; wherever

it went, the enemy scattered, our strength being as [irresistible as] a knife splitting bamboo. We moved from Ch'en-chou to Ch'ang-sha; the latter city was attacked several times, and again we rushed by the city; this also was the result of the Heavenly Father's having secretly willed it so. If the army had entered Ch'ang-sha and had been stationed there long, then the boatmen at I-yang and other places along the river, being unable to avoid the trickery and intimidation of the demons, would have had to flee to distant localities. How then could we have obtained boats for a million brave soldiers, that we might float downstream to capture Wu-ch'ang? From this we can see that our Heavenly Father's power secretly made it so.

From Wu-ch'ang to Chin-ling [Nanking] the land extends as far as a thousand *li;* how strategic and important are the passes and river crossings, and how strong and firm are the cities and moats! To attack and capture the cities seemed difficult; even if victory could have been secured, it appeared that it would take a very long time. Yet in not more than one month's time, we had followed the stream eastward from Wu-ch'ang, passing Kiangsi, crossing Anhwei, and pushing directly up to Chin-ling, without the least resistance. After reaching this provincial capital, we found the height and thickness of the city walls and the vastness of the land to be indeed twice that of other provincial cities; to attack it seemed far more difficult. Who would have known that within ten days one single effort would bring success? Chin-ling was captured with our hands hanging at our sides. Had it not been for our Heavenly Father's power, how could things have been so quick and easy? From this we can again see the Heavenly Father's power to predetermine things. [12b–14a]

There follow accounts of the individual Taiping leaders showing how each triumphed over adversities and suffered great hardships in order to advance the cause.

Even the Eastern King in his holiness and the several Kings in their eminence had to undergo cleansing and polishing and repeatedly demonstrate great fortitude before they could enjoy true happiness. How much more must we elder and younger brothers preserve our fortitude in order that we may seek abundant blessings. Do we not see the Heavenly King's edict which says: "All things are predetermined by the Heavenly Father and the Heavenly Elder Brother; the ten thousand hardships are all the Heavenly Father's and Heavenly Elder Brother's means of testing our hearts; thus each of us must be true-hearted, firm and patient; we must cleave to the Heavenly Father and the Heavenly Elder Brother"? The Heavenly King has also said: "How can it be easy to ascend to Heaven? The first prerequisite is patience of mind and will. You will certainly ascend to Heaven if you are resolute at heart." [17a–b]

Recollecting the past, from the righteous uprising in Chin-t'ien to the capture of Chin-ling, we have received great mercy from our Heavenly Father and Heavenly Elder Brother; we have established our Heavenly Capital and in a few years we have been able to enjoy the great happiness of our Heavenly Father. All this has been due to the work of our Heavenly Father and our Heavenly Elder Brother, who alone can bring such speedy results. Hence, if, with additional efforts toward improvement and perfection, we, with united hearts, combine our strength for the immediate extermination of the demons, our Heavenly Father will display his great powers and instantaneously the seas and lands will be cleared and the hills and rivers united under one command. Then our younger brothers and sisters will be reunited with their families, and blood relations will again be together. How fortunate that will be! [19a–b]

There follows a long section dealing with disobedient and traitorous officers who serve as object lessons of the futility of deserting or betraying the Taiping cause. It is shown how God, who knows and sees all, revealed their wicked designs to the Taiping leaders. Thus their cowardice and self-seeking brought them only the most severe punishment.

We brothers and sisters, enjoying today the greatest mercy of our Heavenly Father, have become as one family and are able to enjoy true blessings; each of us must always be thankful. Speaking in terms of our ordinary human feelings, it is true that each has his own parents and there must be a distinction in family names; it is also true that as each has his own household, there must be a distinction between this boundary and that boundary. Yet we must know that the ten thousand names derive from the one name, and the one name from one ancestor. Thus our origins are not different. Since our Heavenly Father gave us birth and nourishment, we are of one form though of separate bodies, and we breathe the same air though in different places. This is why we say: "All are brothers within the four seas." [10] Now, basking in the profound mercy of Heaven, we are of one family. Brothers and sisters are all of the same parentage; as all are born of one Spiritual Father, why should there be the distinctions of "you and I," or "others and ourselves"? When there is clothing, let all wear it; when there is food, let all eat of it. When someone is ill, others should ask a doctor to treat him and take care of his medicine. We must treat parentless boys and girls and persons of advanced age with more care, bathing them and washing and changing their clothes. Thus we will not lose the idea of sharing joys and sorrows, as well as mutual concern over pain and illness. Safety for the old, sympathy for the young, and compassion for the orphaned, all emerge from the Eastern King's understanding of our Heavenly Father's love for the living and from the Heavenly King's treating all as brothers and fellow beings. [27b–28b]

As for [maintaining] our brothers' peace in the camps, everyone must be kind, industrious, and careful. When the skies are clear the soldiers should be drilled, and when it rains the heavenly books should be read, clearly expounded, and mutually discussed, so that everybody will know the nature of Heaven and forever abide by the true Way. If the demons advance, at the first beat of the signal drums, everyone must hurriedly arm himself with gun, sword, or spear, and hasten to the palace to receive orders. In charging forward, each must strive to be in the front, fearing to be left behind, and none must shirk responsibilities. Thus will we be of one virtue and of one heart. Even if there are a million demons, they will not be hard to exterminate instantly. [28b–29a]

We brothers, our minds having been awakened by our Heavenly Father, joined the camp in the earlier days to support our Sovereign, many bringing parents, wives, uncles, brothers, and whole families. It is a matter of course that we should attend to our parents and look after our wives and children, but when one first creates a new rule, the state must come first and the family last, public interests first and private interests last. Moreover, as it is advisable to avoid suspicion [of improper conduct] between the inner [female] and the outer [male] and to distinguish between male and female, so men must have male quarters and women must have female quarters; only thus can we be dignified and avoid

[10] *Analects*, XII, 5.

confusion. There must be no common mixing of the male and female groups, which would cause debauchery and violation of Heaven's commandments. Although to pay respects to parents and to visit wives and children occasionally are in keeping with human nature and not prohibited, yet it is only proper to converse before the door, stand a few steps apart and speak in a loud voice; one must not enter the sisters' camp or permit the mixing of men and women. Only thus, by complying with rules and commands, can we become sons and daughters of Heaven. [29a–30a]

At the present time, the remaining demons have not yet been completely exterminated and the time for the reunion of families has not yet arrived. We younger brothers and sisters must be firm and patient to the end, and with united strength and a single heart we must uphold God's principles and wipe out the demons immediately. With peace and unity achieved, then our Heavenly Father, displaying his mercy, will reward us according to our merits. Wealth, nobility, and renown will then enable us brothers to celebrate the reunion of our families and enjoy the harmonious relations of husband and wife. Oh, how wonderful that will be! The task of a thousand times ten thousand years also lies in this; the happiness and emoluments of a thousand times ten thousand years also lie in this; we certainly must not abandon it in one day. [37b–38a]

CHAPTER XXVI

REFORM AND REACTION UNDER THE MANCHUS

趙啟澤　　為有康　　同嗣疆

The defeat of the Taipings was only one of the more hopeful signs for the Manchus in the early 1860s, after two decades of defeat and near-disaster for the dynasty. The foreign occupation of Peking in 1860 had been followed by a reorganization of leadership at court, with stronger and more flexible men rallying forces loyal to the dynasty and working toward better relations with the foreign powers. The new diplomatic missions established in the capital and foreign concessions in treaty ports up and down the coast, though forced upon the court originally, had now made it both necessary and possible for the Chinese to come into closer contact with Westerners—contacts which slowly and imperceptibly widened their horizons on the world. In the provinces able commanders like Tseng Kuo-fan, Tso Tsung-t'ang, and Li Hung-chang, who had shown great personal resourcefulness and determination in suppressing the rebels and had even demonstrated a readiness to adopt Western guns and naval vessels for use against the Taipings, continued individually to promote modernization projects which would strengthen their military positions and enhance the basis of their own regional power.

If, to Western observers, these developments suggested some hope for China's future, to the Chinese there were other grounds for encouragement—enough to justify calling this period a "revival" or "restoration" in the life of the nation and the ruling dynasty. In foreign relations, the Chinese could at most be gratified by a respite from the constant pressure of the Western powers; a widening of foreign influence, certainly, was nothing to congratulate themselves upon. In internal affairs, however, they could observe with satisfaction the restoring of peace and stability after several major revolts (besides the Taipings, the Nien rebellion

in Anhwei and Shantung, 1853–1868, and the Muslim rebellions in the
southwest, 1855–1873, and northwestern provinces, 1862–1877); so too
a gradual improvement in local administration, and steps taken to re-
habilitate the economy along more or less traditional lines—the encouragement of agriculture, land reclamation and development, irrigation, flood
control, tax reform, etc. The genuine effectiveness of such time-honored
measures can be appreciated in terms of their contribution to the traditional agrarian economy (upon which, obviously, so many millions of
Chinese depended for their daily life), even if such methods fell far
short of meeting the economic challenge of the West.

To conservative Confucianists there was reassurance in all this, not
only that age-old methods and institutions seemed to stand the test of
these times, but that men of ability and character had appeared who
could make them effective. It was leadership, rather than the techniques
or institutions themselves, in which the Confucianist placed hope. It
was the "gentleman," pursuing virtue and learning rather than power
and profit, who would save China. From such a point of view no more
basic or radical a change could take place than that which transformed
the people inwardly and united them in support of worthy rulers. To
talk of drastic changes in social or political institutions was almost un-
thinkable, and certainly uncalled for.

On this fundamental point there was virtually unanimous agreement,
even among those who felt that the danger from the West prompted
fundamental re-examination and reform. They might believe it necessary
to adopt Western guns and ships—even to master the languages, the
knowledge, the techniques required for the production and use of these
weapons—but such measures would be indispensably linked to a regeneration of the national life, a reassertion of traditional values in government,
a renewed concern for the livelihood of the people, and a kind of moral
rearmament based on self-cultivation and tightened social discipline. A
re-examination in these terms tended, therefore, to focus on two types
of weakness: military inferiority to the West, which called for the employment of new methods, and moral inadequacy with respect to traditional ideals, which called for self-criticism and an intensified effort to
uphold old standards.

SELF-STRENGTHENING AND
THE THEME OF UTILITY

Reform along these lines was most strikingly exemplified in the so-called "Self-strengthening" movement. Its immediate objective was a build-up in military power; its ultimate aim was to preserve and strengthen the traditional way of life. In the following selections are presented the views of men prominently identified as exponents of reform on this basis: namely, that the adoption of Western arms could be justified on grounds of utility and practicality, as a means of defending China and preserving Chinese civilization.

FENG KUEI-FEN
On the Manufacture of Foreign Weapons

Feng Kuei-fen (1809–1874), a classicist, teacher and official, came to recognize the need for modernization and the importance of scientific studies when forced to take refuge in Shanghai from the Taipings and brought into contact with Westerners defending the city. Later as an adviser to some of the leading statesmen of his time, Feng demonstrated an acute grasp of both state and foreign affairs. His essays advocating a wide variety of reforms were highly regarded by some leaders and became increasingly influential toward the end of the century. It was at his suggestion that a school of Western languages and sciences was established in Shanghai in 1863.

Feng had few illusions regarding the ease with which China might undertake reform. He appreciated the difficulty of adopting weapons which presupposed a considerable scientific knowledge and technological development. Even more he recognized the disturbing fact that Western superiority lay not in arms alone but also in leadership. In his eyes, however, the qualities of character and mind displayed by Westerners were simply those long recognized as essential to leadership within the Chinese tradition. The foreigners' example might be edifying, and indeed a reproach to the deplorable state of Chinese public life, but it was not a lesson in the sense that China had anything new to learn from the West. The lesson was simply that she had more to make of her own learning.

Such is the two-pronged attack by Feng on Chinese complacency, as expressed in these excerpts from his book of essays, *Protests from the Study of Chiao-pin* (1861). Note again that when a Confucian reformer seeks to make changes, he must come to grips with the civil service system, which has so pervasive an influence on the Chinese mentality.

[From *Chiao-pin lu k'ang-i, Chih yang-ch'i i,* pp. 58b–63a]

According to a general geography compiled by an Englishman, the territory of China is eight times that of Russia, ten times that of the United States, one hundred times that of France, and two hundred times that of Great Britain. . . . Yet we are shamefully humiliated by the four nations, not because our climate, soil, or resources are inferior to theirs, but because our people are inferior. . . . Now, our inferiority is not something allotted us by Heaven, but is rather due to ourselves. If it were allotted us by Heaven, it would be a shame but not something we could do anything about. Since the inferiority is due to ourselves, it is a still greater shame, but something we can do something about. And if we feel ashamed, there is nothing better than self-strengthening. . . .

Why are the Western nations small and yet strong? Why are we large and yet weak? We must search for the means to become their equal, and that depends solely upon human effort. With regard to the present situation, several observations may be made: in not wasting human talents, we are inferior to the barbarians; in not wasting natural resources, we are inferior to the barbarians; in allowing no barrier to come between the ruler and the people, we are inferior to the barbarians; and in the matching of words with deeds, we are also inferior to the barbarians. The remedy for these four points is to seek the causes in ourselves. They can be changed at once if only the emperor would set us in the right direction. There is no need to learn from the barbarians in these matters. [58b–59a]

We have only one thing to learn from the barbarians, and that is strong ships and effective guns. . . . Funds should be allotted to establish a shipyard and arsenal in each trading port. A few barbarians should be employed, and Chinese who are good in using their minds should be selected to receive instruction so that in turn they may teach many craftsmen. When a piece of work is finished and is as good as that made by the barbarians, the makers should be rewarded with an official *chü-jen* degree, and be permitted to participate in the metropolitan examinations on the same basis as other scholars. Those whose products are of superior quality should be rewarded with the *chin-shih* degree [ordinarily conferred in the metropolitan examinations], and be permitted to participate in the palace examinations like others. The workers should be paid double so that they will not quit their jobs.

Our nation's emphasis on civil service examinations has sunk deep into people's minds for a long time. Intelligent and brilliant scholars have exhausted their time and energy in such useless things as the stereotyped examination essays, examination papers, and formal calligraphy. . . . We should now order one-half of them to apply themselves to the manufacturing of instruments and weapons and to the promotion of physical studies. . . . The intelligence and ingenuity of the Chinese are certainly superior to those of the various barbarians; it is only that hitherto we have not made use of them. When the government above takes delight in something, the people below will pursue it further: their response will be like an echo carried by the wind. There ought to be some people of extraordinary intelligence who can have new ideas and improve on Western methods. At first they may take the foreigners as their teachers and models; then they may come to the same level and be their equals; finally they may move ahead and surpass them. Herein lies the way to self-strengthening. [60a–61a]

It may be argued: "Kuan Chung repeled the barbarians and Confucius acclaimed his virtue; the state of Chu adopted barbarian ways and [Confucius in] the *Spring and Autumn Annals* condemned them. Is not what you are proposing contrary to the Way of the sages?" No, it is not. When we speak of repeling the barbarians, we must have the actual means to repel them, and not just empty bravado. If we live in the present day and speak of repeling the barbarians, we should ask with what instruments we are to repel them. . . . [The answer is that] we should use the instruments of the barbarians, but not adopt the ways of the barbarians. We should use them so that we can repel them.

Some have asked why we should not just purchase the ships and man them with [foreign] hirelings, but the answer is that this will not do. If we can manufacture, repair, and use them, then they are our weapons. If we cannot manufacture, repair, or use them, then they are still the weapons of others. . . . In the end the way to avoid trouble is to manufacture, repair, and use weapons by ourselves. Only thus can we pacify the empire; only thus can we become the leading power in the world;

only thus can we restore our original strength, redeem ourselves from former humiliations, and maintain the integrity of our vast territory so as to remain the greatest country on earth. [61a–62b]

On the Adoption of Western Learning
[From *Chiao-pin lu k'ang-i, Ts'ai hsi-hsüeh i*, pp. 67b–70]

Western books on mathematics, mechanics, optics, light, and chemistry contain the best principles of the natural sciences. In the books on geography, the mountains, rivers, strategic points, customs, and native products of the hundred countries are fully listed. Most of this information is beyond the reach of the Chinese people. . . .

If we wish to use Western knowledge, we should establish official translation bureaus in Canton and Shanghai. Brilliant students not over fifteen years of age should be selected from those areas to live and study in these schools on double allowances. Westerners should be appointed to teach them the spoken and written languages of the various nations, and famous Chinese teachers should be engaged to teach them classics, history, and other subjects. At the same time they should learn mathematics. (Note: All Western knowledge is derived from mathematics. . . . If we wish to adopt Western knowledge, it is but natural that we should learn mathematics). . . . China has many brilliant people. There must be some who can learn from the barbarians and surpass them. [67b–68a]

It is from learning that the principles of government are derived. In discussing good government, the great historian Ssu-ma Ch'ien said (following Hsün Tzu): "Take the latter-day kings as your models." This was because they were nearer in time; their customs had changed from the past and were more similar to the present; and their ideas were not so lofty as to be impracticable. It is my opinion that today we should also take the foreign nations as our examples. They live at the same time and in the same world with us; they have attained prosperity and power by their own efforts. Is it not fully clear that they are similar to us and that their methods can easily be put into practice? If we let Chinese ethics and Confucian teachings serve as the foundation, and let them be supplemented by the methods used by the various nations for the attainment of prosperity and power, would it not be the best of all solutions?

Moreover, during the past twenty years since the opening of trade, a great number of foreign chiefs have learned our written and spoken language, and the best of them can even read our classics and histories. They are generally able to speak on our dynastic regulations and civil administration, on our geography and the condition of our people. On the other hand, our officers from the governors down are completely ignorant of foreign countries. In comparison, should we not feel ashamed? The Chinese officers have to rely upon stupid and preposterous interpreters as their eyes and ears. The mildness or severity of the original statement, its sense of urgency or lack of insistence, may be lost through their tortuous interpretations. Thus frequently a small grudge may develop into a grave hostility. At present the most important political problem of the empire is to control the barbarians, yet the pivotal function is entrusted to such people. No wonder that we understand neither the foreigners nor ourselves, and cannot distinguish fact from untruth. Whether in peace negotiations or in deliberating for war, we are unable to grasp the essentials. This is indeed the underlying trouble of our nation. [69a–70a]

TSENG KUO-FAN AND LI HUNG-CHANG
On Sending Young Men Abroad to Study

Tseng Kuo-fan (1811–1872) and his protege Li Hung-chang (1823–1901) were, in the practical sphere, the outstanding exponents of "self-strengthening" during the latter half of the nineteenth century. Acclaimed as the conqueror of the Taipings, and long viceroy in Central China, Tseng was also admired as a scholar in the classical tradition and as a Confucian "gentleman" who exemplified the traditional virtues in government: industry, frugality, honesty and integrity in office, and loyalty to the dynasty. He was the type of "superior man" whose learning and personal character inspired the devotion of his subordinates and gave Confucianists a confidence that such personal qualities could meet the challenge of the times. Intellectually an eclectic, Tseng minimized doctrinal differences and sought agreement on the ethical bases of action. His support of certain types of modernization for purposes of national defense also reflected a readiness to make compromises for the achievement of practical ends.

In this letter, submitted to the Tsungli Yamen, which handled foreign affairs, in March, 1871, Tseng and Li emphasize not only China's practical need to learn from the West but also the pre-eminent practicality of the Westerners. They are convinced that Western methods can only be mastered through prolonged and intensive study abroad, and propose sending a select group of young men for this purpose. In Japan at this time, the top leaders were themselves visiting the West and preparing to re-educate a whole nation. The aims of Tseng and Li are much more circumscribed—to train an elite corps with a combination of classical Chinese and Western studies, carefully directed and controlled in the interests of the state. Yet even so modest a proposal met with strong opposition at court before it was put into effect in 1872.

[From *Li Wen-chung kung ch'üan-chi, I shu han-kao,* 1:19b–21b]

Last autumn when I [Tseng] was at Tientsin, Governor Ting Jih-ch'ang frequently came to discuss with me proposals for the selection of intelligent youths to be sent to the schools of various Western countries to study military administration, shipping administration, infantry tactics, mathematics, manufacturing, and other subjects. We estimated that after more than ten years their training would have been completed, and they could return to China so that other Chinese might learn thoroughly the superior techniques of the Westerners. Thus we could gradually plan for self-strengthening. . . . After Mr. Pin Ch'un and two other gentlemen, Chih-kang and Sun Chia-ku, had traveled in various countries at imperial command, they saw the essential aspects of conditions overseas, and they found that cartography, mathematics, astronomy, navigation, shipbuilding, and manufacturing are all closely related to military defense. It is the practice of foreign nations that those who have studied abroad and have learned some superior techniques are immediately invited upon their return by academic institutions to teach the various subjects and to develop their fields. Military administration and shipping are considered as important as the learning that deals with the mind and body, and nature and destiny of man. Now that the eyes of the people have been opened, if China wishes to adopt Western ideas and excel in Western methods, we should immediately select intelligent boys and send them to study in foreign countries. . . .

Some may say: "Arsenals have been established in Tientsin, Shanghai and Foochow for shipbuilding and the manufacturing of guns and ammunition. The T'ung-wen College [for foreign languages] has been established in Peking for Manchu and Chinese youths to study under

Western instructors. A language school has also been opened in Shanghai for the training of young students. It seems, therefore, that a beginning has been made in China and that there is no need for studying overseas." These critics, however, do not know that to establish arsenals for manufacturing and to open schools for instruction is just the beginning of our effort to rise again. To go to distant lands for study, to gather ideas for more advantageous use, can produce far-reaching and great results. Westerners seek knowledge for practical use. Whether they be scholars, artisans, or soldiers, they all go to school to study and understand the principles, to practice on the machines, and to participate personally in the work. They all exert themselves to the utmost of their ingenuity, and learn from one another, in the hope that there will be monthly progress and yearly improvement. If we Chinese wish to adopt their superior techniques and suddenly try to buy all their machines, not only will our resources be insufficient to do so, but we will be unable to master the fundamental principles or to understand the complicated details of the techniques, unless we have actually seen and practiced with them for a long time. . . .

We have heard that youths of Fukien, Kwangtung, and Ningpo also occasionally have gone abroad to study, but they merely attempted to gain a superficial knowledge of foreign written and spoken languages in order to do business with the foreigners for the purpose of making a living. In our plan, we must be doubly careful at the beginning of selection. The students who are to be taken to foreign countries will all be under the control of the commissioners. Specializing in different fields, they will earnestly seek for mastery of their subjects. There will be interpreters, and instructors to teach them Chinese literature from time to time, so that they will learn the great principles for the establishment of character, in the hope of becoming men with abilities of use to us.

HSÜEH FU-CH'ENG
On Reform

A one-time secretary and adviser to both Tseng Kuo-Fan and Li Hung-chang, Hsüeh Fu-ch'eng (1838–1894) achieved no high rank or position in the bureaucracy (not having competed in the examinations for the higher civil service degrees). He did, however, become an influential advocate of reform through the circulation of his essays and memorials in official circles, and, besides assisting in the negotiation of the Chefoo Convention (1876), helped to draft plans for a new Chinese navy.

This excerpt is taken from Hsüeh's *Suggestions on Foreign Affairs* (*Ch'ou-yang ch'u-i*), which was submitted to Li in 1879 and forwarded by him to the Tsungli Yamen. Hsüeh argues for reform on the ground that change is inevitable and nothing new to Chinese history. But if he is tempted to accept the idea of progress as a law of history, there is no indication of it here. Rather his premise is the thoroughly traditional one of cyclical or pulsatory change at calculable intervals, which may be for good or ill but in any case must be coped with, as indeed even the sage-kings had to cope with it. A great change in circumstances, therefore, calls for a great change in methods (*fa*, which can also be understood as "laws" or "institutions").

Hsüeh nevertheless contends that changes in method do not mean abandonment of the "immutable" Way of the sages. Indeed it is the use of new methods which will preserve that Way inviolate. Thus a dichotomy is established between ends and means. Here the means Hsüeh has in mind adopting is "the study of machines and mathematics." Consequently the dichotomy is between the Way and "instruments" (*fa* in the sense of methods). How far he would go toward changing *fa* in the sense of basic institutions is left unclear. Where general concepts are used so equivocally—where inevitable change can be understood to imply desired reforms, and methods can mean anything from "instruments" to "institutions"—there is much room for ambiguity and often more scope for rhetoric than logic.

[From *Ch'ou-yang ch'u-i*, in *Yung-an ch'üan chi*, ts'e 12, 46b–49a]

It is the way of Heaven that within several hundred years there are small changes and within several thousand years great changes. . . . In several thousand years [under the early sage-kings] there was change from a primitive world to a civilized world. From the age of the sage-kings through the Three Dynasties there was most truly peace and order. Then the First Emperor of the Ch'in swallowed up the feudal states, abolished the feudal lords, broke up the well-fields, and destroyed the laws of the early kings. Thus it was two thousand years from the time of [the sage-kings] Yao and Shun that the feudal world was changed into a world of [centrally administered] prefectures and districts. . . . As we come down to the present, the European states suddenly rise up and assert themselves overseas because of their knowledge of machinery and mathematics. . . . In ninety thousand *li* around the globe there is no place where they do not send their envoys and establish trade relations. Confronted with this situation, even Yao and Shun would not have been able to close the doors and rule the empire in isolation. And this likewise is now two thousand years from the time of Ch'in and Han. Thus there has been a change from a world in which the Chinese and barbarians were isolated from each other into a world in which China and foreign countries are in close contact. . . . When change in the world is small, the laws governing the world will accordingly undergo small change; when change in the world is great, the laws will accordingly undergo great change. [46b]

Sometimes in the succession of one sage to another there cannot but be changes in the outward forms of government. Sometimes when a sage has to deal with the world, sooner or later there must be changes made. Thus only a sage can pattern himself after another sage, and only a sage can change the laws of another sage. The reason for his making changes is not that he likes change, but that he is obliged to do so by the circumstances of the time. Now there is rapid change in the world. It is my opinion that with regard to the immutable Way we should change the present so as to restore the past [the Way of the sages]; but with regard to changeable laws, we should change the past system to meet present needs. Alas! If we do not examine the differences between the two situations, past and present, and think in terms of practicability, how can we remedy the defects? [47a]

Western nations rely on intelligence and energy to compete with one another. To come abreast of them, China should plan to promote commerce and open mines; unless we change, the Westerners will be rich and we poor. We should excel in technology and the manufacture of machinery; unless we change, they will be skillful and we clumsy. Steamships, trains, and the telegraph should be adopted; unless we change, the Westerners will be quick and we slow. The advantages and disadvantages of treaties, the competence and incompetence of envoys, and the improvement of military organization and strategy should be discussed. Unless we change, the Westerners will cooperate with each other and we shall stand isolated; they will be strong and we shall be weak. [47b]

Some may ask: "If such a great nation as China imitates the Westerners, would it not be using barbarian ways to change China?" Not so. For while in clothing, language, and customs China is different from foreign countries, the utilization of the forces of nature for the benefit of the people is the same in China as in foreign countries. The Western people happen to be the first in adopting this new way of life, but how can we say that they alone should monopolize the secrets of nature? And how do we know that a few decades or a hundred years later China may not surpass them? . . . Now if we really take over the Westerners' knowledge of machinery and mathematics in order to protect the Way of our sage-kings Yao and Shun, Yü and T'ang, Wen and Wu, and the Duke of Chou and Confucius, and so make the Westerners not dare to despise China, I know that if they were alive today, the sages would engage themselves in the same tasks, and their Way would also be gradually spread to the eight bounds of the earth. That is what we call using the ways of China to change the barbarians.

Some may also say: "In making changes one should aim to surpass others and not pursue them. Now the Western methods are superior, and we imitate them; if we follow others helplessly, by what means then are we to surpass them?" This, too, is not so. If we wish to surpass others, it is necessary to know all their methods before we can change; but after we have changed, we may be able to surpass them. We cannot expect to surpass others merely by sitting upright in a dignified attitude. Now if seeing that others are ahead of us we contemptuously say that we do not care to follow them, the result is that we will not be able to move even a small step. Moreover, they have concentrated the ability and energy of several million people, have spent millions of dollars, and have gone through prolonged years and generations before they acquired their knowledge. If we want to excel them in one morning, is it really possible or is it not impossible? A large river may begin with the overflow from small bogs, and a great mound may be built up from overturned baskets of soil. Buddhism came from India and yet it flourished in the East. Mathematics began in China,[1] and yet it has reached its highest development in Western countries. If we compare the ability and wisdom of the Chinese with those of the Westerners, there is no reason to think that we should be unable to surpass them. It all depends on how we exert ourselves.

Alas! There are endless changes in the world, and so there are endless variations in the sages' way of meeting these changes. To be born in the present age but to hold fast to ancient methods, is to be like one who in the age of Shen Nung [when people had learned how to cook] still

[1] A widely held view of which Juan Yüan was a leading exponent. See p. 617.

ate raw meat and drank blood, or like one who lived in the age of the Yellow Emperor [when weapons were available] and yet, in resisting the violence of Ch'ih-yu, struggled against him with bare hands. Such a one would say: "I am following the methods of the ancient sages." But it is hardly possible that he should not become exhausted and fall. Moreover, the laws [or methods] which ought to be changed today can still [in their new form] embody the essence of the laws of the ancient sages. [48a–49a]

WANG T'AO

On Reform

Wang T'ao (1828–1897) represents a new type of reformer on the Chinese scene. In contrast to the great reformers of the past (e.g., Wang Mang, Wang An-shih) who were scholar-officials, and in contrast also to his contemporaries, Feng Kuei-fen and Hsüeh Fu-ch'eng, who wrote as officials and worked closely with statesmen like Tseng Kuo-fan and Li Hung-chang, Wang T'ao was an independent scholar and journalist. Sometimes, indeed, he is called "the father of Chinese journalism." His work was done mainly in the ports of Hongkong and Shanghai, under foreign protection and in close touch with foreigners. For years he assisted the eminent British sinologue, James Legge, in his translations from the Chinese classics, and with Legge's help visited England and Western Europe, observing and writing on developments there. Later, too, Wang visited Japan, where he was well-received as a scholar and reformer. When finally he settled down to a career as journalist, he did so as a man with foreign contacts, a wide knowledge of the outside world, and a freedom to express himself unknown in the past—when not only the right to criticize but even the means (a public press) and the audience (an influential public opinion) were lacking.

The following is taken from an essay of Wang's written about 1870, which anticipates some of Hsüeh Fu-ch'eng's basic points but carries them even further. There is the argument from cyclical change to the need for adapting to the current situation. There is the assertion that Confucius himself would have advocated change under such circumstances. There is the distinction between the Way of the sages, which must be preserved, and the instruments (weapons, methods) of the West which should be adopted for its defense. At the same time, Wang insists that change must go deeper and further than mere imitation of the West in externals, and suggests, however vaguely, that a thorough renovation of society is necessary. Though his specific recommendations here relate primarily to education, eventually he advocated basic governmental change as well. Consequently the ambiguity in Wang's use of the term *pien-fa* for "reform" is even more pronounced than in Hsüeh Fu-ch'eng's essay. Though he speaks of adopting from the West only "instruments," he intends that change should extend not only to technology ("methods") but to *fa* in the sense of "basic institutions." Wang therefore presages, intellectually, the transition from reformism conceived in terms of immediate utility to a more radical view of institutional change.

The following excerpt is preceded by a discussion of previous changes in Chinese history which we have already seen echoed by Hsüeh. Here, however, Wang is consciously re-examining Chinese history to refute the assertion of "Western scholars that China has gone unchanged for 5,000 years." Contending in effect, that China's stagnation was a comparatively recent development, he then goes on to deal with the present situation.

[From *Pien-fa* in *T'ao-yüan wen-lu wai-pien,* 1:11a–15b]

I know that within a hundred years China will adopt all Western methods and excel in them. For though both are vessels, a sailboat differs in speed from a steamship; though both are vehicles, a horse-drawn carriage cannot cover the same distance as a locomotive train. Among weapons, the power of the bow and arrow, sword and spear, cannot be compared with that of firearms; and of firearms, the old types do not have the same effect as the new. Although it be the same piece of work, there is a difference in the ease with which it can be done by machine and by human labor. When new methods do not exist, people will not think of changes; but when there are new instruments, to copy them is certainly possible. Even if the Westerners should give no guidance, the Chinese must surely exert themselves to the utmost of their ingenuity and resources on these things.

However, they are all instruments; they are not the Way, and they cannot be called the basis for governing the state and pacifying the world. The Way of Confucius is the Way of Man. As long as humankind exists, the Way will remain unchanged. The three moral obligations and the five human relations began with the birth of the human race. When a man fulfills his duty as man, he need have no regrets in life. On this is based the teaching of the sages. [1:11a]

I have said before that after a few hundred years the Way will achieve a grand unity. As Heaven has unified the south, north, east, and west under one sky, it will harmonize the various teachings of the world and bring them back to the same source. . . .

Alas! People all understand the past, but they are ignorant of the future.

Only scholars whose thoughts run deep and far can grasp the trends. As the mind of Heaven changes above, so do human affairs below. Heaven opens the minds of the Westerners and bestows upon them intelligence and wisdom. Their techniques and skills develop without bound. They sail eastward and gather in China. This constitutes an unprecedented situation in history, and a tremendous change in the world. The foreign nations come from afar with their superior techniques, contemptuous of us in our deficiencies. They show off their prowess and indulge in insults and oppression; they also fight among themselves. Under these circumstances, how can we not think of making changes? Thus what makes it most difficult for us not to change is the mind of Heaven, and what compels us unavoidably to change is the doings of men. [1:11b–12a]

If China does not make any change at this time, how can she be on a par with the great nations of Europe, and compare with them in power and strength? Nevertheless, the path of reform is beset with difficulties. What the Western countries have today are regarded as of no worth by those who arrogantly refuse to pay attention. Their argument is that we should use our own laws to govern the empire, for that is the Way of our sages. They do not know that the Way of the sages is valued only because it can make proper accommodations according to the times. If Confucius lived today, we may be certain that he would not cling to antiquity and oppose making changes. . . .

But how is this to be done? First, the method of recruiting civil servants should be changed. The examination essays, coming down to the present, have gone from bad to worse and should be discarded. And yet we are still using them to select civil servants. . . .

Second, the method of training soldiers should be changed. Now our army units and naval forces have only names registered on books, but no actual persons enrolled. The authorities consider our troops unreliable, and so they recruit militia who, however, can be assembled but cannot be disbanded. . . . The arms of the Manchu banners and the ships of the naval forces should all be changed. . . . If they continue to hold on to their old ways and make no plans for change, it may be called "using untrained people to fight,"[2] which is no different from driving them to their deaths. . . .

[2] *Mencius*, IV B, 8.

Thirdly, the empty show of our schools should be changed. Now district directors of schools are installed, one person for a small town and two for a large city. It is a sheer waste of government funds, for they have nothing to do. The type of man in such posts is usually degenerate, incompetent, senile, and with little sense of shame. [1:13a–14a]

Fourthly, the complex and multifarious laws and regulations should be changed. . . . The government should reduce the mass of regulations and cut down on the number of directives; it should be sincere and fair and treat the people with frankness and justice. . . .

After the above four changes have been made, Western methods could be used together with others. But the most important point is that the government above should exercise its power to change customs and mores, while the people below should be gradually absorbed into the new environment and adjusted to it without their knowing it. This reform should extend to all things—from trunk to branch, from inside to outside, from great to small—and not merely to Western methods. [1:14b]

Formerly we thought that the foundation of our wealth and strength would be established if only Western methods were stressed, and that the result would be achieved immediately. . . . Now in various coastal provinces there have been established special arsenals to make guns and ships. Young boys have been selected and sent to study abroad. Seen from outside, the effort is really great and impressive. Unfortunately, we are merely copying the superficialities of the Western methods, getting only the name but very little substance. The ships which were formerly built at Foochow were entirely based on the older methods of Western countries, not worth the faint praise of those who know about such things. . . .

The advantage of guns lies in the techniques of discharging them; that of ships in the ability to navigate them. The weapons we use in battle must be effective, but the handling of effective weapons depends upon people. . . . Yet those regarded as able men have not necessarily been able, and those regarded as competent have not necessarily been competent. They are merely mediocrities who accomplish something through the aid of others. Therefore, the urgent task of our nation today lies primarily in the governance of the people, and next in the training of soldiers. And in these two the essential point is to gather men of abilities. Indeed, superficial imitation in concrete things is not so good as arousing intellectual curiosity. The forges and hammers of the factories cannot be compared with the apparatus of people's minds. [1:15a–b]

INSTITUTIONAL REFORM

When we attempt to assess the aims and accomplishments of Chinese reformers in the 1870s and '80s, the comparison to Meiji Japan is almost inevitable. In aims there is a strong general resemblance between the two; in the scope and effectiveness of their reforms a striking difference. Where the Chinese self-strengtheners sought to preserve the Confucian Way through the adoption of Western techniques, Japanese modernizers talked of combining "Eastern ethics and Western science" or spoke of preserving their distinctive "national polity" (*kokutai*) in the midst of an intense program of modernization. Yet, given this general similarity of aims, the process of change in Japan went further and faster than in China, and to a very different result. In the one case there was rapid industrialization, political centralization, educational reform, and social change—all of these involving a much fuller participation of the Japanese people in the national effort and contributing to a degree of unity and strength unprecedented in Japanese history. In China, by the 1890s, it was evident that the self-strengtheners had not only failed to achieve such an effective national unity and concerted action, but had perhaps only contributed further to the processes of disintegration which typically marked the last years of a great dynasty.

The reasons for this obvious difference are complex and profound, and it is not our purpose to examine them here. One relevant observation may be made, however, in distinguishing the Chinese problem from the Japanese. It is the far greater challenge to reform presented by a vast, sprawling China, whose ostensible political unity was perhaps more of a liability than an asset—whose imperial structure, with its centralized administration, bureaucratic organization and procedures, unwieldiness and inflexibility, proved more intractable to reformers in China than did the comparatively decentralized and less stable feudal structure of Japan to the leaders of the Meiji Restoration.

If to Wang T'ao a great nemesis of reform lay in the "multiplicity of governmental regulations and endless number of directives," his complaint represented not only the traditional protest of the Confucian reformer, but a direct recognition that bureaucratic red tape and centralized control left little room for even piecemeal reform. If, in his mind too, the most important thing was for the court to exercise its power and authority in the direction of reform, this came from a realization that, lacking such leadership from above, little initiative could be taken below.

Under these circumstances, reformers might prescribe change for the empire as a whole, but the individual self-strengtheners in positions of limited authority could hardly plan for a truly national program of reform. Within their own spheres of jurisdiction or influence they might inaugurate projects for the modernizing of their personal armies, the manufacturing of arms, the building of ships, the promoting of business, the opening of schools for technical and language training, as well as for the improvement of the more traditional functions of government in China; yet the tendency was for even these worthwhile ventures to take on a strongly bureaucratic character—to become part of an official sub-empire—without, however, enjoying any of the benefits of centralized planning or coordination. The net result is typified by the utter failure of Li Hung-chang's new army and navy, owing to "squeeze," corruption and inefficiency in the supply system, when put to the test by the Japanese in the war of 1894–95. It was this failure that led directly to demands for more drastic change.

K'ANG YU-WEI AND THE REFORM MOVEMENT

China's humiliating defeat in the Sino-Japanese War and the seeming danger of her imminent partition by the foreign powers would have been cause enough for an outcry of alarm and protest. To these were added a growing sense of dissatisfaction and frustration among the younger generation of students, who by now had been exposed to reformist writings and had their eyes opened to the outside world. This group was by no means large. The educated class had always constituted a small minority of Chinese, and those affected by new ideas represented a still smaller fraction. Thus, rather than their numbers, it was their role as recruits or members of the bureaucratic elite, which gave them influence. Significantly, among the leaders of the reform group were several from the Kwangtung region, where, like Hung Hsiu-ch'üan before them and Sun Yat-sen after, they were stimulated by close contact with the West in Hongkong and Canton. Increasingly, toward the end of the century, these young men were being challenged and inspired by the brilliant journalism of a writer like Wang T'ao. Youthful impressions, once wholly formed by the Confucian Classics and native tradition, were now being formed also by the translations of men like Yen Fu (1853–1921), who made available in Chinese the works of Thomas Huxley, John Stuart Mill, Herbert Spencer, and Adam Smith.

More even than by such ideas as evolution, progress, and liberty—radically new though these were and certain to stir intellectual ferment—this generation was disturbed, and profoundly so, just by the shock of events. Not only the handful of active reformers, but officialdom generally, found its pride and self-confidence shaken. This loss of poise and self-assurance may have helped to provide the rare, if momentary, opportunity which innovators seized upon in the famous Hundred Days of Reform in 1898. Yet it also created a deeply felt need among educated Chinese somehow to be reassured that China's cultural identity would not be wholly lost amid these changes—a need which the reformers themselves felt more acutely even than those who opposed them.

K'ang Yu-wei (1858–1927), the dominant figure of the Reform Movement, was born near Canton into a world of crisis. The Taiping Rebellion raised up by K'ang's fellow provincial was still agonizing the empire from within, while from without the British and French, who had moved again into Canton only the year before, were pressing a campaign that would lead to the occupation of Peking itself in 1860.

As the scion of a distinguished gentry-official family, K'ang was provided with an education along traditional lines, but at the age of fifteen he made known his distaste for the business of mastering the "eight-legged essay" so indispensable to success in the civil service examinations. Two years later he was reading about Western geography and in time became a voracious reader of Chinese books on the history and geography of the West. Probably the chief influence on K'ang in these early years was exerted by a teacher of the old school, who aroused in him a passion for classical scholarship and a sense of complete dedication to the Confucian ideals of personal virtue and service to society. An episode recounted in K'ang's *Autobiographical Chronology* shows, nevertheless, that his independence and iconoclasm were already quite marked:

My Master praised highly the writings of Han Yü and so I read and studied the collected works of Han [Yü] and Liu [Tsung-yüan], emulating him in this as well. By this time I had read the books of the philosophers and had learned the [various] methods of [seeking] the Way. Thus I presented myself in person before the Master and said to him that Han Yü's methods of [seeking] the Way were shallow, and that in searching for concrete substance in the writings of all the great names in scholarship down through the Sung, Ming, and the present dynasty, [I had found that] they were all empty and lacking in substance. I ventured to say that when one spoke of the Way, it should be like Chuang Tzu or Hsün Tzu; when one spoke of governing, it should be like Kuan Tzu or Han Fei Tzu; while as regards medicine, the *Su-wen* would constitute a separate subject. But as to Han Yü, he was no more than a literary craftsman skilled in the undulation of broad and sweeping cadences which, while they appealed to the ear, had nothing to do with the Way. Thus his *Yüan-tao* was extremely superficial. . . . The Master, who was usually correct and stern, in this case laughingly chided me for being wrongheaded. From the time he had first seen me he had often cautioned me about my undue feelings of superiority, and after this I was [more] humble, but nevertheless my fellow-students came to be shocked at my intractability.

With the arrival of autumn and winter, I had learned in their broad outlines the general meaning of the important books in the four divisions [of literature]. My intelligence and comprehension became confused, for every day I was buried amid piles of old papers, and I developed a revulsion for them. Then one day I had a new idea. I thought: scholars engaged in textual research, such as Tai Chen, filled their homes with the books that they had written, but in the end what was the use of all this? Thus I gave it up and in my own heart I fancied seeking a place where I might pacify my mind and determine my destiny. Suddenly I abandoned my studies, discarded my books, shut my door, withdrew from my friends, and sat in contemplation, nurturing my mind. My schoolmates thought me very queer, for there had been no one who had done this, inasmuch as the Master upheld the individual's actual practice [of the Confucian virtues] and detested the study of Ch'an [Buddhism]. While I was sitting in contemplation, all of a sudden I perceived that Heaven, earth, and the myriad things were all of one substance with myself, and in a great release of enlightenment I beheld myself a sage and laughed for joy; then suddenly I thought of the sufferings and hardships of all living beings, and I wept in melancholy; abruptly I thought: why should I be studying here and neglecting my parent? and that I should pack up immediately and go back to the thatched hut over my grandfather's grave. The students, observing that I sang and wept for no apparent reason, believed that I had gone mad and was diseased in mind.[3]

This experience of K'ang's was not unusual in the Chinese intellectual tradition. Neo-Confucianists like Wang Yang-ming before him had suddenly found themselves suffocated and overburdened by the kind of exhaustive scholarship Chu Hsi had seemed to encourage—scholarship which often exhausted one's mind and spirit before one began to exhaust the sources. What is significant here for our understanding of K'ang is, first, the evidence of an early tendency toward syncretism, stronger certainly than his sense of orthodoxy; and second, the conception of himself as somehow set apart from the rest of men and, indeed, above them. The impulse toward quietism and mysticism, on the other hand, proved a passing one. After a few months in lonely isolation and meditation, K'ang's sense of a special destiny to save mankind through active involvement in the affairs of the world took command of him. Subsequent visits to Hongkong and Shanghai impressed him with the orderliness and prosperity of Western civilization. Intensifying his pursuit of Western learning, he also became involved in efforts toward practical reform, like his movement to abolish foot-binding. Meanwhile the young reformer had by no means abandoned classical Confucian studies, but had begun to identify himself with the so-called "New Text School" of textual criticism. The purpose of this, for K'ang, was not so much to determine by critical methods what must have been the original teaching of Confucius, but, whether consciously or not, to justify his new view of the sage as essentially a reformer and to discredit all else that passed for Confucianism.

By the mid-1880s K'ang, still only twenty-seven, had already formulated in his mind the ideas which became the basis of his two most famous works, the *Grand Unity* (*Ta t'ung shu*) and *Confucius As a Reformer* (*K'ung Tzu kai-chih k'ao*). By 1887 he had succeeded, after an earlier failure, in winning the second degree in the civil service examinations, and by 1895, the highest regular (*chin-shih*) degree. He had also begun to attract talented students, who helped in the revising and publishing of his works and later in the organizing of reformist societies which spread his ideas and made him the center of violent controversy. Japan, whose defeat of China created an atmosphere of crisis and imminent catastrophe in the late '90s, now became K'ang's model of reform. He urged the court

[3] *K'ang Nan-hai tzu pien nien p'u*, IV, 113-14, as translated by Richard Howard.

to follow the example of Meiji Japan and openly advocated a basic change from absolute monarchy to constitutional rule. Finally an opportunity to put his ideas into effect came when the Kuang-hsü emperor asked him to take charge of the government in June, 1898.

During K'ang's few months of tenure a stream of edicts issued forth from the court, aimed at transforming China into a modern state. The old bureaucracy was to be thoroughly revamped. Education and recruitment would be based on Western studies as well as Chinese; bureaucratic functions would be reorganized to serve modern needs. There would be a public school system and a public press. These, together with popularly elected local assemblies, would prepare the people to take part in eventual parliamentary government. In the economic sphere, too, K'ang had ambitious plans. Bureaus were set up to promote commerce, industry, modern banking, mining, and agricultural development. Lastly, and most importantly, K'ang attempted to reorganize and strengthen the armed forces. Here, however, he ran into serious difficulty trying to bring under central control armies which for decades had been virtually autonomous units loyal to their own commanders.

Had he not failed in this last respect, K'ang might have survived the bitter opposition which his reforms provoked from the entrenched bureaucracy. It was perhaps characteristic of his dogged adherence to principle, if not indeed of a self-righteous and egocentric character, that K'ang reckoned little with such hostility and even less with the surprise and bewilderment felt by many who were simply unaccustomed to rapid change and unable to cope with his radically new ideas. Before many of his plans could take effect, a coup d'etat restored the conservative empress dowager to active control of affairs and drove K'ang's group from power. Some died as martyrs to the cause of reform; others, like K'ang, escaped to become exiles.

Until the dynasty itself collapsed, K'ang continued to write and raise funds overseas in behalf of the movement. After the Revolution of 1911, however, K'ang's "cause" became more and more of a personal one. In a little more than a decade the trend of events and ideas had left him behind. As a constitutional monarchist who still protested his loyalty to the Manchu dynasty, K'ang was now swimming against a strong Republican tide; as a reformer who had always insisted on his fidelity to Confucius, he found himself suddenly surrounded by progressives—a generation that no longer needed to be won over to reform and could not now be won back to Confucius.

The significance of K'ang Yu-wei as a thinker lies in his attempt to provide a Confucian justification for basic institutional reforms. The so-called self-strengtheners had urged reform on the grounds of immediate utility, thinking that Western weapons and techniques could be adopted without proceeding further to any basic changes in Chinese government and society. They spoke of preserving the Confucian Way (Tao) through the use of Western "instruments" (*ch'i*) or "methods" (*fa*). Yet, as men like Wang T'ao came to appreciate, Western power and prosperity rested on something more than technology. To bring China abreast of the modern world, therefore, more radical changes would be needed. Thus reform began to take on a new meaning for them. Change would now extend to *fa* in the sense of institutions as well as *fa* in the sense of methods.

It was here that real trouble arose. According to a hallowed principle of Chinese dynastic rule, the life of a dynasty was bound up with its adherence to the constitution laid down by its founding father (the first emperor). Tampering with its institutions might bring the dynasty down, and supporters of the Manchus could be counted on to resist any such changes. For those more concerned over the Chinese way of life than the fate of the Manchus the problem was even more acute. How far could one go in changing basic institutions while still keeping the Way intact? Would not Confucianism be reduced to a mere set of pious platitudes once its social integument had been destroyed?

K'ang's resolution of this dilemma was a bold one. Rather than permit the sphere occupied by the Confucian Way in Chinese life to be further narrowed and displaced by Western "methods," he would redefine the Way and enlarge its scope so as virtually to include the latter. Instead of making more room for Western institutions alongside Confucianism, he would make room for them inside. This he did by exploiting to the fullest two ideas already put forth by Wang T'ao. The first of these was that the Way of the sages was precisely to meet change with change; Confucius himself had done so, and if alive today would do so again. K'ang provided this theory with an elaborate scriptural justification through his studies of the so-called "forged classics" and his sensational *Confucius As a Reformer*. In terms of its historical influence this was undoubtedly K'ang's main contribution—though not an original one—to the thinking of his times.

Implicit in his notion of reform, however, was a still more momentous idea, since it ran more directly counter to the age-old Confucian view of history and tradition: the idea of progress. It was one thing to assert that the Confucian sage, when faced by one of those cyclically-recurring cycles of degeneration spoken of by Mencius or the *Book of Changes,* took appropriate steps to reform the times, reassert the Way, and restore the institutions of the sage-kings. It was quite another to offer, in place of a return to the Golden Age, a utopia beckoning in the future.

Here again the idea was, among Chinese, originally Wang T'ao's. He had glimpsed a future stage in which the Way would make all things one, a natural result of the process going on around him by which the different nations in the world and their respective ways of life were being brought together by technological progress. He had even referred to it in terms taken from the Confucian *Book of Rites* as the age of Grand Unity or of the Great Commonwealth (*Ta t'ung*). What the *Book of Rites* had spoken of as a golden age at the dawn of history, however, Wang T'ao saw as a vision of the future. And K'ang Yu-wei, in his *Grand Unity,* made this vision the center of his whole world-view. Henceforth, "reform" would never again mean what it had in the past, an adaptation of laws and methods to cyclical change. It was now a wholesale launching of China into the modern world and, beyond that, into a glorious future.

Feng Kuei-fen and Hsüeh Fu-ch'eng, in their writings on reform, had shown deference to China's age-old pretensions to cultural superiority by reassuring their readers that she need not merely follow along behind the Western powers but could overtake and surpass them. K'ang, in the *Grand Unity,* took the lead for China himself by pointing the way into the One World of the future. If China suffered humiliation now for her backwardness, looking ahead, he would be satisfied with nothing less for her than the ultimate in progress. In his world of the future there were to be no national and provincial barriers. Government would virtually cease to exist except in local units fixed arbitrarily on the basis of square degrees of longitude and latitude. Within these units life would be completely communal and completely egalitarian. All distinctions of race, class, clan, and family would also disappear, since they could no longer serve any valid social function. And in place of the differentiated loyalties which had bound men to their particular social group there would be only an undifferentiated feeling of human-kindness or love, which he identified with the Confucian virtue of humanity (*jen*).

Those who recall the layout of Mencius' well-fields, of which K'ang's square degrees of longitude and latitude are so reminiscent; or the neat symmetrical organization of society, set forth so early in the *Rites of Chou* and so late in the plans of the Taiping rebels; or the Chinese fondness for political geometry, reflected even in the plan of capital cities like Ch'ang-an and Peking, will recognize in K'ang's grand design, as even in the communes of Red China later, a quality by no means foreign to native tradition.

If in this respect, then, K'ang's vision of the future still strongly reflects the past, what can be said of his Confucianism? Does it too hold to tradition? Was K'ang either a staunch defender or a creative interpreter of Confucianism? The obvious grounds for placing him still within the Confucian tradition are his emphasis upon the cardinal virtue of *jen* and his efforts to preserve Confucianism as the national religion of the Chinese as something completely inseparable from the Chinese way of life. Against this, most obviously, is his positive rejection of the Confucian family system along with other "divisive" elements in society.

Whatever abuses may have appeared in the family system, however, as it was formulated and practiced down through the centuries, it would still seem difficult to disassociate Confucius completely from it or to preserve Confucianism entirely without it. Without the family virtues and obligations, certainly, the concept of *jen* loses much of its tangible significance, and approaches more nearly—if it does not exactly coincide with—Mo Tzu's principle of undifferentiated universal love. Since Mo Tzu's social ideals resemble K'ang's so closely, the comparison is all the more pointed.

Furthermore, in K'ang's attempt to preserve Confucianism as a kind of national religion, there is something foreign to the spirit of Confucianism itself. The sage's teaching had been offered, and been accepted, as something universal. Its humanistic values were rooted in the nature of man and human society generally. K'ang's defense of it now as the basis of Chinese civilization and as the focus of a new nationalism, while testifying no doubt to his realization that China must have something comparable to the Christianity of the West or the Shinto cult in Japan, nevertheless sacrifices the substance of tradition for the trappings of nationalism. Henceforth Confucianism is to be valued, not on its own terms, but for its Chineseness.

What remains as unquestionably Confucian is K'ang's own sense of dedication to the service of society, his aim of "putting the world in order." Yet even this is not exclusively a Confucian concern (certainly Mo Tzu shared it), nor does his favorite expression for it, "saving the world," hark back only to the sage—there are overtones here, too, of the Buddhist saviors (*bodhisattvas*) and Jesus Christ.

In the light of history K'ang and the reform movement may well appear as the great turning point between old and new in Chinese thought. Confucianism, in his hands, was being launched on a perilous journey, in the course of which much baggage might have to be jettisoned if anything at all was to survive. Confucian traditionalists saw the dangers perhaps better than K'ang. Dropping him as pilot, however, was not the same thing as steering a safe course homeward. The storm now drove all before it, and there was no turning back.

K'ANG YU-WEI

Confucius As a Reformer

K'ang's *K'ung Tzu kai-chih k'ao* (lit., Study of Confucius' Reforms) was started in 1886 and finally published in 1897. It constitutes an extended analysis of the innovations which K'ang believed to have been advocated by Confucius. The following are taken from section introductions which present his general argumentation. As K'ang's subheadings indicate, they purport to show that Confucius' greatness derives from his having written the Six Classics to promote reform in his own time.

[From *K'ung Tzu kai-chih k'ao,* 9:1a; 10:1a-b]

HOW CONFUCIUS FOUNDED HIS TEACHING IN ORDER TO REFORM INSTITUTIONS

Every founder of doctrine in the world reformed institutions and established laws. This is true with Chinese philosophers in ancient times. Chinese principles and institutions were all laid down by Confucius. His disciples received his teachings and transmitted them so that they were carried out in the country and used to change the old customs. [9:1a]

THE SIX CLASSICS ALL WRITTEN BY CONFUCIUS TO REFORM INSTITUTIONS

Confucius was the founder of a doctrine. He was a godlike sage-king. He complements Heaven and earth and nurtures the myriad things. All men, things, and principles are embraced in the Great Way of Confucius. He is, therefore, the most accomplished and perfect sage since the history of mankind. And yet, concerning the Great Way of Confucius, one would search in vain for a single word [under the master's own name]. There are only the *Analects,* which was a record of the master's sayings taken down by his disciples, and the *Spring and Autumn Annals,* which was a kind of old-fashioned gazette copied from ancient documents relative to public events and ceremonies. As to the *Books of Odes, History, Rites, Music,* and *Changes,* they are regarded as the ancient records of Fu Hsi, the Hsia and Shang dynasties, King Wen and the Duke of Chou; thus they have nothing to do with Confucius. If this were true, Confucius would have been merely a wise scholar of later times, no better than Cheng K'ang-ch'eng [127–200] or Chu Hsi [1130–1200, who wrote commentaries on the Confucian classics]. How, then, could he have been called the only model of the human race and the perfect sage of all generations? . . . Before the Han dynasty it was known to all that Confucius was the founder of the doctrine and the reformer of institutions, and that he was the godlike sage-king. . . . Wherein lies the reason for this? It lies in the fact that scholars knew the Six Classics were written by Confucius. This was the opinion of all before the Han dynasty. Only when a scholar recognizes that the Six Classics were written by Confucius can he understand why Confucius was the great sage, the founder of the doctrine, and the model for all ages; and why he alone was called the supreme master. [10:1a–b]

The Three Ages

K'ang's theory of progress is set forth in terms of the Three Ages, a concept of the New Text School for which he derived classical sanction from the Kung-yang commentary on the *Spring and Autumn Annals,* the Li yün section of the *Book of Rites,* and commentaries by the Han scholars Tung Chung-shu and Ho Hsiu. Here we see the ancient cyclical view of history adapted to the modern evolutionary view.

[From *Lun yü chu,* 2:11a–12b]

The meaning of the *Spring and Autumn Annals* consists in the evolution of the Three Ages: the Age of Disorder, the Age of Order, and the Age of Great Peace. . . . The Way of Confucius embraces the evolution of the Three Sequences and the Three Ages. The Three Sequences were used to illustrate the Three Ages, which could be extended to a hundred generations. The eras of Hsia, Shang, and Chou represent the succession of the Three Sequences, each with its modifications and accretions. By observing the changes in these three eras one can know the changes in a hundred generations to come. For as customs are handed down among the people later kings cannot but follow the practices of the preceding dynasty; yet since defects develop and have to be removed, each new dynasty must make modifications and additions to create a new system. The course of humanity progresses according to a fixed sequence. From the clans come tribes, which in time are transformed into nations. And from nations the Grand Unity comes about. Similarly, from the individual man the rule of tribal chieftains gradually becomes established, from which the relationship between ruler and subject is gradually defined. Autocracy gradually leads to constitutionalism, and constitutionalism gradually leads to republicanism. Likewise, from the individual man the relationship between husband and wife gradually comes into being, and from this the relationship between father and son is defined. This relationship of father and son leads to the loving care of the entire race, which in turn leads gradually to the Grand Unity, in which there is a reversion to individuality.

Thus there is an evolution from Disorder to Order, and from Order to Great Peace. Evolution proceeds gradually and changes have their origins. This is true with all nations. By observing the child, one can know the adult and old man; by observing the sprout, one can know the tree when it grows big and finally reaches the sky. Thus, by observing the modifications and additions of the three successive eras of Hsia, Shang, and Chou, one can by extension know the changes in a hundred generations to come.

When Confucius prepared the *Spring and Autumn Annals*, he extended it to embrace the Three Ages. Thus, during the Age of Disorder he considers his own state as the center, treating all other Chinese feudal states as on the outside. In the Age of Order he considers China as the center, while treating the outlying barbarian tribes as on the outside. And in the Age of Great Peace he considers everything, far or near, large or small, as if it were one. In doing this he is applying the principle of evolution.

Confucius was born in the Age of Disorder. Now that communications extend through the great earth and changes have taken place in Europe and America, the world is evolving toward the Age of Order. There will be a day when everything throughout the earth, large or small, far or near, will be like one. There will be no longer any nations, no more racial distinctions, and customs will be everywhere the same. With this uniformity will come the Age of Great Peace. Confucius knew all this in advance.

[From *Chung-yung chu*, 36b]

The methods and institutions of Confucius aim at meeting with the particular times. If, in the Age of Disorder, before the advent of civilization, one were to put into effect the institutions of Great Peace, this would certainly result in great harm. But if, in the Age of Order, one were to continue to cling to the institutions of the Age of Disorder, this too would result in great harm. The present time, for example, is the Age of Order. It is therefore necessary to propagate the doctrines of self-rule and independence, and to discuss publicly the matter of constitutional government. If the laws are not reformed, great disorder will result. . . .

The Need for Reforming Institutions

This memorial to the throne, submitted January 29, 1898, and entitled "Comprehensive Consideration of the Whole Situation," gives the arguments by which K'ang attempted to persuade the Kuang-hsü emperor to inaugurate reforms, which he did a few months later. Note K'ang's equivocal approach to the question of "ancestral institutions."

[From *Ying-ch'ao t'ung-ch'ou ch'üan-chü che*, in *Wu-hsü tsou-kao*, 1b-3b]

A survey of all states in the world will show that those states which undertook reforms became strong while those states which clung to the past perished. The consequences of clinging to the past and the effects of opening up new ways are thus obvious. If Your Majesty, with your discerning brilliance, observes the trends in other countries, you will see that if we can change, we can preserve ourselves; but if we cannot change, we shall perish. Indeed, if we can make a complete change, we shall become strong, but if we only make limited changes, we shall still perish. If Your Majesty and his ministers investigate the source of the disease, you will know that this is the right prescription.

Our present trouble lies in our clinging to old institutions without knowing how to change. In an age of competition between states, to put into effect methods appropriate to an era of universal unification and laissez-faire is like wearing heavy furs in summer or riding a high carriage across a river. This can only result in having a fever or getting oneself drowned. . . .

It is a principle of things that the new is strong but the old weak; that new things are fresh but old things rotten; that new things are active but old things static. If the institutions are old, defects will develop. Therefore there are no institutions that should remain unchanged for a hundred years. Moreover, our present institutions are but unworthy vestiges of the Han, T'ang, Yüan, and Ming dynasties; they are not even the institutions of the [Manchu] ancestors. In fact, they are the products of the fancy writing and corrupt dealing of the petty officials rather than the original ideas of the ancestors. To say that they are the ancestral institutions is an insult to the ancestors. Furthermore, institutions are for the purpose of preserving one's territories. Now that the ancestral territory cannot be preserved, what good is it to maintain the ancestral institutions? . . .

Although there is a desire to reform, yet if the national policy is not fixed and public opinion not united, it will be impossible for us to give up the old and adopt the new. The national policy is to the state just as the rudder is to the boat or the pointer is to the compass. It determines the direction of the state and shapes the public opinion of the country. [1b–2b]

Nowadays the court has been undertaking some reforms, but the action of the emperor is obstructed by the ministers, and the recommendations of the able scholars are attacked by old-fashioned bureaucrats. If the charge is not "using barbarian ways to change China," then it is "upsetting the ancestral institutions." Rumors and scandals are rampant, and people fight each other like fire and water. A reform in this way is as ineffective as attempting a forward march by walking backward. It will inevitably result in failure. Your Majesty knows that under the present circumstances reforms are imperative and old institutions must be abolished. I beg Your Majesty to make up your mind and to decide on the national policy. After the fundamental policy is determined, the methods of implementation must vary according to what is primary and what is secondary, what is important and what is insignificant, what is strong and what is weak, what is urgent and what can wait. . . . If anything goes wrong, no success can be achieved.

After studying ancient and modern institutions, Chinese and foreign, I have found that the institutions of the sage-kings and Three Dynasties [of Hsia, Shang, and Chou] were excellent, but that ancient times were different from today. I hope Your Majesty will daily read Mencius and follow his example of loving the people. The development of the Han, T'ang, Sung, and Ming dynasties may be learned, but it should be remembered that the age of universal unification is different from that of sovereign nations. I wish Your Majesty would study *Kuan Tzu* [4] and follow his idea of managing the country. As to the republican governments of the United States and France and the constitutional governments of Britain and Germany, these countries are far away and their customs are different from ours. Their changes occurred a long time ago and can no longer all be traced. Consequently I beg Your Majesty to adopt the purpose of Peter the Great of Russia as our purpose and to take the Meiji Reform of Japan as the model for our reform. The time and place of Japan's reform are not remote and her religion and customs are somewhat similar to ours. Her success is manifest; her example can be easily followed. [3a-b]

CONSERVATIVE REACTIONS

The great momentum attained by the reform movement after the Sino-Japanese War in 1894 also provoked strong conservative reactions. A stormy debate ensued in which the reformers were charged with subverting the established order and destroying Chinese culture. In Hunan province, where reformers like T'an Ssu-t'ung had organized an academy for the spreading of their ideas, the reaction was particularly forceful. Eminent scholars such as Wang Hsien-ch'ien (1842-1918), outstanding classicist and compiler of the monumental *Tung hua lu* (*Imperial Documents of the Ch'ing Dynasty*), and Yeh Te-hui (1864-1927), famous bibliophile, rallied to the defense of Chinese traditions and Confucianism. In Peking powerful figures led by Jung Lu (1836-1903) fought the reformers with logic and invective until, with the help of the empress dowager they succeeded in bringing the reform movement of 1898 to an abrupt end. Still another brand of opposition was encountered in the great

[4] Early book on political and economic institutions which foreshadows Legalist doctrines.

statesman Chang Chih-tung, who, though himself something of a reformer, wished to hold the line against drastic changes and tried to preserve intact the earlier distinction between traditional Confucian ethics and the Western techniques which should serve only as means for defending the Chinese Way.

Resistance to reform took three main lines. First, the conservatives argued that ancestral institutions should never be changed under any conditions. Said Tseng Lien, one of the conservative writers: "The country belongs to the ancestors; the emperor merely maintains the dynasty for them. He cannot change the permanent laws laid down by the ancestors." This argument, founded upon the tradition of filial piety, was in fact the most formidable obstacle to the reformers, and one which K'ang Yu-wei tried to overcome again and again in his memorials to the throne. It was this same argument which the Grand Councillor, Jung Lu, used so effectively against K'ang.

Secondly, the conservatives argued, on traditional Confucian lines, a good government depended upon men rather than upon laws. It was the moral state of the people that needed improvement, not legal or political institutions. Rather than try to change institutions, one should seek to change or win over the minds of the people. Without men exemplifying superior virtue in the government, this could never be achieved, and in default of it, institutional changes would only bring harm to the country.

Thirdly, as regards the cultivation of these virtues, the traditional teachings of China were definitely superior to those of the West. The Westerners, caring only for money, might build a strong and wealthy country, but would be unable to achieve harmony and unity. Western governments were based upon power; the Chinese government, upon humanity and righteousness. Calculating and self-centered, the Westerners neglected the ethical bases of government, and could offer no sound alternative for the establishment of a harmonious social order.

CH'U CH'ENG-PO
Reforming Men's Minds Comes Before Reforming Institutions

The memorial of the censor Ch'u Ch'eng-po, submitted in 1895 after China's disastrous defeat by Japan, analyzes that failure in a manner much different from the institutional reformers. It is not a failure to change laws and institutions which accounts for the defeat, but precisely that such changes were made without remedying the basic weakness—the incompetence and venality of officials. Since, in fact, graft and corruption among army and navy officers had rendered China's modern weapons useless in battle, Ch'u was on strong ground in arguing the need for official probity and integrity. The implication of this for him was that in the training and recruitment of officials traditional ethical values and moral character should be emphasized over technical qualifications and scientific training (which would have involved still further changes in methods and institutions). Thus, though not wholly opposed to change or to the reforms already undertaken, Ch'u resisted the reform movement's tendency toward progressive displacement of Chinese values—the Confucian Way—by Western methods and institutions.

[From *Chien-cheng t'ang che-kao*, 2:18a–22a]

In the present world our trouble is not that we lack good institutions but that we lack upright minds. If we seek to reform institutions, we must first reform men's minds. Unless all men of ability assist each other, good laws become mere paper documents; unless those who supervise them are fair and enlightened, the venal will end up occupying the places of the worthy. . . .

At the beginning of the T'ung-chih reign (1862–1874), Tseng Kuo-fan, Tso Tsung-t'ang, Shen Pao-chen, Li Hung-chang, and others, because the danger from abroad was becoming daily more serious, strongly emphasized Western learning. In order to effect large-scale manufacture, they built shipyards and machine factories; in order to protect our commercial rights, they organized the China Merchants' Steam Navigation Company and cotton mills; in order to educate persons of talent, they founded the Tung-wen College and other language schools; in order to strengthen training, they established naval and military academies. Countless other enterprises were inaugurated, and an annual expenditure amounting to millions was incurred. Truly no effort was spared in the attempt to establish new institutions after the pattern of the West.

When these enterprises were first undertaken, the regulations and systems were thoroughly considered so as to attain the best. It was asserted then that although China at the outset had to imitate the superior techniques of the West, eventually she would surpass the Western countries. But [in fact] perfunctory execution of these reforms has brought us to the point now where the island barbarians [the Japanese] have suddenly invaded us, and the whole situation of the nation has deteriorated. Was it because there were no reforms or because the reforms were no good? The real mistake was that we did not secure the right men to manage the new institutions. [18a–19a]

In some cases the authorities knew only how to indulge in empty talk; in other cases the officials succeeding those who originated the reforms gradually became lax and let the projects drop. Generally the initial effort was seldom maintained to the end; and while there was much talk, there was little action. . . . If the proposals had been carried out gradually and persistently, China would have long ago become invincible. But these far-reaching plans failed because we only put up an ostentatious façade behind which were concealed the avarice and selfishness [of the officials]. [19b]

In order to create a new impression in the country and to stimulate the lax morale of the people, it is necessary to distinguish between meritorious and unworthy men and to order rewards and punishments accordingly. . . . If this fundamental remedy is adopted, the raising of funds will bring in abundant revenues, and the training of troops will result in a strong army. Institutions that are good will achieve results day by day, while institutions that are not so good can be changed to bring out their maximum usefulness. Otherwise, profit-seeking opportunists will vie with each other in proposing novel theories . . . and there will be no limit to their evil doings. [20b–21a]

As to the present institutions and laws, although in name they adhere to past formulations "respectfully observed," in fact they have lost the essence of their original meaning. If we cling to the vestiges of the past, it will be conforming to externals while departing from the spirit. But if we get at the root, a single change can lead to complete fulfillment of the Way. . . . We should, therefore, make the necessary adjustments in accordance with the needs of the time. If we secure the right persons, all things can be transformed without a trace; but if we do not obtain the right persons, laws and institutions will only serve the nefarious designs of the wicked. [21a–22a]

CHU I-HSIN
Fourth Letter in Reply to K'ang Yu-wei

Chu I-hsin (1846–1894), an official who withdrew from the government to teach and pursue classical studies, prided himself on his Confucian orthodoxy and made no compromises with Westernization. He opposed even the introduction of machines on the ground that, though useful in countries with vast resources and a shortage of manpower, they would only create unemployment in China and thus drive people to desperation and violence.

Chu correctly discerned that the effect of K'ang's ideas (as expressed in *Confucius As a Reformer*) would be not only to change the outward forms of Chinese life but ultimately to undermine traditional Confucian morality itself. The "way" of the West could not be adopted piecemeal: its values and institutions were inseparably related, as were those of China. On the other hand, it was both impossible and undesirable for the Chinese to surrender their own Way—the basis of their whole civilization—for that of the West. The only solution was a return to fixed principles, rejecting expediency and utilitarianism.

[From Su Yü, ed., *I-chiao ts'ung-pien*, 1:11a–13b]

Since ancient times there have been no institutions which might not develop defects. When a true king arises, he makes small changes if the defects are small, and great changes if the defects are great. . . . Thus Confucius said: "Let there be the [right] men and the government will flourish; but without the [right] men, the government will decay and cease." [5] The defects of a government are due to the failings of those who manage the institutions rather than of those who establish them. Now by referring to Confucius as a reformer, your real intention is to facilitate the introduction of new institutions. The accounts of Confucius as a reformer come from apocryphal texts and cannot be wholly believed. But even if the sage had spoken thus, he was only taking a simple pattern and elaborating upon it in order to return to the ancient institutions of the Three Dynasties and sage-kings. How could he have intended to use "barbarian ways to reform China"? [1:11a]

I have heard of "daily renovating one's virtue," [6] but I have never heard of daily renovating one's moral principles. The scholars of the Ch'ien-lung [1736–1795] and Chia-ch'ing [1796–1820] periods regarded moral principle as of great fundamental import. Now, in order to save them from degeneration and loss you do not seek a return to fixed principles, but instead, you talk about their being changed [i.e., of their having been perverted and needing to be reformed]. The barbarians do not recognize the moral obligations between ruler and minister, father and son, elder brother and younger brother, husband and wife. There you have a per-

---

[5] *The Mean*, 20.
[6] *Book of Changes*, Ta-ch'u.

version of principles. Do you mean that the classics of our sages and the teachings of our philosophers are too jejune to follow, and that we must change them so as to have something new? Only if we first have principles can we then have institutions. Barbarian institutions are based on barbarian principles. Different principles make for different customs, and different customs give rise to different institutions. Now, instead of getting at the root of it all, you talk blithely of changing institutions. If the institutions are to be changed, are not the principles going to be changed along with them?

The manufacture of instruments by the workers involves techniques, not principles. As the minds of the people become more and more artful, clever contrivances will daily increase. Once started, there is no resistance to it. Why, therefore, need we fear that our techniques will not become sufficiently refined?

Now, because our techniques have not yet attained the highest level of skillfulness, it is proposed that we should seek to achieve this by changing our institutions as well as our principles. . . . Is this not like rescuing a person from being drowned by pushing him into a deep abyss? Is this not going much too far?

Men's minds are corrupted by utilitarianism. Those who run the institutions will utilize them for self-interest. One institution established only means one more evil added. Consequently, the path to good government is, above all, the rectification of the people's minds and the establishment of virtuous customs. The perfecting of institutions should come next.

Moreover, our institutions are by themselves clear and complete, and it is not necessary to borrow from foreign customs. How can we blame later mistakes on our ancestors and let the theory of utilitarianism be our guide?

Of course, the pitiably stupid people who only follow shadows and listen to echoes cannot be made to understand this. But even a few well-intentioned scholars, going to extremes and believing that the *Books of Odes, History, Rites,* and *Music,* which have been handed down to us by the sages, are not adequate to meet the changing circumstances, take to what is strange and novel and maintain that therein lies the path to wealth and power. But does the reason for the foreigners' being rich and powerful lie in this? Or does it not lie in their having a way which is the source and basis [of their institutions]? And is it not true that a way which is basic and original with them can never be practiced in China, and furthermore that it should absolutely not be practiced by our descendants? [12b-13a]

Mencius said: "The superior man seeks simply to bring back the unchanging standard, and that being rectified, the masses are roused to virtue. When they are so roused, forthwith perversities and wickedness disappear." [7] A review of our history since ancient times will show that herein lies the key to order and disorder. [13b]

YEH TE-HUI
The Superiority of China and Confucianism

In his criticism of the reformers in the late '90s, Yeh Te-hui (1864–1927) attempted to defend not only Confucian ethical ideals but existing institutions. While acknowledging that the West had its points of excellence, worthy of selective emulation, for him they were few indeed compared to what China had to offer. Instead, therefore, of claiming for her simply moral superiority over the West, and thus seeming to retreat from vulnerable institutions into an unimpeachable tradition, Yeh tended to justify the whole existing order—the monarchy, rule by an elite, the civil service examination system, etc.—against democracy and Westernization. With regard to institutions, however, he claimed no more than China's right to keep her own because they were peculiarly suited to her, while in regard to Confucianism he did not hesitate to proclaim its universality and ultimate adoption by the West.

Conservatism of this type, which sanctified the status quo and identified Confucianism so closely with it, helped convince Chinese of the next generation that to overthrow the old dynastic order required the destruction of Confucianism too.

[From Su Yü, ed., I-chiao ts'ung-pien, 3:32b–33a, 35b Ming chiao; 4:12a–13a Yu-hsien chin-yü, 31a Cheng chiai p'ien, 78b–79a Fei yu-hsüeh t'ung-i]

Of all countries in the five continents China is the most populous. It is situated in the north temperate zone, with a mild climate and abundant natural resources. Moreover, it became civilized earlier than all other nations, and its culture leads the world. The boundary between China and foreign countries, between Chinese and barbarians, admits of no argument and cannot be discussed in terms of their strength or our weakness.

Of the four classes of people the scholars are the finest. From the be-

[7] Mencius, VII B, 37.

ginning of the present dynasty until today there have been numerous great ministers and scholars who rose to eminence on the basis of their examination essays and poems. Although special examinations have been given and other channels of recruitment have been opened, it is mostly from the regular civil service examinations that men of abilities have risen up. The Western system of election has many defects. Under that system it is difficult to prevent favoritism and to uphold integrity. At any rate, each nation has its own governmental system, and one should not compel uniformity among them. [4:78b–79a]

An examination of the causes of success and failure in government reveals that in general the upholding of Confucianism leads to good government while the adoption of foreignism leads to disorder. If one keeps to kingly rule [relying on virtue], there will be order; if one follows the way of the overlord [relying on power], there will be disorder. . . .

Since the abdication of Yao and Shun the ruling of China under one family has become institutionalized. Because of China's vast territory and tremendous resources, even when it has been ruled under one monarch, still there have been more days of disorder than days of order. Now, if it is governed by the people, there will be different policies from many groups, and strife and contention will arise. [4:12a–13a]

[Mencius said:] "The people are the most important element in a nation," [8] not because the people consider themselves important, but because the sovereign regards them as important. And it is not people's rights that are important. Since the founding of the Ch'ing dynasty our revered rulers have loved the people as their own children. Whenever the nation has suffered from a calamity such as famine, flood, and war, the emperor has immediately given generous relief upon its being reported by the provincial officials. For instance, even though the treasury was short of funds recently, the government did not raise any money from the people except for the *likin* [9] tax. Sometimes new financial devices are proposed by ministers who like to discuss pecuniary matters, but even if they are approved and carried out by order of the department concerned, they are suspended as soon as it is learned that they are troubling the people. How vastly different is this from the practice of Western countries where taxes are levied in all places, on all persons, for all things, and at all times? [4:31a]

[8] *Mencius*, VII B, 14.   [9] Internal customs duties.

Confucianism represents the supreme expression of justice in the principles of Heaven and the hearts of men. In the future it will undoubtedly be adopted by civilized countries of both East and West. The essence of Confucianism will shine brightly as it renews itself from day to day.

Ethics is common to China and the West. The concept of blood relations and respect for parents prevails also among barbarians. To love life and hate killing is rooted in the human heart. The Confucian ideal is expressed in the *Spring and Autumn Annals,* which aims at saving the world from disorder and treason; proper conduct is defined in the *Book of Filial Piety,* which lays down the moral principles and obligations for all generations to come. And there is the *Analects,* which synthesizes the great laws of the ancient kings. Tseng Tzu, Tzu-hsia, Mencius, and others who transmitted the teaching all mastered the Six Arts and knew thoroughly the myriad changes of circumstances. All that the human heart desires to say was said several thousand years ago. [3:32b–33a]

Chinese scholars who attack Western religion err in false accusation, while those who admire it err in flattery. Indeed, only a superficial Confucianist would say that Westerners have no moral principles, and yet only fools would say that Western religion excels Confucianism. In so far as there is morality, there must be Confucianism. [3:35b]

CHANG CHIH-TUNG

Exhortation to Learn

Chang Chih-tung (1837–1909) was one of the leading figures in the empire during the last days of the Manchus. A brilliant scholar and official, widely esteemed for his personal integrity and patriotism, he was an early supporter of reform and as a provincial administrator promoted many industrial, railway, educational, and cultural projects. When his *Exhortation to Learn* (*Ch'üan-hsüeh p'ien*) was published in 1898, it was hailed by the reformers then in power and given official distribution by the emperor.

Basically, however, Chang was a moderate who coupled gradual reform with a stout adherence to Neo-Confucianism, defense of monarchical institutions, and loyalty to the dynasty. Avoiding extremes, he backed away from the radical measures of K'ang Yu-wei on the one hand, and on the other, from the reactionary policies that led to the Boxer catastrophe in 1900. A combination of moderation and shrewdness thus helped him survive politically to play an influential role at court in the first decade of the new century. During this period he was instrumental both in the enactment of educational and civil service reforms (including abolition of the famous eight-legged essay) and in the attempt to revive Confucianism as a state cult.

Chang's position is summed up in the catch-phrase "Chinese learning for substance, Western learning for function" (*Chung-hsüeh wei t'i, hsi-hsüeh wei yung*). The terms "substance" (*t'i*) and "function" (*yung*) Chang drew from the philosophical lexicon of Sung metaphysics, in which they stood for the ontological and functional aspects of the same reality. A similar distinction was expressed in the dichotomy between the Way or Principle (*tao*) and instruments (*ch'i*), wherein principle is the basis of the instrument and the instrument is the manifestation of the principle. Chang, following the example of earlier reformers who distinguished between the Chinese "Way" (or Chinese moral "principles") and Western instruments, used "substance" in reference to traditional Chinese values, and "function" (i.e., utility, practical application) in reference to the Western methods by which China and its traditional way of life were to be defended in the modern world. In this new formulation "substance" and "function" bore no intrinsic relationship to one another as they had for earlier Neo-Confucianists. Using the terms in an unphilosophic manner, Chang exploited their ambiguity in order to cover a compromise dictated by hard necessity.

There can be no doubt of Chang's genuine traditionalism, in the sense that he held fast to certain established Confucian traditions and sought as much to preserve these values intact as to provide a sanction for needed reforms. He was no K'ang Yu-wei, waving the banner of Confucius while marching off to destroy Confucianism. Nevertheless, his catch-phrases served only for the moment to hide the conflict between old and new. The compatability of "substance" and "function" was a problem now as it had not been for the Sung Neo-Confucianists. Chang, who was not wholly naive about the lengths to which Westernization would go (he insisted, for instance, that Western methods of administration were as essential as Western technology), nor wholly mistaken about the difficulties of establishing political democracy in China, still misjudged the frictions and tensions which modernization would create within the old order. To just such pressures conservative reformism soon fell a victim. As has been said, despotisms are never more endangered than when they begin to make concessions. Two years after the death of this venerable statesman in October, 1909, the Manchu dynasty itself collapsed.

[From *Ch-üan-hsüeh p'ien,* in *Chang Wen-hsiang kung ch-üan-chi,* ts'e 202:iab, iiiab, 2b–3a, 13a–14b, 23a–25a, 27ab; 203:9b, 19b, 22a]

The crisis of China today has no parallel either in the Spring and Autumn period [i.e., the time of Confucius] or in all the dynasties from the Ch'in and Han down through the Yüan and Ming. . . . Our imperial court has shown the utmost concern over the problem, living in anxiety and worry. It is ready to make changes and to provide special opportunities for able ministers and generals. New schools are to be established and special examinations are to be held. All over the land men of serious purpose and sincere dedication have responded with enthusiasm and vigor. Those who seek to remedy the present situation talk of new learning; those who fear lest its acceptance should destroy the true Way hold fast to the teachings of the ancients. Both groups are unable to strike the mean. The conservatives resemble those who give up all eating because they have difficulty in swallowing, while the progressives are like a flock of sheep who have arrived at a road of many forks and do not know where to turn. The former do not know how to accommodate to special circumstances; the latter are ignorant of what is fundamental. Not knowing how to accommodate to special circumstances, the conservatives have no way to confront the enemy and deal with the crisis; not knowing the fundamental, the innovators look with contempt upon the teachings of the sages. Thus those who hold fast to the old order of things despise more and more the innovators and the latter in turn violently detest the conservatives. As the two groups are engaged in mutual recriminations, impostors and adventurers who do not hesitate to resort to falsification and distortion pour out their theories to confuse the people. Consequently students are in doubt as to which course to pursue, while perverse opinions spread all over the country. [202:ia–b]

United Hearts. I have learned of three things that are necessary for saving China in the present crisis. The first is to maintain the state. The second is to preserve the doctrine of Confucius; and the third is to protect the Chinese race. These three are inseparably related. We must protect the state, the doctrine, and the race with one heart, and this is what we mean by united hearts.

In order to protect the race we must first preserve the doctrine, and before the doctrine can be preserved, we must preserve the state and the race. How is the race to be preserved? If we have knowledge, it will be preserved; and by knowledge we mean the doctrine. How is the doctrine to be maintained? It is to be maintained by strength, and strength lies in armies. Thus, if the empire has no power and prestige, the doctrine will not be followed; and if the empire is not prosperous, the Chinese race will not be respected. [202:2b–3a]

The Three Bonds. The subject is bound to the sovereign, the son is bound to the father, and the wife is bound to the husband. . . . What makes a sage a sage, what makes China China, is just this set of bonds. Thus, if we recognize the bond of subject to sovereign, the theory of people's rights cannot stand. If we recognize the bond of son to father, then the theory that father and son are amenable to the same punishment and that funeral and sacrificial ceremonies should be abolished cannot stand. If we recognize the bond of wife to husband, then the theory of equal rights for men and women cannot stand. [202:13ab]

Our sage represented the highest ideal of human relationships. He established in detail and with clarity rules of decorum based on human feelings. Although Westerners have such rules only in abbreviated form, still foreigners have never abandoned the idea of decorum. For the norm of Heaven and the nature of man are about the same in China and in foreign countries. Without these rules of decorum no ruler could ever govern a state, and no teacher could ever establish his doctrine. [202:14b]

Rectifying Political Rights. Nowadays scholars who become vexed with the present order of things are angry at the foreigners for cheating and oppressing us, at the generals for being unable to fight, at the ministers for being unwilling to reform, at the educational authorities for not establishing modern schools, and at the various officials for not seeking to promote industry and commerce. They therefore advocate the theory of people's rights in order to get the people to unite and exert themselves. Alas, where did they find those words that would lead to disorder!

The theory of people's rights will bring us not a particle of good but a hundred evils. Are we going to establish a parliament? Among Chinese scholar-officials and among the people there are still many today who are obstinate and uneducated. They understand nothing about the general situation of the world, and they are ignorant of the affairs of state. They have never heard of important developments concerning the schools, political systems, military training, and manufacture of machinery. Suppose the confused and tumultuous people are assembled in one house, with one sensible man there out of a hundred who are witless, babbling aimlessly, and talking as if in a dream—what use would it be? Moreover, in foreign countries the matter of revenue is mainly handled by the lower house, while other matters of legislation are taken care of by the upper house. To be a member of parliament the candidate must possess a fairly good income. Nowadays Chinese merchants rarely have much capital, and the Chinese people are lacking in long range vision. If any important proposal for raising funds comes up for discussion, they will make excuses and keep silent; so their discussion is no different from nondiscussion. . . . This is the first reason why a parliament is of no use. . . .

At present China is indeed not imposing or powerful, but the people still get along well with their daily work, thanks to the dynastic institutions which hold them together. Once the theory of people's rights is adopted, foolish people will certainly be delighted, rebels will strike, order will not be maintained, and great disturbances will arise on all sides. Even those who advocate the theory of people's rights will not be able to live safely themselves. Furthermore, as the towns will be plundered and the Christian churches burned, I am afraid the foreigners, under the pretext of protecting [their nationals and interests], will send troops and warships to penetrate deeply and occupy our territories. The whole country will then be given to others without a fight. Thus the theory of people's rights is just what our enemies would like to hear spread about. [202:23a–24a]

Recently those who have picked up some Western theories have gone as far as to say that everybody has the right to be his own master. This is even more absurd. This phrase is derived from the foreign books of religion. It means that God bestows upon man his nature and soul and that every person has wisdom and intelligence which enable him to do useful work. When the translators interpret it to mean that every person has the right to be his own master, they indeed make a great mistake.

Western countries, whether they are monarchies, republics, or constitutional monarchies, all have a government, and a government has laws. Officials have administrative laws, soldiers have military laws, workers have labor laws, and merchants have commercial laws. The lawyers learn them; the judges administer them. Neither the ruler nor the people can violate the law. What the executive recommends can be debated by the parliament, but what the parliament decides can be vetoed by the throne. Thus it may be said that nobody is his own master. [202:24b–25a]

Following the Proper Order. If we wish to make China strong and preserve Chinese learning, we must promote Western learning. But unless we first use Chinese learning to consolidate the foundation and to give our purpose a right direction, the strong will become rebellious leaders and the weak, slaves. The consequence will be worse than not being versed in Western learning. . . .

Scholars today should master the Classics in order to understand the purpose of our early sages and teachers in establishing our doctrine. They must study history in order to know the succession of peace and disorder in our history and the customs of the land, read the philosophers and literary collections in order to become familiar with Chinese scholarship and fine writing. After this they can select and utilize that Western learning which can make up for our shortcomings and adopt those Western governmental methods which can cure our illness. In this way, China will derive benefit from Western learning without incurring any danger. [202:27a-b]

[*On Reform*]. It is the human relationships and moral principles that are immutable, but not legal systems; the Way of the sage, not instruments; the discipline of the mind, not technology.

Laws and institutions are what we meet changing situations with; they therefore need not all be the same. The Way is what we establish the foundation upon; it therefore must be uniform. . . . What we call the basis of the Way consists of the Three Bonds and the Four Cardinal Virtues.[10] If these are abandoned, great disorder will occur even before the new laws can be put into effect. But as long as they are preserved, even Confucius and Mencius, if they were to come back to life, could hardly condemn the reforms. [203:19b, 22a]

If we do not change our habits, we cannot change our methods [*fa*]; and if we cannot change our methods, we cannot change our instruments. . . . In Chinese learning the inquiry into antiquity is not important; what is important is knowledge of practical use. There are also different branches of Western learning: Western technology is not important, what is important is Western administration. [202:iiia]

There are five important factors in the administration of the new schools. First, both the old and the new must be studied. By the old we mean the *Four Books,* the five Classics, Chinese history, government, and geography; by the new we mean Western administration, Western technology, and Western history. The old learning is to be the substance; the new learning is to be for application [function]. Neither one should be neglected. Second, both administration and technology should be studied. Education, geography, budgeting, taxes, military preparations, laws and regulations, industry and commerce, belong to the category of Western administration. Mathematics, drawing, mining, medicine, acoustics, op-

---

[10] Decorum, righteousness, integrity, sense of shame.

tics, chemistry, and electricity belong to the category of Western technology. [203:9b]

REFORMISM AT THE EXTREME

In this final section on reform we take up two followers of K'ang Yu-wei who carried Chinese tradition over the brink to which K'ang had led it. They are T'an Ssu-t'ung (1865–1898) who, before his untimely death, sounded the knell of monarchism and Confucian ethics; and Liang Ch'i-ch'ao (1873–1929), the leading reformist-in-exile after 1898, who called for a complete renovation of Chinese life. As opposed to the conservative reformism of Chang Chih-tung, which prevailed in the last decade of Manchu rule, they represent the kind of radical reformism which prepared the ground for revolution in 1911.

T'AN SSU-T'UNG

T'an Ssu-t'ung is one of the most striking figures of the Reform Movement. The non-conformist son of a high official, he loved both independent study and the active life—now delving in books and writing poetry, now practicing swordsmanship, serving as a military officer in the Far West or traveling about as he pleased in search of historic sites and boon companions. He was disinclined toward an official career, and might never have sought office had he not, from his unorthodox studies (embracing Christianity and Buddhism as well as Confucianism and Taoism), developed a passionate interest in the Western world and the modernization of China. Active leadership in the reform movement and study under K'ang Yu-wei led eventually to participation at court in the Hundred Days of Reform. With its failure, he died a "martyr" at the age of thirty-three, risking death in hopes of rescuing the young Kuang-hsü emperor from his enemies.

Not only his martyrdom but his extremism made T'an a far greater hero to the new generation of Chinese than his master, K'ang. Accepting many of K'ang's basic ideas, he became an immediate and outspoken champion of some that K'ang foresaw only as future possibilities. He openly advocated republicanism against the monarchical system which K'ang would have retained and merely reformed. Here T'an cited Huang

Tsung-hsi as native authority for a view to which—not native tradition but—the West had led him. As against loyalty to the Manchus he proclaimed Chinese nationalism, pointing in this case to Wang Fu-chih as its exemplar in the past. T'an also attacked directly and unqualifiedly the traditional Confucian virtues based on specific human relationships which Chang Chih-tung had upheld as the essence of Confucianism and the Chinese way of life. It was these ideas—republicanism, nationalism, and opposition to the Chinese family system—that anticipated main trends in the early twentieth century.

T'AN SSU-T'UNG
On the Study of Humanity

T'an's chief work, The Study of Humanity (Jen-hsüeh, 1898), might more accurately be called On Humanitarianism. It offers an eclectic philosophy with elements drawn ostensibly from Confucianism, Buddhism, and Christianity. The central conception of jen differs little from that of K'ang: a generalized feeling of good will toward men which suggests most the "liberty, equality and fraternity" of the French Revolution, somewhat less Christian "charity" and Buddhist "compassion," and perhaps least of all, the Confucian virtue of "humanity" (jen). Though akin, in certain respects, to the Neo-Confucian concept of jen as a cosmic love which unites man to Heaven and earth, its ethical character is radically altered by T'an's repudiation of the obligations of human relationship, which in the past had given practical significance to jen for Confucianists and Neo-Confucianists alike.

[From T'an Liu-yang ch'üan-chi, Jen-hsüeh, A:37a-b, B:1a-10a]

When Confucius first set forth his teachings, he discarded the ancient learning, reformed existing institutions, rejected monarchism, advocated republicanism, and transformed inequality into equality. He indeed applied himself to many changes. Unfortunately, the scholars who followed Hsün Tzu forgot entirely the true meaning of Confucius' teaching, but clung to its superficial form. They allowed the ruler supreme, unlimited powers, and enabled him to make use of Confucianism in controlling the country. The school of Hsün Tzu insisted that duties based on human relationships were the essence of Confucianism, not knowing that this was a system applicable only to the Age of Disorder. Even for the Age of Disorder, any discussion of the human relationships [11] without reference to

[11] The relationships between ruler and minister, father and son, husband and wife, elder brother and younger brother, and friends.

Heaven would be prejudicial and incomplete, and the evil consequences would be immeasurable. How much worse, then, for them recklessly to have added the three bonds,[12] thus openly creating a system of inequality with its unnatural distinctions between high and low, and making men, the children of Heaven and earth, suffer a miserable life. . . .

For the past two thousand years the ruler-minister relationship has been especially dark and inhuman, and it has become worse in recent times. The ruler is not physically different or intellectually superior to man: on what does he rely to oppress 400 million people? He relies on the formulation long ago of the three bonds and five human relationships, so that, controling men's bodies, he can also control their minds. As Chuang Tzu said: "He who steals a sickle gets executed; he who steals a state becomes the prince." When T'ien Ch'eng-tzu stole the state of Ch'i, he also stole the [Confucian] system of humanity, rightcousness and sage wisdom. When the thieves were Chinese and Confucianists, it was bad enough; but how could we have allowed the unworthy tribes of Mongolia and Manchuria, who knew nothing of China or Confucianism, to steal China by means of their barbarism and brutality! After stealing China, they controlled the Chinese by means of the system they had stolen, and shamelessly made use of Confucianism, with which they had been unfamiliar, to oppress China, to which they had been strangers. But China worshiped them as Heaven, and did not realize their guilt. Instead of burning the books in order to keep the people ignorant [as did the Ch'in], they more cleverly used the books to keep the people under control. Compared with them, the tyrannical emperor of the Ch'in dynasty was but a fool! [A:37a–38a]

At the beginning of the human race, there were no princes and subjects, for all were just people. As the people were unable to govern each other and did not have time to rule, they joined in raising up someone to be the prince. Now "joined in raising up" means, not that the prince selected the people [as for civil service],[13] but that the people selected the prince; it means that the prince was not far above the people, but rather on the same level with them. Again, by "joined in raising up" the prince, it means that there must be people before there can be a prince: the prince is therefore the "branch" [secondary] while the people are the

---

[12] Binding the minister to the ruler, the son to the father, the wife to the husband.
[13] The term "raised up" or "recommended" had been applied to candidates selected for office.

"root" [primary]. Since there is no such thing in the world as sacrificing the root for the branch, how can we sacrifice the people for the prince? When it is said that they "joined in raising up" the prince, it necessarily means that they could also dismiss him. The prince serves the people; the ministers assist the ruler to serve the people. Taxes are levied to provide the means for managing the public affairs of the people. If public affairs are not well managed, it is a universal principle that the ruler should be replaced. . . .

The ruler is also one of the people; in fact, he is of secondary importance as compared to ordinary people. If there is no reason for people to die for one another, there is certainly less reason for those of primary importance to die for one of secondary importance. Then, should those who died for the ruler in ancient times not have done so? Not necessarily. But I can say positively that there is reason only to die for a cause, definitely not reason to die for a prince. [B:1a–b]

In ancient times loyalty meant actually being loyal. If the subordinate actually serves his superior faithfully, why should not the superior actually wait upon his subordinate also? Loyalty signifies mutuality, the utmost fulfillment of a mutual relationship. How can we maintain that only ministers and subjects should live up to it? Confucius said: "The prince should behave as a prince, the minister as a minister." He also said: "The father should behave as a father, the son as a son, the elder brother as an elder brother, the younger brother as a younger brother, the husband as a husband, the wife as a wife." The founder of Confucianism never preached inequality. [B:2b]

As the evils of the ruler-minister relationship reached their highest development, it was considered natural that the relationships between father and son and between husband and wife should also be brought within the control of categorical morality.[14] This is all damage done by the categorizing of the three bonds. Whenever you have categorical obligations, not only are the mouths of the people sealed so that they are afraid to speak up, but their minds are also shackled so that they are afraid to think. Thus the favorite method for controlling the people is to multiply the categorical obligations. [B:7b–8a]

[14] Under the influence of Buddhism and perhaps utilitarianism, T'an viewed the traditional moral values as mere "names" or empty concepts (*ming*) in contrast to reality or actuality (*shih*).

As to the husband-wife relationship, on what basis does the husband extend his power and oppress the other party? Again it is the theory of the three bonds which is the source of the trouble. When the husband considers himself the master, he will not treat his wife as an equal human being. In ancient China the wife could ask for a divorce, and she therefore did not lose the right to be her own master. Since the inscription of the tyrannical law [against remarriage] on the tablet at K'uai-chi during the Ch'in dynasty, and particularly since its zealous propagation by the Confucianists of the Sung dynasty—who cooked up the absurd statement that "To die in starvation is a minor matter, but to lose one's chastity [by remarrying] is a serious matter"—the cruel system of the Legalists has been applied to the home, and the ladies' chambers have become locked-up prisons. [B:7–8]

Among the five human relationships, the one between friends is the most beneficial and least harmful to life. It yields tranquil happiness and causes not a trace of pain—so long as friends are made with the right persons. Why is this? Because the relationship between friends is founded on equality, liberty, and mutual feelings. In short, it is simply because friendship involves no loss of the right to be one's own master. Next comes the relationship between brothers, which is somewhat like the relationship between friends. The rest of the five relationships which have been darkened by the three bonds are like hell. [B:9a]

The world, misled by the conception of blood relations, makes erroneous distinctions between the nearly related and the remotely related, and relegates the relationship between friends to the end of the line. The relationship between friends, however, not only is superior to the other four relationships, but should be the model for them all. When these four relationships have been brought together and infused with the spirit of friendship, they can well be abolished. . . .

People in China and abroad are now talking of reforms, but no fundamental principles and systems can be introduced if the five relationships remain unchanged, let alone the three bonds. [B:9b–10a]

LIANG CH'I-CH'AO

Liang Ch'i-ch'ao, disciple of K'ang Yu-wei and his co-worker in the Reform Movement, escaped to Japan after the failure of K'ang's brief regime and there became perhaps the most influential advocate of reform in the years before the Revolution of 1911. His writings, in a lucid and forceful style, dealt with a wide range of political, social, and cultural issues. To thousands of young Chinese, studying abroad (most of them in Japan) or reading his books and pamphlets on the mainland, he became an inspiration and an idol—a patriotic hero, whose command of Chinese classical learning together with a remarkable sensitivity to ideas and trends in the West, gave him the appearance of an intellectual giant joining Occident and Orient, almost a universal man.

The fortnightly journal, *A People Made New* or *A New People* (*Hsin-min ts'ung-pao*), which Liang published in Yokohama from 1902 to 1905, showed a great change in his thinking. He was now exposed far more to Western influences, and enormously impressed by Japan's progress in contrast to China's repeated failures. Sensing the power of nationalism as the force which galvanized the Western peoples and the Japanese into action, realizing too the apathy and indifference of China's millions toward the abortive palace revolution of 1898 (as, indeed, toward all public affairs), Liang became fully convinced that popular education and the instillment of nationalism were China's greatest needs. Everything in her past culture which seemed an obstacle to national progress was to be cast aside.

Instead of reinterpreting Confucianism to find a sanction for progress, as he and K'ang had done earlier, Liang now put forward a new view of world history strongly colored by Social Darwinism: a struggle for survival among nations and races. Evolution of this fierce, competitive sort, rather than an optimistic view of inevitable progress to the Grand Unity, became the spur to drastic reform. In the 1890s he and K'ang had urged going beyond the mere adoption of Western "methods" and "instruments" to basic institutional reform; now he argued that institutional change itself could only be effected through a transformation of the whole Chinese way of life and particularly its morals, always considered the very essence of Confucianism. Morality was now to serve "the interest of the group," national survival.

But if so much were to be surrendered to the West, what would remain as distinctively Chinese in the new nationalism? Liang's equivocations on this point are evident in the selections which follow.[15] There must be

[15] They are also the subject of searching and detailed analysis by Joseph Levenson in his *Liang Ch'i-ch'ao and the Mind of Modern China* (Cambridge, 1953).

wholesale change, but what is good in China's past should still be preserved (there must, he insists, have been something of value in Chinese civilization which accounts for its survival, even if he cannot specify it here). Clearly, however, Liang's nationalism is now bound up very little with pride in the past and far more with a compulsive hope in China's future progress.

The frustration of Liang's, and China's, hopes is the story of the Republican era. Liang's distaste for violence and his refusal to turn Chinese nationalism against the Manchus made him less suited than Sun Yat-sen to become a great revolutionary leader, and his almost unfailing gift for misjudged compromises stood him in poor stead, after his return from exile, in the rough and tumble of Republican politics and warlordism. In the 1920s, while the revolutionary tide of Sun and the Nationalists rose, Liang withdrew to semi-retirement as a patriarch still revered but little heeded. Disillusioned with his own hopes, and viewing the West after the First World War as the victim of its own aggressiveness and acquistiveness, he took what consolation he could from the superiority of Chinese civilization as an expression of "Eastern spirituality" in contrast to the materialism of the West—an idea which he was neither the first to expound in the new Asia nor the last.

LIANG CH'I-CH'AO
A People Made New
[From Hsin-min shuo, in Yin-ping shih wen-chi, t'se 12:36b, 40a, 40b, 41a, 47a–b; 13:32b–33b]

Since the appearance of mankind on earth, thousands of countries have existed on the earth. Of these, however, only about a hundred still occupy a place on the map of the five continents. And among these hundred-odd countries there are only four or five great powers that are strong enough to dominate the world and to conquer nature. All countries have the same sun and moon, all have mountains and rivers, and all consist of people with feet and skulls; but some countries rise while others fall, and some become strong while others are weak. Why? Some attribute it to geographical advantages. But geographically, America today is the same as America in ancient times; why then do only the Anglo-Saxons enjoy the glory? Similarly, ancient Rome was the same as Rome today; why then have the Latin people declined in fame? Some attribute it to certain heroes. But Macedonia once had Alexander, and yet today it is no longer seen; Mongolia once had Chingis Khan, and yet today it can hardly maintain its existence. Ah! I know the reason. A state is formed by the assembling of people. The relationship of a nation to its people resembles that of the body to its four limbs, five viscera, muscles, veins, and corpuscles. It has never happened that the four limbs could be cut off, the five viscera wasted away, the muscles and veins injured, the corpuscles dried up, and yet the body still live. Similarly, it has never happened that a people could be foolish, timid, disorganized, and confused and yet the nation still stand. Therefore, if we wish the body to live for a long time, we must understand the methods of hygiene. If we wish the nation to be secure, rich, and honored, we must discuss the way for the people's being "made new." [13:36b]

The Meaning of "A People Made New." The term "people made new" does not mean that our people must give up entirely what is old in order to follow others. There are two meanings of "made new." One is to improve what is original in the people and so renew it; the other is to adopt what is originally lacking in the people and so make a new people. Without one of the two, there will be no success. . . .

A nation which can maintain itself in the world must have some peculiar characteristics on the part of its nationals. From morals and laws down to customs, habits, literature, and fine arts, all share an independent spirit which has been handed down from the forefathers to their descendants. Thus the group is formed and the nation develops. This is really the fundamental basis of nationalism. Our people have been established as a nation on the Asian continent for several thousand years, and we must have some special characteristics which are grand, noble, and perfect, and distinctly different from those of other races. We should preserve these characteristics and not let them be lost. What is called preserving, however, is not simply to let them exist and grow by themselves and then blithely say: "I am preserving them, I am preserving them." It is like a tree: unless some new buds come out every year, its withering away may soon be expected. Or like a well: unless there is always some new spring bubbling, its exhaustion is not far away. [12:40a]

If we wish to make our nation strong, we must investigate extensively the methods followed by other nations in becoming independent. We should select their superior points and appropriate them to make up our own shortcomings. Now with regard to politics, academic learning, and techniques, our critics know how to take the superior points of others to make up for our own weakness; but they do not know that the people's virtue, the people's wisdom, and the people's vitality are the great basis of politics, academic learning, and techniques. If they do not take the former but adopt the latter, neglect the roots but tend the branches, it will be no different from seeing the luxuriant growth of another tree and wishing to graft its branches onto our withered trunk, or seeing the bubbling flow of another well and wishing to draw its water to fill our dry well. Thus, how to adopt and make up for what we originally lacked so that our people may be made new, should be deeply and carefully considered. [12:40b]

All phenomena in the world are governed by no more than two principles: the conservative and the progressive. Those who are applying these two principles are inclined either to the one or to the other. Sometimes the two arise simultaneously and conflict with each other; sometimes the two exist simultaneously and compromise with each other. No one can exist if he is inclined only to one. Where there is conflict, there must be compromise. Conflict is the forerunner of compromise.

Those who excel at making compromises become a great people, such as the Anglo-Saxons, who, in a manner of speaking, make their way with one foot on the ground and one foot going forward, or who hold fast to things with one hand and pick up things with another. Thus, what I mean by "a people made new" is not those who are infatuated with Western ways and, in order to keep company with others, throw away our morals, learning, and customs of several thousand years' standing. Nor are they those who stick to old paper and say that merely embracing the morals, learning and customs of these thousands of years will be sufficient to enable us to stand upon the great earth. [12:41a]

On Public Morals. Among our people there is not one who looks on national affairs as if they were his own affairs. The significance of public morality has not dawned on us. Examining into it, however, we realize that the original basis for morality lies in its serving the interests of the group. As groups differ in their degree of barbarism or civilization, so do their appropriate morals vary. All of them, however, aim at consolidating, improving, and developing the group. . . . In ancient times some barbarians considered it moral to practice community of women, or to treat slaves as if they were not human beings. And modern philosophers do not call it immoral because under the particular situation at the time that was the proper thing to do in the interests of the group. Thus morality is founded on the interests of the group. If it is against this principle, even the perfect good can become an accursed evil. Public morality is therefore the basis of all morals. What is beneficial to the group is good; what is detrimental to the interests of the group is bad. This principle applies to all places and to all ages.

As to the external features of morality, they vary according to the degree of progress in each group. As groups differ in barbarism or civilization, so do their public interests and their morals. Morality cannot remain absolutely unchanged. It is not something that could be put into a fixed formula by the ancients several thousand years ago, to be followed by all generations to come. Hence, we who live in the present group should observe the main trends of the world, study what will suit our nation, and create a new morality in order to solidify, benefit, and develop our group. We should not impose upon ourselves a limit and refrain from going into what our sages had not prescribed. Search for public morality and there will appear a new morality, there will appear "a people made new." [12:47a–b]

On Progress. Generally, those who talk about a "renovation" may be divided into two groups. The lower group consists of those who pick up others' trite expressions and assume a bold look in order to climb up the official hierarchy. Their Western learning is stale stuff, their diplomacy relies on bribes, and their travels are moving in the dark. These people, of course, are not worth mentioning. The higher group consists of those who are worried about the situation and try hard to develop the nation and to promote well-being. But when asked about their methods, they would begin with diplomacy, training of troops, purchase of arms and manufacture of instruments; then they would proceed to commerce, mining and railways; and finally they would come, as they did recently, to officers' training, police, and education. Are these not the most important and necessary things for modern civilized nations? Yes. But can we attain the level of modern civilization and place our nation in an invincible position by adopting a little of this and that, or taking a small step now and then? I know we cannot. [13:32b]

Let me illustrate this by commerce. Economic competition is one of

the big problems of the world today. It is the method whereby the powers
attempt to conquer us. It is also the method whereby we should fight
for our existence. The importance of improving our foreign trade has
been recognized by all. But in order to promote foreign trade, it is necessary to protect the rights of our domestic trade and industry; and in order
to protect these rights, it is necessary to issue a set of commercial laws.
Commercial laws, however, cannot stand by themselves, and so it is necessary to complement them with other laws. A law which is not carried
out is tantamount to no law; it is therefore necessary to define the powers
of the judiciary. Bad legislation is worse than no legislation, and so it is
necessary to decide where the legislative power should belong. If those
who violate the law are not punished, laws will become void as soon
as they are proclaimed; therefore, the duties of the judiciary must be
defined. When all these are carried to the logical conclusion, it will be
seen that foreign trade cannot be promoted without a constitution, a
parliament, and a responsible government. Those who talk about foreign
trade today blithely say, "I am promoting it, I am promoting it," and
nothing more. I do not know how they are going to promote it. The
above is one illustration, but it is true with all other cases. Thus I know
why the so-called new methods nowadays are ineffectual. Why? Because
without destruction there can be no construction. . . . What, then, is the
way to effect our salvation and to achieve progress? The answer is that
we must shatter at a blow the despotic and confused governmental system of some thousands of years; we must sweep away the corrupt and
sycophantic learning of these thousands of years. [13:33a–b]

CHAPTER XXVII

THE NATIONALIST REVOLUTION

The Chinese revolution of 1911, which led to the overthrow of the Manchus the following year, was complex in its origins and confused as to its outcome. There is no single trend of thought or political action with which it can be identified. Nevertheless, amid the shifting currents of ideas and events in the two decades following, nationalism and republicanism emerged as perhaps the leading slogans in the political arena; and in the popular mind (if we may so speak of a people just awakening to political consciousness), it was Sun Yat-sen (1866–1925) and his Kuomintang followers who stood out as the most eloquent, though not always the most effective, spokesmen for these concepts. To express their basic aims and hopes is the purpose of the selections which follow. The next chapter will illustrate parallel developments in the intellectual sphere during this same republican era.

SUN YAT-SEN AND THE NATIONALIST REVOLUTION

The origins of the revolutionary movement may be traced back to 1895 when Sun, convinced that the Manchu regime was beyond hope of reforming, attempted his first abortive coup in Canton. As a practitioner of revolution Sun was never a great success, though this was his chosen profession; nor did he, on the other hand, stand out as a brilliant theoretician preparing the ground for revolution by the force and clarity of his ideas. It was rather as a visionary that Sun caught the imagination of Chinese youth—as a man of intense convictions and magnetic personality, who, through his crusading and somewhat quixotic career, dramatized ideas and catalyzed forces far more powerful than he. The first clear sign of this came just after the Russo-Japanese War, which gave great impetus to revolutionary nationalism throughout Asia. Japan was a hotbed of agitation among Chinese in exile and students sent abroad for study under official auspices. Sun, in 1905, joined his secret revolutionary society with other extremist groups to form the League of Common Alliance (*T'ung-meng hui*), out of which later grew the Kuomintang. Through its party organ, the *People's Report* (*Min pao*), this group published a manifesto which stated the aims of the movement, including three from which evolved the Three People's Principles.

One significant feature of this new movement is that it derived its inspiration very largely from Western sources. We have already seen how the thinking of the late nineteenth-century reformers was often decisively influenced by the West, either through its ideas or through the alternatives it confronted them with. In most cases, however, these reformers had been trained in the classical disciplines and prepared themselves for entry into the old elite. Even as reformers they felt a need somehow to reconcile the new with the old. Sun Yat-sen's case is different. His training was almost entirely in Western schools (including secondary education at a mission school in Hawaii). In contrast to generations of office seekers who had passed through the examination halls, this prospective leader of the new China aspired first to a military career and then went to medical school in Hongkong. Knowing little of classical studies, and inclined at first to think them useless, he inspired respect or enthusiasm more by what seemed his practical grasp of world trends than by any Chinese erudition. Moreover, his knowledge of China itself was limited, since his life was mostly spent in a few port cities, in Western outposts like Hongkong and Macao, or in exile abroad.

This is not to say that Sun was wholly Westernized. One whose early years had been spent in a peasant household, whose boyhood hero had been the Taiping leader Hung Hsiu-ch'üan, and whose associations in later life were for the most part with overseas Chinese, could be cut off from the official tradition and Confucian orthodoxy without ceasing in many ways to be Chinese. But it does mean that Sun's aims, primarily political in character and suggested by prevailing modes of thought in the West, were little adapted at the outset either to traditional Chinese attitudes or to the realities of Chinese life. They were inspired rather by a belief that, with the progress of civilization and the advance of science, Western ideas and institutions could be adopted quickly and easily by the Chinese, without regard to their past condition. Yet the bridging of this gap, between China's sluggish past and Sun's high-speed future, proved to be the great despair of the nationalist movement. China, as events after 1911 showed, could not be remade overnight. Sun's own program he was forced to modify, and others after him still faced an enormous task of assimilation and re-evaluation. This, however, is for our later readings to take up.

HU HAN-MIN
The Six Principles of the People's Report

The basic platform of the League of Common Alliance (*T'ung-meng hui*) was set forth in a manifesto issued in the fall of 1905. It reiterated Sun's early anti-Manchu and republican aims, as well as a third, "Equalization of Land Rights," which showed a developing interest in socialistic ideas. The manifesto also stated Sun's plan of revolution in three stages: 1) military government; 2) a provisional constitution granting local self-government; and 3) full constitutional government under a republican system.

A somewhat fuller statement of the League's basic principles was written for the third issue of the party organ, *People's Report,* in April, 1906, by its editor Hu Han-min (1879–1936). The statement carried Sun Yat-sen's endorsement. Three of the six principles set forth here—nationalism, republicanism, and land nationalization—correspond roughly to Sun's famous Three Principles. The other three, not reproduced below, dealt with problems of immediate concern to the revolutionists in Yokohama, as affecting their relations with others, especially the Japanese. The fourth principle asserts the indispensability of a strong, united China to the maintenance of world peace, since it is China's weakness which encourages the great powers to contend for special advantages and risk a catastrophic war. Here the influence of the Japanese statesman, Ōkuma Shigenobu, liberal leader whose support the revolutionists counted heavily upon, is evident. The fifth and sixth principles advocate close collaboration between the Chinese and Japanese, and urge other countries also to support the revolution. Nationalism, at this point, is thus not opposed to foreign intervention but in fact welcomes it—on the right side.

While the Manchu regime is the prime target of the revolutionists' indignation, their actual antagonists in the political struggle are not so much those in power at home as reformers in exile (like Liang Ch'i-ch'ao, then also active in Yokohama) who remain loyal to the dynasty and favor constitutional monarchy. During the first decade of the twentieth century the contest between these two groups, reformist and revolutionary, for the support of Chinese students in Japan was bitter and sometimes violent.

[From Tsou Lu (ed.), *Chung-kuo Kuomintang shih kao*, pp. 442–47]

1. *Overthrow of the Present Evil Government.* This is our first task. That a fine nation should be controlled by an evil one and that, instead of adopting our culture, the Manchus should force us to adopt theirs, is contrary to reason and cannot last for long. For the sake of our independence and salvation, we must overthrow the Manchu dynasty. The Manchus have hurt the Chinese people so much that there has arisen an inseparable barrier between them. Some have argued that the Manchus can be assimilated to Chinese culture as were the Ti, Ch'iang, and Hsien-pi tribes after their invasion of China. We need not discuss the incorrectness of this analogy, but let us ask this question: Were these tribes assimilated to Chinese culture during their rule of China, or were they assimilated after China's regeneration and their defeat and subjugation by the Chinese? Those who advocate assimilation of the Manchus without having them overthrown merely serve as tools of the tyrannical dynasty and are therefore shameless to the utmost. Our nationalism is not to be mixed with political opportunism. What distresses us sorely and hurts us unceasingly is the impossible position of subjugation we are in. If we recover our sovereignty and regain our position as ruler, it is not necessary to eliminate the evil race in order to satisfy our national aspirations. As an inferior minority, the Manchus rule the majority by means of political power. If their regime is overthrown, they will have nothing to maintain their existence. Whether they will flee to their old den [in the North] as did the defeated Mongols, or whether they will be assimilated to the Chinese as were the conquered Ti, Ch'iang and Hsien-pi tribes, we do not know. But unless their political power is overthrown, the Chinese nation will forever remain the conquered people without independence, and, being controlled by a backward nation, will finally perish with it in the struggle with the advanced foreign powers. That is why we say Manchu rule is contrary to reason and cannot last for long.

The Manchu government is evil because it is the evil race which usurped our government, and their evils are not confined to a few political measures but are rooted in the nature of the race and can neither be eliminated nor reformed. Therefore, even if there are a few ostensible reforms, the evils will remain just the same. The adoption of Western constitutional institutions and law will not change the situation . . . [contrary to the view of Liang Ch'i-ch'ao]. [pp. 442–43]

2. *Establishment of a Republic.* That absolute monarchy is unsuitable to the present age requires no argument. Political observers determine the level of a country's civilization by inquiring whether its political system is despotic or not. It is but natural therefore that those who propose new forms of government in the twentieth century should aim at rooting out the elements of absolutism. Revolutions broke out in China one after another in the past, but because the political system was not reformed, no good results ensued. Thus the Mongol dynasty was overthrown by the Ming, but within three hundred years the Chinese nation was again on the decline. For although the foreign rule was overthrown and a Chinese regime was installed in its place, the autocratic form of government remained unchanged, to the disappointment of the people.

According to the general theory of government, the opposite of autocracy is republican government, which, broadly speaking, may be divided into three kinds: first, aristocracy; second, democracy; and third, constitutional democracy. The latter is not only different from aristocracy but also from absolute democracy. People who depend on hearsay all argue that the Chinese nation lacks the tradition of democracy in its history, thus undermining the morale of our patriots. Alas! they are not only ignorant of political science but unqualified to discuss history. The greatest difficulty in establishing a constitutional government, as experienced by other countries, is the struggle of the common people against both the monarch and the nobility. The constitutional government was established without difficulty in America because after its independence there was no class other than the common people. One of the great features of Chinese politics is that since the Ch'in and Han dynasties there has existed no noble class (except for the Mongol and Manchu dynasties when a noble class was maintained according to then alien systems). After the overthrow of the Manchus, therefore, there will be no distinction between classes in China (even the United States has economic classes, but China has none). The establishment of constitutional government will be easier in China than in other countries. . . .

We agree with Herbert Spencer, who compared the difficulty of changing an established political system to that of changing the constitution of an organism after its main body has been formed. Since constitutional democracy can be esablished only after a revolution, it is imperative that following our revolution, only the best and the most public-spirited form of government should be adopted so that no defects will remain. Absolute government, be it monarchical or democratic, is government of injustice and inequality. As to constitutional monarchy, the demarcation between ruler and ruled is definite and distinct, and since their feelings toward each other are different, classes will arise. Constitutional democracy will have none of these defects, and equality will prevail. We can overthrow the Manchus and establish our state because Chinese nationalism and democratic thought are well developed. When we are able to do this, it is inconceivable that, knowing the general psychology of the people, we should abandon the government of equality and retain the distinction between ruler and ruled. [pp. 444–45]

Sun, during his exile in Europe, had been influenced by a variety of socialistic ideas as divergent as German state socialism and Henry George's single tax theories. While Sun's own thinking (and that of his associates) was still somewhat fluid and vague, the provision for "equalization of land rights" in the original *T'ung-meng hui* manifesto was clearly an adaptation of the ideas of Henry George and John Stuart Mill, calling for state appropriation of all future increases in land value but recognizing its present value as the property of the owner. Hu Han-min's version is more extreme (perhaps because of his own dire poverty as a youth). It represents a violent attack on landlordism and calls for complete socialization of the land. Hu also seems to be more conscious of the landlord-tenant problem in rural China than Sun was.

In the preceding section, however, Hu has already asserted that China, in contrast to the West, has no economic classes but only a ruling elite which must be overthrown. Therefore rural landlordism was not, presumably, the primary target in his mind. Whether as an accommodation to Sun or not, it is the urban landlordism attacked by Henry George in the West which appears to be Hu's major concern. In the port cities of China he sees a process developing like that in the West, and his object is to prevent its spread when China modernizes after the coming Revolution.[1]

Note in the following that Hu takes as his point of departure the economic evils of modern society, rather than age-old abuses in China. Note also the sanction for land nationalization which he finds in the ancient well-field system—a symbol for Hu of primitive communism.

[1] On this point, see further Harold Schiffrin, "Sun Yat-sen's Land Policy," in *Journal of Asian Studies*, XVI, No. 4 (August, 1957), pp. 549–64.

3. *Land Nationalization*. The affliction of civilized countries in the modern age is not political classes but economic classes. Hence the rise of socialism. There are many socialist theories, but they all aim at leveling economic classes. Generally speaking, socialism may be divided into communism and collectivism, and nationalization of land is part of collectivism. Only constitutional democracies can adopt collectivism, for there the ruling authority resides in the state and the state machinery is controlled by a representative legislature. Thus there is no inequality involved if a democratic state, in reflecting social psychology, should adopt collectivism in order to promote the welfare of the people. Such, of course, cannot be said of a regime which allows of any political classes.

Not all collectivist theories can be applied to China at her present stage of development. But in the case of land nationalization we already have a model for it in the well-field system of the Three Dynasties, and it should not be difficult to introduce land nationalization as an adaptation of a past system to the present age of political reform. Nationalization of land is opposed to private ownership. It is based on the theory that since land is the essential element in production and is not man-made, any more than sunshine or air, it should not be privately owned.

The landlord system arises from many causes. At first land may be obtained as capital through accumulation of labor and used for productive purposes. Subsequently, as feudal domains develop, land is monopolized, and both capitalists and laborers become dependents of the feudal lords who are the first to receive the crops. The laborers borrow money from the capitalists, and the reason the latter are able to exploit the former is that the former cannot own land. Land values vary from age to age, but as civilization advances, the increase in land value is considerable —an increase not due to any effort on the part of the landlord, but nonetheless enjoyed by him alone. This is not just to harry men in society but completely to make servants of them.

The evil consequences of this system are that the landlord can acquire absolute power in society and thereby absorb and annex more land, that the farmers can be driven out of work, that people may be short of food and thus have to depend on outside supply, and that the entire country may be made poorer while capital and wealth all go to the landlords.

Land in China today, as affected by commercial development in the coastal ports, may in ten years have its value increased more than ten times what it was formerly. We can see from this that after the revolution with the progress of civilization, the same process would be accelerated in the interior. If a system of private monopoly is re-established, then the economic class will perpetuate itself as a political class, but if we make adequate provision against this at the beginning, we can easily plan so that the evil never arises.

There are various measures for carrying out land nationalization, but the main purpose is to deprive the people of the right of landownership while permitting them to retain other rights over land (such as superfices, emphyteusis, easement, etc.). And these rights must be obtained by permission of the state. There will be no private tenancy, nor will there be any permanent mortgage. In this way the power of the landlord will be wiped out from the Chinese continent. All land taxes levied by the state must have the approval of parliament; there will be no manipulations for private profit, nor heavy taxes detrimental to the farmers' interests. Profit from land will be high, but only self-cultivating farmers can obtain land from the state. In this way people will increasingly devote themselves to farming and no land will be wasted. Landlords who in the past have been nonproductive profiteers will now be just like the common people. They will turn to productive enterprises and this will produce striking results for the good of the whole national economy. [pp. 445-47]

SUN YAT-SEN
The Three People's Principles

After the revolution of 1911 Sun Yat-sen reluctantly allowed his secret revolutionary society to be converted into an open political party, the Kuomintang (National People's Party). It accomplished little through parliamentary politics, however, and even when Sun reverted to revolutionary tactics the lack of military support and his failure to obtain sufficient help from Japan or the West kept him from registering any substantial progress. Nevertheless, Sun was impressed and encouraged by the success of the Russian Revolution, and offers of Soviet help induced him in 1923 to reorganize the Kuomintang along Communist organizational lines and to enter upon a period of collaboration with the Soviets and the recently founded Chinese Communist Party. Even so, while making certain tactical adjustments in his propaganda line and adopting a more anti-Western tone, Sun was steadfast in his repudiation of Marxism as such.

The *Three People's Principles* (*San min chu-i*), which served as the basic text of the Nationalist movement, was given its final form in a series of lectures by Sun to party members in 1924, after the Kuomintang's reorganization with Soviet help the year before. It attempted to reformulate the principles put forward in 1905, modifying them in accordance with Sun's subsequent experience and the altered circumstances in which he was making a bid for military and political unification of the country.

Sun's nationalism, in 1905, had been directed mainly against the Manchus. Events after the revolution of 1911, however, proved that ridding China of foreign rule was not enough to assure her future as a nation. Even with the Manchus gone, China was as weak as ever, and still more disunited. Consequently, by 1924 foreign rule had been superseded in Sun's mind by two other issues. First was the Chinese people's need for national solidarity; though possessing all the other requisites of a great nation, they still lacked a capacity for cohesion. Second (and this was perhaps one means of generating the first), Sun found a new target of national indignation: foreign economic imperialism. This was an issue to which Sun acknowledged the Chinese people were not yet alive. Yet it had assumed new significance for him now as the basis for collaboration with the Communists in a national revolution against imperialism. And it reflected Sun's increasing bitterness toward the West for its failure to support him.

The lack of national solidarity Sun saw as in part the legacy of long foreign rule. It was aggravated, however, by a growing cosmopolitanism and internationalism resulting from the West's disenchantment with nationalism after the First World War. Sun, who had once represented the vanguard of nationalism from the West, now found himself fighting a rear guard action in defense of his old cause. He spoke more and more in deprecation of the modern West —its materialism especially—and increasingly sought in Chinese tradition the basis for a nationalism which it had never been made to serve before. In this Sun's political instinct was undoubtedly sound, whatever the deficiencies of his intellectual approach. For nationalism remained in fact a potent issue, in China as in the rest of Asia. Ironically, though, it was to be exploited most effectively by those whose "internationalism" Sun himself condemned—the Communists.

[From *Chung-shan ch'üan-shu*, I, 4–5, 15–16, 28–29, 51–52]

[*China as a Heap of Loose Sand*]. For the most part the four hundred million people of China can be spoken of as completely Han Chinese. With common customs and habits, we are completely of one race. But in the world today what position do we occupy? Compared to the other peoples of the world we have the greatest population and our civilization is four thousand years old; we should therefore be advancing in the front rank with the nations of Europe and America. But the Chinese people have only family and clan solidarity; they do not have national spirit. Therefore even though we have four hundred million people gathered together in one China, in reality they are just a heap of loose sand. Today we are the poorest and weakest nation in the world, and occupy the lowest position in international affairs. Other men are the carving knife and serving dish; we are the fish and the meat. Our position at this time is most perilous. If we do not earnestly espouse nationalism and weld together our four hundred million people into a strong nation, there is danger of China's being lost and our people being destroyed. If we wish to avert this catastrophe, we must espouse nationalism and bring this national spirit to the salvation of the country. [pp. 4–5, Lecture 1]

[*China as a "Hypo-colony"*]. Since the Chinese Revolution, the foreign powers have found that it was much less easy to use political force in carving up China. A people who had experienced Manchu oppression and learned to overthrow it, would now, if the powers used political force to oppress it, be certain to resist, and thus make things difficult for them. For this reason they are letting up in their efforts to control China by political force and instead are using economic pressure to keep us down. . . . As regards political oppression people are readily aware of their suffering, but when it comes to economic oppression most often they are hardly conscious of it. China has already experienced several decades of economic oppression by the foreign powers, and so far the nation has for the most part shown no sense of irritation. As a consequence China is being transformed everywhere into a colony of the foreign powers.

Our people keep thinking that China is only a "semi-colony"—a term by which they seek to comfort themselves. Yet in reality the economic oppression we have endured is not just that of a "semi-colony" but greater even than that of a full colony. . . . Of what nation then is China a colony? It is the colony of every nation with which it has concluded treaties; each of them is China's master. Therefore China is not just the colony of one country; it is the colony of many countries. We are not just the slaves of one country, but the slaves of many countries. In the event of natural disasters like flood and drought, a nation which is sole master appropriates funds for relief and distributes them, thinking this its own duty; and the people who are its slaves regard this relief work as something to which their masters are obligated. But when North China suffered drought several years ago, the foreign powers did not regard it as their responsibility to appropriate funds and distribute relief; only those foreigners resident in China raised funds for the drought victims, whereupon Chinese observers remarked on the great generosity of the foreigners who bore no responsibility to help. . . .

From this we can see that China is not so well off as Annam [under the French] and Korea [under the Japanese]. Being the slaves of one country represents a far higher status than being the slaves of many, and is far more advantageous. Therefore, to call China a "semi-colony" is quite incorrect. If I may coin a phrase, we should be called a "hypo-colony." This is a term that comes from chemistry, as in "hypo-phosphite." Among chemicals there are some belonging to the class of phosphorous compounds but of lower grade, which are called phosphites. Still another grade lower, and they are called hypo-phosphites. . . . The Chinese people, believing they were a semi-colony, thought it shame enough; they did not realize that they were lower even than Annam or Korea. Therefore we cannot call ourselves a "semi-colony" but only a "hypo-colony." [pp. 15–16, Lecture 2]

[*Nationalism and Cosmopolitanism*]. A new idea is emerging in England and Russia, proposed by the intellectuals, which opposes nationalism on the ground that it is narrow and illiberal. This is simply a doctrine of cosmopolitanism. England now and formerly Germany and Russia, together with the Chinese youth of today who preach the new civilization, support this doctrine and oppose nationalism. Often I hear young people say: "The Three Principles of the People do not fit in with the present world's new tendencies; the latest and best doctrine in the world is cosmopolitanism." But is cosmopolitanism really good or not? If that doctrine is good, why is it that as soon as China was conquered, her nationalism was destroyed? Cosmopolitanism is the same thing as China's theory of world empire two thousand years ago. Let us now examine that doctrine and see whether in fact it is good or not. Theoretically, we cannot say it is no good. Yet it is because formerly the Chinese intellectual class had cosmopolitan ideas that, when the Manchus crossed China's frontier, the whole country was lost to them. . . .

We cannot decide whether an idea is good or not without seeing it in practice. If the idea is of practical value to us, it is good; if it is impractical, it is bad. If it is useful to the world, it is good; if it is not, it is no good. The nations which are employing imperialism to conquer others and which are trying to retain their privileged positions as sovereign lords are advocating cosmopolitanism and want the whole world to follow them. [pp. 28–29, Lecture 3]

[*Nationalism and Traditional Morality*]. If today we want to restore the standing of our people, we must first restore our national spirit. . . . If in the past our people have survived despite the fall of the state [to foreign conquerors], and not only survived themselves but been able to assimilate these foreign conquerors, it is because of the high level of our traditional morality. Therefore, if we go to the root of the matter, besides arousing a sense of national solidarity uniting all our people, we must recover and restore our characteristic, traditional morality. Only thus can we hope to attain again the distinctive position of our people.

This characteristic morality the Chinese people today have still not forgotten. First comes loyalty and filial piety, then humanity and love, faithfulness and duty, harmony and peace. Of these traditional virtues, the Chinese people still speak, but now, under foreign oppression, we have been invaded by a new culture, the force of which is felt all across the nation. Men wholly intoxicated by this new culture have thus begun to attack the traditional morality, saying that with the adoption of the new culture, we no longer have need of the old morality.[2] . . . They say that when we formerly spoke of loyalty, it was loyalty to princes, but now in our democracy there are no princes, so loyalty is unnecessary and can be dispensed with. This kind of reasoning is certainly mistaken. In our country princes can be dispensed with, but not loyalty. If they say loyalty can be dispensed with, then I ask: "Do we, or do we not, have a nation? Can we, or can we not, make loyalty serve the nation? If indeed we can no longer speak of loyalty to princes, can we not, however, speak of loyalty to our people?" [pp. 51–52, Lecture 6]

The Principle of Democracy

In 1905 Sun had proclaimed the principle of democracy mainly against the advocates of constitutional monarchy whom he identified with "absolutism." In 1924 his notion of the forms this democracy should take is given more explicit expression, and against a background of personal experience which con-

[2] See Chapter XXVIII.

firmed Sun's longstanding belief in the need for strong political leadership. The result is a plan of government which he believed would insure popular control through electoral processes, yet give a strong executive wide powers to deal with the business of government. The emphasis is on leadership now, not liberty. In fact, argues Sun (thinking again of the Chinese people as a "heap of loose sand"), the struggle of the Chinese people is not for individual liberty, of which they have had an excess, but for the "liberty of the nation." Consequently, he attempts to distinguish between sovereignty, which the people should retain, and the ability to rule, which should be vested in an elite group of experts.

A distinctive feature of Sun's constitutional order is his five branches or powers of the government. These would include the three associated with the American government—executive, legislative and judicial—along with two which were intended as a check on elected officials and their powers of appointment, and for which Sun believed Chinese political tradition provided a unique precedent: a censorate or supervisory organ, and an independent civil service system. These latter he spoke of as if they had indeed been independent organs of the traditional Chinese state, thus enabling him as a nationalist not only to offer a constitution which represented a unique Chinese synthesis but also to redeem Chinese tradition and place it on at least a par with the West. While it cannot be said that Sun's ideas were necessarily given a fair test in Nationalist China, the net effect of this further separation of powers was probably to fragment the power of all but the executive.

The passages which follow illustrate Sun's fondness for analogies drawn from the world of modern machines and applied to political situations.

[From *Chung-shan ch'üan-shu,* I, 117–18, 139–40, 141–42, 143–45, adapted from Price, *San Min Chu I,* pp. 345–46, 350–58]

[*Separation of Sovereignty and Ability*]. How can a government be made all-powerful? Once the government is all-powerful, how can it be made responsive to the will of the people? . . . I have found a method to solve the problem. The method which I have thought of is a new discovery in political theory and is a fundamental solution of the whole problem. . . . It is the theory of the distinction between sovereignty and ability. [pp. 117–18, Lecture 5]

After China has established a powerful government, we must not be afraid, as Western people are, that the government will become too strong and that we will be unable to control it. For it is our plan that the political power of the reconstructed state will be divided into two parts. One is the power over the government; that great power will be placed entirely in the hands of the people, who will have a full degree of sovereignty and will be able to control directly the affairs of state—this political power is popular sovereignty. The other power is the governing power; that great power will be placed in the hands of the government organs, which will be powerful and will manage all the nation's business—this governing power is the power of the government. If the people have a full measure of political sovereignty and the methods for exercising popular control over the government are well worked out, we need not fear that the government will become too strong and uncontrollable. . . .

It is because Europe and America lacked compact and effective methods to control their government that their governmental machines have not, until the present day, been well-developed. Let us not follow in their tracks. Let the people in thinking about government distinguish between sovereignty and ability. Let the great political force of the state be divided into two: the power of the government and the power of the people. Such a division will make the government the machinery and the people the engineer. The attitude of the people toward the government will then resemble the attitude of the engineer toward his machine. The construction of machinery has made such advances nowadays that not only men with mechanical knowledge, but even children without any knowledge of machinery are able to control it. [pp. 139–40, Lecture 6]

[*The Four Powers of the People*]. What are the newest discoveries in the way of exercising popular sovereignty? First, there is suffrage, and it is the only method practiced throughout the so-called advanced democracies. Is this one form of popular sovereignty enough in government? This one power by itself may be compared to the earlier machines which could move forward only but not back.

The second of the newly discovered methods is the right of recall. When the people have this right, they possess the power of pulling the machine back.

These two rights give the people control over officials and enable them to put all government officials in their positions or to remove them from their positions. The coming and going of officials follows the free will of the people, just as the modern machines move to and fro by the free action of the engine. Besides officials, another important thing in a state is law; "with men to govern there must also be laws for governing." What powers must the people possess in order to control the laws? If the people think that a certain law would be of great advantage to them, they should have the power to decide upon this law and turn it over to the government for execution. This third kind of popular power is called the initiative.

If the people think that an old law is not beneficial to them, they should have the power to amend it and to ask the government to enforce the amended law and do away with the old law. This is called the referendum and is a fourth form of popular sovereignty.

Only when the people have these four rights can we say that democracy is complete, and only when these four powers are effectively applied can we say that there is a thorough-going, direct, and popular sovereignty. [pp. 141–42, Lecture 6]

[*The Five-Power Constitution*]. With the people exercising the four great powers to control the government, what methods will the government use in performing its work? In order that the government may have a complete organ through which to do its best work, there must be a five-power constitution. A government is not complete and cannot do its best work for the people unless it is based on the five-power constitution [i.e., a government composed of five branches: executive, legislative, judicial, civil service examination, and censorate]. . . .

All governmental powers were formerly monopolized by kings and emperors, but after the revolutions they were divided into three groups. Thus the United States, after securing its independence, established a government with three coordinate departments. The American system achieved such good results that it was adopted by other nations. But foreign governments have merely a triple-power separation. Why do we now want a separation of five powers? What is the source of the two new features in our five-power constitution?

The two new features come from old China. China long ago had the independent systems of civil service examination and censorate, and they were very effective. The imperial censors of the Manchu dynasty and the official advisers of the T'ang dynasty made a fine censoring system. The power of censorship includes the power to impeach. Foreign countries also have this power, only it is placed in the legislative body and is not a separate governmental power.

The selection of real talent and ability through examinations has been characteristic of China for thousands of years. Foreign scholars who have recently studied Chinese institutions highly praise China's old independent examination system. There have been imitations of the system for the selection of able men in the West. Great Britain's civil service examinations are modeled after the old Chinese system, but they are limited to ordinary officials. The British system does not yet possess the spirit of the independent examination of China.

In old China, only three governmental powers—judicial, legislative, and executive—were vested in the emperor. The other powers of civil service examination and the censorate were independent of the Throne. The old autocratic government of China can also be said to have had three separate departments and so it was very different from the autocratic governments of the West in which all power was monopolized by the king or emperor himself. During the period of autocratic government in China, the emperor did not monopolize the power of examination and the censorate.

Hence, as for the separation of governmental powers, we can say that China had three coordinate departments of government just as the modern democracies. China practiced the separation of autocratic, examination and censorate powers for thousands of years. Western countries have practiced the separation of legislative, judicial, and executive powers for only a little over a century. However, the three governmental powers in the West have been imperfectly applied and the three coordinate powers of old China led to many abuses. If we now want to combine the best from China and the best from other countries and guard against all kinds of abuse, we must take the three Western governmental powers —the executive, legislative and judicial—add to them the Chinese powers of examination and censorate and make a perfect government of five powers. Such a government will be the most complete and the finest in the world, and a state with such a government will indeed be of the people, by the people and for the people. [pp. 143-45, Lecture 6]

The People's Livelihood

The "People's Livelihood" (min-sheng chu-i) joined nationalism and democracy to make up Sun Yat-sen's Three People's Principles in 1906. It was meant to cover the economic side of Sun's program broadly enough so as to embrace a variety of social and economic theories which had attracted Sun's attention. Often he and his followers used min-sheng chu-i as an equivalent for socialism, drawing upon the popularity of this idea in general, while retaining the freedom to interpret it as they chose. For Sun in 1924 its most essential component was still Henry George's single tax. Though paying tribute to Marx as a "social scientist," Sun rejected entirely Marx's theory of class struggle and cited a work little known in the West, *The Social Interpretation of History,* by a Brooklyn dentist, Maurice William, as a conclusive refutation of Marx's economic determinism. Sun also disputed Marx's belief in the steady impoverishment of the worker under capitalism and the latter's imminent collapse. American experience (e.g., Henry Ford) showed that capitalist success and rising living standards for the worker were not mutually exclusive.

Sun exhibited great confidence in China's future, in her ability to catch up with the West and yet avoid its economic woes. China's problem was one of production, not of distribution; and the inequalty of wealth need never arise if economic development were based on his land tax program, which would prevent "unearned increments" from accruing to individuals at the same time that it provided revenues for state investment in industry. Sun envisaged a kind of state socialism, permitting small-scale capitalist enterprise to exist alongside nationalized industries and utilities. But the immediate need was to encourage China's infant industries. Here Sun stressed her emancipation from foreign economic imperialism, the main point of which was to gain customs autonomy, lost through the unequal treaties, and to erect protective tariffs. Foreign investment he was only too ready to promote. His program for agriculture involved mainly technological improvement.

Although Sun's analysis of China's economic problems correctly differentiated it as an undeveloped country from the more advanced industrial societies, his future program was conceived largely in terms of Western economic doctrines or experience. For a man who started life in a peasant household, he showed comparatively little awareness of the peasant's problems, and even less of their potential political significance.

[From *Chung-shan ch'üan-shu,* I, 166, 175–76, 177–79; adapted from Price, pp. 431–34, 437–41]

[*The Principle of Livelihood*]. The Kuomintang some time ago in its party platform adopted two methods by which the principle of livelihood is to be carried out. The first method is equalization of landownership; the second is regulation of capital. [p. 166]

Our first method consists in solving the land question. The methods for solution of the land problem are different in various countries, and each country has its own peculiar difficulties. The plan which we are following is simple and easy—equalization of landownership.

As soon as the landowners hear us talking about the land question and equalization of landownership, they are naturally alarmed as capitalists are alarmed when they hear people talking about socialism, and they want to rise up and fight it. If our landowners were like the great landowners of Europe and had developed tremendous power, it would be very difficult for us to solve the land problem. But China does not have such big landowners, and the power of the small landowners is still rather weak. If we attack the problem now, we can solve it; but if we lose the present opportunity, we will have much more difficulty in the future. The discussion of the land problem naturally causes a feeling of fear among the landowners, but if the Kuomintang policy is followed, present landowners can set their hearts at rest.

What is our policy? We propose that the government shall levy a tax proportionate to the price of the land and, if necessary, buy back the land according to its price.

But how will the price of the land be determined? I would let the landowner himself fix the price. . . . Many people think that if the landowners made their own assessment, they would undervalue the land and the government would lose out. . . . But suppose the government makes two regulations: first, that it will collect taxes according to the declared value of the land; second, that it can also buy back the land at the value declared. . . . According to this plan, if the landowner makes a low assessment, he will be afraid lest the government buy the land at the declared value and make him lose his property; if he makes too high an assessment, he will be afraid of the government taxes according to the value and his loss through heavy taxes. Comparing these two serious possibilities, he will certainly not want to report the value of his land too high or too low; he will strike the mean and report the true market price to the government. In this way neither the landowner nor the government will lose.

After land values have been fixed we should have a regulation by law that from that year on, all increase in land value, which in other countries means heavier taxation, shall revert to the community. This is because the increase in land value is due to improvement made by society and to the progress of industry and commerce. China's industry and commerce have made little progress for thousands of years, so land values have scarcely changed throughout these generations. But as soon as progress and improvement set in, as in the modern cities of China, land prices change every day, sometimes increasing a thousandfold and even ten thousandfold. The credit for the progress and improvement belongs to the energy and enterprise of all the people. Land increment resulting from that progress and improvement should therefore revert to the community rather than to private individuals. [pp. 175–76, Lecture 2]

[*Capital and the State*]. If we want to solve the livelihood problem in China and to "win eternal ease by one supreme effort," it will not be sufficient to depend only on the restriction of capital. The income tax levied in foreign countries is one method of regulating capital. But have these countries solved the problem of the people's livelihood?

China cannot be compared to foreign countries. It is not sufficient for us to regulate capital. Other countries are rich while China is poor; other countries have a surplus of production while China is not producing enough. So China must not only regulate private capital, but she must also develop state capital.

At present our state is split into pieces. How can we develop our state capital? It seems as if we could not find or anticipate a way. But our present disunion is only a temporary state of affairs; in the future we shall certainly achieve unity, and then to solve the livelihood problem we shall need to develop capital and promote industry.

First, we must build means of communication, railroads and waterways, on a large scale. Second, we must open up mines. China is rich in minerals, but alas, they are buried in the earth! Third, we must hasten to develop manufacturing. Although China has a multitude of workers, she has no machinery and so cannot compete with other countries. Goods used throughout China have to be manufactured and imported from other countries, with the result that our rights and interests are simply leaking away. If we want to recover these rights and interests, we must quickly employ state power to promote industry, use machinery in production, and see that all workers of the country are employed. When all the workers have employment and use machinery in production, we will have a great, new source of wealth. If we do not use state power to build up these enterprises but leave them in the hands of private Chinese or of foreign businessmen, the result will be the expansion of private capital and the emergence of a great wealthy class with the consequent inequalities in society. . . .

China is now suffering from poverty, not from unequal distribution of wealth. Where there are inequalities of wealth, the methods of Marx can, of course, be used; a class war can be advocated to destroy the inequalities. But in China, where industry is not yet developed, Marx's class war and dictatorship of the proletariat are impracticable. [pp. 177–79]

The Three Stages of Revolution

The significance of Sun's "Three Stages of Revolution" lies mainly in his doctrine of political tutelage, which represents perhaps the first conscious advocacy of "guided democracy" among the leaders of Asian nationalism. When first enunciated in 1905, it seems to have been Sun's answer to those who argued that the Chinese people, long accustomed to political absolutism and unaccustomed to participation in government, were unprepared for democracy. Sun acknowledged that a period of adjustment or transition would be required, but his early confidence in the people's ability to "learn" democracy is shown by the exact time schedule he had worked out for this process—political tutelage would last just six years.

The following explanation of the Three Stages is taken from *A Program of National Reconstruction,* prepared in 1918, and follows in the main his earlier ideas, though it stresses the difficulties of reconstruction encountered after the revolution. Sun's awareness of these difficulties led to increasing emphasis on the importance of strong leadership in the period of tutelage, somewhat less on the readiness of the people for democracy. In his *Outline of National Reconstruction,* written in 1924 just before his death, he omitted reference to a definite time schedule, as if to concede that the period of tutelage might extend beyond his original expectations.

[From *Chung-shan ch'üan-shu,* Vol. II, *Chien-kuo fang-lüeh,* Part I (also entitled *Sun Wen hsüeh-shuo*), Ch. 6, pp. 37–38, 39–49, 42]

[*The Three Phases of National Reconstruction*]. As for the work of revolutionary reconstruction, I have based my ideas on the current of world progress and followed the precedents in other countries. I have studied their respective advantages and disadvantages, their accomplishments and failures. It is only after mature deliberation and thorough preparation that I have decided upon the Program of Revolution and defined the procedure of the revolution in three stages. The first is the period of military government; the second, the period of political tutelage; and the third, the period of constitutional government.

The first stage is the period of destruction. During this period martial law is to be enforced. The revolutionary army undertakes to overthrow the Manchu tyranny, to eradicate the corruption of officialdom, to eliminate depraved customs, to exterminate the system of slave girls, to wipe out the scourge of opium, superstitious beliefs, and geomancy, to abolish the obstructive *likin* and so forth.

The second stage is a transitional period. It is planned that the provisional constitution will be promulgated and local self-government promoted to encourage the exercise of political rights by the people. The *hsien,* or district, will be made the basic unit of local self-government and is to be divided into villages and rural districts—all under the jurisdiction of the district government.

The moment the enemy forces have been cleared and military operations have ceased in a district, the provisional constitution will be promulgated in the district, defining the rights and duties of citizens and the governing powers of the revolutionary government. The constitution will be enforced for three years, after which period the people of the district will elect their district officers. However, if within the period of three years, the Self-Government Commission of a district can wipe out the evils enumerated above, get more than half of the population to understand the Three Principles of the People and pledge allegiance to the republic, complete the compilation of a census, determine the number of households and carry out constructive measures regarding police, sanitation, education, and highways in accordance with the minimum requirements prescribed in the provisional constitution, the district may also elect its own officials and become a full-fledged self-governing area.

In respect to such self-governing units the revolutionary government will exercise the right of political tutelage in accordance with the provisional constitution. When a period of six years expires after the attainment of political stability throughout the country, the districts which have become full-fledged self-governing units are each entitled to elect one representative to form the National Assembly. The task of the Assembly will be to adopt a five-power constitution and to organize a central government consisting of five branches, namely, the Executive Branch, the Legislative Branch, the Judicial Branch, the Examination Branch, and the Control Branch [Censorate].

When the constitution has been determined, the people of the various districts shall elect by ballot a President to organize the Executive Branch and representatives to organize the Legislative Branch. They are, however, not responsible to the President or to the Legislative Branch. All the five branches will be responsible to the National Assembly. Members of the various branches suspected of delinquency in duty will be impeached by the Control Branch before the National Assembly. Delinquent members of the Control Branch will be directly impeached by the National Assembly and dismissed when found guilty. The function of the National Assembly consists in amending the constitution and checking misconduct on the part of public functionaries. Qualifications of members of the National Assembly and of the five Branches and all other officials will be determined by the Examination Branch.

When the constitution is promulgated and the President and members of the National Assembly are elected, the Revolutionary Government will hand over its governing power to the President, and the period of political tutelage will come to an end.

The third phase is the period of the completion of reconstruction. During this period, constitutional government is to be introduced, and the self-governing body in a district will enable the people directly to exercise their political rights. In regard to the district government, the people are entitled to the rights of election, initiative, referendum, and recall. In regard to the national government, the people exercise the rights of suffrage, while the other rights are delegated to the representatives to the National Assembly. The period of constitutional government will mark the completion of reconstruction and the success of the revolution. This is the gist of the Revolutionary Program. [pp. 37-38]

[*The Necessity of Political Tutelage*]. What is meant by revolutionary reconstruction? It is extraordinary reconstruction and also rapid reconstruction. It differs from ordinary reconstruction which follows the natural course of society and is affected by the trend of circumstances. In a revolution extraordinary destruction is involved, such as the extermination of the monarchical system and the overthrow of absolutism. Such destruction naturally calls for extraordinary reconstruction.

Revolutionary destruction and revolutionary reconstruction complement each other like the two legs of a man or the two wings of a bird. The republic after its inauguration weathered the storm of extraordinary destruction. This, however, was not followed by extraordinary reconstruction. A vicious circle of civil wars has consequently arisen. The nation is on the descendent like a stream flowing downward. The tyranny of the warlords together with the sinister maneuvers of unscrupulous politicians is beyond control. In an extraordinary time, only extraordinary reconstruction can inspire the people with a new mind and make a new beginning of the nation. Hence the Program of Revolution is necessary. . . .

Before their independence the thirteen American colonies had been in an autonomous state and local self-government had developed to a remarkable degree. Consequently, since the founding of the republic, the country has been progressing notably well in the political field. This is because the political structure of the country was built on the foundation of a strongly developed autonomy. . . .

It is not so with France. Although France was an advanced and cultured country in Europe with an intelligent, energetic people, and although for a hundred years before the revolution she had been under the influence of democratic theories and, further, had the American precedent to follow, she was still unable to attain a republican constitutional government with one leap out of revolution. What is the reason? It lies in the fact that her political system had always been an absolute monarchy and that her government had long been centralized; she possessed no new world as an area for development and no self-government as a foundation.

China's defects are similar to those of France, but in addition the knowledge and political ability of our people are far below those of the French. And yet I have hoped to attain a republican constitutional government in one step after the revolution. How could this be brought about? It is to get out of this difficulty that I have devised a transitional period, during which a provisional constitutional government would be established to train the people for local self-government. [pp. 39–40]

It is not to be denied that the Chinese people are deficient in knowledge. Moreover, they have been soaked in the poison of absolute monarchy for several thousand years. . . . What shall we do now? Men of the Yuan Shih-k'ai type argue that the Chinese people, deficient in knowledge, are unfit for republicanism. Crude scholars have also maintained that monarchy is necessary.

Alas! Even an ox can be trained to plow the field and a horse to carry man. Are men not capable of being trained? Suppose that when a youngster was entering school, his father was told that the boy did not know the written characters and therefore could not go to school. Is such reasoning logical? It is just because he does not know the characters that the boy must immediately set about learning them. The world has now come to an age of enlightenment. Hence the growing popularity of the idea of freedom and equality, which has become the main current of the world and cannot be stemmed by any means. China therefore needs a republican government just as a boy needs school. As a schoolboy must have good teachers and helpful friends, so the Chinese people, being for the first time under republican rule, must have a far-sighted revolutionary government for their training. This calls for the period of political tutelage, which is a necessary transitional stage from monarchy to republicanism. Without this, disorder will be unavoidable. [p. 42]

General Theory of Knowledge and Action

Closely linked in Sun's mind to the concept of political tutelage was his theory of knowledge and action. By it Sun attempted to answer those "realists" who, in the years after the revolution, dismissed his grand schemes as impractical because they did not take into account the mentality of the average Chinese or the difficulties of wholesale reform. Curiously, the blame for China's past failure to put his program into effect Sun lays at the door of Wang Yang-ming and his doctrine of the unity of knowledge and action. According to Sun this doctrine had fostered a misconception among the Chinese that "to know is easy and to act is difficult"—an attitude which encouraged lethargy and inaction.

There would seem to be no logical grounds for thus interpreting Wang's teaching, and Sun himself certainly contributed nothing to a clarification of the philosophical issues involved. The points he really is anxious to make are these: 1) knowledge and action can be separated in the sense that some people (like himself) are thinkers, while others are just doers; and 2) the Chinese people as a whole only need faith or confidence in the effectiveness of action; they need not worry about the reasons for acting. The knowledge of a few, the Kuomintang elite, will provide direction for the efforts of the many.

In the passages which follow, note how conscious Sun is of Japan's example of successful modernization and how he assesses the applicability to China of the alleged reasons for this success. Wang Yang-ming's popularity among Japanese reformers is a circumstance which helps to account for his innocent involvement in Sun's controversy over knowledge and action.

[From *Chung-shan ch'üan-shu*, Vol. II, *Chien-kuo fang-lüeh*, Part I (also entitled *Sun Wen hsüeh-shuo*), Ch. 5, pp. 31–33, 36–37]

The doctrine of Wang Yang-ming, who taught the unity of knowledge and action, was intended to encourage men to do good. It may be inferred that Wang also considered it not difficult to know but difficult to act. . . . His efforts at encouraging people to do good are indeed admirable, but his teaching is incompatible with truth. What is difficult he considered easy, and what is easy, difficult. To encourage one to attempt the difficult is tantamount to asking one to act against human nature. . . .

It is said that the renovation of Japan was entirely inspired by the teaching of Wang Yang-ming. The Japanese themselves believe this and pay high tribute to Wang. It should be noted, however, that Japan was still in the feudalistic stage before the [Meiji] Renovation.[3] The people were not yet removed from the tradition of the past and the spirit of initiative and enterprise was not extinct. In the face of foreign aggression, while the official classes were floundering, patriotic citizens felt stirred to action. They advocated support of the emperor in order to resist the foreigners. . . . And when the Japanese failed to expel the foreigners, they immediately changed their course and turned to imitate the way of the foreigners. The Renovation owed its success to their learning from the foreigners. Thus the Japanese effected their reforms without knowing the principle involved. This obviously had nothing to do with Wang's doctrine of the unity of action and knowledge. . . .

While Japan carried out her reforms without seeking to know about them, China would not undertake reform measures until she understood them, and even so she hesitated to act for fear of difficulty. The Chinese have been misled by the teaching that to act is even more difficult than to know. Reformation or change of institutions is a great national event. It is not always possible to comprehend the various measures in advance. Their significance is understood only after they have been carried out. The enterprising and adventurous spirit was mainly responsible for the success of the Japanese Renovation. They did not know what reformation was until they had accomplished it. It was then that they called it the Renovation.

In the case of China, however, she first sought a comprehension of the reform and then made attempts to carry it out. As such knowledge could never be acquired, action was indefinitely postponed. Thus, while the philosophy of Wang Yang-ming failed to discourage enterprising

---

[3] The term Sun uses corresponds to the Japanese *ishin*, often rendered "Restoration." Sun has in mind, not the restoration of imperial rule, but the basic meaning of the term, renovation or reform.

Japan, it did not do anything toward encouraging her. But when such a teaching was advocated in lethargic China, it only did her harm.

In an age of scientific discoveries, Wang's doctrine of the unity of knowledge and action is sound when applied to a particular period or a particular undertaking, but when it is applied to an individual, it is certainly erroneous. With the growth of modern science one's knowledge and one's action are more and more set apart. One who knows does not have to act, and not only that, but one who acts does not have to know. . . .

I have spared no efforts in writing page after page with a view to proving that it is easy to act but difficult to know. It is my strong conviction that this is the necessary course through which China is to be saved. The accumulating weakness and the dying state of the country are due to the misleading effect of the theory that to know is not difficult but to act is difficult. . . . Thus the Chinese shun what is [actually] easy and take to the difficult. At first they seek to know before acting. Then finding that this cannot be accomplished, they feel helpless and give up all thoughts of attempting. Some, imbued with an undaunted spirit, devote their life-long effort to acquiring the knowledge of a certain undertaking. They may have acquired the knowledge and yet hesitate to apply it, being obsessed with the thought that to act is even more difficult. Hence those who do not have the knowledge, of course, fail to act, but even those who have acquired it do not dare to act. It develops that there is nothing that can be attempted in the world. . . .

The advance of civilization is achieved by three groups of persons: first, those who see and perceive ahead, or discoverers; second, those who see and perceive later, or promoters; and third, those who do not see or perceive, or practical workers. From this point of view, China does not lack practical workers, for the great masses of the people are of this kind. Some of my comrades, however, have the habit of saying that so-and-so is [merely] a theoretician, while so-and-so is a practical man. It is a grave fallacy indeed to entertain the idea that a few practical men could reform the nation.

Look at the huge factories, busy boulevards, and imposing buildings of the foreigners in Shanghai. The men of action who performed the work of construction were the Chinese workmen, while the foreigners were the thinkers or planners, who never personally undertook the construction. Hence in the construction of a country it is not the practical workers but the idealists and planners that are difficult to find. . . .

This is the reason for the lack of progress in our national reconstruction after the revolution. I therefore feel the necessity for this thorough refutation, hoping that those who see and perceive late can eventually awake from their error and change their course. In this way they will no longer mislead the world with a theory seemingly right but actually wrong, and no longer hinder the great multitude of practical workers. Herein lies the great hope for the future of our reconstruction.

DEMOCRACY OR ABSOLUTISM: THE DEBATE OVER POLITICAL TUTELAGE

Sun Yat-sen's concept of political tutelage, a key doctrine of the Kuomintang after his death, also remained a continuing issue in Chinese politics. With all the talk about a constitution and preparation for the adoption of democratic institutions, party tutelage still provided the working basis of the new regime and the rationale for Chiang Kai-shek's increasingly strong role as Sun's heir to Kuomintang leadership. The party itself, however, was by no means unanimous in support of this idea. The middle-class and considerably Westernized Chinese which it represented, especially in the commercial ports, included numerous individuals educated abroad or exposed to Western ideas of political democracy. Many of them were poorly reconciled to what seemed a reactionary and dictatorial system of party leadership. Others not identified with the party itself, but active in educational institutions or in journalism, did not hesitate to attack this fundamental premise of the Nanking regime.

The debate which ensued on this issue in the 1930s illustrates a basic dilemma of Kuomintang rule. Though committed to a kind of limited democracy on the theory that the building of national unity must take priority over the extension of political freedom, the party nevertheless allowed its critics just enough freedom to defeat its own purposes— enough so that they could effectively impair the party's authority, not enough so that they felt any indebtedness to the Kuomintang for this privilege.

LO LUNG-CHI
What Kind of Political System Do We Want?

Lo Lung-chi (1896—) was a Western-trained educator and journalist, who wrote this criticism of Sun Yat-sen's doctrine of political tutelage shortly after his return to China, following studies at Wisconsin, at the London School of Economics under Harold Laski, and for the doctorate at Columbia (1928). He later served as editor of influential newspapers in North China, became a leader of the left-wing Democratic League, and was active politically under the Communists. He suffered condemnation as a "rightist," however, during the "Hundred Flowers" campaign in 1957.

By the time Lo wrote this article Communism already offered an important political alternative to the Kuomintang, and Marxist doctrines, such as the withering away of the state, had become a part of his intellectual frame of reference.

[From "Wo-men yao shen-mo yang ti cheng-chih chih-tu," in *Hsin yüeh*, Vol. II (1930), No. 12, pp. 4–13]

We may sincerely say that we do not advocate any high-sounding theory of eliminating the state. We recognize that "to abolish the state through the party" is a blind alley in the twentieth century. In the present world the only road we can take is to maintain the state. *But in taking this road, we want to have the kind of state we cherish and the kind of governmental system we can support.*

On hearing this, the Kuomintang leaders must be delighted and say, "Why, come and join us!"

We admit that the Kuomintang also wants the state. The President of the Kuomintang began his first lecture on the Three Principles of the People by saying: "Gentlemen: I have come here today to speak to you about the Three Principles of the People. What are the Three Principles of the People? They are, by the simplest definition, the principles for our nation's salvation." Whether the Three Principles of the People are the principles for our nation's salvation, or whether the principles for our nation's salvation are necessarily the Three Principles, is a problem outside the scope of the present article. But it is undeniable that those who want to save the state must first recognize the existence of the state. The Kuomintang slogan of "reconstructing the state through the party" is clearly different from the Communist slogan of "abolishing the state through the party." What we cannot lightly lose sight of, however, is the kind of political system the Kuomintang adopts in its reconstructed state.

Let us first discuss with those who talk of "saving" and "reconstructing" the state the following problems: 1) What is the nature of the state? 2) What is the purpose of the state? 3) What should be the strategy for the reconstruction of the state?

Frankly, in the entire *Complete Works of Sun Yat-sen,* no mention has ever been made about such fundamental problems of political philosophy as the nature of the state and the purpose of the state. What concerned Dr. Sun most was the strategy for "national salvation" and "national reconstruction." [4] His weakness—which at the same time was his strength —lay in the fact that in the selection of a strategy his main concern was the attainment of his objectives, not the evaluation of the means. Because he paid no attention to the purpose of the state, he often took "national salvation" or "national reconstruction" for that purpose. Because he was concerned with the end rather than the means, often in the matter of strategy he took a road that was opposed to the nature and purpose of the state. *The strategy of "party above the state" is an illustration.*

To our mind, only when we have a full realization of problems (1) and (2) above can we decide on the strategy. Let us discuss these three problems in the following order:

First, the state is an instrument, and in this respect we are agreed with the Communists. But while the Communists consider the state an instrument of the capitalist class for the oppression of the proletariat, we believe that it is the instrument of the *people as a whole* for the achievement of a certain common purpose through mutual constraints and mutual cooperation.

This seemingly unimportant point should be clearly recognized as the point of departure by all those who talk about political systems. The great trouble of China today is that, on the one hand, the Communists consider the state an instrument of class war and, on the other, those who cry for "national salvation" and "national reconstruction" regard

---

[4] The character for state and nation being the same in Chinese, these slogans also had the meaning of "the state's salvation" and "the state's reconstruction." The emotional appeal of nationalism was used, in this case, for the glorification of the state.

the state as the ultimate purpose itself. For those who consider the state as an end, the people exist for the sake of the state rather than the state for the sake of the people. They do not ask what benefits the state offers the people, but maintain that "national salvation" and "love for the state" are the unconditional duties of the people. And they do not hesitate to employ those weighty words of "national salvation" and "national reconstruction" to silence the people. Thus the people may not be aided in time of famine and calamity, but burdensome taxes must be collected; local peace may not be maintained, but civil war must be fought. Because the state is an end, people become the means for "national salvation" and "national reconstruction." And so the state need not protect the life and property of the people, who become the slaves of the "principle of national salvation"; nor need it support freedom of thought, for schools should become propaganda agencies for the "principle of national salvation." In short, as soon as the banner of "national salvation" and "national reconstruction" is hoisted, all burdensome taxes and levies and all fighting and wars receive new significance. The people can only surrender unconditionally. . . .

When the party is placed above the state, the state becomes the instrument of the party rather than the instrument of the entire people for the attainment of the common purpose. This, of course, is contrary to the nature of the state. Perhaps the Kuomintang people will say that what concerns a revolutionary party is the end rather than the means, and that although the system of "party above the state" may be contrary to the nature of the state, it is this strategy that will achieve the purpose of the state. Let us then examine whether or not the system of "party above the state" can achieve the purpose of the state.

The political systems of other countries today are founded on two different principles: dictatorship and democracy. Dictatorship refers to the political system under which the political power of the state is held by one person, one party, or one class. Democracy refers to the political system under which political power resides in the people as a whole and *all citizens of age can participate directly or indirectly in politics on an equal basis.* The system of "party above the state" or "party authority above state authority" is certainly a dictatorship rather than a democracy.

We must emphatically declare here that we are *absolutely opposed to dictatorship, whether it be dictatorship by one person, one party, or one class. Our reason is very simple: dictatorship is not the method whereby the purpose of the state can be achieved.* Let us explain briefly as follows:

First, the state is the instrument of the people for the attainment of their common purpose through mutual constraint and cooperation. Its function is to protect the rights of the people. We believe that the rights of the people are secure only to the extent that the people themselves have the opportunity to protect them. In the present society, man's public spirit has not developed to such a perfection that we can entrust entirely our political rights to a person, a group, or a class and depend upon him or it to be the guardian of our rights. In practical politics, *he who loses political power will lose all protection of his rights.* . . .

Secondly, . . . The function of the state is to tend and develop the people. In a dictatorship the function of tending and developing is lost. Take, for instance, the cultivation and development of the thought of the people. A dictatorship, whether enlightened or dark, will consider freedom of thought its greatest enemy. The first task it sets itself is to reshape the mind of the people in a single mold by a so-called thought-unification movement. . . . After oppression and persecution under a dictatorship, the people's thought necessarily becomes timid, passive, dependent, senile, and the people themselves may even become pieces of thoughtless machinery.

Thirdly, the state is the instrument of the entire people for the attainment of the common purpose of happiness for all through mutual restraint and cooperation. In order to achieve this purpose the state must furnish the people with an environment of peace, tranquillity, order, and justice. A dictator, be it an individual, a party, or a class, occupies a special position in national politics. This fundamentally rejects political equality as well as justice. The special position of the dictator inevitably incurs the indignation and hatred of the people for their governors, and indignation and hatred are the source of all revolutions. In a society of recurrent revolutions, peace, tranquillity, and order are naturally not to be found. . . .

The Kuomintang itself recognized the inherent evils of dictatorship, but it uses such words as "temporary" and "transitional" to cover the system. The word "temporary" or "transitional" often designates the so-called period of political tutelage. . . .

We believe that the saying, "the more you learn, the more there is to learn," applies equally to politics as to other callings. Man seeks experience and progress in politics unceasingly because there is no limit to them. If the people must have reached a certain ideal stage before they can participate in political activities, then the British and the Americans should also be under political tutelage now. To obtain experience from trial and error, to effect progress from experience—this is the political method of the British and Americans, and this also is the reason why we are opposed to political tutelage. If political tutelage is ever necessary, we believe the rulers—the present tutors—are more urgently in need of training than the people. . . .

Whether during the period of tutelage we should or should not adopt dictatorship with its doctrine of "party above the state" or "party authority above state authority" is another problem. It is our view that because of its inherent evils, dictatorship itself is an unworthy system. To adopt an unworthy system to be our model during the period of political tutelage is diametrically opposed to the purpose of national reconstruction. . . .

TSIANG T'ING-FU

Revolution and Absolutism

The Kuomintang system of one-party rule under a strong leader found a defender, rather than a critic, in another Western-trained (Oberlin and Columbia) scholar, Tsiang T'ing-fu (1895—). A college professor and an authority on political and diplomatic history at the time he wrote this essay, Tsiang became increasingly active as a Nationalist official, as ambassador to the USSR, and later as the Nationalists' permanent representative on the United Nations Security Council (known there as T. F. Tsiang).

> [From "K'ai-ming yü chuan-chih," in *Tu-li p'ing-lun*, No. 80 (December 1933), pp. 2–5]

When the news of the Fukien incident[5] broke out, people throughout the country felt gloomy over the prospects of the nation. China seemed to have reached the stage where neither revolution nor nonrevolution was a solution. . . .

You might say it would be better not to have any revolution, but then

---

[5] The revolt of the left-wing Kuomintang leaders and the 19th Route Army in Fukien province at the end of 1933.

the government would definitely fail to satisfy the wishes of the people. If the government is to satisfy the wishes of the people, you cannot rely on arguments alone. If you are unarmed, no matter how reasonable your arguments are, the government—from the central government above to the district governments below—will at most feel disturbed, but will not pay any attention to you. For if the government does pay attention, either some people within the government or some people outside of it will suffer some loss to their private interests.

Mr. Hu Han-min has recently said that not a single good thing has been done by the government during the past two years. His statement is both overdrawn and inadequate. It is overdrawn because the government did do some good things, but they were of no avail and probably did not outweigh the bad things it had done. The statement is inadequate because the situation described applies not only to the government in the past two years but to the government in the past twenty years. Actually, while China did not have a very good government in the past twenty years, there was no extremely evil government either. Extremely good or extremely bad governments existed at the local level, but not at the national. For even if the central government had intended to do something good, it did not have the capacity to do anything very good. Similarly, even if it had intended to do something bad, it did not have the capacity to do anything bad. This is generally true with the past twenty years during which groups and individuals of various kinds, including Yüan Shih-k'ai and Chiang Kai-shek, assumed control of the government. In my opinion, even northern warlords such as Yüan Shih-k'ai, Tuan Ch'i-jui, Wu P'ei-fu, and Chang Tso-lin were all desirous of doing good, but no good results came out of them. This is because all their energy was spent in dealing with their political enemies. When engaged in dealing with their enemies, they had to sacrifice reconstruction to maintain an army and resort to any dubious means in order to win. The problem is therefore not that of personality but that of circumstances. Given the circumstances, no one could achieve good results. The basic situation of China may be summarized in one sentence: Without a unified political power, there can be no good government. . . .

Viewed from the standpoint of history, this phenomenon is quite natural, and no nation is an exception to it. Advanced Western countries such as England, France, and Russia resembled China in their early stages of development when there was only internal order but not revolution. In England the Wars of the Roses raged in the fifteenth century but no results were achieved. It was toward the end of the fifteenth century that Henry VII unified England and began a century of absolutism under the name of the Tudor dynasty. During these hundred years the British people had a good rest and rehabilitation; as a result, the national state was formed. The seventeenth century saw the culmination of political conflicts in a genuine revolution. Historians are agreed that had there not been any Tudor autocracy in the sixteenth century there could not have been any revolution in the seventeenth century. . . . [Tsiang goes on to cite the Bourbons and the French Revolution, the Romanovs and the Russian Revolution as illustrations of the same point.]

The present situation in China is similar to that of England before the Tudor absolutism, or that of France before the Bourbon absolutism, or that of Russia before the Romanov absolutism. The Chinese too can have only internal disturbance but not genuine revolution. Although we had several thousand years of absolute government, unfortunately, our absolute monarchs, because of environmental peculiarities, did not fulfill their historic duty. The heritage left to the republic by the Manchu dynasty was too poor to be revolutionary capital. In the first place, our state is still a dynastic state, not a national one. Chinese citizens are generally loyal to individuals, families, or localities rather than to the state. Secondly, our absolute monarchs did not leave us a class that could serve as the nucleus of a new regime. In fact, the historic task of the Chinese monarchies was to destroy all the classes and institutions outside the royal family which could possibly become the center of political power. As a result, when the royal family was overthrown, the state became a "heap of loose sand." Thirdly, under the absolutist regime our material civilization lagged far behind. Consequently, when the foreigners took advantage of our trouble after the outbreak of the revolution, we were unable to offer any effective resistance.

In sum, the political history of all countries is divided into two phases: first, the building of a state; and second, the promotion of national welfare by means of the state. Since we have not completed the first phase, it is idle to talk of the second. As a Western saying goes, "the better is often the enemy of the good." The so-called revolution of China today is a great obstacle to our national reconstruction. The Chinese people should adopt an objective attitude and view the civil war as an historical process, just as physicians study physiology. We should foster the unifying force, because it is the vital power of our state organism. We should eliminate the anti-unification force, because it is the virus in our state organism. Our present problem is the existence of our state, not what type of state we should have.

HU SHIH
National Reconstruction and Absolutism

A direct rejoinder to T. F. Tsiang's defense of Kuomintang party dictatorship came from one of the intellectual leaders of republican China, Hu Shih (1891–). Like Lo and Tsiang, he had been educated in the United States (Cornell and Columbia) and become a thoroughgoing exponent of Westernization or modernization in many fields. As such he was often critical of the Kuomintang and of attitudes expressed by Sun Yat-sen or Chiang Kai-shek. Nevertheless, his personal standing as a scholar and thinker was so high both in China and the West that the Nanking government entrusted important diplomatic and educational assignments to him, including (most recently) the presidency of its top academic institution, the Academia Sinica.

[From "Chien-kuo yü chuan-chih," in *Tu-li p'ing-lun*, No. 81 (December 1933), pp. 3–5]

1. Is Absolutism a Necessary Stage for National Reconstruction?

In regard to this problem, there is a basic difference between Mr. Tsiang T'ing-fu's views and mine. As I see it, the history of England, France, and Russia as cited by Mr. Tsiang is only the history of national reconstruction in the three countries. But the scope of national reconstruction is very broad and the factors involved are complex. We cannot single out "absolutism" as the only cause or condition. We may say that the three dynasties (the Tudors of England, the Bourbons of France, and the Romanovs of Russia) were the periods during which their respective states were built, but we cannot prove that the formation of the state in these three countries was due to absolute rule. . . . The birth and propagation of the new English language and literature, the circulation of the English Bible and the Prayer Book, the influence of Oxford and Cambridge universities, the impact of London as England's political, economic, and cultural center, the rapid development of the textile industry, the rise of the middle class—all of these were important factors in the formation of the English national state. Most of these factors did not first appear under the Tudor dynasty; their origins may be traced to the time before the Tudors, although their development was particularly rapid in that century of unity and peace.

What Mr. Tsiang probably means to say is that a unified political power is indispensable to the building of the state. However, his use of the term absolutism to describe the unity of political power easily leads the people to think of a dictatorship with unlimited power. The reign of Henry VIII was the period in which parliamentary power began to rise: members of Parliament were secure from arrest and the king established the new church upon the support of Parliament. Therefore, instead of asserting that absolutism is an indispensable stage for the building of the state, we had better say that unity of political power is the condition. And unity of political power does not depend on completely following the dictatorship of the Romanov dynasty.

2. Why Did Centuries of Absolute Government Fail to Create a National State in China?

Concerning this question, my views are again different from those of Mr. Tsiang. Generally speaking, China had long since become a national state. What we now find defective is that the solidarity and unity of the Chinese national state has proved inadequate for a modern national state. In national consciousness, in unity of language, in unity of history and culture, in unity and continuity of governmental system (including examination, civil service, law, etc.)—in all these, China in the past two thousand years was qualified to be a national state. It is true that there were periods of foreign rule, but during those periods national consciousness became more vigorous and enduring so that eventually there arose national heroes such as Liu Yü, Chu Yüan-chang, Hung Hsiu-ch'üan, and Sun Yat-sen, who led the national revolutions. Indeed, all of the capital for national reconstruction which we have today is the national consciousness passed on to us by our forebears through two thousand years. . . .

As to the three defects pointed out by Mr. Tsiang, they prove only the evil consequences of the former social and political order, but not the lack of a national state in China. First, Mr. Tsiang said: "Chinese citizens are generally loyal to individuals, families, or localities rather than to the state." This is because in the old days the power of the state did not extend directly to the people. When "the emperor was as remote as the sky [from the people]," how could anyone by-pass his family, which exerts an immediate influence on his life, and profess loyalty to the state in the abstract, unless he was highly educated? The famous Burke of eighteenth-century England said: "In order that the people love the state, the state must first be lovable." Can we then say that England in the eighteenth century had not become a national state? The reason the masses of the people today do not love the nation is partly that they are inadequately educated and therefore unable to imagine a state, and partly that the state has not bestowed any benefits upon the people.

CHIANG KAI-SHEK: NATIONALISM AND TRADITIONALISM

Chiang Kai-shek (1887—), who took over leadership after Sun Yat-sen's death, was a devoted follower and admirer of Dr. Sun. He was also a very different man from his mentor. For one thing, Chiang had virtually no Western education, and, knowing no foreign language well, was dependent upon others to interpret the West for him. Consequently his ideas were formed much more within the Chinese tradition, and found their most typical expression in the language and formulas of the past. His experience of foreign lands was also much more limited. The net effect even of his relatively brief travel and study in Japan and later in Soviet Russia was only to increase his consciousness of being a Chinese. Throughout life this consciousness deepened as a result of intensive and prolonged study of Chinese classical literature.

Understandably then, it was the first of Sun's Three Principles, Nationalism, which had the most significance for Chiang. Others of his contemporaries, however, no less intensely nationalistic than he and no less limited in their experience of the outside world, still showed by their eager acceptance of Western standards that the new nationalism could be quite divorced from any real attachment to the values of the past. The contact zone of East and West, in which such a cultural hybrid as Dr. Sun had been produced just a generation before, had moved from Honolulu, Hongkong, Macao, and Yokohama, into the very classrooms of provincial China where Western-style education now prevailed. Chiang himself, in a certain sense, had moved with it. He had, for instance, become a devout Methodist, married a Wellesley-educated girl, attempted to learn English, adopted Western standards of personal hygiene, and made considerable use of Western advisers. All this notwithstanding, his own philosophy of life drew more and more upon Chinese sources of inspiration, and in offering it to the Chinese people as a national way of life, he cut more and more directly across the Westernizing trend of the times.

What Chiang found so essential in Chinese tradition—Confucian ethics—actually represented an important link between him and Dr. Sun. The latter, in his long struggle to organize and lead a national revolution, had come to a new appreciation of the traditional Confucian virtues for which earlier he had found little use. They could serve as a means of achieving social discipline and national cohesion among a people who were otherwise just a "heap of loose sand." Sun thereby found a political value in a system of ethics which had hitherto meant little to him personally. Chiang himself had no less reason, politically, to adopt the same view. He confronted all the same problems of leadership as Sun, and felt the same need for disciplined loyalty among his followers. Moreover, as a military man he must have possessed even keener a sense of the importance of discipline in general.

With Chiang, however, it was more than a question of simply exploiting traditional attitudes which could serve present purposes. It had become a deep personal conviction of his (as it never seems to have been of Sun's) that moral values were the ultimate basis of human life. His own experience of life seems to have taught him the value of self-discipline to the individual, as much as of social discipline to the nation. There is one account, of uncertain reliability, which speaks of his life in Shanghai just after the Revolution as "a period of rather riotous living. . . . With a comfortable income such as he was receiving, there was much chance for moral degeneration. His friends, knowing his temper, and that persuasion would be futile, deplored this; and he would have gone from bad to worse, had it not been for the fact that the second revolutionary war started and kindled again the smoldering ashes of patriotism." [6] Whatever the truth of this may be, there is something intriguing in the idea that Chiang, after a period of youthful dissipation, underwent a process of self-reformation and discovered, on throwing himself again into the

[6] Cf. Emily Hahn, *Chiang Kai-shek*, p. 48.

revolutionary struggle, that he had a personal need for dedication to something greater than himself. For it was this combination of self-discipline and service to the nation, which had perhaps been the means of rescuing him from himself earlier, that Chiang constantly urged upon Chinese youth.

These convictions manifested themselves early in Chiang's public career, and he has never abandoned them. In 1924, as superintendent of the Kuomintang military academy at Whampoa, where Soviet influence was strong and the revolutionary fever ran high, Chiang did not hesitate to base military indoctrination on a text compiled from the moral teachings of the nineteenth-century Neo-Confucianist and Restoration hero, Tseng Kuo-fan. Thus, in contrast to Sun's glorification of the Taiping leader, Hung Hsiu-ch'üan, as a national revolutionary figure, Chiang acclaimed the very suppressor of the Taipings (and a servant of the Manchus) as the finest exemplar of national tradition. In this way the cultivation of personal virtue and nobility of character was stressed over revolutionary fervor.

Ten years later, when Chiang launched his New Life movement as a program for the strengthening of national morale, the Confucian virtues of decorum, righteousness, integrity, and a sense of shame, provided the chief catchwords and main content of this campaign of mass indoctrination. Significantly, the first of these virtues, *li,* implied an acceptance of social discipline, of law and authority, in opposition to the trend from the West toward unfettered individualism. Again, in 1943 when Chiang published his *China's Destiny* to serve as a primer for the party and its Youth Corps, he declared that, with the approaching end of foreign rule and exploitation in China, the great task would be one of internal reconstruction through moral rearmament, Confucian-style. Even in the '50s, after the retreat to Formosa, courses in Neo-Confucian ethical philosophy were compulsory for all students under the Kuomintang regime.

It would be a distortion of Chiang's social philosophy and program to sum it up in terms only of nationalism and Neo-Confucian ethics. He remained committed to all of Dr. Sun's Three Principles, including a large measure of economic planning and state socialism. And if he did not pursue with equal vigor these other aspects of Sun's original program, his justification for the delay in achieving the objectives of People's Rule and People's Livelihood was one provided by Sun himself in the doctrine of political tutelage. Military unification must come first.

Nevertheless, it was here that the incongruity of Chiang's program became apparent. Party tutelage and Chiang's role as near-dictator were premised on the fact that the revolution had not yet been brought to an end. In a revolutionary situation, strong leadership and a quasi-military organization were still indispensable. Yet Chiang, as a revolutionary leader, tried to rally his forces with a conservative ideology. Where messianic zeal was called for, he offered austerity and restraint.

It must be allowed that Chiang's traditionalism was more than a personal idosyncrasy, a quixotic gesture. As our next chapter will show, there were other Chinese at this time—including erstwhile advocates of Westernization, now disillusioned—who joined him in attacking Western individualism and materialism as a threat to the spiritual and moral values of Chinese civilization. Nor was this a purely Chinese phenomenon. Nationalists in India and Japan often shared a revulsion for those aspects of Western life which Chiang found so distasteful in treaty ports like Shanghai. Commercialism, cynicism, soft-living, and self-indulgence seemed to typify the bourgeois culture of the West as transplanted to the soil of Asia. Was this all the West had to offer in place of the traditional values it was destroying? On this point, Chiang's rejection of extreme Western liberalism linked him in spirit with an Indian nationalist like Gandhi, while his *Essentials of the New Life Movement* (from which excerpts are given below), showed at the same time his close kinship with the authors of *Fundamentals of Japan's National Polity* (*Kokutai no hongi*), the official credo of Japanese nationalism in the '30s, who decried as he did the individualism and class antagonism of the West, while extolling the social virtues of Confucianism.[7]

Chiang's traditionalism, it is true, was never conceived as a total opposition to Westernization. The Three People's Principles—nationalism, democracy, and socialism—were basically Western in inspiration, and however much he or Dr. Sun adapted them to their own tastes, the use of such slogans constituted a recognition on their part that Western ideals had an irresistible attraction for twentieth-century Asia. Yet in the face

[7] This is not to say, of course, that the three did not differ considerably in other respects.

of this dominant trend, traditionalism, even when it took the form of an attempted synthesis of East and West and made generous acknowledgement of China's debt to the latter, suffered serious drawbacks as the basis for a national ideology. Quite apart from Chiang's own role as a "revolutionary" leader, the rising demand for material improvement, the great expectations aroused for social progress, and the promise of a freer and easier life for all which Westernization seemed to offer, created a profound dissatisfaction with things as they were, a revolutionary atmosphere in which the response to traditional values and virtues was most often one of impatience.

Nowhere could this be seen more clearly than among the younger generation, and especially the educated. Chiang's own attempts at economic and military modernization created a need for men with training along Western lines, and yet few such men would take Chiang's Confucianism seriously, while many openly resisted it. As our next chapter will show, a considerable gulf had already opened up in the early years of the republic between its intellectual and political leaders. Under Chiang this gulf widened, and while he was by no means wholly responsible for the estrangement, it had become clear that his brand of traditionalism, far from providing a common ground among Chinese, was now itself a source of disunity.

CHIANG KAI-SHEK
Essentials of the New Life Movement

The New Life Movement was inaugurated by Chiang in a speech at Nanchang in September, 1934. Its immediate purpose was to rally the Chinese people for a campaign against the Communists in that region, but a more general aim was to tighten discipline and build up morale in the Kuomintang and nation as a whole. Laxity in public life, official corruption, indiscipline in the ranks of party and army, and apathy among the people were among the weaknesses Chiang tried to overcome by a great moral reformation emphasizing Confucian self-cultivation, a life of frugality, and dedication to the nation. There were exhortations too in behalf of personal hygiene and physical training, as well as injunctions against tobacco and opium-smoking, dancing, spitting on the floor, and leaving coats unbuttoned. In these respects, however, Chiang thought of himself as promoting progress—cleaning up and dressing up China in answer to the type of Westerner who complained about her untidiness and lack of sanitation.

An important influence on the New Life ideology was exerted by Chiang's close adviser and Minister of Education, Ch'en Li-fu (1890—), Western-educated exponent of a modernized Neo-Confucianism. He has been reputed as the "ghost writer" of this text, but has personally denied any part in it.

[From *Hsin sheng-huo yün-tung kang-yao*, in *Tsung-ts'ai yen-lun hsüan-chi*, III, 403–14]

THE OBJECT OF THE NEW LIFE MOVEMENT

Why Is a New Life Needed?

The general psychology of our people today can be described as spiritless. What manifests itself in behavior is this: lack of discrimination between good and evil, between what is public and what is private, and between what is primary and what is secondary. Because there is no discrimination between good and evil, right and wrong are confused; because there is no discrimination between public and private, improper taking and giving [of public funds] occur; and because there is no distinction between primary and secondary, first and last are not placed in the proper order. As a result, officials tend to be dishonest and avaricious, the masses are undisciplined and calloused, the youth become degraded and intemperate, the adults are corrupt and ignorant, the rich become extravagant and luxurious, and the poor become mean and disorderly. Naturally it has resulted in disorganization of the social order and national life, and we are in no position either to prevent or to remedy natural calamities, disasters caused from within, or invasions from without. The individual, society and the whole country are now suffering. If the situation should remain unchanged, it would be impossible even to continue living under such miserable conditions. In order to develop the life of our nation, protect the existence of our society, and improve the livelihood of our people, it is absolutely necessary to wipe out these unwholesome conditions and to start to lead a new and rational life.

THE CONTENT OF THE NEW LIFE MOVEMENT

1. The Principles of the New Life Movement.

The New Life Movement aims at the promotion of a regular life guided by the four virtues, namely, *li, i, lien,* and *ch'ih*.[8] These virtues

---

[8] Standard translations for these terms are: *li*, decorum or rites; *i*, righteousness or duty; *lien*, integrity or honesty; *ch'ih*, sense of shame. Since Chiang defines the terms in what follows, we have kept the romanized forms here.

must be applied to ordinary life in the matter of food, clothing, shelter, and action. The four virtues are the essential principles for the promotion of morality. They form the major rules for dealing with men and human affairs, for cultivating oneself, and for adjustment to one's surroundings. Whoever violates these rules is bound to fail; and a nation which neglects them will not survive.

There are two kinds of skeptics:

First, some hold that the four virtues are merely rules of good conduct. No matter how good they may be, they are not sufficient to save a nation whose knowledge and technique are inferior to others.

Those who hold this view do not seem to understand the distinction between matters of primary and secondary importance. People need knowledge and technique because they want to do good. Otherwise, knowledge and technique can only be instruments of dishonorable deeds. *Li, i, lien,* and *ch'ih* are the principal rules alike for the community, the group, or the entire nation. Those who do not observe these rules will probably utilize their knowledge and ability to the detriment of society and ultimately to their own disadvantage. Therefore, these virtues not only can save the nation, but also can rebuild the nation.

Secondly, there is another group of people who argue that these virtues are merely formal refinements which are useless in dealing with hunger and cold. The argument is probably due to a misunderstanding of the famous teaching of Kuan Tzu,[9] who said: "When one does not have to worry about one's food and clothing, then one cares for personal honor; when the granary is full, then people learn good manners." These skeptics fail to realize that the four virtues are the basic elements of man. If one cannot be a man, what is the use of having abundance of food and clothing? Moreover, Kuan Tzu did not intend to make a general statement; he merely referred to a particular aspect of the subject. In fact, the essence of his statesmanship lay in the pre-eminence given to the four virtues, which he called the four pillars of the nation. When these virtues prevail, even if food and clothing are insufficient, they can be produced by manpower; or, if the granary is empty, it can be filled through human effort. On the other hand, when these virtues are not observed, if food and clothing are insufficient, they will not be made sufficient by fighting and

---

[9] Reputed author of an early text in which these four virtues are spoken of as the pillars of the nation.

robbing; or, if the granary is empty, it will not be filled by stealing and begging. The four virtues, which rectify the misconduct of men, are the proper methods of achieving abundance. Without them, there will be fighting, robbing, stealing, and begging among men. In that event, even if food and clothing are sufficient, even if grain fills the granaries, they cannot be enjoyed by the people. Robbers are usually most numerous in the wealthiest cities of the world. This is an obvious illustration of disorder caused by nonobservance of virtues. People become traitors, Communists and corrupt officials, not because they are driven by hunger and cold, but because they have neglected the cultivation of virtue. The four virtues are so important that they must be adopted as the guiding principles of our life.

2. The Meaning of *Li, I, Lien*, and *Ch'ih*.

Although *li, i, lien*, and *ch'ih* have always been regarded as the foundations of the nation, yet the changing times and circumstances may require that these principles be given a new interpretation. As applied to our life today, they may be interpreted as follows:

Li means regulated attitude.
I means right conduct.
Lien means clear discrimination.
Ch'ih means real self-consciousness.

The word *li* (decorum) means *li* (reason). It becomes natural law, when applied to nature; it becomes a rule, when applied to social affairs; and it signifies discipline, when used in reference to national affairs. A man's conduct is considered regular if it conforms with the above law, rule, and discipline. When one conducts oneself in accordance with the regular manner, one is said to have the regulated attitude.

The word *i* means proper. Any conduct which is in accordance with *li* —i.e., natural law, social rule, and national discipline—is considered proper. To act improperly, or to refrain from acting when one knows it is proper to act, cannot be called *i*.

The word *lien* means clear. It denotes distinction between right and wrong. What agrees with *li* and *i* is right, and what does not agree is wrong. To take what we recognize as right and to forego what we recognize as wrong constitute clear discrimination.

The word *ch'ih* means consciousness. When one is conscious of the fact that his own actions are not in accordance with *li, i, lien,* and *ch'ih,* one feels ashamed. When one is conscious of the fact that others are wrong, one feels disgusted. But the consciousness must be real and thorough so that one will strive to improve what one feels to be a shame and to eliminate what one feels to be disgusting. This is called real self-consciousness.

From the above explanations, it is clear that *ch'ih* governs the motive of action, that *lien* gives the guidance for it, that *i* relates to the carrying out of an action, and that *li* regulates its outward form. The four are interrelated. They are interdependent upon each other in the perfecting of virtue.

THE APPLICATION OF LI, I, LIEN AND CH'IH TO FOOD, CLOTHING,
SHELTER AND ACTION

The means of maintaining our livelihood may be divided into three phases: first, the obtaining of materials; second, the selection of quality; and third, the manner in which these materials are used. Let me explain each separately.

1. The obtaining of materials should be in conformity with the principle of *lien.* Clear discrimination should be exercised between what is ours and what is not. If something does not belong to us, we should not take it. In other words, the materials for our daily life should be acquired through our own labor or through other proper means. Strife should not be encouraged. A parasite is not a good example. Even giving and taking improperly should be avoided. "What really matters is the loss of integrity, not dying from hunger." This famous Confucian saying illustrates the point.

2. The selection of quality should be in conformity with the principle of *i.* Do the proper thing with due regard to special circumstances arising from persons, times, places, and positions. For instance, it is proper for an old man to use silk and to take meat, to be excused from carrying heavy burdens on the road, and to have some leisure; but a young man should be satisfied with moderate food and clothing and be ready to endure hardships. What is proper in winter is not necessarily proper in summer. What is proper in the north is not necessarily proper in the south. Similarly, different positions may influence a situation differently. A ruler, or a military commander, must have authority and rights that are becoming

to his dignity and necessary for his work—authority and rights which should neither be excessive nor inadequate but should be proper to his position and rank.

3. The manner in which materials are used should be in conformity with the principle of *li*, which includes natural law, social rules, and national discipline.

CONCLUSION

In short, the main object of the New Life Movement is to substitute a rational life for the irrational, and to achieve this we must observe *li, i, lien,* and *ch'ih* in our daily life.

1. By observing these virtues, it is hoped that rudeness and vulgarity will be got rid of, and that the life of our people will conform to the standard of art. By art we are not referring to the special enjoyment of the gentry. We mean the cultural standard of all the people, irrespective of sex, age, wealth, and class. It is the boundary line between civilized life and barbarism. It is the only way by which one can achieve the purpose of man, for only by artistically controlling oneself and dealing with others can one fulfill the duty of mutual assistance. . . . A lack of artistic training is the cause of suspicion, jealousy, hatred, and strife that are prevalent in our society today. . . . To investigate things so as to extend our knowledge; to distinguish between the fundamental and the secondary; to seek the invention of instruments; to excel in our techniques—these are the essentials of an artistic life, the practice of which will enable us to wipe out the defects of vulgarity, confusion, crudity, and baseness.

2. By observing these virtues, it is hoped that beggary and robbery will be eliminated, and that the life of our people will be productive. The poverty of China is primarily caused by the fact that there are too many consumers and too few producers. Those who consume without producing usually live as parasites or as robbers. They behave thus because they are ignorant of the four virtues. To remedy this we must make them produce more and spend less. They must understand that luxury is improper and that living as a parasite is a shame.

3. By observing these virtues, it is hoped that social disorder and individual weakness will be remedied and that people will become more military-minded. If a country cannot defend itself, it has every chance of losing its existence. . . . Therefore our people must have military train-

ing. As a preliminary, we must acquire the habits of orderliness, cleanliness, simplicity, frugality, promptness, and exactness. We must preserve order, emphasize organization, responsibility, and discipline, and be ready to die for the country at any moment.

In conclusion, the life of our people will be elevated if we live artistically; we will become wealthy if we live productively; and we will be safe if we lead a military way of life. When we do this, we will have a rational life. This rational life is founded on *li, i, lien,* and *ch'ih.* The four virtues, in turn, can be applied to food, clothing, shelter, and action. If we can achieve this, we will have revolutionized the daily life of our people and laid the foundation for the rehabilitation of our nation.

China's Destiny

China's Destiny appeared in March, 1943, during the darkest period of the war with Japan, when Chinese morale badly needed boosting. Chiang explained at length how his country's difficulties in the past arose from foreign oppression and the consequent deterioration of national life. The recent abrogation of the unequal treaties by Britain and the United States, however, heralded a new era of independence and self-respect for China once the Japanese were defeated. Chiang's great goal was still political and military unification. To achieve this he outlined a five-point program of national reconstruction emphasizing pride in China's past, a return to Confucian virtues, restoration of the traditional system of group-responsibility and mutual aid, and a long-range program of economic development along lines laid down by Sun—industrialization, land "equalization," and state capitalism in a planned and closely controlled economy.

A prime target of Chiang's indignation was the prevalence of foreign ideologies and attitudes among intellectuals, who were accused of yielding and pandering to popular trends. Extreme Western liberalism, almost as much as Communism, came under his fire for encouraging moral anarchy, the pursuit of selfish ambitions, and the quest for private profit or class domination. True enough, Chiang insisted that these tendencies represented not Western civilization itself, properly understood, but only a superficial imitation of the West by shallow-minded Chinese. Nevertheless, exoneration of the West to this extent could only sharpen the indictment of his own countrymen.

As a result, his views tended not only to antagonize Westernized intellectuals in China but even to discourage businessmen, who found private enterprise discredited and offered little place in a planned economy dominated by bureaucratic capitalism. (By contrast, Mao Tse-tung, after 1941, was wooing businessmen with talk of a mixed economy.) Moreover, Chiang's identification of the West with imperialism, exploitation, and profit-seeking helped create a popular image which persisted long after his tributes to his allies and his acknowledgements of Western contributions to China had been forgotten. Thus the Nanking regime itself was embarrassed when, in the postwar struggle with the Communists, it had nowhere else to turn for help but to the West.

[Adapted from *China's Destiny,* tr. by Wang Chung-hui, pp. 72–84, 212–21]

SOCIAL EFFECTS [OF THE UNEQUAL TREATIES]

During the last hundred years, under the oppression of unequal treaties, the life of the Chinese people became more and more degenerate. Everyone took self-interest as the standard of right and wrong, and personal desires as the criterion of good and evil; a thing was considered as right if it conformed to one's self-interest or good if it conformed to one's personal desires. Rascals became influential in the villages, rogues were active in the cities, sacrificing public safety and the welfare of others to satisfy their own interest and desires. In the meantime, extravagant and irresponsible ideologies and political doctrines were freely advanced, either to rationalize self-interest and personal desires or to exploit them for ulterior motives. The rationalizers idolized them as an expression of the self; and the exploiters utilized them as a means of fomenting disturbances in the community, in order to fish in troubled waters. The practice of following in the footsteps of the sages, of emulating the heroes and of being "friends with the ancients" not only tended to disappear, but was even considered mean and despicable. [p. 72]

MORAL EFFECTS

For five thousand years China had always stressed the importance of honest work and frugality. Her people were noted for their simplicity in food and clothing; women occupied themselves with their looms and men with their plows. These good habits, however, were swept clean by the prevalence in the [foreign] concessions of the vices of opium-smoking, gambling, prostitution, and robbery.

China's ancient ethical teachings and philosophies contained detailed and carefully worked out principles and rules for the regulation and maintenance of the social life of man. The structure of our society underwent many changes, but our social life never deviated from the principles governing the relationship between father and son, husband and wife, brother and brother, friend and friend, superior and inferior, man and woman, old and young, as well as principles enjoining mutual help among neighbors and care of the sick and weak.

During the past hundred years, wherever the influence of the concessions was felt, these principles were not only neglected but also despised. Between father and son, husband and wife, brothers and friends, superiors and inferiors, old and young, and among neighbors, the old sentiments of respect and affection and the spirit of mutual help and cooperation were disappearing. Only material interests were taken into consideration and everywhere there was a general lack of moral standards by which to judge oneself. Whenever duty called, people tried to shirk it; whenever there was material profit to be gained, they struggled for it. Truth was concealed between superiors and inferiors, and mutual deception was practiced among friends. The aged and the weak could find no protection, the poor and the sick no relief. Members of the same family were often considered as strangers and fellow countrymen as enemies. In some extreme cases, people even went so far as to "regard rascals as their fathers," and shamelessly served their enemies, thereby violating all principles of family and social relationships without even being aware of their own moral degeneracy. A country which had hitherto attached the greatest importance to decorum and righteousness was now in danger of losing its sense of integrity and honor. What harm these unequal treaties had caused!

The deterioration of national morality also tended to affect the physique of our people. The physical strength of the numberless unemployed in the cities was easily impaired. The health of those merchants who abandoned themselves to a life of extravagance and dissoluteness could not but break down. The most serious thing, however, was the effect upon the health of the youth in the schools. Physical training was not popularized in most of the schools; moral education was also neglected by school masters and teachers. In the meantime, the extravagant and dissolute life outside the school attracted the students, caused them to indulge in evil habits and resulted in the deterioration of their moral character. Infectious and venereal diseases, too, which were rampant in the cities, further undermined their physical constitution. How could these young men, who were unsound in body and mind, help to advance learning, reform social customs, render service to the state and promote enterprises after their graduation? The inevitable result of such a state of affairs was the steady disintegration of our country and the further demoralization of the Chinese nation. [pp. 75–77]

PSYCHOLOGICAL EFFECTS

After the Student Movement of May 4, 1919, two currents of thought, ultra-individualistic liberalism and class-struggle communism, found their way into Chinese academic circles, and later became widespread in the country. On the whole, Chinese academic circles desired to effect a change in our culture, forgetting that it had certain elements which are immutable. With respect to different Western theories they imitated only their superficial aspects and never sought to understand their true significance in order to improve China's national life. The result was that a large number of our scholars and students adopted the superficialities and nonessentials of Western culture and lost their respect for and confidence in our own culture. [pp. 81–2]

Under these circumstances Chinese scholars and politicians who misinterpreted liberalism and abused communism were disposed, openly or indirectly, intentionally or unintentionally, to take a foreign power's stand as their own and to identify a foreign power's interests with theirs. Nay, they even went to the length of putting a favorable color on imperialism and of becoming the tools of aggression. They almost forgot who they were, why they were studying, and what they were doing. Their propaganda and educational activities among the masses were conducted in this mental atmosphere, causing the people to regard as a matter of course the impairment of our state sovereignty and the endangering of our national life. And what is worse, they were unaware that such impairment and endangering were furthered by their blindly following foreign "isms." This truly constituted the greatest crisis in the history of our culture and the most serious menace to the spirit of our people. It is high time for us to wake up and reform ourselves thoroughly. Only thus can we save the nation and ourselves; only thus can we become a self-invigorating people, and build up an independent and free China. [pp. 83–4]

THE DECISIVE FACTOR IN CHINA'S DESTINY

The work of reforming social life and carrying out the program of national reconstruction is one of paramount importance in the process of national revival—a task which requires persistent effort. Individuals, striving singly, will not achieve great results, nor lasting accomplishments. Consequently, all adult citizens and promising youths whether in a town, a district, a province, or in the country at large, should have a common organization with a systematic plan for binding the members together and headquarters to promote joint reconstruction activities and also personal accomplishments. Only by working with such a central organization can individuals live up to Dr. Sun Yat-sen's words: "To dedicate the few score years of our perishable life to the laying of an imperishable foundation for our nation."

In the past our adult citizens have been unable to unite on a large scale or for a long period. They have been derisively compared to "a heap of loose sand" or spoken of as having "only five-minutes' enthusiasm." Now, incapacity to unite is a result of selfishness, and the best antidote for selfishness is public spirit. That unity does not last is due to hypocrisy and the best antidote for hypocrisy is sincerity. With a public spirit, one can take "all men as one's kin and all things as one's company." With sincerity, one can persevere and succeed in the end. Since the Three Principles of the People are based on public good and absolute sincerity, the Kuomintang is all-embracing in spirit while in action it can "abide by the good once it has been chosen"—a fact I have clearly pointed out in my account of the Kuomintang's reorganization.

The principal fault of our youth today, and the cause of their failure and ineffectual living lie essentially in the unsound education they have received. Since they do not follow the guidance of their teachers, or realize the importance of organization as a factor in the success or failure of their life, and since they do not understand what freedom and discipline mean, they are irresponsible in their conduct and unrealistic in their thinking. As soon as they enter society, they feel the lack of ability and confidence to take up any practical work, let alone the task of social and national reconstruction. To make themselves fit for hardships and responsibilities, for social reforms and national reconstruction, it is necessary that their thinking should be scientifically trained and their behavior strictly disciplined. For this reason, immediately after the outbreak of the war of resistance I organized the San Min Chu I [Three People's Principles] Youth Corps to meet the imperative needs of young men and women throughout the country, to give a new life to the Kuomintang, and to furnish a new driving force for the [Chinese] nation. [pp. 212-14]

Given this rare opportunity at the threshold of their life, our youth should calmly plan for their life work in the light of the needs of a modern state. To avoid the mistake of living a misguided and regrettable life, they should never again allow themselves to be led astray by blind and impulsive following of others as in the past. We must realize that the Three Principles represent not only the crystallization of China's time-honored civilization and of her people's highest virtues, but also the inevitable trend of world affairs in this modern age. The San Min Chu I Youth Corps is the central organization of all Chinese youths who are faithful adherents of the Three Principles. All young men and women must therefore place themselves under the guidance of the Corps in order to keep their aims true and to avoid doing harm to themselves and to the nation. It is only by working within the framework of the Corps' program that they can make decisions about their life work in the right direction. Members of the Corps will receive strict training and observe strict discipline. They will promote all phases of the life of the people, and protect the interests of the entire nation. It will be their mission to save the country from decline and disorganization, to wipe out national humiliation, to restore national strength, and to show loyalty to the state and filial devotion to the nation. They should emulate the sages and heroes of history and be the life blood of the people and the backbone of the nation. The youths of the whole nation should not only join the Corps as the starting point of their careers, but should also consider it an honor to be thus enrolled. They should understand that the orders issued by the Corps are aimed at sustaining the collective life of the youth of the whole nation, and that the strong organization of the Corps will enable them to achieve their common objective, namely, the success of our National Revolution in the realization of the Three Principles of the People.

To sum up, the Kuomintang and the San Min Chu I Youth Corps are organic parts of the nation—a fact which need not be dwelt upon at length. But there is one point which should be repeated to my fellow countrymen, namely: that the Kuomintang is the headquarters of our national reconstruction, open to all and to be enjoyed by all. The independence of our nation hinges upon the success of the Kuomintang

Revolution. Without the Kuomintang, there would be no China. In a word, China's destiny is entrusted to the Kuomintang. If the Kuomintang Revolution should fail, China as a nation would have nothing to rely upon. Should this happen, not only would China cease to rank as one of the Four Powers of the world, but she would be at the mercy of other countries. The name of the Chinese Republic would disappear altogether from the map of the world. We should all realize this: Considering the state as an organism as far as its life is concerned, we may say that the Three Principles constitute the soul of our nation, because without these Principles our national reconstruction would be deprived of its guiding spirit. And, considering the state as an organism as far as its functions are concerned, we may say that the Kuomintang is the life blood of our nation and the members of the San Min Chu I Youth Corps may be likened to new blood corpuscles. Without the Kuomintang, China would be deprived of its pivot. If all the revolutionary elements and promising youths in the country really want to throw in their lot with the fate of the country, if they regard national undertakings as their own undertakings and the national life as their own life—then, they should all enlist in the Kuomintang or in the Youth Corps. By so doing, they can discharge the highest duties of citizenship and attain the highest ideal in life. Then and only then can our great mission of national reconstruction be completed. [pp. 219–21]

CHAPTER XXVIII

THE NEW CULTURE
MOVEMENT

The New Culture Movement, as its name implies, was an attempt to destroy what remained of traditional Confucian culture in the Republican era and to replace it with something new. The collapse of the old dynastic system in 1911 and the failure of Yüan Shih-k'ai's Confucian-garbed monarchical restoration in 1916 meant that, politically, Confucianism was almost dead. It had, however, been much more than a political philosophy. It had been a complete way of life, which nationalism and republicanism only supplanted in part. There were some even among republicans who felt that certain aspects of the old culture, Confucian ethics especially, should be preserved and strengthened, lest the whole fabric of Chinese life come apart and the new regime itself be seriously weakened. Others, with far more influence on the younger generation, drew precisely the opposite conclusion. For them nothing in Confucianism was worth salvaging from the debris of the Manchu dynasty. On the contrary, whatever vestiges of the past remained in the daily life and thinking of the people should be rooted out; otherwise the young republic would rest on shaky foundations and its progress would be retarded by a backward citizenry. The new order required a whole new culture. The political revolution had to be followed by a cultural revolution.

During and just after the First World War the intellectual spearhead of this second revolution went on the offensive, launching a movement that reached out in many directions and touched many aspects of Chinese society. Roughly it may be divided into six major phases, presented below in more or less chronological order. They are 1) the attack on Confucianism; 2) the Literary Revolution; 3) the proclaiming of a new philosophy of life; 4) the debate on science and the philosophy of life;

5) the "doubting of antiquity" movement; and 6) the debate on Chinese and Western cultural values. Needless to say, these phases overlapped each other considerably, and certain leading writers figured prominently in more than one phase of the movement.

From its anti-traditionalist character one may infer that the leaders of the movement looked very much to the West. Positivism was their great inspiration, science and materialism were their great slogans, and—in the early years especially—John Dewey and Bertrand Russell were their great idols. The leaders themselves were in many cases Western educated, though not necessarily schooled in the West, since Western-style education was by now established in the East, in Japan, and in the new national and missionary colleges of China. Often college professors themselves, they now had the lecture platform to make use of, as well as the new organs of public journalism and the intellectual and literary reviews which were a novel feature of the modern age. Above all, they had a new audience, young, intense, frustrated by China's failures in the past, and full of eager hopes for the future.

THE ATTACK ON CONFUCIANISM

The open assault on Confucianism, which began in 1916, was led by Ch'en Tu-hsiu (1879–1942), editor of a magazine entitled *The New Youth*. Earlier reformers had attacked at most certain of the concepts of Confucianism, often indeed in the name of a purified and revitalized Confucian belief, or, with less obvious partisanship, combining criticism of certain aspects with praise of others. Ch'en, by contrast, challenged Confucianism from beginning to end, realizing as he did so that he struck at the very heart of the traditional culture. For him, a partisan of "science" and "democracy," Confucianism stood simply for reaction and obscurantism. He identified it with the old regime, with Yüan Shih-k'ai's attempt to restore the monarchy, with everything from the past that, to his mind, had smothered progress and creativity.

Such an uncompromising attack was bound to shock many—those who had taken Confucianism as much for granted as the good earth of China, or those who still held to it consciously, and with some pride, as an expression of cultural nationalism. But there were others upon whom

Ch'en's bold denunciations had an electrifying effect—those, particularly young teachers and students, for whom Confucianism had come to hold little positive meaning as their own education became more Westernized; for whom, in fact, it was now more likely to be felt in their own lives simply as a form of unwanted parental or societal restraint. Young people of this group, with Peking as their center, *The New Youth* as their mouthpiece, and Ch'en as their literary champion, were glad to throw themselves into a crusade against this bugbear from the past, and to proclaim their own coming of age in the modern world by shouting: "Destroy the old curiosity shop of Confucius!"

CH'EN TU-HSIU
The Way of Confucius and Modern Life

Through articles such as this, which appeared in December, 1916, Ch'en Tu-hsiu established himself as perhaps the most influential writer of his time. His popular review, *Hsin ch'ing-nien* (*The New Youth*), had for its Western title "La Jeunesse Nouvelle," reflecting the avant-garde character of its editor, whose higher education had been obtained in a Japanese normal college and later in France. Here the Westernized and "liberated" Ch'en directs his fire at social customs and abuses which seemed to have Confucian sanction but had no place in the modern age. Already the man who was to found the Chinese Communist Party five years later speaks as an economic determinist and moral relativist, but still very much of an individualist.

[From "K'ung Tzu chih tao yü hsien-tai sheng-huo," *Hsin ch'ing-nien*, Vol. II, No. 4 (December 1916), pp. 3–5]

The pulse of modern life is economic and the fundamental principle of economic production is individual independence. Its effect has penetrated ethics. Consequently the independence of the individual in the ethical field and the independence of property in the economic field bear witness to each other, thus reaffirming the theory [of such interaction]. Because of this [interaction], social mores and material culture have taken a great step forward.

In China, the Confucianists have based their teachings on their ethical norms. Sons and wives possess neither personal individuality nor personal property. Fathers and elder brothers bring up their sons and younger brothers and are in turn supported by them. It is said in chapter thirty of the *Book of Rites* that "While parents are living, the son dares not regard his person or property as his own." [27:14] This is absolutely not the way to personal independence. . . .

In all modern constitutional states, whether monarchies or republics, there are political parties. Those who engage in party activities all express their spirit of independent conviction. They go their own way and need not agree with their fathers or husbands. When people are bound by the Confucian teachings of filial piety and obedience to the point of the son not deviating from the father's way even three years after his death [1] and the woman obeying not only her father and husband but also her son,[2] how can they form their own political party and make their own choice? The movement of women's participation in politics is also an aspect of women's life in modern civilization. When they are bound by the Confucian teaching that "To be a women means to submit,"[3] that "The wife's words should not travel beyond her own apartment," and that "A woman does not discuss affairs outside the home,"[4] would it not be unusual if they participated in politics?

In the West some widows choose to remain single because they are strongly attached to their late husbands and sometimes because they prefer a single life; they have nothing to do with what is called the chastity of widowhood. Widows who remarry are not despised by society at all. On the other hand, in the Chinese teaching of decorum, there is the doctrine of "no remarriage after the husband's death."[5] It is considered to be extremely shameful and unchaste for a woman to serve two husbands or a man to serve two rulers. The *Book of Rites* also prohibits widows from wailing at night [XXVII:21] and people from being friends with sons of widows. [IX:21] For the sake of their family reputation, people have forced their daughters-in-law to remain widows. These women have had no freedom and have endured a most miserable life. Year after year these many promising young women have lived a physically and spiritually abnormal life. All this is the result of Confucian teachings of decorum [or rites].

In today's civilized society, social intercourse between men and women is a common practice. Some even say that because women have a tender nature and can temper the crudeness of man, they are necessary in public

---

[1] Referring to *Analects*, I:11.
[2] *Book of Rites*, IX:24.
[3] *Book of Rites*, IX:24.
[4] *Book of Rites*, I:24.
[5] *Book of Rites*, IX:24.

or private gatherings. It is not considered improper even for strangers to sit or dance together once they have been introduced by the host. In the way of Confucian teaching, however, "Men and women do not sit on the same mat," "Brothers- and sisters-in-law do not exchange inquiries about each other," "Married sisters do not sit on the same mat with brothers or eat from the same dish," "Men and women do not know each other's name except through a matchmaker and should have no social relations or show affection until after marriage presents have been exchanged," [6] "Women must cover their faces when they go out," [7] "Boys and girls seven years or older do not sit or eat together," "Men and women have no social relations except through a matchmaker and do not meet until after marriage presents have been exchanged," [8] and "Except in religious sacrifices, men and women do not exchange wine cups." [9] Such rules of decorum are not only inconsistent with the mode of life in Western society; they cannot even be observed in today's China.

Western women make their own living in various professions such as that of lawyer, physician, and store employee. But in the Confucian way, "In giving or receiving anything, a man or woman should not touch the other's hand," [10] "A man does not talk about affairs inside [the household] and a woman does not talk about affairs outside [the household]," and "They do not exchange cups except in sacrificial rites and funerals." [11] "A married woman is to obey" and the husband is the standard of the wife.[12] Thus the wife is naturally supported by the husband and needs no independent livelihood.

A married woman is at first a stranger to her parents-in-law. She has only affection but no obligation toward them. In the West parents and children usually do not live together, and daughters-in-law, particularly, have no obligation to serve parents-in-law. But in the way of Confucius, a woman is to "revere and respect them and never to disobey day or night," [13] "A woman obeys, that is, obeys her parents-in-law," [14] "A woman serves her parent-in-law as she serves her own parents," [15] she "never should disobey or be lazy in carrying out the orders of parents and parents-in-law." "If a man is very fond of his wife, but his parents

[6] *Book of Rites*, I:24.　　　　　　　　　[7] *Book of Rites*, X:12.
[8] *Book of Rites*, X:51.　　　　　　　　　[9] *Book of Rites*, XXVII:17.
[10] *Book of Rites*, XXVII:20.　　　　　　[11] *Book of Rites*, X:12.
[12] *Book of Rites*, IX:24.　　　　　　　　[13] *I-li*, ch. 2; Steele, Vol. I, p. 39.
[14] *Book of Rites*, XLI:6.　　　　　　　　[15] *Book of Rites*, X:3.

do not like her, she should be divorced." [16] (In ancient times there were many such cases, like that of Lu Yü [1125-1210].) "Unless told to retire to her own apartment, a woman does not do so, and if she has an errand to do, she must get permission from her parents-in-law." [17] This is the reason why the tragedy of cruelty to daughters-in-law has never ceased in Chinese society.

According to Western customs, fathers do not discipline grown-up sons but leave them to the law of the country and the control of society. But in the way of Confucius, "When one's parents are angry and not pleased and beat him until he bleeds, he does not complain but instead arouses in himself the feelings of reverence and filial piety." [18] This is the reason why in China there is the saying, "One has to die if his father wants him to, and the minister has to perish if his ruler wants him to". . . .

Confucius lived in a feudal age. The ethics he promoted is the ethics of the feudal age. The social mores he taught and even his own mode of living were teachings and modes of a feudal age. The political institutions he advocated were those of a feudal age. The objectives, ethics, social norms, mode of living, and political institutions did not go beyond the privilege and prestige of a few rulers and aristocrats and had nothing to do with the happiness of the great masses. How can this be shown? In the teachings of Confucius, the most important element in social ethics and social life is the rules of decorum and the most serious thing in government is punishment. In chapter one of the *Book of Rites,* it is said that "The rules of decorum do not go down to the common people and the penal statutes do not go up to great officers." [I:35] Is this not solid proof of the [true] spirit of the way of Confucius and the spirit of the feudal age?

THE LITERARY REVOLUTION

Paralleling the attack on Confucianism was the attack on the classical literary language—the language of Confucian tradition and of the old-style scholar-official. With the abandonment of the "eight-legged essay"

---

[16] *Book of Rites,* X:12.　　　　　　[17] *Book of Rites,* X:13.
[18] *Book of Rites,* X:12.

examinations for the civil service in 1905, the discarding too of the official language, so far removed from ordinary speech, might seem to have been inevitable. This was a time of rising nationalism, which in the West had been linked to the rise of vernacular literatures; an era of expanding education, which would be greatly facilitated by a written language simpler and easier to learn; a period of strong Westernization in thought and scholarship, which would require a more flexible instrument for the expression of new concepts. No doubt each of these factors contributed to the rapid spread of the literary revolution after its launching by Hu Shih, with the support of Ch'en Tu-hsiu, in 1917. And yet it is a sign of the strong hold which the classical language had on educated men, and of its great prestige as a mark of learning, that until Hu appeared on the scene with his novel ideas, even the manifestos of reformers and revolutionaries had kept to the classical style of writing as if there could be no other.

Hu Shih (1891—) had studied agriculture at Cornell on a Boxer Idemnity grant and philosophy at Columbia under John Dewey, of whom he became the leading Chinese disciple. Even before his return home he had begun advocating a new written language for China, along with a complete re-examination and re-evaluation of the classical tradition in thought and literature. Ch'en Tu-hsiu's position as head of the department of literature at Peking National University, and his new political organ, *The New Youth,* represented strong backing for Hu's revolutionary program—a program all the more commanding of attention because its aim was not merely destructive of traditional usage but, ambitiously enough, directed to the stimulation of a new literature and new ideas. Instead of dwelling solely upon the deficiencies of the past, Hu's writings were full of concrete and constructive suggestions for the future. There was hope here, as well as indignation.

Hu's program thus looked beyond the immediate literary revolution, stressing the vernacular as a means of communication, to what came to be known as the literary renaissance. There can be no doubt that this movement stimulated literary activity along new lines, especially in the adoption of forms and genres then popular in the West. Yet there is real doubt that this new literary output was able to fulfill the positive hopes of Hu. It excelled in social criticism, and so contributed further to the processes of social and political disintegration. Also—and this is particularly true of Hu's own work—it rendered great service in the rehabilitation of popular literature from earlier centuries, above all the great Chinese novels. But whether it produced in its own right a contemporary literature of great literary distinction and creative imagination remains a question, a question for historians and critics of the future with a better perspective on these times and on the political movements in which this new generation of writers became so easily caught up.

HU SHIH
A Preliminary Discussion of Literary Reform
[From *Wen-hsüeh kai-liang ch'u-i*, in *Hu Shih wen-ts'un*, Collection I, Ch. 1, pp. 5–16; original version in *Hsin ch'ing-nien*, Vol. II, No. 5 (January 1917), pp. 1–11]

Many people have been discussing literary reform. Who am I, unlearned and unlettered, to offer an opinion? Nevertheless, for some years I have studied the matter and thought it over many times, helped by my deliberations with friends; and the conclusions I have come to are perhaps not unworthy of discussion. Therefore I shall summarize my views under eight points and elaborate on them separately to invite the study and comments of those interested in literary reform.

I believe that literary reform at the present time must begin with these eight items: 1) Write with substance; 2) Do not imitate the ancients; 3) Emphasize grammar; 4) Reject melancholy; 5) Eliminate old clichés; 6) Do not use allusions; 7) Do not use couplets and parallelisms; and 8) Do not avoid popular expressions or popular forms of characters.

1. *Write with substance.* By "substance" I mean: (a) Feeling. . . . Feeling is the soul of literature. Literature without feeling is like a man without a soul. . . . (b) Thought. By thought I mean insight, knowledge, and ideals. Thought does not necessarily depend on literature for transmission but literature becomes more valuable if it contains thought, and thought is more valuable if it possesses literary value. This is the reason why the essays of Chuang Tzu, the poems of T'ao Ch'ien [365–427], Li Po [689–762], and Tu Fu [712–770], the *tz'u* of Hsin Chia-hsüan [1140–1207], and the novel of Shih Nai-an [that is, the *Shui-hu chuan* or *Water Margin*] are matchless for all times. . . . In recent years literary men have satisfied themselves with tones, rhythm, words,

and phrases, and have had neither lofty thoughts nor genuine feeling. This is the chief cause of the deterioration of literature. This is the bad effect of superficiality over substantiality, that is to say, writing without substance. To remedy this bad situation, we must resort to substance. And what is substance? Nothing but feeling and thought.

2. *Do not imitate the ancients.* Literature changes with time. Each period from Chou and Ch'in to Sung, Yüan, and Ming has it own literature. This is not my private opinion but the universal law of the advancement of civilization. Take prose, for example. There is the prose of the *Book of History,* the prose of the ancient philosophers, the prose of [the historians] Ssu-ma Ch'ien and Pan Ku, the prose of the [T'ang and Sung masters] Han Yü, Liu Tsung-yüan, Ou-yang Hsiu, and Su Hsün, the prose of the *Recorded Conversations* of the Neo-Confucianists, and the prose of Shih Nai-an and Ts'ao Hsüeh-ch'in [d. c.1765, author of *The Dream of the Red Chamber*]. This is the development of prose. . . . Each period has changed in accordance with its situation and circumstance, each with its own characteristic merits. From the point of view of historical evolution, we cannot say that the writings of the ancients are all superior to those of modern writers. The prose of Tso Ch'iu-ming [sixth century B.C., author of the *Tso chuan*] and Ssu-ma Ch'ien are wonderful, but compared to the *Tso chuan* and *Records of the Historian,* wherein is Shih Nai-an's *Shui-hu chuan* inferior? . . .

I have always held that colloquial stories alone in modern Chinese literature can proudly be compared with the first class literature of the world. Because they do not imitate the past but only describe the society of the day, they have become genuine literature. . . .

3. *Emphasize grammar.* Many writers of prose and poetry today neglect grammatical construction. Examples are too numerous to mention, especially in parallel prose and the four-line and eight-line verses.

4. *Reject melancholy.* This is not an easy task. Nowadays young writers often show passion. They choose such names as "Cold Ash," "No Birth," and "Dead Ash" as pen names, and in their prose and poetry, they think of declining years when they face the setting sun, and of destitution when they meet the autumn wind. . . . I am not unaware of the fact that our country is facing many troubles. But can salvation be achieved through tears? I hope all writers become Fichtes and Mazzinis and not like Chia I [201–169 B.C.], Wang Ts'an [177–217], Ch'ü Yüan

[343–277 B.C.], Hsieh Kao-yü [1249–1295], etc. [who moaned and complained]. . . .

5. *Eliminate old clichés.* By this I merely mean that writers should describe in their own words what they personally experience. So long as they achieve the goal of describing the things and expressing the mood without sacrificing realism, that is literary achievement. Those who employ old clichés are lazy people who refuse to coin their own terms of description.

6. *Do not use allusions.* I do not mean allusion in the broad sense. These are of five kinds: (a) Analogies employed by ancient writers, which have a universal meaning . . . ; (b) Idioms; (c) References to historical events . . . ; (d) Quoting from or referring to people in the past for comparison . . . ; and (e) Quotations. . . . Allusions such as these may or may not be used.

But I do not approve of the use of allusions in the narrow sense. By using allusions I mean that writers are incapable of creating their own expressions to portray the scene before them or the concepts in their minds, and instead muddle along by borrowing old stories or expressions which are partly or wholly inapplicable. . . .

7. *Do not use couplets and parallelisms.* Parallelism is a special characteristic of human language. This is why in ancient writings such as those of Lao Tzu and Confucius, there are occasionally couplets. The first chapter of the *Tao-te ching* consists of three couplets. *Analects* I:14, I:15 and III:17 are all couplets. But these are fairly natural expressions and have no indication of being forced or artificial, especially because there is no rigid requirement about the number of words, tones, or parts of speech. Writers in the age of literary decadence, however, who had nothing to say, emphasized superficiality, the extreme of which led to the development of the parallel prose, regulated *tz'u,* and the long regulated verse. It is not that there are no good products in these forms, but they are, in the final analysis, few. Why? Is it not because they restrict to the highest degree the free expression of man? (Not a single good piece can be mentioned among the long regulated verse.) To talk about literary reform today, we must "first establish the fundamental" [19] and not waste our useful energy in the nonessentials of subtlety and delicacy. This is why I advocate giving up couplets and rhymes. Even

[19] *Mencius.* VI A:15.

if they cannot be abolished, they should be regarded as merely literary stunts and nothing to be pursued seriously.

There are still people today who deprecate colloquial novels as trifling literature, without realizing that Shih Nai-an, Ts'ao Hsüeh-ch'in, and Wu Chien-jen [1867–1910] [20] all represent the main line of literature while parallel and regulated verse are really trifling matters. I know some will keep clear of me when they hear this.

8. *Do not avoid popular expressions or popular forms of characters.* When Buddhist scriptures were introduced into China, because classical expressions could not express their meanings, translators used clear and simple expressions. Their style already approached the colloquial. Later, many Buddhist lectures and dialogues were in the colloquial style, thus giving rise to the "conversation" style. When the Neo-Confucianists of the Sung dynasty used the colloquial in their *Recorded Conversations,* this style became the orthodox style of scholarly discussion. (This was followed by scholars of the Ming.) By that time, colloquial expressions had already penetrated rhymed prose, as can be seen in the colloquial poems of T'ang and Sung poets. From the third century to the end of the Yüan, North China had been under foreign races and popular literature developed. In prose there were such novels as the *Shui-hu chuan* and *Hsi yu chi (Journey to the West).* In drama the products were innumerable. From the modern point of view, the Yüan period should be considered as a high point of literary development; unquestionably it produced the greatest number of immortal works. At that time writing and colloquial speech were the closest to each other and the latter almost became the language of literature. Had the tendency not been checked, living literature would have emerged in China, and the great work of Dante and Luther [who inaugurated the substitution of a living language for dead Latin] would have taken place in China. Unfortunately, the tendency was checked in the Ming when the government selected officials on the basis of the rigid "eight-legged" prose style and at the same time literary men like the "seven scholars" including Li [Meng-yang, 1472–1529] considered "returning to the past" as highbrow. Thus the once-in-a-millenium chance of uniting writing and speech was killed prematurely, midway in the process. But from the modern viewpoint

[20] Author of the *Erh-shih nien mu-tu chih kuai hsien-chuang (Strange Phenomena Seen in Two Decades).*

of historical evolution, we can definitely say that the colloquial literature is the main line of Chinese literature and that it should be the medium employed in the literature of the future. (This is my own opinion; not many will agree with me today.) For this reason, I hold that we should use popular expressions and words in prose and poetry. Rather than using dead expressions of 3,000 years ago, it is better to employ living expressions of the twentieth century, and rather than using the language of the Ch'in, Han, and the Six Dynasties, which cannot reach many people and cannot be universally understood, it is better to use the language of the *Shui-hu* and *Hsi yu chi* which is understood in every household.

CH'EN TU-HSIU

On Literary Revolution

[From "Wen-hsüeh ko-ming lun," *Hsin ch'ing-nien,* Vol. II, No. 6 (February 1917), pp. 1-4]

The movement of literary revolution has been in the making for some time. My friend Hu Shih is the one who started the revolution of which he is the vanguard. I do not mind being an enemy of all old-fashioned scholars in the country and raising to great heights the banner of "the Army of Literary Revolution" to support my friend. On this banner shall be written these three fundamental principles of our revolutionary army: 1) Destroy the aristocratic literature which is nothing but literary chiseling and flattery, and construct a simple, expressive literature of the people; 2) Destroy the outmoded, showy, classical literature and construct a fresh and sincere literature of realism; 3) Destroy the obscure and abstruse "forest" literature [21] and construct a clear and popular literature of society. . . .

At this time of literary reform, aristocratic literature, classical literature, and forest literature should all be rejected. What are the reasons for attacking these three kinds of literature? The answer is that aristocratic literature employs embellishments and depends on previous writers and therefore has lost the qualities of independence and self-respect; that classical literature exaggerates and piles word after word and has lost the fundamental objective of expressing emotions and realistic descriptions; and that forest literature is difficult and obscure and is claimed to be

[21] An expression of Ch'en's for esoteric literature.

lofty writing but is actually of no benefit to the masses. The form of such literatures is continuous repetition of previous models. It has flesh but no bones, body but no spirit. It is an ornament and is of no actual use. With respect to their contents, their horizon does not go beyond kings and aristocrats, spiritual beings and ghosts, and personal fortunes and misfortunes. The universe, life, and society are all beyond their conception. These defects are common to all three forms of literature. These types of literature are both causes and effects of our national character of flattery, boasting, insincerity, and flagrant disregard of truth and facts. Now that we want political reform, we must regenerate the literature of those who are entrenched in political life. If we do not open our eyes and see the literary tendencies of the world society and the spirit of the time but instead bury our heads in old books day and night and confine our attention to kings and aristocrats, spiritual beings and ghosts and immortals, and personal fortunes and misfortunes, and in so doing hope to reform literature and politics, it is like binding our four limbs to fight Meng Pen [an ancient strong man].

HU SHIH

Constructive Literary Revolution: A Literature of National Speech—A National Speech of Literary Quality

[From "Chien-she ti wen-hsüeh ko-ming lun," *Hsin ch'ing-nien,* Vol. IV, No. 4 (April 1918), pp. 290–306; *Hu Shih wen-ts'un.* Collection I, pp. 56–73]

Since I returned to China last year, in my speeches on literary revolution in various places, I have changed my "eight points" [in the previous selection] into something positive and shall summarize them under four items:

1. Speak only when you have something to say. (A different version of the first of the eight points.)

2. Speak what you want to say and say it in the way you want to say it. (Different version of points 2–6.)

3. Speak what is your own and not that of someone else. (Different version of point 7.)

4. Speak in the language of the time in which you live. (Different version of point 8.)

The literary revolution we are promoting aims merely at the creation of a Chinese literature of national speech. Only when there is such a literature can there be a national speech of literary quality. And only when there is a national speech of literary quality can our national speech be considered a real national speech. A national speech without literary quality will be devoid of life and value and can be neither established nor developed. This is the main point of this essay.

I have carefully gone into the reasons why in the past 2,000 years China has had no truly valuable and living classical-style literature. My own answer is that what writers in this period have written is dead stuff, written in a dead language. A dead language can never produce a living literature. . . .

Why is it that a dead language cannot produce a living literature? It is because of the nature of literature. The function of language and literature lies in expressing ideas and showing feelings. When these are well done, we have literature. Those who use a dead classical style will translate their own ideas into allusions of several thousand years ago and convert their own feelings into literary expressions of centuries past. . . . If China wants to have a living literature, we must use the plain speech that is the natural speech, and we must devote ourselves to a literature of national speech. . . .

Someone says: "If we want to use the national speech in literature, we must first have a national speech. At present we do not have a standard national speech. How can we have a literature of national speech?" I will say, this sounds plausible but is really not true. A national language is not to be created by a few linguistic experts or a few texts and dictionaries of national speech. To create a national speech, we must first create a literature of national speech. Once we have a literature of national speech, we shall automatically have a national speech. This sounds absurd at first but my readers will understand if they think carefully. Who in the world will be willing to learn a national speech from texts and dictionaries? While these are important, they are definitely not the effective means of creating a national speech. The truly effective and powerful text of national speech is the literature of national speech—novels, prose, poems, and plays written in the national speech. The time when these works prevail is the day when the Chinese national speech will have been established. Let us ask why we are now able simply to pick up the brush and write essays in the plain speech style and use several hundred colloquial terms. Did we learn this from some textbook of plain speech? Was it not that we learned from such novels as the *Shui-hu chuan, Hsi yu chi, Hung-lou meng,* and *Ju-lin wai-shi (Unofficial History of Officialdom)*? This type of plain speech literature is several hundred times as powerful as textbooks and dictionaries. . . . If we want to establish anew a standard national speech, we must first of all produce numerous works like these novels in the national speech style. . . .

A literature of national speech and a national speech of literary quality are our basic programs. Let us now discuss what should be done to carry them out.

I believe that the procedure in creating a new literature consists of three steps: 1) acquiring tools, 2) developing methods, and 3) creating. The first two are preparatory. The third is the real step to create a new literature.

1. *The tools.* Our tool is plain speech. Those of us who wish to create a literature of national speech should prepare this indispensable tool right away. There are two ways to do so:

(a) Read extensively literary works written in the plain speech that can serve as models, such as the works mentioned above, the *Recorded Conversations* of the Sung Neo-Confucianists and their letters written in the plain speech, the plays of the Yüan period, and the stories and monologues of the Ming and Ch'ing times. T'ang and Sung poems and *tz'u* written in the plain speech should also be selected to read.

(b) In all forms of literature, write in the plain speech style. . . . Not only those of us who promote the literature of plain speech should do this. I also advise those opposing this literature to do the same. Why? Because if they are not capable of writing in the plain speech style, it means that they are not qualified to oppose this type of literature. . . . I therefore advise them to do a little more writing in this style, write a few more songs and poems in the plain speech, and try to see whether the plain speech has any literary value. If, after trying for several years, they still feel that the plain speech style is not so good as the classical style, it will not be too late for them to attack us. . . .

2. *Methods.* I believe that the greatest defect of the literary men who have recently emerged in our country is the lack of a good literary method. . . . The "new novel" of today is completely devoid of a literary method.

Writers do not have the technique of plot, construction, or description of people and things. They merely write many long and repulsive pieces which are qualified only to fill the space of the second section of a newspaper, but not qualified to have a place in a new literature. Comparatively speaking, the novel is the most developed genre of literature in China in recent years. If even it is in such a poor state, then nothing can be said about other genres like poetry and drama. . . .

Generally speaking, literary methods are of three kinds:

(a) The method of collecting material. . . . I believe that for future literary men the method of collecting material should be about as follows:

(*i*) Enlarge the area from which material is to be collected. The three sources of material, namely, officialdom, houses of prostitution, and dirty society [from which present novelists draw their material] are definitely not enough. At present, the poor man's society, male and female factory workers, ricksha pullers, farmers in the interior districts, small shop owners and peddlers everywhere, and all conditions of suffering have no place in literature [as they should]. Moreover, now that new and old civilizations have come into contact, problems like family catastrophes, tragedies in marriage, the position of women, the unfitness of present education, etc., can all supply literature with material.

(*ii*) Stress actual observation and personal experience. . . .

(*iii*) Use broad and keen imagination to supplement observation and experience. . . .

(b) The method of construction. . . . This may be separated into two steps, namely, tailoring and laying the plot. . . . First, one must find out whether the material should be used for a short or long poem, or for a long novel or a short story, or for a play. . . . While tailoring is to determine what to do, laying the plot is to determine how to do it. . . .

(c) The method of description. . . .

3. *Creation*. The two items, tools and methods, discussed above are only preparations for the creation of a new literature. Only when we have mastered the tools and know the methods can we create a new Chinese literature. As to what constitutes the creation of a new literature, I had better not say a word. In my opinion we in China today have not reached the point where we can take concrete steps to create a new literature, and there is no need of talking theoretically about the tech-

niques of creation. Let us first devote our efforts to the first two steps of preparatory work.

A NEW PHILOSOPHY OF LIFE

The energetic assault on traditional thought and literature focused attention on what should replace Confucianism as a way of looking at the world and at life. Here again, during the years 1918–1919, Ch'en Tu-hsiu and Hu Shih manifested their role as leaders of the whole New Culture Movement. At a time which saw the introduction and lively discussion of the philosophies of Kant, Haeckel, Marx, Nietzsche, Bergson, James, Dewey, Russell, and others, Ch'en and Hu bespoke the dominant belief in science and social progress. In these days Ch'en, reacting strongly against what he conceived to be the social conformism and authoritarianism of Confucian thought, emphasized individualism as the basis of his philosophy. Yet his belief in science and materialism also inclined him strongly to the study of Marxism—an inclination checked to some degree by his interest in the ideas of John Dewey, who lectured widely in China in 1919 and 1920. Hu Shih, for his part, identified himself unequivocally with pragmatism. Nevertheless, in the movement as a whole philosophical allegiances were less clear-cut. It was a period of fermentation and transition, producing also strong counter-currents to trends from the West (as shown in succeeding sections) We can say, however, that the prevailing trend was toward popular acceptance of such slogans as individualism, freedom, progress, democracy, and science.

CH'EN TU-HSIU

The True Meaning of Life
[From "Jen-sheng chen i," in *Hsin ch'ing-nien*, Vol. IV, No. 2 (February 1918), pp. 90–93]

What is the ultimate purpose in life? What should it be, after all? . . . From ancient times not a few people have offered explanations. . . . In my opinion, what the Buddha said is vague. Although the individual's birth and death are illusory, can we say that humanity as a whole is not really existent? . . . The teachings of Christianity, especially, are fabrications out of nothing and cannot be proved. If God can create the human race, who created Him? Since God's existence or nonexistence cannot be proved, the Christian philosophy of life cannot be completely believed in. The rectification of the heart, cultivation of the person, family harmony, national order, and world peace that Confucius and Mencius talked about are but some activities and enterprises in life and cannot cover the total meaning of life. If we are totally to sacrifice ourselves to benefit others, then we exist for others and not for ourselves. This is definitely not the fundamental reason for man's existence. The idea [of altruism] of Mo Tzu is also not free from one-sidedness. The doctrines of Yang Chu [fourth century B.C.?] and Nietzsche fully reveal the true nature of life, and yet if we follow them to their extremes, how can this complex, organized, and civilized society continue? . . .

Because we Chinese have accepted the teachings [of contentment and laissez faire] of Lao Tzu and Chuang Tzu, we have to that extent been backward. Scientists say that there is no soul after a man's death. . . . It is difficult to refute these words. But although we as individuals will inevitably die, it is not easy for the whole race or humanity to die off. The civilization created by the race or humanity will remain. It is recorded in history and will be transmitted to later generations. Is this not the consciousness or memory of our continuation after death?

From the above, the meaning of life as seen by the modern man can be readily understood. Let me state it briefly as follows:

1. With reference to human existence, the individual's birth and death are transitory but society really exists.

2. The civilization and happiness of society are created by individuals and should be enjoyed by individuals.

3. Society is an organization of individuals—there can be no society without individuals. . . . The will and the happiness of the individual should be respected.

4. Society is the collective life of individuals. If society is dissolved, there will be no memory or consciousness of the continuation of the individual after he dies. Therefore social organization and order should be respected.

5. To carry out one's will and to satisfy his desires (everything from food and sex to moral reputation is "desire") are the basic reasons for

the individual's existence. These goals never change. (Here we can say that Heaven does not change and the Way does not change either.)

6. All religions, laws, moral and political systems are but necessary means to preserve social order. They are not the individual's original purpose of enjoyment in life and can be changed in accordance with the circumstances of the time.

7. Man's happiness in life is the result of man's own effort and is neither the gift of God nor a spontaneous natural product. If it were the gift of God, how is it that He was so generous with people today and so stingy with people in the past? If it is a spontaneous, natural product, why is it that the happiness of the various peoples in the world is not uniform?

8. The individual in society is comparable to the cell in the body. Its birth and death are transitory. New ones replace the old. This is as it should be and need not be feared at all.

9. To enjoy happiness, do not fear suffering. Personal suffering at the moment sometimes contributes to personal happiness in the future. For example, the blood shed in righteous wars often wipes out the bad spots of a nation or mankind. Severe epidemics often hasten the development of science.

In a word, what is the ultimate purpose in life? What should it be, after all? I dare say:

During his lifetime, an individual should devote his efforts to create happiness and to enjoy it, and also to keep it in store in society so that individuals of the future may also enjoy it, one generation doing the same for the next and so on unto infinity.

HU SHIH

Pragmatism

[From *Shih-yen chu-i*, in *Hu Shih wen-ts'un*. Collection I, ch. 2, pp. 291–320; originally published in *Hsin ch'ing-nien*, Vol. VI, No. 4 (April 1919), pp. 342–58]

There are two fundamental changes in basic scientific concepts which have had the most important bearings on pragmatism. The first is the change of the scientific attitude toward scientific laws. Hitherto worshipers of science generally had a superstition that scientific laws were unalterable universal principles. They thought that there was an eternal, unchanging "natural law" immanent in all things in the universe and that when this law was discovered, it became scientific law. However, this attitude toward the universal principle has gradually changed in the last several decades. Scientists have come to feel that such a superstitious attitude toward a universal principle could hinder scientific progress. Furthermore, in studying the history of science they have learned that many discoveries in science are the results of hypotheses. Consequently, they have gradually realized that the scientific laws of today are no more than the hypotheses which are the most applicable, most convenient, and most generally accepted as explanations of natural phenomena. . . . Such changes of attitude involve three ideas: 1) Scientific laws are formulated by men; 2) They are hypotheses—whether they can be determined to be applicable or not entirely depends on whether they can satisfactorily explain facts; 3) They are not the eternal, unchanging natural law. There may be such a natural law in the universe, but we cannot say that our hypothecated principles are this law. They are no more than a shorthand to record the natural changes known to us. [pp. 291–94]

Besides this, there was in the nineteenth century another important change which also had an extremely important bearing on pragmatism. This is Darwin's theory of evolution. . . . When it came to Darwin, he boldly declared that the species were not immutable but all had their origins and developed into the present species only after many changes. From the present onward, there can still be changes in species, such as the grafting of trees and crossing of fowls, whereby special species can be obtained. Not only do the species change, but truth also changes. The change of species is the result of adaptation to environment and truth is but an instrument with which to deal with environment. As the environment changes, so does truth accordingly. The concept of loyalty to the emperor during the Hsüan-t'ung era [1909–1911] was no longer the concept of loyalty to the emperor during the Yung-cheng and Ch'ien-lung eras [1723–1795]. Since the founding of the republic, such concepts have been completely cast aside and are useless. Only when we realize that there is no eternal, unchanging truth or absolute truth can we arouse in ourselves a sense of intellectual responsibility. The knowledge that mankind needs is not the way or principle which has an absolute existence but the particular truths for here and now and for particular individuals. Absolute truth is imaginary, abstract, vague, without evidence, and cannot be demonstrated. [pp. 294–95]

THE PRAGMATISM OF JAMES

What we call truth is actually no more than an instrument, comparable to this piece of paper in my hand, this chalk, this blackboard, or this teapot. They are all our instruments. Because this concept produced results, people in the past therefore called it truth and because its utility still remains, we therefore still call it truth. If by any chance some event takes place for which the old concept is not applicable, it will no longer be truth. We will search for a new truth to take its place. . . .

Truth is recognized to be truth because it has helped us ferry the river or make a match. If the ferry is broken down, build another one. If the sailboat is too slow, replace it with a steam launch. If this marriage broker won't do, give him a good punch, chase him out, and ask a dependable friend to make a match.

This is the theory of truth in pragmatism. [pp. 309–10]

THE FUNDAMENTAL CONCEPTS OF DEWEY'S PHILOSOPHY

Dewey is a great revolutionist in the history of philosophy. . . . He said that the basic error of modern philosophy is that modern philosophers do not understand what experience really is. All quarrels between rationalists and empiricists and between idealists and realists are due to their ignorance of what experience is. [p. 316]

Dewey was greatly influenced by the modern theory of biological evolution. Consequently, his philosophy is completely colored by bio-evolutionism. He said that "experiencing means living; and that living goes on in and because of an environing medium, not in a vacuum. . . . The human being has upon his hands the problem of responding to what is going on around him so that these changes will take one turn rather than another, namely, that required by his own further functioning. . . . He is obliged to struggle—that is to say, to employ the direct support given by the environment in order indirectly to effect changes that would not otherwise occur. In this sense, life goes on by means of controlling the environment. Its activities must change the changes going on around it; they must neutralize hostile occurrences; they must transform neutral events into cooperative factors or into an efflorescence of new features." [22]

This is what Dewey explained as experience. [p. 318]

The foregoing are the basic concepts of Dewey's philosophy. Summarized, they are: 1) Experience is life and life is dealing with environment; 2) In the act of dealing with environment, the function of thought is the most important. All conscious actions involve the function of thought. Thought is an instrument to deal with environment; 3) True philosophy must throw overboard the previous toying with "philosophers' problems" and turn itself into a method for solving human problems.

What is the philosophical method for solving human problems? It goes without saying that it must enable people to have creative intelligence, must enable them to envisage a bright future on the basis of present needs, and must be able to create new methods and tools to realize that future. [p. 320]

THE DEBATE ON SCIENCE AND THE PHILOSOPHY OF LIFE

The prevailing glorification of science prompted a reaction in some quarters, which pointed to the inadequacy of science when conceived as a philosophy for dealing with some of the fundamental questions of human life. The debate was touched off by a lecture at Tsing-hua College, near Peking, by Dr. Chang Chün-mai (Carsun Chang, 1886—) who insisted upon the need for a metaphysics as the basis for a genuine philosophy of life. In the controversy which followed (also known as the controversy between metaphysics and science), Chang drew some support from his teacher Liang Ch'i-ch'ao, now much disillusioned with Western materialism and scientism, and from the professional philosopher and translator of Bergson, Chang Tung-sun (1886—). A far larger number of writers, however, immediately rose to attack metaphysics and defend science. Chang's chief opponent was Ting Wen-chiang (1888–1936), a geologist by profession, who stigmatized metaphysics as mere superstition and insisted that there were no genuine problems of philosophy or psychology which lay outside the domain of science or to which science, with the progress of civilization, would not eventually find

[22] John Dewey, *Creative Intelligence* (New York, Henry Holt, 1917), pp. 8–9.

an answer. Many others with a basically materialistic view, from Ch'en Tu-hsiu (now a Marxian and Communist) to Hu Shih and Wu Chih-hui (1865–1953), a writer closely identified with the Kuomintang, joined in the battle. Altogether the writings which dealt with this issue, later compiled in book form, amounted to over 250,000 words. In the end, as far as majority opinion was concerned, the "anti-metaphysics, pro-science" group carried the day. The controversy thus served only to underscore the overwhelming acceptance of pragmatism and materialism among the younger generation of writers and students.

CHANG CHÜN-MAI
The Philosophy of Life

Chang Chün-mai (known in the West as Carsun Chang) was a young professor of philosophy when he delivered this controversial lecture on February 14, 1923. Like so many others of his generation, he had received his higher education in Japan (Waseda University) and Europe. A follower of Liang Ch'i-ch'ao and a believer in the "spiritual" civilization of China, he combined Bergsonian intuitionism with the Neo-Confucian School of the Mind (especially the teachings of Wang Yang-ming). In later years Chang was also politically active as the leader of a "third-force" advocating nationalism and socialism, which had some influence among intellectuals but little mass following.

[From Jen-sheng kuan in Chang Chün-mai et al., K'o-hsüeh yü jen-sheng kuan, I, 4–9]

The central focus of a philosophy of life is the self. What is relative to it is the nonself. . . . But all problems of the nonself are related to human life. Now human life is a living thing and cannot so easily be governed by formulae as can dead matter. The unique character of a philosophy of life becomes especially clear when we compare it with science.

First of all, science is objective whereas a philosophy of life is subjective. The highest standard of science consists in its objective efficacy. Mr. A says so, Mr. B says so, and C, D, E, F all say so. In other words, a general law is applicable to the entire world. . . . A philosophy of life is different. Confucius' doctrine of firm action and Lao Tzu's doctrine of nonaction represent different views. . . . Darwin's theory of struggle and survival and Kropotkin's theory of mutual aid represent different views. All these have their pros and cons and no experiment can be conducted to determine who is right and who is wrong. Why? Because they are philosophies of life; because they are subjective.

Secondly, science is controlled by the logical method whereas a philosophy of life arises from intuition. . . . Science is restricted by method and by system. On the other hand, philosophies of life—whether the pessimism of Schopenhauer and Hartmann or the optimism of Lambert, Nietzsche, and Hegel; whether Confucius' doctrine of personal perfection and family harmony or Buddha's doctrine of renunciation; and whether the Confucian doctrine of love with distinctions or the teaching of universal love of Mo Tzu and Jesus—are not restricted by any logical formula. They are not governed by definitions or methods. They are views held according to one's conscience for the sake of setting a norm for the world and for posterity. This is the reason why they are intuitive.

Thirdly, science proceeds from an analytical method whereas a philosophy of life proceeds from synthesis. The key to science is analysis. . . . A philosophy of life, on the other hand, is synthetic. It includes everything. If subjected to analysis, it will lose its true meaning. For example, the Buddha's philosophy of life is to save all living beings. If one seeks his motive and says that it is due to the Indian love of meditation or to India's climate, to some extent such analysis is reasonable. But it would be a mistake to conclude that Buddhism and all it contains can be explained in terms only of the motives just analyzed. Why? Motives and a philosophy of life are different things. A philosophy of life is a whole and cannot be discovered in what has been divided or mutilated. . . .

Fourthly, science follows the law of cause and effect whereas a philosophy of life is based on free will. The first general law governing material phenomena is that where there is cause, there is effect. . . . Even the relation between body and mind . . . is also the result of cause and effect. But purely psychological phenomena are different, and a philosophy of life is much more so. Why is it that Confucius did not even sit long enough to warm his mat [before hurrying off to serve society] or that Mo Tzu's stove did not have a chance to burn black [before he did likewise]? Why was Jesus crucified, and why did Shakyamuni devote his life to asceticism? All these issued from the free action of conscience and were not determined by something else. Even in an ordinary person, such things as repentance, self-reform, and a sense of responsibility cannot be explained by the law of cause and effect. The master agent is none other than the person himself. This is all there is to it, whether in the case of great men like Confucius, Mo Tzu, the Buddha, and Jesus, or in the case of an ordinary man.

Fifthly, science arises from the phenomenon of uniformity among objects whereas a philosophy of life arises from the unity of personality. The greatest principle in science is the uniformity of the course of nature. Plants, animals, and even inorganic matter can all be classified. Because of the possibility of classification, there is a principle running through all changes and phenomena of a particular class of objects, and therefore a scientific formula for it can be discovered. But in human society some people are intelligent while others are stupid, some are good and some are bad, and some are healthy while others are not. . . . The distinction of natural phenomena is their similarity, while that of mankind is its variety. Because of this variety there have been the "first to be enlightened" and the "hero" as they are called in traditional Chinese terminology and the "creator" and "genius" as they are called in Western terminology. All these are merely intended to show the unique character of human personality.

From the above we can see that the distinguishing points of a philosophy of life are subjectivity, intuitiveness, synthesizing power, free will, and personal unity. Because of these five qualities, the solution of problems pertaining to a philosophy of life cannot be achieved by science, however advanced it may be, but can only be achieved by man himself. . . .

TING WEN-CHIANG
Metaphysics and Science

Ting Wen-chiang (V. K. Ting) was a professor of geology at the University of Peking when he responded to Chang Chün-mai with this article published in April, 1923. Trained at Cambridge and Glasgow universities, he was widely respected for his writings in the fields of geology, mining, geography, etc., but became known also as a leading political pamphleteer. In 1919, a few years before this controversy arose, he had accompanied Liang Ch'i-ch'ao, Carsun Chang, and others on an inspection trip to Europe, from which the latter returned much disillusioned with the materialism of the West. Though Ting's basic outlook was not altered by this experience, from it developed his interest in a wider range of questions—political and philosophical—than his scientific studies had embraced earlier.

[From *Hsüan-hsüeh yü k'o-hsüeh,* in Chang Chün-mai et al., *K'o-hsüeh yü jen-sheng kuan,* I, 1–19]

Metaphysics is a bewildered specter which has been haunting Europe for twenty centuries. Of late it has gradually lost its treacherous occupation and all of a sudden come to China, its body swinging, with all its banners and slogans, to lure and fool the Chinese people. If you don't believe me, look at Chang Chün-mai's "Philosophy of Life." Chang is my friend, but metaphysics is an enemy of science. . . .

Can a philosophy of life and science be separated? . . . Chang's explanation is that philosophies of life are "most diversified" and therefore science is not applicable to them. But it is one thing to say that at present philosophies of life are not unified and quite another thing to say that they can never be unified. Unless you can advance a reason to prove why they can never be unified, we are obliged to find the unity. Furthermore, granted that at present "there are no standards of right and wrong, truth or falsity," [as Chang said], how can we tell that right and wrong and truth and falsity cannot be discovered? Unless we discover them, how are we going to have standards? To find right and wrong and truth and falsity, what other method is there aside from the scientific? . . .

Among those who study biology, who does not know that the problem of the good or evil nature of man and Darwin's theories of struggle and survival are all scientific problems and are problems already solved? But Chang claims that these are subjective and are philosophies of life and cannot be subjected to experiment to show which is right and which is wrong. By merely looking at his inability to separate a philosophy of life from science, we know that they are basically inseparable. [p. 6]

Chang says that a philosophy of life is not controlled by the logical method. Science replies: Whatever cannot be studied and criticized by logic is not true knowledge. He claims that "purely psychological phenomena" lie outside the law of cause and effect. Science replies: Psychological phenomena are at bottom materials of science. If the phenomena you are talking about are real, they cannot go beyond the sphere of science. He has repeatedly emphasized individuality and intuition, but he has placed these outside the logical method and definition. It is not that science attaches no importance to individuality and intuition. But the individuality and intuition recognized by science are those that "emerge from living experience and are based on evidences of experience," [as Hu Shih has said]. Chang has said that a philosophy of life is a synthesis—"It is a whole and cannot be discovered in what has been divided and mutilated." Science replies: We do not admit that there is such a confused, undifferentiated thing. Furthermore, he himself has distinguished the self and the nonself and listed nine items under the latter. Thus he has already analyzed it. He says that "the solution of problems pertaining to a philosophy of life cannot be achieved by science." Science replies: Anything with a psychological content and all true concepts and inferences are materials for science. [pp. 14-15]

Whether we like it or not, truth is truth and falsity is falsity. As truth is revealed, metaphysics becomes helpless. Consequently, the universe that used to belong to metaphysics has been taken over by science. . . . Biology has become a science. . . . Psychology has also declared [its] independence. Thereupon metaphysics has retreated from First Philosophy to ontology but it is still without regret and brags before science, saying: "You cannot study intuition; you cannot study reality outside of sensation. You are corporeal, I am metaphysical. You are dead; I am living." Science does not care to quarrel with it, realizing that the scientific method is all-mighty in the realm of knowledge. There is no fear that metaphysics will not finally surrender. [p. 16]

Metaphysicians only talk about their ontology. We do not want to waste our valuable time attacking them. But young people at large are fooled by them and consider all problems relating to religion, society, government, and ethics to be really beyond the control of the logical method. They think there is really no right or wrong, no truth or falsity. They believe that these problems must be solved by what they call a philosophy of life which they say is subjective, synthesizing, and consisting of free will.

If so, what kind of society will ours be? If so, there will be no need to read or learn, and experience will be useless. We will need only to "hold views according to our conscience," for philosophies of life "all issue from the free action of conscience and are not dictated by something else." In that case, aren't study, learning, knowledge, and experience all a waste of time? Furthermore, there will be no room for discussing any problem, for discussion requires logical formulae, definitions,

and methods, and all these are unacceptable to Chang Chün-mai. . . .
Moreover, everyone has his own conscience. What need is there for anyone to "enlighten" or "set an example" for us? If everyone can "hold
his view" according to his irrational philosophy of life, why should he
regard the philosophies of life of Confucius, the Buddha, Mo Tzu, or
Jesus as superior to his own? And there is no standard of right and
wrong or truth and falsity. Thus a person's philosophy of life may be
self-contradictory, and he may be preaching the doctrine of equality of
the sexes and practicing polygamy at the same time. All he needs to say
is that it is "the free action of his conscience," and he does not have to
bother whether it is logical or not. Whenever it is the free action of conscience, naturally other people must not interfere. Could we live in such
a society for a single day? [pp. 18–19]

WU CHIH-HUI

A New Concept of the Universe and Life
Based on a New Belief

These excerpts are from a long essay by Wu Chih-hui (1865–1953), which
Hu Shih hailed as "the most significant event" in the controversy over science
and metaphysics. "With one stroke of the pen he ruled out God, banished
the soul, and punctured the metaphysical idea that man is the most spiritual of
all things." Wu, an iconoclast who had a reputation as something of a wit
and satirist, is remembered for his declaration, which became a virtual battle-
cry among the anti-Confucianists: "All thread-bound [old-style] books should
be dumped in the lavatory."
    After taking the first steps up the old civil service ladder under the Manchus,
Wu had become involved in the reform movement, and then had studied for
many years in Japan, England and France, where he espoused anarchism.
Acquaintance with Sun Yat-sen led him eventually into the revolutionary
movement. He became a confidant of Sun and Chiang Kai-shek, and in his
later years a sort of elder statesman among the Nationalists.
    [From *I-ko hsin hsin-yang ti yü-chou kuan chi jen-sheng kuan,* in
    Chang Chün-mai *et al., K'o-hsüeh yü jen-sheng kuan,* II, 24–137]

Chang Chün-mai has mobilized his soldiers of science to protect his
specter of metaphysics and engage in warfare with Ting Wen-chiang.
Liang Ch'i-ch'ao has formulated for them "laws of the war of words"
in preparation for stepped up mobilization on both sides and for a pro-

longed struggle. . . . To some extent I feel that even if the struggle lasted for a hundred years, there would be no conclusion. [pp. 24–25]

What philosophy of life have you, oldster? Well, friends, let me tell you. . . .

We need only say that "the universe is a greater life." Its substance involves energy at the same time. To use another term, it may also be called power. From this power the will is produced. . . . When the will comes into contact with the external world, sensations ensue, and when these sensations are welcomed or resisted, feelings arise. To make sure that the feelings are correct, thought arises to constitute the intellect. When the intellect examines again and again a certain feeling to see to it that it is natural and proper or to correct the intellect's own ignorance, this is intuition. [pp. 28–30]

What is the need of any spiritual element or the so-called soul, which never meets any real need anyway? [p. 32]

I strongly believe 1) that the spirit cannot be separated from matter. . . . 2) that the universe is a temporary thing. . . . 3) that people today are superior to people in the past and that people in the future will be superior to people today. . . . 4) that they are so in both good and evil. . . . 5) that the more advanced material civilization becomes, the more plentiful will material goods be, the human race will tend more and more to unity, and complicated problems will be more and more easily solved. . . . 6) that morality is the crystallization of civilization and that there has never been a low morality when civilization reached a higher state. . . . and 7) that all things in the universe can be explained by science. [pp. 112–37]

HU SHIH

Science and Philosophy of Life

[From *Hu Shih wen-ts'un*, Collection II, Ch. 1, pp. 121–39]

The Chinese people's philosophy of life has not yet been brought face to face with science. At this moment we painfully feel that science has not been sufficiently promoted, that scientific education has not been developed, and that the power of science has not been able to wipe out the black smoke that covers the whole country. To our amazement there are still prominent scholars [like Liang Ch'i-ch'ao] who shout, "European science is bankrupt," blame the cultural bankruptcy of Europe on science, deprecate it, score the sins of the scientists' philosophy of life, and do not want science to exert any influence on a philosophy of life. Seeing this, how can those who believe in science not worry? How can they help crying out loud to defend science? This is the motive which has given rise to this big battle of "science versus philosophy of life." We must understand this motive before we can see the position the controversy occupies in the history of Chinese thought. . . .

Chang Chün-mai's chief point is that "the solution of problems pertaining to a philosophy of life cannot be achieved by science." In reply to him, we should make clear what kind of philosophy of life has been produced when science was applied to problems pertaining to a philosophy of life. In other words, we should first describe what a scientific philosophy of life is and then discuss whether such a philosophy of life can be established, whether it can solve the problems pertaining to a philosophy of life, and whether it is a plague on Europe and poison to the human race, as Liang Ch'i-ch'ao has said it is. I cannot help feeling that in this discussion consisting of a quarter of a million words, those who fight for science, excepting Mr. Wu Chih-hui, share a common error, namely, that of not stating in concrete terms what a scientific philosophy of life is, but merely defending in an abstract way the assertion that science *can* solve the problems of a philosophy of life. . . . They have not been willing publicly to admit that the concrete, purely materialistic, and purely mechanistic philosophy of life is the scientific philosophy of life. We say they have not been willing; we do not say they have not dared. We merely say that with regard to the scientific philosophy of life, the defenders of science do not believe in it as clearly and firmly as does Mr. Wu Chih-hui and therefore they cannot publicly defend their view. . . .

In a word, our future war plan should be to publicize our new belief, to publicize what we believe to be the new philosophy of life. The basic ideas of this new philosophy of life have been declared by Mr. Wu. We shall now summarize these general ideas, elaborate and supplement them to some extent, and present here an outline of this new philosophy of life:

1. On the basis of our knowledge of astronomy and physics, we should recognize that the world of space is infinitely large.

2. On the basis of our geological and paleontological knowledge, we should recognize that the universe extends over infinite time.

3. On the basis of all our verifiable scientific knowledge, we should recognize that the universe and everything in it follow natural laws of movement and change—"natural" in the Chinese sense of "being so of themselves"—and that there is no need for the concept of a supernatural Ruler or Creator.

4. On the basis of the biological sciences, we should recognize the terrific wastefulness and brutality in the struggle for existence in the biological world, and consequently the untenability of the hypothesis of a benevolent Ruler who "possesses the character of loving life."

5. On the basis of the biological, physiological, and psychological sciences, we should recognize that man is only one species in the animal kingdom and differs from the other species only in degree but not in kind.

6. On the basis of the knowledge derived from anthropology, sociology, and the biological sciences, we should understand the history and causes of the evolution of living organisms and of human society.

7. On the basis of the biological and psychological sciences, we should recognize that all psychological phenomena are explainable through the law of causality.

8. On the basis of biological and historical knowledge, we should recognize that morality and religion are subject to change, and that the causes of such change can be scientifically discovered.

9. On the basis of our newer knowledge of physics and chemistry, we should recognize that matter is not dead or static but living and dynamic.

10. On the basis of biological and sociological knowledge, we should recognize that the individual—the "small self"—is subject to death and extinction, but mankind—the "Large Self"—does not die and is immortal, and should recognize that to live for the sake of the species and posterity is religion of the highest kind; and that those religions which seek a future life either in Heaven or the Pure Land, are selfish religions.

This new philosophy of life is a hypothesis founded on the commonly accepted scientific knowledge of the last two or three hundred years. We may confer on it the honorable title of "scientific philosophy of life." But to avoid unnecessary controversy, I propose to call it merely "the naturalistic philosophy of life."

"THE DOUBTING OF ANTIQUITY"

Another significant trend of the New Culture Movement which owes its inception to Hu Shih is the new historical and critical approach to the study of Chinese philosophy and literature begun by Hu with his doctoral studies at Columbia. His *Outline of the History of Chinese Philosophy* (*Chung-kuo che-hsüeh shih ta-kang*), published in 1919, is permeated with a spirit of doubt which led him to reject tradition and to study Chinese thought historically and critically. This spirit soon penetrated the whole New Culture Movement. Hu's friend Ch'ien Hsüan-t'ung (1887–1938) and pupil Ku Chieh-kang (1893—) took it up as a concerted "debunking" movement in the early 1920s, which resulted in an almost complete rejection of traditional beliefs in regard to ancient Chinese history, as well as to the loss by the Confucian Classics of whatever sacredness, prestige or authority they still retained.

The attacks of reformers in recent decades had already undermined belief in the political and social ethics of Confucianism among young Chinese. As Nationalists, however, these same reformers had often felt a pride in Chinese antiquity which inclined them to spare it the devastating scrutiny to which they subjected the recent past. Now ancient history too—a domain in which Confucianists had always excelled and which was so vital to their whole world view—was invaded and occupied by modern skepticism.

KU CHIEH-KANG
Preface to Debates on Ancient History (*1926*)
[From *Ku-shih pien,* Vol, I, Pt. I, pp. 40–66]

In those years [1918 ff.] Dr. Hu Shih published many articles. Those articles often provided me with the methods for the study of history. . . . If I can do what Dr. Hu has done in his investigations of the novel *Shui-hu chuan,* discovering the stages through which the story developed and going through the story systematically to show how these stages changed, wouldn't it be interesting! At the same time I recalled that this past spring Dr. Hu published an article on the "well-field" system in the periodical *Construction* [*Chien-she*], using the same critical method of investigation. It shows that ancient history can be investigated by the same method as the investigation of the novel. [p. 40]

As is well known, the history of China is generally considered to be 5,000 years old (or 2,276,000 years according to the apocryphal books!). Actually it is only 2,000 years old if we deduct the history recorded in spurious works and also unauthenticated history based on spurious works. Then we have only what is left after a big discount! At this point I could not help arousing in my mind an ambition to overthrow unauthentic history. At first I wanted only to overthrow unauthentic history recorded in unauthentic books. Now I wanted also to overthrow unauthentic history recorded in authentic works. Since I read the first section of [K'ang Yu-wei's] *Confucius As a Reformer* [*K'ung Tzu kai-chih k'ao*] my thought had been germinating for five or six years, and now for the first time I had a clear conception and a definite plan to overthrow ancient history. What is this plan? Its procedure involves three things to be done. First, the origin and the development of the events recorded in unauthentic histories must be investigated one by one. Secondly, every event in the authentic histories must be investigated to see what this and that person said about it, list what they said and compare them, like a judge examining evidence so that no lie can escape detection. Thirdly, although the words of liars differ, they follow a certain common pattern, just as the rules governing plots in plays are uniform although the stories themselves differ. We can detect the patterns in their ways of telling falsehood. [pp. 42–43]

My only objective is to explain the ancient history transmitted in the tradition of a certain period by the circumstances of that period. . . . Take Po-i [c.1122 B.C.?, who according to tradition preferred starving to death to serving another king]. What was the man really like? Was he the son of the Lord of Ku-chu? We have no way of knowing. But we do know that in the Spring and Autumn period people liked to talk about moral cultivation and upheld the "gentleman" as the standard of molding personal character. Consequently, when Po-i was talked about in the *Analects,* he was described as "not keeping in mind other people's former wickedness" [V:22] and "refusing to surrender his will or degrade himself." [XVIII:8] We also know that in the Contending States period, rulers and prime ministers liked to keep scholars in their service and scholars desperately looked for rulers to serve. For this reason, *The Book of Mencius* says of Po-i that, having heard King Wen was in power, his hopes were aroused and he declared: "Why should I not go and follow him? I hear King Wen is hospitable to the old." [IV A:13, VII A:22] We also know that after the Ch'in united the empire, the concept of absolute loyalty to the ruler became very strong and no one could escape from the mutual obligation between ruler and minister. For this reason, in the *Historical Records* he is recorded as one who bowed before King Wu of Chou to admonish him [not to overthrow King Chou of Shang], and having failed in this mission, chose to follow what he believed to be right, refusing to eat the food produced under the Chou and starving to death in the Shou-yang Mountain.[23] After the Han dynasty the story which had undergone many changes before became stabilized; books had become common, and as a result the personality of Po-i no longer changed in accordance with the varying circumstances of time. We therefore should treat ancient history in the same way as we treat the stories of our own day, for they have all passed from mouth to mouth.

THE CONTROVERSY OVER CHINESE AND WESTERN CULTURES

Intimately related to the debate on science and metaphysics was the controversy over Chinese and Western cultures, which arose from the apparent disillusionment with the West of some who had been the strongest champions of Westernization not long before. In 1919 Liang Ch'i-ch'ao returned from Europe, where he had observed the aftermath of the First World War. The picture he proceeded to give of the West was much in contrast to his earlier view of it as the vanguard of social progress and enlightened civilization. Now he saw it as sick and declining, the victim of its own obsession with science, materialism, and mechanization. The notion of inevitable progress, which had once inspired his belief that China could cut loose from its past and move forward to new greatness, was now bankrupt. Its bankruptcy, however, was all the West's, not Liang's. If Europe fell victim to its own shattered illusions, neither he nor China need suffer in the catastrophe. For the failure of science and

[23] *Shih chi,* ch. 61.

materialism served only to vindicate China and its "spiritual" civilization.

Liang was by no means ready to forego completely the benefits of science and material progress. The failure of the West he saw as resulting from its proclivity toward extremes, its overemphasis on materialism today being an excessive reaction to the exaggerated idealism and spirituality of medieval Europe. China's historical mission had been to preserve a balance between the two, and in the modern world she was specially equipped to reconcile these divergent forces in a new humanistic civilization. Thus Liang arrived at a new syncretism. Whatever was of value in Western science and material progress China could claim for herself and blend with her own spiritual traditions. The latter Liang identified selectively —and here revealed his growing anti-intellectualism—with the idealistic and intuitionist strains of Buddhism and Neo-Confucianism. Clearly Liang wanted the best of both worlds for China, and the better part was clearly Chinese.

Strong support for this view came from Liang Shu-ming (1893–), who likewise saw the superiority of Chinese civilization as lying in its capacity for harmonizing opposing extremes. As in the debate over science and metaphysics, however, the voices of those who spoke for progress and modernism—with Hu Shih again among the leaders—prevailed against the neo-traditionalists. The latter might appeal to national pride or self-respect, and thus swell a growing sense of nationalism, but they could not arrest the steady disintegration of traditional Chinese civilization, which Liang himself had done much to hasten.

LIANG CH'I-CH'AO

Travel Impressions of Europe

[From Lin Chih-chun (comp.), Yin-ping shih ho-chi, Vol. V, chuan-chi No. 23, Pt. i, sec. 13, pp. 35–37]

What is our duty? It is to develop our civilization with that of the West and to supplement Western civilization with ours so as to synthesize and transform them to make a new civilization. . . .

Recently many Western scholars have wanted to import Asia civilization as a corrective to their own. Having thought the matter over carefully, I believe we are qualified for that purpose. Why? In the past, the ideal and the practical in Western civilization have been sharply divided.

Idealism and materialism have both gone to the extreme. Religionists have onesidedly emphasized the future life. Idealistic philosophers have engaged in lofty talk about the metaphysical and mysterious, far, far removed from human problems. The reaction came from science. Materialism swept over the world and threw overboard all lofty ideals. Therefore I once said, "Socialism, which is so fashionable, amounts to no more than fighting for bread." Is this the highest goal of mankind?

Now pragmatism and evolutionism are being promoted, the aim being to embrace the ideal in the practical and to harmonize mind and matter. In my opinion, this is precisely the line of development in our ancient systems of thought. Although the schools of the sages—Confucius, Lao Tzu, and Mo Tzu—are different, their common goal is to unify the ideal and the practical. . . . Also, although Buddhism was founded in India, it really flourished in China. . . . Take Chinese Meditation Buddhism [Ch'an, Zen]. It can truly be considered as practical Buddhism and worldly Buddhism. Certainly it could have developed only outside India, and certainly it can reveal the special characteristics of the Chinese people. It enables the way of renouncing the world and the way of remaining in the world to go hand in hand without conflict. At present philosophers like Bergson and Eucken want to follow this path but have not been able to do so. I have often thought that if they could have studied the works of the Buddhist Idealistic School, their accomplishments would surely have been greater, and if they could have understood Meditation Buddhism, their accomplishments would have been still greater.

Just think. Weren't the pre-Ch'in philosophers and the great masters of the Sui and the T'ang eras our loving and sagely ancestors who have left us a great heritage? We, being corrupted, do not know how to enjoy them and today we suffer intellectual starvation. Even in literature, art, and the rest, should we yield to others? Of course we may laugh at those old folks among us who block their own road of advancement and claim that we Chinese have all that is found in Western learning. But should we not laugh even more at those who are drunk with Western ways and regard everything Chinese as worthless, as though we in the last several hundred years have remained primitive and have achieved nothing? We should realize that any system of thought must have its own period as the background. What we need to learn is the essential spirit of that system and not the conditions under which it was produced, for once we come to the conditions, we shall not be free from the restrictions of time. For example, Confucius said a great deal about ethics of an aristocratic nature which is certainly not suitable today. But we should not take Confucius lightly simply because of this. Shall we cast Plato aside simply because he said that the slavery system should be preserved? If we understand this point, we can study traditional Chinese subjects with impartial judgment and accept or reject them judiciously.

There is another very important matter. If we want to expand our civilization, we must borrow the methods of other civilizations because their methods of study are highly refined. [As Confucius said]: "If one wants a job well done, he must first sharpen his tools."[24] For what other reason was it [than the failure to do this] that while everyone in the past read Confucius and Li Po, no one got anywhere? I therefore hope that our dear young people will, first of all, have a sincere purpose of respecting and protecting our civilization; secondly, that they will apply Western methods to the study of our civilization and discover its true character; thirdly, that they will put our own civilization in order and supplement it with others' so that it will be transformed and become a new civilization; and fourthly, that they will extend this new civilization to the outside world so that it can benefit the whole human race.

LIANG SHU-MING
Eastern and Western Civilizations and Their Philosophies

At a time when Confucianism was being decried everywhere as decadent and outmoded, Liang Shu-ming, originally a Buddhist scholar, caused a stir by his conversion to Confucianism (as represented by the school of Wang Yang-ming). After examining Indian and Western philiosophies, he boldly declared that the future world civilization would be a reconstructed Chinese civilization. Though not unappreciative of certain Western values, such as individualism and science, which he hoped China might some day embrace in a synthesis with her own humanistic values, Liang condemned wholesale imitation of the West as impractical and undesirable. Moreover, unlike conservatives who were tempted to think that modern methods might be employed to defend traditional society, Liang was a genuine traditionalist, ready to dispense with both modernity and the status quo in Chinese society, where these proved incompatible with his Confucian ideals.

[24] *Analects*, XV:9.

According to Liang, the underlying bases of Western democracy—material, social, and spiritual—were totally lacking in China and quite foreign to the Chinese spirit. Consequently political democracy of the Western type could not possibly succeed there. Reformers and revolutionaries who tried arbitrarily to superimpose Western institutions on China failed to recognize the essentially rural and agrarian character of Chinese society. A sound program of reconstruction, Liang believed, could start only at the grass roots and slowly evolve a new socialist society, avoiding the excesses of both capitalism and communism.

To promote such reconstruction of agriculture and rural life, Liang founded an Institute of Rural Reconstruction and a political party, the National Socialists. He became an outspoken critic of the Nationalist regime, and equally so of the Communists later, being one of the few intellectuals who refused to confess his ideological errors.

[From *Tung-hsi wen-hua chi ch'i che-hsüeh*, pp. 54–202]

There are three ways in human life: 1) to go forward; 2) to modify and to achieve harmony, synthesis, and the mean in the self; and 3) to go backward. . . . The fundamental spirit of Chinese culture is the harmony and moderation of ideas and desires, whereas that of Indian civilization is to go backward in ideas and desires [and that of the West is to go forward]. [pp. 54–55]

Generally speaking, Westerners have been too strong and too vigorous in their minds and intellect. Because of this they have suffered spiritually. This is an undeniable fact since the nineteenth century. [p. 63]

Let us first compare Western culture with Chinese culture. First, there is the conquest of nature on the material side of Western culture—this China has none of. Second, there is the scientific method on the intellectual side of Western culture—this also China has none of. And thirdly, there is democracy on the social side of Western culture—this, too, China has none of. . . . This shows negatively that the way of Chinese culture is not that of the West but the second way [mentioned above, namely: achieving the mean]. . . . As to Indian culture . . . religion alone has flourished, subordinating to it philosophy, literature, science, and art. The three aspects of life [material, intellectual, and social] have become an abnormal spiritual development, and spiritual life itself has been an almost purely religious development. This is really most extraordinary. Indian culture has traveled its own way, different from that of the West. Needless to say, it is not the same as that of Chinese culture. [pp. 64–66]

In this respect Chinese culture is different from that of India, because of the weakness of religion as we have already said. For this reason, there is not much to be said about Chinese religions. The most important thing in Chinese culture is its metaphysics, which is applicable everywhere. . . . Chinese metaphysics is different from that of the West and India. It is different in its problems. . . . The problems discussed in the ancient West and ancient India have in fact not existed in China. While the problems of the West and India are not really identical, still they are the same in so far as the search for the reality of the universe is concerned. Where they are the same is exactly where they are decidedly different from China. Have you heard of Chinese philosophers debating monism, dualism, or pluralism, or idealism and materialism? The Chinese do not discuss such static problems of tranquil reality. The metaphysics handed down from the greatest antiquity in China, which constituted the fundamental concept of all learning—great and small, high and low—is that completely devoted to the discussion of change, which is entirely nontranquil in reality. [pp. 114-15]

The first point of the Confucian philosophy of life arising out of this type of Chinese metaphysics is that life is right and good. Basically, this metaphysics speaks in terms of "the life of the universe." Hence it is said that "Change means reproduction and reproduction." [25] Confucius said many things to glorify life, like "The great characteristic of Heaven and earth is to give life," [26] and "Does Heaven speak? All the four seasons pursue their course and all things are continually being produced" [27]. . . . Human life is the reality of a great current. It naturally tends toward the most suitable and the most satisfactory. It responds to things as they come. This is change. It spontaneously arrives at centrality, harmony, and synthesis. Hence its response is always right. This is the reason why the Confucian school said: "What Heaven has conferred is what we call human nature. To fulfill the law of human nature is what we call the Way." [28] As long as one fulfills his nature, it will be all right. This is why it is said that it can be understood and put into practice even by men and women of the simplest intelligence. This knowledge and ability are what Mencius called the knowledge possessed by man without deliberation and

---

[25] *Book of Changes, Hsi tz'u* I, ch. 5; Legge, *Yi King*, p. 356.
[26] *Book of Changes, Hsi tz'u* II, ch. 1; Legge, p. 381.
[27] *Analects*, XVII:19.   [28] *The Mean*, ch. 1.

the ability possessed by him without having been acquired by learning.[29] Today we call it intuition. [pp. 121-25]

This sharp intuition is what Confucius called *jen* [humanity]. . . . Therefore Confucius taught people to "seek *jen*."[30] All human virtues come out of this intuition. . . . Only sharp intuition can enable man to be just right and good in his conduct, and *jen* can produce such a sharp intuition in the highest degree. *Jen* is the substance (*t'i*) and sharp intuition is the function (*yung*). . . . All that Confucianists have sought is a life that is just right. A life that is just right does not consist in rigidly following one particular objective law but in being natural and always achieving the right measure and degree [that is, the mean]. To be rigid surely cannot be just right, and its greatest harm is to hamper the inward springs of life and to violate the law of nature. The Confucianists have believed that a life that is just right is the most natural and most consonant with the changes of the universe—what Confucius called the "operation of the natural law." In this natural change, there is always centrality and harmony. [pp. 126-29]

Clearly, contemporary Western thinkers demand a change in the traditional Western view of life. The tendency they seek is precisely the path of China, the path of Confucianism [namely, intuition or the Confucian *jen*]. . . . The forward path of the West has been entirely devoted to the search for the external, completely casting aside the self and destroying the spirit, so that while the external life is rich and beautiful, the internal life is empty to the point of zero. Therefore Westerners now unanimously make a strenuous effort to rid themselves of the narrow and oppressive world which reason and intellection have imposed on them. . . . In the present world, intuition will rise to replace intellection. [pp. 177-78]

What attitude should we Chinese hold now? What should we select from the three cultures? We may say:

1. We must reject the Indian attitude absolutely and completely.

2. We must accept Western culture as a whole [including conquest of nature, science, and democracy] but make some fundamental changes. That is to say, we must change the Western attitude somewhat [from intellection to intuition].

3. We must renew our Chinese attitude and bring it to the fore, but do so critically. [p. 202]

[29] *Mencius*, VII A:15.   [30] *Analects*, VII:14.

The attitude I want to recommend is what Confucius called "strength." . . . What I ask now is nothing more than our going forward to act, and that activity at its best should issue directly from our feelings. . . . When Confucius said that "to be strong, resolute, simple, and slow in speech is near to humanity," [31] he revealed the nobility of the will of the individual and the richness of our feelings. [pp. 211–13]

HU SHIH
Our Attitude Toward Modern Western Civilization

The most surprising rejoinder to the critics of the West came from Hu Shih, who defended the "materialistic" West on the ground that it was indeed more spiritual than China.

[From *Hu Shih wen-ts'un,* Collection III, Ch. 1, pp. 1–13]

At present the most unfounded and most harmful distortion is to ridicule Western civilization as materialistic and worship Eastern civilization as spiritual. . . . Modern civilization of the West, built on the foundation of the search for human happiness, not only has definitely increased material enjoyment to no small degree, but can also definitely satisfy the spiritual demands of mankind. In philosophy it has applied highly refined methods unceasingly to the search for truth and to investigation into the vast secrets of nature. In religion and ethics, it has overthrown the religion of superstitions and established a rational belief, has destroyed divine power and established a humanistic religion, has discarded the unknowable Heaven or Paradise and directed its efforts to building a paradise among men and Heaven on earth. It has cast aside the arbitrarily asserted transcendence of the individual soul, has utilized to the highest degree the power of man's new imagination and new intellect to promote a new religion and new ethics that is fully socialized, and has endeavored to work for the greatest amount of happiness for the greatest number of people.

The most outstanding characteristic of Eastern civilization is to know contentment, whereas that of Western civilization is not to know contentment.

Contented Easterners are satisfied with their simple life and therefore

[31] *Analects,* XVII:23.

do not seek to increase their material enjoyment. They are satisfied with ignorance and with "not understanding and not knowing" [32] and therefore have devoted no attention to the discovery of truth and the invention of techniques and machinery. They are satisfied with their present lot and environment and therefore do not want to conquer nature but merely be at home with nature and at peace with their lot. They do not want to change systems but rather to mind their own business. They do not want a revolution, but rather to remain obedient subjects.

The civilization under which people are restricted and controlled by a material environment from which they cannot escape, and under which they cannot utilize human thought and intellectual power to change environment and improve conditions, is the civilization of a lazy and non-progressive people. It is truly a materialistic civilization. Such civilization can only obstruct but cannot satisfy the spiritual demands of mankind.

SA MENG-WU, HO PING-SUNG, AND OTHERS

Declaration for Cultural Construction on a Chinese Basis (1935)

The increasing pace of Westernization in the early '30s, especially in the universities, prompted further expressions of fear that Chinese culture might be wholly submerged. This declaration by ten university professors in the magazine *Cultural Construction* deplored the prevailing trend and, in the general vein of Liang Ch'i-ch'ao and Liang Shu-ming, called for a synthesis of Chinese and Western cultures which would nevertheless be distinctively Chinese. Vague though this syncretism was, it attracted enough attention throughout the country so that Hu Shih felt compelled to protest, as he did in the piece which follows the declaration here, this kind of "conservatism . . . hiding under the smoke-screen of compromise."

[From "Chung-kuo pen-wei ti wen-hua chien-she hsüan-yen," in *Wen-hua chien-she*, Vol. 1, No. 4 (January 1935), pp. 3–5]

Some people think we should return to the past. But ancient China is already history, and history cannot and need not be repeated. Others believe that China should completely imitate England and the United States. These viewpoints have their special merits. But China, which is neither England nor the United States, should have her own distinctive characteristics. Furthermore, China is now passing from an agricultural feudal society to an industrial society, and is in a different situation from

[32] *Book of Odes*, Ta ya, Wen wang 7.

England and the United States, which have been completely industrialized.
We therefore definitely oppose complete imitation of them. Besides the
proponents of imitating England and the United States, there are two
other schools of thought, one advocating imitation of Soviet Russia, the
other, of Italy and Germany. But they make the same mistake as those
promoting the imitation of England and the United States; they likewise
ignore the special spatial and temporal characteristics of China. . . .

We demand a cultural construction on the Chinese basis. In the process
of reconstruction, we should realize that:

1. China is China, not just any geographical area, and therefore has her
own spatial characteristics. At the same time, China is the China of today,
not the China of the past, and has her own temporal characteristics. We
therefore pay special attention to the needs of here and now. The necessity to do so is the foundation of the Chinese basis.

2. It is useless merely to glorify ancient Chinese systems and thought.
It is equally useless to curse them. We must examine our heritage, weed
out what should be weeded out, and preserve what should be preserved.
Those good systems and great doctrines which are worthy of praise should
be brought to greater light with all our might and be presented to the
whole world, while evil systems and inferior thoughts which are worthy of
condemnation should be totally eliminated without the slightest regret.

3. It is right and necessary to absorb Western culture. But we should
absorb what is worth absorbing and not, with the attitude of total acceptance, absorb its dregs also.

4. Cultural construction on the Chinese basis is a creative endeavor,
one that is pushing ahead. Its objective is to enable China and the Chinese,
who are backward and have lost their unique qualities in the cultural
sphere, not only to keep pace with other countries and peoples, but also to
make valuable contributions to a world culture.

5. To construct China in the cultural sphere is not to abandon the idea
of the world as a Grand Unity. Rather, it is first to reconstruct China
and make her a strong and complete unit so that she may have adequate
strength to push forward the Grand Unity of the world.

Essentially speaking, China must have both self-recognition and a world
perspective, and must have neither any idea of seclusion nor any determination to imitate blindly. Such recognition is profound and precise recognition. Proceeding on such recognition, our cultural reconstruction

should be: Not to adhere to the past, nor to imitate blindly, but to stand on the Chinese basis, keep a critical attitude, apply the scientific method, examine the past, hold on to the present, and create the future.

HU SHIH

Criticism of the "Declaration for Cultural Construction on a Chinese Basis" (1935)
[From *Hu Shih wen-ts'un*, Collection IV, Ch. 4, pp. 535-40]

At the beginning of the year ten professors, Sa Meng-wu, Ho Ping-sung, et al., issued a declaration on "cultural construction on a Chinese basis." Considerable popular attention in the country has been attracted to it in the last several months. . . . I can't help pointing out that while the ten professors repeatedly uttered the phrase "Chinese basis" and while they declared in so many words that they were "not conservatives," in reality it is their conservative thinking that has been fooling them. The declaration is a most fashionable expression of a reactionary mood prevalent today. Of course, it is out of fashion for people conscientiously to advocate returning to the past and therefore their conservative thinking takes refuge under the smoke-screen of compromise. With respect to indigenous culture, the professors advocated discarding the dregs and preserving the essence, and with respect to the new culture of the world they advocated accepting the good and rejecting the bad and selecting what is best. This is the most fashionable tune of compromise. . . .

The fundamental error of Professors Sa, Ho, and others lies in their failure to understand the nature of cultural change. . . . Culture itself is conservative. . . . When two different cultures come into contact, the force of competition and comparison can partially destroy the resistance and conservatism of a certain culture. . . . In this process of survival of the fittest, there is no absolutely reliable standard by which to direct the selection from the various aspects of a culture. In this gigantic cultural movement, the "scientific method" the ten professors dream of does not work. . . . There is always a limit to violent change in the various spheres of culture, namely, that it can never completely wipe out the conservative nature of an indigenous culture. This is the "Chinese basis" the destruction of which has been feared by numerous cautious people of the past as well as the present. This indigenous basis is found in the life and habits produced by a certain indigenous environment and history. Simply stated, it is the people—all the people. This *is* the "basis." There is no danger that this basis will be destroyed. No matter how radically the material existence has changed, how much intellectual systems have altered, and how much political systems have been transformed, the Japanese are still Japanese and the Chinese are still Chinese. . . . The ten professors need not worry about the "Chinese basis". . . . Those of us who are forward looking should humbly accept the scientific and technological world culture and the spiritual civilization behind it. . . . There is no doubt that in the future the crystallization of this great change will, of course, be a culture on the "Chinese basis."

CHAPTER XXIX

CHINESE COMMUNISM

On the surface Chinese Communism would seem to have little to do with Chinese tradition. From the outset—from the Party's founding in 1921 under the leadership of the iconoclast Ch'en Tu-hsiu—it has been blatantly hostile to Confucian tradition and unashamedly committed to violent overthrow of the old order. Mao Tse-tung too, though he has recognized a kind of native tradition in the peasant rebellions and popular "revolutionary" literature of earlier dynasties, has not thereby acknowledged any debt to the past. For him, recurrent rebellions showed only how the Chinese masses had suffered and protested. They did not show a way out of the historical impasse: the constant re-establishment of dynasticism and warlordism after futile outbursts of popular discontent.

For such an abortive revolutionary tradition Mao could feel pity, but if any lesson was to be learned—and this was Mao's real point—it was the uniqueness of Marxism-Leninism and of the victory which the Communist Party alone had been able to achieve over such an oppressive past. Where earlier failures demonstrated only the need for something totally new to break a deadlock which had spelled frustration and stagnation for all, the ideology and organization of Communism had for the first time given China a revolution worthy of the name.

Yet if, in Communist eyes, the successful Chinese revolution has been so peculiarly a product of superior Marxist science and leadership, Chinese Communism has been also, in the perspective of history, an unmistakable product of the Chinese revolution. For almost a century this revolution had been in the making—perhaps even for longer, if it is taken as part of a much older process, as the latest issue from the ancient womb of dynastic change. But conjoined to the familiar processes of dynastic decay, which might have led to a rebellion typical of the past, was a world revolution of which Communism itself must be considered only one manifestation, a world revolution which, long before Ch'en Tu-hsiu and a handful of intellectuals met to launch the Communist Revolution, had already effected far-reaching and fundamental changes in the Chinese way of life.

It is not our purpose here to assess the forces and factors which contributed to the triumph of Communism in China. The circumstances in which the Party took its rise, however, have a bearing on the relation between Communism and the Chinese tradition. By 1921 the course of revolutionary change was already well advanced. Not only had the Manchu dynasty fallen, but every attempt to restore the old monarchical and dynastic system had met with insuperable resistance. If, therefore, the republican era still looked much like earlier periods of warlordism and decentralization, the possibility had nevertheless vanished of this phase yielding eventually and inexorably to another period of dynastic rule.

With it, however, had not vanished the need for a government strong enough to serve the same purposes—and more: to cope with the enormous problems of China's adjustment to the modern world. In the answers to that need proposed by Sun Yat-sen, anti-Marxist though he was, it is not difficult to discern tendencies with a close affinity to Communism. Whatever Dr. Sun's own intentions, the popularity of his People's Principles (which went almost unchallenged from either Left or Right long after his death) helped create an atmosphere conducive to the acceptance of Communist aims: the People's Livelihood or Socialism, of a state-controlled economy; the People's Rule or Democracy as Sun interpreted it, of rule by a party elite under a strong leader; and Nationalism as adapted by Sun to the Leninist struggle against colonialism, of hostility to and suspicion of the West.

While republican politics floundered in a sea of warlordism and economic dislocation, the estrangement of Chinese intellectuals from traditional ideals and institutions deepened. This process, which began with concessions to Westernization by even would-be defenders of Confucianism, had reached a climax well before the republican revolution with the abandonment of the traditional curriculum for the civil service, long the institutional stronghold of Confucian ideology. If a new political elite were ever to regain the power of the old centralized bureaucracy, it was as unlikely to consist of Confucian scholar-officials as the regime itself was to take the form of monarchy. Instead now of intellectuals serving as defenders of tradition, they had become its most implacable critics. Thus Confucianism had not only lost its bureaucratic function, but even the basis of its intellectual life.

As we have seen in the preceding chapter, the dominant trend of thought in the New Culture Movement was toward Westernization. This was expressed in certain general attitudes which won increasing acceptance among the educated and especially among the younger generation: 1) positivism, as a belief in the value and universal applicability of methods of inquiry developed for the natural sciences; 2) pragmatism, in the sense that the validity of an idea was to be judged primarily by its effectiveness; and 3) materialism, especially as a denial of traditional religious and ethical systems. While each of these attitudes might be held by as liberal a scholar and as eloquent an anti-Communist as Hu Shih, for many others they represented transitional stages on a road that led naturally and easily to Communism—to an acceptance of Marxism as the science of society, of Leninism as the effective method for achieving social revolution, and of dialectical materialism as a philosophy of life.

More than any such intellectual trends, however, what created a receptivity to revolutionary change among the Chinese people as a whole were attitudes of a more general and pervasive character. First among these was the desire for and expectation of a better life, which the material progress of the West had seemed to bring within hope of realization. Second was a new view of history as dominated by forces which would either crush those who fell behind or guarantee a bright future to those who understood and utilized them. Third was the prevailing frustration over China's failure to keep pace with these forces and to fulfill the high expectations of her modern political prophets.

Each of these attitudes contributed to a climate of opinion which called for wholesale change, and in which nothing that was not "revolutionary" could hope to arouse popular enthusiasm. Of this the revolutionary aims of the Kuomintang itself are an eloquent example. But more instructive for present purposes is the inability of the Kuomintang to win support for its brand of revolution from precisely those intellectuals who helped form the minds of the educated elite. We have already seen how quick Western-educated and "liberal-minded" Chinese were to find fault with the Nationalist regime for its failure to exemplify liberal principles and establish political democracy. Yet toward the Communists, whose political aims were still more authoritarian and totalitarian, these same "liberals" sometimes showed far more indulgence. In the revolutionary context of the times it was not difficult for the Communists to gain acceptance as fellow "progressives"—a little extreme perhaps, but nonetheless devoted to the cause of social and economic revolution, to science and technological progress, and above all to the total destruction of the old order.

Yet it was in a more fundamental sense than this that Westernized intellectuals and the exponents of modern Western philosophies helped prepare the way for Communism. Hu Shih had joined hands with Ch'en Tu-hsiu in the attack on traditional values, but nothing pragmatism had to offer in the way of scientific analyses or solutions to the specific problems of modern Chinese society proved intelligible or acceptable to the great masses of Chinese as a substitute for the old value system. Thus if the weakening of traditional ethics did not leave an actual vacuum for Communist doctrine to fill, still the materialistic and utilitarian tendencies of the time offered little resistance to, and could easily be exploited by, the new dogmatism.

Having considered, in an admittedly cursory and no doubt too sweeping fashion, some points in the development of modern Chinese thought from which Chinese Communism took its departure, we shall defer an assessment of its relation to Chinese tradition until the general aims and principles of the movement have been examined. In the selections which follow the presentation of these aims and principles is guided by two basic criteria, which it would be well to keep in mind. First, since this is not intended as a documentary history of Chinese Communism, questions of primarily historical significance are not emphasized. These include questions of strategy and tactics which, though of fundamental importance to an understanding of the Communists' actual rise to power, cannot properly be evaluated except through a more detailed analysis of historical factors than is possible within the scope of this study. Second, this survey centers upon the most important pronouncements of Mao Tse-tung, as the chief exponent of Chinese Communism today. Past leaders and lower-ranking spokesmen are included only where they give expression to ideas that have a significance beyond the importance of their expositors.

Within these limitations the readings attempt to answer the following basic questions:

1. What have been the overall aims of the Chinese Communists, aims for which they have succeeded in gaining the support of both Party members and Chinese outside the Party?

2. In what light have Chinese Communists interpreted their own relation to China's past history and traditions?

3. What are the philosophical premises upon which Communist doctrine claims to be based?

4. What are the ideological factors most vital to the actual practice of Chinese Communism; in other words, what are the basic elements of Communist discipline?

THE NATURE OF THE COMMUNIST REVOLUTION

In this section are presented readings which attempt to answer the first two questions above. They are meant to suggest the overall character and significance of the Communist revolution as its leaders have interpreted them to the Chinese people as a whole. In a second section the theoretical bases of party indoctrination and discipline, directed primarily to the party elite, will be set forth.

LI TA-CHAO
The Victory of Bolshevism

Li Ta-chao (1888–1927) was a Peking University professor and librarian who joined in the intellectual ferment which found expression in Ch'en Tu-hsiu's *New Youth* magazine. He exerted an especially profound influence on his student and library assistant, the youthful Mao Tse-tung. Marxism had attracted comparatively little attention among Chinese, until the success of the October revolution inspired Li to hail it enthusiastically in this article for the November 15 issue of the *New Youth* in 1918. Thereafter he launched a Marxist study club from which recruits were drawn for the founding of the Communist Party in 1921. One of the co-founders of the Party, along with Ch'en Tu-hsiu, Li later was captured in a raid on the Soviet Embassy compound in Peking and executed. Since Ch'en, the original chairman of the

Party, was subsequently expelled and disowned by it, Li came to be honored in his place and to be revered posthumously as the Party's founding father.

Although not yet a convinced Marxist at this time, in this article Li bespeaks a widespread feeling of hope and expectation aroused by the Bolshevik revolution among Chinese bitterly disappointed in the outcome of the Chinese revolution of 1911. Note how he specifically acclaims it as a new and potent religion offering messianic hope for the future.

[From Teng and Fairbank, *China's Response to the West*, pp. 246–49]

"Victory! Victory! The Allies have been victorious! Surrender! Surrender! Germany has surrendered!" These words are on the national flag bedecking every doorway, they can be seen in color and can be indistinctly heard in the intonation of every voice. . . .

But let us think carefully as small citizens of the world, to whom exactly does the present victory belong? Who has really surrendered? Whose is the achievement this time? And for whom do we celebrate? . . .

For the real cause of the ending of the war was not the vanquishing of the German military power by the Allied military power, but the vanquishing of German militarism by German socialism. . . . The victory over German militarism does not belong to the Allied nations; even less does it belong to our factious military men who used participation in the war only as an excuse [for engaging in civil war], or to our opportunistic, cunningly manipulative politicians. It is the victory of humanitarianism, of pacifism; it is the victory of justice and liberty; it is the victory of democracy; it is the victory of socialism; it is the victory of Bolshevism [Chinese text inserts "Hohenzollern" by error]; it is the victory of the red flag; it is the victory of the labor class of the world; and it is the victory of the twentieth century's new tide. Rather than give Wilson and others the credit for this achievement, we should give the credit to Lenin [these names are inserted in English], Trotsky, Collontay [Alexandra Kollontai], to Liebknecht, Scheidemann, and to Marx . . .

Bolshevism is the ideology of the Russian Bolsheviki. What kind of ideology is it? It is very difficult to explain it clearly in one sentence. If we look for the origin of the word, we see that it means "majority." An English reporter once asked Collontay, a heroine in that [Bolshevik] party, what the meaning of "Bolsheviki" was. The heroine answered . . . "Its meaning will be clear only if one looks at what they are doing." According to the explanation given by this heroine, then, "Bolsheviki

means only what they are doing." But from the fact that this heroine had
called herself a Revolutionary Socialist in western Europe, and a Bolshe-
vika in eastern Europe, and from the things they have done, it is clear
that their ideology is revolutionary socialism; their party is a revolutionary
socialist party; and they follow the German socialist economist Marx as
the founder of their doctrine. Their aim is to destroy the national boundaries which are obstacles to socialism at present, and to destroy the system
of production in which profit is monopolized by the capitalist. Indeed,
the real cause of this war was also the destruction of national boundaries.
Since the present national boundaries cannot contain the expansion of the
system of production brought about by capitalism, and since the resources
within each nation are inadequate for the expansion of its productive
power, the capitalist nations all began depending on war to break down
these boundaries, hoping to make of all parts of the globe one single,
coordinated economic organ.

So far as the breaking down of national boundaries is concerned, the
socialists are of the same opinion with them. But the purpose of the
capitalist governments in this matter is to enable the middle class in their
countries to gain benefits; they rely on world economic development by
one class in the victor nations, and not on mutual cooperation among
humanitarian, reasonable organizations of the producers of the world.
This war will cause such a victor nation to advance from the position of
a great power to that of a world empire. The Bolsheviki saw through this
point; therefore they vigorously protested and proclaimed that the present
war is a war of the tsar, of the kaiser, of kings and emperors, that it is a
war of capitalist governments, but it is not their war. Theirs is the war of
classes, a war of all the world's proletariat and common people against
the capitalists of the world. While they are opposed to war itself, they
are at the same time not afraid of it. They hold that all men and women
should work. All those who work should join a union, and there should
be a central administrative soviet in each union. Such soviets then should
organize all the governments of the world. There will be no congress, no
parliament, no president, no prime minister, no cabinet, no legislature,
and no ruler. There will be only the joint soviets of labor, which will
decide all matters. All enterprises will belong to those who work therein,
and aside from this no other possessions will be allowed. They will unite
the proletariat of the world, and create global freedom with their greatest,

strongest power of resistance: first they will create a federation of European democracies, to serve as the foundation of a world federation. This is the ideology of the Bolsheviki. This is the new doctrine of the twentieth-century revolution.

In a report by Harold Williams in the London *Times,* Bolshevism is considered a mass movement. He compares it with early Christianity, and finds two points of similarity: one is enthusiastic partisanship, the other is a tendency to revelation. He says, "Bolshevism is really a kind of mass movement, with characteristics of religion". . . . Not only the Russia of today, but the whole world of the twentieth century probably cannot avoid being controlled by such religious power and swayed by such a mass movement. . . .

Whenever a disturbance in this worldwide social force occurs among the people, it will produce repercussions all over the earth, like storm clouds gathering before the wind and valleys echoing the mountains. In the course of such a world mass movement, all those dregs of history which can impede the progress of the new movement—such as emperors, nobles, warlords, bureaucrats, militarism, capitalism—will certainly be destroyed as though struck by a thunderbolt. Encountering this irresistible tide, these things will be swept away one by one. . . . Henceforth, all that one sees around him will be the triumphant banner of Bolshevism, and all that one hears around him will be Bolshevism's song of victory. The bell is rung for humanitarianism! The dawn of freedom has arrived! See the world of tomorrow; it assuredly will belong to the red flag! . . . The revolution in Russia is but the first fallen leaf warning the world of the approach of autumn. Although the word "Bolshevism" was created by the Russians, the spirit it embodies can be regarded as that of a common awakening in the heart of each individual among mankind of the twentieth century. The victory of Bolshevism, therefore, is the victory of the spirit of common awakening in the heart of each individual among mankind in the twentieth century.

MAO TSE-TUNG
Report on an Investigation of the Hunan Peasant Movement

Under the early leadership of Ch'en Tu-hsiu the Chinese Communist Party followed a policy of collaboration with the Kuomintang dictated by the

Comintern. Since this ended in near-disaster for the Party in 1927 and brought about Ch'en's fall from leadership, Ch'en's writings and ideas do not figure prominently today in the orthodox tradition of Chinese Communist doctrine. By contrast this report on the Hunan Peasant movement by Mao Tse-tung (1893—), who was then of much less importance in the Party hierarchy, has, since his rise to supremacy, come to be regarded as a document of the greatest significance to the development of the revolution.

After taking part in the formation of the Communist Party, Mao had been assigned in 1925 to the organizing of peasants in his native Hunan, where he became convinced of the enormous revolutionary potential of the peasantry. In this report, prepared early in 1927, Mao describes the methods used by the peasant associations, and reveals with undisguised satisfaction the campaign of terror waged against local landlords and officials. These terror tactics became an essential feature of Mao's systematic program of class warfare in areas taken over by the Red Army. Such a condoning of extremism is contrary to the dominant strain in Chinese thought, which favors moderation, compromise, and harmony, but has ample precedent in Chinese political practice and in peasant revolutions like the Taiping Movement. Curiously enough, among the great deeds of the peasants which Mao lists (including the organizing of peasants' associations and cooperatives, tax reduction, price control, etc.) we find prohibitions on gambling, opium smoking, feasting, and wine-drinking, which reflect the strain of native puritanism already encountered in the Taipings.

More significant, in view of the later importance attached to the land problem, is Mao's failure to say anything about the confiscation and redistribution of land among the poor peasants. This period he describes was one of collaboration with the Kuomintang, and the tactics pursued were limited by the Comintern's desire not to offend Kuomintang sensibilities on the question of land expropriation. Mao, concurrently a Kuomintang party official (for a time chief of its Agitprop department and candidate for the Kuomintang Central Committee), was also careful to avoid such offense in writing this report. On the other hand, there is ample evidence, in the passages which follow, of Mao's remarkable capacity to see things through the eyes of the peasant.

[From *Selected Works of Mao Tse-tung*, I, 21–57]

THE IMPORTANCE OF THE PEASANT PROBLEM

During my recent visit to Hunan [1] I conducted an investigation on the spot into the conditions in the five counties of Siangtan, Siangsiang, Hengshan, Liling, and Changsha. In the thirty-two days from January 4 to February 5, in villages and in county towns, I called together for fact-finding conferences experienced peasants and comrades working for the

[1] Hunan was then the storm-center of the peasant movement in China. Unless otherwise noted, footnotes in these selections are from the official text. [Ed.]

peasant movement, listened attentively to their reports, and collected a lot of material. Many of the hows and whys of the peasant movement were quite the reverse of what I had heard from the gentry in Hankow and Changsha. And many strange things there were that I had never seen or heard before. I think these conditions exist in many other places.

All kinds of arguments against the peasant movement must be speedily set right. The erroneous measures taken by the revolutionary authorities concerning the peasant movement must be speedily changed. Only thus can any good be done for the future of the revolution. For the rise of the present peasant movement is a colossal event. In a very short time, in China's central, southern, and northern provinces, several hundred million peasants will rise like a tornado or tempest, a force so extraordinarily swift and violent that no power, however great, will be able to suppress it. They will break all trammels that now bind them and rush forward along the road to liberation. They will send all imperialists, warlords, corrupt officials, local bullies, and bad gentry to their graves. All revolutionary parties and all revolutionary comrades will stand before them to be tested, and to be accepted or rejected as they decide.

To march at their head and lead them? Or to follow at their rear, gesticulating at them and criticising them? Or to face them as opponents?

Every Chinese is free to choose among the three alternatives, but circumstances demand that a quick choice be made. [pp. 21–22]

DOWN WITH THE LOCAL BULLIES AND BAD GENTRY!

All Power to the Peasant Association!

The peasants attack as their main targets the local bullies and bad gentry and the lawless landlords, hitting in passing against patriarchal ideologies and institutions, corrupt officials in the cities, and evil customs in the rural areas. In force and momentum, the attack is like a tempest or hurricane; those who submit to it survive and those who resist it perish. As a result, the privileges which the feudal landlords have enjoyed for thousands of years are being shattered to pieces. The dignity and prestige of the landlords are dashed to the ground. With the fall of the authority of the landlords, the peasant association becomes the sole organ of authority, and what people call "All power to the peasant association" has come to pass. Even such a trifle as a quarrel between man and wife has to be settled at the peasant association. Nothing can be settled in the absence of people from the association. The association is actually dictating in all matters in the countryside, and it is literally true that "whatever it says, goes." The public can only praise the association and must not condemn it. The local bullies and bad gentry and the lawless landlords have been totally deprived of the right to have their say, and no one dares mutter the word "No." To be safe from the power and pressure of the peasant association, the first-rank local bullies and bad gentry fled to Shanghai, the second-rank ones to Hankow, the third-rank ones to Changsha, and the fourth-rank ones and even lesser fry can only remain in the countryside and surrender to the peasant association.

"I'll donate ten dollars, please admit me to the peasant association," one of the smaller gentry would say.

"Pshaw! Who wants your filthy money!" the peasants would reply.

Many middle and small landlords, rich peasants and middle peasants, formerly opposed to the peasant association, now seek admission in vain. Visiting various places, I often came across such people, who solicited my help. "I beg," they would say, "the committeeman from the provincial capital to be my guarantor."

The census book compiled by the local authorities under the Manchu regime consisted of a regular register and a special register; in the former honest people were entered, and in the latter burglars, bandits, and other undesirables. The peasants in some places now use the same method to threaten people formerly opposed to the association: "Enter them in the special register!"

Such people, afraid of being entered in the special register, try various means to seek admission to the association and do not feel at ease until, as they eagerly desire, their names are entered in its register. But they are as a rule sternly turned down, and so spend their days in a constant state of suspense; barred from the doors of the association, they are like homeless people. In short, what was generally sneered at four months ago as the "peasants' gang" has now become something most honorable. Those who prostrated themselves before the power of the gentry now prostrate themselves before the power of the peasants. Everyone admits that the world has changed since last October.

"AN AWFUL MESS!" AND "VERY GOOD INDEED!"

The revolt of the peasants in the countryside disturbed the sweet dreams of the gentry. When news about the countryside reached the cities, the gentry there immediately burst into an uproar. When I first arrived in Changsha, I met people from various circles and picked up a good deal of street gossip. From the middle strata upwards to the right-wingers of the Kuomintang, there was not a single person who did not summarize the whole thing in one phrase: "An awful mess!" Even quite revolutionary people, carried away by the opinion of the "awful mess" school which prevailed like a storm over the whole city, became downhearted at the very thought of the conditions in the countryside, and could not deny the word "mess." Even very progressive people could only remark: "Indeed a mess, but inevitable in the course of the revolution." In a word, nobody could categorically deny the word "mess."

But the fact is, as stated above, that the broad peasant masses have risen to fulfill their historic mission, that the democratic forces in the rural areas have risen to overthrow the rural feudal power. The patriarchal-feudal class of local bullies, bad gentry, and lawless landlords has formed the basis of autocratic government for thousands of years, the cornerstone of imperialism, warlordism and corrupt officialdom. To overthrow this feudal power is the real objective of the national revolution. What Dr. Sun Yat-sen wanted to do in the forty years he devoted to the national revolution but failed to accomplish, the peasants have accomplished in a few months. This is a marvelous feat which has never been achieved in the last forty or even thousands of years. It is very good indeed. It is not "a mess" at all. It is anything but "an awful mess." [pp. 23–25]

THE QUESTION OF "GOING TOO FAR"

There is another section of people who say: "Although the peasant association ought to be formed, it has gone rather too far in its present actions." This is the opinion of the middle-of-the-roaders. But how do matters stand in reality? True, the peasants do in some ways "act unreasonably" in the countryside. The peasant association, supreme in authority, does not allow the landlords to have their say and makes a clean sweep of all their prestige. This is tantamount to trampling the landlords underfoot after knocking them down. The peasants threaten: "Put you in the special register"; they impose fines on the local bullies and bad gentry and demand contributions; they smash their sedan-chairs. Crowds of people swarm into the homes of the local bullies and bad gentry who oppose the peasant association, slaughtering their pigs and consuming their grain. They may even loll for a minute or two on the ivory beds of the young mesdames and mademoiselles in the families of the bullies and gentry. At the slightest provocation they make arrests, crown the arrested with tall paper-hats, and parade them through the villages: "You bad gentry, now you know who we are!" Doing whatever they like and turning everything upside down, they have even created a kind of terror in the countryside. This is what some people call "going too far," or "going beyond the proper limit to right a wrong," or "really too outrageous."

The opinion of this group, reasonable on the surface, is erroneous at bottom.

First, the things described above have all been the inevitable results of the doings of the local bullies and bad gentry and lawless landlords themselves. For ages these people, with power in their hands, tyrannized over the peasants and trampled them underfoot; that is why the peasants have now risen in such a great revolt. The most formidable revolts and the most serious troubles invariably occur at places where the local bullies and bad gentry and the lawless landlords were the most ruthless in their evil deeds. The peasants' eyes are perfectly discerning. As to who is bad and who is not, who is the most ruthless and who is less so, and who is to be severely punished and who is to be dealt with lightly, the peasants keep perfectly clear accounts and very seldom has there been any discrepancy between the punishment and the crime.

Secondly, a revolution is not the same as inviting people to dinner, or writing an essay, or painting a picture, or doing fancy needlework; it cannot be anything so refined, so calm and gentle, or so mild, kind, courteous, restrained, and magnanimous.[2] A revolution is an uprising, an act of violence whereby one class overthrows another. A rural revolution is a revolution by which the peasantry overthrows the authority of the feudal landlord class. If the peasants do not use the maximum of their strength, they can never overthrow the authority of the landlords which has been deeply rooted for thousands of years. In the rural areas, there must be a great fervent revolutionary upsurge, which alone can arouse hundreds and thousands of the people to form a great force. All the actions mentioned above, labeled as "going too far," are caused by the power of the peasants, generated by a great, fervent, revolutionary upsurge in the countryside. Such actions were quite necessary in the second period of the peasant movement (the period of revolutionary action). In this pe-

---

[2] These were the virtues of Confucius, as described by one of his disciples.

riod, it was necessary to establish the absolute authority of the peasants. It was necessary to stop malicious criticisms against the peasant association. It was necessary to overthrow all the authority of the gentry, to knock them down and even trample them underfoot. All actions labeled as "going too far" had a revolutionary significance in the second period. To put it bluntly, it was necessary to bring about a brief reign of terror in every rural area; otherwise one could never suppress the activities of the counter-revolutionaries in the countryside or overthrow the authority of the gentry. To right a wrong it is necessary to exceed the proper limits, and the wrong cannot be righted without the proper limits being exceeded.[3] [pp. 26–27]

VANGUARD OF THE REVOLUTION

The main force in the countryside which has always put up the bitterest fight is the poor peasants. Throughout both the period of underground organization and that of open organization, the poor peasants have fought militantly all along. They accept most willingly the leadership of the Communist Party. They are the deadliest enemies of the local bullies and bad gentry and attack their strongholds without the slightest hesitation. [p. 31]

Without the poor peasants (the "riffraff" as the gentry call them) it would never have been possible to bring about in the countryside the present state of revolution, to overthrow the local bullies and bad gentry, or to complete the democratic revolution. Being the most revolutionary, the poor peasants have won the leadership in the peasant association. . . . This leadership of the poor peasants is absolutely necessary. Without the poor peasants there can be no revolution. To reject them is to reject the revolution. To attack them is to attack the revolution. Their general direction of the revolution has never been wrong. [p. 32]

[3] "Going beyond the proper limit to right a wrong" is an old Chinese phrase. It means that, though the wrong is righted, the proper limit has been exceeded in righting it. This phrase has often been used as a pretext to prevent thorough-going measures and to justify mere patching and tinkering. It implies that the established order of things should not be utterly destroyed, but only certain remedial measures need be introduced for its betterment. Thus it provides a convenient formula for the reformists and the opportunists within the revolutionary ranks. Here Comrade Mao Tse-tung is refuting such people. When he says in the text "To right a wrong, we must go beyond the proper limit; otherwise the wrong cannot be righted," he means that mass revolutionary measures, not reformist-revisionist measures, must be taken to end the old feudal order.

A man in China is usually subjected to the domination of three systems of
authority: 1) the system of the state (political authority), ranging from
the national, provincial, and county government to the township government; 2) the system of the clan (clan authority), ranging from the central and branch ancestral temples to the head of the household; and 3) the
system of gods and spirits (theocratic authority), including the system of
the nether world ranging from the King of Hell to the city gods and local
deities, and that of supernatural beings ranging from the Emperor of
Heaven to all kinds of gods and spirits. As to women, apart from being
dominated by the three systems mentioned above, they are further dominated by men (the authority of the husband). These four kinds of authority—political authority, clan authority, theocratic authority, and the
authority of the husband—represent the whole ideology and institution
of feudalism and patriarchy, and are the four great cords that have bound
the Chinese people and particularly the peasants. We have already seen
how the peasants are overthrowing the political authority of the landlords in the countryside. The political authority of the landlords is the
backbone of all other systems of authority. Where it has already been
overthrown, clan authority, theocratic authority, and the authority of the
husband are all beginning to totter. Where the peasant association is
powerful, the clan elders and administrators of temple funds no longer
dare oppress members of the clan or embezzle the funds. The bad clan
elders and administrators have been overthrown as local bullies and bad
gentry. No ancestral temple dare any longer, as it used to do, inflict cruel
corporal and capital punishments like "beating," "drowning," and "burying alive." The old rule that forbids women and poor people to attend
banquets in the ancestral temple has also been broken. On one occasion the
women of Paikwo, Hengshan, marched into their ancestral temple, sat
down on the seats and ate and drank, while the grand patriarchs could
only look on. At another place the poor peasants, not admitted to the
banquets in the temples, swarmed in and ate and drank their fill, while
the frightened local bullies, bad gentry, and gentlemen in long gowns
all took to their heels.

Theocratic authority begins to totter everywhere as the peasant movement develops. In many places the peasant associations have taken over the temples of the gods as their offices. Everywhere they advocate the appropriation of temple properties to maintain peasant schools and to defray association expenses, calling this "public revenue from superstition." Forbidding superstition and smashing idols has become quite the vogue in Liling. In its northern districts the peasants forbade the festival processions in honor of the god of pestilence. There were many idols in the Taoist temple on Fupo hill, Lukow, but they were all piled up in a corner to make room for the district headquarters of the Kuomintang, and no peasant raised any objection. When a death occurs in a family, such practices as sacrifice to the gods, performance of Taoist or Buddhist rites, and offering of sacred lamps are becoming rare. It was Sun Hsiao-shan, the chairman of the peasant association, who proposed all this, so the local Taoist priests bear him quite a grudge. In the Lungfeng Nunnery in the North Third district, the peasants and school teachers chopped up the wooden idols to cook meat. More than thirty idols in the Tungfu Temple in the South district were burnt by the students together with the peasants; only two small idols, generally known as "His Excellency Pao," [4] were rescued by an old peasant who said, "Don't commit a sin!" In places where the power of the peasants is predominant, only the older peasants and the women still believe in gods, while the young and middle-aged peasants no longer do so. Since it is the young and middle-aged peasants who are in control of the peasant association, the movement to overthrow theocratic authority and eradicate superstition is going on everywhere.

As to the authority of the husband, it has always been comparatively weak among the poor peasants, because the poor peasant women, compelled for financial reasons to take more part in manual work than women of the wealthier classes, have obtained more right to speak and more power to make decisions in family affairs. In recent years rural economy has become even more bankrupt and the basic condition for men's domination over women has already been undermined. And now, with

---

[4] Pao Cheng, commonly known as "His Excellency Pao," was once prefect of Kaifeng, capital of the North Sung dynasty (A.D. 960–1127). He was famous in popular legend as an upright official and a fearless, impartial judge who had a knack for passing true judgments on all the cases he tried.

the rise of the peasant movement, women in many places have set out immediately to organize the rural women's association; the opportunity has come for them to lift up their heads, and the authority of the husband is tottering more and more every day. In a word, all feudal and patriarchal ideologies and institutions are tottering as the power of the peasants rises. In the present period, however, the peasants' efforts are concentrated on the destruction of the landlords' political authority. Where the political authority of the landlords is already completely destroyed, the peasants are beginning their attacks in the other three spheres, namely, the clan, the gods, and the relationship between men and women. At present, however, such attacks have only just "begun" and there can be no complete overthrow of the three until after the complete victory of the peasants' economic struggle. Hence at present our task is to guide the peasants to wage political struggles with their utmost strength, so that the authority of the landlords may be thoroughly uprooted. An economic struggle should also be started immediately in order that the land problem and other economic problems of the poor peasants can be completely solved.[5]

The abolition of the clan system, of superstitions, and of inequality between men and women will follow as a natural consequence of victory in political and economic struggles. If we crudely and arbitrarily devote excessive efforts to the abolition of such things, we shall give the local bullies and bad gentry a pretext for undermining the peasant movement by raising such slogans of counter-revolutionary propaganda as "The peasant association does not show piety towards ancestors," "The peasant association abuses the gods and destroys religion," and "The peasant association advocates the community of women." Clear proof has been forthcoming recently at both Siangsiang in Hunan and Yangsin in Hupeh, where the landlords were able to take advantage of peasant opposition to the smashing of idols. The idols were set up by the peasants, and in time they will pull them down with their own hands; there is no need for anybody else prematurely to pull down the idols for them. The agitational line of the Communist Party in such matters should be: "Draw the bow to the full without letting go the arrow, and be on the alert."[6]

---

[5] This one reference to the land problem is missing from the original version and has apparently been added retrospectively to enhance Mao's stature as a prophet of the peasant revolution who early recognized the importance of this problem. [Ed.]

[6] This metaphor of archery is from Mencius. Here it means that while Communists

The idols should be removed by the peasants themselves, and the temples for martyred virgins and the arches for chaste and filial widowed daughters-in-law should likewise be demolished by the peasants themselves; it is wrong for anyone else to do these things for them.

In the countryside I, too, agitated among the peasants for abolishing superstitions. What I said was:

"One who believes in the Eight Characters [7] hopes for good luck; one who believes in geomancy hopes for the beneficial influence of the burial ground.[8] This year the local bullies, bad gentry, and corrupt officials all collapsed within a few months. Is it possible that till a few months ago they were all in good luck and all under the beneficial influence of their burial grounds, while in the last few months they have all of a sudden been in bad luck and their burial grounds all ceased to exert any beneficial influence on them?

"The local bullies and bad gentry jeer at your peasant association, and say: 'How strange! It has become a world of committeemen; look, you can't even go to the latrines without meeting one of them!' Quite true, in the towns and in the villages, the trade unions, the peasant association, the Kuomintang, and the Communist Party all have their committee members—it is indeed a world of committeemen. But is this due to the Eight Characters and the burial grounds? What a strange thing! The Eight Characters of all the poor wretches in the countryside have suddenly changed for the better! And their burial grounds have suddenly started to exert a beneficial influence!

"The gods? They may quite deserve our worship. But if we had no peasant association but only the Emperor Kuan [9] and the Goddess of Mercy, could we have knocked down the local bullies and bad gentry? The gods and goddesses are indeed pitiful; worshiped for hundreds of years, they have not knocked down for you a single local bully or a single one of the bad gentry!

---

should develop the political consciousness of the peasants to the fullest extent, they should leave it to the peasants' own initiative to abolish superstitious and other bad practices.

[7] A method of fortune-telling in China by studying the two cyclic characters respectively for the year, month, day, and hour of the birth of a person.

[8] This refers to the superstitious belief that the location of the ancestors' graves exerts influence on the fortunes of the descendants. The geomancer claims that he can tell whether the site and its surroundings are auspicious.

[9] Kuan Yu, a warrior in the epoch of the Three Kingdoms (A.D. 196–264), was widely worshiped by the Chinese as the God of Loyalty and War.

"Now you want to have your rent reduced. I would like to ask: How will you go about it? Believe in the gods, or believe in the peasant association?" These words of mine made the peasants roar with laughter. [PP. 45–49]

CULTURAL MOVEMENT

With the downfall of the power of the landlords in the rural areas, the peasants' cultural movement has begun. And so the peasants, who hitherto bitterly hated the schools, are now zealously organizing evening classes. The "foreign-style schools" were always unpopular with the peasants. In my student days I used to stand up for the "foreign-style schools" when, upon returning to my native place, I found the peasants objecting to them. I was myself identified with the "foreign-style students" and "foreign-style teachers," and always felt that the peasants were somehow wrong. It was during my six months in the countryside in 1925, when I was already a Communist and had adopted the Marxist viewpoint, that I realized I was mistaken and that the peasants' views were right. The teaching materials used in the rural primary schools all dealt with city matters and were in no way adapted to the needs of the rural areas. Besides, the primary school teachers behaved badly towards the peasants, who, far from finding them helpful, grew to dislike them. As a result, the peasants wanted old-style rather than modern schools— "Chinese classes," as they call them, rather than "foreign classes"—and they preferred the masters of the old-style school to the teachers in the primary schools.

Now the peasants are energetically organizing evening classes, which they call peasant schools. Many such schools have been opened and others are being established; on the average there is one school to every township. The peasants are very enthusiastic about establishing such schools, and regard only such schools as their own. The funds for evening classes come from the "public revenue from superstitious practices," the funds of ancestral temples and other kinds of public funds or public property that have been lying idle. The county education boards wanted to use these public funds for establishing primary schools, that is, "foreign-style schools" not adapted to the needs of the peasants, while the peasants wanted to use them for peasant schools; as a result of the dispute, both sides got part of the funds, though in certain places the peasants got the whole. As a result of the growth of the peasant movement, the cultural level of the peasants has risen rapidly. Before long there will be tens of thousands of schools sprouting up in the rural areas throughout the whole province, and that will be something quite different from the futile clamor of the intelligentsia and so-called "educators" for "popular education," which for all their hullabaloo has remained an idle phrase. [PP. 56–57]

The Chinese Revolution and the Chinese Communist Party

Along with *On New Democracy* which appeared soon after it (January, 1940), *The Chinese Revolution and the Chinese Communist Party* (December, 1939) is one of two basic texts prepared by Mao to provide a definitive interpretation of the nature and aims of the revolution. Together they represent an adroit analysis of the Party's situation and the strategy to be pursued in the achievement of its objectives, presented in the simple catechetical style, the vigorous and unadorned prose, which are so characteristic of Mao's direct approach to mass indoctrination.

Much had happened since Mao's early days as a peasant organizer in Hunan, when he had become fired with enthusiasm for the revolutionary potentialities of the peasant masses. The lesson of early defeats and disappointments in Hunan and long experience as a practicing revolutionary leader, both in the Kiangsi Soviet and on the Long March to Yenan, are reflected in Mao's analysis of revolutionary strategy. He had devoted much attention to military matters in the early years at Yenan, and had expressed himself at great length on problems of guerilla warfare, military tactics, revolutionary objectives, mass organization and discipline, etc. Some of his main points are summarized in the selections which follow.

At the same time, Mao had been devoting himself to intensive study of Marxism-Leninism and the writings of Stalin. He had prepared texts setting forth the chief theoretical tenets of Communist orthodoxy (excerpts from which are presented in section two of this chapter) and he had given much attention to the proper interpretation of Chinese history and the nature of the Chinese revolution in "orthodox" terms. Indications of this, including Mao's acceptance of Stalin's periodization of Chinese history according to the classical Western pattern (from primitive communism, to slavery, to feudalism, to capitalism) rather than Marx's differentiation of it as a peculiarly Asiatic or Oriental society, are found in the writings below. They present first Mao's view of Chinese history, his characterization of the revolution, and his analysis of revolutionary strategy. Following them are passages from *On New Democracy,* stating the political and economic program Mao had formulated for this stage in the revolution.

It should be remembered that these two works were written in the middle phase of the second United Front period, supposedly based on collaboration with the Kuomintang against the Japanese. With the conclusion of the Moscow-Berlin Pact, signalizing Stalin's accommodation of the Axis powers, the struggle against Japan no longer rated such a high priority. Mao, though still eager to exploit anti-Japanese feeling, felt less of a need to work closely with the Nationalists in the "anti-imperialist" struggle. Accordingly he placed greater stress on the revolution within China and on the Communist Party's leadership of it, as over against the Kuomintang.

[From *Selected Works,* III, 73–86]

THE CHINESE NATION

Developing along the same lines as many other nations of the world, the Chinese nation (chiefly the Hans) first went through some tens of thousands of years of life in classless primitive communes. Up to now approximately 4,000 years have passed since the collapse of the primitive communes and the transition to class society, first slave society and then feudalism. In the history of Chinese civilization, agriculture and handicraft have always been known as highly developed; many great thinkers, scientists, inventors, statesmen, military experts, men of letters, and artists have flourished, and there is a rich store of classical works. The compass was invented in China very long ago. The art of paper-making was discovered as early as 1,800 years ago. Block-printing was invented 1,300 years ago. In addition, movable types were invented 800 years ago. Gunpowder was used in China earlier than in Europe. China, with a recorded history of almost 4,000 years, is therefore one of the oldest civilized countries in the world.

The Chinese nation is not only famous throughout the world for its stamina and industriousness, but also as a freedom-loving people with a rich revolutionary tradition. The history of the Hans, for instance, shows that the Chinese people would never submit to rule by the dark forces and that in every case they succeeded in overthrowing or changing such a rule by revolutionary means. In thousands of years of the history of the Hans, there have been hundreds of peasant insurrections, great or small, against the régime of darkness imposed by the landlords and nobility. And it was the peasant uprisings that brought about most dynastic changes. All the nationalities of China have always rebelled against the foreign yoke and striven to shake it off by means of resistance. They accept a union on the basis of equality, not the oppression of one nationality by another. In thousands of years of history of the Chinese nation many national heroes and revolutionary leaders have emerged. So the Chinese nation is also a nation with a glorious revolutionary tradition and a splendid historical heritage. [pp. 73-74]

ANCIENT FEUDAL SOCIETY

Although China is a great nation with a vast territory, an immense population, a long history, a rich revolutionary tradition, and a splendid historical heritage, yet she remained sluggish in her economic, political, and cultural development after her transition from the slave system into the feudal system. This feudal system, beginning from the Chou and Ch'in dynasties, lasted about 3,000 years. [p. 74]

It was under this feudal system of economic exploitation and political oppression that the Chinese peasants throughout the ages led a slave-like life in dire poverty and suffering. Under the yoke of feudalism they had no freedom of person. The landlords had the right to beat and insult them and even to put them to death at will, while the peasants had no political rights whatever. The extreme poverty and backwardness of the peasants resulting from such ruthless exploitation and oppression by the landlord class is the basic reason why China's economy and social life has remained stagnant for thousands of years. . . .

The ruthless economic exploitation and political oppression of the peasantry by the landlord class forced the peasants to rise repeatedly in revolt against its rule. . . . However, since neither new productive forces, nor new relations of production, nor a new class force, nor an advanced political party existed in those days, and consequently peasant uprisings and wars lacked correct leadership as is given by the proletariat and the Communist Party today, the peasant revolutions invariably failed, and the peasants were utilized during or after each revolution by the landlords and the nobility as a tool for bringing about a dynastic change. Thus, although some social progress was made after each great peasant revolutionary struggle, the feudal economic relations and feudal political system remained basically unchanged.

Only in the last hundred years did fresh changes take place. [pp. 75-76]

PRESENT-DAY COLONIAL, SEMI-COLONIAL AND SEMI-FEUDAL SOCIETY

As mentioned in Section 2, Chinese feudal society lasted for about 3,000 years. It was not until the middle of the nineteenth century that great internal changes took place in China as a result of the penetration of foreign capitalism.

As China's feudal society developed its commodity economy and so carried within itself the embryo of capitalism, China would of herself have developed slowly into a capitalist society even if there had been no influence of foreign capitalism. The penetration of foreign capitalism accelerated this development. [pp. 76–77]

Yet this fresh change represented by the emergence and development of capitalism constitutes only one aspect of the change that has taken place since imperialistic penetration into China. There is another aspect which co-exists with it as well as hampers it, namely, the collusion of foreign imperialism with China's feudal forces to arrest the development of Chinese capitalism. [p. 78]

The contradiction between imperialism and the Chinese nation, and the contradiction between feudalism and the great masses of the people, are the principal contradictions in modern Chinese society. . . . The struggles arising from these contradictions and their intensification inevitably result in the daily-developing revolutionary movements. The great revolutions of modern and contemporary China have emerged and developed on the basis of these fundamental contradictions. [pp. 81–82]

THE CHINESE REVOLUTION

The national revolutionary struggle of the Chinese people has a history of exactly one hundred years dating from the Opium War of 1840, and of thirty years dating from the revolution of 1911. As this revolution has not yet run its full course and there has not yet been any signal achievement with regard to the revolutionary tasks, it is still necessary for all the Chinese people, and above all the Chinese Communist Party, to assume the responsibility for a resolute fight. [pp. 82–83]

Since the character of present-day Chinese society is colonial, semi-colonial and semi-feudal, then what after all are our chief targets or enemies at this stage of the Chinese revolution?

They are none other than imperialism and feudalism, namely, the bourgeoisie of the imperialist countries and the landlord class at home. For these and none other are the principal agents that carry out oppression in Chinese society at the present stage and obstruct its advance. These agents conspire to oppress the Chinese people and, since national oppression by imperialism is the heaviest oppression, imperialism has become the foremost and fiercest enemy of the Chinese people.

Since Japan's armed invasion of China, the principal enemies of the Chinese revolution have been Japanese imperialism and all the collaborators and reactionaries who are in collusion with it, who have either openly capitulated or are prepared to capitulate.

The Chinese bourgeoisie, also actually oppressed by imperialism, once led revolutionary struggles; it played a principal leading role, for instance, in the revolution of 1911, and also joined such revolutionary struggles as the Northern Expedition and the present Anti-Japanese War. In the long period from 1927 to 1937, however, the upper stratum of the bourgeoisie, as represented by the reactionary bloc of the Kuomintang, was in league with imperialism and formed a reactionary alliance with the landlord class, turning against the friends who had helped it—the Communist Party, the proletariat, the peasantry and other sections of the petty bourgeoisie, betraying the Chinese revolution and thereby causing its defeat. [pp. 83–84]

Confronted with such enemies, the Chinese revolution becomes protracted and ruthless in nature. Since the enemies are extremely powerful, the revolutionary forces, unless allowed a long period of time, cannot be massed and steeled into a power that will finally crush them. Since the enemy's suppression of the Chinese revolution is exceedingly ruthless, the revolutionary forces cannot hold their own positions and take over the enemy's unless they steel themselves and develop their tenacity. The view that the forces of the Chinese revolution can be built up in the twinkling of an eye and the Chinese revolutionary struggle can triumph overnight is therefore incorrect.

Confronted with such enemies, the Chinese revolution must, so far as its principal means or the principal form is concerned be an armed rather than a peaceful one. This is because our enemy makes it impossible for the Chinese people, deprived of all political freedoms and rights, to take any peaceful political action. Stalin said, "In China, armed revolution is fighting against armed counter-revolution. This is one of the peculiarities and one of the advantages of the Chinese revolution." [10] This statement is a perfectly correct formulation. The view which belittles armed struggle, revolutionary war, guerrilla war and army work is therefore incorrect.

Confronted with such enemies, the Chinese revolution has also to tackle the question of revolutionary base areas. Since powerful imperialism and its allies, the reactionary forces in China, have occupied China's key cities for a long time, if the revolutionary forces do not wish to compromise with them but want to carry on the struggle staunchly, and if they intend to accumulate strength and steel themselves and avoid decisive battles with their powerful enemy before they have mustered enough strength, then they must build the backward villages into advanced, consolidated base areas, into great military, political, economic, and cultural revolutionary bastions, so that they can fight the fierce enemy who utilizes the cities to attack the rural districts and, through a protracted struggle, gradually win an overall victory for the revolution. In these circumstances, owing to the unevenness in China's economic development (not a unified capitalist economy), to the immensity of China's territory (which gives the revolutionary forces sufficient room to maneuver in), to the disunity inside China's counter-revolutionary camp which is fraught with contradictions, and to the fact that the struggle of the peasants, the main force in the Chinese revolution, is led by the party of the proletariat, the Communist Party, a situation arises in which, on the one hand, the Chinese revolution can triumph first in the rural districts and, on the other hand, a state of unevenness is created in the revolution and the task of winning complete victory in the revolution becomes a protracted and arduous one. It is thus clear that the protracted revolutionary struggle conducted in such revolutionary base areas is chiefly a peasant guerrilla war led by the Chinese Communist Party. To neglect building up revolutionary base areas in the rural districts, to neglect performing arduous work among the peasants, and to neglect guerrilla war, are therefore all incorrect views.

However, to emphasize armed struggle does not mean giving up other

[10] J. V. Stalin, *On the Perspective of the Revolution in China,* as translated in *Political Affairs* (New York. December, 1950), p. 29.

forms of struggle; on the contrary, armed struggle will not succeed unless coordinated with other forms of struggle. And to emphasize the work in rural base areas does not mean giving up our work in the cities and in the vast rural districts under the enemy's rule; on the contrary, without the work in the cities and in other rural districts, the rural base areas will be isolated and the revolution will suffer defeat. Moreover, the capture of the cities now serving as the enemy's main bases is the final objective of the revolution, an objective which cannot be achieved without adequate work in the cities.

This shows clearly that it is impossible for the revolution to triumph in both the cities and the countryside unless the enemy's principal instrument for fighting the people—his armed forces—is destroyed. Thus besides annihilating enemy troops in war, it is important to work for their disintegration.

This shows clearly that, in the Communist Party's propaganda and organizational work in the cities and the countryside long occupied by the enemy and dominated by the forces of reaction and darkness, we must adopt, instead of an impetuous and adventurist line, a line of hiding the crack forces, accumulating strength, and biding our time. In leading the people's struggle against the enemy we must adopt the tactics of advancing slowly but surely, by making the fullest possible use of all forms of open and legal activities permitted by laws and decrees and social customs and basing ourselves on the principles of justifiability, expediency and restraint; vociferous cries and rash actions can never lead to success. [pp. 84-86]

On New Democracy

According to the established Communist (Stalinist) view, China was following in the main the path of other societies from feudalism through a bourgeois-democratic revolution to a socialist revolution led by the proletariat. During the earlier period of Kuomintang-Communist collaboration, the latter acknowledged the "bourgeois" Nationalists as the main force of the so-called democratic revolution. In 1940, however, Mao was unwilling to grant such leadership to the Kuomintang, even though he conceded that the "democratic" revolution had not yet been completed and the socialist revolution still waited upon it. His On New Democracy—based on Leninist and Stalinist doctrines concerning the nature of the bourgeois-democratic revolution in colonial and semicolonial countries, and its relation to the anti-imperialist struggle led by the Soviet Union—was Mao's way of insuring Communist (proletarian) leadership for a new type of democratic revolution.

Politically the New Democracy bears little resemblance to Western democracy but conforms rather to Leninist "democratic centralism," which insures Communist domination of a multi-class coalition. Economically it involves a moderate program of land reform and nationalization of key industries. It was this moderate program which led some Western observers to think of the Communists as simply "agrarian reformers." Yet Mao's writings make it abundantly clear that Communists had no intention of sharing real power and every intention of pushing on to full socialism.

[From *Selected Works,* III, 109–55]

THE CHINESE REVOLUTION IS PART OF THE WORLD REVOLUTION

The historical feature of the Chinese revolution consists in the two steps to be taken, democracy and socialism, and the first step is now no longer democracy in a general sense, but democracy of the Chinese type, a new and special type—New Democracy. How, then, is this historical feature formed? Has it been in existence for the past hundred years, or is it only of recent birth?

If we only make a brief study of the historical development of China and of the world we shall understand that this historical feature did not emerge as a consequence of the Opium War, but began to take shape only after the first imperialist world war and the Russian October Revolution. [pp. 109–10]

Before these events, the Chinese bourgeois-democratic revolution belonged to the category of the old bourgeois-democratic world revolution, and was part of that revolution.

After these events, the Chinese bourgeois-democratic revolution changes its character and belongs to the category of the new bourgeois-democratic revolution and, so far as the revolutionary front is concerned, forms part of the proletarian-socialist world revolution.

Why? Because the first imperialist world war and the first victorious socialist revolution, the October Revolution, have changed the historical direction of the whole world and marked a new historical era of the whole world. [pp. 110–11]

This "world revolution" refers no longer to the old world revolution —for the old bourgeois world revolution has long become a thing of the past—but to a new world revolution, the socialist world revolution. Similarly, to form "part" of the world revolution means to form no longer a part of the old bourgeois revolution but of the new socialist revolution. This is an exceedingly great change unparalleled in the history of China and of the world.

This correct thesis propounded by the Chinese Communists is based on Stalin's theory.

As early as 1918, Stalin wrote in an article commemorating the first anniversary of the October Revolution:

The great world-wide significance of the October Revolution chiefly consists in the fact that:

(1) It has widened the scope of the national question and converted it from the particular question of combating national oppression in Europe into the general question of emancipating the oppressed peoples, colonies, and semi-colonies from imperialism.

(2) It has opened up wide possibilities for their emancipation and the right paths towards it, has thereby greatly facilitated the cause of the emancipation of the oppressed peoples of the West and the East, and has drawn them into the common current of the victorious struggle against imperialism.

(3) It has thereby erected a bridge between the socialist West and the enslaved East, having created a new front of revolutions against world imperialism, extending from the proletarians of the West, through the Russian revolution to the oppressed peoples of the East.[11]

Since writing this article, Stalin has again and again expounded the theoretical proposition that revolutions in colonies and semi-colonies have already departed from the old category and become part of the proletarian-socialist revolution. [pp. 112–13]

The first stage of the Chinese revolution (itself subdivided into many minor stages) belongs, so far as its social character is concerned, to a new type of bourgeois-democratic revolution, and is not yet a proletarian-socialist revolution; but it has long become part of the proletarian-socialist world revolution and is now even an important part of such a world revolution and its great ally. The first step in, or the first stage of, this revolution is certainly not, and cannot be, the establishment of a capitalist society under the dictatorship of the Chinese bourgeoisie; on the contrary, the first stage is to end with the establishment of a new-democratic society under the joint dictatorship of all Chinese revolutionary classes headed by the Chinese proletariat. Then, the revolution will develop into

[11] J. V. Stalin, *Works*, Eng. ed. (Moscow, 1953), IV, 169–70.

the second stage so that a socialist society can be established in China.
[p. 115]

NEW-DEMOCRATIC POLITICS

As to the question of "political structure" [in the New Democracy],
it is the question of the form of structure of political power, the form
adopted by certain social classes in establishing their organs of political
power to oppose their enemy and protect themselves. Without an adequate form of political power there would be nothing to represent the
state. China can now adopt a system of people's congresses—the people's
national congress, the people's provincial congresses, the people's county
congresses, the people's district congresses, down to the people's township congresses—and let these congresses at various levels elect the organs
of government. But a system of really universal and equal suffrage, irrespective of sex, creed, property, or education, must be put into practice
so that the organs of government elected can properly represent each
revolutionary class according to its status in the state, express the people's
will and direct revolutionary struggles, and embody the spirit of New
Democracy. Such a system is democratic centralism.[12] Only a government of democratic centralism can fully express the will of all the revolutionary people and most powerfully fight the enemies of the revolution.
The spirit of "not to be monopolized by a few" must be embodied in the
organizations of the government and the army; without a genuinely
democratic system such an aim can never be attained, and that would
mean a discrepancy between the political structure and the state system.

The state system—joint dictatorship of all revolutionary classes. The
political structure—democratic centralism. This is new-democratic government; this is a republic of New Democracy, the republic of the anti-

---

[12] According to an earlier definition of Mao's, in his report on "The Role of the
Chinese Communist Party in the National War," democratic centralism in the Party
consists in the following principles: 1) that individuals must subordinate themselves
to the organization; 2) that the minority must subordinate itself to the majority; 3)
that the lower level must subordinate itself to the higher level; and 4) that the entire
membership must subordinate itself to the Central Committee. "Whether in the army
or in the local organizations, democracy within the Party is meant to strengthen
discipline and raise fighting capacity, not to weaken them" (*Selected Works*, II, 254–55).
[Ed.]

Japanese united front, the republic of the new Three People's Principles with the three cardinal policies, and the Republic of China true to its name. Today we have a Republic of China in name, but not one in reality; the task today is to bring about the reality that would fit its name. [p. 121]

NEW-DEMOCRATIC ECONOMY

We must establish in China a republic that is politically new-democratic as well as economically new-democratic.

Big banks and big industrial and commercial enterprises shall be owned by this republic.

Enterprises, whether Chinese-owned or foreign-owned, which are monopolistic in character or which are on too large a scale for private management, such as banks, railways, and air lines, shall be operated by the state so that private capital cannot dominate the livelihood of the people: This is the main principle of the control of capital.

This was also a solemn statement contained in the Manifesto of the First National Congress of the Kuomintang during the period of the Kuomintang-Communist cooperation; this is the correct objective for the economic structure of the new-democratic republic. The state-operated enterprises of the new-democratic republic under the leadership of the proletariat are socialist in character and constitute the leading force in the national economy as a whole; but this republic does not take over other forms of capitalist private property, or forbid the development of capitalist production that "cannot dominate the livelihood of the people," for China's economy is still very backward.

This republic will adopt certain necessary measures to confiscate the land of landlords and distribute it to those peasants having no land or only a little land, carry out Dr. Sun Yat-sen's slogan of "land to the tillers," abolish the feudal relations in the rural areas, and turn the land into the private property of the peasants. In the rural areas, rich peasant economic activities will be tolerated. This is the line of "equalization of land ownership." The correct slogan for this line is "land to the tillers." In this stage, socialist agriculture is in general not yet to be established, though the various types of cooperative enterprises developed on the basis of "land to the tillers" will contain elements of socialism. [p. 122]

NEW-DEMOCRATIC CULTURE

A given culture is the ideological reflection of the politics and economy of a given society. There is in China an imperialist culture which is a reflection of the control or partial control of imperialism over China politically and economically. This part of culture is advocated not only by the cultural organizations run directly by the imperialists in China but also by a number of shameless Chinese. All culture that contains a slave ideology belongs to this category. There is also in China a semi-feudal culture which is a reflection of semi-feudal politics and economy and has as its representatives all those who, while opposing the new culture and new ideologies, advocate the worship of Confucius, the study of the Confucian canon, the old ethical code, and the old ideologies. Imperialist culture and semi-feudal culture are affectionate brothers, who have formed a reactionary cultural alliance to oppose China's new culture. This reactionary culture serves the imperialists and the feudal class, and must be swept away. Unless it is swept away, no new culture of any kind can be built up. [p. 141]

SOME ERRORS ON THE QUESTION OF THE NATURE OF CULTURE

So far as national culture is concerned, the guiding role is fulfilled by Communist ideology, and efforts should be made to disseminate socialism and communism among the working class and to educate, properly and methodically, the peasantry and other sections of the masses in socialism. But national culture as a whole is at present not yet socialist.

New-democratic politics, economy, and culture all contain a socialist element, and not an ordinary but a decisive one at that, because they are under the leadership of the proletariat. But taken as a whole, the political, economic and cultural conditions are as yet not socialist but new-democratic. [p. 152]

A NATIONAL, SCIENTIFIC, AND MASS CULTURE

New-democratic culture is national. It opposes imperialist oppression and upholds the dignity and independence of the Chinese nation. It belongs to our own nation, and bears our national characteristics. It unites with the socialist and new-democratic cultures of all other nations and establishes with them the relations whereby they can absorb something from each other and help each other to develop, and form together the new culture of the world; but it can never unite with the reactionary imperialist culture of any nation, for it is a revolutionary national culture. China should absorb on a large scale the progressive cultures of foreign countries as an ingredient for her own culture; in the past we did not do enough work of this kind. We must absorb whatever we today find useful, not only from the present socialist or new-democratic cultures of other nations, but also from the older cultures of foreign countries, such as those of the various capitalist countries in the age of enlightenment. However, we must treat these foreign materials as we do our food, which should be chewed in the mouth, submitted to the working of the stomach and intestines, mixed with saliva, gastric juice, and intestinal secretions, and then separated into essence to be absorbed and waste matter to be discarded—only thus can food benefit our body; we should never swallow anything raw or absorb it uncritically. So-called "wholesale Westernization" [13] is a mistaken viewpoint. China has suffered a great deal in the past from the formalist absorption of foreign things. Likewise, in applying Marxism to China, Chinese Communists must fully and properly unite the universal truth of Marxism with the specific practice of the Chinese revolution; that is to say, the truth of Marxism must be integrated with the characteristics of the nation and given a definite national form before it can be useful; it must not be applied subjectively as a mere formula. Formula-Marxists are only fooling with Marxism and the Chinese revolution, and there is no place for them in the ranks of the Chinese revolution. China's culture should have its own form, namely, a national form. National in form, new-democratic in content—such is our new culture today

New-democratic culture is scientific. It is opposed to all feudal and superstitious ideas, it stands for seeking truth from facts, it stands for objective truth and for the unity between theory and practice. On this point, the scientific thought of the Chinese proletariat can form an anti-imperialist, anti-feudal and anti-superstition united front with the still progressive bourgeois materialists and natural scientists, but it can never

[13] A view advanced by a number of the Chinese bourgeois scholars completely enslaved by antiquated individualist bourgeois Western culture. They recommended so-called "wholesale Westernization," which means imitating the capitalist countries of Europe and America in everything.

form a united front with any reactionary idealism. Communists may form an anti-imperialist and anti-feudal united front for political action with certain idealists and even with religious followers, but we can never approve of their idealism or religious doctrines. A splendid ancient culture was created during the long period of China's feudal society. To clarify the process of development of this ancient culture, to throw away its feudal dross, and to absorb its democratic essence is a necessary condition for the development of our new national culture and for the increase of our national self-confidence; but we should never absorb anything and everything uncritically. We must separate all the rotten things of the ancient feudal ruling class from the fine ancient popular culture that is more or less democratic and revolutionary in character. As China's present new politics and new economy have developed out of her old politics and old economy, and China's new culture has also developed out of her old culture, we must respect our own history and should not cut ourselves adrift from it. However, this respect for history means only giving history a definite place among the sciences, respecting its dialectical development, but not eulogizing the ancient while disparaging the modern, or praising any noxious feudal element. As to the masses of the people and the young students, the essential thing is to direct them not to look backward, but to look forward. [pp. 153–55]

THE TWOFOLD TASK OF THE CHINESE REVOLUTION AND THE CHINESE
COMMUNIST PARTY

[From *Selected Works,* "The Chinese Revolution and the Chinese Communist Party," III, 100–1]

To complete China's bourgeois-democratic revolution (the new-democratic revolution) and to prepare to transform it into a socialist revolution when all the necessary conditions are present—that is the sum total of the great and glorious revolutionary task of the Communist Party of China. All members of the Party should strive for its accomplishment and should never give up half-way. Some immature Communists think that we have only the task of the democratic revolution at the present stage, but not that of the socialist revolution at the future stage; or that the present revolution or the agrarian revolution is in fact the socialist revolution. It must be emphatically pointed out that both views are erroneous. Every Communist must know that the whole Chinese revolutionary movement led by the Chinese Communist Party is a complete revolutionary movement embracing the two revolutionary stages, democratic and socialist, which are two revolutionary processes differing in character, and that the socialist stage can be reached only after the democratic stage is completed. The democratic revolution is the necessary preparation for the socialist revolution, and the socialist revolution is the inevitable trend of the democratic revolution. And the ultimate aim of all Communists is to strive for the final building of socialist society and communist society.

The Dictatorship of the People's Democracy

The Dictatorship of the People's Democracy was written for the Twenty-eighth Anniversary of the Communist Party, July 1, 1949, on the eve of the complete conquest of mainland China. In the main it conforms to the principles laid down in *On New Democracy,* affirming that the new government would continue to represent a coalition of classes under the proletarian leadership of the Communist Party. The present text is noteworthy, however, for its clear definition of what democracy and dictatorship were to represent under the new regime—a definition based on concepts set forth by Lenin much earlier.

After an historical résumé demonstrating the indispensability of Marxism-Leninism and Communist leadership to the Chinese revolution, Mao takes up hypothetical objections to Communism and answers them in his typical catechetical fashion. The key question here concerns its dictatorial character, which Mao does not deny, and the key distinction he draws is a political one, subsuming economic class distinctions, between the "people" (those who accept Communist leadership) and the "reactionaries" (those who do not).

[From Brandt *et al., A Documentary History of Chinese Communism,* pp. 456–58]

PEOPLE'S DEMOCRATIC DICTATORSHIP

"You are dictatorial." Dear sirs, you are right; that is exactly what we are. The experience of several decades, amassed by the Chinese people, tells us to carry out the people's democratic dictatorship. That is, the right of reactionaries to voice their opinions must be abolished and only the people are allowed to have the right of voicing their opinions.

Who are the "people"? At the present stage in China, they are the working class, the peasant class, the petty bourgeoisie, and national bourgeoisie. Under the leadership of the working class and the Communist

Party, these classes unite together to form their own state and elect their own government (so as to) carry out a dictatorship over the lackeys of imperialism—the landlord class, the bureaucratic capitalist class, and the Kuomintang reactionaries and their henchmen representing these classes —to suppress them, allowing them only to behave properly and not to talk and act wildly. If they talk and act wildly their (action) will be prohibited and punished immediately. The democratic system is to be carried out within the ranks of the people, giving them freedom of speech, assembly, and association. The right to vote is given only to the people and not to the reactionaries. These two aspects, namely, democracy among the people and dictatorship over the reactionaries, combine to form the people's democratic dictatorship.

Why should it be done this way? Everybody clearly knows that otherwise the revolution would fail, and the people would meet with woe and the State would perish.

"Don't you want to eliminate state authority?" Yes, but we do not want it at present, we cannot want it at present. Why? Because imperialism still exists, the domestic reactionaries still exist, and classes in the country still exist. Our present task is to strengthen the apparatus of the people's state, which refers mainly to the people's army, people's police, and people's courts, for the defense of the country, and the protection of the people's interests; and with this as a condition, to enable China to advance steadily, under the leadership of the working class and the Communist Party, from an agricultural to an industrial country, and from a new democratic to a socialist and communist society, to eliminate classes and to realize the state of universal fraternity. The army, police, and courts of the state are instruments by which classes oppress classes. To the hostile classes the state apparatus is the instrument of oppression. It is violent, and not "benevolent." "You are not benevolent." Just so. We decidedly will not exercise benevolence towards the reactionary acts of the reactionaries and reactionary classes. Our benevolence applies only to the people, and not to the reactionary acts of the reactionaries and reactionary classes outside the people.

The (function of the) people's state is to protect the people. Only when there is the people's state, is it possible for the people to use democratic methods on a nationwide and all-round scale to educate and reform themselves, to free themselves from the influence of reactionaries at home and abroad (this influence is at present still very great and will exist for a long time and cannot be eliminated quickly), to unlearn the bad habits and ideas acquired from the old society and not to let themselves travel on the erroneous path pointed out by the reactionaries, but to continue to advance and develop towards a socialist and communist society accomplishing the historic mission of completely eliminating classes and advancing towards a universal fraternity.

The methods we use in this field are democratic; that is, methods of persuasion and not coercion. When people break the law they will be punished, imprisoned, or even sentenced to death. But these are individual cases and are different in principle from the dictatorship over the reactionary class as a class.

FUTURE OF THE REACTIONARIES

After their political regime is overthrown the reactionary classes and the reactionary clique will also be given land and work and a means of living; they will be allowed to re-educate themselves into new persons through work, provided they do not rebel, disrupt, or sabotage. If they are unwilling to work, the people's state will compel them to work. Propaganda and educational work will also be carried out among them, and, moreover, with care and adequacy, as we did among captured officers. This can also be called "benevolent administration," but we shall never forgive their reactionary acts and will never let their reactionary activity have the possibility of a free development.

Such re-education of the reactionary classes can only be carried out in the state of the people's democratic dictatorship. If this work is well done the main exploiting classes of China—the landlord and bureaucratic capitalist classes—will be finally eliminated. (Of the exploiting classes) there remain the national bourgeoisie among many of whom appropriate educational work can be carried out at the present stage. When socialism is realized, that is, when the nationalization of private enterprises has been carried out, they can be further educated and reformed. The people have in their hands a powerful state apparatus and are not afraid of the rebellion of the national bourgeois class.

The grave problem is that of educating the peasants. The peasants' economy is scattered. Judging by the experience of the Soviet Union, it requires a very long time and careful work to attain the socialization of agriculture. Without the socialization of agriculture, there will be no complete and consolidated socialism. And to carry out the socialization of agriculture a powerful industry with state-owned enterprises as the main component must be developed. The state of the people's democratic dictatorship must step by step solve this problem (of the industrialization of the country).

THE THEORY AND PRACTICE
OF CHINESE COMMUNISM

This second group of readings is designed to show the theoretical bases of Communist indoctrination and discipline. Since they are intended by their authors for a more specialized audience, the party elite, some of these documents are quite technical and employ a vocabulary that is often abstract and artificial. The ordinary student of Chinese thought may find such treatises almost as forbidding and esoteric as Buddist psychology or Neo-Confucian metaphysics. Nevertheless, the great importance attached to theory by the Chinese Communists cannot be overlooked out of too great a preoccupation with their historical accomplishments. Mao Tse-tung has always been much impressed with Lenin's statement: "Without a revolutionary theory, there can be no revolutionary movement." However contrived that theory may be as an explanation of the revolution itself, there can be no doubt that its acceptance by the Chinese Communists gave them an ideological unity and dynamism that their opponents—Chinese and even Western—sometimes lacked.

MAO TSE-TUNG

On Contradiction

This essay is one of two basic theoretical works by Mao, the other being *On Practice* (which follows it here). Though actually written shortly after the latter, *On Contradiction* is of a more general nature and therefore appears here in logical rather than in chronological order. It was produced by Mao Tse-tung in the early Yenan period and delivered in the form of lectures to the Anti-Japanese Military and Political College in Yenan.

Mao's intensive study at this time of the Communist tradition—from Marx and Engels down through Lenin and Stalin—derives from at least two important considerations. One is the necessity, after years devoted to the practical revolutionary struggle in Hunan and Kiangsi, for improving his own knowledge of basic Communist doctrine in order to present his ideas and policies in orthodox terms. No doubt he suffered some disadvantage in party debates with those who had studied Communist literature more carefully than he—who, while Mao was heavily engaged in the countryside, had given full time in Shanghai or Moscow to mastery of the formal theory and jargon of Marxism-Leninism. Mao's contempt for such "doctrinaires" and "formalists," and their ignorance of revolutionary practice, is manifest in these writings.

Yet Mao's answer to formalism in the Party is not to belittle theory. On the contrary he rises to the challenge with his own formulation of orthodox doctrine deriving from the patristic tradition of Communism, constantly acknowledging his debt to Marx, Engels, Lenin, and Stalin. Mao is far from the defiant rebel, the free-wheeling independent, and far more the prudent practitioner of a science in which he has full faith, the dedicated leader whose practical grasp of disciplined action confirms the importance of ideological orthodoxy. Accordingly, Mao's essay, *On Contradiction,* gives a closely-reasoned and concise summation of those principles which he considers fundamental to Marxism-Leninism, stressing on the one hand their universality, and on the other the particular forms which they must take according to the needs of time and place. For, not to admit the variety of forms which the class struggle must take, would be to limit the universal significance of Communist doctrine—something Mao could never allow.

[From *Selected Works,* II, 17–52]

THE TWO WORLD OUTLOOKS

The dialectical world outlook had already emerged in ancient times both in China and in Europe. But ancient dialectics has something spontaneous and naive about it; being based upon the social and historical conditions of those times, it was not formulated into an adequate theory, hence it could not fully explain the world, and was later supplanted by metaphysics. The famous German philosopher Hegel, who lived from the late eighteenth century to the early nineteenth, made very important contributions to dialectics, but his is idealist dialectics. It was not until Marx and Engels, the great men of action of the proletarian movement, made a synthesis of the positive achievements in the history of human knowledge and, in particular, critically absorbed the rational elements of Hegelian dialectics and created the great theory of dialectical materialism and historical materialism, that a great, unprecedented revolution took place in the history of human knowledge. Later Lenin and Stalin have further developed this great theory. Introduced into China, this theory immediately brought about tremendous changes in the world of Chinese thought.

This dialectical world outlook teaches man chiefly how to observe and analyze skilfully the movement of opposites in various things, and, on the basis of such analysis, to find out the methods of solving the contradictions. Consequently, it is of paramount importance for us to understand concretely the law of contradiction in things.

THE UNIVERSALITY OF CONTRADICTION

For convenience in exposition, I shall deal here first with the universality of contradiction, and then with the particularity of contradiction. Only a brief remark is needed to explain the former, because many people have accepted the universality of contradiction ever since the great creators and continuers of Marxism—Marx, Engels, Lenin, and Stalin—established the materialist-dialectical world outlook and applied materialist dialectics with very great success to many aspects of the analysis of human history and of natural history, to many aspects of changes in society and in nature (as in the Soviet Union); but there are still many comrades, especially the doctrinaires, who are not clear about the problem of the particularity of contradiction. They do not understand that the universality of contradiction resides precisely in the particularity of contradiction. Nor do they understand how very significant it is for our further guidance in revolutionary practice to study the particularity of contradiction in the concrete things confronting us. Therefore, the problem of the particularity of contradiction should be studied with special attention and explained at sufficient length. For this reason, when we analyze the law of contradiction in things, we should first analyze the universality of contradiction, then analyze with special attention the particularity of contradiction, and finally return to the universality of contradiction.

The universality or absoluteness of contradiction has a twofold meaning. One is that contradiction exists in the process of development of all things and the other is that in the process of development of each thing a movement of opposites exists from beginning to end. [pp. 17–19]

Even under the social conditions of the Soviet Union a difference exists between the workers and the peasants; the difference is a contradiction, though, unlike that between labor and capital, it will not become intensified into antagonism or assume the form of class struggle: in the course of socialist construction the workers and the peasants have formed a firm alliance and will gradually solve this contradiction in the process of development from socialism to communism. This is a question of distinction in the character of contradictions, not a matter of the presence or absence of them. Contradiction is universal, absolute, existing in all processes of the development of things, and running through all processes from beginning to end. [p. 21]

THE PARTICULARITY OF CONTRADICTION

It is not only necessary to study the particular contradiction and the quality determined thereby in every great system of forms of motion of matter, but also to study the particular contradiction and the quality of every form of motion of matter at each stage of its long course of development. In all forms of motion, each process of development that is real and not imaginary is qualitatively different. In our study we must emphasise and start from this point.

Qualitatively different contradictions can only be solved by qualitatively different methods. For example: the contradiction between the proletariat and the bourgeoisie is solved by the method of socialist revolution; the contradiction between the great masses of the people and the feudal system is solved by the method of democratic revolution; the contradiction between colonies and imperialism is solved by the method of national revolutionary war; the contradiction between the working class and the peasantry in socialist society is solved by the method of collectivization and mechanization of agriculture; the contradiction within the Communist Party is solved by the method of criticism and self-criticism; the contradiction between society and nature is solved by the method of developing the productive forces. Processes change, old processes and old contradictions disappear, new processes and new contradictions emerge, and the methods of solving contradictions differ accordingly. There is a basic difference between the contradictions solved by the February Revolution and the October Revolution in Russia, as well as between the methods used to solve them. The use of different methods to solve different contradictions is a principle which Marxist-Leninists must strictly observe. The doctrinaires do not observe this principle: they do not understand the differences between the various revolutionary situations, and consequently do not understand that different methods should be used to solve different contradictions; on the contrary, they uniformly adopt a formula which they fancy to be unalterable and inflexibly apply it everywhere, a procedure which can only bring setbacks to the revolution or make a great mess of what could have been done well.

In order to reveal the particularity of contradictions in their totality as well as their interconnection in the process of development of things, that is, to reveal the quality of the process of development of things, we must reveal the particularity of each aspect of the contradiction in the process, otherwise it is impossible to reveal the quality of the process; this is also a matter to which we must pay the utmost attention in our study.

A great thing or event contains many contradictions in the process of its development. For instance, in the process of China's bourgeois-democratic revolution there are the contradiction between the various oppressed classes in Chinese society and imperialism, the contradiction between the great masses of the people and feudalism, the contradiction between the proletariat and the bourgeoisie, the contradiction between the peasantry together with the urban petty bourgeoisie on the one hand, and the bourgeoisie on the other, the contradiction between various reactionary ruling blocs, etc.; the situation is exceedingly complex. Not only do all these contradictions each have their own particularity and cannot be treated uniformly, but the two aspects of every contradiction also have each their own characteristics and cannot be treated uniformly. Not only should we who work for the Chinese revolution understand the particularity of each of the contradictions in the light of their totality, that is, from the interconnection of those contradictions, but we can understand the totality of the contradictions only by a study of each of their aspects. To understand each of the aspects of a contradiction is to understand the definite position each aspect occupies, the concrete form in which it comes into interdependence as well as conflict with its opposite, and the concrete means by which it struggles with its opposite when the two are interdependent and yet contradictory, as well as when the interdependence breaks up. The study of these problems is a matter of the utmost importance. Lenin was expressing this very idea when he said that the most essential thing in Marxism, the living soul of Marxism, is the concrete analysis of concrete conditions.[14] Contrary to Lenin's teaching, our doctrinaires never use their brains to analyze anything concretely; in their writings and speeches they always strike the keynote of the "eight-legged essay" which is void of any content, and have thus brought about in our Party a very bad style in work. [pp. 24–26]

From this it can be seen that in studying the specific nature of any contradiction—contradiction in various forms of motion of matter, contradiction in various forms of motion in every process of development, each aspect of the contradiction in every process of development, contradiction at the various stages of every process of development and each aspect of the contradiction at the various stages of development—in studying the specific nature of all these contradictions, we should be free from any taint of subjective arbitrariness and must make a concrete analysis of them. Apart from a concrete analysis there can be no knowledge of the specific nature of any contradiction. We must all the time bear in mind Lenin's words: the concrete analysis of concrete conditions.

Marx and Engels were the first to supply us with an excellent model of such concrete analysis.

When Marx and Engels applied the law of contradiction in things to the study of the process of social history, they saw the contradiction between the productive forces and the relations of production; they saw the contradiction between the exploiting class and the exploited class, as well as the contradiction produced thereby between the economic foundation and its superstructures, such as politics and ideology; and they saw how these contradictions inevitably lead to different social revolutions in different class societies.

When Marx applied this law to the study of the economic structure of capitalist society, he saw that the basic contradiction of this society is the contradiction between the social character of production and the private character of ownership. It is manifested in the contradiction between the organized character of production in individual enterprises and the unorganized character of production in society as a whole. The class manifestation of this contradiction is the contradiction between the bourgeoisie and the proletariat.

Because of the vastness of the scope of things and the limitlessness of

[14] V. I. Lenin, *Collected Works*, Russian ed. (Moscow, 1950), XXXI, 143.

their development, what in one case is universality is in another changed into particularity. On the other hand, what in one case is particularity is in another changed into universality. The contradiction contained in the capitalist system between the socialization of production and the private ownership of the means of production is something common to all countries where capitalism exists and develops; for capitalism, this constitutes the universality of contradiction. However, this contradiction in capitalism is something pertaining to a certain historical stage in the development of class society in general; as far as the contradiction between the productive forces and the relations of production in class society in general is concerned, this constitutes the particularity of contradiction. But while revealing by analysis the particularity of every contradiction in capitalist society, Marx expounded even more profoundly, more adequately and more completely the universality of the contradiction between the productive forces and the relations of production in class society in general. . . .

When Stalin explained the historical roots of Leninism in his famous work, *The Foundations of Leninism,* he analyzed the international situation in which Leninism was born, together with various contradictions in capitalism which had reached their extreme under the conditions of imperialism, and analyzed how these contradictions made the proletarian revolution a question of immediate action and how they created favorable conditions for a direct onslaught upon capitalism. Besides all these, he analyzed the reasons why Russia became the home of Leninism, how Tsarist Russia represented the focus of all the contradictions of imperialism, and why the Russian proletariat could become the vanguard of the international revolutionary proletariat. In this way, Stalin analyzed the universality of the contradiction in imperialism, showing how Leninism is Marxism of the era of imperialism and the proletarian revolution, and analyzed the particularity of the imperialism of Tsarist Russia in the contradiction of imperialism in general, showing how Russia became the birth-place of the theory and tactics of the proletarian revolution and how in such a particularity is contained the universality of contradiction. This kind of analysis made by Stalin serves us as a model in understanding the particularity and the universality of contradiction and their interconnection. [pp.32–34]

THE PRINCIPAL CONTRADICTION AND THE PRINCIPAL ASPECT OF A CONTRADICTION

As regards the problem of the particularity of contradiction, there are still two sides which must be specially singled out for analysis, that is, the principal contradiction and the principal aspect of a contradiction.

In the process of development of a complex thing, many contradictions exist; among these, one is necessarily the principal contradiction whose existence and development determine or influence the existence and development of other contradictions. [p. 35]

So in studying any process—if it is a complicated process in which more than two contradictions exist—we must do our utmost to discover its principal contradiction. Once the principal contradiction is grasped, any problem can be readily solved. This is the method Marx taught us when he studied capitalist society. When Lenin and Stalin studied imperialism and the general crisis of capitalism, and when they studied Soviet economy, they also taught us this method. [p. 37]

Some people think that this is not the case with certain contradictions. For example: in the contradiction between the productive forces and the relations of production, the productive forces are the principal aspect; in the contradiction between theory and practice, practice is the principal aspect; in the contradiction between the economic foundation and its superstructure, the economic foundation is the principal aspect: and there is no change in their respective positions. This is the view of mechanistic materialism, and not of dialectical materialism. True, the productive forces, practice, and the economic foundation generally manifest themselves in the principal and decisive role; whoever denies this is not a materialist. But under certain conditions, such aspects as the relations of production, theory and the superstructure in turn manifest themselves in the principal and decisive role; this must also be admitted. When the productive forces cannot be developed unless the relations of production are changed, the change in the relations of production plays the principal and decisive role. When, as Lenin put it, "Without a revolutionary theory, there can be no revolutionary movement," [15] the creation and advocacy of the revolutionary theory plays the principal and deci-

---

[15] V. I. Lenin, *What Is To Be Done?*

sive role. When a certain job (this applies to any job) is to be done but there is as yet no directive, method, plan or policy defining how to do it, the directive, method, plan or policy is the principal and decisive factor. When the superstructure (politics, culture and so on), hinders the development of the economic foundation, political and cultural reforms become the principal and decisive factors. In saying this, are we running counter to materialism? No. The reason is that while we recognize that in the development of history as a whole it is material things that determine spiritual things and social existence that determines social consciousness, at the same time we also recognise and must recognise the reaction of spiritual things and social consciousness on social existence, and the reaction of the superstructure on the economic foundation. This is not running counter to materialism; this is precisely avoiding mechanistic materialism and firmly upholding dialectical materialism. [pp. 40–41]

THE IDENTITY AND STRUGGLE OF THE ASPECTS OF A CONTRADICTION

Having understood the problem of the universality and particularity of contradiction, we must proceed to study the problem of the identity and struggle of the aspects of a contradiction.

Identity, unity, coincidence, interpermeation, interpenetration, interdependence (or interdependence for existence), interconnection or cooperation—all these different terms mean the same thing and refer to the following two conditions: first, each of the two aspects of every contradiction in the process of development of a thing finds the presupposition of its existence in the other aspect and both aspects coexist in an entity; second, each of the two contradictory aspects, according to given conditions, tends to transform itself into the other. This is what is meant by identity. [p. 42]

The agrarian revolution we have carried out is already and will be such a process in which the land-owning landlord class becomes a class deprived of its land, while the peasants, once deprived of their land, become small holders of land. The haves and the have-nots, gain and loss, are interconnected because of certain conditions; there is identity of the two sides. Under socialism, the system of the peasants' private ownership will in turn become the public ownership of socialist agriculture; this has already taken place in the Soviet Union and will take place throughout the world. Between private property and public property there is a bridge leading from the one to the other, which in philosophy is called identity, or transformation into each other, or interpermeation.

To consolidate the dictatorship of the proletariat or the people's dictatorship is precisely to prepare the conditions for liquidating such a dictatorship and advancing to the higher stage of abolishing all state systems. To establish and develop the Communist Party is precisely to prepare the condition for abolishing the Communist Party and all party systems. To establish the revolutionary army under the leadership of the Communist Party and to carry on the revolutionary war is precisely to prepare the condition for abolishing war for ever. These contradictory things are at the same time complementary. [p. 45]

THE ROLE OF ANTAGONISM IN CONTRADICTION

"What is antagonism?" is one of the questions concerning the struggle within a contradiction. Our answer is: antagonism is a form of struggle within a contradiction, but not the universal form.

In human history, antagonism between classes exists as a particular manifestation of the struggle within a contradiction. The contradiction between the exploiting class and the exploited class: the two contradictory classes coexist for a long time in one society, be it a slave society, or a feudal or a capitalist society, and struggle with each other; but it is not until the contradiction between the two classes has developed to a certain stage that the two sides adopt the form of open antagonism which develops into a revolution. In a class society, the transformation of peace into war is also like that. [pp. 49–50]

As we have pointed out above, the contradiction between correct ideology and erroneous ideologies within the Communist Party reflects in the Party the class contradictions when classes exist. In the beginning, or with regard to certain matters, such a contradiction need not immediately manifest itself as antagonistic. But with the development of the class struggle, it can also develop and become antagonistic. The history of the Communist Party of the Soviet Union shows us that the contradiction between the correct ideology of Lenin and Stalin and the erroneous ideologies of Trotsky, Bukharin, and others, was in the beginning not yet manifested in an antagonistic form, but subsequently developed into antagonism. A similar case occurred in the history of the Chinese Communist Party. The contradiction between the correct ideology of many of our comrades in the Party and the erroneous ideologies of Ch'en Tu-hsiu, Chang Kuo-t'ao, and others was also in the beginning not manifested in an antagonistic form, but subsequently developed into antagonism. At present the contradiction between the correct ideology and the erroneous ideologies in our Party is not manifested in an antagonistic form and, if comrades who have committed mistakes can correct them, it will not develop into antagonism. Therefore the Party on the one hand must carry on a serious struggle against erroneous ideologies, and on the other hand, must give the comrades who have committed mistakes sufficient opportunity to become aware of them. Under such conditions, struggles pushed to excess are obviously not appropriate. But if those people who have commited mistakes persist in them and increase the gravity of their mistakes, then it is possible that such contradictions will develop into antagonism. [pp. 50–51]

Lenin said: "Antagonism and contradiction are utterly different. Under socialism, antagonism disappears, but contradiction exists." [16] That is to say, antagonism is only a form of struggle within a contradiction but not its universal form; we cannot impose the formula everywhere. [p. 52]

On Practice

Despite its title, which might lead one to expect a discussion of the practical aspects of waging revolution, this essay is actually a highly theoretical discussion of the problem of knowledge and practice in Marxist-Leninist terms. Though not claiming or revealing any originality on Mao's part, it shows again the importance which he attached to the formulation of fundamental philosophical principles as a basis for the preservation of ideological unity. In this case, by emphasizing the inseparability of theory and practice and by condemning any tendency which leaned toward one side or the other, Mao had a formula which could be applied unfailingly to the criticism of opposing policies in any situation. The proper balance between the two was a precarious thing to maintain and only Party leadership could, in the final analysis, judge "objective truth" in such matters. Obedience to it was therefore the only sure means of avoiding the twin heresies of doctrinairism and empiricism.

On Practice, though it deals with a somewhat narrower problem than *On Contradiction*, was actually written before the latter and probably indicates Mao's particular angle of approach to the study of Marxism-Leninism in this period. It has been described as a period of intense Bolshevization or Leninization of the Chinese Communist Party during the years at Yenan, dictated

[16] V. I. Lenin's critical notes on Bukharin's *Economics of the Transitional Period*.

by the necessity of preserving Party orthodoxy against the twofold dangers which arose from collaboration with the Kuomintang and the constant adaptation of policy and strategy to a rapidly changing situation. The official commentary provides some insight into the ideological significance attached to this statement in the context of the times:

"There used to be a group of doctrinaires in the Chinese Communist Party who, disregarding the experience of the Chinese revolution and denying the truth that Marxism is not a dogma but a guide to action, for a long time bluffed people with words and phrases torn out of their context from Marxist works. There was also a group of empiricists who, for a long time clinging to their own fragmentary experience, could neither understand the importance of theory for revolutionary practice nor see the whole of the revolutionary situation, and thus worked blindly, though industriously. The Chinese revolution of 1931–1934 was greatly damaged by the incorrect ideas of these two groups of comrades, particularly by those of the doctrinaires who, wearing the cloak of Marxism, misled large numbers of comrades. This article was written to expose from the viewpoint of Marxist theory of knowledge such subjectivist mistakes in the Party as doctrinairism and empiricism, especially doctrinairism. As its stress is laid on exposing doctrinaire subjectivism which belittles practice, this article is entitled 'On Practice.' These views were originally presented in a lecture at the Anti-Japanese Military and Political College in Yenan." [17]

[From *Selected Works*, I, 283–97]

The Marxists holds that man's social practice alone is the criterion of the truth of his knowledge of the external world. In reality, man's knowledge becomes verified only when, in the process of social practice (in the process of material production, of class struggle, and of scientific experiment), he achieves the anticipated results. If man wants to achieve success in his work, that is, to achieve the anticipated results, he must make his thoughts correspond to the laws of the objective world surrounding him; if they do not correspond, he will fail in practice. If he fails he will derive lessons from his failure, alter his ideas, so as to make them correspond to the laws of the objective world, and thus turn failure into success; this is what is meant by "failure is the mother of success," and "a fall into the pit, a gain in your wit."

The theory of knowledge of dialectical materialism raises practice to the first place, holds that human knowledge cannot be separated the least bit from practice, and repudiates all incorrect theories which deny the im-

[17] *Selected Works*, I, 282.

portance of practice or separate knowledge from practice. Thus Lenin said, "Practice is higher than (theoretical) knowledge because it has not only the virtue of universality, but also the virtue of immediate reality." [18] [pp. 283–84]

Apart from their genius, the reason why Marx, Engels, Lenin, and Stalin could work out their theories is mainly their personal participation in the practice of the contemporary class struggle and scientific experimentation; without this no amount of genius could bring success. The saying "a scholar does not step outside his gate, yet knows all the happenings under the sun" was mere empty talk in the technologically undeveloped old times; and although this saying can be realized in the present age of technological development, yet the people with real firsthand knowledge are those engaged in practice, and only when they have obtained "knowledge" through their practice, and when their knowledge, through the medium of writing and technology, reaches the hands of the "scholar," can the "scholar" know indirectly "the happenings under the sun."

If a man wants to know certain things or certain kinds of things directly, it is only through personal participation in the practical struggle to change reality, to change those things or those kinds of things, that he can come into contact with the phenomena of those things or those kinds of things; and it is only during the practical struggle to change reality, in which he personally participates, that he can disclose the essence of those things or those kinds of things and understand them. [p. 287]

Thus the first step in the process of knowledge is contact with the things of the external world; this belongs to the stage of perception. The second step is a synthesis of the data of perception by making a rearrangement or a reconstruction; this belongs to the stage of conception, judgment, and inference. It is only when the perceptual data are extremely rich (not fragmentary or incomplete) and are in correspondence to reality (not illusory) that we can, on the basis of such data, form valid concepts and carry out correct reasoning.

Here two important points must be emphasized. The first, a point which has been mentioned before, but should be repeated here, is the question of the dependence of rational knowledge upon perceptual knowledge. The person is an idealist who thinks that rational knowledge need not be

[18] V. I. Lenin, *Philosophical Notebooks,* Russian ed. (Moscow, 1947), p. 185.

derived from perceptual knowledge. In the history of philosophy there is the so-called "rationalist" school which admits only the validity of reason, but not the validity of experience, regarding reason alone as reliable and perceptual experience as unreliable; the mistake of this school consists in turning things upside down. The rational is reliable precisely because it has its source in the perceptual, otherwise it would be like water without a source or a tree without roots, something subjective, spontaneous, and unreliable. As to the sequence in the process of knowledge, perceptual experience comes first; we emphasize the significance of social practice in the process of knowledge precisely because social practice alone can give rise to man's knowledge and start him on the acquisition of perceptual experience from the objective world surrounding him. For a person who shuts his eyes, stops his ears, and totally cuts himself off from the objective world, there can be no knowledge to speak of. Knowledge starts with experience—this is the materialism of the theory of knowledge.

The second point is that knowledge has yet to be deepened, the perceptual stage of knowledge has yet to be developed to the rational stage —this is the dialectics of the theory of knowledge.[19] It would be a repetition of the mistake of "empiricism" in history to hold that knowledge can stop at the lower stage of perception and that perceptual knowledge alone is reliable while rational knowledge is not. This theory errs in failing to recognize that, although the data of perception reflect certain real things of the objective world (I am not speaking here of idealist empiricism which limits experience to so-called introspection), yet they are merely fragmentary and superficial, reflecting things incompletely instead of representing their essence. To reflect a thing fully in its totality, to reflect its essence and its inherent laws, it is necessary, through thinking, to build up a system of concepts and theories by subjecting the abundant perceptual data to a process of remodeling and reconstructing—discarding the crude and selecting the refined, eliminating the false and retaining the true, proceeding from one point to another, and going through the outside into the inside; it is necessary to leap from perceptual knowledge to rational knowledge. Knowledge which is such a reconstruction does not become emptier or less reliable; on the contrary, whatever has been

[19] Cf. Lenin, *Philosophical Notebooks,* p. 146: "For the sake of knowing, one must start to know, to study, on the basis of experience and rise from experience to general knowledge."

scientifically reconstructed on the basis of practice in the process of knowledge is something which, as Lenin said, reflects objective things more deeply, more truly, more fully. As against this, the vulgar plodders, respecting experience yet despising theory, cannot take a comprehensive view of the entire objective process, lack clear direction and long-range perspective, and are self-complacent with occasional successes and peep-hole views. Were those persons to direct a revolution, they would lead it up a blind alley.

The dialectical-materialist theory of knowledge is that rational knowledge depends upon perceptual knowledge and perceptual knowledge has yet to be developed into rational knowledge. Neither "rationalism" nor "empiricism" in philosophy recognizes the historical or dialectical nature of knowledge, and although each contains an aspect of truth (here I am referring to materialist rationalism and empiricism, not to idealist rationalism and empiricism), both are erroneous in the theory of knowledge as a whole. The dialectical-materialist process of knowledge from the perceptual to the rational applies to a minor process of knowledge (e.g., knowing a single thing or task) as well as to a major one (e.g., knowing a whole society or a revolution).

But the process of knowledge does not end here. The statement that the dialectical-materialist process of knowledge stops at rational knowledge, covers only half the problem. And so far as Marxist philosophy is concerned, it covers only the half that is not particularly important. What Marxist philosophy regards as the most important problem does not lie in understanding the laws of the objective world and thereby becoming capable of explaining it, but in actively changing the world by applying the knowledge of its objective laws. From the Marxist viewpoint, theory is important, and its importance is fully shown in Lenin's statement: "Without a revolutionary theory there can be no revolutionary movement." [20] But Marxism emphasizes the importance of theory precisely and only because it can guide action. If we have a correct theory, but merely prate about it, pigeon-hole it, and do not put it into practice, then that theory, however good, has no significance.

Knowledge starts with practice, reaches the theoretical plane via practice, and then has to return to practice. The active function of knowledge

[20] V. I. Lenin, *What Is To Be Done?*

not only manifests itself in the active leap from perceptual knowledge to rational knowledge, but also—and this is the more important—in the leap from rational knowledge to revolutionary practice. The knowledge which enables us to grasp the laws of the world must be redirected to the practice of changing the world, that is, it must again be applied in the practice of production, in the practice of the revolutionary class struggle and revolutionary national struggle, as well as in the practice of scientific experimentation. This is the process of testing and developing theory, the continuation of the whole process of knowledge. [pp. 290–93]

But generally speaking, whether in the practice of changing nature or of changing society, people's original ideas, theories, plans, or programs are seldom realized without any change whatever. This is because people engaged in changing reality often suffer from many limitations: they are limited not only by the scientific and technological conditions, but also by the degree of development and revelation of the objective process itself (by the fact that the aspects and essence of the objective process have not yet been fully disclosed). In such a situation, ideas, theories, plans, or programs are often altered partially and sometimes even wholly along with the discovery of unforeseen circumstances during practice. That is to say, it does happen that the original ideas, theories, plans, or programs fail partially or wholly to correspond to reality and are partially or entirely incorrect. In many instances, failures have to be repeated several times before erroneous knowledge can be rectified and made to correspond to the laws of the objective process, so that subjective things can be transformed into objective things, viz., the anticipated results can be achieved in practice. But in any case, at such a point, the process of man's knowledge of a certain objective process at a certain stage of its development is regarded as completed. . . .

It often happens, however, that ideas lag behind actual events; this is because man's knowledge is limited by a great many social conditions. We oppose the die-hards in the revolutionary ranks whose ideas, failing to advance with the changing objective circumstances, manifest themselves historically as "right" opportunism. These people do not see that the struggles arising from contradictions have already pushed the objective process forward, while their knowledge has stopped at the old stage. This characterizes the ideas of all die-hards. With their ideas divorced from social practice, they cannot serve to guide the chariot-wheels of society; they can only trail behind the chariot grumbling that it goes too fast, and endeavor to drag it back and make it go in the opposite direction.

We also oppose the phrase-mongering of the "leftists." Their ideas are ahead of a given stage of development of the objective process: some of them regard their fantasies as truth; others, straining to realize at present an ideal which can only be realized in the future, divorce themselves from the practice of the majority of the people at the moment and from the realities of the day and show themselves as adventurist in their actions. Idealism and mechanistic materialism, opportunism, and adventurism, are all characterized by a breach between the subjective and the objective, by the separation of knowledge from practice. The Marxist-Leninist theory of knowledge, which is distinguished by its emphasis on social practice as the criterion of scientific truth, cannot but resolutely oppose these incorrect ideologies. The Marxist recognizes that in the absolute, total process of the development of the universe, the development of each concrete process is relative; hence, in the great stream of absolute truth, man's knowledge of the concrete process at each given stage of development is only relatively true. The sum total of innumerable relative truths is the absolute truth.[21] [pp. 294–96]

To discover truth through practice, and through practice to verify and develop truth. To start from perceptual knowledge and actively develop it into rational knowledge, and then, starting from rational knowledge, actively direct revolutionary practice so as to remold the subjective and the objective world. Practice, knowledge, more practice, more knowledge; the cyclical repetition of this pattern to infinity, and with each cycle, the elevation of the content of practice and knowledge to a higher level. Such is the whole of the dialectical materialist theory of knowledge, and such is the dialectical materialist theory of the unity of knowing and doing. July, 1937 [p. 297]

LIU SHAO-CH'I
How To Be a Good Communist

Liu Shao-ch'i (1905–   ), a veteran Communist who joined the Party in 1921, the year of its founding, has been one of Mao's closest co-workers and speaks

[21] Cf. V. I. Lenin, *Materialism and Empirio-Criticism*, Chapter II, Section 5.

as a theoretician with an authority second only to Mao. When the People's Republic was established in 1949, he became vice-chairman of the Central People's Government, and after Mao relinquished the chairmanship in 1959, Liu succeeded to it.

How To Be a Good Communist is a basic text of indoctrination for party members, delivered first as a series of lectures in July, 1939, at the Institute of Marxism-Leninism in Yenan. It represents one more aspect of the campaign for tightening Party discipline and strengthening orthodoxy which was pressed in the late '30s and early '40s in order to insure the proper assimilation of new recruits, growing rapidly in number, and the maintenance of Party unity along orthodox Leninist lines.

The original Chinese title of this work is literally *The Cultivation of Communist Party Members*. Both the title and Liu's frequent reference to earlier Chinese concepts of self-cultivation suggest a link with Chinese tradition, though perhaps only a tenuous one. In any case, the crucial factor in Communist cultivation is Party authority and guidance. Though the Party does not conceal its readiness to apply the most stringent sanctions against recalcitrance and deviation, it is highly conscious of the limits to which coercion may be employed in maintaining order and discipline. Wherever possible, it encourages Party members to discipline themselves, and prefers persuasion quietly backed by overwhelming force to outright dictation and naked oppression. A further inducement for Party cadres is the hope of joining the new elite. The prospect of rising to some power and authority in the system encourages them to stomach indoctrination and discipline which otherwise might be quite unpalatable for those who were merely subject to it.

In this, again, there is nothing unique or peculiar to Chinese Communism, but the extension of these methods to the nation as a whole has been a significant element in maintaining ideological unity under the Communist regime.

[From *How To Be a Good Communist*, pp. 15–34]

Comrades! In order to become the most faithful and best pupils of Marx, Engels, Lenin, and Stalin, we need to carry on cultivation in all aspects in the course of the long and great revolutionary struggle of the proletariat and the masses of the people. We need to carry on cultivation in the theories of Marxism-Leninism and in applying such theories in practice; cultivation in revolutionary strategy and tactics; cultivation in studying and dealing with various problems according to the standpoint and methods of Marxism-Leninism; cultivation in ideology and moral character; cultivation in Party unity, inner-Party struggle, and discipline; cultivation in hard work and in the style of work; cultivation in being skillful in dealing with different kinds of people and in associating with the masses of the people; and cultivation in various kinds of scientific knowledge, etc. We are all Communist Party members and so we have a general cultivation in common. But there exists a wide discrepancy today between our Party members. Wide discrepancy exists among us in the level of political consciousness, in work, in position, in cultural level, in experience of struggle, and in social origin. Therefore, in addition to cultivation in general we also need special cultivation for different groups and for individual comrades.

Accordingly, there should be different kinds of methods and forms of cultivation. For example, many of our comrades keep a diary in order to have a daily check on their work and thoughts or they write down on small posters their personal defects and what they hope to achieve and paste them up where they work or live, together with the photographs of persons they look up to, and ask comrades for criticism and supervision. In ancient China, there were many methods of cultivation. There was Tseng Tze [22] who said: "I reflect on myself three times a day." The *Book of Odes* has it that one should cultivate oneself "as a lapidary cuts and files, carves and polishes." Another method was "to examine oneself by self-reflection" and to "write down some mottoes on the right hand side of one's desk" or "on one's girdle" as daily reminders of rules of personal conduct. The Chinese scholars of the Confucian school had a number of methods for the cultivation of their body and mind. Every religion has various methods and forms of cultivation of its own. The "investigation of things, the extension of knowledge, sincerity of thought, the rectification of the heart, the cultivation of the person, the regulation of the family, the ordering well of the state and the making tranquil of the whole kingdom" as set forth in *The Great Learning* [23] also means the same. All this shows that in achieving one's progress one must make serious and energetic efforts to carry on self-cultivation and study. However, many of these methods and forms cannot be adopted by us because most of them are idealistic, formalistic, abstract, and divorced from social practice. These scholars and religious believers exaggerate the function of subjective initiative, thinking that so long as they keep their general "good intentions" and are devoted

[22] A disciple of Confucius.
[23] *The Great Learning* is said to be "a Book handed down by the Confucian school, which forms the gate by which beginners enter into virtue."

to silent prayer they will be able to change the existing state of affairs, change society, and change themselves under conditions separated from social and revolutionary practice. This is, of course, absurd. We cannot cultivate ourselves in this way. We are materialists and our cultivation cannot be separated from practice.

What is important to us is that we must not under any circumstances isolate ourselves from the revolutionary struggles of different kinds of people and in different forms at a given moment and that we must, moreover, sum up historical revolutionary experience and learn humbly from this and put it into practice. That is to say, we must undertake self-cultivation and steel ourselves in the course of our own practice, basing ourselves on the experiences of past revolutionary practice, on the present concrete situation and on new experiences. Our self-cultivation and steeling are for no other purpose than that of revolutionary practice. That is to say, we must modestly try to understand the standpoint, the method and the spirit of Marxism-Leninism, and understand how Marx, Engels, Lenin and Stalin dealt with people. And having understood these, we should immediately apply them to our own practice, i.e., in our own lives, words, deeds, and work. Moreover, we should stick to them and unreservedly correct and purge everything in our ideology that runs counter to them, thereby strengthening our own proletarian and Communist ideology and qualities. That is to say, we must modestly listen to the opinions and criticisms of our comrades and of the masses, carefully study the practical problems in our lives and in our work and carefully sum up our experiences and the lessons we have learned so as to find an orientation for our own work. In addition, on the basis of all these, we must judge whether we have a correct understanding of Marxism-Leninism and whether we have correctly applied the method of Marxism-Leninism, found out our own shortcomings and mistakes and corrected them. At the same time, we must find out in what respects specific conclusions of Marxism-Leninism need to be supplemented, enriched and developed on the basis of well-digested new experiences. That is to say, we must combine the universal truth of Marxism-Leninism with the concrete practice of the revolution.

These should be the methods of self-cultivation of us Communist Party members. That is to say, we must use the methods of Marxism-Leninism to cultivate ourselves. This kind of cultivation is entirely different from other kinds of cultivation which are idealistic and are divorced from social practice.

In this connection, we cannot but oppose certain idle talk and mechanicalism on the question of cultivation and steeling.

First of all, we must oppose and resolutely eliminate one of the biggest evils bequeathed to us by the education and learning in the old society— the separation of theory from practice. In the course of education and study in the old society many people thought that it was unnecessary or even impossible to act upon what they had learned. Despite the fact that they read over and over again books by ancient sages they did things the sages would have been loath to do. Despite the fact that in everything they wrote or said they preached righteousness and morality they acted like out-and-out robbers and harlots in everything they did. Some "high-ranking officials" issued orders for the reading of the *Four Books* and the *Five Classics*,[24] yet in their everyday administrative work they ruthlessly extorted exorbitant requisitions, ran amuck with corruption and killing, and did everything against righteousness and morality. Some people read the *Three People's Principles* over and over again and could recite the *Will of Dr. Sun Yat-sen*, yet they oppressed the people, opposed the nations who treated us on an equal footing, and went so far as to compromise with or surrender to the national enemy. Once a scholar of the old school told me himself that the only maxim of Confucius that he could observe was: "To him food can never be too dainty; minced meat can never be too fine," adding that all the rest of the teachings of Confucius he could not observe and had never proposed to observe. Then why did they still want to carry on educational work and study the teachings of the sages? Apart from utilizing them for window-dressing purposes, their objects were: 1) to make use of these teachings to oppress the exploited and to make use of righteousness and morality for the purpose of hoodwinking and suppressing the culturally backward people; 2) to attempt thereby to secure better government jobs, make money and achieve fame, and reflect credit on their parents. Apart from these objects, their actions were not restricted by the sages' teachings. This was the attitude and return of the "men of letters" and "scholars" of the old society to the

---

[24] The *Four Books* and *Five Classics* are nine ancient Chinese classics of philosophy, history, poetry, etc., of the Confucian Canon.

sages they "worshiped." Of course we Communist Party members cannot adopt such an attitude in studying Marxism-Leninism and the excellent and useful teachings bequeathed to us by our ancient sages. We must live up to what we say. We are honest and pure and we cannot deceive ourselves, the people, or our forefathers. This is an outstanding characteristic as well as a great merit of us Communist Party members. [pp. 15–18]

What is the most fundamental and common duty of us Communist Party members? As everybody knows, it is to establish Communism, to transform the present world into a Communist world. Is a Communist world good or not? We all know that it is very good. In such a world there will be no exploiters, oppressors, landlords, capitalists, imperialists, or fascists. There will be no oppressed and exploited people, no darkness, ignorance, backwardness, etc. In such a society all human beings will become unselfish and intelligent Communists with a high level of culture and technique. The spirit of mutual assistance and mutual love will prevail among mankind. There will be no such irrational things as mutual deception, mutual antagonism, mutual slaughter and war, etc. Such a society will, of course, be the best, the most beautiful, and the most advanced society in the history of mankind. Who will say that such a society is not good? Here the question arises: Can Communist society be brought about? Our answer is "yes." About this the whole theory of Marxism-Leninism offers a scientific explanation that leaves no room for doubt. It further explains that as the ultimate result of the class struggle of mankind, such a society will inevitably be brought about. The victory of Socialism in the U.S.S.R. has also given us factual proof. Our duty is, therefore, to bring about at an early date this Communist society, the realization of which is inevitable in the history of mankind.

This is one aspect. This is our ideal.

But we should understand the other aspect, that is, in spite of the fact that Communism can and must be realized it is still confronted by powerful enemies that must be thoroughly and finally defeated in every respect before Communism can be realized. Thus, the cause of Communism is a long, bitter, arduous but victorious process of struggle. Without such a struggle there can be no Communism. [p. 24]

Comrades! If you only possess great and lofty ideals but not the spirit of "searching for the truth from concrete facts" and do not carry on genuinely practical work, you are not a good Communist Party member. You can only be a dreamer, a prattler, or a pedant. If on the contrary, you only do practical work but do not possess the great and lofty ideals of Communism, you are not a good Communist, but a common careerist. A good Communist Party member is one who combines the great and lofty ideals of Communism with practical work and the spirit of searching for the truth from concrete facts.

The Communist ideal is beautiful while the existing capitalist world is ugly. It is precisely because of its ugliness that the overwhelming majority of the people want to change it and cannot but change it. In changing the world we cannot divorce ourselves from reality, or disregard reality; nor can we escape from reality or surrender to the ugly reality. We must adapt ourselves to reality, understand reality, seek to live and develop in reality, struggle against the ugly reality and transform reality in order to realize our ideals. [pp. 29–30]

At all times and on all questions, a Communist Party member should take into account the interests of the Party as a whole, and place the Party's interests above his personal problems and interests. It is the highest principle of our Party members that the Party's interests are supreme. [p. 31]

If a Party member has only the interests and aims of the Party and Communism in his ideology, if he has no personal aims and considerations independent of the Party's interests, and if he is really unbiased and unselfish, then he will be capable of the following:

1. He will be capable of possessing very good Communist ethics. Because he has a firm outlook he "can both love and hate people." He can show loyalty to and ardent love for all his comrades, revolutionaries, and working people, help them unconditionally, treat them with equality, and never harm any one of them for the sake of his own interests. He can deal with them in a "faithful and forgiving" spirit and "put himself in the position of others." He can consider others' problems from their points of view and be considerate to them. "He will never do to others anything he would not like others to do to him." He can deal with the most vicious enemies of mankind in a most resolute manner and conduct a persistent struggle against the enemy for the purpose of defending the interests of the Party, the class, and the emancipation of mankind. As the Chinese saying goes: "He will worry long before the rest of the world begins to

worry and he will rejoice only after the rest of the world has rejoiced." Both in the Party and among the people he will be the first to suffer hardship and the last to enjoy himself. He never minds whether his conditions are better or worse than others, but he does mind as to whether he has done more revolutionary work than others, or whether he has fought harder. In times of adversity, he will stand out courageously and unflinchingly, and in the face of difficulties he will demonstrate the greatest sense of responsibility. Therefore, he is capable of possessing the greatest firmness and moral courage to resist corruption by riches or honors, to resist tendencies to vacillate in spite of poverty and lowly status, and to refuse to yield in spite of threats or force.

2. He will also be capable of possessing the greatest courage. Since he is free from any selfishness whatever and has never done "anything against his conscience," he can expose his mistakes and shortcomings and boldly correct them in the same way as the sun and the moon emerge bright and full following a brief eclipse. He is "courageous because his is a just cause." He is never afraid of truth. He courageously upholds truth, expounds truth to others, and fights for truth. Even if it is temporarily to his disadvantage to do so, even if he will be subjected to various attacks for the sake of upholding truth, even if the opposition and rebuff of the great majority of the people forces him into temporary isolation (glorious isolation) and even if on this account his life may be endangered he will still be able to stem the tide and uphold truth and will never resign himself to drifting with the tide. So far as he himself is concerned, he has nothing to fear.

3. He will be best capable of acquiring the theory and method of Marxism-Leninism, viewing problems and perceiving the real nature of the situation keenly and aptly. Because he has a firm and clear-cut class standpoint, he is free from personal worries and personal desires which may blur or distort his observation of things and understanding of truth. He has an objective attitude. He tests all theories, truths, and falsehoods in the course of revolutionary practice and is no respecter of persons.

4. He will also be capable of being the most sincere, most candid, and happiest of men. Since he has no selfish desires and since he has nothing to conceal from the Party, "there is nothing which he is afraid of telling others" as the Chinese saying goes. Apart from the interests of the Party

and of the revolution, he has no personal losses or gains or other things to worry about. He can "look after himself when he is on his own." He takes care not to do wrong things when he works independently and without supervision and when there is ample opportunity for him to do all kinds of wrong things. His work will be found in no way incompatible with the Party's interests no matter how many years later it is reviewed. He does not fear criticism from others and he can courageously and sincerely criticize others. That is why he can be sincere, candid and happy.

5. He will be capable of possessing the highest self-respect and self-esteem. For the interests of the Party and of the revolution, he can also be the most lenient, most tolerant, and most ready to compromise, and he will even endure, if necessary, various forms of humiliation and injustice without feeling hurt or bearing grudges. As he has no personal aims or designs, he has no need to flatter others and does not want others to flatter him, either. He has no personal favors to ask of others, so he has no need to humble himself in order to ask help from others. For the interests of the Party and the revolution he can also take care of himself, protect his life and health, raise his theoretical level and enhance his ability. But if for the sake of certain important aims of the Party and of the revolution he is required to endure insults, shoulder heavy burdens and do work which he is reluctant to do, he will take up the most difficult and important work without the slightest hesitation and will not pass the buck.

A Communist Party member should possess all the greatest and noblest virtues of mankind. He should also possess the strict and clear-cut standpoint of the Party and of the proletariat (that is, Party spirit and class character). Our ethics are great precisely because they are the ethics of Communism and of the proletariat. Such ethics are not built upon the backward basis of safeguarding the interests of individuals or a small number of exploiters. They are built, on the contrary, upon the progressive basis of the interests of the proletariat, of the ultimate emancipation of mankind as a whole, of saving the world from destruction and of building a happy and beautiful Communist world. [pp. 32–34]

On Inner-Party Struggle

This essay, delivered by Liu Shao-ch'i as a series of lectures to a Party school in July, 1941, is a kind of sequel to *How To Be a Good Communist* in the series of basic indoctrination texts used for tightening Party organization and morale during the reform campaigns of the early '40s. Where the earlier work focused upon the individual Party member and his self-discipline, attention here is more on the relations among Party members and their conduct within the organization. It is a question then of inner struggle for self-purification of the Party, not of outward struggle for supremacy over others.

The tremendous dynamism of Chinese Communism, especially in this early period, owes no less to its concept of struggle both within and without the Party than to its messianic promises for the future. As a means of keeping Party members in a constant state of alertness, sensitive to the larger interests of the Party rather than to their own, and as a method for overcoming the traditional weakness of hierarchical, bureaucratic organizations—factionalism and favoritism—this kind of ceaseless internal struggle has probably been highly effective. One of its most essential Leninist features is the insistence upon differences in principle as the only valid issues for such struggles. This emphasis on the precise definition of principle and uncompromising adherence to it may seem quite un-Chinese, if we accept the stereotype of the Chinese as having a traditional distaste for rigid dogma and doctrine. Actually, however, Communist principles are far from immutable, and here, as in so many other instances, the Party leadership retains considerable freedom to reinterpret and redefine as it deems necessary.

[From *On Inner-Party Struggle*, pp. 2–69]

INTRODUCTORY REMARKS

Right from the day of its birth, our Party has never for a single moment lived in any environment but that of serious struggle. The Party and the proletariat have constantly lived inside the encirclement of various nonproletarian classes—the big bourgeoisie, the petty bourgeoisie, the peasantry, and even the remnants of feudal forces. All these classes, when they are struggling against the proletariat or when they are cooperating with it, utilize the unstable elements within the Party and the proletariat to penetrate into the heart of the Party and the proletariat and constantly influence the Party and the proletariat in ideology, in living habits, in theory and in action. This is the origin of all kinds of erroneous and undesirable tendencies within the Party. It is the social basis of all kinds of opportunism within the Party, and it is also the source of inner-Party struggles.

Inner-Party struggles are a reflection of the class struggles outside the Party.

From the very day of its inception, our Party has struggled not only against the enemies outside the Party but also against all kinds of hostile and nonproletarian influences inside the Party. These two kinds of strug-

gle are different, but both are necessary and have a common class substance. If our Party did not carry on the latter type of struggle, if it did
not struggle constantly within the Party against all undesirable tendencies,
if it did not constantly purge the Party of every type of nonproletarian
ideology and overcome both "left" and "right" opportunism, then such
nonproletarian ideology and such "left" and "right" opportunism might
gain ground in the Party and influence or even dominate our Party. This
would make it impossible for the Party to consolidate and develop itself or to preserve its independence. This would endanger the Party and
lead to its degeneration. Such nonproletarian ideology and "left" or
"right" opportunism can corrupt our Party, or certain sections of it, and
can even transform the character of our Party or sections of it into that of a
nonproletarian organization. For example, it was in this manner that
the Social-Democratic parties in Europe were corrupted by bourgeois
ideology and transformed into political parties of a bourgeois type, thus
becoming the main social pillars of the bourgeoisie.

Therefore, such inner-Party struggle is absolutely necessary and cannot
be avoided. Any idea of trying to avoid inner-Party struggle, or of refraining from criticizing others' mistakes so that they will not criticize
one's own errors, is totally wrong.

Inner-Party struggles consist principally of ideological struggles. Their
content is made up of the divergencies and antagonisms arising in matters
of ideology and principle. The divergencies and antagonisms among our
comrades on matters of ideology and principle can develop into political
splits within the Party, and, under certain circumstances, even into inevitable organizational splits; but, in character and content, such divergencies and antagonisms are basically ideological struggles.

Consequently, any inner-Party struggle not involving divergencies in
matters of ideology and principle and any conflict among Party members
not based on divergencies in matters of principle is a type of unprincipled struggle, a struggle without content. This kind of struggle without principle or content is utterly unnecessary within the Party. It is
detrimental and not beneficial to the Party. Every Party member should
strictly avoid such struggles. [pp. 2–4]

Comrade Stalin said:

The question here is that contradictions can be overcome only by means of
struggle for this or that principle, for defining the goal of this or that struggle,

for choosing this or that method of struggle that may lead to the goal. We can and we must come to agreement with those within the Party who differ with us on questions of current policy, on questions of a purely practical character. But if these questions involve differences over principle, then no agreement, no "middle" line can save the cause. There is and there can be no "middle" line on questions of principle. The work of the Party must be based either on these or those principles. The "middle" line on questions of principle is a "line" that muddles up one's head, a "line" that covers up differences, a "line" of ideological degeneration of the Party, a "line" of ideological death of the Party. It is not our policy to pursue such a "middle" line. It is the policy of a party that is declining and degenerating from day to day. Such a policy cannot but transform the Party into an empty bureaucratic organ, standing isolated from the working people and becoming a puppet unable to do anything. Such a road cannot be our road.

He added:

Our Party has been strengthened on the basis of overcoming the contradictions within the Party.

This explains the essential nature of inner-Party struggle. [p. 5]

Many comrades did not understand that our inner-Party struggle is a struggle over principle, a struggle for this or that principle, for defining the goal of this or that struggle, for choosing this or that method of struggle that may lead to the goal.

These comrades did not understand that on questions of current policy, on questions of purely practical character, we can and must come to agreement with those within the Party who differ with us. They did not know or understand that on issues involving principle, on questions of defining the goal of our struggles and of choosing the methods of struggle needed to reach such goal they should wage an uncompromising struggle against those in the Party who hold divergent opinions; but on questions of current policy, on questions of a purely practical character, they should come to agreement with those within the Party who hold divergent opinions instead of carrying on an irreconcilable struggle against them, so long as such questions do not involve any difference over principle. [p. 17]

HOW TO CONDUCT INNER-PARTY STRUGGLE

Comrades! Now the question is very clear. It is how to conduct inner-Party struggle correctly and appropriately.

On this question, the Communist Parties of the U.S.S.R. and many other countries have much experience and so has the Chinese Party. Lenin and Stalin have issued many instructions and so has the Central Committee of our Party. Our comrades must make a careful study of these experiences and instructions, which will also be discussed when we come to the question of Party-building. Today I will not touch upon them. I will bring up for the reference of our comrades only the following points, on the basis of the experience of the inner-Party struggle of the Chinese Party.

First of all, comrades must understand that inner-Party struggle is a matter of the greatest seriousness and responsibility. We must conduct it with the strictest and most responsible attitude and should never conduct it carelessly. In carrying out inner-Party struggle we must first fully adopt the correct stand of the Party, the unselfish stand of serving the interests of the Party, of doing better work, and of helping other comrades to correct their mistakes and to gain a better understanding of the problems. We ourselves must be clear about the facts and problems by making a systematic investigation and study. At the same time, we must carry on systematic, well-prepared, and well-led inner-Party struggles.

Comrades must understand that only by first taking the correct stand oneself can one rectify the incorrect stand of others. Only by behaving properly oneself can one correct the misbehavior of others. The old saying has it: "One must first correct oneself before one can correct others." [pp. 55–56]

Secondly, . . . In conducting inner-Party struggle comrades must try their best to assume a sincere, frank, and positive educational attitude in order to achieve unity in ideology and principle. Only in cases where we have no alternative, when it is deemed imperative, may we adopt militant forms of struggle and apply organizational measures. All Party organizations, within appropriate limits, have full right to draw organizational conclusions in regard to any Party member who persists in his errors. The application of Party disciplinary measures and the adoption of organizational measures are entirely necessary under certain circumstances. Such measures, however, cannot be used casually or indiscriminately. Party discipline cannot be upheld simply by the excessive punishment of comrades by Party organizations. The upholding of Party discipline and Party unity does not in the main depend on the punishment of comrades (if they have to be upheld in such a manner it signifies a crisis in the Party), but rather on the actual unity of the Party in ideology and principle, and on the consciousness of the vast majority of the Party members. When we are eventually fully clear regarding ideology and principle, it is very easy for us to draw organizational conclusions, if necessary. It does not take us a minute to expel Party members or announce voluntary withdrawal from the Party. [pp. 58–59]

Thirdly, criticisms directed against Party organizations or against comrades and their work must be appropriate and well-regulated. Bolshevik self-criticism is conducted according to the Bolshevik yardstick. Excessive criticism, the exaggeration of others' errors, and indiscriminate name-calling are all incorrect. The case is not that the more bitter the inner-Party struggle, the better; but that inner-Party struggle should be conducted within proper limits and that appropriateness should be observed. Both over-shooting the target or falling short of it are undesirable. [p. 60]

Fourthly, the holding of struggle meetings, either inside or outside the Party, should in general be stopped. The various defects and errors should be pointed out in the course of summing up and reviewing work. We should first deal with "the case" and then with "the person." We must first make clear the facts, the points at issue, the nature, the seriousness, and the cause of the errors and defects, and only then point out who are responsible for these defects and errors, and whose is the major responsibility and whose is the minor responsibility. [p. 61]

Fifthly, every opportunity to appeal must be given to comrades who have been criticized or punished. As a rule, a comrade should be personally notified of all records or organizational conclusions that may be made about him, and these should be made in his presence. If he does not agree, then after discussion, the case may be referred to a higher authority. (In the case of anyone who expresses dissatisfaction after having been punished the Party organization concerned must refer the case to a higher authority even if the comrade himself does not want to make an appeal.) No Party organization can prevent any comrade who has been punished from appealing to a higher authority. No Party member can be deprived of his right to appeal. No Party organization can withhold any appeal. [p. 62]

On questions of ideology or principle, if agreement cannot be finally reached within the Party organization after discussion, the matter may be settled by a majority decision. After that, the minority who still hold different opinions may have the right to reserve their opinions on condition that they absolutely abide by the decision of the majority in respect to organizational matters and in their activities. [p. 63]

Sixthly, a clear line should be drawn and a proper link should be established between struggles waged inside the Party and those waged outside the Party. [p. 63]

Seventhly, in order to prevent unprincipled disputes within the Party, it is necessary to lay down the following measures:

1. Party members who disagree with the Party's leading body or any Party organization should submit their views and criticisms to the appropriate Party organization and should not talk about it casually among the masses.

2. Party members who disagree with other Party members, or certain responsible Party members, may criticize them in their presence or in certain specific Party organizations and should not talk about it casually.

3. Party members or Party committees of a lower level who disagree with a Party committee of a higher level, may bring the issue to the Party committee of a higher level, or ask it to call a meeting to study the matter, or should refer the matter to a Party committee of a still higher level, but they should not talk about it casually or inform Party committees of a still lower level about the matter.

4. When Party members discover any other Party member doing something wrong and acting in a manner detrimental to the interests of the Party they must report such activities to the appropriate Party organization and should not attempt to cover up the matter or attempt to mutually shield each other.

5. Party members should promote an upright style of work and oppose anything of a deceitful nature, oppose any kind of deceitful talk and actions, and should severely condemn all those who indulge in idle talk, gossiping, prying into others' secrets, and the spreading of rumors. The leading bodies of the Party must from time to time issue instructions forbidding Party members to talk about certain specific matters.

6. The leading bodies at all levels must from time to time summon those comrades who indulge in idle talk and unprincipled disputes and talk with them, correct them and warn them, or subject them to discipline in other ways.

7. Party committees at all levels must respect the opinions set forth by Party members. They should frequently convene meetings to discuss questions and review their work, and provide Party members with ample opportunity to express their opinions.

Unprincipled disputes should in general be forbidden and no judgment should be passed on them, because it is impossible to judge who is right and who is wrong in such unprincipled disputes. [pp. 64–66]

All in all, inner-Party struggle is fundamentally a form of struggle and controversy over ideology and principles. Inside the Party everything must submit to reason, everything must be reasoned out, and everything must have some reason for it, otherwise it will not do. We can do anything without difficulty if we have reasoned it out.

Inside the Party we must cultivate the practice of submitting to reason. The yardstick for determining whether this or that reason is sound is: the interests of the Party and the interests of the proletarian struggle; the subordination of the interests of the part to those of the whole, and the subordination of the immediate interests to long-range interests. All reasons and viewpoints are sound when they are beneficial to the interests of the Party, to the interests of the proletarian struggle, to the long-range interests of the Party as a whole, and to the long-range interests of the proletarian struggle as a whole, otherwise they are not sound. Any struggle that does not submit to reason or that has no reason for it is an unprincipled struggle. [pp. 67–68]

Everything must submit to reason! It would not do if it didn't! It would not do either if we reason incorrectly! It would be even more undesirable if we indulge in empty talk! Of course this is a rather difficult job. But only in this way can we become qualified as Bolsheviks. [p. 69]

MAO TSE-TUNG
Combat Liberalism

If to Liu Shao-ch'i the essence of Marxism-Leninism lay in "principled struggle," to Mao Tse-tung the essence of liberalism lay in indifference to principle. The latter he sees not as a political philosophy but as the want of one, a moral infection which arises from bourgeois individualism and produces selfishness, self-indulgence, slackness, a noncommittal attitude, avoidance of struggle, and a desire for peace-at-any-price. In this respect his views resemble those of Chiang Kai-shek in *China's Destiny* (Mao's piece was actually written earlier, in September, 1937), but they represent a much more severe and sweeping critique. Missing is Chiang's recognition that not all of Western liberalism conformed to this caricature of its weaknesses.

Ironically, Mao's position was enunciated during the early phase of the second United Front period. No doubt one of his purposes was to insure that Party members would not be contaminated and corrupted in the midst of collaboration with Westernized "liberals."

[From *Selected Works*, II, 74–76]

We advocate an active ideological struggle, because it is the weapon for achieving solidarity within the Party and the revolutionary organizations and making them fit to fight. Every Communist and revolutionary should take up this weapon.

But liberalism negates ideological struggle and advocates unprincipled peace, with the result that a decadent, philistine style in work has appeared and certain units and individuals in the Party and the revolutionary organizations have begun to degenerate politically.

Liberalism manifests itself in various ways.

Although the person concerned is clearly known to be in the wrong, yet because he is an old acquaintance, a fellow townsman, a school-friend, a bosom companion, a loved one, an old colleague, or a former subordinate, one does not argue with him on the basis of principle but lets things slide in order to maintain peace and friendship. Or one touches lightly upon the matter without finding a thorough solution, so as to maintain harmony all around. As a result, harm is done to the organization as well as to the individual concerned. This is the first type of liberalism.

To indulge in irresponsible criticism in private, without making positive suggestions to the organization. To say nothing to people's faces, but to gossip behind their backs; or to say nothing at a meeting, but gossip after it. Not to care for the principle of collective life but only for unrestrained self-indulgence. This is the second type.

Things of no personal concern are put on the shelf; the less said the better about things that are clearly known to be wrong; to be cautious in order to save one's own skin, and anxious only to avoid reprimands. This is the third type.

To disobey orders and place personal opinions above everything. To demand special dispensation from the organization, but to reject its discipline. This is the fourth type.

To engage in struggles and disputes against incorrect views, not for the sake of solidarity, progress, or improving the work, but for personal attacks, letting off steam, venting personal grievances, or seeking revenge. This is the fifth type.

Not to dispute incorrect opinions on hearing them, and not even to report counter-revolutionary opinions on hearing them, but to tolerate them calmly as if nothing had happened. This is the sixth type.

Not to engage in propaganda and agitation, to make speeches or carry on investigations and inquiries among the masses, but to leave the masses alone, without any concern for their weal and woe; to forget that one is a Communist, and to behave as if a Communist were merely an ordinary person. This is the seventh type.

Not to feel indignant at actions detrimental to the interests of the masses, not to dissuade or to stop the person responsible for them or to explain things to him, but to allow him to continue. This is the eighth type.

To work half-heartedly without any definite plan or direction; to work perfunctorily and let things drift. "So long as I remain a bonze, I go on tolling the bell." This is the ninth type.

To regard oneself as having performed meritorious service in the revolution and to put on the airs of a veteran; to be incapable of doing great things, yet to disdain minor tasks; to be careless in work and slack in study. This is the tenth type.

To be aware of one's own mistakes yet make no attempt to rectify them, and to adopt a liberal attitude towards oneself. This is the eleventh type.

We can name several more. But these eleven are the principal types.

All these are manifestations of liberalism.

In revolutionary organizations liberalism is extremely harmful. It is a corrosive which disrupts unity, undermines solidarity, induces inactivity, and creates dissension. It deprives the revolutionary ranks of compact organization and strict discipline, prevents policies from being thoroughly carried out, and divorces the organizations of the Party from the masses under their leadership. It is an extremely bad tendency.

Liberalism stems from the selfishness of the petty bourgeoisie, which puts personal interests foremost and the interests of the revolution in the second place, thus giving rise to ideological, political, and organizational liberalism.

Liberals look upon the principles of Marxism as abstract dogmas. They approve of Marxism, but are not prepared to practice it or to practice it in full; they are not prepared to replace their own liberalism with Marxism. Such people have got Marxism, but they have also got liberalism: they talk Marxism but practice liberalism; they apply Marxism to others but liberalism to themselves. Both kinds of goods are in stock and each has its particular use. That is how the minds of certain people work.

Liberalism is a manifestation of opportunism and conflicts fundamentally with Marxism. It has a passive character and objectively has the effect of helping the enemy; thus the enemy welcomes its preservation in our midst. Such being its nature, there should be no place for it in the revolutionary ranks.

We must use the active spirit of Marxism to overcome liberalism with its passivity. A Communist should be frank, faithful and active, looking upon the interests of the revolution as his very life and subordinating his personal interests to those of the revolution; he should, always and everywhere, adhere to correct principles and wage a tireless struggle against all incorrect ideas and actions, so as to consolidate the collective life of the Party and strengthen the ties between the Party and the masses; and he should be more concerned about the Party and the masses than about the individual, and more concerned about others than about himself. Only thus can he be considered a Communist.

All loyal, honest, active and staunch Communists must unite to oppose the liberal tendencies shown by certain people among us, and turn them in the right direction. This is one of the tasks on our ideological front.

On Art and Literature

The so-called *Cheng-feng* movement of Party reform gave particular attention to the rectification of undesirable tendencies in the cultural sphere. In this speech made to a forum on literature and art in Yenan, May, 1942, Mao reasserts the orthodox Communist view that art and literature must subserve the political ends of the revolution, but insists that art cannot be mere propaganda. He acknowledges that aesthetic criteria are distinct from political ones, that political correctness is not enough in works of art, and that they fail if lacking in "artistic quality." He does not, however, pursue the question of how such quality is to be achieved in the aesthetic form if the ideological content is so rigidly controlled, and therefore suggests no remedy for the sterilizing effect which such control has usually had on artistic creativity.

Note the attention given to the special need of cadres, as an elite group, for works of art representing cultural "elevation" rather than mere popularization.

[From *Selected Works*, IV, 69–86]

Comrades! We have met three times during this month. In the pursuit of truth, heated debates have taken place and scores of Party and non-Party comrades have spoken, laying bare the issues and making them concrete. I think this is very profitable to the whole artistic and literary movement.

In discussing any problem we should start from actual facts and not from definitions. We shall be following the wrong method if we first look up definitions of art and literature in the textbooks and then use them as criteria in determining the direction of the present artistic and literary movement or in judging the views and controversies that arise today. We are Marxists and Marxism teaches that in our approach to a problem we should start not from abstract definitions but from objective facts and, by analyzing these facts, determine the way we shall go, our policies and methods. We should do the same in our present discussion of art and literature. . . .

What then is the crux of our problems? I think our problems are basically those of working for the masses and of how to work for them. If these two problems are not solved, or [are] solved inadequately, our artists and writers will be ill-adapted to their circumstances and unfit for their tasks, and will come up against a series of problems from within and without. My conclusion will center round these two problems, while touching upon some other problems related to them.

I

The first problem is: For whom are our art and literature intended?

This problem has, as a matter of fact, been solved long ago by Marxists, and especially by Lenin. As far back as 1905 Lenin emphatically pointed out that our art and literature should "serve the millions upon millions of working people." [25] [pp. 69-70]

II

The question of "whom to serve" having been solved, the question of "how to serve" comes up. To put it in the words of our comrades: Should we devote ourselves to elevation or to popularization? [p. 75]

Though man's social life constitutes the only source for art and literature, and is incomparably more vivid and richer than art and literature as such, the people are not satisfied with the former alone and demand the latter. Why? Because, although both are beautiful, life as reflected in artistic and literary works can and ought to be on a higher level and of a greater power and better focused, more typical, nearer the ideal, and therefore more universal than actual everyday life. Revolutionary art and literature should create all kinds of characters on the basis of actual life and help the masses to push history forward. For example, on the one hand there are people suffering from hunger, cold, and oppression, and on the other hand there are men exploiting and oppressing men—a contrast that exists everywhere and seems quite commonplace to people; artists and writers, however, can create art and literature out of such daily occurrences by organizing them, bringing them to a focal point, and making the contradictions and struggles in them typical—create art and literature that can awaken and arouse the masses and impel them to unite and struggle to change their environment. If there were no such art and literature, this task could not be fulfilled or at least not effectively and speedily fulfilled.

What are popularization and elevation in art and literature? What is the relation between the two? Works of popularization are simpler and plainer and therefore more readily accepted by the broad masses of the people of today. Works of a higher level are more polished and therefore more difficult to produce and less likely to win the ready acceptance of the broad masses of people of today. The problem facing the workers, peasants, and soldiers today is this: engaged in a ruthless and sanguinary struggle against the enemy, they remain illiterate and uncultured as a result of the prolonged rule of the feudal and bourgeois classes and consequently they badly need a widespread campaign of enlightenment, and

[25] See V. I. Lenin, *The Party's Organization and the Party's Literature.*

they eagerly wish to have culture, knowledge, art, and literature which meet their immediate need and are readily acceptable to them so as to heighten their passion for struggle and their confidence in victory, to strengthen their solidarity, and thus to enable them to fight the enemy with one heart and one mind. In meeting their primary need, we are not to "add flowers to a piece of brocade" but "offer fuel to a person in snowy weather." Under the present conditions, therefore, popularization is the more pressing task. It is wrong to despise and neglect this task.

But popularization and elevation cannot be sharply separated. . . . The people need popularization, but along with it they need elevation too, elevation month by month and year by year. Popularization is popularization for the people, and elevation is elevation of the people. Such elevation does not take place in mid-air, nor behind closed doors, but on the basis of popularization. It is at once determined by popularization and gives direction to it. . . . This being the case, the work of popularization in our sense not only constitutes no obstacle to elevation but affords a basis for our work of elevation on a limited scale at present, as well as preparing the necessary conditions for our far more extensive work of elevation in the future.

Besides the elevation that directly meets the need of the masses, there is the elevation that meets their need indirectly, namely, the elevation needed by the cadres. Being advanced members of the masses, the cadres are generally better educated than the masses, and art and literature of a higher level are entirely necessary to them; and it would be a mistake to ignore this. Anything done for the cadres is also entirely done for the masses, because it is only through the cadres that we can give education and guidance to the masses. If we depart from this objective, if what we give to the cadres cannot help them to educate and guide the masses, then our work of elevation will be like aimless shooting, i.e., deviating from our fundamental principle of serving the broad masses of the people. [PP. 77-79]

. . . . .

IV

One of the principal methods of struggle in the artistic and literary sphere is art and literary criticism. It should be developed and, as many comrades have rightly pointed out, our work in this respect was quite inadequate in the past. Art and literary criticism presents a complex problem which requires much study of a special kind. Here I shall stress only the basic problem of criteria in criticism. I shall also comment briefly on certain other problems and incorrect views brought up by some comrades.

There are two criteria in art and literary criticism: political and artistic. According to the political criterion, all works are good that facilitate unity and resistance to Japan, that encourage the masses to be of one heart and one mind, and that oppose retrogression and promote progress; on the other hand, all works are bad that undermine unity and resistance to Japan, that sow dissension and discord among the masses, and that oppose progress and drag the people back. And how can we tell the good from the bad here—by the motive (subjective intention) or by the effect (social practice)? Idealists stress motive and ignore effect, while mechanical materialists stress effect and ignore motive; in contradistinction from either, we dialectical materialists insist on the unity of motive and effect. The motive of serving the masses is inseparable from the effect of winning their approval, and we must unite the two. . . . In examining the subjective intention of an artist, i.e., whether his motive is correct and good, we do not look at his declaration but at the effect his activities (mainly his works) produce on society and the masses. Social practice and its effect are the criteria for examining the subjective intention or the motive. . . . According to the artistic criterion, all works are good or comparatively good that are relatively high in artistic quality; and bad or comparatively bad that are relatively low in artistic quality. Of course, this distinction also depends on social effect. As there is hardly an artist who does not consider his own work excellent, our criticism ought to permit the free competition of all varieties of artistic works; but it is entirely necessary for us to pass correct judgments on them according to the criteria of the science of art, so that we can gradually raise the art of a lower level to a higher level, and to change the art which does not meet the requirements of the struggle of the broad masses into art that does meet them.

There is thus the political criterion as well as the artistic criterion. How are the two related? Politics is not the equivalent of art, nor is a general world outlook equivalent to the method of artistic creation and criticism. We believe there is neither an abstract and absolutely unchangeable political criterion, nor an abstract and absolutely unchangeable artistic criterion, for every class in a class society has its own political and artistic criteria. But all classes in all class societies place the political criterion first and the artistic criterion second. The bourgeoisie always rejects proletarian artistic and literary works, no matter how great their artistic achievement. As for the proletariat, they must treat the art and literature of the past according to their attitude towards the people and whether they are progressive in the light of history. Some things which are basically reactionary from the political point of view may yet be artistically good. But the more artistic such a work may be, the greater harm will it do to the people, and the more reason for us to reject it. The contradiction between reactionary political content and artistic form is a common characteristic of the art and literature of all exploiting classes in their decline. What we demand is unity of politics and art, of content and form, and of the revolutionary political content and the highest possible degree of perfection in artistic form. Works of art, however politically progressive, are powerless if they lack artistic quality. Therefore we are equally opposed to works with wrong political approaches and to the tendency towards so-called "poster and slogan style" which is correct only in political approach but lacks artistic power. We must carry on a two-front struggle in art and literature. [pp. 84–86]

On the Correct Handling of Contradictions Among the People

This speech, popularly known by the catch-phrase "Let A Hundred Flowers Bloom," is one of Mao Tse-tung's most important theoretical statements since the consolidation of Communist power on the mainland of China and since the death of Stalin left Mao as perhaps the dean of Communist theoreticians. It was clearly occasioned in part by the shock of the uprising in Hungary late in 1956, which showed the degree of pent-up dissatisfaction possible under even a seemingly well-established Communist regime. If Mao's gesture was meant to encourage the "letting off of steam," those who took advantage of the offer found, after a brief period of forbearance by the Party, that they would be subjected to severe attack and penalized for their outspokenness.

We are not concerned here with the immediate political or tactical implications of this episode for the period in question or for the Communist world as a whole. In long-range terms its significance would seem to lie, not in any liberalization or loosening of Communist ideological control, but precisely in its reaffirmation of the importance Mao attaches to unity in matters of theory and doctrine. As we have already seen, for Mao and for Liu Shao-ch'i, the principal means of preserving that unity as a dynamic force has been ideological struggle. Yet under conditions of Party dominance the threat of stagnation is always present. Consequently for Mao, always concerned to keep his cohorts in battle-readiness, the question is how to stimulate the airing of contradictions without allowing them to become antagonistic, how to obtain the benefits of struggle without running the risks.

Subsequent reports from Peking have indicated that Mao is still wrestling with this problem and might still find a use for "nonantagonistic" criticism as an outlet for discontent. When, however, the Party stands as sole judge of what is antagonistic or not, and has made such an object lesson of those who unknowingly overstepped the invisible line earlier, it seems unlikely that this particular contradiction can be easily resolved.

This speech was originally delivered on February 27, 1957, before a large audience at a Supreme State Conference. When finally published at the end of June, it had been substantially revised and probably represented a much more guarded statement of policy than the original lecture. The purpose was now less to encourage "fragrant flowers" and more to identify "poisonous weeds."

[From Mao, *Let A Hundred Flowers Bloom,* ed. by G. F. Hudson, pp. 14–50]

TWO DIFFERENT TYPES OF CONTRADICTIONS

Never has our country been as united as it is today. The victories of the bourgeois-democratic revolution and the socialist revolution, coupled with our achievements in socialist construction, have rapidly changed the face of old China. Now we see before us an even brighter future. The days of national disunity and turmoil which the people detested have gone forever. Led by the working class and the Communist Party, and united as one, our 600 million people are engaged in the great work of building socialism. Unification of the country, unity of the people, and unity among our various nationalities—these are the basic guarantees for the sure triumph of our cause. However, this does not mean that there are no longer any contradictions in our society. It would be naive to imagine that there are no more contradictions. To do so would be to fly in the face of objective reality. We are confronted by two types of social contradictions—contradictions between ourselves and the enemy and contradictions among the people. These two types of contradictions are totally different in nature. [pp. 14–15]

The contradictions between ourselves and our enemies are antagonistic ones. Within the ranks of the people, contradictions among the working people are nonantagonistic, while those between the exploiters and the exploited classes have, apart from their antagonistic aspect, a nonantagonistic aspect. Contradictions among the people have always existed, but their content differs in each period of the revolution and during the building of socialism.

In the conditions existing in China today, what we call contradictions among the people include the following:

Contradictions within the working class, contradictions within the peasantry, contradictions within the intelligentsia, contradictions between the working class and the peasantry, contradictions between the working class and peasantry on the one hand and the intelligentsia on the other, contradictions between the working class and other sections of the working people on the one hand and the national bourgeoisie on the other, contradictions within the national bourgeoisie, and so forth. Our People's Government is a government that truly represents the interests of the people and serves the people, yet certain contradictions do exist between the Government and the masses. These include contradictions between the interests of the state, collective interests, and individual interests; between democracy and centralism; between those in positions of leadership and the led, and contradictions arising from the bureaucratic practices of certain state functionaries in their relations with the masses. All these are contradictions among the people; generally speaking, underlying the contradictions among the people is the basic identity of the interests of the people.

In our country, the contradiction between the working class and the national bourgeoisie is a contradiction among the people. The class struggle waged between the two is, by and large, a class struggle within the ranks of the people; this is because of the dual character of the national bourgeoisie in our country. In the years of the bourgeois-democratic revolution, there was a revolutionary side to their character; there was also a tendency to compromise with the enemy—this was the other side. In the period of the socialist revolution, exploitation of the working class to make profits is one side, while support of the Constitution and willingness to accept socialist transformation is the other. The national bourgeoisie differs from the imperialists, the landlords, and the bureaucrat-capitalists. The contradiction between exploiter and exploited which exists between the national bourgeoisie and the working class is an antagonistic one. But, in the concrete conditions existing in China, such an antagonistic contradiction, if properly handled, can be transformed into a nonantagonistic one and resolved in a peaceful way. But if it is not properly handled, if, say, we do not follow a policy of unity, criticizing and educating the national bourgeoisie, or if the national bourgeoisie does not accept this policy, then the contradictions between the working class and the national bourgeoisie can turn into an antagonistic contradiction as between ourselves and the enemy. [pp. 16–18]

There were other people in our country who took a wavering attitude toward the Hungarian events because they were ignorant about the actual world situation. They felt that there was too little freedom under our people's democracy and that there was more freedom under Western parliamentary democracy. They ask for the adoption of the two-party system of the West, where one party is in office and the other out of office. But this so-called two-party system is nothing but a means of maintaining the dictatorship of the bourgeoisie; under no circumstances can it safeguard the freedom of the working people. As a matter of fact, freedom and democracy cannot exist in the abstract; they only exist in the concrete. . . .

Those who demand freedom and democracy in the abstract regard democracy as an end and not a means. Democracy sometimes seems to be an end, but it is in fact only a means. Marxism teaches us that democracy is part of the superstructure and belongs to the category of politics. That is to say, in the last analysis it serves the economic base. The same is true of freedom. Both democracy and freedom are relative, not absolute, and they come into being and develop under specific historical circumstances.

Within the ranks of the people, democracy stands in relation to centralism, and freedom to discipline. They are two conflicting aspects of a single entity, contradictory as well as united, and we should not one-sidedly emphasize one to the denial of the other. Within the ranks of the people, we cannot do without democracy, nor can we do without centralism. Our democratic centralism means the unity of democracy and centralism and the unity of freedom and discipline. Under this system, the people enjoy a wide measure of democracy and freedom, but at the same time they have to keep themselves within the bounds of socialist discipline. All this is well understood by the people. [pp. 21–22]

Marxist philosophy holds that the law of the unity of opposites is a fundamental law of the universe. This law operates everywhere, in the natural world, in human society, and in man's thinking. Opposites in contradiction unite as well as struggle with each other, and thus impel all things to move and change. Contradictions exist everywhere, but as things differ in nature so do contradictions in any given phenomenon or thing; the unity of opposites is conditional, temporary and transitory, and hence relative, whereas struggle between opposites is absolute. Lenin gave a very clear exposition of this law. In our country, a growing number of people have come to understand it. For many people, however, acceptance of this law is one thing and its application, examining and dealing with problems, is quite another. Many dare not acknowledge openly that there still exist contradictions among the people, which are the very forces that move our society forward. Many people refuse to admit that contradictions still exist in a socialist society, with the result that when confronted with social contradictions they become timid and helpless. They do not understand that socialist society grows more united and consolidated precisely through the ceaseless process of correctly dealing with and resolving contradictions. For this reason, we need to explain things to our people, our cadres in the first place, to help them understand contradictions in a socialist society and learn how to deal with such contradictions in a correct way. [p. 26]

ON 'LETTING A HUNDRED FLOWERS BLOSSOM' AND 'LETTING A HUNDRED SCHOOLS OF THOUGHT CONTEND' AND 'LONG-TERM COEXISTENCE AND MUTUAL SUPERVISION'

"Let a hundred flowers blossom" and "let a hundred schools of thought contend," "long-term coexistence and mutual supervision"—how did these slogans come to be put forward?

They were put forward in the light of the specific conditions existing in China, on the basis of the recognition that various kinds of contradictions still exist in a socialist society, and in response to the country's urgent need to speed up its economic and cultural development.

The policy of letting a hundred flowers blossom and a hundred schools of thought contend is designed to promote the flourishing of the arts and the progress of science; it is designed to enable a socialist culture to thrive in our land. Different forms and styles in art can develop freely, and different schools in science can contend freely. We think that it is harmful to the growth of art and science if administrative measures are used to impose one particular style of art or school of thought and to ban another. Questions of right and wrong in the arts and sciences should be settled through free discussions in artistic and scientific circles and in the course of practical work in the arts and sciences. They should not be settled in summary fashion. A period of trial is often needed to determine whether something is right or wrong. In the past, new and correct things often failed at the outset to win recognition from the majority of people and had to develop by twists and turns in struggle. Correct and good things have often at first been looked upon not as fragrant flowers but as poisonous weeds; Copernicus's theory of the solar system and Darwin's theory of evolution were once dismissed as erroneous and had to win through over bitter opposition. Chinese history offers many similar examples. In socialist society, conditions for the growth of new things are radically different from and far superior to those in the old society. Nevertheless, it still often happens that new, rising forces are held back and reasonable suggestions smothered.

The growth of new things can also be hindered, not because of deliberate suppressions but because of lack of discernment. That is why we should take a cautious attitude in regard to questions of right and wrong in the arts and sciences, encourage free discussion, and avoid hasty conclusions. We believe that this attitude will facilitate the growth of the arts and sciences.

Marxism has also developed through struggle. At the beginning, Marxism was subjected to all kinds of attack and regarded as a poisonous weed. It is still being attacked and regarded as a poisonous weed in many parts of the world. However, it enjoys a different position in the socialist countries. But, even in these countries, there are non-Marxist as well as anti-Marxist ideologies. It is true that in China socialist transformation, in so far as a change in the system of ownership is concerned, has in the main been completed, and the turbulent, large-scale, mass class struggles characteristic of the revolutionary periods have in the main concluded. But remnants of the overthrown landlord and comprador classes still exist, the bourgeoisie still exists, and the petty bourgeoisie has only just begun to remold itself. Class struggle is not yet over. . . . In this respect, the question of whether socialism or capitalism will win is still not really settled. Marxists are still a minority of the entire population as well as of the intellectuals. Marxism therefore must still develop through struggle. Marxism can only develop through struggle—this is true not only in the past and present, it is necessarily true in the future also. What is correct always develops in the course of struggle with what is wrong. The true, the good and the beautiful always exist in comparison with the false, the evil and the ugly, and grow in struggle with the latter. As mankind in general rejects an untruth and accepts a truth, a new truth will begin struggling with new erroneous ideas. Such struggles will never end. This is the law of development of truth, and it is certainly also the law of development of Marxism. [pp. 44–46]

People may ask: Since Marxism is accepted by the majority of the people in our country as the guiding ideology, can it be criticized? Certainly it can. As a scientific truth, Marxism fears no criticism. If it did and could be defeated in argument, it would be worthless. In fact, are not the idealists criticizing Marxism every day and in all sorts of ways? As for those who harbor bourgeois and petty-bourgeois ideas and do not wish to change, are not they also criticizing Marxism in all sorts of ways? Marxists should not be afraid of criticism from any quarter. Quite the contrary, they need to steel and improve themselves and win new positions in the teeth of criticism and the storm and stress of struggle. Fighting against wrong ideas is like being vaccinated—a man develops greater immunity from disease after the vaccine takes effect. Plants raised in hot-houses are not likely to be robust. Carrying out the policy of letting a hundred flowers blossom and a hundred schools of thought contend will not weaken but strengthen the leading position of Marxism in the ideological field.

What should our policy be toward non-Marxist ideas? As far as unmistakable counter-revolutionaries and wreckers of the socialist cause are concerned, the matter is easy; we simply deprive them of their freedom of speech. But it is quite a different matter when we are faced with incorrect ideas among the people. Will it do to ban such ideas and give them no opportunity to express themselves? Certainly not. It is not only futile but very harmful to use crude and summary methods to deal with ideological questions among the people, with questions relating to the spiritual life of man. You may ban the expression of wrong ideas, but the ideas will still be there. On the other hand, correct ideas, if pampered in hot-houses without being exposed to the elements or immunized against disease, will not win out against wrong ones. That is why it is only by employing methods of discussion, criticism, and reasoning that we can really foster correct ideas, overcome wrong ideas, and really settle issues. [pp. 47–48]

On the surface, these two slogans—let a hundred flowers blossom and a hundred schools of thought contend—have no class character; the proletariat can turn them to account, and so can the bourgeoisie and other people. But different classes, strata, and social groups each have their own views on what are fragrant flowers and what are poisonous weeds. So what, from the point of view of the broad masses of the people, should be a criterion today for distinguishing between fragrant flowers and poisonous weeds?

In the political life of our country, how are our people to determine what is right and what is wrong in our words and actions? Basing ourselves on the principles of our constitution, the will of the overwhelming majority of our people and the political programs jointly proclaimed on various occasions by our political parties and groups, we believe that, broadly speaking, words and actions can be judged right if they:

1. Help to unite the people of our various nationalities, and do not divide them.

2. Are beneficial, not harmful, to socialist transformation and socialist construction.

3. Help to consolidate, not undermine or weaken, the people's democratic dictatorship.

4. Help to consolidate, not undermine or weaken, democratic centralism.

5. Tend to strengthen, not to cast off or weaken, the leadership of the Communist Party.

6. Are beneficial, not harmful, to international socialist solidarity and the solidarity of the peace-loving peoples of the world.

Of these six criteria, the most important are the socialist path and the leadership of the Party. These criteria are put forward in order to foster, and not hinder, the free discussion of various questions among the people. Those who do not approve of these criteria can still put forward their own views and argue their cases. When the majority of the people have clear-cut criteria to go by, criticism and self-criticism can be conducted along proper lines, and these criteria can be applied to people's words and actions to determine whether they are fragrant flowers or poisonous weeds. These are political criteria. Naturally, in judging the truthfulness of scientific theories or assessing the esthetic value of works of art, other pertinent criteria are needed, but these six political criteria are also applicable to all activities in the arts or sciences. In a socialist country like ours, can there possibly be any useful scientific or artistic activity which runs counter to these political criteria? [pp. 49–50]

CONCLUSION

Having concluded our survey of the Chinese tradition with an examination of Chinese Communism, we return to our initial question: What has the one to do with the other? Does Chinese Communism represent a complete departure from tradition? Is it not, after all, far more Communist than Chinese?

The record to date—certainly as revealed in the writings above—indicates clearly enough the anti-traditionalist character of Chinese Communism. It is not just that revolutionary changes have been effected in Chinese society, and especially in institutions closely bound up with traditional ideologies (the family with Confucianism, for instance), but more directly that a deliberate attempt has been made to efface from Chinese minds whatever influence traditional religious and philosophical systems might still exert upon them.

Then too, above and beyond this overt hostility—Mao's scorn for Confucius and his contempt for religious "superstition"—there is also his positive commitment to a new orthodoxy which must be considered, for it is an orthodoxy which not only dispenses with the sanction of Chinese tradition, but feels little need even to reckon with it. Thus, with minor concessions to popular attitudes and modes of expression, the textbooks of Chinese Communism betray little self-consciousness over their break with the past. Mao's style of writing, his political vocabulary, his sources of authority, and his whole frame of reference are in most respects so foreign to Chinese tradition as to suggest an altogether different orientation of mind. More significant, therefore, than the explicit rejection of the past is the very small place it has occupied in Communist thinking. As Mao himself puts it, the past is of little concern; the important thing for Chinese Communists is to look to the future.

Nevertheless, it would be wrong to imply that Mao's rejection of the past is total. Certain aspects of traditional Chinese culture he does find worthy of admiration, and the new culture fostered by Communism must, he insists, preserve what is valuable in the old at the same time that it discards what is debased. Chinese Communists should therefore "throw away the feudal dross and absorb the democratic essence" of the earlier culture. Without doubt, this concession to history, which Mao says must be "respected" and from which the Chinese "cannot cut themselves adrift," does indeed leave room for future adaptation. In the definition of what is "feudal" and what "democratic," for example, there is a loophole through which much of Chinese tradition could be drawn, if that proved desirable. Indeed the very application of such terms as "feudal" and "democratic" to Chinese history suggests a flexibility of interpretation great enough to permit further adjustments if the need arises.

Allowing this much, the question still remains—and it is a large one—whether at present the Chinese Communists show any inclination toward making such adjustments, and if so, on what basis. Would gestures made toward Chinese tradition reflect a genuine respect for it? Would future adaptations represent the actual influence of traditional values, or rather mere accommodations to national feelings? That the whole process of adaptation or synthesis in regard to Chinese culture might be guided by aims quite foreign to Chinese tradition is a possibility which Mao's own remarks on the subject make very real. There can be no doubt that, in his mind at least, the process of sifting and selecting from Chinese culture should be governed, and most stringently so, by the criteria of Marxism-Leninism. Under such circumstances much that had been honored by tradition would have difficulty gaining recognition, while much else would probably be transformed or contorted beyond recognition.

Examples of the kind of approach which Chinese Communists might take to this problem are not lacking to us. In regard to the classical schools of Chinese philosophy, for instance, there has been a noticeable sympathy among Communist writers for the Taoists, and particularly for "Lao Tzu," as representing an opposition to Confucius and a radical critique of the established order. In such an appreciation, however, the underlying mysticism and quietism of "Lao Tzu" quickly becomes obscured as his new admirers hasten to claim him for the "democratic" tradition.

How much, indeed, of "Lao Tzu" survives when he must serve as spokesman for the oppressed masses, as the voice of social revolution?

Liu Shao-ch'i, on the other hand, offers an example somewhat in contrast in his *How To Be a Good Communist*. Here Confucian sources are drawn upon in explaining the nature and significance of Communist self-cultivation. While obviously Liu adapts traditional concepts to a most untraditional purpose (there is nothing in his sources which would allow for such complete subordination of the individual conscience to political authority, rather than to a presumed set of moral constants), the concepts are still half-recognizable. Confucian cultivation had attempted a delicate adjustment between the claims of the individual and those of his society. With Liu the adjustment is subtle and it involves the individual, but the balance is totally destroyed. The individual life has value now only in social terms (its value to the Party and state), not in human terms (its intrinsic personal worth or "humanity").

Whatever the incidental uses to which tradition has thus been put by Chinese Communists, and whatever allowances must be made for misappropriation (perhaps no more than for previous dynasties, since tradition has been less valued), still even this minimal recognition of the past helps to keep tradition alive. "Lao Tzu" may not be truly appreciated today, but he has survived his misinterpreters before. Liu Shao-ch'i may not quite rank Confucius and Mencius with Lenin and Stalin, and may decide all points of difference in favor of his latter-day sages, but he cannot speak of the two together without doing some honor (among Communists) to the earlier sages. The question is whether tradition kept alive on such a precarious basis will be sufficient for survival in a modern totalitarian society. Minor concessions of this sort could easily be lost in the general destruction of everything that has served to perpetuate tradition in the past.

Apart from such open expressions of the Communist outlook on tradition, there is at least one further approach which might be made to our problem. The evidence may be overwhelming that Chinese Communist thinking has been formed within the tradition of Marxism-Leninism, but is that tradition wholly at variance with the Chinese? In the institutional sphere the character of Communist rule bears strong resemblance to bureaucratic despotisms in the past. May not certain features of Communist thought also have an appeal for the Chinese precisely because they conform to traditional habits of mind or approximate traditional ideals? Here we are on much more speculative ground, but some points of correspondence can at least be suggested:

1. The possibility of achieving the ideal society—perfect peace and order, and eventually a minimum of government—has been a central theme of Chinese political thought for centuries. Where other traditions have placed their final hope in Heaven or Nirvana, the kingdom in which the Confucianists hoped was very much of this world. Again and again Confucian idealism has expressed its belief that such an ideal was attainable, and has inspired numerous (and usually naive) plans for the perfectly ordered and controlled society. The Communists, though condemning Confucian "idealism," have undoubtedly appealed to much the same idealistic hope, as indeed did the similarly anti-Confucian Taipings.

2. In addition to this political idealism, the Communists have probably appealed in their own way to the kind of moral idealism which Confucianism always fostered. The dedication of the Confucian *chün-tzu* to the service of state and society is matched by that demanded of the Communist cadre to the Party and state. Ethically these two forms of idealism rest on very different bases, but Liu Shao-ch'i had good reason to invoke for his cadres Fan Chung-yen's definition of the *chün-tzu* as one who is "first in worrying about the world's troubles and last in enjoying its pleasures." Such a lofty conception corresponded closely to Liu's idea of the good Communist, who accepts rigorous self-discipline and self-denial in the service of the revolution.

3. One aspect of this traditional moral idealism had been its emphasis on the pursuit of what is right rather than of what is profitable. In the past this principle had often been applied to the detriment of commercial activity and to the enhancement of state power in the economic sphere, presumably on the theory that the ruling elite acted in the interests of all but the merchant only in his own. In more recent times, owing to the prevalence of this idea, socialism has enjoyed a discernible advantage over "laissez-faire" liberalism and free enterprise in gaining general acceptance, and the acquisition by the state of great economic powers has conformed to, not violated, the traditional pattern.

4. Closely related to the moral idealism referred to above is the tradi-

tional Confucian ideal of the ruling elite. Despite important ideological differences, the new Communist elite resembles the old one in its combination of ideological and political authority, in its identification with a specific intellectual orthodoxy, and in its claim to qualify for leadership by conforming to a rigorous code of conduct.

It would be possible to list more such correspondences between Communist and Chinese traditions—similarities which can hardly be interpreted as traditional influences on the new ideology, but do suggest the perpetuation of certain general attitudes from the past into the immediate present. Since the list of dissimilarities is even longer and more obvious, we shall not attempt to prepare an inventory here. What is important to recognize ultimately is the superficial character of such resemblances as do exist, in so far as they might seem to bear upon the continuity of Chinese tradition or to endow Communist rule with a traditional character. Chinese Communism may have been the beneficiary of certain deep-rooted attitudes among the people, but it enjoyed this advantage without incurring a corresponding obligation, without binding itself to any of the traditional restraints upon the exercise of great power. As a consequence it has felt free to remake China as it pleased, without reference to traditional values or standards. It has known a degree of authority which yielded nothing to the admonitions of past sages, and it has possessed a degree of control over the lives of men which recognized none of the privileged sanctuaries of private and family life, wherein much that was most noble and gracious and humane in Chinese life had been preserved, even under earlier despotisms.

In the final analysis it must be admitted that the Chinese tradition, if it exists at all today in recognizable form, is in a stage of such rapid and violent flux that predictions have little value. As our introduction and the preceding chapters seek to make clear, this revolutionary process has been in motion since long before the rise of Chinese Communism, and its unsettling effects on tradition have been so severe that any assumption of a continuity in thought or of intellectual influence is extremely dubious. Whether the future belongs to Communism, some modification of it, or something wholly unforeseen, there is no sign yet that the forces of change are spent.

Perhaps this alone may be confidently believed: that a tradition so rich and diverse, and in many ways profound, cannot for long remain submerged. And if the condition of its re-emergence is that it join hands with other traditions, East and West, which share its basic humanistic values, this the Chinese tradition has already shown a capacity to do, for the benefit not of the Chinese alone but of all the world.

CHAPTER DECORATIONS

BIBLIOGRAPHY

Note: Titles of collections which appear more than twice in the list are cited as follows:

KHCPTS   Kuo-hsüeh chi-pen ts'ung-shu. Shanghai, Commercial Press, 1932?–1939?.

PNP   Po-na-pen erh-shih-ssu shih. 820 ts'e. Shanghai, Commercial Press, 1930–1937.

SPPY   Ssu-pu pei-yao. 537 titles in 1372 ts'e. Chung-hua shu-chü, 1927–1935.

SPTK   Ssu-pu ts'ung-k'an. 1st series, 323 titles in 2102 ts'e. Shanghai, Commercial Press, 1920–1922, reprinted in 1929. 3d series. Shanghai, Commerical Press, 1935.

TD   Taishō [shinshū] daizōkyō. Edited by Takakusu Junjirō and Watanabe Kaigyoku. 85 vols. Tokyo, Taishō issai-kyō kankō-kai, 1914–1932.

TSCC   Ts'ung-shu chi-ch'eng. 1384 titles in 2000 vols. Shanghai, Commercial Press, 1935–1937.

Analects. Lun yü. 20 chüan. SPPY. See also Soothill; Waley.

Bernard, Henri, S.J. Matteo Ricci's Scientific Contributions to China. Translated by Edward Chalmers Werner. Peking, Henri Vetch, 1935.

Book of Changes. I ching [Chou i]. 10 chüan. SPPY. See also Legge, Yi King.

Book of History. Shu ching (Shang shu chin-ku wen chu su). KHCPTS. See also Legge, Shoo King.

Book of Odes. Shih ching. Hsüeh-sheng kuo-hsüeh ts'ung-shu ed. Shanghai, Commercial Press, 1926. See also Legge, She King.

Book of Rites. Li chi. 20 chüan. SPPY. See also Legge, Li Ki.

Brandt, Conrad, Benjamin Schwartz, and John K. Fairbank. A Documentary History of Chinese Communism. Cambridge, Mass., Harvard University Press, 1952.

Chang Chih-tung. Ch'üan hsüeh p'ien. In Chang Wen-hsiang kung ch'üan-chi. 229 chüan. Peking, 1928. Chüan 202–203.

Chang Chün-mai. Jen-sheng kuan. In K'o-hsüeh yü jen-sheng kuan, by Chang Chün-mai, Ting Wen-chiang, et al. 2 vols. Shanghai, 1923. Vol. I.

Chang Heng. Hun-t'ien-i. As reconstructed by Hung I-hsüan in Ching-tien chi-lin. 2 ts'e. Ch'en-shih chen-ch'u-t'ang, photolith ed., 1926. Chüan 27:1a-b.

Chang Tsai. Chang Tzu ch'üan-shu. KHCPTS.

—— Cheng meng. In Chang Heng-ch'ü hsien-sheng wen-chi. Cheng-i-t'ang ch'üan-shu ed. Foochow, 1866. Chüan 2–4.

—— Hsi-ming. In Chang Heng-ch'ü hsien-sheng wen-chi. Cheng-i-t'ang ch'üan-shu ed. Foochow, 1866. Chüan 1.

Chang Yen-yüan (ed.). Li-tai ming-hua chi. 10 chüan. Po-ku-chai photolith reprint of Chin-tai pi-shu ed. Shanghai, 1922.

Ch'en Tu-hsiu, "Jen-sheng chen i," Hsin ch'ing-nien, Vol. IV, No. 2 (Peking, February, 1918), pp. 90–93.

—— "K'ung Tzu chih tao yü hsien-tai sheng-huo," Hsin ch'ing-nien, Vol. II, No. 4 (Peking, December, 1916), pp. 3–5.

Cheng Ch'iao. T'ung chih. Shih t'ung ed. 3 vols. Shanghai, Commercial Press, 1936.

Ch'eng Hao. Ming-tao wen-chi. In Ch'eng Hao and Ch'eng Yi, Erh Ch'eng ch'üan-shu. 67 chüan. SPPY.

Ch'eng Hao and Ch'eng Yi. Erh Ch'eng ch'üan-shu. 67 chüan. SPPY. Contains also Erh Ch'eng i-shu and Erh Ch'eng ts'ui-yen.

Ch'eng Yi. Yi-ch'uan wen-chi. In Ch'eng Hao and Ch'eng Yi, Erh Ch'eng ch'üan-shu. 67 chüan. SPPY.

Chi-tsang. San-lun hsüan-i. TD, XLV: 1–11.

Chia I. Hsin shu. 10 chüan. SPTK, 1st series.

Chiang Kai-shek. China's Destiny. Authorized translation by Wang Chung-hui. New York, Macmillan, 1947.

—— [Chiang Chung-cheng]. Tsung-ts'ai yen-lun hsüan-chi. Ko-ming shih-chien yen-chiu-yüan ed. 5 chüan. Taipei, 1952.

Chih-k'ai [Chih-i]. Fa-hua hsüan-i. TD, XXXIII: 693.

—— Mo-ho chih-kuan. TD, XLVI:48–59.

Chin shu. Compiled by Fang Hsüan-ling, et al. PNP.

Chiu T'ang shu. Compiled by Liu Hsü, et al. PNP.

Chou Meng-yen (ed.). Yin-chih wen kuang-i. Yang-chou tsang-ching-yüan ed. 1881.

Chou Tun-yi. T'ai-chi-t'u shuo. In Chou Lien-ch'i chi. Cheng-i-t'ang ch'üan-shu ed. 13 chüan. 1869. Chüan 1.

—— T'ung shu. In Chou Lien-ch'i chi. Cheng-i-t'ang ch'üan-shu ed. 13 chüan. 1869. Chüan 5 and 6.

Chu Hsi. Chih-yüan k'ao-ting t'ung-chien kang-mu. 59 chüan. With T'ung-chien hsü-pien. 27 chüan. Edited by Ch'ien Hsüan. 84 ts'e. Hsi-wu-hsüan reprint of 1697 ed., 1882.

—— [Yü-tsuan] Chu Tzu ch'üan-shu. Compiled by Li Kuang-ti, et al. 32 ts'e. 1714.

Chu Lin. Hung men chih. Shanghai, Chung-hua shu-chü, 1947.

Ch'u Ch'eng-po. Chien-cheng t'ang che-kao. 2 chüan, 2 ts'e. 1905.

Chuang Tzu [Nan-hua chen-ching]. 10 chüan. SPTK, 1st series.

Ch'un-ch'iu yen k'ung t'u. In Ku-wei-shu. Edited by Sun Ku. 8:1a–5b. Shou-shan-ko ts'ung-shu. Compiled by Ch'ien Hsi-tso. Hung-wen shu-chü, 1889. Vol. 4.

Chung yung. No. 31 in Li chi. 20 chüan. SPPY. See also Legge, Li Ki.

de Bary, Wm. Theodore, Stephen Hay, and Royal Weiler (comps.). Sources of Indian Tradition. New York, Columbia, 1958.

Dewey, John. Creative Intelligence. New York, Henry Holt, 1917.

Fa-tsang. Chin-shih-tzu chang. TD, XLV:663–67.

Feifel, Eugene (tr. and ed.). Po Chü-i as a Censor; his memorials presented to Hsien-tsung during the years 808–810. Unpublished Ph.D. dissertation, Columbia University, 1951 [1952].

Feng Kuei-fen. Chiao-pin lu k'ang-i. Chin-ho kuang-jen t'ang editions: 1 ts'e, 1883, 126 leaves; 2 ts'e, n.d., 126 leaves.

Fung Yu-lan. History of Chinese Philosophy. Translated by Derk Bodde. 2 vols. Princeton, Princeton University Press, 1953.

Gallagher, Louis J. (tr.). China in the Sixteenth Century: The Journals of Matthew Ricci: 1583–1610. New York, Random House, 1953.

Great Learning. Ta hsüeh. No. 42 in Li Chi. 20 chüan. SPPY. See also Legge, Li Ki.

Hahn, Emily. Chiang Kai-shek, An Unauthorized Biography. Garden City, New York, Doubleday, 1955.

Han Fei Tzu. SPTK, 1st series.

Han shu. By Pan Ku. PNP.

Han Yü. [Chu wen-kung chiao] Ch'ang-li hsien-sheng wen-chi. SPTK, 1st series.

Hou Han shu. By Fan Yeh. PNP.

Hsi K'ang. Hsi Chung-san chi. 10 chüan. SPPY.

Hsi tz'u. [Great Appendix to] I ching [Chou i]. 10 chüan. SPPY. See also Legge, Yi King.

Hsiao I-shan, comp. T'ai-p'ing t'ien-kuo ts'ung-shu. Series I, 10 ts'e. Kuo-li pien-i kuan, 1936.

Hsin T'ang shu. By Ou-yang Hsiu. In [Ch'in-ting] Erh-shih-ssu shih. Han-fen-lou photo reprint of the Palace ed. of 1739. Shanghai, 1916.

Hsin Wu-tai shih. By Ou-yang Hsiu. PNP.

Hsüan-chuang [Hsüan-tsang]. Ch'eng-wei-shih lun. TD, XXXI: 7, 10, 22, 25, 37, 38.

Hsüeh Fu-ch'eng. Yung-an ch'üan-chi. 12 ts'e. 1888.

Hsün Tzu. 20 chüan. SPTK, 1st series.

Hu Shih, "Ch'an (Zen) Buddhism in China: Its History and Method," Philosophy East and West, Vol. III, No. 1 (April, 1953).

—— "Chien-kuo yü chuan-chih," Tu-li p'ing-lun, No. 81. (Peiping, December, 1933), pp. 3–5.

—— Hu Shih wen-ts'un. Taipei, Yüan-tung Company, 1953.

Huai-nan Tzu. SPTK, 1st series.

Huan K'uan. Yen-t'ieh lun. SPTK, 1st series.

Huang Tsung-hsi. Ming-i tai-fang lu. Wu-kuei-lou ed. 1879.

Huang Tsung-hsi and Ch'üan Tsu-wang. Sung-Yüan hsüeh-an. Ssu-ch'ao
hsüeh-an ed. 2 vols. Shanghai, Shih chieh shu chü, 1936.

Hui-neng. Liu-tsu t'an-ching. TD, XLVIII:337–44.

Hui-ssu. Ta-ch'eng chih-kuan fa-men. TD, XLVI:642–61.

Hui-yüan [Yüan-fa-shih]. Sha-men pu-ching wang-che lun. In Hung-ming chi.
Compiled by Seng-yu. TD, LI:29–32.

Hummel, Arthur W. (ed.). Eminent Chinese of the Ch'ing Period (1644–
1912). 2 vols. The Library of Congress, Washington, D.C., U.S. Government
Printing Office, 1943.

Hung Liang-chi. Hung Pei-chiang shih-wen chi. SPTK, 1st series.

I ching [Chou i]. 10 chüan. SPPY. See also Legge, Yi King.

I-hsüan. Lin-chi Hui-chao ch'an-shih yü-lu. TD, XLVII:497.

I-kuan tao li wen-ta. Author unknown. 1926. (Cornell University Library.)

I-li or Book of Etiquette and Ceremonial. Translated by John Steele. 2 vols.
London, Probsthain, 1917.

Juan Yüan. Ch'ou-jen chuan. In Wen-hsüan-lou ts'ung-shu. Compiled by Juan
Heng. 1842.

K'ang Yu-wei. Chung yung chu. Yen K'ung ts'ung-shu ed. 46 leaves. Preface
dated 1901.

—— K'ang Nan-hai tzu-pien nien-p'u. In Chung-kuo chin-tai-shih tzu-liao
ts'ung-k'an: Wu-hsü pien-fa. Edited by Chien Po-tsan, et al. Shanghai, 1953.

—— K'ung Tzu kai-chih k'ao. Wan-mu ts'ao-t'ang ts'ung-shu ed. 5 ts'e.
Peking, 1920.

—— Lun yü chu. Wan-mu ts'ao-t'ang ts'ung-shu ed. 20 chüan. 1917.

—— Wu-hsü tsou-kao. 1 ts'e. Japanese edition of 1911.

Ko Hung. Pao-p'u Tzu. SPTK, 1st series.

Ku Chieh-kang and Lo Ken-tse. Ku-shih pien. 6 vols. Peiping and Shanghai,
P'o-she and K'ai-ming shu-tien, 1926–1938. Vol. I.

Ku Yen-wu. Ch'iu-ku lu. In Hsing-su ts'ao-t'ang chin-shih ts'ung-shu. Edited
by Chu Chi-jung. 1888. Ts'e 4.

—— Jih-chih lu chi-shih. 32 chüan. SPPY.

—— T'ing-lin shih-wen chi. SPTK, 1st series.

Kung-sun Lung Tzu. SPPY.

K'ung Tzu chia-yü. SPTK, 1st series.

Kuo Hsiang. Commentary on Chuang Tzu (Chuang Tzu Kuo Hsiang chu).
In Chuang Tzu. SPTK, 1st series.

Kuo Ting-tung et al. I-kuan tao i-wen chieh-ta. Tientsin, 1937.

Kuo Yü. 21 chüan. SPPY.

Lao Tzu [Tao-te ching]. 2 chüan. SPPY.

Legge, James (tr.). Li Ki. Oxford, 1885.

—— She King. London, 1871.

—— Shoo King. Hongkong, 1865.

—— Yi King. Oxford, 1882; and in Sacred Books of the East. Edited by F. Max Müller. Oxford, 1899. Vol. XVI.

Levenson, Joseph. Liang Ch'i-ch'ao and the Mind of Modern China. Cambridge, Mass., Harvard University Press, 1953.

Li chi. 20 chüan. SPPY. See also Legge, Li Ki.

Li Chih-tsao. T'ien-hsüeh ch'u-han. Microfilm copy (Columbia University Library) of the 1629 ed. in the National Library of Peking.

Li Hung-chang. Li Wen-chung kung ch'üan-chi. 75 ts'e. Shanghai, Commercial Press, 1921.

Li-huo lun [Mou Tzu]. In Hung-ming chi. Compiled by Seng-yu. TD, LII:1–7.

Li-tai ming-hua chi. Chang Yen-yüan (ed.). 10 chüan, Po-ku-chai photolith reprint of Chin-tai pi-shu ed. Shanghai, 1922.

Liang Ch'i-ch'ao. Yin-ping shih ho-chi. Compiled by Lin Chih-chün. 40 vols. Shanghai, 1936.

—— Yin-ping shih wen-chi. 80 ts'e. Shanghai, Chung-hua shu-chü, 1926.

Liang Shu-ming [Liang Sou-ming]. Tung-hsi wen-hua chi ch'i che-hsüeh. Compiled by Ch'en Cheng and Lo Ch'ang-p'ei. Shanghai, Commercial Press, 1922.

Lieh Tzu [Ch'ung-hsü chih-te chen-ching]. SPTK, 1st series.

Liu Shao-chi [Liu Shao-ch'i]. How To Be a Good Communist. New York, New Century, 1952.

—— On Inner Party Struggle. Peking, Foreign Languages Press, n.d.

Liu-tsu t'an-ching [Nan-tsung tun-chiao tsui-shang ta-ch'eng mo-ho-po-jo-po-lo-mi ching Liu-tsu Hui-neng ta-shih yü Shao-chou Ta-fan-ssu shih-fa t'an-ching]. TD, XLVIII:337–44.

Lo Lung-chi. "Wo-men yao shen-mo yang ti cheng-chih chih-tu," Hsin yüeh, Vol. II, No. 12 (Shanghai, 1930), pp. 4–13.

Lotus of the Wonderful Law, The Scripture of the. Miao-fa lien-hua ching (Saddharmapundarīka Sūtra). TD, IX:8–9, 15.

Lu Chih. Lu Hsüan-kung tsou-i. KHCPTS.

Lu [Chiu-yüan] Hsiang-shan. Hsiang-shan ch'üan-chi. 36 chüan. SPPY.

Lü-shih ch'un-ch'iu. SPTK, 1st series.

Lü Tsu-ch'ien. Lü Tung-lai wen-chi. TSCC.

Lun yü. 20 chüan. SPPY. See also Soothill; Waley.

Ma Tuan-lin. Wen-hsien t'ung k'ao. Shih t'ung ed. Shanghai, Commercial Press, 1936.

Mao Tse-tung. Let a Hundred Flowers Bloom. With notes and an introduction by G. F. Hudson. New York, The New Leader, 1958.

—— Selected Works of Mao Tse-tung. London, Lawrence and Wishart, 1954: Vols. 1 and 2. New York, International Publishers, 1954 and 1956: Vols. 3 and 4.

Meng Tzu (Mencius). 14 chüan. SPTK, 1st series.

Miao-fa lien-hua ching (Saddharmapundarīka Sūtra; The Scripture of the Lotus of the Wonderful Law). TD, IX:8–9, 15.

Mo Tzu. 16 chüan. SPPY.

Mou Tzu. Li-huo lun. In Hung-ming chi. Compiled by Seng-yu. TD, LII:1–7.

Nan-hua chen-ching. Chuang Tzu. 10 chüan. SPTK, 1st series.

Ou-yang Hsiu. Ou-yang Wen-chung kung chi. SPTK, 1st series.

Pan Ku. Han shu. PNP.

Sa Meng-wu, Ho Ping-sung et al. "Chung-kuo pen-wei ti wen-hua chien-she hsüan-yen," Wen-hua chien-she, Vol. I, No. 4 (Shanghai, January, 1935), pp. 3–5.

Saddharmapundarīka Sūtra. Miao-fa lien-hua ching (The Scripture of the Lotus of the Wonderful Law). TD, IX:8–9, 15.

Schiffrin, Harold. "Sun Yat-sen's Land Policy," Journal of Asian Studies, Vol. XVI, No. 4 (August, 1957), pp. 549–64.

Shao Yung. Huang-chi ching-shih shu. SPPY.

Shen-hui. Hsien-tsung chi [entitled Tun-wu wu-sheng po-jo sung in Tun-huang version]. In ch. 30, pp. 6b–8a of Ching-te ch'uan-teng lu. Compiled by Tao-yüan. SPTK, 3d series.

Shih chi. Ssu-ma Ch'ien. PNP.

Shih ching. Hsüeh-sheng kuo-hsüeh ts'ung-shu ed. Shanghai, Commercial Press, 1926. See also Legge, She King.

Shu ching (Shang shu chin-ku wen chu su). KHCPTS. See also Legge, Shoo King.

Soothill, William E. (tr.). The Analects or The Conversations of Confucius with His Disciples and Certain Others. Edited by Lady Hosie. London, Oxford University Press, 1937.

Ssu-ma Ch'ien. Shih chi. PNP.

Ssu-ma Kuang. Tzu-chih t'ung-chien. SPTK, 1st series.

—— Wen-kuo wen-cheng Ssu-ma kung wen-chi. SPTK, 1st series.

Su Hsün. Chia-yu chi. SPTK, 1st series.

Su Shih [Su Tung-p'o]. Ching chin Tung-p'o wen-chi shih-lüeh. SPTK, 1st series.

Su Yü (ed.). I-chiao ts'ung-pien. 6 chüan. Wu-chang reprint of 1898.

Sun Yat-sen [Sun Wen, Sun Chung-shan]. Chung-shan ch'üan-shu. 4 vols. Shanghai, San min t'u-shu kung-ssu, 1946.

—— San Min Chu I, The Three Principles of the People. Translated by Frank W. [Francis Wilson] Price. Edited by L. T. Chen. Chungking, Ministry of Information of the Republic of China, 1943.

Sung shih. In [Ch'in-ting] Erh-shih-ssu shih. Edited by T'o-t'o. Han-fen-lou photo reprint of the Palace ed. of 1739. Shanghai, 1916.

Suzuki, D. T. "Zen: A Reply to Hu Shih," Philosophy East and West, Vol. III, No. 1 (April, 1953).

Suzuki Teitarō and Kimida Rentarō (eds.). Tun huang ch'u-t'u liu tsu t'an-ching. Shanghai, Fo-hsüeh shü-chu, [1934].

Ta hsüeh. No. 42 in Li chi. 20 chüan. SPPY.

T'ai-p'ing t'ien-kuo ts'ung-shu. Compiled by Hsiao I-shan. Series I, 10 ts'e. Kuo-li pien-i kuan, 1936.

T'ai-shang kan-ying p'ien. In Tao-tsang. Photo reprint of Pai-yün-kuan Library Ming ed. Shanghai, Commercial Press, 1924–1926. Vols. 834–39.

T'an-luan. Wang-sheng lun chu. TD, XL:827–36.

T'an Ssu-t'ung. T'an Liu-yang ch'üan-chi. Edited by Ch'en Nai-ch'ien. 6 ts'e. Shanghai, 1924.

Tao-ch'o. An-lo chi. TD, XLVII: 8–11.

Tao-te ching. Lao Tzu. 2 chüan. SPPY.

Tao-yüan (comp.). Ching-te ch'uan teng lu. SPTK, 3d series.

Teng, Ssu-yü, John K. Fairbank, et al. China's Response to the West, A Documentary Survey, 1839–1923. Cambridge, Mass., Harvard University Press, 1954.

Tien-ch'ao t'ien-mu chih-tu. In ts'e 4 of T'ai-p'ing t'ien-kuo ts'ung-shu. Compiled by Hsiao I-shan. Series I, 10 ts'e. Kuo-li pien-i kuan, 1936.

T'ien-ch'ing tao-li shu. In ts'e 5 of T'ai-p'ing t'ien-kuo ts'ung-shu. Compiled by Hsiao I-shan. Series I, 10 ts'e. Kuo-li pien-i kuan, 1936.

T'ien-t'iao shu. In ts'e 1 of T'ai-p'ing t'ien-kuo ts'ung-shu. Compiled by Hsiao I-shan. Series I, 10 ts'e. Kuo-li pien-i kuan, 1936.

Ting Wen-chiang [V. K. Ting]. Hsüan-hsüeh yü k'o-hsüeh. In Chang Chün-mai, q.v.

Ts'ao-shan Pen-chi ch'an-shih yü-lu. TD, XLVII:537–39.

Tsiang T'ing-fu [T. F. Tsiang]. "K'ai-ming yü chuan-chih," *Tu-li p'ing-lun*, No. 81 (Peking, December, 1933), pp. 2–5.

Tsou Lu (ed.). Chung-kuo Kuomintang shih kao. Shanghai, Min-chih shu-chü, 1929.

Ts'ui Shu. K'ao hsin lu t'i-yao. TSCC.

Tsung Ping. Introduction to Landscape Painting (Hua shan-shui hsü). In 6:3b–4b of Li-tai ming-hua chi. Edited by Chang Yen-yüan. 10 chüan. Po-ku-chai photolith reprint of Chin-tai pi-shu ed. Shanghai, 1922.

Tsunoda, Ryusaku, Wm. Theodore de Bary, and Donald Keene (comps.). Sources of Japanese Tradition. New York, Columbia University Press, 1958.

Tung Chung-shu. Ch'un-ch'iu fan-lu. SPTK, 1st series.

Waley, Arthur (tr.). The Analects of Confucius. New York, Macmillan, 1939.

Wang An-shih. Chou-kuan hsin-i. TSCC.

—— Lin-ch'uan hsien-sheng wen-chi. SPTK, 1st series.

Wang Chia. Shih-i-chi. In Han-Wei ts'ung-shu. Compiled by Ch'eng Jung. Han-fen-lou ed. Shanghai, 1925.

Wang Ch'ung. Lun heng. SPTK, 1st series.

Wang Fu-chih. Chou-i wai-chuan. In Ch'uan-shan i-shu. SPTK, 1st series.

—— Huang shu. In Ch'uan-shan i-shu. T'ai p'ing yang shu-tien ed. 1935.

—— Tu T'ung-chien lun. 31 chüan. SPPY.

Wang T'ao. T'ao-yüan wen-lu wai-pien. 6 ts'e. Hongkong, 1883.

Wang Wei. Introduction to Painting (Hsü hua). In 6:5b–6b of Li-tai ming-hua chi. Edited by Chang Yen-yüan. 10 chüan. Po-ku-chai photolith reprint of Chin-tai pi-shu ed. Shanghai, 1922.

Wang Yang-ming [Wang Shou-jen]. Ch'uan hsi lu. In Yang-ming ch'üan-shu. SPPY.

Wei Yüan. Hai-kuo t'u-chih. 24 ts'e. 1876 reprint of the 100-chüan ed.

Wen-hsüan [Liu-ch'en chu Wen-hsüan]. SPTK, 1st series.

Wu Chih-hui. I-ko hsin hsin-yang ti yü-chou chi jen-sheng kuan. In Chang Chün-mai, q.v.

Yang Hsiung. Fa yen. SPTK, 1st series.

Yin-chih wen. Edited by Chou Meng-yen. Yang-chou tsang-ching-yüan ed. 1881.

Yu hsüeh shih. In ts'e 4 of T'ai-p'ing t'ien-kuo ts'ung-shu. Compiled by Hsiao I-shan. Series I, 10 ts'e. Kuo-li pien-i kuan, 1936.

Without the assistance of various publishers, a book of source readings such as this is not possible, and we are grateful for the cooperation of the following: Chinese News Service, New York; Harvard University Press, Cambridge; International Publishers, New York; New Century Publishers, New York; *The New Leader,* New York; Random House, Inc., New York.

INDEX